P9-DFA-958

Introduction to Psychology

Exploration and Application

SEVENTH EDITION

Introduction to Psychology

Exploration and Application

SEVENTH EDITION

Dennis Coon
Department of Psychology
Santa Barbara City College, California

West Publishing Company
Minneapolis/St. Paul New York Los Angeles San Francisco

PRODUCTION CREDITS

COMPOSITION Parkwood Composition
PAGE MAKEUP ARTIST José Delgado

WEST'S COMMITMENT TO THE ENVIRONMENT

In 1906, West Publishing Company began recycling materials left over from the production of books. This began a tradition of efficient and responsible use of resources. Today, up to 95 percent of our legal books and 70 percent of our college and school texts are printed on recycled, acid-free stock. West also recycles nearly 22 million pounds of scrap paper annually—the equivalent of 181,717 trees. Since the 1960s, West has devised ways to capture and recycle waste inks, solvents, oils, and vapors created in the printing process. We also recycle plastics of all kinds, wood, glass, corrugated cardboard, and batteries, and have eliminated the use of Styrofoam book packaging. We at West are proud of the longevity and the scope of our commitment to our environment.

Production, Prepress, Printing and Binding by West Publishing Company

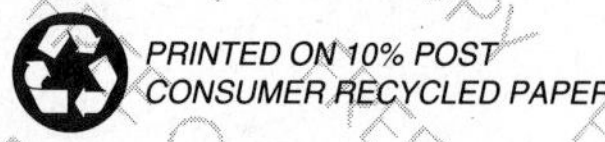

British Library Cataloguing-in-Publication Data. A catalogue record for this book is available from the British Library.

610 Opperman Drive
P.O. Box 64526
St. Paul, MN 55164-0526

Printed in the United States of America

02 01 00 99 98 97 96 95 8 7 6 5 4 3 2 1 0

Library of Congress Cataloging-in-Publication Data

Coon, Dennis.
Introduction to psychology : Exploration and application / Dennis Coon. – 7th ed.
p. cm.
Includes index.
ISBN 0-314-04450-7
1. Psychology. I. Title.
BF121.C625 1995
150–dc20 94-46124
CIP

Contents in Brief

(Contents in Brief–*continued*)

Contents

Chapter 3

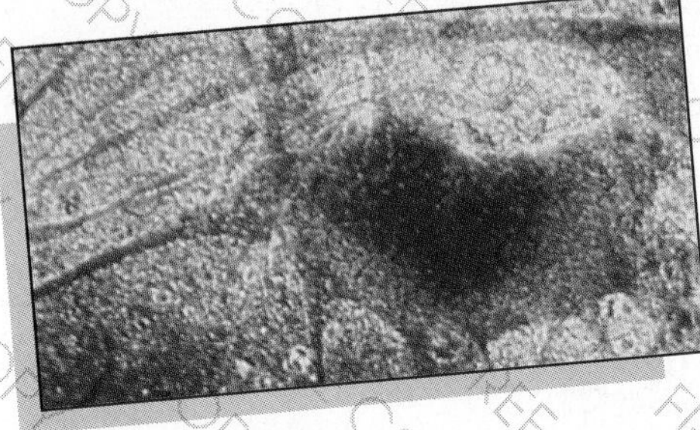

The Brain, Biology, and Behavior 55

Chapter 4

Sensation and Reality 90

Chapter 5

Perceiving the World 123

Chapter 6

States of Consciousness 155

Chapter 7

Chapter 8

Memory 234

Chapter 9

Cognition and Creativity 266

Chapter 10

Motivation and Emotion 297

Chapter 11

Health, Stress, and Coping 338

Chapter 12

Child Development 373

Chapter 13

From Birth to Death: Life-Span Development 413

Chapter 14

Intelligence 449

Chapter 15

Personality 474

Chapter 16

Abnormal Behavior: Deviance and Disorder 511

Chapter 17

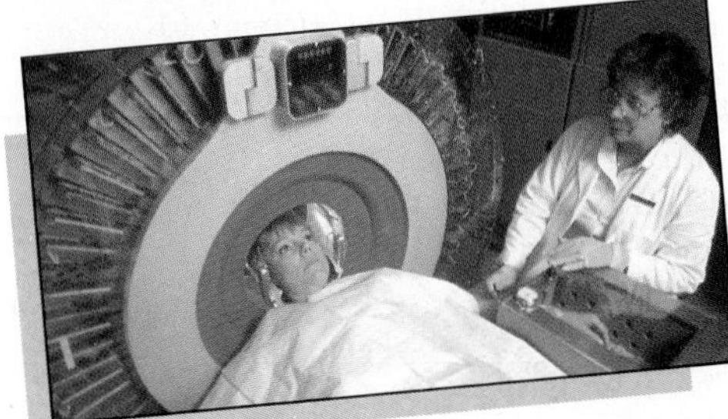

Major Mental Disorders 538

Chapter 18

Therapies 567

Chapter 19

Gender and Sexuality 601

Chapter 20

Social Behavior 632

Chapter 21

Attitudes, Culture, and Human Relations 660

Chapter 22

Preface to the Seventh Edition

To the Student

Psychology is a large and rapidly growing field. It is at once familiar, exotic, commonplace, surprising, and challenging. Most of all, psychology is changing. Indeed, this book can be no more than a "snapshot" of a colorful passing scene. And yet, change makes psychology especially fascinating: What, really, could be more intriguing than our evolving understanding of human behavior?

Psychology is about each of us. Psychology asks, "How can we step outside of ourselves for a more objective look at how we live, think, and act?" Psychologists believe the answer is through careful thought, observation, and inquiry. As simple as that may seem, it is the guiding light for everything that follows in this book.

I sincerely hope that you will find psychology as fascinating as I do. In this text, I have done all that I could imagine to make your first encounter with psychology enjoyable and worthwhile. To help you get off to a good start, Chapter 1 includes a discussion of how to study effectively. The ideas covered there will help you get the most out of this text, class lectures, and your psychology course as a whole. In the remaining chapters, I hope that the delight I have found in my own students' curiosity, insights, imagination, and interests will be apparent. Please view this book as a long letter from me to you. It is, in a very real sense, written about you, for you, and to you.

To the Instructor

This book is designed to promote an interest in human behavior, to facilitate learning psychology, and to encourage critical thinking. If you are already familiar with its format, a description of Seventh Edition changes follows shortly. If the text is unfamiliar, a brief sketch of its design and underlying philosophy is in order.

A Book for Students As an instructor I have learned that selecting a textbook is half the battle in teaching a course. A good text does much of the work of imparting information to students. This frees class time for discussion and it leaves students asking for more. When a book overwhelms students or cools their interest, teaching and learning become uphill battles. For this reason, I have worked hard to make this a clear, readable, and interesting text.

I believe an important question to ask of the introductory course is "What will students remember next year, or in 10 years?" Consequently, *Introduction to Psychology* gives students a clear grasp of major concepts, rather than burying them in details. At the same time, it provides a broad overview that reflects psychology's diversity. I think students will find this book full of intellectual challenge, and teachers will find traditional topics covered to their satisfaction. In addition, I have made a special effort to relate psychology to common experiences and to practical problems of daily life.

A major feature of this book is the *Applications* section in each chapter. These high-interest features bridge the gap between psychological theory and practical applications. I believe students have every right to ask, "Does this mean anything to me? Can I use it? Why should I learn it if I can't?" The Applications sections in this text spell out how students can use the principles of psychology. By doing so, they breathe life into its concepts.

At the end of each chapter you will find a separate *Exploration.* These brief articles cover controversies, current issues, topics from psychology's frontiers, or subjects likely to promote critical thinking and discussion. In essence, they serve as supplemental readings within the text, to provide a taste of changing issues and ideas in psychology. Because Explorations conclude each chapter, they are easy to assign or delete at your discretion.

A Format for Learning

Before this book first appeared, psychology texts made surprisingly little use of cognitive principles to teach psychology. My use of learning aids is based on a belief that students can be guided into more effective study and reading habits while learning course content. Each chapter in this text is built around the well-known SQ3R study-reading formula. In addition to helping students learn psychology, this format promotes valuable study skills. Student response to the format has been very positive, with many students reporting that they transfer SQ3R techniques to other texts as well.

Notice how the time-tested steps of the SQ3R method—*survey, question, read, recite, and review*—underlie the design of each chapter.

Survey A short *Chapter Preview* arouses interest, gives an overview of the chapter, and focuses attention on the task at hand. An outline, titled *In This Chapter*, accompanies the Preview and lists upcoming topics. After that, a list of *Survey Questions* spotlights major issues so that students will read with a purpose.

Question Throughout each chapter, *Guide Questions* act as advance organizers that prime students to look for important ideas as they read. This helps ensure that reading is an active learning experience. Guide Questions also create a dialogue in which student questions and reactions are anticipated. This clarifies difficult points—in a lively give-and-take between questions and responses. And, significantly, many Guide Questions model critical thinking skills, to encourage reflection and inquiry.

Read The readability of each chapter has been carefully controlled for maximum student involvement and comprehension. I have made every effort to keep the text as clear and accessible as possible. To further facilitate comprehension, the text employs a full array of traditional learning aids. These include boldfaced type and phonetic pronunciations for important terms, bulleted summaries, a detailed glossary, summary tables, a complete index, and a robust illustration program. In addition, figure and table references in the text are marked with small geometric shapes so that students can easily return to the point where they were reading. This feature also allows readers to start with a figure or table and easily find the place in the text where it is discussed.

Throughout the text, highlighted margin definitions provide a *running glossary* of key terms. Margin definitions are provided to enhance reading comprehension. For instance, students can use them to differentiate between terms that are easily confused, such as *negative reinforcement* and *punishment*. The running glossary also makes it easy for students to review important terms and concepts before tests.

At several points in each chapter, special accentuated *Highlights* discuss recent research, interesting topics, and original viewpoints. All Highlights are placed exactly where they should be read. Students do not need to search for a separate "box" of information. Highlights are stimulating but nonintrusive supplements to the main text. I have classified them as follows: "A Closer Look At," "Focus on a Controversy," "Research Frontier," "Cultural Diversity," "Using Psychology," "Research Classic," "Truth or Fiction," "Critical Thinking," and "Rate Yourself." As these headings imply, Highlights enrich each chapter and encourage critical thinking.

Recite Every few pages, a *Learning Check* allows students to test their understanding and recall of the preceding discussion. Learning Checks are short, noncomprehensive quizzes that require students to stop and actively process information. Students who miss any questions are encouraged to backtrack and clarify their understanding before reading more. Completing each Learning Check serves as a form of recitation to enhance learning. It also provides feedback so that students can gauge their progress.

A course in psychology naturally contributes to the development of critical thinking abilities. To further facilitate critical thinking, each Learning Check in the Seventh Edition concludes with a *Critical Thinking Question*. These stimulating questions challenge students to think critically and analytically about psychology. Each Critical Thinking Question includes a brief answer with which students can compare their own. Many of these answers are based on recent research and are informative in their own right.

Review As mentioned earlier, an Applications section completes the core of each chapter. Applications show students how psychological concepts relate to practical problems, including problems in their own lives. Through these discussions, students review and extend the ideas they have learned. Applications help reinforce and consolidate learning by illustrating psychology's practicality.

An Exploration follows each Applications section. In most cases, students must be familiar with chapter concepts to fully appreciate an Exploration. This again motivates students to review what they have learned and to broaden their understanding.

To complete the review phase of the SQ3R method, a point-by-point *Chapter Summary* provides a concise synopsis of all major topics. The Chapter Summary is organized around the same Survey Questions posed at the beginning of the chapter. This brings the SQ3R process full-circle and provides closure with respect to the learning objectives of each chapter.

What's New in the Seventh Edition?

Personality development is marked by an intricate interplay of continuity and change. Likewise, the "personality" of *Introduction to Psychology* will seem at times both familiar and novel to those who know it well. Naturally, the Seventh Edition carries forward the best features and topics of previous editions. In addition, I have revised the Seventh Edition in the following ways:

- The text is reorganized from 26 chapters to 22 chapters.
- All discussions of abnormal behavior and other relevant topics are updated to correspond with DSM-IV (1994).
- Numerous research updates appear throughout the text.
- New information on gender and diversity issues augments the text's already substantial coverage of these topics.
- Critical thinking skills are given more emphasis, especially in Chapter 2.
- Each Learning Check now concludes with a Critical Thinking Question, followed by an informative answer.
- A full running glossary now appears in page margins.
- All chapters benefit from improved art and photographs, as well as new cartoons.
- Larger pages allow for added content and new features, while maintaining the text's readability and visual appeal.
- An expanded Glossary, with improved definitions, covers virtually all important terms in the text.

The comments that follow provide more details about some of the changes noted here.

Reorganization For this edition, I combined eight former chapters into four new chapters. In each instance, my goal was to offer a more streamlined presentation of closely-related topics. The old and new chapters are as follows:

- Former Chapters 7 and 8 ("Conditioning and Learning I" and "Conditioning and Learning II") are combined in new Chapter 7, "Conditioning and Learning."
- Former Chapters 11 and 12 ("Motivation" and "Emotion") are combined in new Chapter 10, "Motivation and Emotion."
- Former Chapters 16 and 17 ("Dimensions of Personality" and "Theories of Personality") are combined in new Chapter 15, "Personality."
- Former Chapters 21 and 22 ("Insight Therapies" and "Behavior Therapy") are combined in new Chapter 18, "Therapies."

An added benefit of this reorganization is that many instructors will find it easier to harmonize reading assignments with their course outlines.

Design This revision benefits from further refinements in the chapter format. The treatment of *Highlights* has been improved. *Applications* have been redesigned to more clearly integrate them into the core of each chapter. The new running glossary adds significantly to the text's pedagogy. In addition, new or improved art and photographs supply valuable information at many points in the text.

Critical Thinking The active, questioning nature of the SQ3R method is, in itself, an inducement to think critically. Many of the *Guide Questions* that introduce topics in the text act as models of critical thinking. More important, the *Exploration* for Chapter 1 specifically discusses critical thinking skills. This sets the stage for Chapter 2, "Research Methods and Critical Thinking," which is actually a short course on how to think clearly about behavior. Chapter 9, "Cognition and Creativity," also discusses many topics that focus on thinking skills. In addition, several *Explorations* critically evaluate controversial topics. Throughout the text, many *Highlights* present topics that students should approach with healthy skepticism. And, as mentioned earlier, every Learning Check concludes with a Critical Thinking Question. Taken together, these features will help students gain thinking skills of lasting value.

Human Diversity Student populations increasingly reflect the multicultural, multifaceted nature of contemporary society. The Seventh Edition of *Introduction to Psychology* includes numerous discussions of human diversity, including differences in race, ethnicity, culture, gender, ability, sexual orientation, and age. Too often, such differences needlessly divide people into opposing groups. My intent throughout the text is to discourage stereotyping, prejudice, discrimination, and intolerance. Numerous topics and examples in the Seventh Edition encourage students to appreciate social, physical, and cultural differences and to accept them as a natural part of being human. Nine Highlights, one Application, one Exploration, and large portions of Chapters 13, 19, and 20 are devoted to discussions of human diversity.

New Topics and Updated Coverage

In addition to the improvements already noted, my general goal for this revision was to report psychology's latest ideas, insights, and findings. As this defines a virtual deluge of information, I tried to be very selective about what I included. To make the grade, information had to be conceptually significant or inherently fascinating—or preferably both. Almost every chapter of the Seventh Edition contains new ideas that I believe meet these criteria. I have drawn on hundreds of new references (many as recent as 1994 and some in press) for this revision.

New Highlights Nineteen Highlights in this edition are new or substantially revised. New and revised Highlights include the following titles:

- Ch. 1 Women in Psychology
  The Challenge of Human Diversity
- Ch. 2 Is There a Gender Bias in Psychological Research?
- Ch. 3 The Risky Side of the Brain
- Ch. 4 Pheromones—A Sixth Sense?
- Ch. 5 The "Boiled Frog Syndrome"
- Ch. 6 Eliminating Nightmares
- Ch. 12 The Impact of Poverty
- Ch. 13 Near-Death Experiences—Back from the Brink
- Ch. 15 Personality—When Is the Plaster Set?
- Ch. 16 The Politics of "Madness"
  Are the Mentally Ill Prone to Violence?
- Ch. 17 Psychiatric "Wonder Drugs"
- Ch. 18 "Psych Jockeys" and Telephone Counselors
- Ch. 19 Genes, the Brain, and Sexual Orientation
  Rape Myths and Facts

Other New Contents A new Chapter Preview, "The Time Machine," provides a better introduction to life-span development. Two Applications are substantially revised in this edition. These are "Handedness—If Your Brain Is Right, What's Left?" (Chapter 3) and "Behavioral Self-Management" (Chapter 7). Chapter 8 ends with an important new Exploration titled "The Recovered Memory/False Memory Debate." This provocative new Exploration airs both sides of the debate and reports the latest information on the validity of recovered memories. Chapter 9 also has a new Exploration: "Animal Intelligence," which presents some fascinating new information on apparent symbolic thought by a chimp.

Chapter Notes Publication of DSM-IV alone would have necessitated the revision of *Introduction to Psychology*. I am pleased to report, however, that every chapter of the Seventh Edition has been enhanced. The following list spotlights some of the more prominent new topics that appear in this edition.

- Ch. 1 Brief new coverage of the science and profession of psychology, scientist-practitioner model, psychiatric social workers, cultural psychology, effective note-taking, goal-setting, quality of studying; new Highlight: The Challenge of Human Diversity.
- Ch. 2 New art and examples clarify major elements of the scientific method, correlation, and critical thinking; new table lists basic ethical guidelines for psychological researchers; new Highlight: Is There a Gender Bias in Psychological Research?
- Ch. 3 New art and text provide a more detailed description of the action potential and synapses; new discussion of volume transmission; improved art shows reflex arc, corpus callosum, primary motor and somatosensory cortex, limbic system; brief new coverage of reticular formation, brain size, pineal gland, anabolic steroids; enlarged and updated discussion of handedness; new Highlight: The Risky Side of the Brain; updated Highlight on hypopituitary dwarfism.
- Ch. 4 New art clarifies the nature of elementary visual features, blind spot, rods and cones, organ of Corti, hair cells, olfactory receptors; new Highlight: Pheromones—A Sixth Sense?
- Ch. 5 Improved art clarifies pictorial depth cues, relative size, motion parallax, Ponzo illusion; newly defined Gestalt principle, "common region," presented; new summary of how perceptual principles apply to daily living, "Becoming a Better 'Eyewitness' to Life;" new Highlight: The "Boiled Frog Syndrome."
- Ch. 6 Brief updates on SIDS, caffeine, smoking, alcohol, hallucinogens, marijuana, dream interpretation; new Highlight: Eliminating Nightmares; updated Highlight: Behavioral Remedies for Insomnia.

- Ch. 7 Streamlined discussion of conditioning and learning combines old Chapters 7 and 8; new art explains operant reinforcement; new research on the effects of violence portrayed in the "Power Rangers" TV program; revised discussion of self-management and how to break bad habits.
- Ch. 8 Maintenance rehearsal and elaborative rehearsal now distinguished; types of LTM now discussed in chapter; transfer of training moved to this chapter; important update on flashbulb memories; major new Exploration: The Recovered Memory/False Memory Debate.
- Ch. 9 Brief updates on mental imagery, artificial intelligence, expertise, creative thinking; discussion of animal intelligence collected in a new Exploration, with new information on apparent symbolic thought by a chimp.
- Ch. 10 Combines old Chapters 11 & 12; new information on the role of the hypothalamic nuclei in controlling hunger; new table helps identify eating disorders; new information on jet lag, links between motivation and emotion, facial expressions.
- Ch. 11 Reorganized; new information on behavioral risk factors, health campaigns, wellness, psychoneuroimmunology; updated discussion of psychosomatic disorders; biofeedback now discussed in this chapter; Applications offers new coverage of the *Undergraduate Stress Questionnaire*, information on guided imagery.
- Ch. 12 Research updates on many topics; new tables throughout chapter spell out implications of developmental principles for parents and caregivers; new information on quality of day care, parentese; new Highlight: The Impact of Poverty.
- Ch. 13 New Chapter Preview; updates on ADHD, autism, child abuse, life goals, menopause, adult cognitive development, hospice, euthanasia; new Highlight: Near-Death Experiences.
- Ch. 14 New discussion of aptitude tests places cognitive ability testing in perspective; new table updates Stanford-Binet ability areas and subtests; update on the Larry P. case.
- Ch. 15 New Highlight: Personality—When Is the Plaster Set?; combines old Chapters 16 and 17 for a better integration of personality theories and assessment; updates of twin research, honesty testing.
- Ch. 16 Reorganized discussion of abnormality and psychopathology; discussions of mental disorders and tables revised to match DSM-IV; new table illustrates various levels of dysfunction; new information on sociopathy, rape, phobias, stress disorders; new Highlight: Are the Mentally Ill Prone to Violence?; revised Highlight: The Politics of "Madness."
- Ch. 17 Updates on lead poisoning, the stress-vulnerability model, SAD, schizophrenia, hospitalization, suicide; revised discussion of mood disorders reflects DSM-IV terminology; new Highlight: Psychiatric "Wonder Drugs," critically examines costs and benefits of drug therapy.
- Ch. 18 Reorganized; combines old Chapters 21 and 22 for balanced coverage of insight therapies and behavioral therapies; revised Highlight offers cautions about telephone counselors; updated Application explains how to find competent psychological help.
- Ch. 19 Numerous updates and new art based on data from the *Janus Report* and the 1994 University of Chicago survey on sexual behavior; discussion of androgyny updated and moved to this chapter; major new discussion of sexual orientations; Applications section on sexual dysfunctions completely revised to reflect contemporary terminology, remedies, and data; new Highlight: Genes, the Brain, and Sexual Orientation; new Highlight: Rape Myths and Facts.
- Ch. 20 Research updates on norms, cultural differences in spatial behavior, social comparisons (including upward and downward comparisons), groupthink; interesting new discussion of evolutionary psychology and evolved patterns of mate selection.
- Ch. 21 Updates on cognitive dissonance, cults, stereotypes; enlarged discussion of the effects of TV as a model for prosocial and antisocial behavior.
- Ch. 22 Updates on biodata, personal interviews, employment testing, job enrichment, consumerism; new discussion of pollution and toxic environments; efficient learning of motor skills now discussed in connection with sports psychology.

To summarize, I have tried to update and enhance *Introduction to Psychology* while retaining its existing strengths. I hope that you will be pleased with the final result.

Teaching and Learning Supplements

An enlarged and improved array of supplements accompanies the Seventh Edition of *Introduction to Psychology*. A brief description of each follows. Please contact your West Publishing representative for more information about any of these materials.

Study Guides Two student study guides are available to accompany the Seventh Edition. Like *Introduction to Psychology*, each chapter of the *Study Guide* is structured around the SQ3R method. To facilitate learning, the *Study Guide* provides additional opportunities for practice, self-testing, and elaborative rehearsal. The *Study Guide* emphasizes active learning and high-quality studying.

The *Mastery Study Guide*, by Tom Bond, offers a very thorough review and a chance to practice concepts presented in the text. The MSG includes a list of important terms and individuals, learning objectives (with space for student responses), two tests ("Do You Know the Information," "Can You Apply the Information"), and a fill-in-the-blanks Chapter Review.

Chapter Quizzes New to this edition is a supplement called *Chapter Quizzes*. This collection of quizzes (one quiz per chapter) contains questions similar to the ones found on in-class tests. Students can use the quizzes to practice for tests, to assess their mastery of chapters, or to identify topics needing more attention.

ESL/Developmental Reader's Guide For many students the challenge of learning psychology extends beyond technical terms and concepts. Differences in language and culture can be major barriers to full comprehension. The *ESL/Developmental Reader's Guide* helps clarify idioms and special phrases, cultural and historic allusions, and difficult vocabulary. All terms and phrases in the manual are page referenced to the text and followed by concise definitions. Like a helpful tutor, the *ESL/Developmental Reader's Guide* can answer questions about the meaning of unfamiliar terms and expressions. It is especially suitable for ESL or developmental-skills students.

College Survival Guide The new third edition of Bruce Rowe's *College Survival Guide: Hints and References to Aid College Students* is designed to help students succeed. The guide gives valuable and practical information that students usually must pick up on their own. Rowe reduces students' frustrations and anxieties with tips on how to finance an education, how to manage time, how to study for and take exams, and more. Other sections focus on maintaining concentration, credit by examination, use of the credit/no credit option, cooperative education programs, and the importance of a liberal arts education. The *College Survival Guide* will be especially useful to first-year college students, students reentering college, and non-native students.

Cross-Cultural Perspectives in Psychology How well do the concepts of western psychology apply to non-western cultures? What can we learn about human behavior from cultures different from our own? These, and similar questions lie behind a collection of original articles written by William F. Price and Rich Crapo. *Cross-Cultural Perspectives in Psychology, Second Edition*, draws on examples from around the world to provide a multicultural view of human behavior. Readings begin with an intriguing question about behavior which is then explored through cross-cultural research. *Cross-Cultural Perspectives in Psychology* introduces students to ideas that will challenge their assumptions about behavior. In the process, our own cultural practices are illuminated and placed in perspective.

Psychware *Psychware* is a CAI package to supplement the introductory course. Robert S. Slotnick and the staff of the New York Institute of Technology have developed a stimulating collection of tutorials, simulations, and experiments for use on Apple PCs. Each highly interactive exercise features engaging graphics. By using *Psychware*, students can apply the principles of operant conditioning, they can test their short-term memory, they can explore social behavior or gain insight into Piaget's stages of cognitive development, and much more.

***Mind Scope* Software** This splendid program was created by Robert W. Hendersen. *Mind Scope* consists of 14 computerized exercises in perception, learning, memory, and cognition. The series is designed to help students discover and analyze aspects of their own behavior that might otherwise be hidden from them. In each exercise, students perform a task and record their own responses. By analyzing the results, students are able to see psychological processes illustrated by their own behavior. *Mind Scope* will run on any IBM-compatible microcomputer.

Videotapes West offers a variety of videotapes to enrich classroom presentations. Many video segments pertain directly to major topics in this text, making videotapes excellent lecture supplements. Please contact your West representative for more information about selections from West's *Psychology Video Library*.

***Grade Improvement* Videotape** West's new *Grade Improvement: Taking Charge of Your Learning* videotape is designed for first-year college students or students re-entering college. This upbeat and entertaining video teaches a half-dozen things students can do to enjoy greater success in school. Students learn valuable techniques for active listening, efficient reading, effective note taking, productive studying, improved time management, and more.

***Images of Psychology* Videodiscs** West's exciting new *Images of Psychology: Videodisc Library of Human Behavior* provides a wealth of lecture materials in a compact and convenient format. This two-disc set contains nearly two hours of video material. Video clips range from two to six minutes in length and cover a wide variety of introductory psychology topics. The clips feature material such as original research footage, classic experiments, interviews with prominent psychologists, and investigations of psychological phenomena. The *Videodisc Library* also contains a large collection of still-frame art, charts, tables, animated sequences, and on-screen quizzes.

Videodisc materials can be accessed instantly, in any order, by simply entering a frame number or scanning a barcode. West's companion *Lecture Builder* software allows you to prepare entire laser disc lectures and play them back in class. *Lecture Builder* is available for both Macintosh and Windows environments. The *Images of Psychology Videodisc Library* includes an annotated *Instructor's Manual* by Lonnie Yandell. The manual lists all frames and video segments, describes their contents, and gives suggestions for their use.

Transparency Acetates A revised set of transparencies will again be available to enliven classroom presentations. These transparencies contain over 140 tables, graphs, charts, and drawings—most in color. All of the acetates are reproduced from figures and tables in the text.

***Astound* Software** This state-of-the art presentation program allows you to create and edit presentations using text, animations, graphics, and sound. Transparencies are provided for each major content area. Available images include charts, graphs, illustrations, and topical outlines.

Instructor's Manual The *Instructor's Manual* for this edition was revised by psychologist and master teacher Sandra Ciccarelli. The manual includes updated learning objectives, film suggestions, demonstrations, supplemental lectures, classroom exercises, discussion ideas, and suggested readings. Two special sections created by Kendra Jeffcoat are included in each chapter: "One Minute Motivators" are quick demonstrations, examples, or challenges that can be used to enliven your classroom presentation; the scenarios listed in "Broadening Our Cultural Horizons," will help students examine and role-play diverse cultural values. In addition, the IM contains general teaching strategies and references, two cognitive-diagnostic reading tests devised by Charles Croll and Linda Kovacs, and other helpful materials. An accompanying set of *Worksheets* for all exercises in the IM is available for copying and classroom use, discussion, and activity.

Test Bank Sidney Hochman and Laura Sidorowicz have carefully updated and reorganized the *Test Bank*. This high-quality collection consists of more than 4000 multiple-choice questions, including over 1000 new items. Test items are organized to correspond to learning objectives. In addition, items are page referenced and classified according to question type (factual, conceptual, or applied).

All test items are incorporated into *WESTEST 3.1*, a microcomputer test-generation program. WESTEST allows you to create, edit, store, and print exams. You may randomly generate or selectively choose questions, as well as add your own. WESTEST is now accompanied by *Classroom Management Software*, a program that allows you to record, store, and work with student data.

Guide to Instructional Materials This helpful guide integrates all instructional materials. To facilitate planning and use, the *Guide* is organized by topics to coordinate behavioral objectives, test questions, transparencies, cross-cultural readings, software, videodisc frames, and videotape segments. This is the first place to look when you want to learn what materials apply to a particular chapter of the text.

Summary

I sincerely hope that teachers and students will consider this book and its supporting materials a refreshing change from the ordinary. Writing and revising it has been quite an adventure. In the pages that follow, I think the reader will find an attractive blend of the theoretical and the practical, plus many of the most exciting ideas in psychology.

Acknowledgments

The enterprise of psychology is a cooperative effort requiring the talents and energies of a large community of scholars, teachers, researchers, and students. As with earlier versions of this text, this edition reflects the efforts of a large number of people.

I would like to thank first the many students who sent comments, suggestions, and letters of encouragement.

To the professional users/reviewers who gave their time and expertise I extend my sincere thanks. I deeply appreciate the contributions of all those who have, over the years, supported this text's evolution. I especially wish to thank those who helped make this edition a reality:

Brian Bate
Cuyahoga Community College

Hugh E. Bateman
Jones Junior College

Corinne Crandell
Broome County Community College

Thomas L. Crandell
Broome County Community College

Patrick T. DeBoli
St. John's University

Marie Fox
Metropolitan State College of Denver

David A. Gershaw
Arizona Western College

Cindy Kennedy
Sinclair Community College

Richard R. Klene
University of Cincinnati

Billie Laney
Central Texas College

Elizabeth Levin
Laurentian University

Salvador Macias, III
University of South Carolina, Sumter

Michael Schuller
Fresno City College

I would also like to thank the psychologists whose work and advice has so obviously enhanced this text and its supporting materials: Wayne Bartz, Tom Bond, Sandra Ciccarelli, Rich Crapo, Charles Croll, Robert Fernie, Janice Hartgrove-Freile, Robert Hendersen, Sidney Hochman, Kendra Jeffcoat, Linda Kovacs, William Price, Dick Rasor, Bruce Rowe, Laura Sidorowicz, Robert Slotnick, David Williams, and Lonnie Yandell. It has been a pleasure working with such gifted colleagues. I want to thank Robert W. Fernie, in particular, for excellent counsel and helpful reference materials.

Sadly, this revision coincided with the loss of two outstanding psychologists, each of whom contributed to prior editions of *Introduction to Psychology*. In their dedication to students, clients, community, family, and friends, Ted L. Rosenthal and Michael Sosulski bettered many lives. These exceptional individuals will be missed by all who knew them.

The complexity of revising *Introduction to Psychology* and its supplements continues to be a formidable challenge. The Seventh Edition, more than ever, reflects the talents and hard work of many people. I am indebted to John Orr and his staff for meeting a seemingly impossible schedule. John's brilliance and dedication are evident throughout this book. Thank you, John, for a superb effort. Lee Anne Storey and Matt Thiessen deserve applause for raising the quality of the artwork in this text to new levels. Special thanks to Sheree Mattson for patient photo research, to Suzie DeFazio for meticulous copy editing, and to José Delgado for his graphics skills. I would also like to thank Denis Ralling for excellent, multifaceted editorial support. These individuals and many others at West Educational Publishing have made this text a reality.

Finally, I want to express my continuing gratitude to Clyde H. Perlee, Jr., everyone's favorite Editor in Chief, for his leadership, creativity, and friendship.

Last of all, I would like to thank my wife Sevren, whose understanding, emotional support, and countless hours of help made this book possible.

Dennis Coon

Chapter 1

Psychology: The Search for Understanding

CHAPTER PREVIEW

Why Study Psychology?

You are a universe, a collection of worlds within worlds. Your brain is possibly the most complicated and amazing device in existence. Through its action you are capable of art, music, science, philosophy, and war. Your capacities for love and compassion coexist with your potential for aggression, hatred, and . . . murder? You are the most challenging riddle ever written, a mystery at times even to yourself. You are a unique event in human history. At the same time, you are like everyone who has ever lived. Your thoughts, emotions, and actions, your behavior and conscious experience are the subject of this book.

Look around you. Newspapers, magazines, radio, and television abound with psychological information. Psychology is discussed in homes, schools, businesses, and bars. Psychology is an explosive, exciting, and ever-changing panorama of people and ideas. You can hardly call yourself "educated" without knowing something about it.

There is another reason for studying psychology. Socrates said, "Know thyself," and although we must envy those who have walked on the moon or cruised the ocean's dream-like depths, the ultimate frontier still lies close to home. Psychologist D. O. Hebb

IN THIS CHAPTER

put it this way: "What is psychology all about? Psychology is about the mind: the central issue, the great mystery, the toughest problem of all" (Hebb, 1974).

Psychology is a journey into inner space. This book is a travel guide. Psychologists can't claim to have "the answers" to all your questions. But they can show you the contours of the landscape already explored. More importantly, you may find skills in psychology that will aid you in your own search for answers. Ultimately, the answers must be your own, but studying psychology is a rich starting point.

Survey Questions

- What is psychology? What are its goals?
- How did psychology emerge as a field of knowledge?
- What are the major perspectives in psychology?
- What roles and specialties are found in psychology and related fields?
- Can psychology be applied to improve study skills and grades?
- What is critical thinking? How can it be used to identify false explanations of behavior?

Psychology: Psyche = Mind; Logos = Knowledge or Study

Question: What is psychology?

Psychology is memory, stress, therapy, love, persuasion, hypnosis, perception, death, conformity, creativity, learning, personality, aging, intelligence, sexuality, emotion, and many, many more topics. Psychology has become such an enormous and colorful beast that no short description can do it justice.

It is important to be open-minded as you begin this course. Consider it an adventure, and judge after you have seen what psychology has to offer. By the time you have read this entire book, you will begin to have an overall picture of what psychology is and what psychologists do.

The Science and Profession of Psychology

Psychology is both a **science** and a **profession.** As trained professionals, psychologists use their knowledge and skills to promote human welfare in many areas. Fields such as mental health, education, business, sports, law, and medicine make extensive use of psychological expertise (■ Fig. 1–1).

Many psychologists specialize in the skills needed to do psychotherapy, to collect and analyze data, to

■ **Fig. 1–1** *Psychologists are highly trained professionals. In addition to the psychological knowledge they possess, psychologists learn specialized skills in counseling and therapy, measurement and testing, research and experimentation, statistics, diagnosis, treatment, and many other areas.*

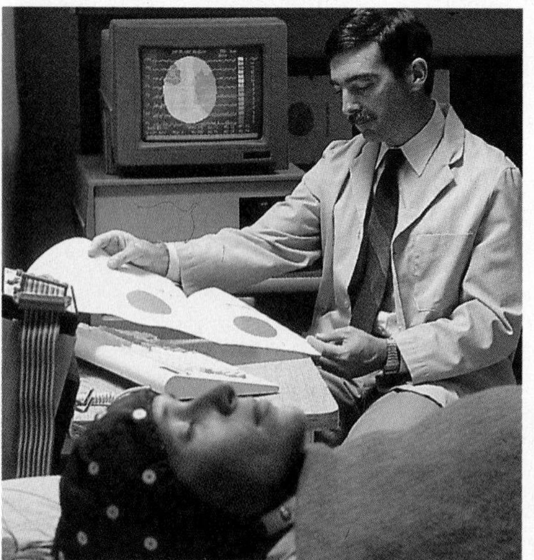

Table 1–1 Comparing Psychology with Related Sciences

Anthropology: The science of human origins, evolution, and cultures.
Biology: The science of life and living organisms: plant, animal, and human.
Psychology: The science of human and animal behavior.
Sociology: The science of the forms and functions of human groups.

administer and interpret psychological tests, to advise parents, to treat sleep disorders, to serve as expert witnesses in courts of law, and a host of other activities. Some psychologists are primarily scientists who apply their research skills to enrich human knowledge. Others are primarily practitioners, who apply psychological knowledge to practical problems. Many psychologists are both scientists and practitioners.

Defining Psychology Later in this chapter we will return to the profession of psychology. For now, let's focus on how psychological knowledge is created. As a science, **psychology** can be defined as, *"the scientific study of human and animal behavior."* (Table 1–1 will help you distinguish psychology from some related sciences.)

Question: What does behavior refer to in the definition of psychology?

Behavior Anything you do—eating, sleeping, talking, thinking, or sneezing—is a behavior. So is dreaming, gambling, taking drugs, watching TV, learning Spanish, basket weaving, or reading this book. The term *behavior* can refer to **covert** (private, internal) activities, such as thinking, as well as **overt** (visible) actions. Psychologists are interested in both visible behavior *and* hidden mental events, such as problem solving, daydreaming, or remembering (Kelly & Saklofske, 1994).

Much of our overt behavior can be studied by direct observation. But how do we study mental activities? Often it takes skillful detective work to *deduce* what is happening internally from what can be observed directly. For example, try answering these questions: Is a horse bigger than a mouse? Is a collie bigger than a German shepherd?

If you are like most people, you answered the first question faster than the second. Why? Most people report that they form mental images of the animals to compare their sizes. A slower answer, therefore, suggests that it is more difficult to compare mental images that are similar in size (Moyer & Bayer, 1976). Although we couldn't actually observe thinking, we were able to learn something interesting about it just the same. When indirect observations consistently point to a conclusion, we can be reasonably certain it is correct.

Empiricism

Question: It seems that psychologists try to be objective in their observations. Is that correct?

Yes. Psychologists are keenly aware that opinions, or claims made by an "authority," may be wrong. They therefore have a special respect for **empirical evidence,** which is information gained from direct observation and measurement. Whenever possible, psychologists settle disputes by collecting **data** (observed facts) that can be verified by two or more independent observers (Kimble, 1989).

Gathering data allows psychologists to compare what each has observed and draw accurate conclusions. Would you say it's true, for instance, that "you can't teach an old dog new tricks"? Why argue about it? A psychologist would get 10 "new" dogs, 10 "used" dogs, and 10 "old" dogs and then try to teach them all new tricks to find out!

The heart of the empirical attitude is summarized by the phrase, "Let's take a look" (Stanovich, 1992). Here's an example: Have you ever wondered if drivers become more hostile and aggressive when the weather gets hot and uncomfortable? Psychologists Douglas Kenrick and Steven MacFarlane (1986) decided to collect some data to investigate. Kenrick and MacFarlane arranged to have a car parked at a green light in a one-lane intersection, in Phoenix, Arizona, where temperatures ranged from 88° to 116°. Then they recorded the number of times other drivers honked at the stalled car, and how long they honked.

The results are shown in Figure 1–2. As you can see, higher temperatures were clearly linked to an increase in the amount of time spent leaning on the horn (which may be why cars come equipped with horns and not cannons). While these findings are not surprising, they do add to our understanding of links between discomfort and aggression.

An empirical approach seems natural in fields like biology and physics. Yet, in psychology, we are often

Psychology The scientific study of human and animal behavior.

Covert behavior A response that is hidden from view.

Overt behavior A response that is directly observable.

Empirical evidence Information gained by direct observation.

Data Observed facts or evidence.

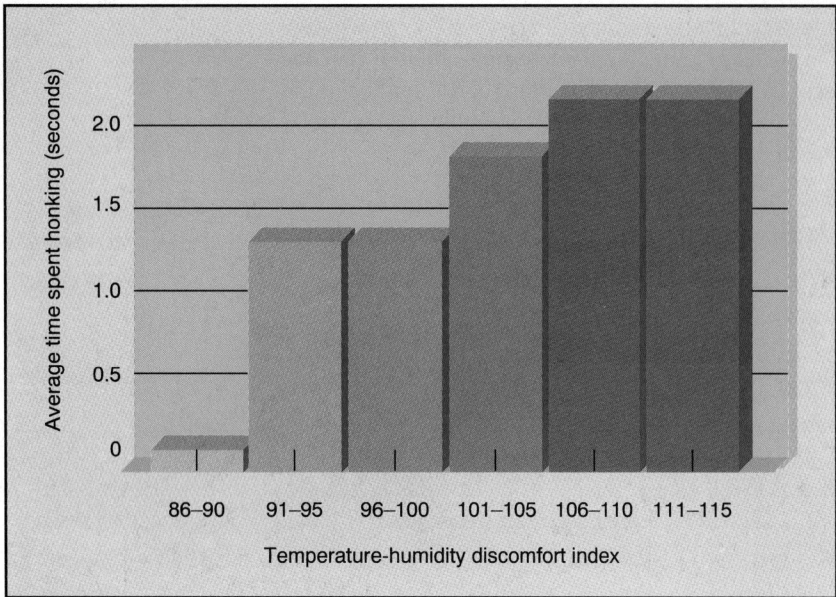

■ **Fig. 1–2** *Results of an empirical study. The graph shows that horn honking by frustrated motorists becomes more likely as air temperature increases. This suggests that physical discomfort is associated with interpersonal hostility. Riots and assaults also increase during hot weather. Here we see a steady rise in aggression as temperatures go higher. However, research done by other psychologists has shown that hostile actions that require physical exertion, such as a fist fight, may become* less *likely at very high temperatures. (Data from Kenrick & MacFarlane, 1986.)*

Scientific observation Orderly observation designed to answer questions about the world.

Research method A systematic procedure for answering scientific questions.

tempted to accept what seems reasonable, rather than what *is*. For example, see if you can tell, from your own experience or common sense, which of the following statements are true. Then we will compare your answers with answers arrived at empirically.

Are These Ideas True or False?

1. If you happened to step on a nail, you would feel it instantly. True or false? (Chapter 3)
2. A one-eyed man could not land an airplane. True or false? (Chapter 5)
3. The apparent size of the moon is greatly magnified by the atmosphere when the moon is low in the sky. True or false? (Chapter 5)
4. When hypnotized, witnesses to crimes can be made to have perfect memory of what they saw. True or false? (Chapter 8)
5. Brain activity almost ceases at various times during sleep. True or false? (Chapter 6)
6. Punishment is the most effective way to reinforce the learning of new habits. True or false? (Chapter 7)
7. All memories are permanent, if only there were some way to retrieve them. True or false? (Chapter 8)
8. People who have high IQs are also usually highly creative. True or false? (Chapter 9)
9. The lie detector (polygraph) is highly accurate at identifying attempts to deceive. True or false? (Chapter 10)
10. Stress is almost always bad for you. True or false? (Chapter 11)
11. Intelligence is completely inherited from one's parents. True or false? (Chapter 14)
12. Those who threaten suicide rarely actually commit suicide. True or false? (Chapter 17)
13. Schizophrenics have two or more distinct personalities. True or false? (Chapter 17)
14. If your car breaks down, you are more likely to get help from a passerby on a busy highway than on a lightly traveled country road. True or false? (Chapter 21)

Scoring this quiz is easy. Empirical research has shown that all of the statements are *false*. (To find out why, you may want to look ahead at the chapters cited in parentheses.) If you missed some questions, don't despair. The point is simply this: Psychology became a science when psychologists began to do experiments, make observations, and seek evidence, and you will become a better observer of human behavior if you do the same (■ Fig. 1–3).

Scientific Observation Empiricism alone is not enough to make a science. True scientific observation must also be *systematic*. **Scientific observation** is structured so that it reveals something about the underlying nature of behavior (Stanovich, 1992). To return to an earlier example, little would be gained if you drove around a city and made haphazard observations of aggressive horn honking. To be scientific, observations must be carefully planned and recorded. In the next chapter we will look more closely at how this is done.

Question: I've heard that psychology isn't scientific. You have said that it is. Is it?

Many fields, such as history, law, art, and business are interested in human behavior. What sets psychology apart is that it applies the scientific method to questions about behavior. This is also what separates scientific psychology from the "pop" psychology often found in commercial books and magazines.

For various reasons, the study of certain topics in psychology is still difficult. Sometimes, psychologists are unable to answer questions because of ethical or practical concerns. More often, lack of a suitable research method causes questions to go unanswered. A **research method** is a systematic procedure for answering scientific questions. For example, at one time the reports of people who say they never dream had to be considered accurate. But with an advance in technology, the EEG (electroencephalograph, or brain-wave machine) was developed. The EEG provides a reliable method for telling when a person is dreaming. People who "never dream," it turns out,

■ **Fig. 1–3** *The variety and complexity of human behavior make psychological investigation challenging. How would you explain the behaviors shown here?*

dream frequently. They also vividly remember their dreams when awakened during one. Through use of the EEG, the study of dreaming has become scientific (■ Fig. 1–4). Today, psychologists continue to find new ways to answer questions about behavior. As they do, they add to psychology's highly useful body of knowledge.

Animals and Psychology

You may have wondered why animals were mentioned in our definition of psychology. It may surprise you to learn that as a group, psychologists are interested in natural laws governing the behavior of *any* living creature—from flatworms to humans. Indeed, specialists known as comparative psychologists may spend their

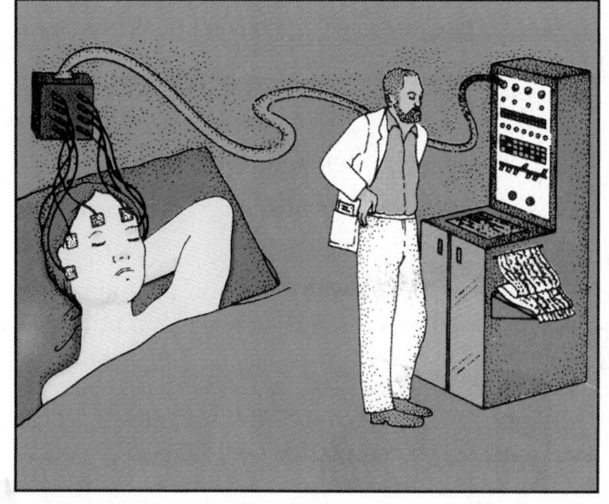

■ **Fig. 1–4** *The scientific study of dreaming was made possible by use of the EEG, a device that records the tiny electrical potentials generated by the brain of a sleeping subject. The EEG converts these electrical potentials to a written record of brain activity. Certain shifts in brain activity, coupled with the presence of rapid eye movements, are strongly related to dreaming. (See Chapter 6 for more information.)*

■ **Fig. 1–5** *Some of the most interesting research with animals has focused on attempts to teach primates to communicate using sign language. (See Chapter 9 for more information.) The risk of anthropomorphizing animals in such research is very high.*

Comparative psychology Study of the behavior of different species, especially animals.

Anthropomorphic fallacy Falsely attributing human thoughts, feelings, or motives to animals.

Animal model An animal used to discover principles that may apply to humans.

entire careers studying rats, cats, dogs, turtles, chimpanzees, or other animals (■ Fig. 1–5). **Comparative psychology** is the study of similarities and differences in the behavior of different species, especially animals.

A subtle trap that must be avoided in animal studies is called the **anthropomorphic fallacy** (AN-thro-po-MORE-fik). This is the error of attributing human thoughts, feelings, or motives to animals.

Question: Why is it risky to attribute motives or emotions to animals?

The temptation to assume that an animal is "angry," "jealous," "bored," or "guilty" can be strong, but it often leads to false conclusions. As an example, let's say I observe gorillas in the wild (where food is plentiful) and conclude that by nature gorillas are not very "greedy." You, on the other hand, place two hungry gorillas in a cage with a banana, stand back to watch the action, and conclude that gorillas are in fact very "greedy." Actually, all we have observed is that competition for food is related to the amount of food available. Allowing the human concept of greed into the picture just clouds our understanding of gorilla behavior. Attributing mischievous motives to a "stubborn" car or computer is a similar thinking error.

Question: Are comparative psychologists the only ones who study animals?

No. Other research psychologists also use animals in experiments. Usually this is done to discover principles that help solve human problems. Studies of topics as diverse as obesity, memory, stress, psychosis, therapy, and aging have been enriched by animal research. More importantly, animals sometimes serve as *models* that provide the only information available on a subject. Of course this has nothing to do with animal fashions: An **animal model** is one whose behavior is used to discover principles that may apply to human behavior. For instance, most of what is known about the brain is based on animal research.

Psychology also benefits animals. Behavioral research has provided ways to avoid the killing of animals, such as coyotes, crows, or deer, that destroy crops or livestock. Likewise, the successful care of endangered species in zoos relies on behavioral research (Miller, 1985). For these and other reasons, animals are very much a part of psychology. In fact, a government panel (which included animal welfare advocates) concluded that in psychology there is often no substitute for ethically done animal research (Fisher, 1986). (The animal rights movement and the ethics of animal research are discussed in the "Exploration" section of Chapter 2.)

Psychology's Goals

What do psychologists hope to achieve? In general, the goals of psychology are to **describe, understand, predict,** and **control** behavior. Beyond this, psychology's ultimate goal is to gather knowledge to benefit humanity (Kimble, 1989).

Description What do psychology's goals mean in practice? Assume that we would like to answer the following questions: What happens when a person has an injury on the right side of the brain? Is there more than one type of memory? How does creative problem solving differ from ordinary thinking? Do autistic children react differently to their parents than to other adults? The answer to each question requires a careful description of behavior, the first goal of psychology. **Description,** or naming and classifying, typically is based on making a detailed record of behavior.

Question: But a description doesn't explain anything, does it?

Right. Useful knowledge begins with accurate description, but descriptions fail to answer the important "why" questions. *Why* do more women attempt suicide, and *why* do more men complete it? *Why* are people more aggressive when they are uncomfortable? *Why* are bystanders often unwilling to help in an emergency?

Understanding Psychology's second goal, **understanding** behavior, is met when we can explain why an event occurs. Understanding usually means that we can state the causes of a behavior. Take the last question as an example. Research on "bystander apathy" has shown that people often fail to help when *other* possible helpers are nearby. Why? Because a "diffusion of responsibility" occurs, so that no one person feels required to pitch in. Generally, the larger the number of potential helpers present, the less likely it is that help will be given (Darley & Latané, 1968). Now we can explain a perplexing problem. (See Chapter 21 for more details.)

Prediction Prediction is psychology's third goal. **Prediction** is the ability to accurately forecast behavior. Notice that the explanation for bystander apathy makes a prediction about the chances of getting help. Anyone who has been stranded by car trouble on a busy freeway will recognize the accuracy of this prediction. Behavioral predictions are often quite useful. For example, psychological research predicts that you will suffer less jet lag if you fly east early in the day and west late in the day. (See Chapter 10 to learn why.) Prediction is especially important in **psychometrics**. The word *psychometrics* means mental measurement. Experts in this area use various tests to predict such things as success in school, work, or a career (■ Fig. 1–6).

Question: Description, explanation, and prediction seem reasonable, but is control a valid goal for psychology?

Control Psychology's most misunderstood goal is control, probably because it sounds like a threat to personal freedom. However, **control** simply means altering conditions that influence behavior in predictable ways. If a psychologist suggests changes in a classroom that help children learn better, the psychologist has exerted control. If the psychologist helps a person overcome a crippling fear of heights, control is involved. Control is also present if behavioral research is used to design an aircraft instrument panel that reduces pilot errors. (The U.S. Federal Aviation Administration estimates that 65 percent of all aircraft accidents are due to human error.)

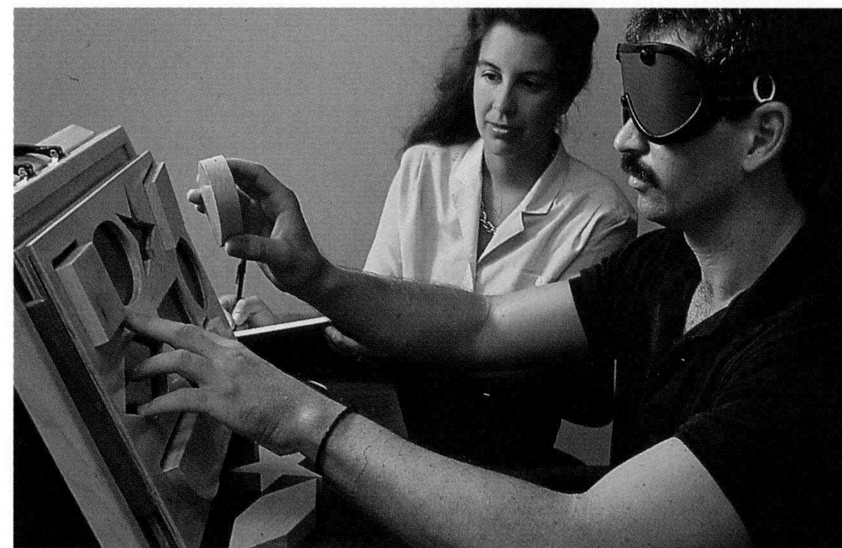

■ **Fig. 1–6** *Some psychologists specialize in administering, scoring, and interpreting psychological tests, such as tests of intelligence, creativity, personality, or aptitude.*

Clearly, psychology can provide the means for changing behavior. But, as is true of knowledge in other areas, psychological principles must be used wisely and humanely (Kipnis, 1987).

In summary, psychology's goals are a natural outgrowth of our desire to understand behavior. For the many topics studied in psychology, the goals boil down to asking:

- What is the nature of this behavior? (description)
- Why does it occur? (explanation)
- Can we predict when it will occur? (prediction)
- What conditions influence or affect it? (control)

Psychometrics Mental measurement or testing.

Learning Check

To improve your memory of this chapter, see if you can answer these questions. If you miss any, skim over the preceding material before continuing, to make sure you understand what you have just read.

1. Psychology is the ______________ study of the ______________ of humans and animals.
2. Information gained through direct observation and measurement is called ______________ evidence.
3. The ______________ fallacy involves attributing human feelings and motives to animals. It is of special concern for ______________ psychologists.
4. Which of the following questions relates most directly to the goal of *understanding* behavior?
   a. Do the scores of men and women differ on tests of thinking abilities?
   b. Why does a blow to the head cause memory loss?
   c. Will productivity in a business office increase if room temperature is raised or lowered?
   d. What percentage of college students suffer from test anxiety?
5. All sciences are interested in the control of the phenomena they study. T or F?

Critical Thinking

Answers: 1. scientific, behavior 2. empirical 3. anthropomorphic, comparative 4. *b* 5. F (Astronomy and archaeology are examples of sciences that do not share psychology's fourth goal.)

■ Fig. 1–7 *Wilhelm Wundt, 1832–1920.*

Philosophy The study of knowledge, reality, and human nature.

Stimulus Any physical energy sensed by an organism.

Introspection To look within; to examine one's own thoughts, feelings, or sensations.

Experimental self-observation Trained introspection combined with objective measurement.

A Brief History of Psychology—Psychology's Family Album

Psychology has a long past but a short history. Psychology's past is centuries old because psychology is an outgrowth of **philosophy,** the study of knowledge, reality, and human nature. In contrast, the history of modern psychology began only about 100 years ago. As sciences go, psychology is the new kid on the block: Easily 9 out of 10 persons to ever work in the field are alive today. Of course, to some students this history is still "not short enough"! Yet, the ideas in psychology's past are intimately tied to the present. To understand where psychology is now, let's take a brief look at its short history.

Into the Lab Psychology's history as a separate science began in 1879 in Leipzig, Germany. There, the "father of psychology," **Wilhelm Wundt** (VILL-helm Voont), created the first psychological laboratory so that he could study *conscious experience.* How, he wondered, are sensations, images, and feelings formed? To find out, Wundt observed and carefully measured *stimuli* of various kinds (lights, sounds, weights). A **stimulus** is any physical energy that has some effect on an organism and that evokes a response (stimulus: singular; stimuli [STIM-you-lie]: plural). Wundt then used **introspection,** or "looking inward," to probe his reactions to various stimuli.

If you stop reading for a moment, and examine your own thoughts, feelings, and sensations, you will have used introspection. Wundt called his approach **experimental self-observation.** It combined *trained* introspection with objective measurement (Blumenthal, 1979). Over the years, he used this method to study vision, hearing, taste, touch, reaction time, memory, feelings, time perception, and many other subjects.

Experimental self-observation was a highly developed skill, much like the skill needed to be a professional wine taster. Wundt's subjects had to make at least 10,000 practice observations before they were allowed to take part in a real experiment (Lieberman, 1979). By using such careful observation and measurement, Wundt got psychology off to a good start (⬬ Table 1–2).

⬬ Table 1–2 The Early Development of Psychology

Approximate Origin	Date	Notable Events
Experimental psychology	1875	■ First psychology course offered by William James
	1878	■ First American Ph.D. in psychology awarded
	1879	■ Wilhelm Wundt establishes first psychology laboratory in Germany
	1883	■ First American psychology lab founded at Johns Hopkins University
	1886	■ First American psychology textbook published by John Dewey
Structuralism	1898	■ Edward Titchener advances psychology based on introspection
Functionalism	1890	■ James publishes *Principles of Psychology*
	1892	■ American Psychological Association founded
Psychoanalytic psychology	1895	■ Sigmund Freud publishes first studies
	1900	■ Freud publishes *The Interpretation of Dreams*
Behaviorism	1906	■ Ivan Pavlov reports his research on conditioning
	1913	■ John Watson presents behavioristic view
Gestalt psychology	1912	■ Max Wertheimer and others advance Gestalt viewpoint
Neo-Freudianism	1914	■ Carl Jung breaks with Freud

Structuralism

Wundt's ideas were carried to the United States by one of his students, a man named Edward B. Titchener (TICH-in-er). In America, Wundt's ideas were called **structuralism** because they dealt with the structure of mental life. The structuralists hoped to develop a sort of "mental chemistry" by *analyzing* experience into basic "elements" or "building blocks."

Question: How could they do that? You can't analyze experience like you can a chemical compound, can you?

Perhaps not, but the structuralists tried, mostly by using introspection. In this approach, a subject might heft an apple and then decide that he or she had experienced the elements "hue" (color), "roundness," and "weight." Another example of the kind of question that might have interested a structuralist is, What basic tastes mix together to create complex flavors as different as liver, lime, bacon, or burnt-almond fudge?

It soon became clear that introspection was a poor way to answer many questions. The biggest problem was that structuralists could only study the contents of their own minds. As a result, they frequently *disagreed.* And when they did, there was no way of settling differences. If two researchers came up with different lists of basic taste sensations, for example, who was to say which was right? Despite such limitations, "looking inward" still has a role in psychology. The study of hypnosis, meditation, drug effects, problem solving, and many other topics would be incomplete if people did not describe their private experiences.

Functionalism

William James, an American psychologist, broadened psychology to include animal behavior, religious experience, abnormal behavior, and a number of other interesting topics (■ Fig. 1–8). James' first book, *Principles of Psychology* (1890), helped establish psychology as a serious discipline in colleges and universities. It was so brilliant that it is still in print today.

The term **functionalism** comes from an interest in how the mind functions to adapt us to our environment. To James, consciousness was an ever-changing *stream* or *flow* of images and sensations—not a set of lifeless building blocks, as the structuralists claimed.

The functionalists were strongly influenced by Charles Darwin. According to Darwin, creatures evolve, through natural selection, in ways that favor their survival. The principle of **natural selection** states that evolution favors plants and animals best suited to their living conditions. Because of natural selection, features that help animals adapt to their environments are retained in evolution. Similarly, the functionalists wanted to find out how thought, perception, habits, and emotions aid human adaptation. In short, they wanted to study the mind *in use.*

■ **Fig. 1–8** *William James, 1842–1910.*

■ **Fig. 1–9** *John B. Watson, 1878–1958.*

Question: What effect did functionalism have on modern psychology?

Functionalism brought the study of animals into psychology by linking human and animal adaptation. It also aided the growth of **educational psychology,** the study of learning, teaching, and related topics. Functionalists stressed that learning makes us more adaptable, and they urged psychologists to help improve education. Today, educational psychologists develop tests and do research on classroom dynamics, teaching styles, and learning. The rise of industrial-organizational psychology was also spurred by Functionalism. **Industrial-organizational psychology** is the application of psychology to work, especially to personnel selection, human relations, and machine design. (See Chapter 22.)

Behaviorism: Stimulus-Response (S-R) Psychology

Functionalism was soon challenged by a new viewpoint called **behaviorism.** Behaviorist John B. Watson objected to defining psychology as the study of the "mind" or "conscious experience" (■ Fig. 1–9). He also considered introspection unscientific. Watson found that he could study animal behavior even though he couldn't ask animals questions, or know what they were thinking. He simply observed the relationship between **stimuli** (events in the environment) and an animal's **responses.** A response is any muscular action, glandular activity, or other identifiable behavior. Why not, he argued, apply the same objectivity to the study of humans?

Structuralism School of psychology that analyzed private experiences into their basic elements.

Functionalism School of psychology concerned with how the mind helps us adapt to our environment.

Natural selection Darwin's theory that evolution favors plants and animals best suited to their living conditions.

Educational psychology The study of learning, teaching, and related topics.

Industrial-organizational psychology The psychology of work and organizations.

Behaviorism The study of overt, observable behavior.

Response Any muscular action, glandular activity, or other identifiable behavior.

Conditioned response A reflex response linked to a new stimulus through learning.

Watson soon adopted Russian physiologist Ivan Pavlov's (ee-VAHN PAV-lahv) **conditioned response** concept to explain most behavior. (A conditioned response is a learned reaction to a particular stimulus.) Watson's enthusiasm for conditioning obviously had reached extremes when he proclaimed, "Give me a dozen healthy infants, well-formed, and my own special world to bring them up in and I'll guarantee to take any one at random and train him to become any type of specialist I might select—doctor, lawyer, artist, merchant-chief, and yes, beggarman and thief" (Watson, 1913).

Question: Would most psychologists agree with Watson's claim?

Today, most would probably consider it an overstatement. Just the same, behaviorism has had a profound effect on modern psychology. One of the best-known modern behaviorists, B. F. Skinner (1904–1990), said, "In order to understand human behavior we must take into account what the environment does to an organism before and after it responds. Behavior is shaped and maintained by its consequences" (Skinner, 1971). Highlight 1–1 delves further into Skinner's views.

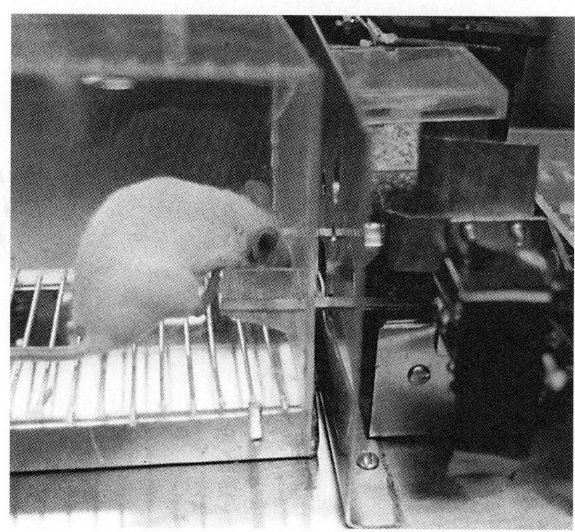

■ **Fig. 1–11** *The Skinner Box is used to study learning in simplified animal experiments.*

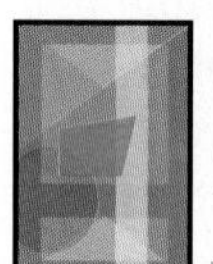

HIGHLIGHT 1–1

A Closer Look At

B. F. Skinner (1904–1990), American Behaviorist

■ **Fig. 1–10**

Burrhus Frederic Skinner, who died in 1990 at age 86, was one of the most fascinating and controversial psychologists of the 20th Century. Skinner believed that our behavior is primarily controlled by the environment, especially by rewards, or positive reinforcers.

To study learning, Skinner created his famous "Skinner Box" (■ Fig. 1–11). This device allowed Skinner to present stimuli to laboratory animals and to record changes in a specific response (see Chapter 7, "Operant Conditioning"). Many of Skinner's ideas grew out of work with rats and pigeons. Nevertheless, he maintained that the same laws of behavior apply to all organisms, including humans.

In his most controversial book, *Beyond Freedom and Dignity,* Skinner claimed that society can no longer afford to rely on the human conceit we call "free will." Instead, he said, we need a "designed culture" in which behavior is guided into desirable patterns by positive reinforcement. (Contrary to common belief, Skinner disliked the use of punishment.) It is essential, he said, to change our behavior before overpopulation, pollution, or nuclear war shatters humanity. As Skinner put it, "We don't need to destroy our environment or escape from it; we need to redesign it." Too often, he believed, we are seduced by misguided rewards into actions that are ultimately destructive.

Among the general public, B. F. Skinner was perhaps best known as the man who taught pigeons to play table tennis (see Chapter 7), as the inventor of teaching machines, and as the creator of a mechanical "baby tender" that looked suspiciously like a big Skinner Box. For 2½ years, Skinner's own daughter Deborah spent several hours a day in the baby tender—a crib-sized chamber with warm filtered air, sound-absorbing walls, special toys, and a large window on one side. "How dehumanizing!" said the critics. But contrary to news reports, Deborah was frequently taken out of the box for cuddling and play. As an adult, she said, "I think I was a very happy baby. Most of the criticisms of the box are by people who don't understand what it was." The same is true of many criticisms of Skinner, which are often based on a misunderstanding of his ideas (DeBell & Harless, 1992).

Of course, not all critics have misunderstood Skinner's views. The behaviorist emphasis on visible behavior clearly tends to ignore thought and private experience. Skinner (1990) steadfastly held that the mind cannot be studied scientifically—which led some critics to the tongue-in-cheek charge that Skinnerian psychology had "lost consciousness." A broader view, called **cognitive behaviorism,** has answered many such criticisms by combining thinking *and* environmental control to explain behavior. Nevertheless, strict behaviorism is alive and well and has many advocates.

Most psychologists would probably agree with the basic idea that human behavior is greatly influenced by learning. Behaviorists deserve credit for discovering much of what we know about learning, conditioning, and the proper use of reward and punishment. A system called **behavior modification** is another valuable product of behaviorism. In behavior modification, learning principles are used to change human behavior, especially problem behaviors such as overeating, phobias, or temper tantrums. (See Chapter 18 for more information.)

Gestalt Psychology

Imagine for a moment that you have just heard a familiar tune, such as "Yankee Doodle," played on a tuba. Next it is played on a high-pitched violin. Even though none of the original sounds are used, the melody will still be recognizable as long as the *relationship* between the notes is the same. Now, what if the original notes were played in the correct order, but at a rate of one per hour? What would we have? Nothing. The separated notes would no longer be a melody. Perceptually, the melody is somehow more than the sum of its parts. It was observations such as this that launched the **Gestalt** school of thought in psychology. Gestalt psychology emphasizes the study of thinking, learning, and perception in whole units, not by analysis into parts.

The German word Gestalt (geh-SHTALT) means "form," "pattern," or "whole." The Gestalt viewpoint was first advanced by the German psychologist Max Wertheimer (VERT-hi-mer) (■ Fig. 1–12). It is a mistake, he said, to analyze psychological events into pieces, or "elements," as the structuralists did. Instead, the Gestaltists tried to study experiences as *wholes.* Their slogan was, "The whole is greater than the sum of its parts" (■ Fig. 1–13).

■ **Fig. 1–12** *Max Wertheimer, 1880–1941.*

As with a melody, many other experiences resist analysis into parts or pieces. For this reason, the Gestalt viewpoint remains influential in the study of

Cognitive behaviorism A system that combines behavioral principles with cognition (thinking, anticipation).

Behavior modification Use of learning principles to change behavior.

Gestalt psychology The study of thinking, learning, and perception in whole units.

■ **Fig. 1–13** *The design you see here is entirely made up of the two elements shown below it. If you stare at the design for a moment, you should quickly see that as a whole it contains patterns and complexities that greatly exceed the sum of its parts.*

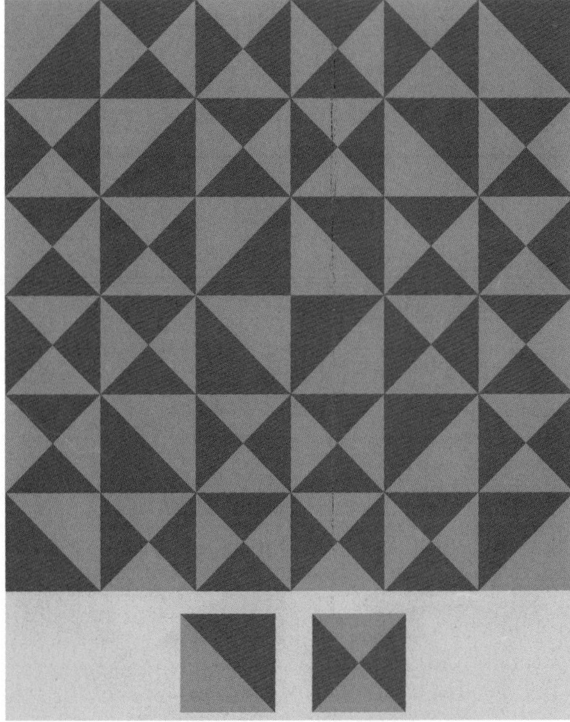

perception and personality. It has also given rise to a type of psychotherapy. If you are curious about what Gestalt therapy is like, look ahead to Chapter 18.

Question: Were all the early psychologists men? So far, no women have been mentioned.

For the most part, men dominated science and education at the turn of the century. Nevertheless, women were active in psychology from its beginning. Highlight 1–2 gives some details.

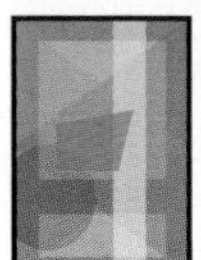

HIGHLIGHT 1–2

Cultural Diversity

Women in Psychology

Histories of psychology abound in "forefathers" but seldom mention women. This situation exists largely because men dominated academic life in the late 1800s. Women, in fact, were actively discouraged from seeking advanced degrees (Bohan, 1990). Even so, by 1906 in America about 1 psychologist in every 10 was a woman. Who were these "foremothers" of psychology? Three who became well known in the field were Mary Calkins, Christine Ladd-Franklin, and Margaret Washburn. Mary Calkins is known for her valuable research on memory. Christine Ladd-Franklin advanced a theory of color vision. And Margaret Washburn wrote an influential textbook on animal behavior, titled *The Animal Mind* (1908).

Christine Ladd-Franklin was the first American woman to complete requirements for the doctorate in psychology, in 1882. However, her degree was not awarded because of a university policy that denied women the doctorate. The first woman to be awarded a Ph.D. in psychology was Margaret Washburn, in 1894. Over the next 15 years many more women followed Washburn's pioneering lead.

Today, the number of males and females receiving doctoral degrees in psychology is roughly equal. (New female Ph.D.s exceeded males 58 percent to 42 percent in 1990.) And in recent years, the number of female psychology graduates at the bachelor's level has far exceeded the number of male psychology graduates. Clearly, psychology has become a profession that is fully open to both men and women. (Sources: Furumoto & Scarborough, 1986; Howard et al., 1986; Metzner et al., 1994; Madigan & O'Hara, 1992.)

■ **Fig. 1–14** *Mary Calkins, 1863–1930.*

■ **Fig. 1–15** *Christine Ladd-Franklin, 1847–1930.*

■ **Fig. 1–16** *Margaret Washburn, 1871–1939.*

Psychodynamic Psychology

As the mainstream of psychology grew more objective and scientific, an Austrian physician named Sigmund Freud was developing his own theory of behavior (■ Fig. 1–17). Freud's point of departure was his belief that mental life is like an iceberg: only a small portion is exposed to view. According to Freud, our behavior is influenced by vast areas of **unconscious** thoughts,

■ **Fig. 1–17** *Sigmund Freud, 1856–1939.*

impulses, and desires, which cannot be known directly. This idea added a new dimension not only to psychology, but to art, literature, and history as well.

Freud theorized that many unconscious thoughts are of a threatening, sexual, or aggressive nature. Hence, they are *repressed* (actively held out of awareness). But sometimes, he said, they are revealed by dreams, emotions, or slips of the tongue. ("Freudian slips" are often humorous, as when a student who is tardy for class says, "I'm sorry I couldn't get here any later.") Freud also insisted that all thoughts, emotions, and actions are *determined* (nothing is an accident). He brought new awareness of the importance of childhood for later personality development ("The child is father to the man"). Most of all, perhaps, Freud is best known for creating a method of psychotherapy called **psychoanalysis,** which is used to explore the unconscious roots of emotional problems (see Chapter 18).

Freud had not held sway for very long before some of his students began to break away from him. These **neo-Freudians** (*neo* means "new" or "recent") accepted the broad features of Freud's theory but modified it to fit their own concepts. Some well-known neo-Freudians are Alfred Adler, Anna Freud (Freud's daughter), Karen Horney (HORN-eye), Carl Jung (yoong), and Otto Rank (rahnk).

Today, Freud's ideas have been altered, revised, and adapted to the point that few strictly psychoanalytic psychologists are left. However, Freud's legacy is still evident in various psychodynamic approaches to psychology. **Psychodynamic theories** focus on the internal motives, conflicts, and unconscious forces that influence our behavior.

Humanistic Psychology

A fairly recent development in psychology is a point of view known as **humanism.** Humanism is sometimes called the "third force" in psychology. (Psychodynamic psychology and behaviorism are the other two.) Humanistic psychologists focus on human experience, problems, potentials, and ideals.

Question: How is the humanistic approach different from others?

Psychologists Carl Rogers, Abraham Maslow, and others developed humanistic psychology as a reply to the negativity they saw in other views (■ Fig. 1–18). Humanists reject the Freudian idea that personality is ruled by unconscious forces. They are also uncomfortable with the behavioristic idea that we are controlled by the environment. Both these views show a strong undercurrent of **determinism,** the idea that behavior is caused by forces beyond our control. In contrast, the humanists stress **free will,** the human ability to freely make choices. Humanists do admit that past experiences affect personality. However, they also believe that people can freely *choose* to live more creative, meaningful, and satisfying lives.

■ **Fig. 1–18** *Abraham Maslow, 1908–1970.*

Humanists helped stimulate interest in needs for love, self-esteem, belonging, self-expression, creativity, and spirituality. Such needs, they believe, are as important as our biological needs for food and water. For example, newborn infants deprived of human love and emotional warmth may die just as surely as they would if deprived of food.

Question: How scientific is the humanistic approach?

Humanists collect data and seek evidence to support their ideas, but for the most part they tend to be less interested in attempts to treat psychology as an objective, behavioral science. Instead, they stress the importance of such *subjective* factors as one's self-image, self-evaluation, and frame of reference.

Self-image refers to your total perception of yourself, including images of your body, personality, and abilities. **Self-evaluation** consists of positive and negative feelings you hold toward yourself. The mental

Unconscious Contents of the mind that are outside direct awareness.

Psychoanalysis A Freudian approach to psychotherapy that explores unconscious conflicts.

Neo-Freudian A theorist who accepts the broad features of Freud's theory but has revised parts of it.

Psychodynamic theory Any theory that emphasizes internal conflicts, motives, and unconscious forces.

Humanism The study of human experience, problems, potentials, and ideals.

Determinism The doctrine that all behavior has prior causes.

Free will The doctrine that humans are capable of freely making choices.

Self-image Total perception of one's body, personality, and capabilities.

Self-evaluation Positive and negative feelings about oneself.

Frame of reference A mental or emotional perspective used for evaluating events.

Self-actualization The on-going process of fully developing one's potentials.

Eclectic Selected from many sources.

Biopsychology The study of biological processes as they relate to behavior.

Cognitive psychology The study of human thinking, knowing, understanding, and information processing.

and emotional perspective you use to judge events is your **frame of reference.** As you can see from these terms, humanists seek to understand how people perceive themselves and experience the world.

A unique feature of the humanistic approach is Maslow's description of **self-actualization.** Self-actualization is the process of developing one's potential fully and becoming the best person one can become. According to the humanists, everyone has this potential. The humanists seek ways to allow it to emerge. (Return to Table 1–2 for a summary of psychology's early development.)

Psychology Today

At one time, schools of thought in psychology were almost like political parties. Loyalty to each view was fierce, and clashes were common. Today, many viewpoints, such as functionalism and Gestalt psychology, have been incorporated into newer, broader perspectives. Also, some early schools of thought, such as structuralism, have disappeared entirely. Certainly, loyalties and specialties still exist. But many psychologists now are **eclectic** (ek-LEK-tik: drawing from many sources) and embrace a variety of theoretical views. Even so, five major perspectives are evident in modern psychology. These are the **behavioristic, humanistic,** and **psychodynamic** views, plus the increasingly important **cognitive** and **biopsychological** perspectives (Table 1–3).

The value of biological approaches for understanding behavior has risen dramatically in recent years. **Biopsychologists** believe that eventually we will be able to explain all behavior in terms of physical mechanisms, such as brain physiology and genetics. This optimism is based on exciting new knowledge about how the brain works and how it relates to thought, feelings, perception, abnormal behavior, and other important topics.

A similar trend is occurring in **cognitive psychology.** *Cognition* means "thinking" or "knowing." Cognitive psychologists study thoughts, expectations, language, perception, problem solving, consciousness, creativity, and other mental processes. Some of these topics were neglected for so many years that psychology can be said to have recently "regained consciousness." Computer models of human thinking have been especially important in spurring recent advances in cognitive psychology.

Each of the five major perspectives in psychology adds to our understanding of human behavior. Consider, for example, a student who has become deeply depressed during her first year at college. Marcia's grades have fallen, she spends much of her time sleeping, and she barely speaks to other students. Let's see what each viewpoint might say about Marcia's depression.

Table 1–3 Five Ways to Look at Behavior

Psychodynamic View
Key Idea: *Behavior is directed by forces within one's personality which are often hidden or unconscious.*
Emphasizes internal impulses, desires, and conflicts—especially those that are unconscious; views behavior as the result of clashing forces within personality; somewhat negative, pessimistic view of human nature.
Behavioristic View
Key Idea: *Behavior is shaped and controlled by one's environment.*
Emphasizes the study of observable behavior and the effects of learning; stresses the influence of external rewards and punishments; neutral, scientific, somewhat mechanistic view of human nature.
Humanistic View
Key Idea: *Behavior is guided by one's self-image, by subjective perceptions of the world, and by needs for personal growth.*
Focuses on subjective, conscious experience, human problems, potentials, and ideals; emphasizes self-image and self-actualization to explain behavior; positive, philosophical view of human nature.
Biopsychological View
Key Idea: *Human and animal behavior is the result of internal physical, chemical, and biological processes.*
Seeks to explain behavior through activity of the brain and nervous system, physiology, genetics, the endocrine system, biochemistry, and evolution; neutral, reductionistic, mechanistic view of human nature.
Cognitive View
Key Idea: *Much human behavior can be understood in terms of the mental processing of information.*
Concerned with thinking, knowing, perception, understanding, memory, decision making, and judgment; explains behavior in terms of information processing; neutral, somewhat computer-like view of human nature.

Psychodynamic psychologist: Because depression is often related to loss, I am interested in the fact that Marcia broke up with her boyfriend shortly before she became depressed. It is possible that her depression is related to feelings of loss, anger, and rejection that she has unconsciously turned inward as self-blame and self-hate.

Behaviorist: I consider it significant that Marcia's grades were mediocre before her depression began, and that they have dropped further. When rewards, such as grades, affection, friendship, or approval are withdrawn, studying and other productive activities can grind to a halt. As Marcia became depressed, her behavior may have changed in ways that made it even less likely that she would be rewarded with successes, praise, and affection.

Humanistic psychologist: Because Marcia got good grades in high school, she may have been unprepared for the greater difficulty of college classes. If viewing herself as an intelligent and competent person is an important part of her self-image, she may be threatened by her poor performance. The break-up with her boyfriend could be a similar threat. I believe that she may be feeling depressed, vulnerable, and confused because of such threats to her self-image and self-esteem.

Biopsychologist: Heredity can influence whether a person is prone to depression. I would like to know if there is a history of depression in Marcia's family. Also, depression can be caused by changes in brain chemistry, regardless of a person's life circumstances. Marcia might have a medical problem that needs treatment.

Cognitive psychologist: Marcia's depression might be explained in part by her thinking patterns. For example, she could be magnifying the importance of bad things that have happened to her recently. She may also have unrealistic beliefs that lead to depression, such as, "I must be completely competent and achieving to be a worthwhile person," or "I must always be loved and approved by every significant person in my life."

As you can see, it is helpful to view human behavior from more than one perspective. This is also true in another sense. We are rapidly becoming a multicultural society, made up of people from many different nations. How has this affected psychology? Highlight 1–3 discusses the challenge of human diversity.

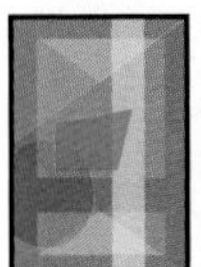

HIGHLIGHT 1–3

Critical Thinking

The Challenge of Human Diversity

Many psychological concepts apply to virtually everyone. Yet, at the same time, much of what we think, feel, and do is influenced by the social and cultural worlds in which we live. For instance, imagine that you are a psychologist and you must judge whether it is abnormal for Linda, a Native American, to believe that spirits live in trees. Clearly, you would be wise to take Linda's cultural background and religious beliefs into account.

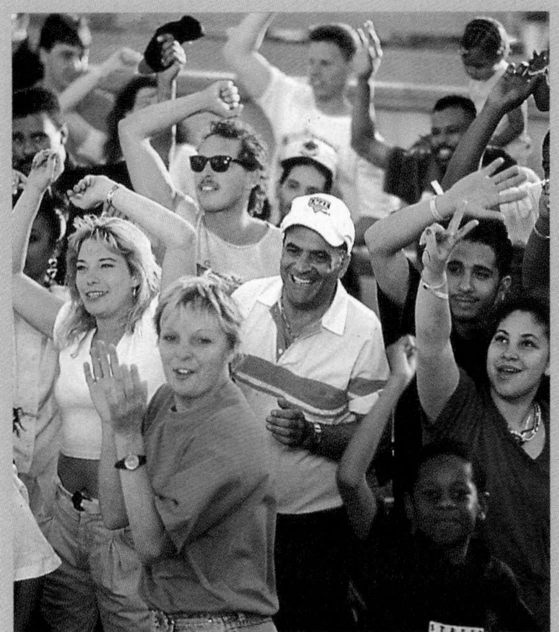

■ **Fig. 1–19** *To fully understand human behavior, personal differences based on age, race, culture, ethnicity, gender, and sexual orientation must be taken into account.*

The same can be said of differences based on age, race, ethnicity, gender, and sexual orientation. To really understand behavior, psychologists must be aware of how people differ, as well as the ways in which we are all alike (■ Fig. 1–19).

Human diversity teaches us to be wary of using false standards when comparing groups. For example, let's say an observer notes that child-rearing practices in Culture A are very "indulgent." What does that tell us? Is child care *inferior* in Culture A? Actually, it probably means that the observer used his or her own culture as a standard for comparison. Child-rearing in Culture A may be more relaxed than it is in our own, but it could be less indulgent than child care in many other cultures.

Recognizing and accepting human diversity helps us better understand ourselves and the behavior of others. Too often, the unstated standard for judging what is "average" or "normal" is the behavior of white, middle-class American males. Becoming aware of personal and cultural differences can enrich your life, as well as your understanding of psychology. (Sources: Denmark, 1994; Graham, 1992; Sampson, 1993; Shweder & Sullivan, 1993; Tavris, 1992.)

In a moment, we will further explore what psychologists do and identify some of their specialties. First, see if you can correctly match the items in the following Learning Check.

Learning Check

Match:

1. ____ Philosophy		A.	Against analysis; studied whole experiences
2. ____ Wundt		B.	"Mental chemistry" and introspection
3. ____ Structuralism		C.	Emphasizes self-actualization and personal growth
4. ____ Functionalism		D.	Interested in unconscious causes of behavior
5. ____ Behaviorism		E.	Gave rise to educational and industrial psychology
6. ____ Gestalt		F.	First woman Ph.D. in psychology
7. ____ Psychodynamic		G.	Studied stimuli and responses, conditioning
8. ____ Humanistic		H.	Part of psychology's "long past"
9. ____ Cognitive		I.	Concerned with thinking, language, problem solving
10. ____ Washburn		J.	Used "experimental self-observation"
11. ____ Biopsychology		K.	Relates behavior to the brain, physiology, and genetics
		L.	Also known as engineering psychology

Critical Thinking

12. Modern sciences like psychology are built on observations that can be verified by two or more independent observers. Did structuralism meet this standard?

Answers: 1. H 2. J 3. B 4. E 5. G 6. A 7. D 8. C 9. I 10. F 11. K 12. No, it did not. The downfall of structuralism was that each observer examined the contents of his or her own mind—which is something that no other person can observe.

Psychologist An individual highly trained in the methods, factual knowledge, and theories of psychology.

Clinical psychologist A specialist who treats or does research on psychological problems.

Counseling psychologist A specialist who treats milder emotional and behavioral disturbances.

Scientist-practitioner model Training of clinical psychologists to do both research and therapy.

Psychiatrist A medical doctor who specializes in treating mental disorders.

Psychologists—Guaranteed Not To Shrink

Question: What is the difference between a psychologist and a psychiatrist?

Answer: About $20 an hour. (And going up.)

There is often confusion about the differences among psychologists, psychiatrists, psychoanalysts, counselors, and other mental health professionals. It is quite inaccurate to think of them all as "shrinks." Each title reflects distinct differences in training and emphasis.

A **psychologist** usually has a master's degree or a doctorate in psychology. These degrees require from 3 to 8 years of postgraduate training in psychological theory and research methods. Depending on their interests, psychologists may teach, do research, give psychological tests, or serve as consultants to business, industry, or the government. Psychologists who treat emotional problems specialize in **clinical** or **counseling psychology** (● Table 1–4).

Counseling psychology was once limited to problems not involving serious mental disorders. Originally, counseling psychology was concerned with helping people understand themselves, plan their lives, and make important choices at work or school. In recent years, however, many counseling psychologists have shifted to doing psychotherapy. As a result, differences between counseling and clinical psychology are beginning to fade (Fitzgerald & Osipow, 1986; Tyler, 1992).

To enter the profession of psychology today, you would probably find it necessary to have a doctorate (Ph.D., Psy.D., or Ed.D.) to be licensed or to qualify for employment. (For more information about job opportunities, see Appendix A, Careers in Psychology, following the last chapter of this text.) Most clinical psychologists hold a Ph.D. degree and follow a **scientist-practitioner model** (O'Sullivan & Quevillon, 1992). That is, they may do either scientific research or therapy. Many do both. Other clinical psychologists earn the Psy.D. (Doctor of Psychology) degree. Training for the Psy.D. emphasizes practical clinical skills, rather than research (Hershey, Kopplin, & Cornell, 1991).

Other Mental Health Professionals

Like clinical psychologists, **psychiatrists** are also interested in treating emotional problems, but they are trained differently. A psychiatrist is a physician. After learning general medicine, psychiatrists specialize in abnormal behavior and psychotherapy. Psychiatrists often become "talking doctors" who spend much of their time doing psychotherapy.

In practice, the major difference between clinical psychologists and psychiatrists is that psychiatrists are trained to treat the physical causes of psychological problems. In the vast majority of cases, they do so by prescribing drugs, something a psychologist cannot do. This distinction may disappear, however. A poll conducted in 1991 found that 68 percent of the psychologists surveyed believe that they should be granted prescription privileges after receiving additional train-

Table 1–4 Kinds of Psychologists and What They Do

Specialty		Typical Activities
Clinical or counseling psychologist	(A*)	Does psychotherapy and personal counseling, helps with emotional and behavioral problems, researches clinical problems, and develops methods of treatment
Industrial-organizational psychologist	(A)	Selects job applicants, does skills analysis, evaluates on-job training, improves work environments and human relations in work setting
Educational psychologist	(A)	Conducts research on classroom dynamics, teaching styles, and learning variables; develops educational tests, evaluates educational programs, acts as consultant for schools
Consumer psychologist	(A)	Researches and tests packaging, advertising, and marketing methods; determines characteristics of product users, conducts public opinion polling
School psychologist	(A)	Does psychological testing, referrals, emotional and vocational counseling of students; detects and treats learning disabilities; improves learning and motivation in the classroom
Developmental psychologist	(A,B)	Carries out basic and applied research on child development, adult developmental trends, and aging; does clinical work with disturbed children; acts as consultant to preschools, programs for the aged, and so forth
Engineering psychologist	(A)	Does applied research on design of machinery, controls, airplanes, automobiles, and so on for business, industry, and the military
Medical psychologist	(A)	Studies the relationship between stress, personality, and disease (heart attacks, high blood pressure, ulcers); manages emotional problems associated with illness or disability
Environmental psychologist	(A,B)	Studies the effects of urban noise pollution, crowding, attitudes toward environment, and human use of space; acts as consultant for design of industrial environments, schools, housing for elderly, and urban architecture
Forensic psychologist	(A)	Studies problems of crime and crime prevention, rehabilitation programs in prisons, courtroom dynamics, psychology and law; selects candidates for police work
Community psychologist	(A)	Treats whole neighborhoods or communities as "clients" by emphasizing prevention, education, and consultation to promote community mental health
Experimental psychologist	(B)	Applies scientific research methods to study of human and animal behavior; may conduct research in the areas of comparative animal behavior, learning, sensation/perception, personality, biopsychology, motivation/emotion, social behavior, or cognition

*Research is typically: applied (A); basic (B); or both.

ing (Bales, 1991). Those who support this change point out that psychologists now do everything psychiatrists do except prescribe drugs. It will be interesting to see if lawmakers agree.

To be a **psychoanalyst,** you must have a moustache and goatee, spectacles, a German accent, and a well-padded couch—or so the TV and movie stereotype goes. Actually, to become an analyst, you must have an M.D. or Ph.D. degree plus further specialized training in the theory and practice of Freudian psychoanalysis. Analysts typically undergo psychoanalysis themselves before applying the method to others. Perhaps because Freud was a medical doctor, psychoanalysis remains more popular among psychiatrists than psychologists. Nevertheless, either a physician or a psychologist may become an analyst by completing more training in this specific type of psychotherapy.

Question: Is psychoanalysis widely used?

Traditional Freudian analysis is expensive and time consuming. This fact is gradually making psychoanalysts something of a rare breed. Today, few psychiatrists and almost no psychologists become analysts, and fewer clients seek analysis. In practice, many psychotherapists find that a flexible and eclectic approach is most effective.

In many states, **counselors** (such as marriage and family counselors, child counselors, or school counselors) also do mental health work. To be a licensed counselor typically requires a master's degree plus one

Psychoanalyst A mental health professional trained to do psychoanalysis.

Counselor An adviser who helps people solve problems with marriage, career, schoolwork, or the like.

Psychiatric social worker A professional who applies social science principles to help patients in clinics and hospitals.

Psychotherapist Anyone who does psychological therapy. Persons who call themselves psychotherapists are not always psychologists.

Basic research Scientific inquiry done to advance basic knowledge, not to solve a practical problem.

Applied research Scientific inquiry done to solve an immediate practical problem.

Experimental psychologist One who scientifically studies human and animal behavior.

Developmental psychologist A psychologist who studies the course of human growth and development.

Learning psychologist A psychologist who studies how learning occurs.

or two years of full-time supervised counseling experience. Almost all of a counselor's postgraduate education is related to practical helping skills. Counselors are not as highly trained as counseling psychologists or clinical psychologists and do not treat serious mental disorders.

Psychiatric social workers play an important role in many mental health programs. Most psychiatric social workers hold an M.S.W. (Master of Social Work) degree. Their training emphasizes the use of social science principles to solve social problems. Psychiatric social workers often work with psychologists and psychiatrists as part of a team in clinics and hospitals. Their typical duties include evaluating patients and their families, conducting group psychotherapy, or visiting a patient's home, school, or job to alleviate problems.

Question: Does a person have to have a license to practice psychology?

Professional Psychologists

Before the American Psychological Association (APA) began a push for licensing and certification, it was possible in many states for virtually anyone to purchase an inexpensive license and "hang out a shingle" as a "psychologist."

Now, to legally become a psychologist, a person must meet rigorous educational requirements. To work as a clinical or counseling psychologist, he or she must have a license issued by a state examining board. However, the law does not prevent you from calling yourself anything else you choose—therapist, rebirther, primal feeling facilitator, cosmic aura balancer, or Rolfer—or from selling your "services" to anyone willing to pay. Beware of people advertising under such self-proclaimed titles. Even if their intentions are honorable, their training may be limited or non-existent. A fully trained, certified counselor or psychologist who chooses to use a particular type of therapy is not the same as someone "trained" solely in that technique.

Psychology, like medicine, has unfortunately attracted a fringe of opportunists, quacks, and charlatans who seek to profit by taking advantage of human needs, fears, and suffering. (See this chapter's "Exploration" section.) What happens when the escapades of these "not-really psychologists" make the news or when a friend or relative has a bad experience with one? Often, psychologists take the blame. This is truly unfortunate. Most psychologists take pride in following a professional code established by the APA that stresses (1) high levels of competence, integrity, and responsibility; (2) respect for people's rights to privacy, dignity, confidentiality, and personal freedom; and above all, (3) protection of the client's welfare. Psychologists are also expected to use their knowledge to contribute to the welfare of society. Many do volunteer work in the communities in which they live ("Ethical," 1992).

How To Be a Psychologist—Let Us Count the Ways

Question: Do all psychologists do therapy and treat abnormal behavior?

No. Even when combined, clinical and counseling psychology account for about 55 percent of psychologists. The rest are found in a large number of other specialties. At present, there are 47 divisions of the APA, each reflecting a special skill area or interest. Some of the major specialties are listed in Table 1–4 (also see ■ Fig. 1–20). Over 40 percent of all psychologists are employed full-time at a college or university. In these settings they teach and may also do research, consulting, or therapy. Some do **basic research,** in which they seek knowledge for the sake of knowledge. For example, you might study memory purely out of interest in understanding how it works. Others who plan to put their findings to immediate practical use do **applied research.** An example would be studying ways to improve the memory of eyewitnesses to crimes. Of course, some psychologists do research of both types.

Question: What kinds of topics would a research psychologist at a university study?

Here is a sampling of typical research topics.

Developmental Psychology "I am interested in development from conception until death. I am trying to learn how people grow and change over time. My interests stretch over the whole life span, but I am especially interested in early childhood. My colleagues and I seek the principles whereby a child develops the ability to think, speak, perceive, and act. Currently, I am studying the effects of stimulating childhood environments on the development of intelligence."

Learning "I'm also interested in how people get to be the way they are, but in a much more abstract sense. I believe that most human behavior is learned. At any given moment, I would describe your behavior as the result of your personal learning history. By studying various kinds of learning, conditioning, and memory in humans and animals, I am helping to construct theories about how learning occurs and what factors affect it. Right now I'm studying how patterns of reinforcement affect learning in pigeons."

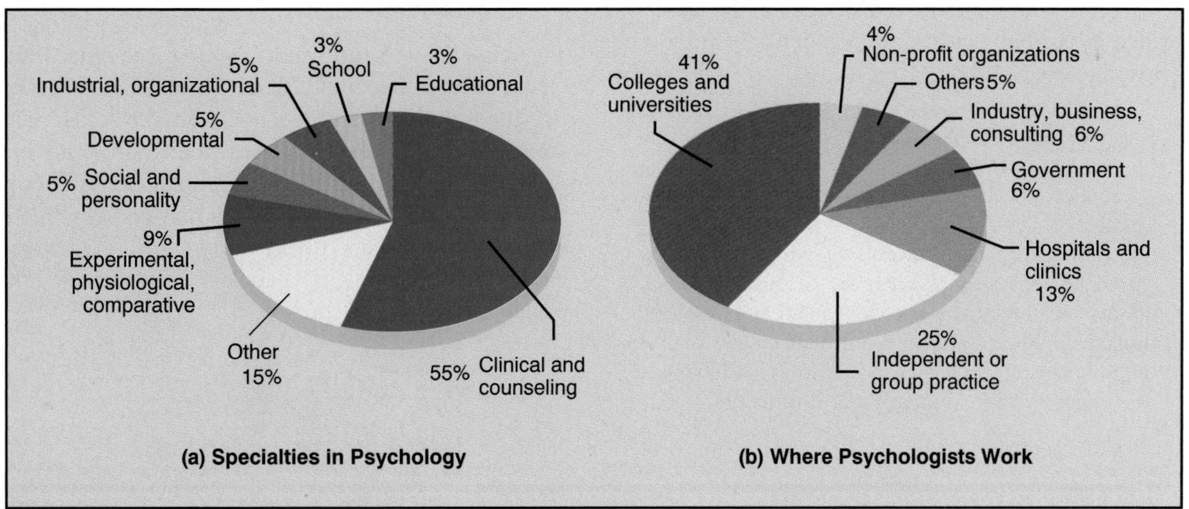

■ **Fig. 1–20** *(a) Specialties in psychology. Percentages are approximate. (b) Where psychologists work (from Pion, 1991). The percentages shown here are based on membership in the American Psychological Association. The APA welcomes both scientists and practitioners. However, some psychological researchers belong to other organizations, such as the American Psychological Society. As a result, the percentage of clinical and counseling psychologists working in the United States may be a little lower than shown in chart a. Nevertheless, it is accurate to say that most psychologists specialize in applied areas and work in applied settings.*

Personality "In many ways my area is both the most rewarding and the most frustrating. Personality theorists draw on the findings of all other research areas, as well as their own work, in an effort to create a total picture of human personality. I concern myself with the structure and dynamics of personality, motivation, and individual differences. I am studying the personality profiles of college students who score high on tests of creativity."

Sensation and Perception "How do we come to know the world? How does information 'get into' our nervous systems? How is it processed and given pattern and meaning? These are my concerns. I am using an information-processing theory called signal detection to study the visual perception of random shapes."

Comparative Psychology "I've always been interested in basic questions about animal behavior. I am especially fascinated by porpoises. For the last three years, I've been studying the porpoise's echolocation ability. We did a lot of testing underwater in pools to determine the animals' sensory limits. In a typical study, we asked porpoises to select between different shapes and surfaces while they were blindfolded. If they chose the right target we rewarded them with food. Their ability to discriminate in this way is superb."

Biopsychology "The brain and nervous system are my meat . . . so to speak. It is my belief that ultimately all other areas in psychology—learning, perception, even personality and abnormal behavior—will be explained by the action of nerve cells and brain chemicals. I have been doing some exciting research on hunger. I find that if I remove part of the hypothalamus in the brain of a rat, the rat will eat and gain weight until it looks like a furry water balloon. If I remove an area just a few millimeters away, the rat will starve to death if not force-fed."

Social Psychology "I study people in a group setting, or under any circumstance in which social factors play a part. Social psychologists in general are interested in attitudes, social influence, riots, conformity, leadership, racism, friendship, and a growing list of other topics. My personal interest is interpersonal attraction. I place two strangers together in a room for a short time and investigate factors that affect their degree of attraction toward each other."

Cultural Psychology "I am especially interested in how cultural forces shape human behavior. While humans everywhere have much in common, we live in cultures that are often strikingly different. The language you speak, the foods you eat, how your parents disciplined you, what laws you must obey, who you regard as "family," whether you eat with a spoon or your fingers—these and countless other details of behavior are strongly influenced by culture. For the last five years I have been comparing early child development in North America, Mexico, India, and Central Africa."

This small sample should give you an idea of the diversity of psychological research. It also hints at some of the kinds of information covered later in this book.

Personality psychologist A psychologist who studies personality traits and dynamics.

Sensation and perception psychologist A psychologist who studies the sense organs and the process of perception.

Comparative psychologist A psychologist who studies and compares the behavior of different species, especially animals.

Biopsychologist A psychologist who studies the relationship between behavior and biological processes, especially activity in the nervous system.

Social psychologist A psychologist interested in human social behavior (behavior influenced by relationships with others).

Cultural psychologist A psychologist who studies the ways in which culture affects human behavior.

A good summary of our discussion so far is provided by psychologists Gary VandenBos and Brenda Bryant:

> Psychologists are explorers and discoverers. They explore the reactions of human beings to small frustrations and great successes, to pleasing colors and the aftermath of disaster, always looking for answers to how and why people think, feel, and behave as they do . . . . The psychologist, regardless of where he or she may work, is always applying what is known in an effort to resolve the unknown. The psychologist, no matter how small the question being asked may appear to be, is looking for the larger answer. (VandenBos & Bryant, 1987)

A Look Ahead

To help you get the most out of psychology, each chapter of this text includes an "Applications" section like the one that follows. These sections discuss ideas you can actually use, now or in the future. Our first Applications section tells how psychology can help you study more effectively, a topic that may come in handy very soon. After that, a final "Exploration" section concludes the chapter with a look at some unscientific explanations of behavior.

LEARNING CHECK

See if you can answer these questions before continuing.

1. Which of the following can prescribe drugs?
   a. a psychologist *b.* a psychiatrist *c.* a psychotherapist *d.* a counselor
2. A psychologist who specializes in treating human emotional difficulties is called a ____________ psychologist.
3. Roughly 40 percent of psychologists specialize in counseling psychology. T or F?

Match the following research areas with the topics they cover.

4. ____ Developmental psychology	A. Attitudes, groups, leadership
5. ____ Learning	B. Conditioning, memory
6. ____ Personality	C. The psychology of law
7. ____ Sensation and perception	D. Brain and nervous system
8. ____ Biopsychology	E. Child psychology
9. ____ Social psychology	F. Individual differences, motivation
10. ____ Comparative psychology	G. Animal behavior
	H. Processing sensory information

11. Who among the following would most likely be involved in the detection of learning disabilities?
    a. a consumer psychologist *b.* a forensic psychologist *c.* an experimental psychologist *d.* a school psychologist

Critical Thinking

12. If the majority of psychologists work in applied settings, why is basic research still of great importance?

Answers: 1. b 2. clinical or counseling 3. F 4. E 5. B 6. F 7. H 8. D 9. A 10. G 11. d 12. Because practitioners benefit from basic psychological research in the same way that physicians benefit from basic research in biology. Discoveries in basic science form the knowledge base that leads to useful applications.

APPLICATIONS: *The Psychology of Studying*

Do you find learning exciting and rewarding? Or painful and intimidating? The second reaction is common even among bright students if they lack basic "tools of the trade." Even if you're not one of those students, you may be able to improve your study skills. Would you like to learn more in less time? There is a good chance you can if you apply the methods described here (■ Fig. 1–21). Students who get good grades tend to work smarter, not longer (Hill, 1990; Dickinson & O'Connell, 1990).

The SQ3R Method—How To Tame a Textbook

Have you ever finished a reading assignment, only to discover later that you remembered little of what you read? This problem plagues students everywhere. But fortunately, an excellent solution exists. Over 50 years ago, educator Francis Robinson developed a superb reading technique called the **SQ3R method.** Robinson's method is simply a way of studying while you read. The symbols S-Q-R-R-R stand for survey, question, read, recite, and review. Following these five steps can help you understand ideas quickly, remember more, and review effectively for tests (Robinson, 1970):

■ **Fig. 1–21** *Effective studying is planned and systematic. The number of hours you spend studying is less important than the quality and efficiency of your learning strategies (Woer & Cavell, 1993).*

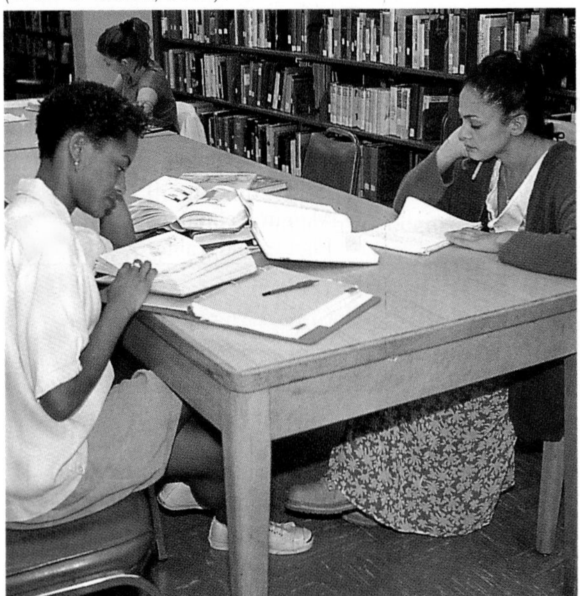

SQ3R method A reading method based on these steps: survey, question, read, recite, and review.

S = *Survey.* Look ahead through a chapter before you begin reading. As you do, read only topic headings, captions for illustrations, and any chapter summary or review. This step should give you an overall picture of what lies ahead.

Q = *Question.* To focus your attention as you read, turn each topic heading into one or more questions. For example, the heading "Stages of Sleep" could raise questions such as: "Is there more than one stage of sleep?" "What are the stages of sleep?" "How do they differ?" Asking questions will increase your interest. Questions also help relate new ideas to what you already know, for better comprehension.

R1 = *Read.* The first R in SQ3R refers to *read.* As you read, try to answer the questions you asked. Read in short "bites," from *one topic heading* to the next, then stop. (If the material is very difficult you may even want to read only a paragraph or two at a time.)

R2 = *Recite.* The second R stands for *recite.* After you have read from one topic heading to the next, you should stop and recite. That is, try to silently answer your questions. Or better yet, summarize what you've read in brief notes. If you can't summarize main ideas in your own words, scan back over the section until you can. Until you can remember what you just read, there's little point to reading more.

After you have read a short "bite" of information, turn the next topic heading into questions. Then read to the next heading. Again, you should look for answers as you read, and you should recite before moving on. Repeat the question-read-recite cycle until you've read the entire chapter.

R3 = *Review.* When you've finished reading, skim back over the chapter, or read your notes. Then check your memory by reciting and quizzing yourself again. Or better yet, get someone to ask you questions about each topic to see if you can answer in your own words. Try to make frequent review a key element of your study habits. (See ■ Figure 1–22.)

Question: Does this method really work?

Experiments show that using the SQ3R method improves both reading comprehension and grades

5. Unless there is a penalty for guessing, be sure to answer every question. Even if you are not sure of an answer, you may be right. If you skip a question it is automatically wrong. When you are forced to guess, don't make the mistake of choosing the longest answer or the letter you've used the least. Both of these strategies produce lower scores than pure random guessing (Shatz, 1986).
6. There is a bit of folk wisdom that says "Don't change your answers on a multiple-choice test. Your first choice is usually right." Careful study of this idea has shown it is *false*. If you change answers you are more likely to gain points than lose them (Geiger, 1991). This is especially true if you feel *very* uncertain of your first answer. ("When in doubt, scratch it out!") When you have strong doubts, your second answer is more likely to be correct. In fact, even if you are only moderately confident about your new answer, you will probably still come out ahead by making the change (Ramsey et al., 1987).
7. Remember that you are searching for the one *best* answer to each question. Some answers may be partly true, yet flawed in some subtle way. When you are in doubt, try rating each multiple-choice alternative on a 1-to-10 scale. The answer with the highest rating is the one for which you are looking.

Essay Tests Essay questions are a weak spot for students who lack organization, fail to support main ideas, or don't write directly to the question. When you take an essay exam try the following:

1. Read the question carefully. Make sure that you note key words, such as *compare, contrast, discuss, evaluate, analyze,* and *describe.* These words all demand a certain emphasis in your answer.
2. Think about your answer before putting words on paper. It's a good idea to make a brief list of the points you want to make. Just list them as they come to mind. Then rearrange your ideas in the order you want to write them. Elaborate plans or outlines are not necessary and will not improve your grade (Torrance et al., 1991).
3. Don't beat around the bush or pad your answer. Be direct. Make a point and support it. Get your list of ideas into words.
4. Look over your essay for errors in spelling and grammar. Save this for last. Your *ideas* are of first importance. You can work on spelling and grammar separately if they affect your grades. (For your convenience, ■ Figure 1–23 provides a checklist summary of the main study skills we have covered so far.)

A Final Word There is a distinction made in Zen between "live words" and "dead words." Live words come from personal experience; dead words are "about" a subject. This book can only be a collection of dead words without your personal involvement. It is designed to help you learn psychology, but it cannot do it for you. You will find many helpful, useful, and exciting ideas in the pages that follow. To make them yours, you must set out to *actively* learn as much as you can. The ideas presented here should get you off to a good start. Good luck!

For more information, consult any of the following books:

Annis, L. F. (1983). *Study Techniques.* Dubuque, IA: Brown.

Burka, J. B., & Yuen, L. M. (1983). *Procrastination: Why You Do It; What To Do About It.* Menlo Park, CA: Addison-Wesley.

Carman, R. A., & Adams, W. R. (1985). *Study Skills: A Student's Guide for Survival.* New York: Wiley.

Deese, J., & Deese, E. K. (1979). *How to Study.* New York: McGraw-Hill.

Ellis, A. & Knaus, W. J. (1977). *Overcoming Procrastination.* New York: Rational Living.

■ **Fig. 1–23** *Study skills checklist.*

Study Skills Checklist

Time Management
- ☐ Make formal schedule
- ☐ Set specific goals

Study Habits
- ☐ Study in specific area
- ☐ Pace study and review
- ☐ Create memory aids
- ☐ Test yourself
- ☐ Overlearn

Reading
- ☐ Use SQ3R method
- ☐ Study while reading
- ☐ Review frequently

Note-taking
- ☐ Listen actively
- ☐ Use LISAN method
- ☐ Review notes frequently

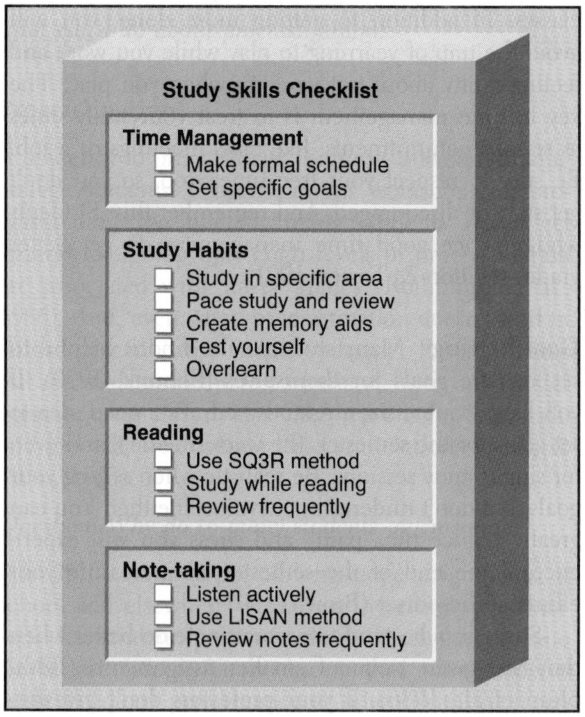

LEARNING CHECK

1. The three *Rs* in SQ3R stand for "read, recite, and review." T or F?
2. When using the LISAN method, students try to write down as much of a lecture as possible so that their notes are complete. T or F?
3. Spaced study sessions are usually superior to massed practice. T or F?
4. According to recent research, you should almost always stick with your first answer on multiple-choice tests. T or F?
5. To use the technique known as overlearning, you should continue to study after you feel you have begun to master a topic. T or F?
6. Procrastination is related to seeking perfection and equating self-worth with grades. T or F?
7. How do the SQ3R method and self-testing relate to the *quality* of study efforts? ***Critical Thinking***

Answers: 1. T 2. F 3. T 4. F 5. T 6. T 7. The SQ3R method and self-testing require you to actively process and remember information. Low quality study techniques involve simply "going through the motions." Information processing remains "shallow" and so does your learning.

EXPLORATION

Critical Thinking—Palms, Planets, and Personality

Most of us would be skeptical when buying a used car. But all too often, we may be tempted to "buy" outrageous claims about topics such as channeling, dowsing, the occult, the Bermuda Triangle, hypnosis, numerology, and so forth. Likewise, most of us easily accept our ignorance of sub-atomic physics. But because we all deal with human behavior every day, we tend to think that we already know what is true and what is false in psychology.

For these, and many more reasons, learning to think critically is one of the lasting benefits of a college education. **Critical thinking** is an ability to evaluate, compare, analyze, critique, and synthesize information. Critical thinkers are willing to ask the hard questions, including those that challenge conventional wisdom. For example, many people believe that punishment (a spanking) is a good way to reinforce learning in children. A critical thinker would immediately ask: "Does punishment work? If so, when? Under what conditions does it not work? What are its drawbacks? Are there better ways to guide learning?" (Halonen, 1986).

Critical Thinking in Psychology

The core of critical thinking is a willingness to take an active role in evaluating ideas. It is, in a sense, the ability to stand outside yourself and reflect on the quality of your own thoughts. Critical thinkers are able to evaluate the quality of the evidence supporting their beliefs and to probe for weaknesses in their reasoning. They recognize that knowledge is not just a static collection of facts. True knowledge is built on thinking skills that allow us to continuously revise and enlarge our understanding of the world. Critical thinking is built upon four basic principles (Gill, 1991; Shore, 1990):

1. *Few "truths" transcend the need for empirical testing.* It is true that religious beliefs and personal values may be held without supporting evidence. But most other ideas can be evaluated by applying the rules of logic and evidence.

2. *Evidence varies in quality.* Judging the quality of evidence is central to critical thinking. Imagine that you are a juror in a courtroom, judging the claims made by two battling lawyers. To judge correctly, you must not just weigh the evidence. You must also critically evaluate the *quality* of the evidence. Then you can give greater weight to the most credible facts.

3. *Authority or claimed expertise does not automatically make an idea true.* Just because someone else, including a teacher, guru, celebrity, or authority is convinced or sincere doesn't mean that you should automatically believe them. It is unscientific and self-demeaning to just take the word of an "expert" without asking, "What evidence convinced her or him? How good is it? Is there a better explanation?"

Critical thinking An ability to evaluate, compare, analyze, critique, and synthesize information.

EXPLORATION

4. *Critical thinking requires an open mind.* You must be willing to consider daring and novel departures in thought, to go wherever the evidence leads. However, it is possible to be "open-minded" to the point where you simply become gullible. Critical thinkers try to strike a balance between open-mindedness and healthy skepticism. Being open-minded means that you are able to consider all possibilities before drawing a conclusion. It is the ability to change your views under the impact of new and more convincing evidence.

To put these principles into action, here are some questions to ask over and over again as you evaluate new information (Bartz, 1990):

1. What claims are being made?
2. What test of these claims (if any) has been made?
3. Who did the test? How good is the evidence?
4. What was the nature and quality of the tests? Are they credible? Can they be repeated?
5. How reliable and trustworthy were the investigators? Do they have conflicts of interest? Do their findings appear to be objective? Has any other independent researcher duplicated the findings?
6. Finally, how much credence can the claim be given? High, medium, low, provisional?

Throughout this course you will have many opportunities to sharpen your thinking skills. In this first Exploration, let's take a critical look at several non-scientific systems that claim to explain behavior.

Table 1–6 Some Key Differences Between Scientists and Pseudo-scientists

	Scientist	Pseudo-scientist
Admits own ignorance; accepts need for more research	Yes	No
Relies on logic	Yes	Sometimes
Advances knowledge by posing and solving new problems	Yes	No
Welcomes new hypotheses and methods	Yes	No
Theories and hypotheses are testable	Yes	Sometimes
Systematically tests concepts by gathering data	Yes	No
Looks for examples that contradict his or her beliefs	Yes	No
Applies objective checking procedures	Yes	No
Settles disputes by experimentation or systematic data collection	Yes	No
Suppresses or distorts unfavorable data	No	Yes
Seeks criticism from others	Yes	No

(Adapted from Bunge, 1984)

Pseudo-psychologies

A **pseudo-psychology** (SUE-doe-psychology) is any dubious and unfounded system that resembles psychology. Many pseudo-psychologies offer elaborate systems that give the appearance of science but are actually false. (*Pseudo* means "false.") Like most pseudo-sciences, pseudo-psychologies change little over time because their followers do not actively seek new data. In fact, they often go to great lengths to avoid evidence that contradicts their beliefs (Kelly & Saklofske, 1994). Scientists, in contrast, actively look for contradictions as a way to advance knowledge (see Table 1–6).

Unlike the real thing, pseudo-psychologies are not based on empirical observation or scientific testing. **Palmistry,** for instance, claims that lines in the hand reveal personality and predict a person's future. Despite the overwhelming evidence against this, palmists can still be found separating the gullible from their money in many cities. A similar false system is **phrenology,** popularized in the nineteenth century by Franz Gall, a German anatomy teacher (Fig. 1–24). Gall believed that personality is revealed by the shape of the skull. However, modern research has shown that bumps on the head have nothing to do with talents or abilities. In fact, the area of the brain that controls hearing was listed on phrenology charts as the center for "combativeness" and "destructiveness"!

At first glance, a pseudo-psychology called **graphology** may seem more reasonable. Graphologists believe that they can identify personality traits and predict job performance from handwriting. Graphology is moderately popular in the United States, where at least 3000 companies use handwriting analysis to evaluate job applicants. This is troubling to psychologists because studies show that graphologists score close to zero in tests of accuracy in rating personality (Ben-Shakhar et al., 1986). In fact, studies show that graphologists do no better than untrained college students in rating personality and job performance (Neter & Ben-Shakhar, 1989; Rafaeli & Klimoski,

Fig. 1–24 *Phrenology was an attempt to assess personality characteristics by examining various areas of the skull. Phrenologists used charts such as the one shown here as guides. Like other pseudo-psychologists, phrenologists made no attempt to empirically verify their concepts.*

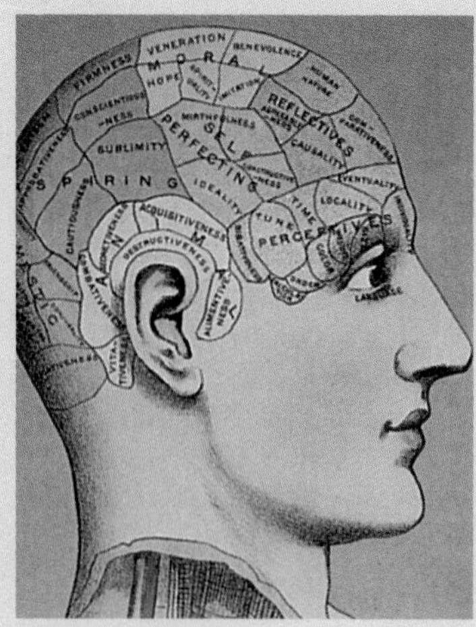

EXPLORATION

1983). (By the way, graphology's failure at revealing personality should be separated from its proven value for detecting forgeries.)

Like other pseudo-psychologies, graphology might seem harmless at first glance. However, this false and unfounded system is sometimes used to determine who is hired, given bank credit, or selected for juries. In these, and similar situations where fairness and honesty are important, pseudo-psychologies can harm people (Barker, 1993; Beyerstein & Beyerstein, 1992).

Question: If the pseudo-psychologies have no scientific basis, how do they survive and why are they popular?

There are several reasons, all of which can be demonstrated by a critique of astrology.

Astrology Astrology is probably the most popular pseudo-psychology. Twenty-five percent of the American public believes in astrology and another 22 percent say they are not sure if the stars and planets can or cannot affect people's lives (Gallup & Newport, 1991).

Astrologers assume that the position of the stars and planets at the time of a person's birth determines personality traits and affects behavior. Like other pseudo-psychologies, astrology has repeatedly been shown to have no scientific validity (Crowe, 1990; Kelly & Saklofske, 1994). The objections to astrology are numerous and devastating, as shown by the following:

Problems in the Stars

1. The zodiac has shifted by one full constellation since astrology was first set up. However, most astrologers simply ignore this shift. (In other words, if astrology calls you a Scorpio you are really a Libra, and so forth.)
2. There is no connection between the "compatibility" of the astrological signs of couples and their marriage and divorce rates.
3. Studies have found no connection between astrological signs and leadership, physical characteristics, career choice, or personality traits.
4. The force of gravity exerted by the physician's body at the moment of birth is greater than that exerted by the stars. Also, astrologers have failed to explain why the moment of birth should be more important than the moment of conception.
5. A study of over 3000 predictions by famous astrologers found that only a small percentage were fulfilled. These "successful" predictions tended to be vague ("There will be a tragedy somewhere in the eastern United States in the spring") or easily guessed from current events. (Sources: "Astrology and Astronomy," 1983; Culver & Ianna, 1979; Kelly & Saklofske, 1994; Pasachoff, 1981; Randi, 1980.)

In short, astrology doesn't work.

Psychologist Richard Crowe (1990) has summarized some of the arguments commonly offered by astrologers to support their beliefs. Counter-arguments based on critical thinking follow each statement. See if you can anticipate the counter-arguments.

- Astrology is ancient and enduring. (Murder has a long tradition too, but that doesn't make it an acceptable philosophy.)
- Astrology is practiced in many cultures. (Wide acceptance does not guarantee truth: Belief in a flat earth was once unanimous.)
- Many great scholars have believed in it. (Many others have not. And those who did believe knew nothing about modern astronomy.)
- The existence of the tides shows that celestial bodies influence events here on earth. (As already explained, the physical effects of celestial bodies on human bodies are trivial.)
- Non-astrologers are not qualified to judge. (Oh? And must one also practice cannibalism in order to judge it?)
- Astrology is an art, not a science. (The claims made by astrologers *can* be tested. Therefore, it is appropriate to look at the evidence for and against astrology.)
- Astrology works. (The statistical evidence suggests otherwise.) (Crowe, 1990; Kelly et al., 1989; Kelly & Saklofske, 1994.)

Question: Then why does astrology often seem to work?

Uncritical Acceptance If you have ever had your astrological chart done, you may have been impressed with its seeming accuracy. Careful reading shows many such charts to be made up of mostly flattering traits. Naturally, when your personality is described in *desirable* terms, it is hard to deny that the description has the "ring of truth." How much acceptance would astrology receive if the characteristics of a birth sign read like this:

> **Virgo:** You are the logical type and hate disorder. Your nitpicking is unbearable to your friends. You are cold, unemotional, and usually fall asleep while making love. Virgos make good doorstops.

Positive Instances Even when an astrological description of personality contains a mixture of good and bad traits it may seem accurate. To find out why, read the following personality description.

Your Personality Profile

You have a strong need for other people to like you and for them to admire you. You have a tendency to be critical of yourself. You have a great deal of unused energy which you have not turned to your advantage. While you have some personality weaknesses, you are generally able to compensate for them. Your sexual adjustment has presented some problems for you. Disciplined and controlled on the

Pseudo-psychology Any false system that purports to explain behavior.

Palmistry False system that claims the palms of the hands reveal personality and predict the future.

Phrenology False system that claims personality traits are revealed by the shape of the skull.

Graphology False system based on the belief that handwriting reveals personality traits.

Astrology False system based on the belief that human behavior is influenced by the stars and planets.

Uncritical acceptance The tendency to believe positive or flattering descriptions of oneself.

EXPLORATION

outside, you tend to be worrisome and insecure inside. At times you have serious doubts as to whether you have made the right decision or done the right thing. You prefer a certain amount of change and variety and become dissatisfied when hemmed in by restrictions and limitations. You pride yourself on being an independent thinker and do not accept other opinions without satisfactory proof. You have found it unwise to be too frank in revealing yourself to others. At times you are extroverted, affable, sociable, while at other times you are introverted, wary, and reserved. Some of your aspirations tend to be pretty unrealistic.*

Does this describe your personality? A psychologist read this summary individually to 79 college students who had taken a personality test. Twenty-nine said it was an "excellent" description of their personality; 30 said it was "good"; 15 said it was "average"; and 5 said it was "poor." Thus, only 5 students out of 79 felt that the description failed to adequately capture their personalities. Another study found that people rated this "personality profile" as more accurate than their actual horoscopes (French et al., 1991).

Reread the description and you will see that it contains both sides of several personality dimensions ("At times you are extroverted . . . while at other times you are introverted . . ."). Its apparent accuracy is an illusion based on the **fallacy of positive instances,** in which a person remembers or notices things that confirm his or her expectations and forgets the rest. The pseudo-psychologies thrive on this effect. For example, you can always find "Leo characteristics" in a Leo. If you looked, however, you could also find "Gemini characteristics," "Scorpio characteristics," or whatever.

*Reprinted with permission of author and publisher from: R. E. Ulrich, T. J. Stachnik, and N. R. Stainton, "Student acceptance of generalized personality interpretations," *Psychological Reports*, 13, 1963, 831–834.

NON SEQUITUR By Wiley

YOU WILL BE TOLD WHAT YOU WANT TO HEAR.
IT WILL BE SO GENERALIZED THAT IT COULD FIT ANYONE.
YOU WILL PAY A RIDICULOUS AMOUNT OF MONEY FOR IT...
TAROT
THE MOST ACCURATE FORTUNE EVER TOLD

The Barnum Effect P. T. Barnum, the famed circus showman, had a formula for success: "Always have a little something for everybody." The **Barnum Effect** refers to a tendency to consider a personal description accurate if it is stated in very general terms. Like the all-purpose personality description, palm readings, fortunes, horoscopes, and other products of pseudo-psychology are stated in such generic terms that they can hardly miss. There is always "a little something for everybody." If you doubt this, read *all 12* of the daily horoscopes found in newspapers for several days. You will find that predictions for other signs fit events as well as those for your own sign do.

Question: Couldn't that be because commercial horoscopes don't take into account a person's specific time of birth?

If they did, they would not be any more accurate, just more convincing. In one experiment, people were given standardized horoscopes. Some had provided only their sign. Others gave the year, month, and day of their birth. All were then given *the same* personality description. The result? Those who had provided more detailed information considered their horoscope more accurate (Snyder & Schenkel, 1975). Thus, the more hocus pocus a fortune teller, palmist, or astrologer goes through, the more believable the results become.

A Final Note Astrology's persistent popularity shows the difficulty many people have separating valid psychology from systems that seem valid but are not. The goal of this discussion, then, has been to make you a more critical observer of human behavior and to clarify what is, and what is not, psychology. In Chapter 2, you will get a chance to further sharpen your critical thinking skills as we investigate the research methods used in psychology. In the meantime, here is what the "stars" say about your future:

> Emphasis now is on education and personal improvement. A learning experience of lasting value awaits you. Take care of scholastic responsibilities before engaging in recreation. Research new possibility. The number 2 figures prominently in your future.

Fallacy of positive instances The tendency to remember or notice information that fits one's expectations.

Barnum Effect The tendency to consider a personal description accurate if it is stated in very general terms.

LEARNING CHECK

1. An important aspect of ____________ ____________ is to seek evidence for and against an idea and to also evaluate the ____________ of that evidence.
2. ____________ is the out-dated theory that personality is revealed by the skull. It was popularized by Franz ____________.
3. The fallacy of positive instances refers to graphology's accepted value for the detection of forgeries. T or F?

EXPLORATION

4. Personality descriptions provided by pseudo-psychologies are stated in general terms, which provide "a little something for everybody." This fact is the basis of the
   a. palmist's fallacy *b.* uncritical acceptance pattern *c.* fallacy of positive instances *d.* Barnum effect

5. Each New Year's Day, so called "psychics" make predictions about events that will occur during the coming year. The vast majority of these predictions are wrong, but the practice continues each year. Can you explain why? ***Critical Thinking***

Answers: 1. critical thinking, quality 2. Phrenology, Gall 3. F 4. *d* 5. Because of the fallacy of positive instances, people only remember predictions that seemed to come true and forget all of the errors. Incidentally, "predictions" that appear to be accurate are usually easily deduced from current events or are stated in very general terms to take advantage of the Barnum Effect.

Chapter Summary

■ ***What is psychology? What are its goals?***

- **Psychology** is a profession and a science. As a science, psychology is defined as the scientific study of behavior.
- Psychology's goals are to **describe, understand, predict,** and **control** behavior.
- Whenever possible, psychologists seek **empirical** (objective and observable) **evidence** based on **scientific observation.**
- Not all psychological questions are answerable, usually because of ethical, practical, technical, or methodological limitations.
- Psychologists study animals as well as people.
- Psychologists may be directly interested in animal behavior or they may study animals as **models** of human behavior.
- One danger in studying animals is the **anthropomorphic fallacy,** the tendency to treat animals as if they had human characteristics.

■ ***How did psychology emerge as a field of knowledge?***

- Historically, psychology is an outgrowth of **philosophy,** an "armchair" approach to understanding human behavior.
- The first psychological laboratory was established in Germany by **Wilhelm Wundt,** who tried to apply scientific methods to the study of conscious experience.
- The first school of thought in psychology was **structuralism,** a kind of "mental chemistry" based on Wundt's ideas and the method of **introspection.**
- Structuralism was followed by **functionalism, behaviorism,** and **Gestalt** psychology.
- The **psychodynamic** approach emphasizes unconscious determinants of behavior. Freud's **psychoanalytic psychology** is an early example of a psychodynamic approach.
- A more recent development is **humanistic** psychology, which emphasizes subjective experience, human potentials, and personal growth.

■ ***What are the major perspectives in psychology?***

- Five main streams of thought that can be seen in modern psychology are **behaviorism, humanism,** the **psychodynamic** approach, **biopsychology,** and **cognitive** psychology.
- Today, there is a strong trend toward an eclectic blending of the best features of many viewpoints within psychology.

■ ***What roles and specialties are found in psychology and related fields?***

- Although **psychologists, psychiatrists, psychoanalysts,** and **counselors** work in the field of mental health, their training and methods differ considerably.
- **Clinical** and **counseling** psychologists, who do psychotherapy, represent only two of dozens of specialties in psychology.
- Other representative areas of specialization are **industrial-organizational, educational, consumer, school, developmental, engineering, medical, environmental, forensic, psychometric,** and **experimental** psychology.
- Psychological research may be **basic** or **applied.** Some common research specialties are comparative, learning, sensation, perception, personality,

physiology, motivation and emotion, social, cognitive, developmental, and cultural psychology.

■ ***Can psychology be applied to improve study skills and grades?***

- The core of **effective study skills** begins with the **SQ3R method,** a way of combining learning with reading.
- All of the following can also add to your studying effectiveness: Active listening and note-taking, a positive attitude toward learning, use of a specific study area, spaced practice, mnemonics, self-testing, overlearning, time management, goal setting, high-quality study methods, and test-taking skills.

■ ***What is critical thinking? How can it be used to identify false explanations of behavior?***

- Psychology makes extensive use of **critical thinking skills.** Critical thinking can be used to evaluate claims made about human behavior, especially the false claims often found in pop psychology and unscientific systems.
- Numerous **pseudo-psychologies** exist. These false systems are frequently confused with valid psychology.
- Belief in pseudo-psychologies is based in part on **uncritical acceptance,** the **fallacy of positive instances,** and the **Barnum effect.**

Questions for Discussion

1. The goals of psychology are a refinement of things we do every day. Can you relate instances in which you have sought to describe, predict, understand, or control behavior? Do you consider control of behavior an acceptable goal for psychology? Why or why not?
2. What do you see as the strengths and weaknesses of each of the five major viewpoints in psychology? What specific human problems do you think that psychologists should study? Which approaches to psychology would be most appropriate for studying the problem you identified?
3. Should psychologists study animals? Most people anthropomorphize pets. How could this be a problem in the objective study of animals? In your opinion, can we learn anything about humans by studying animals?
4. In what ways is your behavior controlled by the environment? Do you believe that you have free will? Is there any way to tell if a "free choice" is really determined by your past?
5. What are the ethical limitations of the goal of "control"? When should the results of psychological studies be used to intervene in individual lives? When is intervention not appropriate?
6. How did you picture psychology and psychologists before reading this chapter? Has your image changed? How accurate are television and movie portrayals of psychologists? What psychological specialty do you consider most interesting at this point?
7. Presently, a number of non-physicians can prescribe certain medications under certain conditions. Examples include optometrists, nurse practitioners, and physician assistants. In your opinion, should psychologists be allowed to prescribe mood-altering drugs?
8. Can you name additional systems of thought that you suspect are pseudo-psychologies? What are their claims? Can you use the points made in the Exploration section to explain their attraction for believers?
9. Return to the quiz at the beginning of the chapter. Why are all the statements false? Explain those that you can.
10. Discuss the limitations of the following widely used "psychological" terms and "insights" (dubbed "psychobabble" by one critic): "I really felt like we were *getting into each other's heads.*" "She's really *together,* you know, really *laid back.*" "You gotta *go with your feelings* and *let it happen* if you don't want to be *uptight.*" "We give each other the *space* to be our *true selves.*" "I'm really *getting in touch with myself.*" "Most problems are due to a lack of *total and honest communication.*"

Chapter 2

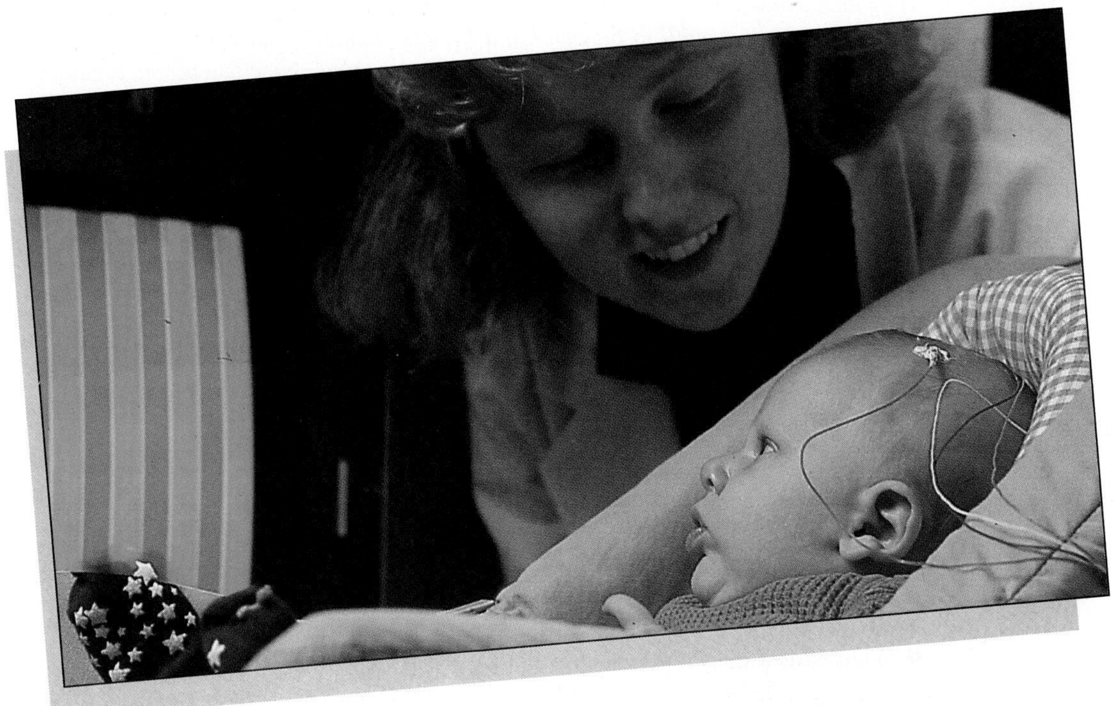

Research Methods and Critical Thinking

CHAPTER PREVIEW

From Common Sense to Controlled Observation

Comment overheard on campus: "I don't know why he bothers taking psychology classes. Psychology is just common sense." Is psychology common sense? Is common sense a good source of information?

Consider some **commonsense statements.** *Let's say that your grandfather has gone back to college. What do people say? "Ah . . . never too old to learn." And what do they say when he loses interest and quits? "Well, you can't teach an old dog new tricks." Let's examine another commonsense statement. It is frequently said that "absence makes the heart grow fonder." Those of us separated from friends and lovers can take comfort in this knowledge—until we remember "Out of sight, out of mind"! Much of what passes for common sense is equally vague and inconsistent. Notice also that most of these B. S. statements work best after the fact. (B. S., of course, stands for* Before Science.*)*

Common sense is not without value; without it, many of us would not be alive. Yet, common sense can often prevent us from seeking better information or seeing the truth.

IN THIS CHAPTER

Albert Einstein reportedly said, "Common sense is the layer of prejudice laid down in our minds before we are 18." In the early stages of the scientific revolution, people laughed at the idea that the world is round. (Anyone with eyes could see that it wasn't.) They laughed at Pasteur when he proposed that microorganisms cause disease. (How could creatures too small to be seen kill a healthy human?) Scientific ideas such as these directly contradicted the common sense of their time. Now few people argue with the findings of sciences such as chemistry, physics, and biology. But many still write off psychology as "just common sense."

Jab a hat pin into your finger. The sensation of pain seems instantaneous. We can go no further with personal observation. However, by using electrical recorders to measure nerve impulses, psychologists have found that such impulses travel at a maximum of 120 meters per second. This is one-third the speed of sound. That's fast, but certainly not instantaneous. Pain messages from the finger take at least a hundredth of a second to reach the brain.

As you can see, psychologists use careful measurement and specialized research techniques to avoid the pitfalls of "common sense." Their techniques are the topic of this chapter.

Survey Questions

- Why is the scientific method important to psychologists?
- How do psychologists collect information?
- How is an experiment performed?
- What other research methods do psychologists use?
- How dependable is psychological information found in the popular press?
- What ethical questions does psychological research raise?

Scientific method Testing a proposition by systematic observation.

Hypothesis An educated guess about relationships or the causes of behavior.

Operational definition The procedures used to define a scientific concept.

Scientific Method—Can a Horse Add?

It is a strange medical fact that adults who often ate Frosted Flakes cereal as children now have half the cancer rate seen in adults who never ate Frosted Flakes. Does this mean that doctors should prescribe Frosted Flakes to growing children? Only a scientifically naive person would draw this conclusion. The observed relationship between childhood diet and cancer is related to an age bias in the group of people studied. Older adults have higher cancer rates than younger adults, and Frosted Flakes weren't available during the childhoods of older people. Thus, Frosted Flakes appear to be related to cancer, when age is the real connection (Tierny, 1987). In many ways, psychologists in search of accurate information must avoid similar traps of faulty observation (■ Fig. 2–1). To do so, they use the **scientific method,** which is based on solid evidence, accurate description and measurement, precise definition, controlled observation, and repeatable results (Bunge, 1984). In its ideal form the scientific method has five elements:

1. Observation
2. Defining a problem
3. Proposing a hypothesis
4. Gathering evidence/testing the hypothesis
5. Theory building

Question: What exactly is a hypothesis?

A **hypothesis** (hi-POTH-eh-sis) is a tentative explanation of an event or observation. In common terms, a hypothesis is a clearly stated and *testable* hunch or educated guess about the causes of behavior. For example, on the basis of your own observation you might hypothesize that "Frustration encourages aggression." How would you test this hypothesis? First you would have to decide how you are going to frustrate people. (This part might be fun.) Then you would have to find a way of measuring whether or not they become more aggressive. (Not so much fun if you plan to be nearby.)

Making specific plans for testing your hypothesis would provide operational definitions of frustration and aggression. **Operational definitions** state the exact *procedures* used to represent a concept. This allows abstract concepts to be tested in real-world terms (■ Fig. 2–2). Thus, you might define frustration as "interrupting an adult before he or she can finish a puzzle and win a $100 prize." And aggression might be "the number of times a frustrated individual insults the person who prevented work on the puzzle."

The major steps of the scientific method can be illustrated with the story of Clever Hans, a "wonder horse" (Rosenthal, 1965). Clever Hans seemed to solve difficult math problems, which he answered by tapping his foot. If you asked Hans, "What is 12 times 2, minus 18," Hans would tap his foot 6 times. Hans was so astonishing that an inquiring scientist decided to

■ Fig. 2–1 *Applying the scientific method to the study of behavior requires careful observation. Here, a student programs a computer to record a rat's responses in a learning experiment.*

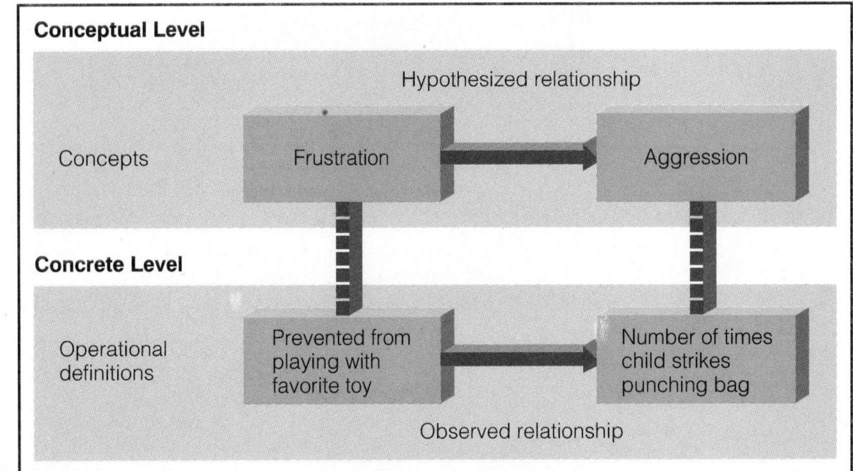

■ Fig. 2–2 *Operational definitions are used to link concepts with concrete observations. Do you think the examples given are reasonable operational definitions of frustration and aggression? Operational definitions vary in how well they represent concepts. For this reason, many different experiments may be necessary to draw clear conclusions about hypothesized relationships in psychology.*

discover how Hans was able to perform. Assume that you are the scientist and that you are just itching to find out how Hans *really* does his trick.

Your investigation of Hans' math skills would probably begin with careful **observation** of both horse and owner while Hans was performing. Assume that these observations fail to reveal any obvious cheating. Then the *problem* becomes more clearly **defined:** What signals Hans to start and stop tapping his foot? Your first **hypothesis** might be that the owner is giving Hans a signal. Your proposed **test** would be to make the owner leave the room. Then someone else could ask Hans questions. Your test would either confirm or deny the owner's role. This **evidence** would support or eliminate the cheating hypothesis. By changing the conditions under which you observe Hans, you have **controlled** the situation to gain more information from your observations.

Incidentally, Hans could still answer when his owner was out of the room. But a brilliant series of controlled observations revealed Hans' secret. If Hans couldn't see the questioner, he couldn't answer. It seems that questioners always *lowered their heads* (to look at Hans' foot) after asking a question. This was Hans' cue to start tapping. When Hans had tapped the correct number, a questioner would always *look up* to see if Hans was going to stop. This was Hans' cue to stop tapping!

Question: What about theory formulation?

Since Clever Hans' ability to do math was an isolated problem, no theorizing was involved. However, in actual research, theory building is quite important. A **theory** interrelates concepts and facts in a way that summarizes the results of a large number of observations. A good theory accounts for existing data, predicts new observations, and guides further research (■ Fig. 2–3). Theories of forgetting, personality, stress, mental illness, and the like, are valuable products of psychological research. Without them, psychologists would drown in a sea of disconnected facts.

We should also add that a good scientific theory, like a good hypothesis, is stated in terms that make it **falsifiable.** In other words, its concepts are defined in ways that allow them to be put to a test. True science focuses on solvable problems. It avoids pie-in-the-sky theorizing that cannot be tested (Stanovich, 1992).

Now let's summarize with a more realistic example of psychological research. All the basic elements of the scientific method are found in the example that follows.

Observation: Suzanne, a psychologist, observes that some managers at a large corporation seem to experience less work-related stress than others do.

Defining a Problem: Suzanne's problem is to identify the ways in which high-stress and low-stress managers are different.

Observation: Suzanne carefully questions groups of managers about how much stress they experience at work. These additional observations suggest that low-stress managers feel more in control of their work.

Proposing a Hypothesis: Suzanne proposes the hypothesis that having control over difficult tasks reduces the amount of stress a person experiences.

Observation Directly gathering data by recording facts or events.

Evidence Facts or data collected to confirm or disconfirm a hypothesis.

Theory A system of ideas that interrelates facts and concepts, summarizes existing data, and predicts future observations.

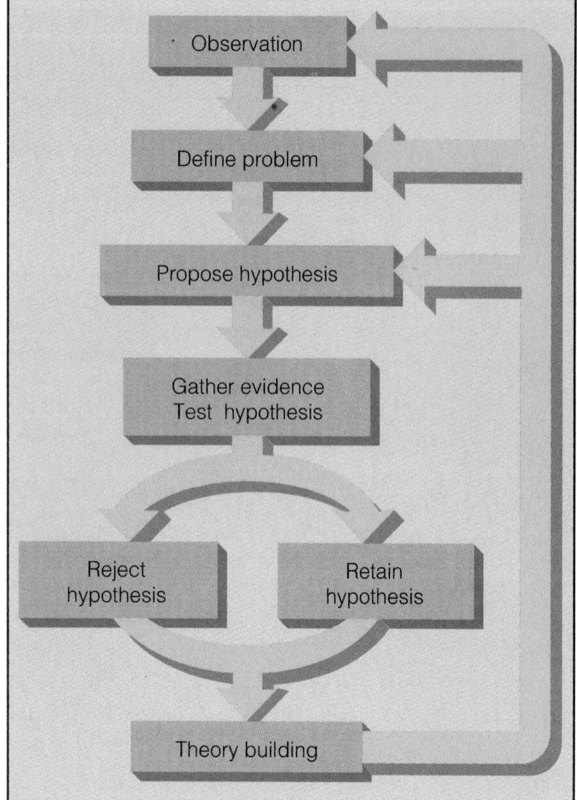

■ **Fig. 2–3** *Psychologists use the logic of science to answer questions about behavior. Specific hypotheses can be tested in a variety of ways, including naturalistic observation, correlational studies, controlled experiments, clinical studies, and the survey method. Psychologists revise their theories to reflect the evidence they gather. New or revised theories then lead to new observations, problems, and hypotheses.*

Natural setting The typical environment in which a person or animal lives.

Gathering Evidence/Testing the Hypothesis: Suzanne designs an experiment in which people must solve a series of very difficult problems. People in one group will solve the problems in an order and at a pace dictated by Suzanne. The other group is allowed to control the order and pace of their problem solving. While working, the second group reports lower levels of stress than the first. This suggests that Suzanne's hypothesis is correct.

Theory Building: Drawing on the results of similar experiments, Suzanne and other psychologists create a theory to explain why having control over a task helps to reduce stress.

Research Methods In their search for accurate information and useful theories, psychologists gather evidence and test hypotheses in many ways: They observe behavior as it unfolds in natural settings (**naturalistic observation**); they make measurements to discover relationships between events (**correlational method**); they use the powerful technique of controlled experimentation (**experimental method**); they study psychological problems and therapies in clinical settings (**clinical method**); and they use questionnaires and surveys to poll large groups of people (**survey method**). Let's see how each of these is used to advance psychological knowledge.

Naturalistic Observation—Psychology Steps Out!

Instead of waiting to haphazardly encounter a behavior of interest, psychologists may set out to **actively observe** subjects in a **natural setting.** A good example of this style of research is the work of Jane Goodall. She and her staff have been observing chimpanzees in Tanzania since 1960. A quote from her book *In the Shadow of Man* captures the excitement of a scientific discovery:

> Quickly focusing my binoculars, I saw that it was a single chimpanzee, and just then he turned my direction. . . . He was squatting beside the red earth mound of a termite nest, and as I watched I saw him carefully push a long grass stem into a hole in the mound. After a moment he withdrew it and picked something from the end with his mouth. I was too far away to make out what he was eating, but it was obvious that he was actually using a grass stem as a tool (■ Fig. 2–4). (van Lawick-Goodall, 1971)

Notice that naturalistic observation only provides *descriptions* of behavior. To *explain* what has been ob-

■ **Fig. 2–4** *A special moment in Jane Goodall's naturalistic study of chimpanzees. A chimp uses a grass stem to extract a meal from a termite nest. Goodall's work also documented the importance of long-term emotional bonds between chimpanzee mothers and their offspring, as well as fascinating differences in the behavior and "personalities" of individual chimps (Goodall, 1990). (Photo by Baron Hugo van Lawick. © National Geographic Society.)*

served often requires more information from other research methods. Just the same, Goodall's discovery forced many scientists to change their definition of humans. Previously, humans had been regarded as the only tool–making animals.

Question: Chimpanzees in zoos use objects as tools. Doesn't that demonstrate the same thing?

Not necessarily. An advantage of naturalistic observation is that the behavior under study has not been tampered with by outside influences. Only by observing chimps in their natural environment can we tell if they use tools without human interference.

Question: But doesn't the presence of human observers in an animal colony affect the animals' behavior?

Effects of the Observer Yes. A major problem with naturalistic studies is the effect of the observer on the observed. The **observer effect** refers to changes in a subject's behavior brought about by an awareness of being observed. Naturalists studying animal colonies must be very careful to keep their distance and avoid the temptation to "make friends" with the animals. Likewise, if you were interested in student-teacher interactions, you couldn't simply walk into a classroom and begin taking notes. A stranger in the room might affect both the students and the teacher. When possible, this problem is minimized by **concealing the observer.**

Observer bias is a closely related problem, in which observers see what they *expect* to see or record only selected details. Teachers in one study were told to watch elementary school children (all normal) who had been labeled as either learning disabled, mentally retarded, emotionally disturbed, or normal. The results were troubling: Ratings teachers gave the children differed markedly, depending on the labels used (Foster & Ysseldyke, 1976). Psychologists doing naturalistic studies make a special effort to minimize observer bias by keeping careful **observational records.**

Despite its problems, naturalistic observation can provide a wealth of information and raise many interesting questions (Sommer, 1977). In most scientific research it is an excellent starting point.

Correlational Studies—In Search of the Perfect Relationship

Let's say that a psychologist notes an association between the IQs of children and their parents, between physical attractiveness and social popularity, between anxiety and test performance, or even between crime and weather conditions. In each instance, two observations or events are **co-related** (linked together in an orderly way). A **correlational study** finds the degree of correlation, or relationship, between two existing traits, behaviors, or events.

Unlike naturalistic observation, correlational studies can be done either in the lab or in the natural environment. First, two factors of interest are measured. Then a statistical technique is used to find their degree of correlation. (See Appendix B for more information.) For example, we could find the correlation between the average number of hours slept each night and daytime anxiety levels. If the correlation is large, knowing the number of hours slept would allow us to predict a person's anxiety level. Likewise, knowing anxiety level would allow prediction of sleep needs.

Question: How is the degree of correlation expressed?

The strength of a relationship can be expressed as a **coefficient of correlation.** This is simply a number falling somewhere between +1.00 and −1.00 (see Appendix B). If the number is zero or close to zero, the association between two measures is weak or nonexistent. For example, the correlation between shoe size and intelligence is zero. (Sorry, size 12 readers.) If the correlation is +1.00, a **perfect positive relationship** exists; if it is −1.00, a **perfect negative relationship** has been discovered.

Correlations in psychology are rarely perfect. But the closer the correlation coefficient is to +1.00 or −1.00, the stronger the relationship. For example, identical twins are likely to have almost identical IQs. In contrast, parents and their children have IQs that are only generally similar. The correlation between IQs of parents and children is .35; that between identical twins is .86.

Question: What do the terms "positive" and "negative" correlation mean?

A positive correlation shows that increases in one measure are matched by increases in the other (or decreases correspond with decreases). For example, there is a positive correlation between high school grades

Observer effect Changes in behavior caused by an awareness of being observed.

Observer bias The tendency of observers to distort their perceptions to match their expectations.

Observational record A formal log of observations.

Correlation An orderly relationship between two events, measures, or variables.

Correlational study A study of the relationship between two or more events, measures, or variables.

Coefficient of correlation A measure of the direction and degree of correlation.

Positive relationship A relationship in which increases in one measure correspond to increases in the other.

Negative relationship A relationship in which increases in one measure correspond to decreases in the other.

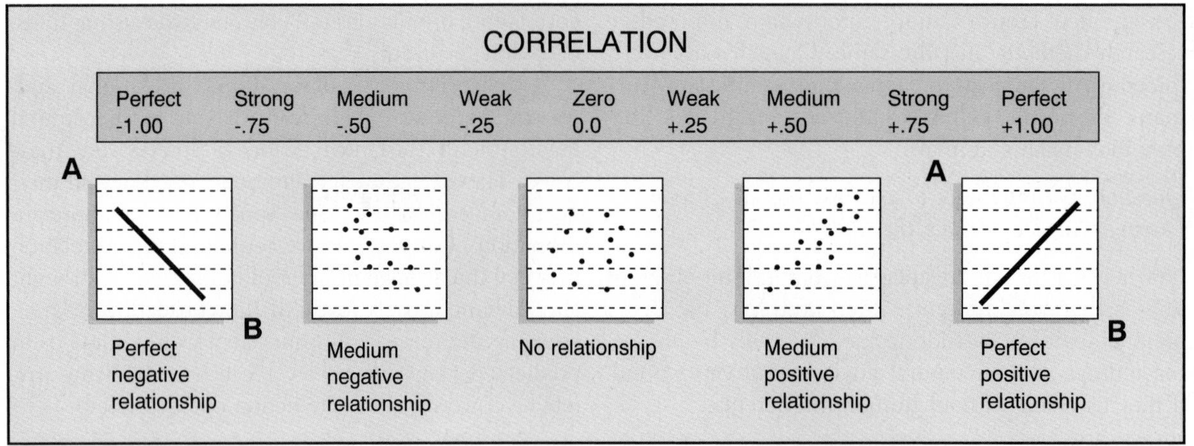

■ **Fig. 2–5** *The correlation coefficient tells how strongly two measures are related. These graphs show a range of relationships between two measures, A and B. If a correlation is negative, increases in one measure are associated with decreases in the other. (As B gets larger, A gets smaller.) In a positive correlation, increases in one measure are associated with increases in the other. (As B gets larger, A gets larger.) The center-left graph ("medium negative relationship") might result from comparing anxiety level (B) with test scores (A): Higher anxiety is associated with lower scores. The center graph ("no relationship") would result from plotting a person's shoe size (B) and his or her IQ (A). The center-right graph ("medium positive relationship") could be a plot of the number of hours pilots went without sleep (B) and the number of errors each made when tested on a flight simulator (A). In this case, longer periods without sleep are associated with a greater number of errors.*

and college grades; students who do better in high school tend to do better in college (and the reverse). In a negative correlation, *increases* in the first measure are associated with *decreases* in the second (■ Fig. 2–5). We might observe, for instance, that the higher the air temperature, the lower the activity level of animals in a zoo.

Question: Would that show that air temperature causes changes in activity level?

It might seem so, but we cannot be sure without performing an experiment. Correlational studies help us discover relationships and make useful predictions. However, correlation *does not demonstrate causation.* (There is an exception, but it involves an advanced technique beyond the scope of this book.) Just because one thing *appears* to be related to another does not mean that a cause-and-effect connection exists. The animals' activity might be affected by seasonal changes in weight, hormone levels, or even the feeding schedule at the zoo.

Here is another example of mistaking correlation for causation: What if a psychologist discovered that the blood of schizophrenic patients contained a certain chemical not found in people functioning normally? Would this show that the chemical *causes* schizophrenia? Again, it may seem so, but schizophrenia could cause the chemical to form. Or, both schizophrenia and the chemical might be caused by some unknown third factor, such as the typical diet in mental hospitals. Just because one thing *appears* to cause another does not *confirm* that it does. This fact can be seen clearly in the case of obviously non-causal relationships. For example, there is a correlation between the number of churches in American cities and the number of bars; the more churches, the more bars. Does this mean that drinking makes you religious? Does it mean that religion makes you thirsty? No one, of course, would leap to such conclusions about cause and effect in this instance. But in less obvious situations, it's tempting. (The real connection is simply that both the number of churches and the number of bars is related to the population size of cities.) Highlight 2–1 delves further into correlational relationships.

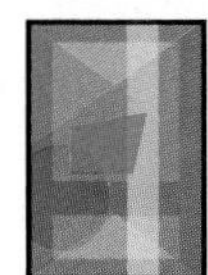

HIGHLIGHT 2–1

A Closer Look At

Relationships in Psychology

Do students who study more get better grades? To answer this question we could record the number of hours different students study each week. Then we could match hours studied with grades earned. Suppose we find that low amounts of study time correspond to low grades and high amounts of studying are linked with high grades. If this were the case, there would be a **positive relationship** between studying and grades. Similarly, we might discover that students who watch many hours of television each day tend to get lower grades than those who watch few hours. (This is the well-known TV zombie effect.) This time, a **negative relationship** would exist. That is,

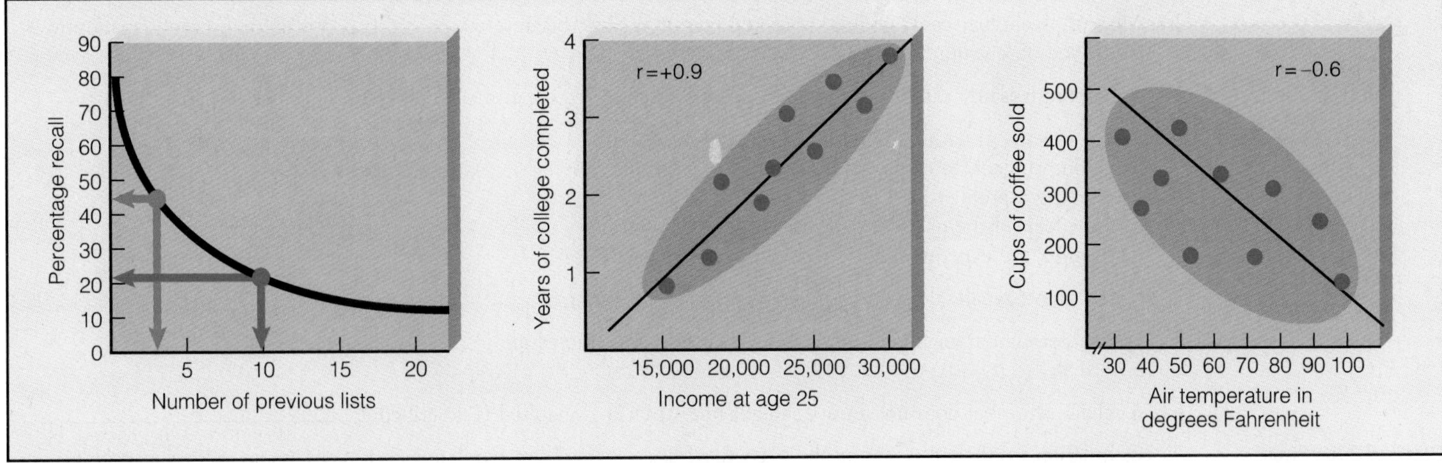

■ **Fig. 2–6** *Effects of interference on memory. A graph of the approximate relationship between percentage recalled and number of different word lists memorized. (Adapted from Underwood, 1957)*

■ **Fig. 2–7** *The relationship between years of college completed and personal income (hypothetical data).*

■ **Fig. 2–8** *The relationship between air temperature and amount of coffee consumed (hypothetical data.)*

low viewing times go with high grades, and high viewing times go with low grades. Obviously, these examples are only hypothetical. However, when real patterns of this sort can be identified, they have great value. Relationships summarize large amounts of data and allow prediction as well.

Drawing graphs of relationships often helps clarify their nature. For example, ■ Figure 2–6 shows the results of a memory experiment. Before being tested, subjects learned from 1 to 20 word lists. The question was, How well would they remember the last list? The graph shows that when no other lists were memorized, 80 percent of the test list was remembered. When 3 other lists were memorized, scores on the last list dropped to 43 percent (blue arrows). When 10 other lists were memorized, recall fell even further, to 22 percent (red arrows). Overall, there was a negative relationship between the number of lists memorized and recall of the last list. (The meaning of this finding is discussed in Chapter 8. For now, let's just say that you shouldn't memorize the telephone book before studying for a test.)

Some graphs reveal a **linear** (straight-line) **relationship.** Others are **curvilinear** (kur-vih-LIN-ee-er), consisting of a curved line, like Figure 2–6. In either case, relationships need not be perfect to be useful. Suppose, for instance, that we randomly select 10 people. We then compare the number of years of college completed with each person's income at age 25. If we were to obtain results like those shown in ■ Figure 2–7, it would be clear that there is a strong positive relationship between education and earnings. Recall that such a correlation does not prove that earnings are increased by education. Nevertheless, a pattern like this might be of great interest to a high school student thinking about whether to attend college.

The shaded area and the colored line in Figure 2–7 show that the relationship is approximately linear, but not perfect. (If it were perfect, all the dots would lie on the colored line.) The correlation coefficient (*r*) also shows that the relationship is strong, and positive, but not perfect. (How often do you find a perfect relationship?) If the relationship were perfect, the coefficient would be 1.00.

For comparison, ■ Figure 2–8 plots more hypothetical data. Assume that the manager of a college cafeteria has recorded the amount of coffee sold on 10 different days, as well as the air temperature on each day. Notice again that the relationship appears to be linear. However, this time it is negative. Also note how the shaded area and the correlation coefficient both indicate a weaker relationship. Even so, knowing the correlation between temperature and coffee drinking would help anyone planning how much "mud" to brew each morning. On a higher plane, psychologists seek to identify relationships concerning memory, perception, stress, aging, therapy, and a host of similar topics. Much of this book is a summary of such relationships.

Linear relationship A relationship that forms a straight line when graphed.

Curvilinear relationship A relationship that forms a curved line when graphed.

The best way to be confident that a cause-and-effect relationship exists is to perform a controlled experiment. You'll learn how in the next section. But before you read more, check your progress by answering the questions that follow.

Learning Check

1. Most of psychology can rightfully be called common sense because psychologists prefer naturalistic observation to controlled observation. T or F?
2. A hypothesis is any careful observation made in a controlled experiment. T or F?
3. Two problems in naturalistic observation are
   a. getting subjects to cooperate and identifying correlations
   b. defining a problem and proposing a hypothesis
   c. the effects of the observer and observer bias
   d. running the experiment and making careful records
4. Correlation typically does not demonstrate causation. T or F?
5. Which correlation coefficient represents the strongest relationship?
   a. −0.86 *b.* +0.66 *c.* +0.10 *d.* +0.09
6. A relationship that does not form a straight line when it is graphed is described as ______________.

Critical Thinking

7. Correlation coefficients measure the strength of linear (straight-line) relationships. Why might it be a mistake to assume that a low correlation means two variables are unrelated?

Answers: 1. F 2. F 3. c 4. T 5. a 6. curvilinear 7. Because the relationship could be very strong, yet curvilinear. In such cases, a psychologist might find that the correlation coefficient is zero, even though a significant relationship exists.

Experiment A formal test of a fact or principle.

Experimental subjects Humans or animals whose behavior is investigated in an experiment.

Experimental group In an experiment, subjects exposed to the independent variable.

Control group In an experiment, subjects exposed to all conditions *except* the independent variable.

Variable Any condition that can change; a measure, event, or state that may vary.

The Psychology Experiment—Where Cause Meets Effect

One of the most powerful research tools is the experiment. An **experiment** is a formal trial undertaken to confirm or disconfirm a fact or principle. Psychologists carefully control conditions in an experiment to identify cause-and-effect relationships. To perform a psychological experiment you would do the following:

1. Directly vary a condition you think might cause changes in a behavior.
2. Create two or more groups of subjects. These groups should be alike in all ways *except* the condition you are varying.
3. Record whether varying the condition has any effect on behavior.

Assume, for example, that you want to find out if hunger affects memory. First, you would form two groups of people. Then you could give one group a memory test while its members are hungry. The second group would take the same test after eating a meal. By comparing average memory scores for the two groups, you could tell if hunger affects memory.

As you can see, the simplest psychological experiment is based on two groups of **subjects** (animals or people). One group is called the **experimental group;** the other becomes the **control group.** The control group and the experimental group are treated exactly alike except for the one condition you intentionally vary. This condition is called the *independent variable.*

A **variable** is any condition that can change, and that might affect the outcome of the experiment. Identifying causes and effects in an experiment involves three types of variables:

1. **Independent variables** are the conditions altered or varied by the experimenter. The size, amount, or value of an independent variable is set by the experimenter and does not depend on any other condition. Independent variables are suspected *causes* for differences in behavior.
2. **Dependent variables** measure the results of the experiment. Dependent variables reveal the *effects* that independent variables have on behavior. Such effects are often revealed by measures of performance, such as test scores.
3. **Extraneous variables** are conditions that a researcher wishes to prevent from affecting the outcome of the experiment.

We can apply these terms to our hunger/memory experiment in this way: Hunger is the independent variable—we want to know if hunger affects memory. Memory (defined by scores on the memory test) is the dependent variable—we want to know if the ability to memorize depends on how hungry a person is. All other conditions that could affect memory scores, such as hours slept the night before, intelligence, or difficulty of the test, are extraneous variables.

Let's examine another simple experiment. Suppose you notice that you seem to study better while listening to music. This suggests the hypothesis that music

improves learning. We could test this idea experimentally by forming two groups of people. One group studies with music. The other studies without music. Then we could compare their scores on a test. The group exposed to music is the experimental group because the independent variable (music) is present. The group not exposed to music is the control group.

Question: Is a control group really needed? Can't people just study with music on to see if they do better?

Without a control group it would be impossible to tell if music had any effect on learning. The control group provides a *point of reference* for comparison with scores of the experimental group. If the average test score of the experimental group is higher than that of the control group, it can be concluded that music improves learning efficiency. If the average is lower than the control group's average, we will know that music slows learning. If there is no difference, we know that the independent variable has no effect on learning.

In the experiment described, the amount learned (indicated by scores on the test) is the **dependent variable.** We are asking the question, Does the independent variable *affect* the dependent variable? (Does music affect or influence learning?) Another way to think of this is that the results of an experiment are measured by the dependent variable, which *depends* on the independent variable. (The amount learned depends on whether or not music accompanies study.)

Question: How do we know that the people in one group aren't more intelligent than those in the other group?

It's true that personal differences among subjects might influence the outcome of an experiment. However, these can be controlled by *randomly assigning* subjects to the two groups. **Random assignment** means that a subject has an equal chance of being a member of either the experimental group or the control group. Random assignment helps ensure that personal differences are evenly balanced across the two groups. In our musical experiment, random assignment could be done by simply flipping a coin for each subject: Heads, and the subject is in the experimental group; tails, it's the control group. Even in fairly small groups, this results in few differences in the number of people in each group who are geniuses or dunces, hungry, hung over, tall, music lovers, or whatever.

Other **extraneous,** or outside, variables—such as the amount of study time, the sex of subjects, the temperature in the room, the time of day, the amount of light, and so forth—must also be prevented from affecting the outcome of an experiment. But how? Usually this is done by making all conditions except the independent variable *exactly* alike for both groups. When all conditions are the same for both groups—*except* the presence or absence of music—then a difference in the amount learned *must* be caused by the music (■ Fig. 2–9).

Now let's summarize more formally. In a psychology experiment two or more groups of subjects are treated differently with respect to the independent variable. In all other ways they are treated the same. That is, extraneous variables are equalized for all groups in the experiment. This prevents conditions we are not interested in from affecting the results of the experiment. The effect of the independent variable (or variables) on some behavior (the dependent variable) is then measured. In a carefully controlled experiment,

Independent variable In an experiment, the condition tested as a possible cause of changes in behavior.

Dependent variable In an experiment, the condition (usually a behavior) that is affected by the independent variable.

Random assignment Using chance (for example, flipping a coin) to assign subjects to the experimental and control groups.

Extraneous variable In an experiment, any condition prevented from influencing the outcome.

■ **Fig. 2–9** *Elements of a simple psychological experiment to assess the effects of music during study on test scores.*

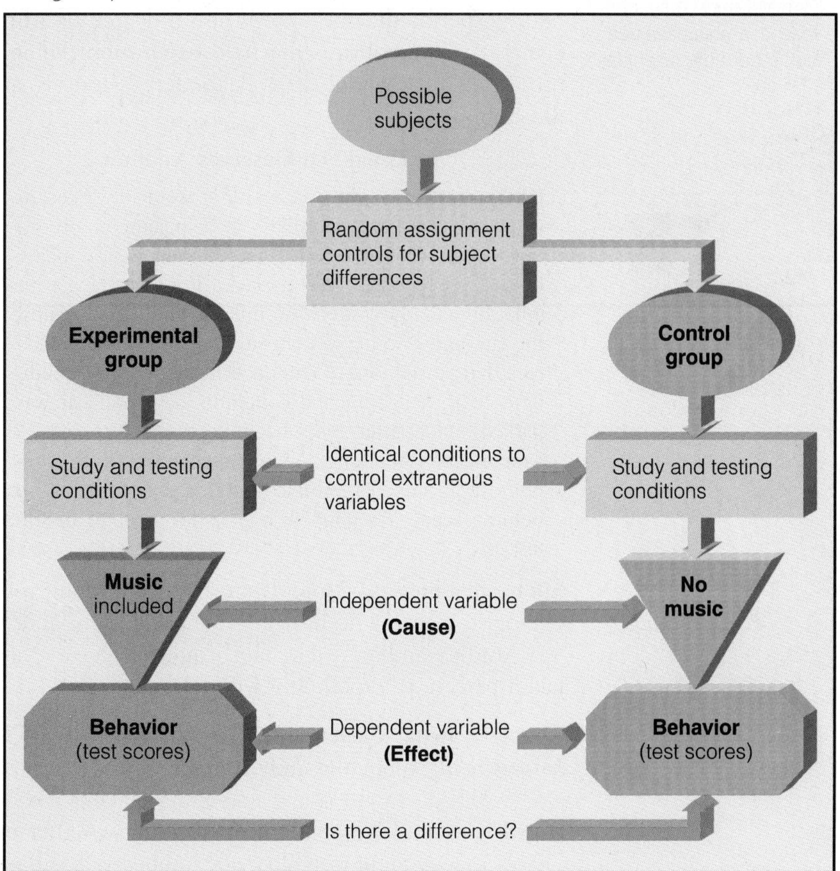

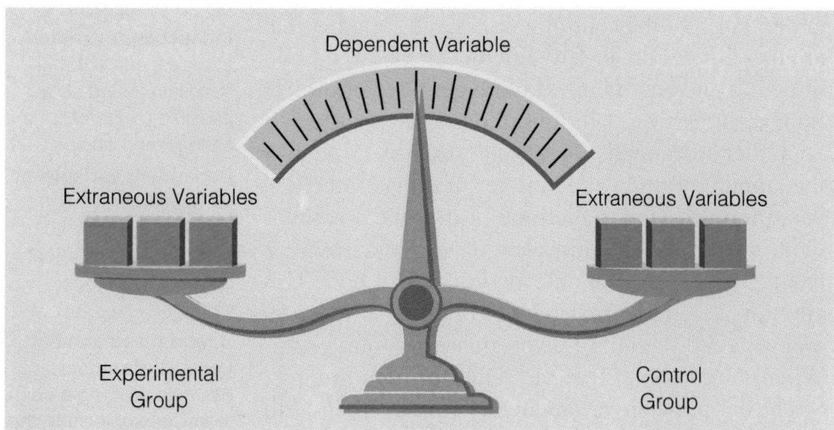

■ Fig. 2–10 *Experimental control is achieved by balancing or equalizing extraneous variables for the experimental group and the control group. Then, when the independent variable is applied to the experimental group, any change in the dependent variable must be caused by the independent variable.*

Field experiment An experiment conducted in a natural setting.

Statistical significance Experimental results that would rarely occur by chance alone.

Replication Repeating observations or experiments to confirm prior conclusions.

Parascience A system that resembles science but is not truly scientific.

differences in the independent variable can be the only possible **cause** for any **effect** noted in the dependent variable. This allows clear cause-and-effect connections to be identified (■ Fig. 2–10).

Question: Experiments seem to set up artificial situations. Do experimental findings have anything to do with the real world?

Field Experiments There are many advantages to being able to "custom design" conditions in a laboratory experiment. But there is also a degree of artificiality. An alternative is the **field experiment,** which uses the "real world" as a laboratory. Here is an illustration:

One Good Flat Deserves Another

James Bryan and Mary Test (1971) were interested in whether people are more likely to help someone in distress when they have just seen someone else being helped. To find out, they parked a Ford Mustang with a flat tire on a busy street. An inflated tire leaned against the car, and a young woman stood nearby. Of the 2000 cars that passed, only 35 stopped in this control condition. In the experimental condition, a second car was parked one-quarter mile back from the test car. A woman stood watching a man change a tire on the second car. Of the 2000 vehicles that first passed this staged helping scene, 58 stopped to help the woman in the test car.

Such "real-life" experiments are popular among psychologists as a way to bridge the gap between laboratory studies and everyday life. You may have even taken part in an experiment without knowing it!

Question: Is the difference between 35 helpers and 58 helpers really enough to draw a conclusion?

Significance The problem of deciding whether or not an independent variable made a difference is handled statistically. Reports in psychology journals almost always include the statement, "Results were **statistically significant.**" What this means is that the obtained results would occur very rarely *by chance alone.* To be statistically significant, a difference must be large enough so that it would occur by chance in less than 5 experiments out of 100. (See Appendix B for more information.) Of course, research findings also become more convincing when they can be duplicated or repeated, as discussed in Highlight 2–2.

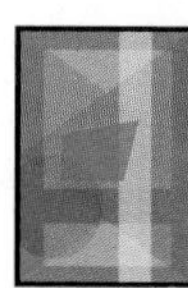

HIGHLIGHT 2–2

Critical Thinking

Replication and Parascience

The question, "Could you repeat that, please?" takes on special meaning in psychology. A key element in any science is the ability to **replicate** (repeat) observations or experiments. In contrast, a failure to replicate observations is a major failing of **parascience** (that which resembles science, but is not truly scientific). A good example is the idea that plants have feelings. This claim, which received wide media coverage, was largely based on "experiments" performed by Cleve Backster, a polygraph expert. (The polygraph is commonly referred to as a lie detector; see Chapter 10.)

Backster claimed that plants wired to a lie detector responded to music, threats (such as a lighted match), and other stimuli. However, when scientists tried to repeat the experiments, using either identical or improved methods, the results were completely negative (Galston & Slayman, 1983).

A long list of other purported wonders—from "pyramid power" to dowsing to moon madness—have likewise disappeared in the light of careful scrutiny. Psychology, too, has admittedly had its share of unrepeatable results. What separates psychology and other sciences from parascience is that they are self-correcting.

When a finding cannot be repeated, the scientific response is, "We don't believe the result." Maintaining such high standards can be frustrating at times. Among other things, it requires a willingness to change one's beliefs as new or better evidence comes along. Yet, the end result is highly satisfying. High standards of evidence and a demand for repeatability ensure that science moves slowly, but surely, toward the truth (Lett, 1990).

Placebo Effects—Sugar Pills and Salt Water

Assume that we want to perform an experiment to see if Dexedrine (a powerful central nervous system stimulant) affects learning. An accurate test of the drug will *not* occur if, before studying, members of the experimental group are given a Dexedrine pill and control group members get nothing.

Question: Why not? The experimental group gets the drug and the control group doesn't. If there is a difference in learning scores, it must be due to the action of the drug, right?

No, because an error has been made: The drug is not the only difference between the experimental group and the control group. Members of the experimental group swallow a pill, and control subjects do not. Without using a **placebo** (plah-SEE-bo), it is impossible to tell if the drug affects learning. It might be that those who swallow a pill expect to do better. This alone might alter their performance, even if the pill has no chemical effect.

Question: What is a placebo? Why would it make a difference?

A placebo is a fake pill or injection. A placebo's benefits come from what it suggests to a person, rather than from what it contains. Sugar pills and saline (salt-water) injections are common placebos (■ Fig. 2–11).

Although they have little or no direct chemical effect, placebos can have a tremendous *psychological* impact. As an example of how powerful the **placebo effect** can be, one study showed that an injection of saline solution was 70 percent as effective as morphine in reducing pain for hospital patients (Beecher, 1959). This fact is well known to physicians. For years they have prescribed placebos for complaints that they feel have no physical basis. Placebos appear to relieve pain because they cause the pituitary gland to release chemicals called **endorphins.** Endorphins are similar to painkilling opiate drugs such as morphine. The body also naturally releases endorphins at times of stress and bodily injury (Lipman et al., 1990).

To control for placebo effects, a psychologist doing drug research could use a **single-blind** arrangement. In this approach *all* subjects get a pill or injection. The experimental group gets the real drug and the control group gets a placebo. Thus, subjects are *blind* as to whether they are receiving the drug. Any difference between the two groups must be caused by the drug.

But this is not enough. *Experimenters* must also be blind as to whether they are giving the drug or a placebo to a particular subject. **Double-blind experiments** prevent the researcher from unconsciously influencing subjects' reactions. Typically, someone else prepares the pills or injections, so that the experimenters don't know until after testing who got what.

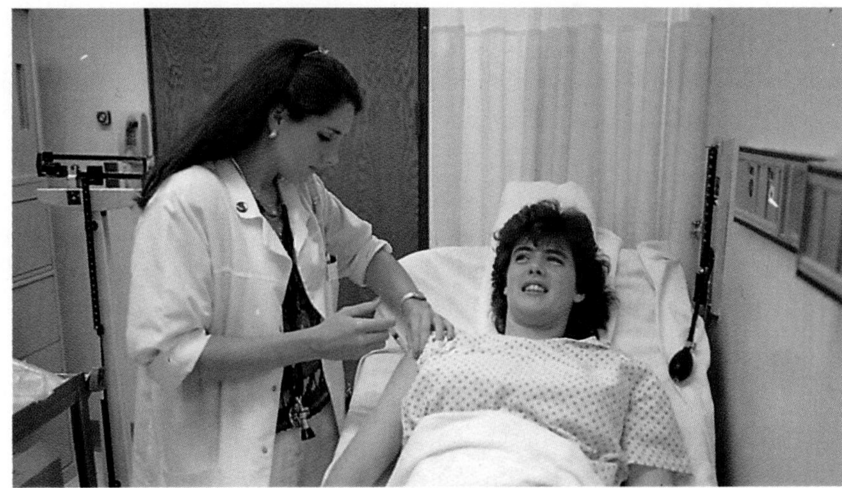

■ **Fig. 2–11** *The placebo effect is a major factor in medical treatments. Would you also expect the placebo effect to occur in psychotherapy? (It does, which complicates studies on the effectiveness of new therapies.)*

Question: How could the researcher influence the subject?

The Experimenter Effect Psychologists face an interesting problem not shared by physicists and chemists. Human subjects are very sensitive to hints from an experimenter about what is expected of them. The **experimenter effect** refers to changes in subjects' behavior caused by the unintended influence of an experimenter's actions. It can have a powerful impact on a person's behavior (Rosenthal, 1976).

The experimenter effect even applies outside the laboratory, where expectations have been shown to influence people in interesting ways. Psychologist Robert Rosenthal (1973) reports a typical example: At the U.S. Air Force Academy Preparatory School 100 airmen were randomly assigned to one of five math classes. Their teachers were unaware of this random assignment. Instead, the teachers were told that their students were selected for high or low levels of ability. Students in the classes labeled "high-ability" improved much more in math scores than those in "low-ability" classes. Yet, initially, the classes were all of equal ability.

Apparently, the teachers subtly communicated their expectations to the students through tone of voice, body language, and by offering encouragement or criticism. This, in turn, created a **self-fulfilling prophecy** that affected the students' performance. A self-fulfilling prophecy is a prediction that prompts people to act in ways that make the prediction come

Placebo A substance that resembles a drug but has no chemical effect.

Placebo effect Changes in behavior caused by belief that one has taken a drug.

Endorphins Chemicals produced by the pituitary gland that are similar to opiate drugs such as morphine.

Single-blind experiment A test in which subjects do not know if they are in the experimental group.

Double-blind experiment A test in which neither subjects nor experimenters know which subjects are in the experimental group.

Experimenter effect Changes in subjects' behavior unintentionally caused by the experimenter's actions.

Self-fulfilling prophecy A prediction that prompts people to act in ways that make the prediction come true.

true. In this instance, students tended to perform as they expected to perform. Even though educators should know better, self-fulfilling prophesies continue to influence large numbers of students (Jussim & Eccles, 1992).

In short, people sometimes become what we prophesy for them. It is wise to remember that others tend to live *up* or *down* to our expectations of them.

Learning Check

1. Anything that can change (vary) and that might affect the behavior of subjects is called a ________.
2. To understand cause and effect, a simple psychological experiment is based on creating two groups: the ________ group and the ________ group.
3. There are three types of variables to consider in an experiment: ________ variables (which are manipulated by the experimenter); ________ variables (which measure the outcome of the experiment); and ________ variables (factors not of interest in a particular experiment).
4. A researcher performs an experiment to learn if room temperature affects the amount of aggression displayed by college students under crowded conditions in a simulated prison environment. In this experiment, the independent variable is
   a. room temperature *b.* the amount of aggression *c.* crowding *d.* the simulated prison environment
5. A procedure used to control both the placebo effect and the experimenter effect in drug experiments is the
   a. correlation method *b.* extraneous prophecy
   c. double-blind technique *d.* random assignment of subjects

Critical Thinking

6. How would you determine if sugary breakfasts affect children's activity levels and their ability to learn in school?

Answers: 1. variable 2. experimental, control 3. independent, dependent, extraneous 4. *a* 5. *c* 6. An actual experiment on this question used a double-blind design in which children were given a breakfast drink containing either 50 grams of sucrose (sugar), a placebo (aspartame), or only a very small amount of sucrose. Observed changes in activity levels and in scores on a learning task did not support the view that sugar causes major changes in children's behavior (Rosen et al., 1988).

Case study An in-depth focus on all aspects of a single person.

Natural clinical test An accident or other natural event that provides psychological data.

Frontal lobotomy The destruction of neural tissue in frontal areas of the brain.

The Clinical Method—Data by the Case

Many experiments that might be revealing are impractical, unethical, or impossible to perform. In instances such as these, information may be gained from **case studies.** A case study is an in-depth focus on all aspects of a single subject. Case studies are used heavily by clinical psychologists.

Case studies may sometimes be thought of as **natural clinical tests** of the effects of unusual variables. Gunshot wounds, brain tumors, accidental poisonings, and similar disasters have provided much information on the functioning of the human brain. One remarkable case from the history of psychology is reported by Dr. J. M. Harlow (1868). Phineas Gage, a young foreman on a work crew, had a 13-pound steel rod blown through the front of his brain by an excavating charge (■ Fig. 2–12). Amazingly, he survived the accident, but not without undergoing a profound personality change. Dr. Harlow carefully recorded all details of what was perhaps the first in-depth case study of an accidental **frontal lobotomy** (the destruction of front brain matter).

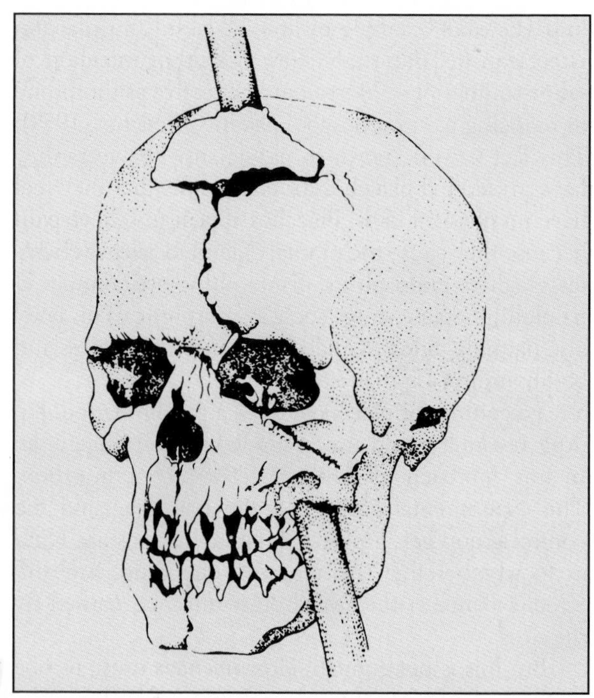

■ Fig. 2–12 *Some of the earliest information on the effects of damage to frontal areas of the brain came from a case study of the accidental injury of Phineas Gage.*

Over 120 years later, a Los Angeles carpenter named Michael Melnick was the victim of a similar freakish accident. Melnick fell from the second story of a house under construction and impaled his head on a steel reinforcing rod. Incredibly, he recovered completely, with no sign of lasting ill effects ("Man tells," 1981). Melnick's very different reaction to a similar injury shows why psychologists prefer controlled experiments and often use lab animals for studies of the brain. Case studies lack formal control groups. This, of course, limits the conclusions that can be drawn from clinical observations. Nonetheless, when a purely psychological problem is under study, the clinical method may be the *only* source of information.

A classic psychological case study is *The Three Faces of Eve* (Thigpen & Cleckley, 1957). Eve White was a mild, restrained suburban housewife who in the course of psychotherapy revealed a second, separate personality. This second personality, Eve Black, was the antithesis of Eve White. Eve Black was childish, mischievous, and erotically flirtatious. Eve Black knew about Eve White and openly talked about the times she had disobeyed her parents or gotten drunk and had then "gone into" Eve White. After Eve Black's escapades, Eve White faced her punishment or bore her hangover. But she did so with bewilderment because she did not know of Eve Black's existence. Eventually, this duality was resolved when a third personality—who called herself Jane—emerged. Jane ultimately separated from Eve White's husband and began a relatively stable new life marked by the slow development of a progression of other personalities. Now in her late 50s, the former Eve White no longer suffers from *multiple personality disorder.*

The careful recording of all pertinent facts in cases like Eve's is essential to psychology. Multiple personality is a rare event, which cannot be produced experimentally. (Multiple personality is discussed further in Chapter 16.)

Survey Method—Here, Have a Sample

Sometimes psychologists would like to ask everyone in the world a few well-chosen questions: "Have you ever smoked marijuana?" "Have you engaged in premarital sexual intercourse?" "What is your marital status now, and were your parents ever separated or divorced?" "Do you favor legal abortion?" The answers to questions such as these can reveal much about significant psychological events in the lives of large groups of people. But since it is impractical to question everyone, psychologists use the **survey method.**

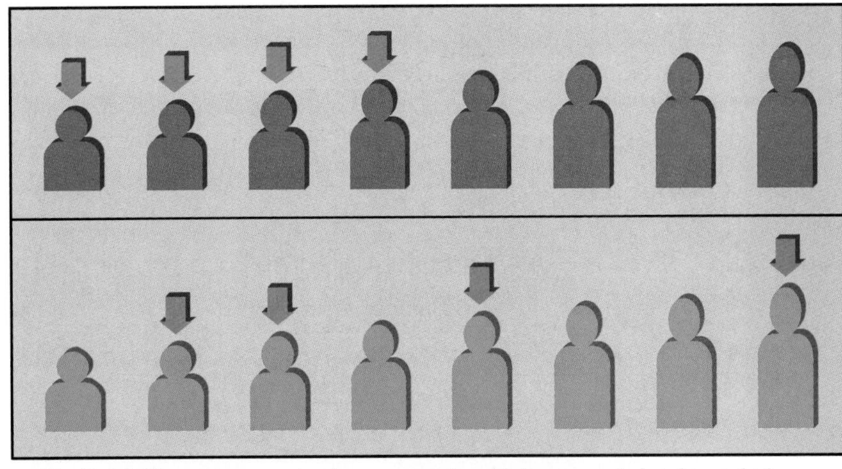

■ **Fig. 2–13** *If you were conducting a survey in which a person's height might be an important variable, the upper, non-random sample would be very unrepresentative. The lower sample, selected using a table of random numbers, better represents the group as a whole.*

In a survey, people in a representative sample are asked a series of carefully worded questions. A **representative sample** includes the same proportion of men, women, young, old, professionals, blue-collar workers, Republicans, Democrats, whites, blacks, Latinos, Asians, and so on, as found in the **population** as a whole. Ultimately, we are interested in an entire group, or population. But by selecting a smaller segment, or sample, we can draw conclusions about the entire group without polling each and every person. Representative samples are often obtained by *randomly* selecting who will be included (■ Fig. 2–13).

Survey questions must be carefully phrased because their wording can greatly affect how people answer. In a survey conducted in 1991, during the Persian Gulf War, people were asked if they were concerned about the "collateral damage" caused by allied bombing in Iraq. When this military euphemism for civilian deaths was used, 55 percent of those polled said they were concerned. In contrast, when people were asked if they were concerned about "the number of civilian casualties and other unintended damage," 82 percent said yes (Rosenstiel, 1991).

A careful survey can provide an accurate picture of how large segments of the general population feel about current issues. However, some psychologists have questioned—tongue in cheek—psychology's claim that its conclusions apply to people in general. The distinguished psychologist Edward Tolman once noted how much of American psychology is based on two sets of subjects: rats and college sophomores. Tolman urged his colleagues to remember that rats certainly are not people and that college sophomores may not be!

In recent years, 93 percent of human subjects in psychology experiments were recruited from introduc-

Multiple personality A rare mental disorder in which a person manifests two or more personalities.

Survey method The use of public polling techniques to answer psychological questions.

Representative sample A small group that accurately reflects a large population.

Population An entire group of animals or people belonging to a particular category (for example, all college students or all married women).

Gender bias A tendency for researchers to base conclusions solely on subjects of one gender (usually males).

Biased sample A sample that does not accurately reflect the population from which it was drawn.

Courtesy bias The tendency to give "polite" answers so as not to hurt an interviewer's feelings.

tory psychology courses (Sieber & Saks, 1989). The majority of these subjects were white members of the middle class (Graham, 1992). This doesn't automatically invalidate the results of psychology experiments. But it may place some limitations on their meanings. Highlight 2–3 further explores a related problem.

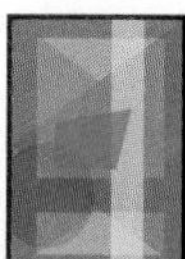

HIGHLIGHT 2–3

Cultural Diversity

Is There a Gender Bias in Psychological Research?

Many doctors recommend that adults take an aspirin a day to help prevent heart attack. Both men and women patients are given this advice. The problem? Not a single woman was included in the sample on which the advice is based. Although females make up more than half the population, they continue to be neglected in psychological and medical research (Denmark, 1994).

Owing to a **gender bias** that favors male subjects, researchers must often *assume* that conclusions based on men also apply to women. But without directly studying women, it is impossible to know how often this assumption is wrong. A related problem occurs when researchers combine results from men and women. Doing so can hide important male-female differences. Similar biases exist concerning the race, ethnicity, age, and sexual orientation of participants in psychological research (Denmark, 1994).

The solution to such problems is straightforward: Whenever possible, researchers need to include a wider array of people in their studies. In recognition of human diversity, many researchers are doing just that.

Question: How accurate is the survey method?

Modern surveys like the Gallup and Harris polls are quite accurate. The Gallup poll has erred in its election predictions by only 1.5 percent since 1954. This high level of accuracy has not always existed. During the 1936 presidential election, a well-known magazine, the *Literary Digest*, predicted that Alfred Landon would defeat Franklin Roosevelt by a large margin. Roosevelt defeated Landon by a landslide!

Question: How could the poll have been so wrong?

The answer lies in the way the sample was taken. Most people in the poll were contacted by *telephone*. In 1936, during the Great Depression, people who had phones were much more wealthy than average, and the wealthy favored Landon. Thus, the telephone sample was **biased** (slanted or distorted) rather than representative. Today, similar problems afflict surveys done by magazines and on-line information services, such as Prodigy and CompuServe. If only subscribers can be polled, the resulting sample may be biased.

Even when questions are carefully stated and the sample is representative, a survey may be limited by another problem. If a psychologist were to ask you detailed questions about your sexual history and current sexual behavior, how accurate would your replies be? Would you be self-conscious and perhaps not completely frank? Or might you have a tendency to exaggerate? Replies to survey questions are not always *accurate* or *truthful*. Many people show a distinct **courtesy bias,** or tendency to give answers that are agreeable and socially acceptable. For example, pollsters working on an election found that black persons talking to white interviewers were less likely to admit support for an African-American candidate. Similarly, white persons talking to black interviewers were more likely to claim support for the African-American candidate (McKean, 1984).

Despite their limitations, surveys frequently produce useful information. For instance, in recent years working women have complained of sexual harassment at their jobs. How widespread is this problem? In 1981, psychologist Barbara Gutek found that 53 percent of women had experienced some form of sexual harassment at work (Gutek, 1981). A more recent survey obtained a figure of 45 percent (Janus & Janus, 1993). These results suggest that sexual harassment has declined slightly, perhaps because of greater public awareness of the problem. Although such information does not solve the problem of sexual harassment, it is a first step toward understanding it and remedying it.

Summary—Science and Critical Thinking

Question: Is so much emphasis on research really necessary in psychology?

In a word, yes. As we have seen, science is a powerful way of asking questions about the world and getting trustworthy answers. More importantly, we might ask, What is the alternative to using the scientific method? In most areas of knowledge, including psychology, wiping out scientific advances would mean a return to the Dark Ages. Your awareness of this fact, along with your understanding of research methods, should help make you a more critical observer of human behavior. Table 2–1 summarizes many of the important ideas we have covered.

Table 2–1 Comparison of Psychological Research Methods

	Advantages	Disadvantages
Naturalistic observation	Behavior is observed in a natural setting; much information is obtained, and hypotheses and questions for additional research are formed	Little or no control is possible; observed behavior may be altered by the presence of the observer; observations may be biased; causes cannot be conclusively identified
Correlational method	Demonstrates the existence of relationships; allows prediction; can be used in lab, clinic, or natural settings	Little or no control possible; relationships may be coincidental; cause-and effect relationships cannot be confirmed
Experimental method	Clear cause-and effect relationships can be identified; powerful controlled observations can be staged; no need to wait for natural event	May be somewhat artificial; some natural behavior not easily studied in laboratory (field experiments may avoid these objections)
Clinical method	Takes advantage of "natural clinical trials" and allows investigation of rare or unusual problems or events	Little or no control is possible; does not provide a control group for comparison; subjective interpretation is often necessary; a single case may be misleading or unrepresentative
Survey method	Allows information about large numbers of people to be gathered; can address questions not answered by other approaches	Obtaining a representative sample is critical and can be difficult to do; answers may be inaccurate; people may not do what they say or say what they do

In many ways, scientific thinking is a refinement of the critical thinking skills described in Chapter 1. Of course, thinking critically about behavior is not easy. A special trap to watch for is called the **my-side bias.** This is the tendency to pay more attention to evidence that supports your existing beliefs and to avoid contradictory evidence. To minimize the my-side bias, critical thinkers actively look for reasons why their ideas might be wrong or incomplete (Baron, 1993).

As you seek to understand your own behavior and that of others, it is valuable to ask yourself frequently: "How might my initial conclusions be wrong? What counter-arguments can I think of? What contradictory evidence might cause me to draw a new conclusion? Remember, too, that critical thinking can help you resist persuasion based on faulty logic, irrational thinking, or invalid conclusions. Searching for contradictory evidence and arguments is a wonderful antidote to misguided persuasion by advertisers, gurus, pundits, politicians, "experts," medical quacks, and sometimes, even psychologists and educators!

My-side bias The tendency to pay attention to evidence and arguments that support one's existing beliefs.

A Look Ahead To complete our discussion, this chapter's Applications section offers a critical look at information reported in the popular press. Unfortunately, these reports abound with sloppy thinking, misinformation, and pie-in-the-sky theories. The first words that spring to your lips when you read outlandish claims should be, "Prove it." The Applications section gives some pointers on what to look for. After that we'll explore the ethics of psychological research. You should find these topics an interesting way to conclude our look at research in psychology.

LEARNING CHECK

1. Case studies can often be thought of as natural tests and are frequently used by clinical psychologists. T or F?
2. For the survey method to be valid, a representative sample of people must be polled. T or F?
3. The phenomenon of multiple personality would most likely be investigated by use of
   a. a representative sample *b.* field experiments *c.* the double-blind procedure *d.* case studies
4. A problem with the survey method is that answers to questions may not always be ______________ or ______________.
5. A psychologist conducting a survey at a shopping mall (The Gallery of Wretched Excess) flips a coin before stopping passersby. If the coin shows heads, he interviews the person; if it shows tails he skips that person. Has the psychologist obtained a random sample? ***Critical Thinking***

Answers: 1. T 2. T 3. *d* 4. accurate, truthful 5. The psychologist's coin flips *might* produce a reasonably good sample of people *at the mall*. The real problem is that people who go to the mall may be mostly from one part of town, from upper income groups, or from some other non-representative group. The psychologist's sample is likely to be seriously flawed.

APPLICATIONS: *Psychology in the News—Reading the Popular Press*

The popularity of psychology has spurred extensive coverage of psychological research and theories in magazines and newspapers. Unfortunately, much of what is written is based on wishful thinking rather than science. Here are some suggestions for separating high quality information from misleading fiction.

Suggestion 1: Be skeptical. Psychological reports in the popular press tend to be made uncritically and with a definite bias toward reporting sensational findings. Remember, saying "That's incredible" means "That's not believable"—which is quite often true.

Example: Some years ago, stories appeared reporting research on "dermo-optical perception." According to these reports, people had been found who could identify colors and read print (even under glass) while blindfolded. These feats supposedly were performed using the fingertips. Many articles treated them as evidence of a "sixth sense," or "X-ray eyes."

Martin Gardner, a scientist whose hobby is magic, suggests that such "abilities" are based on what stage magicians call a "nose peek." Gardner says that it is impossible to prepare a blindfold (without doing damage to the eyes) that does not leave a tiny space on each side of the nose through which a person can peek. In accordance with this criticism, the phenomenal abilities reported in the first dermo-optical perception experiments disappeared each time the opportunity to peek was controlled (Gardner, 1966).

Here is another indication of the need to be skeptical. Psychologist Philip Zimbardo tells with amusement about mentioning to a reporter that in two mental hospitals in which Zimbardo worked, women patients seemed to use more obscenities than male patients did. Zimbardo emphasizes that this was nothing more than a casual statement. Clearly, it was not based on data of any kind. Yet, when it was reported in *The New York Times*, it became an "observation" that he had "noted" over a long period of time. When *Newsweek* reported the *Times* article, the relationship that was "noted" became one that had been "found." Ultimately, *Playboy*'s version stated, "a number of psychologists, *The New York Times* reports, have found that women of every social level have become increasingly uninhibited in their use of obscene language" (Playboy, 1969). Zimbardo was the only authority mentioned to confirm this amazing "fact" (Ruch & Zimbardo, 1971)!

Suggestion 2: Consider the source of information. It should come as no surprise that information given to sell a product often reflects a desire for profit rather than the objective truth. Here is a typical advertising claim: "Government tests have proved that no pain reliever is stronger or more effective than Brand X aspirin." A statement like this usually means that there was *no difference* between the product and others tested. No other pain reliever was stronger or more effective, but none was weaker either.

Keep the source in mind when reading the claims of makers of home biofeedback machines, sleep-learning devices, subliminal tapes, and the like. Remember also that psychological services may be merchandised as well. Be wary of expensive courses that promise instant mental health and happiness, increased efficiency, memory, ESP or psychic ability, control of the unconscious mind, an end to the smoking habit, and so on. Usually they are promoted with a few testimonials and many unsupported claims.

Psychic claims should be viewed with special caution. Stage mentalists make a living by deceiving the public. Understandably, they are highly interested in promoting belief in their non-existent powers. Psychic phenomena, when (and if) they do occur, are quite unpredictable. It would be impossible for a mentalist to do three shows a night, six nights a week without consistently using deception.

Question: I've seen some amazing things on TV. Could you give an example of how I may have been fooled?

Here is a typical stage mentalist's routine. The mentalist picks an audience member "at random" and begins telling him personal things that "the mentalist could not possibly know." How does the mentalist do it? Easy! One of the mentalist's assistants stood in line outside the theater and eavesdropped on conversations before the show. The assistant then made careful note of where the audience member was seated. The seating location and the overheard information were then passed to the mentalist. The mentalist then announces, "You have an aunt . . . Aunt Bessy . . . she has been very ill . . . you were thinking about her earlier this evening . . . you had a flat tire on the way here this evening."

Suggestion 3: Ask yourself if there was a control group. The key importance of a control group in any experiment is frequently overlooked by the unsophisticated—an error to which you are no longer susceptible! The popular press is full of reports of "experiments" performed without control groups: "Talking to Plants Speeds Growth"; "Special Diet Controls Hyperactivity in Children"; "Food Shows Less Spoilage in Pyramid Chamber"; "Graduates of Firewalking Seminar Risk their Soles."

Consider the last example for a moment. In recent years, expensive commercial courses have been promoted to teach people to walk barefoot on hot coals. (Why anyone would want to do this is itself an interesting question.) Firewalkers supposedly protect their feet with a technique called "neurolinguistic programming." Many people have paid good money to learn the technique, and most do manage a quick walk on the coals. But is the technique necessary? And is anything remarkable happening? We need a comparison group!

Fortunately, physicist Bernard Leikind has provided one. Leikind showed with volunteers that anyone (with reasonably callused feet) can walk over a bed of coals without being burned. The reason is that the coals, which are light, fluffy carbon, transmit little heat when touched (■ Fig. 2–14). The principle involved is similar to briefly putting your hand in a hot oven. If you touch a pan, you will be burned because metal transfers heat efficiently. But if your hand stays in the heated air you'll be fine because air transmits little heat (Mitchell, 1987). Mystery solved.

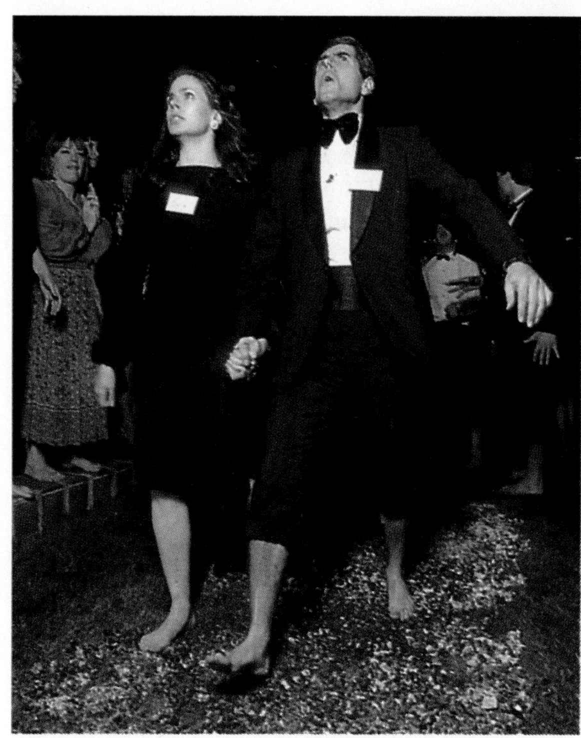

■ **Fig. 2–14** *Firewalking is based on simple physics, not on any form of supernatural psychological control. The temperature of the coals may be as high as 1200° F. However, coals are like the air in a hot oven: they are very inefficient at transferring heat during brief contact.*

Suggestion 4: Look for errors in distinguishing between correlation and causation. An earlier discussion should make it clear that it is dangerous to presume that one thing has *caused* another on the basis of correlation. In spite of this, you will see many claims based on questionable correlations. Recently a nutritionist was quoted in the news as saying that drinking excessive amounts of milk may cause juvenile delinquency. (This must have been a real hit with the National Dairy Association.) On what did he base this conclusion? Adolescent males who are often in trouble, he said, drink greater than average amounts of milk.

This correlation is certainly interesting. But in no way does it demonstrate that milk causes delinquency. It could easily be, for instance, that young males who mature early are more likely to be aggressive or get into trouble. Maturing early involves rapid growth. And rapid growth promotes hunger. It is entirely possible that this is the only link between milk and delinquency. Or perhaps some other unknown factor is involved.

Here's another example of mistaking correlation for causation. Jeanne Dixon, a popular astrologer, once answered a group of prominent scientists—who had declared that there is no scientific foundation for astrology—by saying, "They would do well to check the records at their local police stations, where they will learn that the rate of violent crime rises and falls with lunar cycles" (Dixon, 1975). Dixon, of course, believes that the moon affects human behavior.

Question: If it is true that violent crime is more frequent at certain times of the month, doesn't that prove her point?

Far from it. Increased crime could be due to darker nights, the fact that bills fall due at the first of the month, or any number of similar factors. More importantly, direct studies of the alleged "lunar effect" have shown that it doesn't occur (Rotton & Kelly, 1985). Moonstruck criminals, along with "moon madness," are a fiction (Coates, Lehle, & Cottington, 1989).

Suggestion 5: Be sure to distinguish between observation and inference. If you see a person *crying* is it correct to assume that he or she is *sad?* Although it seems reasonable to make this assumption, it is actually quite risky. We can observe objectively that the person is crying, but to *infer* sadness may be in error. It could be that the individual has just peeled five pounds of onions. Or maybe he or she just won a million-dollar lottery or is trying contact lenses for the first time.

Psychologists, politicians, physicians, scientists, and other experts often go far beyond the available facts in their claims. This does not mean that their inferences, opinions, and interpretations have no value; the opinion of an expert on the causes of mental illness, criminal behavior, learning problems, or whatever can be revealing. But be careful to distinguish between fact and opinion. Here is an example that illustrates why this is important.

> A 54-year-old schizophrenic patient was rewarded for holding a broom that was given to her by a ward attendant. If she held the broom, she was given a cigarette by another attendant. The purpose of this experiment was to determine if rewards should be used to alter the patient's listless behavior (she had been hospitalized for 23 years and refused to do anything on the ward). Soon the patient spent much of her time holding the broom. At this point, two psychiatrists were invited to observe the patient through a one-way mirror. One psychiatrist's interpretation of the broom-holding behavior was that it was a symbolic expression of deep-seated unfulfilled desires. According to him, the broom could be a symbol for (1) "a child that gives her love and she gives him in return her devotion," (2) "a phallic symbol," or (3) "the scepter of an omnipotent queen" (Ayllon et al., 1965).

The psychiatrist *observed* that the patient spent much of her time holding a broom. He *inferred* that this behavior had deep psychological meaning. In fact, she held the broom for one reason: She received cigarettes for doing so!

Suggestion 6: Beware of over-simplifications, especially those motivated by monetary gain. Courses or programs that offer a "new personality in three sessions," "six steps to love and fulfillment in marriage," or newly discovered "secrets of unlocking the powers of the mind" should be immediately suspect.

An excellent example of over-simplification is provided by a brochure entitled, "Dr. Joyce Brothers Asks: How Do You Rate as a 'Superwoman'?" Dr. Brothers, a "media" psychologist who has no private practice and is not known for research, wrote the brochure as a consultant for the Aerosol Packaging Council of the Chemical Specialties Manufacturers Association. A typical suggestion in this brochure tells how to enhance a marriage: "Sweep him off to a weekend hideaway. Tip: When he's not looking spray a touch of your favorite *aerosol* cologne mist on the bedsheets and pillows" (italics added). Sure, Joyce.

Suggestion 7: Remember, "for example" is no proof. After reading this chapter you should be sensitive to the danger of selecting single examples. If you read, "Law student passes state bar exam using sleep-learning device," don't rush out to buy one. Systematic research has shown that these devices are of little or no value (Wood et al., 1992). A corollary to this suggestion is to ask, Are the reported observations important or widely applicable?

Examples, anecdotes, single cases, and testimonials are all potentially deceptive. Unfortunately, *individual cases* tell nothing about what is true *in general* (Stanovich, 1992). For instance, studies of large groups of people show that smoking increases the likelihood of lung cancer. It doesn't matter if you know a lifelong heavy smoker who is 94 years old. The general finding is the one to remember.

Summary We are all bombarded daily with such a mass of new information that it is difficult to absorb it. The available knowledge, even in a limited area like psychology, biology, medicine, or contemporary rock music, is so vast that no single person can completely know and comprehend it. With this situation in mind, it becomes increasingly important that you become a critical, selective, and informed consumer of information.

LEARNING CHECK

1. Newspaper accounts of dermo-optical perception have generally reported only the results of carefully designed psychological experiments. T or F?
2. Stage mentalists and psychics often use deception in their acts. T or F?
3. Blaming the lunar cycle for variations in the rate of violent crime is an example of mistaking correlation for causation. T or F?

APPLICATIONS: *Continued*

4. Psychiatric interpretations of a patient's broom-holding behavior (described earlier) show the importance of using a control group in experiments. T or F?
5. In what way is reading the popular press like being a jury member in a courtroom trial? *Critical Thinking*

Answers:

1. F 2. T 3. T 4. F 5. In both instances it is important to not only study the evidence supporting various claims, but also to evaluate the *quality* of that evidence.

EXPLORATION

Research Ethics—Smile, You're on Candid Camera!

Several years ago, social psychologist Philip Zimbardo and his associates set up a simulated prison at Stanford University. Their goal was to probe the effects of imprisonment on otherwise healthy individuals. Students were recruited to play the roles of prisoners and guards. Much to everyone's surprise, the two-week experiment had to be called off 6 days after it began. The "guards" had become so sadistic that 4 of the 10 "prisoners" suffered severe emotional reactions, including crying, depression, anxiety, and rage (Zimbardo et al., 1973). (This experiment is discussed further in Chapter 20.)

The Stanford prison experiment is only one of several to raise serious ethical questions. Were the participants permanently harmed? Did the information gained justify the emotional costs? Are such experiments dehumanizing? Questions like these have drawn attention to three issues to which researchers must be particularly sensitive. These are: *deception, invasion of privacy,* and *lasting harm.* Each issue is illustrated by the following experiments. See if you think they are ethical.

Deception

In many experiments the true interests of a researcher are hidden by deception. This approach is often considered necessary to obtain genuine reactions. For example, a researcher interested in guilt once led subjects to believe that they had broken an expensive piece of machinery. During the experiment, the machine suddenly popped loudly, released a plume of smoke, and sputtered to a stop. As embarrassed subjects were about to leave, the experimenter asked them to sign a petition he was supposedly circulating. The petition called for a doubling of tuition fees at the school. Almost all control subjects had refused to sign the same petition. However, because of their guilt, more than 50 percent of the experimental subjects signed (Rubin, 1970). Was deception really necessary to answer the researcher's question?

Invasion of Privacy A second area of debate concerns the extent to which invasion of privacy should be allowed in psychological research. One study that has been both criticized and defended involved secret observation of men in a rest room. Psychologist Eric Knowles was interested in the stress caused by "personal space" invasions. An observer concealed himself in a toilet stall in a public rest room and used a hidden periscope to monitor activity at the urinals. As predicted, urination took longer to begin when an assistant occupied a urinal next to the unsuspecting subject (Middlemist et al., 1976; Koocher, 1977). This finding is interesting, but does it justify the invasion of privacy used to obtain it?

Lasting Harm Do psychological experiments ever do lasting harm to participants? This is perhaps the most serious ethical question of all. A classic experiment on obedience to authority illustrates the problem. In the study, subjects thought they were giving painful and dangerous electrical shocks to another person (Milgram, 1974). (No shocks were actually given; see Chapter 20.) Belief that they were hurting someone proved extremely stressful for most subjects. Many left the experiment shaken and upset. Some presumably suffered guilt and distress for some time afterward.

This experiment may sound clearly unethical, but the researcher, Stanley Milgram, did follow-up studies on the participants. Most felt positive about their experience and claimed they were glad they had taken part. Many added that they had learned something of value about themselves. But what about the few who felt otherwise? As in medical research, there are no easy answers to the ethical questions raised by psychology.

Most students find the studies just described interesting and informative. How can the search for knowledge be properly balanced with human rights? As a reply to this question, the American Psychological Association has adopted guidelines that state in part: "Psychologists must carry out investigations with respect for the people who participate and with concern for their dignity and welfare." To ensure that this is the case, most college psychology departments have ethics committees that oversee proposed research. Nevertheless, no easy answers exist for the ethical questions raised by some research. How do *you* think a psychologist should decide if his or her research is ethical?

Becoming a Subject The ethics of research may turn out to be highly pertinent for many students. As mentioned earlier, college students are frequently asked to serve as subjects in psychology experiments. If you become a subject, what should you expect? First of all, count on having an interesting and educational experience. There is no better way to learn how research is done than to observe it firsthand. Beyond that, you have a right to expect that your reactions will remain confidential; that you will be debriefed about the purpose of the research; that you will receive an interpretation of your responses or test results; and finally, that the results of the research project will be made available to you (Blanck et al., 1992; Fisher & Fyrberg, 1994). (See ● Table 2–2.)

Psychological research can be truly fascinating. If you do participate as a subject, you may end up wanting to try experiments or answer questions of your own. Many careers in psychology were launched in just this way.

The Ethics of Animal Research

Research with animals can also raise difficult ethical questions. In recognition of this fact, Principle 10 of the *Ethical Principles of Psychologists* states:

> An investigator of animal behavior strives to advance understanding of basic behavioral principles and/or to contribute to the improvement of human health and welfare. In seeking these ends, the investigator ensures the welfare of animals and treats them humanely. Laws and regulations notwithstanding, an animal's immediate protection depends upon the scientist's own conscience. ("Ethical," 1992)

Behind this statement lies a storm of controversy. Opinions about the ethics of animal research range widely—from medical researchers who routinely conduct animal experiments to vegetarian animal rights activists who raid labs to "liberate" animals. It is not possible here to discuss all of the arguments for and against animal research. However, a brief sketch of the debate may serve as a starting point for further thought.

At one extreme are members of the animal liberation movement. These individuals believe that animals have a right to live without human interference. Animal liberators oppose animal research of all kinds, the raising of animals for food, hunting, rodeos, zoos, and circuses. They regard behavioral research as worthless and cruel, and want to abolish it entirely (Herzog, 1990). At the other extreme are scientists who believe human welfare always takes precedence over animal welfare. These individuals feel that they have a moral imperative to improve the human condition and save human lives. Doing so, they believe, inescapably involves animal research ("Scientists," 1989).

Question: Is there a middle ground?

The majority of scientists, 80 percent of the general public, and many animal welfare advocates, take a more moderate position. These individuals accept the necessity for scientific experiments. They note, for instance, that creating vaccines to end the crippling polio epidemics of the 1950s would have been impossible without animal research. They also recognize that animals, as well as humans, benefit from knowledge gained from scientific research. Moderates primarily seek to ensure humane treatment of animals and to minimize the use of animals where possible. As animal activist Phyllis Macy (1990) says:

> What is called for here is not the cessation of research with animals, but a different attitude toward their use. . . . Research with animals should above all be humane. This means respecting another creature's aspirations for life and capacity for pain. On this variable, all animals, including humans, are equal. We earn respect for ourselves by respecting life around us.

It is probably fair to say that the animal rights movement has called needed attention to the abuse of animals for such purposes as testing cosmetics and other commercial products. It has also encouraged development of alternatives to animal research. Part of the middle ground in this debate, if indeed one exists, is the agreed-upon value of finding alternatives that minimize the use of animals. For example, it may be possible to use computer simulations of animal behavior for teaching and preliminary research. Also, use of animals could be limited to critical studies. But, again questions arise: Who is to say what research is worthwhile? Is it possible to guess where new knowledge will lead? Might a seemingly minor finding unleash a breakthrough?

Think About It No easy answers exist for the ethical questions raised by animal research. However, as noted in Chapter 1, a government report on behavioral research concluded, "The chance that alternatives will completely replace animals

● **Table 2–2 Basic Ethical Guidelines for Psychological Researchers**

- Do no harm.
- Accurately describe risks to potential subjects.
- Ensure that participation is voluntary.
- Minimize any discomfort to participants.
- Maintain confidentiality.
- Do not unnecessarily invade privacy.
- Use deception only when absolutely necessary.
- Remove any misconceptions caused by deception (debrief).
- Provide results and interpretations to participants.
- Treat participants with dignity and respect.

EXPLORATION

in the future is nil" ("Research," 1989). In light of this, how would you answer the following questions?

- When is the use of animals necessary? When are replacements acceptable?
- If use of animals is necessary, can their numbers be reduced?
- If use of animals is necessary, and the numbers cannot be decreased, what are the moral and ethical implications?
- Could animal subjects be treated more humanely than they are now?
- What groups are best qualified to make decisions in this area? ("Animal rights," 1990)

Learning Check

1. Deception is regarded as a necessary part of almost all psychology experiments. T or F?
2. Most of the subjects who participated in Milgram's obedience experiment felt that they had not been harmed. T or F?
3. The major ethical question raised by the Stanford prison experiment concerned an invasion of privacy. T or F?
4. In the United States, the American Psychological Association must rule on whether or not an experiment is ethical before it is performed. T or F?
5. Principle 10 of the *Ethical Principles of Psychologists* states that humane treatment of animals ultimately depends on each scientist's own conscience. T or F?
6. Perhaps the most basic of all ethical requirements in psychological research involves the accurate reporting of results. Can you explain why? ***Critical Thinking***

Answers: 1. F 2. T 3. F 4. F 5. T 6. To advance scientific knowledge and human welfare, psychologists must report the results of their studies honestly—even when the results contradict the researcher's beliefs or expectations. It takes a high level of integrity to do psychological research and follow the evidence wherever it leads.

Chapter Summary

- ***Why is the scientific method important to psychologists?***

- The **scientific method** is used to improve upon common sense and avoid the pitfalls of informal observation.
- Important elements in a scientific investigation include **observing, defining a problem,** proposing a **hypothesis, gathering evidence/testing the hypothesis,** and forming a **theory.**
- Before they can be investigated, psychological concepts must be given **operational definitions.**

- ***How do psychologists collect information?***

- **Naturalistic observation** is a starting place in many investigations. Three problems with this approach are the effects of the observer on the observed, observer bias, and an inability to explain observed behavior.
- In the **correlational method,** relationships between two traits, responses, or events are measured. Then a **correlation coefficient** is computed to gauge the strength of the relationship. Correlations allow prediction, but they are usually insufficient to demonstrate cause-and-effect connections.
- **Relationships** in psychology may be **positive** or **negative, linear** or **curvilinear.** Relationships are often clarified by graphing.
- Cause-and-effect relationships are best identified by **controlled experiments.**

- ***How is an experiment performed?***

- In an experiment, two or more groups of subjects are formed. These groups differ only with regard to the **independent variable** (condition of interest as a cause in the experiment).
- Effects on the **dependent variable** are then measured. All other conditions **(extraneous variables)** are held constant.
- It must be possible to **replicate** (repeat) observations or experiments for them to be meaningful.
- In experiments testing drugs, a **placebo** (fake pill or injection) must be used to control for the effects of expectations. Drug research also frequently employs

a **double-blind** procedure so that neither subjects nor experimenters know who is receiving a drug.

- A related problem is the **experimenter effect.** This is the tendency for experimenters to subtly and unconsciously influence the outcome of an experiment. Expectations can create a **self-fulfilling prophecy,** in which a person changes in the direction of the expectation.

■ ***What other research methods do psychologists use?***

- The **clinical method** employs **case studies,** which are in-depth records of a single subject. Case studies provide important information on topics that would not be studied any other way.
- In the **survey method,** people in a **representative sample** are asked a series of carefully worded questions. Responses to these questions provide information on the attitudes and psychological functioning of large groups of people.

■ ***How dependable is psychological information found in the popular press?***

- Information in the popular media varies greatly in quality and accuracy. It is wise to approach such information with skepticism and caution. This is especially true with regard to the **source of information, uncontrolled observation, correlation and causation, inferences, over-simplification,** and **single examples.** Critical thinking will help you cut through the misinformation.

■ ***What ethical questions does psychological research raise?***

- Psychological research raises a number of ethical questions. Three **ethical issues** of particular importance in human research are: **deception, invasion of privacy,** and **lasting harm.**
- Animal research also poses ethical dilemmas. Debates concerning animal welfare are based on personal values and morals and are therefore not easily resolved. The American Psychological Association strongly endorses the humane treatment of research animals.

Questions for Discussion

1. Can you think of some "commonsense" statements (other than those already mentioned) that contradict each other? Why do you think such contradictions go unnoticed?
2. There is a loophole in the statement, "I've been taking vitamin C tablets, and I haven't had a cold all year." What is it?
3. Let's say you are interested in investigating the unspoken rules that govern the spacing of people in public places. What research techniques would you use? Can you propose some field experiments that might be performed?
4. What type of correlation would you expect to find between noise levels and productivity in an office? Between income and education? Between physical attractiveness and frequency of dating? Between class attendance and grades? Between use of alcohol by parents and their children? How would you demonstrate a causal link in any of these cases?
5. Regarding self-fulfilling prophecies, how have the expectations of teachers, parents, or friends affected your expectations for yourself? If you have attended a school with slow, normal, and accelerated classes, what advantages and disadvantages do you see in such a system?
6. In your opinion, is it dishonest or unethical for a physician to administer placebos to patients? Why or why not?
7. Clinical cases are often described in the popular press. What could be the benefits and negative effects of this kind of publicity?
8. Have you ever taken part in a survey? On the basis of your participation, how accurate do you think surveys are? What are the flaws of typical "person on the street" surveys often done by local newspapers?
9. Compared to things done regularly by the government, the military, business, and educational institutions, most psychology experiments are pretty tame. With this in mind, what is your position on the ethical questions raised by human research?
10. Do you consider the experiments described in the Exploration section ethical? What changes would you make if you were repeating the experiments?
11. Compared with their despised relatives in the streets, laboratory rats are well caged, cared for, and fed. Why do you think that animal activists haven't protested the wholesale poisoning of sewer rats and other "pest" animals? To what extent are an animal's chances of gaining protection based on how "cute" it is?
12. Psychologist Harold Herzog (1991) has pointed out that the owners of dogs and cats "imprison" these animals for their own pleasure. They also place their pets' interests ahead of the animals that are raised to make pet food. "Is this really so different," he asks, "from researchers who place the interests of sick animals or humans ahead of those animals that are subjects of research designed to find ways of alleviating suffering?" What do you think?

Chapter 3

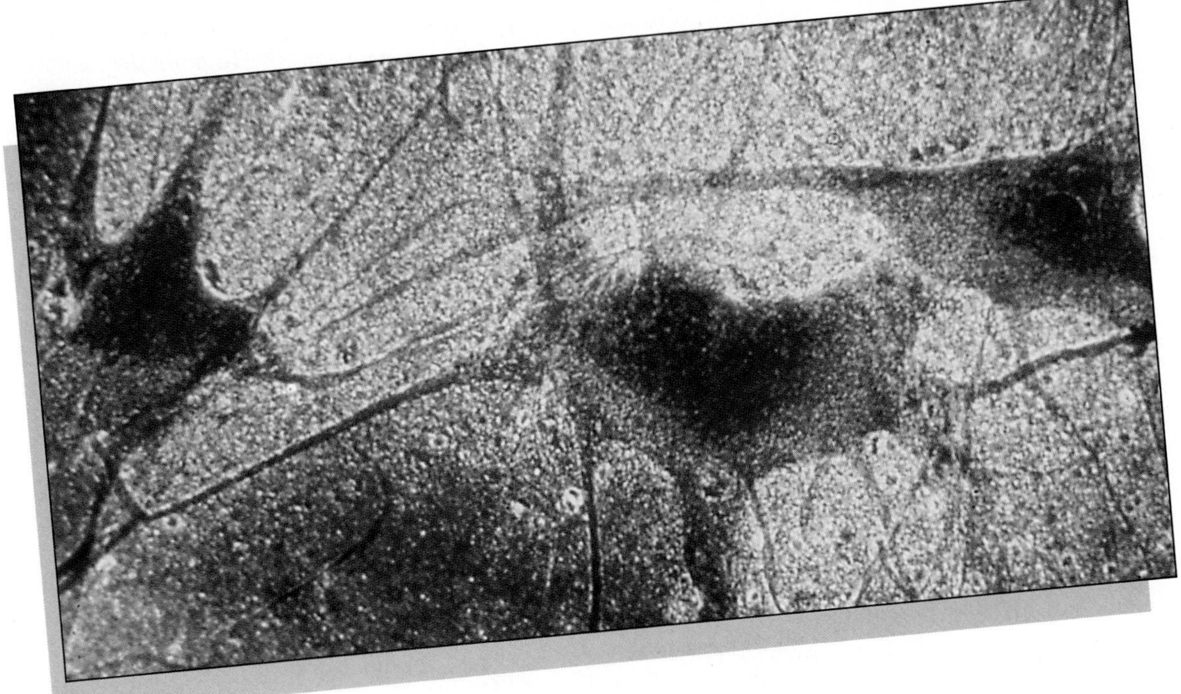

The Brain, Biology, and Behavior

CHAPTER PREVIEW

Worlds Within Worlds Within Worlds

Imagine yourself smaller than the period at the end of this sentence. Then join me as we enter a bizarre microscopic world. Surrounding us is a tangle of spidery branches, delicate fibers, and transparent globes. As we watch, pulsing waves of electrical energy flash through the fibers, scattering in thousands of directions. Meanwhile, all is bathed in a swirling sea of exotic chemicals. We are indeed in a strange realm. Yet there is beauty here, and mind-bending complexity—for we have just entered that most amazing of all computers, the human brain.

Crack open the fragile shell of the skull and you find, in the truest sense, "worlds within worlds within worlds." The human brain is about the size of a large grapefruit. Weighing a little over 3 pounds, it consists of some 100 billion nerve cells called ***neurons*** *(NEW-rons).*

Neurons specialize in carrying and processing information. They also activate muscles and glands. Thus, everything you think, do, or feel can be traced back to these tiny cells. The mass of neurons we call the brain allows humans to make music of exquisite beauty, to seek a cure for cancer, or to read a book like this one.

IN THIS CHAPTER

Neurons Individual nerve cells.

Each neuron in the brain's "enchanted loom" is linked to as many as 15,000 others. This network makes it possible to combine and store an exceedingly large amount of information. In fact, there may be more possible pathways between neurons in a single human brain than there are atoms in the entire universe!

Scientists have long known that the brain is the organ of consciousness and action. Yet only recently have they been able to demonstrate it directly. To prove the point, researcher José Delgado once entered a bullring with a cape and a radio transmitter. The bull charged. Delgado retreated. At the last possible instant the speeding bull stopped short. Why? Because Delgado's radio activated electrodes (metal wires) implanted deep within the bull's brain. These, in turn, stimulated "control centers" that brought the bull to a halt.

***Biopsychology** is the study of how biological processes, especially activity in the brain and nervous system, relate to behavior. It is clear that answers to many age-old questions of mind, consciousness, and knowledge lie buried within the brain (Carlson, 1991). Let us enter this fascinating realm for a closer look at our biological heritage and human potential.*

Survey Questions

- How do nerve cells operate and communicate?
- What are the functions of major parts of the nervous system?
- How is the brain organized and what do its higher structures do?
- Why are the brain's association areas important? What happens when they are injured?
- What kinds of behaviors are controlled by the subcortex?
- Does the glandular system affect behavior?
- In what ways do right- and left-handed individuals differ?
- How do biopsychologists study the brain?

Biopsychology The study of how biological activity, especially in the brain and nervous system, relates to behavior.

Dendrites Neuron fibers that receive incoming messages.

Soma The main body of a neuron or other cell.

Axon Fiber that carries information away from the cell body of a neuron.

Axon terminals Branching fibers at the ends of axons.

Ion An electrically charged molecule.

Resting potential The electrical charge of a neuron at rest.

Threshold The point at which a nerve impulse is triggered.

Neurons—Building a "Biocomputer"

As biopsychologist Paul MacLean once remarked, the towering question today is whether we can master the brain before we blow ourselves to smithereens through our mastery of physics and chemistry. Unraveling the mysteries of the brain begins with neurons, the basic units of the human "biocomputer." A single neuron is not very smart. Yet, when neurons join in vast networks, they produce intelligence and consciousness.

Question: How do neurons carry information?

Parts of a Neuron

The nervous system is made up of long "chains" of neurons. No two neurons are exactly alike in size or shape, but most have four basic parts (■ Fig. 3–1). Notice first the **dendrites** (DEN-drytes), which look like the roots of a tree. The dendrites specialize in receiving messages from other neurons. The cell body, or **soma** (SOH-mah), also accepts incoming information, which it collects and combines. Every so often, these messages cause the soma to send a nerve impulse down a long thin fiber called an **axon** (AK-sahn).

Most axons branch at their ends to form **axon terminals.** These branches link with the dendrites and somas of other neurons. In this way, information passes from neuron to neuron. Some axons are only about 0.1 millimeter long. (That's about the width of a pencil line.) Other axons stretch up to a meter through the adult nervous system. Like miniature cables, axons carry messages from the sensory organs to the brain, from the brain to muscles or glands, or simply from one neuron to the next.

The Nerve Impulse

Each neuron is like a tiny biological battery ready to be discharged. Electrically charged molecules called **ions** (EYE-ons) are found in differing numbers inside and outside of each nerve cell. As a result, a tiny difference in electrical charge exists across the cell membrane (outer casing). The inside of human neurons measures about minus 70 millivolts compared to outside the cell (■ Fig. 3–2). (A millivolt is one-thousandth of a volt.) This electrical charge is called the **resting potential.**

Messages arriving from other neurons alter the resting potential until it reaches a **threshold,** or trigger point, for firing. The threshold for human neurons is about minus 50 millivolts (see Fig. 3–2). When a neu-

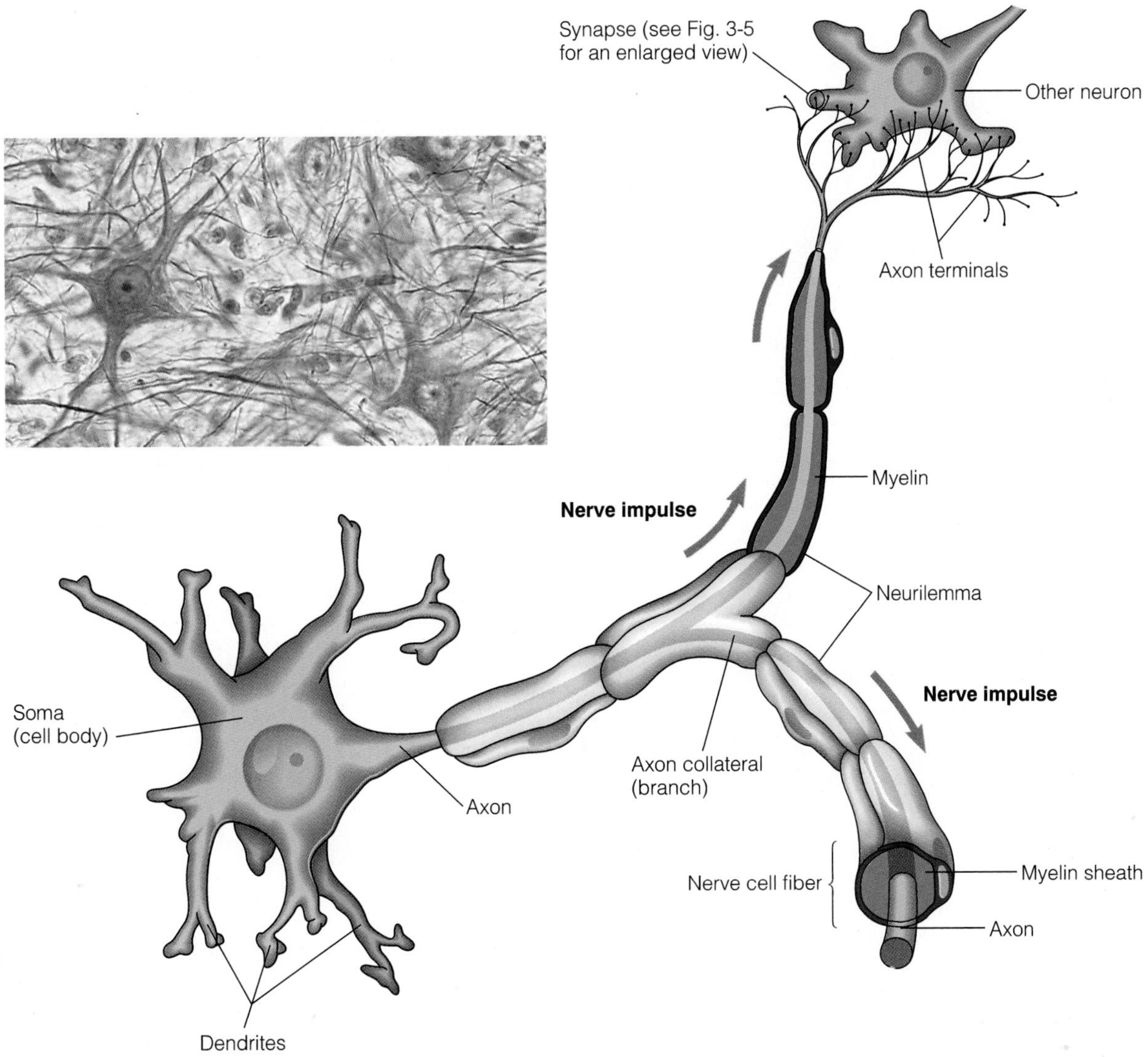

■ **Fig. 3–1** *An example of a neuron, or nerve cell, showing several of its important features. The right foreground shows a nerve cell fiber in cross section, and the upper left inset gives a more realistic picture of the shape of neurons. The nerve impulse usually travels from the dendrites and soma to the branching ends of the axon. The neuron shown here is a motor neuron. Motor neurons originate in the brain or spinal cord and send their axons to the muscles or glands of the body.*

■ **Fig. 3–2** *Activity in an axon can be measured by placing electrical probes inside and outside the axonal membrane. At rest, the inside of an axon is about minus 60 to 70 millivolts, compared with the outside. Electrochemical changes in a nerve cell generate an action potential. When positively charged sodium ions (Na+) rush into the cell, its interior briefly becomes positive. This is the action potential. After the action potential, an outward flow of positive potassium ions (K+) restores the negative charge inside the axon. (See Figures 3–3 and 3–4 for further explanation.)*

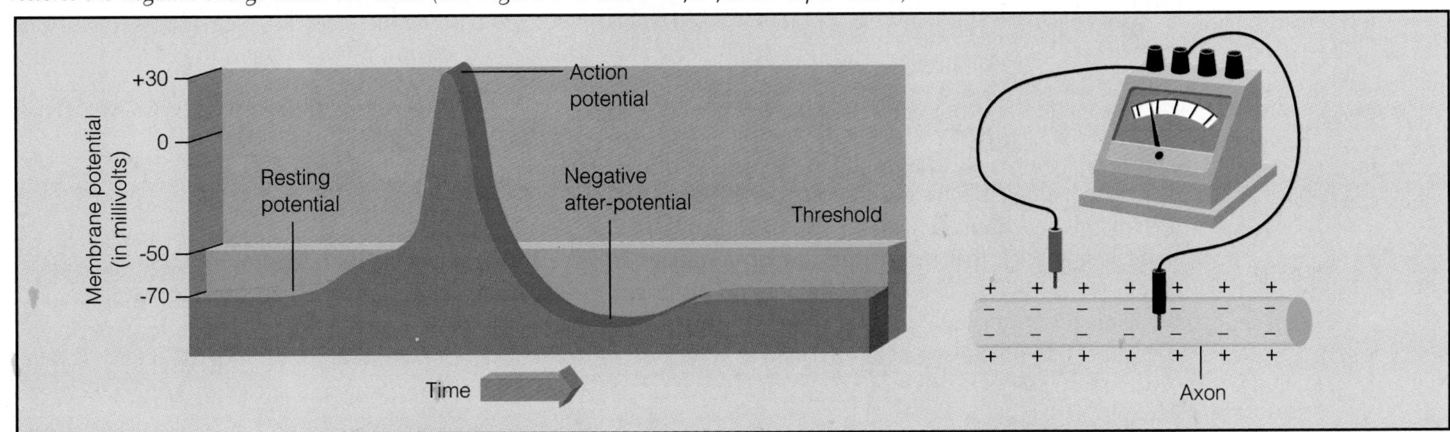

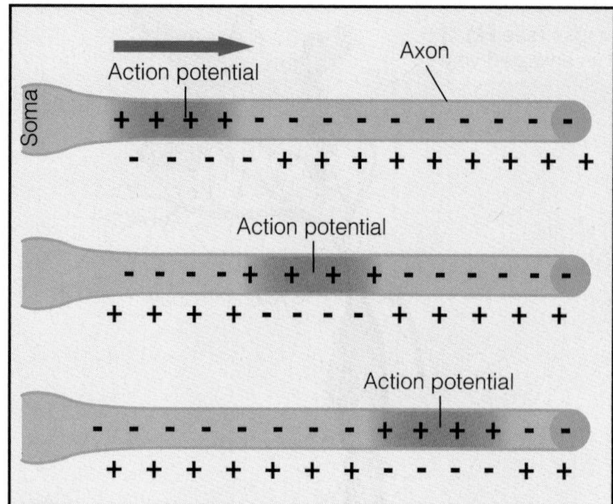

■ **Fig. 3–3** *The inside of an axon normally has a negative electrical charge. The fluid surrounding an axon is normally positive. As an action potential passes along the axon, these charges reverse, so that the interior of the axon briefly becomes positive.*

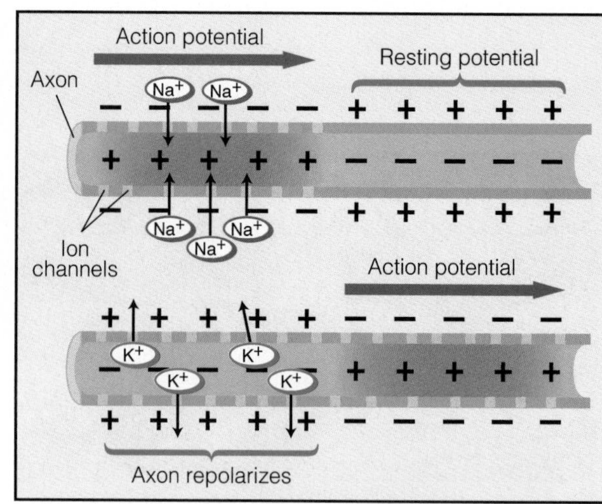

■ **Fig. 3–4** *Cross-sectional views of an axon. The right end of the top axon is at rest, with a negatively charged interior. An action potential begins when the ion channels open and sodium ions (Na+) enter the axon. In this drawing the action potential would travel rapidly along the axon, from left to right. In the lower axon the action potential has moved to the right. After it passes, potassium ions (K+) flow out of the axon. This quickly renews the negative charge inside the axon, so it can fire again. Sodium ions that enter the axon during an action potential are pumped back out more slowly. Their removal restores the original resting potential.*

Action potential The nerve impulse.

Ion channels Channels through the axon membrane.

Negative after-potential A drop in electrical charge below the resting potential.

Myelin A fatty layer coating some axons.

ron reaches this point, a nerve impulse, or **action potential,** sweeps down the axon (■ Fig. 3–3).

The action potential occurs because tiny tunnels, called **ion channels,** pierce the axon membrane. These channels are normally closed by molecular "gates." During an action potential, the gates pop open and allow sodium ions (Na+) to rush into the axon (Carlson, 1991). This happens first near the soma. Then, as the action potential moves along, the gates open, one after another, down the length of the axon (■ Fig. 3–4). At this very instant, millions of action potentials are firing in your brain.

The threshold for firing makes the action potential an **all-or-nothing** event; an impulse occurs completely or not at all. You might find it helpful to picture the axon as a row of dominoes set on end. Tipping over the dominoes is an all-or-nothing event. Once the first domino drops, a wave of falling dominoes will zip rapidly to the end of the line. Similarly, when a nerve impulse is triggered near the soma, a wave of activity (the action potential) travels down the axon to the axon terminals.

After each nerve impulse, the cell briefly drops below its resting level. This drop is called a **negative after-potential.** It is due to an outward flow of potassium ions (K+) that occurs while the membrane gates are open (Fig. 3–4). After each nerve impulse, the neuron must recharge. It does this by shifting ions back across the cell membrane until the resting potential is restored. Using our model, that means the row of dominoes is quickly set up again, beginning at the soma. This leaves the axon ready for another wave of activity very soon after an action potential reaches the end of the axon.

It takes about one-thousandth of a second for a neuron to fire an impulse and return to its resting level. For this reason, a maximum of about 1000 nerve impulses per second is possible. However, firing rates of 1 per second to 300 or 400 per second are more typical (Steven, 1979).

Question: How fast do nerve impulses travel along the axon?

Impulses travel at about 2.5 meters (roughly, 8 feet) per second in small, thin axons and up to 100 meters per second (about 225 miles per hour) in large axons. The larger the diameter of an axon, the faster it conducts. The speed of nerve impulses is also higher when **myelin** (MY-eh-lin) is present. Myelin is a fatty layer that covers some axons. Where the myelin is broken by small gaps, nerve impulses move faster by jumping from gap to gap.

As you can see, nerve impulses are far from instantaneous. If someone steps on your toes, it takes one-fiftieth of a second for your brain to get the message!

Question: How does information move from one neuron to another?

Synapses and Neurotransmitters

We have seen that the nerve impulse is primarily an electrical event. That's why electrically stimulating the brain affects behavior. (A good example is José Delgado's "electronic bullfighting" described in the Chapter Preview.) In contrast, communication between neurons is primarily *chemical.*

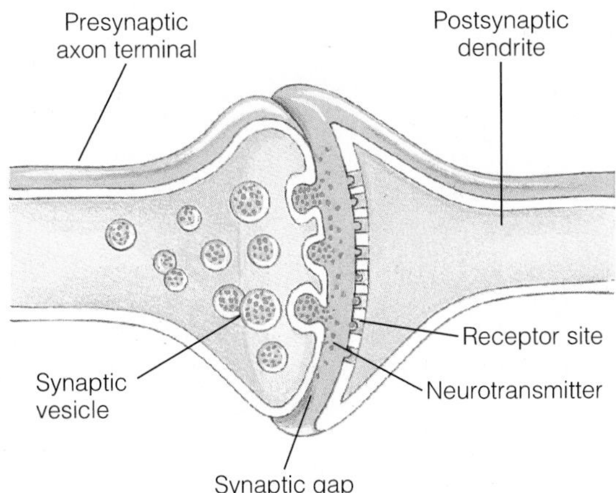

■ **Fig. 3–5** *A highly magnified view of a synapse like that shown in Fig. 3–1. In a typical chemical synapse, neurotransmitters are stored in tiny sacs called synaptic vesicles. When a nerve impulse arrives at an axon terminal, the vesicles move to the surface and release neurotransmitters. These transmitter molecules cross the synaptic gap to affect the next neuron. The size of the gap is exaggerated here; it is actually only about one-millionth of an inch. Transmitter molecules vary in their effects: Some excite the next neuron and some inhibit its activity. In insects and lower animals electrical synapses sometimes occur. In this case, a nerve impulse in one neuron may directly alter the electrical charge in the next neuron, without any reliance on chemical messengers (Agnati et al., 1992).*

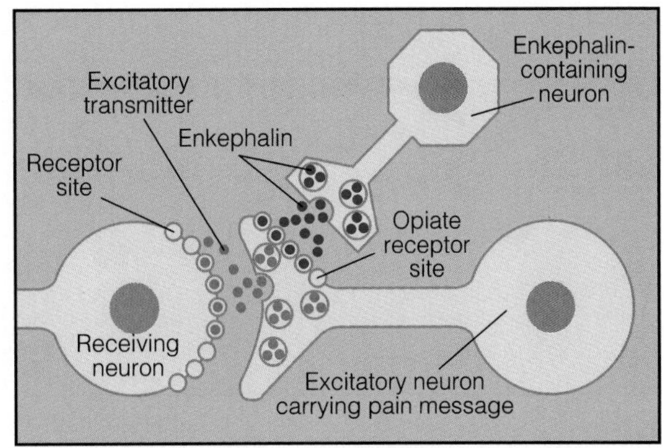

■ **Fig. 3–6** *This simplified diagram shows how natural opiates may operate in the brain to relieve pain. Neurons carrying pain messages appear to have receptor sites for opiate-like transmitters called enkephalins. Release of enkephalins by "regulator" neurons suppresses activity in pain-carrying neurons. This suppression blocks or reduces the flow of pain messages.*

The point of contact between neurons is called a **synapse** (SIN-aps) (■ Fig. 3–5). When a nerve impulse reaches the tips of the axon terminals, it causes chemicals called **neurotransmitters** (NUE-roh-TRANS-mit-ers) to be released into the synaptic gap. Transmitter molecules cross the gap and attach to special **receptor sites** on the soma or dendrites of the next neuron (Fig. 3–5). Receptor sites are tiny areas on the surface of a cell that are sensitive to neurotransmitters. Transmitters also activate receptor sites on muscles and glands.

Question: Does the release of a neurotransmitter immediately trigger an action potential in the next neuron?

Not always. Transmitters may excite the next neuron (move it closer to firing) or *inhibit* it (make an impulse less likely). At any instant, a neuron may receive messages from hundreds or thousands of other neurons. If several "exciting" messages arrive close in time, and they are not canceled by "inhibiting" messages, the neuron reaches its trigger point. This means that chemical messages are *combined* before a neuron "decides" to fire its all-or-nothing action potential. Multiply these events by 100 billion neurons and 100 trillion synapses and you have an amazing computer—one that fits into a space smaller than a shoe box.

There are now more than 30 known or suspected neurotransmitters in the brain. Among the more important "chemical messengers" are acetylcholine, adrenaline, noradrenaline, serotonin, dopamine, histamine, and various amino acids. So, in addition to acting like an electronic computer, the brain is also a sort of chemical factory. The large variety of transmitter chemicals is one reason why thousands of drugs affect behavior.

Many drugs operate by imitating, duplicating, or blocking the actions of neurotransmitters. For example, a transmitter called **acetylcholine** (ah-SEET-ul-KOH-leen) normally activates muscles. However, the drug **curare** (cue-RAH-ree) also attaches to receptor sites on muscles. This prevents acetylcholine from reaching the sites (Thompson, 1985). As a result, a person or animal given curare will be paralyzed—a fact known to South American Indians of the Amazon River Basin, who use curare as an arrow poison.

Neural Regulators A stunning series of recent discoveries has revealed a new class of brain transmitters. These are called **neuropeptides** (NUE-roh-PEP-tides), or simply brain peptides (Agnati et al., 1992).

Neuropeptides do not carry messages directly. Instead, these chemicals seem to *regulate* the activity of other neurons. An example of a brain peptide in action is shown in ■ Figure 3–6. As you can see in the drawing, some neurons have specific receptor sites for opiate drugs such as morphine.

Question: Why would the brain have opiate receptors? After all, the human body isn't born with opium in it.

This is exactly the question that started a search for natural opiate-like peptides in the brain. Scientists found that the brain produces opiate-like neural regulators called **enkephalins** (en-KEF-ah-lins) to relieve pain and stress (Iversen, 1979). Related chemicals called **endorphins** (en-DORF-ins) are released by the

Synapse The microscopic space between two neurons, over which messages pass.

Neurotransmitter Any chemical released by a neuron that alters activity in other neurons.

Receptor sites Areas on the surface of neurons and other cells that are sensitive to neurotransmitters or hormones.

Acetylcholine The neurotransmitter released by neurons to activate muscles.

Curare A drug that competes with acetylcholine, causing paralysis.

Neuropeptides Brain chemicals that regulate the activity of neurons.

Enkephalins Opiate-like brain chemicals that regulate pain and reactions to stress.

Endorphins Chemicals that are similar in structure and pain-killing effect to opiate drugs such as morphine.

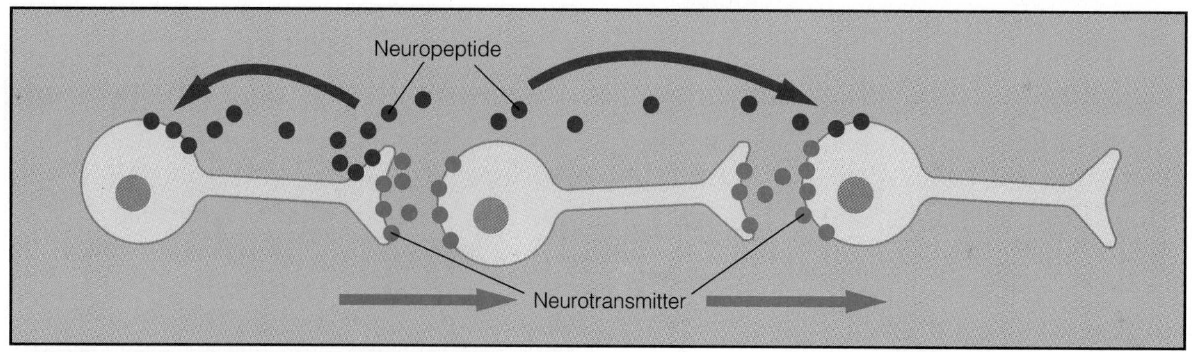

■ **Fig. 3–7** *Some neurons release only neurotransmitters. These nerve cells create fast, reliable message pathways in the brain. Other neurons release neuropeptides which directly regulate the activity of specific target neurons. (See Fig. 3–6.) A third class of neurons releases both neurotransmitters and neuropeptides. As you would expect, the neurotransmitters are released directly into the synaptic gap. Neuropeptides, in contrast, are released at some distance from the synapse. As the drawing shows, brain peptides can travel through the extra-cellular fluid surrounding neurons. Although they move slowly, neuropeptides can have far-reaching effects on neighboring neurons, resulting in changes in emotion and behavior (Agnati et al., 1992).*

Volume transmission The spread of neuropeptides into groups of neurons, affecting their behavior.

Nerve A bundle of neuron fibers.

Neurilemma A layer of cells that encases some axons.

pituitary gland (Thompson, 1985). It now appears that phenomena as diverse as "runner's high," the placebo effect, and acupuncture may be explained by the action of enkephalins and endorphins. (See Chapter 4 for more information.)

When you touch something hot, you jerk your hand away. The neural messages for this action are carried by neurotransmitters. At the same time, pain may cause the brain to release enkephalins and endorphins. These chemical regulators reduce the pain so that it is not too disabling (Thompson, 1985).

Relaying messages across synapses is fast and efficient. Information travels in well-defined pathways like train tracks connecting cities. In contrast, neuropeptides seem to "leave the track" in order to influence surrounding nerve cells. The action of neuropeptides is more like a radio broadcast: When a peptide is released, large groups of neurons may be affected. This process is called **volume transmission** (Agnati et al., 1992).

Rather than merely crossing the synaptic gap, some neuropeptides are carried through the fluid-filled space surrounding neurons. Messages carried in this way can be received by any nerve cell that has an appropriate receptor. A neuropeptide can affect the neuron that released it (autoregulation), a neighboring cell, or a distant cell (■ Fig. 3–7).

Neuropeptides can have long-term effects on how excitable a target neuron is. The neuron's metabolism or growth may even be affected. In these ways, release of peptides from a few neurons can alter the pattern of activity in large areas of the brain. By regulating the general level of activity in brain circuits, neuropeptides appear to influence sleep and wakefulness, alertness, moods, memory, pain, hunger, pleasure, sexual behavior and other basic processes (Agnati et al., 1992). Ultimately, brain peptides may help explain depression, schizophrenia, drug addiction, and other puzzling problems.

The Nervous System—Wired for Action

Picture two people playing catch with a Frisbee. To an outside observer this activity appears interesting, but certainly not amazing. Yet, consider what is going on inside the body: To toss the Frisbee or catch it, a huge amount of information must be sensed, interpreted, and directed to countless muscle fibers. The neural circuits of the body are ablaze with activity. Let's explore the "wiring diagram" that makes this possible.

Neurons and Nerves

Question: Are neurons the same as nerves?

No. Neurons are tiny individual cells. Nerves can be seen with the unaided eye. Rather than being single cells, **nerves** are large bundles of neuron fibers (axons and dendrites). Many nerves have a whitish color because they are made up mainly of axons coated with myelin. A thin layer of cells called the **neurilemma** (NUE-rih-LEM-ah) is also wrapped around most nerve cell fibers outside the brain and spinal cord. (Return to Fig. 3–1.)

The neurilemma is important because it forms a "tunnel" through which damaged nerve cell fibers can grow when repairing themselves. If you were to accidentally sever a finger, and if it were sewn back on, there is a good chance the nerves would regenerate. In fact, you could expect feeling to creep back at a rate of about one millimeter per day.

The *brain* and *spinal cord* cannot normally grow new neurons to replace any that are lost, so they must last a lifetime. If the spinal cord is torn, cut, or crushed, a person may permanently lose use of the body below the point of injury. Also, if the cell body of a neuron is destroyed *anywhere* in the nervous system, the cell's axon and dendrites will die, too. This is the cause of polio, a crippling disease in which the cell bodies of neurons controlling muscles are destroyed. Highlight 3–1 discusses a fascinating exception to the preceding statements.

Central nervous system The brain and spinal cord.

Peripheral nervous system All parts of the nervous system outside the brain and spinal cord.

HIGHLIGHT 3–1

Research Frontier

Brain Grafts and Nerve Regeneration

Transplanting brain tissue may sound like science fiction. Nevertheless, some brain grafts are already being done. It seems likely that other types will someday be used to correct a variety of brain diseases and injuries.

If brain cells that die are lost forever, can they be replaced artificially? There is growing evidence that in some cases the answer is yes. Damage can sometimes be repaired with grafts of healthy brain cells (Kimble, 1990). In one experiment, the brains of rats were damaged in an area that affects learning. Some of the rats then received implants of healthy brain tissue in the damaged region. Others remained untreated. Next, a maze-learning test was conducted, with encouraging results: Rats that received implants did significantly better than those left untreated (Labbe et al., 1983). In addition, the grafts appeared to have "taken," or actually linked up with existing brain tissue.

Implants may also provide a cure for some brain-centered diseases. For instance, the crippling effects of Parkinson's disease are caused by a loss of brain cells that release dopamine. (Recall that dopamine is a transmitter substance.) In recent years, a number of human patients with severe Parkinson's disease have had dopamine-producing cells grafted into their brains. Some of these patients have improved greatly (Lindvall et al., 1990).

A problem with brain grafts is that they are unlikely to be accepted by the body unless immature fetal cells are used. However, reliance on fetal cells raises grave ethical concerns. Is there a way to resolve this dilemma? In a stunning breakthrough, researchers have succeeded in growing normal, mature brain cells in the laboratory (Ronnett et al., 1990). Thus, cultured neurons may soon be available to help repair brain injuries and to treat Parkinson's disease (■ Fig. 3–8).

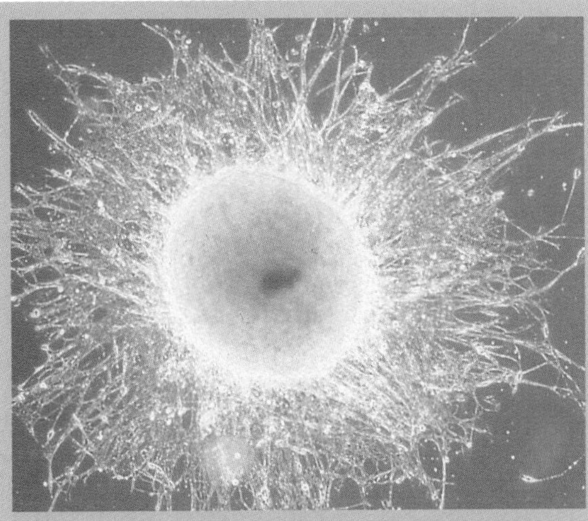

■ **Fig. 3–8** *Scientists predict that damaged neurons in the brain and spinal cord will someday be regenerated with a combination of growth-promoting substances and chemicals that block growth inhibitors. Here, a cultured nerve cell bathed in nerve growth factor (a growth-promoting protein) has been coaxed into sprouting new nerve endings (Weiss, 1989).*

Obviously, it's a little early to think about seeking a brain graft to get you through final exams. Transplants remain highly experimental. Just the same, brain grafting may make it possible to repair some brain and spinal injuries that are now irreversible. Imagine what that could mean to a person confined to a wheelchair or someone suffering the after-effects of a stroke.

Progress is also being made in coaxing regrowth of damaged neurons in the brain and spinal cord. For example, Swiss scientists recently found a way to trigger regrowth of up to a half inch in the severed spinal cords of rats (Schnell & Schwab, 1990). Although it is unwise to raise false hopes, such studies suggest that regrowth and repair of the nervous system is moving closer to reality.

The Nervous System

Taken as a whole, the nervous system is a single unified structure. Dividing it into smaller parts, however, makes it easier to understand. As seen in ■ Fig. 3–9, the **central nervous system** can be distinguished from the **peripheral nervous system.** The central nervous system (CNS) consists of the brain and spinal cord. The brain is the central "computer" of the nervous system. It communicates with the rest of the body

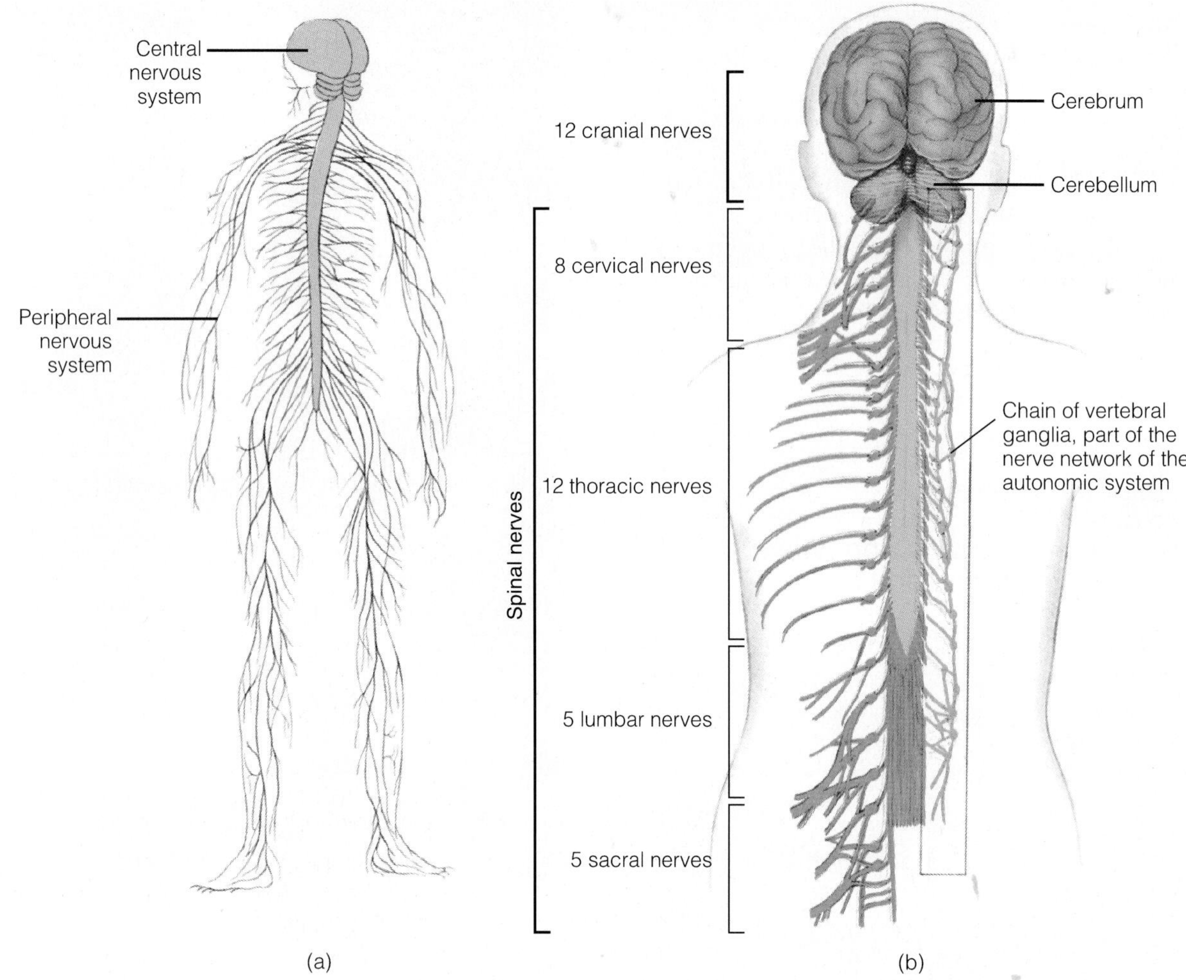

■ **Fig. 3–9** (a) *Central and peripheral nervous systems.* (b) *Spinal nerves, cranial nerves, and the autonomic nervous system. (The cranial nerves, which exit the brain on its underside, are not visible in this drawing.)*

Somatic system The system of nerves linking the spinal cord with the body and sense organs.

Autonomic system The system of nerves carrying information to and from the internal organs and glands.

Sympathetic system A branch of the ANS that arouses the body.

Parasympathetic system A branch of the ANS that quiets the body.

through the spinal cord and the peripheral nervous system (and in other ways as well).

Question: How are the CNS and the peripheral nervous system related?

The Peripheral Nervous System The peripheral system (PNS) is composed of nerves that carry information to and from the CNS. The peripheral system has two subparts: (1) the **somatic** system, which carries messages to and from the sense organs and skeletal muscles and (2) the **autonomic** system, which serves the internal organs and glands of the body (■Fig. 3–10). In general, the somatic system controls voluntary behavior and the autonomic system controls involuntary activities. Thus, messages carried by the somatic system can make your hand move, but they cannot change your heart rate. Likewise, messages carried by the autonomic system can stimulate digestion, but they cannot help you write a letter.

The autonomic nervous system (ANS) can be subdivided into the **sympathetic** and **parasympathetic** branches. Both branches are related to emotional responses, such as crying, sweating, heart rate, and other involuntary behavior (■Fig. 3–11). The ANS, along with the somatic system, coordinates the inner and outer worlds of the body. If a large and angry-looking dog lunges at you, the somatic system helps control the muscles for running. At the same time, the autonomic system raises blood pressure, quickens the heart, and so forth.

Question: How do the branches of the autonomic system differ?

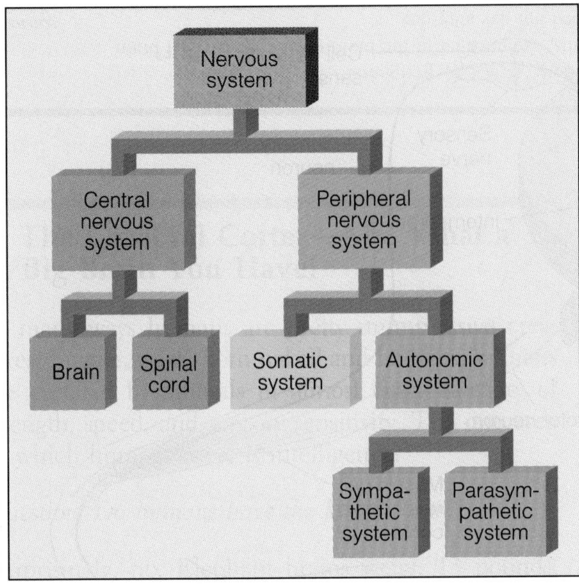

■ **Fig. 3–10** *Subparts of the nervous system.*

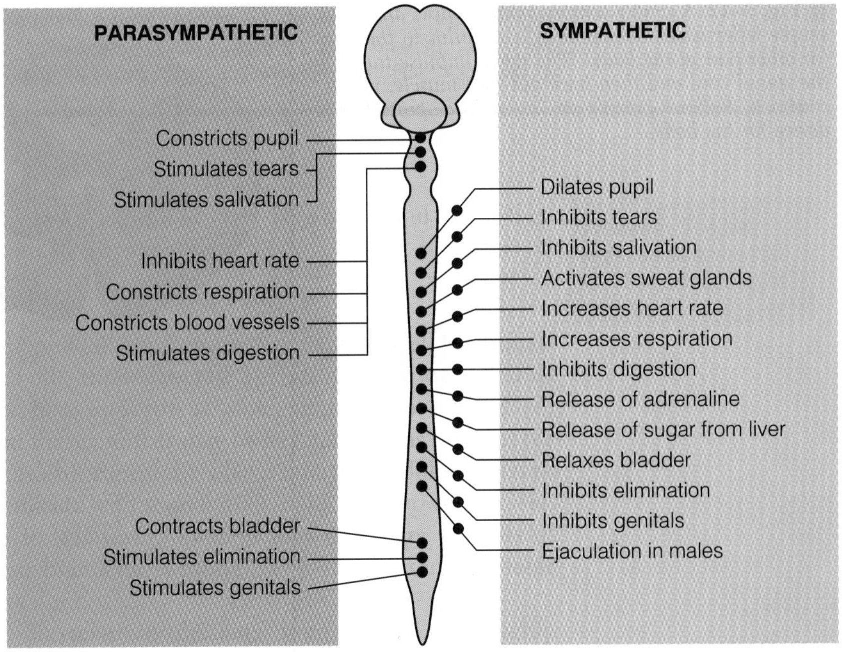

■ **Fig. 3–11** *Sympathetic and parasympathetic branches of the autonomic nervous system. Both branches control involuntary actions. The sympathetic system generally activates the body. The parasympathetic system generally quiets it. The sympathetic branch relays through a chain of ganglia (clusters of cell bodies) outside the spinal cord.*

The sympathetic branch is an "emergency" system that prepares the body for "fight or flight" during times of danger or emotion. In essence, it arouses the body for action. The parasympathetic or "sustaining" branch, on the other hand, is most active *soon after* a stressful or emotional event. Its role is to quiet the body and return it to a lower level of arousal (Thompson, 1985). It also helps maintain vital functions such as heart rate, breathing, and digestion at moderate levels. Of course, both branches of the ANS are active at all times. Their activity combines to determine if the body is aroused or quieted. (See Chapter 10 for more information on the autonomic system.)

The Spinal Cord The spinal cord is important because it is responsible for some low-level behaviors, such as reflexes. The spinal cord also acts like a cable connecting the brain to other parts of the body. If you were to cut through the spinal cord, you would see columns of **white matter.** This nerve tissue is made up of axons that leave the spinal cord to form peripheral nerves. Return to Figure 3–9b and you will see that there are 30 pairs of these **spinal nerves** leaving the spinal cord, plus one pair leaving the bottom tip. The 31 pairs, together with 12 more pairs of nerves that leave the brain directly (the **cranial nerves**), place the entire body in sensory and motor communication with the brain.

Question: How is the spinal cord related to behavior?

Within the spinal cord itself, the simplest behavior pattern, known as a **reflex arc,** can be carried out without any help from the brain (see ■ Fig. 3–12). Imagine that one of our Frisbee players steps on a thorn. This is detected in the foot by a **sensory neuron,** and a message (in the form of an action potential) is fired off to the spinal cord.

The sensory neuron synapses with a **connector neuron** (or **interneuron**) inside the spinal cord. The connector neuron in turn activates another nerve cell (in this case a **motor neuron**) that leads back to muscle fibers. The muscle fibers are made up of **effector cells,** which contract and cause the foot to withdraw. Note that brain activity is not required for a reflex arc. The body can react to protect itself without calling on the brain. (However, the spinal cord informs the brain of the action it has taken.)

In reality, even a simple reflex usually triggers more complex activity. For example, muscles of the limb on the opposite side of the body must contract to support the shift in weight. Even this can be done by the spinal cord, but it involves many more cells and several levels of the spinal nerves.

Perhaps you have realized how adaptive it is to have a spinal cord capable of responding on its own. Such automatic responses leave the brain of our Frisbee ace free to deal with more important information—such as the location of trees, lampposts, and attractive onlookers—as he or she makes a grandstand catch.

White matter Areas of the nervous system that appear white due to the presence of myelin.

Spinal nerves Major nerves that carry sensory and motor messages in and out of the spinal cord.

Cranial nerves Major nerves that leave the brain without passing through the spinal cord.

Reflex arc The simplest behavior, in which a stimulus provokes an automatic response.

Sensory neuron A nerve cell that carries messages from the senses toward the CNS.

Connector neuron A nerve cell that serves as a link between two others.

Motor neuron A nerve cell that carries motor commands from the CNS to muscles and glands.

Effector cells Cells in muscles and glands capable of producing some type of response.

LEFT BRAIN
- Language
- Speech
- Writing
- Calculation
- Time sense
- Rhythm
- Ordering of complex movements

RIGHT BRAIN
- Non-verbal
- Perceptual skills
- Visualization
- Recognition of patterns, faces, melodies
- Recognition and expression of emotion
- Spatial skills
- Simple language comprehension

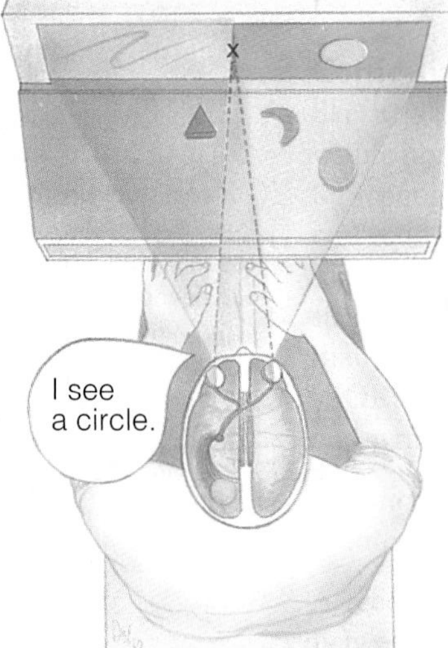

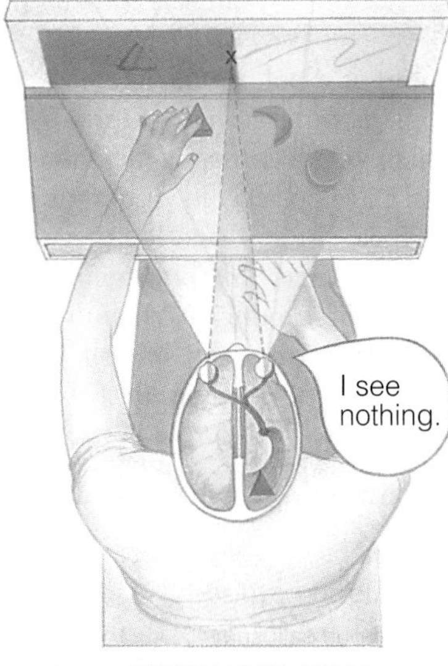

LEFT HEMISPHERE RIGHT HEMISPHERE

■ **Fig. 3–17** *If a circle is flashed to the left brain and a split-brain patient is asked to say what he or she saw, the circle is easily named. The person can also pick out the circle by touching shapes with the right hand, out of sight under a tabletop (shown semi-transparent in the drawing). However, the left hand will be unable to identify the shape. If a triangle is flashed to the right brain, the person cannot say what was seen (speech is controlled by the left hemisphere). The person will also be unable to identify the correct shape by touch with the right hand. Now, however, the left hand will have no difficulty picking out the hidden triangle. Separate testing of each hemisphere reveals distinct specializations, as listed above. (Figure adapted from an illustration by Edward Kasper in McKean, 1985.)*

using the left hand, out of sight. The left hand draws a dollar sign. If the person is then asked to point with the right hand to a picture of what the hidden left hand drew, he or she will point to a question mark (Sperry, 1968). In short, for the split-brain person, one hemisphere may not know what is happening in the other. This has to be the ultimate case of the "right hand not knowing what the left hand is doing"! ■ Figure 3–17 provides another example of split-brain testing.

Question: Earlier it was stated that the hemispheres differ in abilities; in what ways do they differ?

Right Brain/Left Brain The brain divides its work in interesting ways. For example, language is a specialty of the left hemisphere. Roughly 95 percent of all adults use the left side of the brain for speaking, writing, and understanding language. (The figures are 97 percent for right-handed persons and 68 percent for left-handers—see the Applications section for details.) In addition, the left hemisphere is superior at math, at judging time and rhythm, and at ordering or coordinating complex movements (especially those needed for speech) (Corballis, 1980).

In contrast, the right hemisphere responds to only the simplest language and numbers. Working with the right hemisphere is a little like talking to a child who only understands a dozen words or so. To answer questions, the right hemisphere must point to objects or make other non-verbal responses (see Fig. 3–17).

At one time the right brain was regarded as the "minor" hemisphere. But we now know that it has talents of its own. The right hemisphere is superior at perceptual skills such as recognizing patterns, faces, and melodies. It is also involved in detecting and expressing emotion. The right brain is better at visualization and at "manipulo-spatial" skills, such as arranging blocks to match a pattern, putting together a puzzle, or drawing a picture (Hellige, 1990).

The superiority of the right hemisphere at spatial tasks leads to another intriguing split-brain observation. A common test of spatial ability involves solving a geometric puzzle. On this test the split-brain patient's left hand can typically perform quite well, but the right hand cannot. As Robert Ornstein (1972) reports,

> Professor Sperry often shows an interesting film clip of the right hand attempting to solve the problem and failing, whereupon the patient's left hand cannot restrain itself and "corrects" the right—as when you know the answer to a problem and watch me making mistakes, and cannot refrain from telling me the answer.

Question: Do people normally solve puzzles with just their right hemisphere? Do they do other things with only the left?

No. The entire brain is active at all times. It's true that some tasks may make *more* use of one hemisphere or the other. But direct studies of brain activity show that both hemispheres are activated for virtually all tasks. What changes is the *balance* of activity between the two hemispheres (see Highlight 3–3). There is no scientific basis for the idea that people rely on only one hemisphere or the other for thinking (Hellige, 1990).

It is possible, of course, to prefer right- or left-brain modes of thought. A recent study found that students who prefer right-brain thinking tend to major in such subjects as music, journalism, art, oral communication, and architecture. A left-brain preference was associated with majors in such subjects as management, computer science, mathematics, nursing, criminal justice, and education (Monfort et al., 1990).

In general, the left hemisphere is mainly involved with *analysis* (breaking information into parts). It also processes information *sequentially* (in order, one item after the next). The right hemisphere appears to process information simultaneously and *holistically* (all at once) (Springer & Deutsch, 1989). However, in most "real world" tasks, the hemispheres share the work. Each does the parts it does best and shares information with the other side of the brain. That's why popularized courses that claim to teach "right-brain thinking" ignore the fact that everyone already uses the right brain for thinking (Hellige, 1990).

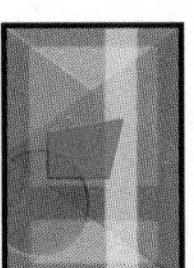

HIGHLIGHT 3–3

Using Psychology

The Risky Side of the Brain

If you pay attention to information from your right ear or the right side of vision, your left brain will become more active. The reverse is true for leftward attention and right brain activity (De Toffol et al., 1992).

How could you apply these facts in everyday life? One way is to attend to information from the right side when you want to emphasize the talents of the left hemisphere. For example, to judge the timing or rhythm of a musical passage, turn your right ear toward the music. To better appreciate its melody, turn your left ear toward the music. Here's another example: To evaluate a drawing, place the drawing to the left in your visual field. (That is, look to the right of the drawing.) Doing so will facilitate right-hemisphere processing and improve your sensitivity to shapes. (Refer to the specialized abilities in Fig. 3–17 for other possibilities.)

One of the most useful differences between the right and left hemispheres involves decision making. Psychologist Roger Drake and others have found that people are more willing to make risky decisions when their left hemisphere is more active than the right. The right hemisphere is associated with a more cautious cognitive style (Drake & Seligman, 1989; Drake & Ulrich, 1992; Miller & Milner, 1985).

Professor Drake suggests that when you want to persuade a friend to be careful, you should speak to the person from his or her left side. That way, you will activate the more cautious right hemisphere. On other occasions you may want to advise a friend to take more risks, such as joining a club, seeking out new friends, or applying for a job. At such times you will be more effective if you place yourself on your friend's right side. Doing so will emphasize stimuli that activate the left hemisphere and the tendency to take a risk (Drake, 1994).

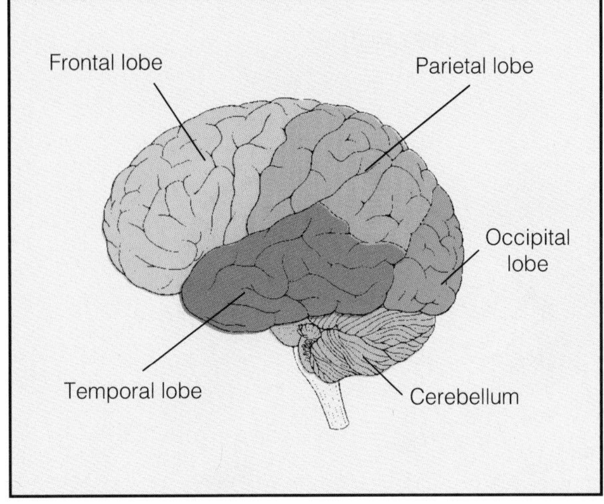

■ **Fig. 3–18** *The lobes of the cerebral cortex are defined by several larger and more prominent fissures on the surface of the cerebrum.*

Lobes of the Cerebral Cortex

In addition to the hemispheres, the cerebral cortex can be divided into several smaller areas, or **lobes** (see ■ Fig. 3–18).

Question: What is known about the function of the lobes?

The functions of areas on each of the lobes have been "mapped" by clinical and experimental studies. For example, the surface of the cortex can be activated by touching it with a small electrified needle or wire called an **electrode.** When this is done to a patient undergoing brain surgery (using only local painkillers), the patient can report what effect the stimulation had. (This chapter's Exploration tells more about methods of brain mapping.) The functions of the cortex have also been identified by clinical studies of changes in personality, behavior, or sensory capacity caused by brain diseases or injuries. Let us consider the outcome of such studies (see ■ Fig. 3–19).

Lobes of cerebral cortex Areas on the cortex bordered by major fissures.

Electrode Any wire, needle, or metal plate used to electrically stimulate nerve tissue or to record its activity.

Occipital lobes Portion of the cerebral cortex where vision registers in the brain.

Primary visual area Main area of the cerebral cortex that processes visual information.

The Occipital Lobes The occipital lobes (awk-SIP-ih-tal), located at the back of the brain, are the **primary visual area** of the cortex. Patients with *tumors* (cell growths that interfere with brain activity) in the occipital lobes experience blind spots in areas of their vision.

Question: Do the visual areas of the cortex correspond directly to what is seen?

Visual images are mapped onto the cortex, but the map is greatly stretched and distorted (Carlson, 1991). It is important to avoid thinking of the visual area as being like a little TV screen in the brain. Visual information creates complex patterns of activity in nerve cells; it does *not* make a TV-like image.

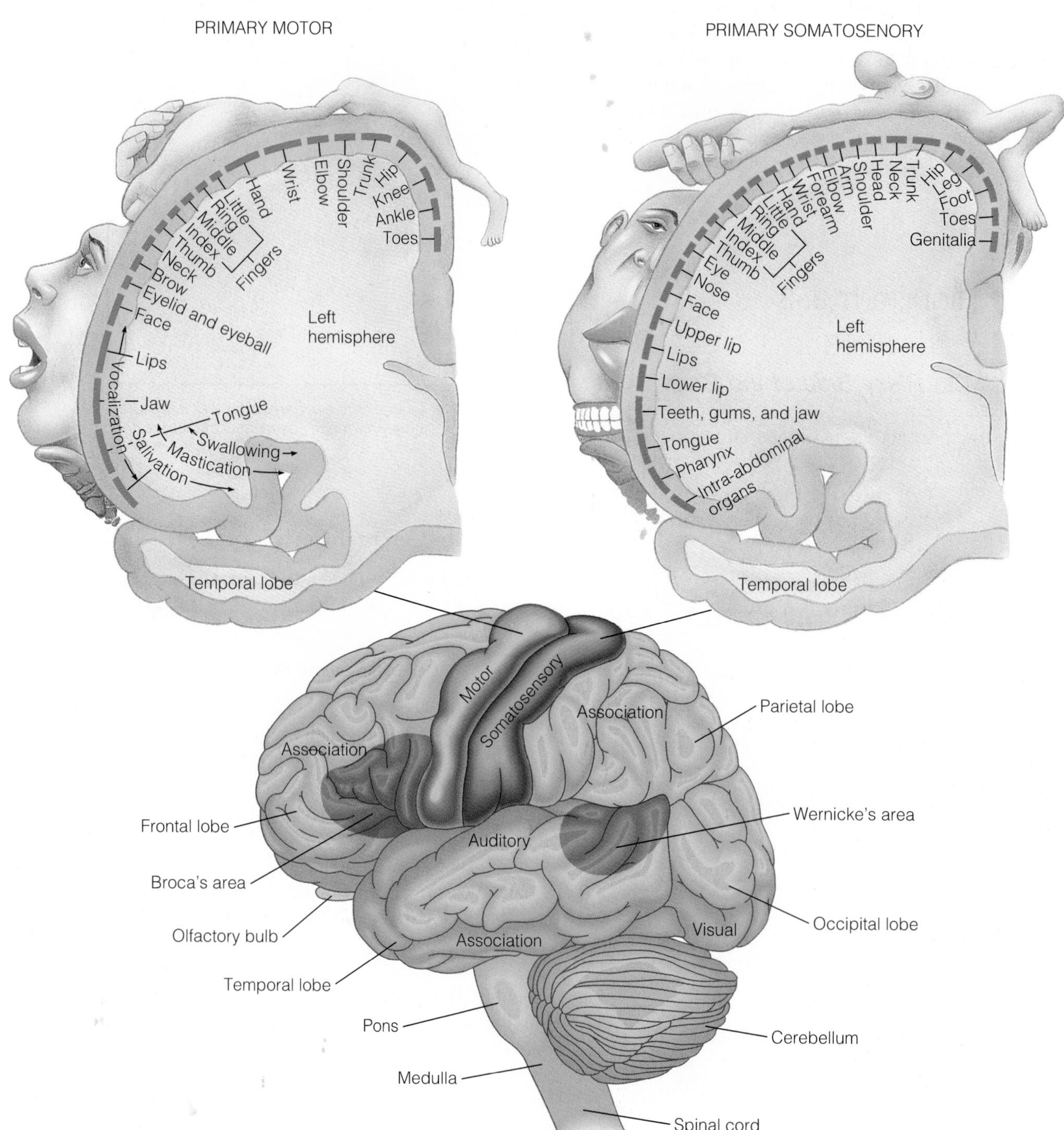

■ **Fig. 3–19** *The lobes of the cerebral cortex and the primary sensory, motor, and association areas on each. The top diagrams show (in cross section) the relative amounts of cortex "assigned" to the sensory and motor control of various parts of the body. (Each cross section, or "slice," of the cortex has been turned 90 degrees so that you see it as it would appear from the back of the brain.)*

Parietal lobes Area of the brain where bodily sensations register.

Somatosensory area A receiving area for bodily sensations.

The Parietal Lobes The parietal lobes (puh-RYE-ih-tal) are located just above the occipital lobes. Touch, temperature, pressure, and other somatic, or bodily sensations are channeled to the **somatosensory area** (SO-mat-oh-SEN-so-ree) on the parietal lobes. The correspondence between areas of the parietal lobes and parts of the body is not perfect. The distorted body in Figure 3–19 shows that as a map of sensations, the cortex reflects the *sensitivity* of body areas, not their size. For example, the lips are large in the drawing because of their great sensitivity, while the back and trunk, which are less sensitive, are much smaller.

The Temporal Lobes The temporal lobes are located on each side of the brain. Auditory information projects directly to the temporal lobes, making them the main site where hearing registers. If we were to stimulate the **primary auditory area** of a temporal lobe, our subject would "hear" a series of sounds. These sounds would increase in pitch as we moved from the top to the bottom. Stimulating in another direction, we would find an orderly change in loudness (Carlson, 1991). This indicates that sound qualities are clearly mapped on the surface of the cortex.

For most people, the left temporal lobe also contains a language "center." (For five percent of all people, the area is on the right temporal lobe.) Damage to the temporal lobe can severely limit ability to use language. (More on this later.)

The Frontal Lobes The frontal lobes perform a mixture of functions. An important arch of tissue, called the **motor cortex,** runs laterally over the top of the brain. This area directs the body's muscles. If the motor cortex is stimulated with an electrical current, muscles in various parts of the body will twitch. Like the somatosensory area, the motor cortex corresponds to the importance of bodily areas, not to their size. The hands, for example, get more area than the feet (see Fig. 3–19). The larger area of motor cortex devoted to our hands is what makes them so dexterous.

More complex behaviors are also related to the frontal lobes. Damage to the frontal lobes in humans tends to alter personality and emotionality. Intellectual tasks based on reasoning or planning also seem to rely on the frontal lobes. Patients with frontal lobe damage often get "stuck" on such tasks and repeat the same wrong answers over and over (Springer & Deutsch, 1989). Frontal lobe damage in childhood leads to a lowered adult IQ and significant social impairment (Kolb, 1989).

Question: The sensory and motor areas leave a lot of the cortex unaccounted for. What do the remaining areas do?

Associative Areas In the human brain, primary sensory and motor areas make up only a small part of the cerebral cortex. All other areas, including parts of all the lobes, are called the **association cortex.** The size and relative amount of association cortex increase strikingly as one ascends the evolutionary scale (Thompson, 1985).

The association cortex seems to process and combine information from the various senses. It is probably also related to higher mental abilities. The frontal lobes' link with thinking skills is a good example of such abilities. Additional clues to the workings of the association cortex come from studies of humans with brain injuries.

■ **Fig. 3–20** *Spatial neglect. A patient with right-hemisphere damage was asked to copy three model drawings. Notice the obvious neglect of the left side in his drawings. Similar instances of neglect occur in many patients with right-hemisphere damage. (From* Left Brain, Right Brain, *Revised Edition by S. P. Springer and G. Deutsch, copyright 1981, 1985, 1989. Reprinted with the permission of W. H. Freeman and Company.)*

Brain Injuries

As mentioned earlier, damage to motor areas on the right brain may paralyze the left side of the body; this is reversed for damage to the left brain. Damage to the right hemisphere may also cause a curious problem called **neglect.** Affected patients pay no attention to the left side of visual space. Often, the patient will not eat food on the left side of a plate. Some even refuse to acknowledge a paralyzed left arm as their own. (See ■ Fig. 3–20.) Surprisingly, left hemisphere damage usually does not produce similar neglect of the right side of space (Springer & Deutsch, 1989).

Brain injuries may also impair the special abilities of the left and right hemispheres. A person with damage in the left brain may lose the ability to speak, read, write, or spell. Yet, the same person may remain able to draw or hum with skill. Persons with right brain damage may get lost while driving, or they may have difficulty understanding diagrams and pictures. Yet, they can speak and read as before.

Regarding emotions, a person with left brain damage may not understand what you say, but he or she

Temporal lobes Areas that include sites where hearing registers.

Primary auditory area Main area on the temporal lobes where hearing registers.

Frontal lobes A brain area associated with the control of movement and higher mental functions.

Motor cortex A brain area associated with control of movement.

Association cortex All areas of the cerebral cortex that are not sensory or motor in function.

Neglect Ignoring one side of vision or of the body after damage to a brain hemisphere.

Broca's area A language area related to grammar and pronunciation.

Wernicke's area An area related to language comprehension.

Aphasia Impaired language ability resulting from brain damage.

Agnosia An inability to grasp the meaning of stimuli, such as words, objects, or pictures.

Facial agnosia An inability to recognize familiar faces.

will pick up your emotional tone. With right hemisphere damage, the person can understand what is said, but may not recognize if it is spoken in an angry or humorous way (Geschwind, 1975).

Question: Is it fair to say that damage to the left hemisphere is generally more serious?

Generally it is, because speech and language are so essential. However, if you are an artist, the right brain may be the "major hemisphere" from your point of view. It has been observed, for instance, that painters can still paint after left brain damage. But an artist with right brain damage may neglect the left side of the canvas, distort outlines, or portray bizarre and repulsive subject matter. Also, because the right hemisphere is important for recognizing faces and emotion, damage to the right side of the brain can seriously impair a person's ability to relate to others.

Aphasia Two areas of the cortex are particularly related to language. One, called **Broca's area** (BRO-cahs), lies on the left frontal lobe. The second, known as **Wernicke's area** (VER-nick-ees), is found on the left temporal lobe (see Fig. 3–19). Injury to either area can cause **aphasia** (ah-FAZE-yah), meaning an impaired ability to use language.

Question: What kinds of impairment take place?

Persons with damage in Broca's area can read, and they can understand the speech of others, but they have great difficulty speaking or writing themselves. Typically, their grammar and pronunciation are poor and their speech is slow and labored. For example, the person may say "bife" for bike, "seep" for sleep, or "zokaid" for zodiac. Generally the person knows what he or she wants to say but can't seem to utter the words (Geschwind, 1979).

In Wernicke's aphasia, the person has problems with the *meaning* of words, not grammar or pronunciation. Whereas someone with Broca's aphasia might say "tssair" when shown a picture of a chair, a Wernicke's patient might say "stool." People with injuries to Wernicke's area often speak in incredibly roundabout ways to avoid using certain nouns. While discussing her son's career one patient said, "Well he was two years away, away down for nothing. He didn't do it and got out and said I want to go over there and . . . how to do things, what he's doing now" (Goodglass, 1980).

It is obvious that both Broca's area and Wernicke's area are crucial for normal language use. It is not surprising to find, then, that they are interconnected in the brain.

"Mindblindness" One of the most fascinating results of brain injury is **agnosia** (ag-KNOW-zyah). This condition is sometimes referred to as "mindblindness" because it involves an inability to identify seen objects. If shown a candle, for instance, someone with an agnosia might describe it as a long narrow object tapering at the top. The person might even draw it accurately and still fail to name it. However, if the person is allowed to feel the candle, he or she will name it immediately (Benton, 1980).

Question: Are agnosias limited to objects?

No. A fascinating form of "mindblindness" is **facial agnosia,** the inability to identify familiar persons. For instance, one patient with facial agnosia was unable to recognize her husband or mother when they visited her in the hospital, and she could not identify pictures of her children. However, when visitors spoke she knew them immediately from their voices (Benton, 1980).

The study of facial agnosias shows that a brain area devoted to recognizing others is located on the underside of the occipital lobes. These areas appear to have no other function. Why would part of the brain be set aside solely for recognizing faces? From an evolutionary standpoint it is not really so surprising. After all, we are social animals, for whom facial recognition is very important (Geschwind, 1979). This specialization is one more example of what a marvelous organ of consciousness we possess.

Learning Check

See if you can successfully match the following.

1. ____ Corpus callosum
2. ____ Occipital lobes
3. ____ Parietal lobes
4. ____ Temporal lobes
5. ____ Frontal lobes
6. ____ Association cortex
7. ____ Aphasias
8. ____ Corticalization
9. ____ Left hemisphere
10. ____ Right hemisphere
11. ____ "Split brain"
12. ____ Agnosia

A. Visual area
B. Language, speech, writing
C. Motor cortex and abstract thinking
D. Spatial skills, visualization, pattern recognition
E. Speech disturbances
F. Causes sleep
G. Increased ratio of cortex in brain
H. Bodily sensations
I. Treatment for severe epilepsy
J. Inability to identify seen objects
K. Fibers connecting the cerebral hemispheres
L. Cortex that is not sensory or motor in function
M. Hearing

13. If you wanted to increase the surface area of the cerebrum so that more cerebral cortex would fit within the skull, how would you do it? *Critical Thinking*

Answers: 1. K 2. A 3. H 4. M 5. C 6. L 7. E 8. G 9. B 10. D 11. I 12. J 13. One solution would be to gather the surface of the cortex into folds, just as you might if you were trying to fit a large piece of cloth into a small box. This, in fact, is probably why the cortex is more convoluted (folded or wrinkled) in higher animals.

The Subcortex—At the Core of the (Brain) Matter

Question: What do brain areas below the cortex do?

A person can lose large portions of the cerebrum and still survive. As a matter of fact, if damage is limited to the less crucial areas of the cortex, little visible change may take place. Not so with the brain areas below the cortex. Most of these are so indispensable that damage may endanger a person's life.

Question: Why are the lower brain areas so important?

Below the cerebral cortex and completely covered by it are structures known as the **subcortex.** The subcortex can be divided into three general areas called the **brainstem** or **hindbrain,** the **midbrain,** and the **forebrain.** (The forebrain also includes the cerebral cortex, which we have already discussed because of its size and importance.) For our purposes the midbrain can be viewed primarily as a link between the brain structures above and below it. Therefore, let us focus on the forebrain and the hindbrain to appreciate their importance (see ■Fig. 3–21).

Subcortex All brain structures below the cerebral cortex.

Brainstem Lowest portions of the brain, including the cerebellum, medulla, and reticular formation.

Midbrain Brain area that links the forebrain and the brainstem.

Forebrain The highest brain areas, including the hypothalamus, thalamus, corpus callosum, and cerebrum.

■ **Fig. 3–21** *This simplified drawing shows the main structures of the human brain and describes some of their most important features. (You can use the color code in the foreground to identify which structures are parts of the forebrain, midbrain, and hindbrain.)*

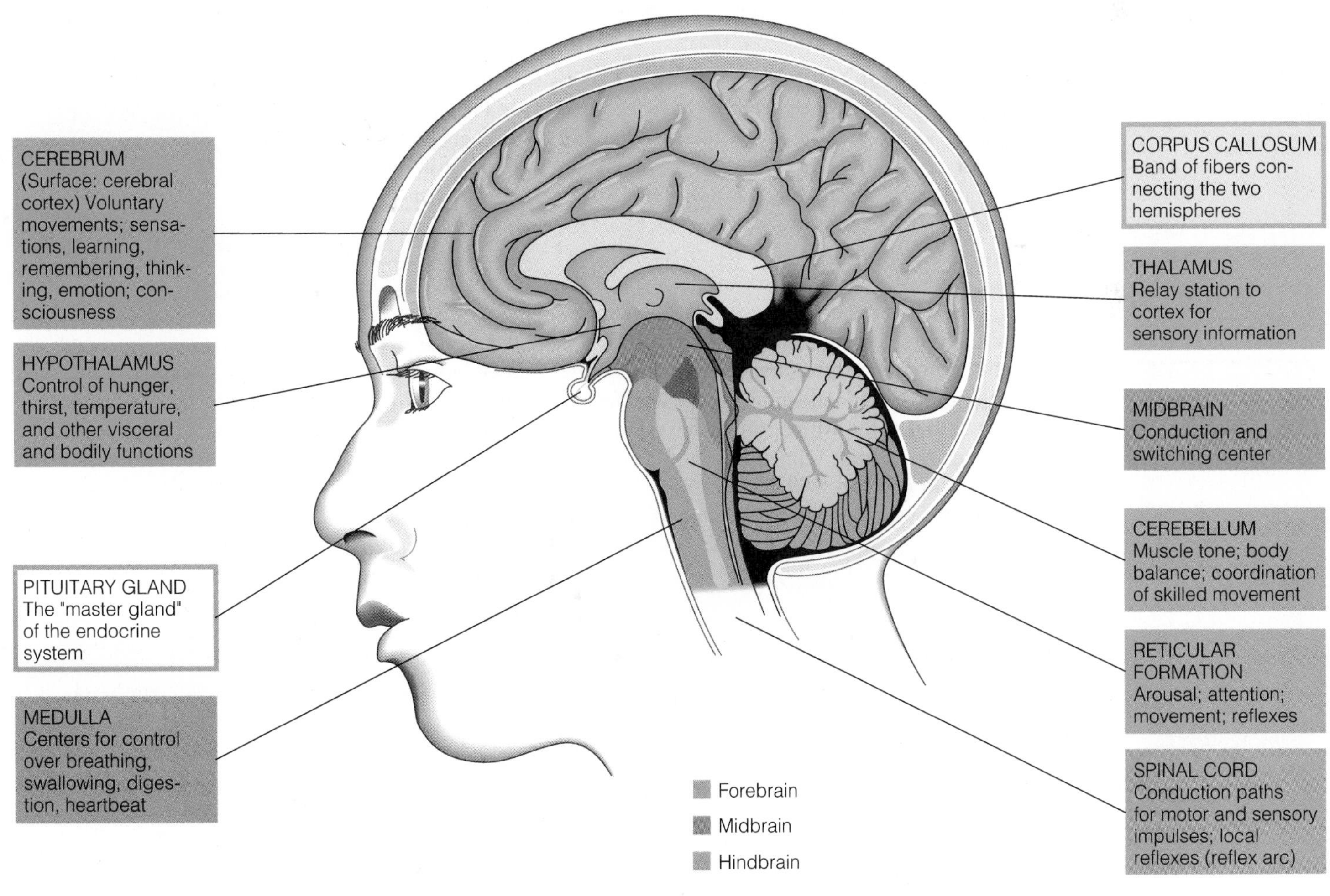

Medulla Structure linking the brain and spinal cord that controls vital life functions.

Cerebellum A brain structure that controls posture and coordination.

Reticular formation A network within the medulla and brainstem; associated with attention, alertness, and some reflexes.

Reticular activating system (RAS) A part of the reticular formation that activates the cerebral cortex.

Thalamus A central brain structure that relays sensory information to the cerebral cortex.

Hypothalamus A small area that regulates emotional behaviors and motives.

Limbic system A system in the forebrain that is closely linked with emotional response.

The Hindbrain

As the spinal cord enters the skull to join the brain, it widens into the brainstem. The brainstem consists mainly of the **medulla** (meh-DUL-ah) and the **cerebellum** (ser-ah-BEL-uhm). The *medulla* contains centers important for the reflex control of vital life functions, including heart rate, breathing, swallowing, and the like. Various drugs, diseases, or injuries can disrupt the medulla enough to end or endanger life. That's why a karate chop to the back of the neck, like those depicted in movies, can be extremely dangerous.

The *cerebellum,* which looks like a small cerebral cortex, lies at the base of the brain. The cerebellum is closely connected to many areas in the brain and spinal cord. It primarily regulates posture, muscle tone, and muscular coordination. The cerebellum also plays a role in the storage of memories for skills and habits (Thompson, 1991). (See Chapter 8 for more information on "skill memory.")

Question: What happens if the cerebellum is injured?

Without an intact cerebellum, tasks like walking, running, or playing catch are impossible. The first symptoms of a crippling disease called *spinocerebellar degeneration* are tremor, dizziness, and muscular weakness. Eventually, victims have difficulty standing, walking, or even feeding themselves.

Reticular Formation A *network* of fibers and cell bodies called the **reticular** (reh-TICK-you-ler) **formation** (RF) lies within a cavity inside the medulla and the brainstem. The RF exerts influence on messages entering and leaving the brain. As a result, the RF affects attention, movement, some reflexes, and alertness.

As nerve impulses flow into the brain, the RF gives priority to some messages, while excluding others. In this way, the RF influences *attention.* The reticular formation also modifies out-going commands to the body. Muscle tone, posture, and movements of the eyes, face, head, body, and limbs are all affected by the RF. In addition, the RF controls reflexes involved in breathing, sneezing, coughing, and vomiting (Stalheim-Smith & Fitch, 1993).

Maintaining vigilance, alertness, and wakefulness is another important task of the reticular formation (Carlson, 1991). Incoming messages from the sense organs branch into a part of the RF called the **reticular activating system** (RAS). The RAS bombards the cortex with stimulation, keeping it active and alert.

Researchers have found that destroying a small area of the RAS causes a coma resembling sleep. In contrast, electrical stimulation of the same area instantly awakens sleeping animals. The RF is also very responsive to stimulant drugs, such as amphetamine, which produce arousal and wakefulness (Carlson, 1991).

The sleepy driver who snaps to attention when an animal appears in the middle of the road can thank the reticular activating system for arousing the rest of the brain. If you're getting sleepy while reading this chapter, try pinching your ear—a little pain will cause the RAS to momentarily arouse your cortex.

The Forebrain

Like gemstones of nerve tissue, two of the most important parts of the body lie buried deep within the center of the brain. The **thalamus** (THAL-uh-mus) and an area just below it called the **hypothalamus** (HI-po-THAL-uh-mus) are part of the forebrain (see Fig. 3–21).

Question: How could these be any more important than other areas already described?

The thalamus is a small football-shaped structure that acts as a final "switching station" for sensory messages on their way to the cortex. Information from vision, hearing, taste, and touch relay through the thalamus. Sensory messages undergo initial analysis there as well. Injury to even small areas of the thalamus can cause deafness, blindness, or loss of any other sense, except smell. (Sensory information from the sense of smell is sent directly to the cortex, on the underside of the brain, without passing through the thalamus.)

The human hypothalamus is about the size of a small grape. Small as it may be, the hypothalamus is a kind of master control center for emotion and many basic motives (Carlson, 1991). The hypothalamus affects behaviors as diverse as sex, rage, temperature control, hormone release, eating and drinking, sleep, waking, and emotion. The hypothalamus is a "crossroads" that connects with many other areas of the cortex and subcortex. As such, it acts as a "final path" for many kinds of behavior leaving the brain. You might think of the hypothalamus as the last area in the brain where many behaviors are organized or "decided on." (See Chapter 10 for a discussion of the role of the hypothalamus in hunger and thirst.)

The Limbic System The hypothalamus, parts of the thalamus, and several structures buried within the cortex form the **limbic system** (■ Fig. 3–22). The limbic system has an unmistakable role in producing *emotion* and motivated behavior. Rage, fear, sexual response, and other instances of intense arousal can be obtained from various points in the limbic system. For example, cats can be made aggressive by electrically stimulating the limbic system. Typically, they will crouch, hiss, expose their claws, lean forward, and tense their muscles—all characteristic of defense or attack. Highlight 3–4 provides more information on research of this type.

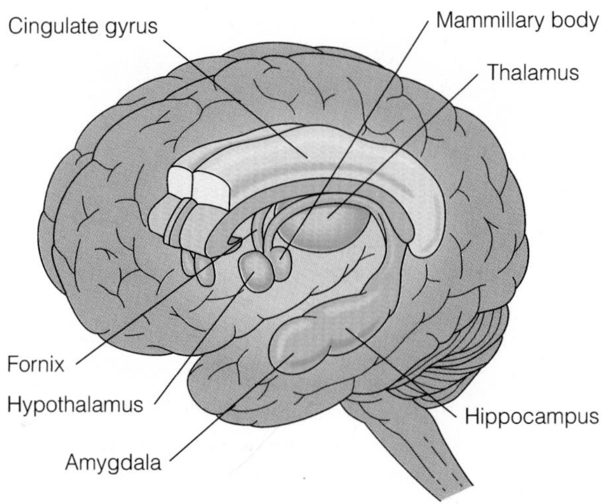

■ **Fig. 3–22** *Parts of the limbic system are shown in this highly simplified drawing. Although only one side is shown, the hippocampus and the amygdala extend out into the temporal lobes at each side of the brain. The limbic system is a sort of "primitive core" of the brain strongly associated with emotion.*

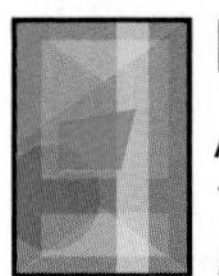

HIGHLIGHT 3–4

A Closer Look At

Electrical Stimulation of the Brain

Electrical stimulation of the brain (ESB) is used to explore brain-behavior connections. ESB allows an animal (or person) to function normally while the experimenter turns various brain areas on and off. As we saw in the Chapter Preview, ESB can even be done at a distance, with a radio transmitter and receiver.

ESB begins with the implantation of thin metal electrodes deep within the brain. Each electrode is used to electrically activate a specific brain area. ESB calls forth behavior with astonishing power, instantly bringing about aggression, alertness, escape, eating, drinking, sleeping, movement, euphoria, memories, speech, tears, and more.

Electrical activation of parts of the limbic system often produces emotional responses. During medical testing one woman reacted with a sudden outburst of anger when the amygdala (ah-MIG-dah-luh) was stimulated, saying "I feel like I want to get up from this chair! Please don't let me do it! I don't want to be mean! I want to get something and just tear it up!" (King, 1961). When the temporal lobe was activated, another patient giggled, became flirtatious, and said she enjoyed the stimulation very much. Soon, she expressed a desire to marry the therapist! When stimulation ceased, she again became quiet, reserved, and proper.

It might seem that ESB could be used to control a person like a robot. But in most cases, the details of emotions and behaviors elicited by ESB are modified by the individual's personality and by the situation. Fortunately, it would be impossible for a ruthless dictator to enslave people by "radio controlling" their brains. ESB is better thought of as a tool for probing the brain, and, in the future, as a potential treatment for epilepsy, uncontrollable violence, and other brain-based problems. Using ESB, researchers are creating a three-dimensional map or "atlas" of brain functions. The atlas shows the pattern of sensory, motor, and emotional responses that can be elicited from various parts of the brain. It promises to be a valuable guide for medical treatment, as well as for further exploration of the brain (Yoshida, 1993).

Electrical stimulation of the brain (ESB) Direct electrical stimulation and activation of brain tissue.

Hippocampus A part of the limbic system associated with storing memories.

During evolution, the limbic system was the earliest layer of the forebrain to develop. In lower, relatively primitive animals, the limbic system helps organize the appropriate response to stimuli: feeding, fleeing, fighting, or reproduction (Thompson, 1985). In humans, the link to emotion remains. However, some parts of the limbic system have taken on additional, higher-level functions. For example, one part appears to be important for forming lasting memories (Squire, 1992). This is the **hippocampus** (HIP-oh-CAMP-us), found at the core of the temporal lobes. A link between the hippocampus and memory may explain why stimulating the temporal lobes can produce memory-like or dream-like experiences. (See Chapter 8 for more information on this point.)

One of the most exciting discoveries in biopsychology was the finding that animals will learn to press a lever to deliver a rewarding dose of electrical stimulation to the limbic system (Olds & Milner, 1954). Since the original discovery, many additional areas of the limbic system have been shown to act as reward, or "pleasure," pathways in the brain. Many are found in the hypothalamus, where they overlap with areas associated with drives such as thirst, sex, and hunger (Olds, 1977). (See Chapter 7.) Commonly abused drugs, such as cocaine, amphetamine, heroin, nicotine, marijuana, and alcohol activate many of the same pleasure pathways. This appears to explain, in part, the rewarding properties of such drugs (Wise & Rompre, 1989).

Punishment, or "aversive," areas have also been found in the limbic system. When these areas are stimulated, animals show discomfort and will work to turn off the stimulation. Since a great deal of human and animal behavior is directed by seeking pleasure and

Redundancy Duplication of function by brain structures.

Plasticity The brain's capacity for revising its organization.

Endocrine system Glands whose secretions pass directly into the bloodstream or lymph system.

Hormone A glandular secretion that affects bodily functions or behavior.

avoiding pain, these discoveries continue to fascinate psychologists.

The Brain in Perspective—Beyond the Biocomputer

We have seen that the human brain is an impressive assembly of billions of sensitive cells and nerve fibers. The brain controls vital bodily functions, keeps track of the external world, issues commands to the muscles and glands, responds to current needs, creates the magic of consciousness, and regulates its own behavior—*all* at the same time. Each of these basic needs is met by the action of one or more of the three main brain divisions: Control of vital bodily functions is carried out by the hindbrain (with some assistance from the hypothalamus in the forebrain); gathering sensory information and issuing motor commands takes place at all three levels of the brain; and response selection, learning, memory, and higher thought processes are controlled by the forebrain, particularly the cortex and its association areas.

Redundancy A final note of caution is now in order. For the sake of simplicity we have assigned functions to each "part" of the brain as if it were a computer. This is only a half-truth. In reality the brain is a vast information-processing system. Incoming information scatters to structures all over the brain and converges again as it goes out to muscles and glands. The overall system acts in ways that go far beyond any view that considers only "parts" or "brain centers" (Thompson, 1985). To say the least, the brain is much, much more complicated than implied here.

■ Fig. 3–23 *Locations of the endocrine glands in the male and female.*

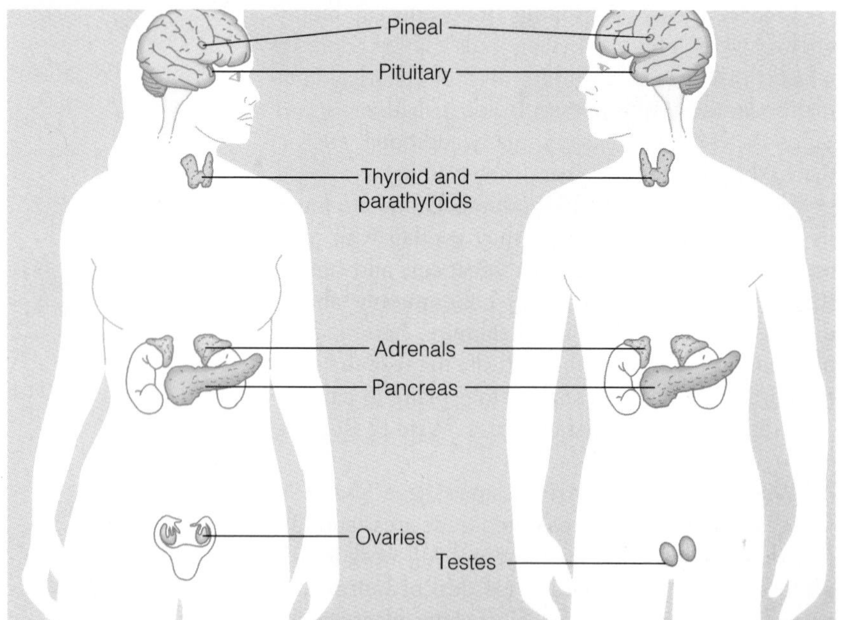

One reason the brain is so complex is because it has tremendous **redundancy,** or duplication, throughout. The brain may use dozens of areas to do what any one area could manage alone. Because of such redundancy, the brain has an impressive ability to compensate for some types of injury.

Question: Does it make any difference at what age a person experiences a brain injury?

Plasticity Yes. In response to brain damage, children often show greater **plasticity** (flexibility) of brain organization than adults. For example, when there is severe damage to the left hemisphere, children under age two usually can shift language processing to the right side of the brain. If damage occurs between ages two and five, language areas remain in the left brain but shift to new locations (Kolb, 1989). A more dramatic example of plasticity occurs when a person is born without a corpus callosum. As adults these people can answer questions from both hemispheres, write with both hands, draw with both hands, and solve block-design puzzles with both hands (Sperry, 1974). In general, brain plasticity appears to be based on increased branching of dendrites (Kolb, 1989). After age 10, such plasticity becomes rare.

Potential In the final analysis, the brain is both highly vulnerable and amazingly resilient. Brain damage before age five almost always lowers adult IQ (Kolb, 1989). Yet, in one astounding case a child had the entire left hemisphere of his brain removed at age five. As an adult he was paralyzed on the right side and blind in his right visual field. But he was able to speak, read, write, and comprehend so well that he maintained a double major in college and has an above-average IQ (Smith & Sugar, 1975). Such recoveries suggest that full use of the brain's potential may still lie ahead. At the same time that injuries help us understand the brain's limitations, they also raise questions about how the undamaged brain might be used more fully. Perhaps future breakthroughs will allow us to enhance memory, intelligence, or thinking abilities. For now, it is exciting to think that the brain hasn't yet yielded all its secrets.

The Endocrine System—Slow but Sure Messenger Service

The nervous system is not the only communication network in the body. The **endocrine system** (IN-duh-krin) is the second great communication system. The endocrine system is made up of a number of glands that pour chemicals directly into the bloodstream or lymph system (see ■Fig. 3–23). These chemicals, called **hormones,** are carried throughout the body, where they affect internal activities and behavior. Hormones are chemically related to neurotransmitters. Like transmitters, hormones activate cells in the body. To respond, the cells must have receptor sites for the hormone (Carlson, 1991).

Question: How do hormones affect behavior?

Although we are seldom aware of them, hormones affect us in a multitude of ways. Here is a brief sample: Hormone output from the adrenal glands rises during stressful situations; androgens ("male" hormones) are related to the sex drive in both males and females; hormones secreted during times of high emotion intensify memory formation; at least some of the emotional turmoil of adolescence is due to elevated hormone levels; different hormones predominate when you are angry, rather than fearful (Hoyenga & Hoyenga, 1984). Since this is just a sample, let's consider some additional effects hormones have on the body and behavior.

The **pituitary** is a pea-sized structure hanging from the base of the brain (return to Fig. 3–23). One of the pituitary's more important roles is regulation of growth. During childhood, the pituitary secretes a hormone that speeds body development. If too little **growth hormone** is released, a person may remain far smaller than average (see Highlight 3–5). Too much growth hormone produces giantism (■ Fig. 3–24). Secretion of too much growth hormone late in the growth period causes enlargement of the arms, hands, feet, and facial bones. This condition is called **acromegaly** (AK-row-MEG-uh-lee). Acromegaly produces unusually prominent facial features, which some people have used as a basis for careers as character actors, wrestlers, and the like.

Highlight 3–5

Focus On A Controversy

A Short Topic

Children who lag far behind in growth may suffer lasting emotional scars from rejection by peers or adults. One common cause of limited growth is insufficient growth hormone. If this condition is not treated, a child may fall 6 to 12 inches behind age-mates in height. As adults, some of these individuals will be **hypopituitary dwarfs** (HI-po-pih-TU-ih-ter-ee). Such persons are perfectly proportioned, but tiny. Should they receive medical treatment?

For many years, dwarfism could be treated only with injections of human growth hormone. Supplies were extracted from the pituitary glands of human cadavers—a painstaking and expensive process. Now, a cheaper synthetic growth hormone is available. (Treatment still costs from $10,000 to $20,000 per child per year.) Regular injections of growth hormone can raise a hypopituitary child's height by several inches, usually to the short side of average.

Growth hormone therapy is usually safe. However, it does raise ethical concerns. Some experts believe that it is wrong to treat shortness as a medical problem. Also, some parents and children are bitterly disappointed when the child fails to grow as much as expected. In addition, some short children adjust poorly to becoming more "ordinary." Many go from playing with younger children to being ignored by age-mates.

The greatest risk comes from parents who pressure physicians to increase the growth of "normal short" children. If a child's body produces normal amounts of growth hormone, drugs typically will not make the child taller as an adult. Such children grow *faster* when given growth hormone, but not taller. Nevertheless, thousands of "normal short" children are being given growth hormone injections.

With all this in mind, perhaps it is fair to say that the success of growth hormone therapy should be measured by increased emotional well-being—not merely by an increase in stature (Adler, 1992; Franklin, 1984; Roan, 1993).

Pituitary gland The "master gland" whose hormones influence other endocrine glands.

Giantism Excessive bodily growth caused by too much growth hormone.

Acromegaly Enlargement of the arms, hands, feet, and face caused by excess growth hormone late in the human growth period.

Hypopituitary dwarfism Shortness and smallness caused by too little growth hormone.

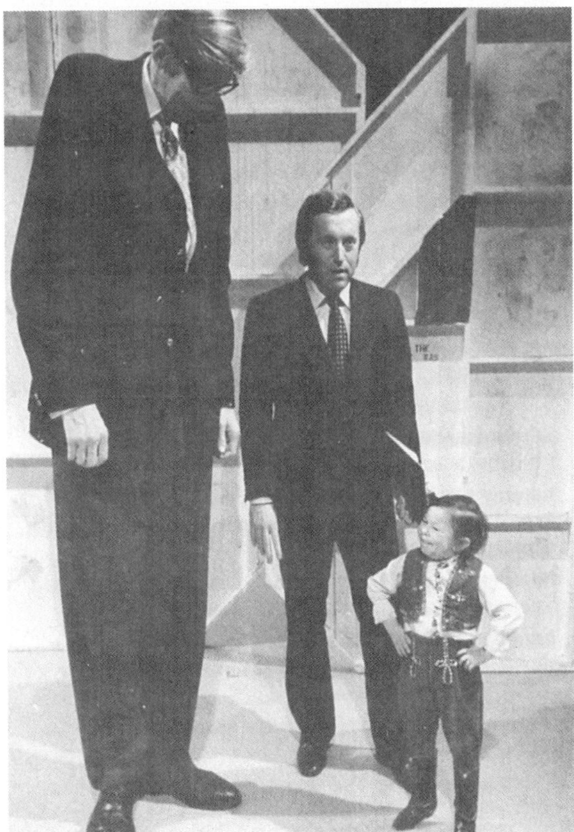

■ Fig. 3–24 *Underactivity of the pituitary gland may produce a dwarf; overactivity a giant.*

The pituitary also regulates the functioning of other glands (especially the thyroid, adrenal glands, and ovaries or testes). These glands in turn regulate such bodily processes as metabolism, responses to stress, and reproduction. In women, the pituitary also controls the production of milk during pregnancy. Because of its many effects, the pituitary is often called the "master gland." But the master has a master: The pituitary is directed by the hypothalamus, which lies above it in the brain. In this way, the hypothalamus affects glands throughout the body. This, then, is the major link between the brain and the glandular system (Carlson, 1991).

The **pineal gland** (pin-EE-ul), was once considered a useless remnant of evolution. In certain fishes, frogs, and lizards, the gland is associated with a well-developed light-sensitive organ, or so-called "third eye." In humans, the function of the pineal gland is just now coming to light (so to speak). The gland releases a hormone called **melatonin** (mel-ah-TONE-in) in response to daily variations in light. Melatonin levels in the bloodstream start to rise at dusk and peak around midnight. They fall again as morning approaches. This light-driven cycle helps control body rhythms and sleep cycles. People who are totally blind sometimes suffer from sleep disorders because their melatonin cycle is upset. (See Chapter 10 for information on melatonin and jet lag.)

The **thyroid gland** is found in the neck, on each side of the windpipe. The thyroid regulates **metabolism**—the rate at which energy is produced and expended in the body. As a consequence, it can have a sizable effect on personality. A person with an overactive thyroid (termed **hyperthyroidism**) tends to be thin, tense, excitable, and nervous. An underactive thyroid (**hypothyroidism**) in an adult can cause inactivity, sleepiness, slowness, and overweight. In infancy, hypothyroidism limits development of the nervous system and can cause severe mental retardation (see Chapter 14).

When you are frightened or angry, a number of important actions take place in your body to prepare it for action: Your heart rate and blood pressure rise; stored sugar is released into the bloodstream for quick energy; the muscles tense and receive more blood; and the blood is prepared to clot more quickly in case of injury. As we discussed earlier, these changes are brought about by the autonomic nervous system. Specifically, the sympathetic branch of the ANS causes the hormones **adrenaline** and **noradrenaline** to be released by the adrenal glands. (As mentioned earlier, the same substances also act as neurotransmitters.)

The **adrenal glands** are located just under the back of the rib cage, atop the kidneys. The **adrenal medulla,** or inner core of the adrenal glands, is the source of adrenaline and noradrenaline. The **adrenal cortex,** or outer "bark" of the adrenal glands, produces a second set of hormones called corticoids (KOR-tih-coids). One of their jobs is to regulate salt balance in the body. A deficiency of certain corticoids can evoke a powerful craving for the taste of salt in humans (Beach, 1975). The corticoids also help the body adjust to stress, and they are a secondary source of sex hormones. (For a full discussion of the role of sex glands in development, see Chapter 19.)

An oversecretion of the adrenal sex hormones can cause **virilism,** in which a woman grows a beard or a man's voice becomes so low it is difficult to understand. Oversecretion in children may cause **premature puberty,** resulting in full sexual development. One of the most remarkable cases on record is that of a five-year-old Peruvian girl who gave birth to a son (Strange, 1965).

While we are on the topic of sex hormones there is a related issue worth mentioning. One of the principal androgens or "male" hormones is testosterone, which is supplied in small amounts by the adrenal glands. (The testes are the main source of testosterone in males.) Perhaps you have heard about the use of anabolic steroids by athletes who want to "bulk up" or promote muscle growth. Most of these drugs are synthetic versions of testosterone.

Although many athletes believe otherwise, there is no evidence that steroids improve performance, and they may cause serious side effects. Problems include voice deepening or baldness in women and shrinkage

Pineal gland Gland in the brain that helps regulate body rhythms and sleep cycles.

Melatonin Hormone released by the pineal gland in response to daily cycles of light and dark.

Thyroid gland Endocrine gland that helps regulate the rate of metabolism.

Hyperthyroidism Faster metabolism and excitability caused by an overactive thyroid gland.

Hypothyroidism Slower metabolism and sluggishness caused by an underactive thyroid gland.

Adrenaline An adrenal hormone that tends to arouse the body; associated with fear.

Noradrenaline An adrenal hormone that tends to arouse the body; associated with anger.

Adrenal glands Endocrine glands that arouse the body, regulate salt balance, adjust the body to stress, and affect sexual functioning.

Adrenal medulla The inner core of the adrenal glands; a source of adrenaline and noradrenaline.

Adrenal cortex The outer layer of the adrenal glands; source of hormones that affect salt intake, reactions to stress, and sexual development.

Virilism The development of male sexual characteristics in a female.

Premature puberty The development of sexual maturity in childhood.

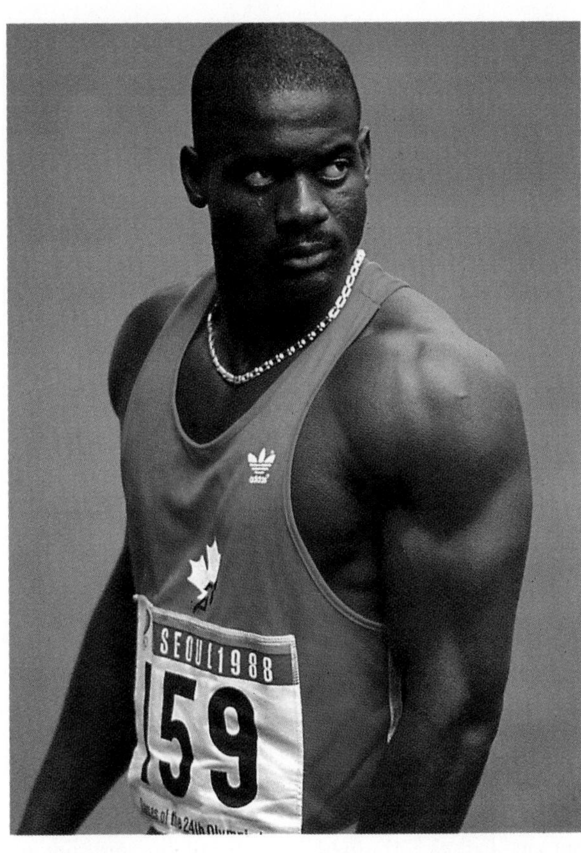

■ **Fig. 3–25** *Canadian sprinter Ben Johnson won a gold medal in the 100 meter dash at the 1988 Olympic Games. Johnson was then disgraced and stripped of the medal after testing positive for anabolic steroids.*

of the testicles, sexual impotence, or breast enlargement in men. Also common are an increased risk of heart attack and stroke, liver damage, and stunted growth when steroids are used by younger adolescents. For some users steroids may cause mania or suicidal depression, antisocial behavior ("roid rage"), and near-psychotic reactions (Harrison & Katz, 1987). Understandably, all major sports organizations ban the use of anabolic steroids (■ Fig. 3–25).

In this brief discussion of the endocrine system we have considered only a few of the more important glands. Nevertheless, this should give you an appreciation of how completely behavior and personality are tied to the ebb and flow of hormones in the body.

A Look Ahead In the upcoming Applications section, we will return to the nervous system to see how hand preference relates to the brain. The final Exploration contrasts time-tested research methods with trailblazing new ways to explore the brain. Included are some fascinating images of the brain's inner workings.

Learning Check

Here is a chance to check your memory of the preceding discussions.

1. Three major divisions of the brain are the brainstem or ________________, the ________________, and the ________________.
2. Reflex centers for heartbeat and respiration are found in the
   a. cerebellum *b.* thalamus *c.* medulla *d.* RF
3. A portion of the reticular formation, known as the RAS, serves as an ________________ system in the brain.
   a. activating *b.* adrenal *c.* adjustment *d.* aversive
4. The ________________ is a final relay, or "switching station," for sensory information on its way to the cortex.
5. ESB is done primarily by electrically stimulating the spinal cord. T or F?
6. Stimulation of the amygdala causes a person to become hostile and aggressive. T or F?
7. "Reward" and "punishment" areas are found throughout the ________________ system, which is also related to emotion.
8. Undersecretion from the thyroid can cause
   a. dwarfism *b.* giantism *c.* overweight *d.* mental retardation
9. The body's ability to resist stress is related to the action of the adrenal ________________.
10. If your brain were removed, replaced by another, and moved to a new body, which would you consider to be yourself, your old body with the new brain, or your new body with the old brain? ***Critical Thinking***

Answers: 1. hindbrain, midbrain, forebrain 2. *c* 3. *a* 4. thalamus 5. F 6. T 7. limbic 8. *c*, *d* (in infancy) 9. cortex 10. While there is no "correct" answer to this question, your personality, knowledge, personal memories, and self-concept all derive from brain activity—which makes a strong case for your old brain in a new body being more nearly the "real you."

APPLICATIONS: *Handedness—If Your Brain Is Right, What's Left?*

In the English language, "what's right is right," but what's left may be wrong. We have left-handed compliments, leftovers, people with "two left feet," those who are left behind, left out, and . . . left-handed. On the other hand (so to speak), we have the right way, the right whale, the right angle, the "right-hand man" (or woman), righteousness, and . . . the right-handed.

The Sinister Hand Left-handedness has a long and undeserved bad reputation. Southpaws have been accused of being clumsy, stubborn (for refusing to use their right hand), and maladjusted. One 1930s psychologist described the left-handed as "Awkward in the house, and clumsy in their games, they are fumblers and bunglers at whatever they do." But as any lefty will tell you, and modern psychology has confirmed, none of this is true. The supposed clumsiness of lefties is merely a result of living in a right-handed world: If it can be gripped, turned, folded, held, or pulled, it's probably designed for the right hand. Even toilet handles are on the right side.

What causes handedness? Why are there more right-handed than left-handed people? How do left-handed and right-handed people differ? Does being left-handed really create problems? Are there any benefits to being left-handed? The answers to most of these questions lead us back to the brain, where handedness begins. Let's see what research has revealed about handedness, the brain, and you.

Hand Dominance To begin with, you might find it interesting to compare your hands by copying the following design on a piece of paper. Try it once with your right hand and once with your left.

You probably noticed a definite superiority when you used your dominant hand. The interesting thing about this exercise is that there's no real difference in the strength or dexterity of the hands themselves. The agility of your dominant hand is an outward expression of superior motor control on one side of your brain (Herron, 1980).

The preceding exercise implies that you are either entirely right-handed or entirely left-handed. But handedness is not clear-cut for everyone. Rather, it is a matter of degree (Coren, 1992). To better assess your handedness, circle an answer for each of the questions that follow.

Are You Right- or Left-Handed?

1. Which hand do you normally use to write? Right Left Either
2. Which hand would you use to throw a ball at a target? Right Left Either
3. Which hand do you use to hold your toothbrush? Right Left Either
4. Which hand do you use to hold a knife when cutting food? Right Left Either
5. With which hand do you hold a hammer when hitting a nail? Right Left Either
6. When you thread a needle, which hand holds the thread? Right Left Either

To find your score, count the number of "Rights" you circled and multiply by three. Then multiply the number of "Eithers" by two. Next count the number of "Lefts" you circled. Now add all three totals and compare the result with the following scale (Adapted from Coren, 1992).

17–18	Strongly right-handed
15–16	Moderately right-handed (mixed)
13–14	Mildly right-handed (mixed)
12	Ambidextrous
10–11	Mildly left-handed (mixed)
8–9	Moderately left-handed (mixed)
6–7	Strongly left-handed

A majority of people (about 77 percent) are strongly right- or left-handed. The rest show some inconsistency in hand preference. As Table 3–1 indicates, such differences can affect performance in some sports (also see Fig. 3–26).

Table 3–1 Sports and Handedness

Sport	Handedness Advantage
Boxing	Left
Fencing	Left
Basketball	Mixed and ambidextrous
Ice hockey	Mixed and ambidextrous
Field hockey	Mixed and ambidextrous
Tennis	Strong left or strong right
Squash	Strong left or strong right
Badminton	Strong left or strong right

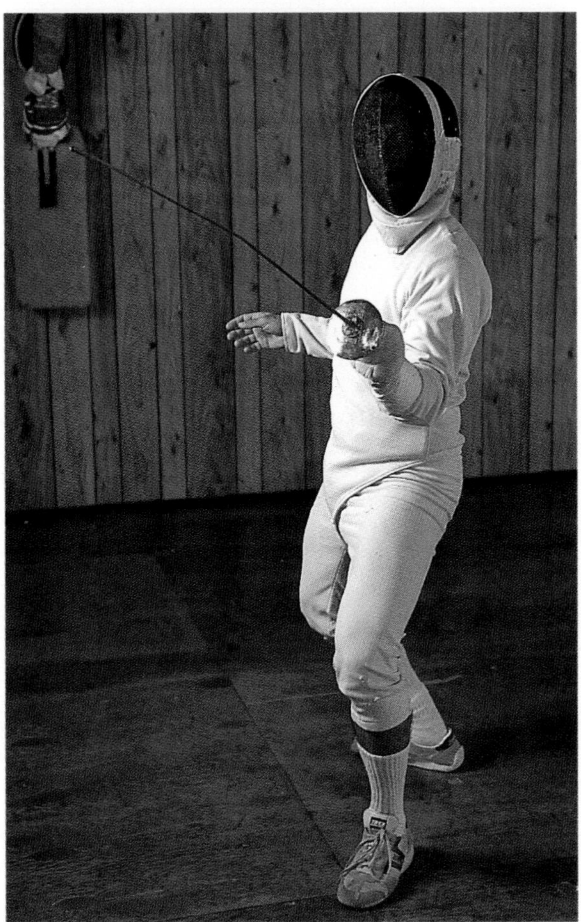

■ Fig. 3–26 *Left-handers have an advantage in sports such as fencing and boxing. Most likely, their movements are less familiar to opponents, who usually face right-handers. Contrary to what many people believe, left-handers have no overall advantage in baseball.*

Question: If a person is strongly left-handed does that mean the right hemisphere is dominant?

Not necessarily. It's true that the right hemisphere controls the left hand, but a left-handed person's language-producing, dominant hemisphere may be on the opposite side of the brain.

Brain Dominance About 97 percent of right-handers process speech in the left hemisphere and are left-brain dominant (■ Fig. 3–27). A good 68 percent of left-handers produce speech from the left hemisphere, just as right-handed people do. About 19 percent of all lefties and 3 percent of righties use their right brain for language. Approximately 12 percent of left-handers use both sides of the brain for language processing. All totaled, 94 percent of the population uses the left brain for language (Coren 1992).

Brain dominance The language-producing cerebral hemisphere.

Handedness A preference for the right or left hand in most activities.

Question: Is there any way for a person to tell which of his or her hemispheres is dominant?

One interesting clue is based on the way you write. Right-handed individuals who write with a straight hand, and lefties who write with a hooked hand, are usually left-brain dominant for language. Left-handed people who write with their hand below the line, and righties who use a hooked position, are usually right-brain dominant (Levy & Reid, 1976; Pines, 1980). Are your friends right brained or left brained? (See ■ Fig. 3–28.)

Before you leap to any conclusions, be aware that writing position is not a foolproof sign of brain organization. The only sure way to determine brain dominance is to do a medical test that involves briefly anesthetizing one cerebral hemisphere at a time (Springer & Deutsch, 1989).

Question: How common is left-handedness, and what causes it?

Handedness Animals show definite hand (or paw) preferences. However, in most animal groups—even monkeys—there is a 50–50 split of right- and left-"handedness." Among humans the split is about 90–10, with right-handedness being most common. The prevalence of right-handedness in humans probably reflects the left brain's specialization for language production (Coren, 1992).

In the past, left-handed children were often forced to use their right hand for writing, eating, and other

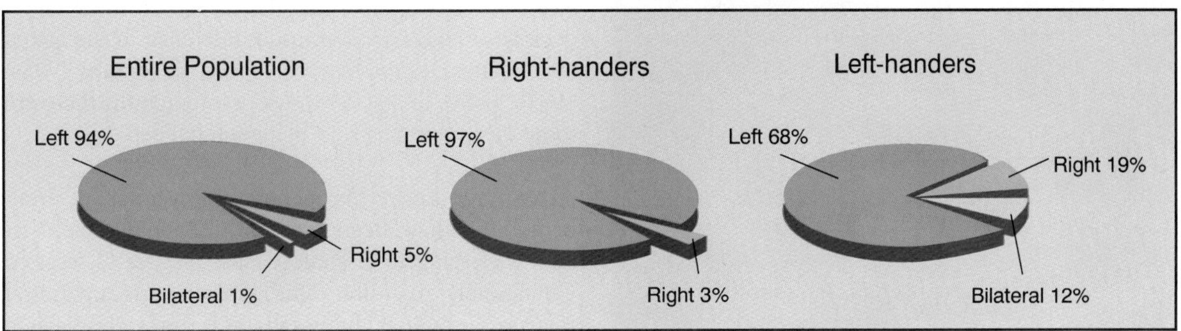

■ Fig. 3–27 *Language is controlled by the left side of the brain in the majority of right- and left-handers.*

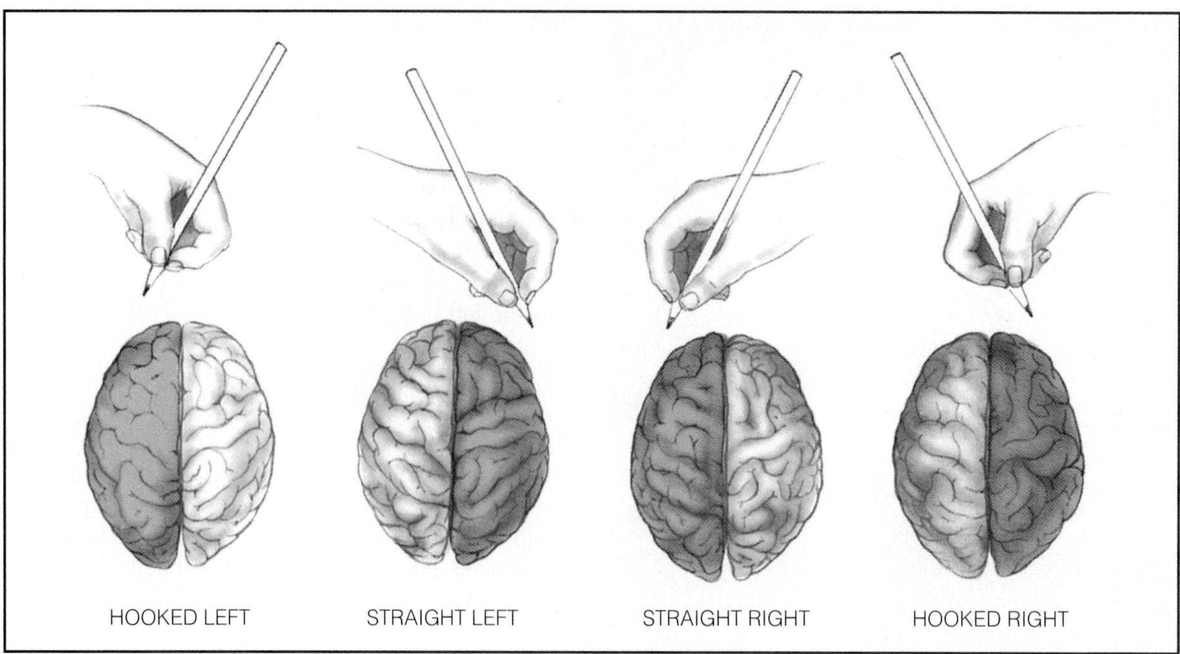

■ **Fig. 3–28** *Research suggests that the hand position used in writing may indicate which brain hemisphere is used for language. (Redrawn from an illustration by M. E. Challinor.)*

skills. But as fetal ultrasound images show, clear hand preferences are apparent even before birth (Hepper, 1990). (See ■ Fig. 3–29.) This suggests that handedness cannot be dictated. Parents should never try to force a left-handed child to use the right hand. To do so may invite speech or reading problems.

Question: Is handedness inherited from parents?

Hand preferences are not directly inherited like eye-color or skin color. What is inherited is the *degree* of handedness. If your parents are strongly handed you probably have a strong hand preference too—even though your dominant hand may not match theirs. If your parents are ambidextrous or mixed handed, you probably are too (Coren, 1992).

■ **Fig. 3–29** *In this ultrasound image, a four-month-old fetus sucks her right thumb. A study by psychologist Peter Hepper suggests that she will continue to prefer her right hand after she is born and that she will be right-handed as an adult.*

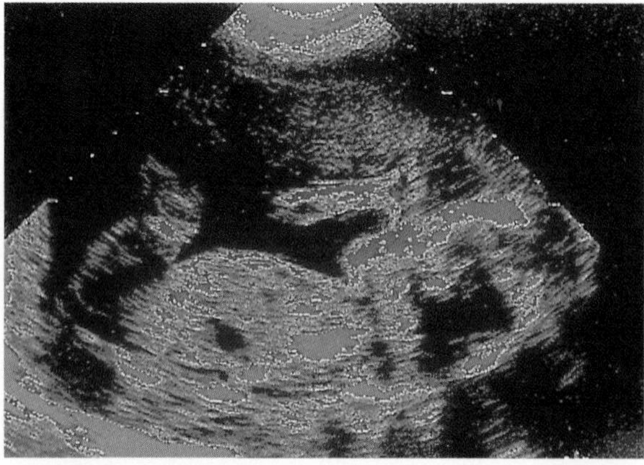

Question: Are there any drawbacks to being left-handed?

A minority of lefties owe their hand preference to birth traumas (such as prematurity, low birth weight, and breech birth). These individuals have a higher incidence of allergies, learning disorders, and other problems (Betancur et al., 1990). But genetic left-handedness, which accounts for most lefties, shows no correlation to general intelligence (McManus et al., 1988). Many people have been alarmed by news reports that lefties tend to die younger than right-handed persons (Coren & Halpern, 1991). However, three rather decisive studies have found no difference in the age at which left- and right-handed persons die (Harris, 1993a, 1993b; Salive et al., 1993). More importantly, there are some clear advantages to being left-handed.

Advantage Left Throughout history a notable number of artists have been lefties, from Leonardo da Vinci and Michelangelo to Pablo Picasso and M. C. Escher. Conceivably, since the right hemisphere is superior at imagery and visual abilities, there is some advantage to using the left hand for drawing or painting (Springer & Deutsch, 1989). At the least, lefties are definitely better at visualizing three-dimensional objects. This may be why there are more left-handed architects, artists, and chess players than would be expected (Coren, 1992).

One striking feature of lefties is that they are generally less **lateralized** than the right-handed (Hellige, 1990). This means that there is less distinct specialization in the two sides of their brains. In fact, even the physical size and shape of their cerebral hemispheres are more alike. If you are a lefty you can take pride in the fact that your brain is less lopsided than the brains of your right-handed friends (Corballis, 1980)! In general, left-handers are more symmetrical on almost everything, including eye dominance, fingerprints—even foot size (Corballis, 1980).

In some situations less lateralization may be a real advantage. For instance, individuals who are moderately left-handed or ambidextrous seem to have better than average pitch memory, which is a basic musical skill (Deutsch, 1978). Correspondingly, more musicians are ambidextrous than would normally be expected. It's not clear, however, if those who are musically gifted were initially less lateralized or if playing music develops both hands or possibly both sides of the brain (Springer & Deutsch, 1989).

Math abilities may also benefit from fuller use of the right hemisphere. Students who are extremely gifted in math are much more likely to be left-handed or ambidextrous (Benbow, 1986). Even where ordinary arithmetic skills are concerned, lefties seem to excel (Annett & Manning, 1990). The clearest advantage of being left-handed shows up when there is a brain injury. Because of their milder lateralization, left-handed individuals typically experience less language loss after damage to either brain hemisphere, and they recover more easily (Geschwind, 1979). Maybe having "two left feet" isn't so bad after all.

Lateralization Specialization in the abilities of the brain hemispheres.

LEARNING CHECK

1. About 97 percent of left-handed people process language on the left side of the brain, the same as right-handed people do. T or F?
2. Left-handed individuals who write with their hand below the line are likely to be right-brain dominant. T or F?
3. Most animals, like most humans, show a preference for the right limb. T or F?
4. In general, left-handed individuals show less lateralization in the brain and in fact throughout the body. T or F?
5. Recent studies have shown conclusively that left-handed people tend to die younger than members of the right-handed population. T or F?
6. Reports that left-handed people tend to die younger were flawed in an important way: The average age of people in the left-handed group was younger than that of subjects in the right-handed group. Why would this make a difference in the conclusions drawn?

Critical Thinking

Answers: 1. F 2. T 3. F 4. T 5. F 6. Because we can't tell if handedness or average age accounts for the difference in death rates. For example, if we start with a group of 20- to 30-year-old people, in which some die, the average age of death has to be between 20 and 30. If we start with a group of 30- to 40-year-old people, in which some die, the average age of death has to be between 30 and 40. Thus, the left-handed group might have an earlier average age at death simply because members of the group were younger to start with.

EXPLORATION

Charting the Brain's Inner Realms

On the table in front of you lies a small, mysterious, and powerful computer. Your assignment is to discover how it works. How will you proceed? The challenge is much like the one scientists face in studying the brain. You'll find a box of tools and a flashlight next to the computer. Ready. Begin.

The Computer Your first step might be to take apart the computer. This would allow you to tell in general what is connected with what.

The Brain Similarly, researchers use **dissection** (dih-SEK-shun: separation into parts) to identify major brain parts and pathways. Dissection is often aided by chemically **staining** thin slices of brain tissue so smaller details become visible. However, like taking a computer apart, dissection and staining tell relatively little about the purpose or *function* of parts of the brain.

The Computer What parts of the computer supply its memory? Control its keyboard? Activate its screen? Do the computing? To begin answering such questions, you could remove one part inside the computer at a time. By observing what effect removing the part has you could learn something about its purpose.

The Brain Using similar logic, many studies in biopsychology are based on **ablation** (ab-LAY-shun: surgical removal) of parts of the brain. (Don't try this at home.) When ablation is followed by a change in behavior or capacity, we gain insight into the purpose of the missing structure. But many studies may be necessary before we can be confident about the function of each part.

The Computer In time, it will become instructive to cut only a single wire or to remove only one tiny electrical part of the computer.

The Brain **Deep lesioning** (LEE-zhun-ing) is the comparable procedure in brain research. In deep lesioning, a thin wire electrode, insulated except at the tip, is lowered into a selected target area inside the brain (■ Fig. 3–30). An electric current is then used to destroy a small amount of brain tissue. Again, observed changes in behavior give clues about the function of the lesioned area. Using a weaker current, it is also possible to *activate* target areas, rather than remove them. This is called ESB, as described earlier in Highlight 3-4.

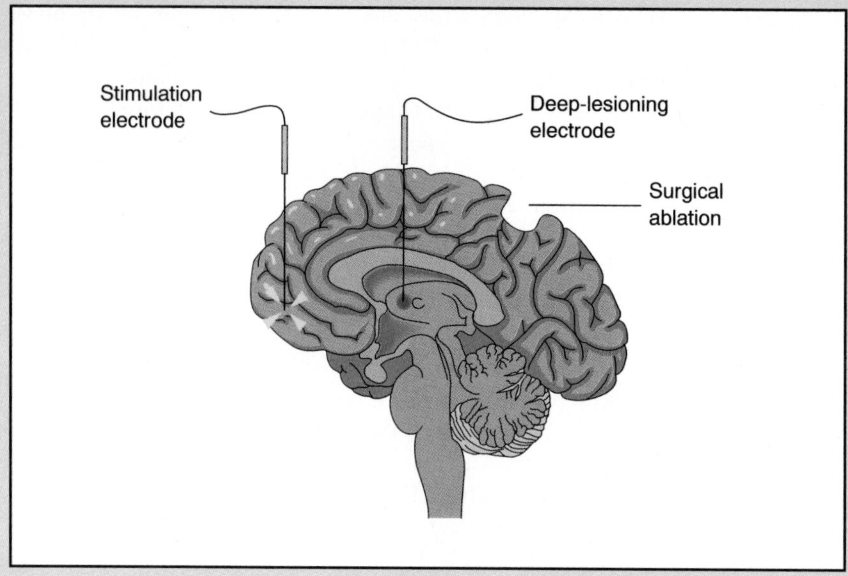

■ Fig. 3–30 *The functions of brain structures can be explored by selectively activating or removing them. Brain research is often based on electrical stimulation, but chemical stimulation is also used at times.*

The Computer As you delve deeper into the computer, you eventually will want to directly measure its electrical signals. Using electrical measuring devices, you record activity in various circuits of the computer *while it is on and functioning.*

The Brain Likewise, researchers use electrodes to record the firing of large populations of neurons within the brain. Even more revealing, perhaps, are *micro-electrode recordings.* A **micro-electrode** is a tiny glass tube filled with a salty, electrically conducting fluid. The tip of a micro-electrode is small enough to detect the activity of a *single* neuron. Watching the action potentials of a single neuron provides a fascinating, fine-grain glimpse into the origins of behavior.

Up to this point, our "mystery computer" has merely served as a model to clarify the nature of conventional brain research. The remainder of this Exploration explains how computers are being used to enrich biopsychology by creating vivid images of the brain and its activity.

New Images of the Living Brain

Many of the brain's riddles have been solved with the methods just described. Yet, each technique lets us see only a small part of the whole picture. What would it be like to be able to "peek" inside an intact brain while a person is thinking, perceiving, and reacting? Computer-enhanced images are now making this age-old dream possible. Let's look through some of these newly opened "windows" into the human biocomputer.

CT Scan Computerized X-ray scanning equipment has virtually revolutionized the study of brain diseases and injuries. At best, conventional X-rays produce only shadowy images of soft tissues like the

EXPLORATION

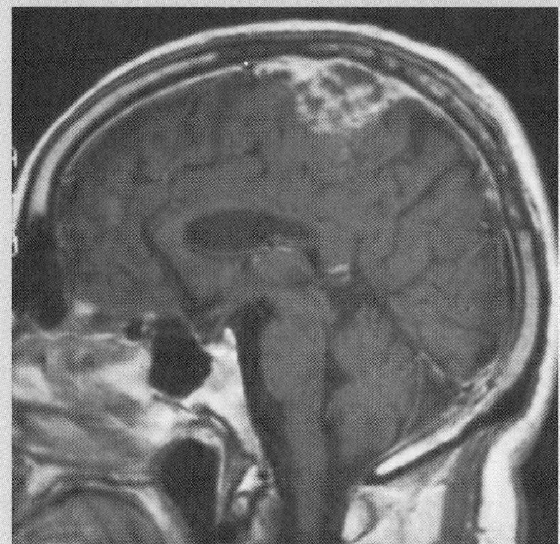

■ **Fig. 3–31** *An MRI scan shows a tumor in the cerebrum (see arrow). Notice how it is possible to display a precise "slice" from the middle of the three-dimensional MRI data.*

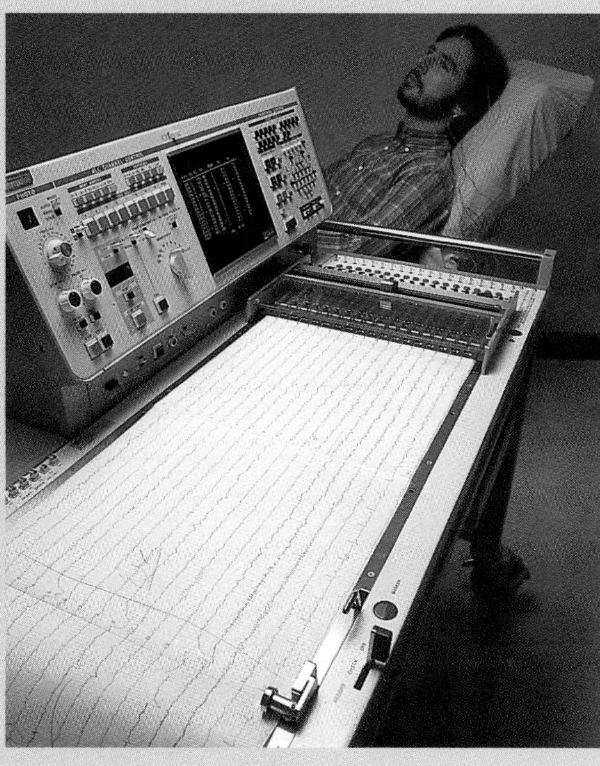

■ **Fig. 3–32** *A conventional EEG record of brain-wave patterns.*

brain. **Computed tomographic** (CT) scanning is a specialized type of X-ray that does a much better job of making the interior of the brain visible. In a CT scan, the head is placed inside a large doughnut-shaped metal ring. Next, very thin X-ray beams are passed through the head from points all around the ring. The X-ray information is collected by a computer and formed into an image of the brain. A CT scan can reveal the effects of strokes, injuries, tumors, and other brain disorders (Larson, 1990). These, in turn, can be related to changes in a person's behavior.

MRI Scan **Magnetic resonance imaging** (MRI) uses a very strong magnetic field, rather than X-rays, to produce an image of the body's interior. During an MRI scan, the body is placed inside a magnetic field. Each hydrogen atom in the body responds to the magnetism. A detector surrounding the body measures the atoms' responses. Processing by a computer then creates a composite, three-dimensional representation of the brain or body. Any two-dimensional plane, or slice, of the body can be selected electronically from the MRI data and displayed as an image on a computer screen (Larson, 1990). This allows scientists to peer into the living brain almost as if it were transparent (■ Fig. 3–31).

A newer method, called **functional MRI,** goes one step further by making brain *activity* visible. For example, an area of the motor cortex will be highlighted in a functional MRI image when a person taps her fingers. Such images are allowing scientists to pinpoint areas in the brain responsible for thoughts and actions (Naeye, 1994).

Electroencephalography (EEG) Electroencephalography (ee-LEK-tro-in-SEF-ah-LOG-ruh-fee) measures the waves of electrical activity produced by the brain. Small disk-shaped metal electrodes are placed at various locations on a person's scalp. Electrical impulses from the brain are detected by the electrodes and sent to an **electroencephalograph.** The EEG amplifies these very weak signals (brain waves) and records them on a moving sheet of paper (■ Fig. 3–32). Various brain-wave patterns can help identify the presence of tumors, epilepsy, and other diseases. The EEG also reveals changes in brain activity during sleep, daydreaming, hypnosis, and other mental states (see Chapter 6).

For all its value, an "old-fashioned" EEG is like trying to guess what's happening inside a busy factory by standing outside with your ear pressed against the wall. The EEG allows us to detect an overall rise or fall of brain activity, but only very general patterns are apparent.

Dissection Separation of tissues into their parts.

Staining Chemically treating tissues to make their details more visible.

Ablation Surgical removal of tissue.

Deep lesioning Removal of tissue within the brain by use of an electrode.

Micro-electrode An electrode small enough to record the activity of a single neuron.

CT scan Computed tomography scan; a computer-enhanced X-ray image of the brain or body.

MRI scan Magnetic resonance imaging; a computer-enhanced three-dimensional image of the brain or body, based on the body's response to a magnetic field.

Functional MRI An MRI scan that records brain activity.

Electroencephalograph (EEG) A device that detects, amplifies, and records electrical activity in the brain.

EXPLORATION

MANSCAN Computers have recently brought the EEG a step closer to the dream of "seeing" brain activity. Neuroscientist Alan Gevins (1989) and his colleagues have developed a new technique they call the **mental activity network scanner,** or MANSCAN. It consists of a soft helmet that records EEG data from 124 points, rather than the typical 16 to 30. A computer tracks brain wave activity and maps it onto a three-dimensional MRI scan of the brain (Weiss, 1990). While a person performs a mental task, MANSCAN takes 250 "snapshots" of brain waves per second. After processing and analysis, the computer creates a diagram of brain activity (■ Fig. 3-33). MANSCAN is providing new information on memory, mental fatigue, coordination, and language use (Gevins et al., 1990).

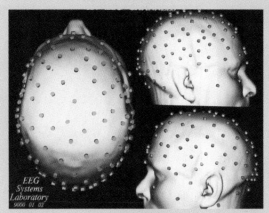

■ **Fig. 3-33** (Top) *The MANSCAN device records EEG data from 124 points on the head.* (Bottom) *A computer combines EEG data with an MRI scan to produce three-dimensional "maps" of thinking and other brain activity. Colors are used to show the time delay between points of peak activity. Wider arrows indicate greater similarity of activity between two points. In this example, notice how different the patterns are for a task requiring immediate memory* (right) *and one not requiring it* (left).

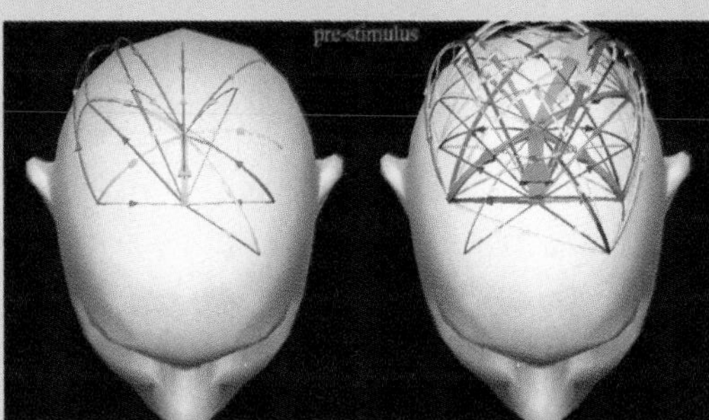

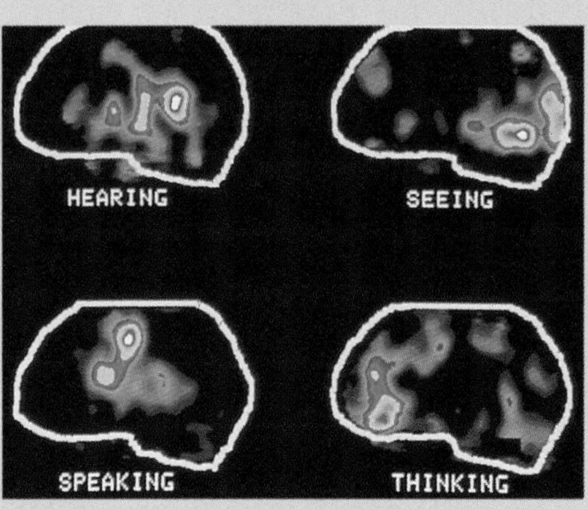

■ **Fig. 3-34** *These PET images show scans of the left side of the brain made while a person heard a word, saw a word, repeated a word aloud, and said a word related to the one that was seen (Petersen et al., 1988).*

PET Scan Positron emission tomography (PET) images of the brain are perhaps the most remarkable of all. As described earlier in Highlight 3-2, a PET scan detects positrons (sub-atomic particles) emitted by weakly radioactive glucose (sugar) as it is consumed by the brain. Since the brain runs on glucose, a PET scan shows which brain areas are using more energy. Higher energy use is assumed to correspond with higher activity. By placing positron detectors around the head and sending data to a computer it is possible to create a moving, color picture of changes in brain activity (Fig. 3-14 is a good example).

Rainbow-hued PET scan images are mapping human brain activity with a precision never before possible. In a further refinement, tiny amounts of a radioactive oxygen compound are injected into a person's bloodstream. This "tagged" oxygen remains active for only a few minutes. Tagged glucose, in comparison, is active for several hours.

Each dose of oxygen allows a brief PET scan to be made. Each of these "snapshots" of the brain can be compared with others in a way that isolates a fleeting moment of brain activity. For example, let's say that a person is reading a word while one of the PET images is being made. An average of several PET images, each made while the person is doing other tasks, can be *subtracted* from the one made while the person was reading. This cancels out generalized activity in the PET image and spotlights only the area most involved with reading (Petersen et al., 1988).

As you can see in ■ Figure 3-34, tagged-oxygen PET scans reveal that very specific brain areas are active when you are reading a word, hearing a word, saying a word, or thinking about the meaning of a word. PET images of this type can also be superimposed on an MRI scan. The MRI scan shows the brain in detail and the PET scan tells which areas are linked with various abilities (■ Fig. 3-35).

MANSCAN Mental activity network scanner; a specialized type of EEG recording.

PET scan Positron emission tomography; a computer generated image of brain activity, based on glucose consumption in the brain.

EXPLORATION

Images of the Future Neuroscientists and medical researchers are still learning how to make full use of computerized imaging techniques. At the same time, newer techniques are being added to their arsenal. One is called MEG, which stands for magnetoencephalography. A MEG scan uses exotic electronic devices to detect the exceedingly weak magnetic fields created when neurons fire (Heppenheimer, 1990). MEG is giving the clearest views yet of human brain activity. It is just a matter of time until even brighter beacons are flashed into the shadowy inner world of thought.

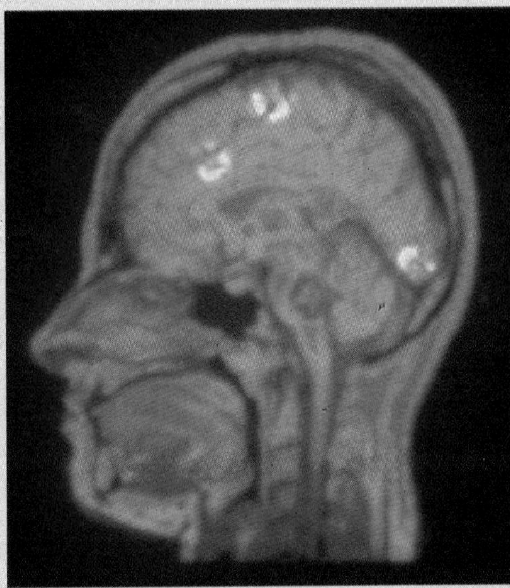

■ **Fig. 3–35** *The bright spots you see here were created by a PET scan. They are similar to the spots in Figure 3–27. However, here they have been placed over an MRI scan so that the brain's anatomy is visible. The three bright spots are areas in the left brain related to language. The spot on the right is active during reading. The top-middle area is connected with speech. The area to the left, in the frontal lobe is linked with thinking about a word's meaning ("The Mind," 1989).*

LEARNING CHECK

1. In brain research, making a micro-electrode recording is the first step in deep lesioning studies. T or F?
2. Both CT scans and MRI scans are based on X-ray data that is assembled into an image by a computer. T or F?
3. The MANSCAN technique combines EEG information with an MRI scan. T or F?
4. In a PET scan, brain areas that are using more glucose or oxygen are assumed to be more active than surrounding areas. T or F?
5. Deep lesioning is used to ablate an area in the hypothalamus of a rat. After the operation, the rat seems to lose interest in food and eating. Why would it be a mistake to conclude that the ablated area is a "hunger center"? ***Critical Thinking***

Answers: 1. F 2. F 3. T 4. T 5. Because other factors might explain the apparent loss of appetite. For example, the taste or smell of food might be affected, or the rat might simply have difficulty swallowing. It is also possible that hunger originates elsewhere in the brain and the ablated area merely relays messages that cause the rat to eat.

Chapter Summary

■ ***How do nerve cells operate and communicate?***

- The brain and nervous system are made up of linked nerve cells called **neurons.** Neurons are arranged in long chains and dense networks. They pass information from one to another through **synapses.**
- The basic conducting fibers of neurons are **axons,** but **dendrites** (a receiving area), the **soma** (the cell body and also a receiving area), and **axon terminals** (the branching ends of an axon) are also involved in communication.
- The firing of an **action potential** (nerve impulse) is basically electrical, whereas communication between neurons is chemical or electrical. Chemical synapses are most numerous in nature, but some electrical synapses exist.
- In chemical synapses, neurons release chemicals called **neurotransmitters.** These cross to **receptor sites** on the receiving cell, causing it to be excited or inhibited.
- Transmitters called **neuropeptides** appear to regulate activity in the brain. Through **volume conduction** their effects can be widespread.

Peripheral vision Vision at the edges of the visual field.

Tunnel vision Vision restricted to the center of the visual field.

Trichromatic theory Theory of color vision based on three cone types: red, green, and blue.

Opponent-process theory Theory of color vision based on three coding systems (red or green, yellow or blue, black or white).

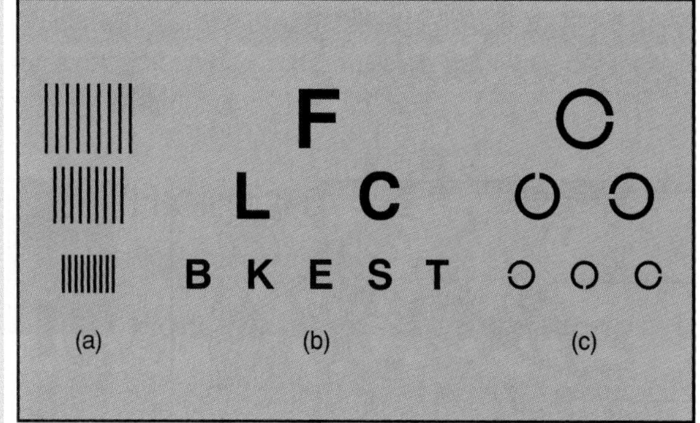

■ Fig. 4–10 *Tests of visual acuity. Here are some common tests of visual acuity. In (a), sharpness is indicated by the smallest grating still seen as individual lines. The Snellen chart (b) requires that you read rows of letters of diminishing size until you can no longer distinguish them. The Landolt rings (c) require no familiarity with letters. All that is required is a report of which side has a break in it. Normal acuity is designated as 20/20 vision: At 20 feet in distance, you can distinguish what the average person can see at 20 feet. If your vision is 20/40, you can only see at 20 feet what the average person can see at 40 feet. If your vision is 20/200, you need glasses! Vision that is 20/12 would mean that you can see at 20 feet what the average person must be 8 feet nearer to see, indicating better than average acuity. American astronaut Gordon Cooper, who claimed to see railroad lines in northern India from 100 miles above, had 20/12 acuity.*

If you look at your thumbnail at arm's length, its image just about covers the fovea. Like a newspaper photograph made of many small dots, the tightly packed cones of the fovea produce the greatest visual acuity. In other words, vision is sharpest when an image falls on the fovea. Acuity steadily decreases as images are moved to the edge of the retina.

■ Figure 4–10 describes a widely used rating system for acuity. If vision can be corrected to no better than 20/200 acuity, a person is considered legally blind. With 20/200 vision, the world is seen as nothing but a blur.

Question: What is the purpose of the rest of the retina?

Peripheral Vision Areas outside the fovea also get light. This creates a large region of **peripheral** (side) **vision.** The rods are most numerous about 20 degrees from the center of the retina, so much peripheral vision is rod vision. Fortunately, the rods are quite sensitive to *movement.* Thus, while the eye gives its best acuity to the center of vision, it maintains a radar-like scan for movement in side vision. Seeing "out of the corner of the eye" is important for sports, driving, and walking down dark alleys. Those who have lost peripheral vision suffer from **tunnel vision,** a condition much like wearing blinders.

Sailors, pilots, astronomers, and military spotters have long made use of another interesting fact about peripheral vision. Although the rods give poor acuity, they are many times more responsive to light than the cones are. Since most rods are 20 degrees to each side of the fovea, the best night vision is obtained by looking *next* to an object you wish to see. Test this yourself some night by looking at, and next to, a very dim star.

Color Vision—There's More to It than Meets the Eye

What would you say is the brightest color? Red? Yellow? Blue? Actually, there are two answers to this question, one for the rods and one for the cones. The rods and cones differ in *maximal color sensitivity,* a difference that has practical importance. The cones are most sensitive to the *yellowish-green* region of the spectrum. In other words, if all colors are tested in daylight (with each reflecting the same total amount of light) then yellowish green appears *brightest.* The increased use of yellow fire trucks and the Day-Glo yellow vests worn by roadside work crews reflects this fact (■ Fig. 4–11).

Question: To what color are the rods most sensitive?

Remember that the rods do not produce color sensations. If very dim colored lights are used, no color will be seen. Even so, one light will appear brighter than the others. When tested this way, the rods are most sensitive to *blue-green* lights. Thus, at night or in dim light, when rod vision prevails, the brightest-colored light will be one that is blue or blue-green. For this reason, police and highway patrol cars in many states now have blue emergency lights for night work. Also, you may have wondered why the taxiway lights at airports are blue. It seems like a poor choice, but blue is actually highly visible to pilots.

Color Theories

Question: How do the cones produce color sensations?

No short answer can do justice to the complexities of color vision, but briefly, here is the best current explanation. The **trichromatic theory** (TRY-kro-MAT-ik) of color vision holds that there are three types of cones, each most sensitive to a specific color: red, green, or blue. Other colors are assumed to result from combinations of these three, whereas black and white sensations are produced by the rods.

A basic problem with the trichromatic theory is that four colors seem psychologically primary: red, green, blue, and yellow. A second view, known as the **opponent-process theory,** attempts to explain why you can't have a reddish green or a yellowish blue. According to this theory, the visual system analyzes color

■ **Fig. 4–11** *Yellow-green fire trucks are far more visible in daylight because their color matches the cones' sensitivity peak. However, many cities continue to prefer red trucks because of tradition.*

■ **Fig. 4–12** *Negative afterimages. Stare at the dot near the middle of the flag for at least 30 seconds. Then look immediately at a plain sheet of white paper or a white wall. You will see the American flag in its normal colors. Reduced sensitivity to yellow, green, and black receptors in the eye, caused by prolonged staring, results in the appearance of complementary colors. Project the afterimage of the flag on other colored surfaces to get additional effects.*

into "either-or" messages. It is assumed that the visual system can produce messages for either red or green, yellow or blue, black or white. Coding one color in a pair (red for instance) seems to block the opposite message (green), so a reddish green is impossible, but a yellowish red (orange) can occur.

According to opponent-process theory, fatigue caused by making one response produces an **afterimage** of the opposite color as the system recovers. To see an afterimage of this type, look at ■ Figure 4–12 and follow the instructions given there.

Question: Which color theory is correct?

Both! The three-color theory applies to the retina, where three types of light-sensitive **visual pigments** have been found. As predicted, each pigment is most sensitive to a different wavelength of light. The three peaks of sensitivity fall in roughly the red, green, and blue regions. As a result, the three types of cones fire nerve impulses at different rates when various colors are viewed (■ Fig. 4–13). In further support of the three-color theory, researchers have confirmed that each cone contains only one pigment and that each pigment is controlled by its own gene (Nathans et al., 1986).

In contrast, the opponent-process theory seems to explain events recorded in the optic pathways *after* information leaves the eye. So both theories are "correct." One explains what happens in the eye itself. The other explains how visual information is analyzed on its way to the brain. Together they explain color vision.

Afterimage Visual sensation that persists after a stimulus is removed.

Visual pigments Light-sensitive chemicals found in the rods and cones.

■ **Fig. 4–13** *Firing rates of blue, green, and red cones in response to different colors. The larger the colored circle, the higher the firing rates. Colors are coded by activity in all three types of cones in the normal eye. (Adapted from Goldstein, 1989.)*

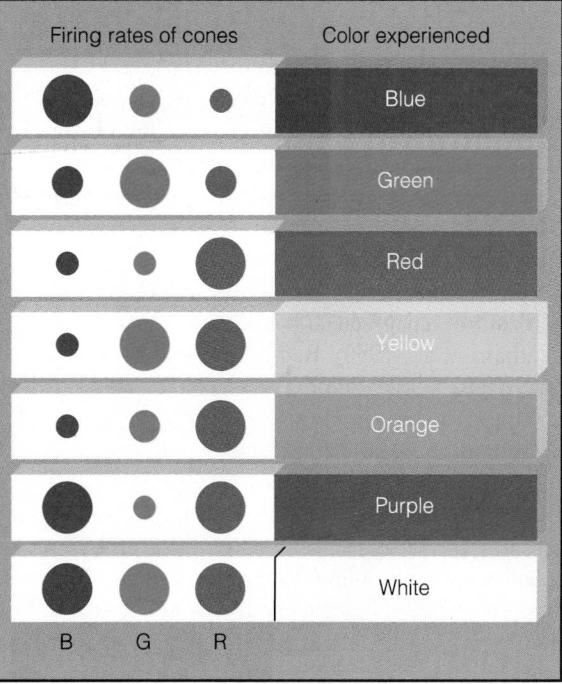

(a)

(b)

(c)

■ Fig. 4–14 *Color blindness and color weakness. (a) Photograph illustrates normal color vision. (b) Photograph is printed in blue and yellow and gives an impression of what a red-green color-blind person sees. (c) Photograph simulates total color blindness. If you are totally color-blind, all three photos will look nearly identical.*

Color blindness A total inability to perceive colors.

Color weakness An inability to distinguish some colors.

Ishihara test A test for color blindness and color weakness.

Dark adaptation Increased retinal sensitivity to light.

Color Blindness and Color Weakness

Do you know anyone who regularly draws hoots of laughter by wearing clothes of wildly clashing colors? Or someone who sheepishly tries to avoid saying what color an object is? If so, you probably know someone who is color-blind.

Question: What is it like to be color-blind? What causes color blindness?

A person who is completely **color-blind** sees the world as if it were a black and white movie. How do we know? In a few rare cases, people have been color-blind in only one eye and can compare (Hsia & Graham, 1965). Two colors of equal brightness look exactly alike to the color-blind individual. The color-blind person either lacks cones or has cones that do not function normally (Rushton, 1975).

Total color blindness is rare. **Color weakness,** or partial color blindness, is more common. Approximately 8 percent of the male population (but less than 1 percent of women) are red-green color-blind. (Another form of color weakness, involving yellow and blue, is extremely rare.)

Color blindness is caused by changes in the genes that control red, green, and blue pigments in the cones (Nathans et al., 1986). Red-green color blindness is a recessive, sex-linked trait. This means that it is carried on the X, or female chromosome. Women have two X chromosomes, so if they receive only one defective color gene, they still have normal vision. Color-blind men, however, have only one X chromosome, so they can inherit the defect from their mothers (who are usually not color-blind themselves). The red-green color-blind individual sees both reds and greens as the same color, usually a yellowish brown (Rushton, 1975) (see ■ Fig. 4–14).

Question: Then how can color-blind individuals drive? Don't they have trouble with traffic lights?

Red-green color-blind individuals have normal vision for yellow and blue, so their main problem is telling red lights from green. In practice, this is not difficult. In the United States and Canada, the red light is always on top, and the green light is brighter than the red. Also, to help remedy this problem, most modern traffic signals have a "red" light that has a background of yellow light mixed with it, and a "green" light that is really blue-green.

Question: How can a person tell if he or she is color-blind?

A common test for color blindness and weakness is the **Ishihara test.** In the test, numbers and other designs made of dots are placed on a background also made of dots. The background and the numbers are of different colors (red and green, for example). A person who is color-blind sees only a jumble of dots. The person with normal color vision can detect the presence of the numbers or designs. ■ Figure 4–15 is a replica of the Ishihara test. You should not consider Figure 4–15 a true test of color vision, but it may give you some idea of whether or not you are color-blind. The real test is highly accurate (Birch & McKeever, 1993).

Dark Adaptation—Let There Be Light!

Question: What happens to the eyes when they adapt to a dark room?

Dark adaptation is the dramatic increase in light sensitivity that occurs after entering the dark. Consider

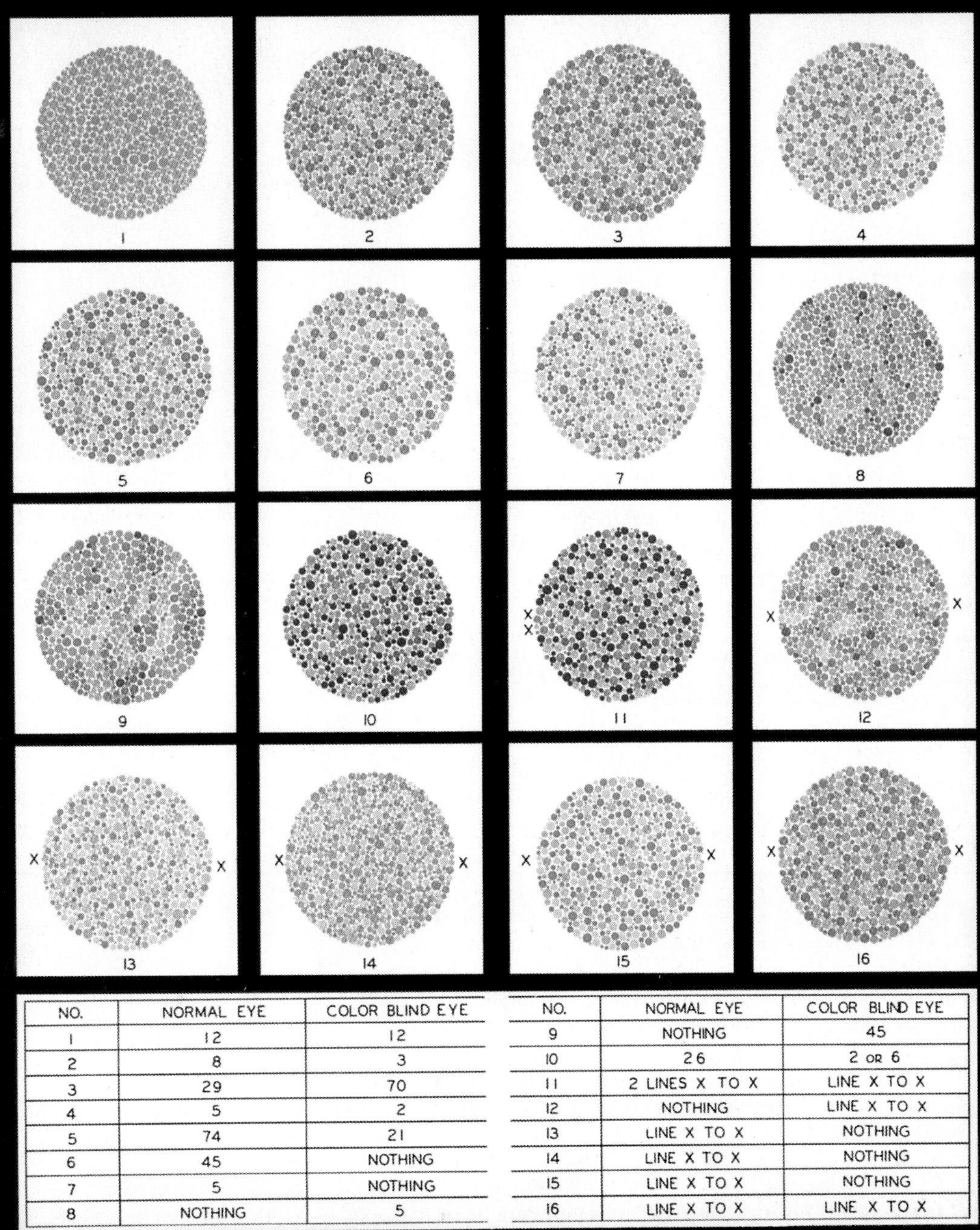

NO.	NORMAL EYE	COLOR BLIND EYE	NO.	NORMAL EYE	COLOR BLIND EYE
1	12	12	9	NOTHING	45
2	8	3	10	26	2 OR 6
3	29	70	11	2 LINES X TO X	LINE X TO X
4	5	2	12	NOTHING	LINE X TO X
5	74	21	13	LINE X TO X	NOTHING
6	45	NOTHING	14	LINE X TO X	NOTHING
7	5	NOTHING	15	LINE X TO X	NOTHING
8	NOTHING	5	16	LINE X TO X	LINE X TO X

■ **Fig. 4–15** *Replica of a test for color blindness.*

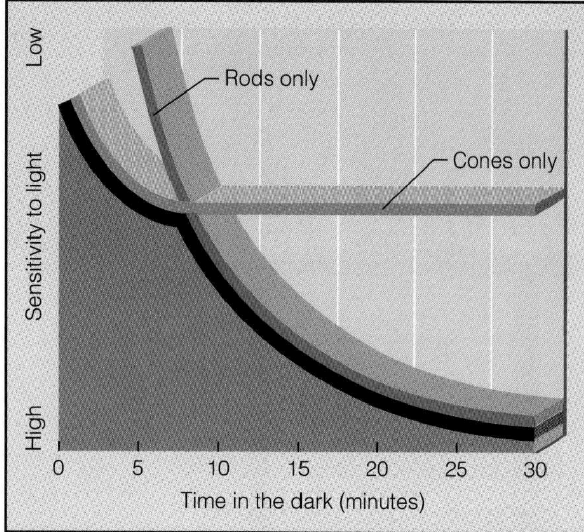

■ Fig. 4–16 *Typical course of dark adaptation. The black line shows how the threshold for vision lowers as a person spends time in the dark. (A lower threshold means that less light is needed for vision.) The green line shows that the cones adapt first, but they soon cease adding to light sensitivity. Rods, shown by the red line, adapt more slowly. However, they continue to add to improved night vision long after the cones are fully adapted.*

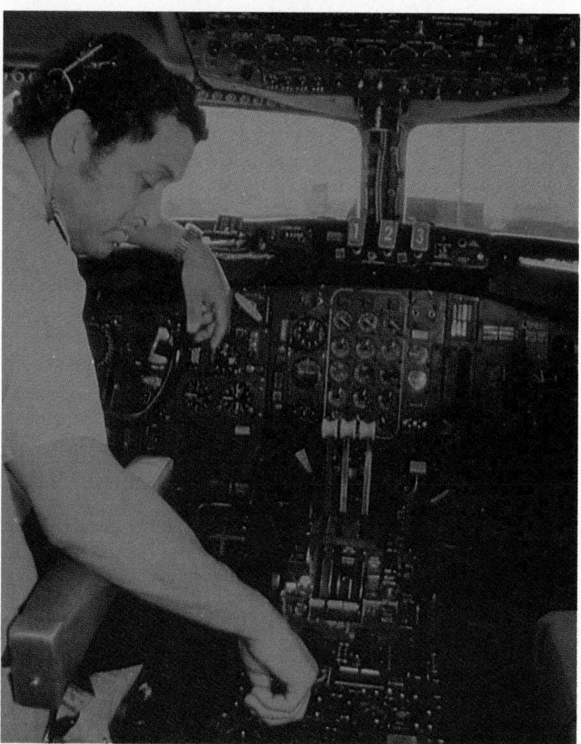

■ Fig. 4–17 *Red light allows dark adaptation to occur because it provides little or no stimulation to the rods.*

Rhodopsin The light-sensitive pigment in the rods.

walking into a theater. If you enter from a brightly lighted lobby, you practically need to be led to your seat. After a short time, however, you can see the entire room in detail (including the couple kissing over in the corner). Studies of dark adaptation show that it takes about 30 to 35 minutes of complete darkness to reach maximum visual sensitivity (■ Fig. 4–16). When dark adaptation is complete, the eye can detect lights 10,000 times weaker than those to which it was originally sensitive.

Question: What causes dark adaptation?

Like the cones, the rods also contain a light-sensitive **visual pigment.** When struck by light, visual pigments bleach, or break down chemically. (The afterimages caused by flashbulbs are a direct result of this bleaching.) To restore light sensitivity, the visual pigments must recombine, which takes time. Night vision is due mainly to an increase of the rod pigment, **rhodopsin** (row-DOP-sin). When completely dark-adapted, the human eye is almost as sensitive to light as the eye of an owl.

Before artificial lighting, gradual adaptation at sunset posed few problems. Now we are often caught in temporary semi-blindness. Usually this isn't dangerous, but it can be. Even though dark adaptation takes a long time, it can be wiped out by just a few seconds of viewing bright light. Try this demonstration:

See (and Don't See) for Yourself

Spend 15 or 20 minutes in a darkened room. At the end of this time, you should be able to see clearly. Now, close your left eye and cover it tightly with your hand. Turn on a bright light for 1 or 2 seconds and look at it with your right eye. With the light off again, compare the vision in your two eyes, first opening one and then the other. You will be completely blinded in your right eye.

This experience should convince you to avoid looking at the headlights of approaching cars during night driving. Under normal conditions, glare recovery takes about 20 seconds, plenty of time for an accident. After a few drinks, it may take 30 to 50 percent longer, because alcohol dilates the pupils, allowing more light to enter. Note, too, that dark adaptation occurs more slowly as we grow older. This is one reason why injuries caused by falling in the dark become more common among the elderly (McMurdo & Gaskell, 1991).

Question: Is there any way to speed up dark adaptation?

The rods are *insensitive* to extremely red light. To take advantage of this lack of sensitivity, submarines and airplane cockpits are illuminated with red light. So are the ready rooms for fighter pilots and ground crews (■ Fig. 4–17). In each case, this allows people to move quickly into the dark without having to adapt. Because the red light doesn't stimulate the rods, it is as if they had already spent time in the dark.

Question: Can eating carrots really improve vision?

One of the "ingredients" of rhodopsin is **retinal,** which the body makes from vitamin A. (Retinal is also called retinene.) When too little vitamin A is available, less rhodopsin is produced. Thus, a person lacking vitamin A may develop **night blindness.** In night blindness, the person sees normally in bright light while using the cones, but becomes totally blind at night when the rods must function. Carrots are an excellent source of vitamin A, so they could improve night vision for someone suffering a deficiency, but not the vision of anyone with an adequate diet (Carlson, 1991).

Learning Check

After such an extended discussion of vision you may find it helpful to review the following questions.

1. The ________________ ________________ is made up of electromagnetic radiation with wavelengths between 400 and 700 nanometers.
2. Match:

____ Myopia	A.	Farsightedness
____ Hyperopia	B.	Elongated eye
____ Presbyopia	C.	Farsightedness due to aging
____ Astigmatism	D.	Lack of cones in fovea
	E.	Misshapen cornea or lens

3. In dim light, vision depends mainly on the ________________. In brighter light, color and fine detail are produced by the ________________.
4. The fovea has the greatest visual acuity due to the large concentration of rods found there. T or F?
5. Hubel and Wiesel found that cells in the visual cortex of the brain function as ________________ ________________.
6. The term 20/20 vision means that a person can see at 20 feet what can normally be seen from 20 feet. T or F?
7. When using the cones, the most visible color is
   a. reddish orange *b.* blue-green *c.* yellow-orange *d.* yellowish green
8. The eyes become more sensitive to light at night because of a process known as ________________ ________________.
9. Sensory transduction in the eye takes place first in the cornea, then in the lens, then in the retina. T or F? ***Critical Thinking***

Answers:

1. visible spectrum 2. B, A, C, E 3. rods, cones 4. F 5. feature detectors 6. T 7. *d* 8. dark adaptation 9. False. The cornea and lens bend and focus light rays, but they do not change light to another form of energy. No change in the *type* of energy takes place until the retina converts light to nerve impulses.

Hearing—Good Vibrations

Rock, classical, jazz, country, pop—whatever your musical taste, you have probably been moved or soothed by the riches of sound. Hearing also provides the brain with a wealth of information not available through the other senses, such as the approach of an unseen car or the information imparted by spoken language. Hearing collects information from all around the body. Vision, in all its glory, is limited to stimuli in front of the eyes (unless, of course, your "shades" have rear-view mirrors attached).

Question: What is the stimulus for hearing?

If you throw a stone into a quiet pond, a circle of waves will spread in all directions. In much the same way, sound travels as a series of invisible waves of **compression** (peaks) and **rarefaction** (RARE-eh-fak-shun, valleys) in the air. Any vibrating object—a tuning fork, the string of a musical instrument, or the vocal cords—will produce **sound waves** by setting air molecules in motion. Other materials, such as fluids or solids, will also carry sound. But sound does not travel in a vacuum. Movies that show characters reacting to the "roar" of alien starships or to titanic battles in deep space are in error.

The **frequency** of sound waves (the number of waves per second) corresponds to the perceived **pitch** of a sound. The **amplitude,** or physical "height," of a sound wave tells how much energy it contains. Psychologically, amplitude corresponds to sensed **loudness** (■ Fig. 4–18).

Question: How are sounds converted to nerve impulses?

What we call the "ear" is only the **pinna** (PIN-ah), or visible, external part of the ear. In addition to being a good place to hang earrings or balance pencils, the

Retinal Part of the chemical compound that makes up rhodopsin (also known as retinene).

Night blindness Blindness under conditions of low illumination.

Sound wave Cyclic, wave-like movement of air molecules.

Pitch Higher or lower tones; related to the frequency of sound waves.

Loudness The intensity of a sound; determined by the amplitude of sound waves.

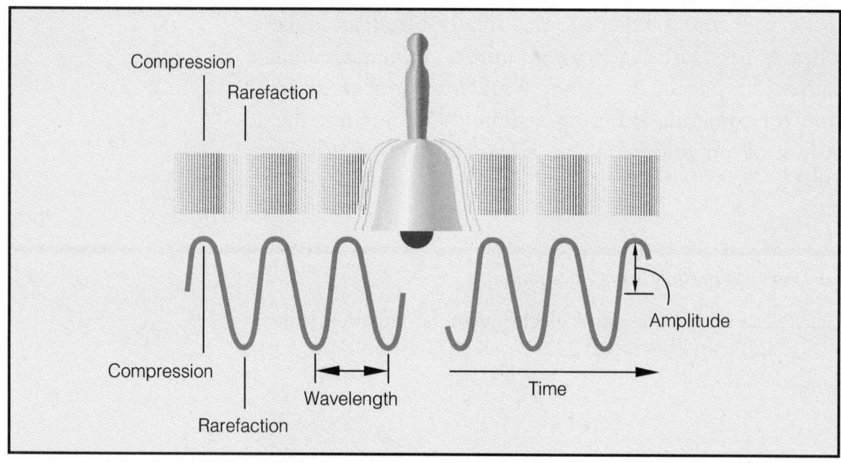

■ **Fig. 4–18** *Waves of compression in the air, or vibrations, are the stimulus for hearing. The frequency of sound waves determines their pitch. The amplitude determines loudness.*

pinna acts like a funnel to concentrate sounds. After they are guided into the ear, sound waves collide with the **eardrum (tympanic membrane),** which is like a tight drumhead within the ear canal. The sound waves set the eardrum in motion. This, in turn, causes three small bones called the **auditory ossicles** (OSS-ih-kuls) to vibrate (■ Fig. 4–19). The ossicles are the malleus (MAL-ee-us), incus, and stapes (STAY-peas). Their common names are the hammer, anvil, and stirrup. The stapes is attached to a second membrane, or drumhead, called the **oval window.** As the oval window moves back and forth, it makes waves in a fluid within the **cochlea** (KOCK-lee-ah).

The cochlea is really the organ of hearing, since it is here that waves in the fluid are detected by tiny **hair cells.** The hair cells are part of a structure called the **organ of Corti** (KOR-tee) which runs down the middle of the cochlea (■ Fig. 4–20). A set of **stereocilia** (STER-ee-oh-SIL-ih-ah) or "bristles" atop each hair cell brush against the tectorial membrane when waves

Tympanic membrane The eardrum.

Auditory ossicles Three small bones that link the eardrum to the cochlea.

Oval window A membrane on the cochlea connected to the third auditory ossicle.

Cochlea The snail-shaped organ that makes up the inner ear.

Hair cells Receptor cells within the cochlea that transduce vibrations into nerve impulses.

Organ of Corti Center part of the cochlea, containing hair cells, canals, and membranes.

Stereocilia Bristle-like structures on hair cells.

■ **Fig. 4–19** *Anatomy of the ear. The entire ear is a mechanism for changing waves of air pressure into nerve impulses. Inset in the foreground shows that as the stapes moves the oval window, the round window bulges outward, allowing waves to ripple through fluid in the cochlea. The waves move membranes near the hair cells, causing cilia or "bristles" on the tips of the cells to bend. The hair cells then generate nerve impulses carried to the brain. (See enlarged cross sections of cochlea and Figure 4–20.)*

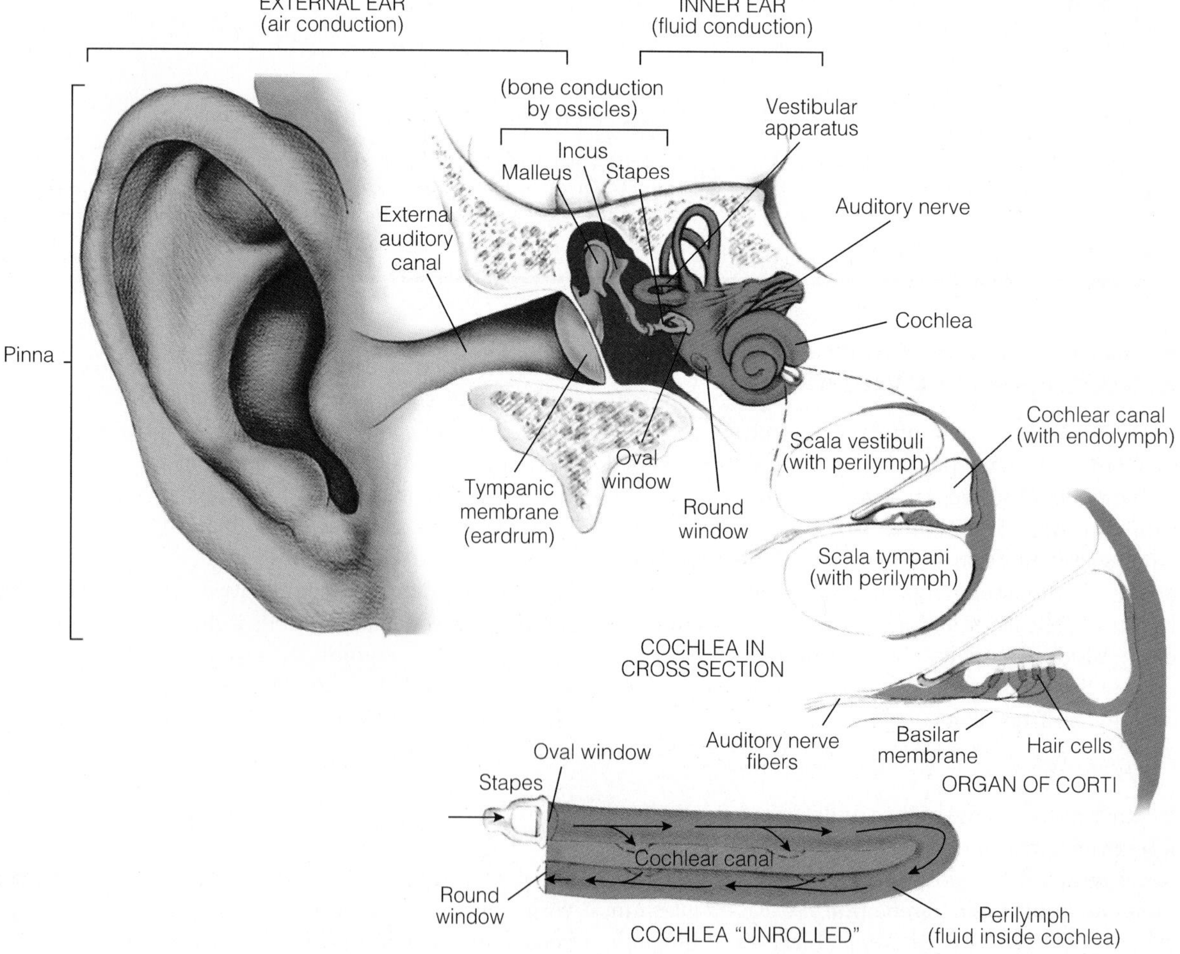

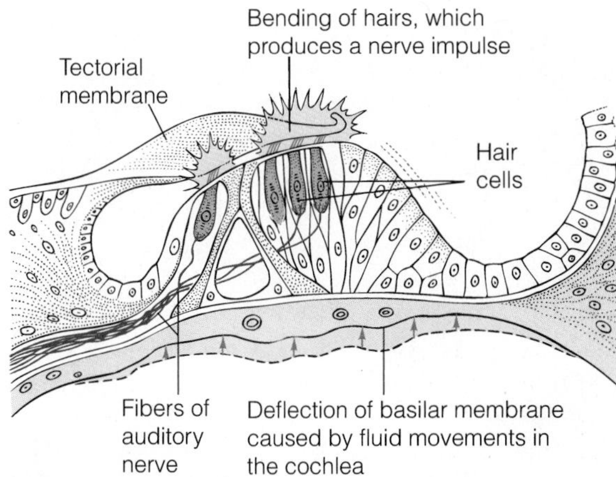

■ **Fig. 4–20** *A closer view of the hair cells shows how movement of fluid in the cochlea causes the bristling "hairs" or cilia to bend, generating a nerve impulse.*

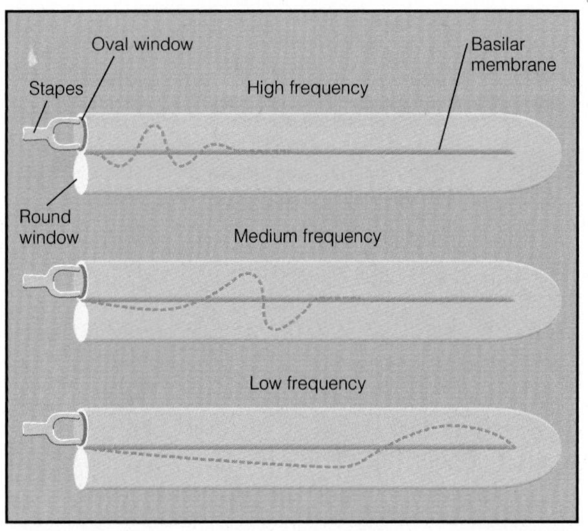

■ **Fig. 4–21** *Here we see a simplified side view of the cochlea "unrolled." Remember that the basilar membrane is the elastic "roof" of the lower chamber of the cochlea. The organ of Corti, with its sensitive hair cells, rests atop the basilar membrane. The colored line shows where waves in the cochlear fluid cause the greatest deflection of the basilar membrane. (The amount of movement is exaggerated in the drawing.) Hair cells respond most in the area of greatest movement, which helps identify sound frequency.*

ripple through the fluid surrounding the organ of Corti. As the stereocilia are bent, nerve impulses are triggered which then flow to the brain.

Question: How are higher and lower sounds detected?

The **frequency theory** of hearing states that as pitch rises, nerve impulses of the same frequency are fed into the auditory nerve. That is, an 800 hertz tone produces 800 nerve impulses per second. This explains how sounds up to about 4000 hertz reach the brain. But higher tones require a different explanation. The **place theory** of hearing states that high tones register most strongly at the base of the cochlea (near the oval window). Lower tones, on the other hand, mostly move hair cells near the outer tip of the cochlea (■ Fig. 4–21). Pitch is therefore signaled by the area of the cochlea most strongly activated. Place theory also explains why hunters sometimes lose hearing in a narrow pitch range. "Hunter's notch," as this is called, occurs when hair cells are damaged in the area activated by the pitch of gunfire.

Question: What causes other types of deafness?

Deafness There are three principal types of deafness. **Conduction deafness** occurs when the eardrums or ossicles are damaged or immobilized by disease or injury. Such damage reduces the transfer of sounds to the inner ear. In many cases, conduction deafness can be overcome by a hearing aid, which makes sounds louder and clearer.

Nerve deafness is a hearing loss resulting from damage to the hair cells or auditory nerve. Hearing aids are of no help in this case, because auditory messages are blocked from reaching the brain. However, a new artificial hearing system is making it possible for some persons with nerve deafness to break through the wall of silence (Highlight 4–3).

HIGHLIGHT 4–3

Using Psychology

Artificial Hearing

Researchers have recently found that in many cases of "nerve" deafness, the nerve is actually intact. This has spurred development of **cochlear implants** that bypass hair cells and stimulate the auditory nerves directly (■ Fig. 4–22).

■ **Fig. 4–22** *A cochlear implant, or "artificial ear."*

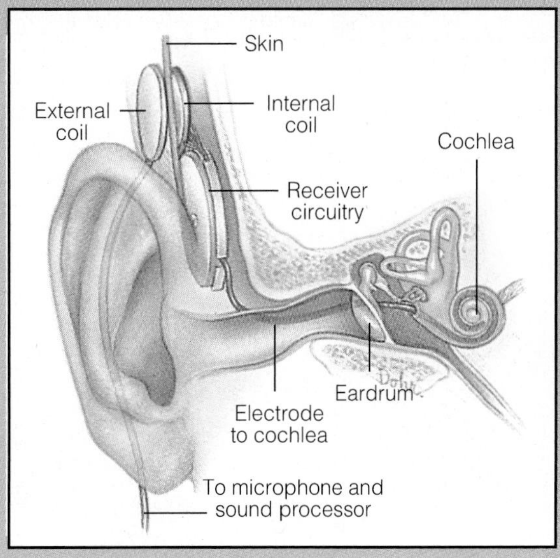

Frequency theory Holds that tones up to 4000 hertz are converted to nerve impulses that match the frequency of each tone.

Place theory Theory that higher and lower tones excite specific areas of the cochlea.

Conduction deafness Poor transfer of sounds from the eardrum to the inner ear.

Nerve deafness Deafness caused by damage to the hair cells or auditory nerve.

Stimulation deafness Damage caused by exposing the hair cells to excessively loud sounds.

Temporary threshold shift A temporary, partial loss of hearing.

As you can see, wires from a microphone carry electrical signals to an external coil. A matching coil under the skin picks up the signals and carries them to one or more areas of the cochlea. Early implants allowed patients to hear only low-frequency sounds, such as a dog's bark or the horn of a speeding car. Newer multi-channel models make use of place theory to separate higher and lower tones. This has allowed some formerly deaf persons to hear human voices and other higher frequency sounds. About 60 percent of all multi-channel implant patients can understand some spoken words (Cohen, Waltzman, & Fisher, 1993).

At present, artificial hearing remains crude. All but the most successful implant patients describe the sound as "like a radio that isn't quite tuned in." In fact, 30 percent of all adults who have tried implants have given up on them. But the implants are improving. And even now it is hard to argue with enthusiasts like Kristen Cloud. Shortly after Kristen received an implant, she was able to hear a siren and avoid being struck by a speeding car (Williams, 1984). She says simply, "The implant saved my life."

■ **Fig. 4–23** *A highly magnified electron microscope photo of the cilia (yellow bristles) on the top of human hair cells. (Colors are artificial.)*

A particular type of nerve deafness, called **stimulation deafness,** is of special interest, because many jobs, hobbies, and pastimes can cause it. Stimulation deafness occurs when very loud sounds damage hair cells in the cochlea (as in hunter's notch). Each of us starts life with about 32,000 hair cells (■ Fig. 4–23). However, we begin losing them the moment we are born. By age 65 more than 40 percent are gone.

If you work in a noisy environment or enjoy loud music, motorcycling, snowmobiling, hunting, or similar pursuits, you may be risking stimulation deafness. The hair cells, which are about as thick as a cobweb, are very fragile and easily damaged. Once dead, they are never replaced: When you abuse them you lose them.

Question: How loud must a sound be to be hazardous?

The danger of hearing loss depends on both the loudness of sound and how long you are exposed to it. Daily exposure to 85 decibels or more may cause permanent hearing loss. Even short periods at 120 decibels (a rock concert) may cause a **temporary threshold shift,** or temporary loss of hearing. Brief exposure to 150 decibels (jet airplane nearby) can cause permanent deafness.

You might find it interesting to check the decibel ratings of some of your activities in ■ Figure 4–24 as

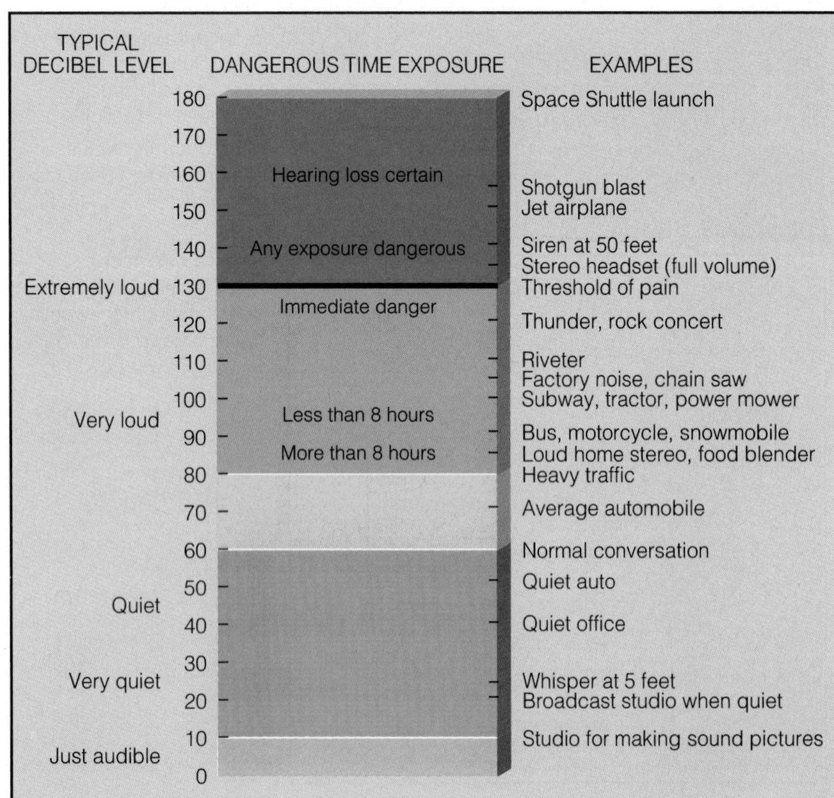

■ **Fig. 4–24** *The loudness of sound is measured in decibels. Zero decibels is the faintest sound most people can hear. Sound in the range of 110 decibels is uncomfortably loud. Prolonged exposure to sounds above 85 decibels may damage the inner ear. Rock music, which may rate 120 decibels, is known to have caused hearing loss in musicians and may affect audiences as well. Sounds of 130 decibels pose an immediate danger to hearing.*

a way of estimating hearing risk. Don't be fooled by the numbers, though. Decibels are plotted on a logarithmic scale (like earthquake intensity!). Every 20 decibels increases the amount of energy in a sound by a factor of 10. In other words, a rock concert at 120 decibels is not just twice as powerful as a normal voice at 60 decibels. It is actually 1000 times stronger.

Music, as well as noise, can do damage. People who sit directly in front of the speaker columns at highly amplified musical concerts run considerable risk of hearing loss. Dancing or aerobic exercise heightens the risk by diverting blood flow from the inner ear to the extremities. Rock musicians Neil Young and David Lee Roth have been sued by fans who claim their hearing was damaged at concerts. Walkman-style stereo headphones also present a danger. Many can reach 115 decibels or more. If you can hear the sound from the headset on the person standing next to you, the volume is probably damaging the user's ears. "Boom box" car stereos present similar dangers.

If a ringing sensation known as **tinnitus** (tin-NYE-tus) follows exposure to loud sounds, chances are that hair cells have been damaged (Dunkle, 1982; McFadden & Wightman, 1983). Almost everyone has tinnitus at times, especially with increasing age. But after repeated sounds that produce this warning, you can expect to become permanently hard-of-hearing. The next time you are exposed to a very loud sound, remember Figure 4–24 and take precautions against damage. (Remember, too, that for temporary ear protection, fingers are always handy.)

Smell and Taste—The Nose Knows When the Tongue Can't Tell

Unless you are a wine taster, a perfume blender, a chef, or a gourmet, you may think of **olfaction** (smell) and **gustation** (taste) as least important among the senses. Certainly a person could survive without these two **chemical senses.** Just the same, the chemical senses occasionally prevent poisonings and they add pleasure to our lives. Let's see how they operate.

Tinnitus A ringing or buzzing sensation in the ears.

Olfaction The sense of smell.

Gustation The sense of taste.

Chemical senses Senses, such as smell and taste, that respond to chemical molecules.

Anosmia Loss or impairment of the sense of smell.

The Sense of Smell

The receptors for smell respond primarily to gaseous molecules carried in the air. As air enters the nose, it passes over roughly 5 million nerve fibers embedded in the lining of the upper nasal passages. Airborne molecules passing over the exposed fibers trigger nerve signals that are sent to the brain (■ Fig. 4–25).

Question: How are different odors produced?

This is still something of a mystery. One hint comes from the fact that it is possible to develop a sort of "smell blindness" for a single odor. This loss, called an **anosmia** (an-NOSE-me-ah), suggests that olfactory nerve fibers have specific receptors for different odors. Indeed, scientists have noticed that molecules having a particular odor are quite similar in shape. Specific shapes have been identified for the following odors: *floral* (flower-like), *camphoric* (camphor-like), *musky* (Have you ever smelled a sweaty musk ox?), *minty* (mint-like), and *etherish* (like ether or cleaning fluid).

■ **Fig. 4–25** *Receptors for the sense of smell (olfaction). Olfactory nerve fibers respond to gaseous molecules. Receptor cells are shown in cross section at left of part* (a).

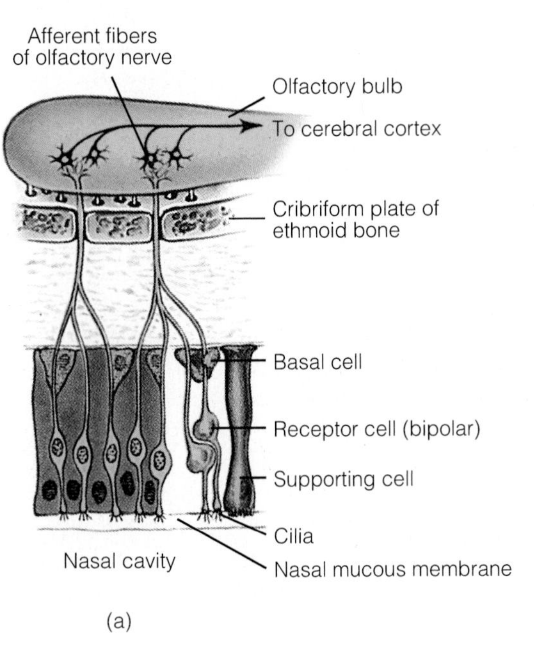

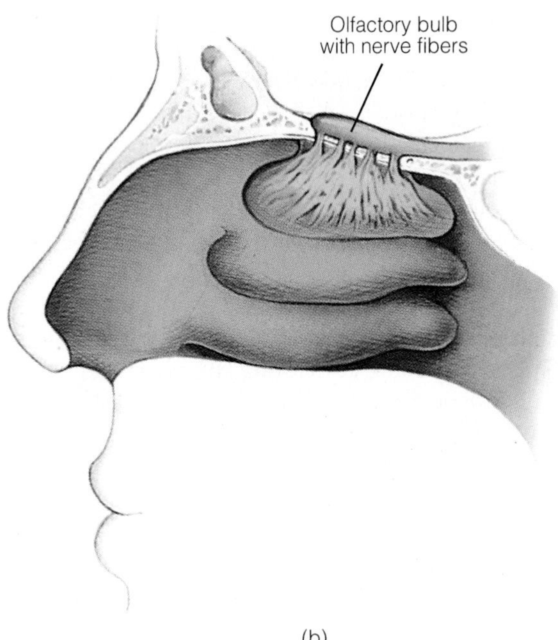

Lock and key theory Holds that odors are related to the shapes of chemical molecules.

Pheromone An airborne chemical signal.

Vomeronasal organ A sensory organ sensitive to pheromones.

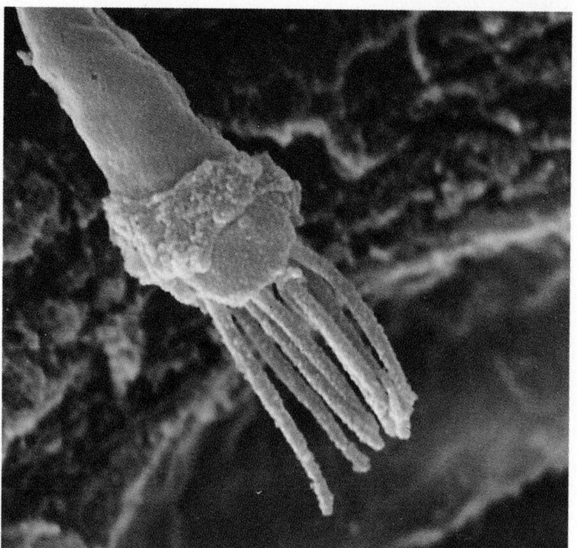

■ Fig. 4–26 *This extreme close-up of an olfactory receptor cell shows the thread-like fibers which project into the air flow inside the nose. Receptor proteins on the surface of the fibers are sensitive to different airborne molecules. Nerve impulses are triggered when gaseous molecules match the structure of specific proteins in a lock-and-key fashion.*

This does not mean, however, that there are five different olfactory receptors, like the three types of cones in vision (Gesteland, 1986). At least 1000 types of receptors for smell exist (■ Fig. 4–26). Each receptor is probably sensitive to a particular type of molecule. Activity in combinations of receptors may explain why we can identify roughly 10,000 different odors (Buck & Axel, 1991; Freedman, 1993).

It is currently believed that there are different shaped "holes," or "pockets," on the odor receptors. Like a piece fits in a puzzle, a molecule produces an odor when it matches a hole of the same shape. This is called the **lock and key theory.** Scents are also identified, in part, by the *location* of receptors in the nose activated by an odor. And finally, the number of activated receptors tells the brain how strong an odor is (Freeman, 1991).

A recent large-scale test found that 1.2 percent of the population cannot smell at all (Gilbert & Wysocki, 1987). People with total anosmia typically find that olfaction is not such a minor sense after all. One anosmic individual, for instance, failed to notice that his apartment building was on fire. He was awakened just in time by neighbors, not by the smell of smoke (Monmaney, 1987). Even in everyday terms, anosmia can be a real loss. Many anosmics are unable to cook, and they may be poisoned by spoiled food.

Question: What causes anosmia?

Risks include infections, allergies, and blows to the head (which may tear the olfactory nerves). Exposure to chemicals such as ammonia, photo-developing chemicals, and hair-dressing potions can also cause anosmia. If you value your sense of smell, be careful what you breathe.

Could the nose be the home of another, poorly understood chemical sense? Highlight 4–4 examines a sensory mystery.

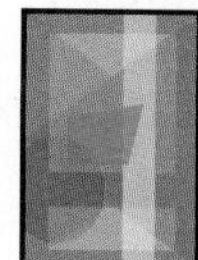

HIGHLIGHT 4–4

Research Frontier

Pheromones—A Sixth Sense?

In the animal kingdom, a class of chemicals known as **pheromones** (FAIR-oh-monz) greatly affect mating, sexual behavior, recognition of family members, and territorial marking. For example, when a female pig is exposed to the pheromones in a male pig's breath, she immediately becomes sexually receptive.

The chemical messages carried by pheromones are sensed by the **vomeronasal organ** (VNO) (voh-MARE-oh-NAZE-ul). Until recently, humans were assumed to have only a vestigial VNO or none at all. Now, however, scientists believe they have located the VNO in humans.

The suspected human vomeronasal organ looks like a small pit inside the nose (one on each side of the septum). These pits are lined with nerve cells and respond to chemicals that are suspected pheromones.

Question: What would a pheromone smell like?

Pheromones are not smelled, felt, seen, tasted, or heard. In humans, pheromones would most likely produce vague feelings, such as well-being, attraction, aversion, unease, or anxiety. When people say that their relationships are influenced by good or bad "chemistry," there may be some truth to it. Pheromones could add to the intoxicating feelings of romantic attraction or the sourness of instant dislike. (Men shouldn't expect

"Boar's Breath" cologne to be offered anytime soon, however.)

Evidence for the existence of human pheromones remains preliminary and controversial. Nevertheless, the possibilities are intriguing. For instance, human pheromones may explain why the menstrual cycles of women who live together tend to become synchronized. It's also possible that pheromones may one day be used to decrease anxiety, curb hunger, or relieve premenstrual discomforts. Only further study will tell if searching for a sixth sense makes sense. (Sources: Monti-Bloch & Grosser, 1991; Stensaas et al., 1991; Wright, 1994.)

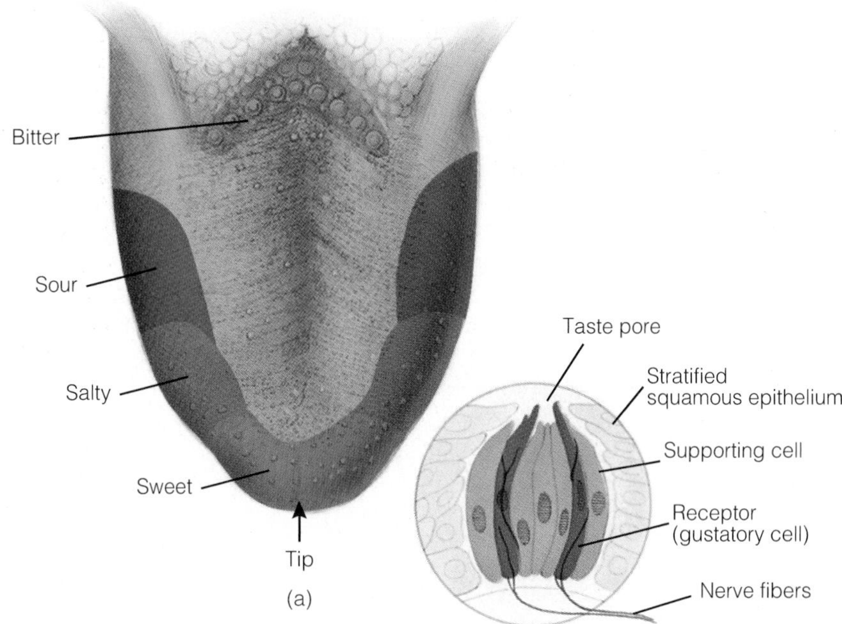

■ **Fig. 4–27** *Receptors for taste: (a) Position of receptors (taste buds) especially sensitive to four taste qualities. (b) Detail of a taste bud within the tongue. The buds also occur in other parts of the digestive system.*

Taste

There are at least four basic taste sensations: *sweet, salt, sour,* and *bitter.* We are most sensitive to bitter, less sensitive to sour, even less sensitive to salt, and least sensitive to sweet. This order may have helped prevent poisonings when most humans foraged for food, because bitter and sour foods are more likely to be inedible.

Question: If there are only four tastes, how can there be so many different flavors?

Flavors seem more varied than suggested by the four taste qualities because we tend to include sensations of texture, temperature, smell, and even pain ("hot" chili peppers) along with taste. Smell is particularly important in determining flavor. Small bits of apple, potato, and onion "taste" almost exactly alike when the nose is plugged. So do gourmet jelly beans! It is probably no exaggeration to say that subjective flavor is one half smell. This is why food loses its "taste" when you have a cold.

The four primary tastes are detected by **taste buds** located mainly on the top of the tongue, but also at other points inside the mouth (■ Fig. 4–27). As food is chewed, it dissolves and enters the taste buds, where it sets off nerve impulses to the brain. Like the skin senses, taste receptors are not equally distributed. Look at Figure 4–27 and you will see that some areas of the tongue are more sensitive to certain tastes than others. Like smell, some tastes appear to be based on a lock-and-key match between molecules and intricately shaped receptors. Saltiness and sourness, however, appear to be triggered by a direct flow of atoms into the tips of taste cells.

Question: People seem to have very different tastes. Why is that?

Some differences are genetic. The chemical phenylthiocarbamine (FEEN-il-thi-oh-CAR-bah-meen), or PTC, tastes bitter to about 70 percent of those tested and has no taste for the other 30 percent. More generally, taste sensitivity is related to how many taste buds you have on your tongue. Some people have as few as 500 taste buds, while others have as many as 10,000. Those with many taste buds are "supertasters" who need only half as much sugar in their coffee to make it sweet (Pennisi, 1992).

The sense of taste also varies with age. Taste cells have a life of only several days. With aging, cell replacement slows down, so the sense of taste diminishes (Beidler, 1963). This is why many foods you disliked in childhood have now become acceptable. Children who will not eat broccoli, spinach, liver, and so on, may be having a very different taste experience than the adult urging the child to eat. Aside from this fact, however, most taste preferences are acquired. Would you eat the coagulated secretion of the modified skin glands of a cow after it had undergone bacterial decomposition? If you would, you are a *cheese* fancier!

Taste bud The receptor organ for taste.

Somesthetic sense Sensations produced by the skin, muscles, joints, viscera, and organs of balance.

The Somesthetic Senses—Flying by the Seat of Your Pants

A gymnast "flying" through a routine on the uneven bars may rely as much on the **somesthetic senses** as on vision. Even the most routine activities, such as walking, running, or passing a sobriety test, would be impossible without somesthetic information from the body.

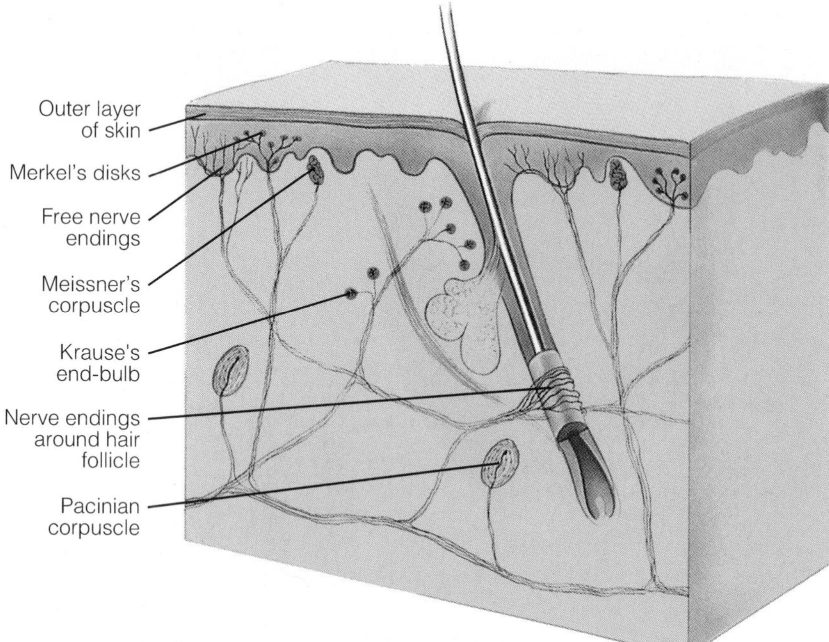

■ Fig. 4–28 *The skin senses include touch, pressure, pain, cold, and warmth. This drawing shows different forms the skin receptors can take. Other shapes were once recognized, but most turned out to be variations of the shapes shown. The only clearly specialized receptor is the Pacinian corpuscle, which is highly sensitive to pressure. Free nerve endings are receptors for pain and any of the other sensations. For reasons that are not clear, cold is sensed near the surface of the skin, and warmth is sensed deeper. (Carlson, 1991.)*

Skin senses The senses of touch, pressure, pain, heat, and cold.

Kinesthetic senses The senses of body movement and positioning.

Vestibular senses The senses of balance, position in space, and acceleration.

Skin receptors Sensory organs for touch, pressure, pain, cold, and warmth.

Visceral pain Pain originating in the internal organs.

Referred pain Pain that is felt in one part of the body, but comes from another.

Somatic pain Pain from the skin, muscles, joints, and tendons.

Warning system Pain based on large nerve fibers; warns that bodily damage may be occurring.

Question: What are the somesthetic senses?

The somesthetic senses (*soma* means "body," *esthetic* means "feel") include the **skin senses** (touch), the **kinesthetic senses** (receptors in the muscles and joints that detect body position and movement), and the **vestibular senses** (receptors in the inner ear used to maintain balance). (The vestibular senses also contribute to motion sickness, as discussed in this chapter's Exploration.) Because of their importance, let us focus on the skin senses.

Skin receptors produce at least five different sensations: *light touch, pressure, pain, cold,* and *warmth.* Receptors with particular shapes appear to specialize somewhat in various sensations (■ Fig. 4–28). However, the surface of the eye, which only has free nerve endings, can produce all five sensations (Carlson, 1991). Altogether, the skin has about 200,000 nerve endings for temperature, 500,000 for touch and pressure, and 3 million for pain.

Question: Does the number of receptors in an area of skin relate to its sensitivity?

Yes. Your skin could be "mapped" by applying heat, cold, touch, pressure, or pain to points all over your body. Such testing would show that the skin receptors are found in varying numbers, and that sensitivity generally matches the number of receptors in a given area. As a rough-and-ready illustration, try this two-point touch test:

> The density of touch receptors on various body areas can be checked by having a friend apply two pencil points to the skin with varying distances between them. Without looking, you should respond "one" or "two" each time. Record the distance between the pencils each time you feel two points.

You should find that two points are recognizable when they are 1/10 inch apart on the fingertips, 1/4 inch on the nose, and 3 inches at the middle of the back. Generally speaking, important areas such as the lips, tongue, face, hands, and genitals have a higher density of receptors.

Question: There are many more pain receptors than other kinds. Why is pain so heavily represented, and does the concentration of pain receptors also vary?

Like the other skin senses, pain receptors vary in their distribution. There are an average of about 232 pain points per square centimeter behind the knee, 184 per centimeter on the buttocks (an area preferred by many parents for spankings), 60 on the pad of the thumb, and 44 on the tip of the nose (Geldard, 1972). (Is it better then, to be pinched on the nose than behind the knee? It depends on what you like!)

Pain fibers are also found in the internal organs of the body. Stimulation of these fibers causes **visceral pain.** Curiously, visceral pain is often felt on the surface of the body, at a site some distance from the point of origin (Chiras, 1991). For example, a person having a heart attack may feel pain in the left shoulder, arm, or even the little finger. Experiences of this type are called **referred pain** (■ Fig. 4–29).

Pain from the skin, muscles, joints, and tendons is known as **somatic pain.** Somatic pain carried by *large* nerve fibers is sharp, bright, fast, and seems to come from specific body areas. This is the body's **warning system.** Give yourself a small jab with a pin and you will feel this type of pain. As you do this, notice that warning pain quickly disappears. Much as we may dislike warning pain, it is usually a signal that the body has been, or is about to be, damaged. Without warning pain, we would be unable to detect or prevent injury (Melzack & Dennis, 1978). Children who are born with a rare inherited insensitivity to pain repeatedly burn themselves, break bones, bite their tongues, and become ill without knowing it.

A second type of somatic pain is carried by *small* nerve fibers. This type is slower, nagging, aching, widespread, and very unpleasant. It gets worse if the pain stimulus is repeated. This is the body's **reminding system** (Melzack & Dennis, 1978). A sad thing about the reminding system is that it often causes agony even when the reminder is useless, as in ter-

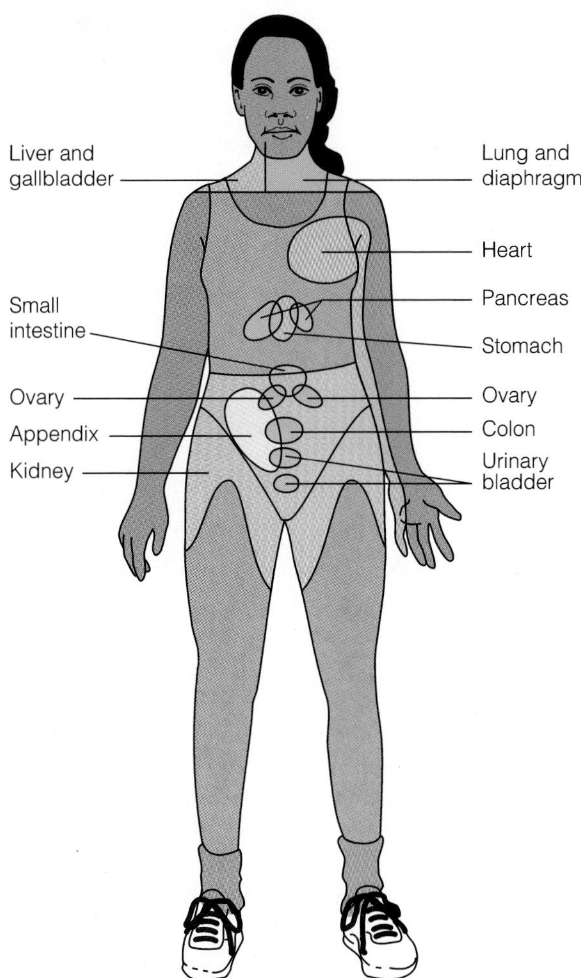

■ **Fig. 4–29** *Visceral pain often seems to come from the surface of the body, even though its true origin is internal. Referred pain is believed to result from the fact that pain fibers from internal organs enter the spinal cord at the same location as sensory fibers from the skin. Apparently, the brain misinterprets the visceral pain messages as impulses from the body's surface (Chiras, 1991).*

minal cancer, or when pain continues after an injury has healed. Later in the chapter we will return to pain to learn how it can be controlled. If you got carried away with the pin demonstration, maybe you should read ahead now!

Adaptation, Attention, and Gating—Tuning In and Tuning Out

Each of the senses we have described is continuously active. Even so, many sensory events never reach awareness. One reason for this is *sensory adaptation*, a second is *selective attention*, and a third is *sensory gating*. Let's see how information is filtered by these processes.

Sensory Adaptation Think about walking into a house where fried fish, sauerkraut, and head cheese were prepared for dinner. (Some dinner!) You would probably pass out at the door, yet people who had been in the house for some time would be unaware of the food odors because of **sensory adaptation.** Sensory adaptation refers to a decrease in sensory response to a constant or unchanging stimulus.

Fortunately, the olfactory (smell) receptors are among the most quickly adapting. When exposed to a constant odor, they send fewer and fewer nerve impulses to the brain until the odor is no longer noticed. Adaptation to sensations of pressure from a wristwatch, waistband, ring, or glasses is based on the same principle. Sensory receptors generally respond best to *changes* in stimulation. As David Hubel says, "We need above all to know about changes; no one wants or needs to be reminded 16 hours a day that his shoes are on" (Hubel, 1979).

Question: If change is necessary to prevent sensory adaptation, why doesn't vision undergo adaptation like the sense of smell does? If you stare at something, it certainly doesn't go away.

The rods and cones, like other receptor cells, would respond less to a constant stimulus were it not for the fact that the eye normally makes thousands of tiny movements every minute. These are caused by tremors in the eye muscles known as **physiological nystagmus** (nis-TAG-mus). Although they are too small to be seen, these movements shift visual images from one receptor cell to another.

Constant shifting of the eyes ensures that images always fall on fresh, unfatigued receptors. Evidence for this comes from experiments in which subjects are fitted with a special contact lens that has a miniature slide projector attached to it (■ Fig. 4–30a). Since the projector follows the exact movements of the eye, an image can be stabilized on the retina. When this is done, projected geometric designs fade from view within a few seconds (Pritchard, 1961). You can get the same effect by staring at Figure 4–30b. Since the lighter circle does not form a distinct edge, the retina adapts to the brightness difference and the circle gradually disappears.

Selective Attention The so-called "seat-of-your-pants phenomenon" also relates to the functioning of sensory systems. As you sit reading this chapter, receptors for touch and pressure in the seat of your pants are sending nerve impulses to your brain. Even though these sensations have been present all along, you were probably not aware of them until just now. The seat-of-your-pants phenomenon is an example of **selective attention.** We are able to "tune in on" any of the many sensory messages bombarding us while exclud-

Reminding system Pain based on small nerve fibers; reminds the brain that the body has been injured.

Sensory adaptation A decrease in sensory response to an unchanging stimulus.

Physiological nystagmus An involuntary tremor of the eye.

Selective attention Voluntarily focusing on a specific sensory input.

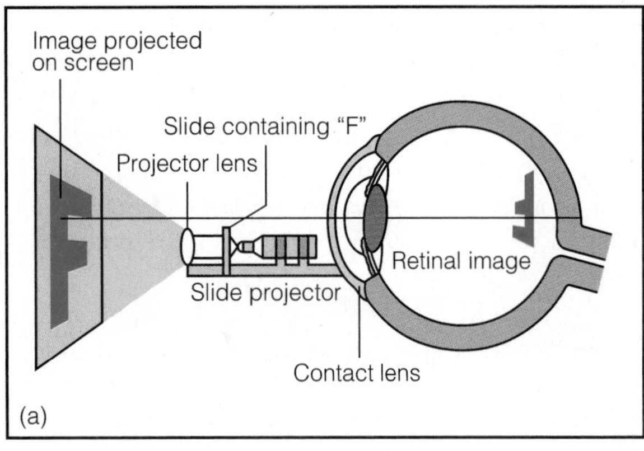

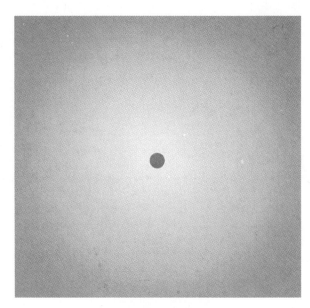

■ Fig. 4–30 *Stabilized images. (a) Miniature slide projector attached to a contact lens moves each time the eye moves. As a result, the projected image disappears in a few seconds because it does not move on the retina. (b) A similar effect occurs when changes in brightness do not define a distinct edge. In this case, eye movements cannot prevent adaptation. Therefore, if you stare at the dot, the lighter area will disappear. (After Cornsweet, 1970.)*

Sensory gating Alteration of sensory messages in the spinal cord.

Gate control theory Proposes that pain messages pass through neural "gates" in the spinal cord.

Acupuncture Chinese medical art of relieving pain and illness by inserting thin needles into the body.

Beta-endorphin A natural, pain-killing brain chemical similar to morphine.

ing others. Another familiar example of this is the "cocktail party effect." When you are in a group of people, surrounded by voices, you can still select and attend to the voice of the person you are facing. Or if that person gets dull, you can eavesdrop on conversations all over the room. (Be sure to smile and nod your head occasionally!)

Question: What makes this possible?

Selective attention appears to be based on the ability of various brain structures to select and divert incoming sensory messages (see Chapter 3). But what about messages that haven't reached the brain? Is it possible that some are blocked while others are allowed to pass? Evidence suggests there are **sensory gates** that control the flow of incoming nerve impulses in just this way.

Sensory Gating of Pain A fascinating example of sensory gating is provided by Ronald Melzack and Patrick Wall, who study "pain gates" in the spinal cord (Melzack & Wall, 1983). Melzack and Wall noticed, as you may have, that one type of pain will sometimes cancel another. This suggests that pain messages from different nerve fibers pass through the same neural "gate" in the spinal cord. If the gate is "closed" by one pain message, other messages may not be able to pass through.

Question: How is the gate closed?

Messages carried by large, fast nerve fibers seem to close the spinal pain gate directly. Doing so can prevent slower, "reminding system" pain from reaching the brain. Pain clinics use this effect by applying a mild electrical current to the skin. Such stimulation, felt only as a mild tingling, can greatly reduce more agonizing pain (Long, 1991).

Messages from small, slow fibers seem to take a different route. After going through the pain gate, they pass on to a "central biasing system" in the brain. Under some circumstances, the brain then sends a message back down the spinal cord, closing the pain gates (Melzack & Dennis, 1978). (See ■ Figure 4–31.) Melzack and Wall believe that their **gate control theory** explains the painkilling effects of acupuncture (■ Fig. 4–32). As the acupuncturist's needles are twirled, heated, or electrified, they activate small pain fibers. These relay through the biasing system to close the gates to intense or chronic pain (Melzack & Wall, 1983). Controlled studies have shown that acupuncture produces short-term pain relief for 50–80 percent of patients tested (Brockhaus & Elger, 1990; Richardson & Vincent, 1986).

Acupuncture has an interesting side effect not predicted by sensory gating. People given acupuncture often report feelings of light-headedness, relaxation, or euphoria. How are these feelings explained? The answer seems to lie in the body's ability to produce opiate-like chemicals. To combat pain, the brain causes the pituitary gland to release a chemical called **beta-endorphin** (BAY-tah-en-DOR-fin: from *endo*, "within" and *orphin*, "opiate"), which is similar to morphine (Snyder & Childers, 1979). Endorphins are related to a class of brain chemicals known as enkephalins, discussed in Chapter 3.

Receptor sites for endorphins are found in large numbers in the limbic system and other brain areas associated with pleasure, pain, and emotion (Feldman & Quenzer, 1984). Both acupuncture and electrical

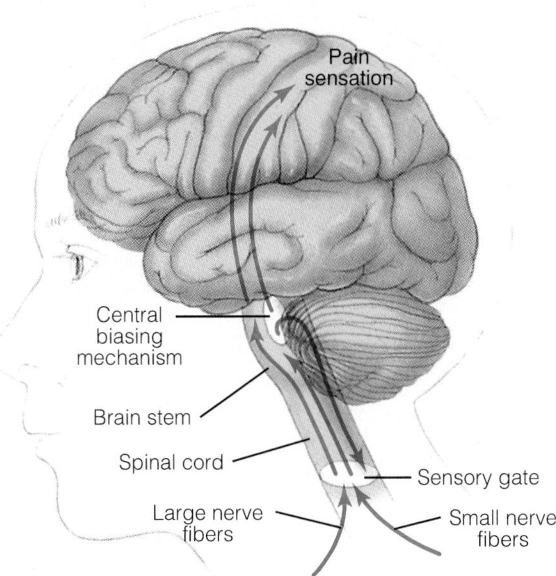

■ **Fig. 4–31** *Diagram of a sensory gate for pain. A series of pain impulses going through the gate may prevent other pain messages from passing through. Or pain messages may relay through a "central biasing mechanism" that exerts control over the gate, closing it to other impulses.*

stimulation cause a build-up of endorphins in the brain. In other words, the nervous system makes its own "drugs" to block pain. Actually, this ties in nicely with the idea of pain gates. The central biasing system, which closes pain gates in the spinal cord, is highly sensitive to morphine and other opiate painkillers (Melzack & Wall, 1983).

The discovery of endorphins and their painkilling effect has caused quite a stir in psychology. At long last it may be possible to explain a number of puzzling phenomena. For example, the painkilling effect of placebos (fake pills or injections) appears to be based on a rise in beta-endorphin levels (Lipman et al., 1990). A release of endorphins also appears to underlie "runner's high," masochism, acupuncture, and the euphoria sometimes associated with childbirth and painful initiation rites. In each instance there is reason to believe that pain and stress cause the release of endorphins. These in turn induce feelings of pleasure or euphoria similar to morphine intoxication (Kruger & Liebskind, 1984; Ulett, 1992).

The "high" often felt by long-distance runners serves as a good example of the endorphin effect. In one experiment, subjects were tested for pain tolerance. After running 1 mile, each was tested again. In the second test, all could withstand pain about 70 percent longer than before. The runners were then given naloxone, a drug that blocks the effects of endorphins. Following another 1-mile run the subjects were tested again. This time they had lost their earlier protection

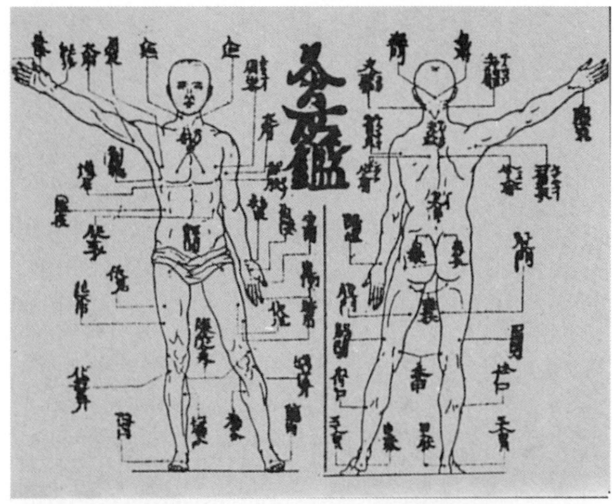

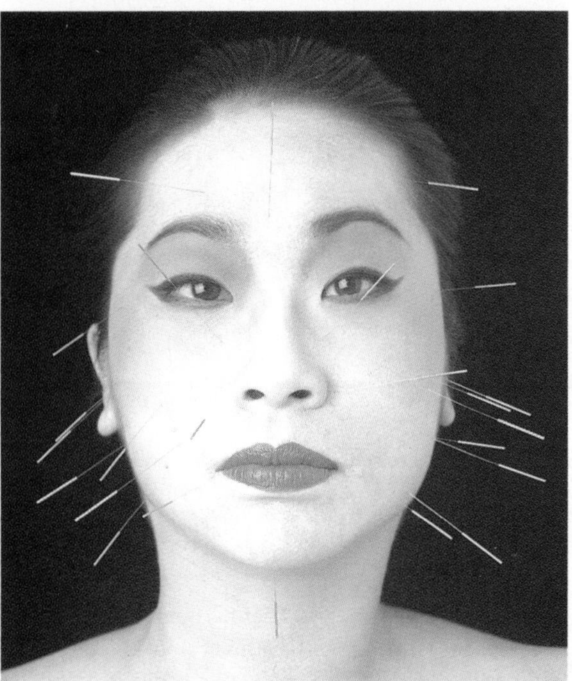

■ **Fig. 4–32** (top) *An acupuncturist's chart.* (bottom) *Thin stainless steel needles are inserted into areas defined by the chart. Modern research has begun to explain the painkilling effects of acupuncture (see text). Acupuncture's claimed ability to cure diseases is more debatable.*

from pain (Haier et al., 1981). People who say they are "addicted" to running may be closer to the truth than they realize. And more importantly, we may at last have an explanation for those hardy souls who take hot saunas followed by cold showers!

A Look Ahead The severity of pain is also affected by a variety of psychological factors. Since you may not want to try acupuncture or electrical stimulation to control everyday pain, the following Applications describes several practical ways to reduce pain. After that, we will explore the sense of balance—and motion sickness. Before we turn to these topics, here's a Learning Check.

Learning Check

1. Which of the following is not important for the transduction of sound?
   a. pinna *b.* ossicles *c.* phosphenes *d.* oval window *e.* hair cells
2. Daily exposure to sounds with a loudness of ____________ decibels may cause permanent hearing loss.
3. Cochlear implants have been used primarily to overcome
   a. conduction deafness *b.* stimulation deafness *c.* nerve deafness *d.* tinnitus
4. Olfaction appears to be at least partially explained by the ____________ ____ ____________ theory of molecule shapes and receptor sites.
5. From the standpoint of survival, we are fortunate that bitter tastes register primarily on the tip of the tongue. T or F?
6. Which of the following is a somesthetic sense?
   a. gustation *b.* olfaction *c.* rarefaction *d.* kinesthesis
7. Warning pain is carried by ____________ nerve fibers.
8. Sensory adaptation refers to an increase in sensory response that accompanies a constant or unchanging stimulus. T or F?
9. The brain-centered ability to influence what sensations we will receive is called
   a. sensory gating *b.* central adaptation *c.* selective attention *d.* sensory biasing
10. The painkilling effects of acupuncture appear to result from ____________ ____________ and the release of beta-endorphin.

Critical Thinking

11. What precautions would you need to take to test claims that acupuncture reduces pain?

Answers: 1. *c* 2. 85 3. *c* 4. lock and key 5. F 6. *d* 7. large 8. F 9. *c* 10. sensory gating 11. At the very least, you would have to control for the placebo effect by giving fake acupuncture to control group members. However, true double-blind studies of acupuncture are difficult to do. Acupuncturists know if they are giving a placebo treatment or the real thing, which means they might unconsciously influence subjects.

APPLICATIONS: *Controlling Pain—This Won't Hurt a Bit*

There are many indications that pain may be controlled psychologically. In India, fakirs pierce their cheeks with needles or sit on beds of spikes. In other cultures, people endure tattooing, stretching, cutting, burning, and the like, with little apparent pain. How is such insensitivity achieved? There is no evidence that these people lack normal pain responses. Very likely the answer lies in four factors that can be used by anyone to alter the amount of pain felt in a particular situation. These are: (1) **anxiety,** (2) **control,** (3) **attention,** and (4) **interpretation.**

Anxiety The basic sensory message of pain can be separated from emotional reactions to it (Melzack, 1978). Fear or high levels of anxiety almost always increase pain (■ Fig. 4–33). A dramatic reversal of this effect is the surprising lack of pain displayed by soldiers wounded in battle. Being excused from further combat apparently produces a flood of relief. This emotional state leaves many soldiers insensitive to wounds that would agonize a civilian (Melzack & Wall, 1983).

Control A moment's reflection should convince you that the most upsetting pain is that over which you have no control. Loss of control seems to increase pain by increasing anxiety and emotional distress. People who are allowed to regulate, avoid, or control a painful stimulus suffer less (Craig, 1978). In general, the more control one *feels* over a painful stimulus, the less pain experienced (Kruger & Liebskind, 1984).

Attention Distraction can also radically reduce pain. Pain, even though it is highly persistent, can be selectively "tuned out" (at least partially), just like any other sensation. Subjects in one experiment who were exposed to intense pain experienced the greatest relief when they were distracted by the task of reading letters aloud (Dubreuil, Endler, & Spanos, 1988). In another

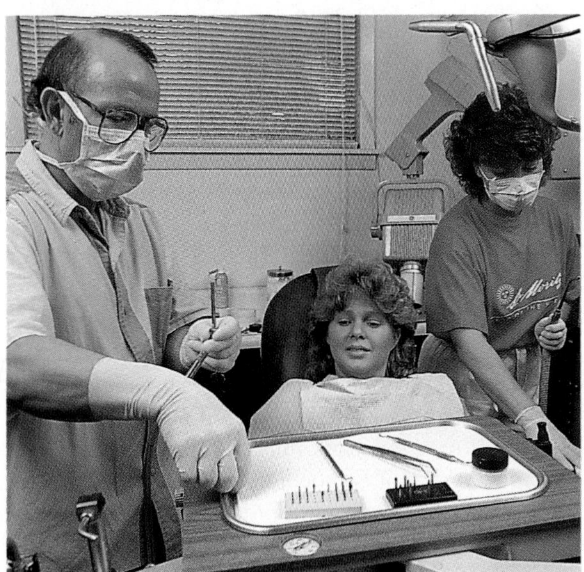

■ **Fig. 4–33** *Pain is a complex experience. In addition to producing a physical sensation, pain messages activate areas of the brain associated with emotion. If you are fearful or anxious, the emotional part of pain will be magnified, and you will feel more intense pain. Reducing fear and anxiety is one of several things you can do to diminish pain.*

experiment, pain was lessened when subjects concentrated on trying to name all their high school courses and teachers (Ahles et al., 1983). For the same reason, you may have temporarily forgotten about a toothache or similar pain while absorbed in a movie or book. Concentrating on pleasant, soothing images can be especially helpful (Fernandez & Turk, 1989). Instead of listening to the whirr of a dentist's drill, for example, you might imagine that you are lying in the sun at a beach, listening to the roar of the surf.

Interpretation The meaning or interpretation given a painful stimulus also affects pain (Keefe, 1982). For example, if you give a child a swat on the behind while playing, you'll probably get a burst of laughter. Yet the same swat given as punishment may bring tears (Bresler & Trubo, 1979). The effects of interpretation have also been demonstrated in the lab (Devine & Spanos, 1990). For example, in one experiment it was found that thinking of pain as pleasurable (denying the pain) greatly increased pain tolerance (Neufeld, 1970).

Coping with Pain

Question: How can these facts be applied?

In a sense, they have already been applied to childbirth. **Prepared childbirth training,** which promotes birth with a minimum of drugs or painkillers, uses all four factors. To prepare for natural childbirth, the expectant mother learns in great detail what to anticipate at each stage of labor. This greatly relieves her fears and anxieties. During labor, she attends to sensations that mark her progress and she adjusts her breathing accordingly. Her attention is shifted to sensations other than pain, resulting in less discomfort (Leventhal et al., 1989). Also, her positive attitude is maintained by use of the term *contractions* rather than *labor pains.* Finally, because of her months of preparation and her active participation, she feels *in control* of the situation.

Prepared childbirth training System for preparing women and their partners for childbirth.

Natural childbirth techniques reduce pain by an average of about 30 percent. Many women find this reduction quite helpful. However, it is important to remember that labor can produce very severe pain. A woman should not feel guilty if she needs painkillers during labor. Many women who have had prepared childbirth training still end up asking for an epidural block (Melzack, 1984).

With more moderate pain, reduced anxiety, redirected attention, and added control can make quite a difference. In any situation where pain can be anticipated (a trip to the doctor, dentist, and so on), lowered anxiety may be achieved by making sure that you are *fully informed.* Be sure that everything that will happen or could happen to you is explained. Also, be sure to fully discuss any fears you have. If you are physically tense, the use of relaxation exercises can help lower your level of arousal. Relaxation methods involve tensing and then releasing muscles in various parts of the body. A typical technique is described in detail in the Applications section of Chapter 18. (The desensitization procedure described there may also help reduce anxiety.)

Distraction and Reinterpretation Some dentists are now equipped to help you shift attention away from pain. Patients are actively distracted with video games and headphones carrying music. In other situations, focusing on some external object may help you shift attention away from pain. Pick a tree outside a window, a design on the wall, or some other stimulus and examine it in great detail. Prior practice in meditation can be a tremendous aid to such attention shifts. (Meditation techniques are described in Chapter 11.) Research suggests that distraction of this type works best for mild or brief pain. For chronic or strong pain, reinterpretation is more effective (McCaul & Malott, 1984).

Question: Is there any way to increase control over a painful stimulus?

APPLICATIONS: *Continued*

Counterirritation Using mild pain to block more intense or long-lasting pain.

Counterirritation Practically speaking, the choices may be limited. You may be able to arrange a signal with a doctor or dentist that will give you control over whether a painful procedure will continue. A second possibility is more unusual. Ronald Melzack's gate control theory of pain suggests that sending *mild* pain messages to the spinal cord and brain may effectively close the neurological gates to more severe or unpredictable pain. Medical texts have long recognized this effect. Physicians have found that intense surface stimulation of the skin can control pain from other parts of the body. Likewise, a brief, mildly painful stimulus can relieve more severe pain. Such procedures, known as **counterirritation,** are evident in some of the oldest techniques used to control pain: applying ice packs, hot-water bottles, mustard packs, vibration, or massage to other parts of the body (Kakigi et al., 1993; Melzack, 1974).

These facts suggest a way to minimize pain that is based on increased control, counterirritation, and the release of endorphins. If you pinch yourself, you can easily *create and endure* pain equal to that produced by many medical procedures (receiving an injection, having a tooth drilled, and so on). The pain doesn't seem too bad because you have control over it, and it is predictable.

This fact can be used to *mask* one pain with a second painful stimulus that is under your control. For instance, if you are having a tooth filled, try pinching yourself or digging a fingernail into a knuckle while the dentist is working. Focus your attention on the pain you are creating, and increase its intensity anytime the dentist's work becomes more painful. This suggestion may not work for you, but casual observation suggests that it can be a useful technique for controlling pain in some circumstances. Generations of children have used it to take the edge off a spanking.

LEARNING CHECK

1. Like heightened anxiety, increased control tends to increase subjective pain. T or F?
2. In one experiment, subjects given the task of reading letters aloud experienced less pain than subjects who paid attention to the pain stimulus. T or F?
3. Imagining a pleasant experience can be an effective way of reducing pain in some situations. T or F?
4. The concept of counterirritation holds that relaxation and desensitization are key elements of pain control. T or F?

Critical Thinking

5. What measures would you take to ensure that an experiment involving pain is ethical?

Answers: 1. F 2. T 3. T 4. F 5. Experiments that cause pain must be handled with care and sensitivity. Participation must be voluntary; the source of pain must be non-injurious; and subjects must be allowed to quit at any time.

EXPLORATION

Sensation in Space—Adapting to an Alien Environment

On television, astronauts are often shown playfully enjoying the acrobatics made possible by weightlessness (■ Fig. 4–34). But adapting to life in space is not as easy or pleasant as such images imply (Johnson, 1984). Indeed, if you were to ride into space, it is about 70 percent likely that your first experience in orbit would be throwing up (Davis, et al., 1988). Over one-half of all astronauts have suffered from **space adaptation syndrome,** or "space sickness."

Question: Is space sickness like seasickness?

Space Sickness Space sickness is a type of motion sickness. Like seasickness, car sickness, and airsickness, its first signs are dizziness and mild disorientation. However, space sickness usually does not produce the pallor, "cold sweating," and nausea so common on earth. In most types of motion sickness, these signs warn that vomiting is about to occur. But in space, vomiting is usually sudden and unexpected. Seeing another astronaut drift by upside down or viewing the earth at an odd angle is often all it takes to trigger repeated vomiting (Connors et al., 1985). Space sickness is especially intense because weightlessness drastically alters sensations the brain receives from the head, muscles, and joints (Lackner & DiZio, 1993).

■ **Fig. 4–34** *Weightlessness presents astronauts with a real challenge in sensory adaptation.*

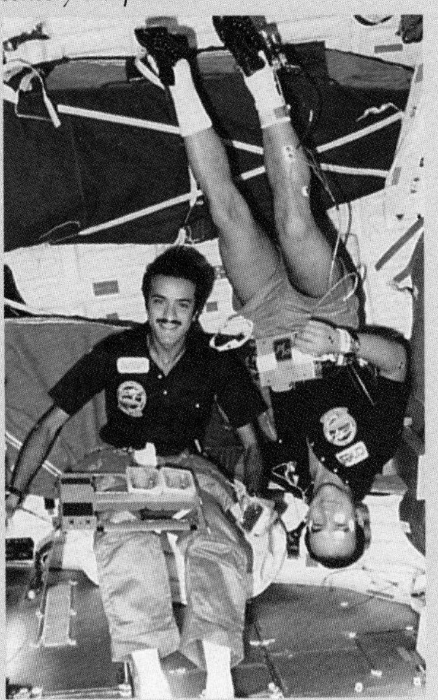

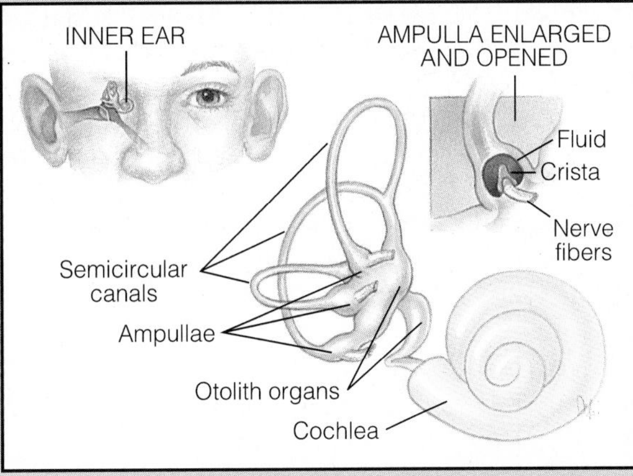

■ **Fig. 4–35** *The vestibular system. (See text for explanation.)*

The Vestibular System

Question: What causes motion sickness?

Motion sickness is directly related to the vestibular system (■Fig. 4–35). Fluid-filled sacs called **otolith organs** (OH-toe-lith) contain tiny crystals in a soft, gelatin-like mass. The tug of gravity or rapid head movements can cause the mass to shift. This, in turn, stimulates hair-like receptor cells, allowing us to sense gravity and movement through space.

Three fluid-filled tubes called the **semicircular canals** are also part of the vestibular system. If you could climb inside these tubes, you would find that head movements cause the fluid to swirl about. As the fluid moves, it bends a small "flap," or "float," within a wider part of the canal called the **ampulla** (am-PULL-ah). This bending again stimulates hair cells and signals head rotation.

Motion Sickness The most widely accepted explanation of motion sickness is the **sensory conflict theory.** According to this theory, dizziness and nausea occur when sensations from the vestibular system fail to match information received from the eyes and body (Yardley, 1992).

You can create an example of sensory conflict by turning around repeatedly until you become dizzy. Doing so sets the fluid spinning in the semicircular canals. When you stop, the fluid continues to swirl about, so the brain thinks your head is still moving.

On solid ground, information from the vestibular system, vision, and kinesthesis usually matches. However, in a heaving, pitching boat, car, or airplane, a serious mismatch can occur—causing disorientation and heaving of another kind.

Space adaptation syndrome Motion sickness caused by weightlessness.

Otolith organs Vestibular structures sensitive to movement, acceleration, and gravity.

Semicircular canals Fluid-filled vestibular canals; the sensory organs for balance.

Crista A floating structure that detects fluid movement in the semicircular canals.

Ampulla Enlarged area in a semicircular canal; contains a crista.

Sensory conflict theory Attributes motion sickness to mismatched information from vision, the vestibular system, and kinesthesis.

EXPLORATION

Question: Why would sensory conflict cause nausea?

According to the most popular theory, you can blame (or thank) evolution. Many poisons disturb the coordination of messages from the vestibular system, vision, and the body. Therefore, we may have evolved so that we react to sensory conflict by vomiting to expel poison. The value of this reaction, however, may be of little comfort to anyone who has ever been "green" and miserable with motion sickness.

In space, sensory conflict can be especially intense. During weightlessness, merely pulling on one's shoes can result in a backward somersault. Under such conditions, the otolith organs send unexpected signals to the brain, and head movements are no longer confirmed by the semicircular canals. Few of the messages the brain receives from the vestibular system and kinesthetic receptors agree with a lifetime of past experience (Yardley, 1992).

Question: How long does it take to adapt to weightlessness?

Space sickness usually disappears in 2 or 3 days. Recent research suggests that this adaptation occurs because astronauts shift to using visual cues instead of vestibular information. Later, this same shift can cause "earth sickness." Immediately after returning to earth (especially after very long missions), some astronauts have experienced dizziness and nausea. All had considerable difficulty in standing with their eyes closed for the first day or two (von Baumgarten et al., 1984).

How to Minimize Motion Sickness

Researchers trying to prevent space sickness have learned a great deal about what helps and what doesn't. The following points may be of some aid to you here on earth (Jackson, 1994).

- Medical treatment for space sickness has concentrated on drugs. The most successful so far is scopolamine, which is available by prescription. Non-prescription "sea sickness" pills also offer some protection. Alcohol and other intoxicating drugs, however, usually make motion sickness worse.
- Soviet cosmonauts have had some success with a system that limits head movements for the first two days in space. In a boat, car, or airplane, it helps to move your head as little as possible (Jackson, 1994). You may even want to place a towel around your neck to restrict head movement. (If it doesn't help, you may soon find another use for it.)
- To minimize sensory conflict, stay out of the cabin on boats. In cars and airplanes, try closing your eyes. Or as an alternative, fixate your eyes on an unmoving point (such as the horizon) or look above the horizon at the unmoving sky (Stern et al., 1990).
- If possible, you should lie down. The otoliths are less sensitive to vertical movements when you are horizontal, and your head will move less.
- Anxiety intensifies motion sickness. Some of the astronauts have had success at learning to focus their attention on pleasant, distracting thoughts or calming images. If you do the same, be sure to also breathe slowly and deeply. Breathing can, in fact, be a good focus for attention (Jackson, 1994; Nicogossian & Parker, 1982).
- Relaxation helps minimize motion sickness. You may find it valuable to learn relaxation exercises that you can use when needed (Jackson, 1994). (Relaxation methods are described in Chapter 18 of this book.)

Space sickness is only one of the behavioral challenges of space travel. In fact, the long-term effects of space flight are still largely unknown. Although space missions seem relatively routine, astronauts remain true pioneers in a strange and alien sensory environment.

LEARNING CHECK

1. At least 170 out of every 200 astronauts have suffered from space sickness. T or F?
2. Head movements are detected primarily in the semicircular canals, gravity by the otolith organs. T or F?
3. Sensory conflict theory appears to explain space sickness, but it does not seem to apply to other types of motion sickness. T or F?
4. The drug amphetamine has been used successfully to prevent motion sickness. T or F?

Critical Thinking

5. Drivers are less likely to become car sick than passengers are. Why do you think drivers and passengers differ in susceptibility to motion sickness?

Answers: 1. F 2. T 3. F 4. F 5. Drivers experience less sensory conflict because they control the car's motion. This allows them to anticipate the car's movements and to coordinate their head and eye movements with those of the car.

Chapter Summary

- *In general, how do sensory systems function?*

- Sensory organs **transduce** physical energies into nerve impulses.
- Because of **selectivity,** limited **sensitivity, feature detection,** and **coding** patterns, the senses act as **data reduction systems.**
- Sensory response can be partially understood in terms of **localization of function** in the brain.

- *What are the limits of our sensory sensitivity?*

- The minimum amount of physical energy necessary to produce a sensation defines the **absolute threshold.** The amount of change necessary to produce a **just noticeable difference** in a stimulus defines a **difference threshold.** The study of thresholds and related topics is called **psychophysics.**
- Threatening or anxiety-provoking stimuli may raise the threshold for recognition, an effect called **perceptual defense.**
- Any stimulus below the level of conscious awareness is said to be **subliminal.** There is evidence that **subliminal perception** occurs, but subliminal advertising is largely ineffective.

- *How is vision accomplished?*

- The **visible spectrum** consists of electromagnetic radiation in a narrow range.
- The eye is in some ways like a camera, but ultimately, it is a **visual system,** not a photographic one. Individual cells in the visual cortex of the brain act as **feature detectors** to analyze visual information.
- Four common visual defects, correctable with glasses, are **myopia** (nearsightedness), **hyperopia** (farsightedness), **presbyopia** (loss of accommodation), and **astigmatism.**
- The **rods** and **cones** are **photoreceptors** making up the **retina** of the eye. The rods specialize in night vision, black and white reception, and motion detection. The cones, found exclusively in the **fovea** and otherwise toward the middle of the eye, specialize in color vision, **acuity** (perception of fine detail), and daylight vision. Much **peripheral vision** is supplied by the rods.

- *How do we perceive colors?*

- The rods and cones differ in color sensitivity. *Yellowish green* is brightest for cones; *blue-green* for the rods (although they will see it as colorless). Color vision is explained by the **trichromatic theory** in the retina and by the **opponent-process theory** in the visual system beyond the eyes.
- Total **color blindness** is rare, but 8 percent of males and 1 percent of females are red-green color-blind or color-weak. Color blindness is a **sex-linked trait** carried on the X chromosome. The **Ishihara test** is used to detect color blindness.
- **Dark adaptation,** an increase in sensitivity to light, is caused by increased concentration of visual pigments in both the rods and the cones, but mainly by **rhodopsin** recombining in the rods. Vitamin A deficiencies may cause **night blindness.**

- *What makes hearing possible?*

- **Sound waves** are the stimulus for hearing. They are transduced by the **eardrum, auditory ossicles, oval window, cochlea,** and ultimately, the **hair cells.**
- The **frequency theory** and **place theory** of hearing together explain how pitch is sensed.
- Three basic types of deafness are **nerve deafness, conduction deafness,** and **stimulation deafness.**

- *How do the chemical senses operate?*

- **Olfaction** (smell) and **gustation** (taste) are **chemical senses** responsive to airborne or liquefied molecules. It is also suspected that humans are sensitive to **pheromones,** although the evidence for this sense remains preliminary.
- The **lock and key** theory partially explains smell. In addition, the location of the olfactory receptors in the nose helps identify various scents.
- Specific areas on the tongue are more responsive to sweet, salty, sour, and bitter tastes. Taste also appears to be based in part on lock-and-key coding of molecule shapes.

- *What are the somesthetic senses and why are they important?*

- The **somesthetic senses** include the **skin senses, vestibular senses,** and **kinesthetic senses** (receptors that detect muscle and joint positioning).
- The skin senses include **touch, pressure, pain, cold,** and **warmth.** Sensitivity to each is related to the number of receptors found in an area of skin.
- Distinctions can be made among various types of pain, including **visceral pain, somatic pain, referred pain, warning system pain,** and **reminding system pain.**

- *Why are we more aware of some sensations than others?*

- Incoming sensations are affected by **sensory adaptation** (a reduction in the number of nerve impulses sent), by **selective attention** (selection and diversion of messages in the brain), and by **sensory**

had seen a few moments before, in broad daylight, as a huge, vicious, horrible-looking creature. The man was not a stranger. He was a neighbor of mine. I had seen him dozens of times before. I know him by name. He is a rather small man.

The last chapter discussed sensation, the process of bringing information into the nervous system. This chapter is about **perception,** *or how we assemble sensations into usable patterns that provide a "picture" or model of the world. As we perceive events, the brain actively selects, organizes, and integrates sensory information. These mental processes are so automatic, it may take drastic misperceptions to call attention to them. Perception creates faces, melodies, works of art, illusions, and on occasion, "murders" out of the raw material of sensation. Let's see how this takes place.*

Survey Questions

- What are perceptual constancies, and what is their role in perception?
- What basic principles do we use to group sensations into meaningful patterns?
- How is it possible to see depth and judge distance?
- What effect does learning have on perception?
- How is perception altered by attention, motives, values, and expectations?
- How reliable are eyewitness reports?
- Is extrasensory perception possible?

Perception The mental process of organizing sensations into meaningful patterns.

Size constancy The perceived size of an object remains constant, despite changes in its retinal image.

Perceptual Constancies—Taming an Unruly World

What would it be like to have your vision restored after a lifetime of blindness? In reality, a first look at the world can be disappointing. A newly sighted person must *learn* to identify objects, to read clocks, numbers, and letters, and to judge sizes and distances (Senden, 1960). Indeed, learning to "see" can be quite frustrating (■ Fig. 5–1).

Richard Gregory (1990) describes the experiences of Mr. S. B., a 52-year-old cataract patient who had been blind since birth. After an operation restored his sight, Mr. S. B. struggled to use his vision. At first, for instance, he could only judge distance in familiar situations. One day he was found crawling out of a hospital window to get a closer look at traffic on the street. It's easy to understand his curiosity, but he had to be restrained. His room was on the fourth floor!

Question: Why would Mr. S. B. try to crawl out of a fourth-story window? Couldn't he at least tell distance from the size of the cars?

No, because using size to judge distance requires familiarity with the appearance of objects. Try holding your left hand a few inches in front of your eyes and your right hand at arm's length. The image of your right hand should be about half the size of your left hand. Still, because you have viewed your hands from different distances countless times, you know your right hand did not suddenly shrink. This is called **size constancy:** The perceived size of an object remains the same, despite changes in the size of the image it casts on the retina. Even newborn babies show some evidence of size constancy (Slater, Mattock, & Brown, 1990).

■ **Fig. 5–1** *Visual perception involves finding meaningful patterns in complex stimuli. If you look closely at this painting by the artist Yvaral, you will see that it is entirely made up of small, featureless squares. An infant or newly-sighted person would see only a jumble of meaningless colors. But because the squares form a familiar pattern, you should easily see Marilyn Monroe's face. (Or is that Madonna?) ("Marilyn Numerisée," 1990, courtesy Circle Gallery.)*

To perceive your hand accurately, you had to draw on past experience. Some perceptions are so basic they seem to be **native** (inborn). An example is the ability to see a line on a piece of paper. However, much perception is **empirical,** or based on prior experience (Julesz, 1975). For instance, Colin Turnbull (1961) tells of the time he took a Pygmy from the dense rain forests of Africa to the vast African plains. The Pygmy had never before seen objects at a great distance. Hence, the first time he saw a herd of buffalo in the distance, he thought it was a swarm of insects. Imagine his confusion when he was then driven toward the animals. He concluded that witchcraft was being used to fool him because the "insects" seemed to grow into buffalo before his eyes.

Perhaps you have also experienced the failure of size constancy in unfamiliar situations. When viewed from aloft, in an airplane, houses, cars, and people no longer seem normal in size; instead, they begin to look like toys. Thus, we can summarize that size constancy, while being innate, is also molded by experience.

Shape constancy is another interesting effect: The perceived shape of an object is unaffected by changes in the shape of its image on the retina. Shape constancy can be demonstrated by looking at this page from directly overhead and then from an angle. Obviously, the page is rectangular, but most of the time the image that reaches your eye is distorted. Even though the book's image changes, your perception of its shape remains constant. (For additional examples, see ■ Fig. 5–2.) In a movie theater, preserving shape constancy becomes difficult if you sit in the front row or near the front and to the side. Nevertheless, most people are able to tolerate a fair amount of shape distortion, as long as all objects on the screen are similarly distorted (Cutting, 1987). On the highway, alcohol intoxication impairs size and shape constancy, adding to the accident rate among drunk drivers (Farrimond, 1990).

Let's say that you are outside in bright sunlight. Beside you is a friend wearing a gray skirt and a white blouse. Suddenly a cloud shades the sun. It might seem that the blouse would grow dimmer, but it still appears to be bright white. This happens because the blouse continues to reflect a larger *proportion* of light than nearby objects. The principle of **brightness constancy** states that the apparent brightness of an object stays the same under changing conditions of light. However, this holds true only if the blouse and surrounding objects are all illuminated by the same amount of light. You could make a part of your friend's gray skirt look whiter than the shaded blouse by shining a very bright spot of light on the skirt.

To summarize, the energy patterns reaching our senses are constantly changing, even when they come from the same object. Size, shape, and brightness constancy rescue us from a confusing world in which objects would seem to shrink and grow, change shape as if made of rubber, and light up or fade like neon lamps. Gaining these constancies was only one of the hurdles Mr. S. B. faced in learning to see. In the next section, we will consider some others.

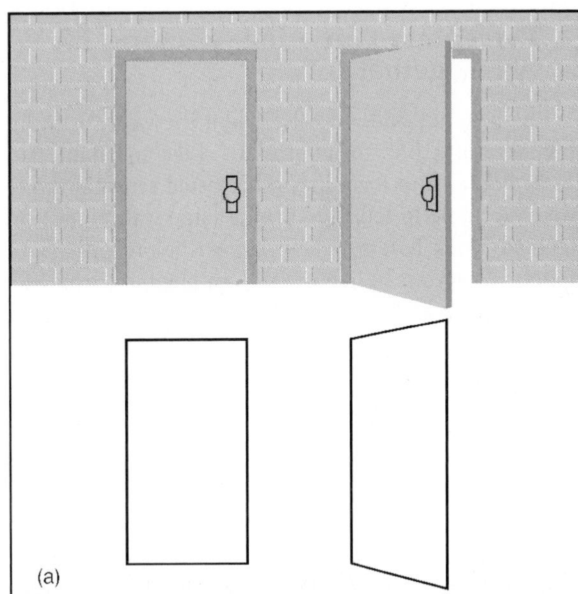

(b)

■ **Fig. 5–2** *Shape constancy. (a) When a door is open its image actually forms a trapezoid. Shape constancy is indicated by the fact that it is still perceived as a rectangle. (b) With great effort you may be able to see this design as a collection of flat shapes. However, if you maintain shape constancy the distorted squares strongly suggest the surface of a sphere. (From Spherescapes-1 by Scott Walter and Kevin McMahon, 1983.)*

Shape constancy The perceived shape of an object is unaffected by changes in its retinal image.

Brightness constancy The apparent (or relative) brightness of objects remains the same as long as they are illuminated by the same amount of light.

Figure-ground organization Part of a stimulus appears to stand out as an object (figure) against a less prominent background (ground).

Reversible figure A stimulus pattern in which figure-ground organization can be reversed.

Illusory figure An implied shape that is not actually bounded by an edge or an outline.

Perceptual Grouping—Getting It All Together

William James said, "To the infant the world is just a big, booming, buzzing confusion." Like an infant, Mr. S. B. had to find meaning in his visual sensations. He was soon able to tell time from a large wall clock and to read block letters he had known before only from touch. At a zoo, he recognized an elephant from descriptions he had heard. However, handwriting meant nothing to him for more than a year after he regained sight, and many objects remained meaningless until he touched them. Thus, while Mr. S. B. had visual *sensations*, his ability to *perceive* remained limited.

Question: How are sensations organized into meaningful perceptions?

Figure and Ground The simplest organization involves grouping some sensations into an object, or *figure*, that stands out on a plainer background. **Figure-ground** organization is probably inborn, since it is the first perceptual ability to appear after cataract patients regain sight (Hebb, 1949). Even 7-month-old babies respond to figure-ground patterns (Dannemiller & Braun, 1988). In normal figure-ground perception, only one figure is seen. In **reversible figures**, however, figure and ground can be switched. In ■ Fig. 5–3 it is equally possible to see either a wineglass figure on a dark background or two face profiles on a white background. As you shift from one pattern to the other, you should get a clear sense of what figure-ground organization means.

■ **Fig. 5–3** *A reversible figure-ground design. Do you see two faces in profile, or a wineglass?*

Gestalt Principles

Question: What causes the formation of a figure?

The Gestalt psychologists (see Chapter 1) studied this question in detail. Even if you were seeing for the first time, they concluded, a number of factors would bring some order to your perceptions (■ Fig. 5–4).

1. **Nearness.** Stimuli that are near each other tend to be grouped together (see Fig. 5–4a). Thus, if three people stand near each other and a fourth person stands 10 feet away, the adjacent three will be seen as a group and the distant person as an outsider.
2. **Similarity.** "Birds of a feather flock together," and stimuli that are similar in size, shape, color, or form tend to be grouped together (see Fig. 5–4b). For instance, picture two bands marching side by side. If their uniforms are different colors, the bands will be seen as two separate groups, not as one large group.
3. **Continuation, or continuity.** Perceptions tend toward simplicity and continuity. In Figure 5–4c it is easier to visualize a wavy line on a squared-off line than it is to see a complex row of shapes.
4. **Closure.** Closure refers to the tendency to *complete* a figure, so that it has a consistent overall form. Each of the drawings in Figure 5–4d has one or more gaps, yet each is perceived as a recognizable figure. The "shapes" that appear in the middle of the two right drawings in Figure 5–4d are called **illusory figures** (Parks, 1984). Illusory figures are implied shapes that are not actually bounded by an edge or an outline. Even young children see these implied shapes, despite knowing that they are "not really there." Illusory figures reveal that our tendency to form shapes—even with minimal cues—is powerful.
5. **Contiguity.** A principle that can't be shown in Fig. 5–4 is contiguity, or nearness in time *and* space. Contiguity is often responsible for the perception that one thing has *caused* another (Michotte, 1963). A psychologist friend of the author's demonstrates this principle in class by knocking on his head with one hand while knocking on a wooden table (out of sight) with the other. The knocking sound is perfectly timed with the movements of his visible hand. This leads to the irresistible perception that his head is made of wood.

In addition to these classical principles, psychologist Stephen Palmer recently demonstrated one more way in which we organize perceptions (Palmer, 1992).

6. **Common region.** As you can see in Figure 5–4e, stimuli that are found within a common region or area tend to be seen as a group. On the basis of similarity and nearness, the stars in Figure 5–4e should be one group and the dots another. However, the colored backgrounds define regions that create three groups of

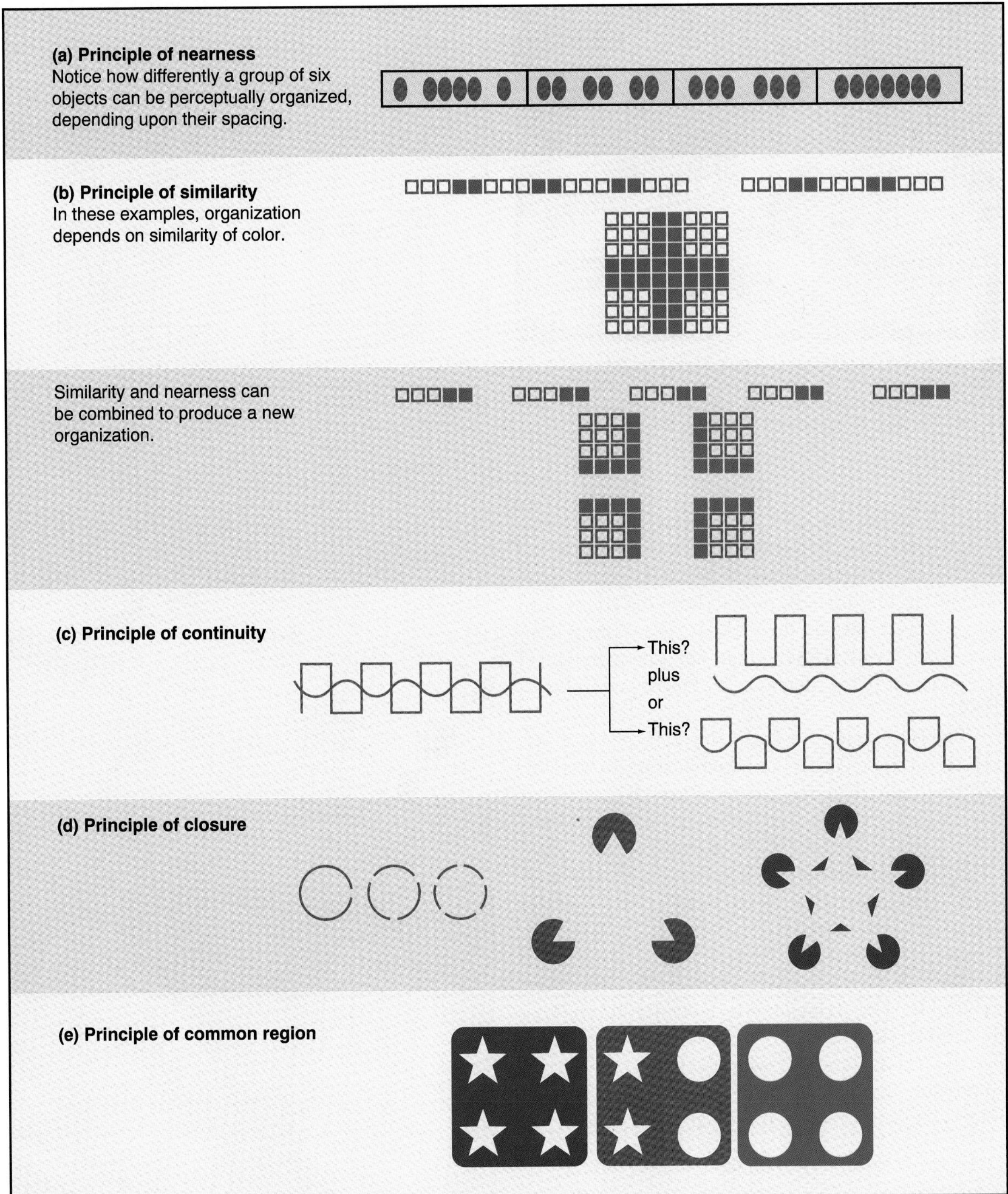
(a) Principle of nearness
Notice how differently a group of six objects can be perceptually organized, depending upon their spacing.
(b) Principle of similarity
In these examples, organization depends on similarity of color.
Similarity and nearness can be combined to produce a new organization.
(c) Principle of continuity
This?
plus
or
This?
(d) Principle of closure
(e) Principle of common region

■ **Fig. 5–4** *Perceptual grouping illustrations.*

objects (four stars, two stars plus two dots, and four dots). Perhaps the principle of common region explains why we tend to mentally group together people from a particular country, state, province, or geographic region.

Clearly, our day-to-day perceptions are shaped by the Gestalt principles for grouping stimuli. In addition, learning and past experience also greatly affect perceptual organization. For example, contrast Mr. S. B.'s immediate recognition of letters to his inability to read handwriting. Also, take a moment and look for the camouflaged animal pictured in ■Figure 5–5. **Camouflage** patterns are those that break up figure-ground organization. If you had never seen similar animals before, could you have located this one? Mr. S. B. would have been at a total loss to find meaning in such a picture.

Camouflage Designs that break up figure-ground organization.

■ **Fig. 5–5** *A challenging example of perceptual organization. Once the camouflaged insect (known as a giant walkingstick) becomes visible, it is almost impossible to view the picture again without seeing the insect.*

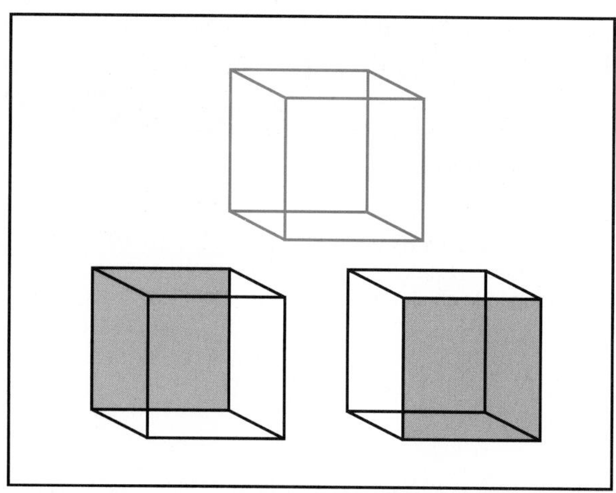

■ **Fig. 5–6** *Necker's cube. Visualize the top cube as a wire box. If you stare at the cube, its organization will change. Sometimes it will seem to project upward, like the lower left cube; other times it will project downward. The difference lies in how the brain interprets the same information.*

Perceptual hypothesis An initial guess regarding how to organize (perceive) a stimulus pattern.

Ambiguous stimuli Patterns that allow more than one perceptual organization.

Impossible figure A stimulus pattern that cannot be organized into a stable perception.

In a way, we are all detectives, seeking patterns in what we see. In this sense, a meaningful pattern represents a **perceptual hypothesis,** or initial guess about how to organize sensations. Have you ever seen a "friend" in the distance, only to have the friend turn into a stranger as you drew closer? Pre-existing ideas and expectations *actively* guide our interpretation of sensations in many situations (McBurney & Collings, 1984).

The active nature of organizing perceptions is perhaps most apparent for **ambiguous stimuli** (patterns allowing more than one interpretation). If you look at a cloud, you may discover dozens of ways to organize its contours into fanciful shapes and scenes. Even clearly defined stimuli may permit more than one interpretation. Stare at the design in ■ Figure 5–6 if you doubt the active nature of perception. In some instances, a stimulus may offer such conflicting information that perceptual organization becomes impossible. For example, the tendency to make a three-dimensional object out of a drawing is frustrated by the "three-pronged widget" (■ Fig. 5–7), an **impossible figure.** Such patterns cannot be organized into stable, consistent, or meaningful perceptions.

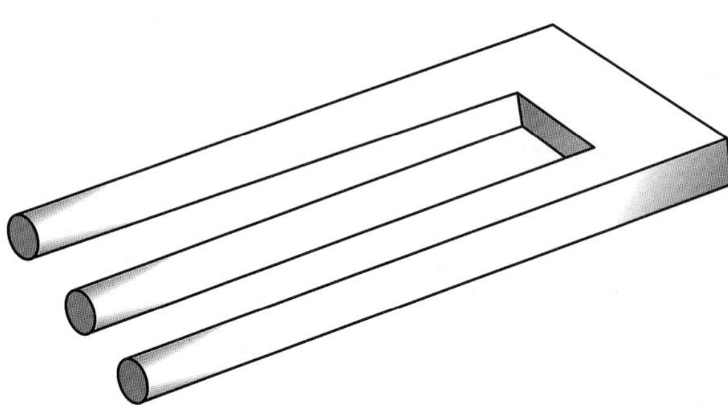

■ **Fig. 5–7** *An impossible figure—the "three-pronged widget."*

Question: Is the ability to understand drawings learned?

Humans almost always appear to understand lines that represent the *edges of surfaces.* We also have no problem with a single line used to depict the *parallel edges* of a narrow object, such as a rope. One thing that we *do not* easily recognize is lines showing color boundaries on the surface of an object (Kennedy, 1983).

To illustrate the last point, let's pay a brief visit to the Songe, a small tribe in Papua New Guinea. Before they were tested, the Songe had never made or seen line drawings—not even doodles scratched on the ground. As a test, the Songe were shown drawings like those in ■ Figure 5–8. When this was done, they easily recognized the hand and the parrot from simple outlines. But lines showing color boundaries confused

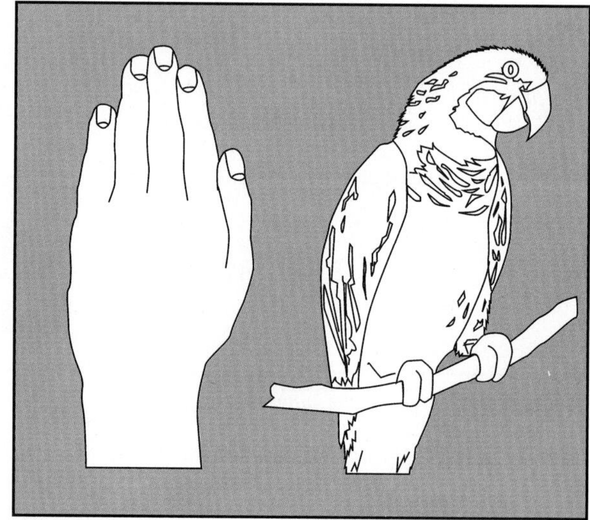

■ **Fig. 5–8** *Stimuli similar to those used by Kennedy (1983) to study the kinds of information universally recognized in drawings. (See text for explanation.)*

them. The half-moons on the fingernails, for example, made them think that the nails had been damaged and new ones were growing in. Similarly, they thought that the parrot must have been cut repeatedly. They thought this even though the lines in the drawing match color markings of parrots found in Songe territory (Kennedy, 1983).

One of the most amazing feats of perceptual organization deserves a separate discussion. In the next section we will explore our capacity to create three-dimensional space from flat retinal images.

LEARNING CHECK

Try these questions before reading more.

1. Which among the following are subject to basic perceptual constancy?
   a. figure-ground organization *b.* size *c.* ambiguity *d.* brightness
   e. continuity *f.* closure *g.* shape *h.* nearness
2. The first and most basic perceptual organization to emerge when sight is restored to a blind person is:
   a. continuity *b.* nearness constancy *c.* recognition of numbers and letters *d.* figure-ground
3. At times, meaningful perceptual organization represents a ______________________, or "guess," held until the evidence contradicts it.
4. The design known as Necker's cube is a good example of an impossible figure. T or F?
5. There is evidence that humans universally recognize line drawings depicting the edges of ______________________ and narrow parallel lines.
6. People who have taken psychedelic drugs, such as LSD or mescaline often report that the objects and people they see appear to be changing in size, shape, and brightness. This suggests that such drugs disrupt what perceptual process?

Critical Thinking

Answers: 1. *b, d, g* 2. *d* 3. hypothesis 4. F 5. surfaces 6. Perceptual constancies (size, shape, and brightness).

Depth Perception—What If the World Were Flat?

Depth perception is the ability to see three-dimensional space and to accurately judge distances. Without depth perception, you would be unable to drive a car or ride a bicycle, play catch, shoot baskets, thread a needle, or simply navigate around a room. The world would look like a flat surface.

Question: Mr. S. B. had trouble with depth perception after his sight was restored. Is depth perception learned?

Some psychologists (nativists) hold that depth perception is inborn. Others (the empiricists) view it as learned. Most likely, depth perception is partly learned and partly innate. Some evidence on the issue comes from work with the **visual cliff** (■ Fig. 5–9). The visual cliff is basically a glass-topped table. On one side a checkered surface lies directly beneath the glass. On the other side, the checkered surface is 4 feet below. This makes the glass look like a tabletop on one side and a cliff, or drop-off, on the other.

To test for depth perception, 6- to 14-month-old infants were placed in the middle of the visual cliff. This gave them a choice of crawling to the shallow side or the deep side. (The glass prevented them from doing any "skydiving" if they chose the deep side.) Most infants chose the shallow side. In fact, most refused the deep side even when their mothers tried to call them toward it (Gibson & Walk, 1960).

Question: If infants were at least 6 months old when they were tested, isn't it possible that they learned to perceive depth?

Yes, it is. However, other tests have shown that human depth perception consistently emerges at about 4 months of age (Aslin & Smith, 1988). For example, psychologist Jane Gwiazda fitted infants with goggles that make some designs stand out three-dimensionally while others remain flat. By watching head movements, Gwiazda could tell when babies first become aware of "3-D" designs. As in other tests, this occurs at age 4 months. The nearly universal emergence of depth perception at this time suggests that it depends more on brain development than it does on individual learning. It is very likely that at least a basic level of depth perception is innate.

Question: Then why do some babies crawl off tables or beds?

Depth perception The ability to see three-dimensional space and to accurately judge distances.

Visual cliff An apparatus that looks like the edge of an elevated platform or cliff.

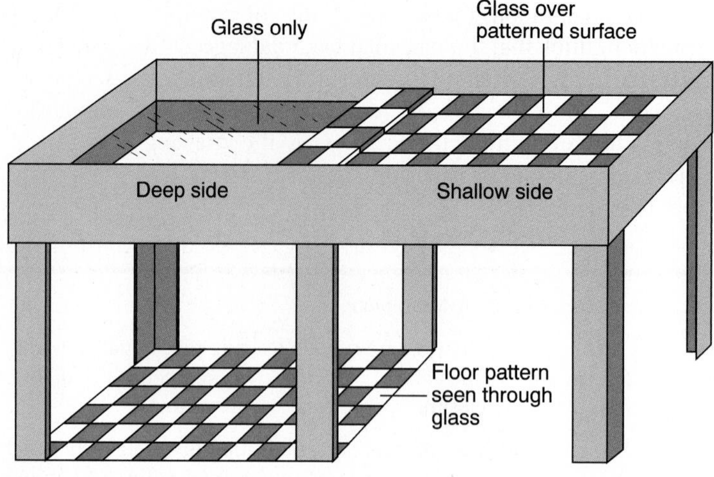

■ **Fig. 5–9** *Human infants and newborn animals refuse to go over the edge of the visual cliff.*

Depth cues Perceptual features that impart information about distance and three-dimensional space.

Monocular depth cues Depth cues that can be sensed with one eye.

Binocular depth cues Depth cues that require two eyes.

Accommodation Changes in the shape of the lens of the eye.

Convergence The simultaneous turning inward of the two eyes.

Retinal disparity Small discrepancies in images on the right and left retinas.

As soon as infants become active crawlers, they refuse to cross the deep side of the visual cliff (Campos et al., 1978). But even babies who perceive depth may not be able to catch themselves if they slip. A lack of coordination—not an inability to see depth—probably explains most "crash landings" after about 4 months of age.

Question: How do adults perceive depth?

A number of **depth cues** combine to produce our experience of three-dimensional space. Depth cues are features of the environment and messages from the body that supply information about distance and space. Some cues will work with just one eye (**monocular cues**), while others require two eyes (**binocular cues**).

Muscular Cues As their name implies, muscular cues come from within the body. One such cue is **accommodation**, a monocular cue for depth perception. You may recall from Chapter 4 that the lens in each eye must bend or bulge to focus nearby objects. Sensations from muscles attached to the lens are channeled back to the brain. Differences in these sensations help us judge distances within about 4 feet of the eyes. Beyond 4 feet, accommodation has a limited effect on depth perception. (It does, however, contribute to an interesting illusion described later under the heading "The Moon Illusion.") Obviously, accommodation is more important to a watchmaker or a person trying to thread a needle than it is to a basketball player or someone driving an automobile.

A second bodily source of information about depth is **convergence**, a binocular cue. When you look at a distant object, the lines of vision from your eyes are parallel. However, when you look at something 50 feet or less in distance, your eyes must converge (turn in) to focus the object (■ Fig. 5–10).

You are probably not aware of it, but whenever you estimate a distance under 50 feet (as when you approach a stop sign, play catch, or zap flies with your personal laser), you are using convergence. How? Again there is a relationship between muscle sensations and distance. Convergence is controlled by a group of muscles attached to the eyeball. These muscles feed information on eye position to the brain to help it judge distance. You can feel convergence by exaggerating it: Focus on your fingertip and bring it toward your eyes until they almost cross. At that point you can feel the sensations from the muscles that control eye movement.

Stereoscopic Vision The most basic source of depth perception is **retinal disparity**, also a binocular cue. Retinal disparity is based on the simple fact that the eyes are about 2.5 inches apart. Because of this,

■ **Fig. 5–10** *The eyes must converge, or turn in toward the nose, to focus close objects.*

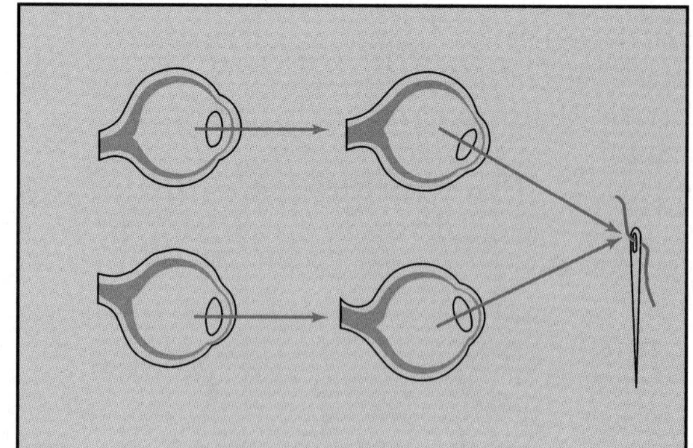

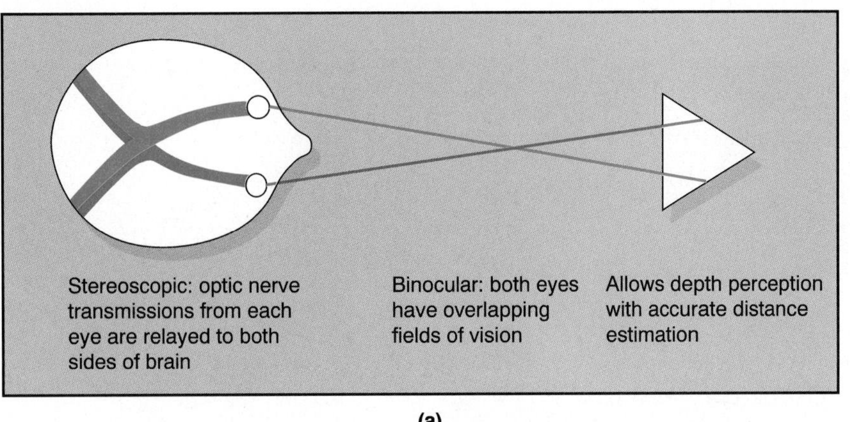
Stereoscopic: optic nerve transmissions from each eye are relayed to both sides of brain
Binocular: both eyes have overlapping fields of vision
Allows depth perception with accurate distance estimation

(a)

(b)

(c)

■ **Fig. 5–11** *(a) Stereoscopic vision. (b) The photographs show what the right and left eyes would see when viewing a vase. Hold a file card or small piece of paper (4 or 5 inches tall) vertically between the two photos. Place the bridge of your nose on the card so that each eye sees only one photo. Relax your eyes so that they sight along parallel lines, as if looking at something in the distance. Then try to fuse the vases into one image. The third dimension appears like magic. (c) Now do the same with the random dot stereogram, but with your eyes 8 or 10 inches from the page. With luck you will see a diamond shape hovering over the background. (See text for explanation.) Most readers will not be able to get the effect without using a prism to perfectly fuse the right and left dot squares. (Julesz, 1971; reprinted by permission of the University of Chicago Press.)*

each eye receives a slightly different view of the world. When the two images are *fused* into one overall image, **stereoscopic vision** occurs. The result is a powerful sensation of depth (■ Fig. 5–11).

Stereoscopic vision Perception of space and depth caused chiefly by the fact that the eyes receive different images.

Retinal disparity can be used to produce 3-D movies by filming with two cameras separated by several inches. Later, both images are simultaneously projected on a screen. Audience members wear glasses that filter out one of the images to each eye. Since each eye gets a separate image, normal stereoscopic vision is duplicated. Try the following demonstration of retinal disparity and fusion.

Totally Tubular

Roll a piece of paper into a tube. Close your left eye. Hold the tube to your right eye like a telescope. Look through the tube at some object in the distance. Place your left hand against the tube halfway down its length and in front of your left eye. Now open your left eye. You should see a "hole" in your hand. You couldn't expect a professional photographer to do a better job of blending the two images than your brain and visual system does automatically.

Question: How does retinal disparity produce depth?

Perceiving depth is more than a simple blending of two images or "pictures" of the world. In Figure 5–11c you will find two squares of random dots. Notice that they contain no lines, edges, or distinct patterns. Just the same, when these **random dot stereograms** are properly viewed (one to each eye), a center area seems to float above the background. Researcher Bela Julesz believes the designs show that the brain is very sensitive to any **mismatch** of information from the eyes. In Figure 5–11c, depth comes from shifting dots in the center of one square so they do not match dots in the

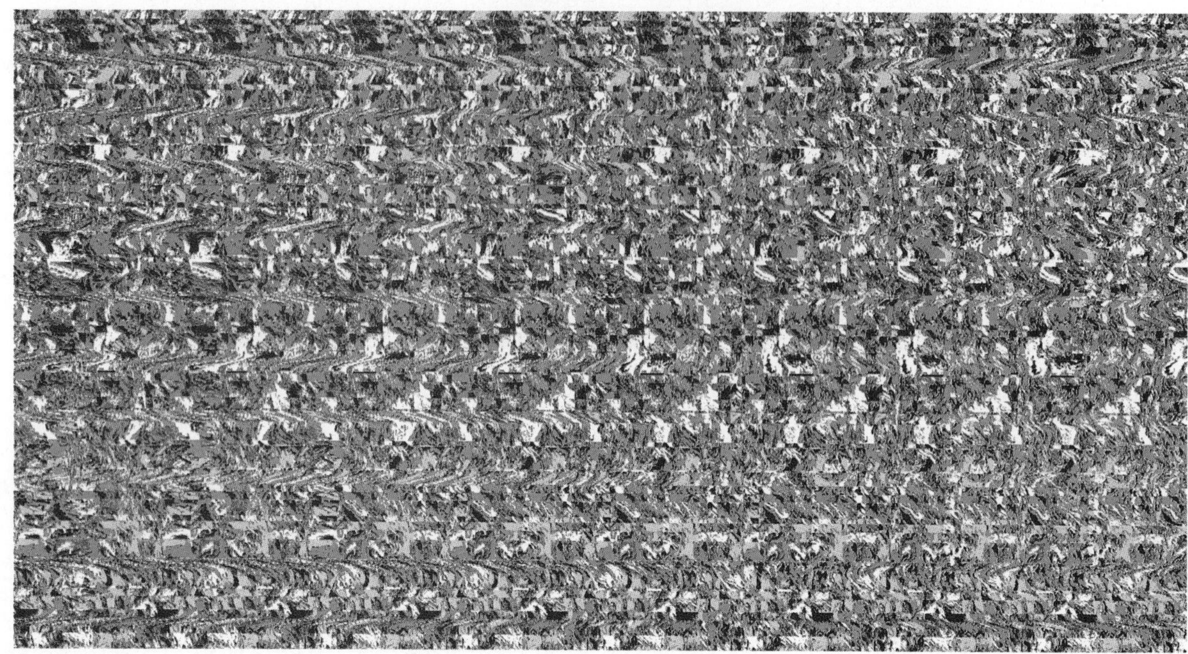

■ **Fig. 5–12** *This popular style of computer-generated art creates a 3-D illusion by superimposing two random dot patterns. Mismatches between the two patterns create a sensation of depth. To get the 3-D effect, hold the stereogram about 6 to 8 inches from the end of your nose. Relax your eyes and look* through *the art, as if you were focusing on something in the distance. If you're patient, you may see a 3-D maze. (Stereogram © Anything Enterprises, 1994.)*

other square (Julesz, 1971; Ross, 1976). (Also see ■ Figure 5–12.)

To a large extent, three-dimensional space is woven from countless tiny differences between what the right and left eyes see. Direct studies of the brain have shown that visual areas do, in fact, contain cells that detect disparities (Ohzawa, DeAngelis, & Gregory, 1990).

Question: If disparity is so important, can a person with one eye perceive depth?

A one-eyed person lacks convergence and retinal disparity, and accommodation is helpful mainly for judging short distances. This means that a person with only one eye will have limited depth perception. Try driving a car or riding a bicycle some time with one eye closed. You will find yourself braking too soon or too late, and you will have difficulty estimating your speed. ("But officer, my psychology text said to . . . .") Despite this, you will be able to drive, although it will be more difficult than usual. A person with one eye can even successfully land an airplane—a task that depends strongly on depth perception.

It is tempting to assume that higher animals perceive depth much as we do. While this is sometimes true, there are many exceptions. Highlight 5–1 explores some examples of how a "bird's-eye" view of the world might differ from our own.

Highlight 5–1

A Closer Look At

Stereoscopic Vision—A Bird's-Eye View

Harness yourself to a hang-glider, step off a cliff, and soar. No matter how exhilarating, your flight still wouldn't provide a true "bird's-eye" view. Scientist Jerry Waldvogel has found that many birds see the world in ways that would seem strange to a human. For example, pigeons, ducks, and hummingbirds can see ultraviolet light, which adds an extra color to their visual palette. Homing pigeons and many migrating birds can perceive the polarization of light. This aids navigation by allowing the birds to see geometric patterns in sunlight.

It might seem that birds also would have acute stereoscopic vision, and some do. But most birds are prey for other animals. When you spend life as a potential meal, it's important to be able to detect approaching predators. Accordingly, nature has given many birds an unusually wide field of view (■ Fig. 5–13b). An extreme case is the American woodcock, a bird that can survey a 360 degree panorama without moving its eyes or head. The trade-off for this wide-angle view is a

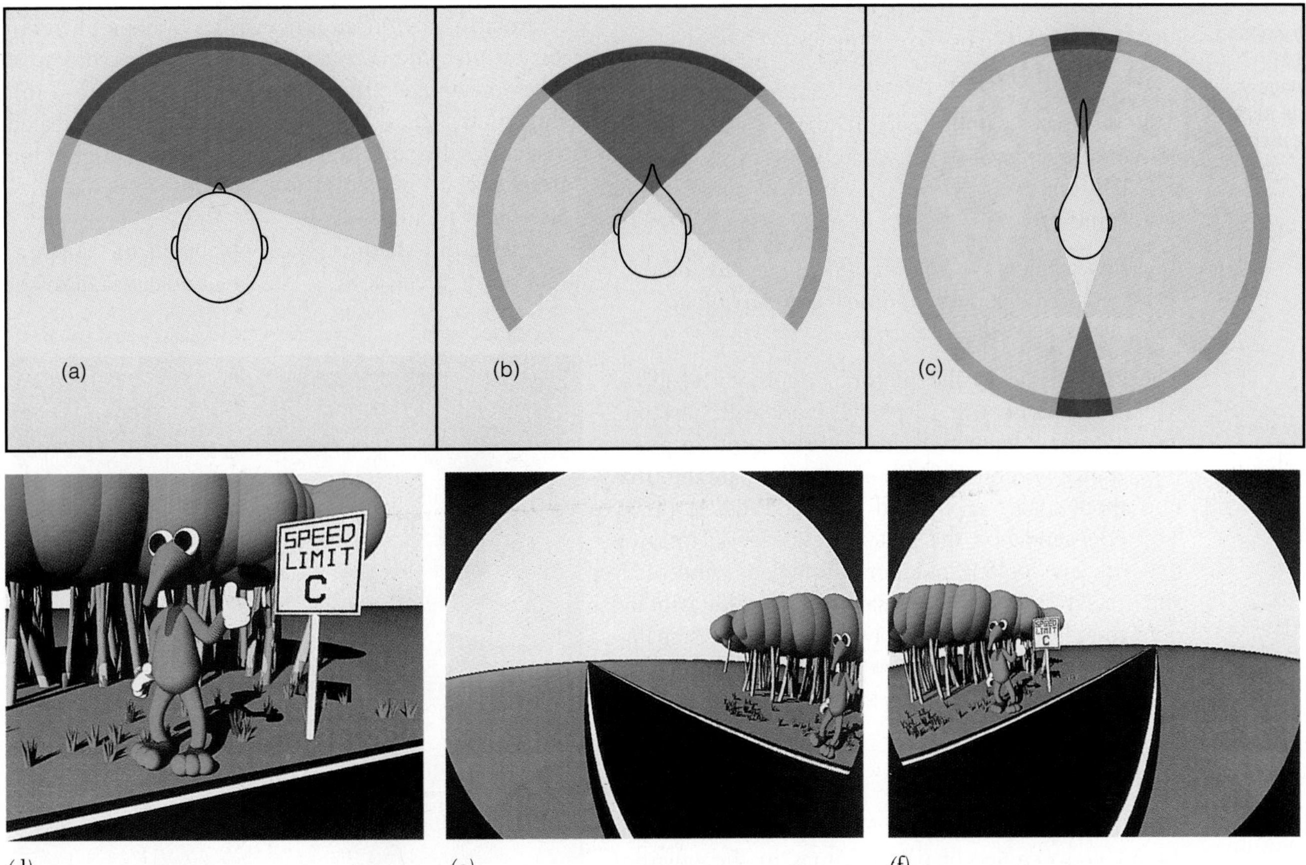

■ **Fig. 5–13** *(a) When viewed from above the head, a human's field of view for the right and left eyes contains a large area of overlapping, stereoscopic vision (darker shading). (b) The barn swallow's vision, like that of many birds, covers a much wider field of view than ours. Although the swallow's area of binocular vision is smaller than a human's, the swallow has sharper peripheral vision. (c) A bird called the American woodcock can see all the way around its head. Binocular vision is limited to a narrow band, but an extremely wide field of view helps the woodcock detect predators. (Adapted from Waldvogel, 1990). (d) This image, created by Ping-Kang Hsiung (1990), shows how an imaginary scene would look to a person standing across the road from a rather strange hitch-hiker. (e) (f) This is what a woodcock's left and right eyes would see if the bird were at the same point as the human in view* d. *(Computer graphics courtesy of Dr. Hsiung.)*

very limited area of binocular vision (Fig. 5–13c). But to the woodcock, an ability to spot hungry predators is probably more valuable than depth perception.

What does the world look like to a woodcock? You can put away the hang-glider: Computer scientist Ping-Kang Hsiung (1990) has used a method known as optical ray-tracing to simulate the woodcock's view (Fig. 5–13e, 5–13f). Of course, it is impossible to know if this is truly how the woodcock sees the world. But Hsiung's remarkable images are a close approximation. As you can see in Figure 5–13, even a pretty foxy predator would have trouble sneaking up on a woodcock.

Specialized adaptations are found in the eyes of other animals as well. Most of these variations, which are the result of evolution, have a purpose. For example, falcons can clearly see objects during a 150-mile-per-hour swoop that would be a blur to us. Scientists theorize that human depth perception is also an evolutionary holdover—from life in the tree-tops. Along with opposable thumbs and extensive shoulder rotation, we have inherited well-developed binocular vision. The superb depth perception that helped our distant ancestors swing from branch to branch now helps us swing at a softball or avoid erratic drivers in traffic. Perhaps it's too bad that a little of the woodcock's wide-angle vision didn't get thrown in as well. (Source: Waldvogel, 1990.)

Pictorial depth cues Features found in paintings, drawings, and photographs that impart information about space, depth, and distance.

Pictorial Cues for Depth—A Deep Topic

A good movie, painting, or photograph can create a convincing sense of depth where none exists. And, as noted, a one-eyed person can learn to gauge depth with some success.

Question: How is the illusion of depth created on a two-dimensional surface, and how is it possible to judge depth with one eye?

The answers lie in the **pictorial depth cues,** all of which are monocular (they will work with just one eye). Pictorial depth cues are features found in paintings, drawings, and photographs that impart information about space, depth, and distance (Haber, 1980). To understand how the pictorial cues work, imagine that you are looking outdoors through a window. If you traced everything you saw through the window onto the glass, you would have an excellent drawing, with convincing depth. If you then analyzed what was on the glass you would find the following features.

Pictorial Depth Cues

1. **Linear perspective.** This cue is based on the apparent convergence of parallel lines in the environment. If you stand between two railroad tracks, they appear to meet near the horizon. Since you know they are parallel, their convergence implies great distance (■ Fig. 5–14a).

2. **Relative size.** If an artist wishes to depict two objects of the same size at different distances, the artist makes the more distant object smaller (Fig. 5–14b). Films such as *Star Wars* and *Return of the Jedi* created sensational illusions of depth by rapidly changing the image size of planets, space stations, and starships. (Also see ■ Figure 5–15.)

3. **Light and shadow.** Most objects in the environment are lighted in ways that create clear patterns of

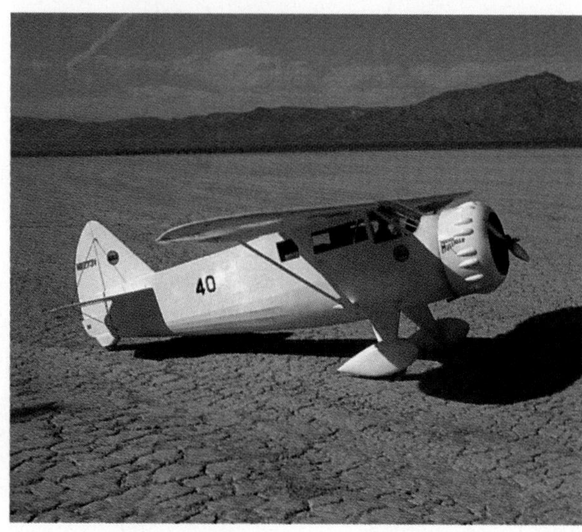

■ **Fig. 5–15** *On a dry lake bed, relative size is just about the only depth cue available for judging the camera's distance from this vintage aircraft. What do you estimate the distance to be? For the answer, look ahead to Figure 5–19.*

■ **Fig. 5–14** *(a) Linear perspective. (b) Relative size. (c) Light and shadow. (d) Overlap. (e) Texture gradients. Drawings in the top row show fairly "pure" examples of each of the pictorial depth cues. In the bottom row, the pictorial depth cues are used to assemble a more realistic scene.*

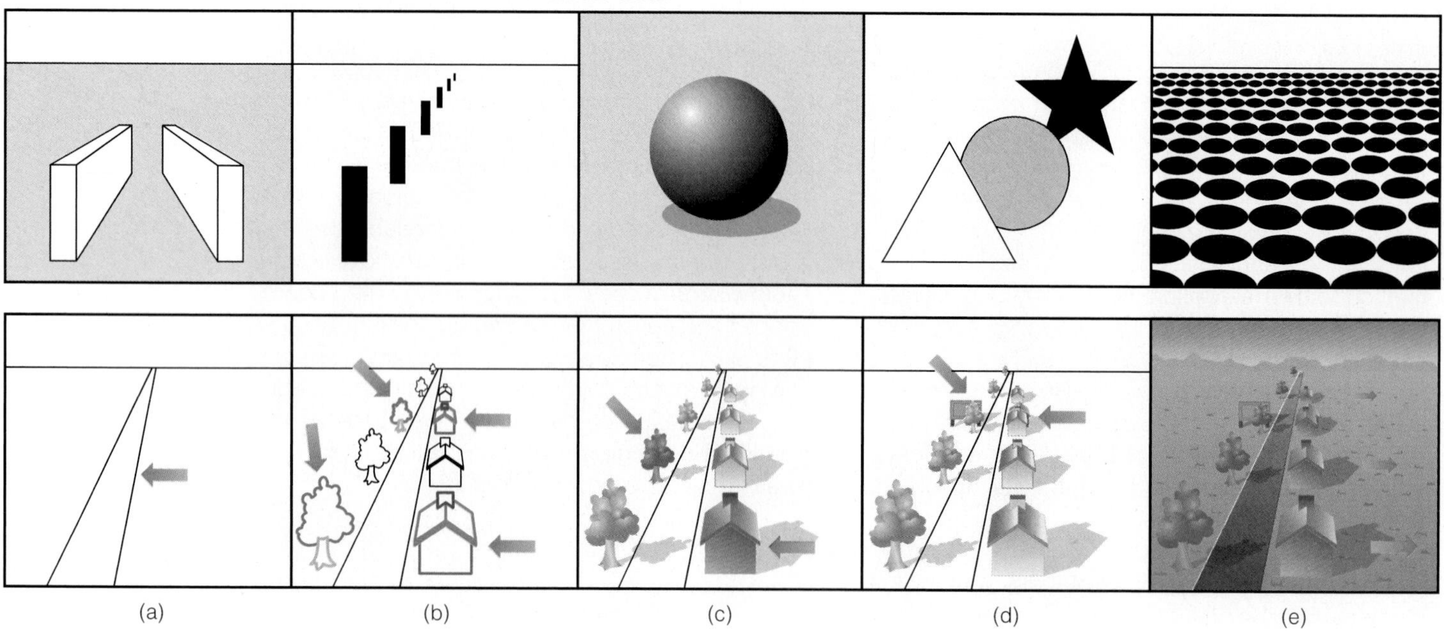

light and shadow. Copying such patterns of light and shadow can give a two-dimensional design a three-dimensional appearance (Fig. 5–14c).

4. **Overlap.** Overlap (also known as *interposition*) is a depth cue that occurs when one object partially blocks another object. Hold your hands up and have a friend try to tell from across the room which is nearer. Relative size will give the answer if one hand is much nearer to your friend than the other. But if one hand is only slightly closer than the other, your friend may have difficulty—until you slide one hand in front of the other. Overlap then removes any doubt (Fig. 5–14d).

5. **Texture gradients.** Changes in texture also contribute to depth perception. If you stand in the middle of a cobblestone street, the street will look coarse near your feet. However, its texture will get smaller and finer if you look into the distance (Fig. 5–14e).

6. **Aerial perspective.** Smog, fog, dust, and haze add to the apparent distance of an object. Because of aerial perspective, objects seen at great distance tend to be hazy, washed-out in color, and lacking in detail. This is true even in clear air, but it is increasingly the case in our mechanized society. As a matter of fact, aerial haze is often most noticeable when it is missing. If you have traveled the wide open spaces of states such as Colorado or Wyoming, you may have seen mountain ranges that looked only a few miles away, and then were shocked to find that you were actually viewing them through 50 miles of crystal-clear air.

7. **Relative motion.** Relative motion, also known as *motion parallax* (PAIR-ah-lax), can be seen by looking out a window and moving your head from side to side. Notice that objects near you appear to move a sizable distance as your head moves. In comparison, trees, houses, and telephone poles at a greater distance appear to move slightly in relation to the background. Distant objects like hills, mountains, or clouds don't seem to move at all.

When combined, pictorial cues can create a powerful illusion of depth. (Also, see ⬬ Table 5–1 for a summary of all the depth cues we have discussed.)

Question: Is motion parallax really a pictorial cue?

Strictly speaking it is not, except in movies, television, or animated cartoons. However, when parallax is present, depth is almost always perceived. Much of the apparent depth of a good movie comes from the relative motion of objects captured by the camera. People who can only see with one eye depend heavily on motion parallax. Often, they make frequent head movements to exaggerate parallax and improve depth perception.

■ Figure 5–16 illustrates an interesting feature of motion parallax. Imagine that you are riding in a bus and watching the passing scenery. Your gaze is more or less at a right angle to the direction of travel. Under these conditions, nearby objects will appear to rush *backward*. Those farther away, such as distant mountains, will seem to move very little or not at all. Objects that are more remote, such as the sun or moon, will appear to move in the *same* direction as you are traveling. (This is why the moon appears to "follow" you when you take a stroll at night.) To convincingly recreate motion parallax in cartoons, animators draw scenes in several layers, each of which is moved appropriately during filming.

Question: Are pictorial depth cues universal, like the understanding of basic drawings noted earlier?

⬬ **Table 5–1 Summary of Visual Depth Cues**

Binocular Cues	• Convergence • Retinal disparity
Monocular Cues	• Accommodation • Pictorial depth cues Linear perspective Relative size Light and shadow Overlap Texture gradients Aerial perspective Relative motion (motion parallax)

■ **Fig. 5–16** *The apparent motion of objects viewed during travel depends on their distance from the observer. Apparent motion can also be influenced by an observer's point of fixation. At middle distances, objects closer than the point of fixation appear to move backward; those beyond the point of fixation appear to move forward. Objects at great distances, such as the sun or moon, always appear to move forward.*

Moon illusion The apparent change in size that occurs as the moon moves from the horizon (large moon) to overhead (small moon).

Apparent distance hypothesis An explanation of the moon illusion stating that the horizon seems more distant than the night sky.

Not entirely. Some cultures use only selected pictorial cues to represent depth. People in these cultures may not easily recognize other cues (Deregowski, 1972). For example, researcher William Hudson tested members of remote tribes who do not use relative size to show depth in drawings. These people perceive simplified drawings as two-dimensional designs. As you can see in ■ Figure 5–17, they do not assume, as we do, that a larger image means that an object is closer. Of course, members of non-Western cultures can learn to interpret drawings of depth if they are given a chance to practice (Mshelia & Lapidus, 1990).

Question: How do the depth perception cues relate to daily experience?

The Moon Illusion Like the bodily depth cues, we constantly use the pictorial cues to sense depth and judge distances. Cues of both types also combine to produce an intriguing illusion. When the moon is on the horizon, it tends to look as large as a silver dollar. When it is directly overhead, it looks like a dime, very much smaller than it did earlier the same evening. Contrary to what some people believe, the moon's image is not magnified by the atmosphere. If you take a photograph of the moon and measure its image, you will find that it is not larger when it is near the horizon. But the moon *looks* larger when it's low in the sky. This is because the **apparent distance** of the moon is greater when it is near the horizon than when it is overhead (Kaufman & Rock, 1989).

Question: But if it seems farther away, shouldn't it look smaller?

No. When the moon is overhead, there are few depth cues around it. In contrast, when you see the moon on the horizon, it is behind houses, trees, telephone poles, and mountains. These objects add numerous depth cues, which cause the horizon to seem more distant than the sky overhead. The moon illusion is so powerful that it can occur in photographs if they contain depth cues (Coren & Aks, 1990).

To better understand the moon illusion, picture two balloons, one 10 feet away and the second 20 feet away. Suppose the more distant balloon is inflated until its image matches the image of the nearer balloon. How do we know the more distant balloon is larger? Because its image is the same size as a balloon that is closer. Similarly, the moon makes the same-size image on the horizon as it does overhead. However, the horizon seems more distant because more depth cues are present. As a result, the horizon moon must be perceived as larger (Rock, 1962). (See ■ Figure 5–18.)

This explanation is known as the **apparent distance hypothesis.** You can test it by removing depth cues while looking at a horizon moon. Try looking at the moon through a rolled-up paper tube, or make your hands into a "telescope" and look at the next large moon you see. It will immediately appear to shrink when viewed without depth cues.

Question: How exactly does apparent distance change the moon's perceived size?

Researchers have discovered that the moon illusion is directly related to changes in accommodation (Iavec-

■ **Fig. 5–17** *A Hudson test picture. Two-dimensional perceivers assume the hunter is trying to spear the distant elephant rather than the nearby antelope. Some acquaintance with conventions for representing depth in pictures and photographs seems necessary. (From "Pictorial Perception and Culture" by J. B. Deregowski. © 1972 by Scientific American, Inc. All rights reserved.)*

■ **Fig. 5–18** *The Ponzo illusion may help you understand the moon illusion. Picture the two white bars as resting on the railroad tracks. In the drawing, the upper bar is the same length as the lower bar. However, because the upper bar appears to be farther away than the lower bar, we perceive it as longer. The same logic applies to the moon illusion.*

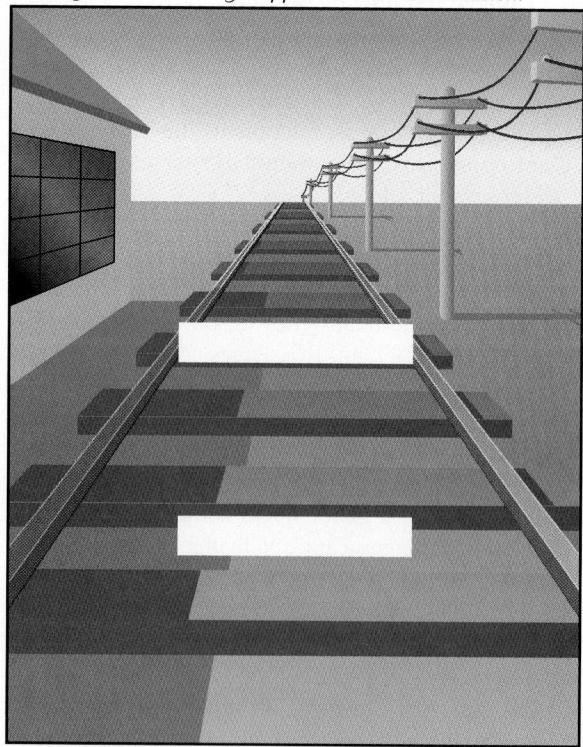

chia et al., 1983; Roscoe, 1985). Extra depth cues near the horizon cause the eyes to focus on a more distant point than they do when you look overhead. Such changes in accommodation appear to provide the brain with a "yardstick" for judging the size of images, including that of the moon.

LEARNING CHECK

If you have difficulty with any of these questions, skim back over the previous material.

1. The visual cliff is used to test for infant sensitivity to linear perspective. T or F?
2. Write an *M* or a *B* after each of the following to indicate if it is a monocular or binocular depth cue.
   accommodation ______ convergence ______ retinal disparity ______ linear perspective ______
   motion parallax ______ overlap ______ relative size ______
3. Which of the depth cues listed in question 2 are based on muscular feedback? ____________.
4. Interpretation of pictorial depth cues requires no prior experience. T or F?
5. The moon's image is greatly magnified by the atmosphere near the horizon. T or F?
6. What hearing ability would you say is most closely related to stereoscopic vision? ***Critical Thinking***

Answers:

1. F 2. accommodation (M), convergence (B), retinal disparity (B), linear perspective (M), motion parallax (M), overlap (M), relative size (M) 3. accommodation or convergence 4. F 5. F 6. If you close your eyes, you can usually tell the direction and perhaps the location of a sound source, such as a hand-clap. Locating sounds in space is heavily dependent on having two ears, just as stereoscopic vision depends on having two eyes.

Perceptual Learning—What If the World Were Upside Down?

England is one of the few countries in the world where people drive on the left side of the road. In view of this reversal, it is not unusual for visitors to step off curbs in front of cars—after carefully looking for traffic in the *wrong* direction. This problem is so common, in fact, that crosswalks near tourist attractions in London are stenciled with the words, "Look right"! As this example suggests, learning has a powerful impact on perception, something we have already seen in other ways.

Perceptual habits Established patterns of perceptual organization and attention.

Question: How does learning affect perception?

Perceptual Habits One way learning affects perception is through ingrained patterns of organization and attention, referred to as **perceptual habits.** Stop for a moment and look at ■ Fig. 5–20. The left face

■ **Fig. 5–19** *Before you can use familiar size to judge distance, objects must actually be the size you assume they are. Either these men are giants, or the model airplane was closer than you may have thought when you looked at Figure 5–15.*

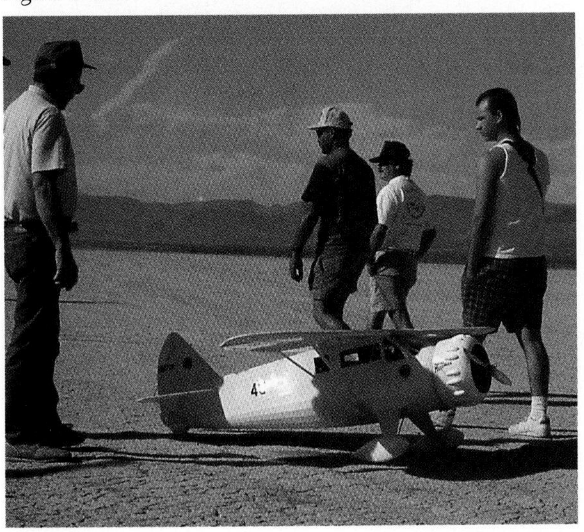

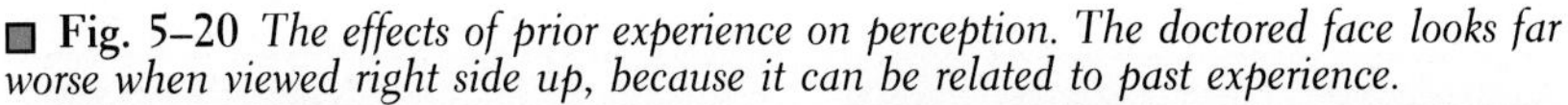

■ **Fig. 5–20** *The effects of prior experience on perception. The doctored face looks far worse when viewed right side up, because it can be related to past experience.*

■ Fig. 5–21

Ames room A distorted room that appears normal when viewed from a specific location.

Perceptual features Important elements of a stimulus, such as lines, shapes, edges, spots, colors.

looks somewhat unusual, to be sure. But the distortion seems mild—until the page is turned upside down. Viewed normally, the face looks quite grotesque. Why is there a difference? Apparently, most people have little experience with upside-down faces. Perceptual learning, therefore, has less impact on our perceptions of an upside-down face. With a face in normal position, you know what to expect and where to look. Also, you tend to see the entire face as a recognizable pattern. When a face is inverted, we are forced to perceive its individual features separately (Bartlett & Searcy, 1993).

Before we continue, read aloud the short phrase in ■ Figure 5–21. Did you read "Paris in the spring"? If so, look again. The word *the* appears twice in the phrase. Because of past experience with the English language, good readers often overlook the repeated word. Again, the effects of perceptual learning are apparent.

Magicians make use of perceptual habits when they use sleight of hand to distract observers while performing tricks. Another kind of "magic" is related to consistency in the environment. It is usually safe to assume that a room is shaped roughly like a box. This need not be true, however. When viewed from a certain point, a lopsided room can be made to appear square. This is done by carefully distorting the proportions of the walls, floor, ceiling, and windows. One such room, called an **Ames room,** after the man who designed it, presents a unique problem for the perceptual habits of an observer (■ Fig. 5–22).

Since the left corner of the Ames room is farther from a viewer than the right, a person standing in that corner looks very small, whereas one standing in the nearer, shorter right corner looks very large. If a person walks from the left corner of the room to the right, observers are faced with a conflict. They can maintain shape constancy by perceiving the room as square, or they can maintain size constancy by refusing to see the person "grow." Most people choose shape constancy and see people "shrink" and "grow" before their eyes.

As mentioned in the previous chapter, the brain is especially sensitive to **perceptual features** such as lines, shapes, edges, spots, and colors. At least some of this sensitivity appears to be learned. Colin Blakemore and Graham Cooper of Cambridge University raised kittens in a room with only vertical stripes on the walls. Another set of kittens saw only horizontal stripes. When returned to normal environments, the "horizontal" cats could easily jump onto a chair, but when walking on the floor, they bumped into chair legs. "Vertical" cats, on the other hand, easily avoided chair legs, but they missed when trying to jump to horizontal surfaces. The cats raised with vertical stripes were "blind" to horizontal lines, and the "horizontal" cats acted as if vertical lines were invisible (Lewin, 1974). Other experiments show that there is an actual decrease in brain cells tuned to the missing features (Grobstein & Chow, 1975).

Question: Would it be possible, then, for an adult to adapt to a completely new perceptual world?

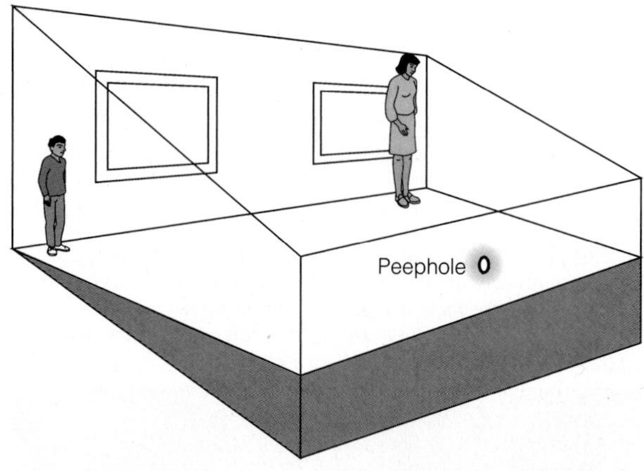

■ **Fig. 5–22** *The Ames room. From the front, the room looks normal; actually, the right-hand corner is very short, and the left-hand corner is very tall. In addition, the left side of the room slants away from viewers. The diagram shows the shape of the room and reveals why people appear to get bigger as they cross the room toward the nearer, shorter right corner.*

Inverted Vision An answer comes from experiments in which people wore lenses that invert visual images. In one experiment, a subject wore goggles that turned the world upside down and reversed objects from right to left. At first, even the simplest tasks—walking, eating, and so forth—were incredibly difficult (■ Fig. 5–23). Imagine trying to reach for a door handle and watching your hand shoot off in the wrong direction.

Subjects also reported that head movements made the world swing violently through space, causing severe headaches and nausea. Yet, after several days they began to adapt to inverted vision. Their success, while not complete, was impressive. Such a high degree of adaptation is related to superior human learning abilities. If the eyes of goldfish are surgically turned upside down, the fish swim in circles and rarely adapt (Sperry, 1956).

Question: Did everything turn upright again for the humans?

No. While they wore the goggles, their visual images remained upside down. But subjects learned to perform most routine activities, and their inverted world began to seem relatively normal. In later experiments, subjects wearing inverting lenses were able to successfully drive cars. One subject even flew an airplane after a few weeks of adaptation (Kohler, 1962). These feats are like driving or flying upside down, with right and left reversed. Some ride!

■ **Fig. 5–23** *Inverted vision. Adaptation to complete inversion of the visual world is possible, but challenging.*

Interacting with a new visual world through **active movement** seems to be a key to rapid adaptation. In one experiment, people wore glasses that grossly distorted vision. Those who walked on their own adapted more quickly than subjects pushed around in a wheeled cart (Held, 1971). Why does movement help? Probably because commands sent to the muscles can be related to sensory feedback (McBurney & Collings, 1984). Remaining immobile would be like watching a weird movie over which you have no control. There would be little reason for any perceptual learning to occur (■ Fig. 5–24).

Context Information surrounding a stimulus.

Frame of reference An internal perspective relative to which events are perceived and evaluated.

Adaptation level An internal or mental "average" or "medium" point that is used to judge amounts.

Adaptation Level An important factor affecting perception is the external **context** in which a stimulus is judged. Context is the information surrounding a stimulus. For example, a man 6 feet in height will look "tall" when surrounded by others of average height, and "short" among a group of professional basketball players. In ■ Figure 5–25, the center circle is the same size in both designs. But like the man in different company, context alters the circle's apparent size. The importance of context is also shown by ■ Figure 5–26. What do you see in the middle? If you read across, context causes it to be organized as a 13. Reading down makes it a B.

In addition to external contexts, we all have *internal* **frames of reference,** or standards by which stimuli are judged. If you were asked to lift a 10-pound weight, would you label it light, medium, or heavy? The answer to this question depends on your **adaptation level** (Helson, 1964). This is your own personal "medium point," or frame of reference. Each person's adaptation level is constantly modified by ex-

■ **Fig. 5–25** *Are the center dots in both figures the same size?*

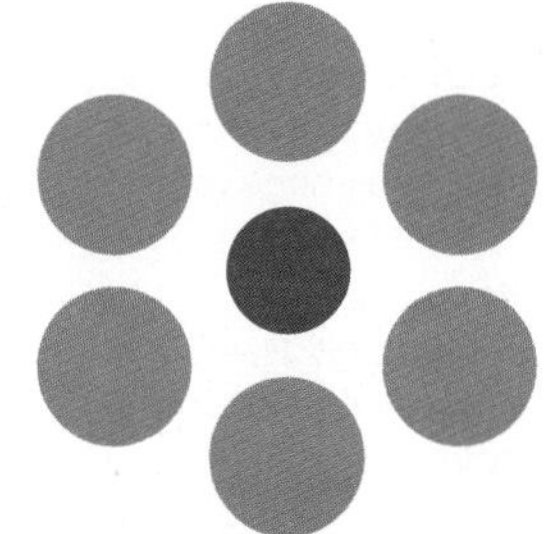

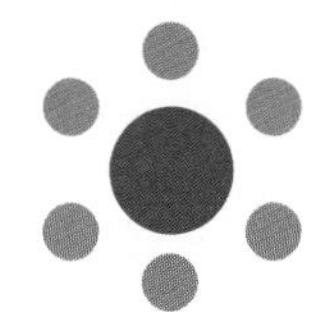

■ **Fig. 5–24** *Even small distortions of the visual world may necessitate perceptual learning. For example, the apparent size, distance, and curvature of objects is distorted underwater. Experiments confirm that professional divers gradually correct for these distortions as they gain experience with them (Vernoy, 1989).*

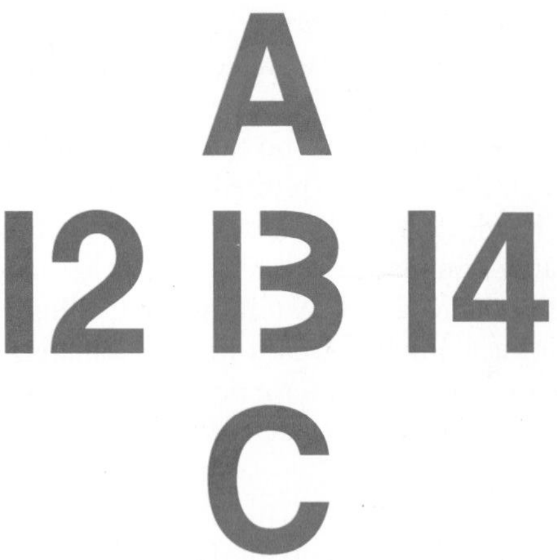

Fig. 5–26 *Context alters the meaning of the middle figure.*

A

12 13 14

C

Illusion A misleading or distorted perception.

Hallucination An imaginary sensation—such as seeing, hearing, or smelling something that does not exist in the external world.

Stroboscopic movement Illusion of movement in which an object is shown in a rapidly changing series of positions.

perience. If most of the weights you lift in day-to-day life *average* around 10 pounds, you will call a 10-pound weight medium. If you are a watchmaker and spend your days lifting tiny watch parts, you will probably call a 10-pound weight heavy. If you work as a furniture mover, your adaptation level will exceed 10 pounds, and you will call a 10-pound weight light. (If you are an aging rock star, you will no doubt call everything "heavy," man).

Illusions Perceptual learning is responsible for a number of **illusions,** or misleading perceptions. In an illusion, length, position, motion, curvature, or direction is consistently misjudged (Gillam, 1980). Illusions differ from **hallucinations** in that illusions distort stimuli that actually exist. People who are hallucinating perceive objects or events that have no external reality (for example, they hear voices that are not there). If you think you see a 3-foot-tall butterfly, you can confirm you are hallucinating by trying to touch its wings. To detect an illusion, it is often necessary to measure a drawing or apply a straight-edge to it.

Illusions are a fascinating challenge to our understanding of perception. On occasion, they also have practical uses. An illusion called **stroboscopic movement** (strobe-oh-SKOP-ik) puts the "motion" in motion pictures. The strobe lights sometimes used on dance floors reverse this illusion. Each time the strobe flashes, it "freezes" dancers in particular positions. However, if the flashes are speeded up sufficiently, normal motion is seen. In a similar way, movies project a rapid series of "snapshots" on the screen, so the gaps in motion are imperceptible.

Question: Can other illusions be explained?

Not in all cases, or to everyone's satisfaction. Generally speaking, size and shape constancy, habitual eye movements, continuity, and perceptual habits combine in various ways to produce the illusions in Figure 5–27. Rather than attempt to explain all of

Fig. 5–27 *Some interesting perceptual illusions.*

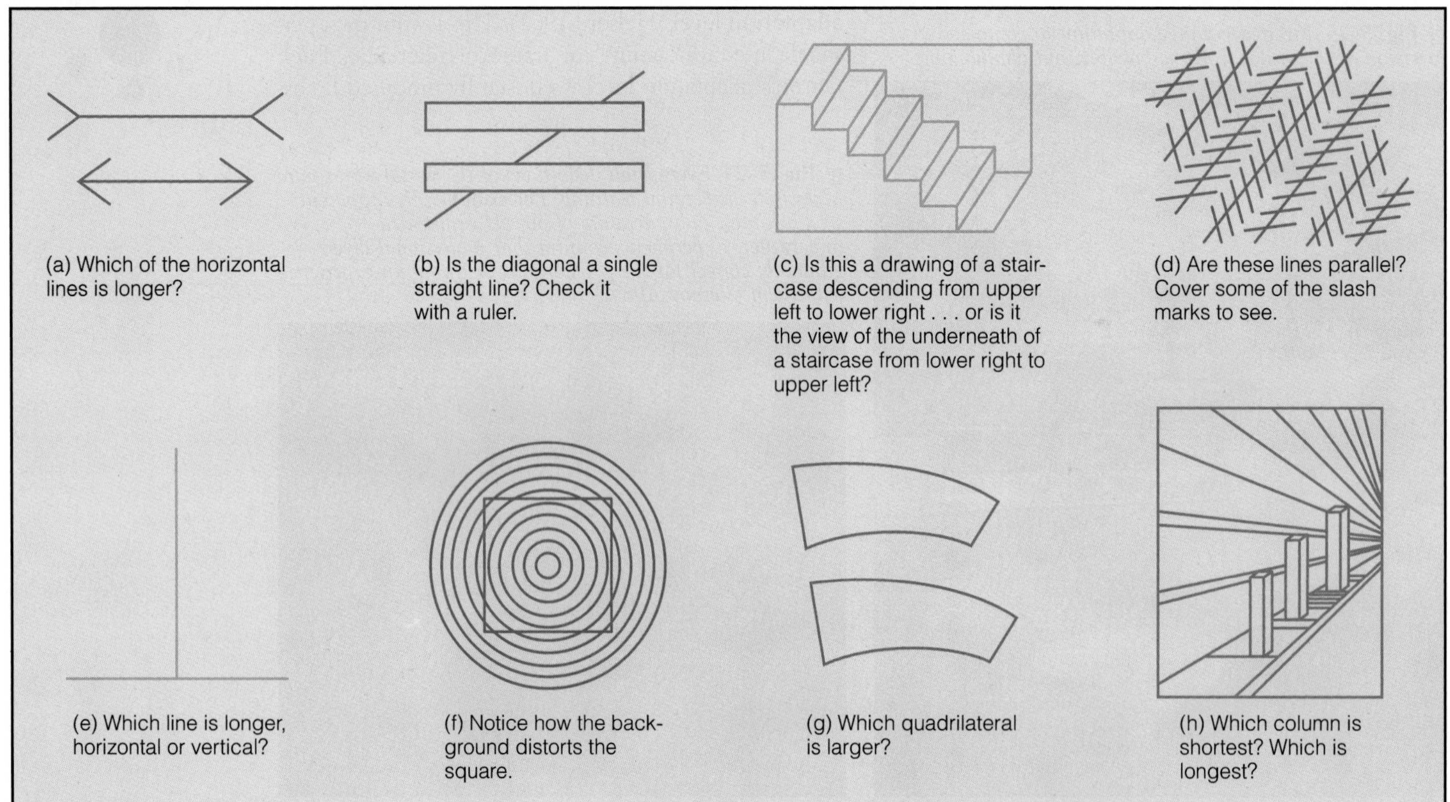
(a) Which of the horizontal lines is longer?
(b) Is the diagonal a single straight line? Check it with a ruler.
(c) Is this a drawing of a staircase descending from upper left to lower right . . . or is it the view of the underneath of a staircase from lower right to upper left?
(d) Are these lines parallel? Cover some of the slash marks to see.
(e) Which line is longer, horizontal or vertical?
(f) Notice how the background distorts the square.
(g) Which quadrilateral is larger?
(h) Which column is shortest? Which is longest?

the pictured illusions, let's focus on one deceptively simple example.

Consider the drawing in Figure 5–27a, the familiar **Müller-Lyer illusion** (MUE-ler-LIE-er). In this illusion, the horizontal line with arrowheads appears shorter than the line with V's on each end. A quick measurement will show that they are the same length. How can we explain this illusion? Evidence suggests it is based on a lifetime of experience with the edges and corners of rooms and buildings. Richard Gregory (1990) believes you see the horizontal line with the V's as if it were the corner of a room viewed from inside (■ Fig. 5–28). The line with arrowheads, on the other hand, suggests the corner of a room or building seen from outside.

Earlier, to explain the moon illusion, we said that if two objects make images of the same size, the more distant object must be larger. This is known formally as **size-distance invariance.** Gregory believes the same concept explains the Müller-Lyer illusion. That is, if the V-tipped line looks farther away than the arrowhead-tipped line, then you must compensate by seeing the V-tipped line as longer. This explanation of the Müller-Lyer illusion presumes that you have had years of experience with straight lines, sharp edges, and corners—a pretty safe assumption in our culture.

Question: Is there any way to show that past experience causes the illusion?

If we could test someone who saw only curves and wavy lines as a child, we would know if experience with a "square" culture is important. Fortunately, a group of people in South Africa, the Zulus, live in a "round" culture. In their daily lives, Zulus rarely encounter a straight line: Their huts are shaped like

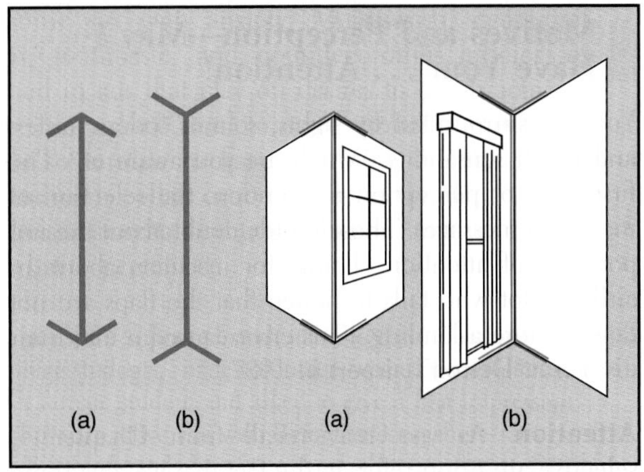

■ **Fig. 5–28** *Why does line (b) in the Müller-Lyer illusion look longer than line (a)? Probably because it looks more like a distant corner than a nearer one. Since the vertical lines form images of the same length, the more "distant" line must be perceived as larger.*

rounded mounds and arranged in a circle, tools and toys are curved, and there are no straight roads or square buildings.

Question: What happens if a Zulu looks at the Müller-Lyer design?

The typical Zulu does not experience the illusion. At most, he or she sees the V-shaped line as *slightly* longer than the other (Gregory, 1990). This seems to confirm the importance of past experience and perceptual habits in determining our view of the world. But, like many topics in psychology, room for debate remains. The Müller-Lyer illusion also seems to be partly based on directly misperceiving the location of the ends of the lines (Morgan, Hole, & Glennerster, 1990). Thus, it could be that both apparent size and mislocating the ends of the lines causes the illusion.

Müller-Lyer illusion Two equal-length lines tipped with inward or outward pointing V's appear to be of different lengths.

Size-distance invariance The strict relationship between the distance an object lies from the eyes and the size of its image.

Learning Check

1. Perceptual habits may become so ingrained that they lead us to misperceive a stimulus. T or F?
2. Perceptual learning seems to program the brain for sensitivity to important ______________ of the environment.
3. The Ames room is used to test for adaptation to inverted vision. T or F?
4. An important factor in adaptation to inverted vision is
   a. learning new categories *b.* active movement
   c. overcoming illusions *d.* the horizontal-vertical invariance
5. Size-distance relationships appear to underlie which two illusions? ______________ and ______________
6. An adaptation level represents a personal "medium point," or internal ______________ ______________.

Critical Thinking

7. What size object do you think you would have to hold at arm's length to cover up a full moon?

Answers: 1. T 2. features 3. F 4. b 5. moon illusion and Müller-Lyer illusion 6. frame of reference 7. The most popular answers range from a quarter to a softball. Actually, a pea held in the outstretched hand will cover a full moon (Kunkel, 1993). If you listed an object larger than a pea, be aware that perceptions, no matter how accurate they seem, may distort reality.

APPLICATIONS: *Perception and Objectivity—Believing Is Seeing*

Have you ever seen the sun set? You may think you have. Yet, in reality, we know that the sun does not "set." Instead, our viewing angle changes as the earth turns, until the sun is obscured by the horizon. Want to try the alternative? This evening, stand facing the west. With practice, you can learn to feel yourself being swept backward on the rotating surface of the earth as you watch an unmoving sun recede in the distance (Fuller, 1969).

Perceptual reconstruction A mental model of external events.

Weapon focus The tendency of crime victims to fix their attention on an attacker's weapon.

This radical shift in perspective illustrates the limitations of "objective" observation. As with most other perceptions, seeing a "sunset" is an active and creative **reconstruction** of events. As we have seen, perception reflects the needs, expectations, attitudes, values, and beliefs of the perceiver. In this light, the phrase "seeing is believing" must be modified. Clearly, we see what we believe, as well as believe what we see.

In some cases, subjective perception nurtures the personal vision valued in art, music, poetry, and scientific innovation. Often, though, it is a real liability.

Eyewitness In the courtroom, eyewitness testimony can be a key element in establishing guilt or innocence. The claim, "I saw it with my own eyes," carries a lot of weight with a jury. But to put it bluntly, eyewitness testimony is frequently wrong. Juries are most swayed by witnesses who are certain that their testimony is accurate. Yet, in fact, a person's confidence in his or her testimony has almost no bearing on its accuracy (Wells, 1993)! In addition, misleading questions about what a person saw can greatly decrease eyewitness accuracy *and* confidence (Smith & Ellsworth, 1987).

Psychologists interested in perception are gradually convincing lawyers, judges, and police officers of the fallibility of eyewitness testimony. Even so, thousands of people have been wrongfully convicted in the United States alone (Loftus, 1993). In one typical court case, a police officer testified that he saw the defendant shoot the victim as both stood in a doorway 120 feet away. Measurements made by a psychologist showed that at that distance, light from the dimly lit doorway was extremely weak—less than a fifth of that from a candle. To further show that identification was improbable, a juror stood in the doorway under identical lighting conditions. None of the other jurors could identify him. The defendant was acquitted (Buckhout, 1974).

Unfortunately, perception rarely provides an "instant replay" of events. Even in broad daylight, eyewitness testimony is untrustworthy. After a horrible DC-10 airliner crash in Chicago in 1979, 84 pilots who saw the accident were interviewed. Forty-two said the DC-10's landing gear was up, and 42 said it was down! As one investigator commented, the best witness may be a "kid under 12 years old who doesn't have his parents around." Adults, it seems, are easily swayed by their expectations.

Perceptions formed when a person is surprised, threatened, or under stress are especially prone to distortion. That's why witnesses to crimes so often disagree. As a dramatic demonstration of this problem, an assault was staged on a college campus in which a professor was attacked by an actor. Immediately after the event, 141 witnesses were questioned in detail. Their descriptions were then compared to a videotape made of the staged "crime." The total accuracy score for the group (on features such as appearance, age, weight, and height of the assailant) was only *25 percent* of the maximum possible (Buckhout, 1974).

Question: Wouldn't the victim of a crime remember more than a mere witness?

A revealing experiment found that eyewitness accuracy is virtually the same for witnessing a crime (seeing a pocket calculator stolen) as it is for being a victim (seeing one's own watch stolen) (Hosch & Cooper, 1982). Jurors who place more weight on the testimony of victims may be making a serious mistake. Also, it is worth repeating that witnesses who are confident in their testimony are no more likely to be accurate than those who have doubts (Smith, Kassin, & Ellsworth, 1989).

In many crimes, victims fall prey to the phenomenon of **weapon focus.** Understandably, victims often fix their entire attention on the knife, gun, or other weapon used by an attacker. In doing so, they fail to perceive details of appearance, dress, or other clues to identity (Steblay, 1992).

Additional factors affecting eyewitnesses are summarized in ● Table 5–2. (Inaccuracies in memory also affect eyewitness testimony; see Chapter 8 for more information.)

Implications How often are everyday perceptions as inaccurate or distorted as those of an emotional eyewitness? The answer we have been moving toward is, very frequently. Bearing this in mind may help you be more tolerant of the views of others and more cautious about your own objectivity. It may also encourage more frequent **reality testing** on your part.

Question: What do you mean by reality testing?

Reality Testing In any situation having an element of doubt or uncertainty, reality testing involves obtaining additional information to check your perceptions. Even simple designs like those in ■ Figure 5–33 are easily misperceived. One of the designs in the drawing is a continuous line; the other is not. Most people cannot see this difference spontaneously. Instead, they must carefully trace and compare the two designs as a check on pure perception (Julesz, 1975).

Psychologist Sidney Jourard once offered a more pertinent example of reality testing. One of Jourard's students believed her roommate was stealing from her. The student gradually became convinced of her roommate's guilt, but said nothing. As her distrust and anger grew, their relationship turned cold and distant. Finally, at Jourard's urging, she confronted her roommate. The roommate cleared herself immediately and expressed relief when the puzzling change in their relationship was explained (Jourard, 1974). With their friendship reestablished, the true culprit was soon caught. (The cleaning woman did it!)

If you have ever concluded that someone was angry, upset, or unfriendly without checking the accuracy of your perceptions, you have fallen into a subtle trap. Personal objectivity is an elusive quality, requiring frequent reality testing to maintain. At the very least, it pays to ask a person what he or she is feeling when you are in doubt. Undoubtedly, most of us could learn to be better "eyewitnesses" to daily events.

● Table 5–2 Factors Affecting the Accuracy of Eyewitness Perceptions

Sources of Error	Summary of Findings
1. Stress	Very high levels of stress impair the accuracy of eyewitness perceptions.
2. Weapon focus	The presence of a weapon impairs an eyewitness's ability to accurately identify the culprit's face.
3. Exposure time	The less time an eyewitness has to observe an event, the less accurately he or she will perceive and remember it.
4. Accuracy-confidence	An eyewitness's confidence is not a good predictor of his or her accuracy.
5. Cross-racial perceptions	Eyewitnesses are better at identifying members of their own race than they are at identifying people of other races.
6. Post-event information	Eyewitness testimony about an event often reflects not only what was actually seen but also information obtained later on.
7. Color perception	Judgments of color made under monochromatic light (such as an orange street light) are highly unreliable.
8. Wording of questions	An eyewitness's testimony about an event can be affected by how the questions put to that witness are worded.
9. Unconscious transference	Eyewitnesses sometimes identify as a culprit someone they have seen in another situation or context.
10. Trained observers	Police officers and other trained observers are no more accurate as eyewitnesses than the average person.
11. Time estimation	Eyewitnesses tend to overestimate the duration of events.
12. Attitudes, expectations	An eyewitness's perception and memory for an event may be affected by his or her attitudes and expectations.

(Adapted from Kassin, Ellsworth, & Smith, 1989)

■ **Fig. 5–33** *The limits of pure perception. Even simple designs are easily misperceived. The drawing on the left is a continuous line; the one on the right is not. Most people cannot see this difference without carefully tracing the lines. (Adapted from patterns devised by Marvin Minsky and Seymour Papert.)*

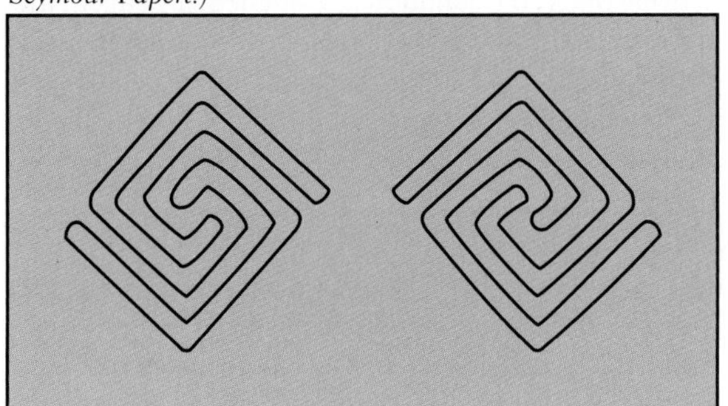

Reality testing Obtaining additional information to check on the accuracy of perceptions.

Question: Do some people perceive things more accurately than others?

Perceptual Awareness Humanistic psychologist Abraham Maslow (1969) believed that some people are unusually accurate in perceptions of themselves

Dishabituation A reversal of habituation.

and of others. Maslow characterized these people as especially alive, open, aware, and mentally healthy. He found that their perceptual styles were marked by immersion in the present, a lack of self-consciousness, freedom from selecting, criticizing, or evaluating, and a general "surrender" to experience. The kind of perception Maslow described is like that of a mother with her newborn infant, a child at Christmas, or two people in love.

Other researchers have tested Zen masters for habituation to repeated stimuli. The results indicate that Zen masters fail to show the expected habituation (Kasamatsu & Hirai, 1966). This finding lends some credibility to claims that Zen masters perceive a tree as vividly after seeing it 500 times as they did the first time.

Attention Whereas the average person has not reached perceptual restriction of the "if you've seen one tree, you've seen them all" variety, the fact remains that most of us tend to look at a tree and classify it into the perceptual category of "trees in general" without really appreciating the miracle standing before us. How then can we bring about a **dishabituation** of perception (without going through years of meditative discipline, as a Zen master does)? The deceptively simple answer is: Pay attention.

The following quote summarizes the importance of attention:

> One day a man of the people said to Zen Master Ikkyu: "Master, will you please write for me some maxims of the highest wisdom?"
>
> Ikkyu immediately took his brush and wrote the word "Attention."
>
> "Is that all?" asked the man. "Will you not add something more?"
>
> Ikkyu then wrote twice running: "Attention. Attention."
>
> "Well," remarked the man rather irritably, "I really don't see much depth or subtlety in what you have just written."
>
> Then Ikkyu wrote the same word three times running: "Attention. Attention. Attention." Half angered, the man demanded, "What does that word 'Attention' mean anyway?"
>
> And Ikkyu answered gently: "Attention means attention." (Kapleau, 1966)

To this we can add only one thought, provided by the words of poet William Blake: "If the doors of perception were cleansed, man would see everything as it is, infinite."

Becoming a Better "Eyewitness" to Life

Here's a summary of ideas from this chapter to help you maintain and enhance perceptual accuracy.

1. *Remember that perceptions are reconstructions of reality.* Learn to regularly question your own perceptions. Are they accurate? Could another interpretation fit the facts? What assumptions are you making? Could they be false? How might your assumptions be distorting your perceptions?
2. *Break perceptual habits and interrupt habituation.* Each day, try to do some activities in new ways. For example, take different routes when you travel to work or school. Do routines, such as brushing your teeth or combing your hair, with your non-preferred hand. Try to look at friends and family members as if they are persons you just met for the first time.
3. *Shift adaptation levels and broaden frames of reference by seeking out-of-the-ordinary experiences.* The possibilities here range from trying foods you don't normally eat, to reading opinions very different from your own. Experiences ranging from a quiet walk in the woods to a trip to an amusement park may be perceptually refreshing.
4. *Beware of perceptual sets.* Anytime you pigeonhole people, objects, or events, there is a danger that your perceptions will be distorted by expectations or pre-existing categories. Be especially wary of labels and stereotypes. Try to see people as individuals and events as unique, one-time occurrences.
5. *Be aware of the ways in which motives and emotions influence perceptions.* It is difficult to avoid being swayed by your own interests, needs, desires, and emotions. But be aware of this trap and actively try to see the world through the eyes of others. Taking the other person's perspective is especially valuable in disputes or arguments. Ask yourself, "How does this look to her or him?"
6. *Make a habit of engaging in reality testing.* Actively look for additional evidence to check the accuracy of your perceptions. Ask questions, seek clarifications, and find alternate channels of information. Remember that perception is not automatically accurate. You could be wrong—we all are frequently.
7. *Pay attention.* Make a conscious effort to pay attention to other people and your surroundings. Don't drift through life in a haze. Listen to others with full concentration. Watch their facial expressions. Make eye contact. Try to get in the habit of approaching perception like you are going to have to testify later about what you saw and heard.

LEARNING CHECK

1. Most perceptions can be described as active reconstructions of external reality. T or F?
2. Inaccuracies in eyewitness perceptions obviously occur in "real life," but they cannot be reproduced in psychology experiments. T or F?
3. Accuracy scores for facts provided by witnesses to staged crimes may be as low as 25 percent correct. T or F?
4. Victims of crimes are more accurate eyewitnesses than are impartial observers. T or F?
5. *Reality testing* is another term for dishabituation. T or F?
6. Return for a moment to the incident described in the Chapter Preview. What perceptual factors were involved in the first version of the "murder"? How did the girl affect what was seen? ***Critical Thinking***

Answers: 1. T 2. F 3. T 4. F 5. F 6. The girl's misperception, communicated so forcefully to other eyewitnesses, created a powerful expectancy that influenced what they perceived. Also, the stressful or emotional nature of the incident encouraged misperception.

EXPLORATION

Extrasensory Perception—Do You Believe in Magic?

In a quiet laboratory, Uri Geller, a self-proclaimed "psychic," has agreed to demonstrate his claimed abilities to communicate by mental telepathy, to detect hidden objects, and to predict future events. In the course of testing, Geller was supposedly able to select from a row of 10 film canisters, the one that contained an object, correctly guess the number that would come up on a die shaken in a closed box 8 out of 8 times, and reproduce drawings sealed in opaque envelopes.

Question: Was Geller cheating, or was he using some ability beyond normal perception?

There is now little doubt that Geller was cheating (Randi, 1980). But how? The answer lies in a discussion of **extrasensory perception (ESP)**—the purported ability to perceive events in ways that cannot be explained by accepted perceptual principles.

Parapsychology

Parapsychology is the study of ESP and other **psi phenomena** (*psi* is pronounced like *sigh*), or events that seem to defy accepted scientific laws. Parapsychologists seek answers to the questions raised by three basic forms that ESP could take. These are:

1. **Clairvoyance.** The ability to perceive events or gain information in ways that appear unaffected by distance or normal physical barriers.
2. **Telepathy.** Extrasensory perception of another person's thoughts, or more simply, an ability to read someone else's mind.
3. **Precognition.** The ability to perceive or accurately predict future events. Precognition may take the form of *prophetic dreams* that foretell the future.

While we are at it, we might as well toss in another purported psi ability:

4. **Psychokinesis.** The ability to exert influence over inanimate objects by willpower ("mind over matter"). (Psychokinesis cannot be classed as a type of perception, extrasensory or otherwise, but it is frequently studied by parapsychologists.)

Question: Have parapsychologists confirmed the existence of ESP and other psi abilities?

American psychologists as a group are highly skeptical about psi abilities. But the general public remains split on the issue. A national poll conducted in 1991 found that 49 percent of all American adults believe in ESP (Gallup & Newport, 1991). If

Extrasensory perception The purported ability to perceive events in ways that cannot be explained by known sensory capacities.

Parapsychology The study of extranormal psychological events, such as extrasensory perception.

Psi phenomena Events that seem to lie outside the realm of accepted scientific laws.

Clairvoyance The purported ability to perceive events at a distance or through physical barriers.

Telepathy The purported ability to directly know another person's thoughts.

Precognition The purported ability to accurately predict future events.

Psychokinesis The purported ability to mentally alter or influence objects or events.

you doubt ESP, then you should know that some experiments seem to support its existence. If you are among those who believe in ESP, then you should know why the scientific community doubts many of these experiments!

Coincidence Anyone who has ever had an apparent clairvoyant or telepathic experience may find it hard to question the existence of ESP. Yet, the difficulty of excluding *coincidence* makes natural ESP occurrences less conclusive than they might seem. For example, consider a typical psychic experience. During the middle of the night, a woman away for a weekend visit suddenly had a strong impulse to return home. When she arrived she found the house on fire with her husband asleep inside (Rhine, 1953). An experience like this is striking, but it does not confirm the existence of ESP. If, by coincidence, a hunch turns out to be correct, it may be *reinterpreted* as a premonition or case of clairvoyance (Marks & Kammann, 1979). If it is not confirmed, it will simply be forgotten. Most people don't realize it, but such coincidences occur so often that we should *expect* them, not consider them strange or mysterious (Alcock, 1990). There is evidence that believers in ESP are more prone to falsely see cause-and-effect links in everyday coincidences (Brugger, Landis, & Regard, 1990).

The formal study of psi events owes much to the late J. B. Rhine. Rhine established the first parapsychological laboratory at Duke University and spent the rest of his life trying to document ESP. To avoid problems of coincidence and after-the-fact interpretation of "natural" ESP events, Rhine tried to study ESP more objectively. Many of his experiments made use of the **Zener cards** (■ Fig. 5–34). In a typical clairvoyance test, subjects tried to guess the symbols on the cards as they were turned up from a shuffled deck. Pure guessing in this test will produce an average score of 5 "hits" out of 25 cards.

Unfortunately, some of Rhine's most dramatic early experiments used badly printed Zener cards that allowed the symbols to show faintly on the back. It is also very easy to cheat, by marking cards with

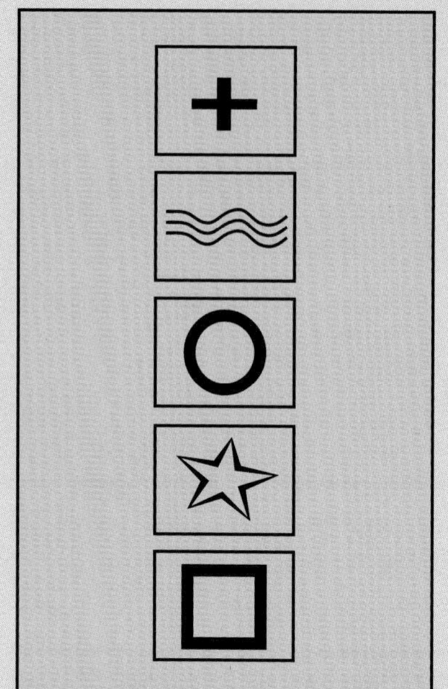

■ **Fig. 5–34** *ESP cards used by J. B. Rhine, an early experimenter in parapsychology.*

a fingernail or by noting marks on the cards caused by normal use. Even if this were not the case, there is evidence that early experimenters sometimes unconsciously gave subjects cues about the cards with their eyes, facial gestures, or lip movements. In short, none of the early studies in parapsychology were done in a way that eliminated the possibility of fraud or "leakage" of helpful information (Alcock, 1990).

Modern parapsychologists are now well aware of the need for double-blind experiments, maximum security and accuracy in record keeping, meticulous control, and repeatability of experiments (Rhine, 1974a). In the last 10 years, hundreds of experiments have been reported in parapsychological journals. Many of them seem to support the existence of psi abilities.

Question: Then why do most psychologists remain skeptical about psi abilities?

For one thing, fraud continues to plague the field. Walter J. Levy, who was former director of Rhine's laboratory, was caught faking records. So have some others who got positive results. Even honest scientists have been fooled by various frauds and cheats, so there is reason to remain skeptical and on guard. The greatest danger may lie in errors by sincere, but self-deceiving, investigators (Hyman, 1989). As one critic put it, positive ESP results usually mean "Error Some Place" (Marks, 1990). The more closely psi experiments are examined, the more likely it is that claimed successes will evaporate (Alcock, 1990; Hyman, 1989).

Statistics and Chance A major criticism of psi research has to do with inconsistency. For every study with positive results, there are others that fail (Hansel, 1980). It is rare—in fact, almost unheard of—for a subject to maintain psi ability over any sustained period of time (Jahn, 1982; Schmeidler, 1977). ESP researchers consider this "decline effect" an indication that parapsychological skills are very fragile and unpredictable (Rhine, 1977). But critics argue that subjects who only temporarily score above chance have just received credit for a **run of luck,** or statistically unusual outcome. When the run is over, it is not fair to assume that ESP is temporarily gone. We must count *all* attempts.

To understand the run-of-luck criticism, consider an example. Say that you flip a coin 100 times and record the results. You then flip another coin 100 times, again recording the results. The two lists are compared. For any 10 pairs of flips, we would expect heads or tails to match 5 times. Let's say that you go through the list and find a set of 10 pairs where 9 out of 10 matched. This is far above chance expectation. But does it mean that the first coin "knew" what was going to come up on the second coin? The idea is obviously silly.

Now, what if a person guesses 100 times what will come up on a coin. Again, we might find a set of 10 guesses that matches the results of flipping the coin. Does this mean that the person, for a time, had precognition—then lost it? Parapsychologists tend to believe the answer is yes. Skeptics assume that nothing more than random matching occurred, as in the two-coin example.

EXPLORATION

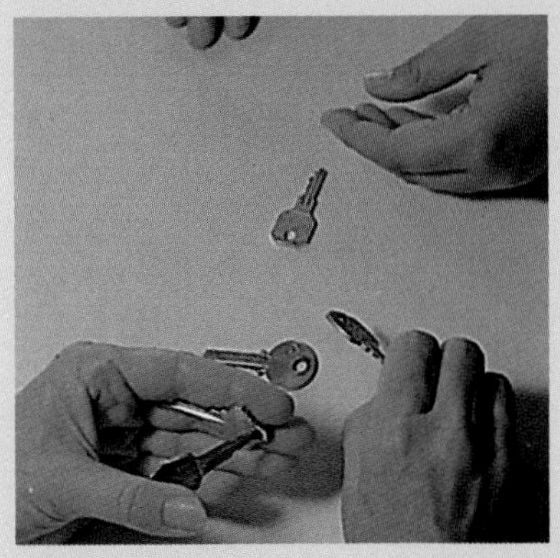
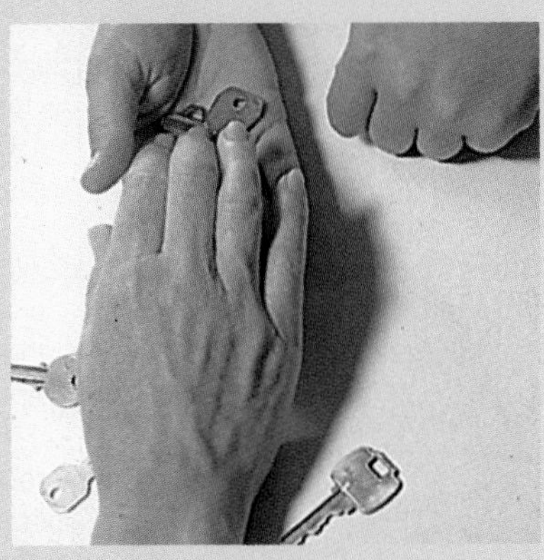

■ Fig. 5–35 *Fake psychokinesis. (a) The performer shows an observer several straight keys. While doing so, he bends one of the keys by placing its tip in the slot of another key. Normally, this is done out of sight, behind the "psychic's" hand. It is clearly shown here so you can see how the deception occurs. (b) Next, the "psychic" places the two keys in the observer's hand and closes it. By skillful manipulation, the observer has been kept from seeing the bent key. The performer then "concentrates" on the keys to "bend them with psychic energy." (c) The bent key is revealed to the observer. "Miracle" accomplished! (Adapted from Randi, 1983.)*

Research Methods

Unfortunately, many of the most spectacular findings in parapsychology simply cannot be **replicated** (repeated) (Hyman, 1989). More importantly, improved research methods usually result in fewer positive results. Proponents of parapsychology feel that they can point to experiments that meet all possible criticisms. But in virtually every case, the results cannot be repeated by doubters.

Believers in ESP, such as ex-astronaut Edgar Mitchell, claim that other factors explain negative results: "The scientist has to recognize that his own mental processes may influence the phenomenon he's observing. If he's really a total skeptic, the scientist may well turn off the psychic subject." This may sound convincing, but skeptics consider it unfair. With Mitchell's argument in effect, anyone attempting an objective experiment can only get two results: He or she may find evidence of ESP or be accused of having suppressed it. This makes it impossible to disprove ESP to believers, even if it truly does not exist.

Reinterpretation is also a problem in psi experiments. For example, Mitchell claimed he did a successful telepathy experiment from space. Yet news accounts never mentioned that on some trials Mitchell's "receivers" scored above chance, while on others they scored *below* chance. The second outcome, Mitchell decided, was also a "success" because it represented intentional "psi missing." But, as skeptics have noted, if both high scores and low scores count as successes, how can you lose?

Stage ESP

Skeptics and serious researchers in ESP both agree on one point. If psychic phenomena do occur, they cannot be controlled well enough to be used by entertainers. **Stage ESP** (like stage magic) is based on a combination of sleight of hand, deception, and patented gadgets (■Fig. 5–35). A case in point is Uri Geller, a former nightclub magician who "astounded" audiences—and some scientists—from coast to coast with apparent telepathy, psychokinesis, and precognition.

Geller's performance on tests was described earlier. Not mentioned is what University of Oregon professor Ray Hyman calls the "incredible sloppiness" of these tests. One example is Geller's reproductions of sealed drawings. These, it turns out, were done in a room next to the one where the drawings were made. Original reports of Geller's alleged "ability" failed to mention that there was a hole in the wall between the two rooms, through which Geller might have heard discussions of the pictures being drawn. Also unreported was the fact that Geller's friend Shipi Stang was present at every test. Geller's manager has since testified that Stang frequently acted as Geller's accomplice in trickery (Alcock, 1990). Is it a coincidence that when a picture of a rocket ship was drawn, Stang hummed the theme music from the motion picture *2001: A Space Odyssey*? A similar lack of control pervaded every other test. In the "die in the box" tests, for instance, Geller was allowed to hold the box, shake it, and have the honor of opening it (Randi, 1980; Wilhelm, 1976). Why weren't such pertinent details reported?

Sensational and uncritical reporting of apparent paranormal events is widespread. Hundreds of books, articles, and television programs are produced each year by people who have become wealthy promoting unsupported claims. If a person did have psychic powers, he or she would not have to make a living by entertaining, giving demonstrations, or making

Zener cards A deck of 25 cards bearing various symbols and used in parapsychological research.

Run of luck A statistically unusual outcome (as in getting 5 heads in a row when flipping a coin) that could still occur by chance alone.

Replicate To reproduce or repeat.

Stage ESP The simulation of ESP for the purpose of entertainment.

EXPLORATION

personal appearances. A quick trip to the gaming tables of Las Vegas would allow the person to retire for life.

Conclusion After close to 130 years of investigation, it is still impossible to say conclusively whether psi events occur. As we have seen, a close look at psi experiments often reveals serious problems of evidence, procedure, and scientific rigor (Alcock, 1990; Hyman, 1989; Marks & Kammann, 1979; Swets et al., 1988). It is also interesting to note that a survey of leading parapsychologists and skeptics found that almost all in both groups said their belief in psi had decreased (Blackmore, 1989). Yet, being a skeptic does not mean a person is against something. It means that you are unconvinced. The purpose of this discussion, then, has been to counter the *uncritical* acceptance of psi events that is rampant in the media.

Question: What would it take to scientifically demonstrate the existence of ESP?

Quite simply, a set of instructions that would allow any competent, unbiased observer to produce a psi event under standardized conditions (Moss & Butler, 1978). Undoubtedly, some intrepid researchers will continue their attempts to supply just that. Others remain skeptics, and some consider 130 years of inconclusive efforts reason enough to abandon the concept of ESP (Marks, 1990; Swets et al., 1988). At the least, it seems essential to be carefully skeptical of evidence reported in the popular press or by researchers who are uncritical "true believers." (But then, you already knew I was going to say that, didn't you!)

Learning Check

1. Four purported psi events investigated by parapsychologists are clairvoyance, telepathy, precognition, and ____________________.
2. The ____________ cards were used by J. B. Rhine in early tests of ESP.
3. Natural, or "real life," occurrences are regarded as the best evidence for the existence of ESP. T or F?
4. Skeptics attribute positive results in psi experiments to statistical runs of luck. T or F?
5. Replication rates are very high for ESP experiments. T or F?

Critical Thinking

6. A "psychic" on television offers to fix broken watches for viewers. Moments later, dozens of viewers call the station to say that their watches miraculously started running again. What have they overlooked?

Answers:

1. psychokinesis 2. Zener 3. F 4. T 5. F 6. When psychologists handled watches awaiting repair at a store, 57 percent began running again, with no help from a "psychic." Believing the "psychic's" claim also overlooks the impact of big numbers: If the show reached a large audience, at least a few "broken" watches would start working merely by chance.

Chapter Summary

■ ***What are perceptual constancies, and what is their role in perception?***

- **Perception** is the process of assembling sensations into a usable mental representation of the world.
- In vision, the image projected on the retina is constantly changing, but the external world appears stable and undistorted because of **size, shape,** and **brightness constancy.**

■ ***What basic principles do we use to group sensations into meaningful patterns?***

- The most basic organization of sensations is a division into **figure and ground** (object and background).
- A number of factors contribute to the organization of sensations. These are **nearness, similarity, continuity, closure, contiguity, common region,** and combinations of the preceding. Basic elements of line drawings appear to be universally recognized.
- A perceptual organization may be thought of as a **hypothesis** held until evidence contradicts it. Perceptual organization shifts for **ambiguous stimuli. Impossible figures** resist stable organization altogether.

■ ***How is it possible to see depth and judge distance?***

- **Depth perception** (the ability to perceive three-dimensional space and judge distances) is present in basic form soon after birth (as shown by testing with the **visual cliff** and other methods).

- Depth perception depends on the **muscular cues** of **accommodation** (bending of the lens) and **convergence** (inward movement of the eyes). **Stereoscopic vision** is created mainly by **retinal disparity** and the resulting overlap and **mismatch** of visual sensations.
- A number of **pictorial cues** also underlie depth perception. These are **linear perspective, relative size, light and shadow, overlap, texture gradients, aerial haze,** and **relative motion** (motion parallax). All are monocular depth cues (only one eye is needed to make use of them).
- The **moon illusion** is at least partially explained by the **apparent distance hypothesis,** which emphasizes the greater number of depth cues present when the moon is on the horizon. Changes in accommodation also contribute to the moon illusion.

■ ***What effect does learning have on perception?***

- Organizing and interpreting sensations is greatly influenced by **perceptual habits.** Studies of **inverted vision** show that even the most basic organization is subject to a degree of change. **Active movement** speeds adaptation to a new perceptual environment.
- Perceptual judgments are not made in a vacuum. They are almost always related to **context,** or to an internal **frame of reference** called the **adaptation level.**
- One of the most familiar of all illusions, the **Müller-Lyer illusion,** seems to be related to perceptual learning, linear perspective, **size-distance invariance** relationships, and mislocating the endpoints of the figure.

■ ***How is perception altered by attention, motives, values, and expectations?***

- **Attention** is **selective,** and it may be **divided** among various activities. Attention is closely related to **stimulus intensity, repetition, contrast, change,** and **incongruity.**
- Attention is accompanied by an **orientation response.** When a stimulus is repeated without change, the orientation response undergoes **habituation.**
- Personal **motives** and **values** often alter perceptions by changing the evaluation of what is seen or by altering attention to specific details.
- Perceptions may be based on **top-down** or **bottom-up processing** of information.
- Attention, prior experience, suggestion, and motives combine in various ways to create **perceptual sets,** or expectancies. These prepare a person to perceive or misperceive in a particular way.

■ ***How reliable are eyewitness reports?***

- Perception is an active **reconstruction** of events. This is one reason why **eyewitness testimony** is surprisingly unreliable. Eyewitness accuracy is further damaged by **weapon focus,** and a number of similar factors.
- Perceptual accuracy is enhanced by **reality testing, dishabituation,** and conscious efforts to **pay attention.** It is also valuable to break perceptual habits, to broaden frames of reference, to beware of perceptual sets, and to be aware of the ways in which motives and emotions influence perceptions.

■ ***Is extrasensory perception possible?***

- **Parapsychology** is the study of purported **psi phenomena,** including **clairvoyance, telepathy, precognition,** and **psychokinesis.**
- Research in parapsychology remains controversial owing to a variety of problems and shortcomings. The bulk of the evidence to date is against the existence of ESP. **Stage ESP** is based on deception and tricks.

Questions for Discussion

1. Which of the perceptual "constancies" or "organizational tendencies" would be most difficult to live without? Why?
2. Do you think your perceptions of an argument or fight with a friend, parent, spouse, or lover are accurate? What perceptual factors might affect your viewpoint?
3. Bicyclists and motorcyclists often complain that automobile drivers act as if cyclists are invisible. What perceptual factors might cause drivers to "look right at" cyclists without seeing them?
4. Which occupations would be dangerous for a person lacking depth perception?
5. A professional basketball player is at the free-throw line for the last shot in a tied championship game. What depth cues are available to him? A professional golfer is making the last putt for a $10,000 prize; what depth cues is she using? A pilot is landing at an unfamiliar airport; what cues are available to her? You are looking through a microscope with one eye; what depth cues can you use?

6. Describe a situation you have misperceived. What influenced your perceptions?
7. What role might habituation play in industrial accidents (especially on production lines) and in driving on arrow-straight superhighways? What changes would you make in work procedures or highway design to combat habituation?
8. In view of the Chapter Preview and Applications, how dependable do you think eyewitness testimony is in a courtroom? What factors other than accuracy of original perceptions might contribute to inaccuracies in testimony?
9. Serious family, national, cultural, and international conflicts develop because of differing perceptions. Describe a conflict you have observed and tell how perceptual processes contributed to the conflict.
10. If you believe that ESP occurs, what would it take to convince you that it does not? If you do not believe that ESP occurs, what would it take to convince you that it does?

Chapter 6

States of Consciousness

CHAPTER PREVIEW

Living Nightmares

January 1959, in New York's Times Square: To raise money for charity, disc jockey Peter Tripp has agreed to go without sleep for 200 hours. All too soon Tripp's fight to stay awake turns brutal. After 100 hours, he begins to have visual hallucinations: He sees cobwebs in his shoes and watches in terror as a tweed coat becomes a suit of "furry worms." When Tripp goes to a hotel to change clothes, a dresser drawer seems to burst into flames.

After 170 hours, Tripp's agony becomes almost unbearable. He struggles with the simplest thought, reasoning, and memory problems. His brain-wave patterns look like those of sleep, and he is no longer sure who he is. By the end of 200 hours, Tripp is unable to distinguish between his waking nightmares, hallucination, and reality (Luce, 1965).

The Womb Tank *We shift now to a scene far removed from Peter Tripp's ordeal. Some years ago, physician John Lilly pioneered the use of an unusual* sensory deprivation *environment. Subjects in Lilly's experiments wore darkened goggles and floated naked in a tank of body-temperature water (Lilly, 1972). As they drifted weightlessly in this "womb-like" environment, subjects were cut off from smell, touch, vision, hearing, and taste sensations.*

IN THIS CHAPTER

Question: What effect does sensory deprivation have?

Under such conditions, subjects often lose track of time and find it hard to concentrate. Some also undergo strange alterations in consciousness. For example, one subject in another experiment screamed in panic, "There is an animal having a long slender body with many legs. It's on the screen, crawling in back of me!" (Heron, 1957).

As you can see, both sleep loss and sensory deprivation have a major impact on consciousness. *In the discussion of consciousness that follows, we will begin with the familiar realms of sleep and dreaming and then move to points beyond.*

Survey Questions

- What is an altered state of consciousness?
- What are the effects of sleep loss or changes in sleep patterns?
- Are there different stages of sleep?
- How does dream sleep differ from dreamless sleep?
- What are the causes of sleep disorders and unusual sleep events?
- Can insomnia be prevented?
- Do dreams have meaning?
- How is hypnosis done, and what are its limitations?
- How does sensory deprivation affect consciousness?
- What are the effects of the more commonly used psychoactive drugs?
- How can dreams be used to promote personal understanding?
- Why is drug abuse so widespread?

Consciousness Mental awareness of sensations, perceptions, memories, and feelings.

Waking consciousness A state of normal, alert awareness.

Altered state of consciousness A condition of awareness distinctly different in quality or pattern from waking consciousness.

States of Consciousness—The Many Faces of Awareness

To be conscious means to be aware. **Consciousness** consists of all the sensations, perceptions, memories, and feelings that you are aware of at any given instant. As William James noted, consciousness is an ever-changing "stream," or flow of awareness. We spend most of our lives in ordinary **waking consciousness,** which is organized, meaningful, and clear. Waking consciousness is perceived as real, and it is marked by a familiar sense of time and place (Marsh, 1977). But as James also noted, states of consciousness related to fatigue, delirium, hypnosis, drugs, and ecstasy differ markedly from "normal" awareness. All people experience at least some altered states of awareness, such as sleep, dreaming, and daydreaming. In everyday life, changes in consciousness may accompany long-distance running, listening to music, making love, or other circumstances.

Question: *It's clear that there are many altered states of consciousness. How are they distinguished from normal awareness?*

Altered States of Consciousness

An **altered state of consciousness** (ASC) is a distinct change in the *quality* and *pattern* of mental activity. Typically there are shifts in perceptions, emotions, memory, time sense, thinking, feelings of self-control, and suggestibility (Tart, 1975, 1986). Definitions aside, most people know when they have experienced an ASC.

Question: *Are there other causes of ASCs?*

The list of causes is nearly endless. In addition to those already mentioned, we could add: sensory overload (for example, a light show, Mardi Gras crowd, or mosh pit), monotonous stimulation (meditation and "highway hypnotism" on long drives are good examples), unusual physical conditions (high fever, hyperventilation, dehydration, sleep loss, near-death experiences), sensory deprivation, and many other possibilities. As Highlight 6–1 points out, altered states of awareness may have important cultural significance.

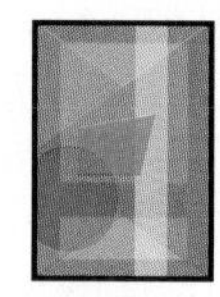

HIGHLIGHT 6–1

Cultural Diversity

States of Consciousness in Other Cultures

People throughout history have sought ways to alter consciousness. A dramatic example is the sweat lodge ritual of the Sioux Indians. During the ritual, several men sit in total darkness inside a small chamber heated by a bed of coals. Cedar smoke, bursts of steam, and the aroma of sage fill the air. The men chant rhythmically. The heat builds. At last they can stand it no more. The door is thrown open. Cooling night breezes rush in. And then? The cycle begins again—often to be repeated 4 or 5 times more. Among the Sioux this ritual is viewed as a cleansing of mind and body. When it is especially intense, it brings altered awareness and personal revelation.

Some altered states are sought primarily for pleasure, as is often true of drug intoxication. Yet as the Sioux example illustrates, many cultures regard changes in consciousness as pathways to enlightenment. Almost every known religion has accepted at least some altered states as a source of mystical experience. Accepted avenues have ranged from fasting, meditation, prayer, isolation, sleep loss, whirling, and chanting, to self-inflicted pain and psychedelic substances. In many cultures, the special powers attributed to medicine men, shamans, or healers are believed to come from an ability to enter a trance and communicate with spirits. Often, rituals that help form tribal bonds among community members are accentuated by altered states of consciousness (■ Fig. 6–1).

In short, all cultures recognize and accept some alterations of consciousness. However, the meanings given various states vary greatly—from signs of "madness" and "possession" by spirits, to life-enhancing breakthroughs. Thus, cultural conditioning greatly affects what altered states a person recognizes, seeks, considers normal, and attains (Ward, 1989).

■ **Fig. 6–1** *In many cultures, rituals of healing, prayer, purification, or personal transformation are accompanied by altered states of consciousness.*

In this chapter we will focus on sleep, dreaming, hypnosis, stimulus deprivation, and the effects of drugs (psychoactive chemicals). To get right to the questions raised by the Chapter Preview, let's begin with the most familiar altered states of consciousness: sleep and dreaming.

Sleep—A Nice Place to Visit

Each of us will spend some 25 years of life in a strange state of semi-consciousness called sleep. Contrary to common belief, humans are not totally unresponsive during sleep. Studies show that you are more likely to awaken if your own name is spoken, instead of another (Webb, 1978). Likewise, a sleeping mother may ignore a jet thundering overhead, but wake at the slightest whimper of her child. Some people can even do simple tasks while asleep. In one experiment, subjects learned to avoid an electric shock by touching a switch each time a tone sounded. Eventually, they could do it without waking. (This is much like the basic survival skill of turning off your alarm clock without waking.) Of course, sleep does impose limitations. There is no evidence, for instance, that a person can learn math, a foreign language, or other complex skills while asleep—especially when the snooze takes place in class (Wood et al., 1992).

Because of its many contradictions, sleep has always aroused curiosity. What do we know about this daily retreat from the world?

Biological rhythm Any cycle of biological activity, such as sleep and waking cycles or changes in body temperature.

Microsleep A brief shift to the brain-wave patterns of sleep.

The Need for Sleep

Question: How strong is the need for sleep?

Sleep expert Wilse Webb (1975) calls sleep a "gentle tyrant." Webb considers sleep an **innate biological rhythm** that can never be entirely sidestepped. But if flexibility is needed, sleep will give way temporarily, especially at times of great danger. As one comic put it, "The lion and the lamb shall lie down together, but the lamb will not be very sleepy." You could choose, then, to stay awake for an extended period. But there are limits. A rare disease that prevents its victims from sleeping always ends the same way: The patient falls into a stupor, followed by coma, followed by death (Oliwenstein, 1993).

In one set of experiments, animals were placed on treadmills over a pool of water to minimize sleep. Even so, sleep won out. The animals soon began to drift into repeated microsleeps (Goleman, 1982). A **microsleep** is a brief shift in brain activity to patterns

Sleep deprivation Being deprived of desired or needed amounts of sleep.

Sleep-deprivation psychosis A major disruption of mental and emotional functioning brought about sleep loss.

normally recorded during sleep. Microsleeps also occur in humans: When you drive, it is well worth remembering that a microsleep can lead to a macro-accident. Even a driver whose eyes are open can be asleep for a few seconds.

Question: How long could a person go without sleep?

Sleep Deprivation With few exceptions, 4 days or more without sleep becomes hell for anyone, but longer sleepless periods are possible. The world record for staying awake is held by Randy Gardner—who at age 17 went 268 hours (11 days) without sleep. Surprisingly, Randy needed only 14 hours of sleep to recover (Dement, 1972). It is usually not necessary to completely replace lost sleep. As Randy found, most symptoms of sleep loss are reversed by a single night's rest.

What are the costs of sleep loss? Age and personality make a big difference. Randy Gardner remained clear-headed to the end of his vigil, whereas Peter Tripp's behavior became quite bizarre. In general, there is little impairment on complex mental tasks after 2 or 3 days without sleep. But most people do decline in their ability to pay attention, remain vigilant, and follow simple routine (Mikulincer, 1989).

As you may know, sleep loss doesn't have to be total to take a toll. For example, players in a marathon, week-long tennis match averaged about 3 hours of sleep per night. After the match, the players' scores declined on tests of memory and perceptual-motor coordination (Edinger et al., 1990). (Maybe they kept playing because neither could remember who was ahead?)

If you were mildly deprived of sleep you would probably be able to rouse yourself for more complex or challenging tasks. What usually suffers most is low-level, boring, self-motivated tasks. As Wilse Webb says, "It's not your thinking or memory that goes, it's your will to continue; you would prefer to be asleep" (Goleman, 1982). For a driver, pilot, or machine operator, this may be enough to spell disaster.

Greater sleep loss sometimes causes a temporary **sleep-deprivation psychosis** like Peter Tripp suffered. Confusion and disorientation, delusions (false or distorted beliefs), and hallucinations are typical signs of this reaction. Hallucinations may be visual, like Tripp's "coat of furry worms," or tactile, such as feeling cobwebs on the face. Fortunately, such "crazy" behavior is less common than once thought. Hallucinations and delusions are rarely evident before 60 hours of continuous wakefulness. The most common reactions to extended sleep loss are inattention, staring, trembling hands, drooping eyelids, increased pain sensitivity, and a reduced sense of well-being (Naitoh et al., 1989; Webb, 1978).

Calvin and Hobbes by Bill Watterson

Sleep Patterns

Question: Sleep was described as an innate biological rhythm. What does that mean?

Rhythms of sleep and waking are so steady that they continue for many days, even when clocks and light-dark cycles are removed. However, under such conditions, humans eventually shift to a sleep-waking cycle that averages 25 *hours*, not 24 (Sulzman, 1983). This finding suggests that external time markers, especially light and dark, help tie our sleep rhythms to a normal 24-hour day (■Fig. 6–2). Otherwise, many of us would drift into our own unusual sleep cycles.

Question: What is the normal range of sleep?

According to medical records there is a man in England who gets by on only 15 minutes to an hour of sleep each night—and feels perfectly fine. However, this is quite rare. Only 8 percent of the population are **short sleepers,** averaging 5 hours of sleep or less per

■ **Fig. 6–2** *Sleep rhythms. Bars show periods of sleep during the fourth, fifth, and sixth weeks of an experiment with a human subject. During unscheduled periods, the subject was allowed to select times of sleep and lighting. The result was a sleep rhythm of about 25 hours. Notice how this free-running rhythm began to advance around the clock. When periods of darkness were scheduled (colored area), the rhythm quickly resynchronized with 24-hour days. (Adapted from Czeilser, 1981.)*

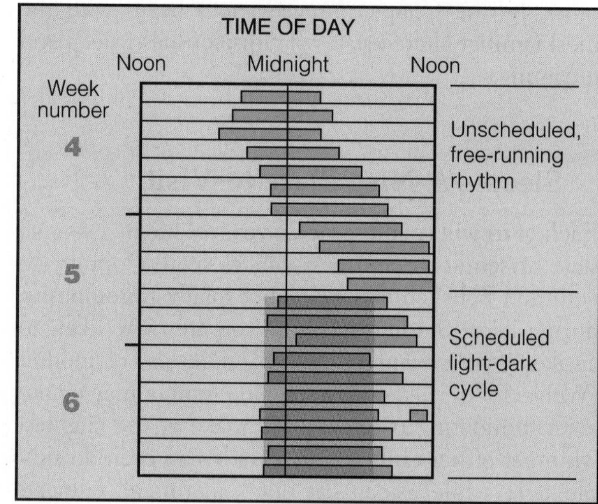

night. On the other end of the scale, **long sleepers** tend to be people who worry a lot during the day (McCann & Stewin, 1988). The majority of people sleep on a familiar 7- to 8-hour-per-night schedule. It is quite normal, however, to sleep as little as 5 hours per night or as much as 11. Urging everyone to sleep 8 hours would be like advising everyone to wear medium-size shoes.

Question: Do elderly people need more sleep?

They may need it, but they seldom get it. As people age they usually sleep less. People over the age of 50 average only 6 hours of sleep a night. In contrast, infants spend up to 20 hours a day sleeping, usually in 2- to 4-hour cycles. As they mature, most children go through a "nap" stage and eventually settle into a steady cycle of sleeping once a day (■ Fig. 6–3). Some people, of course, maintain the afternoon "siesta" as an adult pattern. Perhaps we all should. Experts now regard midafternoon sleepiness as a natural part of the sleep cycle. There appears to be a strong biological readiness to fall asleep during the afternoon. Brief, well-timed naps, therefore, may be the key to maintaining alertness in people like truck drivers and hospital interns who often must fight drowsiness (Goleman, 1989).

It is very tempting to try to reduce sleep time. However, people on *shortened* cycles—for example, 3 hours of sleep to 6 hours awake—often can't get to sleep when the cycle calls for it (Webb, 1978). The underlying sleep rhythm simply won't cooperate. This is why astronauts continue to sleep on their normal earth schedule while in space. Adapting to *longer* than normal days is more promising. Such days can be tailored to match natural **sleep patterns,** which have a ratio of *2 to 1* between time awake and time asleep. One study showed that 28-hour "days" work for some people. Unfortunately, subjects did poorly on longer 38-hour cycles (24 hours awake and 12 hours asleep) (Webb, 1978). Most people couldn't use the entire 12-hour sleep period, so they repeatedly lost sleep. As with sleep needs, we see again that sleep is a "gentle tyrant." Sleep patterns may be bent and stretched, but they rarely yield entirely to human whims (Akerstedt et al., 1993).

Stages of Sleep—The Nightly Roller-Coaster Ride

Question: What causes sleep?

Early sleep experts thought that some substance related to fatigue must accumulate in the bloodstream and cause sleep. But studies of Siamese twins (individuals whose bodies are joined at birth) show that this is false. One twin can frequently be observed sleeping while the second is awake (■ Fig. 6–4). During waking hours, a sleep-promoting chemical collects in the brain and spinal cord, *not* in the blood. If this substance is extracted from one animal and injected into another, the second animal will fall asleep (Pappenheimer, 1976). Notice, however, that this explanation for sleep is incomplete. For example, how do we account for the well-rested student who must fight to stay awake during a boring lecture?

Whether you are awake or asleep depends on the *balance* between opposed sleep and waking systems in the brain. One consists of circuits and transmitter chemicals that promote sleep. The second is a network

Sleep patterns The order and timing of daily sleep and waking periods.

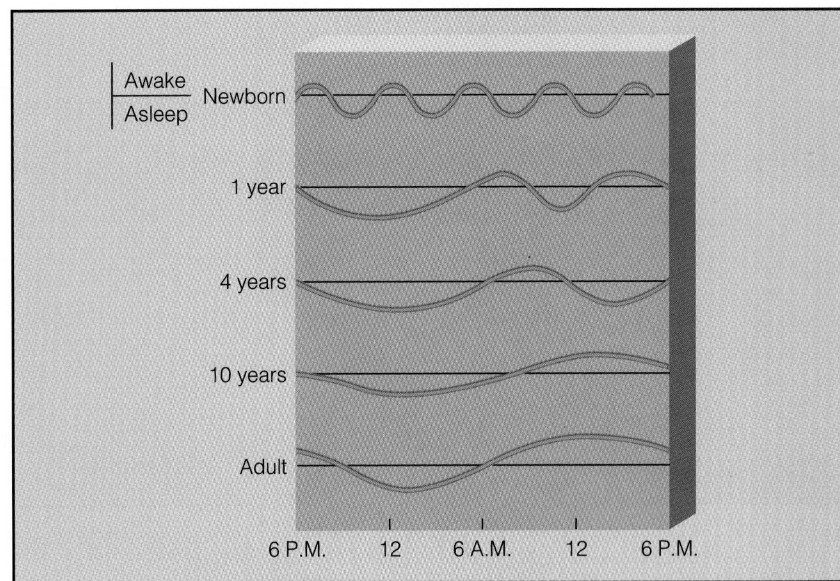

■ **Fig. 6–3** *Development of sleep patterns. Short cycles of sleep and waking gradually become the night-day cycle of an adult. While most adults don't take naps, midafternoon sleepiness is a natural part of the sleep cycle. (After Williams, 1964.)*

■ **Fig. 6–4** *These Siamese twins share the same blood supply, yet one sleeps while the other is awake. (Photo by Yale Joel, Life Magazine. © 1954 Time, Inc.)*

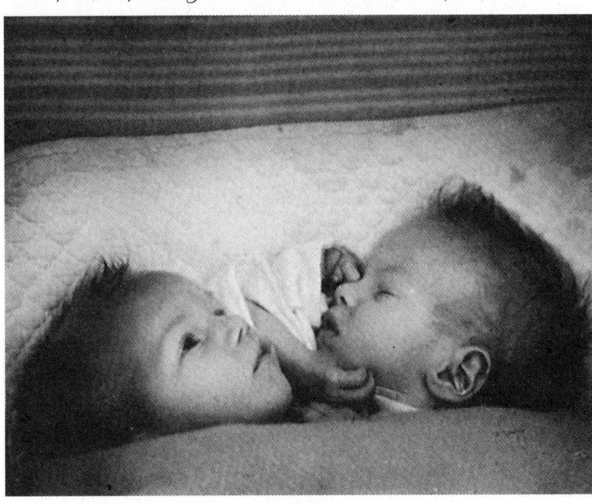

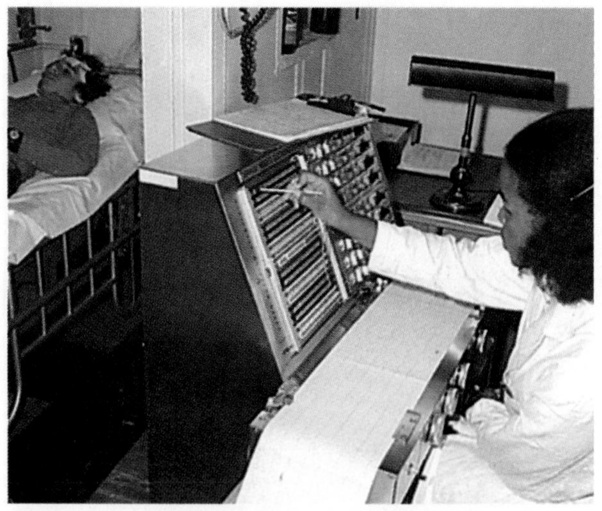

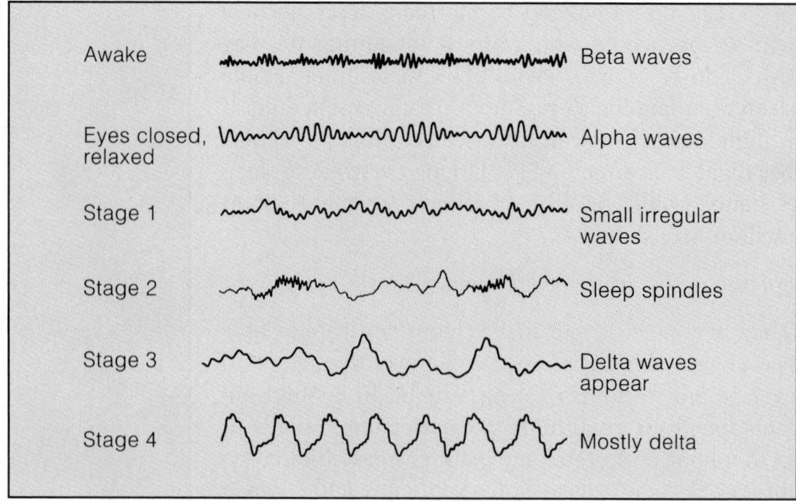

■ Fig. 6–5 (a) *Photograph of an EEG recording session. The man in the background is asleep.* (b) *Changes in brain-wave patterns associated with various stages of sleep. Actually, most wave types are present at all times, but they occur more or less frequently in various sleep stages.*

Sleep stages Levels of sleep identified by brain-wave patterns and behavioral changes.

Electroencephalograph (EEG) A device designed to detect, amplify, and record electrical activity in the brain.

Light sleep Stage 1 sleep, marked by small irregular brain waves and some alpha waves.

Hypnic jerk A reflex muscle twitch throughout the body that often occurs as one is falling asleep.

Myoclonus Restless spasms of the leg muscles that disturb sleep.

Sleep spindles Distinctive bursts of brain-wave activity that indicate a person is asleep.

Delta waves Large, slow brain waves that occur in deeper sleep (stage 3 and stage 4).

Deep sleep Stage 4 sleep; the deepest form of normal sleep.

of brain cells that respond to a different set of chemicals and inhibit sleep. These two systems see-saw back and forth, as they vie for the upper hand. Depending on which system is dominant, the brain is switched from sleep to wakefulness and back again. Rather than "shutting down" during sleep, the brain changes the *pattern* of its activity, not the amount (Steriade & McCarley, 1990).

Question: What happens when you fall asleep?

Stages of Sleep

The changes that come with sleep can be measured with an **electroencephalograph** (e-LEK-tro-en-SEF-uh-lo-graf), or brain-wave machine, commonly called an **EEG.** The brain gives off tiny electrical signals that can be amplified and recorded (see the Exploration in Chapter 3 for more information). When you are awake and alert, the EEG shows a pattern of small fast waves called **beta** (■ Fig. 6–5). Immediately before sleep the EEG record shifts to a pattern of larger and slower waves called **alpha.** (Alpha waves also occur when a person is relaxed and thoughts are allowed to drift.) As the eyes close, breathing becomes slow and regular, the pulse rate slows, and body temperature drops.

Stage 1 As you lose consciousness and enter **light sleep,** your heart rate slows even more. Breathing becomes more irregular; the muscles of your body relax. This sometimes triggers a reflex muscle contraction called a **hypnic jerk** (HIP-nik: sleep), which is quite normal. (Have no fear, then, about admitting to your friends that you fell asleep with a hypnic jerk.) Muscle spasms in the legs that occur later, during sleep itself, are called **myoclonus** (MY-oh-KLOE-nus). This problem, also known as **restless legs syndrome,** causes about 15 to 20 percent of all cases of insomnia.

In stage 1 sleep the EEG is made up mainly of small, irregular waves with some alpha. Persons awakened at this time may or may not say they were asleep.

Stage 2 As sleep deepens, the EEG begins to show short bursts of activity called **sleep spindles,** and body temperature drops further (see Fig. 6–5). Sleep spindles seem to mark the true boundary of sleep. Within 4 minutes after spindles appear, the majority of persons who are awakened say they were asleep (Bonnet & Moore, 1982).

Stage 3 In stage 3, a new brain wave called **delta** begins to appear. Delta waves are very large and slow. Delta waves signal deeper sleep and a further loss of consciousness.

Stage 4 **Deep sleep** is reached about an hour after sleep begins. In stage 4 the brain-wave pattern becomes almost pure delta waves, and the sleeper is in a state of oblivion. If you sound a loud noise during stage 4, the sleeper will awaken in confusion and may not remember the noise.

After spending some time in stage 4, the sleeper returns (through stages 3 and 2) to stage 1. Further shifts between deeper and lighter sleep occur throughout the night (■ Fig. 6–6).

Two Basic States of Sleep

If you watch a person who is asleep, you will soon notice that the sleeper's eyes occasionally move under

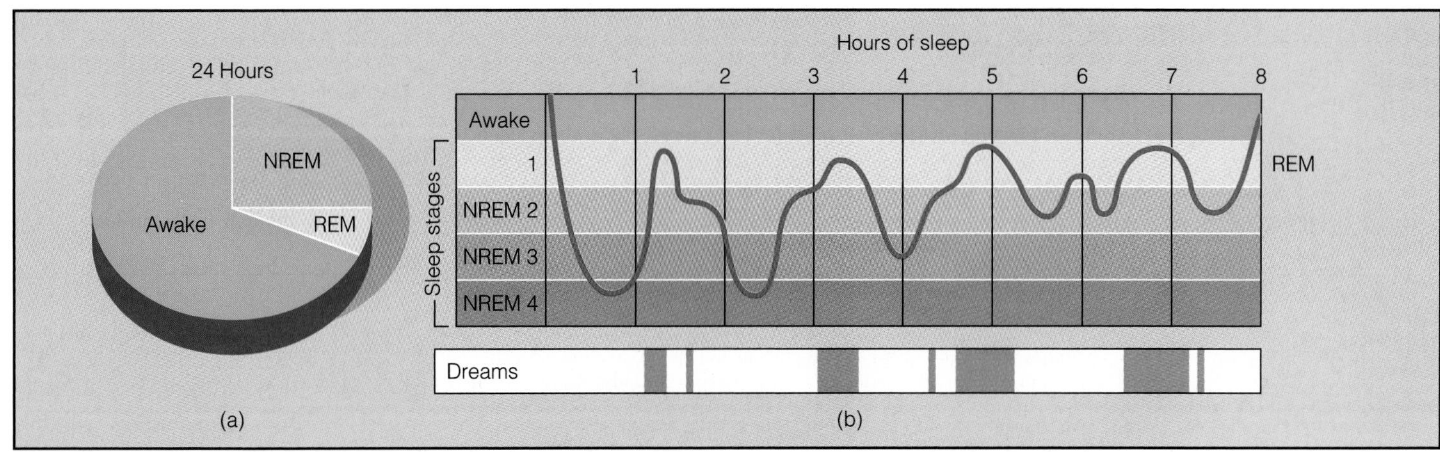

■ **Fig. 6–6** (a) *Average proportion of time adults spend daily in REM sleep and NREM sleep. REM periods add up to about 20 percent of total sleep time.* (b) *Typical changes in stages of sleep during the night. Notice that dreams mostly coincide with REM periods.*

the eyelids. These **rapid eye movements** (or **REMs**) are strongly associated with dreaming (Fig. 6–6). Roughly 85 percent of awakenings made during ongoing REMs produce reports of vivid dreams. **REM sleep** is also easy to observe in pets, such as dogs and cats. Watch for eye and facial movements and for irregular breathing. (You can forget about your pet iguana, though. Reptiles show no signs of REM sleep.)

REM and NREM Sleep The two most basic states of sleep now appear to be REM sleep with its associated dreaming and **non-REM (NREM) sleep,** which occurs mainly during stages 2, 3, and 4 (Hobson & Stickgold, 1994). NREM sleep is dream free about 90 percent of the time. It is true that people awakened during NREM sleep sometimes say they were dreaming. However, dreams reported during REM sleep are usually longer, clearer, more detailed, and more "dream-like" (Foulkes & Schmidt, 1983). Your first period of stage 1 sleep is usually free of REMs and dreams. Stage 1 sleep during the rest of the night is usually accompanied by rapid eye movements.

NREM sleep seems to help us recover from fatigue built up during the day. It increases with exercise or physical exertion (Horne & Staff, 1983). In comparison, REM sleep increases when a person is subjected to added daytime stress. REM sleep totals only about 90 minutes per night (about the same as a feature movie). Yet, its link with dreaming makes it as important as NREM sleep. REM sleep may rise dramatically when there is a death in the family, trouble at work, a marital conflict, or other emotionally charged events (Hartmann, 1973).

Question: What happens to the body when a person dreams?

REM Sleep and Dreaming REM sleep is a time of high emotion. The heart beats irregularly, and blood pressure and breathing waver. Both males and females appear to be sexually aroused: Males usually have an erection, and genital blood flow increases in women. This occurs for all REM sleep, so it is not strictly related to erotic dreams. When an erotic dream does occur, evidence of sexual arousal increases.

With all this emotional activity, you might expect that your muscles would be active during dreaming. The reverse is true, however. During REM sleep the body becomes quite still, as if the person were paralyzed. Imagine for a moment the results of acting out some of your recent dreams. Very likely, REM-sleep paralysis prevents some hilarious—and dangerous—nighttime escapades. When REM paralysis fails, some people thrash violently about, leap out of bed, and may attack their bedpartners. This recently recognized problem is called **REM behavior disorder** (Chase & Morales, 1990).

In a moment we will survey some additional sleep problems—if you are still awake. First, here are a few questions to test your memory of our discussion so far.

Rapid eye movements (REMs) Swift eye movements during sleep.

REM sleep Sleep marked by rapid eye movements and a return to stage 1 EEG patterns.

NREM sleep Non-rapid eye movement sleep characteristic of stages 2, 3, and 4.

REM behavior disorder A failure of normal muscle paralysis, leading to violent actions during REM sleep.

Learning Check

1. Altered states of consciousness are defined mainly by changes in patterns of alertness. T or F?
2. A momentary shift in brain activity to a pattern characteristic of sleep is referred to as
   a. delta sleep *b.* light sleep *c.* microsleep *d.* deprivation sleep
3. Delusions and hallucinations typically continue for several days after a sleep-deprived individual returns to normal sleep. T or F?

4. Older adults, and particularly the elderly, sleep more than children do because the elderly are more easily fatigued. T or F?

5. Most studies of sleep patterns show a consistent ratio of 2 to 1 between time awake and time asleep. T or F?

6. Rapid eye movements (REMs) indicate that a person is in deep sleep. T or F?

7. Alpha waves are to presleep drowsiness as ________ ________ are to stage 4 sleep.

Critical Thinking

8. Why might it be better for the unscheduled human sleep-waking cycle to average more than 24 hours, instead of less?

Answers:

1. F 2. c 3. F 4. F 5. T 6. F 7. delta waves 8. Sleep experts theorize that the 25-hour average leaves a little "slack" in the cycle. External time markers can then retard the bodily cycle slightly to synchronize it with light-dark cycles. If the bodily cycle were shorter than 24 hours, we all might have to "stretch" every day to adjust.

Somnambulist One who sleepwalks.

Sleeptalking Speaking while asleep.

Night terror A very frightening NREM sleep episode.

Sleep Disturbances—Showing Nightly: Sleep Wars!

Sleep clinics treat thousands of people each year who suffer from sleep disorders or complaints. Let's see what has been learned about a few of the most common problems. (See Table 6–1.)

Sleepwalking and Sleeptalking

Like many sleep disturbances, sleepwalking is eerie and fascinating. **Somnambulists** (som-NAM-bue-lists) avoid obstacles, descend stairways, climb trees, and on rare occasions may step out of windows or in front of automobiles. The sleepwalker's eyes are usually open, but a blank face, a lack of recognition, and shuffling feet show that the person is still asleep. Parents who are sleepwalkers or sleeptalkers tend to have children with the same problems. This suggests that these disturbances are partially hereditary (Abe et al., 1984). A parent who finds a child sleepwalking should gently guide the child back to bed. Awakening a sleepwalker does no harm, but it is not necessary.

Question: Does sleepwalking occur during dreaming?

It might seem that sleepwalkers are acting out dreams. But remember that people are normally immobilized during REM sleep. EEG studies have shown that somnambulism occurs during NREM stages 3 and 4. **Sleeptalking** also occurs mostly in NREM stages of sleep. A link with the deeper stages of sleep seems to explain why sleeptalking makes little sense and why sleepwalkers are confused and remember little when awakened (DSM-IV, 1994).

Nightmares and Night Terrors

Stage 4 sleep is also the realm of **night terrors.** These severely frightening episodes are quite different from ordinary, garden-variety nightmares (Table 6–2). A

Table 6–1 Sleep Disturbances—Things that Go Wrong in the Night

Disturbance	Description
Insomnia	Difficulty in getting to sleep or staying asleep; also, not feeling rested after sleeping.
Myoclonus ("restless legs" syndrome)	Restless and annoying twitching movements in the leg muscles that disturb sleep.
Narcolepsy	Sudden, irresistible, daytime sleep attacks that may last anywhere from a few minutes to a half hour. Victims may fall asleep while standing, talking, or even driving.
Sleep apnea	During sleep, breathing stops for 20 seconds or more until the person wakes a little, gulps in air, and settles back to sleep; this cycle may be repeated hundreds of times per night.
Sleep-wake schedule disorder	A mismatch between the sleep-wake schedule demanded by a person's bodily rhythm and that demanded by the environment.
REM behavior disorder	A failure of normal muscle paralysis, leading to violent actions during REM sleep.
Nightmare disorder	Vivid, recurrent nightmares that significantly disturb sleep.
Sleep terror disorder	Repeated occurrence of night terrors that significantly disturb sleep.
Sleepwalking disorder	Repeated incidents of leaving bed and walking about while asleep.
Sleep drunkenness	A slow transition to clear consciousness after awakening; sometimes associated with irritable or aggressive behavior.
Hypersomnia	Excessive daytime sleepiness. (Can result from depression, insomnia, narcolepsy, sleep apnea, sleep drunkenness, nocturnal myoclonus, drug abuse, and other problems.)

(DSM-IV, 1994; Hauri & Linde, 1990.)

Table 6–2 Was It a Nightmare or a Night Terror?

	Nightmare	Night Terror
Stage of sleep	■ REM	■ NREM
Activity	■ Slight or no movement	■ Violent body movement, sits up, cries out, may run
Emotion	■ Fear or anxiety	■ Terror and disorganizing panic
Mental state when awakened	■ Coherent, can be calmed	■ Incoherent, disoriented, cannot be calmed, may be hallucinating
Physiological changes	■ No perspiration	■ Perspires heavily
Recall	■ Dream activity usually remembered	■ Amnesia for episode

(Adapted from Woods & Greenhouse, 1974.)

nightmare is simply a bad dream that takes place during REM sleep. Nightmares are usually brief and remembered in detail. Surprisingly, nightmares have little connection with daytime anxieties. For most people, nightmares occur, on average, about twice a month (Wood & Bootzin, 1990).

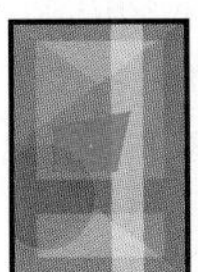

HIGHLIGHT 6–2

Using Psychology

Eliminating Nightmares

A bad nightmare can be worse than any horror movie. You can leave a theater, but often we remain trapped in our most terrifying dreams. Yet bad as they may be, most nightmares, even those that repeat, can be banished by following three simple steps. First, write down your nightmare, describing it in detail. Next, change the dream any way you wish, being sure to spell out the details of the new dream. The third step is to mentally rehearse the changed dream before you fall asleep again (Krakow & Neidhardt, 1992).

This method is called **imagery rehearsal.** It may work by making upsetting dreams familiar while a person is awake and feeling safe. Or perhaps it mentally "reprograms" future dream content. In any case, the technique has proved helpful for many people.

During stage 4 night terrors, a person suffers total panic and may hallucinate frightening dream images into the room itself. The attack may last 15 or 20 minutes. When it is over, the person awakens drenched in sweat, but only vaguely remembers the terror itself. Since night terrors occur during NREM sleep (when the body is not immobilized), the victim may sit up, scream, get out of bed, or run around the room. Night terrors are most common in childhood, but they continue to plague some adults throughout their lives (DSM-IV, 1994).

Narcolepsy

One of the most dramatic sleep problems is **narcolepsy** (NAR-koe-lep-see). Narcoleptics suffer from sudden, irresistible sleep attacks. These last anywhere from a few minutes to a half hour. The attacks are so overpowering that victims may fall asleep while standing, talking, or even driving. Emotional excitement, especially laughter, commonly triggers narcolepsy. Most victims also suffer from **cataplexy** (CAT-uh-plex-see), a sudden temporary paralysis of the muscles, leading to complete body collapse.

Question: Sudden paralysis sounds like what happens during dreaming. Does that suggest a connection between narcolepsy and REM sleep?

Yes. When monitored on an EEG, narcoleptics tend to fall directly into REM sleep. (Recall that the first REM period normally occurs about 90 minutes after sleep begins.) Also, direct recordings in the brainstem have identified cells that are highly active during both cataplexy and REM sleep (Siegel et al., 1991). In other words, the narcoleptic's sleep attacks and paralysis seem to occur when REM sleep intrudes into the waking state.

Fortunately, narcolepsy is rare. It tends to run in families, which suggests that it too is hereditary. This has been confirmed by breeding several generations of narcoleptic dogs (Guilleminault et al., 1976). (These dogs, by the way, are simply outstanding at learning the trick "Roll over and play dead.") There is no known cure for narcolepsy, but stimulant drugs may cut down the frequency of attacks. Scheduling a long nap each day also helps narcoleptics manage their sleep attacks (Mullington & Broughton, 1993).

Nightmare An upsetting dream.

Imagery rehearsal Mental review of desired dream images.

Narcolepsy A sudden, irresistible sleep attack.

Cataplexy A sudden temporary paralysis of the muscles.

Insomnia Difficulty in getting to sleep or staying asleep.

Drug-dependency insomnia Insomnia that follows withdrawal from sleeping pills.

Temporary insomnia A brief episode of insomnia.

Tryptophan A sleep promoting amino acid.

Chronic insomnia Insomnia that persists for more than three weeks.

Stimulus control Linking a particular response with specific stimuli.

Insomnia

While some people sleep when they don't want to, a far greater number have trouble getting enough sleep. About 32 percent of adults report some degree of insomnia. Roughly 15 to 20 percent have a serious or chronic problem (Hopson, 1986). **Insomnia** includes difficulty in going to sleep, frequent nighttime awakenings, waking too early, or a combination of these problems.

Americans spend more than one-half billion dollars each year on sleeping pills. There is real irony in this expense. Non-prescription sleeping pills such as *Sominex*, *Nytol*, and *Sleep-eze* have little or no sleep-inducing effect. Even worse are most prescription *sedatives.* These drugs (usually barbiturates) decrease both stage 4 sleep and REM sleep, which drastically lowers sleep quality. In addition, a drug tolerance rapidly builds so that the initial dosage quits working. Many users become "sleeping-pill junkies" who need an ever-greater number of pills to get to sleep. The result is **drug-dependency insomnia,** a serious problem. Victims must be painstakingly withdrawn from their sleeping pills. Otherwise, terrible nightmares and "rebound insomnia" may drive them back to drug use.

Question: If sleeping pills are a poor way to treat insomnia, what can be done?

Actually, a drug called triazolam (try-AS-o-lam) appears to help in some cases of insomnia (Seidel et al., 1984). However, even triazolam has drawbacks, and it too can cause rebound insomnia on the first few nights after it is withdrawn. Rather than using drugs, it is often far better to learn behavioral techniques to treat insomnia (Jacobs et al., 1993).

Types and Causes of Insomnia **Temporary insomnia** caused by worry, stress, or excitement usually sets up a cycle in which heightened physical arousal blocks sleep. Then, frustration and anger cause more arousal, which further delays sleep. Delayed sleep causes more frustration, and so on. A good way to beat this cycle is to avoid fighting it. It is usually best to get up and do something useful or satisfying when you have difficulty sleeping (reading a textbook might not be a bad choice of useful activities).

Some insomniacs undergo a drop in blood sugar during the night. The restlessness and hunger this causes can be avoided by having a small snack before sleeping. Also, scientists have discovered that the amino acid **tryptophan** (TRIP-tuh-fan) can help people sleep—especially those who sleep poorly, rather than those who are just slow in getting to sleep (Lindsley et al., 1983). Interestingly, tryptophan can be found in a glass of milk. So grandma was right after all! But she apparently didn't know that an egg-tuna-cottage cheese-soybean-cashew-chicken-turkey-banana sandwich would be even better for inducing sleep. All of the listed foods are also high in tryptophan. (Sales of tryptophan as a food supplement were temporarily banned when it seemed to be causing a rare blood disease in some users. However, the problem was traced to impurities in tryptophan made by a single Japanese company.)

Question: What about more serious cases of insomnia?

Chronic insomnia is said to exist if sleeping problems last for more than three weeks. Treatment for chronic insomnia usually begins with a careful analysis of a person's sleep history. Possible sources of insomnia, such as depression, anxiety, medical problems, lifestyle, stress, and sleep habits are carefully assessed (Hauri & Linde, 1990).

The first thing that anyone suffering from insomnia should do is to reduce consumption of caffeine, alcohol, and tobacco. Some insomniacs benefit from relaxation training to lower arousal before sleep. (See the Applications section in Chapter 18 for more information about relaxation.) **Stimulus control** strategies are also helpful. For example, patients are told to strictly avoid doing anything other than sleeping when they go to bed. They are not to study, eat, watch TV, read, or even think in bed. In this way, only sleeping becomes associated with retiring (Bootzin, 1973; Hauri & Linde, 1990).

One of the best ways to combat insomnia is also the simplest. Many insomniacs have scattered sleep habits. For these people, adopting a regular schedule helps establish a firm body rhythm and greatly improves sleep. Patients are told to get up and go to sleep at the same time each day, including weekends. (Many people disturb their sleep rhythms by sleeping in late and staying up late over the weekend.) These and other ways of combating insomnia are summarized in Highlight 6–3.

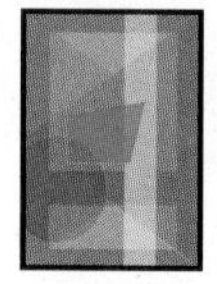

HIGHLIGHT 6–3

Using Psychology

Behavioral Remedies for Insomnia

All of the approaches listed here are helpful for treating insomnia (Hopson, 1986). With a little experimenting, you should be able to find a combination that works for you. Of the methods listed, sleep restriction and stimulus control are the most effective (Lacks & Morin, 1992).

Stimulants Avoid stimulants such as coffee and cigarettes. Remember too that alcohol, while not a stimulant, impairs sleep quality.

Worries Schedule time in the early evening to write down worries or concerns and what you will do about them the next day.

Relaxation Learn a physical or mental strategy for relaxing, such as progressive muscle relaxation (see Chapter 18), meditation (see Chapter 11), or blotting out worries with calming images. Strenuous exercise during the day promotes sleep, but it is usually too stimulating in the evening. Very light evening exercise may be helpful, however (Jacobs et al., 1993).

Sleep Restriction Even if you miss an entire night's sleep, do not sleep late in the morning, nap more than an hour, sleep during the evening, or go to bed early the following night. Try to restrict sleep to your normal bedtime hours. That way, you will avoid fragmenting your sleep rhythms (Lacks & Morin, 1992).

Stimulus Control Link only sleep with your bedroom so that it does not trigger worrying: (1) Go to bed only when you are feeling sleepy. (2) Awaken at the same time each morning. (3) Avoid non-sleep activities in bed. (4) Always leave the bedroom if sleep has not occurred within 10 minutes. (5) Do something else when you are upset about not being able to sleep (Lacks & Morin, 1992).

Paradoxical intention To remove the pressures of trying to get to sleep, try instead to keep your eyes open (in the dark) and stay awake as long as possible (Horvath & Goheen, 1990). This allows sleep to overtake you unexpectedly and lowers performance anxiety. Never try to go to sleep. Arrange to let it happen.

Sleep Apnea

Some sage once said, "Laugh and the whole world laughs with you; snore and you sleep alone." Most nightly "wood sawing" is harmless, but it can signal a serious problem. A person who snores loudly, with short silences and loud gasps or snorts, may suffer from **sleep apnea** (AP-nee-ah). In sleep apnea, breathing stops for periods of 20 seconds to 2 minutes. As the need for oxygen becomes intense, the person wakes a little and gulps in air. He or she then settles back to sleep; but soon, breathing stops again. This cycle is repeated hundreds of times a night (Larson, 1990). As you might guess, apnea victims complain of daytime sleepiness known as **hypersomnia** (hi-per-SOM-nee-ah) (DSM-IV, 1994).

Sleep apnea Repeated interruption of breathing during sleep.

Hypersomnia Extreme daytime sleepiness.

Sudden infant death syndrome The sudden, unexplained death of an apparently healthy infant.

Question: What causes sleep apnea?

Some apnea occurs because the brain stops sending signals to the diaphragm to maintain breathing. Another cause is blockage of the upper air passages. In either case the person can breathe normally during the day, so he or she may be unaware of the problem. Apnea should be suspected any time very loud snoring is present. In addition to the misery it causes, apnea seriously endangers health. Persons who suspect they are apneic should seek treatment at a sleep clinic. The most effective treatments are weight loss, surgery for breathing obstructions, and use of a breathing mask called a CPAP (Continuous Positive Airway Pressure) to aid breathing during sleep (Hauri & Linde, 1990).

SIDS Sleep apnea is especially dangerous in infancy, when it is suspected as one cause of **sudden infant death syndrome** (SIDS), or "crib death." SIDS is the most frequent cause of death for infants under one year of age. Each year one out of every 500 babies is a victim of SIDS. In the "typical" crib death, a slightly premature or small baby with some signs of a cold or cough is bundled up and put to bed. A short time later, when parents return to the crib, the child is dead.

Doctors think that some cases of SIDS are caused by apnea due to immature breathing centers in the brainstem (Thoman et al., 1988). Others suspect a defect that stalls the heart during sleep. Sometimes it appears that direct blockage of the nose is responsible. Most infants will cry, flail, and kick if the nose is blocked for a few seconds—responses that can save them if they roll face-down. But a few babies remain passive when breathing is blocked. These infants run a much higher risk of crib death (Lipsett, 1980).

Babies at risk for SIDS must be carefully watched for the first 6 months of life. To aid parents in this task, a special monitor may be used that sounds an alarm when breathing or pulse becomes weak (■ Fig. 6–7). The list that follows gives some danger signals for SIDS (Einspieler et al., 1988). Be aware, however, that SIDS can also strike babies who show none of these signs.

Some Warning Signs for SIDS

- The mother is a teenager or smoker.
- The baby is premature.
- The baby has a shrill, high-pitched cry.
- The baby engages in "snoring," breath-holding, or frequent awakening at night.
- The baby breathes mainly through an open mouth.
- The baby remains passive when its face rolls into a pillow or blanket and moves little during sleep.

REM rebound The occurrence of extra rapid eye movement sleep following REM sleep deprivation.

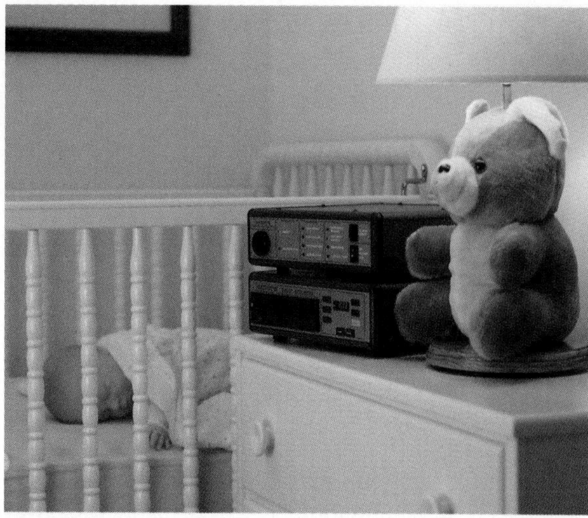

■ **Fig. 6–7** *Infants at risk for SIDS are often attached to devices that monitor breathing and heart rate during sleep. An alarm sounds to alert parents if either pulse or respiration falters. SIDS rarely occurs after an infant is one year old. Babies at risk for SIDS should be placed on their sides, as shown here, or on their backs. (Photo courtesy of Healthdyne, Inc.)*

"Back to Sleep" Pop quiz: Should babies be placed face-down or face-up in bed? Another major risk factor for SIDS is the position in which babies sleep. Doctors used to advise parents to place infants face down in bed. Now, experts believe that healthy infants are better off sleeping on their backs or sides. (Premature babies and those with respiratory problems or who often vomit, however, may still need to sleep face down. Ask a pediatrician for guidance.) Since this advice was first publicized, there has been a 50 percent drop in SIDS deaths. Remember, "*back* to sleep" is the safest position for most infants (Willinger et al., 1994).

Dreams—A Separate Reality?

When researchers Nathaniel Kleitman and Eugene Aserinsky discovered REM sleep in 1952, they ushered in a "Golden Era" of dream inquiry. To conclude our discussion of sleep, let's consider some age-old questions about dreaming.

Question: Does everyone dream? Do dreams occur in an instant?

Most people dream 4 or 5 times a night, but not all people remember their dreams. "Non-dreamers" are often shocked by their dreams when first awakened during REM sleep. Dreams are usually spaced about 90 minutes apart. The first dream lasts only about 10 minutes; the last averages 30 minutes and may run as long as 50. Dreams, therefore, occur in real time, not as a "flash" (Blackmore, 1991).

Question: How important is dream sleep? Is it essential for normal functioning?

REM Sleep Deprivation To answer these questions, dream researcher William Dement awakened volunteers each time they entered REM sleep. People kept from dreaming several nights in a row showed an increased tendency to dream. By the fifth night, many had to be awakened 20 or 30 times to prevent REM sleep. When undisturbed sleep was finally allowed, the volunteers dreamed extra amounts. This effect, called a **REM rebound,** explains why alcoholics often have horrible nightmares after they quit drinking (Dement, 1960). Alcohol suppresses REM sleep and sets up a powerful rebound effect when it is withdrawn. It's worth remembering that while alcohol and other depressant drugs may help a person get to sleep, they often greatly reduce sleep quality.

While they were deprived of dream sleep, Dement's volunteers complained of lapses in memory and concentration, and they felt more anxious during the day. For a time, it looked like people deprived of dreaming might go crazy. But sleep researchers now refer to this idea as the "REM myth." Later experiments showed that missing *any* sleep stage can cause a rebound for that stage. In general, daytime disturbances are related to the *total amount* of sleep lost, not to the type of sleep lost (Glovinsky et al., 1990).

Functions of REM Sleep What then, is the purpose of REM sleep? Early in life, dreaming may stimulate the developing brain. Newborn babies spend about 50 percent of their sleeping time in REM sleep. This amounts to a hearty 8 or 9 hours a day of dream time. In adulthood, REM sleep may serve other purposes. For one thing, REM sleep increases after learning, so it may help restore brain chemicals needed for learning and memory (Hartmann, 1981; Stern, 1981). REM sleep also seems to help sort and integrate memories formed during the day (see Highlight 6–4). Dreams may prevent sensory deprivation during sleep and aid the processing of emotional events. Although we have much to learn, it seems clear that REM sleep and dreaming are valuable for keeping the brain in good working order.

HIGHLIGHT 6–4

Research Frontier

REM Sleep and Memory

No one has to remember to dream. But do we dream to remember? In animals, REM sleep seems to help the brain store daytime experiences that are important for survival. Specifically, REM sleep boosts activity in the hippocampus, an area of the brain crucial for memory. In mammals, this appears to be a basic characteristic of the brain.

Though it's a long leap from animals to humans, your own dreams may help you sort out and retain everyday "survival" strategies. Sleep biologist Johnathan Winson believes it is no accident that our dreams center on fears, insecurities, strengths, ambitions, failures, sexual feelings, desires, hates, jealousies, and love (Winson, 1990). Such concerns relate strongly to primal motives and emotions.

Question: What about more abstract memories? Does dreaming aid learning in college, for example?

According to researcher Carlyle Smith it does. In one study, for instance, college students did two mental tasks, one easy and the other difficult. For the easy task, students merely memorized a list of paired words. The difficult task was a logic game that required some tricky mental gymnastics. Later, students spent the night in a sleep lab. Some were awakened each time they entered REM sleep. Others were awakened only during NREM periods. A third group was kept awake all night. The lucky fourth group was allowed to sleep undisturbed.

The following day, all four groups performed equally well on the easy memory task. But on the hard task, those who lost REM sleep did much worse than the other groups (Chollar, 1989). To succeed at the logic game, students had to create new mental strategies and remember what worked. In short, REM sleep seems to aid the development of memories that help us cope with the world (Dujardin et al., 1990; Smith & Lapp, 1991). Speaking very loosely, it's as if the dreaming brain were reviewing messages left during the day on a telephone answering machine, in order to decide which are worth keeping.

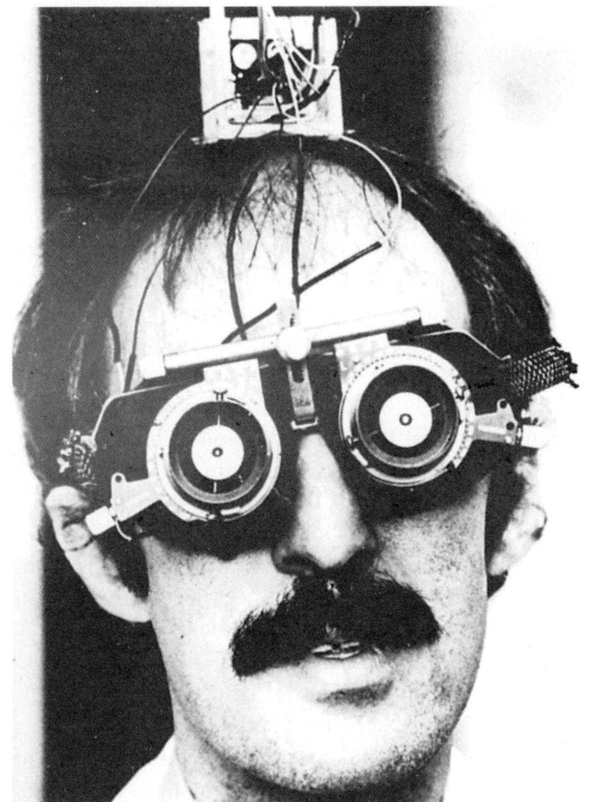

■ **Fig. 6–8** *Dr. John Herman of the University of Texas may look like he just stepped out of the movie* Star Wars, *but he is actually involved in dream research. Dr. Herman is wearing goggles that electronically monitor eye movements during sleep. Use of such devices has greatly extended our understanding of dreaming.*

Dream Worlds

Calvin Hall, a noted authority on dreams, collected and analyzed over 10,000 dreams (Hall, 1966; Hall et al., 1982). Hall found that most dreams reflect everyday events. The favorite dream setting is familiar rooms in a house. Action usually takes place between the dreamer and two or three other emotionally important people—friends, enemies, parents, or employers. Dream actions are also mostly familiar: running, jumping, riding, sitting, talking, and watching. About half of the recorded dreams had sexual elements. Dreams of flying, floating, and falling occur less frequently. Researchers have also found that if you're dreaming more now, you may be enjoying it less. Unpleasant emotions such as anxiety, fear, anger, and sadness are more frequent in dreams than pleasant emotions (Merritt et al., 1994). As you may have noticed, when dreams depart from the ordinary and become bizarre, we are more likely to remember them (Cipolli et al., 1993).

Dream Theories

Question: How meaningful are dreams?

Most theorists agree that dreams reflect our waking thoughts, fantasies, and emotions (Cartwright & Lamberg, 1992; Winget & Kramer, 1979). Thus, a better question might be, How deep should we dig in interpreting dreams? Some theorists believe that dreams have deeply hidden meanings. Others regard dreams as meaningless. Let's examine both views.

Psychodynamic Dream Theory Sigmund Freud's book *The Interpretation of Dreams* (1900) opened a

Wish fulfillment Freudian belief that many dreams express unconscious desires.

Psychodynamic theory Any theory of behavior that emphasizes internal conflicts, motives, and unconscious forces.

Dream symbols Images in dreams that serve as visible signs of hidden ideas, desires, impulses, emotions, relationships, and so forth.

Activation-synthesis hypothesis Theory that relates dream content to motor commands in the brain, which are made, but not carried out during sleep.

whole new world of psychological investigation. After analyzing his own dreams, Freud concluded that many dreams represent **wish fulfillment.** Thus, a student who is angry at a teacher may dream of embarrassing the teacher in class; a lonely person may dream of romance; or a hungry child may dream of food.

Although Freud's **psychodynamic** view of dreaming is attractive, there is evidence against it. For example, volunteers in a study of the effects of prolonged starvation showed no particular increase in dreams about food and eating (Keys, 1950). Freud's response, no doubt, would have been that dreams rarely express needs so directly. One of Freud's key insights is that dreams represent thoughts expressed in *images* or pictures, rather than in words (Globus, 1987).

Freud believed that the conscience relaxes during sleep, allowing dreams to express *unconscious* desires and conflicts in disguised **dream symbols.** For instance, death might be symbolized by a journey, children by small animals, or sexual intercourse by horseback riding or dancing. Similarly, a woman sexually attracted to her best friend's husband might dream of stealing her friend's wedding ring and placing it on her own hand, an indirect symbol of her true desires. (For a discussion of dream analysis in psychotherapy, see Chapter 18.)

Question: Do all dreams have hidden meanings?

Probably not. Even Freud realized that some dreams are trivial or unimportant "day residues," or carryovers from ordinary waking events. Also, you may be relieved to learn that Freud's is not the only approach to dream interpretation.

The Activation-Synthesis Hypothesis At the other end of the scale from Freud stands a radically different view of dreaming offered by scientists Allan Hobson and Robert McCarley (1977). After studying REM sleep in cats, Hobson and McCarley believe that dreams are made in this way: During REM sleep, certain brain cells are activated that normally control eye movements, balance, and actions. However, messages from the cells are blocked from actually reaching the body, so no movement occurs. But the cells continue to tell higher brain areas of their activities. Struggling to interpret this information, the brain searches through stored memories and manufactures a dream. Hobson and McCarley call this explanation of dreaming the **activation-synthesis hypothesis.** Hobson (1988) explains that "the brain is turned on (activated) during sleep and then generates and integrates (synthesizes) its own sensory and motor information."

Question: How does this help explain dream content?

Let's use the classic chase dream as an example. In such dreams we feel we are running but not going anywhere as a pursuer bears down on us. Hobson and McCarley suggest that in such dreams the brain is being told that the body is running, but it gets no feedback from the motionless body to confirm it. As it tries to make sense of this information, the brain creates a chase drama. From this perspective, dreams have no "latent" or hidden meanings. They are merely a different type of thought that occurs during sleep (Hobson, 1988).

The activation-synthesis hypothesis certainly seems to explain some dream experiences. However, it does not tell us much about how dreams function in the mental life of humans. Many psychologists continue to believe that dreams have deeper meaning (Cartwright & Lamberg, 1992; Globus, 1987; Winget & Kramer, 1979). Moreover, there seems little doubt that dreams can make a difference in our lives: Veteran sleep researcher William Dement once dreamed that he had lung cancer. In the dream a doctor told Dement he would die soon. At the time, Dement was smoking two packs of cigarettes a day. He says, "I will never forget the surprise, joy, and exquisite relief of waking up. I felt reborn." Dement quit smoking the following day (Hales, 1980).

In recent years the idea that dreams can only be interpreted by professionals has given way to acceptance of the personal nature of dream meanings. As a result, many psychologists now urge people to collect and interpret their own dreams. Later in this chapter, the Applications section offers some practical suggestions for doing just that.

Learning Check

1. Night terrors, sleepwalking, and sleeptalking all occur during stage 1, NREM sleep. T or F?
2. Narcolepsy and cataplexy are both associated with ______________ sleep.
3. Sleep ______________ is suspected as one cause of SIDS.
4. Which of the following is *not* a behavioral remedy for insomnia?
   a. daily hypersomnia *b.* stimulus control *c.* progressive relaxation *d.* paradoxical intention
5. The favored setting for dreams is
   a. work *b.* school *c.* outdoors or unfamiliar places *d.* familiar rooms
6. Unpleasant emotions such as fear, anger, and sadness are more frequent in dreams than pleasant emotions. T or F?

7. According to the activation-synthesis model of dreaming, dreams are constructed from ______________ to explain messages received from nerve cells controlling eye movement, balance, and bodily activity.

8. REM sleep seems to contribute to learning, especially to the formation of memories associated with ______________ that aid survival or coping.

9. Even without being told that somnambulism is an NREM event, you could have predicted that sleepwalking doesn't occur during dreaming. Why? ***Critical Thinking***

Answers: 1. F 2. REM 3. apnea 4. *a* 5. *d* 6. T 7. memories 8. strategies 9. Because people are immobilized during REM sleep and REM sleep is strongly associated with dreaming. This makes it unlikely that sleepwalkers are acting out dreams.

Hypnosis—Look into My Eyes

"Your body is becoming heavy. Your eyes are so tired you can barely keep them open. You feel warm and relaxed and very heavy. You are so tired you can't move. Relax. Let go. Relax. Close your eyes and relax." These are the last words a textbook should ever say to you, and the first a professional hypnotist might say.

Hypnosis, like dreaming, has an aura of mystery surrounding it. In reality, hypnosis is not nearly so mysterious as it might seem. **Hypnosis** is an *altered state of consciousness, characterized by narrowed attention and an increased openness to suggestion.* Not all psychologists agree with this definition. Some regard hypnosis as no more than a blend of conformity, relaxation, imagination, obedience, suggestion, and role-playing (Spanos, 1990; Kirsch et al., 1992). Either way, the point is that hypnosis can be explained by normal psychological principles. It is not "magical."

Interest in hypnosis began in the 1700s with Franz Mesmer (whose name is the basis for the term **mesmerize**). Mesmer, an Austrian physician, believed that he could cure diseases by passing magnets over the body. Mesmer's mysterious "treatments" are related to hypnosis because they made heavy use of the power of suggestion. For a time, mesmerism enjoyed quite a following. In the end, however, Mesmer's theories of "animal magnetism" were rejected and he was branded a quack and a fraud.

The term *hypnosis* was coined by an English surgeon named James Braid. The Greek word *hypnos* means "sleep," and Braid used it to describe the hypnotic state. Today we know that hypnosis is *not* sleep, since EEG records during hypnosis are similar to those obtained when a person is awake. Confusion about this point remains because some hypnotists give the suggestion, "Sleep, sleep."

Question: Can anyone be hypnotized?

Hypnotic Susceptibility Approximately 8 people out of 10 can be hypnotized, but only 4 out of 10 will be good hypnotic subjects. People who are imaginative, prone to fantasy, and who easily become absorbed in tasks are often highly responsive to hypnosis (Crawford et al., 1993; Silva & Kirsch, 1992). But people who lack these traits may also be hypnotized. If you are willing to be hypnotized, chances are good that you could be.

Hypnotic susceptibility can be measured by making a series of suggestions and counting the number to which a person responds. A typical hypnotic test is the **Stanford Hypnotic Susceptibility Scale** shown in Table 6–3. (Also see Fig. 6–9.) Notice that the scale progresses from easier to more difficult tasks. If you were to score high on the scale today, you probably would do the same years from now. Hypnotizability is very stable over time (Piccione, et al., 1989).

Question: How is hypnosis done? Could anyone be hypnotized against his or her will?

Inducing Hypnosis There are as many different hypnotic routines as there are hypnotists. Still, there are factors common to all techniques. They all encourage a person (1) to focus attention on what is being said, (2) to relax and feel tired, (3) to "let go" and accept suggestions easily, and (4) to use vivid imagination (Tart, 1975).

A person who is deeply hypnotized may relax "reality testing" so that normal "willpower," or self-control, is reduced. But at first, a person must cooperate to become hypnotized. Many theorists believe that all hypnosis is really **self-hypnosis.** In other words, the hypnotist simply acts as a guide to help the person achieve an altered state of mind that could be reached alone.

Question: What does it feel like to be hypnotized?

You might be surprised at some of your actions during hypnosis, and you might have mild feelings of floating, sinking, anesthesia, or separation from your body. Personal experiences vary widely. However, in all but the deepest hypnosis, people remain aware of what is going on.

A key element in hypnosis is the **basic suggestion effect.** Hypnotized persons feel that suggested actions

Hypnosis An altered state of consciousness characterized by narrowed attention and increased suggestibility.

Mesmerize To hypnotize.

Hypnotic susceptibility One's capacity for becoming hypnotized.

Hypnotic susceptibility scale Any test designed to assess an individual's capacity for being hypnotized.

Self-hypnosis A state of hypnosis attained without the aid of a hypnotist; autosuggestion.

Basic suggestion effect The tendency of hypnotized persons to carry out suggested actions as if they were involuntary.

Table 6–3 Stanford Hypnotic Susceptibility Scale

Suggested Behavior	Criterion of Passing
1. Postural sway	Falls without forcing
2. Eye closure	Closes eyes without forcing
3. Hand lowering (left)	Lowers at least 6 inches by end of 10 seconds
4. Immobilization (right arm)	Arm rises less than 1 inch in 10 seconds
5. Finger lock	Incomplete separation of fingers at end of 10 seconds
6. Arm rigidity (left arm)	Less than 2 inches of arm bending in 10 seconds
7. Hands moving together	Hands at least as close as 6 inches after 10 seconds
8. Verbal inhibition (name)	Name unspoken in 10 seconds
9. Hallucination (fly)	Any movement, grimacing, acknowledgment of effect
10. Eye catalepsy	Eyes remain closed at end of 10 seconds
11. Posthypnotic (changes chairs)	Any partial movement response
12. Amnesia test	Three or fewer items recalled

(Adapted from Weitzenhoffer & Hilgard, 1959.)

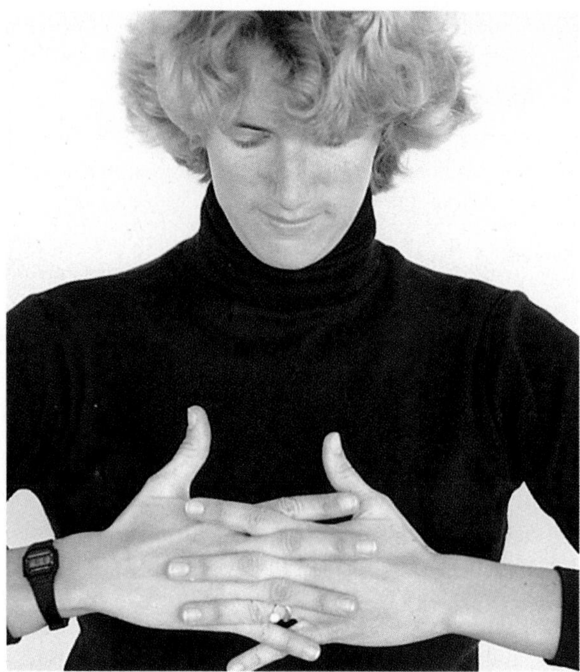

Fig. 6–9 *In one test of hypnotizability, subjects attempt to pull their hands apart after hearing suggestions that their fingers are "locked" together.*

Hidden observer A detached part of the hypnotized person's awareness that silently observes events.

or experiences are *automatic*—they seem to just "happen" without effort (Kihlstrom, 1985). Here is how one person described his hypnotic session:

> I felt lethargic, my eyes going out of focus and wanting to close. My hands felt real light . . . . I felt I was sinking deeper into the chair . . . . I felt like I wanted to relax more and more . . . . My responses were more automatic. I didn't have to *wish* to do things so much or *want* to do them . . . . I just did them . . . . I felt floating . . . very close to sleep (Hilgard, 1968).

Hypnosis may also cause a *dissociation* or "split" in awareness. To illustrate, researcher Ernest Hilgard asks hypnotized subjects to plunge one hand into a painful bath of ice water. Subjects told to feel no pain say they feel none. The same subjects are then asked if there is any part of their mind that does feel pain. With their free hand, many write, "It hurts," or "Stop it, you're hurting me," while they continue to act pain-free (Hilgard 1977, 1978). One part of the hypnotized person says there is no pain and acts as if there is none. Another part, which Hilgard calls the **hidden observer,** is aware of the pain but remains in the background.

Question: What can (and cannot) be achieved with hypnosis?

Effects of Hypnosis Many abilities have been tested for responsiveness to hypnosis. In some cases, the evidence is incomplete or conflicting. Even so, the following conclusions seem justified (Kihlstrom, 1985):

1. **Superhuman acts of strength.** Hypnosis has no more effect on physical strength than instructions that encourage a subject to make his or her best effort.
2. **Memory.** There is some evidence that hypnosis can enhance memory. However, it also frequently increases the number of false memories as well (Dywan & Bowers, 1983). For this reason, many states now bar persons who have been hypnotized from testifying in court cases. (See Chapter 8 for more information.)
3. **Pain relief.** Hypnosis can relieve pain (Hilgard & Hilgard, 1983). Therefore, it can be especially useful in situations where chemical painkillers cannot be used or are ineffective. One such situation is control of phantom limb pain. (Phantom limb pains are re-

curring pains that amputees sometimes feel coming from the missing limb.)

4. **Age regression.** Through hypnosis, subjects have been "regressed" to childhood. Some theorists feel that regressed subjects are only acting child-like. Doubt is also cast by the fact that age-regressed persons continue to use knowledge they could only have learned as adults. The validity of age regression, therefore, remains doubtful (Kihlstrom, 1985).

5. **Sensory changes.** Hypnotic suggestions concerning sensations are among the most effective. Given the proper instructions, a person can be made to smell a small bottle of ammonia and respond as if it were a wonderful perfume. It is also possible to alter color vision, hearing sensitivity, time sense, perception of illusions, and many other sensory responses (Kihlstrom, 1985).

Hypnosis seems to have greatest value as a tool for inducing relaxation, as a way of controlling pain (in dentistry and childbirth, for example), and as an adjunct to psychological therapy and counseling (Overholser, 1988). In general, hypnosis is better at changing subjective experience than at modifying behavior, such as smoking or overeating. Hypnotic effects are useful, but seldom amazing (Gibson & Heap, 1991).

Stage Hypnosis

On stage the hypnotist intones, "When I count to three, you will imagine that you are on a train to Disneyland, and growing younger and younger as the train approaches." Responding to these suggestions, grown men and women begin to giggle and squirm like children on their way to a circus.

Question: How do entertainers use hypnosis on stage to get people to do strange things?

They don't. Little or no hypnosis is needed to do a good stage hypnosis act. T. X. Barber, an authority on hypnosis, says that stage hypnotists make use of several features of the stage setting to perform their act (Barber, 1970).

1. **Waking suggestibility.** We are all more or less open to suggestion, but on stage people are unusually cooperative because they don't want to "ruin the act." As a result, they will readily follow almost any instruction given by the entertainer.

2. **Selection of responsive subjects.** Participants in stage hypnotism (all *volunteers*) are first "hypnotized" as a group. Thus, anyone who doesn't yield to instructions is eliminated.

3. **The hypnosis label disinhibits.** Once a person has been labeled "hypnotized," he or she can sing, dance, act silly, or whatever, without fear of embarrassment. On stage, being "hypnotized" takes away personal responsibility for one's actions.

4. **The hypnotist as a "director."** After volunteers loosen up and respond to a few suggestions, they find that they are suddenly the stars of the show. Audience response to the antics on stage brings out the "ham" in many people. All the "hypnotist" needs to do is direct the action.

5. **The stage hypnotist uses tricks.** Stage hypnosis is about 50 percent taking advantage of the situation and 50 percent deception. Here is a common deception:

> One of the more impressive stage tricks is to rigidly suspend a person between two chairs. This is astounding only because the audience does not question it. Anyone can do it, as is shown in the photographs and instructions in ■ Figure 6–10. Try it!

To summarize, hypnosis is real, and it can significantly alter private experience. Hypnosis is a useful

Stage hypnosis Use of hypnosis to entertain; often, merely a simulation of hypnosis.

Disinhibition A reduction or removal of inhibitions.

■ Fig. 6–10 *Arrange three chairs as shown. Have someone recline as shown. Ask him to lift slightly while you remove the middle chair. Accept the applause gracefully! (Concerning hypnosis and similar phenomena, the moral, of course, is "Suspend judgment until you have something solid to stand on.")*

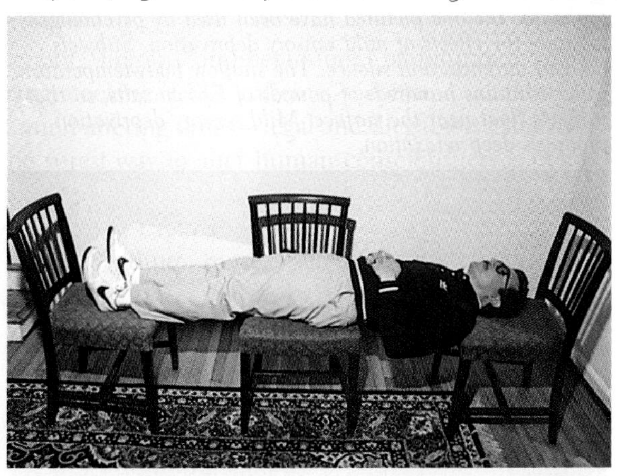

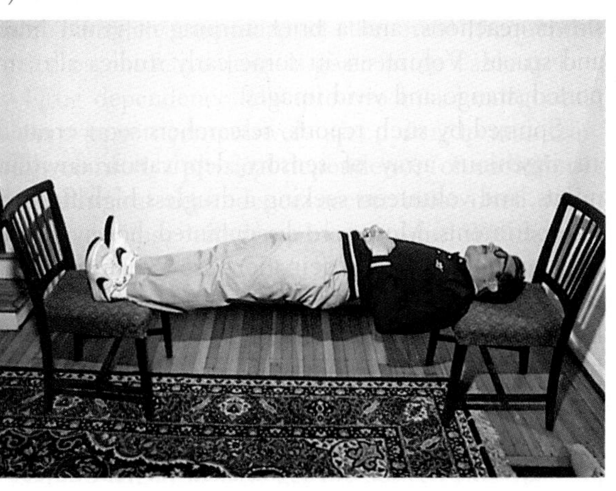

Table 6–4 Comparison of Psychoactive Drugs

Name	Classification	Medical Use	Usual Dose	Duration of Effect
Alcohol	Sedative-hypnotic	Solvent, antiseptic	Varies	1–4 hours
Amphetamines	Stimulant	Relief of mild depression, control of appetite and narcolepsy	2.5–5 milligrams	4 hours
Barbiturates	Sedative-hypnotic	Sedation, relief of high blood pressure, hyperthyroidism	50–100 milligrams	4 hours
Benzodiazepines	Anxiolytic	Tranquilizer	2–100 milligrams	1–8 hours
Caffeine	Stimulant	Counteract depressant drugs, treatment of migraine headaches	Varies	Varies
Cocaine	Stimulant, local anesthetic	Local anesthesia	Varies	Varied, brief periods
Codeine	Narcotic	Ease pain and coughing	30 milligrams	4 hours
Heroin	Narcotic	Pain relief	Varies	4 hours
LSD	Hallucinogen	Experimental study of mental function, alcoholism	100–500 milligrams	10 hours
Marijuana (THC)	Relaxant, euphoriant; in high doses, hallucinogen	Treatment of glaucoma	1–2 cigarettes	4 hours
Mescaline	Hallucinogen	None	350 micrograms	12 hours
Methadone	Narcotic	Pain relief	10 milligrams	4–6 hours
Morphine	Narcotic	Pain relief	15 milligrams	6 hours
PCP	Anesthetic	None	2–10 milligrams	4–6 hours, plus 12 hour recovery
Psilocybin	Hallucinogen	None	25 milligrams	6–8 hours
Tobacco (nicotine)	Stimulant	Emetic (nicotine)	Varies	Varies

(Question marks indicate conflict of opinion. It should be noted that illicit drugs are frequently adulterated and thus pose unknown hazards to the user.)

Psychological dependence Drug dependence that is based primarily on emotional or psychological needs.

When a person develops a **psychological dependence,** he or she feels that a drug is necessary to maintain emotional or psychological well-being. Usually, this is based on an intense craving for the drug and its rewarding qualities (Feldman & Quenzer, 1984). Make no mistake, however: Psychological dependence may affect a drug user as powerfully as physical addiction does. This is why some psychologists prefer to define addiction more broadly as any compulsive habit pattern. By this definition, a person who has lost control over his or her drug use, for whatever reason, is addicted (Marlatt et al., 1988).

Note in Table 6–4 that the drugs most likely to lead to physical dependence are alcohol, amphetamines, barbiturates, cocaine, codeine, heroin, methadone, morphine, and tobacco. Using *any* of the drugs listed in Table 6–4 can result in psychological dependence. Note too that people who take drugs intravenously, especially those who share needles, are at high risk for developing AIDS (see Chapter 19).

Table 6–4 Comparison of Psychoactive Drugs (continued)

Effects Sought	Long-Term Symptoms	Physical Dependence Potential	Psychological Dependence Potential	Organic Damage Potential
Sense alteration, anxiety reduction, sociability	Cirrhosis, toxic psychosis, neurologic damage, addiction	Yes	Yes	Yes
Alertness, activeness	Loss of appetite, delusions, hallucinations, toxic psychosis	Yes	Yes	Yes
Anxiety reduction, euphoria	Addiction with severe withdrawal symptoms, possible convulsions, toxic psychosis	Yes	Yes	Yes
Anxiety relief	Irritability, confusion, depression, sleep disorders	Probably	Yes	No
Wakefulness, alertness	Insomnia, heart arrhythmias, high blood pressure	No?	Yes	Yes
Excitation, talkativeness	Depression, convulsions	Yes	Yes	Yes
Euphoria, prevent withdrawal discomfort	Addiction, constipation, loss of appetite	Yes	Yes	No
Euphoria, prevent withdrawal discomfort	Addiction, constipation, loss of appetite	Yes	Yes	No*
Insightful experiences, exhilaration, distortion of senses	May intensify existing psychosis, panic reactions	No	No?	No?
Relaxation; increased euphoria, perceptions, sociability	Possible lung cancer, other health risks	No	Yes	Yes
Insightful experiences, exhiliration, distortion of senses	May intensify existing psychosis, panic reactions	No	No?	No?
Prevent withdrawal discomfort	Addiction, constipation, loss of appetite	Yes	Yes	No
Euphoria, prevent withdrawal discomfort	Addiction, constipation, loss of appetite	Yes	Yes	No*
Euphoria	Unpredictable behavior, suspicion, hostility, psychosis	Debated	Yes	Yes
Insightful experiences, exhiliration, distortion of senses	May intensify existing psychosis, panic reactions	No	No?	No?
Alertness, calmness, sociability	Emphysema, lung cancer, mouth and throat cancer, cardiovascular damage, loss of appetite	Yes	Yes	Yes

*Persons who inject drugs under non-sterile conditions run a high risk of contracting AIDS, hepatitis, abscesses, or circulatory disorders.

Patterns of Abuse Some drugs, of course, have a higher potential for abuse than others. Heroin is certainly more dangerous than caffeine. However, this is only one side of the picture. Often, it is as useful to classify drug-taking *behavior* as it is to rate drugs. For example, some people remain social drinkers for life, whereas others become alcoholics within weeks of taking their first drink. In this sense, drug use can be classified as **experimental** (short-term use based on curiosity), **social-recreational** (occasional social use for pleasure or relaxation), **situational** (use to cope with a specific problem such as boredom or staying awake for night work), **intensive** (daily use with elements of dependence), or **compulsive** (intense use and extreme dependence) (National Commission of Marihuana and Drug Abuse, 1973). The last three categories of drug-taking tend to be damaging no matter what drug is used. The discussion that follows focuses on the drugs most often abused by college students.

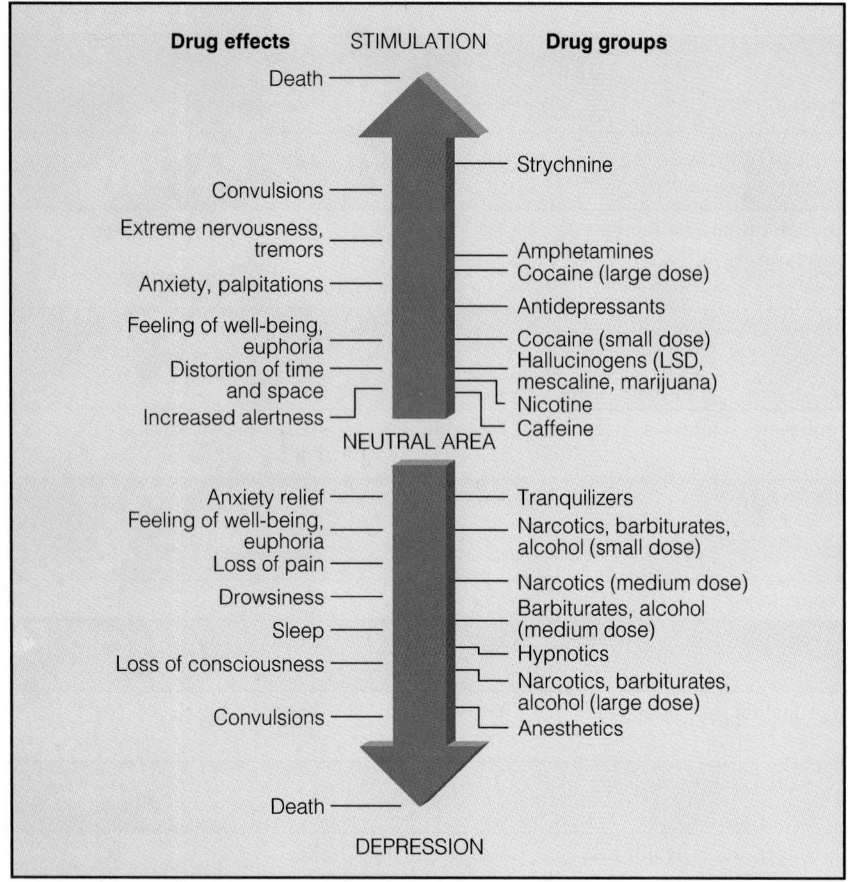

■ Fig. 6–12 *Spectrum and continuum of drug action. Many drugs can be rated on a stimulation-depression scale according to their effects on the central nervous system. Although LSD, mescaline, and marijuana are listed here, the stimulation-depression scale is less relevant to these drugs. The principal characteristic of such hallucinogens is their mind-altering quality.*

Amphetamines A class of synthetic drugs having stimulant effects on the nervous system.

Amphetamine psychosis A severe disruption of psychological functioning caused by abuse of amphetamines.

Cocaine A crystalline drug derived from coca leaves; used as a central nervous system stimulant and local anesthetic.

Uppers—Amphetamines, Cocaine, Caffeine, Nicotine

Amphetamines form a large group of synthetic stimulants. Drugs commonly available in this group are *Dexedrine*, *Methedrine*, and *Benzedrine*. Amphetamines were once widely prescribed to aid weight loss or to combat mild depression. Both practices are now frowned on because patients often become dependent on their legal amphetamines. The only fully legitimate medical uses of amphetamines are to treat narcolepsy, childhood hyperactivity, and overdoses of depressant drugs. Illicit use of amphetamines is widespread among individuals seeking an easy way to stay awake and by those who think drugs can improve mental or physical performance.

Amphetamines rapidly produce a drug tolerance. Most abusers who begin with 1 or 2 pills a day progress to taking dozens a day to get the same effect. Eventually, some users switch to injecting Methedrine ("speed") directly into the bloodstream. The true speed freak typically goes on binges lasting several days, after which he or she "crashes" from lack of sleep and food.

Question: How dangerous are amphetamines?

Abuse Amphetamine use poses many dangers. To stay high, the abuser must take more and more of the drug as the body's tolerance grows. Higher doses can cause nausea, vomiting, high blood pressure, fatal heart arrhythmias, and crippling strokes. Also, it is important to realize that amphetamines speed the use of bodily resources; they do not magically supply energy. Hence, the after-effects of an amphetamine binge can be dangerous and uncomfortable. Possible effects include extreme fatigue, depression, terrifying nightmares, confusion, uncontrolled irritability, and aggression. Repeatedly overextending one's body with stimulants may lead to severe weight loss, sores and non-healing ulcers, tooth grinding, chronic chest infections, liver disease, high blood pressure, and in some cases, brain hemorrhage.

Amphetamines can also cause a loss of contact with reality known as **amphetamine psychosis.** Affected users feel threatened and suffer from paranoid delusions that someone is out to get them. Acting on these delusions, the speed freak may become violent, resulting in self-injury or injury to others. Amphetamine psychosis is probably caused by damage to a brain structure called the habenula (Ellison, 1992).

A potent new smokable form of crystal methamphetamine has recently added to the problem of stimulant abuse. The drug, known as "ice" on the street, is highly addictive. Like "crack," the smokable form of cocaine, it produces an intense high without the use of needles. Also like crack (discussed in a moment), crystal methamphetamine leads very rapidly to compulsive abuse and severe drug dependence.

Cocaine

Cocaine is a powerful central nervous system stimulant extracted from the leaves of the coca plant. Cocaine produces feelings of alertness, euphoria, well-being, power, boundless energy, and pleasure (Gawin, 1991).

Cocaine has a long history of use and misuse. At the turn of the century, dozens of non-prescription potions and cure-alls contained cocaine (■ Fig. 6–13). It was during this time that Coca-Cola was indeed the "real thing." From 1886 until 1906, when the Pure Food and Drug Act was passed, Coca-Cola contained cocaine (which has since been replaced with caffeine). Today, cocaine is one of the most widely abused drugs. An estimated 4 to 5 million Americans use it at least once a month, and half of all Americans between the ages of 25 and 30 have tried cocaine (Gawin, 1991).

Among college students, there has been a 4-fold increase in cocaine use, compared to 15 years ago (Patterson, et al. 1988).

Question: How does cocaine differ from amphetamines?

The two are very much alike in their effects on the central nervous system. The main difference is that amphetamine effects may last several hours; cocaine is quickly metabolized, so its effects last only about 15 to 30 minutes (Woods et al., 1987).

Question: How dangerous is cocaine?

Abuse Cocaine is one of the most dangerous drugs of abuse. Even casual or first-time users run a risk because cocaine can cause convulsions, heart attack, or a stroke (Cregler & Mark, 1986; Isner, 1986). The highly publicized death of All-American basketball star Len Bias is a case in point (■ Fig. 6–14). The most tragic cocaine victims are children who were exposed to the drug before birth. Just one hit of cocaine taken by a pregnant woman can cause defects in her fetus. At birth, "crack babies" are very excitable and jittery if their mother recently used cocaine (Lester et al., 1991). Otherwise, they are sluggish and depressed. By the time cocaine babies start school, they often suffer from tremors, hyperactivity, listlessness, slowed language learning, and disorganized thinking (Fackelmann, 1991). Many will never be normal.

When rats and monkeys are given free access to cocaine, they find it irresistible. Many, in fact, end up dying of convulsions from self-administered overdoses of the drug (Hammer & Hazelton, 1984). Cocaine increases activity in brain pathways sensitive to the chemical messengers dopamine (DOPE-ah-meen) and noradrenaline (nor-ah-DREN-ah-lin). Noradrenaline arouses the brain, and added dopamine produces a "rush" of pleasure. This combination is so powerfully rewarding that those who use cocaine run a high risk of becoming dependent and compulsive abusers.

A person who stops using cocaine does not experience the physical withdrawal symptoms typical of drugs such as heroin. But cocaine has its own withdrawal pattern and can be just as addicting. First, there is a jarring "crash" of mood and energy following a cocaine binge. Within a few days, the person enters a long period of fatigue, anxiety, paranoia, boredom, and anhedonia (an-he-DAWN-ee-ah: an inability to feel pleasure). This occurs because the brain adapts to cocaine abuse in ways that upset its chemical balance, causing depression when cocaine is withdrawn (Hurley, 1989).

During withdrawal, cravings for cocaine are intense: The person feels wretched and also vividly remembers the intense pleasure of previous cocaine highs. The urge to use cocaine grows overwhelming.

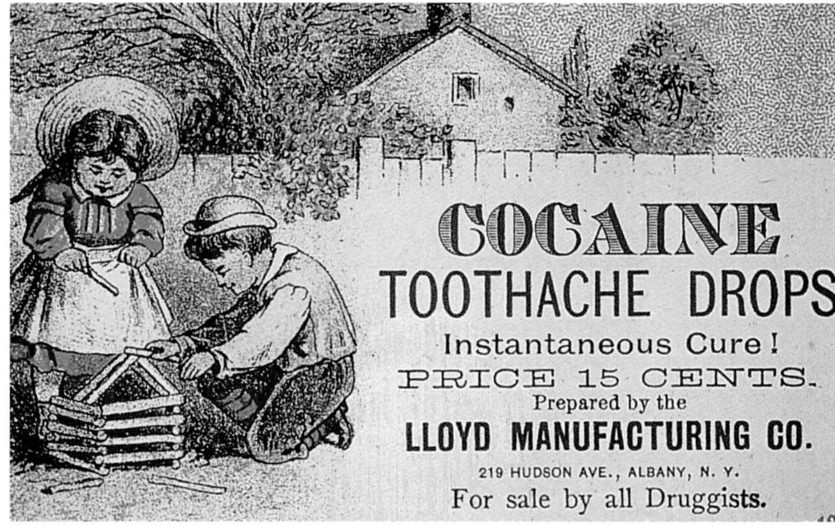

■ **Fig. 6–13** *Cocaine was the main ingredient in many non-prescription elixirs before the turn of the century. Today cocaine is recognized as a powerful and dangerous drug. Its high potential for abuse has damaged the lives of countless users.*

So, while cocaine does not fit the classic pattern of physical addiction, there is little doubt about its potential for compulsive abuse (Byck, 1987). Even a person who gets through the withdrawal period may crave cocaine months or years after last using it (Gawin, 1991).

Cocaine's rate of abuse would probably be even higher were it not for its absurdly high price. Many authorities estimate that if cocaine were cheaper, 9 out

■ **Fig. 6–14** *The future looked bright in 1986 when college basketball star Len Bias was chosen to play for the Boston Celtics. Thrilled by his hard-earned achievement, and perhaps feeling invincible, Bias tried cocaine, probably for the first time. Hours later his dream perished. Bias was dead from cardiac arrest at age 22.*

Caffeine A natural drug with stimulant properties; found in coffee and tea and added to artificial beverages and medicines.

Caffeinism Excessive consumption of caffeine, leading to dependence and a variety of physical and psychological complaints.

Nicotine A potent stimulant drug found primarily in tobacco; nicotine is a known carcinogen.

of 10 users would progress to compulsive use. In fact, rock cocaine (or "crack"), which is cheaper, produces very high abuse rates among those who try it. Here are some increasingly serious signs of cocaine abuse (Pursch, 1983).

- **Compulsive use.** If cocaine is available—say, at a party—you will undoubtedly use it. You can't say no to it.
- **Loss of control.** Once you have had some cocaine, you will keep using it until you are exhausted or the cocaine is gone.
- **Disregarding consequences.** You don't care if the rent gets paid, your job is endangered, your lover disapproves, or your health is affected, you'll use cocaine anyway.

It is becoming clear that cocaine's capacity for abuse and social damage rivals or exceeds that of such unglamorous drugs as opium and heroin. Anyone who thinks he or she may be developing a cocaine problem should seek advice at a drug clinic or a Cocaine Anonymous meeting. From 30 to 90 percent of cocaine abusers who remain in treatment programs succeed in breaking their coke addiction (Gawin, 1991).

Caffeine

Caffeine is the most frequently used psychoactive drug in the United States. Caffeine stimulates the brain by blocking chemicals that normally inhibit or slow nerve activity (Julien, 1988). Its effects become apparent with doses as small as 50 milligrams (the amount found in about one half cup of brewed coffee). Physically, caffeine causes sweating, talkativeness, tinnitus (ringing in the ears), and hand tremors (Hughes et al., 1991). Psychologically, caffeine suppresses fatigue or drowsiness and increases feelings of alertness; some people have a hard time starting a day without it.

How much caffeine did you consume today? It is common to think of coffee as the major source of caffeine, but there are many others. Caffeine is found in tea, many soft drinks (especially colas), chocolate, and cocoa. Over 2000 non-prescription drugs also contain caffeine, including stay-awake pills, cold remedies, and many name-brand aspirin products. Table 6–5 gives the approximate caffeine content of several foods.

Question: Are there any serious drawbacks to using caffeine?

Abuse Serious abuse of caffeine may result in an unhealthy dependence known as **caffeinism**. Insomnia, irritability, loss of appetite, chills, racing heart, and elevated body temperature are all signs of caffeinism. It is not uncommon to find that individuals with these symptoms are drinking 15 or 20 cups of coffee a day.

Table 6–5 Average Caffeine Content of Various Foods

Instant coffee (5 ounces), 64 milligrams
Percolated coffee (5 ounces), 108 milligrams
Drip coffee (5 ounces), 145 milligrams
Decaf. coffee (5 ounces), 3 milligrams
Black tea (5 ounces), 42 milligrams
Canned ice tea (17 ounces), 30 milligrams
Cocoa drink (6 ounces), 8 milligrams
Chocolate drink (8 ounces), 14 milligrams
Sweet chocolate (1 ounce), 20 milligrams
Colas (12 ounces), 50 milligrams
Soft drinks (12 ounces) 0–52 milligrams

Even in the absence of caffeinism, there are some caffeine-related health risks. Caffeine encourages the development of breast cysts in women, and it contributes to bladder cancer, heart problems, and high blood pressure. Health authorities urge pregnant women to give up caffeine entirely because of a suspected link between caffeine and birth defects. Also, caffeine can double or triple the risk of miscarriages (Grady, 1986; Infante-Rivard et al., 1993).

It is customary in our culture to think of caffeine as a non-drug. But as this discussion shows, it is wise to remember that it *is* a drug and use it in moderation. As few as 2.5 cups of coffee a day (or the equivalent) can be a problem. People who consume even such modest amounts of caffeine may experience anxiety, depression, fatigue, headaches, and flu-like symptoms during withdrawal (Silverman et al., 1992).

Nicotine

Nicotine is a natural stimulant found mainly in tobacco. Next to caffeine, it is the most widely used psychoactive drug (Julien, 1988).

Question: How does nicotine compare with other stimulants?

Nicotine is a potent drug. It is so toxic that it is sometimes used as an insecticide! In large doses it causes stomach pain, vomiting and diarrhea, cold sweats, dizziness, confusion, and muscle tremors. In very large doses, nicotine may cause convulsions, respiratory failure, and death. For a non-smoker, 50 to 75 milligrams of nicotine taken in a single dose could be lethal. (Chain-smoking about 17 to 25 cigarettes will produce this dosage.)

Most first-time smokers get sick on 1 or 2 cigarettes. In contrast, a heavy smoker may inhale 40 cigarettes a day without feeling ill. This difference indicates that regular smokers build a tolerance for nicotine.

The real reason dinosaurs became extinct

■ Fig. 6–15 *Actress Lilly Tomlin took up smoking for a role in the movie "Shadows and Fog" and developed a 4-pack-a-day habit. As Tomlin's experience shows, the best way to avoid developing a nicotine addiction is to not begin smoking in the first place.*

Question: Is it true that nicotine can be addicting?

Abuse A 1988 report by the U.S. surgeon general concluded that nicotine is addicting (■ Fig. 6–15). For many smokers, withdrawal from nicotine causes headaches, sweating, cramps, insomnia, digestive upset, irritability, and a sharp craving for cigarettes. These symptoms may last from 2 to 6 weeks and may be worse than heroin withdrawal. Indeed, relapse patterns are nearly identical for alcoholics, heroin addicts, cocaine abusers, and smokers who try to quit (Brownell et al., 1986; Koop, 1988a). Relapse is especially likely to occur if a smoker becomes depressed during withdrawal—as many do (Hughes, 1992).

Question: How serious are the health risks of smoking?

Impact on Health A burning cigarette releases more than 6800 different chemicals. Many of these are potent *carcinogens* (car-SIN-oh-jins, cancer-causing substances). In addition, nicotine itself may be cancer causing. Lung cancer and other cancers caused by smoking are now considered the single most preventable cause of death in the United States. Among men, 97 percent of lung cancer deaths are caused by smoking. For women, 74 percent of all lung cancers are due to smoking, a rate that has risen sharply in recent years. Altogether, smoking is responsible for about one third of all cancer deaths. Skeptics take note: Wayne McLaren, who portrayed the rugged "Marlboro Man" in cigarette ads, died of lung cancer at age 51. Here are some sobering facts about smoking:

Smoking Facts

- Every cigarette reduces a smoker's life expectancy by 7 minutes.
- Smoking is the number one cause of deaths in the United States—more than the number of deaths from alcohol, drugs, car accidents, and AIDS combined.
- In the United States alone, smoking-related costs total $50 billion a year. Taxpayers pick up the bill for 43 percent of this total.
- Forty percent of all smokers who develop throat cancer try smoking again.
- Each year, only 1 out of 15 smokers who tries to quit smoking succeeds.
- Some tobacco companies manipulate nicotine levels in their cigarettes to keep smokers addicted.
- Daily exposure to second-hand smoke at home or work causes a 24 to 39 percent increase in cancer risk to non-smokers.

If you think smoking is harmless, or the link between smoking and cancer is unproved, you're kidding yourself. As one expert says, "The scientific link between tobacco smoking and cancer is now as firmly established as any link between cause and effect in a human disease is likely to be" (Reif, 1981). By the way, urban cowboys and Skol bandits, similar conclusions apply to smokeless tobacco (chewing tobacco and

Barbiturate One of a large group of sedative drugs.

Sedative A substance that calms, tranquilizes, or induces sleep by depressing activity in the nervous system.

Drug interaction A combined effect of two drugs that exceeds the addition of one drug's effects to the other.

snuff). Users of smokeless tobacco run a 4 to 6 times higher risk of developing oral cancer. Smokeless tobacco also causes shrinkage of the gums, contributes to heart disease, and probably is as addicting as cigarettes (Christian & McDonald, 1987; Foreyt, 1987).

Smokers don't just risk their own health, they also endanger those who live and work nearby. A massive study by the U.S. government concluded in 1993 that secondary smoke causes 20 percent of all lung cancers. Non-smoking women who are married to smokers suffer a 30 percent increase in their risk of developing lung cancer. Babies born to mothers who smoked during and after pregnancy are 3 times more likely to die of sudden infant death syndrome (also see Fig. 6–7). It is particularly irresponsible of smokers to expose young children to second-hand smoke (Abramson, 1993).

Dynamics of Smoking Smokers, unless they have a death wish, must be getting something out of smoking. Most claim that smoking helps them concentrate, feel sociable, or calm down. But psychologist Stanley Schachter asserts, "The heavy smoker gets nothing out of smoking. He smokes only to prevent withdrawal" (Schachter, 1978). Schachter has shown that smoking does not improve the mood or the performance of heavy smokers compared to non-smokers. On the other hand, heavy smokers who are *deprived* of nicotine feel worse and perform worse than non-smokers.

Schachter has also shown that heavy smokers adjust their smoking to keep bodily levels of nicotine constant. Thus, when smokers are given lighter cigarettes, they smoke more. Also, if they are under stress (which speeds the removal of nicotine from the body), they smoke more (Schachter, 1978). The link between stress and nicotine probably explains why students smoke more during stressful periods such as final exams, or at parties, which are also stressful.

Question: Is it better for a person to quit smoking abruptly or taper down gradually?

Quitting Smoking For many years, smokers were advised to quit cold-turkey. The current view is that quitting all at once isn't as effective as tapering off. Going cold-turkey makes quitting an all-or-nothing proposition. Smokers who smoke even one cigarette after "quitting forever" tend to feel they've failed and might as well resume smoking. Those who quit gradually accept that success may take many attempts, spread over several months.

Here are some helpful strategies for quitting smoking: (1) Delay having a first cigarette in the morning. Then try to delay a little longer each day. (2) Gradually reduce the total number of cigarettes you smoke each day. (3) Quit completely, but for just one week. Then quit again, a week at a time, for as many times as necessary to make it stick (Pierce, 1991).

Whatever approach is taken, quitting smoking is not easy. It does help, though, if you get a spouse or partner to support your effort (Cohen & Lichtnestein, 1990). Also, as we have noted, anyone trying to quit should be prepared to make several attempts before succeeding (Brownell et al., 1986). But the good news is tens of millions of people have quit.

Downers—Barbiturates and Alcohol

Question: How do downers differ from the stimulant drugs?

The most widely used downers, or depressant drugs, are alcohol and barbiturates. These drugs are so much alike in their effects that barbiturates are sometimes referred to as "solid alcohol." Let's examine the properties of each.

Barbiturates

Barbiturates are **sedative** drugs that depress activity in the brain. Medically, they are used to calm patients or to induce sleep. In mild doses, barbiturates have an effect similar to alcohol intoxication, but an overdose can easily cause coma or death. Barbiturates combined with alcohol are particularly risky. When mixed, the effects of both drugs are multiplied by a **drug interaction** (one drug enhances the effect of another).

Barbiturates are often taken in excess amounts because a first dose may be followed by others as the user becomes uninhibited or forgetful. Over the years, Marilyn Monroe, Judy Garland, and a number of other well-known persons have died of barbiturate overdoses. An overdose of barbiturates first causes unconsciousness. Then it so severely depresses the brain centers controlling heartbeat and breathing that death results.

Abuse The most frequently abused downers are short-acting barbiturates such as *Seconal* and *Tuinal*. Closely related to these (and to alcohol) is the non-barbiturate drug *methaqualone* (*Quaalude*, *Sopor*, and *Parest* are its trade names). These drugs seem to be preferred because they take effect quickly, and the rush of intoxication only lasts from 2 to 4 hours. Like the other depressants, repeated use can cause a physical dependence and emotional depression. Many suicides have been linked with the use of depressant drugs.

All too often, the short-acting depressants are gulped down with alcohol or added to a "spiked" punch bowl. This is the combination that left a young woman named Karen Ann Quinlan in a coma that lasted 10 years, ending with her death in 1985. It is no exaggeration to restate that mixing barbiturates with alcohol can be fatal.

Alcohol

Alcohol is the common name for ethyl alcohol, the intoxicating element in fermented and distilled liquors. Contrary to popular belief, alcohol is not a stimulant. Lively behavior at drinking parties is actually due to the fact that alcohol is a central nervous system **depressant.** As ■ Figure 6–16 shows, small amounts of alcohol reduce inhibition and produce feelings of relaxation and euphoria. Larger amounts of alcohol cause ever-greater impairment of the brain until the drinker loses consciousness. Alcohol also does not act as an aphrodisiac. It usually impairs sexual performance, particularly in males. As William Shakespeare observed long ago, drink "provokes the desire, but it takes away the performance."

Question: Some people become aggressive and want to argue or fight when they are drunk. Others become relaxed and friendly. How can the same drug have such different effects?

When a person is drunk, thinking and perception become dulled or shortsighted, a condition that has been called **alcohol myopia** (my-OH-pea-ah). Only the most obvious and immediate stimuli catch a drinker's attention. Worries and "second thoughts" that would normally restrain behavior are banished from the drinker's mind. This is why many behaviors become more extreme when a person is drunk. Alcohol also reduces anxiety and temporarily makes people feel better about themselves (Steele & Josephs, 1990). It's easy to see why alcohol is such a seductive drug.

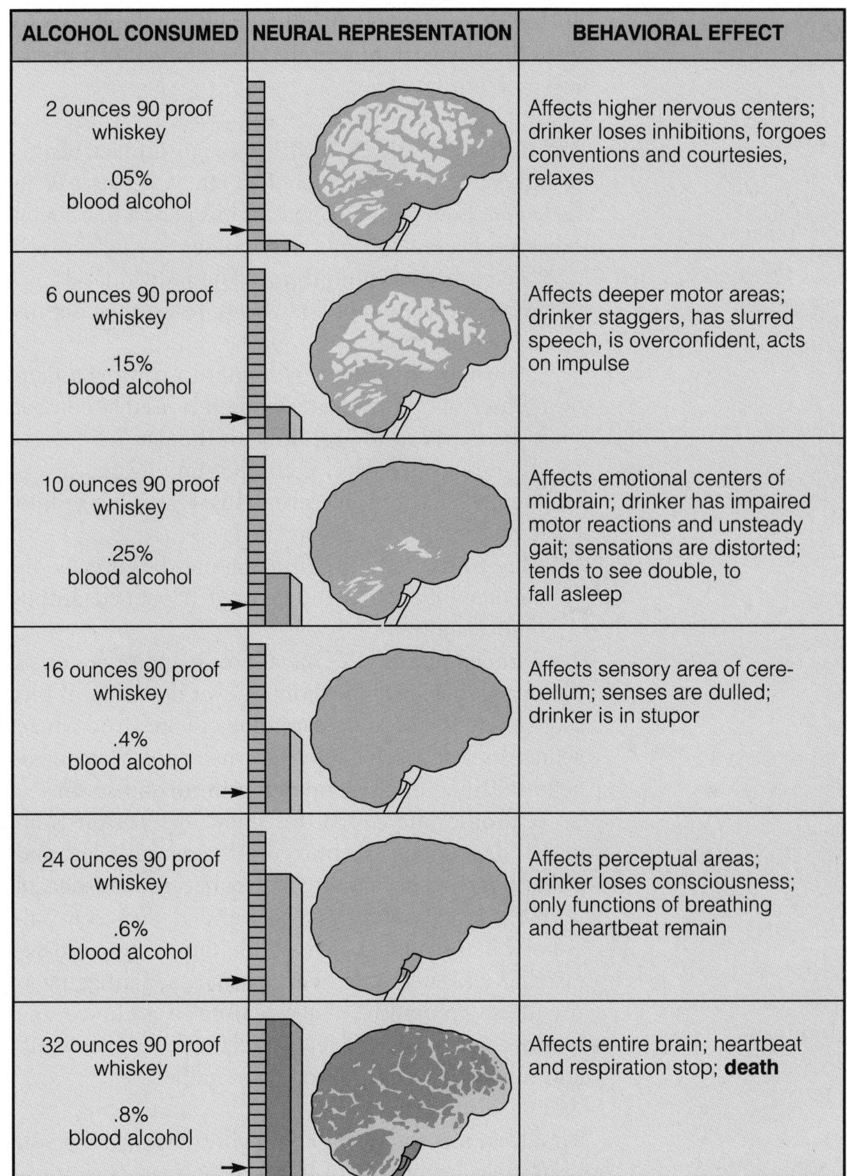

ALCOHOL CONSUMED
NEURAL REPRESENTATION
BEHAVIORAL EFFECT
2 ounces 90 proof whiskey
.05% blood alcohol
Affects higher nervous centers; drinker loses inhibitions, forgoes conventions and courtesies, relaxes
6 ounces 90 proof whiskey
.15% blood alcohol
Affects deeper motor areas; drinker staggers, has slurred speech, is overconfident, acts on impulse
10 ounces 90 proof whiskey
.25% blood alcohol
Affects emotional centers of midbrain; drinker has impaired motor reactions and unsteady gait; sensations are distorted; tends to see double, to fall asleep
16 ounces 90 proof whiskey
.4% blood alcohol
Affects sensory area of cerebellum; senses are dulled; drinker is in stupor
24 ounces 90 proof whiskey
.6% blood alcohol
Affects perceptual areas; drinker loses consciousness; only functions of breathing and heartbeat remain
32 ounces 90 proof whiskey
.8% blood alcohol
Affects entire brain; heartbeat and respiration stop; death

■ **Fig. 6–16** *The behavioral effects of alcohol are related to blood alcohol content and the resulting suppression of higher mental function. Arrows indicate the typical threshold for legal intoxication in the United States. (From Jozef Cohen,* Eyewitness Series in Psychology, *p. 44. Copyright © by Rand McNally and Company. Reprinted by permission.)*

Abuse Alcohol, America's favorite depressant, breeds this country's biggest drug problem. Over 160 million Americans use alcohol, and an estimated 20 million of these have a serious drinking problem. A particularly alarming trend is a dramatic increase in alcohol abuse among adolescents and young adults. A national survey of college students found that 17 percent (more than 1 out of 6) are heavy drinkers. For college males, the figure was 25 percent, or 1 out of 4 male students (Olmstead, 1984). Children of alcoholics must be very cautious about drinking. As adults, these people have an elevated risk of becoming alcohol abusers themselves (Blane, 1988).

Women also face some special risks of alcohol abuse. For one thing, alcohol is absorbed faster and metabolized more slowly by women's bodies. The result is that women get intoxicated from less alcohol than men do. Women who drink are also more prone to liver disease, osteoporosis, and depression. As few as 3 drinks a week may increase a woman's risk of breast cancer by 50 percent. In addition, women who abuse alcohol are more likely to face social rejection and stigma than men who drink similar amounts (Gomberg, 1993).

Question: What are the signs of alcohol abuse?

Recognizing Problem Drinking Because alcohol abuse is such a common problem, it is important to recognize the danger signals of growing dependency. The progression from a social drinker to an alcohol

Alcohol Common name for ethyl alcohol, the intoxicating element in fermented and distilled liquors.

Alcohol myopia Shortsighted thinking and perception that occurs during alcohol intoxication.

abuser to an alcoholic is often subtle. Jellinek (1960) gives these typical steps in the development of a drinking problem.

1. **Initial phase.** At first, the social drinker begins to turn more often to alcohol to relieve tension or to feel good. Four danger signals in this period that signal excessive dependence on alcohol are:

Increasing consumption. The individual drinks more and more and may begin to worry about his or her drinking.

Morning drinking. Morning drinking is a dangerous sign, particularly when it is used to combat a hangover or to "get through the day."

Regretted behavior. The person engages in extreme behavior while drunk that leaves her or him feeling guilty or embarrassed.

Blackouts. Abusive drinking may be revealed by an inability to remember what happened during intoxication.

2. **Crucial phase.** A crucial turning point comes as the person begins to lose control over drinking. At this stage, there is still some control over when and where a first drink is taken. But one drink starts a chain reaction leading to a second and a third, and so on.
3. **Chronic phase.** At this point, the person is alcohol dependent. Victims drink compulsively and continuously. They rarely eat, they become intoxicated from far less alcohol than before, and they crave alcohol when deprived of it. Work, family ties, and social life all deteriorate. The person's self-drugging is usually so compulsive that when given a choice, the bottle comes before friends, relatives, employment, and self-esteem. The person is an addict.

To add to this summary, Highlight 6–5 may help you form a clearer picture of the development of a drinking problem.

HIGHLIGHT 6–5

A Closer Look At

The Development of a Drinking Problem

Early Warnings

You are beginning to feel guilty about your drinking.

You drink more than you used to and tend to gulp your drinks.

You try to have a few extra drinks before or after drinking with others.

You have begun to drink at certain times or to get through certain situations.

You drink to relieve feelings of boredom, depression, anxiety, or inadequacy.

You are sensitive when others mention your drinking.

You have had memory blackouts or have passed out while drinking.

Signals Not To Be Ignored

There are times when you need a drink.

You drink in the morning to overcome a hangover.

You promise to drink less and are lying about your drinking.

You often regret what you have said or done while drinking.

You have begun to drink alone.

You have weekend drinking bouts and Monday hangovers.

You have lost time at work or school because of drinking.

You are noticeably drunk on important occasions.

Your relationship to family and friends has changed because of your drinking.

Moderated Drinking Many people who are social-recreational drinkers could do a far better job of managing their use of alcohol. Almost everyone has been to a party or social gathering spoiled by someone who drank too much too fast. Those who avoid overdrinking have a better time, and so do their friends. But how do you avoid drinking too much? After all, as one wit once observed, "The conscience dissolves in alcohol." Psychologists Roger Vogler and Wayne Bartz (1982; 1992) provide a partial answer.

Vogler and Bartz observe that drinking makes you feel good while blood alcohol is rising and remains below a level of about 0.05. In this range, people feel relaxed, euphoric, and sociable. At higher levels they go from moderately intoxicated to thoroughly drunk. Later, as blood alcohol begins to fall, those who overdrink become sick and miserable. ⬬ Table 6–6 shows the approximate amount per hour that can be consumed without exceeding the 0.05 blood alcohol level. (Even at this level, driving may be affected.) By pacing themselves, those who choose to drink can remain comfortable, pleasant, and coherent during a long party or other event. In short, if you drink, it might be wise to learn your "magic" number from Table 6–6.

It takes skill to regulate drinking in social situations, where the temptation to drink can be strong. If you choose to drink, here are some guidelines that may be helpful. (Adapted from Vogler & Bartz, 1992.)

Table 6–6 Drinking in Moderation

Your Weight (pounds)	Approximate number of drinks per hour to stay below 0.05 blood alcohol.*	
	Male	*Female*
100	0.75	0.60
120	1.00	0.75
140	1.25	0.90
160	1.30	1.00
180	1.50	1.10
200	1.60	1.20
220	1.80	1.35

One drink = 12 ounces beer,
4 ounces wine,
2.5 ounces brandy, or
1.25 ounces 80 proof liquor.

*Table entries are approximate, owing to individual differences in metabolism, recency of meals, and other factors. Estimates are from tables prepared by Vogler and Bartz (1982; 1992).

Paced Drinking

1. Think about your drinking beforehand and plan how you will manage it.
2. Drink slowly, eat while drinking, and make every other drink (or more) a non-alcoholic beverage.
3. Limit drinking primarily to the first hour of a social event or party. Pace your drinking using the information from Table 6–6.
4. Practice how you will politely but firmly refuse drinks.
5. Learn how to relax, meet people, and socialize without relying on alcohol.

Treatment Treatment for alcohol dependence begins by sobering up the person and cutting off the supply. This phase is referred to as **detoxification.** It frequently produces all the symptoms of drug withdrawal and can be extremely unpleasant for the alcoholic. The next step is to try to restore the person's health. Continued heavy use of alcohol usually causes severe damage to body organs and the nervous system. Food, vitamins, and medical care cannot fully reverse the damage, but a reasonable state of health can be obtained. When alcoholics have "dried out" and health has been restored, they may be treated with tranquilizers, antidepressants, or psychotherapy. Unfortunately, the success of these procedures has been limited.

One mutual-help approach that has been fairly successful is Alcoholics Anonymous (AA). AA acts on the premise that it takes a former alcoholic to understand and help a current alcoholic. Participants at AA meetings admit that they have a problem, share feelings, and resolve to stay "dry" one day at a time. Other group members provide support for those struggling to end dependency. (Cocaine Anonymous and Narcotics Anonymous use the same approach.)

Eighty-one percent of those who remain in AA over 1 year get through the following year without a drink (Sexias, 1981). AA's success rate may simply reflect the fact that members participate voluntarily, meaning they have admitted that they have a serious problem (McLatchie & Lomp, 1988). Sadly, it seems that alcohol abusers will often not face their problems until they have "hit rock bottom." If they are willing, though, AA presents a practical approach to the problem.

Two newer groups offer a rational, non-spiritual approach to alcohol abuse that better fits the needs of some people. These are Rational Recovery and Secular Organizations for Sobriety (SOS). Other alternatives to AA include medical treatment, group therapy, and individual psychotherapy (Institute of Medicine, 1990). There is a strong tendency for abusive drinkers to deny that they have a problem. Nevertheless, the sooner they seek help the better.

Detoxification In the treatment of alcoholism, the withdrawal of the patient from alcohol.

Marijuana The leaves and flowers of the hemp plant, *Cannabis sativa.*

Hashish Resinous material high in THC, scraped from the leaves of the hemp plant.

Cannabis sativa The hemp plant, from which marijuana and hashish are derived.

THC Tetrahydrocannabinol, the main active chemical in marijuana.

Hallucinogen Any substance that distorts sensory impressions.

Marijuana—What's in the Pot?

If you pick any three Americans at random, one will have tried marijuana at least once. More than 18 million Americans may be regular users, which puts marijuana in a league with tobacco and alcohol. **Marijuana** and **hashish** are derived from the hemp plant *Cannabis sativa.* The main active chemical in Cannabis is tetrahydrocannabinol, or **THC** for short. THC is a mild **hallucinogen** (hal-LU-sin-oh-jin)—a substance that alters sensory impressions.

Hallucinogens The drug LSD (lysergic acid diethylamide) is perhaps the best known hallucinogen. Even when taken in tiny amounts, LSD can produce hallucinations and psychotic-like disturbances in thinking and perception (■Fig. 6–17). Two other common hallucinogens are mescaline (peyote) and psilocybin ("magic mushrooms"). Incidentally, the drug PCP (phencyclidine) can have hallucinogenic effects. However, PCP, which is an anesthetic, also has stimulant and depressant effects. This potent combination can cause extreme agitation, disorientation, violence—and too often, tragedy. All of the hallucinogens, including marijuana, affect neurotransmitter systems that carry messages between brain cells (Palfai & Jankiewicz, 1991).

Marijuana Marijuana's typical psychological effects include a sense of euphoria or well-being, relaxation, altered time sense, and perceptual distortions. At high dosages, however, paranoia, hallucinations, and delusions can occur (Palfai & Jankiewicz, 1991). All con-

■ **Fig. 6–17** *Artists have tried at times to capture the effects of hallucinogens. Here, an artist depicts a visual experience he had while under the influence of LSD.*

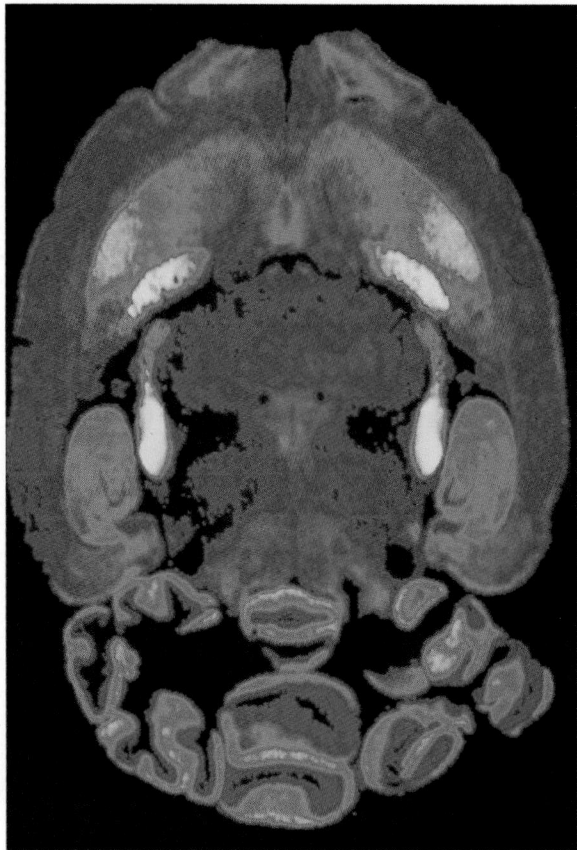

■ **Fig. 6–18** *This thin slice of a rat's brain has been washed with a radioactive THC-like drug. Yellowish areas show where the brain is rich in THC receptors. In addition to the cortex, or outer layer of the brain, THC receptors are found in abundance in areas involved in the control of coordinated movement. Naturally occurring chemicals similar to THC may help the brain cope with pain and stress. However, when THC is used as a drug, high doses can cause paranoia, hallucinations, and dizziness (Fackelmann, 1993).*

sidered, marijuana intoxication is relatively subtle by comparison to drugs such as LSD or alcohol (Kelly et al., 1990). Despite this, it is now well established that driving a car or operating machinery while high on marijuana can be extremely hazardous. As a matter of fact, driving under the influence of any intoxicating drug is dangerous.

There have been no overdose deaths from marijuana use reported in the United States. However, enough is now known about the effects of marijuana to make it clear that it cannot be considered harmless. Particularly worrisome is the fact that THC accumulates in the body's fatty tissues, especially in the brain and reproductive organs. Even if a person smokes marijuana just once a week, the body is never entirely free of THC. Scientists recently located a specific receptor site on the surface of brain cells where THC binds to produce its effects (■ Fig. 6–18). These receptor sites are found in large numbers in the cerebral cortex, which is the seat of human consciousness (Matsuda et al., 1990).

Question: Does marijuana produce physical dependence?

Studies of long-term heavy users of marijuana in Jamaica, Greece, and Costa Rica failed to find any physical dependence (Carter, 1980; Rubin & Comitas, 1975; Stefanis et al., 1977). Marijuana's potential for abuse lies primarily in the realm of psychological dependence, not addiction (■ Fig. 6–19).

Question: There have been very alarming reports in the press about the dangers of marijuana. Are they accurate?

Dangers of Marijuana Use As one pharmacologist put it, "Those reading only *Good Housekeeping* would have to believe that marijuana is considerably more dangerous than the black plague." Unfortunately, an evaluation of marijuana's risks has been clouded by emotional debate. Let's see if we can make a realistic appraisal.

In the past it was widely reported that marijuana causes brain damage, mental illness, and a loss of motivation. These are serious charges, but each has been criticized for being based on poorly done or inconclusive research (Brecher, 1975a; Julien, 1988; NIDA, 1976; Zinberg, 1976). In addition, major studies in Jamaica, Greece, and Costa Rica failed to find any serious health problems or mental impairment in long-term marijuana smokers (Carter, 1980; Rubin & Comitas, 1975; Stefanis et al., 1977). Does this mean that marijuana gets a clean bill of health? Not really. As is true of alcohol, some adults become highly dependent on marijuana. The use of any drug, including marijuana, can seriously impair mental, physical, and emotional development (Pandina et al., 1990). In addition, long-term marijuana users tend to show some impairments of learning, memory, and thinking abilities. These effects, while subtle, can be a serious problem for frequent users (Block & Ghoneim, 1993).

Health Risks After many years of conflicting information, some of marijuana's health hazards are being clarified. After an extensive review of research, the National Academy of Sciences concluded that marijuana's long-term effects include several health risks.

1. In regular users, marijuana causes chronic bronchitis and pre-cancerous changes in lung cells. At present no direct link between marijuana and lung cancer has been proved, but it is suspected. Marijuana smoke contains 50 percent more cancer-causing hydrocarbons than does tobacco smoke. Some doctors estimate that smoking several "joints" a week is the equivalent of smoking a dozen cigarettes a day. Other researchers have found that "smokers of only a few joints a day have as much microscopic damage to the cells lining the airways as smokers of more than a pack of cigarettes a day" (Tashkin et al., 1988).
2. Marijuana temporarily lowers sperm production in males, and some studies show more abnormal sperm in men who use it. This could be a problem for a man who is marginally fertile and wants to have a family (Palfai & Jankiewicz, 1991).
3. In experiments with female monkeys, THC causes abnormal menstrual cycles and disrupts ovulation. Other animal studies show that THC causes a higher rate of miscarriages and that it can reach the developing fetus. As is true for so many other drugs, it appears that marijuana should be avoided during pregnancy.
4. THC can suppress the body's immune system, possibly increasing the risk of disease (Turkington, 1986).
5. In animals, marijuana causes genetic damage within cells of the body. It is not known to what extent this happens in humans, but it does suggest that marijuana can be detrimental to health (Zimmerman & Zimmerman, 1990).

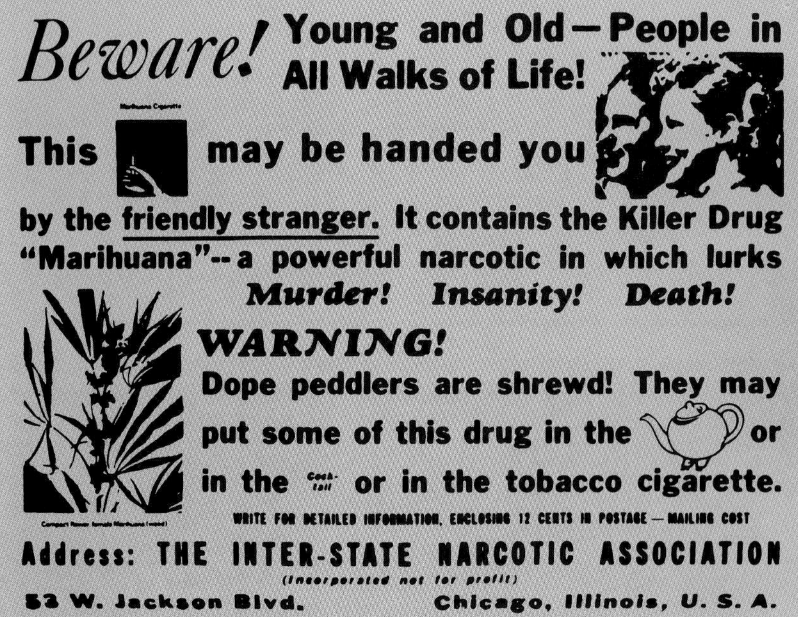

■ Fig. 6–19 *An outdated anti-marijuana poster demonstrates the kind of misinformation that has long been attached to this drug. Research is beginning to sort out what risks are associated with continued use of marijuana.*

When the preceding findings are compared with the studies of veteran marijuana users, it is clear that no one can say with certainty that marijuana is extremely harmful or completely safe. Although much is still unknown, marijuana appears to be in a class with two other potent drugs—tobacco and alcohol. Only future research will tell for sure "what's in the pot."

A Look Ahead Of the many states of consciousness we have discussed, dreaming remains one of the most familiar—and the most surprising. Are there lessons to be learned from dreams? What personal insights lie hidden in the ebb and flow of dream images? The following Applications section probes such questions. After that, in the Exploration, we will conclude by wrestling with the question, Why do people abuse drugs and what can be done about it?

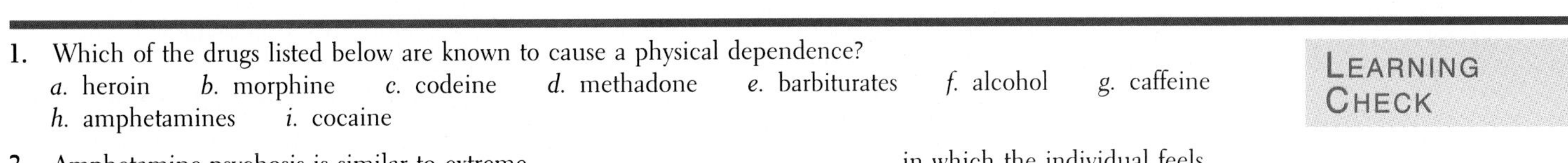

LEARNING CHECK

1. Which of the drugs listed below are known to cause a physical dependence?
a. heroin *b.* morphine *c.* codeine *d.* methadone *e.* barbiturates *f.* alcohol *g.* caffeine *h.* amphetamines *i.* cocaine
2. Amphetamine psychosis is similar to extreme ______________________, in which the individual feels threatened and suffers from delusions.
3. Cocaine is very similar to which of the following in its effects on the central nervous system?
a. Quaaludes *b.* codeine *c.* Cannabis *d.* amphetamine

4. The combination of ________________ and alcohol can be fatal.
5. One drink starts a chain reaction leading to a second and a third in the crucial phase of problem drinking. T or F?
6. In terms of sheer numbers, this country's biggest drug problem centers on abuse of
   a. marijuana *b.* alcohol *c.* tobacco *d.* heroin
7. Most experts now acknowledge that marijuana is physically addicting. T or F?

Critical Thinking

8. The United States government, which helps fund anti-smoking campaigns and smoking-related health research also continues to subsidize tobacco growers. Can you explain this contradiction?

Answers: 1. All but *g* 2. paranoia 3. *d* 4. barbiturates or driving 5. T 6. *b* 7. F 8. Neither can I.

APPLICATIONS: *Exploring and Using Your Dreams*

At one time or another almost everyone has had a dream that seemed to have deep meaning. In view of this, it seems appropriate to return to dreaming in this Applications section. Let's start with Freud's approach to dream interpretation. Recall that Freud regarded dreams as disguised expressions of unconscious desires and conflicts. How are these deeper dream meanings revealed?

Dream processes Mental filters that hide the true meanings of dreams.

Condensation Combining several people, objects, or events into a single dream image.

Displacement Directing emotions or actions toward safe or unimportant dream images.

Symbolization The non-literal expression of dream content.

Secondary elaboration Making a dream more logical and complete while remembering it.

Interpreting Your Dreams

To unlock dreams, Freud identified four **dream processes** that he believed disguise the hidden meanings of dream images. The first is called **condensation.** Through condensation, a single character in a dream may represent several people at once. A character in a dream that looks like a teacher, acts like your father, talks like your mother, and is dressed like your employer might be a condensation of authority figures in your life.

A second way of disguising dream content is **displacement.** Displacement may cause the most important emotions or actions of a dream to be redirected toward safe or seemingly unimportant images. Thus, a student angry at his parents might dream of accidentally wrecking their car instead of directly attacking them.

A third dream process is **symbolization.** As mentioned earlier, Freud believed that dreams are often expressed in images that are symbolic rather than literal in their meanings. To uncover the meaning of dreams it helps to ask what feelings or ideas a dream image might symbolize. Let's say, for example, that a student dreams of coming to class naked. A literal interpretation would be that the student is an exhibitionist! A more likely symbolic meaning might be that the student feels vulnerable in the class or is unprepared for a test (■ Fig. 6–20).

■ **Fig. 6–20** *Dream images may contain symbolic messages, as well as literal meanings. If you find yourself wearing a mask in a dream, for instance, it could relate to important roles that you play at school, work, or home. It could also mean that you want to hide or that you are looking forward to a costume party. To accurately interpret a dream it is important to learn your own "vocabulary" of dream images and meanings. Keeping a dream diary is the first step toward gaining valuable insights.*

A process called **secondary elaboration** is the fourth method by which the meaning of dreams is disguised. Secondary elaboration is the tendency to make a dream more logical, and to add details when remembering it. The fresher a dream memory is, the more useful it is likely to be.

Looking for condensation, displacement, symbolization, and secondary elaboration may help you unlock your dreams. But there are simpler ways to proceed. Dream theorist Calvin Hall (1974) prefers to think of dreams as plays and the dreamer as a playwright. Hall does admit that the images and ideas in dreams tend to be more primitive than those experienced while awake. Nevertheless, much can be learned by simply considering the **setting, cast of characters, plot,** and **emotions** portrayed in a dream.

Another dream researcher, Rosalind Cartwright suggests that dreams are primarily "feeling statements." According to her, the overall **emotional tone** of a dream is a major clue to its meaning. Is the dream comical, threatening, joyous, or depressing? Were you lonely, jealous, frightened, in love, or angry? Cartwright encourages use of everyday dream life as a source of personal enrichment and personal growth (Cartwright & Lamberg, 1992).

In many ways, dreams can be thought of as a message *from* yourself *to* yourself. Thus, the way to understand dreams is to remember them, write them down, look for the messages they contain, and become deeply acquainted with *your* own symbol system. Here's how.

How To Catch a Dream

1. Before retiring, plan to remember your dreams. Keep a pen and paper or a tape recorder beside your bed.
2. If possible, arrange to awaken gradually without an alarm. Natural awakening is almost always soon after a REM period.
3. If you rarely remember your dreams, you may want to set an alarm clock to go off an hour before you usually awaken. Although less desirable than awakening naturally, this method may let you catch a dream.
4. Upon awakening, lie still and review the dream images with your eyes closed. Try to recall as many details as possible.
5. If you can, make your first dream record (whether by writing or by tape) with your eyes closed. Opening your eyes will disrupt dream recall.
6. Review the dream again and record as many additional details as you can remember. Dream memories disappear quickly. Be sure to describe feelings as well as the plot, characters, and actions of the dream.
7. Put your dreams into a permanent dream diary. Keep dreams in chronological order and review them periodically. This procedure will reveal recurrent themes, conflicts, and emotions. It almost always produces valuable insights.
8. Remember, a number of drugs suppress dreaming (see Table 6–7).

Table 6–7 Effects of Selected Drugs on Dreaming

Drug	Effect on REM Sleep
Alcohol	Decrease
Amphetamines	Decrease
Barbiturates	Decrease
Caffeine	None
Cocaine	Decrease
LSD	Slight increase
Marijuana	Slight decrease or no effect
Opiates	Decrease
Valium (Diazepam)	Decrease

Dream Work Because each dream has several possible meanings or levels of meaning, there is no fixed way to work with it. Telling the dream to others and discussing its meaning can be a good start. Describing it may help you relive some of the feelings in the dream, and family or friends may be able to offer interpretations you would be blind to yourself. Watch for verbal or visual puns and other playful elements in dreams. If, for example, you dream that you are in a wrestling match and your arm is pinned behind your back, it may mean that you feel someone is "twisting your arm" in real life.

The meaning of most dreams will yield to a little detective work. Rosalind Cartwright suggests asking a series of questions about dreams you would like to understand (Cartwright and Lamberg, 1992).

Probing Dreams

1. Who was in the dream? Do you recognize any of the characters?
2. What was happening? Were you active in the dream or watching it transpire? Did someone else do something to you?
3. Where did the action of the dream take place? Have you seen the setting or any part of it in real life, or was it a fantasy scene?
4. What was the time frame? What was your age in the dream?
5. Who is responsible for what happened in the dream?
6. Who are you in your dreams? Are you someone you would like to be or someone you'd rather not be?

If you still have trouble seeing the meaning of a dream, you may find it helpful to use a technique developed by Fritz Perls. Perls, the originator of Ge-

Lucid dream A dream in which the dreamer feels awake and capable of normal thought and action.

stalt therapy, considered most dreams a special message about what's missing in our lives, what we avoid doing, or feelings that need to be "re-owned." Perls felt that dreams are a way of filling in gaps in personal experience (Perls, 1969).

An approach that Perls found helpful is to "take the part of" or "speak for" each of the characters and objects in the dream. In other words, if you dream about a strange man standing behind a doorway, you would speak aloud to the man, then answer for him. To use Perls' method, you would even speak for the door, perhaps saying something like, "I am a barrier. I keep you safe, but I also keep you locked inside. The stranger has something to tell you. You must risk opening me to learn it."

A particularly interesting dream exercise is to continue a dream as waking fantasy so that it may be concluded or carried on to a more meaningful ending. As the world of dreams and your personal dream language become more familiar, you will doubtless find many answers, paradoxes, intuitions, and insights into your own behavior.

Using Your Dreams

Dream theorist Gordon Globus (1987) believes that some of our most creative moments take place during dreaming. Even unimaginative people, he notes, may create amazing worlds each night in their dreams. For many of us, this rich ability to create is lost in the daily rush of sensory input. How might we tap the creative power of dreams that is so easily lost during waking?

Dreams and Creativity History is full of cases where dreams have been a pathway to creativity and discovery. A striking example is provided by Dr. Otto Loewi, a pharmacologist and winner of a Nobel Prize. Loewi had spent years studying the chemical transmission of nerve impulses. A tremendous breakthrough in his research came when he dreamed of an experiment three nights in a row. The first two nights he woke up and scribbled the experiment on a pad. But the next morning, he couldn't tell what the notes meant. On the third night, he got up after having the dream. This time, instead of making notes he went straight to his laboratory and performed the crucial experiment. Loewi later said that if the experiment had occurred to him while awake he would have rejected it.

Loewi's experience gives some insight into using dreams to produce creative solutions. Inhibitions are reduced during dreaming, which may be especially useful in solving problems that require a fresh point of view.

Being able to take advantage of dreams for problem solving is improved if you "set" yourself before retiring. Before you go to bed, try to think intently about a problem you wish to solve. Steep yourself in the problem by stating it clearly and reviewing all relevant information. Then use the suggestions listed in the previous section to catch your dreams. While this method is not guaranteed to produce a novel solution or a new insight, it is certain to be an adventure. About half of a group of college students using this method for one week recalled a dream that helped them solve a personal problem (Barrett, 1993).

Lucid Dreaming If you would like to press further into the territory of dreams, you may want to learn lucid dreaming. During a **lucid dream** the dreamer "wakes" within an ordinary dream and feels capable of normal thought and action. Lucid dreamers know they are dreaming, but they feel fully conscious within the dream world (La Berge, 1985). If you ask yourself, "Could this be a dream?" and answer "Yes," you are having a lucid dream (Blackmore, 1991).

Stephen La Berge and his colleagues at the Stanford University Sleep Research Center have used a unique approach to show that lucid dreams are real and that they occur during REM sleep. In the sleep lab, lucid dreamers agree to make prearranged signals when they become aware they are dreaming. One such signal is to look up abruptly in a dream, causing a distinct upward eye movement. Another signal is to clench the right and left fists (in the dream) in a prearranged pattern. Corresponding muscle changes in the wrists can then be recorded electrically. Such signals show very clearly that lucid dreaming and voluntary action in dreams is possible (La Berge, 1981, 1985; La Berge et al., 1981; Moss, 1989).

Question: How would a person go about learning to have lucid dreams?

La Berge found he could greatly increase lucid dreaming by following this simple routine: When you awaken spontaneously from a dream, take a few minutes to try to memorize it. Next, engage in 10 to 15 minutes of reading or any other activity requiring full wakefulness. Then while lying in bed and returning to sleep, say to yourself, "Next time I'm dreaming, I want to remember I'm dreaming." Finally, visualize yourself lying in bed asleep while in the dream you just rehearsed. At the same time, picture yourself realizing that you are dreaming. Follow this routine each time you awaken (substitute a dream memory

APPLICATIONS: *Continued*

from another occasion if you don't awaken from a dream).

Question: Why would anyone want to have more lucid dreams?

Researchers are interested in lucid dreams because they provide a new tool for understanding dreaming. Using subjects who can signal while they are dreaming may make it possible to explore dreams with first-hand data from the dreamer's world itself (La Berge, 1985).

On a more personal level, lucid dreaming can convert dreams into a nightly "workshop" for emotional growth. Consider, for example, a recently divorced woman who kept dreaming that she was being swallowed by a giant wave. Rosalind Cartwright asked the woman to try swimming the next time the wave engulfed her. She did, with great determination, and the nightmare lost its terror. More importantly, her revised dream made her feel that she could cope with life again. For reasons such as this, people who have lucid dreams tend to feel a sense of emotional well-being (Wolpin et al., 1992). So, day or night, don't be afraid to dream a little.

LEARNING CHECK

1. In secondary elaboration, one dream character stands for several others. T or F?
2. Calvin Hall's approach to dream interpretation emphasizes the setting, cast, plot, and emotions portrayed in a dream. T or F?
3. Rosalind Cartwright stresses that dreaming is a relatively mechanical process having little personal meaning. T or F?
4. Both alcohol and LSD cause a slight increase in dreaming. T or F?
5. "Taking the part of" or "speaking for" dream elements is a dream interpretation technique originated by Fritz Perls. T or F?
6. Recent research shows that lucid dreaming occurs primarily during NREM sleep or micro-awakenings. T or F?
7. If you were dreaming right now, how could you prove it? *Critical Thinking*

Answers: 1. F 2. T 3. F 4. F 5. T 6. F 7. In waking consciousness, our actions have consequences that produce immediate sensory feedback. Dreams lack such external feedback (Tart, 1986). Thus, trying to walk through a wall or doing similar tests would reveal if you were dreaming.

EXPLORATION

Drug Abuse—Many Questions, Few Answers

Why do people use drugs? People seek drug experiences for a variety of reasons, ranging from curiosity and a desire to belong to a group to a search for meaning or an escape from feelings of inadequacy. The best predictors of adolescent drug use and abuse are peer drug use, parental drug use, delinquency, parental maladjustment, poor self-esteem, social nonconformity, and stressful life changes (Marlatt et al., 1988).

For many young people, drug abuse is just one part of a general pattern of problem behavior. A study that followed children from preschool to age 18 found that adolescents who abuse drugs tend to be maladjusted, alienated, impulsive, and emotionally distressed. The study makes it clear that drug abuse is a symptom, rather than a cause, of personal and social maladjustment (Shedler & Block, 1990).

The Dynamics of Drug Abuse Many abusers turn to drugs in a self-defeating attempt to cope with life. All of the frequently abused drugs produce immediate feelings of pleasure. The negative consequences follow much later. This combination of immediate pleasure and delayed punishment allows abusers to feel good on demand. In time, of course, most of the pleasure goes out of drug abuse, and the abuser's problems get

EXPLORATION

worse. But if an abuser merely feels *better* (however briefly) after taking a drug, drug taking can become compulsive (Barrett, 1985).

Drug Expectancies Closely related to a drug's actual effects are users' beliefs and expectations about drugs. Patterns of drinking alcohol offer a good example of how expectations promote abuse. For example, Brown, Goldman, and Christiansen (1985) studied the expectations people have about drinking. Drinkers were asked about alcohol's effect on general good feelings, sexual performance, social and physical pleasure, self-assertion, relaxation, and feelings of power. The study found that heavy drinkers expect far more positive effects and fewer negative consequences from drinking alcohol than light drinkers do. Children who learn such expectancies are likely to become problem drinkers in adolescence (Christiansen et al., 1989). The three most dangerous beliefs are:

- Alcohol makes experiences more positive.
- Alcohol facilitates social behavior.
- Alcohol improves thinking and physical performance.

Cultural Values There is a widespread tendency to think of drugs as a magic way to produce good feelings by avoiding, minimizing, or escaping negative situations. Some observers believe that drug use is so deeply ingrained in modern society that "we are addicted to addiction. This is to say that, with few exceptions we subscribe to the premise that life cannot be lived without drugs." We are so used to having our own way that we have come to believe "we should be able to will ourselves to be calm, cheerful, thin, industrious, creative—and moreover, to have a good night's sleep." Some critics believe that the medical profession, well meaning but misguided, has accepted these premises wholeheartedly and unnecessarily encourages legal drug use. Indeed, one psychologist observed:

> Depression, social inadequacy, anxiety, apathy, marital discord, children's misbehavior, and other psychological and social problems of living are now being redefined as medical problems, to be solved by physicians with prescription pads. (Rogers, 1971)

Perhaps physicians and the general public alike can be partially excused for placing undue faith in the value of drugs. Each group is the target of multimillion-dollar advertising campaigns aimed at encouraging drug use. Even the lowly aspirin is pushed as a means of relieving "nervous tension." Advertisements directed at physicians encourage overuse of drugs even more blatantly. An ad pictures a distraught mother with a child and asks, "Her kind of pressures last all day . . . shouldn't her tranquilizer?" Another reads:

> School, the dark, separation, dental visits, monsters. The everyday anxiety of children sometimes gets out of hand. A child can usually deal with his anxieties. But sometimes the anxieties overpower the child. Then he needs your help. Your help may include Vistaril.

Drugs, of course, have legitimate uses and have alleviated much suffering. The problem is that drugs strong enough to ease pain, induce sleep, end depression, or otherwise alter consciousness have a high potential for abuse. Rather than sounding the alarm about illicit drug use, politicians and public health officials need to pay more attention to the far more widespread abuse of legally prescribed drugs (MacCoun, 1993).

Drug abuse in Western nations has reached epidemic proportions in recent years. Problems once restricted to drug-related subcultures and the urban poor are now seen regularly among high school and college students and among the vast middle classes. In the United States, one survey found that nearly 40 percent of doctors under age 40 admitted that they use marijuana or cocaine to get high with friends (McAuliffe, 1986)!

Question: What, if anything, should be done about drug abuse?

Prevention Traditional approaches have emphasized limiting drug supplies, strict law enforcement, and legal penalties. Limiting supplies has been relatively successful in the case of some drugs. But drug abuse and the legality of a drug are two separate issues. This distinction becomes clear when it is recognized that one of the most potent, destructive, and potentially dangerous drugs available is alcohol. By the government's own standards, alcohol should be at the top of the list of controlled substances. Yet it is legal.

Facts such as these have led some observers to conclude that anyone who seeks drug-induced consciousness alteration will find a drug, legal or illegal, to achieve it. Psychiatrist Thomas Szasz (1985) believes that it is futile for the government to attempt to "legislate morality" by regulating what drugs a person chooses to take. Szasz suggests that current drug regulations have an effect similar to the prohibition of alcohol in the United States in the 1920s. That is, they encourage a black market, organized crime, disrespect for the law, and occasional poisonings from adulterated drugs. As Szasz points out, "tobacco is not legally considered a drug, marijuana is, gin is not, but Valium is . . . ."

After an extensive review of research on drugs, drug abuse, and drug laws, the magazine *Consumer Reports* drew the same conclusion and added these recommendations (Brecher, 1972):

- Stop publicizing the horrors of the "drug menace." Scare publicity has functioned not as warnings, but to popularize drugs and as a lure to recreational drug use.
- Stop misclassifying drugs. Our current legal classification system treats alcohol and nicotine—two of the most harmful drugs—essentially as non-drugs, while marijuana is equated with heroin—a shocking and harmful bit of foolishness. Cocaine is still listed as a narcotic when it is clearly a stimulant. A scientifically based legal system must replace the current politically based one.

Think About It Whereas it is true that drug *use* is essentially a "victimless crime," the fact remains that *abuse* of drugs—legal or illegal—represents a serious loss in the productivity and mental health of self-drugged citizens.

EXPLORATION

The point of view expressed by Szasz is obviously controversial. Many in fact, believe that the answer to drug problems is to be found in stricter penalties and law enforcement. And yet, a sober look at drug abuse makes it clear that some psychoactive drugs are almost always available. In general, Americans tend to overlook the frequency of abuse of legal drugs such as tranquilizers or alcohol and overestimate the misuse of illegal drugs (MacCoun, 1993).

Although billions of dollars have been spent on drug enforcement, there has been an increase in the overall level of drug use in the United States. On the other hand, there has been no increase in use of marijuana in states that have relaxed penalties for its possession to a fine (Thies & Register, 1993). In the Dutch city of Amsterdam, drug addiction is treated as a medical problem rather than a criminal offense (Engelsman, 1989). Methadone is freely available to heroin addicts and little effort is made to prevent the use of "soft drugs" such as marijuana. Contrary to what critics predicted, the proportion of younger addicts in Amsterdam has fallen during the last decade. Many European countries and American cities would envy this trend. Given such facts, some experts believe that prevention through education and early intervention—rather than tougher enforcement—is the answer to drug problems (MacCoun, 1993). What do you think?

Learning Check

1. Advertising campaigns directed at physicians tend to overstate the need for treating behavioral problems with drugs. T or F?
2. Heavy drinkers of alcohol learn from experience to expect more negative consequences from alcohol's effects. T or F?
3. Thomas Szasz believes that it is time for the government to take a lead in "legislating morality" with regard to drug use. T or F?
4. Current laws in the United States have been accused of misclassifying some drugs. T or F?
5. The immediate reinforcing effects of drugs and the delayed negative consequences are believed to play a major role in drug abuse. T or F?
6. Why do you think there is such a contrast between the laws regulating marijuana and those regulating alcohol and tobacco? *Critical Thinking*

Answers: 1. T 2. F 3. F 4. T 5. T 6. Drug laws in Western societies reflect cultural values and historical patterns of use. Inconsistencies in the law often cannot be justified on the basis of pharmacology, health risks, or abuse potential.

Chapter Summary

■ ***What is an altered state of consciousness?***

- States of awareness that differ from normal, alert, waking consciousness are called **altered states of consciousness** (ASCs). Altered states are especially associated with sleep and dreaming, hypnosis, sensory deprivation, and psychoactive drugs.
- Cultural conditioning greatly affects what altered states a person recognizes, seeks, considers normal, and attains.

■ ***What are the effects of sleep loss and changes in sleep patterns?***

- Sleep is an **innate biological rhythm** essential for survival. Higher animals and people deprived of sleep experience involuntary **microsleeps.**
- Moderate sleep loss mainly affects vigilance and performance on routine or boring tasks. Extended sleep loss can (somewhat rarely) produce a temporary **sleep-deprivation psychosis.**
- **Sleep patterns** show some flexibility, but 7 to 8 hours remains average. The amount of daily sleep decreases steadily from birth to old age. Once-a-day **sleep patterns,** with a 2-to-1 ratio of waking and sleep, are most efficient for most people.

■ ***Are there different stages of sleep?***

- Sleep occurs in four **stages.** Stage 1 is **light sleep,** and stage 4 is **deep sleep.** The sleeper alternates between stages 1 and 4 (passing through stages 2 and 3) several times each night.

ıapter 7

Conditioning and Learning

IN THIS CHAPTER

Antecedents and consequences
Classical conditioning
Operant conditioning
Types of reinforcement
Patterns of reinforcement
Stimulus control
Punishment
Two-factor learning
Feedback
Cognitive learning
Observational learning
Applications:
Behavioral self-management
Self-regulated learning
Exploration:
Biological influences on learning

CHAPTER PREVIEW

What Did You Learn in School Today?

When your aging author was in college, we discovered a "game" that could be played with the plumbing in the dorms. When a toilet was flushed while someone was taking a shower, the cold water pressure dropped suddenly. This caused the shower to become scalding hot. Naturally, the shower victim screamed in terror as his reflexes caused him to leap back in pain. Soon we discovered that if we flushed all *the toilets at once, the effects were multiplied many times over!*

The sound of a flushing toilet has to be one of the world's most uninspiring stimuli. But for a time, a whole flock of college students twitched involuntarily whenever they heard a toilet flush. Their new reactions to a formerly neutral stimulus resulted from classical conditioning, *a special type of learning. Details about classical conditioning are explored in this chapter.*

Now consider another learning situation: Let's say that you are at school and you feel like you are "starving to death." Locating a vending machine, you deposit your last two quarters to buy a candy bar. You press the button, and . . . nothing happens. Being civilized and in complete control, you press the other buttons, try the coin return, and look for an attendant. Still nothing. Your stomach growls. Being no longer either civilized or self-controlled, you give the machine a little kick (just to let it know how you feel). Then, as you turn away, the machine begins to whirr and out pops a candy bar plus 25 cents change. Once this happens, chances are good that you will repeat the "kicking response" in the future. If it pays off several times more, kicking vending machines may become a regular feature of your behavior. In this case, learning is based on operant conditioning *(also called* instrumental learning*).*

Classical and operant conditioning underlie much human learning. In fact, conditioning reaches into every corner of our lives. You should certainly find it useful to learn more about it. Are you ready to learn more about learning? If so, read on! This chapter explores conditioning and other forms of learning.

Survey Questions

- What is learning?
- How does classical conditioning occur?
- Does conditioning affect emotions?
- How does operant conditioning occur?
- Are there different kinds of operant reinforcement?
- How are we influenced by patterns of reward?
- What does punishment do to behavior?
- In what ways are classical conditioning and operant conditioning alike?
- What is feedback and how does it affect learning?
- What is cognitive learning?
- Does learning occur by imitation?
- How does conditioning apply to practical problems?
- How does biology influence learning?

What Is Learning?—Does Practice Make Perfect?

Most of our daily activities are either wholly learned or directly affected by learning. Imagine what you would be like if you suddenly lost everything you had ever learned. What could you do? You would be unable to read, write, or speak. You couldn't feed yourself, find your way home, drive a car, play the bassoon, or "party." Needless to say, you would be totally incapacitated. (Dull, too!)

Question: Learning is obviously important. What's a formal definition of learning?

Learning is a *relatively permanent change in behavior that can be attributed to experience.* Notice that this definition excludes temporary changes caused by motivation, fatigue, maturation, disease, injury, or drugs. Each of these can alter behavior, but none qualifies as learning.

Many of our likes, dislikes, and emotional responses are acquired by classical conditioning. Other aspects of behavior, such as what you eat, or how often you study, are affected by operant conditioning. Learning in both types of conditioning is based on *reinforcement.*

Reinforcement **Reinforcement** refers to any event which increases the probability that a response will occur again. A **response** is an identifiable behavior. Responses may be observable actions, such as blinking, eating a piece of candy, or turning a door handle; or, they may be internal events, such as an increase in heart rate.

Let's say you want to teach a dog to sit up when you whistle. To reinforce a correct response, you could whistle, and then give the dog a small bit of food if it sits up. If the dog does nothing when you whistle, you would withhold the food. Similarly, you could teach a child to be neat by praising her for picking up her toys. Learning also occurs in ways quite different than these examples imply. For instance, if a girl gets stung by a bee, she may learn to fear bees. In this case, the girl's fear is reinforced by the pain she feels immediately after seeing the bee. Later we will see how such varied experiences lead to learning.

Learning Any relatively permanent change in behavior that can be attributed to experience.

Reinforcement Any event that increases the probability that a particular response will occur.

Antecedents Events that precede a response.

Consequences Effects that follow a response.

Classical conditioning A form of learning in which reflex responses are associated with new stimuli.

Antecedents and Consequences Unlocking the secrets of learning begins with noting what happens just before, and just after, a response. Events before a response are called **antecedents.** Those that follow a response are called **consequences.** Paying careful attention to the "before and after" of learning is a key to understanding it.

Classical Conditioning The focus in classical conditioning is on what happens before a response. We begin with a stimulus that reliably triggers a response. Imagine, for example, that a puff of air (the stimulus)

Reflex An innate, automatic response to a stimulus; for example, an eye blink.

Operant conditioning Learning based on the consequences of responding.

Neutral stimulus A stimulus that does not evoke a response.

Conditioned stimulus A stimulus that evokes a response because it has been repeatedly paired with an unconditioned stimulus.

Unconditioned stimulus A stimulus innately capable of eliciting a response.

is aimed at your eye. The air puff will make you blink (a response) every time. Blinking is a **reflex** or automatic, non-learned response. Now, assume that we sound a horn (another stimulus) just before each puff of air hits your eye. If the horn and the air puff occur together many times, what happens? Soon, the horn alone will make you blink. How do we know that learning has occurred? Because before conditioning, you didn't blink when the horn sounded. Similarly, if your mouth waters each time you eat a cookie, you may learn to salivate when you merely *see* a cookie, a picture of cookies, a cookie jar, or other stimuli that have consistently preceded salivation.

In classical conditioning, *antecedent events* become *associated* with one another: A stimulus that does not produce a response is linked with one that does. (A horn is associated with an air puff, for example.) Learning is evident when the new stimulus also elicits (brings forth) responses (■ Fig. 7–1).

Operant Conditioning Operant conditioning involves learning that is affected by *consequences*. Each time a response is made, it may be followed by a reinforcer (such as food), by punishment, or by nothing.

■ Fig. 7–1 *In classical conditioning, a stimulus that does not produce a response is paired with a stimulus that does elicit a response. After many such pairings, the stimulus that previously had no effect begins to produce a response. In the example shown, a horn precedes a puff of air to the eye. Eventually the horn alone will produce an eye blink. In operant conditioning, a response that is followed by a reinforcing consequence becomes more likely to occur on future occasions. In the example shown, a dog learns to sit up when it hears a whistle.*

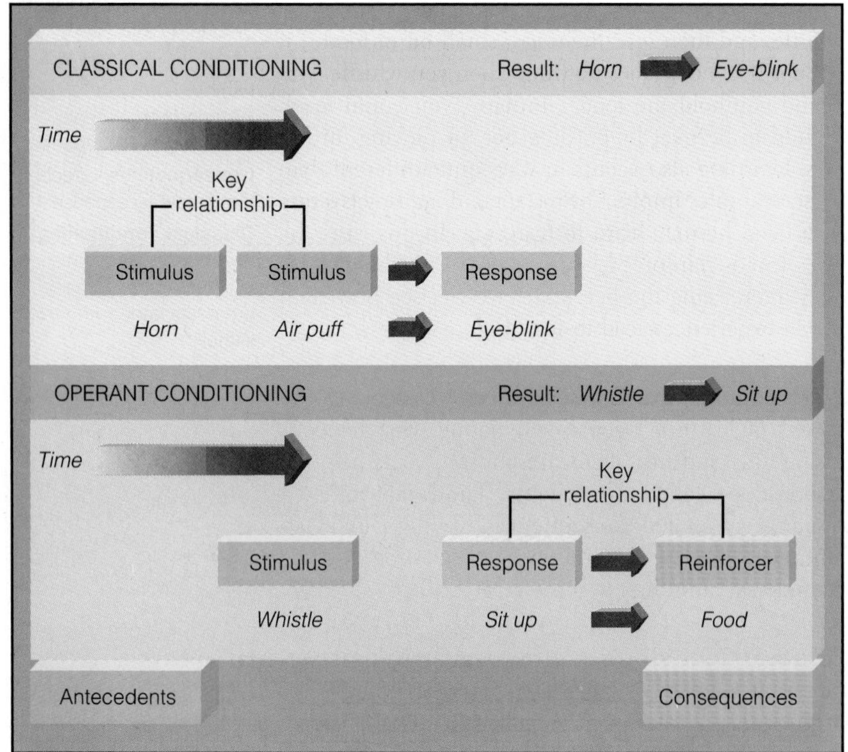

These results determine whether a response is likely to be made again (Fig. 7–1). For example, if you wear a particular shirt or blouse and get lots of compliments (reinforcement), you are likely to wear it more often. If people snicker, insult you, call the police, or scream (punishment), you will probably wear it less often.

Now that you have an idea of what happens in the two basic kinds of learning, let's look at classical conditioning in more detail.

Classical Conditioning—Does the Name Pavlov Ring a Bell?

Question: How was classical conditioning discovered?

At the beginning of the twentieth century, something happened in the lab of the Russian physiologist **Ivan Pavlov** that brought him lasting fame. The event was so unastounding that a lesser man might have ignored it: Pavlov's dogs drooled at him.

Actually, Pavlov was studying digestion. To observe salivation, he placed meat powder or some tidbit on a dog's tongue. After doing this many times, Pavlov noticed that his dogs were salivating *before* the food reached their mouths. Later, the dogs even began to salivate at the mere sight of Pavlov entering the room. Was this misplaced affection? Pavlov knew better. Salivation is normally a reflex (automatic, non-learned) response. In order for the animals to salivate at the mere sight of food, some form of learning had to be taking place. Pavlov called this type of learning **conditioning.** Because of its importance in psychology's history, it is now called **classical conditioning** (also known as **Pavlovian conditioning** or **respondent conditioning**).

Question: How did Pavlov study conditioning?

Pavlov's Experiment After Pavlov observed that meat powder causes reflex salivation, he began his classic experiments (■ Fig. 7–2). To begin, he rang a bell. At first, the bell was a *neutral stimulus.* (It did not produce any salivation.) Immediately after Pavlov rang the bell, he placed meat powder on the dog's tongue. Each time Pavlov rang the bell, he followed it with meat powder, which always caused salivation. Pavlov repeated the sequence many times: bell, meat powder, salivation; bell, meat powder, salivation.

Eventually (as conditioning took place), Pavlov's bell alone began to cause salivation (■ Fig. 7–3). By association, the bell, which before had no effect on salivation, began to produce the same response that food did. This was shown by sometimes ringing the bell and observing that the dog salivated when no food was present.

Psychologists use several terms to describe these events. The bell in Pavlov's experiment starts out as a **neutral stimulus (NS)** (a stimulus that does not evoke a response). In time, the bell becomes a **conditioned stimulus (CS)**; that is, a stimulus to which the dog has *learned* to respond. The meat powder is an **unconditioned stimulus (US)** (because the dog did not have to learn to respond to it). Unconditioned stimuli typically produce reflexive responses or involuntary emotional reactions. Since a reflex is "built in," it is called an **unconditioned** (non-learned) **response (UR).** Salivation is the UR in Pavlov's study. When the bell alone causes salivation, we would say that salivation has become a **conditioned** (learned) **response (CR)** (see Fig. 7–3).

Question: Are all these terms really necessary?

Yes, because they help us see similarities in various instances of classical conditioning. Let's summarize the terms using an earlier example:

Before Conditioning	**Example**
US → UR	Puff of air → eye blink
NS → no effect	Horn → no effect
After Conditioning	**Example**
CS → CR	Horn → eye blink

Now, let's use the terms to explain the effects of the shower and flushing toilet, described in the Chapter Preview. The unconditioned, or non-learned, response was a reflexive jump away from the hot water. The unconditioned stimulus was the hot water. The conditioned stimulus was the sound of a flushing toilet. That is, the flushing sound was at first neutral. But as a result of conditioning, it became capable of eliciting a reflex.

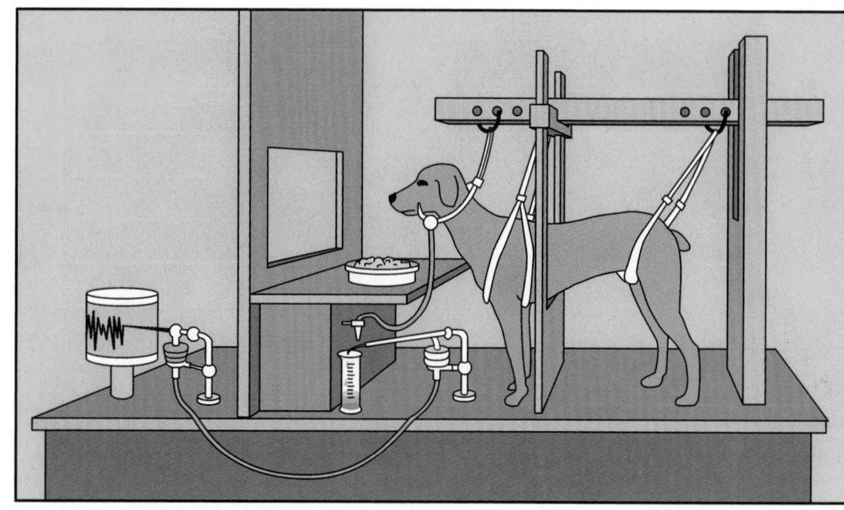

■ **Fig. 7–2** *A classical conditioning apparatus. In Pavlov's early experiments, placing a dish of food in front of the dog was paired with various other stimuli for conditioning. A tube carried saliva from the dog's mouth so that Pavlov could measure it later. The apparatus shown here is more elaborate than the one Pavlov used. In this case, the dog's salivation is recorded by the device pictured to the left.*

Elements of Conditioning—Teach Your Little Brother to Salivate

Several interesting events occur during classical conditioning. To observe them, you could ring a bell, squirt lemon juice into a child's mouth, and condition salivation to the bell. The child's reactions might then be used to explore other aspects of conditioning.

Acquisition During **acquisition,** or training, a conditioned response must be **reinforced,** or strengthened (■ Fig. 7–4). Classical conditioning is reinforced whenever the CS is followed by, or paired with, an unconditioned stimulus (US). For our child, the bell is the CS; salivating is the UR; and the US is the sour lemon juice. To reinforce salivating to the bell, we must pair

Unconditioned response An innate reflex response elicited by an unconditioned stimulus.

Conditioned response A learned response elicited by a conditioned stimulus.

Acquisition The period in conditioning during which a response is reinforced.

Respondent reinforcement Reinforcement that occurs when an unconditioned stimulus closely follows a conditioned stimulus.

■ **Fig. 7–3** *The classical conditioning procedure. Notice that the UR and CR appear to be the same. For practical purposes, you can think of them as the same response. However, the CR is usually a little weaker than the UR. This difference shows that the CR is, in fact, a learned response, not an innate reflex.*

Before conditioning	During conditioning (acquisition)	Test for conditioning
Time Bell (NS) - - - → No salivation Meat powder (US) → Salivation (UR) Reflex	Bell (CS) Associated Meat powder (US) → Salivation (UR) Reflex	Bell (CS) → Salivation (CR) Conditioned reflex

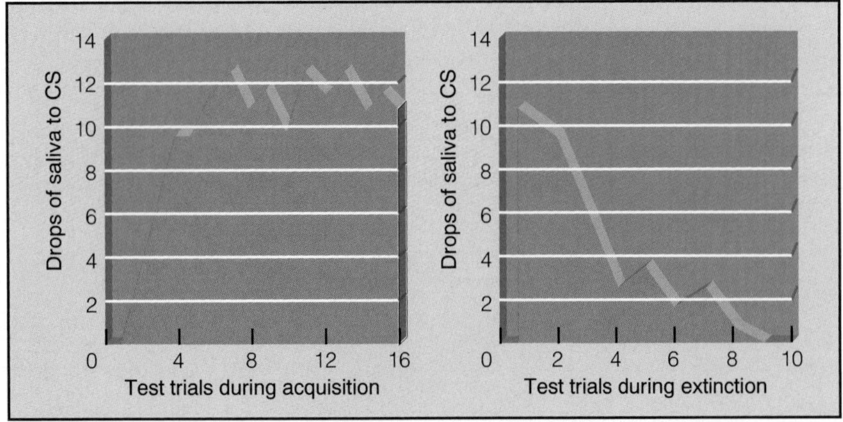

■ **Fig. 7–4** *Acquisition and extinction of a conditioned response. (After Pavlov, 1927.)*

Higher-order conditioning Classical conditioning in which a conditioned stimulus is used to reinforce further learning; that is, a CS is used as if it were a US.

Extinction The weakening of a conditioned response through removal of reinforcement.

Spontaneous recovery The reappearance of a learned response after its apparent extinction.

Stimulus generalization The tendency to respond to stimuli similar to, but not identical to, a conditioned stimulus.

the bell with the lemon juice. Conditioning will be most rapid if the US follows *immediately* after the CS. With most reflexes, the optimal delay between CS and US is from one-half second to about 5 seconds (Schwartz, 1989).

Higher-Order Conditioning After a response is learned, it can bring about **higher-order conditioning.** In higher-order conditioning a well-learned CS is used to reinforce further learning. In other words, the CS is strong enough to be used like an unconditioned stimulus. Let's illustrate again with our salivating child. As a result of earlier learning, the bell now makes the boy salivate. (No lemon juice is needed.) To go a step further, you could clap your hands and then ring the bell.

■ **Fig. 7–5** *Higher-order conditioning takes place when a well-learned conditioned stimulus is used as if it were an unconditioned stimulus.*

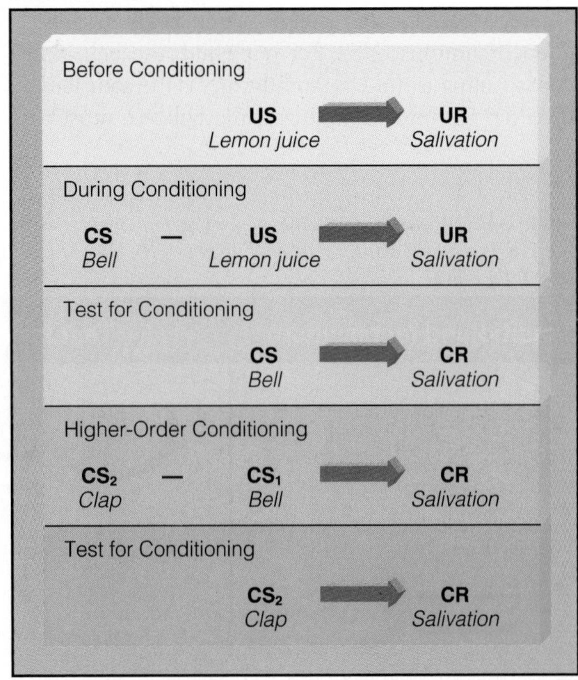

(Again, no lemon juice would be used.) Through higher-order conditioning, the child would soon learn to salivate when you clapped your hands (■ Fig. 7–5). (This little trick could be a real hit with friends and neighbors.)

Higher-order conditioning extends learning one or more steps beyond the original conditioned stimulus. Many advertisers use this effect by pairing images that evoke good feelings (such as people smiling and having fun) with pictures of their products. Obviously, they hope that you will learn, by association, to feel good when you see their products.

Question: After conditioning has occurred, what would happen if the US no longer followed the CS?

Extinction and Spontaneous Recovery If the US never again follows the CS, conditioning will **extinguish.** If the bell (in our example) is rung many times and not followed by lemon juice, the child's tendency to salivate to the ringing of the bell will be *inhibited* (or suppressed). Thus, we see that classical conditioning can be weakened by removing reinforcement (see Fig. 7–4). This process is called **extinction.**

Question: If conditioning takes a while to build up, shouldn't it take time to reverse?

Yes. In fact, several extinction sessions may be necessary to completely reverse conditioning. If you ring the bell until the child quits responding, it might seem that extinction is complete. However, ringing the bell the next day will probably cause the child to respond again at first. This reaction is called **spontaneous recovery.** Spontaneous recovery occurs when a *period of rest* follows extinction. Spontaneous recovery explains why a person who has had a terrifying car accident may need many slow, calm rides before fear is completely extinguished.

Generalization Once a person or an animal learns to respond to a conditioned stimulus, other stimuli *similar* to the CS may also trigger a response. For example, we might find that our conditioned child salivates to the sound of a ringing telephone or doorbell, an effect called **stimulus generalization** (Kimble, 1961). Stimulus generalization greatly affects our behavior. For instance, think about what happens when you meet someone new. If the person looks like one of your friends, enemies, or a former lover, your initial feelings toward the person may be influenced by generalization.

The value of stimulus generalization is easy to see. Consider the child who burns a finger while playing with matches. Learning principles predict that the sight of a lighted match will become a conditioned stimulus for fear. But will the child fear only matches? Because of stimulus generalization, the child should

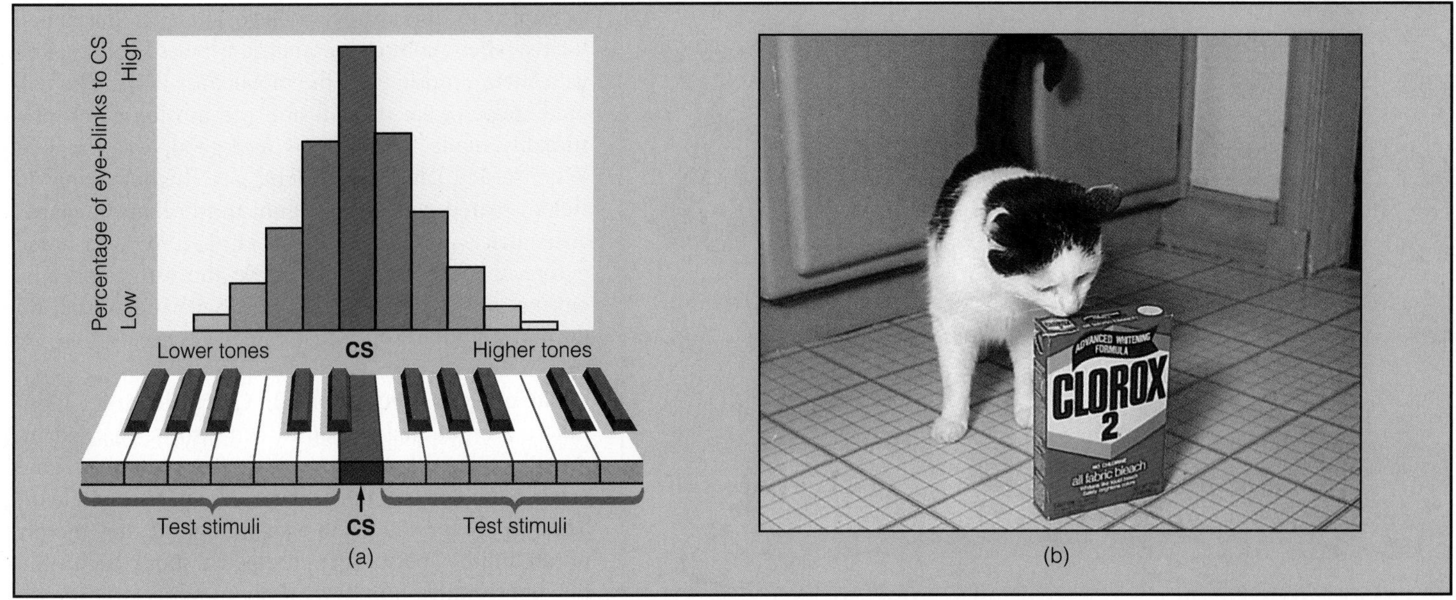

■ **Fig. 7–6** (a) *Stimulus generalization. Stimuli similar to the CS also elicit a response.* (b) *This cat has learned to salivate when it sees a cat food box. Because of stimulus generalization, it also salivates when shown a similar-looking detergent box.*

also show a healthy fear of flames from lighters, fireplaces, stoves, and so forth. It's fortunate that generalization extends learning to new settings and similar situations. Were it not for this, we would all be far less adaptable.

As you may have guessed, stimulus generalization does have limits. Responses gradually decrease as stimuli become less like the original CS (Siegel et al., 1968). In other words, if you condition a person to blink each time you play a particular note on a piano, blinking will decline as you play higher or lower notes. If the notes are *much* higher or lower, the person will not respond at all (■ Fig. 7–6).

Discrimination Let's consider one more idea with our salivating child (who by now must be ready to hide in the closet). Suppose the child is again conditioned with a bell as the CS. As an experiment, we occasionally sound a buzzer instead of the bell, but never follow it with the US (lemon juice). At first, the buzzer will produce salivation (because of generalization). But after hearing the buzzer several times more, the child will stop responding to it. The child has now learned to *discriminate*, or respond differently, to the bell and the buzzer. In essence, the child's generalized response to the buzzer has been extinguished.

Stimulus discrimination is an important part of learning. As an example, you might remember the feelings of anxiety or fear you had as a child when your mother's or father's voice changed to its you're-about-to-get-swatted tone. (Or the dreaded, "Give-me-that-Game-Boy" tone.) Most children quickly learn to discriminate voice tones associated with pain from those associated with praise or affection.

Classical Conditioning in Humans—An Emotional Topic

Question: How much human learning is based on classical conditioning?

In its simplest form, classical conditioning depends on reflex responses. Recall that a *reflex* is a dependable, inborn stimulus-and-response connection. For example, pain causes reflex withdrawal of various parts of the body. The pupil of the eye reflexively narrows in response to bright lights. Various foods cause salivation. It is entirely possible for humans to associate any of these—or other—reflex responses with a new stimulus. At the very least, you have probably noticed how your mouth waters when you see or smell a bakery. You may have even salivated to pictures of food (a picture of a lemon is great for this).

Conditioned Emotional Responses Of larger importance, perhaps, are the more subtle ways that conditioning affects us. In addition to simple reflexes, more complex *emotional*, or "gut," responses may be conditioned to new stimuli. For instance, if your face reddened as part of your emotional reaction to being punished as a child, you may blush now as an adult when you are embarrassed or ashamed. Or think about associating pain with a dentist's office during your first visit. On later visits, did your heart pound and your palms sweat *before* the dentist began?

Many *involuntary*, autonomic nervous system responses ("fight-or-flight" reflexes) are linked with new stimuli and situations by classical conditioning (Mazurski et al., 1993). Of course, this also applies to an-

Stimulus discrimination The learned ability to respond differently to similar stimuli.

■ Fig. 7–7 *Hypothetical example of a CER becoming a phobia. A child approaches dog* (a) *and is frightened by it* (b). *Fear generalizes to other household pets* (c) *and later to virtually all furry animals* (d).

Phobia An intense and unrealistic fear of some specific object or situation.

Conditioned emotional response An emotional response that has been linked to a previously non-emotional stimulus by classical conditioning.

Desensitization Reducing fear or anxiety by repeatedly exposing a person to emotional stimuli while the person is deeply relaxed.

Vicarious classical conditioning Classical conditioning brought about by observing another person react to a particular stimulus.

imals. One of the most common mistakes people make with pets (especially dogs) is hitting them if they do not come when called. Calling the animal then becomes a conditioned stimulus for fear and withdrawal. No wonder the pet disobeys when called on future occasions. Parents who belittle, scream at, or physically abuse their children make the same mistake.

Phobias (FOE-bee-ahs) are another common example of emotional conditioning. A phobia is a fear that persists even when no realistic danger exists. Persons with fears of dogs, water, heights, thunder, fire, bugs, elevators, or whatever, can often trace their fears to a time when they were frightened, injured, upset, or in pain while exposed to the feared object or stimulus. Reactions of this type, called **conditioned emotional responses (CERs),** may be broadened into phobias by stimulus generalization (■ Fig. 7–7). In fact, a therapy called **desensitization,** is now used to *extinguish* fears, anxieties, and phobias. This is done by gradually exposing the phobic person to feared stimuli while he or she tries to remain calm and relaxed. (Desensitization is described in detail in Chapter 18.)

Undoubtedly, many of our likes, dislikes, and fears are acquired as conditioned emotional responses. For example, in one study, college students developed CERs when colored geometric shapes were paired with theme music from the movie *Star Wars*. The colored shapes were the CS and the music, which presumably made the students feel good, was the US. When tested later, the students gave higher ratings to shapes paired with the pleasant music than to shapes associated with silence (Bierly et al., 1985). As noted before, advertisers try to achieve the same effect by pairing products with pleasant images and music. So do many students on a first date.

Vicarious, or Secondhand, Conditioning Conditioned emotional responses can also be learned indirectly, a fact that adds to their impact on us. One experiment, for example, showed that people will learn to respond emotionally to a signal light if they merely watch another person get an electric shock each time the light comes on. Even though subjects never directly received a shock, they developed a CER to the light just the same (Bandura & Rosenthal, 1966). Children who learn to fear thunder by watching their parents react to it have undergone similar conditioning.

Vicarious classical conditioning, as it is called, occurs when we observe another person's emotional reactions to a stimulus and, by doing so, learn to respond emotionally to the same stimulus. Such learning affects feelings in many situations. For example, "horror" movies probably add to fears of snakes, caves, spiders, heights, and other terrors. If movies can affect us, we might expect the emotions of parents, friends, and relatives to have even more impact. How, for instance, does a city child learn to fear snakes and to respond emotionally to mere pictures of them? Being told that "snakes are dangerous" may not explain the child's *emotional* response. More likely, such fears are learned by observing others as they react fearfully when the word *snake* is mentioned or a snake image appears on television (Ollendick & King, 1991).

The emotional attitudes we develop toward certain types of food, political parties, ethnic groups, escalators—whatever—are conditioned not only by direct experience but vicariously as well. Parents may do well to look in a mirror if they wonder how or where a child has "picked up" a particular fear or emotional attitude.

Learning Check

Be sure you can answer these questions before continuing.

1. Classical conditioning takes place when one ________________ stimulus is associated with another; operant conditioning is based on the ________________ that follow a response.
2. Classical conditioning, studied by the Russian physiologist ________________, is also referred to as ________________ conditioning.

3. Classical conditioning is strengthened or reinforced when the ________ follows the ________.
a. CS, US *b.* US, CS *c.* UR, CR *d.* CS, CR

4. Training that inhibits (or weakens) a conditioned response is called ________________.

5. When a conditioned stimulus is used to reinforce the learning of a second conditioned stimulus, higher-order conditioning has occurred. T or F?

6. Psychologists theorize that many phobias begin when a CER generalizes to other, similar situations. T or F?

7. Conditioning brought about by observing pain, joy, or fear in others is called ________________ conditioning.

8. Lately you have been getting a shock of static electricity every time you touch a door handle. You begin to notice a hesitation in your door-opening movements. Can you analyze this situation in terms of classical conditioning? ***Critical Thinking***

Answers:
1. antecedent, consequences 2. Pavlov, respondent or Pavlovian 3. *b* 4. extinction 5. T 6. T 7. vicarious
8. Door handles have become conditioned stimuli that elicit the reflex withdrawal and muscle tensing that normally follows getting a shock.

Operant Conditioning—Can Pigeons Play Ping-Pong?

As stated earlier, in **operant conditioning** we learn to associate responses with their consequences. The basic principle of operant conditioning (or instrumental learning) is simple: Acts that are followed by reinforcing consequences tend to be repeated. Pioneer learning theorist Edward L. Thorndike called this the **law of effect.** According to Thorndike, learning is strengthened each time a response is followed by a satisfying state of affairs. Think of the earlier example of the vending machine. What effect did kicking the machine have? It produced food and money, so the odds of repeating the "kicking response" increased.

As we have seen, classical conditioning tends to be passive and involuntary. It simply "happens to" the learner when a US closely follows a CS. In operant conditioning, the learner actively "operates on" the environment. Thus, operant conditioning refers mainly to learning *voluntary* responses. For example, waving your hand in class is a learned operant response. It is reinforced by gaining the teacher's attention. (See ● Table 7–1 for a further comparison of classical and operant conditioning.)

The idea that reward affects learning is certainly nothing new to parents (and other trainers of small animals). However, parents, as well as teachers, politicians, supervisors, and even you, may use reward in ways that are haphazard, inexact, or misguided. A case in point is the very term *reward.* To be correct, it is better to say *reinforcer.* Why? Because "rewards" do not always increase responding. If you give licorice candy to a child as a "reward" for good behavior, it will work only if the child likes licorice. What is reinforcing for one person may not be for another. Therefore, as a practical rule of thumb, psychologists define an **operant reinforcer** as any event that follows a response and increases its probability (■ Fig. 7–8).

● Table 7–1 Comparison of Classical and Operant Conditioning

	Classical Conditioning	Operant Conditioning
Nature of response	Involuntary, reflex	Spontaneous, voluntary
Reinforcement	Occurs *before* response (conditioned stimulus paired with unconditioned stimulus)	Occurs *after* response (response is followed by reinforcing stimulus or event)
Role of learner	Passive (response is *elicited* by US)	Active (response is *emitted*)
Nature of learning	Neutral stimulus becomes a CS through association with a US	Probability of making a response is altered by consequences that follow it

Acquiring an Operant Response

Most laboratory studies of operant learning take place in some form of **conditioning chamber,** also called a Skinner box (after B. F. Skinner, who invented it to study operant conditioning) (■ Fig. 7–9). A look into a typical Skinner box will clarify the process of operant conditioning.

The Adventures of Mickey Rat

A hungry rat is placed in a small cage-like chamber. The walls are bare except for a metal lever and a tray into which food pellets can be dispensed (see Fig. 7–9).

Frankly, there's not much to do in a Skinner box. This fact increases the chances that our subject will make the response we want to reinforce, which is pressing the bar. Hunger also ensures that the animal will be motivated to seek food and to actively *emit,* or freely

Operant conditioning Learning based on the consequences of responding.

Law of effect Responses that lead to desirable effects are repeated; those that produce undesirable results are not.

Operant reinforcer Any event that increases the probability or frequency of responses it follows.

Conditioning chamber An apparatus for the study of operant conditioning in animals; a Skinner box.

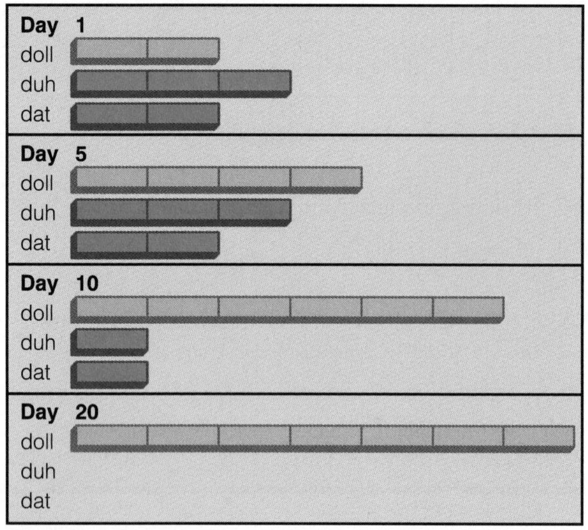

■ **Fig. 7–8** *Assume that a child who is learning to talk points to her favorite doll and says either "doll," "duh," or "dat" when she wants it. Day 1 shows the number of times the child uses each word to ask for the doll (each block represents one request). At first, she uses all three words interchangeably. To hasten learning, her parents decide to give her the doll only when she names it correctly. Notice how the child's behavior shifts as operant reinforcement is applied. By Day 20, saying "doll" has become the most probable response.*

Response-contingent reinforcement Reinforcement given only when a particular response is made.

give off, a variety of responses. Now let's take another look at our subject.

Further Adventures of Mickey Rat

For a while our subject walks around, grooms, sniffs at the corners, or stands on his hind legs—all typical rat behaviors. Then it happens. He places his paw on the lever to get a better view of the top of the cage. *Click!* The lever depresses, and a food pellet drops into the tray. The rat walks to the tray, eats the pellet, then grooms himself. Up and exploring the cage again, he leans on the lever. *Click!* After a trip to the food tray, he returns to the bar and sniffs it, then puts his foot on it. *Click!* Soon the rat settles into a smooth pattern of frequent bar pressing.

■ **Fig. 7–9** *The Skinner box. This simple device, invented by B. F. Skinner, allows controlled study of operant conditioning. When a rat presses the bar, a pellet of food or a drop of water is automatically released. (Photographs of Skinner boxes appear in Chapter 1, Figure 1–11 and Chapter 2, Figure 2–1.)*

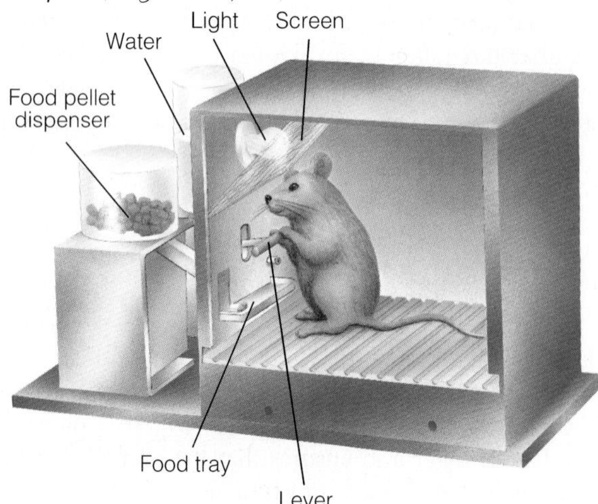

Notice that the rat did not acquire a new skill in this situation. He could already depress the bar. Reinforcement only alters how *frequently* he presses the bar. In operant conditioning, reinforcement is used to alter the frequency of responses, or to mold them into new patterns.

A good example of how operant reinforcement can change behavior is shown in ■ Figure 7–10. The results are from an effort to teach a severely disturbed 9-year-old child to say "Please," "Thank you," and "You're welcome." As you can see, during the initial, baseline period, the child rarely used the word *please*. Typically, he just grabbed objects he desired and became angry if he couldn't have them. However, when he was reinforced for saying "Please," he soon learned to use the word nearly every time he wanted something. When the child said "Please" he was reinforced in three ways: he received the object he requested (a crayon, for example); he was given a small food treat, such as piece of candy, popcorn, or a grape, and he was praised for his good behavior (Matson et al., 1990).

Operant reinforcement is most effective when it is **response contingent** (kon-TEN-jent). That is, it must be given *only* after the desired response. If the child in the preceding study had received reinforcers haphazardly, his behavior wouldn't have changed at all. In situations ranging from studying, to working hard on the job, contingent reinforcement also affects the *performance* of responses (■ Fig. 7–11). Highlight 7–1 discusses an interesting application of this principle.

HIGHLIGHT 7–1

Using Psychology

Life in an Operant Community

In 1948, B. F. Skinner published *Walden Two,* a utopian novel about a model community based on behavioral engineering. Would such a community work? On a small scale, the answer appears to be yes. One such operant community organized at the University of Kansas was quite successful. College students took part in an Experimental Living Project in which 30 men and women shared a large house (Miller, 1976). In this "community," work, leadership, and self-government were tied directly to behavioral principles.

Worksharing provides a good example of the project's operant approach. Basic jobs such as preparing food and cleaning were divided into approximately 100 tasks. Each task was described in terms of its expected end result. Residents performed all of the tasks themselves, and one community member checked daily to see that each job was completed. (This role was rotated.) To maintain job performance, credits were assigned for each of the tasks. At the end of the month, residents who had collected 400 credits got a sizable rent reduction.

This system was very effective in maintaining day-to-day work habits. As anyone who has shared living quarters knows, good intentions are no guarantee that the chores will get done. More importantly, residents rated the project as superior to dormitory living and similar alternatives. Most were highly satisfied with the system (Miller, 1976). The Experimental Living Project is a good example of the possibilities of applying conditioning principles to human behavior.

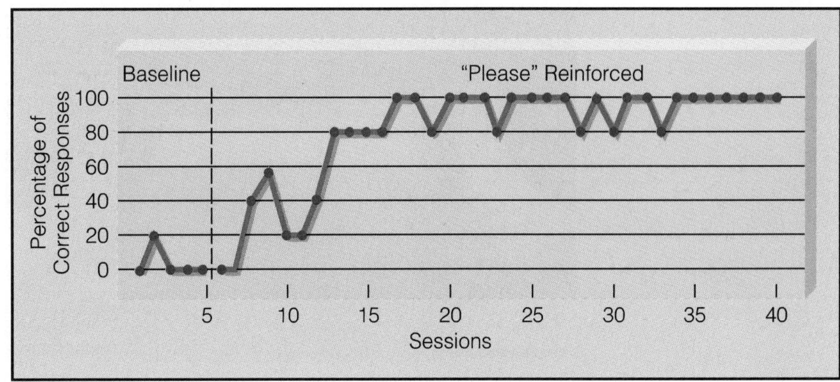

■ **Fig. 7–10** *Reinforcement and human behavior. The percentage of times that a severely disturbed child said "Please" when he wanted an object increased dramatically when he was reinforced for making a polite request. Reinforcement produced similar improvements in saying "Thank you" and "You're welcome," and the boy applied these terms in new situations as well. (Adapted from Matson et al., 1990.)*

Shaping How is it possible to reinforce responses that rarely occur? Even in a barren Skinner box, it might be a long time before a rat accidentally pressed the bar and ate a food pellet. We might wait forever for more complicated responses to occur. For example, you would have to wait a long time for a duck to accidentally walk out of its cage, turn on a light, play a toy piano, turn off the light, and walk back to its cage. If this is what you wanted to reward, you would never get the chance.

Question: Then how are the animals on TV and at amusement parks taught to perform complicated tricks?

The answer lies in **shaping,** which is the gradual molding of responses to a final desired pattern. Let's look again at our subject, Mickey Rat.

Mickey Rat Shapes Up

Assume that the rat has not yet learned to press the bar. He also shows no signs of interest in the bar. Instead of waiting for the first accidental bar press, we can shape his behavior patterns. At first, we settle for just getting him to face the bar. Any time he turns toward the bar, he is reinforced with a bit of food. Soon Mickey spends much of his time facing the bar. Next, we reinforce him every time he takes a step toward the bar. When he turns toward the bar, then walks away, nothing happens. But when he faces the bar and takes a step forward, *click!* His responses are being shaped.

By changing the rules about what makes a successful response, we can gradually train the rat to approach the bar and press it. We can reinforce responses that come closer and closer to the final desired pattern until it occurs. The principle of shaping, then, is that **successive approximations** (ever closer matches) to the desired response are reinforced. B. F. Skinner once taught two pigeons to play Ping-Pong in this way (■ Fig. 7–12).

Shaping applies to humans, too. Let's say, for example, that you want to study more, clean the house more often, or exercise more. Success in each case would be aided if you set a series of gradual, daily goals and rewarded yourself for each small step in the right direction (Watson & Tharp, 1993). Similarly, a child learning to tie her shoes could be praised first for slip-

Shaping Gradually molding responses to a final desired pattern.

Successive approximations A series of steps or ever-closer matches to a desired response pattern.

■ **Fig. 7–11** *Mean number of innings pitched by major league baseball players before and after signing long-term guaranteed contracts. The performance of 38 pitchers who signed multi-year contracts for over $100,000 per season is shown. When salary was no longer contingent on good performance, there was a rapid decline in innings pitched and in the number of wins. During the same 6-year period, the performance of pitchers on 1-year contracts remained fairly steady. (Data from O'Brian et al., 1981.)*

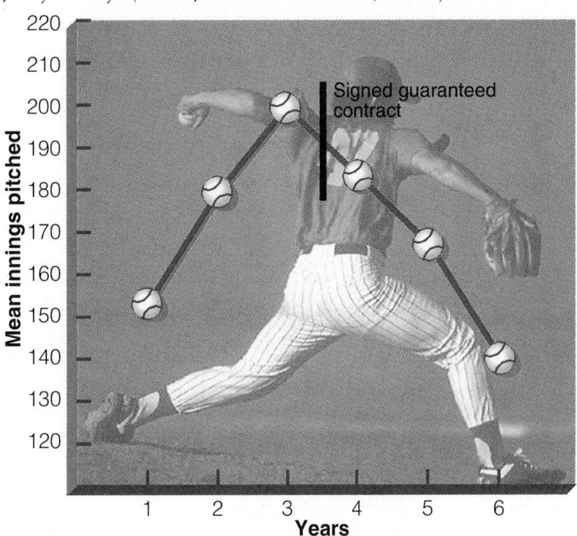

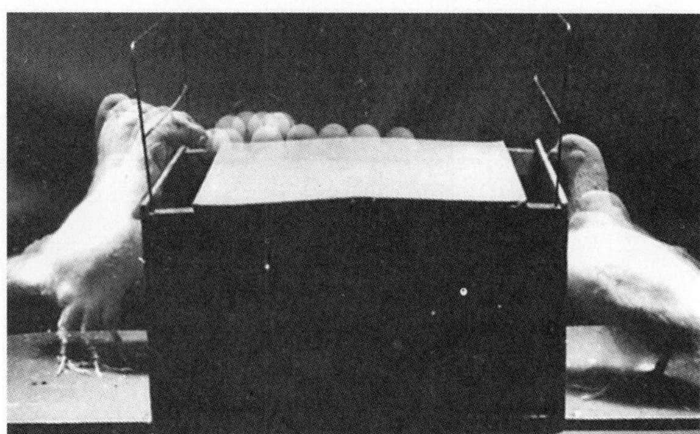

■ Fig. 7–12 *Operant conditioning principles were used to train these pigeons to play Ping-Pong.*

Operant extinction The weakening or disappearance of a non-reinforced operant response.

Negative attention seeking Using misbehavior to gain attention.

Positive reinforcement Occurs when a response is followed by a reward or other positive event.

Negative reinforcement Occurs when a response is followed by an end to discomfort or by the removal of a unpleasant event.

Punishment Any event that follows a response and *decreases* its likelihood of occurring again.

Response cost Removal of a positive reinforcer after a response is made.

ping her shoes on for you to tie; then for slipping them on and tying a simple knot; and finally for putting them on and tying a bow.

Operant Extinction

Would a rat's bar pressing stop if food delivery ended? Yes, but not immediately. Just as acquiring an operant response takes time, so does **operant extinction.** If a learned response is not reinforced, it gradually drops out of behavior. For example, if a particular TV program repeatedly bores you, watching the program will probably extinguish over time. Operant extinction, therefore, refers to the same general concept as extinction in classical conditioning.

Even after extinction seems complete, there may be a return of the previously reinforced response. If a rat is removed from a Skinner box after extinction and given a short rest, the rat will begin pressing the bar when returned to the Skinner box.

Question: Does extinction take as long the second time?

If reinforcement is still withheld, a rat's bar pressing will extinguish again, usually more quickly. The brief return of an operant response after extinction is another example of *spontaneous recovery* (mentioned earlier regarding classical conditioning). Spontaneous recovery seems to be very adaptive. After a rest period, the rat responds again in a situation that produced food in the past: "Just checking to see if the rules have changed!"

Reinforcement and extinction are often combined to change behavior. For example, attention and approval from parents are very powerful reinforcers for most children. As a result, parents often unknowingly reinforce **negative attention seeking** in their children. Generally, children are *ignored* when they are playing quietly. Instead, they get attention as they become louder and louder, when they yell "Hey, Mom!" at the top of their lungs, when they throw tantrums, show off, or break something. Granted, the attention they get is often a scolding, but it is still attention, and it still reinforces attention seeking. Parents report dramatic improvements when they *ignore* their children's disruptive behavior and praise or attend to children who are quiet or playing constructively.

Negative Reinforcement

Until now, we have stressed **positive reinforcement,** which occurs when a pleasant or desired event follows a response. How else could operant learning be reinforced? The time has come to consider the "flip side" of operant conditioning: **Negative reinforcement** occurs when making a response *removes* an *unpleasant* event. Like positive reinforcement, negative reinforcement also increases responding. However, it does so by *ending discomfort.*

Let's say that you have a headache and take an aspirin. Your aspirin taking will be negatively reinforced if the headache stops. Likewise, a rat could be taught to press a bar to get food (positive reinforcement) or the rat could be given a mild shock that lasts until it is *turned off* by a bar press (negative reinforcement). Either way, bar pressing would increase. Why? Because it leads to a desired state of affairs (food or an end to pain). Often, positive and negative reinforcement combine. If you are uncomfortably hungry, eating a meal is reinforced by the good-tasting food (positive reinforcement) and by an end to nagging hunger (negative reinforcement).

Punishment

Many people mistake negative reinforcement for punishment. However, **punishment** is any event that follows a response and *decreases* its likelihood of occurring again. As noted, negative reinforcement *increases* responding. The difference can be seen in a hypothetical example. Let's say you live in an apartment and your neighbor's stereo is blasting so loudly that your ears hurt. If you pound on the wall and the volume suddenly drops (negative reinforcement), future wall pounding will be more likely. But if you pound on the wall and the volume increases (punishment), or if the neighbor comes over and pounds on you (more punishment), pounding on the wall becomes less likely.

As another example, consider a drug addict undergoing withdrawal. Taking the drug will temporarily end painful withdrawal symptoms. Drug taking is therefore negatively reinforced. If, on the other hand, the drug made the pain worse (punishment), the addict would quickly stop taking it.

Question: Isn't it also punishing to have privileges, money, or other positive things taken away for making a particular response?

Yes. Punishment also occurs when a reinforcer or positive state of affairs is removed, such as losing privileges. This second type of punishment is called **response cost** (Cautela & Kearney, 1986). Parents who take away TV privileges or "ground" their teenage children for misbehavior are applying response cost. Parking tickets and other fines are also based on response cost. Because punishment is such an important topic we will explore it more later. For your convenience, Table 7–2 summarizes four basic consequences of making a response.

Table 7–2 Behavioral Effects of Various Consequences

	Consequence of making a response	Example	Effect on response probability
Positive reinforcement	Positive event begins	Food given	Increase
Negative reinforcement	Negative event ends	Pain stops	Increase
Punishment	Negative event begins	Pain begins	Decrease
Punishment (response cost)	Positive event ends	Food removed	Decrease
Non-reinforcement	Nothing	—	Decrease

Operant Reinforcers—What's Your Pleasure?

For humans, an effective operant reinforcer may be anything from an M&M candy to a pat on the back. In categorizing such reinforcers, useful distinctions can be made among *primary reinforcers, secondary reinforcers, generalized reinforcers,* and *prepotent responses.* Operant reinforcers of all types have a large impact on our lives. Let's examine them in more detail.

Primary Reinforcers

A **primary reinforcer** is natural, or unlearned. As a result, primary reinforcers are almost universally effective for a given species. Primary reinforcers are usually rooted in biology and produce comfort, end discomfort, or fill an immediate physical need. Food, water, and sex are obvious primary reinforcers. Every time you open the refrigerator, walk to a drinking fountain, turn up the heat, or make a trip to an ice cream parlor, your actions reflect the effect of primary reinforcement.

In addition to obvious examples, there are other less natural primary reinforcers. One of the most unusual (and powerful) is **intra-cranial stimulation** (ICS). ICS involves direct stimulation of "pleasure centers" in the brain (Olds & Fobes, 1981) (Fig. 7–13).

Wiring a Rat for Pleasure

Use of brain stimulation for reward requires the permanent implantation of tiny electrodes in specific areas of the brain. A rat "wired for pleasure" can be trained to press the bar in a Skinner box to deliver electrical stimulation to its own brain. Some rats will press the bar thousands of times per hour to obtain brain stimulation. After 15 or 20 hours of constant pressing, animals sometimes collapse from exhaustion. When they revive, they begin pressing again. If the reward circuit is not turned off, an animal will ignore food, water, and sex in favor of bar pressing.

Many natural primary reinforcers, including most commonly abused drugs, activate the same pleasure pathways in the brain that make ICS so powerful. One shudders to think what might happen if brain implants were easy and practical to do. (They are not.) Every company from *Playboy* to General Motors would have a device on the market, and we would have to keep a closer watch on politicians than usual!

Primary reinforcers Unlearned reinforcers; usually those that satisfy physiological needs.

Intra-cranial stimulation Direct electrical stimulation and activation of brain tissue.

Secondary reinforcer A learned reinforcer; often one that gains reinforcing properties by association with a primary reinforcer.

Secondary Reinforcers

In some traditional societies, learning is still strongly tied to food, water, and other primary reinforcers. Most of us, however, respond to a much broader range of rewards and reinforcers. Money, praise, attention, approval, success, affection, grades, and similar rewards, all serve as *learned* or **secondary reinforcers.**

Fig. 7–13 *In the apparatus shown in* (a), *the rat can press a bar to deliver mild electric stimulation to a "pleasure center" in the brain. Humans also have been "wired" for brain stimulation, as shown in* (b). *However, in humans, this has been done only as an experimental way to restrain uncontrollable outbursts of violence. Implants have not been done merely to produce pleasure. (See Chapter 3 for more information on ICS.)*

(a)

(b)

Social reinforcers Reinforcers, such as attention and approval, provided by other people.

Token reinforcer A tangible secondary reinforcer such as money, gold stars, poker chips, and the like.

Question: How does a secondary reinforcer gain its ability to promote learning?

Some secondary reinforcers are simply associated with a primary reinforcer. This can be shown in the following way.

The Push-Button Rat

A rat caged in a Skinner box has learned through operant conditioning to press the bar for food pellets. Each rewarded bar press is also followed by a brief auditory tone. After a period of training in which bar pressing, food, and the tone are associated, the rat is moved to a new cage. This cage has no bar, but it does have a button mounted on the wall. If the rat pushes the button, the tone sounds, but no food is delivered. Even though no primary reinforcement (food) is given, the rat learns to press the button to turn on the tone. Because it was associated with food, the tone has become a secondary reinforcer.

As we have noted, learned desires for attention and approval, which are called **social reinforcers,** often influence human behavior. This fact can be used in a classic, if somewhat mischievous, demonstration of the effects of secondary reinforcement.

Shaping a Teacher

For this demonstration, approximately one half (or more) of the students in a classroom must participate. First, a target behavior should be selected. This should be something like "lecturing from the right side of the room." (Keep it simple, in case your teacher is a slow learner.) Begin training in this way: Each time the instructor turns toward the right side of the room or takes a step in that direction, participating students should look *really* interested. Also, smile, ask questions, lean forward, and make eye contact. If the teacher turns to the left or takes a step in that direction, participating students should lean back, yawn, check out their split ends, close their eyes, or generally look bored. Soon, without being aware of why, the instructor should be spending most of his or her time each class period lecturing from the right side of the classroom.

This trick has been a favorite of psychology graduate students for decades. For a time, one of my professors delivered all of his lectures from the right side of the room while toying with the cords from the venetian blinds. (We added the cords the second week!) The point to remember from this example is that attention and approval can change the behavior of children, family members, friends, roommates, and co-workers. Be aware of what you are reinforcing.

Tokens Secondary reinforcers that can be *exchanged* for primary reinforcers gain their value more directly. Printed money obviously has little or no value of its own. You can't eat it, drink it, or sleep with it. However, it can be exchanged for food, water, lodging, and other necessities. In a series of classic experiments, chimpanzees were taught to work for **tokens.** Chimps were first trained to put poker chips into a "Chimp-O-Mat" vending machine that dispensed a few grapes or raisins for each chip. After the animals had learned to exchange tokens for food, they would learn new tasks to earn chips. Value of the tokens was maintained by occasionally allowing the chimps to use the "Chimp-O-Mat" (■Fig. 7–14) (Wolfe, 1936; Cowles, 1937).

One problem with primary reinforcers is that people and animals receiving them may quickly *satiate* (SAY-she-ate). (To be satiated means to be fully satisfied or to have reduced desire.) If, for example, you want to use candy to reinforce a retarded child for correctly naming things, the child might only show interest while hungry.

A major advantage of tokens is that they do not lose reinforcing value as quickly as primary reinforcers do. That's why tokens (plastic chips, gold stars, and the like) have been useful in work with troubled children, adolescents, and adults in special programs, as well as in educating the mentally retarded (■Fig. 7–15). Tokens are even used at times in ordinary elementary school classrooms.

Wherever tokens are used, the goal is to provide an immediate, tangible reward for learning. Typically, tokens may be exchanged for food, desired goods, special privileges, or trips to movies, amusement parks, and so forth. (See Chapter 18 for more information on the use of tokens in therapy.) Many parents have found that discipline problems with younger children can be greatly reduced through the use of tokens. For

■ **Fig. 7–14** *Poker chips normally have little or no value for chimpanzees, but this chimp will work hard to earn them once he learns that the "Chimp-O-Mat" will dispense food in exchange for chips.*

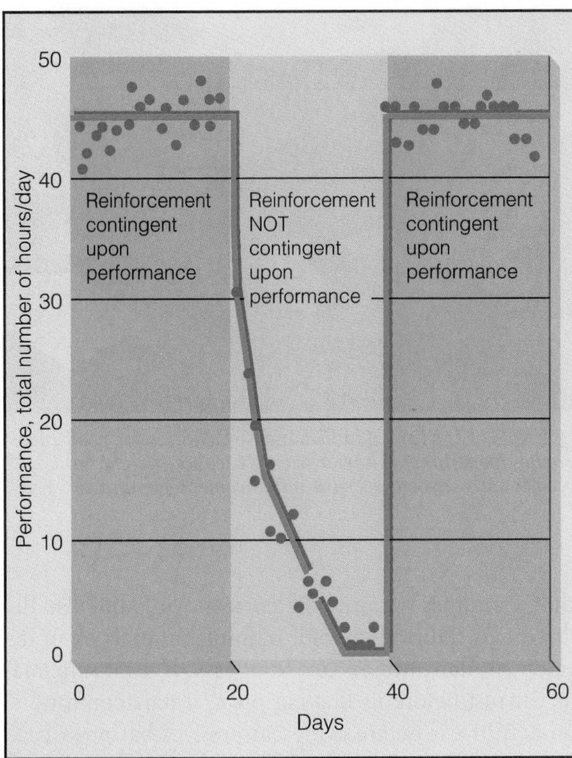

■ **Fig. 7–15** *Reinforcement in a token economy. This graph shows the effects of using tokens to reward socially desirable behavior in a mental hospital ward. Desirable behavior was defined as cleaning, bed making, attending therapy sessions, and so forth. Tokens earned could be exchanged for basic amenities such as meals, snacks, coffee, game-room privileges, or weekend passes. The graph shows more than 24 hours per day because it represents the total number of hours of desirable behavior performed by all patients in the ward. (Adapted from Aylion & Azrin, 1965.)*

example, children can earn points or gold stars during the week for good behavior. If they earn enough tokens they are allowed on Sunday to choose one item out of a "grab bag" of small treats.

Generalized Reinforcers

Question: People sometimes hoard money even when all their needs are met. Why is that?

Interestingly, the chimps working for tokens also tended to hoard them, even when they were hungry. This and similar observations suggests that in time, secondary reinforcers may become independent of their link to primary reinforcers. In other words, secondary reinforcers sometimes become **generalized reinforcers.** Money is a good example of a generalized reinforcer. Not only can money be exchanged for primary reinforcers, it may also lead to other secondary reinforcers, such as prestige, attention, approval, status, or power. This property makes its value so general in our society that people sometimes pursue and hoard money just for the sake of having it.

Prepotent Responses Discovering what will serve as a reinforcer can sometimes be tricky. Praise, candy, or a pat on the back may be reinforcing for one person but not for another. One way out of this dilemma is to apply the **Premack principle.** The idea, advanced by David Premack (1965), is that any frequent (or "prepotent") response can be used to reinforce an infrequent response. Let's say you love music and listen to it frequently. In contrast, you hate to take out the trash and rarely do it. If this is the case, listening to music can be used to reinforce taking out the trash. By requiring yourself to take out the trash before turning on music, you will boost the infrequent response. As another example, making access to video games contingent on good behavior is a very effective reinforcer for children who often play the games (Buckalew & Buckalew, 1983).

If you are interested in applying reinforcement to change your own behavior (your study habits, for instance), remember that anything you do frequently (watching television, talking with friends, listening to music) can serve as a reinforcer.

Generalized reinforcer A secondary reinforcer that has become independent of direct association with primary reinforcers.

Premack principle Any high frequency response can be used to reinforce a low frequency response.

Delay of Reinforcement

Reinforcement is most effective when there is a short time lapse between a response and its consequences. For rats in a Skinner box, very little learning occurs when the delay between bar pressing and receiving food reaches 50 seconds. If the food reward is delayed more than about 90 seconds, no learning occurs (Perin, 1943) (■Fig. 7–16). In general, you will be most successful if you present a reinforcer *immediately* after a response you wish to change. Thus, a child who is helpful or

■ **Fig. 7–16** *The effect of delay of reinforcement. Notice how rapidly the learning score drops when reward is delayed. Animals who were learning to press a bar in a Skinner box showed no signs of learning if food reward followed a bar press by more than 100 seconds. (Perin, 1943.)*

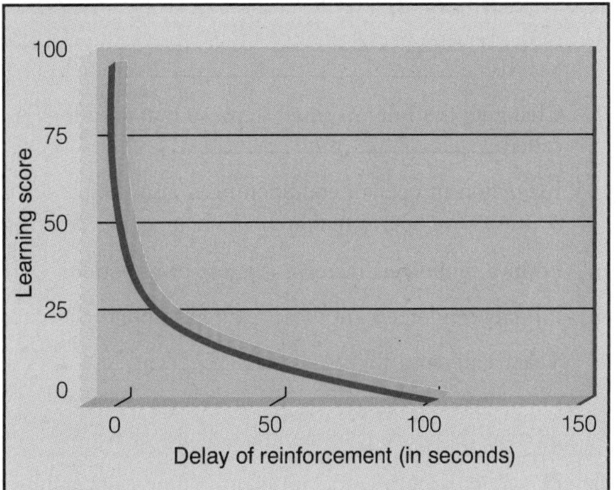

Response chaining The assembly of separate responses into a series of actions that lead to reinforcement.

Superstitious behavior A behavior repeated because it seems to produce reinforcement, even though it is actually unnecessary.

courteous should be praised immediately for her good behavior.

Response Chaining Leslie worked hard all semester to get an A grade in her biology class. Why didn't the delay in reinforcement prevent her from learning? First, as a human Leslie can anticipate future reward. Second, she was reinforced by good quiz and test grades all through the semester. Third, a single reinforcer can often maintain a long *chain* of responses. A simplified example of **response chaining** is provided by Barnabus, a rat trained by psychologists at Brown University.

The Great Barnabus

By carefully working from the last response to the first, Barnabus was trained to make an ever longer chain of responses to obtain a single food pellet. When in top form, Barnabus was able to climb a spiral staircase, cross a narrow bridge, climb a ladder, pull a toy car with a chain, get into the car, pedal it to a second staircase, climb the staircase, wriggle through a tube, climb onto an elevator and descend to a platform, press a lever to receive a food pellet, and . . . start over! (Pierrel & Sherman, 1963.)

Many of the things we do every day involve similar response chains. The long series of events necessary to prepare a meal, for instance, is rewarded by the final eating. A violin maker may spend three months carrying out thousands of steps for the final reward of hearing the first note from an instrument. Dialing a telephone is a short but familiar response chain.

Superstitious Behavior Operant reinforcers affect not only the response they follow, but also other responses that occurred shortly before. This helps account for the learning of many human superstitions. If a golfer taps her club on the ground three times and then hits an unusually fine shot, the success of the shot reinforces not only the correct swing, but also the three taps. During operant training, animals often develop similar unnecessary responses. If a rat scratches its ear just before its first bar press, it may continue to scratch its ear before every bar press. A bar press is all that is needed to produce food, but the animal may continue to "superstitiously" scratch its ear each time, as if this were necessary.

■ **Fig. 7–17** *Many gamblers rely on charms for good luck. Such superstitious behavior occurs because the charm is occasionally associated with reinforcement (winning).*

Superstitious acts probably *appear* to pay off to the person or animal. If you get the large half of a wishbone and have good fortune soon after, you may credit the wishbone for your luck (■ Fig. 7–17). If you walk under a ladder and then break a leg, you may avoid ladders in the future. Each time you avoid a ladder and nothing bad occurs, your **superstitious behavior** is reinforced. Belief in magic can also be explained along such lines. Rituals to bring rain, ward off illness, or produce abundant crops very likely earned the faith of participants by occasionally appearing to succeed. Besides, better safe than sorry!

Learning Check

1. Responses in operant conditioning are ________________, whereas those in classical conditioning are passive, ________________ responses.
2. Changing the rules in small steps, so that an animal (or person) is gradually trained to respond as desired, is called ________________.
3. Extinction in operant conditioning is also subject to ________________ of a response.
   a. successive approximations *b.* shaping *c.* automation *d.* spontaneous recovery
4. Positive reinforcers increase the rate of responding and negative reinforcers decrease it. T or F?
5. Primary reinforcers are those learned through classical conditioning. T or F?
6. Tokens are basically ________________ reinforcers.
7. Superstitious responses are those that are
   a. shaped by secondary reinforcement *b.* extinguished *c.* prepotent *d.* unnecessary to obtain reinforcement

Critical Thinking

8. How could you use operant conditioning to encourage people to pick up litter?

Answers: 1. voluntary or emitted, involuntary or elicited 2. shaping 3. *d* 4. F 5. F 6. secondary 7. *d* 8. One strategy is to hold drawings for various prizes, such as movie or concert passes. Turning in a specific amount of litter is rewarded with one chance (a token) in the drawing. Giving refunds for cans and bottles is another way to reinforce recycling of litter.

Partial Reinforcement—Las Vegas, a Human Skinner Box?

SERENDIPITY *(n):* To discover one thing while looking for another

B. F. Skinner, so the story goes, was studying operant conditioning when he ran short of food pellets. In order to continue, he arranged for a pellet to reward every other response. Thus began the formal study of **schedules of reinforcement.**

Schedules are plans for determining which responses will be reinforced. Until now, we have treated operant reinforcement as if it were continuous. **Continuous reinforcement** means that a reinforcer follows every correct response. This is fine for the lab, but it has little to do with the real world. Most of our responses are more inconsistently rewarded. In daily life, operant learning is usually based on **partial reinforcement,** in which reinforcers do not follow every response.

Partial reinforcement may be given in several patterns, each of which affects responding. In addition to these specific effects (to be discussed in a moment), there is a general effect: *Responses acquired by partial reinforcement are highly resistant to extinction.* For some obscure reason, lost in the lore of psychology, this is called the **partial reinforcement effect.**

Question: How does getting reinforced part of the time make a habit stronger?

If you have ever visited Las Vegas or a similar gambling mecca, you may have been amused by row after row of people pulling slot machine handles. To gain insight into partial reinforcement effects, imagine that you are making your first visit to Las Vegas. You put a dollar in a slot machine and pull the handle. Ten dollars spills into the tray. "I think I like this game," you say to yourself. Using one of your newly won dollars, you pull the handle again. Another payoff! Let's say this continues for 15 minutes. Every pull is followed by a payoff. Then, without your knowing it, someone turns off the payoff mechanism. Suddenly each pull is followed by nothing. Obviously, you would respond several times more before giving up. However, when continuous reinforcement is followed by extinction, the message soon becomes clear: No more payoffs.

Contrast this with partial reinforcement. Again, imagine that this is your first encounter with a slot machine. You begin by putting a dollar in the machine five times without a payoff. You are just about to quit, but decide to play one more. Bingo! The machine returns $20. After this, payoffs continue on a partial schedule; some are large, and some are small. All are unpredictable. Sometimes you hit 2 in a row, and sometimes 10 or 20 pulls go unrewarded.

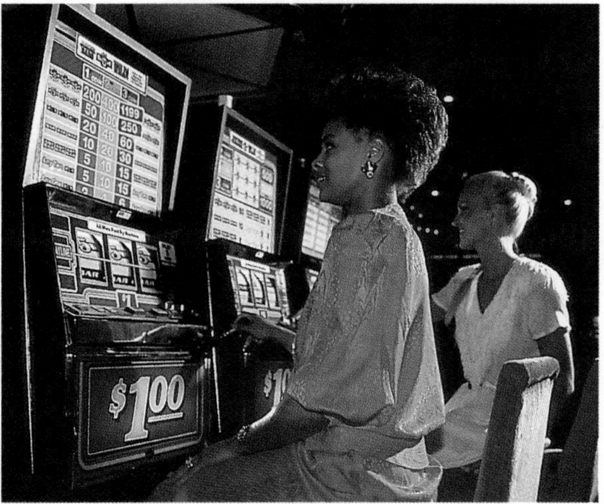

■ **Fig. 7–18** *The one-armed bandit (slot machine) is a dispenser of partial reinforcement.*

Now let's say the payoff mechanism is turned off again. How many times do you think you would respond this time before your handle-pulling behavior extinguished? Since you have developed the expectation that any play may be "the one," it will be hard to resist just one more play . . . and one more . . . and one more. Also, since partial reinforcement includes long periods of non-reward, it will be harder to discriminate between periods of reinforcement and extinction. It is no exaggeration to say that the partial reinforcement effect has left many people penniless. Even psychologists visiting Las Vegas often get "cleaned out"—and they should know better!

Schedule of reinforcement A rule or plan for determining which responses will be reinforced.

Continuous reinforcement A schedule in which every correct response is followed by a reinforcer.

Partial reinforcement A pattern in which only a portion of all responses are reinforced.

Partial reinforcement effect Responses acquired with partial reinforcement are more resistant to extinction.

Fixed ratio schedule A set number of correct responses must be made to get a reinforcer. For example, a reinforcer is given for every 4 correct responses.

Schedules of Partial Reinforcement

The patterns in which partial reinforcement could be given are limitless. Let's consider the four most basic possibilities, which have some interesting effects on us.

Fixed Ratio (FR) What would happen if a reinforcer only followed every other response? Or what if we followed every third, fourth, fifth, or other number of responses with reinforcement? Each of these patterns is a **fixed ratio (FR) schedule.** The ratio of re-

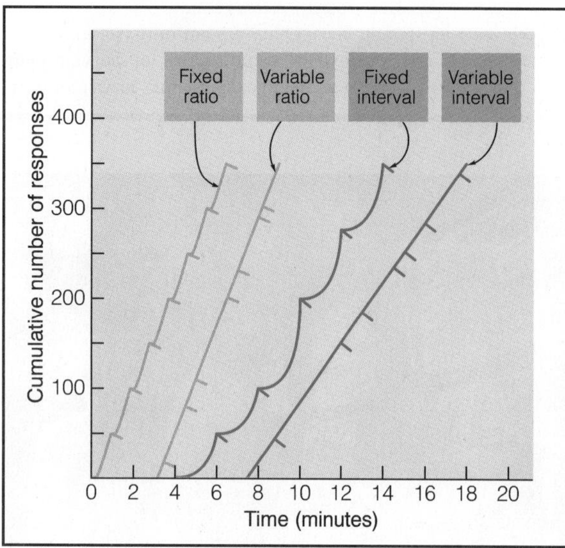

■ **Fig. 7–19** *Typical response patterns for reinforcement schedules. Results such as these are obtained when a cumulative recorder is connected to a Skinner box. The recorder consists of a moving strip of paper and a mechanical pen that jumps upward each time a response is made. At any given time, the graph line on a cumulative recorder shows the total number of responses made up to that point. (When the pen reaches the top of the paper it drops to the bottom and starts over.) Rapid responding causes the pen to draw a steep line; a horizontal line indicates no response. Small tick marks on the lines show when a reinforcer was given.*

Variable ratio schedule A varied number of correct responses must be made to get a reinforcer. For example, a reinforcer is given after 3 to 7 correct responses; the actual number changes randomly.

Fixed interval schedule A reinforcer is given only when a correct response is made after a set amount of time has passed since the last reinforced response. Responses made during the time interval are not reinforced.

Variable interval schedule A reinforcer is given for the first correct response made after a varied amount of time has passed since the last reinforced response. Responses made during the time interval are not reinforced.

inforcers to responses is fixed: FR-2 means that every other response is rewarded; FR-3 means that every third response is reinforced; in an FR-10 schedule, exactly 1 out of every 10 responses would produce a reinforcer.

Fixed ratio schedules produce *very high rates of response* (■ Fig. 7–19). A hungry rat on an FR-10 schedule will quickly run off 10 responses, pause to eat, and will then run off 10 more. A similar situation occurs when factory or farm workers are paid on a piecework basis. When a fixed number of items must be produced for a set amount of pay, work output is high.

Variable Ratio (VR) A **variable ratio (VR) schedule** is a slight variation on fixed ratio. Instead of reinforcing, for example, every fourth response (FR-4), a person or animal on a VR-4 schedule gets rewarded *on the average* every fourth response. Sometimes 2 responses must be made to obtain a reinforcer, sometimes it's 5 responses, sometimes 4, and so on. The actual number of responses required varies, but it averages out to 4 (in this example). Variable ratio schedules also produce high rates of responding.

Question: VR schedules seem less predictable than FR. Does that have any effect on extinction?

Yes. Since reinforcement is less predictable, VR schedules tend to produce greater resistance to extinction than fixed ratio schedules. Playing a slot machine is an example of behavior maintained by a variable ratio schedule. Another would be a child asking for a "treat" at the supermarket. The number of times the child must ask before getting reinforced varies, so the child becomes quite persistent. Golf, tennis, and many other sports are also reinforced on a variable ratio basis: An average of perhaps 1 good shot in 5 or 10 may be all that's needed to create a sports fanatic.

Fixed Interval (FI) In another pattern, reinforcement is given only when a correct response is made after a fixed amount of time has passed since the last reinforced response. Responses made *during* the time interval are not reinforced. The first correct response made *after* the time period has passed is reinforced. Thus, a rat on an FI-30-second schedule has to wait 30 seconds *after the last reinforced response* before pressing the bar will pay off again. The rat can press the bar as often as it wants during the interval, but it will not be rewarded. **Fixed interval (FI) schedules** produce *moderate response rates.* These are marked by spurts of activity mixed with periods of inactivity. Animals working on an FI schedule seem to develop a keen sense of the passage of time. For example:

Mickey Rat Takes a Break

Mickey Rat, trained on an FI-60-second schedule, has just been reinforced for a bar press. What does he do? He saunters around the cage, grooms himself, hums, whistles, reads magazines, and polishes his nails. After 50 seconds, he walks to the bar and gives it a press—just testing. After 55 seconds, he gives it two or three presses, but there's still no payoff. Fifty-eight seconds, and he settles down to rapid pressing, 59 seconds, 60 seconds, and he hits the reinforced press. After one or two more presses (unrewarded), he wanders off again for the next interval.

Question: Is getting paid weekly an FI schedule?

Pure examples of fixed interval schedules are rare, but getting paid each week at work does come close. Notice, however, that most people do not work faster just before payday, as an FI schedule predicts. A closer parallel would be having a report due every 2 weeks for a class. Right after turning in a paper, your work would probably drop to zero for a week or more. Then, as the next due date draws near, a work frenzy occurs. Another fixed interval example is checking a Thanksgiving turkey in the oven. Typically, the frequency of checking increases as the time for the turkey to be done draws near (Schwartz, 1989).

Variable Interval (VI) Variable interval (VI) schedules are a variation on fixed intervals. Here, reinforcement is given for the first correct response made after a varied amount of time. On a VI-30-second schedule, reinforcement is available after an interval that av-

erages 30 seconds. VI schedules produce *slow, steady rates* of response and tremendous resistance to extinction. When you dial a phone number and get a busy signal, reward (getting through) is on a VI schedule. You may have to wait 30 seconds or 30 minutes. If you are like me, you will doggedly dial over and over again until you get a connection. Success in fishing is also on a VI schedule—which may explain the bulldog tenacity of many anglers (Schwartz, 1989).

In the "real world" two or more schedules of reinforcement may be in effect at once. When this is done intentionally, it can be used to engineer desired behavior. For example, let's say that a business owner who pays employees an hourly wage wants to increase productivity. How could the owner make more effective use of reinforcement? Continued use of fixed interval rewards (a salary) would guarantee a basic level of income for employees. To reinforce extra effort, the owner could add some fixed ratio reinforcement (such as incentives, bonuses, commissions, or profit sharing) to employees' pay.

Stimulus Control—Putting Habits on a Leash

When you are driving, your behavior at intersections is controlled by the red or green light. In similar fashion, many of the stimuli we encounter each day act like stop or go signals that guide our behavior. This is called **stimulus control.** To state the idea more formally, antecedent stimuli (events that come before a response) also affect operant conditioning.

Return for a moment to Figure 7–1. As you can see, whistling (an antecedent stimulus) was used to signal a dog that it would receive food—if it sat up. In general, a response tends to come under the control of stimuli that are present when the response is reinforced. Notice how this works with our friend Mickey Rat.

Lights Out for Mickey Rat

While learning the bar-pressing response, Mickey has been in a Skinner box illuminated by a bright light. During several training sessions, the light is alternately turned on and off. When the light is on, a bar press will produce food. When the light is off, bar pressing goes unrewarded. We soon observe that the rat presses vigorously when the light is on and ignores the bar when the light is off.

In this example, the light tells what consequences will follow if a response is made. A similar situation would be a child learning to ask for candy when his mother is in a good mood, but not asking at other times. In operant conditioning, stimuli that precede a rewarded response tend to influence *when* and *where* the response will occur in the future. Evidence for stimulus control could be shown in our example by turning the food delivery *on* when the light is *off*. A well-trained animal might never discover that the rules had changed.

Generalization Two important aspects of stimulus control are **generalization** and **discrimination.** Let's return to the example of the vending machine (from the Chapter Preview) to illustrate these concepts. First, generalization.

Question: Is generalization the same in operant conditioning as it is in classical conditioning?

Basically, yes. Responses followed by reinforcement tend to be made again when similar antecedents are present. Assume, for instance, that you have been reliably rewarded for kicking one particular vending machine. Your kicking response tends to occur in the presence of that machine. It has come under stimulus control.

Now let's say that there are three other machines on campus identical to the one that pays off. Because they are similar, your kicking response will very likely transfer to them. If each of these machines also pays off when kicked, your kicking response may *generalize* to other machines only mildly similar to the original. Similar generalization explains why children may temporarily call all men *daddy*—much to the embarrassment of their parents.

Discrimination Meanwhile, back at the vending machine . . . . As stated earlier, to **discriminate** means to respond differently to different stimuli. Because one vending machine reinforced your kicking response, you began kicking other identical machines (generalization). Because these also paid off, you began kicking similar machines (more generalization). If kicking these new machines has no effect, the kicking response that generalized to them will extinguish because of non-reinforcement. Thus, your response to machines of a particular size and color is consistently rewarded, whereas the same response to different machines is extinguished. You have learned to discriminate between antecedent stimuli that signal reward and non-reward. As a result, your response pattern will shift to match these **discriminative stimuli** (■ Fig. 7–20). Highlight 7–2 provides a further look at how discriminations are formed.

Stimulus control Stimuli present when an operant response is reinforced tend to control when and where the response is made.

Operant stimulus generalization The tendency to respond to stimuli similar to those which preceded operant reinforcement.

Operant stimulus discrimination The tendency to make a response when stimuli previously associated with reward are present and to withhold the response when stimuli associated with non-reward are present.

Discriminative stimuli Stimuli that precede rewarded and non-rewarded responses in operant conditioning.

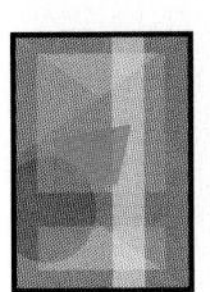

HIGHLIGHT 7–2

A Closer Look At

Stimulus Control—The Cat's Meow

The role of discriminative stimuli may be clarified by an interesting feat achieved by Jack, a psy-

■ **Fig. 7–20** *Stimulus control. Operant shaping was used to teach Flo, the pictured walrus, first to cover her face (left) and then to douse her trainer. A fish is her reward. Notice the trainer's hand signal, which serves as a discriminative stimulus to control Flo's performance. (Photographs © 1984,* Los Angeles Times.*)*

chologist friend of the author's. Jack decided to teach his cat to say its name. Here is how he proceeded. First he gave the cat a pat on the back. If the cat meowed in a way that sounded anything like its name, Jack immediately gave the cat a small amount of food. If the cat made this unusual meow at other times, it received nothing. This process was repeated many times each day.

By gradual shaping, the cat's meow was made to sound very much like its name. Also, this peculiar meow came under stimulus control: When it received a pat on the back, the cat said its name; without the pat, it remained silent or meowed normally. Psychologists symbolize a stimulus that precedes reinforced responses as an S+. Discriminative stimuli that precede unrewarded responses are symbolized as S− (Schwartz, 1989). Thus, the accompanying diagram summarizes the cat's training.

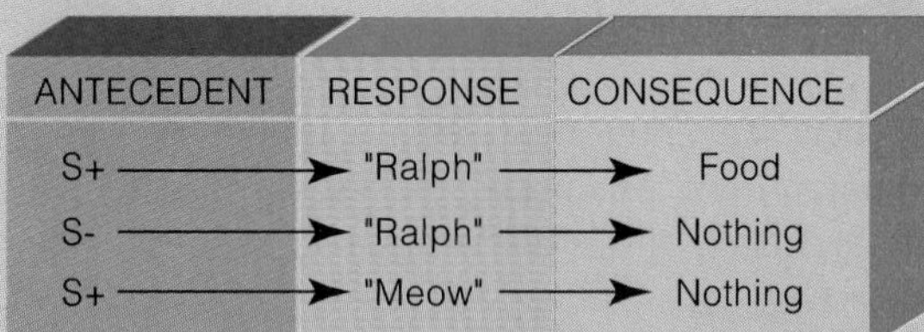

I should add at this point that I was unaware that Jack had a new cat or that he had trained it. I went to visit him one night and met the cat on the front steps. I gave the cat a pat on the back and said, "Hi kitty, what's your name?" Imagine my surprise when the cat immediately replied, "Ralph"!

A discriminative stimulus that most drivers are familiar with is a police car on the freeway. This stimulus is a clear signal that a specific set of reinforcement contingencies applies. As you have probably observed, the presence of a police car brings about rapid reductions in driving speed, lane changes, tail-gating, and, in Los Angeles, gun battles.

Stimulus discrimination is also aptly illustrated by the "sniffer" dogs used at airports and border stations to locate drugs and explosives. Operant discrimination training is used to teach these dogs to recognize contraband. During training, the dogs are reinforced only for approaching containers baited with drugs or explosives (■ Fig. 7–21). Stimulus discrimination clearly has a tremendous impact on human behavior. Learning to recognize different automobile brands, birds, animals, wines, types of music, and even the answers on psychology tests all depends, in part, on operant discrimination learning.

■ **Fig. 7–21** *Operant discrimination training is used to sharpen the skills of "detective" dogs.*

Learning Check

1. When a reward follows every response, it is called
   a. continuous reinforcement *b.* fixed reinforcement *c.* ratio reinforcement *d.* controlled reinforcement
2. Partial reinforcement tends to produce slower responding and reduced resistance to extinction. T or F?
3. The schedule of reinforcement associated with playing slot machines and other types of gambling is
   a. fixed ratio *b.* variable ratio *c.* fixed interval *d.* variable interval
4. If you are able to pass a classroom test scheduled every 3 weeks, your studying is reinforced on a ______________ ______________ schedule of reinforcement. If you must study for unannounced pop quizzes, studying is reinforced on a ______________ ______________ schedule. The style of testing that would probably produce the most consistent daily studying is ______________ ______________.
5. Two aspects of stimulus control are ______________ and ______________.
6. Responding tends to occur in the presence of discriminative stimuli associated with reinforcement and tends not to occur in the presence of discriminative stimuli associated with non-reinforcement. T or F?
7. Stimulus generalization refers to making an operant response in the presence of stimuli similar to those that preceded reinforcement. T or F?
8. How could you use conditioning principles to teach a dog or a cat to come when called? ***Critical Thinking***

Answers: 1. *a* 2. F 3. *b* 4. fixed interval, variable interval, variable interval (pop quizzes) 5. generalization, discrimination 6. T 7. T 8. An excellent way to train a pet is to give a distinctive call or whistle each time you feed the animal. This makes the signal a secondary reinforcer and a discriminative stimulus for reward (food).

Punishment—Putting the Brakes on Behavior

For better or worse, punishment is one of the more popular ways to control behavior. Spankings, reprimands, loss of privileges, fines, jail sentences, firings, failing grades, and the like all reveal widespread use of punishment (■ Fig. 7–22). Clearly, the story of learning is unfinished without a return to punishment.

■ **Fig. 7–22** *Punishment has long been used to suppress undesirable behavior.*

Edict of Louis XI, King of France
A.D.1481

"Anyone who sells butter containing stones or other things (to add to the weight) will be put into our pillory, then said butter will be placed on his head until entirely melted by the sun. Dogs may lick him and people offend him with whatever defamatory epithets they please without offense to God or King. If the sun is not warm enough, the accused will be exposed in the great hall of the gaol in front of a roaring fire, where everyone will see him."

Recall that **punishment** lowers the probability that a response will occur again. To be most effective, punishment must be given *contingently* or only after an undesired response occurs.

Punishers, like reinforcers, are best defined by observing their effects on behavior. Any consequence that reduces the occurrence of a behavior is, by definition, a punisher. It is not always possible to know ahead of time what will act as a punisher for a particular individual. For example, when Jason got a reprimand from his mother for throwing toys, he stopped doing it. In this instance, the reprimand was a punisher. However, Chris is starved for attention of any kind from his parents, who both work. For Chris, a reprimand, or even a spanking, might actually reinforce toy throwing. Remember, too, that a punisher can be either the onset of an unpleasant event, or the removal of a positive state of affairs (response cost) (■ Fig. 7–23).

Punishment Decreasing the likelihood that a response will occur again.

Punisher Any event that decreases the probability or frequency of responses it follows.

Variables Affecting Punishment

Question: How effective is punishment at weakening a response?

Many people assume that punishment stops undesired behavior. Is this always true? Psychologists have learned that the effect of punishers depends greatly on their *timing, consistency,* and *intensity.* Punishment suppresses behavior best when it occurs as a response is being made, or *immediately* afterward (timing), and when it is given *each time* a response occurs (consis-

■ Fig. 7–23 *Punishers are consequences that lower the probability that a response will be made again. Receiving a traffic citation is directly punishing because the driver is delayed and reprimanded. Paying a fine and higher insurance rates add to the punishment, in the form of response cost.*

tency). Thus, a dog that has developed a habit of constantly barking can be effectively (and humanely) punished if water is sprayed on its nose each time it barks. Ten to 15 such treatments are usually enough to greatly reduce barking. This would not be the case if punishment were applied occasionally or long after the barking stopped. If you discover that your dog ate a rug while you were gone, punishing the dog hours later will do little good. Likewise, the commonly heard childhood threat, "Wait 'til your father comes home, then you'll be sorry," does more to make father an ogre than it does to effectively punish an undesirable response.

Severe punishment Intense punishment; punishment capable of suppressing a response for long periods.

Mild punishment Punishment that has a relatively weak effect, especially punishment that only temporarily slows responding.

Non-reinforcement Withholding reinforcement after selected responses (extinction training).

Severe punishment can be extremely effective in stopping behavior. If Beavis, a 3-year-old, sticks his finger in a light socket and gets a shock, that may be the last time he *ever* tries it. More often, however, punishment only temporarily *suppresses* a response. If the response is still reinforced, punishment may be especially ineffective. Responses suppressed by **mild punishment** usually reappear later. If 7-year-old Alissa sneaks a snack from the refrigerator before dinner and is punished for it, she may pass up snacks for a short time. But since snack sneaking was also rewarded by the sneaked snack, she will probably try sneaky snacking again, sometime later.

■ Fig. 7–24 *The effect of punishment on extinction. Immediately after punishment, the rate of bar pressing is suppressed, but by the end of the second day, the effects of punishment have disappeared. (After B. F. Skinner,* The Behavior of Organisms. *© 1938. D. Appleton-Century Co., Inc. Reprinted by permission of Prentice-Hall, Inc.)*

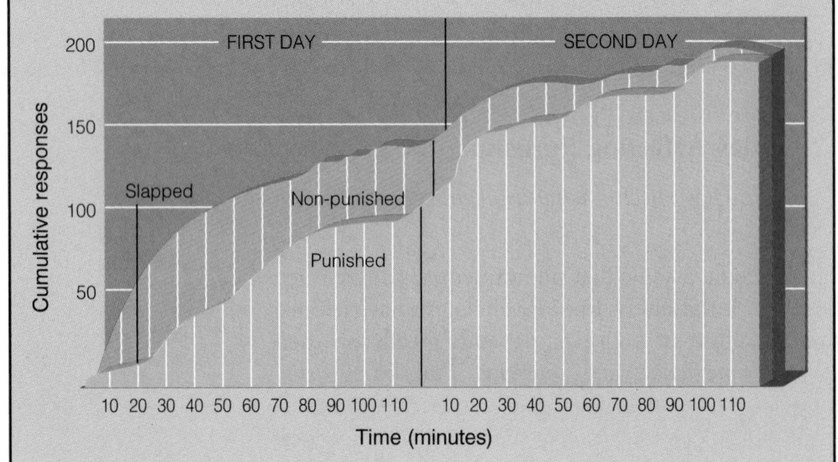

This fact was demonstrated experimentally by slapping rats on the paw as they were bar pressing in a Skinner box. Two groups of well-trained rats were placed on extinction. One group was punished with a slap for each bar press, while the other group was not. It might seem that the slap would cause bar pressing to extinguish more quickly. Yet, this was not the case, as you can see in ■ Figure 7–24. Punishment temporarily slowed responding, but it did not cause more rapid extinction. Slapping the paws of rats or children has little permanent effect on a reinforced response. It is worth stating again, however, that intense punishment may permanently suppress a response. Experiments show that actions as basic as eating can be suppressed. Animals severely punished while eating may never eat again (Bertsch, 1976).

Question: Then should punishment be used to control behavior?

Using Punishment Wisely

Parents, teachers, animal trainers, and the like have three basic tools to control simple learning: (1) *Reinforcement* strengthens responses; (2) *non-reinforcement* causes responses to extinguish; (3) *punishment* suppresses responses (■ Fig. 7–25). These tools work best in combination. (Of course, behavioral methods are only one element of effective child management. The Applications section in Chapter 13 describes other techniques.)

If punishment is used at all, it should always be mild. But remember that mild punishment will be ineffective if reinforcers are still available in the situation. That's why it is best to also reward an alternate, desired response. For example, a child who has a habit of taking toys from her sister should not just be reprimanded for it. She should also be praised for cooperative play and sharing her toys with others. Punishment tells a person or an animal that a response was "wrong." However, it does not say what the "right" response is, so it *does not teach new behaviors.* If reinforcement is missing from the formula, punishment becomes less effective.

In a situation that poses immediate danger, such as when a child reaches for something hot or a dog runs into the street, mild punishment may prevent disaster. Punishment in such cases works best when it produces actions *incompatible* with the response you want to suppress. Let's say a child reaches toward a stove burner. Would a swat on the bottom serve as an effective punisher? Probably so. It would be better, however, to slap the child's outstretched hand so it will be *withdrawn* from the source of danger. Remember, too, that temporarily taking away positive reinforcers (response cost) is an effective, non-physical form of punishment.

Highlight 7–3 provides some additional tips on using punishment.

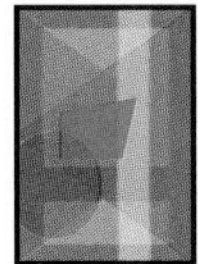

HIGHLIGHT 7–3

Using Psychology

If You Must Punish, Here's How

There are times when punishment may be necessary to manage the behavior of an animal, child, or even another adult. If you feel that you must punish, here are some tips to keep in mind.

1. *Don't use punishment at all if you can discourage misbehavior in other ways.* Make liberal use of positive reinforcement, especially praise, to encourage good behavior. Also, try extinction first: See what happens if you ignore a problem behavior; or shift attention to a desirable activity and then reinforce it with praise.

2. *Apply punishment during, or immediately after, misbehavior.* Of course, immediate punishment is not always possible. With older children and adults, you can bridge the delay by clearly stating what act you are punishing. If you cannot punish an animal *immediately,* wait for the next instance of misbehavior.

3. *Use the minimum punishment necessary to suppress misbehavior.* Often, a verbal rebuke or a scolding is enough. Avoid harsh physical punishment. (Never slap a child's face, for instance.) Taking away privileges or other positive reinforcers (response cost) is usually best for older children and adults. Frequent punishment may lose its effectiveness, and harsh or excessive punishment has serious negative side effects (discussed in a moment).

4. *Be consistent.* Be very clear about what you regard as misbehavior. Punish every time the misbehavior occurs. Don't punish for something one day and ignore it the next. If you are usually willing to give a child three chances, don't change the rule and explode without warning after a first offense. Both parents should try to punish their children for the same things and in the same way.

5. *Expect anger from a punished person.* Briefly acknowledge this anger, but be careful not to reinforce it. Be willing to admit your mistake if you wrongfully punish someone or if you punished too severely.

6. *Punish with kindness and respect.* Allow the punished person to retain self-respect. For instance, do not punish a person in front of others, if at all possible. A strong, trusting relationship tends to minimize behavior problems.

Ideally, others should *want* to behave well to get your praise, not because they fear punishment.

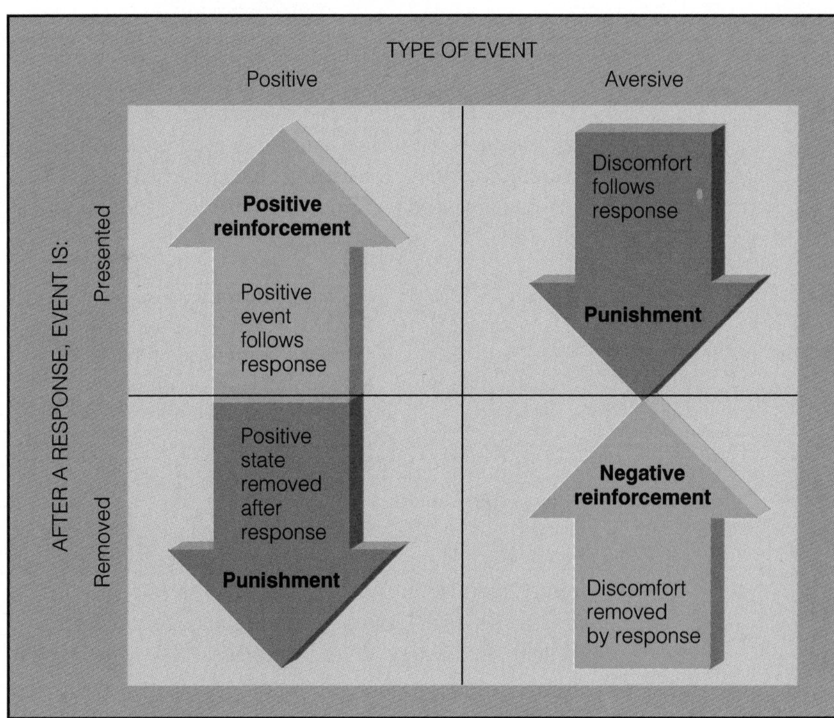

■ **Fig. 7–25** *Types of reinforcement and punishment. The impact of a consequence depends on whether it is pleasant or aversive (painful or unpleasant) and whether it is presented or removed after a response is made. Each square defines one possibility. For example, the upper left box shows that positive reinforcement occurs when a positive event is presented after a response is made. Arrows pointing upward indicate that responding is increased; downward-pointing arrows indicate that responding is decreased. (Adapted from Kazdin, 1975.)*

Side Effects of Punishment

Question: What are the drawbacks of using punishment?

The basic problem with punishment is that it is usually *aversive* (painful or uncomfortable). As a result, people and situations associated with punishment tend, through classical conditioning, to also become aversive (feared, resented, or disliked). This association, perhaps, is why children so often choose school windows to break when other targets are also available. The aversive

Escape learning Learning to make a response in order to end an aversive (painful or uncomfortable) stimulus.

Avoidance learning Learning to make a response in order to postpone or prevent discomfort.

nature of punishment makes it especially poor for teaching children to eat politely or for toilet training.

Escape and Avoidance A second major problem is that aversive stimuli usually encourage **escape learning** and **avoidance learning.** Escape learning is based on negative reinforcement, as the following example shows.

> A dog is placed in a two-compartment cage called a shuttle box. If the dog is shocked while in one of the compartments, it will quickly learn to jump to the other compartment to *escape* the shock. If a buzzer is sounded 10 seconds each time before the shock is turned on, the dog will soon learn to associate the buzzer with shock. It will then *avoid* pain by jumping *before* the shock begins. (Solomon & Wynne, 1953)

Avoidance learning appears to involve *both* classical and operant conditioning (Levis, 1989). In a shuttle box a dog first learns, through classical conditioning, to fear the buzzer. (The buzzer is a CS, which is followed by shock, a US for pain and fear.) Each time the buzzer sounds, the dog becomes fearful. But, by jumping to the "safe" compartment the dog can end the unpleasant fear it feels. Therefore, learning to jump *before* the onset of the shock is negatively reinforced by fear reduction. This is the operant part of avoidance learning. (A combination of classical and operant conditioning is called two-factor learning, a topic we will discuss soon.)

Many newer automobiles have an unpleasant buzzer that sounds if the ignition key is turned before the driver's seat belt is fastened. Most drivers quickly learn to fasten the belt to stop the annoying sound. This is another example of escape conditioning based on negative reinforcement. Avoidance conditioning is evident when a driver learns to buckle up *before* the buzzer sounds (Cautela & Kearney, 1986). However, not everyone reaches this point. The buzzer also stops if you simply wait long enough, which negatively reinforces some drivers for patiently ignoring it.

Once avoidance is learned it is very persistent. The electric shock in a shuttle box can be turned off, yet the dog will continue to leap from the compartment each time the buzzer sounds. This fact is rather puzzling: If the buzzer is never followed by shock, why doesn't fear of the buzzer extinguish? The dog, it seems, has learned to *expect* that the buzzer will be followed by shock. If the dog leaves before the shock would normally occur, it gets no new information to change the expectancy (Schwartz, 1989).

In a moment we will explore additional ways in which expectancies affect learning. But first, let's complete our discussion of punishment.

Question: How do escape and avoidance learning relate to punishment?

Escape and avoidance learning are a regular part of daily experience. For instance, if you work with a loud and obnoxious person, you may at first escape from conversations with him; later you may learn to avoid him altogether. Each time you sidestep him, your avoidance is reinforced by a sense of relief. In many situations involving frequent punishment, similar desires to escape and avoid are activated. For example, children who run away from punishing parents (escape) may soon learn to lie about their behavior (avoidance) or to spend as much time away from home as possible (also an avoidance response).

Aggression A third problem with punishment is that it can greatly increase *aggression.* Many animals react to pain by attacking whomever or whatever else is around (Azrin et al., 1965). A common example of this effect is the faithful dog that nips its owner during a painful procedure at the veterinarian's office.

We also know that one of the most common responses to frustration is aggression (■ Fig. 7–26). Generally speaking, punishment is painful, frustrating, or both. Punishment, therefore, sets up a powerful environment for learning aggression. When a child is spanked, the child may feel angry, frustrated, and hostile. What if the child then goes outside and hits a brother, sister, or a neighbor? The danger is that hitting someone may feel good because it releases anger and frustration. If so, aggression has been rewarded and will tend to occur again in other frustrating situations. One study found that overly aggressive adolescent boys had been severely punished for aggression at home. Since aggression was suppressed at home, parents were often surprised to learn that their "good boys" were in trouble at school for fighting and other forms of aggression (Bandura & Walters, 1959).

■ **Fig. 7–26** *Frustration and aggression are frequent side effects of punishment.*

Should You Punish or Not? To summarize, the most common error in using punishment is to rely on it alone to manage behavior. The overall emotional adjustment of a child or pet disciplined mainly by reward is usually superior to one disciplined mainly by punishment. Frequent punishment makes a person or an animal unhappy, confused, anxious, aggressive, and fearful of the source of punishment. Children who are harshly punished by parents or teachers learn to dislike parents and teachers. They also tend to dislike and avoid activities associated with punishment (schoolwork or household chores, for instance).

Parents and teachers should be aware that using punishment can be "habit forming." When children are being noisy, messy, disrespectful, or otherwise misbehaving, the temptation to punish can be strong. The trouble is that punishment often works. When it does, a sudden end to the adult's irritation acts as a negative reinforcer. This encourages the adult to use punishment more often in the future (Alberto & Troutman, 1990). Immediate silence may be "golden," but its cost can be very high in terms of a child's emotional health.

On rare occasions it may be reasonable to use very mild physical punishment with 3- to 5-year-old children (see Chapter 13 Applications). Otherwise, it would seem that the adage "Spare the rod and spoil the child" should at least be changed to "Use the rod sparingly or spoil the child" and perhaps to simply "Spare the rod."

LEARNING CHECK

1. A punisher can be either the ______________ of an unpleasant event, or the removal of a ______________ state of affairs.
2. Three factors that greatly influence the effects of punishment are timing, consistency, and ______________ .
3. Mild punishment tends to only temporarily ______________ a response that is also reinforced.
   a. enhance *b.* aggravate *c.* replace *d.* suppress
4. Three undesired side effects of punishment are: (1) conditioning of fear and resentment, (2) encouragement of aggression, and (3) the learning of escape or ______________ responses.
5. Using punishment can be "habit forming" because putting a stop to someone else's irritating behavior can ______________ ______________ the person who applies the punishment.
6. Using the concept of partial reinforcement, can you explain why inconsistent punishment is especially ineffective? ***Critical Thinking***

Answers: 1. onset, positive 2. intensity 3. *d* 4. avoidance 5. negatively reinforce 6. An inconsistently punished response will continue to be reinforced on a partial schedule, which makes it even more resistant to extinction.

Conditioning in Perspective—Great Expectations

His eyes, driven and blazing, dart from side to side. His left hand twitches, dances, rises, and strikes, hitting its target again and again. At the same time, his right hand furiously spins in circular motions. Does this describe some strange neurological disorder? Actually, it depicts 10-year-old Mark as he plays his favorite video game, an animated skateboarding adventure!

How did Mark learn the complex movements to excel at this unusual task? After all, he was not rewarded with food or money for correct responses. The answer lies in the fact that Mark's video game provides two key elements that underlie learning: a *responsive environment* and *information.* Whenever you move one of the controls on a video game, the machine responds instantly with sounds, animated actions, and a higher or lower score. The machine's responsiveness and the information flow it provides can be very motivating for players trying to master the game. The same principle applies to many other learning situations: If you are trying to learn to use a computer, to play a musical instrument, to cook, or to solve math problems, reinforcement comes from knowing that you succeeded at getting a desired result.

Until now we have discussed learning as if it were fairly mechanical. It is now time to explore learning at a higher level. An important theme to watch for is that learning is based on information.

Two-Factor Learning

Two-factor learning Learning that involves both classical conditioning and operant conditioning.

An ice cream truck approaches with its bell ringing. A boy named Justin hears the bell and thinks about ice cream. As he does, his mouth waters. Justin runs to the truck, buys an ice cream and eats it. What kind of learning is this? If it seems to you that both classical and operant conditioning are present in this example, you are right.

In the real world, classical and operant conditioning are often intertwined. This is called **two-factor**

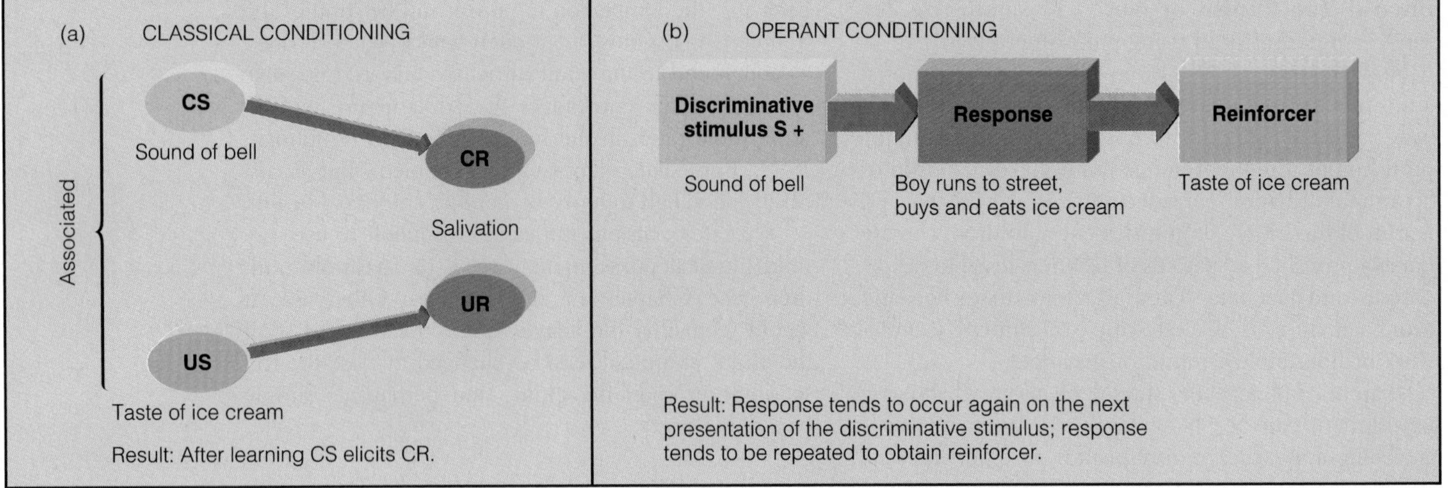

■ **Fig. 7–27** *Two-factor learning.*

Informational view Perspective that explains learning in terms of information imparted by events in the environment.

Expectancy An anticipation concerning future events or relationships.

Feedback Information returned to a person about the effects a response has had; also known as knowledge of results.

learning. As you can see in ■ Figure 7–27 Justin's behavior reflects both kinds of learning. As a result of classical conditioning, Justin will salivate each time he hears the truck's bell. Also, the bell is a discriminative stimulus (S+) signaling that reward is available if certain responses are made. When he hears the bell, Justin will run to the truck to buy and eat an ice cream (operant conditioning). Justin's involuntary responses are altered by classical conditioning, while his voluntary behavior is shaped by operant conditioning.

Question: Other than the fact that they often occur together, do operant and classical conditioning have anything in common?

Information At one time, psychologists pictured conditioning as a mechanical "stamping in" of responses. Now, many think of learning in terms of *information processing.* According to this **informational view,** learning creates mental **expectancies** (or expectations) about events. (Avoidance learning, described earlier, is an example.) Once acquired, expectancies alter behavior. For example, researcher Robert Rescorla (1987) explains classical conditioning this way: The conditioned stimulus reliably precedes the unconditioned stimulus; because it does, the CS *predicts* the US. When the CS is present, the brain *expects* the US to follow. Therefore, the brain prepares the body to respond to the US.

In our example, whenever Justin hears the bell or sees the truck, his mouth waters to prepare for eating ice cream. Similarly, when you are about to get a shot with a hypodermic needle, your muscles tighten and there is a catch in your breathing as your body prepares for pain. Notice that the CS gives valuable *information* about the US before the US appears. Pavlovian conditioning is not a "stupid" process that links any two stimuli that happen to occur together. Rather, conditioning occurs as we seek information about the world (Rescorla, 1988).

If you think about it, operant reinforcers also supply information. In operant conditioning, we learn to *expect* that a certain response will have a certain effect at certain times (Bolles, 1979). From this point of view, reward tells a person or an animal that a response was "right" and worth repeating. Likewise, stimuli or events prior to actions tell what response to make to get a reinforcer. Thus, when Justin hears the bell, he *expects* that running to the truck and paying for an ice cream will lead to eating it. If his expectation changes, his behavior will, too. Picture what would happen if the ice cream truck changed its route and Justin repeatedly ran out to find, instead, a garbage truck with its safety bell ringing. Rapid extinction would follow as Justin's expectancy changed from "bell means ice cream" to "bell means garbage."

The adaptive value of information helps explain why much human learning occurs without obvious reinforcement by food, water, and the like. We readily learn responses that merely have a desired effect or that bring a goal closer. Let's explore this idea further.

Feedback

Imagine that you are asked to throw darts at a target. Each dart must pass over a screen that prevents you from telling if you hit the target. If you threw 1000 darts this way, we would expect little improvement in your performance, because no *feedback* is provided. **Feedback** (information about what effect a response had) is particularly important in human learning. Recall, for instance, that Mark's video game did not explicitly reward him for correct responses. Yet, because it provided feedback, rapid learning took place.

The value of feedback (also called **knowledge of results,** or **KR**) is one of the most useful lessons to be gained from studies of learning. Increased feedback almost always improves learning and performance (Lee & Carnahan, 1990).

Question: How can feedback be applied?

There are many methods already in wide use. If you want to learn to play a musical instrument, to sing, to speak a second language, or to deliver a speech, tape-recorded feedback can be very helpful. In sports, videotapes are used to improve everything from tennis serves to pick-off moves in baseball. If you would like to make a similar use of feedback, it's worth knowing that taped replays are most helpful when a skilled coach directs attention to key details (Salmoni et al., 1984).

Learning Aids Feedback is valuable in education, too. In recent years, operant learning and feedback have been combined in two interesting ways. These are programmed instruction and computer-assisted instruction.

Question: How do these techniques make use of feedback?

Feedback is most effective when it is *frequent, immediate,* and *detailed.* **Programmed instruction** teaches students in a format that requires precise answers about information as it is presented. This method gives ample feedback to keep learners from practicing errors. It also has the advantage of letting students work at their own pace. (The Learning Check that follows this discussion is done in a programmed format so you can see what one looks like.)

In **computer-assisted instruction (CAI)**, students work at individual computer terminals. The computer displays lessons on a screen, and students type answers. In addition to giving immediate feedback, the computer can analyze each answer. This allows use of a **branching program** that supplies extra information and asks extra questions when errors are made. The newest CAI programs, which use artificial intelligence (see Chapter 9), can even give hints about why an answer was wrong and what is needed to correct it (Fath, Mitchell, & Govindaraj, 1990).

Elementary school children seem to do especially well with "computer tutors" because of the rapid feedback and individualized pacing. Adults benefit too: CAI speeds training in the military, business, and college (Alessi & Trollip, 1985; Dossett & Hulvershorn, 1983; Kulik et al., 1980). Although the final level of skill or knowledge is no higher than that gained by conventional methods, CAI can save time and effort (Wexley, 1984). In general, people tend to do better with CAI because they don't feel like they are being watched and evaluated by a teacher (Schneider & Shugar, 1990). This allows students to freely make mistakes and learn from them.

The simplest computerized instruction consists of self-paced **drill and practice.** In this format, students answer questions similar to those in printed workbooks, but they instantly get correct answers. In addition, the computer can give extra feedback, such as how fast you worked, your percentage correct, or how your work compared with previous scores (Lepper, 1985).

Higher-level CAI programs include **instructional games** and **educational simulations.** Instructional games use stories, competition with a partner, sound effects, and game-like graphics to increase the learner's interest and motivation (■ Fig. 7–28). In educational simulations, students face problems in an imaginary situation or "microworld." By seeing the effects of their choices, students discover basic principles of physics, biology, psychology, or other subjects. Recently, interactive videodiscs have added a new dimension to CAI. **Interactive videodisc instruction** provides a stimulating

Knowledge of results Informational feedback.

Programmed instruction Any learning format that presents information in small amounts, gives immediate practice, and provides continuous feedback to learners.

Computer-assisted instruction (CAI) Learning aided by computer-presented information and exercises.

Branching program A computer program that gives learners corrective information and exercises based on the nature of their errors.

Drill and practice A basic CAI format, typically consisting of questions and answers.

Instructional games Educational computer programs designed to resemble games in order to motivate learning.

Educational simulations Computer programs that simulate real-world settings or situations to promote learning.

Interactive videodisc instruction Computerized multimedia instruction.

■ **Fig. 7–28** *Computer-assisted instruction. The screen on the left shows a typical drill-and-practice math problem, in which students must find the hypotenuse of a triangle. The center screen presents the same problem as an instructional game to increase interest and motivation. In the game, a child is asked to set the proper distance on a ray gun in the hovering space ship to "vaporize" an attacker. The screen on the right depicts an educational simulation. Here, students place a "probe" at various spots in a human brain. They then "stimulate," "destroy," or "restore" areas. As each area is altered, it is named on the screen, and the effects on behavior are described. This allows students to explore basic brain function on their own.*

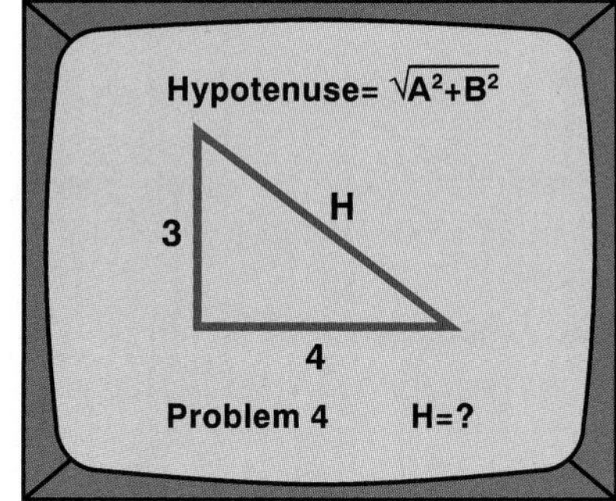

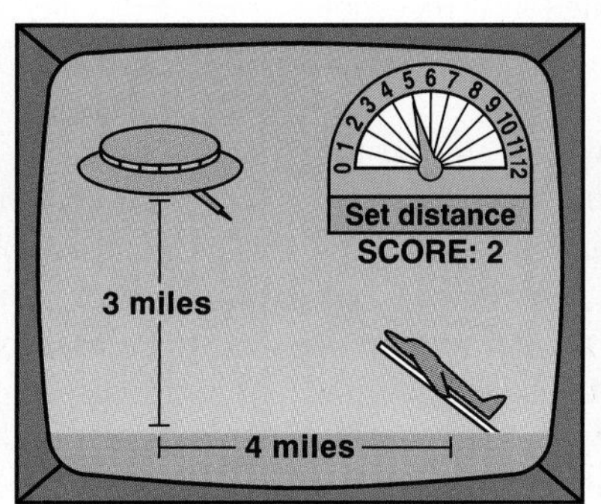

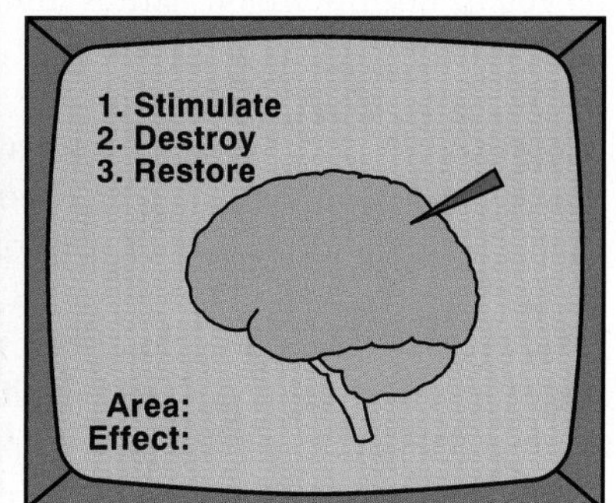

mixture of text, still photos, motion video, and sound, as well as built-in feedback and coaching (Tannenbaum & Yukl, 1992).

Psychologists are actively exploring the advantages and limitations of computer-assisted instruction. It seems likely that their efforts will improve not only education, but our understanding of human learning as well.

LEARNING CHECK

To give you an idea of what programmed instruction is like, this Learning Check is presented in a programmed format. To use it, cover the words on the left, and then uncover each answer after you have filled in a blank.

classical factor classical expectancies knowledge results feedback drill practice	In many learning situations, __________ and operant conditioning occur simultaneously. This circumstance is referred to as two-__________ learning. Often, a reinforcer that strengthens an operant response also serves as an unconditioned stimulus for __________ conditioning. The informational view of learning states that both classical and operant conditioning create mental __________ that alter behavior. Much human learning is based on informational feedback about the effects a response has had. Feedback is also known as KR or __________ of __________. Programmed instruction is self-paced and gives immediate __________ to the learner. The simplest form of computer-assisted instruction is __________ and __________.

Cognitive learning Higher level learning involving thinking, knowing, understanding, and anticipation.

Cognitive map Internal images or other mental representations of an area (maze, city, campus, and so forth) that underlie an ability to choose alternate paths to the same goal.

Latent learning Learning that occurs without obvious reinforcement and that remains unexpressed until reinforcement is provided.

Cognitive Learning—Beyond Conditioning

Question: Is all learning just a connection between stimuli and responses?

Some learning can be thought of this way. But, as we have seen, even basic conditioning has "mental" elements. As a human, you can anticipate future reward or punishment and react accordingly. (You may wonder why this doesn't seem to work when a doctor or dentist says, "This won't hurt a bit." Here's why: They lie!) There is no doubt that human learning includes a large *cognitive*, or mental, dimension. We are greatly affected by information, expectations, perceptions, mental images, and the like.

Loosely speaking, **cognitive learning** refers to understanding, knowing, anticipating, or otherwise making use of information-rich higher mental processes. Cognitive learning extends beyond basic conditioning into the realms of memory, thinking, problem solving, and language. Since these topics are covered in later chapters, our discussion here is limited to a first look at learning beyond conditioning.

Cognitive Maps How do you navigate around the town you live in? Is it fair to assume that you have simply learned to make a series of right and left turns to get from one point to another? It is far more likely that you have developed an overall mental picture of how the town is laid out. This **cognitive map** (internal representation of spatial relationships) acts as a guide even when you must detour or take a new route. Even the lowly rat—not exactly a mental giant—learns *where* food is found in a maze, not just which turns to make to reach the food (Tolman, 1946).

In a sense, cognitive maps also apply to other kinds of knowledge. For instance, it could be said that you have been developing a "map" of psychology while reading this book. This may be why students sometimes find it helpful to draw pictures of how they envision concepts fitting together.

Latent Learning Cognitive learning is also revealed by **latent** (hidden) **learning.** That is, learning sometimes occurs without obvious reinforcement. The learning remains hidden until reinforcement is provided. Here's an example from a classic animal study: Two groups of rats are allowed to explore a maze. Rats in one group find food at the far end of the maze. Soon, they learn to rapidly make their way through the maze when released. Rats in the second group are unrewarded and show no signs of learning. But later, when the "uneducated" rats are given food, they suddenly run the maze as well as the rewarded group (Tolman & Honzik, 1930). Although there was no outward sign of it, the unrewarded rats had learned their way around the maze. Their learning, therefore, remained latent at first (■ Fig. 7–29).

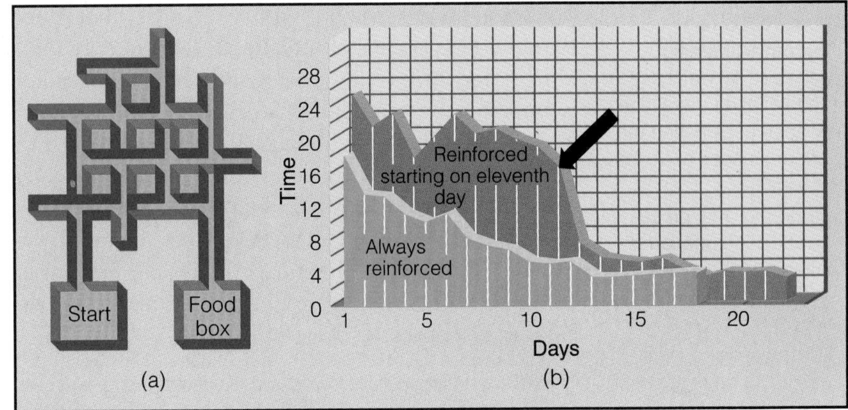

■ **Fig. 7–29** *Latent learning.* (a) *The maze used by Tolman and Honzik to demonstrate latent learning by rats.* (b) *Results of the experiment. Notice the rapid improvement in performance that occurred when food was made available to the previously unreinforced animals. This indicates that learning had occurred, but that it remained hidden or unexpressed. (Adapted from Tolman & Honzik, 1930.)*

Question: How did they learn if there was no reinforcement?

It seems that satisfying curiosity can be enough to reward learning (Harlow & Harlow, 1962). In humans, latent learning is probably related to higher-level abilities, such as anticipating future reward. For example, if you give an attractive classmate a ride home, you may make mental notes about how to get to his or her house, even if a date is only a remote future possibility.

Discovery Learning Much of what is meant by cognitive learning is summarized by the word *understanding.* Each of us has, at times, learned ideas by *rote* (repetition and memorization). Although rote learning is efficient, many psychologists believe that learning is more lasting and flexible when people *discover* facts and principles on their own (Lepper, 1985). In **discovery learning,** skills are gained by insight and understanding instead of by rote.

Question: As long as learning occurs, what difference does it make?

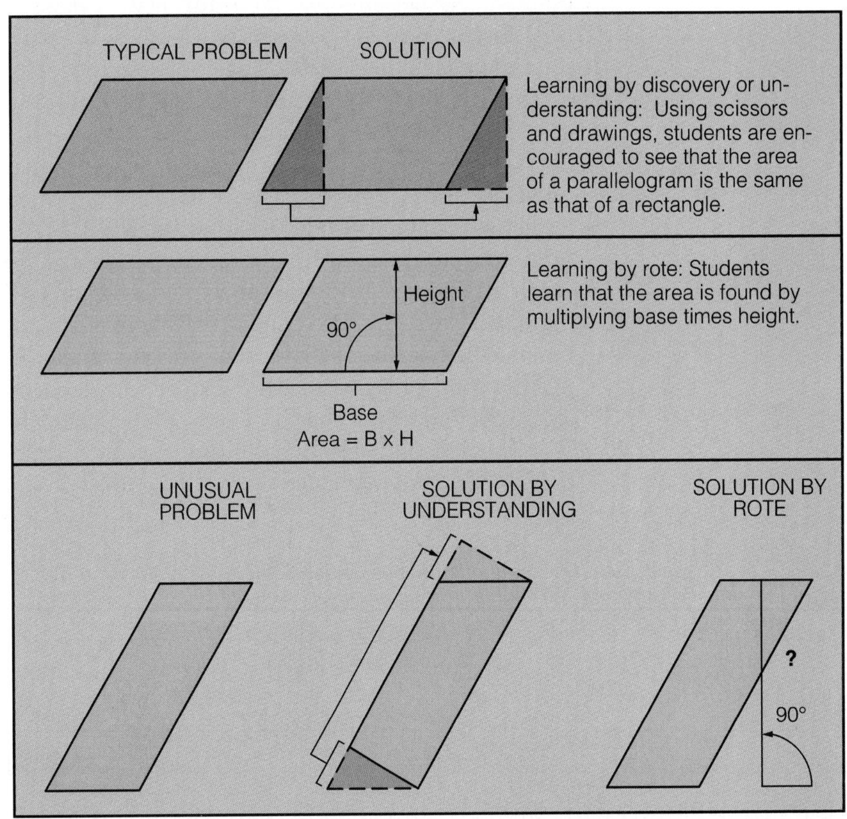

■ **Fig. 7–30** *Learning by understanding and by rote. For some types of learning, understanding may be superior, although both types of learning are useful. (After Wertheimer, 1959.)*

■ Figure 7–30 illustrates the difference. Two groups of students were taught to calculate the area of a parallelogram. Some were encouraged to see that a "piece" of a parallelogram could be "moved" to create a rectangle. Later, they were better able to solve unusual problems than were students who simply memorized a rule (Wertheimer, 1959). As this suggests, discovery learning tends to produce better understanding of new problems and situations (Lepper, 1985). Discovery learning is particularly valuable if a person has to try new strategies or discover new solutions to problems during learning (McDaniel & Schlager, 1990). Rote learning is undeniably direct and efficient. However, in many situations it is worthwhile to cultivate insight and deeper understanding, even if learning by discovery takes longer.

Discovery learning Learning based on insight or understanding rather than on a mechanical application of rules.

Modeling—Do as I Do, Not as I Say

The class watches intently as a skilled potter pulls a spinning ball of clay into the form of a vase. There is

Observational learning Learning achieved by watching and imitating the actions of another or noting the consequences of those actions.

Modeling Any process in which information is imparted by example, before direct practice is allowed.

Model A person who serves as an example in observational learning.

little doubt that many skills are learned by what Albert Bandura (1971) calls **observational learning,** or **modeling.** Modeling is any process in which information is imparted by example, before direct practice is allowed (Rosenthal & Steffek, 1990). The value of learning by observation is obvious: Imagine trying to *tell* someone how to tie a shoe, do a dance step, crochet, or play a guitar. Bandura believes that anything that can be learned from direct experience can be learned by observation. Often, this allows a person to skip the tedious trial-and-error stage of learning (■ Fig. 7–31).

Question: It seems obvious that we learn by observation, but how does it occur?

Observational Learning

By observing a **model** (someone who serves as an example), a person may (1) learn new responses, (2) learn to carry out or avoid previously learned responses (depending on what happens to the model for doing the same thing), or (3) learn a general rule that can be applied to various situations.

For observational learning to occur, several things must take place. First, the learner must pay *attention* to the model and *remember* what was done. (A beginning auto mechanic might be interested enough to watch an entire tune-up, but unable to remember all the steps.) Next, the learner must be able to *reproduce* the modeled behavior. (Sometimes this is a matter of practice, but it may be that the learner will never be able to perform the behavior. I may admire the feats of world-class gymnasts, but with no amount of practice could I ever reproduce them.) If a model is *successful* at a task or *rewarded* for a response, the learner is more likely to imitate the behavior. In general, models who are attractive, rewarded, admired, or high in status also tend to be imitated (Bandura & Walters, 1963). Finally, once a new response is tried, normal *reinforcement determines if it will be repeated thereafter.* (Notice the similarity here to latent learning, described earlier.)

■ Fig. 7–31 *Observational learning often imparts large amounts of information that would be difficult to obtain by reading instructions or memorizing rules.*

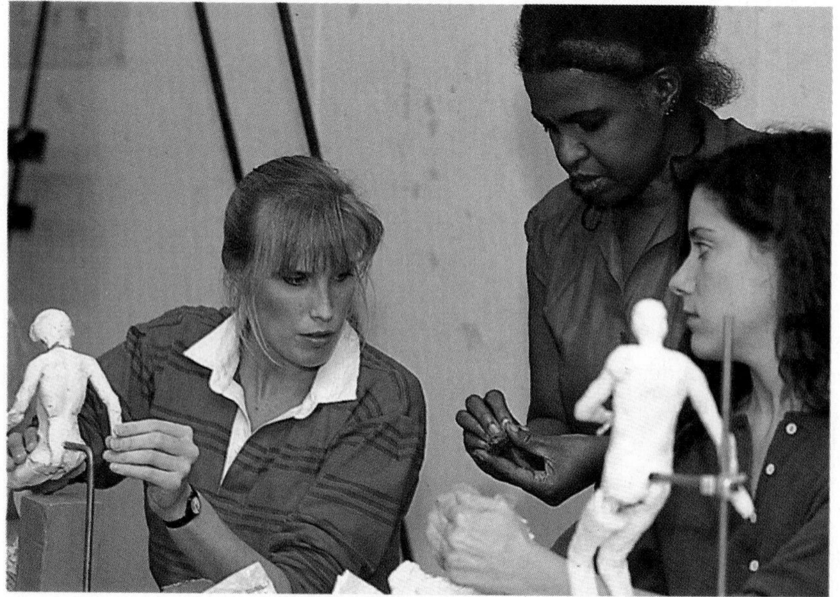

Imitating Models Modeling has a powerful effect on behavior. In a classic experiment, children watched an adult attack a large blowup "Bo-Bo the Clown" doll. Some children saw an adult sit on the doll, punch it, hit it with a hammer, and kick it around the room. Others saw a color movie of these actions. A third group saw a cartoon version of the aggression. Later, the children were frustrated (by having some attractive toys taken away from them) and then allowed to play with the Bo-Bo doll. Most imitated the attack they had seen the adult perform (■ Fig. 7–32). Some even added new aggressive acts of their own! Interestingly, the cartoon was only slightly less effective in encouraging aggression than the live adult model and the filmed model (Bandura et al., 1963).

Question: Then do children blindly imitate adults?

No. Remember that observational learning equips a person to duplicate a response, but whether it is actually imitated depends on whether the model was rewarded or punished for what was done. Nevertheless, research shows that when parents tell a child to do one thing, but model a completely different response, children tend to imitate what the parents *do*, and *not* what they *say* (Bryan & Walbek, 1970). Thus, through modeling, children learn not only attitudes, gestures, emotions, and personality traits, but fears, anxieties, and bad habits as well.

Consider a typical situation. Little Shawn-Erin-Ringo-Jeremy Jones has just been interrupted at play by his younger brother, Mildew. Angry and frustrated, he screams at Mildew. This behavior interrupts his father's TV watching. Father promptly spanks little Shawn-Erin-Ringo-Jeremy, saying, "This will teach you to hit your little brother." And it will. Because of modeling effects, it is unrealistic to expect a child to "Do as I say, not as I do." The message the father has given the child is clear: "You have frustrated me; therefore, I will hit you." The next time little Shawn-Erin-Ringo-Jeremy is frustrated, it will be no surprise if he imitates his father and hits his brother.

Question: Can television serve as a model for observational learning?

Yes it can. As a convicted criminal once told *TV Guide* magazine, "TV taught me how to steal cars, how to break into establishments, how to go about robbing

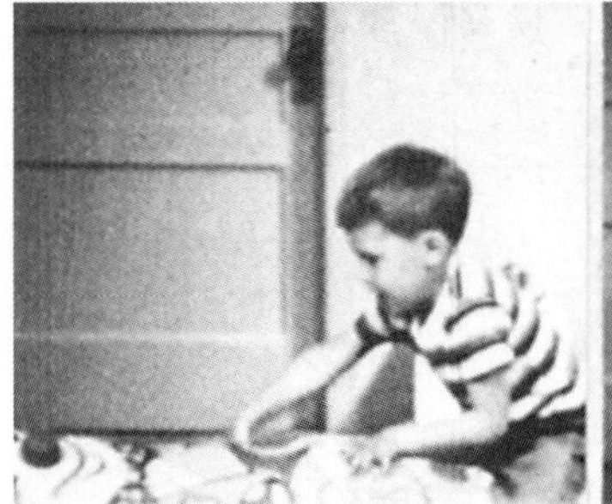

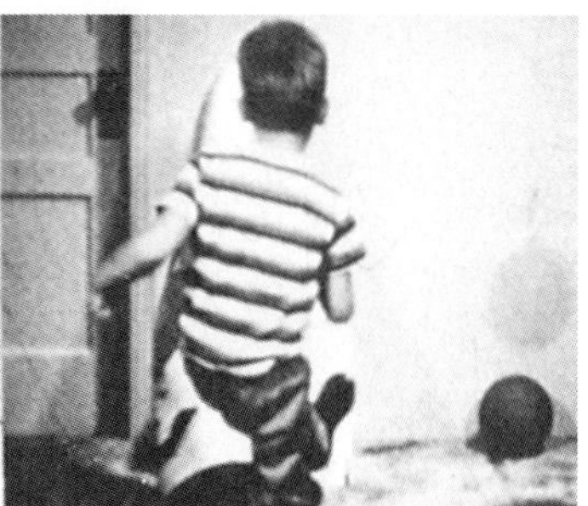

■ **Fig. 7–32** *A nursery school child imitates the aggressive behavior of an adult model he has just seen in a movie. (Photos courtesy of Albert Bandura.)*

people, even how to roll a drunk. Once after having watched 'Hawaii Five-O,' I robbed a gas station. The show showed me how to do it."

Modeling and Television The potential impact of TV can be found in these figures: By the time the average person has graduated from high school, he or she will have viewed some 15,000 hours of TV, compared with only 11,000 hours spent in the classroom. In that time, such viewers will have seen some 18,000 murders and countless acts of robbery, arson, bombing, torture, and beatings (■ Fig. 7–33). It's true that TV programming in the United States has improved somewhat during the last decade. Overall, however, violent acts, dynamite blasts, gun battles, high-speed car wrecks, stereotypes, and sexism still prevail (Kubey & Csikszentmihaly, 1990). Children watching Saturday morning cartoons see a chilling 26 or more violent acts each hour (Pogatchnik, 1990). Teenage mutant ninja turtles, indeed!

At this point, hundreds of studies, involving well over 10,000 children, have been completed. The vast majority point to the same conclusion: "If large groups of children watch a great deal of televised violence, they will be more prone to behave aggressively" (Heath, Bresolin, & Rinaldi, 1989; Joy et al., 1986; Levinger, 1986; National Institute of Mental Health, 1982). In other words, not all children will become more aggressive, but many will. Incidentally, the same conclusion applies to violent video games (Schutte et al., 1988).

■ **Fig. 7–33** *Televised violence may promote observational learning of aggression. A study conducted in 1993 found that 1,846 acts of violence occurred in a single day of television programming in the United States. The worst offenders were music videos, "reality" shows, cartoons, and promotions for violent movies.*

Question: Is it fair to say, then, that televised violence causes aggression in viewers, especially children?

No. That would be an exaggeration. Televised violence can make aggression more *likely*, but it does not invariably "cause" it to occur (Freedman, 1984; Levinger, 1986). Many other factors affect the chances that hostile thoughts will be turned into actions (Berkowitz, 1984). Among children, one such factor is the extent to which a child *identifies* with aggressive characters (Huesmann et al., 1983). That's why it is so sad to find TV *heroes* behaving aggressively, as well as villains (■ Fig. 7–34). Youngsters who believe that aggression is an acceptable way to solve problems, who believe that TV portrayals of violence are realistic, and who identify with TV characters are most likely to copy televised aggression (Eron, 1986). For another look at the effects of TV violence, see Highlight 7–4. For further information also consult Chapter 21.

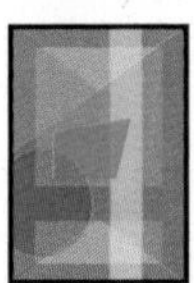

HIGHLIGHT 7–4

Research Frontier

Life after TV—A Natural Experiment

North American children and adults spend the majority of their leisure time watching TV. What effect does this have on behavior? A study by Canadian psychologists offers a fascinating look at life with the tube. A team of researchers found a town in northwestern Canada that did not receive TV broadcasts. Discovering that the town was

■ **Fig. 7–34** *A recent study investigated the effects on children's aggressive behavior of a popular children's TV program, "The Mighty Morphin Power Rangers." In each episode, the "Power Rangers" "morph" into super-heroes who use karate and other violent actions to conquer monsters. The study found that after watching an episode of the Power Rangers, a group of 7-year-old children committed 7 times more aggressive acts than a control group that did not watch the program. The aggressive children hit, kicked, and karate chopped their peers, often directly imitating the "Power Rangers" (Matillo, Nesbitt, & Boyatzis, in press).*

about to get TV, the research team seized a rare opportunity. Tannis Williams and her team carefully tested residents of the town just before TV arrived and again two years later. This natural experiment revealed that after TV came to town:

■ Reading development among children declined (Corteen & Williams, 1986).
■ Children's scores on tests of creativity dropped (Harrison & Williams, 1986).
■ Children's perceptions of sex roles became more stereotyped (Kimball, 1986).

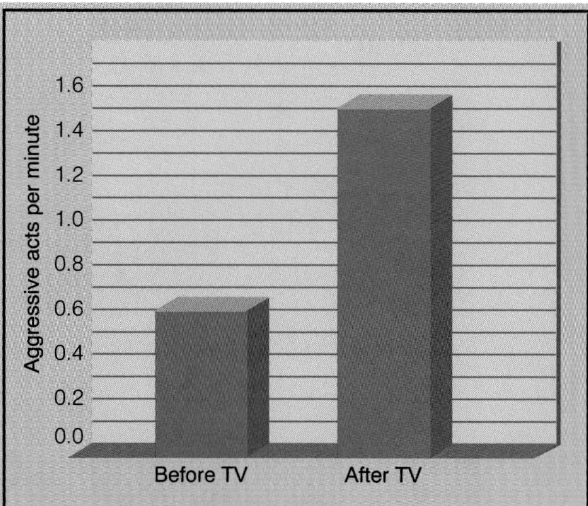

■ **Fig. 7–35** *This graph shows the average number of aggressive acts per minute before and after television broadcasts were introduced into a Canadian town. The increase in aggression after television watching began was significant. Two other towns that already had television were used for comparison. Neither showed significant increases in aggression during the same time period. (Data compiled from Joy et al., 1986.)*

■ There was a significant increase in both verbal and physical aggression (■Fig. 7–35). This occurred for both boys and girls, and it applied equally to children who were high or low in aggression before they began watching TV (Joy et al., 1986).

The last result comes as no surprise. Researchers have consistently found that television has a strong impact on aggression. In view of such findings, it is understandable that Canada, Norway, and Switzerland have restricted the amount of permissible violence on television (Levinger, 1986). Should all countries do the same?

A Look Ahead Perhaps the best way to appreciate learning is to observe how reinforcement affects your own behavior. With this in mind, the upcoming Applications section proposes a personal experiment in operant conditioning. We'll also consider steps you can take to better manage your learning at school. Following that, we will explore biological influences on learning. Don't miss these coming attractions!

Learning Check

1. Higher level learning that involves understanding or knowing is known as ______________ learning.
2. In humans, extinction of a conditioned response can be influenced by expectation. T or F?
3. An internal representation of spatial relationships is referred to as a ______________ ______________.
4. Learning that suddenly appears when a reward or incentive for performance is given is called
 a. discovery learning *b.* latent learning *c.* rote learning *d.* reminiscence

5. Psychologists use the term ______________ to describe observational learning.

6. If a model is successful, rewarded, attractive, or high in status, his or her behavior is
   a. difficult to reproduce *b.* less likely to be attended to
   c. more likely to be imitated *d.* subject to positive transfer

7. Children who observed a live adult behave aggressively became more aggressive; those who observed movie and cartoon aggression did not. T or F?

8. Televised aggression causes young viewers to behave more aggressively. T or F?

9. Children who watch many aggressive programs on television tend to be more aggressive than average. Why doesn't this observation prove that televised aggression causes aggressive behavior? ***Critical Thinking***

Answers: 1. cognitive 2. T 3. cognitive map 4. *b* 5. modeling 6. *c* 7. F 8. F (It makes aggression more likely but does not cause it to occur.) 9. Because the observation is based on a correlation. Children who are already aggressive may choose to watch more aggressive programs, rather than being made aggressive by them. It took experimental studies to verify that televised aggression promotes aggression by viewers.

APPLICATIONS: *Behavioral Self-Management*

This discussion could be the start of one of the most personal "Applications" in this book. There is now little doubt that self-administered reward affects behavior (Watson & Tharp, 1993). Many people have learned to use reinforcement to alter or manage their own behavior. At the very least, self-management can make you more aware of your behavior and what controls it.

This, then, is an invitation to carry out a self-management project of your own. Would you like to increase the number of hours you spend studying each week? Would you like to exercise more, attend more classes, concentrate longer, or read more books? All these activities and many others can be improved by following the rules described here.

Self-Managed Behavior—A Rewarding Project

Managing your own behavior can be achieved by adapting the principles of operant conditioning for personal use.

1. **Choose a target behavior.** Identify the activity you want to change.
2. **Record a baseline.** Record how much time you currently spend performing the target activity, or count the number of desired or undesired responses you make each day.
3. **Establish goals.** Your goals may be stated as increases or decreases in a target behavior. Remember the principle of shaping and set gradual, realistic goals for each successive week. Also, set daily goals that add up to the weekly goal.
4. **Choose reinforcers.** If you meet your daily goal, what reward will you allow yourself? Daily rewards might be watching television, eating a candy bar, socializing with friends, playing a musical instrument, or whatever you enjoy. Also establish a weekly reward. If you reach your weekly goal, what reward will you allow yourself? A movie? A dinner out? A weekend hike?
5. **Record your progress.** Keep accurate records of the amount of time you spend each day on the desired activity or the number of times you make the desired response.
6. **Reward successes.** If you meet your daily goal, collect your reward. If you fall short, be honest with yourself and skip the reward. Do the same for your weekly goal.
7. **Adjust your plan.** As you learn more about your behavior, change goals and reinforcers as needed. Overall progress will reinforce your attempts at self-management.

Target behavior A response selected for modification.

Baseline A record of the initial frequency of a target behavior.

Here is a sample of one student's plan for getting more aerobic exercise by walking, swimming, and biking:

1. *Target behavior:* Number of hours spent exercising each week.
2. *Recorded baseline:* An average of 17 minutes per day, for a weekly total of 2 hours.
3. *Goal for the first week:* Increase exercise time to 25 minutes per day; weekly goal of 3 hours total exercise time.

Self-recording Self-management based on keeping records of response frequencies.

Behavioral contract A formal agreement stating behaviors to be changed and consequences that apply.

Goal for second week: Increase to 35 minutes per day and 4 hours per week.
Goal for third week: Increase to 45 minutes per day and 5 hours per week.
Ultimate goal: To reach and maintain 1 hour per day, 7 hours per week of aerobic exercise.
4. *Daily reward for reaching goal:* One half hour of guitar playing in the evening; no playing if the goal is not met. Weekly reward for reaching goal: going to a movie or buying a compact disc.

If you have trouble finding rewards, or if you don't want to use the entire system, remember that anything done often can serve as reinforcement (the Premack principle). For example, if you watch television every night and want to keep your house cleaner, make it a rule not to turn on the set until you have cleaned for 30 minutes (or whatever length of time you choose).

Self-Recording Even if you find it difficult to give and withhold the rewards in your program, you are likely to succeed. Simply knowing that you are reaching a desired goal can be reward enough. The key to any self-management program is accurate record keeping. This concept is demonstrated by a study in which some students in an introductory psychology course recorded study time and graphed their daily and weekly study behavior. Even though no extra rewards were offered, students who were asked to record their study time earned better grades than those who were not required to keep records (Johnson & White, 1971).

Good Ways to Break Bad Habits

Question: How can I use learning principles to break a bad habit?

By using the methods we have discussed, you can reinforce yourself for *decreasing* unwanted behaviors, such as swearing, nail-biting, criticizing others, smoking, drinking coffee, excess TV watching, or any other behavior you choose to target. However, breaking bad habits may require some additional techniques. Here are four strategies to help you change bad habits.

Alternate Responses A good strategy for change is to try to get the same reinforcement with a new response.

Example: Marta often tells jokes at the expense of others. Her friends sometimes feel hurt by her sharp-edged humor. Marta senses this and wants to change. What can she do? Usually, Marta's joke telling is reinforced by attention and approval. She could just as easily get the same reinforcement by giving other people praise or compliments. Making a change in her behavior should be easy because she will continue to receive the reinforcement she seeks.

Extinction Try to discover what is reinforcing a unwanted response and remove, avoid, or delay the reinforcement (Ferster et al., 1962).

Example: Tiffany has developed a habit of taking longer and longer "breaks" to watch TV when she should be studying. Obviously, TV watching is reinforcing her break taking. To improve her study habits, Tiffany could delay reinforcement by studying at the library or some other location a good distance from her TV.

Response Chains Break up response chains that precede an undesired behavior. The key idea is to scramble the chain of events that leads to an undesired response (Watson & Tharp, 1993).

Example: Almost every night Steve comes home from work, turns on the TV, and eats a whole bag of cookies or chips. He then takes a shower and changes clothes. By dinner time he has lost his appetite. Steve realizes he is substituting junk food for dinner. Steve might resolve the problem by breaking the response chain that precedes dinner. For instance, he could shower immediately when he gets home or he could avoid turning on the television until after dinner.

Cues and Antecedents Try to avoid, narrow down, or remove stimuli that elicit the bad habit.

Example: Raul wants to cut down on smoking. He has taken many smoking cues out of his surroundings by removing ashtrays, matches, and extra cigarettes from his house, car, and office. Raul should try narrowing antecedent stimuli even more. He could begin by smoking only in the lounge at work, never in his office or in his car. He could then limit his smoking to home. Then to only one room at home. Then to one chair at home. If he succeeds in getting this far, he may want to limit his smoking to only one unpleasant place, such as a bathroom, basement, or garage (Goldiamond, 1971).

Contracting

If you try any of the techniques described here and have difficulty sticking with them, you may want to try **behavioral contracting.** In a behavioral contract, you state a *specific* problem behavior you want to control, or a goal you want to achieve. Also state the rewards you will receive, privileges you will forfeit, or punishments you must accept. The contract should be typed and signed by you and a person you trust.

A behavioral contract can be quite motivating, especially when mild punishment is part of the agreement. Here's an example reported by Nurnberger and Zimmerman (1970): A student working on his Ph.D. had completed all requirements but his dissertation, yet for 2 years had not written a single page. A contract was drawn up for him in which he agreed to meet weekly deadlines on the number of pages he would complete. To make sure he would meet the deadlines, he wrote postdated checks. These were to be forfeited if he failed to reach his goal for the week. The checks were made out to organizations he despised (the Ku Klux Klan and American Nazi Party). From the time he signed the contract until he finished his degree, the student's work output was greatly improved.

Effective learning at school poses a special set of challenges. The next section describes some additional steps you can take to increase your chances of success.

Self-Regulated Learning—Academic All-Stars

Rick is passing his college classes—but just barely. Yet, elsewhere his capacity for learning is impressive. On his own, Rick is teaching himself advanced music theory, computer-synthesized music techniques, and music history.

Why is there such a big difference in Rick's apparent learning ability? The answer is that in the realm of music, Rick is an *active, goal-oriented* learner: He continuously identifies gaps in his knowledge and seeks new learning experiences to fill them. In contrast, Rick's learning at school has been haphazard and passive.

How could Rick make college work more like his voluntary learning of music? An approach known as self-regulated learning might be a good start.

Psychologist Barry Zimmerman (1990) calls the active pursuit of knowledge **self-regulated learning.** Self-regulated learners use planning and feedback to guide their efforts. They are self-starters who persist until they get it right. Even if you are a good student, you may find some ways to improve your learning skills in the guidelines which follow.

Set Learning Goals Try to begin each learning session with specific goals in mind. What knowledge or skills are you trying to master? What do you hope to accomplish?

It's best to state each of your learning goals as a clear-cut outcome. For example, your goal for a single study session might be, "I want to be able to define, in my own words, all of the boldface terms in this chapter." A weekly goal might read, "My goal is to spend 5 hours this week working on my term paper for sociology."

Be sure to set long-term, intermediate, and short-term goals. Distant payoffs such as grades, graduation, or a rewarding career may not be much help when you are tempted by distractions. (Many students have never met a distraction they didn't like.) Short-term, day-by-day goals make it easier to maintain motivation, because you can clearly see your progress (Schunk, 1990).

Plan a Learning Strategy How will you accomplish your goals? Formal assignments made by your teachers may not be enough. Or, they may not be ideal for you. Make daily, weekly, and monthly plans for learning. Then put them into action.

Be Your Own Teacher Effective learners engage in frequent **self-instruction.** In other words, they act, in a sense, as their own teachers.

Typically, self-instruction takes the form of a silent dialogue, in which you guide your own learning with instructions or questions. For example, when you are reading, you might ask yourself at the end of each paragraph, "What is the main idea here? How does it connect with what came before? What are the implications of this idea? How does this information relate to what I already know? What details should I remember?" It is also important to ask often, "Do I really understand this information? Where are the gaps and weaknesses in my knowledge? What needs more attention? Do I need to consult other sources of information or ask for clarification in class?"

Being very honest with yourself is one of the challenges of self-instruction. It's easy to fall prey to a false sense of mastery when there are actually holes in your knowledge.

Monitor Your Progress Monitoring your own progress may be the most important aspect of effective learning. Virtually all researchers agree that self-regulated learning depends on feedback about learning effectiveness.

Self-regulated learning Active, self-guided learning.

Self-instruction Use of silent questions and instructions to structure learning.

Exceptional learners actively seek feedback in both formal and informal ways. They keep records of their progress toward learning goals (pages read, hours of studying, assignments completed, and so forth). They quiz themselves, use study guides, and find other ways to check their understanding while learning.

If you would like to add more feedback to your study routine, you might find it helpful to simply rate your work on a scale of 1 to 10. Such ratings can be used both daily and weekly to monitor personal progress. Ratings can be applied to specific classes, assignments, readings, papers, or skills that were listed in your learning goals. It can also be helpful to keep a daily journal or diary in which you make informal notes about your progress. Sometimes this is all the feedback necessary to stay on course and regulate learning.

Use Self-Reinforcement When you meet your daily, weekly, or monthly performance standards, reward your efforts in some way.

Of course, self-reinforcement can be tangible and explicit, such as rest breaks, food, new clothes, attending a party, or going to a movie (as described earlier). But be aware that self-praise also rewards learning. Being able to say "Hey, I did it!," or "Good work!" and know that you deserve it can be very reinforcing. In the long run, success, feelings of accomplishment, and personal satisfaction provide the real payoffs for self-regulated learning.

Evaluate Your Progress and Goals It is a good idea to frequently evaluate your performance records and goals.

If you are not making good progress toward long-range goals, do you need to revise your short-term performance targets? Are there specific classes or areas of your work that need more attention? Do you need to make adjustments in how you study? Even informal self-evaluations can be helpful. While studying, self-regulated learners take time to say to themselves, "I know this material," or "I did poorly when I tried to summarize. I'd better review and take better notes."

Take Corrective Action If you discover areas that need attention, ask yourself, "What changes can I make to improve?"

Taking corrective action may demand a change in how you use your time. It may require changes in your learning environment, to deal with distractions such as watching TV, daydreaming, talking to friends, or testing the structural integrity of the walls with your stereo system. You may need to improve your study skills (Chapter 1) or your ability to memorize information (Chapter 8). Adjustments may be called for in self-reinforcement. If you discover that you are lacking necessary knowledge or skills, ask for help, take advantage of tutoring programs, or look for sources of information beyond your courses and textbooks. (Table 7–3 summarizes the main elements of self-regulated learning.)

Table 7–3 Elements of Self-Regulated Learning

- Set specific, objective learning goals
- Plan learning efforts and use learning strategies
- Use self-instruction to guide studying
- Use feedback and record keeping to monitor progress
- Reinforce your own efforts and successes
- Periodically evaluate your progress and goals
- Make adjustments as needed in all of the preceding

Whatever changes you make, keep in mind that you may also need to reassess your learning goals. It's best to learn for personal satisfaction. But to be practical, you must also adjust your performance standards to meet or exceed those set by your professors.

Empowerment Getting an "education" cannot possibly teach you everything you will ever need to know. The true value of attending college lies in learning to educate yourself. Knowing how to regulate and control learning can be a key to life-long enrichment and personal empowerment.

Getting Help

Attempting to manage or alter your own behavior may be more difficult than it sounds. If you feel you need more information, consult either of the books listed here. You will also find helpful advice in the Applications section of Chapter 18. If you do try a self-modification project, but find it impossible to reach your goal, be aware that professional advice is available.

For more information about behavioral self-management, consult:

Watson, D. L. and Tharp, R. G. *Self-directed behavior.* Pacific Grove, CA: Brooks/Cole, 1993.

Williams, R. L. and Long, J. D. *Toward a self-managed life style.* Boston, MA: Houghton Mifflin, 1991.

APPLICATIONS: *Continued*

LEARNING CHECK

1. After a target behavior has been selected for reinforcement, it's a good idea to record a baseline so you can set realistic goals for change. T or F?
2. Self-recording, even without the use of extra rewards, can bring about desired changes in target behaviors. T or F?
3. The Premack principle states that behavioral contracting can be used to reinforce changes in behavior. T or F?
4. A self-management plan should make use of the principle of shaping by setting a graduated series of goals. T or F?
5. An essential element of self-regulated learning is the use of ______________ to monitor progress toward learning goals.
6. Self-instruction refers to the process of comparing short-term performance to long-term goals. T or F?
7. Effective self-reinforcement in self-regulated learning can be either explicit and pre-arranged or informal. T or F?
8. Adjustments in personal ______________ ______________ must take external performance standards into account.
9. How does setting daily goals in a behavioral self-management program help maximize the effects of reinforcement? ***Critical Thinking***

Answers: 1. T 2. T 3. F 4. T 5. feedback 6. F 7. T 8. performance goals 9. Daily performance goals and rewards reduce the delay of reinforcement, which maximizes its impact.

EXPLORATION

Biological Constraints on Learning—Snakes, Spiders, and the Reluctant Raccoon

The weaverbird is a curious creature that ties a special grass knot to hold its nest together. How does it learn to make the knot? It doesn't! Weaverbirds raised in total isolation for several generations still tie the knot the first time they build a nest.

Knot tying in the weaverbird is a **fixed action pattern** (**FAP**). A FAP is an instinctual chain of movements found in almost all members of a species. Like other **innate** (inborn) **behaviors,** fixed action patterns help animals meet major needs in their lives (picture a cat's face-washing routine, for instance). More complicated behaviors, like the maternal instinct in lower animals, combine both fixed action patterns and various reflexes.

Question: Do humans have instincts?

Humans do not have instincts as most psychologists define them. To qualify as instinctual, a behavior must be innate, complex, and "species specific." **Species-specific behaviors** are those that occur with little variation in almost all members of a species. Species-specific behaviors appear to be "wired into" the nervous system. Other than reflexes, no human behaviors are so rigidly programmed. However, that doesn't mean that human learning isn't affected by innate behavior.

All species, including humans, engage in a large number of clearly recognizable **species-typical behaviors.** For example, pigeons typically peck at things when they are hungry. If you want to train a pigeon to peck a button to receive food, the pigeon will learn quickly. Likewise, if you want to teach a pigeon to flap its wings to escape an electric shock, learning will be rapid. But, just try to teach a pigeon to flap its wings to receive food or to peck a button to turn off a shock to its feet. In both cases little or no learning will take place.

Such observations suggest that there are **biological constraints,** or limits, to learning—especially for animals. Some associations between stimuli and responses or between responses and consequences are easily learned; others can be acquired only with great difficulty. For example, many people find it very difficult to do the follow-

Fixed action pattern (FAP) An instinctual chain of movements found in almost all members of a species.

Innate behavior Inborn, unlearned behavior.

Species-specific behavior Behavior patterns that occur with little variation in almost all members of a species.

Species-typical behavior Behavior patterns that are typical of a species, but not automatic.

Biological constraints Biological limits on what an animal or person can easily learn.

ing: Move the tip of your right foot in a *clockwise* circle on the floor; at the same time, hold your right hand out at waist level and move it in a *counterclockwise* circle, parallel to the floor. Even for a substantial reward, you might find it hard to learn these biologically atypical movements. Perhaps we appreciate gifted musicians and athletes, in part, because they succeed at learning responses that are biologically constrained.

Biological constraints affect both classical conditioning and operant conditioning, as shown by the examples which follow.

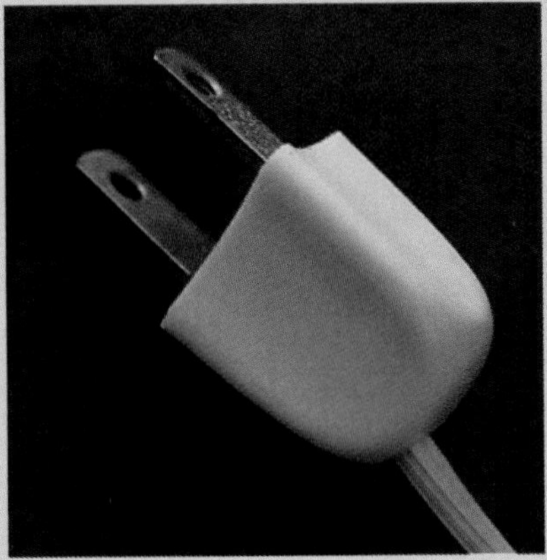

■ **Fig. 7–36** *Which of these stimuli do you think would make a better conditioned stimulus for learned fear? Why did you choose as you did? Fear-relevant stimuli are much more effective conditioned stimuli for learned fears (Ohman & Soares, 1993).*

Conditioned Fears

Through classical conditioning, it is possible to learn to fear or dislike just about anything. Is it possible, however, that some fears are easier to learn than others (■ Fig. 7–36)? Martin Seligman's (1972) **prepared fear theory** holds that it is. Seligman believes that we are prepared by evolution to readily develop fears to certain stimuli, such as snakes and spiders. Other common objects are more likely to cause pain or harm (a hammer, light socket, or skis, for example). Even so, phobias are less likely to develop for such objects than for spiders or snakes. Seligman also believes that our readiness to learn such fears makes them highly resistant to extinction.

Why should fears of "crawly things" be easier to acquire? According to Seligman's theory, such stimuli posed dangers earlier in human history. Through natural selection, they have become highly effective conditioning stimuli. Experiments in which fear was conditioned to images of spiders, snakes, neutral shapes, and electrical plugs offer some support for Seligman's theory (Hugdahl & Karker, 1981). Maybe with further evolution, humans will develop proper fears of light sockets and skis, too!

The Reluctant Raccoon

B. F. Skinner's success in shaping pigeons to play Ping-Pong was aided by the fact that pigeons naturally peck objects. At one time, psychologists assumed that almost any voluntary response could be taught by operant conditioning. But in recent years, it has become clear that operant responses are also subject to biological constraints. For example, two noted psychologists, Keller and Marion Breland, went into business training animals for television shows, zoo displays, and amusement parks. Along with their successes came some revealing failures (Bailey & Bailey, 1993).

In one instance, the Brelands tried to condition a raccoon to put coins in a piggy-bank for an advertisement. Instead, the raccoon repeatedly rubbed the coins together in a miserly-looking fashion (Breland & Breland, 1961). No amount of reinforcement would change this behavior. The Brelands ran into similar snags with other animals. In each case an innate behavior pattern hindered learning. They called this problem **instinctive drift:** Learned responses tend to "drift" toward innate ones. The "miserly" behavior of the raccoon was simply an innate food-washing response. In view of such observations, it is wise to remember that the laws of learning operate within a framework of biological limits and possibilities (Adams, 1980).

Think about It

An advantage of biologically programmed behavior is that it prepares animals and humans to survive in their natural environments. A disadvantage is that evolution is slow. Natural selection prepares a species only for a future which resembles the biological past (Skinner, 1990). Under normal circumstances, animals are superbly adapted to their surroundings. But throw them a curve by changing the environment in unexpected ways and their behavior may suddenly look very "stupid." For example, if a spider begins spinning a cocoon and its silk glands are removed, it will continue to make all 6400 spinning movements to complete the job. Then it will lay eggs in the non-existent cocoon. We are indeed fortunate that an overriding feature that emerged in human evolution is our capacity to learn.

Prepared fear theory Holds that people and animals are prepared by evolution to readily learn fears of certain stimuli.

Instinctive drift The tendency of learned responses to shift toward innate response patterns.

EXPLORATION

Learning Check

1. An instinctual chain of responses found in nearly all members of a species is called a ______ ______ ______.
2. Biological constraints on learning reflect underlying potentials and limitations imposed by prior conditioning. T or F?
3. A child rapidly learned to fear a neighbor's dog that knocked her down, growled, and showed its teeth. Yet, the same child seems to have no fear of the cars passing by her house. This difference may be explained by ______ ______ theory.
4. Instinctive drift can be said to have occurred any time an unlearned stimulus triggers a reflex. T or F?
5. Biologically based patterns of behavior evolve very slowly. Changes based on learning occur very quickly. Can you identify a dimension of human behavior that helps bridge this gap? *Critical Thinking*

Answers: 1. fixed action pattern 2. F 3. prepared fear 4. F 5. B. F. Skinner argued that cultures evolve far more quickly than organisms do. Cultures, therefore, help humans survive and adapt by passing on time-tested behavior patterns.

Chapter Summary

What is learning?

- **Learning** is a relatively permanent change in behavior due to experience. Learning that results from conditioning depends on **reinforcement.**
- **Classical,** or **respondent,** conditioning and **instrumental,** or **operant,** conditioning are two basic types of learning. In classical conditioning, a previously neutral stimulus begins to elicit a response through **association** with another stimulus. In operant conditioning, the pattern of voluntary responses is altered by **consequences.**

How does classical conditioning occur?

- Classical conditioning, studied by **Pavlov,** occurs when a **neutral stimulus** (NS) is associated with an **unconditioned stimulus** (US). The US causes a reflex called the **unconditioned response** (UR). If the NS is consistently paired with the US, it becomes a **conditioned stimulus** (CS) capable of producing a response by itself. This response is a **conditioned** (learned) **response** (CR).
- When the conditioned stimulus is followed by the unconditioned stimulus, conditioning is **reinforced** (strengthened).
- **Higher-order** conditioning occurs when a well-learned conditioned stimulus is used as if it were an unconditioned stimulus, bringing about further learning.
- When the CS is repeatedly presented alone, conditioning is **extinguished** (weakened or inhibited). After extinction seems to be complete, a rest period may lead to the temporary reappearance of a conditioned response. This is called **spontaneous recovery.**
- Through **stimulus generalization,** stimuli similar to the conditioned stimulus will also produce a response. Generalization gives way to **stimulus discrimination** when an organism learns to respond to one stimulus, but not to similar stimuli.

Does conditioning affect emotions?

- Conditioning applies to visceral or emotional responses as well as simple reflexes. As a result, **conditioned emotional responses** (CERs) also occur. Irrational fears called **phobias** may be CERs. Conditioning of emotional responses can occur **vicariously** (secondhand) as well as directly.

How does operant conditioning occur?

- Operant conditioning occurs when a voluntary action is followed by a **reinforcer.** Reinforcement in operant conditioning increases the frequency or probability of a response. This result is based on the **law of effect.**
- Complex operant responses can be taught by reinforcing **successive approximations** to a final desired response. This is called **shaping.**
- If an operant response is not reinforced, it may **extinguish** (disappear). But after extinction seems complete, it may temporarily reappear (**spontaneous recovery**).

■ ***Are there different kinds of operant reinforcement?***

- In **positive reinforcement,** reward or a pleasant event follows a response. In **negative reinforcement,** a response that ends discomfort becomes more likely. **Primary reinforcers** are "natural," physiologically–based rewards. **Intra-cranial stimulation** of "pleasure centers" in the brain can also serve as a primary reinforcer.
- **Secondary reinforcers** are learned. They typically gain their reinforcing value by association with primary reinforcers or because they can be exchanged for primary reinforcers. **Tokens** and money gain their reinforcing value in this way.
- Money may be exchanged for so many other reinforcers that it sometimes becomes a **generalized reinforcer. Prepotent,** or frequent, responses, can be used to reinforce low-frequency responses.

■ ***How are we influenced by patterns of reward?***

- **Delay** of reinforcement greatly reduces its effectiveness, but long **chains** of responses may be built up so that a single reinforcer maintains many responses. **Superstitious behaviors** often become part of response chains because they *appear* to be associated with reinforcement.
- Reward or reinforcement may be given **continuously** (after every response), or on a **schedule of partial reinforcement.** Partial reinforcement produces greater resistance to extinction.
- The four most basic schedules of reinforcement are **fixed ratio, variable ratio, fixed interval,** and **variable interval.**
- Stimuli that precede a reinforced response tend to control the response on future occasions (**stimulus control**).
- Two aspects of stimulus control are **generalization** and **discrimination.** In generalization, an operant response tends to occur when stimuli similar to those preceding reinforcement are present. In discrimination, responses are given in the presence of **discriminative stimuli** associated with reinforcement (**S+**) and withheld in the presence of stimuli associated with non-reinforcement (**S−**).

■ ***What does punishment do to behavior?***

- **Punishment** decreases responding. Punishment occurs when a response is followed by the onset of an aversive event or by the removal of a positive event (**response cost**).
- Punishment is most effective when it is **immediate, consistent,** and **intense. Mild punishment** tends only to temporarily suppress responses that are also reinforced or were acquired by reinforcement.
- The undesirable side effects of punishment include the **conditioning of fear;** the learning of **escape** and **avoidance responses;** and the encouragement of **aggression.**

■ ***In what ways are classical conditioning and operant conditioning alike?***

- Many real-world situations involve **two-factor learning,** a combination of classical conditioning and operant conditioning.
- From an **informational view,** conditioning creates **expectancies,** which alter response patterns. In classical conditioning, the CS creates an expectancy that the US will follow. Learning in operant conditioning is based on the expectation that a response will have a specific effect.

■ ***What is feedback and how does it affect learning?***

- **Feedback,** or **knowledge of results,** aids learning and improves performance. It is most effective when it is **immediate, detailed,** and **frequent.**
- **Programmed instruction** breaks learning into a series of small steps and provides immediate feedback. **Computer-assisted instruction (CAI)** does the same, but has the added advantage of providing alternate exercises and information when needed. Three variations of CAI are **drill and practice, instructional games,** and **educational simulations.**

■ ***What is cognitive learning?***

- **Cognitive learning** involves higher mental processes, such as understanding, knowing, or anticipating. Evidence of cognitive learning is provided by **cognitive maps** and **latent learning. Discovery learning** emphasizes insight and understanding, in contrast to **rote learning.**

■ ***Does learning occur by imitation?***

- Much human learning is achieved through observation, or modeling. **Observational learning** is influenced by the personal characteristics of the **model** and the success or failure of the model's behavior.
- Television characters can act as powerful models for observational learning. Televised violence increases the likelihood of aggression by viewers.

■ ***How does conditioning apply to practical problems?***

- Operant principles can be readily applied to manage behavior in everyday settings. When managing one's own behavior, **self-reinforcement, self-recording, feedback,** and **behavioral contracting** are all helpful.
- Four strategies that can help change bad habits are reinforcing alternate responses, promoting extinction, breaking response chains, and avoiding antecedent cues.

- In school, **self-regulated learners** typically do all of the following: They set learning goals, plan learning strategies, use self-instruction, monitor their progress, evaluate themselves, reinforce successes, and take corrective action when required.

■ ***How does biology influence learning?***

- Many animals are born with **innate** behavior patterns far more complex than **reflexes.** These are organized into **fixed action patterns** (FAPs), which are stereotyped, **species-specific** behaviors.
- Learning in animals is limited at times by various **biological constraints** and **species-typical** behaviors. According to **prepared fear theory,** some stimuli are especially effective conditioned stimuli. Many responses are subject to **instinctive drift** in operant conditioning. Human learning is subtly influenced by many such biological potentials and limits.

Questions for Discussion

1. Over the years, balloons have occasionally popped in your face when you were blowing them up. Now you squint and feel tense whenever you blow up a balloon. What kind of conditioning is this? What schedule of reinforcement contributed to the conditioning? How could you extinguish the response?
2. In what ways do advertisers attempt to combine both classical and operant conditioning to get us to buy their products?
3. You are in charge of a group of fifth-grade children that meets regularly for recreation. Other members of the group have excluded a younger girl and a very shy boy from activities. How could you use reinforcement principles to improve this situation? (Include techniques aimed at both the excluded children and the group.)
4. What role has reinforcement had in your selection of a major? Friends? A job? The clothes you wore to school today?
5. You have a friend who checks the coin return slot every time he/she walks by a phone booth. Very rarely is a coin discovered. How do you explain this behavior?
6. From your point of view, what would be the ideal way to be paid at a job? Should pay be weekly, hourly, daily? Should it be tied to work output? Should rewards other than money be offered? If you owned a business what would you consider the ideal way to pay your employees?
7. Corporal punishment has been banned in many schools. In your opinion, what would be the pros and cons of banning corporal punishment in homes?
8. From an operant conditioning perspective, why is it important for parents to "catch kids being good" and praise them?
9. A child in the grocery store has a temper tantrum. The embarrassed father scolds the child and then quiets her by giving her a candy bar. Is this punishment or reinforcement? What kind? What other options did Dad have to keep this behavior from happening again in the future? Who is conditioning whom in such circumstances?
10. A child is frightened by a large dog while he is walking to school. From that day forward, he walks two blocks out of his way to skirt the yard where the dog is kept. The people who own the dog move away, but the child continues to take the long way to school. Can you analyze the child's avoidance learning?
11. Describe a behavior you learned by observation. What were the advantages of learning in this way? What were the disadvantages? What changes would have made the model you observed more effective?
12. What kind of an experiment would you do to assess the effects that viewing TV violence has on small children? What ethical questions would you need to answer?
13. In what ways could instinctive drift be adaptive for an animal? In what ways could it be maladaptive? In what ways does human learning show signs of biological constraints?

Chapter 8

Memory

IN THIS CHAPTER

Stages of memory
Short-term memory
Long-term memory
Measuring memory
Exceptional memory
Theories of forgetting
Forming memories
How to improve memory
Applications:
Mnemonic systems
Exploration:
The recovered-memory debate

CHAPTER PREVIEW

"What the Hell's Going on Here?"

February, 1978. Steven Kubacki is cross-country skiing on the ice of Lake Michigan. He stops for a moment, pausing to enjoy the winter solitude. It's cold; colder in fact than he had realized. Steven decides to turn back. In a few minutes comes a new realization: He is lost. Wandering on the ice, he grows numb and very, very tired.

Put yourself in Steven Kubacki's shoes, and you will appreciate the shock of what happened next. Steven clearly recalls wandering lost and alone on the ice. Immediately after that, he remembers waking up in a field. But as he looked around, Steven knew something was wrong. It was spring! The backpack beside him contained running shoes, swimming goggles, and a pair of glasses—all unfamiliar. As he looked at his clothing—also unfamiliar—Steven thought to himself, "What the hell's going on here?" Fourteen months had passed since he left to go skiing (Loftus, 1980). How did he get to the field? Where did the strange gear come from? Steven couldn't say. He had lost over a year of his life to total amnesia.

As Steven Kubacki's amnesia vividly shows, life without memory would be meaningless. Imagine the terror and confusion of having all of your memories wiped out, from birth to the present. You would have no identity, no knowledge, no life history, no recognition of friends or family. Your past would be a total blank. In a very real sense, we are our memories.

This chapter discusses memory and forgetting. As an inquiring person, you should find the information interesting. Also included is a large section on improving memory skills. As a student, you should find this discussion particularly helpful. Almost anyone (including you) can learn to use memory more effectively.

Survey Questions

- How do we store information in memory?
- Is there more than one type of memory?
- What are the features of each type of memory?
- Is there more than one type of long-term memory?
- How is memory measured?
- What are "photographic" memories?
- What causes forgetting?
- How accurate are everyday memories?
- What happens in the brain when memories are formed?
- How can memory be improved?
- What is the "recovered-memory" debate?

Stages of Memory—Do You Have a Mind Like a Steel Trap? Or a Sieve?

"A dusty storehouse of facts." That's how many people think of memory. In reality, **memory** is an *active system* that receives, stores, organizes, alters, and recovers information (Baddeley, 1990). In some ways memory acts like a computer (■ Fig. 8–1). Incoming information is first **encoded,** or changed into a usable form. This step is like typing data into a computer. Next, information is **stored,** or held in the system. (As we will see in a moment, human memory can be pictured as three separate storage systems.) Finally, memories must be **retrieved,** or taken out of storage, to be useful. If you're going to remember all of the 9,856 new terms that will appear on your next psychology exam, you must successfully encode, store, and retrieve them.

Question: What are the three separate memory systems just mentioned?

Psychologists have identified three stages of memory. To be stored for a long time, information must pass through all three (■ Fig. 8–2).

Sensory Memory

Let's say a friend asks you to pick up several things at a market. How do you remember them? Incoming information first enters **sensory memory.** Sensory memory holds, for a few seconds or less, an exact copy of what is seen or heard. For instance, if you look at an object and then close your eyes, an **icon** (EYE-kon), or fleeting image, will persist for about one-half second afterward. Without sensory memory, a movie would look like a flickering series of still pictures. Similarly, information you hear is held as a brief **echo** in sensory memory for up to 2 seconds.

■ **Fig. 8–1** *In some ways, a computer acts like a mechanical memory system. Both systems process information, and both allow encoding, storage, and retrieval of data.*

Let's say that your attention wanders as your friend names the last item on her shopping list. You automatically ask, "What did you say?" But before she can answer, you realize that you know what the last item is. An ability to mentally "play back" what someone else just said is based on echoic memory (Eysenck & Keane, 1990).

In general, sensory memory holds information just long enough to transfer it to the second memory system.

Memory The mental system for receiving, storing, organizing, altering, and recovering information.

Encoding Converting information into a form in which it will be retained in memory.

Storage Holding information in memory.

Retrieval Recovering information stored in memory.

Sensory memory The first stage of memory, which holds an explicit and literal record of incoming information for a few seconds or less.

Icon A mental image or representation.

Echo A brief continuation of activity in the auditory system after a sound is heard.

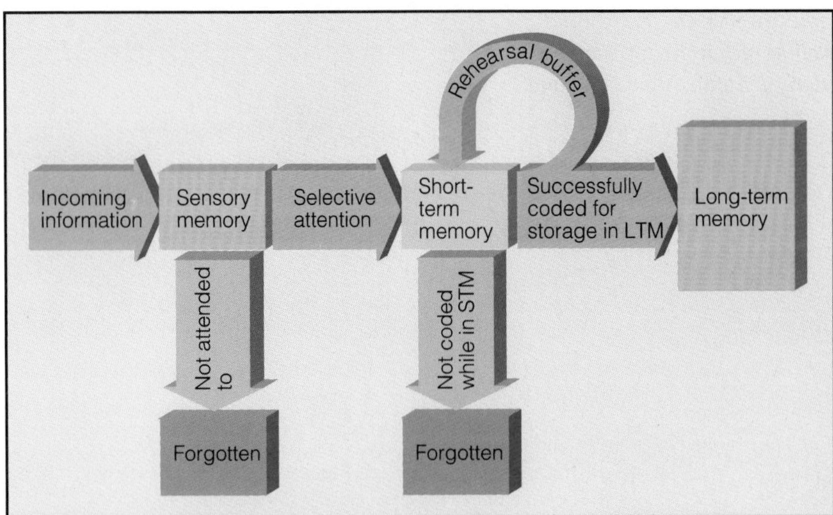

■ Fig. 8–2 *Remembering is thought to involve at least three steps. Incoming information is first held for a second or two by sensory memory. Information selected by attention is then transferred to temporary storage in short-term memory. If new information is not rapidly encoded, or rehearsed, it is forgotten. If it is transferred to long-term memory, it becomes relatively permanent, although retrieving it may be a problem. The preceding is a useful, but highly simplified,* model *of memory; it may not be literally true of what happens in the brain (Eysenck & Keane, 1990).*

Selective attention Voluntarily focusing on a selected portion of sensory input.

Short-term memory (STM) The memory system used to hold small amounts of information for relatively brief time periods.

Working memory Another name for short-term memory, especially as it is used for thinking and problem solving.

Long-term memory (LTM) The memory system used for relatively permanent storage of meaningful information.

Short-Term Memory

Not everything seen or heard is kept in memory. Let's say a radio is playing in the background as your friend reads you her shopping list. Do you remember what the announcer says too? Probably not, because *selective attention* (discussed in Chapters 4 and 5) controls what information moves on to **short-term memory** (**STM**). Short-term memories are also brief, but longer lasting than sensory memories. Paying attention to your friend's words will place the shopping list in short-term memory (while allowing you to ignore the voice on the radio saying, "Buy Burpo Butter").

Question: How are short-term memories encoded?

Short-term memories can be stored as images. But more often they are stored by *sound*, especially in recalling words and letters (Anderson, 1990). If you are introduced to Tim at a party and you forget his name, you are more likely to call him by a name that *sounds like* Tim (Jim or Tom, for instance) than a name that sounds different, such as Bob or Mike. Your friend with the shopping list will be lucky if you don't bring home peas instead of cheese and soap instead of soup!

Short-term memory acts as a *temporary* storehouse for *small amounts* of information. Unless the information is important, it is quickly "dumped" from STM and forever lost. Short-term memory prevents our minds from collecting useless names, dates, telephone numbers, and other trivia. At the same time, it provides a **working memory** where we do much of our thinking. Dialing a phone number, doing mental arithmetic, remembering a shopping list, and the like, all rely on STM.

As you may have noticed when dialing a telephone, STM is very sensitive to *interruption*, or *interference*. You've probably had this happen with STM: You look up a number and walk to the phone repeating it to yourself. You dial the number and get a busy signal. Returning a few minutes later, you find that you must look up the number again. This time as you are about to dial, someone asks you a question. You answer, turn to the phone, and find that you have forgotten the number.

Question: If short-term memory is brief, easily interrupted, and limited in "size," how do we remember for greater lengths of time?

Long-Term Memory

Information that is important or *meaningful* is transferred to the third memory system, called long-term memory. In contrast to STM, **long-term memory** (**LTM**) acts as a permanent storehouse for information. LTM contains everything you know about the world—from aardvark to zucchini, math to Monopoly, facts to fantasy. And yet, there appears to be no danger of running out of room in LTM. LTM has a nearly limitless storage capacity. In fact, the more you know, the easier it becomes to add new information to memory. This is the reverse of what we would expect if LTM could be "filled up" (Eysenck & Keane, 1990). It is also one of many powerful reasons for getting an education.

Question: Are long-term memories also encoded as sounds?

No. Information in LTM is stored on the basis of *meaning* and importance, not by sound. If you make an error in LTM, it will probably be related to meaning. For example, if you are trying to recall the word BARN from a memorized list, you are more likely to mistakenly say SHED or FARM than BORN.

When new information enters STM, it is related to knowledge stored in LTM. This gives the new information meaning and makes it easier to store in LTM. As an example, try to memorize this story:

> With hocked gems financing him, our hero bravely defied all scornful laughter. "Your eyes deceive," he had said, "An egg, not a table, correctly typifies this unexplored planet." Now three sturdy sisters sought proof. Forging along, days became weeks as many doubters spread fearful rumors about the edge. At last from nowhere welcome winged creatures appeared, signifying momentous success. (Adapted from Dooling & Lachman, 1971)

This odd story emphasizes the impact of meaning on memory. People given the title of the story were able to remember it far better than those not given a title. See if the title helps you as much as it did them. The title is "Columbus Discovers America."

Dual Memory Most of our daily memory chores are handled by STM and LTM. To summarize their connection, picture short-term memory as a small desk at the front of a huge warehouse full of filing cabinets (LTM). As information enters the warehouse, it is first placed on the desk. Since the desk is small, it must be quickly cleared off to make room for new information. Some items are simply tossed away because they are unimportant. Meaningful or important information is placed in the permanent files (long-term memory).

When we want to use knowledge from LTM to answer a question, the information is returned to STM. Or, in our analogy, a folder is taken out of the files (LTM) and moved to the desk (STM), where it can be used. Computer users may prefer to think of STM as being like RAM and LTM as being like a hard disk. However, in the human brain it is unlikely that short- and long- term memories are stored at different locations. STM and LTM are more likely different stages in the storage of information (Best, 1992).

Now that you have a general picture of STM and LTM it is time to explore both in more detail. The discussions that follow should add to your understanding.

LEARNING CHECK

Match: **A.** Sensory memory **B.** STM **C.** LTM

1. ____ Working memory
2. ____ Holds information for a few seconds or less
3. ____ Stores an icon or echo
4. ____ Permanent, unlimited capacity
5. ____ Temporarily holds small amounts of information
6. ____ Selective attention determines its contents
7. STM is improved by interruption, or interference, because attention is more focused at such times. T or F?

Critical Thinking

8. Parents sometimes warn children not to read comic books, fearing that they will learn less in school if they "fill their heads up with junk." Why is this warning unnecessary?

Answers: 1. B 2. A 3. A 4. C 5. B 6. B 7. F 8. Because the more information you have in long-term memory, the greater the possibilities for linking new information to it. Generally, the more you know, the more you can learn—even if some of what you know is "junk."

Short-Term Memory—Do You Know the Magic Number?

Question: How much information can be held in short-term memory?

For an answer, read the following numbers once. Then close the book and write as many as you can in the correct order.

8	5	1	7	4	9	3

This is called a **digit-span test.** If you were able to correctly repeat this series of 7 digits, you have an average short-term memory. Now try to memorize the following list of digits, reading them only once.

7	1	8	3	5	4	2	9	1	6	3	4

This series was probably beyond your short-term memory capacity. Psychologist George Miller found that short-term memory is limited to what he calls the "magic number" **seven** (plus or minus two) **bits** of information (Miller, 1956). A *bit* is a single "piece" of information—a single digit, for example. It is as if short-term memory has 7 "slots" or "bins" into which separate items can be placed. Actually, 7 bits is the average *upper limit* for short-term memory. For many kinds of information, 5 bits is more typical (Barsalou, 1992).

When all of the "slots" in STM are filled, there is no room for new information. Picture how this works at a party: Let's say your hostess begins introducing

Digit-span test A test of attention and short-term memory in which a string of digits is recalled.

Information bits Meaningful units of information, such as numbers, letters, words, or phrases.

Memory structure The pattern of associations among bits of information stored in memory.

Network model A model of memory that views it as an organized system of linked information.

Redintegration The process of reconstructing an entire complex memory after first observing or remembering only a part of it.

Question: Couldn't hypnosis be used to avoid such problems?

News stories often give the impression that it can. Is this true? Highlight 8–1 examines this intriguing question.

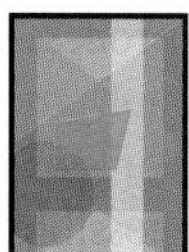

HIGHLIGHT 8–1

Focus On A Controversy

Hypnosis, Imagination, and Memory

In 1976, near Chowchilla, California, 26 children were abducted from a school bus and held captive for a ransom. Under hypnosis, the bus driver recalled the license plate number of the kidnappers' van. This memory helped break the case and led to the children's rescue. Such successes seem to imply that hypnosis can improve memory. But does it? Read on, and judge for yourself.

Research has shown that a hypnotized person is more likely than normal to use imagination to fill in gaps in memory. Also, when hypnotized subjects are given false information, they tend to weave it into their memories (Sheehan & Statham, 1989). It has been shown that "leading" questions asked during hypnosis can alter memories (Sanders & Simmons, 1983). And even when a memory is completely false, the hypnotized person's confidence in it can be unshakable (Laurence & Perry, 1983). Most telling of all is the fact that hypnosis increases false memories more than it does true ones. Eighty percent of the new memories produced by hypnotized subjects in one experiment were *incorrect* (Dywan & Bowers, 1983).

Overall, it can be concluded that hypnosis does not greatly improve memory (Kassin et al., 1989; Murray-Smith, 1990). It is true that hypnosis sometimes uncovers more information (Watkins, 1989). However, when it does there is no sure way to tell which memories are true and which are false. Clearly, hypnosis is not the "magic bullet" against forgetting that some police investigators hoped it would be.

Organization

Long-term memory records a seemingly infinite amount of information in a lifetime. How is it possible to quickly find specific memories? The answer is that each person's "memory index" is highly organized.

Question: Do you mean that information is arranged alphabetically, as in a dictionary?

Not a chance! If I ask you to name a black and white animal that lives on ice, is related to a chicken, and cannot fly, you don't have to go from aardvark to zebra to find the answer. You will probably only think of black and white birds living in the Antarctic. Which of these cannot fly? *Voila*, the answer is penguin.

The arrangement of information in LTM may be based on rules, images, categories, symbols, similarity, formal meaning, or personal meaning (Baddeley, 1990). In recent years, psychologists have begun to develop a picture of the **structure,** or arrangement, of memories. One example will serve to illustrate this research.

You are given the following two statements, to which you must answer yes or no: *A canary is an animal. A canary is a bird.* Which do you answer more quickly? Collins and Quillian (1969) found that *A canary is a bird* produced a faster yes than *A canary is an animal.* Why should this be so? Many psychologists believe that a **network model** of memory explains why. According to them, LTM is organized as a network of linked ideas (■Fig. 8–5). When ideas are "farther" apart, it takes a longer chain of associations to connect them. The more two items are separated, the longer it takes to answer. In terms of information links, *canary* is probably "close" to *bird* in your "memory files." *Animal* and *canary* are farther apart. Remember though, this has nothing to do with alphabetical order. We are talking about organization based on linked meanings.

Redintegrative Memories Networks of associated memories may help explain a common experience: Imagine finding a picture taken on your sixth birthday or tenth Christmas. As you look at the photo, one memory leads to another, which leads to another, and another. Soon you have unleashed a flood of seemingly forgotten details. This memory process is called **redintegration** (ruh-DIN-tuh-GRAY-shun).

Redintegrative memories seem to spread through the "branches" of memory networks. Many people find that such memories are also touched off by distinctive odors out of the past—from a farm visited in childhood, Grandma's kitchen, the seashore, a doctor's office, the perfume or after-shave of a former lover, and so on. The key idea in redintegration is that one memory serves as a cue to trigger another. As a result, an entire past experience may be reconstructed from one small recollection.

Types of Long-Term Memory

Question: How many types of long-term memory are there?

As we have seen, *memory* is an umbrella term that includes both short-term and long-term memory. Be-

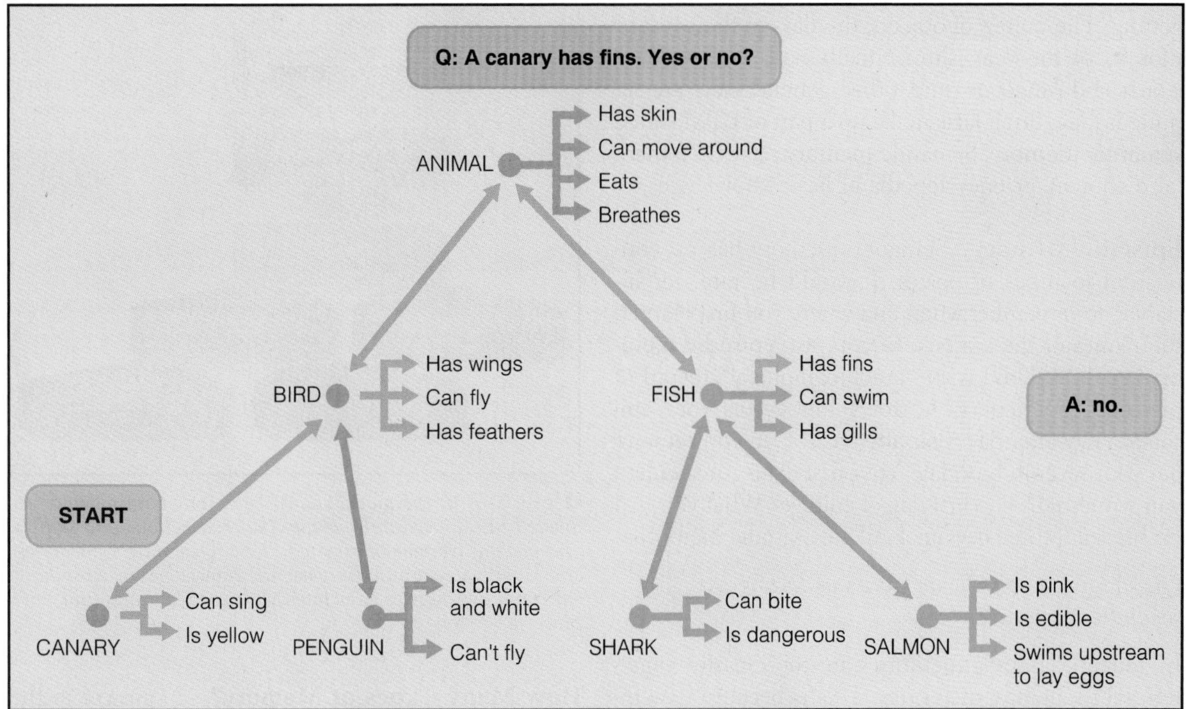

■ **Fig. 8–5** *A hypothetical network of facts about animals shows what is meant by the structure of memory. Small networks of ideas such as this are probably organized into larger and larger units and higher levels of meaning. (Adapted from Collins & Quillian, 1969.)*

yond this, it is becoming clear that more than one type of long-term memory exists. Let's probe a little further into the mysteries of memory.

Skill Memory and Fact Memory A curious thing happens to many people who develop amnesia. Amnesic patients may be unable to learn a telephone number, an address, or a person's name. And yet, the same patients may learn to solve complex puzzles in the same amount of time as normal subjects (Squire & Zola-Morgan, 1988) (■ Fig. 8–6). These and other observations have led many psychologists to conclude that long-term memories fall into at least two categories. One of these might be called **procedural memory** (or skill memory). The other is called **declarative memory** (also sometimes called fact memory).

Procedural memory includes basic conditioned responses and learned actions like those involved in typing, solving a puzzle, or swinging a golf club. Memories such as these can be fully expressed only as actions (or "know-how"). It is likely that skill memories register in "lower" brain areas, especially the cerebellum (Squire et al., 1992). They represent the more basic "automatic" elements of conditioning, learning, and memory (Thompson, 1991).

Declarative memory involves remembering specific information, such as names, faces, words, dates, and ideas. Declarative memories are expressed as words or symbols. For example, knowing that Steven Spielberg directed both *Close Encounters of the Third Kind* and *Schindler's List* is a declarative memory. This is the type of memory that a person with amnesia lacks and that most of us take for granted. Some psychologists believe that declarative memory can be further divided into two other types, called semantic and episodic memory (Tulving, 1989).

Procedural memory Long-term memories of conditioned responses and learned skills.

Declarative memory That part of long-term memory containing factual information.

Semantic Memory Most of our basic *factual knowledge* about the world is almost totally immune to for-

■ **Fig. 8–6** *The tower puzzle. In this puzzle, all the colored disks must be moved to another post, without ever placing a larger disk on a smaller one. Only one disk may be moved at a time, and a disk must always be moved from one post to another (it cannot be held aside). An amnesic patient learned to solve the puzzle in 31 moves, the minimum possible. Even so, each time he began, he protested that he did not remember ever solving the puzzle before and that he did not know how to begin. Evidence like this suggests that memories for skills are distinct from memories for facts.*

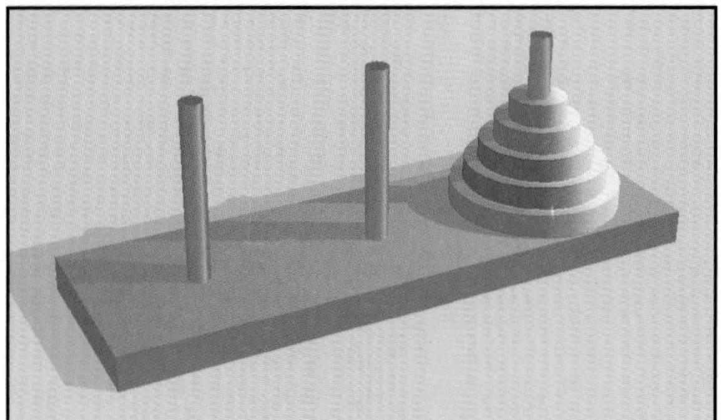

Semantic memory A subpart of declarative memory that records impersonal knowledge about the world.

Episodic memory A subpart of declarative memory that records personal experiences that are linked with specific times and places.

getting. The names of objects, the days of the week or months of the year, simple math skills, the seasons, words and language, and other general facts are all quite lasting. Such facts make up a part of LTM called **semantic memory.** Semantic memory serves as a mental dictionary or encyclopedia of basic knowledge.

Episodic Memory Semantic memory has no connection to times or places. It would be rare, for instance, to remember when and where you first learned the names of the seasons. In contrast, **episodic memory** (ep-ih-SOD-ik) is an "autobiographical" record of personal experiences. It stores life events (or "episodes") day after day, year after year. Can you remember your seventh birthday? Your first date? An accident you witnessed? The first day of college? What you had for breakfast three days ago? All are episodic memories.

Question: Are episodic memories as lasting as semantic memories?

In general, episodic memories are more easily forgotten than semantic memories. This is because new information constantly pours into episodic memory. Stop for a moment and remember what you did last summer. That was an episodic memory. Notice that you now remember that you just remembered something. You have a new episodic memory in which you remember that you remembered while reading this text! It's easy to see how much we ask of our memory system.

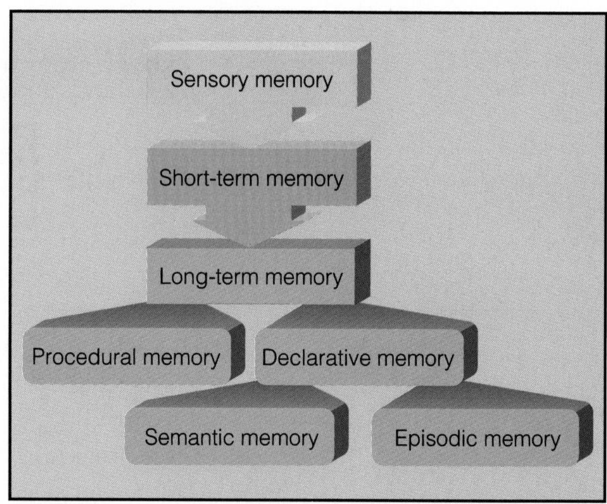

■ **Fig. 8–7** *In the model shown here, long-term memory is divided into procedural memory (learned actions and skills) and declarative memory (stored facts). Declarative memories can be either semantic (impersonal knowledge) or episodic (personal experiences associated with specific times and places).*

How Many Types of Memory? In answer to the question posed at the beginning of this section, it is very likely that three kinds of long-term memories exist: procedural, semantic, and episodic (Mitchell, 1989; Squire et al., 1993) (■ Fig. 8–7). However, the relationship among them is still actively debated. While the debate continues—and other types may be discovered in the future—it appears that some pieces of the puzzle called memory are falling into place.

Learning Check

1. The digit-span test is commonly used to measure LTM. T or F?
2. There is evidence that STM lasts about 18 seconds, without rehearsal. T or F?
3. Information is best transferred from STM to LTM when a person engages in
   a. maintenance chunking *b.* maintenance recoding
   c. elaborative networking *d.* elaborative rehearsal
4. Constructive processing is often responsible for creating pseudo-memories. T or F?
5. Electrical stimulation of the brain has shown conclusively that all memories are stored permanently, but not all memories can be retrieved. T or F?
6. Memories elicited under hypnosis are more vivid, complete, and reliable than normal. T or F?
7. ______________________ of related information are an example of the structure or organization found in LTM.
8. Procedural memories are stored in STM, whereas declarative memories are stored in LTM. T or F?
9. Episodic memories are almost totally immune to forgetting. T or F?

Critical Thinking

10. Telephone companies are aware of the limitations of short-term memory. In what way is this evident?

Answers: 1. F 2. T 3. *d* 4. T 5. F 6. F 7. Networks 8. F 9. F 10. Local numbers are broken into a 3-digit chunk and a 4-digit chunk. Long-distance numbers consist of a 3-digit chunk (the area code) plus a 3-digit chunk and a 4-digit chunk. If telephone numbers weren't recoded this way, a long-distance number would be 10 single digits—too many for most people's short-term memory.

Measuring Memory—The Answer Is on the Tip of My Tongue

Initially, it might seem that you either remember something or you don't. But a moment of thought should convince you that this is not always true. For instance, have you ever recognized someone you only saw once before and thought you had completely forgotten? If so, you have used a form of partial memory called *recognition.* Partial memory is also demonstrated by the **tip-of-the-tongue state.** This is the experience of having an answer or a memory just out of reach—on the "tip of your tongue."

In one study of the tip-of-the-tongue state, university students read the definitions of words such as *sextant, sampan,* and *ambergris.* Students who "drew a blank" and couldn't name a defined word were asked to give whatever other information they could about it. Often, they could accurately guess the first and last letter and even the number of syllables of the word they were seeking. They were also able to give words that sounded like or meant the same thing as the defined word (Brown & McNeill, 1966). A related finding is that people can often tell beforehand if they are likely to remember something (Nelson, 1987). This ability is based on a state called the **feeling of knowing.** Feeling-of-knowing reactions are easy to observe on television game shows, where they occur just before contestants are allowed to answer.

Because memory is not an all-or-nothing event, there are several ways of measuring it. Three commonly used **memory tasks** are *recall, recognition,* and *relearning.* Let's see how they differ.

Recall

What is the name of the first song on your favorite compact disc? Who won the World Series last year? Who wrote *Hamlet?* If you can answer these questions you are demonstrating recall. To **recall** means to supply or reproduce facts or information. Tests of recall often require *verbatim* (word-for-word) memory. If you study a poem or a speech until you can recite it without looking, you are recalling it. If you complete a fill-in-the-blank question, you are using recall. When you take an *essay* exam and provide facts and ideas without prompting you are also using recall, even though you didn't learn your essay verbatim. Essay tests tend to be difficult because they offer few cues to aid memory.

The order in which information is memorized has an interesting effect on recall. To experience it, try to memorize the following list, reading it only once:

BREAD, APPLES, SODA, HAM, COOKIES, RICE, LETTUCE, BEETS, MUSTARD, CHEESE, ORANGES, ICE CREAM, CRACKERS, FLOUR, EGGS

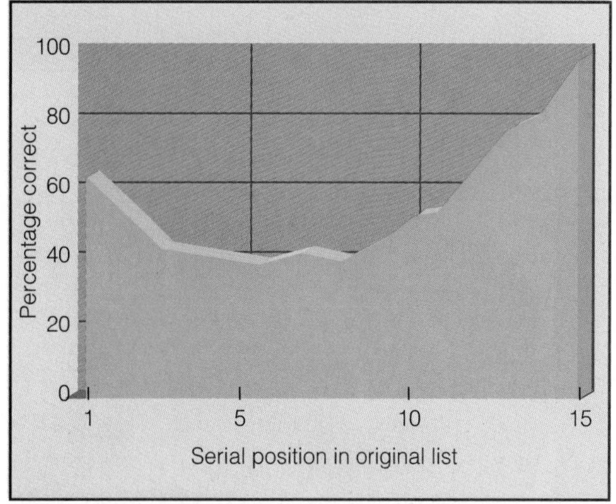

■ **Fig. 8–8** *The serial position effect. The graph shows the percentage of subjects correctly recalling each item in a 15-item list. Recall is best for the first and last items. (Data from Craik, 1970.)*

If you are like most people, you will have the most difficulty recalling items from the middle of the list. ■ Figure 8–8 shows the results of a similar test. Notice that the greatest number of errors is found for middle items. This is called the **serial position effect.** The last items on a list appear to be remembered best because they are still in STM. The first items are also remembered because they entered an "empty" short-term memory where they could be rehearsed and moved to long-term memory (Medin & Ross, 1992). The middle items are neither held in short-term memory nor moved to long-term memory, so they are often lost.

Tip-of-the-tongue state Feeling that a memory is available, while being unable to retrieve it.

Feeling of knowing Ability to predict beforehand whether one will be able to remember something.

Memory task Any task designed to test or assess memory.

Recall To supply or reproduce memorized information with a minimum of external cues.

Serial position effect The tendency to make the most errors in remembering the middle items of an ordered list.

Recognition Memory in which previously learned material is correctly identified.

Recognition

If you tried to write down all the facts you could remember from a class taken last year, you might conclude that you had learned very little. However, a more sensitive test based on **recognition** could be used. For instance, you could be given a *multiple-choice* test on facts and ideas from the course. Since multiple-choice tests only require you to recognize the correct answer, we would probably find evidence of considerable learning.

Recognition memory can be amazingly accurate for pictures, photographs, or other visual input. One investigator showed subjects 2560 photographs at a rate of one every 10 seconds. Subjects were then shown 280 pairs of photographs. One in each pair was from the first set of photos and the other was similar but new. Subjects could tell with 85 to 95 percent accuracy which photograph they had seen before (Haber, 1970). This finding may explain why people so often say, "I may forget a name, but I never forget a face."

Recognition is usually superior to recall. This is why police departments use photographs or a lineup

■ **Fig. 8–9** *Police lineups make use of the sensitivity of recognition memory.*

Distractors False items grouped with a correct item to test recognition memory (for example, the wrong answers on a multiple-choice test).

False positive A false sense of recognition.

Relearning Learning again something that was previously learned. Used to measure memory of prior learning.

Savings score The amount of time saved (expressed as a percentage) when relearning information.

Explicit memory A memory that a person is aware of having; a memory that is consciously retrieved.

Implicit memory A memory that a person does not know exists; a memory that is retrieved unconsciously.

to identify criminal suspects (■Fig. 8–9). Witnesses who disagree in their recall of a suspect's height, weight, age, or eye color often agree completely when recognition is all that is required. Identification is also more accurate when witnesses are allowed to hear suspects' voices as well as see their faces (Melara et al., 1989).

Question: Is recognition always superior?

It depends greatly on the kind of **distractors** used. These are false items included with an item to be recognized. If the distractors are very similar to the correct item, memory may be poor. A reverse problem sometimes occurs when only one choice looks like it could be correct. This can produce a **false positive,** or false sense of recognition. For example, there have been instances in which witnesses described a criminal as black, tall, or young. Then a lineup was held in which a suspect was the only African American among whites, the only tall suspect, or the only young person (Loftus, 1980). Under such circumstances a false identification is very likely. A better method is to have all the distractors resemble the description given by witnesses. This reduces false-positives and increases accurate identifications (Wells et al., 1993).

Relearning

In a classic experiment on memory, a psychologist read a short passage in Greek to his son. This was done daily when the boy was between 15 months and 3 years of age. At age 8, the boy was asked if he remembered the Greek passage. He showed no evidence of recall. He was then given selections from the passage he heard and selections from other Greek passages. Could he recognize the one he heard as an infant? "It's all Greek to me!" he said, indicating no recognition (and drawing a frown from everyone in the room).

Had the psychologist stopped, he might have concluded that no memory of the Greek remained. However, the child was then asked to memorize the original quotation and others of equal difficulty. This time his earlier learning became evident. The boy memorized the passage he had heard in childhood 25 percent faster than the others (Burtt, 1941). As this experiment suggests, relearning is typically the most sensitive measure of memory.

When a person is tested by **relearning,** how do we know a memory still exists? As with the boy described, relearning is measured by a **savings score.** Let's say it takes you one hour to memorize all the names in a telephone book. (It's a small town.) Two years later you relearn them in 45 minutes. Because you "saved" 15 minutes, your savings score would be 25 percent (15 divided by 60 times 100). Savings of this type are a good reason for studying a wide range of subjects. It may seem that time spent learning algebra, history, or a foreign language is wasted because so much is lost within a year or two. But if you ever need such information, you will find you can relearn it in far less time.

Implicit Memory

Psychologists have recently discovered that many memories remain outside of conscious awareness. For example, if you know how to type, it is apparent that you know where the letters are on the keyboard. But how many typists could correctly label blank keys in a drawing of a typewriter? Many people find that they cannot directly remember such information, even though they "know" it.

Who were the last three Presidents of the United States? What did you have for breakfast today? What is the title of Michael Jackson's best-selling album? Answering each of these questions requires the use of **explicit memory.** Explicit memories are past experiences that a person is aware he or she has brought to mind. Recall, recognition, and the tests you take in school rely on explicit memories. In contrast, **implicit memories** lie outside of awareness (Roediger, 1990). That is, we are not aware that a memory or record of past experience exists. Nevertheless, implicit memories—such as unconsciously knowing where the letters are on a typewriter—greatly influence our behavior (Bower, 1990).

Question: If a memory is outside of awareness, how can it be shown to exist?

Priming Implicit memory was first noticed in studies of patients who were suffering memory loss as a result of brain injuries. Let's say, for example, that a patient is shown a list of common words, such as *chair, tree, lamp, table,* and so on. A few minutes later, the patient is asked to recall words from the list. Sadly, he has no memory of the words. Now, instead of asking the patient to explicitly recall the list, we could "prime" his memory by giving him the first two letters of each word. "We'd like you to say a word that begins with these letters," we tell him. "Just say whatever comes to mind." Of course, many words could be made from each pair of letters. For example, the first item (from chair) would be the letters CH. The patient could say "child," "chalk," "chain," "check," or many other words. Instead, he says "chair," a word from the original list. The patient is not aware that he is remembering the list, but as he gives a word for each letter pair, almost all are from the list. Apparently, the letters **primed** (activated) hidden memories, which then influenced his answers.

Similar effects have been found for people with normal memories. As the preceding example implies, implicit memories are often revealed by giving a person limited cues, such as the first letter of words or partial drawings of objects. Typically, the person believes that he or she is just saying whatever comes to mind. Nevertheless, information seen or heard previously affects his or her answers (Roediger, 1990). Some nutritionists like to say, "You are what you eat." In the realm of memory it appears that we are what we experience—to a far greater degree than once realized.

■ **Fig. 8–10** *Test picture like that used to identify children with eidetic imagery. To test your eidetic imagery, look at the picture for 30 seconds. Then look at a blank surface and try to "project" the picture onto it. If you have good eidetic imagery, you will be able to see the picture in detail. Return now to the text and try to answer the questions there. (Redrawn from an illustration in Lewis Carroll's* Alice in Wonderland.)

Eidetic Imagery—Picture This!

Question: What is a photographic memory? How is it different from the types of memory already described?

Eidetic (eye-DET-ik) **imagery,** known informally as photographic memory, occurs when a person has visual images clear enough to be "scanned" or retained for at least 30 seconds. In other words, eidetic images are similar to the after-images you might have for a moment after looking at a flashbulb or a brightly lit neon sign (Kunzendorf, 1989). Eidetic imagery occurs most often in childhood, with about 8 children out of 100 having eidetic images.

In one series of tests, children were shown a picture from *Alice in Wonderland* (■ Fig. 8–10). To test your eidetic imagery, look at the picture and read the instructions there. Now, let's see how much you remember. Can you say (without looking again) which of Alice's apron strings is longer? Are the cat's front paws crossed? How many stripes are on the cat's tail? After the picture was removed from view, one 10-year-old boy was asked what he saw. He replied, "I see the tree, gray tree with three limbs. I see the cat with stripes around its tail." Asked to count the stripes, the boy replied, "There are about 16" (a correct count!). The boy then went on to describe the remainder of the picture in striking detail (Haber, 1969).

Don't be disappointed if you didn't do too well when you tried your eidetic skills. Most eidetic imagery disappears during adolescence and becomes rare by adulthood (Kunzendorf, 1989). Actually, this change may not be too much of a loss. The majority of eidetic memorizers have no better long-term memory than average.

Priming Facilitating the retrieval of an implicit memory by providing cues related to the memory.

Eidetic imagery The ability to retain a "projected" mental image long enough to use it as a source of information.

Internal Images

Eidetic images are "projected" out in front of a person. That is, they are best "seen" on a plain surface, such as a blank piece of paper. Many psychologists believe that a second type of imagery is also used in memory

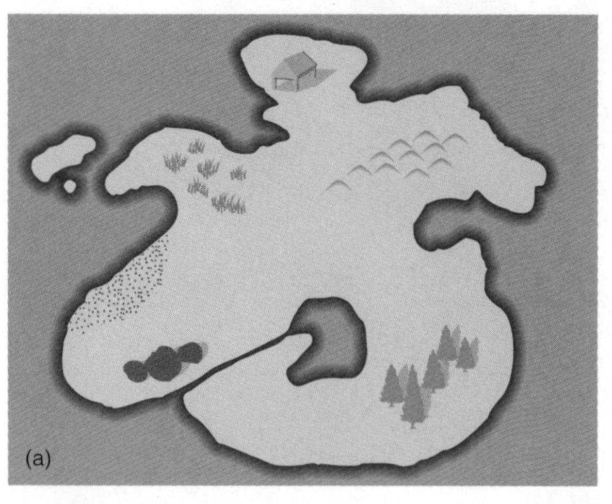

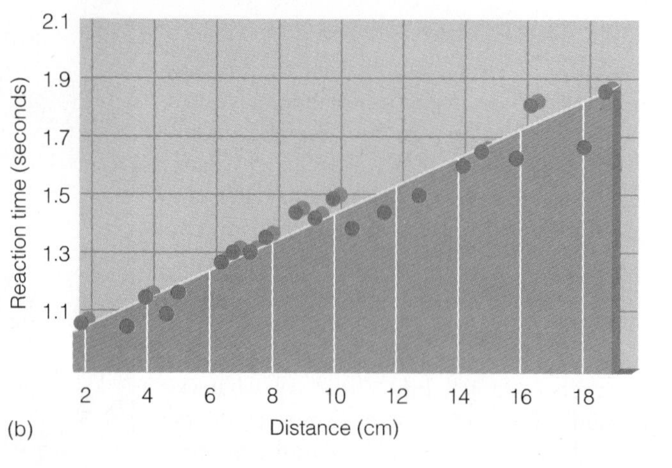

■ **Fig. 8–11** (a) *"Treasure map" similar to the one used by Kosslyn, Ball, and Reisler (1978) to study images in memory.* (b) *This graph shows how long it took subjects to move a visualized spot various distances on their mental images of the map. (See text for explanation.)*

Internal images Mental images or representations used in memory and thinking.

(Barsalou, 1992). Can you remember how many doors there are in your house or apartment? To answer a question like this, many people form **internal images** of each room and count the doorways they visualize.

Kosslyn, Ball, and Reisler (1978) found an interesting way to show that memories do exist as images. Subjects first memorized a sort of treasure map similar to the one shown in ■ Figure 8–11a. They were then asked to picture a black dot moving from one object, such as one of the trees, to another, such as the hut at the top of the island. Did subjects really form an image to do this task? It seems they did. As shown in Figure 8–11b, the time it took to "move" the dot was directly related to actual distances on the map.

Interestingly, word memories sometimes impair our recall of remembered images. For example, university students in one study saw a person's face on a videotape. Later, some of the students were asked to describe the face. Those who did were *less* accurate at recognizing a picture of the face on a test (Schooler & Engstler-Schooler, 1990). Where the memory of images is concerned, some things are better left unsaid!

Exceptional Memory Some people may have such vivid internal images that they too have a "photographic memory." A notable example was reported by A. R. Luria (1968) in his book, *The Mind of a Mnemonist.* Luria studied a man (Mr. S) who had practically unlimited memory for visual images. Mr. S could remember almost everything that ever happened to him with incredible accuracy. When Luria tried to test Mr. S's memory by using longer and longer lists of words or numbers, he discovered that no matter how long the list, Mr. S was able to recall it without error.

As fantastic as it might sound to a struggling student, Mr. S's memory caused great difficulty. He remembered so much that he could not separate important facts from trivia. For instance, if he were tested on the contents of this chapter after reading it, he might remember not only every word, but all the images each word made him think of and all the sights, sounds, and feelings that occurred as he was reading. Finding the answer for a specific question, writing a logical essay, or even understanding a single sentence was very difficult for him.

Psychologists used to think that exceptional memory was a biological gift and could not be learned. However, as Highlight 8–2 explains, research has raised questions about this conclusion.

HIGHLIGHT 8–2

Focus On A Controversy

Can Exceptional Memory Be Learned?

At first, a student volunteer we will call Steve could remember 7 digits—a typical score for a college student. Could he improve with practice? For 20 months psychologist William Chase guided Steve as he practiced memorizing ever longer lists of digits. Ultimately, Steve was able to memorize around 80 digits, like this sample:

9284204805084226895399019025291280799970

6606574717310601080585269726026357332135

How did Steve reach such lofty heights of memory? He worked by chunking digits into meaningful groups containing 3 or 4 digits each.

Steve's avid interest in long-distance running helped greatly. For instance, to him the first three digits above represented 9 minutes and 28 seconds, a good time for a two-mile run. When running times wouldn't work, Steve used other associations, such as ages or dates, to chunk digits (Ericsson & Chase, 1982). By using similar memory systems, other people have trained themselves to equal Steve's feat (Bellezza et al., 1992).

Chase and psychologist Anders Ericsson believe that Steve's performance shows that exceptional memory is merely a learned extension of normal memory. They believe this is true even of people who have phenomenal memories like Mr. S (the man studied by Luria and described earlier). As further evidence, they note that Steve's short-term memory did not improve during his months of practice. For example, he could still memorize only 7 consonants.

Steve's phenomenal memory for numbers grew as he figured out ways to encode digits so he could rapidly store them in LTM. Researchers studying Rajan Mahadevan have drawn similar conclusions about his spectacular memory for long strings of digits. In 1981 Rajan earned a place in the *Guinness Book of World Records* by reciting the first 31,811 digits of pi! Yet, like Steve, Rajan's memory for most other types of information is average. His exceptional memory seems to be based on highly practiced strategies for encoding and storing digits (Thompson et al., 1993).

The idea that Mr. S had a normal memory is, perhaps, open to debate. Mr. S could memorize, with equal ease, strings of digits, meaningless consonants, mathematical formulas, and poems in foreign languages. His memory was so powerful that he had to devise ways to *forget*—such as writing information on a piece of paper and then burning it.

In sum, there is evidence that exceptional memory can be learned. It's an open question, however, about whether some exceptional memories, like Mr. S's, are based on unusually vivid images or other rare abilities.

LEARNING CHECK

Unless you have a memory like Mr. S's, it might be a good idea to see if you can answer these questions before reading on.

1. Four techniques for measuring or demonstrating memory are ____________ ____________ ____________ ____________
2. Multiple-choice tests primarily require ____________ memory.
3. Essay tests require ____________ of facts or ideas.
4. As a measure of memory, a savings score is associated with
   a. recognition *b.* eidetic images *c.* relearning *d.* reconstruction
5. Tests of ____________ memory are designed to reveal the influences of information that is stored, but which remains unconscious.
6. Children with eidetic imagery typically have no better than average long-term memory. T or F?
7. Mr. S had great difficulty remembering faces. Can you guess why? ***Critical Thinking***

Answers:

1. recall, recognition, relearning, priming 2. recognition 3. recall 4. *c* 5. implicit 6. T 7. Mr. S's memory was so specific that faces seemed different and unfamiliar if he saw them from a new angle or if a face had a different expression on it than when Mr. S last saw it.

Forgetting—Why We, Uh, Let's See; Why We, Uh . . . Forget!

Question: Why are some memories lost so quickly? For example, why is it hard to remember information a week or two after taking a test in class?

Generally speaking, most forgetting occurs immediately after memorization. In a famous set of experiments, **Herman Ebbinghaus** (1885) tested his own memory at various times after learning. Ebbinghaus wanted to be sure he would not be swayed by prior learning, so he memorized **nonsense syllables.** These are meaningless 3-letter words such as GEX, CEF, and WOL. The importance of using meaningless words is shown by the fact that VEL, FAB, and DUZ are no longer used on memory tests. Subjects who recognize these words as detergent names find them very easy to remember.

Nonsense syllables Invented three-letter words used to test learning and memory.

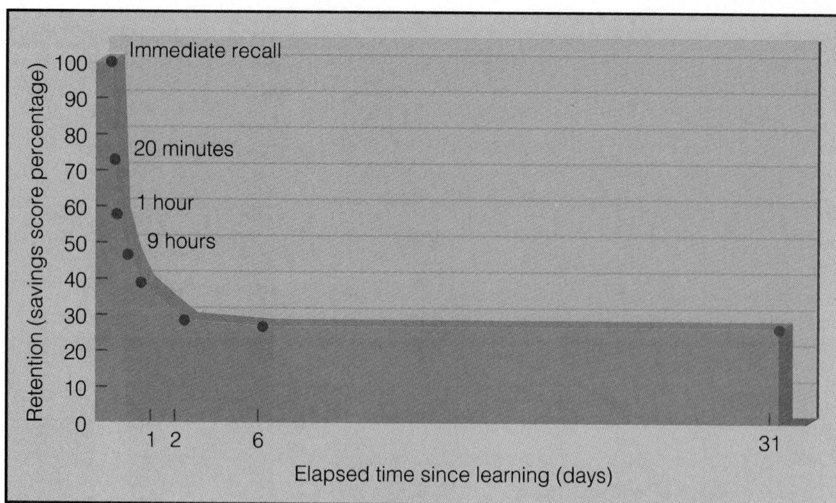

■ **Fig. 8–12** *The curve of forgetting. This graph shows the amount remembered (measured by relearning) after varying lengths of time. Notice how rapidly forgetting occurs. The material learned was nonsense syllables. Forgetting curves for meaningful information also show early losses followed by a long gradual decline, but overall, forgetting occurs much more slowly. (After Ebbinghaus, 1885.)*

Curve of forgetting A graph that shows the amount of memorized information remembered after varying lengths of time.

Encoding failure Failure to store sufficient information to form a useful memory.

Memory traces Physical changes in nerve cells or brain activity that store memories.

Memory decay The fading or weakening of memories assumed to occur when memory traces become weaker.

Disuse Theory that memory traces weaken when memories are not periodically used or retrieved.

By waiting various lengths of time before testing himself, Ebbinghaus plotted a **curve of forgetting** (■ Fig. 8–12). Because of the great care Ebbinghaus took in his work, these findings remain valid today. Notice that forgetting is rapid at first and is then followed by a slow decline.

As a student, you should note that forgetting is minimized when there is little delay between review and taking a test. However, don't take this as a reason for cramming. The error most students make is to cram *only.* If you cram, you don't have to remember for very long, but you may not learn enough in the first place. If you use short, daily study sessions and, in addition, review intensely before a test, you will get the benefit of good preparation and a minimum time lapse.

Question: The Ebbinghaus curve shows less than 30 percent remembered after only two days have passed. Is forgetting really that rapid?

No, not always. Meaningful information is not lost nearly as quickly as nonsense syllables. For example, it took students who completed a university psychology course about 3 years to forget 30 percent of the facts they had learned. After that, little more forgetting occurred (Conway et al., 1992). In fact, as learning grows stronger, some knowledge may become nearly permanent (Bahrick, 1984). Semantic memories and implicit memories (both mentioned earlier) appear to be very lasting (Bower, 1990).

"I'll never forget old, old . . . oh, what's his name?" Forgetting is both frustrating and embarrassing. Why *do* we forget? The Ebbinghaus curve gives a general picture of forgetting, but it doesn't explain it. For explanations we must search further.

ANIMAL CRACKERS

By Rog Rowen

Encoding Failure

Whose head is on a U.S. penny? Which way is it facing? What is written at the top of a penny? Can you accurately draw and label a penny? In an interesting experiment, Nickerson and Adams (1979) asked a large group of students to draw a penny. Few could. Well then, could the students at least recognize a drawing of a real penny among fakes? (See ■ Figure 8–13.) Again, few could.

The most obvious reason for forgetting is also the most commonly overlooked. In many cases we "forget" because of **encoding failure.** That is, a memory was never formed in the first place. Obviously, few of us ever encode the details of a penny. If you are bothered by frequent forgetting, it is wise to ask yourself, "Have I been storing the information in the first place?" When 140 college professors were asked what strategies they use to improve their memory, the most frequently recommended technique was to *write things down* (Park, et al., 1990). Making notes ensures that information will not be lost from short-term memory before you can store it more permanently.

Decay

One view of forgetting holds that **memory traces** (changes in nerve cells or brain activity) fade, weaken, or **decay,** over time. Decay appears to be a factor in the loss of sensory memories. Such fading also applies to short-term memory. Information stored in STM seems to initiate a brief flurry of activity in the brain that quickly dies out (Shiffrin & Cook, 1978). Short-term memory therefore operates like a "leaky bucket": New information constantly pours in, but it rapidly fades away and is replaced by still newer information.

Disuse Is it possible that the decay of memory traces also explains long-term forgetting? That is, could long-term memory traces fade from **disuse** and eventually become so weak they cannot be retrieved? As tempting as this theory may be, there are reasons to doubt it. One reason already mentioned is the recovery of seemingly forgotten memories through redintegration, relearning, and priming. Another is that disuse fails to explain why some unused memories fade, while others are carried for life. A third contradiction will be recognized by anyone who has spent time with the elderly. People growing senile may become so forgetful that they can't remember what happened a week ago. Yet at the same time your Uncle Oscar's recent memories are fading, he may have vivid memories of trivial and long-forgotten events from the past. "Why, I remember it as clearly as if it were yesterday," he will say, forgetting that the story he is about to tell is one he told earlier the same day. In short, disuse alone does not adequately explain long-term forgetting.

Question: If decay and disuse don't fully explain forgetting, what does?

There are several additional possibilities. Let's briefly consider each.

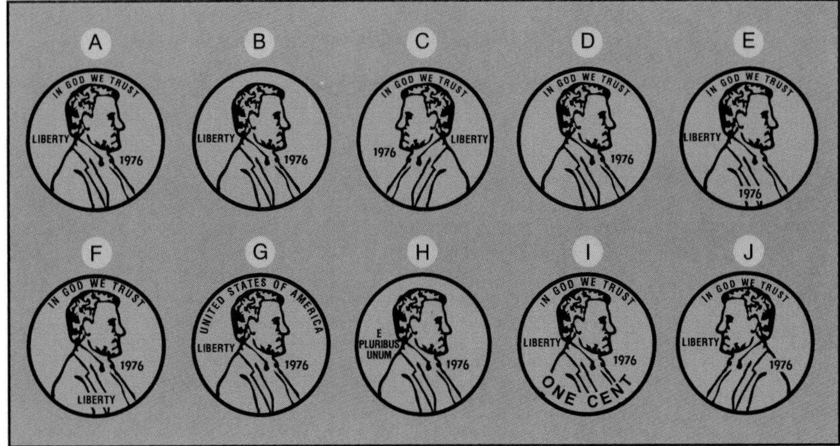

■ Fig. 8–13 *Some of the distractor items used in a study of recognition memory and encoding failure. Penny A is correct but was seldom recognized. Pennies G and J were popular wrong answers. (Adapted from Nickerson & Adams, 1979.)*

Cue-Dependent Forgetting

Often, memories appear to be *available*, but not accessible. An example is having an answer on the "tip of your tongue." You know the answer is there, but it remains just "out of reach." This situation indicates that many memories are "forgotten" because **cues** present at the time of learning are absent when the time comes to retrieve information. For example, if you were asked, "What were you doing on Monday afternoon of the third week in September two years ago?" your reply might be, "Come on. How should I know?" However, if you were reminded, "That was the day the courthouse burned," or "That was the day Mary had her automobile accident," you might remember immediately. The presence of such cues almost always enhances memory (■ Fig. 8–14). In theory, memory will be best if you study in the same room where you will be tested. Since this is often impossible, try to visualize the room where you will be tested, while you are studying. Doing so can enhance memory later (Jerabek & Standing, 1992).

State-Dependent Learning Nearly everyone has heard the story about the drunk who misplaced his wallet and had to get drunk again to find it. Although this tale is often told as a joke, it is not too farfetched. The *bodily state* that exists during learning can be a strong cue for later memory (Overton, 1985). Being very thirsty, for instance, might make you remember events that took place on another occasion when you were thirsty. Because of such effects, information learned under the influence of a drug is best remembered when the drugged state occurs again. This is known as **state-dependent learning.**

A similar effect may apply to emotional states. For instance, Gordon Bower (1981) found that people who learned a list of words while in a happy mood recalled them better when they were again happy. People who learned while they felt sad remembered best when they were sad (■ Fig. 8–15). Similarly, if you are in a happy mood you are more likely to remember recent happy events (Salovey & Singer, 1989). If you are in a bad mood you will tend to have unpleasant memories (Eich, et al., 1990). Such links between emotional cues and memory could explain why couples who quarrel often end up remembering—and rehashing—old arguments.

Memory cue Any stimulus associated with a particular memory. The presence of such cues usually enhances memory retrieval.

State-dependent learning Memory influenced by one's bodily state at the time of learning and at the time of retrieval. Improved memory occurs when the bodily states match.

■ Fig. 8–14 *External cues like those found in a photograph, a scrapbook, or a walk through an old neighborhood often aid recall of seemingly lost memories. For many veterans, finding a familiar name engraved in the Vietnam Veterans Memorial unleashes a flood of memories.*

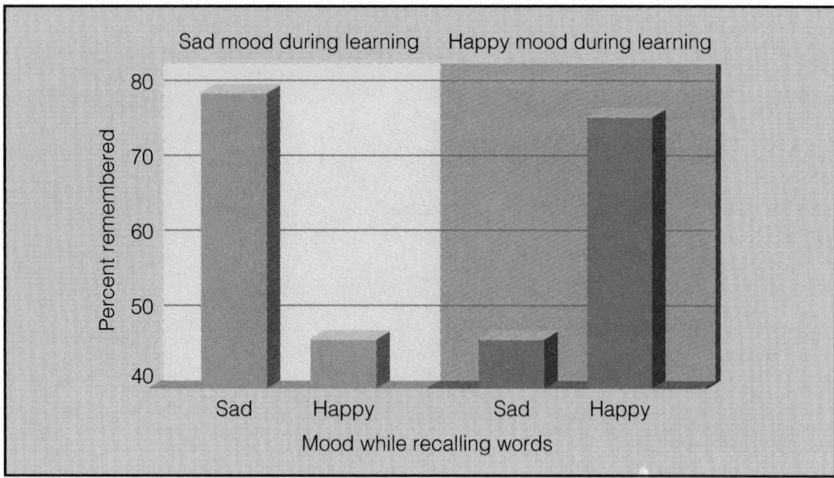

■ **Fig. 8–15** *The effect of mood on memory. Subjects best remembered a list of words when their mood during testing was the same as their mood was when they learned the list. (Adapted from Bower, 1981.)*

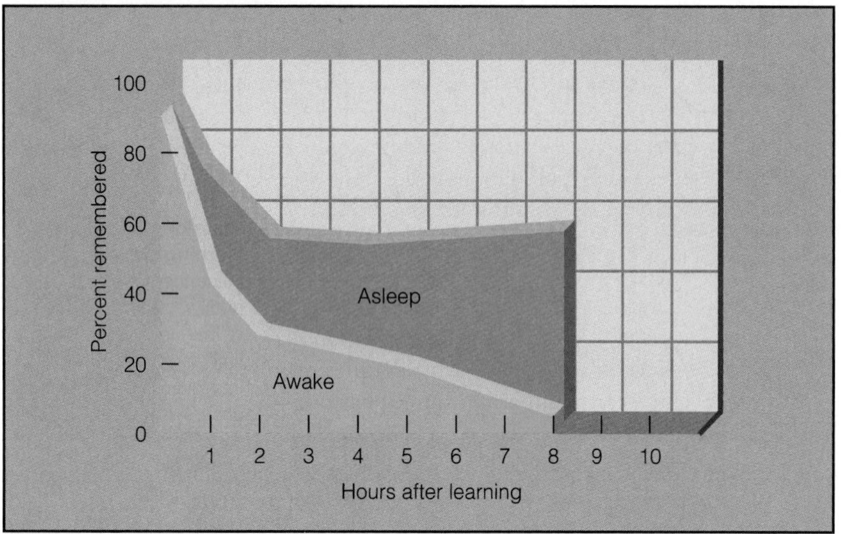

■ **Fig. 8–16** *The amount of forgetting after a period of sleep or of being awake. Notice that sleep causes less memory loss than activity that occurs while one is awake. (After Jenkins & Dallenbach, 1924.)*

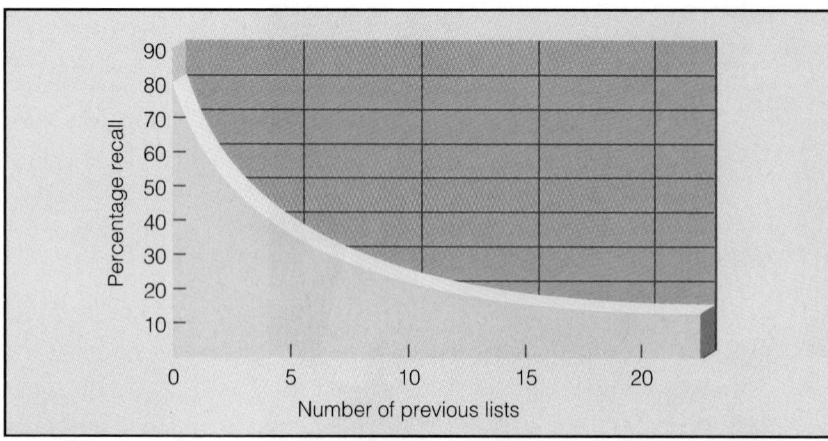

■ **Fig. 8–17** *Effects of interference on memory. A graph of the approximate relationship between percentage recalled and number of different word lists memorized. (Adapted from Underwood, 1957.)*

Interference

Further understanding of forgetting comes from an experiment in which college students learned lists of nonsense syllables. After studying, students in one group slept for 8 hours and were then tested for memory of the lists. A second group remained awake for 8 hours and went about business as usual. When members of the second group were tested, they remembered *less* than the group that slept (■ Fig. 8–16). This difference is based on the fact that new learning can *interfere* with previous learning (Shiffrin, 1970). **Interference** refers to the tendency for new memories to impair retrieval of older memories, and the reverse. It seems to apply to both short-term and long-term memories.

It is not completely clear if new memories alter existing memory traces or if they make it harder to "locate" (retrieve) earlier memories. In any case, there is no doubt that interference is a major cause of forgetting (Johnson & Hasher, 1987). College students who memorized 20 lists of words (one list each day) were able to recall only 15 percent of the last list. Students who learned only one list remembered 80 percent (Underwood, 1957) (■ Fig. 8–17).

Order Effects The sleeping college students remembered more because **retroactive** (RET-ro-AK-tiv) **interference** was held to a minimum. Retroactive interference refers to the tendency for new learning to inhibit retrieval of old learning. Avoiding new learning prevents retroactive interference from occurring. This fact doesn't exactly mean you should hide in a closet after you study for an exam. However, you should avoid studying other subjects until the exam. Sleeping after study can help you retain memories, and reading, writing, or even watching TV may cause interference.

Retroactive interference is easily demonstrated in the laboratory by this arrangement:

Experimental group:	Learn A	Learn B	Test A
Control group:	Learn A	Rest	Test A

Imagine yourself as a member of the experimental group. In task A, you learn a list of telephone numbers. In task B, you learn a list of Social Security numbers. How do you do on a test of task A (the telephone numbers)? If you do not remember as much as the control group that learns *only* task A, then retroactive interference has occurred. The second thing learned has interfered with memory of the first thing learned; the interference went "backward," or was "retroactive" (■ Fig. 8–18).

Proactive (pro-AK-tiv) **interference** is a second basic source of forgetting. Proactive interference occurs when prior learning inhibits recall of later learning. A test for proactive interference would take this form.

Experimental group:	Learn A	Learn B	Test B
Control group:	Rest	Learn B	Test B

If the experimental group remembers less than the control group on a test of task B, then learning task A has interfered with memory of task B.

Question: Then proactive interference goes "forward"?

Yes. For instance, if you cram for a psychology exam and then later the same night cram for a history exam, your memory for the second subject studied (history) will be less accurate than if you had studied only history. (Because of retroactive interference, your memory for psychology would probably also suffer.) The greater the similarity in the two subjects studied, the more interference takes place. The moral, of course, is don't procrastinate in preparing for exams.

The interference effects we have described apply primarily to memories of verbal information, such as the contents of this chapter. When you are learning a skill, similarity can sometimes be beneficial, rather than disruptive. The next section explains how this occurs.

Transfer of Training

Two people begin taking mandolin lessons. One already plays the violin. The other is a trumpet player. All other things being equal, which person will initially do better in learning the mandolin? If you chose the violin player you have an intuitive grasp of what *positive transfer* is. (The strings on a mandolin are tuned the same as a violin.) **Positive transfer** is said to have taken place when mastery of one task aids mastery of a second task. Another example would be learning to balance and turn on a bicycle before learning to ride a motorcycle or motor scooter. Likewise, skateboarding skills transfer to snowboarding.

Question: Is there such a thing as negative transfer?

There is indeed. In **negative transfer,** skills developed in one situation conflict with those required to master a new task. Learning to back a car with a trailer attached is a good example. Normally, when you are backing a car, the steering wheel is turned in the direction you want to go, the same as when moving forward. However, with a trailer attached, the steering wheel must be turned opposite from the direction you want the trailer to go. This situation results in negative transfer, and often creates comical scenes at campgrounds and boat launching ramps.

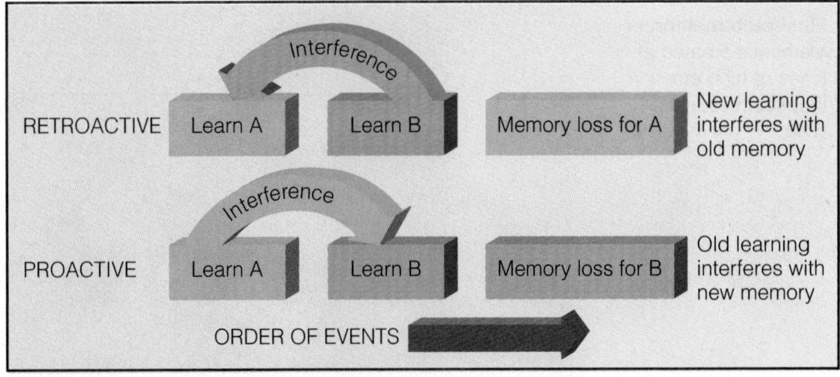

■ **Fig. 8–18** *Retroactive and proactive interference. The order of learning and testing shows whether interference is retroactive (backward) or proactive (forward).*

On a more serious note, many tragic crashes caused by negative transfer finally led to greater standardization of airplane cockpits. Fortunately, negative transfer is usually brief, and it occurs less often than positive transfer (Drowatzky, 1975). Negative transfer is most likely to occur when a new response must be made to an old stimulus. If you have ever encountered a pull-type handle on a door that must be pushed open, you will appreciate this point.

Repression

Take a moment from reading and scan over the events of the last few years of your life. What kinds of things most easily come to mind? Many people find that they tend to remember happy, positive events better than disappointments and irritations (Linton, 1979). A clinical psychologist would call this tendency **repression,** or motivated forgetting. Through repression, painful, threatening, or embarrassing memories are held out of consciousness by forces within one's personality. The forgetting of past failures, upsetting childhood events, the names of persons you dislike, or appointments you don't want to keep may reveal repression.

Adults who were sexually abused as children may repress all memory of their mistreatment. Some are startled when their repressed memories are brought to the surface by psychotherapy or other events (■Fig. 8–19). (This chapter's Exploration discusses some important cautions about the "recovery" of repressed memories.)

Question: If I try to forget a test I have failed, am I repressing it?

No. Repression can be distinguished from **suppression,** an active, conscious attempt to put something out of mind. By not thinking about the test, you have merely suppressed a memory. If you choose to, you can remember the test. Clinicians consider true repression an *unconscious* event. When a memory is repressed we are unaware that forgetting has even oc-

Interference The tendency for new memories to impair retrieval of older memories, and the reverse.

Retroactive interference The tendency for new memories to interfere with the retrieval of old memories.

Proactive interference The tendency for old memories to interfere with the retrieval of newer memories.

Positive transfer Mastery of one task aids learning or performing another.

Negative transfer Mastery of one task conflicts with learning or performing another.

Repression Unconsciously pushing unwanted memories out of awareness.

Suppression A conscious effort to put something out of mind or to keep it from awareness.

Flashbulb memories Memories created at times of high emotion that seem especially vivid.

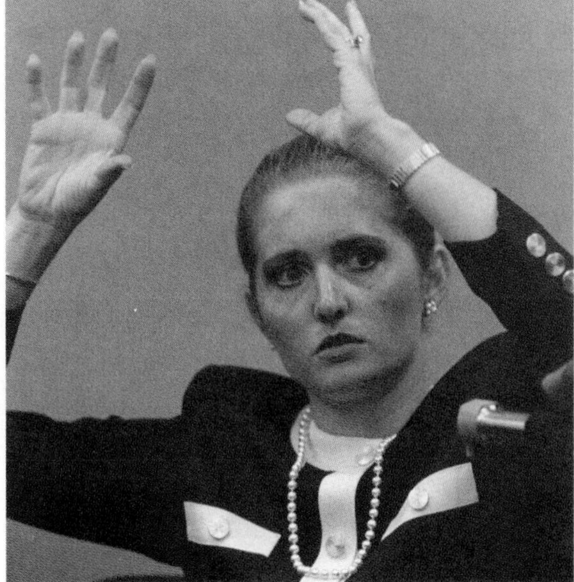

■ **Fig. 8–19** *In an apparent instance of repression, Eileen Franklin-Lipsker testified in court in 1990 that her father, George T. Franklin abducted, raped, and killed 8-year-old Susan Nason in 1969. Franklin-Lipsker witnessed her best friend's slaying but repressed the horror for 20 years after her father threatened to kill her if she told anyone. The memory finally surfaced one day as she looked into the eyes of her own young daughter. As discussed in this chapter's Exploration, there is reason to believe that some "recovered" memories of this type are false. Trying to separate true memories from fantasies has become a major headache for psychologists and the courts.*

■ **Fig. 8–20** *People who survive earthquakes almost always have flashbulb memories of the event. Typically, people vividly remember where they were when the quake started, what they thought as it was occurring, and how they reacted to it.*

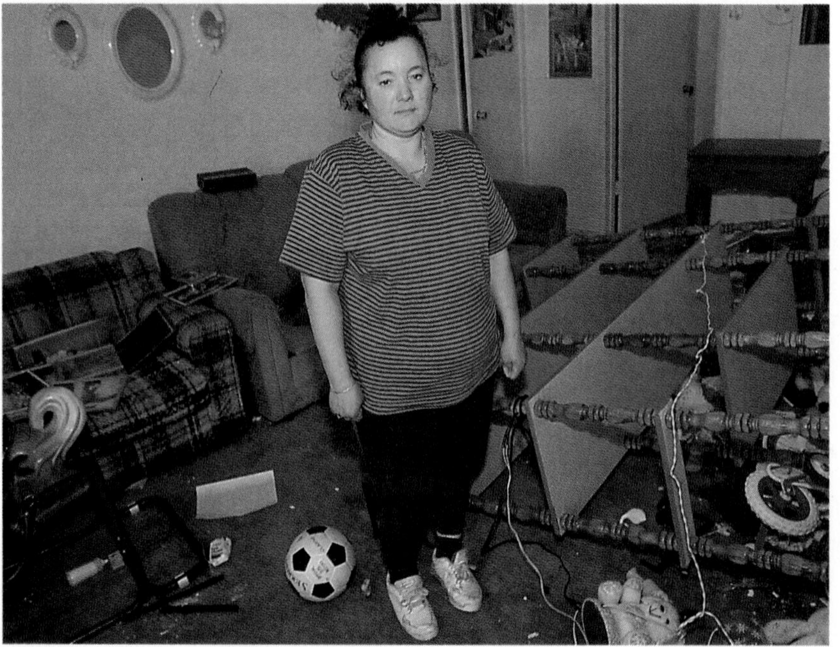

curred. (See Chapter 11 for more information on repression.)

Flashbulb Memories

Why are some traumatic events vividly remembered while others are repressed? Psychologists use the term **flashbulb memories** to describe images that seem to be frozen in memory at times of personal tragedy, accident, or other emotionally significant events. Depending on your age, you may have a "flashbulb" memory for the Pearl Harbor attack, the assassinations of John F. Kennedy and Martin Luther King, or the *Challenger* space shuttle disaster (■ Fig. 8–20). Flashbulb memories are most often formed when an event is surprising, important, or emotional (Rubin, 1985). They are frequently associated with public tragedies, but memories of positive events may also have "flashbulb" clarity.

Flashbulb memories seem to be very detailed and they often focus primarily on how you reacted to the event. ● Table 8–1 lists some memories that had "flashbulb" clarity for at least 50 percent of a group of college students. How vivid are the memories they trigger for you? (Note again that both positive and negative events are listed.)

The term *flashbulb memories* was first used to describe memories that seemed to be especially intense

● **Table 8–1 Bright Flashes of Memory**

Memory Cue	Percentage of Students with Flashbulb Memories
A car accident you were in or witnessed	85
When you first met your college roommate	82
The night of your high school graduation	81
The night of your senior prom (if you went or not)	78
An early romantic experience	77
A time you had to speak in front of an audience	72
When you first got your college admissions letter	65
Your first date—the moment you met him/her	57
When President Reagan was shot in Washington	52

(From Rubin, 1985.)

and permanent. It has become clear, however, that such memories are not always accurate (Harsch & Neisser, 1989). For example, a recent study examined memories formed during the Persian Gulf War. One year later, the flashbulb memories people had about the bombing of Iraq were no more accurate than ordinary memories formed the same day. More than anything else, what sets flashbulb memories apart is that we tend to place great *confidence* in them—even when they are wrong (Weaver, 1993). Perhaps that's because such memories act as prominent landmarks in our lives. We usually review emotionally-charged events over and over and tell others about them. Also, public events such as wars, earthquakes, and assassinations reappear many times in the news, which highlights them in memory (Wright, 1993).

Memory Formation—Some "Shocking" Findings

One possibility overlooked in our discussion of forgetting is that memories may be lost as they are being formed. For example, a head injury may cause a "gap" in memories preceding the accident. **Retrograde amnesia,** as this is called, involves forgetting events that occurred *before* an injury or the onset of disease. (In contrast, **anterograde amnesia** involves forgetting events that occur *after* an injury or trauma.) Retrograde amnesia can be understood if we assume that it takes a certain amount of time to move information from short-term to long-term memory. The forming of a long-term memory is called **consolidation** (Squire et al., 1993). You can think of consolidation as being somewhat like writing your name in wet concrete. Once the concrete is set, the information (your name) is fairly lasting, but while it is setting, it can be wiped out (amnesia) or scribbled over (interference).

Consider a classic experiment on consolidation, in which a rat is placed on a small platform. The rat steps down to the floor and receives a painful electric shock. After one shock, the rat can be returned to the platform repeatedly, but it will not step down. Obviously, the rat remembers the shock. Would it remember if consolidation were disturbed?

Interestingly, one way to prevent consolidation is to give a different kind of shock called **electroconvulsive shock (ECS)** (Jarvik, 1964). ECS is a mild electric shock to the brain. It does not harm the animal, but it does destroy any memory that is being formed. If each painful shock (the one the animal remembers) is followed by ECS (which wipes out memories during consolidation), the rat will step down over and over. Each time, ECS will erase the memory of the painful shock. (ECS has been employed as a psychiatric treatment for severe depression in humans. Used in this way, electroshock therapy also causes memory loss. See Chapter 17 for details.)

Question: What would happen if ECS were given several hours after the learning?

Recent memories are more easily disrupted than older memories (Gold, 1987). If enough time is allowed to pass between learning and ECS, the memory is unaffected. Apparently, consolidation is already completed. This is why people with mild head injuries usually only lose memories from just before the accident, while older memories remain intact (Baddeley, 1990). Likewise, you would forget more if you studied, stayed awake 8 hours, and then slept 8 hours than you would if you studied, slept 8 hours, and were then awake for 8 hours. Both cases involve the passage of 16 hours. However, in the second instance forgetting is reduced because more consolidation takes place before interference begins.

Question: Can memory be improved with drugs?

Drugs, Memory, and Consolidation The possibility of chemically improving memory has long intrigued psychologists. We have known for some time that various stimulating drugs speed up consolidation if given just after learning (McGaugh, 1983). Note, however, that this only reduces the time during which interference can take place; it does not magically improve memory. Also, the drugs involved (metrazol, strychnine, nicotine, caffeine, and amphetamine) must be given in carefully controlled dosages. If the dosage is too high by even a small amount, memory will be *disrupted.*

Question: What effect does alcohol have on memory?

Memory losses are common when a person overindulges in alcohol. This may be due, in part, to state dependent learning. At higher levels of intoxication, alcohol seems to directly impair encoding and consolidation of memories. A person suffering an alcohol blackout may lose anywhere from a few minutes to several hours of memory (Loftus, 1980). Research makes it clear that studying while drunk is an excellent way to *lower* test scores (Birnbaum et al., 1978). Even intoxicated eyewitnesses to crimes, which are usually memorable events, suffer impaired memory for what they saw (Yuille & Tollestrup, 1990).

Question: What part of the brain causes consolidation?

From STM to LTM

Actually, many areas of the brain are responsible for memory, but the **hippocampus** is of particular importance. This structure, buried deep within the brain, seems to act as a sort of "switching station" between short-term and long-term memory. The hippocampus

Retrograde amnesia Loss of memory for events that preceded a head injury or other amnesia-causing event.

Anterograde amnesia Loss of the ability to form or retrieve memories for events that occur after an injury or trauma.

Consolidation Process by which relatively permanent memories are formed in the brain.

Electroconvulsive shock An electric current passed directly through the brain, producing a convulsion.

Hippocampus A brain structure associated with emotion and the transfer of information from short-term memory to long-term memory.

Engram A memory trace.

is essential for memories of facts and information, rather than for skills and habits (Squire, 1992).

Humans who have had hippocampal damage show a striking inability to store new memories. A patient described by Brenda Milner is typical. Two years after an operation that affected the hippocampus, a 21-year-old patient continued to give his age as 27, and reported that it seemed that the operation had just taken place (Milner, 1965). His memory of events before the operation remained clear, but he found forming new long-term memories almost impossible. (He suffered, in other words, from anterograde amnesia.) When his parents moved to a new house a few blocks away on the same street, he could not remember the new address, and he read the same magazines over and over again without finding them familiar. If you were to meet this man, he would seem fairly normal, since he still has short-term memory. But if you were to leave the room and return 15 minutes later, he would act as if he had never seen you before (Milner, 1965). Years ago his favorite uncle died, but he suffers the same grief anew each time he is told of the death. Lacking the ability to form new lasting memories, he lives eternally in the present.

The Brain and Memory Somewhere within the 3-pound mass of the human brain lies all we know: zip codes, faces of loved ones, history, favorite melodies, the taste of an apple, and much, much more. Where is this information? Karl Lashley, a pioneering brain researcher, set out in the 1920s to find an **engram**, or memory trace. Lashley taught animals to run mazes and then removed parts of their brains to see how memory of the maze changed. After 30 years he had to concede defeat: Engrams are not located in any one area of the brain. It mattered little which part of the brain's cortex he removed. Only the *amount* removed correlated to memory loss. This conclusion may remain true for specific memories. However, some areas of the cerebral cortex *are* more important to memory than others (Tulving, 1989). ■ Figure 8–21 explains why.

Question: Then how are memories recorded in the brain?

Scientists studying simple animals are beginning to identify the exact ways in which individual nerve cells record information. There is now much evidence that learning alters the electrical activity, structure, and chemistry of the brain (McGaugh, 1983). For example, Eric Kandel and his colleagues have studied learning in the marine snail *Aplysia* (■ Fig. 8–22). Kandel has found that learning in *Aplysia* (ah-PLEEZ-yah) occurs when certain nerve cells in a circuit alter the amount of transmitter chemicals they release (Kandel, 1976). Such changes determine which circuits get stronger and which become weaker. It has also been shown that an increase in receptor sites for transmitter chemicals occurs during learning (Lynch & Baudry, 1984).

On the basis of such breakthroughs, scientists are now studying a bewildering array of chemicals and brain processes that affect memory. If this research succeeds, it may be possible to help the millions of persons who suffer from memory impairment. Will researchers ever produce a "memory pill" for those with normal memory? Some neuroscientists are confident that memory can be and will be artificially enhanced. At present, however, the possibility of something like a "physics pill" or a "math pill" seems especially remote.

■ **Fig. 8–21** *Patterns of blood flow in the cerebral cortex (wrinkled outer layer of the brain) change as areas become more or less active. Thus, blood flow can be used to draw "maps" of brain activity. This drawing, which views the brain from the top, shows the results of measuring cerebral blood flow while people were thinking about a semantic memory* (a) *or an episodic memory* (b). *In the map, green indicates areas that are more active during semantic thinking. Reds show areas of greater activity during episodic thinking. The brain on the right shows the difference in activity between views* a *and* b. *The resulting pattern suggests that the front of the cortex is related to episodic memory. Back areas are more associated with semantic memory (Tulving, 1989).*

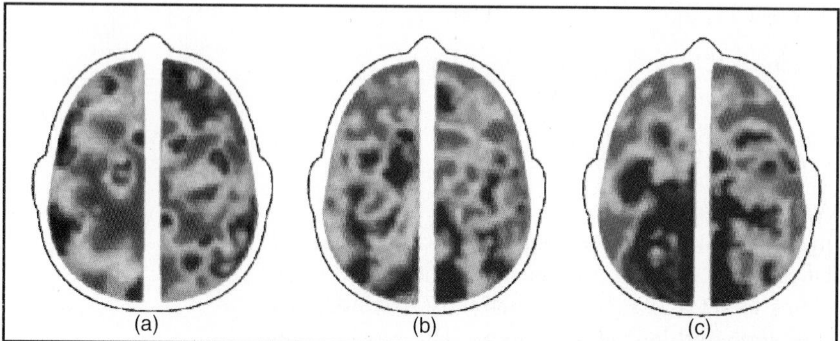

■ **Fig. 8–22** *An* Aplysia. *The relatively simple nervous system of this sea animal allows scientists to study memory as it occurs in single nerve cells.*

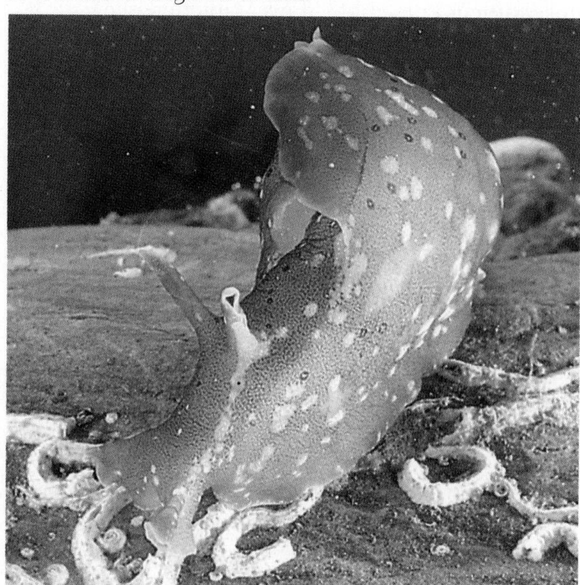

LEARNING CHECK

1. According to the Ebbinghaus curve of forgetting, we forget slowly at first and then a rapid decline occurs. T or F?
2. Which explanation seems to account for the loss of short-term memories?
   a. decay *b.* disuse *c.* repression *d.* interference
3. When memories are available but not accessible, forgetting may be cue dependent. T or F?
4. When learning one thing makes it more difficult to recall another, forgetting may be caused by ______________ .
5. You are asked to memorize long lists of telephone numbers. You learn a new list each day for 10 days. When tested on list 3, you remember less than a person who only learned the first three lists. Your larger memory loss is probably caused by
   a. disuse *b.* retroactive interference
   c. regression *d.* proactive interference
6. ______________________ ______________________ is said to occur when skills learned in one situation conflict with those required to master a new task.
7. Repression is thought of as a type of motivated forgetting. T or F?
8. Retrograde amnesia results when consolidation is speeded up. T or F?
9. Researchers have clearly established that engrams are stored in the hippocampus. T or F?
10. You must study French, Spanish, psychology, and biology in one evening. What do you think would be the best order in which to study these subjects so as to minimize interference? ***Critical Thinking***

Answers: 1. F 2. *a* and *d* 3. T 4. interference 5. *b* 6. Negative transfer 7. T 8. F 9. F 10. Any order that separates French from Spanish and psychology from biology would work (for instance: French, psychology, Spanish, biology).

Improving Memory—Keys to the Memory Bank

While you're waiting around for the development of a memory pill, let's focus on some ways of improving your memory skills right now.

Knowledge of Results Learning proceeds best when feedback, or knowledge of results, allows you to check to see if you are learning. Feedback also helps you identify ideas that need extra practice. In addition, knowing that you have remembered or answered correctly can be rewarding. A prime means of providing feedback for yourself when studying is *recitation*.

Recitation If you are going to remember something, eventually you will have to retrieve it. Recitation refers to summarizing aloud while you are learning. Recitation forces you to practice retrieving information. When you are reading a text, you should stop frequently and try to remember what you have just read by restating it in your own words. In one experiment, the best memory score of all was earned by a group of students who spent 80 percent of their time reciting and only 20 percent reading (Gates, 1958). Maybe students who talk to themselves aren't crazy after all.

Rehearsal The more you rehearse information as you read, the better you will remember it (Muth, et al., 1988). But remember that maintenance rehearsal alone is not very effective. Elaborative rehearsal, in which you look for meaning and connections to existing knowledge, is far better. It's also helpful to frequently ask yourself "why" questions as you read (Woloshyn et al., 1990). Thinking about facts helps link them together in memory.

Selection The Dutch scholar Erasmus said that a good memory should be like a fish net: It should keep all the big fish and let the little ones escape. If you boil down the paragraphs in most textbooks to one or two important terms or ideas, your memory chores will be more manageable. Practice very selective marking in your texts and use marginal notes to further summarize ideas. Most students mark their texts too much instead of too little. If everything is underlined, you haven't been selective. And, very likely, you didn't pay much attention to what you read in the first place (Peterson, 1992).

Organization Assume that you must memorize the following list of words: *north, man, red, spring, woman, east, autumn, yellow, summer, boy, blue, west, winter, girl, green, south.* This rather difficult list could be reorganized into *chunks* as follows: *north-east-south-west, spring-summer-autumn-winter, red-yellow-green-blue, man-woman-boy-girl.* This simple reordering made the second list much easier to learn when college students were tested on both lists (Deese & Hulse, 1967). In another experiment, students who made up stories us-

Knowledge of results During learning, feedback about the correctness of responses or other aspects of performance.

Recitation As a memory aid, repeating aloud information one wishes to retain.

Rehearsal Silently repeating or mentally reviewing information to improve memory.

Whole learning Studying an entire package of information (such as a complete poem) at once.

Part learning Separately studying subparts of a larger body of information (such as sections of a textbook chapter).

Serial position effect The tendency for the greatest number of memory errors to occur in the middle portion of a list.

Memory cues Any stimuli linked with particular memories.

Overlearning Study or learning that continues after initial mastery of skills or information.

Spaced practice A practice schedule that alternates study periods with brief rests.

Massed practice A practice schedule in which studying continues for long periods, without interruption.

ing long lists of words to be memorized learned the lists better than those who didn't (Bower & Clark, 1969). Organizing class notes and summarizing chapters can be helpful when studying (Dickinson & O'Connell, 1990). It may even be helpful to summarize your summaries, so that the overall organization of ideas becomes clearer and simpler.

Whole versus Part Learning If you have to memorize a speech, is it better to try to learn it from beginning to end? Or in smaller parts like paragraphs? Generally it is better to practice whole packages of information rather than smaller parts. This is especially true for fairly short, organized information. An exception is that learning parts may be better for extremely long, complicated information. Try to study the largest *meaningful* amount of information possible at one time.

For very long or complex material, try the *progressive part method.* In this approach, you break a learning task into short sections. At first, you study part A until it is mastered. Next, you study parts A and B; then A, B, and C; and so forth. This is a good way to learn the lines of a play, a long piece of music, or a poem (Ash & Holding, 1990). After the material is learned, you should also practice it by starting at points other than A (at C, D, or B, for example). This helps prevent getting "lost" or going blank in the middle of a performance.

Serial Position Whenever you must learn something in *order,* be aware of the *serial position effect.* As you will recall, this is the tendency to make the most errors in remembering the middle of a list. If you are introduced to a long line of people, the names you are likely to forget will be those in the middle, so you should make an extra effort to attend to them. The middle of a list, poem, or speech should also be given special attention and extra practice. Try to break long lists of information into short sub-lists, and make the middle sub-lists the shortest of all.

Cues The best cues for remembering are those that were present during encoding (Reed, 1992). For example, students in one study had to recall a list of 600 words. As they read the list (which they did not know they would be tested on), the students gave three other words closely related in meaning to each listed word. In a test given later, the words each student supplied were used as cues to jog his or her memory. The students recalled an astounding 90 percent of the original word list (Mantyla, 1986). Once again, this shows why it often helps to *elaborate* information as you learn. When you study, try to use new names, ideas, or terms in several sentences. Also, form images that include the new information, and relate it to knowledge you already have (Pressley et al., 1988). Your goal should be to knit meaningful cues into your memory code to help you retrieve information when you need it.

Overlearning Numerous studies have shown that memory is greatly improved when study is continued beyond bare mastery. In other words, after you have learned material well enough to remember it once without error, you should continue studying. Overlearning is your best insurance against going blank on a test because of nervousness.

Spaced Practice To keep boredom and fatigue to a minimum, try alternating short study sessions with brief rest periods. This pattern, called **spaced practice,** is generally superior to **massed practice,** in which little or no rest is given between learning sessions (Naveh-Benjamin, 1990). By improving attention and consolidation, three 20-minute study sessions can produce more learning than one hour of continuous study.

Perhaps the best way to make use of spaced practice is to *schedule* your time. If most students were to keep a totally honest record of their weekly activities, they would probably find that very few hours were spent really studying. To make an effective schedule, designate times during the week before, after, and between classes when you will study particular subjects. Then treat these times just as if they were classes you had to attend.

Sleep Remember that sleeping after study reduces interference. Since you obviously can't sleep after every study session or study everything just before you sleep, your study schedule (see Spaced Practice) should include ample breaks between subjects. Using your breaks and free time in a schedule is as important as living up to your study periods.

Review If you have spaced your practice and overlearned, review will be like icing on your study cake. Reviewing shortly before an exam cuts down the time during which you must remember details that may be important for the test. When reviewing, hold the amount of new information you try to memorize to a minimum. It may be realistic to take what you have actually learned and add a little more to it at the last minute by cramming. But remember that more than a little new learning may interfere with what you already know.

Using a Strategy to Aid Recall Successful recall is usually the result of a planned *search* of memory (Reed, 1992). For example, one study found that students were most likely to recall names that eluded them if they made use of partial information (Reed & Bruce, 1982). The students were trying to answer questions such as, "He is best remembered as the scarecrow in the Judy Garland movie *The Wizard of Oz*." (The answer is Ray Bolger.) Partial information that helped students remember included impressions about the length of the name, letter sounds within the name, similar names, and related information (such as the names of other characters in the movie). A similar helpful strategy is to go through the alphabet, trying each letter as the first sound of a name or word you are seeking.

Using a variety of cues, even partial ones, opens more paths to a memory. Highlight 8–3 gives further hints for recapturing context and jogging memories.

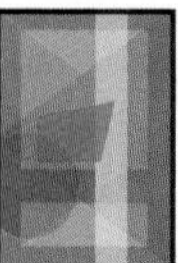

HIGHLIGHT 8–3

Using Psychology

Memory Detectives

You may not think of yourself as a "memory detective," but active probing often helps improve recall. A case in point is the *cognitive interview,* a technique used to jog the memory of eyewitnesses. The cognitive interview was created by R. Edward Geiselman and Ron Fisher to help police detectives. When used properly, it produces 35 percent more correct information than standard questioning (Geiselman et al., 1986).

By following four simple steps, you can apply cognitive principles to your own memory. The next time you are searching for a "lost" memory—one that you know is in there somewhere—try the following search strategies.

1. Say or write down *everything* you can remember that relates to the information you are seeking. Don't worry about how trivial any of it seems; each bit of information you remember can serve as a cue to bring back others.

2. Try to recall events or information in different orders. Let your memories flow out backward or out of order, or start with whatever impressed you the most.

3. Recall from different viewpoints. Review events by mentally standing in a different place. Or try to view information as another person would remember it. When taking a test, for instance, ask yourself what other students or your professor would remember about the topic.

4. Mentally put yourself back in the situation where you learned the information. Try to mentally re-create the learning environment or relive the event. As you do, include sounds, smells, details of weather, nearby objects, other people present, what you said or thought, and how you felt as you learned the information (Fisher & Geiselman, 1987).

These strategies help re-create the context in which information was learned, and they provide multiple memory cues. If you think of remembering as a sort of "treasure hunt," you might even learn to enjoy the detective work.

A Look Ahead Psychologists still have much to learn about the nature of memory and how to improve it. For now, one thing stands out clearly: People who have good memories excel at organizing information and making it meaningful. With this in mind, the Applications for this chapter tells how you can combine organization and meaning into a powerful method for improving memory. In the Explorations section, we will examine the growing controversy concerning the purported recovery of long-repressed memories of childhood sexual abuse.

LEARNING CHECK

1. To improve memory, it is reasonable to spend as much or more time reciting as reading. T or F?
2. Organizing information while studying has little effect on memory because long-term memory is already highly organized. T or F?
3. The progressive part method of study is best suited to long and complex learning tasks. T or F?
4. Sleeping immediately after studying is highly disruptive to the consolidation of memories. T or F?
5. As new information is encoded and rehearsed it is helpful to elaborate on its meaning and connect it to other information. T or F?
6. What advantages would there be to taking notes as you read a textbook, as opposed to underlining words in the text? ***Critical Thinking***

Answers: 1. T 2. F 3. T 4. F 5. T 6. Note taking is a form of recitation, it encourages elaborative rehearsal, facilitates the organization and selection of important ideas, and your notes can be used for review.

APPLICATIONS: *Mnemonics—Memory Magic*

Question: Some stage performers use memory as part of their acts. Do they have eidetic imagery?

Various "memory experts" entertain by giving demonstrations in which they memorize the names of everyone at a banquet, the order of all the cards in a deck, long lists of words, or other seemingly impossible amounts of information. Such feats may seem like magic, but if they are, you can have a magic memory too. These tricks are performed through the use of **mnemonics** (nee-MON-iks). A mnemonic is any kind of memory system or aid. In some cases, mnemonic strategies increase recall ten-fold (Patten, 1990).

Mnemonic Any kind of memory system or aid.

Some mnemonic systems have become so common that almost everyone knows them. If you are trying to remember how many days there are in a month, you may find the answer by reciting, "Thirty days hath September . . . ." Physics teachers often help their students remember the colors of the spectrum by giving them the mnemonic "Roy G. Biv": **R**ed, **O**range, **Y**ellow, **G**reen, **B**lue, **I**ndigo, **V**iolet. The budding sailor who has trouble telling port from starboard may remember that port and left both have four letters or may remind himself, "I *left* port." And what beginning musician hasn't remembered the notes represented by the lines and spaces of the musical staff by learning "F-A-C-E" and "**E**very **G**ood **B**oy **D**oes **F**ine."

Mnemonic techniques are ways of avoiding *rote* learning (learning by simple repetition). The superiority of mnemonic learning as opposed to rote learning has been demonstrated many times. For example, Bower (1973) asked college students to study 5 different lists of 20 unrelated words. At the end of a short study session, subjects were asked to recall all 100 items. Subjects using mnemonics remembered an average of 72 items, whereas a control group using simple, or rote, learning remembered an average of 28.

Stage performers rarely have naturally superior memories. Instead, they make extensive use of memory systems to perform their feats. Few of these systems are of practical value to you as a student, but the principles underlying mnemonics are. By practicing mnemonics you should be able to greatly improve your memory with little effort.

Here, then, are the basic principles of mnemonics.

1. **Use mental pictures.** There are at least two kinds of memory, *visual* and *verbal.* Visual pictures, or images, are generally easier to remember than words. Turning information into mental pictures is therefore very helpful (Kroll et al., 1986; Paivio, 1969).
2. **Make things meaningful.** Transferring information from short-term to long-term memory is aided by making it meaningful. If you encounter technical terms that have little or no immediate meaning for you, *give* them meaning, even if you have to stretch the term to do so. (This point is clarified by the examples following this list.)
3. **Make information familiar.** Connect it to what you already know. Another way to get information into long-term memory is to connect it to information already stored there. If some facts or ideas in a chapter seem to stay in your memory easily, associate other more difficult facts with them.
4. **Form bizarre, unusual, or exaggerated mental associations.** Forming images that make sense is better in most situations (Reed, 1992). However, when associating two ideas, terms, or especially mental images, you may sometimes find that the more outrageous and exaggerated the association, the more likely you are to remember (Iaccino & Sowa, 1989). Bizarre images can make stored information more *distinctive* and therefore easier to retrieve (Riefer & Rouder, 1992). Bizarre images mainly help improve immediate memory (Zoller et al., 1989). Nevertheless, they can be a first step toward retaining information (■ Fig. 8–23).

■ **Fig. 8–23** *Mnemonics can be an aid in preparing for tests. However, because mnemonics help most in the initial stages of storing information, it is important to follow through with other learning strategies.*

APPLICATIONS: *Continued*

A sampling of typical applications of mnemonics should make these four points clear to you.

Example 1 Let's say you have 30 new vocabulary words to memorize in Spanish. You can proceed by rote memorization (repeat them over and over until you begin to get them), or you can learn them with little effort by using the **keyword method** (Pressley, 1987). To remember that the word *pajaro* (pronounced PAH-hah-ro) means bird, you can link it to a "key" word in English: *Pajaro* (to me) sounds like "parked car-o." Therefore, to remember that *pajaro* means bird, I will visualize a parked car jam-packed full of birds. I will try to make this image as vivid and exaggerated as possible, with birds flapping and chirping and feathers flying everywhere. Similarly, for the word *carta* (which means "letter"), I will imagine a shopping *cart* filled with postal letters.

If you link similar keywords and images for the rest of the list, you may not remember them all, but you will get most without any more practice. As a matter of fact, if you have formed the *pajaro* and *carta* images just now, it is going to be almost impossible for you to ever see these words again without remembering what they mean. The keyword method is also superior when you want to work "backward" from an English word to a foreign vocabulary word (Hogben & Lawson, 1992).

Question: What if I think that pajaro *means "parked car" when I take my Spanish test?*

This is why you should form one or two extra images so that the important feature (bird, in this case) is repeated.

Example 2 Let's say you have to learn the names of all the bones and muscles in the human body for biology. You are trying to remember that the jawbone is the *mandible*. This one is easy because you can associate it to a *man nibbling*, or maybe you can picture a *man dribbling* a basketball with his jaw (make this image as ridiculous as possible). If the muscle name *latissimus dorsi* gives you trouble, familiarize it by turning it into *"the ladder misses the door, sigh."* Then picture a ladder glued to your back where the muscle is found. Picture the ladder leading up to a small door at your shoulder. Picture the ladder missing the door. Picture the ladder sighing like an animated character in a cartoon.

Question: This seems like more to remember, not less; and it seems like it would cause you to misspell things.

Mnemonics are not a complete substitute for normal memory; they are an aid to normal memory. Mnemonics are not likely to be helpful unless you make extensive use of *images.* Your mental pictures will come back to you easily. As for misspellings, mnemonics can be thought of as a built-in hint in your memory. Often, when taking a test, you will find that the slightest hint is all you need to remember correctly. A mnemonic image is like having someone leaning over your shoulder who says, "Psst, the name of that muscle sounds like 'ladder misses the door, sigh.' " If misspelling continues to be a problem, try to create memory aids for spelling, too.

Here are two more examples to help you appreciate the flexibility of a mnemonic approach to studying.

Keyword method As an aid to memory, using a familiar word or image to link two items.

Example 3 Your art history teacher expects you to be able to name the artist when you are shown slides as part of exams. You have seen many of the slides only once before in class. How will you remember them? As the slides are shown in class, make each artist's name into an object or image. Then picture the object *in* the paintings done by the artist. For example, you can picture Van Gogh as a *van* (automobile) *going* through the middle of each Van Gogh painting. Picture the van running over things and knocking things over. Or, if you remember that Van Gogh cut off his ear, picture a giant bloody ear in each of his paintings.

Example 4 If you have trouble remembering history, try to avoid thinking of it as something from the dim past. Picture each historical personality as a person you know right now (a friend, teacher, parent, and so on). Then picture these people doing whatever the historical figures did. Also, try visualizing battles or other events as if they were happening in your town or make parks and schools into countries. Use your imagination.

Question: How can mnemonics be used to remember things in order?

Here are three techniques that are helpful.

1. **Form a chain.** To remember lists of ideas, objects, or words in order, try forming an exaggerated association (mental image) connecting the first item to the second, then the second to the third, and so on. To remember the following short list in order—*elephant, doorknob, string, watch, rifle, oranges*—picture a full-sized *elephant* balanced on a *doorknob* playing with a *string* tied to him. Picture a *watch* tied to the

string, and a *rifle* shooting *oranges* at the watch. This technique can be used quite successfully for lists of 20 or more items. In a recent test, people who used a linking mnemonic did much better at remembering lists of 15 and 22 errands (Higbee et al., 1990). Try it next time you go shopping and leave your list at home.

2. **Take a mental walk.** Ancient Greek orators had an interesting way to remember ideas in order when giving a speech. Their method was to take a mental walk along a familiar path. As they did, they associated topics with the images of statues found along the walk. You can do the same thing by "placing" objects or ideas along the way as you mentally take a familiar walk.

3. **Use a system.** Many times, the first letters or syllables of words or ideas can be formed into another word that will serve as a reminder of order. "Roy G. Biv" is an example. As an alternative, learn the following: 1 is a bun, 2 is a shoe, 3 is a tree, 4 is a door, 5 is a hive, 6 is sticks, 7 is heaven, 8 is a gate, 9 is a line, 10 is a hen. To remember a list in order, form an image associating bun with the first item on your list. For example, if the first item is *frog*, picture a "frog-burger" on a bun to remember it. Then, associate shoe with the second item, and so on.

If you have never used mnemonics, you may still be skeptical, but give this approach a fair trial. Most people find they can greatly extend their memory through the use of mnemonics. For example, college students who used the keyword method to learn medical terms scored significantly higher than those using conventional memory (Troutt-Ervin, 1990). But remember, mnemonics only supplement the memory tips given earlier; they do not replace them. Like most things worthwhile, remembering takes effort.

LEARNING CHECK

1. Memory systems and aids are referred to as ______________________.
2. Which of the following is least likely to improve memory?
   a. using exaggerated mental images
   b. forming a chain of associations
   c. turning visual information into verbal information
   d. associating new information to information that is already known or familiar
3. Picturing your knee moaning as it tries to remember something could serve as a mnemonic for the term mnemonic. T or F?
4. Bower's 1973 study showed that, in general, mnemonics only improve memory for related words or ideas. T or F?

Critical Thinking

5. How could you use mnemonics to make the nonsense syllables LAZ, CEF, and WOL easier to remember?

Answers: 1. mnemonics 2. c 3. T 4. F 5. How about, the "LAZy CHEF is a WOLF"?

EXPLORATION

The Recovered Memory/False Memory Debate

The idea that early traumatic memories are often deeply repressed has gained wide acceptance. Perhaps too wide. "Recovered" memories of childhood sexual abuse are surfacing by the thousands in therapists' offices, incest recovery groups, celebrity confessions, TV talk shows, and courtrooms.

Question: How valid are memories of sexual abuse that return to awareness long after childhood?

Psychologists are currently debating this question. To grasp the nature of their debate, consider the following sketches.

Laura's Story Laura visits a psychotherapist for help with depression and marital difficulties. The therapist tells Laura that her symptoms suggest she was sexually abused as a child. At first, Laura insists that she doesn't remember any abuse. But with the therapist's guidance, Laura begins to bring disturbing memory fragments to the surface. Eventually, in a horrifying rush of flashbacks, Laura remembers her father raping her.

Through hypnosis, dream analysis, guided visualization, and an incest survivors group, Laura recovers other lost memories of childhood sexual abuse. In doing so, she takes the first painful steps toward healing the long-hidden cause of her problems.

Kathy's Story Kathy seeks help from a psychotherapist for depression and marital difficulties. Unbeknownst to her, Kathy has blundered into a "memory mill" run by an incompetent therapist who believes that sexual abuse is the root of nearly all problems. During the very first session, the therapist tells Kathy that she was sexually abused as a child. Kathy resists this idea, saying that she has no memory of any abuse. But gradually, as she submits to hypnosis, dream analysis, guided visualization, and participation in an incest survivors group, Kathy begins to have detailed memories of childhood abuse.

Kathy's "recovered memories" are actually pure fantasy, spawned by her therapist's suggestions. Nevertheless, she believes them completely. Kathy accuses her father of sexual abuse and breaks all ties with him. Kathy's father loses his job and her family is shattered. Yet, there is no way of proving Kathy's memories are false.

Recovered Memories?

Laura's and Kathy's stories represent two extremes of the recovered-memory debate. Advocates of recovered-memory therapy view it as an antidote for the long-buried pain of childhood incest and sexual abuse. Critics see it as a nightmare of malpractice that can create false memories and destroy families. Let's examine some points of the debate.

Point Many adults who suffer from depression, low self-esteem, sexual problems, and other complaints, have documented histories of sexual abuse. Recovered-memory therapists think it is reasonable to suspect hidden abuse when a person like Laura or Kathy has similar problems.

Counterpoint Critics believe that the purported symptoms of hidden abuse are dubious at best. For example, signs of abuse listed in one pop-psychology book include "too much or too little trust of others, high risk-taking or an inability to take risks, too much interest in sex or too little." On the basis of such vague symptoms, and others like them, almost anyone could be suspected of harboring hidden memories of abuse.

Point Most victims of childhood sexual abuse vividly remember having been molested. That's why skeptics doubt that many victims repress the experience. Childhood memories of other atrocities, such as seeing a family member killed, are usually carried for life. The problem for most victims of abuse is that they can't forget what happened to them, not that they don't remember it.

Counterpoint Proponents of recovered memory theorize that sexual abuse is a special case, because the abuse is repeated and extremely threatening. To cope with ongoing abuse the child must repress it, they say.

Reply Critics reply that children who survived the Holocaust in Nazi concentration camps vividly remember the experience. Again, their problem is an inability to forget repeated atrocities, not a failure to remember.

Point From 10 to 60 percent of early sexual abuse victims say that there was a time in their lives when they "forgot" about having been abused.

Counterpoint Estimates of repression rates are probably inflated. Books, survivors groups, celebrity testimonials, and media coverage have led many people to believe that "recovered" memories are common.

Point Memory experts argue that countless studies have shown that everyday memories are unreliable and easily altered. A patient guided by an incompetent therapist might confuse dreams with memories, unconsciously transforming fantasies and old resentments into a forgotten molestation.

Counterpoint Defenders of recovered-memory therapy reply that only minor details of memory are altered in lab experiments. They believe that personally important or traumatic memories cannot be created through suggestion.

Reply In fact, memory researcher Elizabeth Loftus has shown that false memories are easy to create. Loftus arranged for older relatives to tell college students false stories about how the students got lost in a shopping mall as children. When they were later asked to recall further details, the students described elaborate memories of the fictitious incidents.

Loftus also cites a study of children who were not at their elementary school when a sniper shot at youngsters on the playground. Despite being absent, many of

EXPLORATION

the children later reported intricate memories of the event.

Point Suggestion and fantasy are major elements of most of the techniques used to recover repressed memories, such as hypnosis and guided visualization. A person seeking an explanation for his or her suffering may be especially susceptible to suggestion. Certainly, some memories that are brought to awareness by suggestion are genuine. However, there is no way to distinguish real memories from false memories.

Counterpoint Defenders of recovered memories state that therapists rarely wield enough power or influence over patients to impose false memories on them. They believe that false complaints are rare. Most survivors unfairly blame themselves, not their abusers.

Point Psychologist Margaret Singer has interviewed 50 people who once believed they had recovered repressed memories of abuse but now think they were mistaken. All say that their therapists were far more sure than they were that their parents had molested them. An increasing number of recovered-memory patients have retracted their accusations. Some have joined their families in suing the therapists and clinics they claim led them astray (■ Fig. 8–24).

Counterpoint Recovered-memory advocates believe that those who recant may *prefer* to believe their troubling memories are not true. Accusations of incest and sexual abuse cause great pain and are followed by many pressures to recant.

Reply Skeptics reply that there are equally strong pressures to not retract an accusation. Once a charge of sexual abuse has been made public it is very difficult for an accuser to admit he or she was wrong. Researchers have identified many instances in which "recovered" traumatic memories were shown to be absolutely false.

Summary

As you can see, persuasive arguments exist on both sides of the recovered-memory debate. There is evidence that memories of sexual abuse are sometimes repressed, or at least suppressed for periods of time. Likewise, there is little doubt that some "recovered" memories are pure fantasy. Clearly there is a need to strike a balance between uncovering and treating real repressed trauma and doing damage by fabricating memories.

■ **Fig. 8–24** *Gary Ramona lost his marriage and his $400,000-a-year job as a business executive when his 19-year-old daughter Holly alleged that he molested her throughout her childhood. Ramona sued Holly's therapists, claiming that they had been irresponsible. To prove to Holly that her memories were true, the therapists gave her the drug sodium amytal, and told her that it was a "truth drug." (Sodium amytal is a hypnotic drug that induces a twilight state of consciousness. People do not automatically tell the truth while under its influence.) After reviewing the evidence for 2 months, a jury awarded Gary Ramona $500,000 in damages in May, 1994.*

Question: What can therapists do to help protect their clients from creating false memories?

Some preliminary suggestions follow.

Suggestions for Therapists

1. Mental health professionals should re-evaluate their work. Therapists who too readily assume that problems must be caused by childhood sexual abuse are probably harming some of their clients.
2. Therapists must not push clients to find "hidden" memories. If a therapist strongly suspects hidden trauma, he or she might ask a client to jog memories in some neutral way, such as by reviewing old family photographs. But this should be done without suggesting what kind of memories the person will find.
3. Therapists should be extremely cautious about using techniques that can foster false memories. Clients should be warned that such techniques may cause them to misinterpret dreams or fantasies as genuine memories. The American Medical Association, American Psychiatric Association, and American Psychological Association, have all issued cautions concerning misapplications of techniques used to find repressed memories.
4. Therapists should not encourage clients to join incest survivors groups until they are reasonably certain that sex abuse actually happened. The shared recollections of group members can be highly persuasive and may promote false memories.
5. Therapists should maintain a healthy skepticism regarding recovered memories. "Memories" of sexual abuse may be symbolic, rather than literally true. For instance, they may reveal that a client felt emotionally "raped" in childhood, not that the person was actually molested. In the absence of firm supporting evidence, there is no way to tell if a memory is real or not.

Question: What can individuals who suspect they were sexually abused do to avoid making false accusations?

Suggestions for Consumers

1. If you think you may have been sexually abused but aren't sure, consult an experienced psychotherapist. (See the Applications section of Chapter 18 for information on finding a competent therapist.) Never put yourself in the hands of a self-described "recovered-memory therapist."
2. Be wary of any therapist who tells you within the first few sessions that you were probably sexually abused as a child.

EXPLORATION

3. If a therapist pressures you to believe that you were sexually abused, discuss your concerns with the therapist. If the pressure continues, report the experience to the therapist's professional association and consider changing therapists.

4. Beware of anyone who treats failure to recall abuse as evidence of abuse. One popular book on abuse states that: "If you think you were abused and your life shows the symptoms, then you were," and "If you don't remember your abuse, you are not alone. Many women don't have memories . . . this doesn't mean they weren't abused." Both are dangerously misleading ideas.

5. Maintain a healthy skepticism regarding recovered memories. Remember, unless a memory can be independently confirmed, there is no way to tell if it is real or not real.

6. Before making accusations of abuse against anyone, seek confirming evidence. If none is available, consider consulting another therapist before acting on your memories. In the absence of firm evidence you should be cautious about accusing anyone based on recovered memories alone.

Sources: Baker, 1992; Byrd, 1994; Gardner, 1993; Gold et al., 1994; Herman, 1992; Kendall-Tackett & Simon, 1992; Loftus, 1993, 1994; Tavris, 1993; Terr, 1991.

LEARNING CHECK

1. Hypnosis, dream analysis, and guided verbalization are methods that are commonly used to "recover" repressed memories. T or F?
2. A reasonable conclusion to be drawn from the recovered-memory debate is that creating false memories is so rare as to be nearly impossible. T or F?
3. Like sexual abuse, memories of other types of severe trauma in childhood are almost always repressed. T or F?
4. Advocates of recovered-memory therapy believe that lab studies which show that memories can be altered by suggestion do not apply to childhood memories of sexual abuse. T or F?
5. People who have renounced their "recovered" memories generally admit that they were guilty of persuading skeptical therapists that their memories were real. T or F?
6. If you think you were abused and your life shows the symptoms, then you were. T or F?
7. Why does the use of hypnosis to unlock repressed memories limit the credibility of any "memories" that may be "recovered"? *Critical Thinking*

Answers: 1. F 2. F 3. F 4. T 5. F 6. F 7. As stated earlier in this chapter, hypnosis tends to increase the occurrence of false memories. Also, people often have unshakable confidence in false memories that are retrieved under hypnosis.

Chapter Summary

- ***How do we store information in memory?***
- **Memory** is an active system that **encodes, stores,** and **retrieves** information.
- ***Is there more than one type of memory?***
- Humans appear to have three interrelated memory systems. These are **sensory memory, short-term memory** (STM, also called **working memory**), and **long-term memory** (LTM).
- ***What are the features of each type of memory?***
- Sensory memory is exact, but very brief. Through **selective attention,** some information is transferred to STM.
- STM has a capacity of about **seven bits** of information, but this can be extended by **chunking,** or **recoding.** Short-term memories are brief and very sensitive to **interruption,** or **interference;** however, they can be prolonged by **maintenance rehearsal.**
- LTM functions as a general storehouse of information, especially *meaningful* information. **Elaborative rehearsal** helps transfer information from STM to LTM. Long-term memories are *relatively permanent,* or lasting. LTM seems to have an almost *unlimited storage* capacity.
- LTM is subject to **constructive processing,** or ongoing revision and updating. LTM is highly *organized* to allow retrieval of needed information. The

Chapter 9

Cognition and Creativity

IN THIS CHAPTER

What is cognition?
Mental imagery
Concepts
Language
Problem solving
Artificial intelligence
Insight and creativity
Intuition
Applications:
Improving thinking
Exploration:
Animal intelligence

CHAPTER PREVIEW

Chess, Anyone?

David Levy was in trouble. It was the fourth game of a six-game chess match, and Levy was trying a new strategy. If he lost the match, Levy would forfeit $2500 of his own money. Game 1 was a tie. Levy won games 2 and 3. Now in game 4, he was losing. What was wrong? In the earlier games Levy relied on the kind of wide-open maneuvering that had made him an International Master. In contrast, his opponent's strength was a powerful short-term, or tactical, style of play. Maybe "powerful" isn't the right word. Unbeatable is closer to the truth, as Levy soon learned. For the moment, David Levy had met his match. He watched silently as the robot arm of Chess 4.7 made its final move, winning game 4.

Chess 4.7 is a computer program. It once won the Minnesota Open Chess Tournament—against humans. However, David Levy, the reigning Scottish champion, proved to be a tougher opponent. After losing game 4, Levy quickly returned to his original style of play—and won the match.

More recently, world chess champion Garri Kasparov triumphed over Deep Thought, presently the most advanced chess program. Kasparov said the computer was "fully aggressive" but that its "mind was too straight and too primitive." While computers have the raw power to plan up to 20 chess moves in advance (by considering billions of possibilities), they can still be beaten by strategy and foresight.

Such victories symbolize one of the most unique of all human capacities, the ability to think intelligently and creatively. We know how computers "think" because we created them. But how do we explain a chess master's creativity and problem-solving ability? Or yours? Thinking, problem solving, and creativity are the challenging topics of this chapter.

Survey Questions

- What is the nature of thought?
- In what ways are images related to thinking?
- How are concepts learned? Are there different kinds of concepts?
- What is the role of language in thinking?
- Can animals be taught to use language?
- What do we know about problem solving?
- What is artificial intelligence?
- What is the nature of creative thinking?
- How is creativity defined and measured?
- How accurate is intuition?
- What can be done to improve thinking and promote creativity?
- Do animals think?

What Is Thinking?—It's All in Your Head!

Thinking takes many forms, including daydreaming, problem solving, and reasoning (to name but a few). Stated more formally, **thinking,** or **cognition,** refers to mentally processing information (images, concepts, words, rules, and symbols) (■ Fig. 9–1). Studying thinking is similar to figuring out how a computer works by repeatedly asking, "I wonder what would happen if I did this?" But in **cognitive psychology** the "computer" is the brain, and thinking is the "programming" we seek to understand.

Although an ability to think is not limited to humans, imagine trying to teach an animal to match the feats of Shakuntala Devi, who holds the "world record" for mental calculation. Devi once multiplied two 13-digit numbers (7,686,369,774,870 times 2,465,099,745,779) in her head, giving the answer in 28 seconds (Morain, 1988). (That's 18,947,668,177,995,426,773,730 if you haven't already figured it out yourself.)

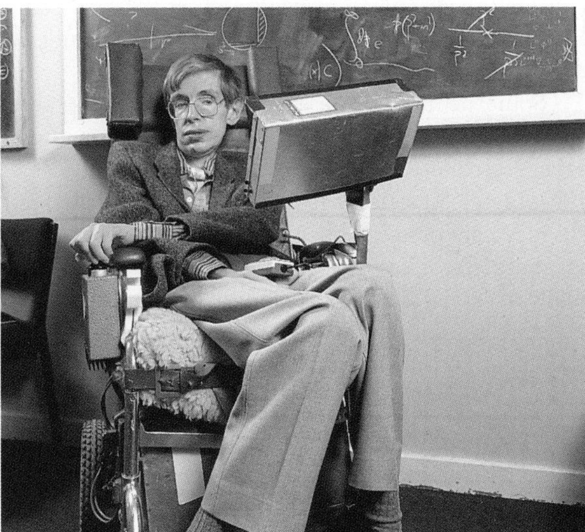

■ **Fig. 9–1** *The power of thought is beautifully expressed by Stephen W. Hawking, a theoretical physicist and one of the best-known scientific minds of modern times. Now in his late 40s, Hawking has suffered since age 13 from amyotrophic lateral sclerosis, a disabling condition also known as Lou Gehrig's disease. Today, he can only control his left hand, and he cannot speak. Nevertheless, his brain remains fiercely active. With courage and determination, he has used his intellect to advance our understanding of the universe.*

Cognition The process of thinking or mentally processing information (images, concepts, words, rules, and symbols).

Cognitive psychology The study of thinking, knowing, understanding, problem solving, and information processing.

Internal representation Any image, concept, precept, symbol, or process used to mentally represent information.

Image Most often, a mental representation that has picture-like qualities.

Concept A generalized idea representing a class of related objects or events.

Language Words or symbols and rules for combining them for thinking and communication.

Some Basic Units of Thought

At its most basic, thinking is the **internal representation** of a problem or situation. (Picture a chess player who mentally tries out several possible moves before actually touching a chess piece.) The power of being able to internally represent problems is dramatically illustrated by Chess Grand Master Miguel Najdorf, who once simultaneously played 45 chess games, while *blindfolded.* It is estimated that over 3600 different positions arose during this exhibition.

How did Najdorf perform his feat? Like most people, he probably used the following basic units of thought: (1) **images,** (2) **concepts,** and (3) **language,** or **symbols.** All three ways of representing information

Synesthesia Experiencing one sense in ways normally associated with another sense; for example, "seeing" colors when a sound is heard.

Mental rotation The ability to change the position of an image in mental space.

may be combined in complex thinking. Indeed, in some situations people need all the help they can get. To accomplish their mental feats, blindfolded chess players rely on visual images, kinesthetic (muscular) images involving "lines of force," concepts ("Game 2 is an English opening"), and the special notational system, or "language," of chess.

In a moment we will explore the units of thought identified here. Be aware, however, that thinking involves attention, pattern recognition, memory, decision making, intuition, knowledge, and more. This chapter is only a sample of what cognitive psychologists study.

Mental Imagery—Does a Frog Have Lips?

Ninety-seven percent of all people have visual images and 92 percent have auditory images. Over 50 percent have imagery that includes movement, touch, taste, smell, and pain. When we speak of images, we usually think of mental "pictures" (Kosslyn, 1990). But as you can see, images may involve the other senses as well. For example, your image of a bakery may include its delicious odor, as well as its appearance.

Some people have a rare form of imagery called **synesthesia** (sin-es-THEE-zyah). For these individuals, images cross normal sensory barriers (Cytowic, 1993). For instance, a synesthetic individual listening to music may experience a burst of colors or tastes, as well as sound sensations. Despite such variations, it is generally accepted that most people use images to think, remember, and to solve problems (Kosslyn, 1990). Table 9–1 lists the most common uses for mental images.

Properties of Mental Images

In recent years Stephen Kosslyn and other researchers have added greatly to our understanding of mental imagery. For instance, Kosslyn discovered that mental images are not flat, like photographs. To sample Kosslyn's work, think about the following question: Does a frog have lips and a stubby tail? Unless you often kiss frogs, you will probably tackle this question by using mental images. To answer, most people report that they picture a frog, "look" at its mouth, and then **mentally rotate** the frog to check its tail (Kosslyn, 1983).

It can be seen that mental images of objects are not necessarily flat, and they can be moved about as needed (■ Fig. 9–2). As Highlight 9–1 explains, images of entire three-dimensional spaces may be created just from descriptions, like those in a novel.

Table 9–1 Common Uses of Mental Images

Mental images are most frequently used for the following purposes.
▪ **To make a decision or solve a problem.** *Examples:* Choosing what clothes to wear; figuring out how to arrange furniture in a room.
▪ **To help understand a verbal description.** *Examples:* Mentally picturing what a person is talking about; picturing a scene described in a novel.
▪ **To change feelings.** *Examples:* Thinking of pleasant images to get out of a bad mood; imagining oneself as thin to help stay on a diet.
▪ **To help explain or describe something.** *Example:* Visualizing a scene at a party to describe it to a friend.
▪ **To improve a skill or to prepare for some action.** *Examples:* Using images to improve a swimming stroke; mentally rehearsing how you will ask for a raise.
▪ **To aid memory.** *Example:* Picturing Mr. Cook wearing a chef's hat, so you can remember his name.

(Kosslyn et al., 1990).

HIGHLIGHT 9–1

Research Frontier

3-D Images—Now Showing in Imaginations Everywhere

Detective Psyche slowly pushed open the window and stepped into the dingy room. On the opposite wall, above a rumpled bed, a mirror reflected her image, startling her. "This is creepy," she thought. Psyche's eyes drifted from the mirror to the floor at her right. Was that someone's shadow spilling under the closed door?

When you read a description of a particular scene, how do you remember the locations of objects? Psychologists Nancy Franklin and Barbara Tversky (1990) believe that we don't merely remember words, such as "mirror above bed." Typically, they say, we form a mental model, or spatial image, of how objects are arranged. To explore the nature of such images, Franklin and Tversky had people read descriptions of realistic three-dimensional environments. Settings included an opera, a hotel lobby, a barn, a lagoon, and other sites. In each scene, five objects were located above, below, ahead, behind, and to the right or left of the person. In the barn scene, for example, the objects were a saddle, a rake, a pail, a lantern, and shears.

Subjects imagined themselves in each environment and were asked about the locations of the five objects. Periodically, they were asked to change position in the imagined scene ("Turn 90 degrees to the right" or "Face the pail"). Franklin and Tversky found that even though subjects were not told to form mental pictures, all used mental imagery to locate the objects. Most, in fact, reported that they mentally "turned" and "looked at" objects to answer questions about them.

Perhaps the most interesting finding was that it is easier to locate objects in some positions than in others. Subjects were quickest at locating objects above or below themselves. Next came objects in front, followed by objects behind themselves. Most difficult of all was finding objects placed to the right or left. This insight into how we construct mental images may aid the design of such things as airplane cockpits or nuclear power plant controls. For instance, to minimize confusion about the location of controls, it would be better to concentrate on the up-down dimension instead of right-left positioning.

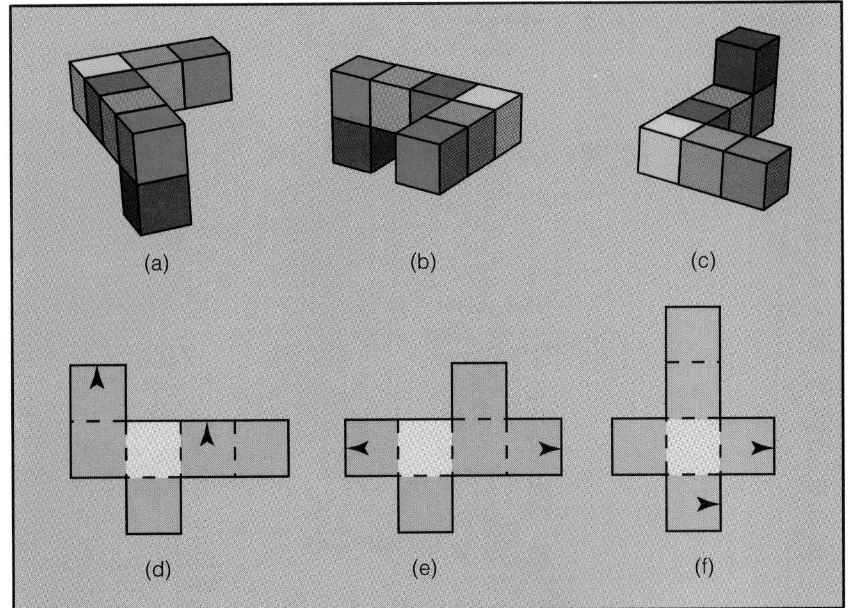

■ Fig. 9–2 *Imagery in thinking.* (Top) *Subjects were shown a drawing similar to* (a) *and drawings of how* (a) *would look in other positions, such as* (b) *and* (c). *Subjects could recognize* (a) *after it had been "rotated" from its original position. However, the more* (a) *was rotated in space, the longer it took to recognize it. This result suggests that subjects actually formed a three-dimensional image of* (a) *and rotated the image to see if it matched. (Shepard, 1975.)* (Bottom) *Try your ability to manipulate mental images: Each of these shapes can be folded to make a cube; in which do the arrows meet? (After Kosslyn, 1985.)*

Question: What happens in the brain when a person has visual images?

"Reverse Vision" Seeing something in your "mind's eye" is closely related to seeing real objects. Information from the eyes normally activates the primary visual area of the brain, creating an image (■ Fig. 9–3). Other brain areas then help us recognize the image by relating it to memories and stored knowledge. When you form a mental image, the system works in reverse. A stimulus, such as an odor, a song, or a question, activates memories in higher brain areas. These areas send signals back to the visual cortex, where once again, an image is created (Farah, 1988; Farah et al., 1989).

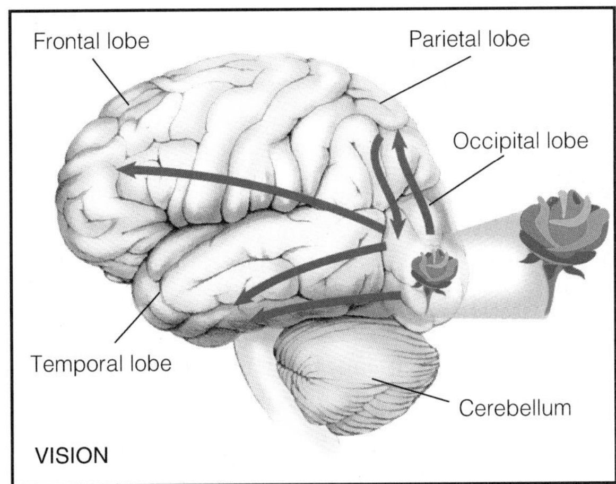

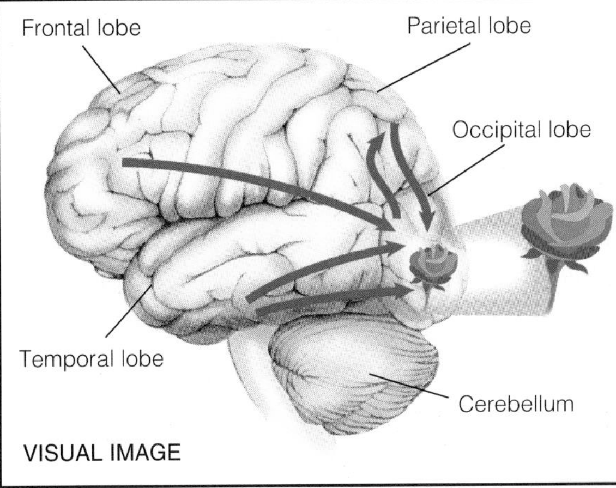

■ Fig. 9–3 *When you see a flower, its image is represented by activity in the primary visual area of the cortex, at the back of the brain. Information about the flower is also relayed to other brain areas. If you form a mental image of a flower, information follows a reverse path. The result, once again, is activation of the primary visual area.*

Question: How are images used to solve problems?

Using Mental Images **Stored images** can be retrieved from memory in order to apply prior experience to problem solving. If you were asked the question, "How many uses can you think of for an old automobile tire?" you might begin by picturing all the uses you have already seen. To generate more original solutions, **created images** may be used. Thus, an artist may completely picture a proposed sculpture before

Stored image A mental image retained in memory and retrieved when appropriate.

Created image A mental image that has been assembled or invented rather than simply remembered.

Kinesthetic imagery Images created by produced, remembered, or imagined muscular sensations.

Micromovements Tiny, nearly imperceptible movements associated with changes in muscle tension and activity.

■ **Fig. 9–4** *The* Church of the Sacred Family *in Barcelona, Spain, was designed by Antonio Gaudi. Could a person lacking mental imagery design such a masterpiece? Three people out of 100 find it impossible to produce mental images and 3 out of 100 have very strong imagery. Most artists, architects, designers, sculptors, and film makers have excellent visual imagery.*

beginning work (■ Fig. 9–4). Research shows that people who have good imaging abilities tend to score higher on tests of creativity (Shaw & Belmore, 1983). In fact, some of history's most original intellects relied heavily on mental images in their thinking. Examples include Albert Einstein, Thomas Edison, Lewis Carroll, and Winston Churchill (West, 1991).

Does the "size" of a mental image make any difference in thinking? To find out, first picture a cat sitting beside a housefly. Now try to "zoom in" on the cat's ears so you see them clearly. Next, picture a rabbit sitting beside an elephant. How quickly can you "see" the rabbit's front feet? Did it take longer than picturing the cat's ears?

When a rabbit is pictured with an elephant, the rabbit's image must be small because the elephant is large. Using such tasks, Kosslyn (1975) found that the smaller an image is, the harder it is to "see" its details. To put this finding to use, try forming over-sized images of things you want to think about. For example, to understand electricity, picture the wires as large pipes with electrons the size of golf balls moving through them; to understand the human ear, explore it (in your mind's eye) like a large cave; and so forth.

Kinesthetic Imagery

Question: How do muscular responses relate to thinking?

It is surprising to realize that, in a sense, we think with our bodies as well as our heads. We often represent things in a kind of **kinesthetic imagery** created by actions or *implicit* (unexpressed) actions (Oyama & Ichikawa, 1990). For example, people who "talk" with their hands are using gestures to help themselves think as well as to communicate.

A great deal of information is contained in kinesthetic sensations (feelings from the muscles and joints). As a person talks, these sensations help structure the flow of ideas. If you try to tell a friend how to knead bread dough, you may find it impossible to resist moving your hands as you describe the proper motion. Or, try answering this question: Which direction must you turn the hot water handle in your kitchen to turn the water off? Most people have not simply memorized the words "Turn it clockwise," or "Turn it counterclockwise." Instead you will probably "turn" the faucet in your imagination before answering. You may even find yourself making the hand motions required for turning the handle before you answer.

Kinesthetic images are especially important in music, sports, dance, martial arts, and other movement-oriented skills. People with good kinesthetic imagery learn such skills faster than those with poor imagery (Goss et al., 1986).

Most thinking is accompanied by muscular tension and **micromovements** throughout the body. In one classic study, a man was asked to imagine that he was hitting a nail with a hammer. As he did, a burst of activity was recorded in the muscles of his unmoving arm (Jacobson, 1932). The same thing happens when weight lifters imagine lifting a dumbbell (Hale, 1982). If you would like to demonstrate the link between muscular activity and thinking, ask a friend who was in a sports event to describe what occurred. Along with a description, you will probably get an "instant replay" of the high points!

Concepts—I'm Positive, It's a Whatchamacallit

A **concept** is an idea that represents a class of objects or events. Concepts are powerful tools because they allow us to think more *abstractly*, free from distracting details. Imagine, for instance, that you have shown a five-year-old child two big toy frogs and four little frogs. You then ask the child, "Are there more frogs or more baby frogs?" When kindergarten children were asked this question, most erred and said, "More baby frogs."

Then the concept of a *family* was brought into the problem ("This is a family of frogs. Are there more frogs or more baby frogs?") Adding the concept dramatically reduced the children's thinking errors (Markman & Seibert, 1976).

Question: How are concepts learned?

Concept Formation

Concept formation is the process of classifying information into meaningful categories. At its most basic, concept formation is based on experience with **positive** and **negative instances** of the concept. This is not as simple as it might seem. Imagine a child learning the concept of *dog.*

Dog Daze

A child and her father go for a walk. At a neighbor's house, they see a medium-sized dog. The father says, "See the dog." As they pass the next yard, the child sees a cat and says, "Dog!" Her father corrects her, "No, that's a *cat.*" The child now thinks, "Aha, dogs are large and cats are small." In the next yard, she sees a Pekingese and says, "Cat!" "No, that's a dog," replies her father.

The child's confusion is understandable. At first she might even mistake a Pekingese for a dust mop. However, with more positive and negative instances, the child will eventually recognize everything from Great Danes to Chihuahuas as examples of the same category—dogs.

As adults, we more often acquire concepts by learning or forming **rules.** For example, a *triangle* must be a closed shape with three sides made of straight lines. Rule learning is generally more efficient than examples, but examples remain important (Rosenthal & Zimmerman, 1978). It is unlikely that memorizing a series of rules would allow an uninitiated listener to accurately categorize *punk, hip hop, fusion, salsa, heavy metal, grunge rock,* and *rap* music.

Types of Concepts

Question: Are there different kinds of concepts?

Yes, several general types of concepts have been identified. A **conjunctive concept** refers to a class of objects having more than one feature in common. Conjunctive concepts are sometimes called "and" concepts: To belong to the concept class, an item must have "this feature *and* this feature *and* this feature." For example, a *motorcycle* must have two wheels *and* an engine *and* handle bars.

Relational concepts classify objects on the basis of their relationship to something else or by the relationship between features of an object. *Larger, above, left, north,* and *upside down* are all relational concepts. Another example is *sister,* which is defined as "a female considered in her relation to another person having the same parents."

Disjunctive concepts refer to objects that have at least one of several possible features. These are "either-or concepts." To belong, an item must have "this feature *or* that feature *or* another feature." For example, in the game of baseball, a *strike* is *either* a swing and a miss *or* a pitch down the middle *or* a foul ball. The either-or quality of disjunctive concepts makes them difficult to learn.

Prototypes When you think of the concept *bird,* do you make a mental list of features that birds have? Probably not. In addition to rules and features, we frequently use **prototypes,** or ideal models, to identify concepts (Rosch, 1977; Smith, 1989). A robin, for instance, is a model bird, whereas an ostrich is not. What this tells us is that not all examples of a concept are equally representative. For example, which of the drawings in ■ Figure 9–5 best represents a cup? At some point, a cup that is made taller or wider becomes a vase or a bowl. How do we know when the line is crossed? Probably, we mentally compare objects to an "ideal" cup, like number 5. The upshot is that identifying concepts is difficult when we cannot come up with a prototype relevant to what we see. What, for example, are the objects shown in ■ Figure 9–6?

Connotative Meaning Generally speaking, concepts have two types of meaning. The **denotative meaning** of a word or concept is its exact definition. The **connotative meaning** is its emotional or personal meaning. For example, the denotative meaning of the word *naked* (having no clothes) is the same for a nudist as it is for a movie censor, but we could expect their connotations to differ.

Question: Can you give a clearer statement of what a connotative meaning is?

■ **Fig. 9–5** *When does a cup become a bowl or a vase? Deciding if an object belongs to a conceptual class is aided by relating it to a prototype, or ideal example. Subjects in one experiment chose number 5 as the "best" cup. (After Labov, 1973.)*

Concept formation The process of classifying information into meaningful categories by direct experience, rule learning, or exposure to prototypes (idealized models).

Positive instance In concept learning, an object or event that belongs to the concept class.

Negative instance In concept learning, an object or event that does not belong to the concept class.

Conceptual rule A formal rule for deciding if an object or event is an example of a particular concept.

Conjunctive concept A class of objects that have two or more features in common. (For example, to qualify as an example of the concept an object must be both red *and* triangular.)

Relational concept A concept defined by the relationship between features of an object or between an object and its surroundings (for example, "greater than," "lopsided").

Disjunctive concept A concept defined by the presence of at least one of several possible features. (For example, to qualify an object must be either blue *or* circular.)

Prototype An ideal, or model, used as a prime example of a particular concept.

Denotative meaning The exact, dictionary definition of a word or concept; its objective meaning.

Connotative meaning The subjective, personal, or emotional meaning of a word or concept.

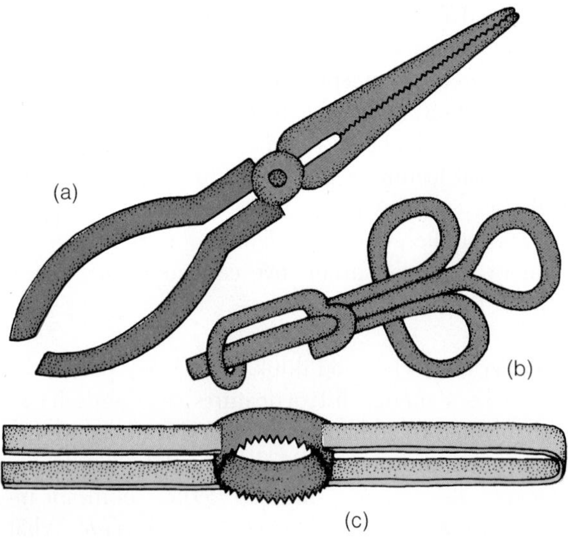

■ **Fig. 9–6** *Use of prototypes in concept identification. Even though its shape is unusual, item* (a) *can be related to a model (an ordinary set of pliers) and thus recognized. But what are items* (b) *and* (c)*? If you don't recognize them, look ahead to Fig. 9–8. (After Bransford & McCarrell, 1977.)*

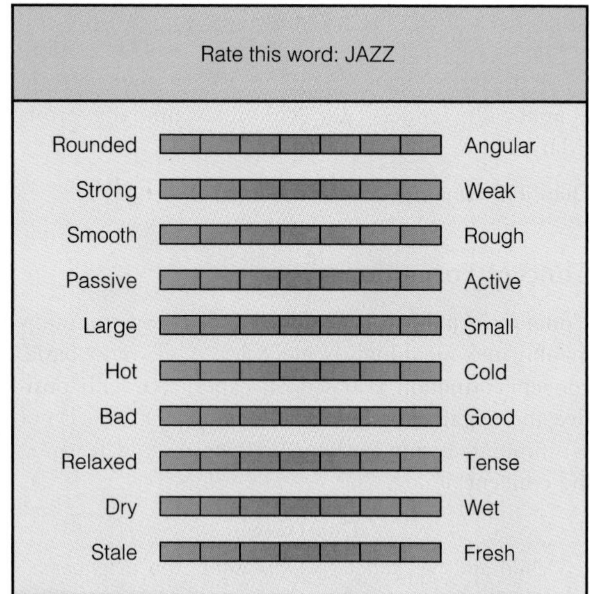

■ **Fig. 9–7** *This is an example of Osgood's semantic differential. The connotative meaning of the word* jazz *can be established by rating it on the scales. Mark your own rating by placing dots or X's in the spaces. Connect the marks with a line; then have a friend rate the word and compare your responses. It might be interesting to do the same for* rock and roll, disco, *and* classical. *You also might want to try the word* psychology. *(From C. E. Osgood. Copyright © 1952 American Psychological Association. Reprinted by permission.)*

Semantic differential A measure of connotative meaning obtained by rating words or concepts on several dimensions.

Researcher Charles Osgood used a method called the **semantic differential** to measure connotative meaning (■ Fig. 9–7). When words or concepts are rated on a series of scales, most of their connotative meaning boils down to the dimensions *good-bad, strong-weak,* and *active-passive.* (Sounds like a good movie title, doesn't it: *The Good the Bad the Strong the Weak the Active and the Passive.*) Because concepts vary on these dimensions, words or phrases with roughly the same denotative meaning may have very different connotations. For example, I am *conscientious;* you are *careful;* he is *nit-picking!*

Learning Check

1. List three basic units of thought:
   ____________ ____________ ____________
2. Synesthesia is the use of kinesthetic sensations as a vehicle for thought. T or F?
3. Humans appear capable of forming three-dimensional images that can be moved or rotated in mental space. T or F?
4. When a person forms a three-dimensional image of an environment, it is easiest to remember if an object is placed to the right or left of center. T or F?
5. Our reliance on imagery in thinking means that problem solving is impaired by micromovements. T or F?
6. A *mup* is defined as anything that is small, blue, and hairy. *Mup* is a ____________ concept.
7. The connotative meaning of the word *naked* is "having no clothes." T or F?

Critical Thinking

8. It takes longer to answer the question, "Does a frog have lips and a stubby tail?" than the question, "Does a frog have lips?" Can you think of an explanation other than mental rotation to explain this difference?
9. A Democrat and a Republican are asked to rate the word *democratic* on the semantic differential. Under what conditions would their ratings be most alike?

Answers: 1. images, concepts, and language or symbols (others could be listed) 2. F 3. T 4. F 5. F 6. conjunctive 7. F 8. The first question could simply be more difficult. The difficulty of questions must be carefully matched in studies of mental imagery. 9. If they both assume the word refers to a form of government, not a political party or a candidate.

Language—Don't Leave Home without It

As we have seen, thinking sometimes takes place without language. Everyone has had the experience of searching for a word to express an idea that exists as a vague image or feeling. Nevertheless, most thinking leans heavily on language, because it allows the world to be **encoded** into symbols that are easy to manipulate.

Study of the meaning of words and language is called **semantics.** It is here that the link between language and thought becomes most evident. Suppose, on an intelligence test, you were asked to circle the word that does not belong in this series:

SKYSCRAPER CATHEDRAL TEMPLE PRAYER

If you circled *prayer*, you answered as most people do. Now try another problem, again circling the odd item:

CATHEDRAL PRAYER TEMPLE SKYSCRAPER

Had you seen only this question, you probably would have circled *skyscraper*. There is a subtle change in meaning caused by reordering the words (Judson & Cofer, 1956, cited by Mayer, 1992).

Semantic problems often arise when a word has dual, or unclear, meaning: Does the sentence "Tom was seated by the waiter" mean the waiter gave Tom a seat? Or that Tom was seated beside the waiter? Choice of words may directly influence thought by shifting meaning: Has one country's army "invaded" another? Or "effected a protective incursion"? Is the city reservoir "half full" or "half empty"? Would you rather eat "prime beef" or "dead cow"?! (See ■ Fig. 9–9.)

Cross-culturally, semantic problems often arise when one language is translated into another. Perhaps the San Jose, California, public library can be excused for displaying a large banner that was supposed to say, "You are welcome" in a native Philippine language.

■ **Fig. 9–8** *Context can substitute for a lack of appropriate prototypes in concept identification.*

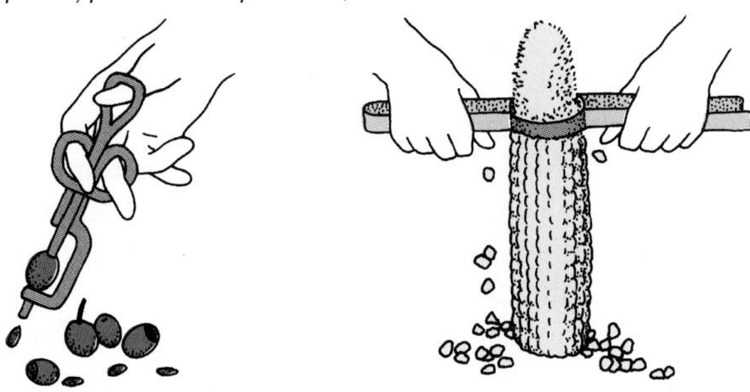

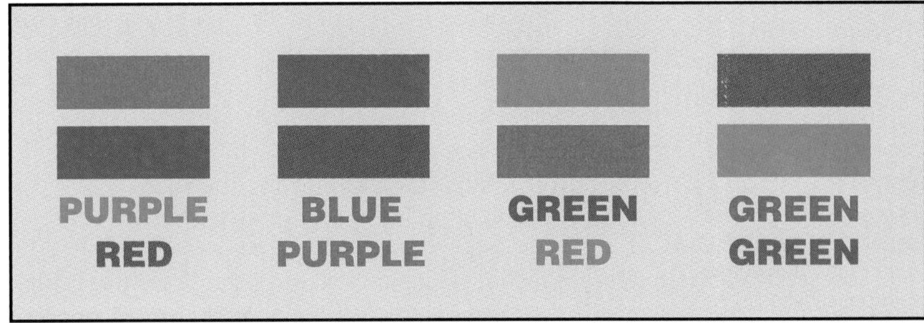

■ **Fig. 9–9** *The Stroop interference task. Test yourself by naming the colors in the top two rows as quickly as you can. Then name the colors of the ink used to print the words in the bottom two rows (do not read the words themselves). The greater difficulty of naming colors in the bottom rows shows how intimately thought is linked to language. The meaning of words has a powerful impact on our response to them. (After Tzeng & Wang, 1983.)*

The banner actually meant, "You are circumcised." Likewise, we may forgive Pepsi for translating "Come alive, you Pepsi generation," into Thai as "Pepsi brings your ancestors back from the dead." However, in more important circumstances, such as in international diplomacy, avoiding semantic confusion may be vital.

Question: What does it take to make a language?

The Structure of Language First of all, a language must provide *symbols* that can stand for objects and ideas. The symbols we call words are built out of **phonemes** (FOE-neems: basic speech sounds) and **morphemes** (MOR-feems: speech sounds collected into meaningful units, such as syllables or words). For instance, in English the sounds *m, b, w,* and *a* cannot form a syllable *mbwa*. In Swahili, they can. The units of speech can be arranged in countless ways. Consider the possibilities with just four morphemes: *reach, to, able,* and *un*. From these, we can make *able to, unable to, reach to, to reach, able to reach, unable to reach, reachable, unreachable, reachable to, unreachable to, unto, unto Able.*

As a second point, a language must have a **grammar,** or set of rules, for making sounds into words and words into sentences. One part of grammar, known as **syntax,** consists of rules for word order in sentences. Syntax is important because rearranging words almost always changes the meaning of a sentence: "Dog bites man" versus "Man bites dog."

Traditional grammar is concerned with "surface" language—the sentences we actually speak. The revolutionary ideas of linguist Noam Chomsky focus instead on the unspoken rules we use to change core ideas into various sentences. Chomsky (1986) argues that we do not learn all the sentences we might ever say. Rather, we actively *create* them by applying **transformation rules** to universal, core patterns. Such rules allow us to change a simple sentence into other voices or forms. For example, the core sentence "Dog bites

Encoding Changing information into a form that allows it to be stored in memory and manipulated in thought.

Semantics The study of meanings in language.

Phonemes The basic speech sounds of a language.

Morphemes The smallest meaningful units in a language, such as syllables or words.

Grammar A set of rules for combining language units into meaningful speech or writing.

Syntax Rules for ordering words when forming sentences.

Transformation rules Rules for changing a simple declarative sentence to other voices or forms (past tense, passive voice, and so forth).

American Sign Language A language system of hand gestures used by deaf and hearing-impaired persons.

Productivity The capacity of language for generating new ideas and possibilities.

man" can be transformed to the following patterns (and others as well):

Past: The dog bit the man.
Passive: The man was bitten by the dog.
Negative: The dog did not bite the man.
Question: Did the dog bite the man?

Children show evidence of using transformation rules when they form sentences such as "I runned home." The child has applied the past tense rule to the irregular verb *to run*.

There is a tendency to think of languages only as systems of spoken sounds and written symbols. However, as Highlight 9–2 explains, language is not limited to speech.

■ **Fig. 9–10** *ASL has only 3000 root signs, compared with roughly 600,000 words in English. However, variations in signs make ASL a highly expressive language. For example, the sign LOOK-AT can be varied in ways to make it mean look at me, look at her, look at each, stare at, gaze, watch, look for a long time, look at again and again, reminisce, sightsee, look forward to, predict, anticipate, browse, and many more variations.*

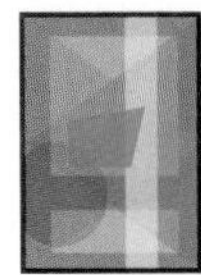

HIGHLIGHT 9–2

Cultural Diversity

A Voice for the Deaf

At age 24, Ildefonso, who was born deaf, had never communicated with another human, except by mime. Then at last, after much hard work with a sign language teacher, Ildefonso had a breakthrough: He understood the link between a cat and the gesture for it. At that magic moment, he grasped that the idea "cat" could be communicated to another person, just by signing the word. For Ildefonso, it marked the end of his terrible isolation from others.

Ildefonso's long-awaited breakthrough was made possible by **American Sign Language** (ASL). Contrary to what many people think, ASL is not pantomime or a code. It is a true language, like German, Spanish, or Japanese. In fact, ASL is not understood by those who use other gestural languages, such as French Sign, Chinese Sign, Yiddish Sign, or Old Kentish Sign.

In the hands of a master, sign can be rigorous, poetic, philosophical, and analytic. For some expressions, it is superior to speech. In the last 10 years psychologists and linguists have realized that our biological tendency to learn a language does not specify if it should be spoken or gestural. Similar universal language patterns are evident in both speech and sign. Of course, ASL has a *spatial* grammar, syntax, and semantics all its own (■ Fig. 9–10). Just the same, signing children pass through the same stages of language development at about the same age as speaking children do.

Sign languages naturally arise out of a need to communicate visually. But they also embody a personal identity and define a distinct community. Sign is the true voice of the deaf and hearing impaired. Those who "speak" sign share not just a language, but a rich culture as well. (Sources: Meier, 1991; Petitto & Marentette, 1991; Sacks, 1990; Schaller, 1991)

The third, and perhaps most essential, characteristic of language is that it is **productive.** The great strength of any true language is that it can produce new thoughts or ideas. Because symbols do not resemble the things they represent, words or signs can be rearranged to produce an infinite variety of meaningful sentences. Some are silly: "Please don't feed me to the goldfish." Some are profound: "We hold these truths to be self-evident, that all men are created equal." In either case, it is the productive quality of language that makes it such a powerful tool for thought.

Question: Do animals use language?

Animals do communicate. The cries, gestures, and mating calls of animals have broad meanings immediately understood by other animals of the same species (Premack, 1983). For the most part, however, natural animal communication is quite limited. Even apes and monkeys make only a few dozen distinct cries, which carry messages such as "attack," "flee," or "food here." More importantly, animal communication seems to lack the productive quality of human language. For example, when a monkey gives an "eagle distress call," it means something like, "I see an eagle." The monkey has no way of saying, "I don't see an eagle," or "Thank heavens that wasn't an eagle," or "That sucker I saw yesterday was some huge eagle" (Glass et al., 1979).

Question: Could an animal be taught to use language?

Psychologists have made several interesting attempts to teach animals to use language. Let's consider some of their successes and failures.

Talking Chimps

Early attempts to teach chimps to talk were a dismal failure. The world record was held by Viki, a chimp who could say only four words (*mama, papa, cup,* and *up*) after six years of intensive training (Fleming, 1974; Hayes, 1951). (Actually, all four words sounded something like a belch.) Obviously, chimps lack the vocal control needed to speak. The first real success came when Beatrice and Allen Gardner realized that chimps might be able to learn a gestural language. Using operant conditioning and imitation, the Gardners set out to teach a female chimp named Washoe to use American Sign Language.

To the Gardners' delight, Washoe's communication skills blossomed rapidly as her vocabulary grew. Soon she began to put together primitive sentence strings like "Come-gimme sweet," "Out please," "Gimme tickle," and "Open food drink." Washoe has a vocabulary of about 240 signs and can put together six-word sentences (Gardner & Gardner, 1969; Rose, 1984).

A female chimp named Sarah was another well-known pupil of human language. David Premack (1970) taught Sarah to use 130 "words" consisting of plastic chips arranged on a magnetized board (■ Fig. 9–11). From the beginning of her training, Sarah was required to use proper word order. She learned to answer questions, to label things "same" or "different," to classify objects by color, shape, and size, and to construct compound sentences (Premack & Premack, 1983). One of Sarah's most outstanding achievements was the use of sentences involving **conditional relationships:** "If Sarah take apple, then Mary give Sarah chocolate." "If Sarah take banana, then Mary no give Sarah chocolate."

Question: Can it be said with certainty that the chimps understand such interchanges?

Most researchers working with chimps believe that they have indeed communicated with them. Especially striking are the chimps' spontaneous responses. Washoe once "wet" on psychologist Roger Fouts' back while riding on his shoulders. When Fouts asked, with some annoyance, why she had done it, Washoe signed, "It's funny!"

■ **Fig. 9–11** *After reading the message "Sarah insert apple pail banana dish" on the magnetic board, Sarah performed the actions as directed. (From "Teaching Language to an Ape" by Ann J. Premack and David Premack. Copyright © 1972 by Scientific American, Inc. All rights reserved.)*

Criticisms Such interchanges are impressive. But communication and actual language use are two different things. Several psychologists have expressed doubt that apes can really use language. For one thing, the chimps rarely "speak" without prompting. Many of their seemingly original sentences turn out to be responses to questions or imitations of signs the teacher made. Also, it appears that the apes may be simply performing chains of *operant responses* to get food, play, or other "goodies" (Savage-Rumbaugh et al., 1979; Terrace, 1985). By using such responses, the apes then manipulate their trainers to get what they want.

Conditional statement A statement that contains a qualification, often of the *if-then* form.

You might say that the critics think that the apes have made monkeys out of their trainers. However, psychologists Roger and Debbi Fouts believe they can answer such criticisms. An analysis they performed of some 6000 conversations between chimps showed that only 5 percent had anything to do with food. The Fouts also videotaped conversations between chimps that took place when no humans were present to cue them (Fouts et al., 1984). Another recent study of chimps using a special symbol system (described in the next section) found that the chimps do not merely imitate humans. During "conversations" with humans, the chimps use symbols to express agreement, excitement, to make requests or promises, and to select alternatives. In short, they hold real conversations, in which information is exchanged symbolically (Greenfield & Savage-Rumbaugh, 1993). So, maybe the chimps will make monkeys out of the critics.

Lexigram A geometric shape used as a symbol for a word.

Mechanical solution A problem solution achieved by trial and error or by a fixed procedure.

Problems with Syntax At this point, numerous chimps, a gorilla named Koko, and an assortment of dolphins and sea lions have learned to communicate with word symbols of various kinds. Yet, even if some criticisms can be answered, linguists such as Noam Chomsky remain unconvinced that animals can truly use language. The core issue is that problems with syntax (word order) have plagued almost all animal language experiments. For example, when a chimp named Nim Chimpsky (no relation to Chomsky) wanted an orange, he would typically signal a grammarless string of words: "Give orange me give eat orange me eat orange give me eat orange give me you." This might be communication, but it is not language.

Recently, the flames of controversy have been fanned again by Kanzi, a pygmy chimpanzee studied by Duane Rumbaugh and Sue Savage-Rumbaugh. Kanzi communicates using gestures and push-buttons on a computer keyboard. Each of the 250 buttons is marked with a **lexigram**, or geometric word-symbol (■ Fig. 9–12). Using the lexigrams, Kanzi can create primitive sentences several words long. He can also understand about 650 spoken sentences. During testing, Kanzi hears spoken words over headphones, so his caretakers cannot prompt him (Savage-Rumbaugh et al., 1990).

Kanzi's sentences consistently follow correct word order. His syntax is good even for new word combinations he has never made before. Like a child learning language, Kanzi picked up some ordering rules from his caregivers. However, he has developed other patterns on his own. For example, Kanzi almost always places two action symbols in the order he wants to carry them out, such as "chase tickle" or "chase hide." That is, he uses symbols to plan and communicate the order of actions. Psycholinguist Patricia Marks Greenfield says that Kanzi's use of grammar is on a par with that of a 2-year-old child (Savage-Rumbaugh et al., 1993).

■ **Fig. 9–12** *Kanzi's language learning has been impressive. He can comprehend spoken English words. He can identify lexigram symbols when he hears corresponding words. He can use lexigrams when the objects they refer to are absent and he can, if asked, lead someone to the object. All these skills were acquired through observation, not conditioning (Savage-Rumbaugh et al., 1990).*

Kanzi's ability to invent a simple grammar may help us better understand the roots of human language. It is certainly the strongest answer yet to the critics. On the other hand, Chomsky insists that if chimps were biologically capable of language they would have made use of it on their own. Although the issue is far from resolved, such research promises to unravel some of the mysteries of language learning. In fact, it has already been helpful for teaching language to aphasic children (children with serious language impairment) and severely retarded children (Savage-Rumbaugh et al., 1990).

Problem Solving—Getting an Answer in Sight

We have reviewed some of the basic ways that we mentally represent information so that it can be manipulated and used to solve problems. It is now time to take a direct look at problem solving. A good way to start is to solve a problem. Give this one a try.

> A famous ocean liner (the *Queen Ralph*) is steaming toward port at 20 miles per hour. It is 50 miles from shore when a sea gull takes off from its deck and flies toward port. At the same instant, a speedboat leaves port at 30 miles per hour. The bird flies back and forth between the speedboat and the *Queen Ralph* at a speed of 40 miles per hour. How far will the bird have flown when the two boats pass?

If you don't immediately see the answer to this problem, read it again. (The answer is revealed shortly in Insightful Solutions.)

We all do a tremendous amount of problem solving every day. Problem solving can be as commonplace as figuring out how to make a non-poisonous meal out of leftovers or as significant as developing a cure for cancer. In either case, we begin with an awareness that an answer probably exists and that by proper thinking, a solution can be found. A number of different approaches to problem solving can be identified.

Mechanical Solutions

A **mechanical solution** may be achieved by **trial and error** or by **rote.** If I forget the combination to my bike lock, I may be able to discover it by trial and error. In an era of high-speed computers, many trial-and-error solutions are best left to machines. A computer could generate all possible combinations of the five numbers

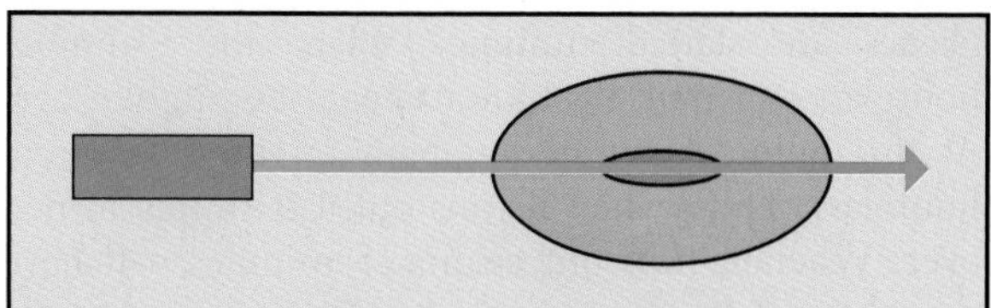

■ **Fig. 9–13** *A schematic representation of Duncker's tumor problem. The dark spot represents a tumor surrounded by healthy tissue. How can the tumor be destroyed without injuring surrounding tissue? (After Duncker, 1945.)*

on my lock in a split second. (Of course it would take me a long time to try them all.)

When a problem is solved by rote, thinking is guided by a learned set of rules. If you have a good background in mathematics, you may have solved the problem of the bird and the boats by rote. I hope you didn't. There is an easier solution.

Solutions by Understanding

Many problems cannot be solved mechanically or by habitual modes of thought. In this case, a higher level of thinking based on **understanding** is necessary. A classic series of studies on thinking of this type was performed by German psychologist Karl Duncker (1945). Duncker gave college students this problem:

> A person has an inoperable stomach tumor. A device is available that produces rays which at high intensity will destroy tissue (both healthy and diseased). How can the tumor be destroyed without damaging surrounding tissue? (Students were also shown the sketch in ■ Fig. 9–13.)

Question: What did this problem show about problem solving?

Duncker asked the students to think aloud as they worked, and found that there were two phases to successful problem solving. First, students had to discover the **general properties** of a correct solution. This phase was complete when they realized that the intensity of the rays had to be lowered on their way to the tumor. Then, in the second phase, they proposed a number of **functional** (workable) **solutions** and selected the best one. (One correct solution is to focus weak rays on the tumor from several angles. Another solution is to rotate the person's body so that the exposure of healthy tissue is minimized.)

It might help to summarize with a more familiar example. Almost everyone who has tried the Rubik's cube puzzle begins at the mechanical, *trial-and-error* level. If you want to take the easy route, printed instructions are available that give the steps for a *rote* solution. In time, those who persist begin to *understand* the *general properties* of the puzzle. After that, they can solve it consistently.

Heuristics

"You can't get there from here." Or so it often seems when facing a problem. Solving problems often requires a strategy. If the number of alternatives is small, a **random search strategy** may work. This is another example of trial-and-error problem solving in which all possibilities are tried. Imagine, for example, that you are traveling and decide to look up an old friend, J. Smith, in a city you are visiting. You open the phone book and find 47 J. Smiths listed. Of course, you could dial each number until you find the right one. "Forget it," you say to yourself. "Is there any way I can narrow the search?" "Oh, yeah! I remember hearing that Janet lives by the beach." Then you take out a map and call only the numbers with addresses near the waterfront (Ellis & Hunt, 1983).

The approach used in this example is a **heuristic** (hew-RIS-tik) or problem-solving strategy. Typically, a heuristic is a "rule of thumb" that reduces the number of alternatives that a thinker must consider. This raises the odds of success, although it does not guarantee a solution can be found. Nevertheless, heuristics certainly help. Here are some strategies that often work:

- Try to identify how the current state of affairs differs from the desired goal. Then find steps that will reduce the difference.
- Try working backward from the desired goal to the starting point or current state.
- If you can't reach the goal directly, try to identify an intermediate goal or subproblem that at least gets you closer.
- Represent the problem in other ways, with graphs, diagrams, or analogies, for instance.
- Generate a possible solution and test it. Doing so may eliminate many alternatives, or it may clarify what is needed for a solution.

Ideal Problem Solving Perhaps the most valuable heuristic of all is having a *general* thinking strategy. Psychologist John Bransford and his colleagues list five steps that they believe lead to effective problem solving: **i**dentify, **d**efine, **e**xplore, **a**ct, and **l**ook and learn (Bransford et al., 1986; Bransford & Stein, 1984). Notice that the first letters of the steps spell *ideal.*

To apply the ideal thinking strategy you should *identify* the problem, *define* it clearly, and then *explore* possible solutions and relevant knowledge. Next, you must *act* by trying a possible solution or hypothesis. Finally, you should *look* at the results and *learn* from them. Of course, each attempted solution may identify further subproblems. These can again be tackled with

General solution A solution that states the requirements for success, but not in enough detail for further action.

Functional solution A detailed, practical, and workable solution.

Random search strategy Trying possible solutions to a problem in a more or less random order.

Heuristic Any strategy or technique that aids problem solving, especially by limiting the number of possible solutions to be tried.

A sudden mental reorganization of a problem that makes the solution obvious.

Selective encoding Selecting information relevant to a problem while ignoring useless or distracting information.

Selective combination The ability to connect seemingly unrelated items of information.

Selective comparison The ability to relate a present problem to similar problems solved in the past or to prior experience.

Fixation The tendency to repeat wrong solutions or faulty responses, especially as a result of becoming blind to alternatives.

Functional fixedness A rigidity in problem solving caused by an inability to see new uses for familiar objects.

the "ideal" steps until a final satisfactory solution is found.

Insightful Solutions During problem solving we say that **insight** has occurred when an answer suddenly appears after a period of unsuccessful thought. An insight is usually so *rapid* and *clear* that we often wonder how the solution could have been missed. Insight usually involves a reorganization of the elements of a problem. Seeing the problem in a new way makes its solution seem obvious.

Let's return now to the problem of the boats and the bird. The best way to solve it is by insight. Because the boats will cover the 50-mile distance in exactly one hour, and the bird flies 40 miles per hour, the bird will have flown 40 miles when the boats meet. No math is necessary if you have insight into this problem.

In an interesting experiment, college students rated how "warm" (close to an answer) they felt while solving insight problems. Students who had insights usually jumped directly from "cold" to the correct answer. In contrast, those who gradually felt "warmer" and then "very warm" usually gave wrong answers (Metcalfe, 1986). The surprising message in this study is that you may be headed for a mistake if an insight is *not* rapid.

Question: What, really, does it mean to have an insight?

The Nature of Insight Psychologists Robert Sternberg and Janet Davidson (1982) have studied people as they solve problems that require insight or "leaps of logic." According to them, insight involves three abilities. The first is **selective encoding,** which refers to selecting information that is relevant to a problem, while ignoring distractions. For example, consider the following problem:

> If you have white socks and black socks in your drawer, mixed in the ratio of 4 to 5, how many socks will you have to take out to make sure of having a pair of the same color?

A person who fails to recognize that "mixed in a ratio of 4 to 5" is irrelevant information will be less likely to come up with the correct answer of three socks.

Insight also relies on **selective combination,** or bringing together seemingly unrelated bits of useful information. Try this sample problem:

> With a 7-minute hourglass and an 11-minute hourglass, what is the simplest way to time the boiling of an egg for 15 minutes?

The answer requires using both hourglasses in combination. First, the 7-minute and the 11-minute hourglasses are started running. When the 7-minute hourglass runs out, it's time to begin boiling the egg. At this point, 4 minutes remain on the 11-minute hourglass. Thus, when it runs out it is simply turned over. When it runs out again, 15 minutes will have passed.

A third source of insights is **selective comparison.** This is the ability to compare new problems with old information or with problems already solved. A good example is the hat rack problem, in which subjects must build a structure that can support an overcoat in the middle of a room. Each person is given only two long sticks and a C-clamp to work with. The solution, shown in ■ Figure 9–14, is to clamp the two sticks together so that they are wedged between floor and ceiling. If you were given this problem, you would be more likely to solve it if you first thought of the way pole lamps are wedged between floor and ceiling.

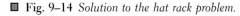

Fixations The ease with which problems are solved is related to a variety of factors. One of the most important barriers to problem solving is called **fixation.** Fixation is the tendency to get "hung up" on wrong solutions or to become blind to alternatives. A prime example of fixation is **functional fixedness.** Functional fixedness is the inability to see new uses (functions) for familiar objects or for objects that have been used in a particular way. If you have ever used a dime as a screwdriver, you've overcome functional fixedness.

Question: How does functional fixedness affect problem solving?

Karl Duncker, who coined the term *functional fixedness,* performed a clever study to demonstrate it. Duncker challenged students to mount a candle on a vertical board so that the candle could burn normally. Duncker gave each student three candles, some

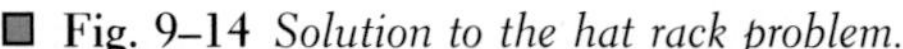

■ **Fig. 9–14** *Solution to the hat rack problem.*

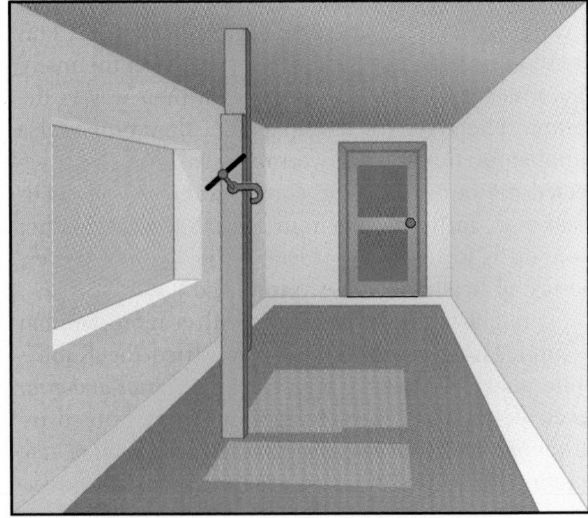

matches, some cardboard boxes, some thumbtacks, and other items. Half of Duncker's subjects received these items *inside* the cardboard boxes. The others were given all the items, including the boxes, spread out on a tabletop.

Duncker found that when the items were in the boxes, solving the problem was very difficult. This is because the boxes were seen as *containers*, not as items that might be part of the solution. (If you haven't guessed the solution, check ■ Fig. 9–15.) Undoubtedly, we could avoid many fixations if we took a more flexible approach to categorizing the world (Langer & Piper, 1987). For instance, creativity could be facilitated in Duncker's container problem by saying, "This *could be* a box," instead of, "This *is* a box."

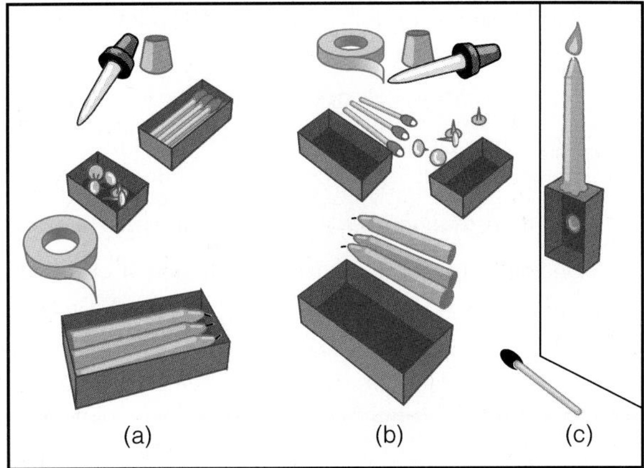

■ **Fig. 9–15** *Materials for solving the candle problem were given to subjects in boxes* (a) *or separately* (b). *Functional fixedness caused by condition* (a) *interfered with solving the problem. The solution to the problem is shown in* (c).

Common Barriers to Problem Solving

Functional fixedness is just one of the mental blocks that prevent insight. Here's an example of another: A $5 bill is placed on a table and a stack of objects is balanced precariously on top of the bill. How can the bill be removed without touching or moving the objects? A good answer is to split the bill on one of its edges. Gently pulling from opposite ends will tear the bill in half and remove it without toppling the objects. Many people fail to see this solution because they have learned not to destroy money (Adams, 1986). Notice again the impact of placing something in a category, in this case, "things of value" (which should not be destroyed). The list that follows identifies other common mental blocks and fixations that can hinder problem solving.

1. **Emotional barriers:** Inhibition and fear of making a fool of oneself, fear of making a mistake, inability to tolerate ambiguity, excessive self-criticism.

Example: An architect is afraid to try an unconventional design because she fears that other architects will think it is frivolous.

2. **Cultural barriers:** Values that hold that fantasy is a waste of time; that playfulness is for children only; that reason, logic, and numbers are good; that feelings, intuitions, pleasure, and humor are bad or have no value in the serious business of problem solving.

Example: A corporate manager wants to solve a business problem, but becomes stern and angry when members of his marketing team joke playfully about possible solutions.

3. **Learned barriers:** Conventions about uses (functional fixedness), meanings, possibilities, taboos.

Example: A cook doesn't have any clean mixing bowls and fails to see that he could use a frying pan as a bowl.

4. **Perceptual barriers:** Habits leading to a failure to identify important elements of a problem.

Example: A beginning artist concentrates on drawing a vase of flowers without seeing that the "empty" spaces around the vase are part of the composition, too.

In the last 10 years, studies of thinking have benefitted greatly from computer models of problem solving. Before we explore this topic, it might be a good idea to see if you can answer the following Learning Check questions (without help from a computer).

LEARNING CHECK

1. True languages are ________________ because they can be used to generate new possibilities.
2. The basic speech sounds are called ________________; the smallest meaningful units of speech are called ________________.
3. One of the chimpanzee Sarah's most outstanding achievements was the construction of sentences involving
   a. negation *b.* conditional relationships *c.* adult grammar *d.* unprompted questions
4. Critics consider "sentences" constructed by apes to be simple ________________ responses having little meaning to the animal.
5. Insight refers to rote, or trial-and-error, problem solving. T or F?

6. The first phase in problem solving by understanding is to discover the general properties of a correct solution. T or F?

7. Problem-solving strategies that guide the search for solutions are called ______________________ .

8. A common element underlying insight is that information is encoded, combined, and compared
a. mechanically *b.* by rote *c.* functionally *d.* selectively

9. The term *fixation* refers to the point at which a helpful insight becomes fixed in one's thinking. T or F?

Critical Thinking

10. Do you think that it is true that "a problem clearly defined is a problem half solved"?

Answers:

1. productive 2. phonemes, morphemes 3. *b* 4. operant 5. F 6. T 7. heuristics 8. *d* 9. F 10. Although that might be an overstatement, it is true that clearly defining a starting point and the desired goal can serve as a heuristic in problem solving.

Artificial intelligence Any artificial system (often a computer program) that is capable of human-like problem solving or intelligent responding.

Artificial Intelligence—I Compute, Therefore I Am

It's been a long time since Johann Sebastian Bach, the eighteenth-century German composer, last wrote any music. But listeners can be forgiven if they briefly mistake music created by Kemal Ebcioglu for Bach's work. Ebcioglu devised a computer program that writes harmonies remarkably similar to Bach's. Ebcioglu analyzed Bach's music and came up with 350 rules that govern the harmonization process. The resulting program displays what is known as *artificial intelligence.* Its compositions sound like reasonably good classical music. This shows the power of artificial intelligence. Small but glaring defects in the music and a certain lack of inspiration reveal its shortcomings (Maugh, 1988).

Artificial intelligence (AI) refers to computer programs capable of doing things that require intelligence when done by people (Best, 1992). Artificial intelligence is based on the fact that many tasks—from harmonizing music to medical diagnosis—can be reduced to a set of rules applied to a body of information. AI is valuable in situations where speed, vast memory, and persistence are required. In fact, AI programs are better at some tasks than humans.

AI and Cognition

Artificial intelligence provides a way to probe some of the oldest questions about the mind, such as how we comprehend language, make decisions, and solve problems. Increasingly, cognitive psychologists are using AI as a research tool in two basic ways: computer simulations and expert systems.

■ Fig. 9–16 *Two composers. The one on the left was a genius who wrote sublime, multi-voiced harmonies. The one on the right has created reasonably good, if uninspired, music. Computer models of thought can approximate intelligent human behavior. However, rule-based computer "thinking" still lacks the flexibility, creativity, and common sense of human intelligence.*

In **computer simulations,** programs are used to simulate human behavior, especially thinking, decision making, or problem solving. Here, the computer acts as a "laboratory" for testing models of cognition. If a computer program behaves as humans do (including making the same errors), then the program may be a good model of how we think (Mayer, 1992).

Most computer-based models of human problem solving are based on some form of **means-ends analysis.** In a means-ends analysis, the computer compares the current state of affairs to the desired end state (or goal). The program then searches for steps that can be taken to reduce this difference. After each step, the program tests to see if the difference is greater or less than before. This cycle is repeated until the problem is solved. Models such as this may seem removed from real life, but much human thinking and problem solving has a means-ends quality to it (Anderson, 1993). The following quotation provides an everyday example:

> I want to take my son to nursery school. What's the difference between what I have and what I want? Distance. What changes distance? My car. My car won't start. What is needed to make it start? A new battery. What has new batteries? An auto repair shop. I need to have the shop come to my house and put in a new battery. But the shop doesn't know I need a battery. What is the problem? Communication. What allows communication? A telephone. (And so on.) (Adapted from Newell & Simon, 1972)

Expert systems are a second major form of AI. Such programs display advanced knowledge of a specific topic or skill. Expert systems have demystified some areas of human ability by converting complex skills to clearly stated rules that a computer can follow. Expert systems have been created to predict the weather, to analyze geological formations, to diagnose disease, to tell when to buy and sell stocks, to play chess, to read text, to do psychotherapy, and to perform many other tasks.

Experts and Novices Working with artificial intelligence has helped especially to clarify differences between novices and experts. Research on chess masters, for example, shows that their skills are based on specific **organized knowledge** and **acquired strategies.** In other words, becoming a star performer does not come from some general strengthening of the mind. Master chess players don't necessarily have better memories than beginners (except for realistic chess positions). (See ■ Figure 9–17.) And, typically, they don't explore more moves ahead than lesser players.

What does set master players apart is their ability to recognize *patterns* that suggest what lines of play should be explored next (Best, 1992). This helps eliminate a large number of possible moves. The chess master, therefore, does not waste time exploring unproductive pathways. Experts are better able to see the true nature of problems and to define them in terms of general principles (Anderson, 1993).

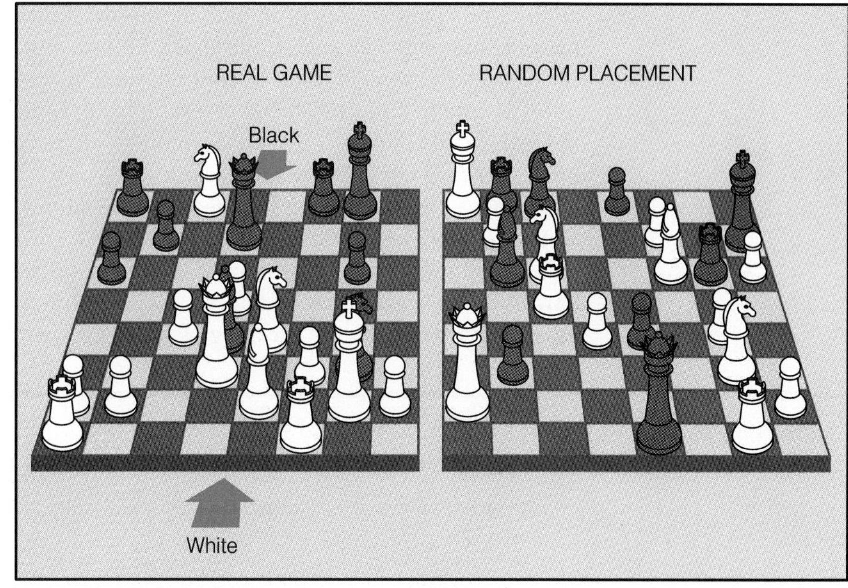

■ **Fig. 9–17** *The left chessboard shows a realistic game. The right chessboard is a random arrangement of pieces. Expert chess players can memorize the left board at a glance, yet they are no better than beginners at memorizing the random board. Expert performance at most thinking tasks is based on acquired strategies and knowledge. If you would like to excel at a profession or a mental skill, plan on adding to your knowledge every day (Holyoak, 1990).*

Expertise also allows more **automatic processing,** or fast, fairly effortless thinking based on experience with similar problems. Automatic processing frees attention and "space" in short-term memory that can be used to work on the problem. At the highest skill levels, expert performers tend to rise above a reliance on rules and plans. Their decisions, thinking, and actions become rapid and fluid. Thus, when a chess master recognizes a pattern on the chessboard, the most desirable tactic comes to mind almost immediately (Dreyfus & Dreyfus, 1986).

Limitations What the preceding tells us is that experts in one area do not automatically become better problem solvers elsewhere. Nor do they become generally smarter (Bransford et al., 1986). The same conclusion applies to artificial intelligence. Expert systems have been hailed as a possible remedy for human errors in tasks such as air traffic control, the operation of nuclear power plants, and the control of weapons systems. However, the truth is that expert systems are "idiot geniuses." They are very adept within a narrow range of problem solving, but they are "stone stupid" at everything else.

Eventually, AI may lead to robots that recognize voices and that speak and act "intelligently" (Best,

Computer simulations Computer programs that mimic some aspect of human thinking, decision making, or problem solving.

Means-ends analysis An analysis of how to reduce the difference between the present state of affairs and a desired goal.

Expert systems Computer programs designed to respond as a human expert would; programs based on the knowledge and rules that underlie human expertise in specific topics.

Organized knowledge Orderly and highly refined information about a particular topic or skill.

Acquired strategies Learned tactics for swiftly solving the problems encountered in one's area of expertise.

Automatic processing Thinking that can be done with little conscious effort or attention.

1992). But cognitive scientists are becoming aware that machine "intelligence" is ultimately "blind" outside its underlying set of rules. In contrast, human cognition is much more flexible. For example, u cann understnd wrds thet ar mizpeld. Computers are very literal and easily stymied by such errors.

Humans are able to take into account exceptions, context, and interpretations as they think. We also make commitments and take responsibility for our actions. A rule-driven expert system processes information without regard for the meaning of actions. Expert systems may never be able to anticipate the infinite number of possible events that could occur. As a result, their actions might be disastrous in unanticipated situations (Denning, 1988).

Clearly, artificial intelligence will play an increasingly visible role in cognitive research and in our lives. However, it is not likely to soon replace the human touch in many areas. Although Bach might have been fascinated by AI, it is doubtful that his musical magic will be eclipsed by a machine.

Learning Check

1. Two aspects of artificial intelligence are computer simulations and automatic processing. T or F?
2. Computer simulations are often used to test models of human cognition. T or F?
3. Organized knowledge, acquired strategies, and automatic processing are all characteristics of human expertise. T or F?
4. Expert systems can be described as broadly intelligent because their rules and heuristics apply to almost any problem solving situation. T or F?

Critical Thinking

5. Is it ever accurate to describe a machine as "intelligent"?

Answers: 1. F 2. T 3. T 4. F 5. As stated, rule-driven expert systems may appear "intelligent" within a narrow range of problem solving. However, they are idiots at everything else. This is usually not what we have in mind when discussing human intelligence.

Creative Thinking—Fluency, Flexibility, and Originality

As we have noted, problem solving may be the result of thinking that is mechanical, insightful, or based on understanding. To this we can add that thought may be **inductive** (going from specific facts or observations to general principles) or **deductive** (going from general principles to specific situations). Thinking may also be **logical** (proceeding from given information to new conclusions on the basis of explicit rules) or **illogical** (intuitive, associative, or personal).

Question: What distinguishes creative thinking from more routine problem solving?

Creative thinking involves all these styles of thought (in varying combinations) *plus* fluency, flexibility, and originality (Guilford, 1950). The meaning of these terms can be illustrated with an example. Let's say that you would like to find a creative use (or uses) for the millions of automobile tires discarded each year. The creativity of your suggestions could be rated in this way: **Fluency** is defined as the total number of suggestions you are able to make. **Flexibility** is defined as the number of times you shift from one class of possible uses to another. **Originality** refers to how novel or unusual your suggestions are. By totaling the number of times you showed fluency, flexibility, and originality, we could rate the creativity of your thinking on this problem. Speaking more generally, we would be rating your capacity for **divergent thinking** (Wallach, 1985).

Divergent thinking is the most widely used measure of creative problem solving. In routine problem solving or thinking, there is one correct answer, and the problem is to find it. This leads to **convergent**

Inductive thought Thinking in which a general rule or principle is inferred from a series of specific examples; for instance, inferring the laws of gravity by observing many falling objects.

Deductive thought Thought that applies a general set of rules to specific situations; for example, using the laws of gravity to predict the behavior of a single falling object.

Logical thought Drawing conclusions on the basis of formal principles of reasoning.

Illogical thought Thought that is intuitive, haphazard, or personal.

Fluency The total number of solutions produced on a test of creativity.

Flexibility The number of different types of solutions produced on a test of creativity.

Originality A rating of how novel or unusual problem solutions are.

Divergent thought Thinking that produces many ideas or alternatives.

Convergent thought Thinking directed toward discovery of a single established correct answer.

thought (lines of thought converge on the correct answer). Divergent thinking is the reverse, in which many possibilities are developed from one starting place (Wallach, 1985).

Divergent thinking is also a characteristic of daydreaming. Before we discuss divergent thinking further, let's take a brief detour into the realm of fantasy (if you're not there already).

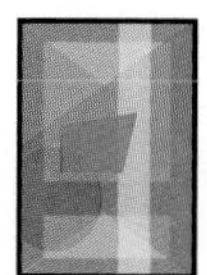

HIGHLIGHT 9–3

A Closer Look At

Daydreams, Fantasy, and Creativity

Has your reading of this chapter been interrupted by a **daydream?** Psychologist Eric Klinger (1990) fitted volunteers with electronic pagers and asked them to record what they were doing or thinking whenever he "beeped" them. Surprisingly, Klinger found that about half of our waking thoughts are occupied by daydreams. What do we know about this unique mental state?

Content In general, daydreams mirror our desires, fears, and anxieties in a fairly direct way. Eric Klinger says that, "When you're happy you have happy daydreams, when you're sad you have sad daydreams, and when you're angry you have angry daydreams." Because daydreams are fairly straightforward in meaning, they can be a good source of personal insights. Sleeping dreams, in contrast, tend to be more complex and difficult to analyze (Klinger, 1990).

Two of the most common daydream plots are the **conquering hero** and the **suffering martyr** themes. In a conquering hero fantasy, the daydreamer gets the starring role as a famous, rich, or powerful person: a celebrity, athlete, musician, famous surgeon, brilliant lawyer, or magnificent lover. Themes such as these seem to reflect needs for mastery and escape from the frustrations of everyday life. Suffering martyr daydreams center on feelings of being neglected, hurt, rejected, or unappreciated by others. In such fantasies, others end up regretting their past actions and realizing what a *wonderful person* the daydreamer was all along.

Benefits Daydreams often fill a need for stimulation during routine or boring tasks. They also improve our ability to delay immediate pleasures so that future goals can be achieved. And in everyday terms, fantasy can be an outlet for frustrated impulses. If you have a momentary urge to kill the fool in front of you on the highway, substituting fantasy for action may avert disaster (Biblow, 1973).

Perhaps the greatest value of fantasy is its contribution to creativity. In the imaginative realm of fantasy, nothing is impossible—a quality allowing for tremendous fluency and flexibility of thought. For most people, fantasy and daydreaming are associated with positive emotional adjustment, lower levels of aggression, and greater mental flexibility or creativity (Klinger, 1990; Singer, 1974). Perhaps this is why Albert Einstein was, in his own words, "disorderly and a dreamer."

Tests of Creativity

There are several tests of divergent thinking. In the **Unusual Uses Test,** a person is asked to think of as many uses for an object (such as the tires mentioned earlier) as possible. In the **Consequences Test,** the object is to answer a question such as, "What would be the results if everyone suddenly lost the sense of balance and could no longer stay in an upright position?" Subjects try to list as many reactions as possible. In the **Anagrams Test,** subjects are given a word such as *creativity* and asked to make as many new words as possible by rearranging the letters. Each of these tests can be scored for fluency, flexibility, and originality. (For an example of other tests of divergent thought, see ■Fig. 9–18.) Tests of divergent thinking apparently tap something quite different from intelligence. Generally there is little correlation between such tests and IQ test scores (Wallach, 1985).

Daydream A vivid waking fantasy.

Conquering hero daydream Fantasy in which the daydreamer is a hero.

Suffering martyr daydream Fantasy in which the daydreamer is at first unappreciated, then revealed to be a wonderful person.

Unusual Uses Test A test of creativity based on thinking of new uses for a common object.

Consequences Test A test of creativity based on listing the consequences that would follow a basic change in the world.

Anagrams Test A test of creativity based on making as many new words as possible from the letters in a given word.

Question: Isn't creativity more than divergent thought? What if a person comes up with a large number of useless answers to a problem?

A good question. Divergent thought is definitely an important part of creative thinking, but there is more to it. To be creative, the solution to a problem must be more than novel, unusual, or original. It must also be *practical* if it is an invention and *sensible* if it is an idea (Finke, 1990). This is the dividing line between a "harebrained scheme" and a "stroke of genius" (■Figs. 9–19 and ■9–20). In other words, the creative person brings reasoning and critical thinking to bear on novel ideas once they are produced (Snow, 1986).

Question: Is there any pattern to creative thinking?

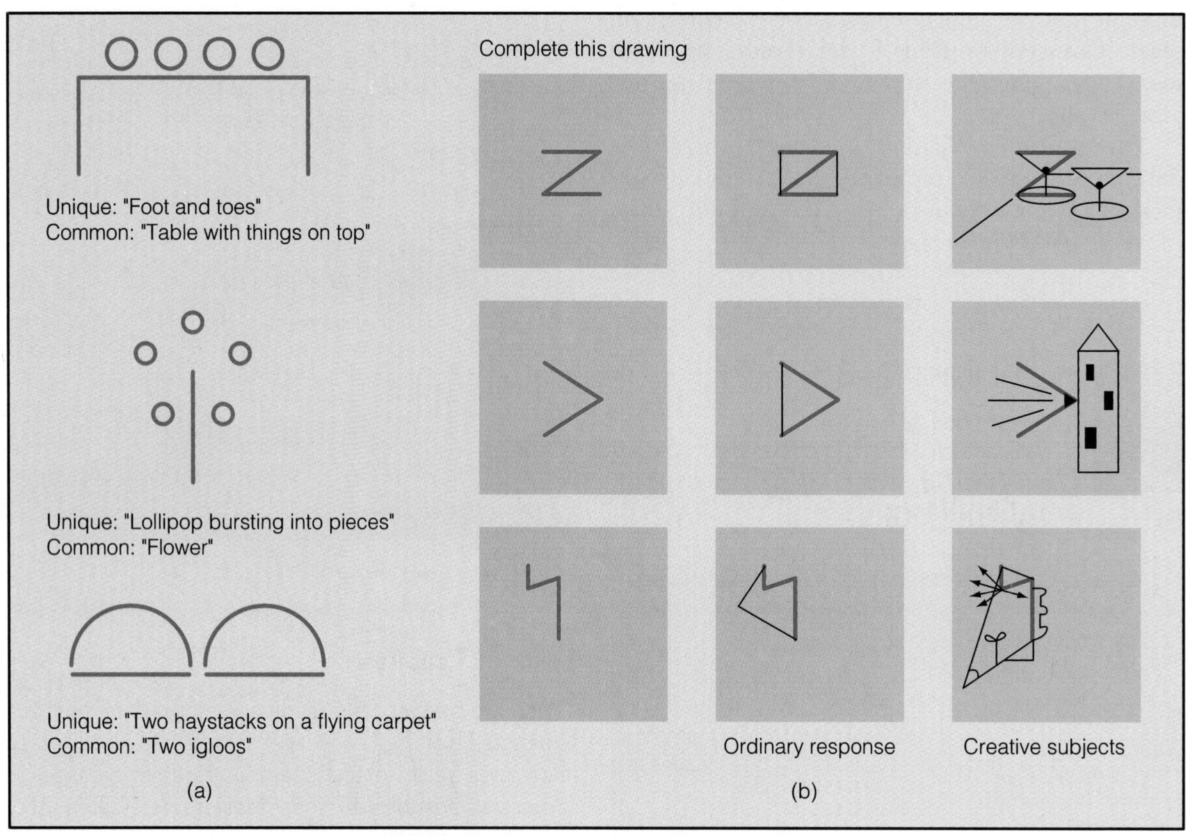

■ **Fig. 9–18** *Some tests of divergent thinking. Creative responses are more original and more complex.* [(a) *after Wallach & Kogan, 1965;* (b) *after Barron, 1958.*]

Stages of Creative Thought

A good summary of the sequence of events in creative thinking proposes five stages that usually occur:

1. **Orientation.** As a first step, the problem must be defined and important dimensions identified.
2. **Preparation.** In the second stage, creative thinkers saturate themselves with as much information pertaining to the problem as possible.
3. **Incubation.** Most major problems produce a period during which all attempted solutions will have proved futile. At this point, problem solving may proceed on a subconscious level: While the problem seems to have been set aside, it is still "cooking" in the background.

■ **Fig. 9–19** *Creative ideas combine originality with feasibility. (Adapted from McMullan & Stocking, 1978.)*

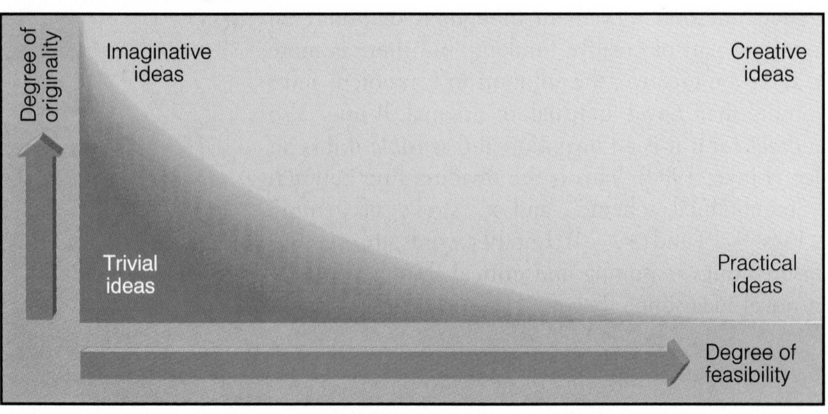

■ **Fig. 9–20** *Hat-tipping device. According to the patent, it is for "automatically effecting polite salutations by the elevation and rotation of the hat on the head of the saluting party when said person bows to the person or persons saluted." In addition to being original or novel, a creative solution must fit the demands of the problem. Is this a creative solution to the "problem" of hat tipping?*

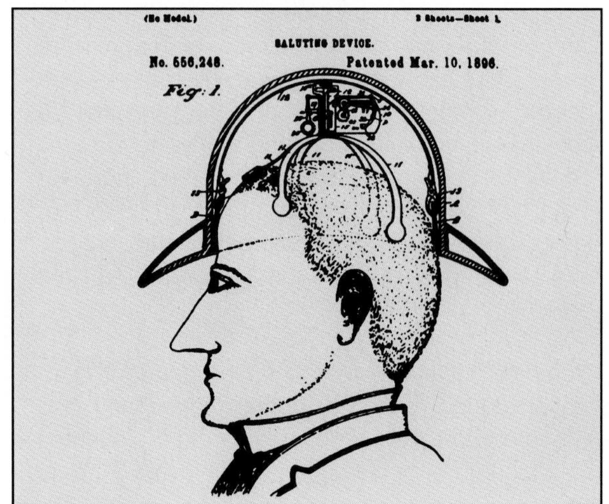

4. Illumination. The stage of incubation is often ended by a rapid insight or series of insights. These produce the "Aha!" experience, often depicted in cartoons as a light bulb appearing over the thinker's head.

5. Verification. The final step is to test and critically evaluate the solution obtained during the stage of illumination. If the solution proves faulty, the thinker reverts to the stage of incubation.

Of course, creative thought is seldom so neat. Nevertheless, the stages listed are a good summary of the typical sequence of events.

You may find it helpful to attach the stages to the following more or less true story. Legend has it that the king of Syracuse (a city in ancient Greece) once suspected that his goldsmith had substituted cheaper metals for some of the gold in a crown and had pocketed the difference. Archimedes, a famous mathematician and thinker, was given the problem of discovering whether the king had been cheated.

Archimedes began by defining the problem (*orientation*): "How can I determine what metals have been used in the crown without damaging it?" He then checked all known methods of analyzing metals (*preparation*). All involved cutting or melting the crown, so he was forced to temporarily set the problem aside (*incubation*). Then one day as he stepped into his bath, Archimedes suddenly knew he had the solution (*illumination*). He was so excited he is said to have run naked through the streets shouting, "Eureka, eureka!" (I have found it, I have found it!).

On observing his own body floating in the bath, Archimedes realized that different metals of equal weight would displace different amounts of water. A pound of brass, for example, occupies more space than a pound of gold, which is denser. All that remained was to test the solution (*verification*). Archimedes placed an amount of gold (equal in weight to that given the goldsmith) in a tub of water. He marked the water level and removed the gold. He then placed the crown in the water. Was the crown pure gold? If it was, it would raise the water to exactly the same level. Unfortunately, the purity of the crown and the fate of the goldsmith are to this day unknown!

The preceding account is a good general description of creative thinking. However, creative thinking can be highly complex. Rather than springing from sudden insights, much creative problem solving is **incremental** (Weisenberg, 1986). That is, it is the end result of many small steps. This is certainly true of many inventions, which build on earlier ideas (■ Fig. 9–21).

Some authors believe that truly exceptional creativity requires a rare combination of thinking skills, personality, and a supportive social environment. This mix, they believe, accounts for creative giants such as Edison, Freud, Mozart, Picasso, Tolstoy, and others (Tardif & Sternberg, 1988).

■ **Fig. 9–21** *The development of modern aircraft has been highly creative and quite rapid. Even so, it has been marked more by incremental progress than by dramatic breakthroughs.*

Question: What makes a person creative?

The Creative Personality

According to the popular stereotype, highly creative people are eccentric, introverted, neurotic, socially inept, unbalanced in their interests, and frequently, on the edge of madness. Although some well-known artists and musicians cultivate a public image to fit the

military strategy, investing and finance, international relations, and more. In each area, people are learning to think twice before they decide. With practice, you, too, can learn to spot errors like those described. Remember, short cuts to answers often short-circuit clear thinking—a point we will pursue in the upcoming Applications section. After that, the Explorations section delves briefly into the fascinating topic of animal intelligence.

LEARNING CHECK

1. Fluency, flexibility, and originality are characteristics of
   a. convergent thought *b.* deductive thinking *c.* creative thought *d.* trial-and-error solutions
2. List the typical stages of creative thinking in the correct order.
   ____________ ____________ ____________
   ____________ ____________
3. An ability to organize, abstract, and synthesize ideas blocks creativity; these are non-creative qualities. T or F?
4. To be creative, an original idea must also be practical or feasible. T or F?
5. Intelligence and creativity are highly correlated; the higher a person's IQ, the more likely he or she is to be creative. T or F?
6. Kate is single, outspoken, and very bright. As a college student, she was deeply concerned with discrimination and other social issues and participated in several protests. Which statement is more likely to be true?
   a. Kate is a bank teller. *b.* Kate is a bank teller and a feminist.
7. The probability of two events occurring together is lower than the probability of either one occurring alone. T or F?
8. Usually, the broadest way of ____________ a problem yields the most rational decisions.

Critical Thinking

9. A coin is flipped four times with one of the following results: *(a)* H T T H, *(b)* T T T T, *(c)* H H H H, *(d)* H H T H. Which sequence would most likely precede getting a head on the fifth coin flip?

Answers: 1. *c* 2. orientation, preparation, incubation, illumination, verification 3. F 4. T 5. F 6. *a* 7. T 8. framing 9. The chance of getting a head on the fifth flip is the same in each case. Each time you flip a coin, the chance of getting a head is 50 percent, no matter what happened before. However, many people intuitively think that *b* is the answer because a head is "overdue," or that *c* is correct because the coin is "on a roll" for heads.

APPLICATIONS: Steps to Better Thinking and Problem Solving

At one time or another, we all experience difficulties in thinking and problem solving. The following should alert you to some of the more common problems.

Rigid Mental Set Try the problems pictured in ■ Figure 9–22. If you have difficulty, try asking yourself what assumptions you are making. The problems are designed to demonstrate the limiting effects of a mental set. (The answers to these problems, along with an explanation of the sets that prevent their solution, are found in ■ Fig. 9–24.) In addition to the assumptions and mental sets we bring to a problem, problems themselves may produce a disruptive set. A simple example is the following:

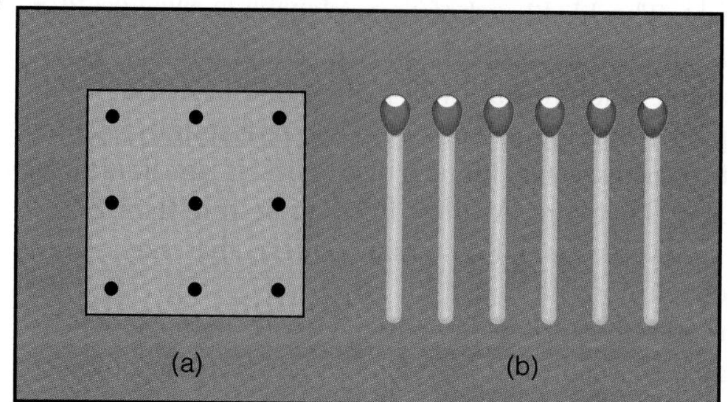

■ **Fig. 9–22** (a) *Nine dots are arranged in a square. Can you connect them by drawing four continuous straight lines without lifting your pencil from the paper?* (b) *Six matches must be arranged to make four triangles. The triangles must be the same size, with each side equal to the length of one match. (The solutions to these problems appear in Fig. 9–24.)*

The name Polk is pronounced "poke," the word folk is pronounced "foke," and the white of an egg is pronounced ____________. Here is another example: See if you can unscramble each set of letters to make a word that uses all the letters:

MEST ____________
LFAE ____________
DUB ____________
STKAL ____________
OTOR ____________
LTEPA ____________

Now try a new list:

FINEK ____________
OPONS ____________
KROF ____________
PUC ____________
SDIH ____________
LTEPA ____________

Did you notice that the last problem was the same in each case? Many people don't and end up solving the problem twice. To complete the first list (*stem, leaf, bud, stalk, root*), the item LTEPA is usually unscrambled at *petal*. In the second list (*knife, spoon, fork, cup, dish*), LTEPA becomes *plate* for many people.

Now that you have been forewarned about the danger of faulty assumptions, see if you can correctly answer the following questions.

1. Argentines do not have a fourth of July. T or F?
2. How many birthdays does the average person have?
3. A farmer had 19 sheep. All but 9 died. How many sheep did the farmer have left?
4. It is not unlawful for a man living in Winston-Salem, North Carolina, to be buried west of the Mississippi River. T or F?
5. Some months have 30 days, some have 31. How many months have 28 days?
6. I have two coins that together total 30 cents. One of the coins is not a nickel. What are the two coins?
7. It would be far better to have an elephant eat you than a gorilla. T or F?

These questions are designed to cause thinking errors. Here are the answers:

1. F. Of course they have a fourth of July. What would they do, go from the third to the fifth? 2. One, celebrated each year. 3. Nineteen—9 alive and 10 dead. 4. F. It is against the law to bury a living person anywhere. 5. All of them. 6. A quarter and a nickel. One of the coins is not a nickel, but the other one is! 7. F. It would be better to have the elephant eat the gorilla. (Read it again.)

If you got caught on any of the questions, consider it an additional reminder of the value of actively challenging the assumptions you are making in any instance of problem solving.

Syllogism A format for analyzing logical arguments.

Problems with Logic A major thinking difficulty centers on the process of *logical reasoning.* Simple sequences of logical thought can be arranged as a set of *premises* (assumptions) and a *conclusion.* This format is called a **syllogism.** A syllogism can be evaluated for the *validity* of its reasoning and for the *truth* of its *conclusion.* It is entirely possible to draw true conclusions using faulty logic or to draw false conclusions using valid logic. The following examples show how this is possible.

Syllogism I

All humans are mortal. (**Major premise**)
All women are humans. (**Minor premise**)
Therefore, all women are mortal. (**Conclusion**)

Comment: As you can see from ■ Figure 9–23, the logic of this syllogism is valid. Since our premises are true, this means the conclusion is true. The diagram shows all women included within the boundaries of mortals.

Syllogism II

All women are humans.
All humans are mortal.
Therefore, all mortals are women.

Comment: In this example, the conclusion drawn is false because the reasoning is invalid. The diagram for Syllogism I shows that all mortals are not women. Notice how little the syllogism has to be changed to produce a false conclusion. Now consider Syllogism III.

■ Fig. 9–23

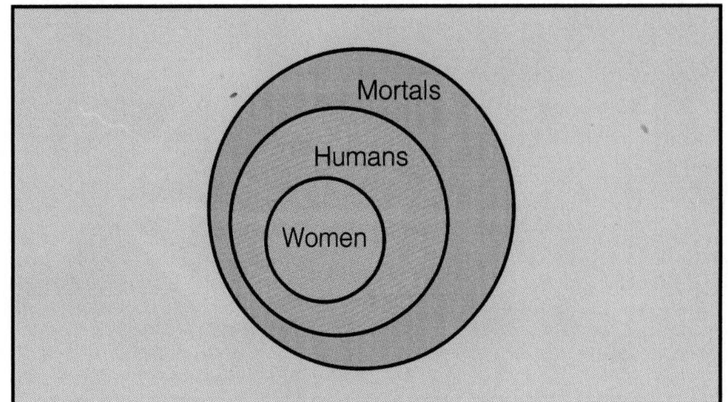

All-or-nothing thinking Classifying things in black and white terms.

Stereotype An inaccurate and oversimplified image of members of a social group.

Syllogism III

All psychologists are weird.
Mary is a psychologist.
Therefore, Mary is weird.

Comment: In this case the reasoning is valid, but the conclusion is false because the first premise is false. All psychologists are *not* weird. (Honest!) Now let's consider one more syllogism.

Syllogism IV

All ducks have wings.
All birds have wings.
Therefore, all ducks are birds.

Comment: This syllogism shows the importance of paying close attention to logic. The reasoning appears to be valid since the conclusion is true, but substitute *bats* or *airplanes* for *ducks* and see how the conclusion reads. It is a good idea to get in the habit of questioning the logic used by politicians, advertisers, and psychologists, too, for that matter.

Over-simplification It may be an over-simplification to say so, but over-simplification is another basic source of thinking errors. There are two types of over-simplification that are particularly troublesome. The first is **all-or-nothing thinking.** Classifying things as absolutely right or wrong, good or bad, acceptable or unacceptable, or honest or dishonest prevents appreciation of the complexity of most life problems.

The second problem is thinking in terms of **stereotypes.** Stereotypes are particularly troublesome when human relationships are involved (see Chapter 21). An overly simplified, inaccurate, or rigid picture of men, African Americans, women, conservatives, liberals, police officers, or any other group of people leads to muddled thinking about individual members of the group. Try to look for this and other errors in your own thinking habits.

■ **Fig. 9–24** *Problem solutions.* (a) *The dot problem can be solved by extending the lines beyond the square formed by the dots. Most people assume incorrectly that they may not do this.* (b) *The match problem can be solved by building a three-dimensional pyramid. Most people assume that the matches must be arranged on a flat surface.*

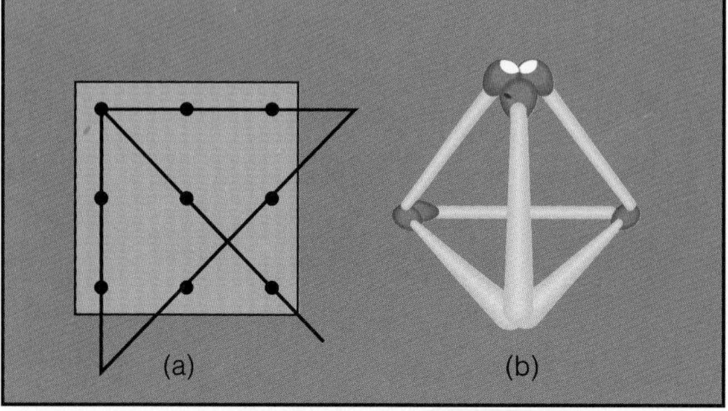

Enhancing Creativity—Brainstorms

Thomas Edison once explained his creativity by saying, "Genius is 1 percent inspiration and 99 percent perspiration." Many studies of creativity show that "genius" owes as much to persistence and dedication as it does to inspiration (Hunt, 1982). Once it is recognized that creativity can be hard work, then something can be done to enhance it. Here are some suggestions on how to begin (from Hayes, 1978, and indicated sources).

1. Define the problem broadly. Whenever possible, enlarge the definition of a problem. For instance, assume your problem is: Design a better doorway. This is likely to lead to ordinary solutions. Why not change the problem to: Design a better way to get through a wall? Now your solutions will be more original. Best of all might be to state the problem as: Find a better way to define separate areas for living and working. This could lead to truly creative solutions (Adams, 1986).

Let's say that you are the leader of a group interested in designing a new can opener. Wisely, you ask the group to think about *opening* in general, rather than about can openers. This was just the approach used in developing the pop-top can. As the design group discussed the concept of opening, one member suggested that nature has its own openers, like the soft seam on a pea pod. Instead of a new can-opening tool, the group invented the self-opening can (Stein, 1974) (■ Fig. 9–25).

2. Create the right atmosphere. A variety of experiments show that people make more original, spontaneous, and imaginative responses when exposed to others (models) doing the same (Amabile, 1983). If you want to become more creative, spend more time around creative people. This is the premise underlying much education in art, theater, dance, and music.

3. Allow time for incubation. Trying to hurry or to force a problem's solution may simply encourage fixation on a dead-end. Most experts agree that creativity takes time. Creative thinking depends on having a chance to revise or elaborate initial solutions, even those based on rapid insight (Tardif & Sternberg, 1988). In one experiment, subjects were asked to list as many consequences as possible that would follow if people no longer needed to eat. Most subjects rapidly produced several ideas and then ran dry. After working for a time, some subjects were interrupted and required to do another task for 20 minutes. Then they returned to the original question. The interruption improved their scores, even though they worked no longer than the control group (Fulgosi & Guilford, 1968).

4. Seek varied input. Remember, creativity requires divergent thinking. Rather than digging deeper with logic, you are attempting to shift your mental "prospecting" to new areas. As an example of this strategy, Edward de Bono (1970) recommends that you randomly look up words in the dictionary and relate each to the problem. Often this activity will trigger a fresh perspective or open a new avenue. For instance, let's say you are asked to come up with new ways to clean oil off a beach, and you draw a blank. Following de Bono's suggestion, you would read the following randomly selected words, relate each to the problem, and see what thoughts are triggered: *weed, rust, poor, magnify, foam, gold, frame, hole, diagonal, vacuum, tribe, puppet, nose, link, drift, portrait, cheese, coal.*

5. Look for analogies. As the principle of selective comparison (described earlier) suggests, many "new" problems are really old problems in new clothing (Siegler, 1989). Representing a problem in a variety of ways is often the key to solution. Most problems become easier to solve when they are effectively represented. For example, consider this problem:

> Two backpackers start up a steep trail at 6 A.M. They hike all day, resting occasionally, and arrive at the top at 6 P.M. The next day they start back down the trail at 6 A.M. On the way down they stop several times and vary their pace. They arrive back at 6 P.M. On the way down, one of the hikers, who is a mathematician, tells the other that she has realized that they will pass a point on the trail at exactly the same time as they did the day before. Her non-mathematical friend finds this hard to believe, since on both days they have stopped and started many times and changed their pace. The problem: Is the mathematician right?

Perhaps you will see the answer to this problem immediately. If not, think of it this way: What if there were two pairs of backpackers, one going up the trail, the second coming down, and both hiking on the *same day?* It becomes obvious that the two pairs of hikers will pass each other at some point on the trail. Therefore, they will be at the same place at the same time. The mathematician was right (adapted from Hayes, 1978).

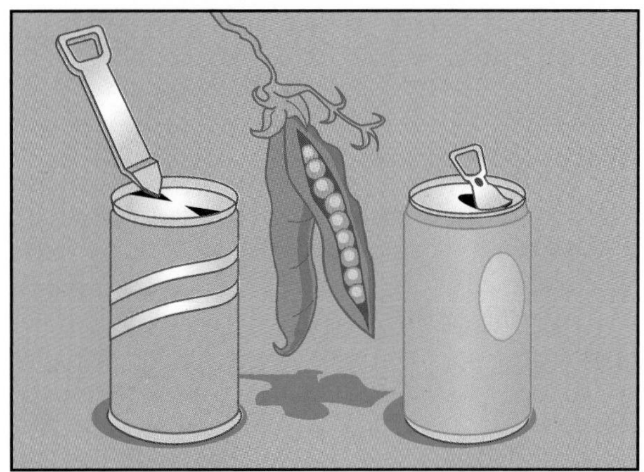

■ Fig. 9–25

6. Delay evaluation. Various studies suggest that people are most likely to be creative when they are given the freedom to play with ideas and solutions without having to worry about whether they will be evaluated. In the first stages of creative thinking, it is important to avoid criticizing your efforts. Worrying about the correctness of solutions tends to inhibit creativity (Amabile, 1983). This idea is expanded in the discussion that follows.

An alternative approach to enhancing creativity is called *brainstorming.* Although brainstorming is a group technique, it can be applied to individual problem solving as well.

Brainstorming Method of creative thinking that separates the production and evaluation of ideas.

Cross-stimulation effect In group problem solving, the tendency of one person's ideas to trigger ideas from others.

Brainstorming

The essence of **brainstorming** is that *production* and *criticism* of ideas are kept separate. To encourage divergent thinking in group problem solving, each person is encouraged to produce as many ideas as possible without fear of criticism or evaluation (Buyer, 1988). Some of the most successful brainstorming takes place on computer networks, where each person's fears of being evaluated are minimized (Dennis & Valacich, 1993).

Only at the end of a brainstorming session are ideas reconsidered and evaluated. As ideas are freely generated, an interesting **cross-stimulation effect** takes place in which one participant's ideas trigger ideas from others. The four basic rules for successful brainstorming are:

1. Criticism of an idea is absolutely barred. All evaluation is to be deferred until after the session.
2. Modification or combination with other ideas is encouraged. Don't worry about giving credit for ideas or keeping them neat. Mix them up!
3. Quantity of ideas is sought. In the early stages of brainstorming, quantity is more important than quality. Try to generate lots of ideas.

4. Unusual, remote, or wild ideas are sought. Let your imagination run amok!

Question: How is brainstorming applied to individual problem solving?

The essential point to remember is to *suspend judgment.* Ideas should first be produced without regard for logic, organization, accuracy, practicality, or any other evaluation. In writing an essay, for instance, you would begin by writing ideas in any order, the more the better, just as they occur to you. Later you would go back and reorganize, rewrite, and criticize your efforts.

As an aid to following rules 2, 3, and 4 of the brainstorming method, you might find this checklist helpful for encouraging original thought. It can be used to see if you have overlooked a possible solution (adapted from Parnes, 1967).

Creativity Checklist

1. **Redefine.** Consider other uses for all elements of the problem. (This is designed to alert you to fixations that may be blocking creativity.)
2. **Adapt.** How could other objects, ideas, procedures, or solutions be adapted to this particular problem?
3. **Modify.** Imagine changing anything and everything that could be changed.
4. **Magnify.** Exaggerate everything you can think of. Think on a grand scale.
5. **Minify.** What if everything were scaled down? What if all differences were reduced to zero? "Shrink" the problem down to size.
6. **Substitute.** How could one object, idea, or procedure be substituted for another?
7. **Rearrange.** Break the problem into pieces and shuffle them.
8. **Reverse.** Consider reverse orders and opposites, and turn things inside out.
9. **Combine.** This one speaks for itself.

By making a habit of subjecting a problem to each of these procedures, you should be able to greatly reduce the chances that you will overlook a useful, original, or creative solution.

LEARNING CHECK

1. In evaluating a syllogism, it is possible to draw a true conclusion with faulty logic, or a false conclusion with valid logic. T or F?
2. Stereotyping is an example of over-simplification in thinking. T or F?
3. Exposure to creative models has been shown to enhance creativity. T or F?
4. In brainstorming, each idea is critically evaluated as it is generated. T or F?
5. Defining a problem broadly produces a cross-stimulation effect that can inhibit creative thinking. T or F?

Critical Thinking

6. What mode of thinking does the "Creativity Checklist" (redefine, adapt, modify, magnify, and so forth) encourage?

Answers: 1. T 2. T 3. T 4. F 5. F 6. divergent thinking

EXPLORATION

Animal Intelligence

uestion: To what extent are animals capable of thought?

Most pet owners can supply stories of apparent thinking in animals. A friend might say, "Wow, you should have seen Studebaker figure out how to get into the closet where I hid the dog food." Are animals actually thinking in such situations? In a rudimentary sense they are. Animals demonstrate an ability to mentally represent situations in **delayed response problems.** For example, a hungry animal could be allowed to watch as food is hidden under one of three goal boxes. After a delay, the animal is released. Can it select the correct box? If the delay is brief, the answer is yes. At times, animal behavior implies far higher levels of thought. In fact, German psychologist Wolfgang Köhler (VOOLF-gong KEAR-ler) believed that animals such as chimpanzees are capable of insight.

EXPLORATION

To test for insight, Köhler challenged Sultan, his brightest chimp, with a **multiple-stick problem.** In this problem several sticks of increasing length were arranged between the cage and a banana (■ Fig. 9–26). To reach the banana, Sultan had to use the first stick to retrieve the second stick (which was longer than the first). The second stick could then be used to get an even longer stick, which could then be used to reach the banana (Köhler, 1925).

When confronted with this problem, Sultan looked at the banana, then at the sticks . . . then at the banana. Picking up the first stick, Sultan smoothly and without further hesitation solved the problem and raked in the banana.

Psychologists have long debated whether Köhler's chimps actually displayed insight. However, in recent years evidence for animal intelligence and thinking ability has continued to grow—but not without controversy.

■ **Fig. 9–26** *Psychologist Wolfgang Köhler believed that the solution of a multiple-stick problem revealed a capacity for insight in chimpanzees.*

How Intelligent Are Animals?

Evidence for the idea that animals are capable of intelligent thought is varied and, to many researchers, convincing:

- ■ Monkeys can learn to select, from among three objects, the one that differs from the other two.
- ■ When a container of sugar water is moved a set distance farther from a beehive each day, the bees begin to go to the new location *before* the water is moved.
- ■ Pigeons can learn to select photographs of humans from a group of photos that includes various objects.
- ■ A chimp named Lana has learned to remove one, two, or three objects from a computer screen, after first being shown the numbers 1, 2, or 3.

Do such examples really demonstrate thinking by animals? Some psychologists say yes; some say no. What would it take, then, to verify animal thinking? Psychologist Donald Griffin suggests that we must observe behavior that is *versatile* and *appropriate* to changing circumstances. He also believes that thinking is implied by actions that appear to be planned with an awareness of likely results (Griffin, 1992). As one example, sea otters select suitably sized rocks and use them to hammer shellfish loose for eating. They then use the rock to open the shell (■ Fig. 9–27).

■ **Fig. 9–27** *Does the seemingly intelligent behavior of sea otters and other animals reflect thinking ability, instinct, or conditioning? The evidence remains inconclusive, so psychologists disagree.*

As convincing as such examples may seem, they have been challenged. For instance, Epstein, Lanza, and Skinner conditioned pigeons to duplicate seemingly insightful behavior like that claimed for higher animals. Other psychologists, however, reply that the pigeons only achieved the *appearance* of thinking, because their behavior was strongly guided by reinforcement.

As stated before, it seems reasonable to assume that animals do think. However, debate is sure to continue about the limits of their intelligence and about whether specific examples demonstrate thinking, instinct, or conditioning.

Delayed response problem A task in which an animal must remember the solution to a problem for a set amount of time before responding.

Multiple-stick problem A task in which progressively longer sticks are used to reach a desired object.

EXPLORATION

Psychologist Sarah Boysen recently added to the debate about animal cognition in a fascinating experiment. Boysen and her colleagues taught a chimp named Sheba to count and to recognize numbers from 0 to 8. When Boysen decided to test Sheba's understanding of *more* and *less,* a striking thing happened. Boysen placed two plates of gumdrops in front of Sheba, one holding more gumdrops than the other. Sheba was allowed to select one of the plates. Naturally enough, Sheba selected the plate with more candy. When she did, that plate was given to another chimpanzee. Sheba became visibly agitated at this foul turn of events.

The gumdrop test was repeated many more times. Nonetheless, Sheba could not learn to choose the plate with less candy on it. At that point, Boysen decided to place numbers on the plates, rather than gumdrops. The number Sheba chose determined how many gumdrops the second chimp would receive (■ Fig. 9–28). Almost immediately, Sheba learned to point to the smaller number. Clearly, she knew the rule: If she chose the larger number the larger amount of candy was given away and she kept the smaller amount; if she pointed to the smaller number, she got to keep the larger amount of candy.

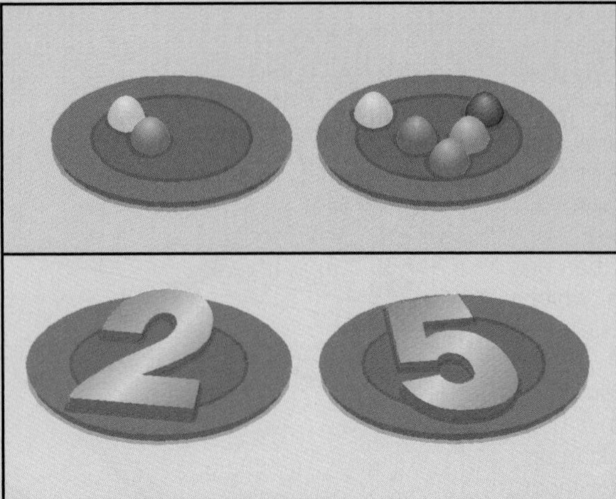

■ **Fig. 9–28** *Typical stimuli used in testing chimpanzees for comprehension of the concepts* less *and* more. *The chimps could not resist choosing the larger amount of candy, even when that choice meant they got the smaller amount of candy and another chimp got the larger amount. The use of numeric symbols freed the chimps to choose the smaller amount of food for the other chimp.*

Further testing revealed that knowing the rule and acting on it were two different things. Whenever gumdrops were used, Sheba could not choose the smaller number. When numerals were used, she could. Sheba's behavior suggests that chimpanzees can learn, at a very basic level, to think symbolically. (Symbolic thought uses language or symbols to represent the external world.)

Sheba's inability to choose correctly when faced with plates of candy is intriguing. Very likely, chimps living in the wild are genetically programmed to collect food as efficiently as possible. Only when they have learned to use symbols are chimps freed from the immediate and powerful allure of a plate of gumdrops. In addition to providing insight into the mind of a chimpanzee, Sheba's behavior emphasizes the tremendous advantage that we humans have as symbol using animals.

(Sources: Boysen & Berntson, 1989; Epstein et al., 1981; Griffin, 1992; Herrnstein, 1979; Premack, 1983; Rose, 1984; Rumbaugh et al., 1989.)

LEARNING CHECK

1. There is evidence that chimpanzees are capable of insightful solutions to problems, but some psychologists remain unconvinced that true insight is involved. T or F?
2. Rudimentary thinking abilities are revealed when animals successfully solve ______________________ ______________________ problems, which involve mentally representing an external situation.
3. Köhler's ape Sultan was apparently able to solve problems involving numbers and amounts. T or F?
4. Psychologist Donald Griffin suggests that animal cognition is revealed by behavior which is *versatile* and *appropriate* to changing circumstances. T or F?
5. In tests involving the concepts *more* and *less,* Sheba the chimpanzee was only able to perform correctly when the amounts were represented ______________________.

Critical Thinking

6. Chimpanzees and other apes are intelligent and entertaining animals. If you were doing research on their cognitive abilities, what major problem would you have to guard against?

Answers: 1. T 2. delayed response 3. F 4. T 5. symbolically 6. The problem of anthropomorphizing (ascribing human characteristics to animals) is especially difficult to avoid when researchers spend many hours interacting with chimps.

Chapter Summary

- ***What is the nature of thought?***

- Thinking is the manipulation of **internal representations** of external stimuli or situations.
- Three basic units of thought are **images, concepts,** and **language** or **symbols.**

- ***In what ways are images related to thinking?***

- Most people have internal images of one kind or another. Images may be **stored** or **created.** Sometimes they cross normal sense boundaries in a type of imagery called **synesthesia.**
- The size of images used in problem solving may change and they may be three-dimensional.
- **Kinesthetic images** are created by memory of actions or by **implicit actions. Kinesthetic sensations** and **micromovements** seem to help structure the flow of thought for many people.

- ***How are concepts learned? Are there different kinds of concepts?***

- A **concept** is a generalized idea of a class of objects or events.
- **Concept formation** may be based on **positive** and **negative instances** or more commonly, on **rule learning.** In practice, concept identification frequently makes use of **prototypes,** or general models of the concept class.
- Concepts may be classified as **conjunctive** ("and" concepts), **disjunctive** ("either-or" concepts), or **relational.**
- The **denotative** meaning of a word or concept is its dictionary definition. **Connotative** meaning is personal or emotional. Connotative meaning can be measured with the **semantic differential.**

- ***What is the role of language in thinking?***

- Language allows events to be **encoded** into **symbols** for easy mental manipulation. Thinking in language is influenced by meaning. The study of meaning is called **semantics.**
- Language carries meaning by combining a set of symbols or signs according to a set of rules (**grammar**), which includes rules about word order (**syntax**). A true language is **productive,** and can be used to generate new ideas or possibilities.

- ***Can animals be taught to use language?***

- Animal communication is relatively limited because it lacks symbols that can be rearranged easily.
- Attempts to teach chimpanzees systems such as **American Sign Language** suggest to some that primates are capable of language use. Others question this conclusion. Studies that make use of **lexigrams** provide the best evidence yet of animal language use.

- ***What do we know about problem solving?***

- The solution to a problem may be arrived at **mechanically** (by **trial and error** or by **rote** application of rules), but mechanical solutions are frequently inefficient or ineffective, except where aided by computer.
- Solutions by **understanding** usually begin with discovery of the **general properties** of an answer. Next comes proposal of a number of **functional solutions.**
- Problem solving is frequently aided by **heuristics.** These are strategies that typically narrow the search for solutions. The **ideal strategy** is a general heuristic.
- When understanding leads to a rapid solution, it is said that **insight** has occurred. Three elements of insight are **selective encoding, selective combination** and **selective comparison.**
- Insight and other problem solving can be blocked by **fixation. Functional fixedness** is a common fixation, but **emotional blocks, cultural values, learned conventions,** and **perceptual habits** are also problems.

- ***What is artificial intelligence?***

- **Artificial intelligence** refers to any artificial system that can perform tasks that require intelligence when done by people.
- Two principal areas of artificial intelligence research are **computer simulations** and **expert systems.**
- Computer simulations of human problem solving are usually based on a **means-ends analysis.**
- Expert human performance and problem solving is based on **organized knowledge** and **acquired strategies,** rather than some general improvement in thinking ability.
- Artificial intelligence is helping scientists explore the nature of human thought, knowledge, and expertise.

- ***What is the nature of creative thinking?***

- To be creative, a solution must be practical and sensible as well as original. Creative thinking requires **divergent** thought, characterized by **fluency, flexibility,** and **originality.** Tests of creativity measure these qualities.
- **Daydreaming and fantasy** are a source of much divergent thinking.

- Five stages often seen in creative problem solving are **orientation, preparation, incubation, illumination,** and **verification.** Not all creative thinking fits this pattern. Much creative activity is based on **incremental problem solving.**
- Studies suggest that **creative persons** share a number of identifiable characteristics, most of which contradict popular stereotypes. There appears to be little or no correlation between IQ and creativity.

■ ***How accurate is intuition?***

- Intuitive thinking often leads to errors. Wrong conclusions may be drawn when an answer seems highly **representative** of what we already believe is true.
- A second problem is ignoring the **base rate** (or **underlying probability**) of an event.
- Clear thinking is usually aided by stating or **framing** a problem in broad terms.

■ ***What can be done to improve thinking and to promote creativity?***

- Major sources of thinking errors include **rigid mental set, faulty logic,** and **oversimplification.**
- Various strategies, including **brainstorming,** tend to enhance creative problem solving.

■ ***Do animals think?***

- Animals reveal a rudimentary capacity for thought when they solve **delayed response problems** and, in some cases, problems that appear to require understanding or **insight.**
- There is also evidence that higher animals, such as chimpanzees, can learn to use rudimentary symbolic thought. For the moment, however, some psychologists remain unconvinced about such abilities.

Questions for Discussion

1. If you suddenly lost your ability to mentally represent external problems, what changes would you have to make in your behavior?
2. In what ways does a large vocabulary make a person a more effective thinker?
3. Describe a time when you have used imagery to solve a problem. What are the advantages and disadvantages of imagery in comparison to other modes of thought?
4. In what ways might bilingualism increase thinking ability? In what ways might it be a problem?
5. How do differences in connotative meaning contribute to arguments and misunderstandings? Do you think connotative meaning could or should be standardized?
6. The text states that animals communicate, but may not use language in the human sense. Do you agree? Do you think that Washoe's use of ASL qualifies as language? What about Kanzi's use of lexigrams?
7. Think of the most creative person you know. What is that person like? How does he or she differ from your less creative acquaintances?
8. From your point of view, how does creativity differ from intelligence?
9. In your opinion, should measures of divergent or creative thinking be used to select students for college admission? Why or why not?
10. You are the president of an advertising company. You want to hire a new account executive who is extremely creative. How would you go about identifying this person?
11. What effects would you expect the following to have on fantasy: television; highly realistic toys; free or unstructured time; high levels of stress or anxiety; skits, role taking, or acting; sensory deprivation; sensory overload?
12. Can you provide a real-life example of each of Kahneman and Tversky's concepts (representativeness, base rates, and framing)?
13. What perceptual habits could contribute to barriers in problem solving?
14. To what kinds of tasks do you think artificial intelligence should be applied? Would you be comfortable with computerized medical diagnosis, for instance? What about the launch of a nuclear attack?

Chapter 10

Motivation and Emotion

CHAPTER PREVIEW

Flight of the *Gossamer Albatross*

What would it feel like to pedal an airplane over the English Channel? Cyclist Bryan Allen found out the hard way by serving as pilot and "engine" for the first human-powered flight from England to France. Allen pedaled a delicate aircraft, the Gossamer Albatross, *in a grueling three-hour flight. The flight took Allen to the limits of endurance as he fought head winds, thirst, leg cramps, and exhaustion. The following excerpts are from Allen's (1979) account:*

> *6:59* A.M. *At last, word comes over the radio . . . . "We have France in sight—four miles to go . . . . "*
>
> *Four miles or four hundred. I'm fading now and know it. Gradually the head winds have been building up . . . I talk to myself . . . Don't give up now, you can do it! As I waver between hope and despair, the radio crackles again:*
>
> *"Altitude six inches, six inches; get it up, you've got to get it up!"*
>
> *7:29* A.M. *One mile. Less distance than I had flown* Gossamer Condor *two years before for the original Kremer prize. Then, however, there were no head winds or turbulence, no thirst, no cramps . . . . Despite the cramps, I struggle back up to five feet. "Against all hope," I repeat to myself, "against all hope."*

IN THIS CHAPTER

Types of motives
Hunger and eating
Thirst, sex, and pain
Stimulus motives
Arousal and body rhythms
Learned motives
Achievement motivation
Motives in perspective
Elements of emotion
Sudden death and lying
Emotional expressions
Theories of emotion
Applications:
Behavioral dieting
Exploration:
Types of love

7:36 A.M. *Four hundred yards to shore . . . . One hundred yards now. I am running on reserves I never knew I had . . . .*

Motivation and Emotion *This chapter is about the motives and emotions underlying Bryan Allen's behavior—and your own. Bryan Allen's final burst of effort ("I am running on reserves I never knew I had") is but one example of the many links between emotion and motivation. Our discussion begins with basic motives, such as hunger and thirst, and ends with a look at how emotions affect us. While emotions can be the spice of life, they are sometimes the spice of death as well.*

Survey Questions

- What is motivation? Are there different types of motives?
- What causes hunger? Overeating? Eating disorders?
- Is there more than one type of thirst?
- In what ways are pain avoidance and the sex drive unusual?
- How does arousal relate to motivation?
- What are social motives? Why are they important?
- Are some motives more basic than others?
- What happens during emotion?
- Can "lie detectors" really detect lies?
- How accurately are emotions expressed by "body language" and the face?
- How do psychologists explain emotions?
- Can psychology be applied to weight control?
- What is the nature of love?

Motivation Mechanisms that initiate, sustain, and direct activities.

Need An internal deficiency that may energize behavior.

Drive The psychological expression of a motive; for example, hunger, thirst, or a drive for success.

Response Any muscular action, glandular activity, or other identifiable behavior.

Goal The target of a motivated chain of behaviors.

Motivation—Forces That Push and Pull

We move. We seek different goals, some more vigorously than others. The same goal may be pursued for different reasons, or different goals may be pursued for the same reasons. We use the concept of motivation to explain each of these basic aspects of behavior. To be more specific, **motivation** refers to the *dynamics* of behavior—the ways in which our actions are initiated, sustained, and directed.

Question: Can you clarify that?

Yes. Let's relate the concept of motivation to a simple sequence of activity:

> Liz is studying (psychology, of course) in the library. She begins to feel hungry and has difficulty concentrating. Her stomach growls. She grows restless and decides to buy an apple from a vending machine. The machine is empty, so she goes to the cafeteria. Closed. She returns to the library, packs up her books, and drives home, where she prepares a meal and eats. At last her hunger is satisfied, and she again resumes studying.

Liz's food seeking was *initiated* by her bodily need for food; it was *sustained* because her need was not immediately met; and her activities were *directed* by possible sources of food. Notice too that her food seeking was *terminated* by achieving her goal.

A Model of Motivation

Many motivated activities can be thought of as beginning with a **need.** The need that initiated Liz's search was a depletion of substances within the cells of her body. Needs cause a psychological state or feeling, called a **drive,** to develop. (The drive was hunger, in Liz's case.) Drives activate a **response** (or series of actions) designed to attain a **goal** that will satisfy the need. Meeting the need temporarily ends the motivational sequence. Thus, a simple model of motivation can be shown in this way:

→ NEED → DRIVE → RESPONSE → GOAL
(NEED REDUCTION) ←

Question: Why use the terms need *and* drive*? Aren't they the same thing?*

Both terms are necessary because the strength of needs and drives can differ. If you were to begin fasting, your bodily need for food would increase daily, but you would probably be less "hungry" on the seventh day of fasting than you were on the first. Your need steadily increases, but the hunger drive comes and goes.

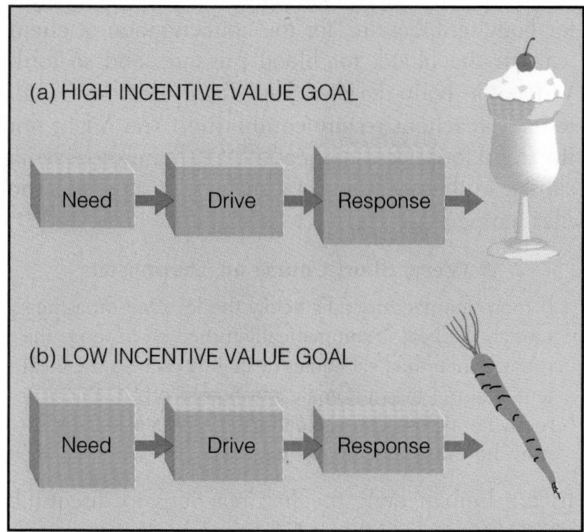

■ Fig. 10–1 *Needs and incentives interact to determine drive strength* (left). (a) *Moderate need combined with a high-incentive goal produces a strong drive.* (b) *Even when a strong need exists, drive strength may be moderate if a goal's incentive value is low. It is important to remember, however, that incentive value lies "in the eye of the beholder"* (photo). *No matter how hungry, few people would be able to eat the pictured grubworms.*

Before we assume that we have a complete model of motivation, let us observe Liz's eating behavior on another occasion:

> For dinner, Liz has just eaten soup, salad, a large steak, a large baked potato, one-half of a loaf of bread, two pieces of cheesecake, and four cups of coffee. After the meal she remarks about her discomfort from overeating. Soon after, Liz's roommate arrives with a strawberry pie. Liz exclaims that strawberry pie is her favorite dessert and proceeds to eat three good-sized pieces and has a cup of coffee to wash them down.

Is this hunger? Certainly we can believe that Liz's extra-large meal was enough to satisfy her biological needs for food.

Question: How does this change the model of motivation?

Incentives The story illustrates that motivated behavior can be energized by the "pull" of external stimuli, as well as by the "push" of internal needs. The pull exerted by a goal is called its **incentive value.** Some goals are so desirable (strawberry pie, for example) that they motivate behavior in the absence of an internal need. Other goals are so low in incentive value that they will be rejected even though they might meet the internal need. Fresh, live grubworms, for instance, are considered a delicacy in some parts of the world, but it is doubtful that you would eat one no matter how hungry you might be.

In most instances, actions are energized by both internal needs *and* external incentives. In addition, a strong state of need may make a less attractive incentive into a desirable goal. You may never have eaten a grubworm, but chances are good that you have eaten some pretty horrible leftovers when the refrigerator was bare. Incentives also help account for motives that do not seem to have any identifiable internal need, such as drives for success, status, or approval (■ Fig. 10–1).

Incentive value A goal's value above and beyond its ability to fill a need.

Primary motives Innate motives based on biological needs.

Stimulus motives Innate needs for stimulation and information.

Secondary motives Motives based on learned needs and drives.

Types of Motives For the purpose of study, motives can be divided into three major categories:

1. **Primary motives** are based on biological needs that must be met for survival. The most important primary motives are hunger, thirst, pain avoidance, and the need for air, sleep, elimination of wastes, and regulation of body temperature. Primary motives are innate.
2. **Stimulus motives** also appear to be innate, but they are not necessary for survival. Their purpose seems to be to provide the nervous system with useful information and stimulation. Examples of stimulus motives include activity, curiosity, exploration, manipulation, and physical contact.
3. **Learned,** or **secondary, motives** account for the great diversity of human activities suggested by the

Homeostasis A steady state of bodily equilibrium.

Chapter Preview. Behavior like Bryan Allen's flight over the English Channel is probably best understood in terms of learned motives or goals. Many secondary motives are related to acquired needs for power, affiliation (the need to be with others), approval, status, security, and achievement. The important motives of fear and aggression also appear to be subject to learning.

Primary Motives and Homeostasis—Keeping the Home Fires Burning

How important is food in your life? Water? Sleep? Air? Temperature regulation? For most of us, satisfying these biological needs is so routine that we tend to overlook how much of our behavior they direct. But exaggerate any of these needs through famine, shipwreck, poverty, near-drowning, or bitter cold, and their powerful grip on behavior becomes evident. We are, after all, still animals in many ways.

Biological drives are essential because they maintain **homeostasis** (HOE-me-oh-STAY-sis), or bodily equilibrium (Cannon, 1932).

Question: What is homeostasis?

The term *homeostasis* means "standing steady," or "steady state." Within the body there are "ideal" levels for body temperature, for the concentration of chemicals in the blood, for blood pressure, and so forth. When the body deviates from these ideal levels, automatic reactions restore equilibrium. You might find it helpful to think of homeostatic mechanisms as being similar to the operation of a *thermostat* set at a particular temperature.

A (Very) Short Course on Thermostats

If room temperature falls below the level set on a thermostat, the heat is automatically turned on to warm the room. When the heat equals or slightly exceeds the ideal temperature, it is automatically turned off. In this way room temperature is maintained in a state of equilibrium hovering around the ideal level.

In the human body the first reactions to disequilibrium are also automatic. For example, if you become too hot, blood flow to your body surfaces increases and you begin to perspire, thus lowering body temperature. We become aware of the need to maintain homeostasis only when we are driven by continued disequilibrium to seek shade, warmth, food, or water.

Since hunger is one of the most interesting and better understood of the primary drives, let's examine it before we discuss biological drives in general. Before reading about hunger, you may find it helpful to complete the Learning Check that follows.

Learning Check

1. Motives ______________, sustain, and ______________ activities.
2. Needs provide the ______________ of motivation, whereas incentives provide the ______________.

Classify the following needs or motives by placing the correct letter in the blank.

A. Primary motive B. Stimulus motive C. Secondary motive

3. _____ curiosity
4. _____ status
5. _____ sleep
6. _____ thirst
7. _____ achievement
8. _____ physical contact
9. The maintenance of bodily equilibrium is called thermostasis. T or F?
10. A goal high in incentive value may create a drive in the absence of any internal need. T or F?

Critical Thinking

11. Many people mistakenly believe that they suffer from "hypoglycemia" which is often blamed for fatigue, difficulty concentrating, irritability, and other symptoms. Why is it unlikely that many people actually have hypoglycemia?

Answers: 1. initiate, direct 2. push, pull 3. B 4. C 5. A 6. A 7. C 8. B 9. F 10. T 11. Because of homeostasis: Blood sugar is normally maintained within narrow bounds. While blood sugar levels fluctuate enough to affect hunger, true hypoglycemia is an infrequent medical problem.

Hunger—Pardon Me, That's Just My Hypothalamus Growling

Question: What causes hunger?

When you feel hungry, you probably associate a desire for food with sensations from your stomach. This, sensibly enough, is where the search for hunger began. In an early study, Cannon and Washburn (1912) decided to see if the contractions of an empty stomach cause hunger. To do this, Washburn trained himself to swallow a balloon. The balloon was then inflated inside his stomach, through an attached tube. This allowed Washburn's stomach contractions to be recorded (■ Fig. 10–2). Cannon and Washburn observed that when Washburn's stomach contracted, he felt "hunger pangs." They concluded that hunger is "nothing more than stomach contractions." (Unfortunately, this proved to be an inflated conclusion.)

Perhaps you already guessed that something more than the stomach is involved in hunger. For many people, hunger produces an overall feeling of weakness or shakiness that seems unrelated to the stomach. And, while eating *is* limited when the stomach is distended (full), it can be shown that the stomach is not essential for experiencing hunger (Martin, White, & Hulsey, 1991).

Question: How has that been demonstrated?

For one thing, cutting the sensory nerves from the stomach (so that stomach sensations can no longer be felt) does not abolish hunger in animals. Even more convincing is the fact that many people have had their stomachs removed surgically. These people continue to feel hungry and to eat regularly.

It would seem that some *central* factor must be the cause of hunger. One important element now appears to be the level of sugar in the blood. If insulin is injected in a human, it causes **hypoglycemia** (HI-po-gly-SEE-me-ah: low blood sugar) and stimulates feelings of hunger and stomach contractions (Hoyenga & Hoyenga, 1984). Strange as it may seem, the liver also affects hunger.

Question: The liver?

Yes, the liver. The liver responds to a lack of bodily "fuel" by sending nerve impulses to the brain, thus triggering the desire to eat (Martin, White, & Hulsey, 1991).

Question: What part of the brain controls hunger?

When you are hungry, many parts of the brain are affected, so no single "hunger center" exists. However, one area of importance is the **hypothalamus** (HI-po-THAL-ah-mus), located near the base of the brain (■ Fig. 10–3).

Cells in the hypothalamus are sensitive to levels of sugar (and perhaps other substances) in the blood. The hypothalamus also receives messages from the liver and the stomach (Martin, White, & Hulsey, 1991). These messages combine to produce hunger. One area of the hypothalamus seems to be part of a **feeding system** in the brain. If the *lateral hypothalamus* is "turned on" with an electrified probe, even a well-fed animal will immediately begin eating. (The term *lateral* simply means the sides of the hypothalamus. See ■ Figure 10–4.) If the same area is destroyed, the animal will refuse to eat and will die if not force-fed (Thompson, 1985).

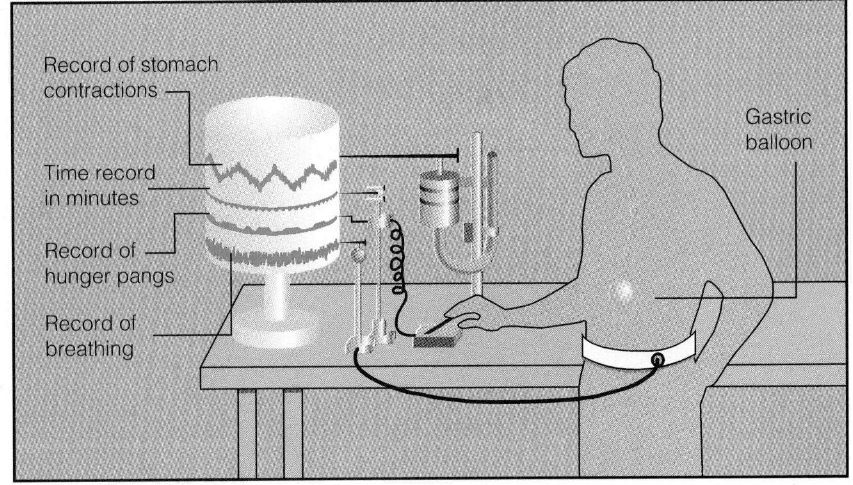

■ **Fig. 10–2** *In Cannon's early study of hunger, a simple apparatus was used to simultaneously record hunger pangs and stomach contractions. (After Cannon, 1934.)*

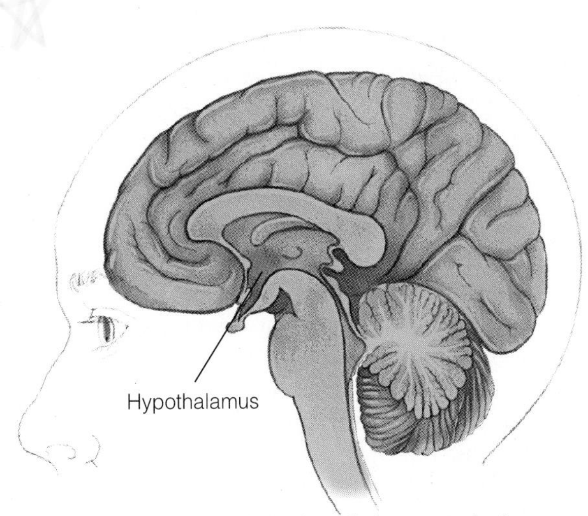

■ **Fig. 10–3** *Location of the hypothalamus in the human brain.*

A second area within the hypothalamus seems to be part of a **satiety system** (or "stop system") for eating. If the *ventromedial hypothalamus* (VENT-ro-MEE-dee-al) is destroyed, dramatic overeating results. (*Ventromedial* refers to the bottom middle of the hypothalamus.) Rats with such damage will overeat until they are totally obese. Some balloon up to weights of 1000 grams or more and get so large that they can barely move (■ Fig. 10–5). A normal rat weighs about 180 grams. To picture this weight gain in human terms, envision someone you know who weighs 180 pounds growing to a weight of 1000 pounds.

A third area of importance in the hypothalamus is the *paraventricular nucleus* (PAIR-uh-ven-TRICK-you-ler) (Fig. 10–4). This area helps keep blood sugar levels steady. As a result, it seems to be involved in both

Hypoglycemia Below-normal blood sugar level.

Hypothalamus A small brain area that regulates many aspects of motivation and emotion, especially hunger, thirst, and sexual behavior.

Feeding system Areas on each side of the hypothalamus that initiate eating when stimulated.

Satiety system Areas on the bottom middle of the hypothalamus that terminate eating.

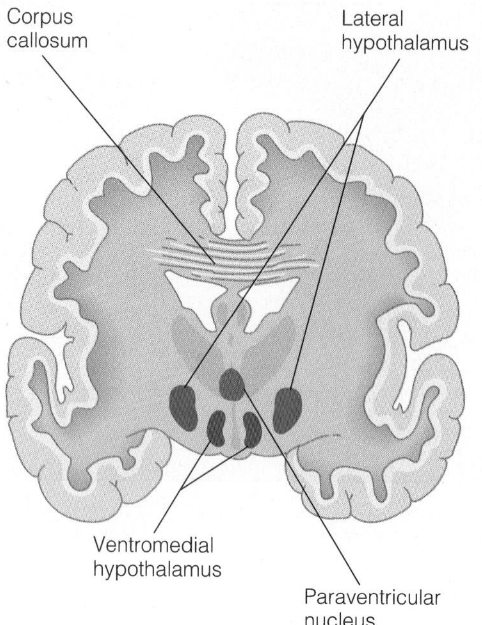

■ Fig. 10–4 *This is a cross section through the middle of the brain (viewed from the front of the brain). Indicated areas of the hypothalamus are associated with hunger and the regulation of body weight.*

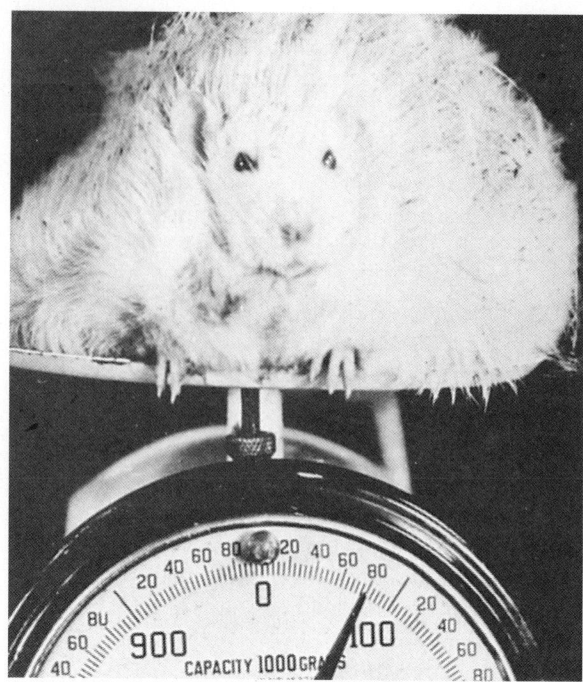

■ Fig. 10–5 *Damage to the hunger satiety system in the hypothalamus can produce a very fat rat, a condition called hypothalamic* hyperphagia *(Hi-per-FAGE-yah: overeating). This rat weighs 1080 grams. (The pointer has gone completely around the dial and beyond.) (Photo courtesy of Neal Miller.)*

Set point A proportion of body fat that tends to be maintained by changes in hunger and eating.

External eating cue Any external stimulus that tends to encourage hunger or to elicit eating.

starting *and* stopping eating. The paraventricular nucleus is very sensitive to a substance called neuropeptide Y (NPY). If large amounts of NPY are present in the paraventricular nucleus, an animal will eat until it cannot hold another bite. The discovery of NPY and related substances may soon make chemical control of hunger possible. If so, treatments for eating disorders, such as extreme obesity and self-starvation, could follow (Martin, White, & Hulsey, 1991).

It should come as no surprise that there is more to hunger than simple "start" and "stop" systems in the brain. Fat stored in the body also influences hunger. The body has a **set point** for the *proportion* of body fat it maintains. That is, the set point acts like a "thermostat" for body fat. Your personal set point is the weight you maintain when you are making no effort to gain or lose weight. When your body goes below its set point, you are likely to feel hungry most of the time (Martin, White, & Hulsey, 1991). Incidentally, the set point helps explain why people often gain weight when they stop smoking. Nicotine lowers the set point. Quitting smoking allows the set point—and body weight—to rise (Perkins, 1993).

Question: Do people have different set points?

Yes. Set points appear to be partly inherited and partly affected by childhood feeding patterns. The role of heredity is shown by studies of adopted children. If a child's birth parents are overweight, the child is likely to become obese too (Stunkard et al., 1986). This suggests that genes greatly influence adult weight. Also, the set point tends to be higher for people who were overfed as children. Adults whose weight problems began in childhood tend to have *more* fat cells and *larger* fat cells in the body. What about a person who does not become overweight until adulthood? In that case, the fat cells grow larger, but they usually do not increase in number. Thus, weight problems that begin in childhood are much more difficult to control.

Obesity

Question: Why do people overeat?

Set points are only one piece in a complex puzzle that scientists are still trying to solve. Their search is fueled by the fact that obesity is a major health risk and, for many, a source of social stigma and low self-esteem (Brownell, 1982) (■ Fig. 10–6).

If eating were controlled only by internal needs, fewer people would overeat. As noted earlier, however, the sight or aroma of food often makes people want to eat, even when they do not feel hungry. It seems that many people are sensitive to **external eating cues** (signs and signals linked with food) (Rodin, 1978). If you are sensitive to external cues, you are most likely to eat when food is attractive, highly visible, and easy to obtain (Schachter & Rodin, 1974). (Have you ever overeaten at a holiday party or buffet?) People of all weights can be found who are unusually sensitive to

■ **Fig. 10–6** *Professional football player William (Refrigerator) Perry cools off after a practice session. Perry has received much notoriety because of his size and his good humor about it. However, when Perry arrived at training camp weighing 377 pounds, he admitted that he had a problem and entered a program for eating disorders. Obesity can be a serious health problem and is ultimately no laughing matter.*

external eating cues, so this is not strictly a problem of the obese (Rodin, 1981). Just the same, eating cues do appear to be a factor in some overeating. For example, psychologist Judith Rodin found that externally responsive girls were most likely to gain weight at a 2-month summer camp (Rodin, 1978).

It is highly likely that **diet** also contributes to overeating. Placing animals on a "supermarket" diet, for instance, can lead to gross obesity. In one experiment, rats were given meals of chocolate chip cookies, salami, cheese, bananas, marshmallows, milk chocolate, peanut butter, and fat. Rats on this diet gained almost three times as much weight as control animals that ate only laboratory rat chow (Sclafani & Springer, 1976). (Rat chow is a dry mixture of several bland grains. If you were a rat, you'd probably eat more cookies than rat chow, too!) We humans also appear to be sensitive to dietary content. In general, *sweetness*, high *fat content*, and *variety* tend to encourage overeating (Ball & Grinker, 1981; Lucas & Sclafani, 1990). It seems that our culture may provide the worst possible kinds of foods for those with a tendency toward obesity.

It is tempting to assume that fatness comes from constant overeating, but this is a myth. Studies by Albert Stunkard (1980) and Judith Rodin (1978) show that overeating occurs mainly when a person is gaining weight. Once excess weight is gained, it can be maintained with a normal diet. An added problem is that as people gain weight, many reduce their activity level and burn fewer calories. As a result, some overweight persons may continue to gain weight while consuming fewer calories than their slimmer neighbors (Ball & Grinker, 1981).

Question: Is it true that people also overeat when they are emotionally upset?

Yes. People with weight problems are just as likely to eat when they are anxious, angry, or sad, as when hungry (Schotte et al., 1990). Furthermore, unhappiness often accompanies obesity in our fat-conscious culture. The result is a pattern of overeating that leads to emotional distress and still more overeating. This cycle makes weight control extremely difficult.

To summarize, overeating results from a complex interplay of internal and external influences, diet, emotions, genetics, exercise, and many other factors. To answer the question we began with, people become obese in different ways and for different reasons. Clearly, scientists are still a long way from winning the "battle of the bulge." (For another perspective on overeating, see Highlight 10–1.)

Diet The types and amounts of food and drink regularly consumed over a period of time.

Weight cycling Repeated swings between losing and gaining weight.

Metabolic rate The rate at which energy is consumed by bodily activity.

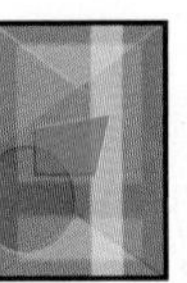

Highlight 10–1

A Closer Look At

The Paradox of Yo-Yo Dieting

If dieting works, why are hundreds of "new" diets published each year? The answer is that while dieters do lose weight, most regain it soon after the diet ends. Indeed, many people experience a rebound that can push weight higher than before the diet began. Why should this be so? It appears that dieting (starving) alters the physiology of the body (Katahn & McMinn, 1990; Seligman, 1994).

In effect, dieting causes the body to become highly efficient at *conserving* calories and storing them as fat (Bennett & Gurin, 1982). Any diet may have this effect, but "yo-yo dieting," or repeated weight loss and gain, is especially troublesome. Frequent **weight cycling** caused by dieting tends to slow the body's **metabolic rate** (the rate at which energy is used up). This makes it harder to lose weight each time a person diets and easier to regain weight when the diet ends (Brownell et al., 1986; Brownell, 1988). Frequent changes in weight also increase susceptibility to heart disease and premature death (Lissner et al., 1991).

Apparently, evolution prepared us to save energy when food is scarce and to stock up on fat when food is plentiful. Briefly starving yourself,

■ **Fig. 10–7** *Fans cheered as daytime TV host Oprah Winfrey lost 67 pounds on a commercial diet. Over the next year, viewers watched in morbid fascination as Oprah regained all of the weight she had lost. Oprah's rebound came as no surprise to psychologists. Numerous studies show that you can lose weight on almost any diet. However, you will almost certainly gain it back in a few years (Seligman, 1994).*

Cultural values The values attached to various objects and activities by people in a given culture.

Taste aversion An active dislike for a particular food; frequently created when the food is associated with illness or discomfort.

Bait shyness An unwillingness on the part of animals to eat a particular food; often caused by a taste aversion.

Self-selection feeding Free choice concerning the foods eaten.

therefore, may have little lasting effect on weight (■ Fig. 10–7). To avoid ineffectively bouncing between feast and famine requires a permanent change in basic eating habits—a topic we will return to in this chapter's Applications.

Other Factors in Hunger

As research on overeating suggests, "hunger" is affected by more than bodily needs for food. Let us consider some additional factors of interest.

Cultural Factors Learning to think of some foods as desirable and others as revolting obviously has much to do with eating habits. In the United States we would never consider eating the eyes out of the steamed head of a monkey, but in some parts of the world this dish is considered a real delicacy. By the same token, our willingness to eat meat, cows, and fish would be considered barbaric in many cultures. Thus, **cultural values** greatly affect the incentive value of various foods.

Taste Even tastes for "normal" foods may vary considerably. One experiment revealed that the hungrier you are, the more pleasant a sweet food tastes (Cabanac & Duclaux, 1970). It is also interesting to note that a **taste aversion** can be easily learned if a food causes sickness or is merely associated with nausea (Jacobsen et al., 1993). Not only will such foods be avoided, they too can become nauseating. A friend of the author's, who once became ill after eating a cheese Danish (well, actually, *several*), has never again been able to come face to face with this delightful pastry.

Question: If getting sick occurs long after eating, how does it become associated with the food eaten?

A good question. Taste aversions are a type of classical conditioning. As stated in Chapter 7, a long delay between the CS and US usually prevents conditioning. For this reason, psychologists theorize that we have a biological tendency to associate an upset stomach with food eaten earlier. Such learning usually helps protect both animals and people (Garcia et al., 1974). Yet, sadly, many human cancer patients suffer taste aversions long after the nausea of their drug treatments has passed (Jacobsen et al., 1993).

If you like animals, you will be interested in an imaginative approach to an age-old problem. In many rural areas, predators are poisoned, trapped, or shot on sight by livestock owners. These practices have nearly wiped out the timber wolf, and in some areas the coyote faces a similar end. How might the coyote be saved without an unacceptable loss of livestock?

In a classic experiment, coyotes were given lamb tainted with lithium chloride. Coyotes who took the bait rapidly became nauseated and vomited. After one or two such treatments, they developed **bait shyness**—a lasting distaste for the tainted food (Gustavson & Garcia, 1974). If applied consistently, taste aversion conditioning might solve many predator-livestock problems for less money than traditional methods (■ Fig. 10–8). (Perhaps this technique could even be used to protect roadrunners from the Wiley Coyote!)

Taste aversions may also help people avoid severe nutritional imbalances. For example, if you go on a fad diet and eat only grapefruit, you will eventually begin to feel ill. In time, associating your discomfort with grapefruit could create an aversion to it and restore some balance to your diet.

One classic study on **self-selection feeding** found that human infants ate a balanced diet when given a free choice of foods (Davis, 1928). Since the infants sometimes went on food jags, the overall balance of their eating may have been based, in part, on the process just described. It should be noted, however, that the "wisdom of the body" is quite limited. Babies in the study were only allowed to choose from fresh, unseasoned, unsweetened foods. If candy had been a choice, the infants might have gorged themselves on it (Story & Brown, 1987). We humans seem to have an innate preference for sweet and fatty foods—juicy steaks and fried chicken, cookies, cakes and so on (Katahn, 1984). Thus, an appetite for candy and junk food

■ **Fig. 10–8** *Like humans and other animals, coyotes develop taste aversions when food is associated with nausea.*

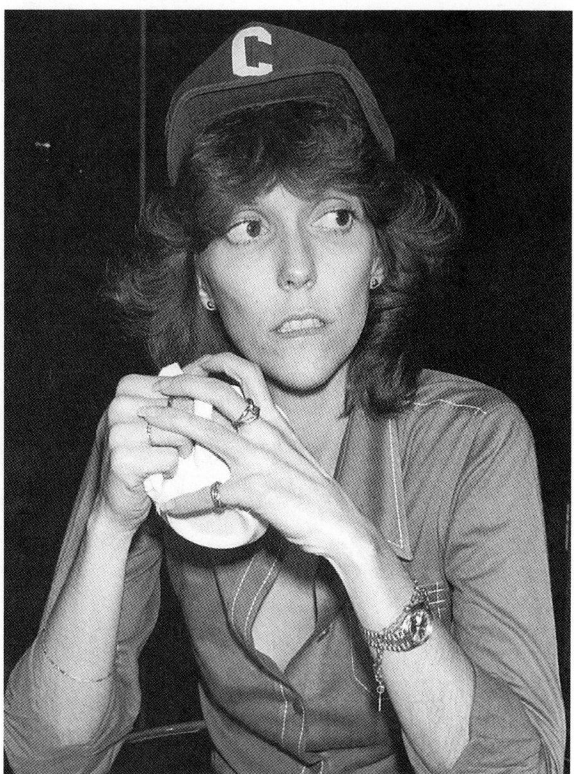

■ **Fig. 10–9** *Anorexia nervosa can be far more dangerous than many people realize. This haunting photo shows popular singer Karen Carpenter shortly before her death. Carpenter died of starvation-induced heart failure. More recently, Christy Henrich, a former member of the U.S. National Gymnastics Team, died at age 22. Henrich, too, suffered from anorexia. Many more victims of eating disorders die each year (Witherspoon, 1994).*

Anorexia nervosa Active self-starvation or a sustained loss of appetite that has psychological origins.

Bulimia nervosa Excessive eating (gorging) usually followed by self-induced vomiting and/or taking laxatives.

can easily override the weaker tendency to eat a balanced diet.

Eating Disorders

Under the sheets of her hospital bed Krystal looks like a starved skeleton. If her self-destructive course cannot be changed, Krystal may die of malnutrition. Serious cases of undereating like Krystal's are called **anorexia nervosa** (AN-uh–REK-see-yah ner-VOH-sah). Victims of anorexia, who are mostly adolescent females (5 to 10 percent are male), suffer devastating weight loss from self-inflicted starvation.

Question: Do anorexics lose their appetite?

No, many anorexics continue to feel hunger, and yet they struggle to starve themselves. The problem is best described as a *relentless pursuit of excessive thinness.* Often, the problem starts with "normal" dieting that gradually begins to dominate the person's life. In time, anorexics suffer physical weakness, absence of menstrual cycles, and a dangerous risk of infection. Five to eight percent (more than 1 in 20) die of malnutrition or related health problems (■ Fig. 10–9). ● Table 10–1 lists the symptoms of anorexia nervosa.

Bulimia nervosa (bue-LIHM-ee-yah), also known as the binge-purge syndrome, is a second major eating disorder. Bulimics gorge on food, then induce vomiting or take laxatives to avoid gaining weight (see Table 10–1). Like anorexia, bulimia is far more prevalent in

● **Table 10–1 Recognizing Eating Disorders**

Anorexia nervosa
■ Body weight below 85 percent of normal for one's height and age. ■ Refusal to maintain body weight in normal range. ■ Intense fear of becoming fat or gaining weight, even though underweight. ■ Disturbance in one's body image or perceived weight. ■ Self-evaluation is unduly influenced by body weight. ■ Denial of seriousness of abnormally low body weight. ■ Absence of menstrual periods. ■ Purging behavior (vomiting or misuse of laxatives or diuretics).
Bulimia nervosa
■ Normal or above normal weight. ■ Recurring binge eating. ■ Eating within an hour or two an amount of food that is much larger than most people would consume. ■ Feeling a lack of control over eating. ■ Purging behavior (vomiting or misuse of laxatives or diuretics). ■ Excessive exercise to prevent weight gain. ■ Fasting to prevent weight gain. ■ Self-evaluation is unduly influenced by body weight.

DSM–IV, 1994

Extracellular thirst Thirst caused by a reduction in the volume of fluids between body cells.

women than in men. Approximately 5 percent of college women are bulimic and as many as 61 percent have milder eating problems (Mintz & Betz, 1988; Ollendick & Hart, 1985). Bingeing and purging can also cause serious health problems. Typical risks include sore throat, hair loss, muscle spasms, kidney damage, dehydration, erosion of tooth enamel, swelling of the salivary glands, menstrual irregularity, loss of sex drive, and even heart attack.

Question: What causes anorexia and bulimia?

Causes Both anorexics and bulimics have unrealistic views of their body size and exaggerated fears of becoming fat. Many victims overestimate their body size by 25 percent or more. Almost all continue to see themselves as "fat" when in fact they are wasting away (■ Fig. 10–10) (Williamson et al., 1989). In some cases, body image can actually change after a meal. For example, after eating nothing more than a candy bar and a soft drink, bulimic women thought they had grown larger. It's no wonder that bulimic women often panic and attempt to purge themselves of food (McKenzie et al., 1993).

Control is another issue for people with eating disorders. Anorexics are usually described as "perfect" daughters—helpful, considerate, conforming, and obedient. Many seem to be trying to have perfect control in one area of their lives, by being perfectly slim. Bulimics also seem to be concerned with control. Typically they are obsessed with thoughts of weight, food, eating, and ridding themselves of food. Most feel guilt, shame, self-contempt, and anxiety after a binge. Vomiting reduces this anxiety, which makes purging highly reinforcing for many bulimics. Depression is also a factor in some eating disorders (Nagel & Jones, 1992).

Treatment Eating disorders are serious, health- and life-threatening problems that rarely disappear on their own. In almost all cases, victims need professional help. Treatment for anorexia usually begins with a carefully controlled medical diet to restore weight and health. Next, the client enters counseling to work on the personal conflicts and family issues that led to weight loss. For bulimia, psychologists have had some success with behavioral counseling. This approach includes careful self-monitoring of food intake and work on extinguishing the urge to vomit after eating.

Although much progress is being made in treating eating disorders, most anorexics do not seek help, and many actively resist it. Bulimics will sometimes seek treatment, but usually not until their eating habits become intolerable. In either case, it may take strong urging by family or friends to get victims into treatment. (Additional sources: DSM-IV, 1994; Moore, 1981; Rosen & Leitenburg, 1982; Schlessier-Stroop, 1984.)

■ **Fig. 10–10** *Women with abnormal eating habits were asked to rate their body shape on a scale similar to the one you see here. As a group, they chose ideal figures much thinner than what they thought their current weights were. (Most women say they want to be thinner than they currently are, but to a lesser degree than women with eating problems.) Notice that the women with eating problems chose an ideal weight that was even thinner than what they thought men prefer. This is not typical of most women. In this study, only women with eating problems wanted to be thinner than what they thought men find attractive (Zellner, Harner, & Adler, 1989).*

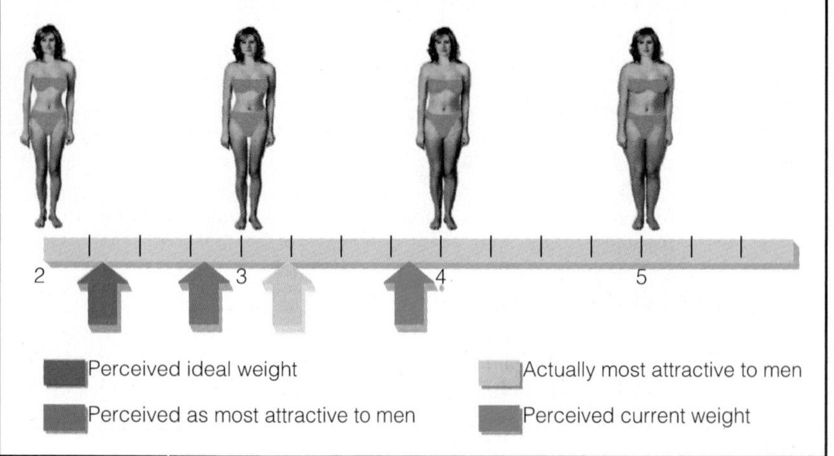

Primary Motives Revisited—Thirst, Sex, and Pain

Most other primary motives show patterns of control similar to those observed in hunger. For example, thirst is only partially related to dryness of the mouth and throat. When drugs are used to keep the mouth constantly wet or dry, thirst and water intake remain normal. Like hunger, thirst appears to be regulated by the hypothalamus, where separate *thirst* and *thirst satiety* systems are found. Also like hunger, thirst is strongly affected by individual learning and by cultural values.

Thirst

You may not have noticed, but there are actually two kinds of thirst. **Extracellular thirst** occurs when water is lost from the fluids surrounding the cells of your body. Bleeding, vomiting, diarrhea, sweating, and drinking alcohol cause this type of thirst (Houston, 1985). When a person loses both water and minerals in any of these ways—especially by perspiration—a slightly salty liquid may be more satisfying than plain water.

Question: Why would a thirsty person want to drink salty water?

The reason is that before the body can retain water, minerals lost through perspiration (mainly salt) must be replaced. In lab tests, animals greatly prefer salt water after salt levels in their bodies are lowered (Stricker & Verbalis, 1988). Similarly, some nomadic peoples of the Sahara Desert prize blood as a beverage, probably because of its saltiness. (Maybe they should try Gatorade?)

A second type of thirst occurs when you eat a salty meal. In this instance your body does not lose fluid. Instead, *excess* salt causes fluid to be drawn out of cells. As the cells "shrink," **intracellular thirst** is triggered. Thirst of this type is best quenched by plain water.

The drives for food, water, air, sleep, and elimination are all fairly similar in that they are generated by a combination of activities in the body and the brain, are modified by learning and culture, and are influenced by external factors. Two unusual primary drives are the sex drive and the drive to avoid pain.

Question: How is the drive to avoid pain different?

Pain

Drives such as hunger, thirst, and sleepiness come and go in a fairly regular cycle each day. Pain avoidance, by contrast, is an **episodic drive** (ep-ih-SOD-ik). That is, it occurs in distinct episodes, because it is aroused only when damage to the body takes place. Most of the primary drives cause us to actively seek a desired goal (food, drink, warmth, and so forth). The goal of the pain avoidance drive is the elimination of pain.

It may surprise you to discover that the drive to avoid pain is partly learned. Some people, for instance, feel they must be "tough" and not show any discomfort; others complain loudly at the smallest ache or pain. As you might expect, the first attitude raises pain tolerance, and the second lowers it (Kleinke, 1978). Such attitudes explain why members of some societies endure cutting, burning, whipping, tattooing, and piercing of the skin that would agonize the typical member of our society (■ Fig. 10–11).

The Sex Drive

The sex drive is an unusual motive. In fact, many psychologists do not think of sex as a primary motive because sex (contrary to anything your personal experience might suggest) is not necessary for *individual* survival. It is necessary, of course, for *group* survival among humans and other creatures.

In lower animals the sex drive is directly related to the action of bodily hormones. Female mammals, other than humans, are interested in mating only when their fertility cycles are in the stage of **estrus,** or "heat" (caused by secretion of the hormone **estrogen** into the bloodstream). Hormones are important in the male animal as well. In most lower animals, castration will abolish the sex drive. But in contrast to the female, the normal male animal is almost always ready to mate. His sex drive is primarily aroused by the behavior of a receptive female. In many species, mating is therefore closely tied to the fertility cycle of the female.

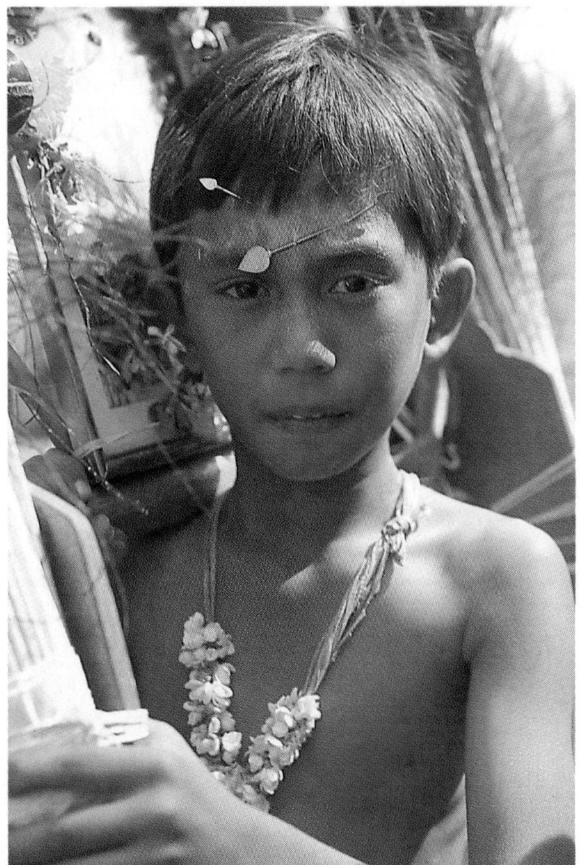

■ **Fig. 10–11** *Tolerance for pain and the strength of a person's motivation to avoid discomfort are greatly affected by cultural practices and beliefs.*

Question: How much do hormones affect the sex drive in humans?

The link between hormones and the sex drive grows weaker as we ascend the biological scale. Hormones do affect the human sex drive, but only to a limited degree. For example, one careful study found no connection between female sexual activity and the monthly menstrual cycle (Udry & Morris, 1977). In humans, mental, cultural, and emotional factors determine sexual expression. However, our liberation from hormones is not total. Human males show a loss of sex drive after castration, and some women lose sexual desire when using birth control pills (McCauley & Ehrhardt, 1976).

Human sexual behavior and attitudes are discussed in detail in Chapter 19. For now it is enough to note that the sex drive is largely **non-homeostatic.** In humans, the sex drive can be aroused at virtually any

Intracellular thirst Thirst triggered when fluid is drawn out of cells due to an increased concentration of salts and minerals outside the cells.

Episodic drive A drive that occurs in distinct episodes associated with particular conditions (for example, pain avoidance, sexual motivation).

Estrus Changes in the reproductive organs and sexual drives of animals that create a desire for mating; particularly used to refer to females in heat.

Estrogen Any of a number of female sex hormones.

Non-homeostatic drive A drive that is relatively independent of physical deprivation cycles or bodily need states.

Exploration drive Drive to investigate unfamiliar areas of the environment.

Manipulation drive Drive to investigate objects by touching and handling them.

Curiosity drive Drive assumed to underlie a wide range of investigative and stimulus-seeking behaviors.

time by almost anything. It therefore shows no clear relationship to deprivation (the amount of time since the drive was last satisfied). Certainly, an increase in desire may occur as time passes. But on the other hand, recent sexual activity does not prevent sexual desire from occurring again. Notice, too, that people may seek to arouse the sex drive as well as to reduce it. This unusual quality makes the sex drive capable of motivating a wide range of behaviors. It also explains why sex is used to sell almost everything imaginable.

The non-homeostatic quality of the sex drive can be shown in this way: An animal is allowed to copulate until it seems to have no further interest in sexual behavior. Then a new sexual partner is provided. Immediately the animal resumes sexual activity. This pattern is called the *Coolidge effect* after former U.S. president Calvin Coolidge. What, you might ask, does Calvin Coolidge have to do with the sex drive? The answer is found in the following story.

While touring an experimental farm, Coolidge's wife reportedly asked if a rooster mated just once a day. "No ma'am," she was told, "he mates dozens of times each day." "Tell that to the president," she said, with a faraway look in her eyes. When President Coolidge reached the same part of the tour, his wife's message was given to him. His reaction was to ask if the dozens of matings were with the same hen. No, he was told, different hens were involved. "Tell *that* to Mrs. Coolidge," the president is said to have replied.

Learning Check

1. Systems for the control of hunger and thirst are linked with the ______________ of the brain.
2. The hunger satiety system in the hypothalamus signals the body to start eating when it receives signals from the liver or detects changes in blood sugar. T or F?
3. Varied diets containing high levels of sweets and fats encourage overeating only for people who tend to eat when they are anxious. T or F?
4. Bait shyness occurs when
   a. a specific hunger develops
   b. the set point for body fat is altered
   c. the hypothalamus is activated electrically
   d. a taste aversion is formed
5. People who diet frequently tend to benefit from practice: They lose weight more quickly each time they diet. T or F?
6. Anorexia nervosa is also known as the binge-purge syndrome. T or F?
7. Thirst may be either intracellular or ______________ .
8. Pain avoidance is an ______________ drive.
9. Sexual behavior in animals is largely controlled by estrogen levels in the female and the occurrence of estrus in the male. T or F?

Critical Thinking

10. Kim, who is overweight, is highly sensitive to external eating cues. How might her wristwatch contribute to her overeating?

Answers: 1. hypothalamus 2. F 3. F 4. *d* 5. F 6. F 7. extracellular 8. episodic 9. F 10. The time of day can influence eating, especially for externally cued eaters, who tend to get hungry at mealtimes, irrespective of their internal needs for food.

Stimulus Drives—Skydiving, Horror Movies, and the Fun Zone

It is sometimes said that curiosity killed the cat, but nothing could be further from the truth. Drives for **exploration, manipulation,** or simply for **curiosity** clearly aid survival. As mentioned earlier, such drives might be explained by the life-and-death necessity of keeping track of sources of food, danger, and other important details of the environment. However, curiosity drives seem to go beyond such needs.

Monkey Business

In an experiment, monkeys confined to a dimly lit box learned to perform a simple task in order to open a window that allowed them to view the outside world (Butler & Harlow, 1954). In a similar experiment, monkeys quickly learned to solve a mechanical puzzle made up of interlocking metal pins, hooks, and hasps (Butler, 1954) (■ Fig. 10–12). In both situations, no external reward was offered for exploration or manipulation.

The puzzle-solving monkeys seemed to work for the sheer fun of it. An interest in video games, chess, cross-

■ Fig. 10–12 *Monkeys happily open locks that are placed in their cage. Since no reward is given for this activity, it provides evidence of the existence of stimulus needs. (Photo courtesy of Harry F. Harlow.)*

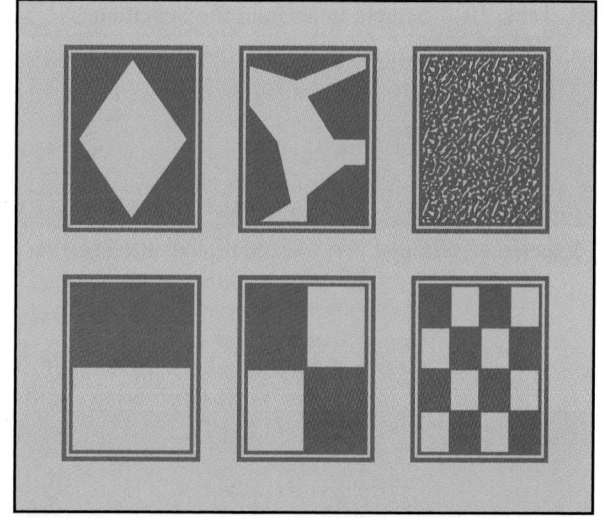

■ Fig. 10–13 *Daniel Berlyne studied curiosity in infants by showing them these designs. Babies looked first at the more complex patterns on the right. (From* Science, 153, *25–33. Copyright © 1966 by the American Association for the Advancement of Science.)*

word puzzles, Rubik's cube, and the like offers a human parallel. Curiosity—the drive to *know*—also seems to be powerful in humans. Scientific investigation, intellectual curiosity, and other advanced activities may express this basic drive.

Closely related to curiosity is the drive for sensory stimulation. It is well known that humans and animals demand and actively seek stimulation (Reykowski, 1982). As discussed in Chapter 6, people who have undergone prolonged or severe **sensory deprivation**—for example, prisoners, arctic explorers, radar operators, and truck drivers—often report sensory distortions and disturbed thinking.

The drive for stimulation can even be observed in infants. When babies are shown printed designs (■ Fig. 10–13), they spend more time looking at complex patterns than at simpler ones (Berlyne, 1966). Indeed, human infants seem to have an almost limitless appetite for stimulation. By the time a child can walk, few things in the home have not been tasted, touched, viewed, handled, or, in the case of toys, destroyed!

Question: Are stimulus drives homeostatic?

Arousal Theory

By combining homeostasis with drives for stimulation, we get a useful model of human behavior. The **arousal theory** of motivation states that there are ideal levels of arousal for various activities. It further assumes that people try to keep arousal near these ideal levels (Hebb, 1966).

Question: What do you mean by arousal?

Arousal refers to activation of the body and the nervous system. Arousal is zero at death; it is low during sleep; it is moderate during normal daily activities; and it is high at times of excitement, emotion, or panic. Arousal theory assumes that an individual becomes uncomfortable when arousal is too low ("I'm bored.") or when it is too high, as in fear, anxiety, or panic ("The dentist will see you now."). Curiosity and stimulation seeking can be interpreted as attempts to raise the level of arousal when it is too low. Most adults vary their activities to maintain a comfortable level of activation. Music, parties, athletics, conversation, sleep, and the like are mixed to keep arousal at moderate levels, thus preventing both boredom and overstimulation.

Question: Do people vary in their needs for stimulation?

Sensation Seekers The city dweller who visits the country complains that it is "too quiet," and seeks some "action." The country dweller finds the city "hectic," "overwhelming," or "too much," and seeks peace and quiet. Arousal theory also assumes that each of us learns to seek a personal "ideal" or preferred level of arousal. Marvin Zuckerman (1990) has devised a test to measure such differences. The *Sensation-Seeking Scale* (SSS), as he calls it, includes statements like the samples shown in ● Table 10–2 (from Zuckerman et al., 1978).

High and low sensation seeking probably reflects differences in how each person's body responds to new, unusual, surprising, or intense stimulation (Zuckerman, 1990). People who score high on the full-length version of this test tend to be extroverted, independent individuals who value change (■ Fig. 10–14). They also report more sexual partners than low scorers; they are more

Sensory deprivation Any major reduction in the amount or variety of sensory stimulation.

Arousal theory Assumes that people prefer to maintain "ideal," or comfortable, levels of arousal.

Arousal The overall level of excitation or activation in a person or animal.

Sensation seeking A personality trait of persons who prefer high levels of stimulation.

EXPLORATION

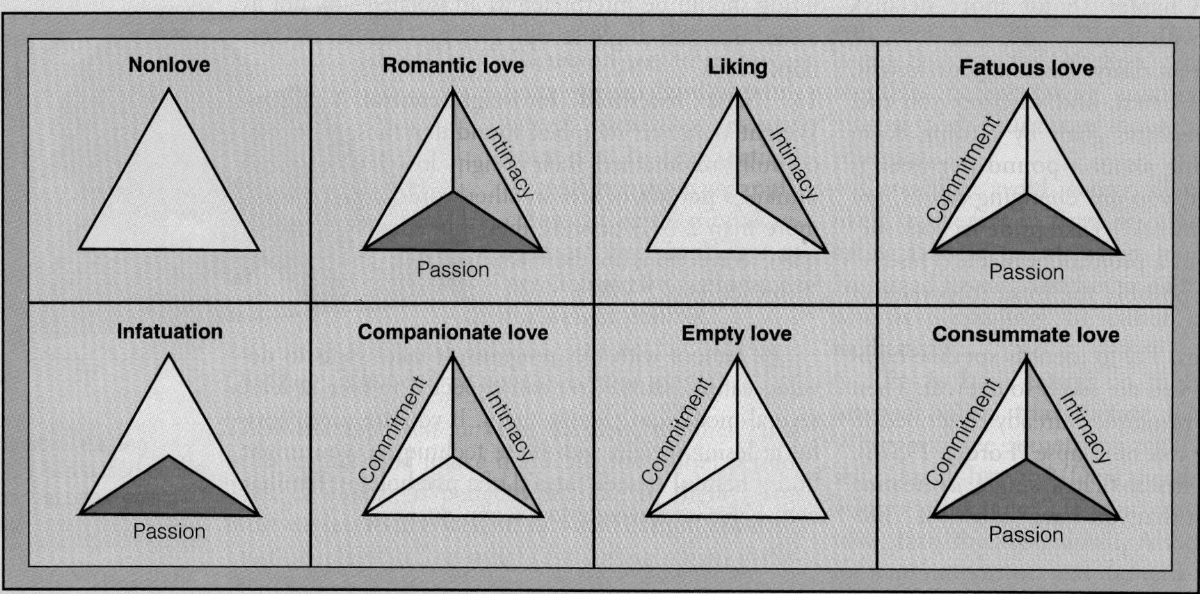

■ Fig. 10–34 *Sternberg's triangular theory of love.*

We will return to these types in a moment, but first let's briefly explore love's three "ingredients."

Intimacy A relationship has intimacy, or closeness, if affection, sharing, communication, and support are present. Intimacy grows steadily at first, but in time it levels off. After it does, people in long-term relationships may gradually lose sight of the fact that they are still very close and mutually dependent.

Passion Passion refers mainly to *physiological arousal.* This arousal may be sexual, but it includes other sources too. As discussed earlier in this chapter, arousal, no matter what its cause, may be interpreted as passion in a romantic relationship (Bersheid & Walster, 1974b). This is probably why passionate love often occurs against a backdrop of danger, adversity, or frustration—especially in soap operas and romance novels! Passion is the primary source of love's *intensity.* It's not surprising, then, that romance inspires the strongest feelings of love. In contrast, love for siblings is least intense (Sternberg & Grajeck, 1984).

Commitment The third side of the love triangle consists of your decision to love another person and your degree of long-term commitment to them. Commitment starts at zero before you meet a person and it grows steadily as you get acquainted. Like intimacy, commitment tends to level off. However, it may waver up and down with a relationship's good times and bad times. Commitment drops rapidly when a relationship is in serious trouble.

Seven Flavors of Love

The presence or absence of intimacy, passion, and/or commitment produces eight triangles. The first defines **non-love,** a total absence of all three elements.

In **liking,** you feel close to a person and communicate well with her or him. However, you do not feel any passion or deep commitment to the person. A likable classmate might fall into this category.

Romantic love mixes intimacy (closeness and sharing) with passion (often in the form of physical attraction). Despite its intensity, romantic love does not involve much commitment at first. Think, for example, of a summer romance that ends in a relatively easy parting of ways.

Fatuous love describes commitments made rapidly on the basis of physical attraction (passion), but without much emotional intimacy. Fatuous love is of the boy-meets-girl-and-they-get-married-a-month-later type. Relationships started this way risk failure because lovers make a commitment before they really get to know each other well.

Infatuation is an even more superficial form of love. In this case a person is inflamed with passion, but shares no intimacy or commitment with the beloved. In time, of course, infatuation may lead to more lasting kinds of love.

Companionate love refers to affection and deep attachment that is built on respect, shared interests, and firm friendship. Companionate love is lower key emotionally. However, it is steady and long term and tends to grow in time. Companionate love is the "kind of affection we feel for those with whom our lives are deeply intertwined" (Walster & Walster, 1978).

Couples sometimes reach a point where there is little passion or intimacy left in their relationship. If they stay together merely out of commitment or habit, they experience **empty love.**

Consummate love occurs when two people are passionate, committed to one another, and emotionally close. Complete, balanced love of this kind occurs only in very special relationships. When all three factors are present, a relationship is more likely to be lasting (Whitley, 1993).

EXPLORATION

How Do I Love Thee? The categories described here are certainly not the last word on love. Undoubtedly, other kinds of love also exist. In addition, Sternberg's theory may place too much emphasis on passion. In most relationships, intimacy and commitment are a bigger part of love than passion is (Clark & Reis, 1988; Tucker & Aron, 1993).

Our culture also tends to place much emphasis on passion as the main basis for "falling" in love. However, this overlooks the fact that the passionate, breathless stage of love typically lasts only about 6 to 30 months (Walster & Walster, 1978). What happens when this period ends? Quite often, people separate.

There is a degree of danger in expecting to live forever on a romantic cloud. People who are primarily caught up in passionate love may neglect to build a more lasting relationship. Rather than down-playing companionate love, it is helpful to realize that lovers must also be friends. High quality relationships are frequently based on secure, companionate love (Hecht et al., 1994). In fact, consummate love is basically a blending of romantic love and companionate love.

You may be tempted to match the love triangles with your own relationships. If you do apply the theory, remember that relationships vary greatly and that few are perfect (Trotter, 1986). In another study, Sternberg and Michael Barnes (1986) found that relationships are generally satisfying if you think the other person feels about you the way you would *like* for her or him to feel about you.

Some politicians have belittled the study of love as "unscientific." But in a world often wracked by violence, hatred, and despair, what could be more important than understanding the elusive state we call love?

Liking Intimacy without passion or commitment.

Romantic love Intimacy plus passion.

Fatuous love Passion with commitment, but lacking intimacy.

Infatuation Passion without commitment or intimacy.

Companionate love Intimacy and commitment without passion.

Empty love Commitment without intimacy or passion.

Consummate love Passion, intimacy, and commitment.

Learning Check

1. Essentially, all types of love can be described as a passion for another person. T or F?
2. According to Sternberg's theory, all forms of love involve commitment to another person or to a relationship. T or F?
3. Passion is the primary element of infatuation. T or F?
4. Fatuous love can be defined as commitment based on passion but lacking in intimacy. T or F?
5. The passionate stage of love usually lasts only 6 to 30 weeks. T or F?
6. Passionate love tends to decline at each of three major transitions in marriage. Based on your own observations of relationships, what do you think they are? ***Critical Thinking***

Answers: 1. F 2. F 3. T 4. T 5. F 6. The transitions are: From engagement to marriage; from childlessness to parenthood; and from children living at home to an empty nest (Tucker & Aron, 1993).

Chapter Summary

■ ***What is motivation? Are there different types of motives?***

- Motives **initiate, sustain,** and **direct** activities. Motivation typically involves the sequence **need, drive, goal,** and **goal attainment** (need reduction).
- Behavior can be activated either by **needs** (push) or by **goals** (pull). The attractiveness of a goal and its ability to initiate action are related to its **incentive value.**
- Three principal types of motives are **primary motives, stimulus motives,** and **secondary motives.** Most primary motives operate to maintain **homeostasis.**

■ ***What causes hunger? Overeating? Eating disorders?***

- Hunger is influenced by a complex interplay between fullness of the stomach, blood sugar levels, metabolism in the liver, and fat stores in the body. The most direct control of eating is effected by the **hypothalamus,** which has areas that act like **feeding** and **satiety** systems.
- Other factors influencing hunger are the body's **set point,** external **eating cues,** the attractiveness and variety of **diet, emotions,** learned **taste preferences** and **taste aversions,** and **cultural values.**

- **Anorexia nervosa** (self-inflicted starvation) and **bulimia nervosa** (gorging and purging) are two prominent eating disorders. Both problems tend to involve conflicts about self-image, self-control, and anxiety.

■ ***Is there more than one type of thirst?***

- Like hunger, thirst and other basic motives are affected by a number of bodily factors, but are primarily under the central control of the hypothalamus. Thirst may be either **intracellular** or **extracellular.**

■ ***In what ways are pain avoidance and the sex drive unusual?***

- Pain avoidance is unusual because it is **episodic** as opposed to **cyclic.** Pain avoidance and pain tolerance are partially learned. The sex drive is also unusual in that it is **non-homeostatic.**

■ ***How does arousal relate to motivation?***

- The stimulus motives include drives for **exploration, manipulation, change,** and **sensory stimulation.**
- Drives for stimulation are partially explained by **arousal theory,** which states that an ideal level of bodily arousal will be maintained if possible. The desired level of arousal or stimulation varies from person to person, as measured by the *Sensation-Seeking Scale.*
- Optimal performance on a task usually occurs at *moderate* levels of arousal. This relationship is described by an **inverted U function.** The **Yerkes-Dodson law** further states that for simple tasks the ideal arousal level is higher, and for complex tasks it is lower.
- **Circadian rhythms** of bodily activity are closely tied to sleep, activity, and energy cycles. Time zone travel and shift work can seriously disrupt sleep and bodily rhythms. Biorhythm theory is a false system unrelated to circadian rhythms.

■ ***What are social motives? Why are they important?***

- **Social motives** are learned through socialization and cultural conditioning. Such motives account for much of the diversity of human motivation. **Opponent-process theory** explains the operation of some acquired motives.
- One of the most prominent social motives is the **need for achievement (nAch).** High nAch is correlated with success in many situations, with occupational choice, and with *moderate* risk taking.
- There is evidence that at times both men and women experience a **fear of success.** This is especially true if achievement is seen as conflicting with social acceptance.

■ ***Are some motives more basic than others?***

- Maslow's **hierarchy of motives** categorizes needs as **basic** and **growth oriented.** Lower needs in the hierarchy are assumed to be **prepotent** (dominant) over higher needs. Self-actualization, the highest and most fragile need, is reflected in **meta-needs.**
- Higher needs in Maslow's hierarchy are closely related to the concept of **intrinsic motivation.** In many situations, **extrinsic motivation** (that which is induced by obvious external rewards) can reduce intrinsic motivation, enjoyment, and creativity.

■ ***What happens during emotion?***

- Emotions are linked to many basic **adaptive behaviors.** Other major elements of emotion are **physiological changes** in the body, **emotional expressions,** and **emotional feelings.**
- The following are considered to be **primary emotions:** *fear, surprise, sadness, disgust, anger, anticipation, joy,* and *acceptance.* Other emotions seem to represent mixtures of the primaries.
- Physical changes associated with emotion are caused by the action of **adrenaline,** a hormone released into the bloodstream, and by activity in the **autonomic nervous system** (ANS).
- The **sympathetic branch** of the ANS is primarily responsible for arousing the body, the **parasympathetic branch** for quieting it. Sudden death due to prolonged and intense emotion is probably related to a **parasympathetic rebound.** Heart attacks caused by sudden intense emotion are more likely due to sympathetic arousal.

■ ***Can "lie detectors" really detect lies?***

- The **polygraph,** or "lie detector," measures emotional arousal by monitoring *heart rate, blood pressure, breathing rate,* and the *galvanic skin response (GSR).* The accuracy of the lie detector has been challenged by many researchers.

■ ***How accurately are emotions expressed by "body language" and the face?***

- Basic emotional expressions, such as smiling or baring one's teeth when angry, appear to be unlearned. **Facial expressions** appear to be central to emotion.
- Body gestures and movements (body language) also express feelings, mainly by communicating **emotional tone.** Three dimensions of facial expressions are **pleasantness-unpleasantness, attention-rejection,** and **activation.** The study of body language is know as **kinesics.**
- Lying can sometimes be detected from changes in **illustrators** or **emblems** and from signs of **general arousal.**

■ ***How do psychologists explain emotions?***

- The **James-Lange theory** of emotion says that emotional *experience* follows the bodily reactions of emotion. In contrast, the **Cannon-Bard theory** says that bodily reactions and emotional experience occur at the same time and that emotions are organized in the brain.
- Schachter's **cognitive theory** of emotion emphasizes the importance of *labels*, or interpretations, applied to feelings of bodily arousal. Also important is the process of **attribution,** in which bodily arousal is attributed to a particular person, object, or situation.
- The **facial feedback hypothesis** holds that sensations and information from emotional expressions help define what emotion a person is feeling.
- Contemporary views of emotion place greater emphasis on the effects of **cognitive appraisals** of situations. Also, all of the elements of emotion are seen as interrelated and interacting.

■ ***Can psychology be applied to weight control?***

- Because of the limitations of traditional dieting, changing basic eating patterns and habits is usually more effective. **Behavioral dieting** brings about such changes by use of self-control techniques.

■ ***What is the nature of love?***

- Sternberg's **triangular theory** describes love as a combination of **passion, intimacy,** and **commitment.** Combinations of these three factors produce **non-love, liking, infatuation, romantic love, fatuous love, companionate love, empty love,** and **consummate love.**

Questions for Discussion

1. Discuss some of the factors that contribute to overeating at Thanksgiving or a similar holiday feast.
2. It is noon in July in the desert. You have been sweating in the sun and enjoying the warmth. You are suddenly thirsty. Why? What should you do about it?
3. The sex drive is not essential for individual survival, and it can be easily interrupted by any of the other primary drives. Why do you think so much energy is directed toward sexuality in our culture?
4. In what ways have you observed the stimulus motives at work in human behavior? Does learning contribute to curiosity or needs for stimulation?
5. Why doesn't jet lag occur for flights that only go north or south?
6. Does the American emphasis on competition (in your opinion) encourage achievement or discourage it? (Consider the effects, for example, when only one person can be considered the "winner" in many situations.)
7. In *Lady Windermere's Fan*, playwright Oscar Wilde said, "In this world there are only two tragedies. One is not getting what one wants, and the other is getting it. The last is the real tragedy." What do you think Wilde meant? Where does your motivation come from?
8. If you had a guaranteed income, would you "work?" What do you think you would spend your time doing? For how long? What, if anything, does this reveal about intrinsic motivation?
9. How has our culture contributed to eating problems such as obesity, anorexia nervosa, and bulimia? In some cultures, a degree of fatness is considered desirable as a hedge against starvation. Do we label people "fat" when they are perfectly healthy?
10. Do you consider yourself more emotional or less emotional than average? What role has learning played in the development of your emotional life? (Consider the influence of family, friends, and culture.)
11. There is an element of truth to each of the theories of emotion. What parts of each seem to apply best to your own emotions?
12. What would be the advantages and disadvantages of being emotionless? (You might use Mr. Spock from the "Star Trek" movies as a model for answering this question.)
13. In your opinion, what added limits, if any, should be placed on the use of lie detection devices by businesses? By the military? By government?
14. Did you learn "body language" from your parents? How similar are your facial and hand gestures to theirs?
15. How do you define love? Do you believe that Sternberg's theory captures the essence of love? Why do you think our culture places so much emphasis on passion as the basis for falling in love? What are the consequences of this emphasis?

Chapter 11

Health, Stress, and Coping

IN THIS CHAPTER

Health psychology
Behavioral risk factors
Health-promoting behaviors
Stress
Frustration
Conflict
Defense mechanisms
Learned helplessness
Stress and health
Applications:
Stress management
Exploration:
Meditation and relaxation

CHAPTER PREVIEW

How To Build a Human Time Bomb

When he was arrested, John was sitting atop a 30-ton bulldozer, staring into space. Behind him lay a mile-long path of destruction: John had cut a broad, straight path through yards, roads, and fields. The path led back to his house where the dozer was usually kept. Why did he do it? John explained that his father had denied him use of the family car that morning. Hours later, his anger exploded.

Question: What would cause someone to react so drastically to a family disagreement?

In John's case, the answer is that he was frustrated—*very frustrated! Perhaps you have been as frustrated as John must have been when he climbed into the driver's seat. For example, picture yourself looking for a parking space in a crowded lot. Imagine that you are late for a test and have already been delayed by an irritating traffic jam. After 15 minutes of frantic searching, you finally spy an empty space, but as you start toward it, a Volkswagen darts around the corner and into "your" space. A car behind you begins to honk impatiently. Your car's radiator boils over. In such a situation, you might be seized by a colossal desire to run over anything in sight—other cars, pedestrians, lampposts, trees, and flower beds. Few people actually carry out such impulses, but the feeling is common. Aggressive urges frequently accompany frustration (Berkowitz, 1988).*

Question: Is frustration the same as anger?

No. Frustration *can be defined as a negative emotional state that occurs when one is prevented from reaching a goal. John's desire to use the family car was blocked by his father. Similarly, in the imaginary parking lot, the goal of finding a parking space was blocked by the presence of other cars.*

Frustration is just one of the many causes of stress. *Stress occurs whenever a challenge or a threat forces a person to* adjust or adapt. *Stress is a normal part of life. But when stress is severe or prolonged it can do tremendous damage to one's health. Stress is an example of a* behavioral *factor that directly affects personal health and well-being. In the first part of this chapter we will explore a variety of behavioral risks to your health. Then, we will look more closely at what stress is and how it affects us. After that, we will stress effective ways of coping with stress.*

Health psychology Study of the ways in which psychological principles can be used to prevent illness and promote health.

Behavioral medicine The study of behavioral factors in medicine, physical illness, and medical treatment.

Lifestyle disease A disease related to health-damaging personal habits.

Behavioral risk factors Behaviors that increase the chances of disease or injury or that shorten life expectancy.

Survey Questions

- What is health psychology? How does behavior affect health?
- What is stress? What factors determine its severity?
- What causes frustration and what are typical reactions to it?
- Are there different types of conflict? How do people react to conflict?
- What are defense mechanisms?
- What do we know about coping with feelings of helplessness and depression?
- How is stress related to health and disease?
- What are the best strategies for managing stress?
- Is meditation useful for coping with stress?

Health Psychology—Here's to Your Good Health

Most people agree that health is important—especially their own. Yet, almost one-half of all deaths in the United States are primarily due to unhealthy behavior or lifestyles. A new specialty called **health psychology** aims to do something about it. The core of this approach is the use of psychological principles to promote health and to prevent illness (Taylor, 1990). Psychologists working in the allied field of **behavioral medicine** apply psychological knowledge to medical problems. Their interests include the control of pain, adjustment to chronic illness, adherence to doctors' instructions, stress-related diseases, and similar topics (Feuerstein et al., 1986).

Behavioral Risk Factors

Around the turn of the century, people primarily died from infectious diseases and accidents. Today, people generally suffer and die from **lifestyle diseases,** such as heart disease, stroke, lung cancer, and similar problems (McGinnis & Foege, 1993). (See ■ Figure 11–1.) Clearly, some behaviors and lifestyles promote health, whereas others increase the likelihood of illness and death. As the cartoon character Pogo put it, "We have met the enemy and he is us."

Question: What kinds of behavior are you referring to as unhealthy?

Although some causes of poor health are beyond our control, psychologists have identified a number of **behavioral risk factors** that *can* be controlled. Each of the following factors increases the chances of accident,

■ **Fig. 11–1** *The nine leading causes of death in the United States are shown in this graph. As you can see, eight of the top nine causes are directly related to behavioral risk factors (infection is the exception). At least 45 percent of all deaths can be traced to unhealthful behavior. The percentage of day-to-day health problems related to unhealthful behavior is even higher. (Data from McGinnis & Foege, 1993.)*

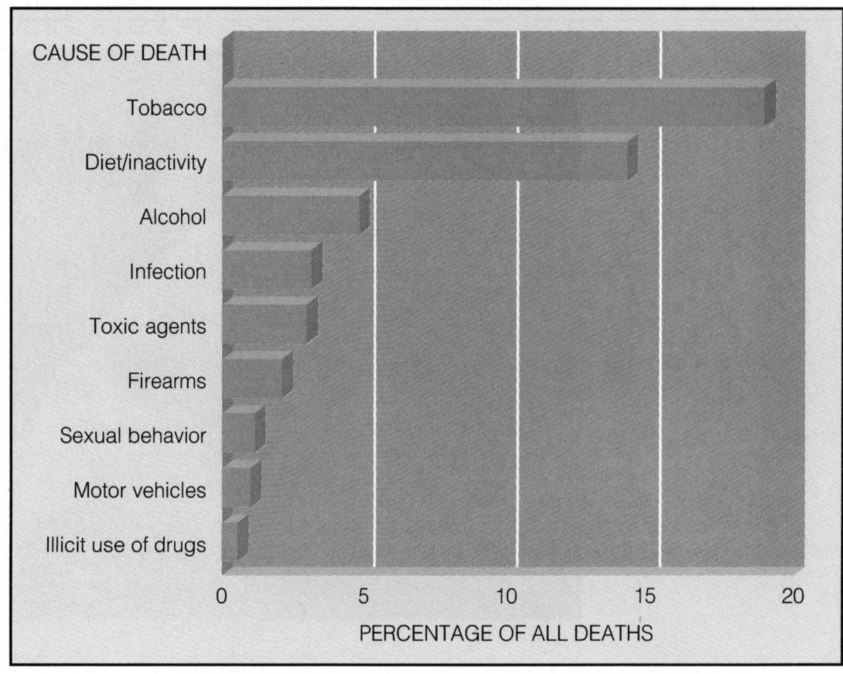

Disease-prone personality A personality style associated with poor health; marked by persistent negative emotions, including anxiety, depression, and hostility.

Health-promoting behavior Any practice that tends to help maintain or promote good health.

disease, and early death: high levels of stress, untreated high blood pressure, cigarette smoking, abuse of alcohol or other drugs, overeating, underexercise, risky sexual behavior, exposure to toxic substances, violence, and driving at excessive speeds (Dubbert, 1992; Matarazzo, 1984). A general **disease-prone personality** type may also exist. People who have this pattern tend to be chronically depressed, anxious, and hostile. They are also frequently ill (Taylor, 1990).

Lifestyle In your mind's eye, fast-forward an imaginary film of your life all the way to old age. Do it twice—once with a lifestyle including a large number of behavioral risk factors, and the second time without them. It should be obvious that when countless small risks add up, they dramatically raise the chance of illness. If stress is a frequent part of your life, visualize your body seething with emotion, day after day after day. If you smoke, picture a lifetime's worth of cigarette smoke blown through your lungs in a week or a day. If you drink, take a lifetime of alcohol's assaults on the brain, stomach, and liver and squeeze them into a month: Your body would be poisoned, ravaged, and soon dead. If you eat a high-fat, high-cholesterol diet, fast-forward a lifetime of heart-killing plaque building up in your arteries (■ Fig. 11–2).

Although it may sound like it, this discussion is not meant to be a sermon. It is merely a reminder that risk factors do make a difference. To make matters worse, unhealthy lifestyles almost always create multiple risks (Feuerstein et al., 1986). That is, people who smoke are also likely to drink excessively. Those who overeat usually do not get enough exercise. And so on (Matarazzo, 1984).

Health-Promoting Behaviors

To help prevent disease and promote well-being, health psychologists first try to remove behavioral risk factors. All the medicine or surgery in the world may not be enough to restore health without changes in behavior. We all know someone who has had a heart attack or lung disease and who cannot or will not change the habits that have contributed to their illness (Matarazzo, 1984).

Beyond this, psychologists are also interested in increasing behaviors that actively promote health. **Health-promoting behaviors** include such obvious practices as getting regular exercise, maintaining a balanced diet, and managing stress. Health-promoting behaviors can also be as simple as using seat belts in a car—a practice that greatly ups life expectancy!

Common sense suggests that basic health practices should extend a person's life. But do they? A major study done in Alameda County, California provides an answer (Belloc, 1973; Belloc & Breslow, 1972; Breslow & Enstrom, 1980). In this study, nearly 7000 people were given a detailed health questionnaire that focused on 7 basic health practices. In ensuing years the health and death records of these people were closely watched. Before we discuss the results, you might find it interesting to check the items listed here that apply to you.

Basic Health-Promoting Behaviors

1. I get 7 to 8 hours of sleep a night.
2. I am currently at or near the ideal weight for my height.
3. I have never smoked cigarettes.
4. I use alcohol moderately or not at all.

■ Fig. 11–2 *In the long run, behavioral risk factors and lifestyles do make a difference in health and life expectancy.*

5. I get regular physical exercise.
6. I eat breakfast almost every day.
7. I never or rarely eat between meals.

The authors of this study found that men who engaged in all 7 health practices had a death rate almost 4 times lower than that of men who engaged in 0 to 3 practices. The comparable death rate for women who engaged in all 7 practices was 2 times lower than that for women who engaged in 0 to 3 practices. To state the results another way, a 45-year-old male who regularly engages in only 3 of the behaviors has a remaining life expectancy of about 22 years. A man of the same age who maintains 6 or 7 of the health practices has a remaining life expectancy of 33 years. That's a 50 percent increase in life expectancy.

Later work showed that the first 5 practices are the most important for predicting health. You should note, however, that these are not the only elements of a healthy lifestyle. They are just the ones investigated in this particular study. In addition to improving physical health, such practices are closely related to an overall sense of psychological well-being (Wetzler & Ursano, 1988).

Prevention and Health Campaigns Smoking has been called the largest preventable cause of death in the U.S. It is clearly the single most lethal behavioral risk factor (McGinnis & Foege, 1993). As such, smoking provides a good example of the behavioral possibilities for preventing illness.

Question: What have health psychologists done to lessen the risks?

Recent attempts to "immunize" youths against pressures to start smoking provide a glimpse of health psychology in action. The smoker who says, "Quitting is easy, I've done it dozens of times" states a basic truth—giving up smoking is very difficult. In fact, only 1 smoker in 10 has long-term success. Thus, the best way to deal with smoking may be to prevent it before it becomes a lifelong habit. A study of 7th, 9th, and 10th grade students found that habitual smoking develops slowly. This makes it possible to expose young people to **refusal skills training** and other prevention efforts (Botvin & Botvin, 1992; Hirschman & Leventhal, 1989). In one prevention program, junior high students were given "standard" information on the unhealthy effects of smoking. Then, to add to the program's impact, the students *role-played* ways to resist pressures from peers, adults, and cigarette advertisements. Follow-up checks indicated that students who did the role-playing were only half as likely to begin smoking as were students in a control group (Hurd et al., 1980).

In addition to small projects like the one described, health psychologists have had success with **community health campaigns.** These are education projects designed to lessen a combination of major risk factors. Health campaigns help make people aware of risks such as stress, alcohol abuse, high blood pressure, high cholesterol, smoking, sexually transmitted diseases, or excessive sun exposure. This is followed by efforts to motivate people to change their behavior. Many campaigns provide **role models** who show people how to improve their own health. They also direct people to community services for health screening, advice, and treatment (Cheadle et al., 1992–93). People may be reached through the mass media, public schools, health fairs, their place of work, or self-help programs (Calvert & Cocking, 1992; Schooler et al., 1993). Highlight 11–1 offers an example of one such effort.

Refusal skills training Program that teaches youths how to resist influences to begin smoking (can also be applied to other drugs, such as alcohol or cocaine).

Community health campaign A community-wide education program that provides information about factors that affect health and what to do about them.

Role model A person who serves as a positive example of desirable behavior.

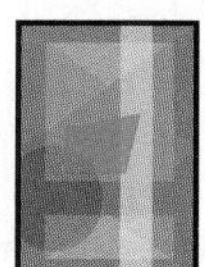

HIGHLIGHT 11–1

Using Psychology

Health Campaigns—Have a Heart

A good example of a community health campaign in action is the Stanford Heart Disease Prevention Program (Meyer et al., 1980). In the Stanford project, a media campaign about risk factors in heart disease—smoking, diet, and exercise—was com-

■ **Fig. 11–3** *The page shown here is reproduced from a booklet prepared as part of a public health campaign conducted in southern Arizona. Such campaigns promote health by calling attention to psychological risk factors and by telling what to do about them. (From Marques et al., 1982.)*

A Way to Change Your Habits:

SELF MONITORING

Before you can make any changes, you need to know how much of something you are already doing, such as smoking, eating or exercising.

We have all known people who kept gaining weight on their diets while swearing up and down that they never eat. Their problem was that they were not keeping track of how much they were really eating.

Here are the steps to help you find out what you are doing. Just keeping track may help you decide to make a change.

STEP 1:
Decide which habit you want to watch.

CAUTION: *Keep track of only one habit at a time. You should not try to quit smoking, lose weight and increase your exercise all at the same time.*

Wellness A positive state of good health; more than the absence of disease.

bined with special group "workshops" for high-risk individuals. The program's success can be seen in the fact that after 2 years, the number of smokers decreased by 17 percent in two test communities. Compare this figure with the 12 percent *increase* observed in similar, untreated communities.

Such progress may seem modest, but it is, in fact, worthwhile, cost effective, and highly promising (Foreyt, 1987; Miller, 1983). Overall, results of the project show a 15 percent reduction in risk of heart disease in the target cities (Farquhar et al., 1984). All you have to do is picture someone you love staying healthy or living longer to appreciate the value of such efforts.

Wellness Health is not just an absence of disease. People who are truly healthy attain a positive state of **wellness** or well-being. Maintaining wellness is a lifelong pursuit and, hopefully, a labor of love. People who attain optimal wellness are both physically and psychologically healthy. They also enjoy supportive relationships with others, they do meaningful work, and they live in a clean environment. Many of these aspects of wellness are addressed in other chapters of this book. In this chapter we will give special attention to the role that stress plays in health and sickness. As stated earlier, stress management is a major activity of health psychologists (Feuerstein et al., 1986). Understanding stress and learning to control it can improve not only your health, but the quality of your life as well. For these reasons, a discussion of stress and stress management follows.

Learning Check

1. Adjustment to chronic illness and the control of pain are topics that would more likely be of interest to a specialist in __________ __________ rather than to a health psychologist.
2. With respect to health, which of the following is *not* a major behavioral risk factor?
   a. overexercise *b.* cigarette smoking *c.* stress *d.* high blood pressure
3. Eating breakfast almost every day and rarely eating between meals proved to be the two most important health-promoting behaviors in the Alameda County study. T or F?
4. Health psychologists tend to prefer __________ rather than modifying habits (like smoking) that become difficult to break once they are established.
5. The disease-prone personality is marked by __________, anxiety, and hostility.

Critical Thinking

6. The general public is increasingly well informed about health risks and healthful behavior. Can you apply the concept of reinforcement to explain why so many people fail to act on this information?

Answers: 1. behavioral medicine 2. *a* 3. F 4. prevention 5. depression 6. Many health payoffs are delayed by months or years, greatly lessening the immediate rewards for healthful behavior.

Stress The mental and physical condition that occurs when a person must adjust or adapt to the environment.

Stress reaction The physical response to stress, consisting mainly of bodily changes related to autonomic nervous system arousal.

Stress—Thrill or Threat?

It is common to assume that stress is always bad or that a complete lack of stress is ideal. However, as stress researcher Hans Selye (1976) observed, "To be totally without stress is to be dead." As stated in the Chapter Preview, **stress** occurs any time we must adjust or adapt to the environment. Naturally, unpleasant events such as work pressures, marital problems, or financial troubles produce stress. But so do travel, sports, a new job, mountain climbing, dating, and other pleasant activities. Even if you aren't a thrill seeker, a healthy lifestyle may include a fair amount of stress.

Your body's **stress reaction** begins with the same autonomic nervous system arousal that occurs during emotion. If you were standing at the top of a wind-whipped ski jump for the first time, and you found it stressful, we would observe a rapid surge in your heart rate, blood pressure, respiration, muscle tension, and other ANS responses. *Short-term* stresses of this kind can be uncomfortable, but they rarely do any damage. (Your landing might be another matter, however.) Later we will describe *long-term* physical changes that accompany prolonged stress. These changes can do much harm.

Question: Other than when it is long lasting, why is stress sometimes damaging and sometimes not?

Stress reactions are complex. Let's examine some of the chief factors that determine whether or not stress is harmful.

When Is Stress a Strain?

It goes almost without saying that some events are more likely to be **stressors** than others. Police officers, for instance, suffer from a high rate of stress-related diseases. The threat of injury or death, plus occasional confrontations with drunk or belligerent citizens, takes a toll. A major factor here is the *unpredictable* nature of police work. An officer who stops to issue a traffic ticket never knows if a cooperative citizen or an armed fugitive is waiting in the car.

An interesting experiment involving three groups of rats shows how a lack of predictability adds to stress. In the experiment, one group was given shocks preceded by a warning tone. A second group got shocks without warning. The third group received no shocks, but heard the tone. After a few weeks, the animals that received unpredictable shocks had severe ulcers. Those given predictable shocks showed little or no ulceration. Those receiving no shocks had no stomach ulcers (Weiss, 1972).

Pressure is another element in stress, especially job stress. **Pressure** occurs when activities must be speeded up, when deadlines must be met, when extra work is added unexpectedly, or when a person must work near maximum capacity for long periods (Weiten, 1988). Most students who have survived final exams are familiar with the effects of pressure.

Question: What if I set deadlines for myself? Does it make a difference where the pressure comes from?

Yes. People generally feel more stress in situations over which they have little or no **control** (Taylor, 1990). For example, Douglas DeGood (1975) subjected college students to an unpleasant shock-avoidance task. Some subjects were allowed to select their own rest periods, while others rested at times selected for them. Subjects allowed to control their own rest periods showed lower stress levels (as measured by blood pressure) than those given no choice (■ Fig. 11–4).

To summarize, when emotional "shocks" are *intense* or *repeated*, *unpredictable*, *uncontrollable*, and linked to *pressure*, stress will be magnified and damage is likely to result. At work, chronic stress sometimes results in *burnout*, a pattern of emotional exhaustion described in Highlight 11–2.

■ **Fig. 11–4** *Although it may not seem so, assembly line work can be quite stressful, due to the lack of control employees have over the pace of work.*

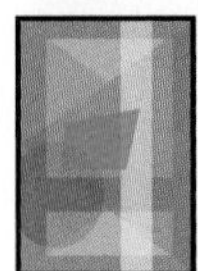

HIGHLIGHT 11–2

A Closer Look At

Burnout—The High Cost of Caring

Margo, a young nurse, realizes with dismay that she has changed from a caring person at work to a cynic who has "lost all patience with her patients" and wishes they would "go somewhere else to be sick." Reactions like Margo's are clear signs of job **burnout,** a condition that exists when an employee is physically, mentally, and emotionally drained. What does it mean to be "burned out"? Psychologist Christina Maslach (1982) has identified three aspects of the problem (Lee & Ashford, 1990).

First of all, burnout involves *emotional exhaustion.* Affected persons are fatigued, tense, and apathetic. Many suffer from various physical complaints. They feel "used up" and have an "I don't give a damn anymore" attitude toward work.

A second aspect of burnout is *depersonalization,* or detachment from others. "Burned-out" workers coldly treat clients as if they were objects and find it difficult to care about them.

The third aspect of burnout is a feeling of *reduced personal accomplishment.* Workers who have burned out do poor work and feel helpless, hopeless, or angry. Their self-esteem suffers and they yearn to change jobs or careers.

Burnout may occur in any job, but it is a marked problem in emotionally demanding helping professions, such as nursing, teaching, social work, child care, counseling, or police work (Matthews, 1990; Poulin & Walter, 1993) (■ Fig. 11–5).

It's ironic that the same work that produces burnout can also be highly challenging and rewarding. If our society wishes to keep caring people in the helping professions, several changes

Stressor A specific condition or event in the environment that challenges or threatens a person.

Pressure A stressful condition that occurs when a person must respond at, or near, maximum capacity for long time periods.

Control With regard to stress, the ability to exert some influence over a threat or challenge.

Burnout A job-related condition of mental, physical, and emotional exhaustion.

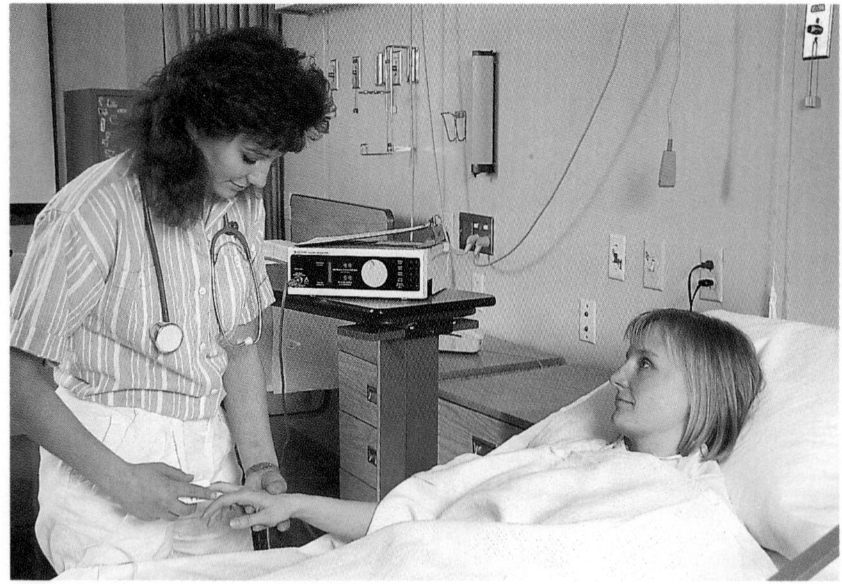

■ **Fig. 11–5** *The helping professions require empathy, caring, and emotional involvement. As a result, caregivers risk depleting their emotional resources and ability to cope. Over time, this can lead to burnout.*

Support group A group formed to provide emotional support for its members through discussion of shared stresses and concerns.

Threat An event or situation perceived as potentially harmful to one's well-being.

Primary appraisal Deciding if a situation is relevant to oneself and if it is a threat.

Secondary appraisal Deciding how to cope with a threat or challenge.

may be needed. A good start would be to redesign jobs to create a better balance between demands and satisfactions. Building stronger social support systems at work could also help. A good example is the growing use of **support groups** by nurses and other caregivers. Such groups allow workers to give and receive emotional support as they talk about feelings, problems, and stresses (Garside, 1993). Ultimately, however, the best solution may be for each of us to show greater understanding of the stresses felt by those whose work requires caring about the needs of others (Capner & Caltabiano, 1993).

Appraising Stressors

As important as *external* events may be, they are not the whole story where stress is concerned. As noted in Chapter 10, emotion is greatly affected by the way in which a situation is appraised. This is why some people are stressed by events that others view as a thrill or a challenge. Ultimately, stress depends on how a situation is perceived. I have a friend who would find it stressful to listen to five of his son's rap albums in a row. He has a son who would find it stressful to listen to one of his father's opera albums. To know if a person is stressed, we must know what meaning the person places on events. As we will see in a moment, whenever a stressor is appraised as a **threat**, an especially powerful stress reaction follows (Lazarus, 1991a).

"Am I Okay or in Trouble?" Situation: You have been selected to give a speech to 300 people. Or, a doctor tells you that you must undergo a dangerous and painful operation. Or, the one true love of your life walks out the door. What would your emotional response to these events be? How do you cope with an emotional threat?

According to Richard Lazarus (1991a), there are two important steps in managing a threatening situation. The first is a **primary appraisal,** in which you decide if a situation is relevant or irrelevant, positive or threatening. In essence, this appraisal answers the question, "Am I okay or in trouble?" Then you make a **secondary appraisal,** during which you assess your resources and choose a way to meet the threat or challenge. ("What can I do about this situation?") The way a situation is "sized up" therefore becomes very important to coping with it. Public speaking, for instance, can be appraised as an intense threat or as a challenge and a chance to perform. Emphasizing the threat—by imagining failure, rejection, or embarrassment—obviously invites disaster (Lazarus, 1993).

The Nature of Threat What does it mean to feel threatened by a stressor? Certainly in most day-to-day situations it does not mean that you think your life is in danger. Threat has more to do with the idea of control. As psychologist Michael Gazzaniga says, "Animals and people are particularly prone to stress when they can't—or think they can't—control their immediate environment" (Gazzaniga, 1988). In short, a *per-*

THE FAR SIDE By GARY LARSON

"The fuel light's on, Frank! We're all going to die! ... Wait, wait. ... Oh, my mistake—that's the intercom light."

ceived lack of control is just as important as actual lack of control in causing us to feel threatened. If your answer to the question, "What can I do about this situation?" is "nothing," you are likely to feel emotionally stressed.

Your personal sense of control in any situation also comes from believing that you can reach desired goals. Or, to state it another way, it is threatening for a person to feel that he or she lacks *competence* to cope with a particular demand (Bandura, 1986). Thus, the intensity of the body's stress reaction often depends on what we think and tell ourselves about stressors. This is why it can be valuable to train yourself to think in ways that avoid triggering the body's stress response. (Some strategies for controlling upsetting thoughts are described in this chapter's Applications section.)

Coping with Threat

Assume that you have appraised a situation as threatening. What will you do next? There are two major choices. **Problem-focused coping** is aimed at managing or altering the distressing situation itself. In **emotion-focused coping,** people try instead to control their emotional reactions to the situation (Lazarus, 1993).

Question: Couldn't both types of coping occur together?

Yes. Sometimes the two types of coping aid one another. Say, for example, that a woman feels anxious as she steps to the podium to give a speech. If she does some deep breathing to reduce her anxiety (emotion-focused coping) she will be better able to glance over her notes to improve her delivery (problem-focused coping).

It is also possible, unfortunately, for the two types of coping to clash. For instance, if you have to make a difficult decision, you may suffer unbearable emotional distress. In such circumstances there is a temptation to make a quick and ill-advised choice, just to end the emotional suffering. Doing so may allow you to cope with your emotions, but it shortchanges problem-focused coping. In general, problem-focused coping tends to be especially useful when you are facing a controllable stressor—that is, a situation you can actually do something about. Emotion-focused efforts are best suited to managing stressors that you cannot control (Lazarus, 1993; Taylor, 1990). To improve your chances of coping effectively, the stress-fighting strategies described in this chapter include a mixture of both techniques.

We will soon return to another look at stress and its effects. But first, let's examine two major (and all too familiar) causes of stress: frustration and conflict.

Frustration—Blind Alleys and Lead Balloons

Question: What causes frustration?

Obstacles of many kinds cause frustration. A useful distinction can be made between *external* and *personal* sources of frustration. **External frustration** is based on conditions outside of the individual that impede progress toward a goal. All of the following are external frustrations: getting stuck with a flat tire; having a marriage proposal rejected; finding the cupboard bare when you go to get your poor dog a bone; finding the refrigerator bare when you go to get your poor tummy a T-bone; finding the refrigerator gone when you return home; being chased out of the house by your starving dog. In other words, external frustrations are based on *delay*, *failure*, *rejection*, *loss*, and other direct blocking of motives.

Notice that external obstacles can be either *social* (slow drivers, tall people in theaters, people who cut into lines) or *non-social* (stuck doors, a dead battery, rain on the day of the game). If you ask 10 of your friends what has frustrated them recently, most will probably mention someone's behavior ("My sister wore one of my dresses when I wanted to wear it," "My supervisor is unfair," "My history teacher grades too hard"). As social animals, we humans are highly sensitive to social sources of frustration.

Frustration usually increases as the **strength, urgency,** or **importance** of a blocked motive increases. An escape artist submerged in a tank of water and bound with 200 pounds of chain would become *quite* frustrated by the jamming of a trick lock. Remember too that motivation becomes stronger as we near a goal. As a result, frustration is more intense when a person runs into an obstacle very close to a goal. If you've ever missed an A grade by 2 points, you were probably very frustrated. If you've missed an A by 1 point—well, frustration builds character, right?

A final factor affecting frustration is summarized by the old phrase "the straw that broke the camel's back." The effects of *repeated* frustrations can accumulate until a small irritation sets off an unexpectedly violent response. The boy who bulldozed the countryside (see the Chapter Preview) probably had been frustrated many times before by his father.

Personal frustrations are based on personal characteristics. If you are 4 feet tall and aspire to be a professional basketball player, you very likely will be frustrated. If you want to go to medical school, but can earn only D grades, you will likewise be frustrated. In both examples, frustration is actually based on personal limitations. Yet, failure may be *perceived* as externally caused. We will return to this point in the Applications

Problem-focused coping Directly managing or remedying a stressful or threatening situation.

Emotion-focused coping Managing or controlling one's emotional reaction to a stressful or threatening situation.

External frustration A negative emotional state caused by external conditions that block satisfaction of a need or progress toward a goal.

Personal frustration A negative emotional state caused by personal characteristics that block satisfaction of a need or progress toward a goal.

Aggression Any response made with the intent of harming some person or object.

Persistence Repeated, more vigorous efforts and more varied responding.

Displaced aggression Redirecting aggression to a target other than the actual source of one's frustration.

Scapegoating Selecting a person or group of people to take the blame for conditions not of their making; habitual redirection of aggression toward some person or group.

section. In the meantime, let's look at some typical reactions to frustration.

Reactions to Frustration

Aggression is one of the most frequent responses to frustration (Berkowitz, 1988). The frustration-aggression link is so common, in fact, that experiments are hardly necessary to show it. A glance at almost any newspaper will provide examples such as the one that follows.

Justifiable Autocide

Burien, Washington (AP)—Barbara Smith committed the assault, but police aren't likely to press charges. Her victim was a 1964 Oldsmobile which failed once too often to start.

When Officer Jim Fuda arrived at the scene, he found one beat-up car, a broken baseball bat and a satisfied 23-year-old Seattle woman.

"I feel good," Ms. Smith reportedly told the officer. "That car's been giving me misery for years and I killed it."

Question: Does frustration always cause aggression? Aren't there other reactions?

Although the connection is strong, frustration does not always provoke aggression. Later, in Chapter 21, we will explore factors that influence when and where aggression is likely to occur. For now, it is enough to note that aggression is not usually the first, or only, reaction to frustration. More often, frustration is met first with **persistence.** This is characterized by more **vigorous efforts** and more **varied responses** (■ Fig. 11–6). For example, if you put your last quarter in a vending machine and find that pressing the button has no effect, you will probably press harder and faster (vigorous effort). Then you will press all the other buttons (varied response). Persistence may help you get *around* a barrier in order to reach your goal. However, if the machine *still* refuses to deliver, or return your quarter, you may become aggressive and kick the machine (or at least tell it what you think of it).

Persistence can be very adaptive. Overcoming a barrier ends the frustration and allows the need or motive to be satisfied. The same is true of aggression that removes or destroys a barrier. Picture a small band of primitive humans, parched by thirst but separated from a water hole by a menacing animal. It is easy to see that attacking the animal may ensure their survival. In modern society such direct aggression is seldom acceptable. If you find a long line at the drinking fountain, aggression is hardly an appropriate response. Because direct aggression is disruptive and generally discouraged, it is frequently *displaced.*

Question: How is aggression displaced? Does displaced aggression occur often?

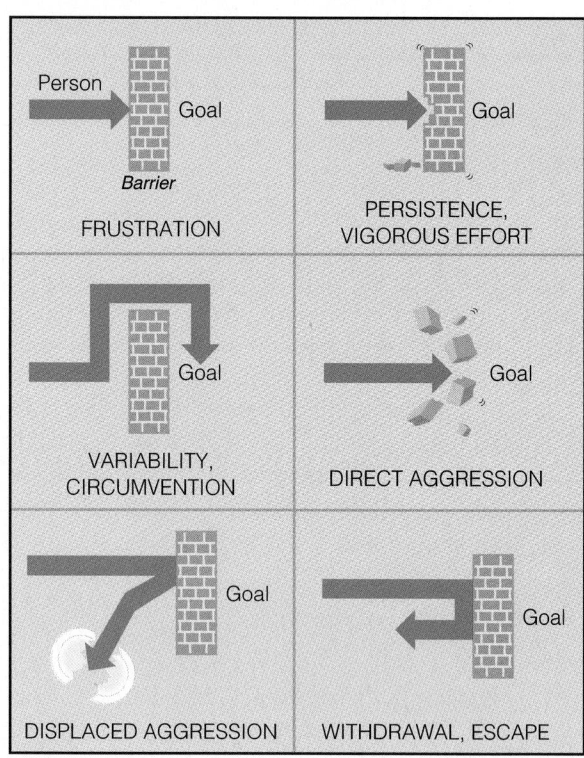

■ **Fig. 11–6** *Frustration and common reactions to it.*

Directing aggression toward a source of frustration may be impossible, or it may be too dangerous. If you are frustrated by your boss at work or by a teacher at school, the cost of direct aggression may be too high (losing your job or failing a needed class). Instead, the aggression may be displaced, or *redirected,* toward whomever or whatever is available.

Targets of **displaced aggression** tend to be safer, or less likely to retaliate, than the original source of frustration. Bulldozing the countryside when the real source of frustration was one's father is a clear case of displaced aggression. Sometimes long *chains* of displacement occur, in which one person displaces aggression to the next. For instance, a businesswoman who is frustrated by high taxes reprimands an employee, who swallows his anger until he reaches home and then yells at his wife, who in turn yells at the children, who then tease the dog. The dog chases the cat, who later knocks over the canary cage (■ Fig. 11–7).

Psychologists attribute much hostility and destructiveness in our society to displaced aggression. A disturbing example is the finding that when unemployment increases, so does child abuse (Steinberg et al., 1981). A pattern known as **scapegoating** is particularly damaging. A scapegoat is a person who has become a habitual target of displaced aggression. A tragic example of scapegoating on a large scale is the

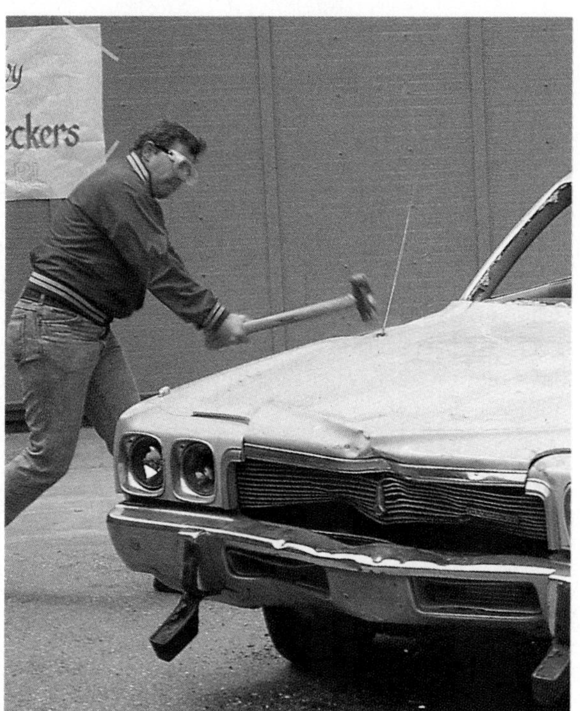

■ **Fig. 11–7** *Some organizations raise money by charging people for the "privilege" of smashing a junk car with a sledge hammer. Are some participants displacing aggressive urges related to frustration in other areas of their lives?*

fact that in the United States between 1880 and 1930 there was a strong correlation between the price of cotton and the number of lynchings of blacks in the South. As the price of cotton went down (and frustration increased), the number of lynchings increased (Dollard et al., 1939). Despite recent progress, many minority groups continue to suffer from hostility based on scapegoating. Think, for example, about the hostility expressed toward recent immigrants to this country during times of economic recession or hardship.

Question: I have a friend who dropped out of school to hitchhike around the country. He seemed very frustrated before he quit. What type of response to frustration is that?

Another major reaction to frustration is **escape,** or **withdrawal.** It is stressful and unpleasant to be frustrated. If other reactions do not reduce feelings of frustration, a person may try to escape. Escape may mean actually leaving a source of frustration (dropping out of school, quitting a job, leaving an unhappy marriage), or it may mean *psychologically* escaping. Two common forms of psychological escape are *apathy* (pretending not to care) and the *use of drugs* such as cocaine, alcohol, marijuana, or narcotics. (See Fig. 11–6 for a summary of common reactions to frustration.)

Conflict—Yes, No, Yes, No, Yes, No, Well, Maybe

Conflict occurs whenever a person must choose between *incompatible* or *contradictory* needs, desires, motives, wishes, or external demands. Choosing between college and work, marriage and single life, or study and failure are conflicts many students face. There are four basic forms of conflict. As we will see, each has its own effects and characteristics (■ Figs. 11–8 and ■ 11–9).

Approach-Approach Conflicts The simplest conflict comes from having to choose between two *positive,* or desirable, alternatives. Choosing between tutti-frutti-coconut-mocha-champagne-ice and orange-marmalade-peanut butter-coffee-swirl at the ice cream parlor may throw you into a temporary conflict. However, if you really like both choices, your decision will be quickly made. Even when more important decisions are at stake, **approach-approach conflicts** tend to be the easiest to resolve. The old fable about the mule that died of thirst and starvation while standing between a bucket of water and a bucket of oats is obviously unrealistic. When both options are positive, the scales of decision are easily tipped one direction or the other.

Avoidance-Avoidance Conflicts Being forced to choose between two *negative,* or undesirable, alternatives creates an **avoidance-avoidance conflict.** A per-

Escape Reducing discomfort by leaving frustrating situations or by psychologically withdrawing from them.

Conflict A stressful condition that occurs when a person must choose between incompatible or contradictory alternatives.

Approach-approach conflict Choosing between two positive, or desirable, alternatives.

Avoidance-avoidance conflict Choosing between two negative, or mutually undesirable, alternatives.

■ **Fig. 11–8** *Three basic forms of conflict. For this woman, choosing between pie and ice cream is a minor approach-approach conflict; deciding whether to take a job that will require weekend work is an approach-avoidance conflict; and choosing between paying higher rent and moving is an avoidance-avoidance conflict.*

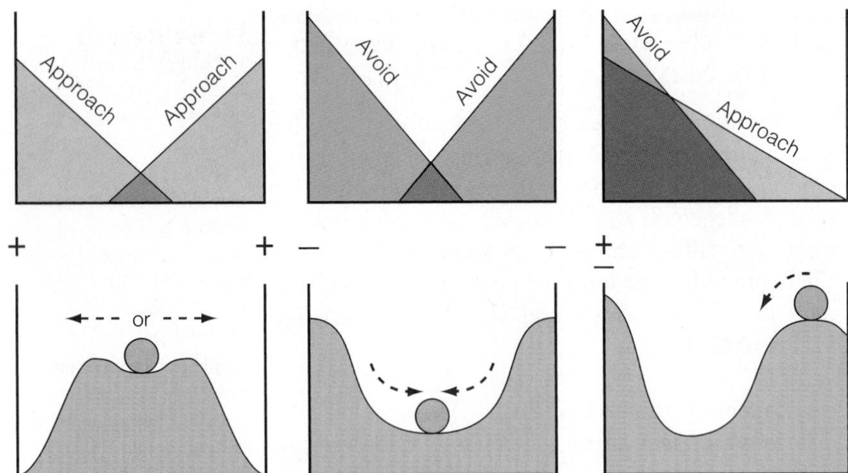

■ Fig. 11–9 *Conflict diagrams. As shown by the colored areas in the graphs, desires to approach and to avoid increase near a goal. The effects of these tendencies are depicted below each graph. The "behavior" of the ball in each example illustrates the nature of the conflict above it. An approach conflict* (left) *is easily decided. Moving toward one goal will increase its attraction* (graph) *and will lead to a rapid resolution. (If the ball moves in either direction, it will go all the way to one of the goals.) In an avoidance conflict* (center), *tendencies to avoid are deadlocked, resulting in inaction. In an approach-avoidance conflict* (right), *approach proceeds to the point where desires to approach and avoid cancel each other. Again, these tendencies are depicted* (below) *by the action of the ball. (Graphs after Miller, 1944.)*

Approach-avoidance conflict Being attracted to and repelled by the same goal.

Ambivalence Mixed positive and negative feelings or simultaneous attraction and repulsion.

son in an avoidance conflict is caught between "the devil and the deep blue sea" or between "the frying pan and the fire." In real life, avoidance-avoidance conflicts involve such dilemmas as choosing between studying and failure, unwanted pregnancy and abortion, the dentist and tooth decay, a monotonous job and poverty, or dorm food and starvation.

Question: Suppose I don't object to abortion. Or suppose that I consider any pregnancy sacred and not to be tampered with?

Like many other stressful situations, these examples can be defined as conflicts only on the basis of personal needs and values. If a woman wants to end a pregnancy and does not object to abortion, she experiences no conflict. If she would not consider abortion under any circumstances, there is no conflict.

Double avoidance conflicts often have a "damned if you do, damned if you don't" quality. In other words, both choices are negative, but *not choosing* may be impossible or equally undesirable. To illustrate, imagine the plight of a person trapped in a hotel fire 20 stories from the ground. Should the person jump from the window and almost surely die on the pavement? Or should the person try to dash through the flames and almost surely die of smoke inhalation and burns? When faced with a choice such as this, it is easy to see why people often *freeze*, finding it impossible to decide or take action. A trapped individual may first think about the window, approach it, and then back away after looking down 20 stories. Next, the person may try the door and again back away as heat and smoke billow in. In actual disasters of this sort, people are often found dead in their rooms, victims of an inability to take action.

Indecision, inaction, and freezing are not the only reactions to double avoidance conflicts. Since avoidance conflicts are stressful and rarely solved, people sometimes pull out of them entirely. This reaction, called *leaving the field*, is another form of escape. It may explain the behavior of a student the author knew who could not attend school unless he worked. However, if he worked he could not earn passing grades. His solution after much conflict and indecision? He joined the navy.

Approach-Avoidance Conflicts Approach-avoidance conflicts are also difficult to resolve. Since people seldom escape them, they are in some ways more troublesome than avoidance conflicts. A person in an **approach-avoidance conflict** is "caught" by being attracted to, and repelled by, the same goal or activity. Attraction keeps the person in the situation, but its negative aspects cause turmoil and distress. For example, a high school student arrives to pick up his date for the first time. He is met at the door by her father, who is a professional wrestler—7 feet tall, 300 pounds, and entirely covered with hair. The father gives the boy a crushing handshake and growls that he will break him in half if the girl is not home on time. The student considers the girl attractive and has a good time. But does he ask her out again? It depends on the relative strength of his attraction and his fear. Almost certainly he will feel *ambivalent* about asking her out again, knowing that another encounter with her father is involved.

Ambivalence (mixed positive and negative feelings) is a central characteristic of approach-avoidance conflicts. Ambivalence is usually translated into *partial approach* (Miller, 1944). Since our student is still attracted to the girl, he may spend time with her at school and elsewhere. But he may not actually date her again. Some more realistic examples of approach-avoidance conflicts are planning marriage to someone your parents strongly disapprove, wanting to be an actor but suffering stage fright, wanting to buy a car but not wanting to make monthly payments, wanting to eat when overweight, and wanting to go to school but hating to study. Many of life's important decisions have approach-avoidance dimensions.

Question: Aren't real-life conflicts more complex than the ones described here?

Yes. In reality, conflicts are rarely as clear-cut as those described. People in conflict are usually faced with several dilemmas at once, so several types of conflict are intermingled. The fourth type of conflict moves us closer to this realistic state of affairs.

Multiple Conflicts You are offered two jobs: One has good pay but poor hours and dull work; the second has interesting work and excellent hours, but low pay. Which do you select? This situation is more typical of the choices we must usually make. It offers neither completely positive nor completely negative options. It is, in other words, a **double approach-avoidance conflict,** in which each alternative has both positive and negative qualities.

As with single approach-avoidance conflicts, people faced with double approach-avoidance conflicts feel ambivalent about each choice. This causes them to **vacillate,** or waver, between the alternatives. Just as you are about to choose one such alternative, its undesirable aspects tend to loom large. So, what do you do? You swing back toward the other choice. If you have ever been romantically attracted to two people at once—each having qualities you like and dislike—then you have probably experienced vacillation. Another example that may be familiar is trying to decide between two college majors, each with advantages and disadvantages.

In real life it is very common to face **multiple approach-avoidance conflicts** in which several alternatives each have positive and negative features. An example would be trying to choose which automobile to buy among several brands. On a day-to-day basis, most multiple approach-avoidance conflicts are little more than an annoyance. When they involve major life decisions, such as choosing a career, a school, a mate, or a job they can add greatly to the amount of stress experienced.

Double approach-avoidance conflict Being simultaneously attracted to and repelled by each of two alternatives.

Vacillation Wavering in intention or feelings.

Multiple approach-avoidance conflict Being simultaneously attracted to and repelled by each of several alternatives.

LEARNING CHECK

Be sure you can answer these questions before continuing.

1. Greater perceived control over a stressor is usually associated with a reduction in the amount of stress experienced. T or F?
2. Emotional exhaustion, depersonalization, and reduced accomplishment are characteristics of job ______________.
3. Stress tends to be greatest when a situation is appraised as a ______________ and a person does not feel ______________ to cope with the situation.
4. According to Lazarus, coping with threatening situations can be both problem-focused and ______________ focused.
5. Which of the following is *not* a common reaction to frustration?
a. ambivalence *b.* aggression *c.* displaced aggression *d.* persistence
6. Sampson Goliath is 7 feet tall and weighs 300 pounds. He has failed miserably in his aspirations to become a jockey. The source of his frustration is mainly ______________.
7. As a reaction to frustration, apathy may be viewed as a form of ______________.
8. Inaction and freezing are most characteristic of avoidance-avoidance conflicts. T or F?
9. Approach-avoidance conflicts produce mixed feelings called ______________.
10. Which do you think would produce more stress: (a) Appraising a situation as mildly threatening but feeling like you are totally incompetent to cope with it? Or, (b) appraising a situation as very threatening but feeling that you have the resources and skills to cope with it? *Critical Thinking*

Answers: 1. T 2. burnout 3. threat, competent 4. emotion- 5. *a* 6. personal 7. escape 8. T 9. ambivalence 10. There is no correct answer because individual stress reactions vary greatly. However, the secondary appraisal of a situation often determines just how stressful it is. Feeling incapable of coping is very threatening all by itself.

Psychological Defense—Mental Karate?

Threatening situations are often accompanied by an unpleasant emotion known as **anxiety.** A person who is anxious feels tense, uneasy, apprehensive, worried, and vulnerable. This can lead to emotion-focused coping that is *defensive* in nature (Lazarus, 1991b). Since anxiety is unpleasant and uncomfortable, we are usually motivated to avoid it. Anxiety caused by stressful situations or by our own shortcomings and limitations may be lessened by the use of **psychological defense mechanisms.**

Question: What are psychological defense mechanisms and how do they reduce anxiety?

A defense mechanism is any technique used to avoid, deny, or distort sources of threat or anxiety. Defense mechanisms are also used to maintain an idealized self-image so that we can comfortably live with our-

Anxiety Apprehension, dread, or uneasiness similar to fear but based on an unclear threat.

Psychological defense mechanisms Habitual and often unconscious psychological strategies used to reduce anxiety.

JUMP START® By Robb Armstrong

Denial Protecting oneself from an unpleasant reality by refusing to perceive it or believe it.

Repression Unconsciously preventing painful or dangerous thoughts from entering awareness.

Reaction formation Preventing dangerous impulses from being expressed in behavior by exaggerating opposite behavior.

selves. Many of the defenses were first identified by Sigmund Freud, who assumed they operated *unconsciously*. Often, defense mechanisms create large "blind spots" in awareness, as when an extremely stingy person fails to recognize that he or she is a tightwad. Everyone has at one time or another used such defenses. Let's consider some of the most common. (A more complete listing is given in ● Table 11–1.)

Denial One of the most basic defense mechanisms is **denial.** Denial means to protect oneself from an unpleasant reality by refusing to accept it or believe it. Denial is closely linked with death, illness, and similar painful and threatening experiences. For instance, if you were told that you had only three months to live, how would you react? Your first thoughts might be "Aw, come on, someone must have mixed up the X-rays" or "The doctor must be mistaken" or simply "It can't be true!" Similar denial and disbelief are common reactions to the unexpected death of a friend or relative: "It's just not real. I don't believe it. I just don't believe it!"

● Table 11–1 Psychological Defense Mechanisms

Compensation	Counteracting a real or imagined weakness by emphasizing desirable traits or seeking to excel in the area of weakness or in other areas.
Denial	Protecting oneself from an unpleasant reality by refusing to perceive it.
Fantasy	Fulfilling unmet desires in imagined achievements or activities.
Intellectualization	Separating emotion from a threatening or anxiety-provoking situation by talking or thinking about it in impersonal "intellectual" terms.
Isolation	Separating contradictory thoughts or feelings into "logic-tight" mental compartments so that they do not come into conflict.
Projection	Attributing one's own feelings, shortcomings, or unacceptable impulses to others.
Rationalization	Justifying your behavior by giving reasonable and "rational," but false, reasons for it.
Reaction formation	Preventing dangerous impulses from being expressed in behavior by exaggerating opposite behavior.
Regression	Retreating to an earlier level of development or to earlier, less demanding habits or situations.
Repression	Unconsciously preventing painful or dangerous thoughts from entering awareness.
Sublimation	Working off unmet desires, or unacceptable impulses, in activities that are constructive.

Repression Freud noticed that his patients had tremendous difficulty recalling shocking or traumatic events from childhood. It seemed that powerful forces were holding these painful memories from awareness. Freud called this **repression.** Apparently, we protect ourselves by repressing thoughts or impulses that are painful or threatening. Feelings of hostility toward a loved one, the names of disliked people, and past failures and embarrassments are common targets of repression.

Reaction Formation **Reaction formation** is a defense in which impulses are not only repressed, but are also held in check by exaggerated opposite behavior. For example, a mother who unconsciously resents her children may, through reaction formation, become absurdly overprotective and overindulgent. Her real thoughts of "I hate them" and "I wish they were gone" are replaced by "I love them" and "I don't know what I would do without them." The mother's hostile impulses are traded for "smother" love, so that she won't have to admit her dislike of her children. The basic idea in a reaction formation is that the individual acts out an opposite behavior to block threatening impulses or feelings.

Regression In its broadest meaning, **regression** refers to any return to earlier, less demanding situations or habits. Most parents who have a second child have to put up with at least some regression by the older child. Threatened by a new rival for attention, an older child may regress to childish speech, bed-wetting, or infantile play after the new baby arrives. However, regression is usually less severe. The child at summer camp who gets homesick and longs for the security of familiar surroundings is undergoing mild regression. An adult who throws a temper tantrum or a married adult who "goes home to mother" is also regressing.

Projection **Projection** is an unconscious process that protects us from the anxiety that would occur if we were to discern our own faults or unacceptable traits. A person who is *projecting* tends to see his or her own shortcomings or unacceptable impulses in others. Projection lowers anxiety by exaggerating negative traits in others while directing attention away from one's own failings.

The author once worked for a greedy shop owner who cheated many of his customers. This same man considered himself a pillar of the community and a good Christian. How did he justify to himself his greed and dishonesty? He believed that everyone who entered his store was bent on cheating *him* any way they could. In reality, few, if any, of his customers shared his motives, but he projected his own greed and dishonesty onto them.

Rationalization Every teacher is familiar with this strange phenomenon: On the day of an exam, an incredible wave of disasters sweeps through the city. An amazing number of mothers, fathers, sisters, brothers, aunts, uncles, grandparents, friends, relatives, and pets become ill or die. Motors suddenly fall out of automobiles. Books are lost or stolen. Alarm clocks go belly-up and ring no more.

The making of excuses comes from a natural tendency to explain one's behavior. When the explanation offered is reasonable, rational, and convincing—but not the real reason—we say a person is *rationalizing*. **Rationalization** provides us with reasons for behavior we ourselves find somewhat questionable. Here is a typical example of rationalization. A student who fails to turn in an assignment made at the beginning of the semester explains:

> My car broke down two days ago and I couldn't get to the library until yesterday. Then I couldn't get all the books I needed because some were checked out, but I wrote what I could. Then last night, as the last straw, the ribbon in my typewriter broke, and since all the stores were closed, I couldn't finish the paper on time.

If asked why he left the assignment until the last minute (the real reason for its being late), the student would probably offer another set of rationalizations. If these are questioned, the student may become emotional as he is forced to see himself without the protection of his rationalizations.

Question: All of the defense mechanisms described seem pretty undesirable. Do they have a positive side?

People who overuse defense mechanisms become less adaptable, because they consume great amounts of emotional energy to control anxiety and to maintain an unrealistic self-image. Defense mechanisms do have value, however. Often, they help keep us from being overwhelmed by immediate threats. This can provide time for a person to learn to cope in a more effective, problem-focused manner. If you recognize some of your own behavior in the descriptions here, it is hardly a sign that you are hopelessly defensive. As noted earlier, most people make occasional use of defense mechanisms.

Two defense mechanisms that have a more positive quality are *compensation* and *sublimation.*

Compensation **Compensatory reactions** are defenses against feelings of inferiority. A person who has a defect or weakness (real or imagined) may go to unusual lengths to overcome the weakness or to compensate for it by excelling in other areas. One of the pioneers of "pumping iron" in America is Jack LaLanne. LaLanne made a successful career out of body building in spite of the fact that he was thin and sickly as a young man. Or perhaps it would be more accurate to say *because* he was thin and sickly. There are dozens of examples of compensation at work. A childhood stutterer may excel in debate at college. Franklin D. Roosevelt's outstanding achievements in politics came after he was stricken with polio. As a child, Helen Keller was unable to see or hear, but she became an outstanding thinker and writer. Doc Watson, Ray Charles, Stevie Wonder, Ronnie Milsap, and a number of other well-known musicians are blind.

Sublimation A defense called **sublimation** (sub-lih-MAY-shun) is defined as working off frustrated desires (especially sexual desires) in activities that are constructive and accepted by society. Freud believed that art, music, dance, poetry, scientific investigation, and other creative activities can serve to rechannel sexual energies into productive behavior. Freud also felt that almost any strong desire can be sublimated. For example, a very aggressive person may find social acceptance as a professional soldier, boxer, or football player (■ Fig. 11–10). Greed may be refined into a successful business career. Lying may be sublimated into storytelling, creative writing, or politics.

Regression Retreating to an earlier stage of development or to earlier, less demanding habits or situations.

Projection Attributing one's own feelings, shortcomings, or unacceptable impulses to others.

Rationalization Justifying personal behavior by giving reasonable and "rational" but false reasons for it.

Compensation Counteracting a real or imagined weakness by emphasizing desirable traits or seeking to excel in the area of weakness or in other areas.

Sublimation Working off frustrated desires or unacceptable impulses in substitute activities that are constructive or accepted by society.

■ **Fig. 11–10** *For some players—and fans—football probably allows sublimation of aggressive urges.*

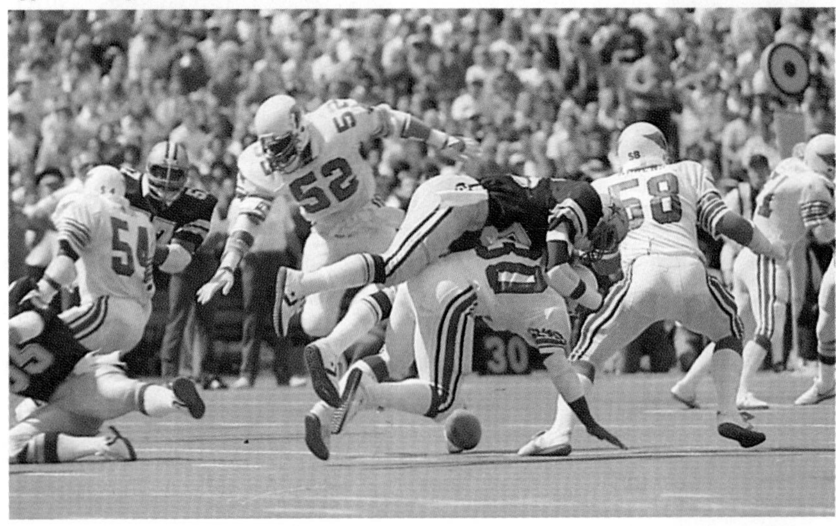

Learned helple
A learned inabili
overcome obsta
to avoid punishr
learned passivit
inaction to avers
stimuli.

Depression A s
deep desponder
marked by apatl
emotional negat
behavioral inhibi

Fig. 11–11 *I*
shortly before the
the dog, the dog
Dogs soon learn
a shock (d). *Dog*
to avoid it.

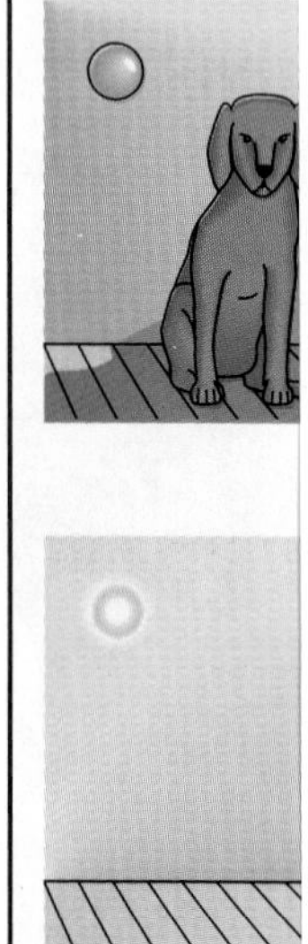

a minor fluctuation in mood is involved when five conditions exist:

Recognizing Depression

1. You have a consistently negative opinion of yourself.
2. You engage in frequent self-criticism and self-blame.
3. You place negative interpretations on events that usually wouldn't bother you.
4. The future looks bleak and negative.
5. You feel that your responsibilities are overwhelming.

Combating Depression Beck and Greenberg (1974) suggest you should begin by making a *daily schedule* for yourself. Try to schedule activities to fill up every hour during the day. It is best to start with easy activities and progress to more difficult tasks. Check off each activity as it is completed. In this way, you will begin to break the self-defeating cycle of feeling helpless and falling further behind (depressed students spend much of their time sleeping). A series of small accomplishments, successes, or pleasures may be all that you need to get going again. However, if you are lacking skills needed for success in college, ask for help in getting them. Don't remain "helpless."

Beck and Greenberg also believe that feelings of worthlessness and hopelessness are supported by self-critical or negative thoughts. They recommend writing down such thoughts as they occur, especially those that immediately precede feelings of sadness. After you have collected these thoughts, write a rational answer to each. For example, the thought "No one loves me" should be answered with a list of those who do care. (See Chapter 18 for more information.) One more point to keep in mind is this: When events begin to improve, try to accept it as a sign that better times lie ahead. An increase in positive events is most likely to end depression if you view them as stable and continuing, rather than temporary and fragile (Needles & Abramson, 1990).

Attacks of the "college blues" are common and should be distinguished from more serious cases of depression. Severe depression is a serious problem that can lead to suicide or a major impairment of emotional functioning. In such cases it would be wise to seek professional help.

LEARNING CHECK

1. The psychological defense known as denial refers to the natural tendency to explain or justify one's actions. T or F?
2. Fulfilling frustrated desires in imaginary achievements or activities defines the defense mechanism of
a. compensation *b.* isolation *c.* fantasy *d.* sublimation
3. In compensation, one's own undesirable characteristics or motives are attributed to others. T or F?
4. Of the defense mechanisms, two that are considered relatively constructive are
a. compensation *b.* denial *c.* isolation *d.* projection *e.* regression *f.* rationalization *g.* sublimation
5. Depression in humans is similar to ____________ ____________ observed in animal experiments.
6. At any given time, over one-half of the college student population suffers symptoms of depression. T or F?
7. Frequent self-criticism and self-blame are a natural consequence of doing college work. T or F?
8. Countering negative, self-critical thoughts only calls attention to them and makes depression worse. T or F?

Critical Thinking

9. Learned helplessness is closely related to which of the factors that determine the severity of stress?

Answers: 1. F 2. *c* 3. F 4. *a, g* 5. learned helplessness 6. F 7. F 8. F 9. Feelings of incompetence and lack of control.

Stress and Health—Unmasking a Hidden Killer

At a university medical school, Dr. Thomas Holmes and his associates confirmed something long suspected: Stressful events can reduce the body's natural defenses against disease. Stress, therefore, can increase the likelihood of illness (Holmes & Masuda, 1972). Holmes found that disaster, depression, and sorrow often precede illness. More surprising is the finding that almost any major *change* in one's life requires adjustment and may increase susceptibility to accidents and illness.

Question: How would I know if I were subjecting myself to too much stress?

Life Events and Stress

Holmes and his associates developed a rating scale to estimate the health hazards faced when stresses add up. Their **Social Readjustment Rating Scale (SRRS)** is reprinted in ● Table 11–2. Notice that the effect of life events is expressed in **life change units (LCUs).**

As you read the scale, notice too that a positive life event may be as costly as a disaster. Marriage rates 50 life change units, even though it is usually a happy event. Notice also that many items read "Change in . . . ." This means that an improvement in life conditions can be as costly as a decline.

To use the scale, add up the LCUs for all life events you have experienced during the last year and compare the total to the following standards.

0–150:	No significant problems
150–199:	Mild life crisis (33 percent chance of illness)
200–299:	Moderate life crisis (50 percent chance of illness)
300 or more:	Major life crisis (80 percent chance of illness)

According to Holmes, there is a high chance of illness or accident in the near future when one's LCU total exceeds 300 points.

A more conservative rating of stress can be obtained by totaling LCU points for only the previous 6 months. Studies of U.S. Navy personnel produced the figures shown here for 6-month totals (Rahe, 1972).

LCUs	Average number of illnesses reported for 6-month period
0–100	1.4
300–400	1.9
500–600	2.1

Question: Many of the listed life changes don't seem relevant to young adults or college students. Does the SRRS apply to these people?

The SRRS tends to be more appropriate for older, more established adults. However, research has shown that the health of college students is also affected by stressful events, such as entering college, changing majors, or the breakup of a steady relationship (Crandall, Preisler, & Aussprung, 1992).

Evaluation The SRRS is not a foolproof way to rate stress, and some studies have failed to confirm the

Social Readjustment Rating Scale (SRRS) A scale that rates the impact of various life events on the likelihood of illness.

Life change units (LCUs) Numerical values assigned to each life event on the SRRS; used to predict the likelihood of illness.

● **Table 11–2 Social Readjustment Rating Scale (SRRS)**
The SRRS lists significant life events and offers a rating of their contribution to susceptibility to illness.

Rank	Life Event	Life Change Units	Rank	Life Event	Life Change Units
1	Death of spouse	100	22	Change in responsibilities at work	29
2	Divorce	73	23	Son or daughter leaving home	29
3	Marital separation	65	24	Trouble with in-laws	29
4	Jail term	63	25	Outstanding personal achievement	28
5	Death of a close family member	63	26	Spouse begins or stops work	26
6	Personal injury or illness	53	27	Begin or end school	26
7	Marriage	50	28	Change in living conditions	25
8	Fired at work	47	29	Revision of personal habits	24
9	Marital reconciliation	45	30	Trouble with boss	23
10	Retirement	45	31	Change in work hours or conditions	20
11	Change in health of family member	44	32	Change in residence	20
12	Pregnancy	40	33	Change in school	20
13	Sex difficulties	39	34	Change in recreation	19
14	Gain of new family member	39	35	Change in church activities	19
15	Business readjustment	39	36	Change in social activities	18
16	Change in financial state	38	37	Take out loan less than $20,000	17
17	Death of close friend	37	38	Change in sleeping habits	16
18	Change to different line of work	36	39	Change in number of family get-togethers	15
19	Change in number of arguments with spouse	35	40	Change in eating habits	15
20	Take out mortgage or loan for major purchase	31	41	Vacation	13
21	Foreclosure of mortgage or loan	30	42	Christmas	12
			43	Minor violation of the law	11

Hassle Any distressing, day-to-day annoyance; also called a microstressor.

Acculturative stress Stress caused by the many changes and adaptations required when a person moves to a foreign culture.

LCU-illness link (Weinberger, 1987). Furthermore, it is debatable whether positive life events are always stressful (Feuerstein et al., 1986). Perhaps the most important criticism of the scale is based on a point made earlier: People differ greatly in their reactions to the same event. For such reasons, the SRRS is, at best, only a rough index of stress. Nevertheless, it's hard to ignore a study in which people were deliberately exposed to the virus that causes common colds. The results were nothing to sneeze at: If a person had a high stress score, he or she was much more likely to actually get a cold (Cohen et al., 1993).

To summarize, a high LCU score should be taken seriously. If your score goes much over 300, an adjustment in your activities or lifestyle may be needed. Remember, "To be forewarned is to be forearmed."

Question: There must be more to stress than major life changes. Isn't there a link between ongoing stresses and health?

The Hazards of Hassles In addition to their immediate impact, major life changes often create a kind of "ripple effect." That is, countless daily frustrations and irritations spring from the original event. In addition, many of us face ongoing stresses at work or at home that do not involve major life changes. In view of these facts, psychologist Richard Lazarus and his associates studied the impact of minor but frequent stresses. Lazarus (1981) aptly refers to such stresses as **hassles,** or **microstressors.** Hassles are defined as distressing daily annoyances. They range from traffic jams to losing classroom notes; from an argument with a roommate to an employer's unrealistic demands.

In a year-long study, Lazarus had 100 men and women keep track of the frequency and severity of the hassles they endured. Subjects in the study also filled out questionnaires about their physical and mental health. As Lazarus had suspected, frequent and severe hassles turned out to be better predictors of day-to-day emotional and physical health than major life events were. However, major life events did predict changes in health 1 or 2 years after the events took place. It appears that daily hassles are closely linked to immediate health and psychological well-being (Chamberlain & Zika, 1990; Ruffin, 1993). Major life changes have more of a long-term impact.

In follow-up work, Lazarus and others found that the personal importance of hassles affects the amount of stress they produce (Lazarus et al., 1985). Microstressors that are viewed as central to one's self-worth are many times more likely to cause trouble. For many people, central hassles are linked to work, family, and relationships. But as psychologist Rand Gruen notes, "Taking care of paperwork or being organized can be central for some people" (Fisher, 1984). This observation again emphasizes that stress occurs in people, not in the environment. Stress is always related to personality, values, perceptions, and personal resources (Moos & Swindle, 1990).

Question: What can be done about a high LCU score or feeling excessively hassled?

A good response is to use stress management skills. For serious problems, stress management should be learned directly from a therapist or at a stress clinic. When ordinary stresses are involved, there is much you can do on your own. This chapter's Applications section will give you a start. In the meantime, take it easy!

One way to guarantee that you will experience a large number of life changes and hassles is to live in a foreign culture. Highlight 11–4 offers a brief glimpse into some of the consequences of culture shock.

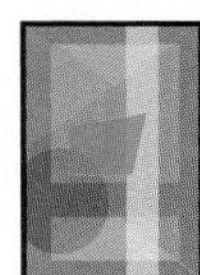

HIGHLIGHT 11–4

Cultural Diversity

Acculturative Stress—Stranger in a Strange Land

How stressful is it to be a "stranger in a strange land"? Around the world, an increasing number of emigrants and refugees must adapt to dramatic changes in language, dress, values, and social customs. For many, the result is a period of culture shock or **acculturative stress,** marked by confusion, anxiety, hostility, depression, alienation, physical illness, or identity confusion (■ Fig. 11–12).

The severity of acculturative stress is related, in part, to how a person adapts to a new culture. Four main patterns are:

- Integration—maintain your old cultural identity but participate in the new culture
- Separation—maintain your old cultural identity and avoid contact with the new culture
- Assimilation—adopt the new culture as your own and have contact with its members
- Marginalization—reject your old culture but suffer rejection by members of the new culture

To illustrate each pattern, let's consider a family that has migrated to the United States from the imaginary country of Farlandia.

The father favors integration. He is learning English and wants to get involved in American life. At the same time, he is a leader in the Farlandian-American community and spends much of his leisure time with other Farlandian-Americans. His level of acculturative stress is low.

The mother only speaks Farlandish and only interacts with other Farlandian-Americans. She remains almost completely separate from American society. Her stress level is high.

The teenage daughter is annoyed by hearing Farlandish spoken at home, by her mother's serving only Farlandian food, and by having to spend her leisure time with her extended Farlandian family. She would prefer to speak English and to be with her American friends. Her desire to assimilate creates moderate stress.

The son doesn't particularly value his Farlandian heritage, yet he is rejected by his schoolmates because he speaks with a Farlandian accent. He feels trapped between two cultures. His position is marginal and his stress level is high.

To summarize, those who feel marginalized tend to be highly stressed; those who seek to remain separate are also highly stressed; those who pursue integration into their new culture are minimally stressed; and those who assimilate are moderately stressed. (Sources: Berry, 1990; Rogler, Cortes, Malgady, 1991; Williams & Berry, 1991.)

■ **Fig. 11–12** *One of the best antidotes for acculturative stress is a society that tolerates or even celebrates ethnic diversity. While some people find it hard to accept new immigrants, the fact is, nearly everyone's family tree includes people who were once strangers in a strange land.*

Psychosomatic Disorders

As we have seen, chronic or repeated stress can damage physical health, as well as upset emotional well-being. Prolonged stress reactions are closely related to a large number of psychosomatic (SIKE-oh-so-MAT-ik) illnesses. In **psychosomatic disorders** (*psyche:* mind; *soma:* body), psychological factors contribute to actual bodily damage or to damaging changes in bodily functioning. Psychosomatic problems, therefore, are *not* the same as *hypochondria.* **Hypochondriacs** (HI-po-KON-dree-aks) *imagine* that they suffer from diseases. There is nothing imaginary about asthma, a migraine headache, or high blood pressure. Severe psychosomatic disorders can be fatal. The person who says, "Oh it's *just* psychosomatic" misunderstands the seriousness of stress-related diseases.

Question: Are stomach ulcers psychosomatic?

For many years, stomach ulcers were thought to be primarily caused by stress. However, recent medical research has traced some ulcers to bacterial infections of the stomach. This does not rule out the possibility that ulcers may occasionally be psychosomatic. However, it is more likely that a person suffering from stomach pain has functional dyspepsia. This psychosomatic disorder causes ulcer-like pain, but does not make holes in the stomach lining (Whitehead, 1992).

The most common psychosomatic problems are gastrointestinal and respiratory (dyspepsia and asthma, for example), but many others exist. Typical problems include eczema (skin rash), hives, migraine headaches, rheumatoid arthritis, hypertension (high blood pressure), colitis (ulceration of the colon), and heart disease. Actually, these are only the major problems. Lesser health complaints are also frequently stress related. Typical examples include muscle tension, headaches, neckaches, backaches, indigestion, constipation, chronic diarrhea, fatigue, insomnia, premenstrual problems, and sexual dysfunctions (Brown, 1980; de Benedittis et al., 1990). (■ See Fig. 11–13). For some of these problems biofeedback may be helpful. Highlight 11–5 explains how.

Psychosomatic disorders Illnesses in which psychological factors contribute to bodily damage or to damaging changes in bodily functioning.

Hypochondriac A person who is excessively preoccupied with minor bodily problems or who complains about illnesses that appear to be imaginary.

Biofeedback Information about bodily activities; aids voluntary regulation of bodily states.

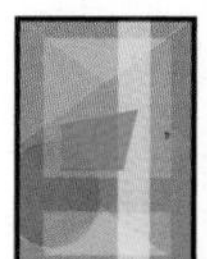

HIGHLIGHT 11–5

Using Psychology

Biofeedback—Electronic Yoga?

Psychologists have discovered that people can learn to control bodily activities once thought to be involuntary. This is done by applying the principle of feedback to bodily control, a process called **biofeedback.** If I were to say to you, "Raise the temperature of your right hand," you probably couldn't, because you wouldn't know if you were succeeding. To make your task easier, we could attach a sensitive thermometer to your hand. The thermometer could be wired so that an increase

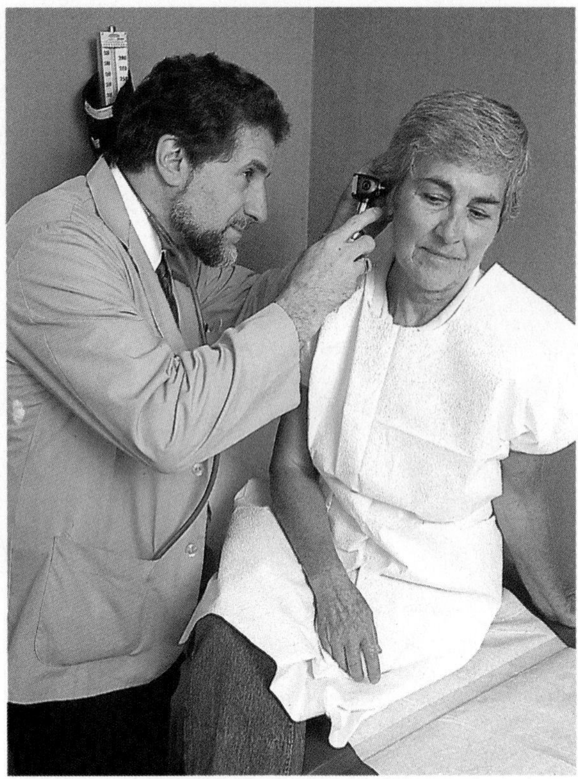

■ Fig. 11–13 *It is estimated that at least half of all patients who see a doctor have a psychosomatic disorder or an illness that is complicated by psychosomatic symptoms.*

■ Fig. 11–14 *Biofeedback training involving muscle tension and blood flow has been used to relieve headaches and to promote relaxation. Here, a biofeedback signal is routed back to the patient through headphones, allowing him to alter bodily activities not normally under voluntary control.*

in temperature would activate a signal light. Then, all you would have to do is try to keep the light on as much as possible. With practice and the help of biofeedback, you could learn to raise your hand temperature at will.

Biofeedback holds promise as a way to treat psychosomatic problems (■ Fig. 11–14). For example, Elmer and Alyce Green have successfully trained people to treat migraine headaches with biofeedback. Sensors are taped to patients' hands and foreheads. Patients then learn to redirect blood flow away from the head to their extremities. Since migraine headaches involve excessive blood flow to the head, biofeedback helps patients to reduce the frequency of their headaches (Gauthier et al., 1994; Lisspers & Ost, 1990).

Early successes led many to predict that biofeedback would offer a cure for psychosomatic illnesses, anxiety, phobias, drug abuse, chronic pain, and a long list of other problems. In reality, biofeedback has proved helpful, but not an instant cure (Amar, 1993). Biofeedback can help relieve muscle-tension headaches, migraine headaches, and chronic pain (Flor & Birbaumer, 1993; Gauthier et al., 1994; Lissers & Ost, 1990). It shows promise for lowering blood pressure and controlling heart rhythms (Larkin et al., 1990; McGrady, 1994). The technique has been used with some success to control epileptic seizures and hyperactivity in children (Potashkin & Beckles, 1990; Sterman, 1977). Insomnia also responds to biofeedback therapy (Barowsky et al., 1990).

How does biofeedback help? Some researchers believe that many of its benefits arise from *general relaxation.* Others stress that there is no magic in biofeedback itself. The method simply acts as a "mirror" to help a person perform tasks involving *self-regulation* (Green & Shellenberger, 1986; Norris, 1986). Just as a mirror does not comb your hair, biofeedback does not do anything by itself. It can, however, help people make desired changes in their behavior (Amar, 1993).

Question: Does biofeedback apply to brain activity?

Alpha Control Alpha waves are one of several brain wave patterns that can be recorded with the EEG (electroencephalograph; see Chapter 6). Using an EEG, psychologist Joseph Kamiya developed a system that signals subjects with a tone or light whenever they produce alpha waves (Kamiya, 1968). Subjects typically report that high levels of alpha are linked with sensations of pleasure, relaxation, passive alertness, or peaceful images.

Some researchers have successfully used alpha-wave biofeedback to reduce anxiety in emotionally troubled patients (Rice et al., 1993). However, questions remain about the ability of alpha training to promote deep relaxation. Research has shown that for some people increased alpha waves are related to relaxation; but for others alpha waves occur at times of *heightened* arousal. For the moment, it seems that we have not yet reached the age of "electronic yoga" or "instant bliss." This is especially true of low-cost home "alpha-feedback" machines. These devices are so inaccurate that many "blissed out" users are actually listening to electrical noise from their house wiring, rather than their own brain waves (Beyerstein, 1985). Likewise, commercial programs that claim to teach people to produce alpha waves are essentially worthless (Beyerstein, 1990). Although biofeedback is a useful therapy, it must be applied skillfully to be of value (Amar, 1993).

■ **Fig. 11–15** *Individuals with Type A personalities feel a continuous sense of anger, irritation, and hostility.*

It would be a mistake to assume that stress is the sole cause of psychosomatic diseases. Usually, several factors combine to produce damage. These include hereditary differences, specific organ weaknesses, and learned reactions to stress. Personality also enters the picture. As mentioned earlier, there may be a general disease-prone personality. To a degree, there are also "headache personalities," "asthma personalities," and so on. The best documented of such patterns is the "cardiac personality"—a person at high risk for heart disease.

Type A Two noted cardiologists, Meyer Friedman and Ray Rosenman, offer a glimpse at how some people create unnecessary stress. In a landmark study of heart problems, Friedman and Rosenman (1974) classified people into two categories: **Type A personalities** (those who run a high risk of heart attack) and **Type B personalities** (those who are unlikely to have a heart attack). Friedman and Rosenman then did an 8-year follow-up, finding more than twice the rate of heart disease in Type A's than in Type B's (Rosenman et al., 1975).

Question: What is the Type A personality like?

Type A people are hard-driving, ambitious, highly competitive, achievement oriented, and striving (■ Fig. 11–15). Type A people believe that with enough effort they can overcome any obstacle, and they "push" themselves accordingly.

Perhaps the most telltale signs of a Type A personality are *time urgency* and chronic *anger* or *hostility*. Type A's seem to chafe at the normal pace of events. They hurry from one activity to another, racing the clock in self-imposed urgency. As they do, they feel a constant sense of frustration and anger. Feelings of anger and hostility, in particular, are strongly related to increased risk of heart attack (Denollet, 1993). One study found that 15 percent of a group of 25-year-old doctors and lawyers who scored high on a hostility test were dead by age 50.

Type A personality A personality type with an elevated risk of heart disease; characterized by time urgency, anger, and hostility.

Type B personality All personality types other than Type A; a low cardiac-risk personality.

Question: Some news reports have stated that Type A behavior is not a factor in heart attacks. Why is that?

It's true that some studies have failed to show a link between Type A behavior and heart attacks. However, many of these failures appear to be a result of using less accurate ways to classify people as A's and B's. (Friedman and Rosenman did probing interviews to classify people. Many later studies have used paper-and-pencil tests.) There is also growing evidence that anger or hostility may be the core *lethal factor* of Type A behavior (Chesney & Rosenman, 1985; Denollet, 1993; Friedman & Booth-Kewley, 1987). Placing such disputes aside, hundreds of studies *have* supported the validity of the Type A concept. At this point, it still seems that Type A's would be wise to take their increased health risks seriously (Miller et al., 1991; Sprafka et al., 1990).

Question: How are Type A people identified?

Characteristics of Type A people are summarized in the short self-identification test presented in ● Table 11–3. If most of the list applies to you, you may be a Type A. However, confirmation of your type would require more powerful testing methods.

A large-scale study of heart attack victims found that modifying Type A behavior significantly reduces

Table 11–3 Characteristics of the Type A Person

Check the items that apply to you. Do you:

______	Have a habit of explosively accentuating various key words in ordinary speech even when there is no need for such accentuation?
______	Finish other persons' sentences for them?
______	*Always* move, walk, and eat rapidly?
______	Quickly skim reading material and prefer summaries or condensations of books?
______	Become easily angered by slow-moving lines or traffic?
______	Feel an impatience with the rate at which most events take place?
______	Tend to be unaware of the details or beauty of your surroundings?
______	Frequently strive to think of or do two or more things simultaneously?
______	Almost always feel vaguely guilty when you relax, vacation, or do absolutely nothing for several days?
______	Tend to evaluate your worth in quantitative terms (number of A's earned, amount of income, number of games won, and so forth)?
______	Have nervous gestures or muscle twitches, such as grinding your teeth, clenching your fists, or drumming your fingers?
______	Attempt to schedule more and more activities into less time and in so doing make fewer allowances for unforeseen problems?
______	Frequently think about other things while talking to someone?
______	Repeatedly take on more responsibilities than you can comfortably handle?

Shortened and adapted from Meyer Friedman and Ray H. Rosenman, *Type A Behavior and Your Heart* (New York: Knopf, 1983).

the rate of repeat heart attacks (Friedman et al., 1984). Since our society places a premium on achievement, competition, and mastery, it is not surprising that many people develop Type A personalities. The best way to avoid the self-made stress this causes is to adopt behavior that is the opposite of that listed in Table 11–3 (Suinn, 1982). It is entirely possible to succeed in life without sacrificing your health or happiness in the process. People who frequently feel angry and hostile toward others may benefit from the advice of Redford Williams, a physician interested in Type A behavior. Highlight 11–6 summarizes his advice. (For more hints on combating Type A behavior, consult Friedman and Rosenman, *Type A Behavior and Your Heart* or Redford Williams, *The Trusting Heart.*)

Highlight 11–6

Using Psychology

Strategies for Reducing Hostility

According to Redford Williams, reducing hostility involves three goals. First, you must stop mistrusting the motives of others. Second, you must find ways to reduce how often you feel anger, indignation, irritation, and rage. Third, you must learn to be kinder and more considerate of others. Based on his clinical experience, Williams (1989) recommends 12 strategies for reducing hostility and increasing trust.

1. Become aware of your angry, hostile, and cynical thoughts by logging them in a notebook. Record what happened, what you thought and felt, and what actions you took. Review your hostility log at the end of each week.

2. Admit to yourself and to someone you trust that you have a problem with excessive anger and hostility.

3. Interrupt hostile, cynical thoughts whenever they occur. (The Applications for Chapter 18 explains a thought-stopping method you can use for this step.)

4. When you have an angry, hostile, or cynical thought about someone, silently look for the ways in which it is irrational or unreasonable.

5. When you are angry, try to mentally put yourself in the other person's shoes.

6. Learn to laugh at yourself and use humor to defuse your anger.

7. Learn reliable ways to relax. Two methods are described in this chapter's Applications section. Another can be found in the Applications for Chapter 18.

8. Practice trusting others more. Begin with situations where no great harm will be done if the person lets you down.

9. Make an effort to listen more to others and to really understand what they are saying.

10. Learn to be assertive, rather than aggressive in upsetting situations. (See Chapter 21 for information about self-assertion skills.)

11. Rise above small irritations by pretending that today is the last day of your life.

12. Rather than blaming people for mistreating you, and becoming angry over it, try to forgive them. We all have shortcomings.

Question: How do Type A people who do not develop heart disease differ from those who do?

Hardy Personality Psychologists Salvatore Maddi and Suzanne Kobasa (1984) studied people who have what they call a **hardy personality.** Such people seem to be unusually resistant to stress. Maddi and Kobasa's studies began with a comparison of two groups of managers at a large utility company. All of the managers held high-stress positions. Yet, some tended to get sick after stressful events, while others were rarely ill. How did the people who were thriving differ from their "stressed-out" colleagues? Both groups seemed to have traits typical of the Type A personality, so that wasn't the explanation. They were also quite similar in most other respects. The main difference was that the hardy group seemed to hold a world view that consisted of the following:

1. They had a sense of personal *commitment* to self, work, family, and other stabilizing values.
2. They felt that they had *control* over their lives and their work.
3. They had a tendency to see life as a series of *challenges,* rather than as a series of threats or problems.

These traits seemed to allow the hardy personality to transcend stresses. Basically, hardy persons react to stressors with less arousal and negative emotion than their non-hardy neighbors do. Non-hardy persons tend to exaggerate the negative impact of life experiences (Rhodewalt & Zone, 1989; Wiebe, 1991). The message is clear that a willingness to commit yourself to active coping can do much to change stress into a healthy challenge.

A very basic question remains unanswered in our discussion of stress. How does stress, and our response to it, translate into bodily damage? The answer seems to lie in the body's defenses against stress, a pattern known as the *general adaptation syndrome.*

The General Adaptation Syndrome

Study of the **general adaptation syndrome** (G.A.S.) began when Canadian physiologist Hans Selye (1976) noticed that the first symptoms of almost any disease or trauma (poisoning, infection, injury, or stress) are almost identical. After more research, Selye concluded that the body responds in the same way to any stress, be it infection, failure, embarrassment, adjustment to a new job, trouble at school, or a stormy romance.

Question: What pattern does the body's response to stress take?

The G.A.S. consists of three stages: an *alarm reaction,* a *stage of resistance,* and a *stage of exhaustion* (Selye, 1976).

In the **alarm reaction,** the body mobilizes its resources to cope with added stress. The pituitary gland secretes a hormone that causes the adrenal glands to step up their output of adrenaline and noradrenaline. As these hormones are dumped into the bloodstream, some bodily processes are speeded up and others are slowed so that bodily resources are applied where they are needed.

We should all be thankful that our bodies instantly and automatically respond to emergencies. But brilliant as this automatic emergency system is, it can also cause problems (Wilson, 1986). In the first phase of the alarm reaction, people have such symptoms as headache, fever, fatigue, sore muscles, shortness of breath, diarrhea, upset stomach, loss of appetite, and lack of energy. Notice that these are also the symptoms of being sick, of stressful travel, of high-altitude sickness, of final exam week, and (possibly) of falling in love!

Soon the body's defenses are stabilized, and symptoms of the alarm reaction disappear. Physically, the body has made adjustments to resist stress. However, the outward appearance of normality comes at a high cost. During the **stage of resistance,** the body is better able to cope with the original source of stress (■ Fig. 11–16), but its resistance to other stresses is lowered. For example, animals placed in an extremely cold environment become more resistant to the cold, but more susceptible to infection. It is during the stage of resistance that the first signs of psychosomatic disorders begin to appear.

If stress continues, the **stage of exhaustion** may be reached. In this stage the body's resources are exhausted and the stress hormones are depleted. Unless a way of relieving stress is found, the result will be a psychosomatic disease, a serious loss of health, or complete collapse.

The stages of the G.A.S. may sound melodramatic if you are young and healthy or if you have never

Hardy personality A personality style associated with superior stress resistance.

General adaptation syndrome (G.A.S.) A series of bodily reactions to prolonged stress; occurs in three stages: alarm, resistance, and exhaustion.

Alarm reaction First stage of the G.A.S., during which bodily resources are mobilized to cope with a stressor.

Stage of resistance Second stage of the G.A.S., during which bodily adjustments to stress stabilize, but at a high physical cost.

Stage of exhaustion Third stage of the G.A.S., at which time the body's resources are exhausted and serious health consequences occur.

■ **Fig. 11–16** *The General Adaptation Syndrome. During the initial alarm reaction to stress, resistance falls below normal. It rises again as bodily resources are mobilized, and it remains high during the stage of resistance. Eventually, resistance falls again as the stage of exhaustion is reached. (From* The Stress of Life *by Hans Selye. Copyright © 1956, 1976 by Hans Selye. Used by permission of McGraw-Hill Book Company.)*

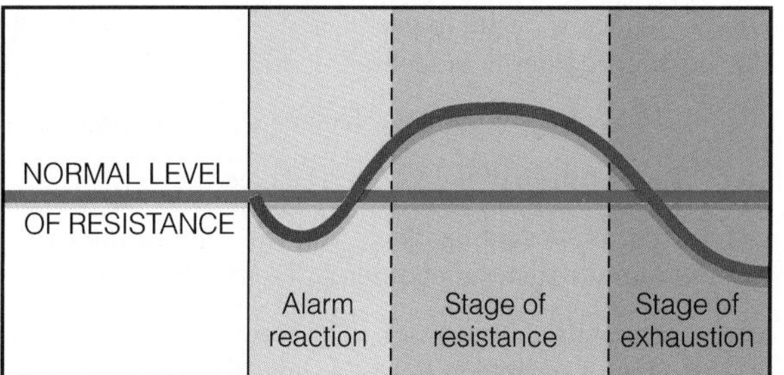

Immune system System that mobilizes bodily defenses (such as white blood cells) against invading microbes and other disease agents.

Psychoneuroimmunology Study of the links among behavior, disease, and the immune system.

endured prolonged stress. However, stress should not be taken lightly. When Selye examined animals in the later stages of the G.A.S., he found enlargement and discoloration of their adrenal glands, intense shrinkage of the thymus, spleen, and lymph nodes, and deep bleeding stomach ulcers. In addition to such direct effects, stress can disrupt the body's **immune system,** making people more vulnerable to illness (Ader & Cohen, 1993) (see Highlight 11–7).

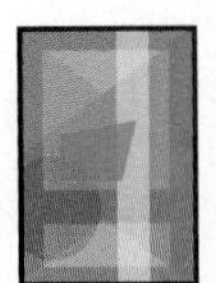

HIGHLIGHT 11–7

Research Frontier

Stress, Illness, and the Immune System

Health experts have uncovered fascinating evidence that the body and the brain work together as a kind of "health care system." The body's immune system is regulated, in part, by the brain. Because of this link, stress and upsetting emotions may affect the immune system in ways that increase susceptibility to disease (Ader & Cohen, 1993). (By the way, this area of research is called **psychoneuroimmunology.** Try dropping that into a conversation sometime if you want to observe a stress reaction!)

Psychologists have found that the immune system is weakened in students during major exam times, and by divorce, bereavement, a troubled marriage, job loss, depression, and similar stresses (Herbert & Cohen, 1993; Kiecolt-Glaser & Glaser, 1988; Stein et al., 1990). Findings such as these suggest that stress leads to illness by affecting the immune system. This is probably why the "double whammy" of getting sick when you are trying to cope with prolonged or severe stress is so common (Ader & Cohen, 1993).

Question: Could reducing stress help prevent illness?

Yes. Various psychological approaches, such as support groups, relaxation exercises, guided imagery, and stress management training can actually boost immune system functioning (Kiecolt-Glaser & Glaser, 1992). By doing so, they help promote and restore health. There is even evidence that such measures improve the chances of survival following life-threatening diseases, such as cancer (Andersen et al., 1994). No one is immune to stress. Nevertheless, it's reassuring to know that managing stress can help protect your immune system and health.

A Look Ahead The work we have reviewed here has drawn new attention to the fact that each of us has a personal responsibility for maintaining and promoting health (Patton et al., 1986). In the Applications section that follows, we will look at what you can do to better cope with stress and the health risks that it entails. The concluding Exploration looks at meditation as a potential stress-reducing technique. But first, the following Learning Check may help you maintain a healthy grade on your next psychology test.

LEARNING CHECK

1. Holmes' SRRS appears to predict long-range changes in health, whereas the frequency and severity of daily microstressors is closely related to immediate ratings of health. T or F?
2. Ulcers, migraine headaches, and hypochondria are all frequently psychosomatic disorders. T or F?
3. Which of the following is *not* classified as a psychosomatic disorder?
   a. hypertension *b.* colitis *c.* eczema *d.* thymus
4. Biofeedback is a type of meditation in which the body is made very quiet so that bodily functioning can be detected. T or F?
5. Two major elements of biofeedback training appear to be relaxation and self-regulation. T or F?
6. Evidence is beginning to suggest that the most important feature of the Type A personality is a sense of time urgency rather than feelings of anger and hostility. T or F?
7. A sense of commitment, challenge, and control characterizes the hardy personality. T or F?
8. The first stage of the G.A.S. is called the ________________ reaction.
9. Whereas stressful incidents suppress the immune system, stress management techniques have almost no effect on immune system functioning. T or F?
10. Acculturative stress tends to be minimal when a person who has moved to a different country maintains a high degree of separation from the new "host" culture. T or F?

11. In addition to being stress-resistant, persons with hardy personalities appear to be good at avoiding a problem discussed earlier in this chapter. Can you name it? *Critical Thinking*

Answers: 1. T 2. F 3. d 4. F 5. T 6. F 7. T 8. alarm 9. F 10. F 11. Learned helplessness.

APPLICATIONS: *Stress Management*

As promised, this section describes techniques for managing stress. Before you continue, you may want to assess your level of stress again, this time using a scale developed for undergraduate students. (See Table 11–4.) Like the SRRS, high scores on the *Undergraduate Stress Questionnaire* (USQ) are associated with greater susceptibility to illness (Crandall, Preisler, & Aussprung, 1992).

The USQ is scored by simply counting the number of items you checked. (Notice that the questionnaire is a mixture of major life events and daily hassles.) The scale below is an approximate guide to the meaning of your score. But remember, stress is an internal state. If you are good at coping with stressors, a high score may not be a problem for you.

0–7	Low
8–15	Below average
16–23	Average
24–31	Above average
32–39	High
40+	Very high

Now that you have a picture of your current level of stress, what can you do about it? The simplest way of coping with stress is to modify or remove its source—by leaving a stressful job, for example. Obviously this is often impossible, which is why learning to manage stress is so important.

As shown in Figure 11–17, stress triggers *bodily effects, upsetting thoughts,* and *ineffective behavior.* Also shown is the fact that each element worsens the others in a vicious cycle. Indeed, the basic idea of the "Stress Game" is that once it begins, *you lose*—unless you take action to break the cycle. The information that follows tells how.

Managing Bodily Reactions

Much of the immediate discomfort of stress is caused by the body's fight-or-flight emotional response. The body is ready to act, with tight muscles and a pounding heart. When action is prevented, we merely remain "uptight." A sensible remedy is to learn a reliable, drug-free way of relaxing.

Stress management The application of behavioral strategies to reduce stress and improve coping skills.

Meditation A mental technique for quieting the mind and body.

Progressive relaxation A method for producing deep relaxation of all parts of the body.

Exercise Because stress prepares the body for action, its effects can be dissipated by using the body. Any full-body exercise can be effective. Swimming, dancing, jumping rope, yoga, most sports, and especially walking are valuable outlets (Rosenthal, 1993). Be sure to choose activities that are vigorous enough to relieve tension, yet enjoyable enough to be done repeatedly. Exercising for stress management is most effective when it is done daily (Wheeler & Frank, 1988). Remember, though, that this refers to light exercise, such as walking. If you do more vigorous exercise to maintain aerobic fitness, 3 to 4 times a week is about right.

Meditation Many stress counselors recommend meditation for quieting the body and promoting relaxation. We will consider meditation techniques and their effects in the upcoming Exploration section. For now, it is enough to note that meditation is easy to learn—taking an expensive commercial course is unnecessary.

Meditation is one of the most effective ways to relax (Eppley, Abrams, & Shear, 1989). But be aware that listening to or playing music, taking nature walks, enjoying hobbies, and the like can be meditations of sorts. Anything that reliably interrupts upsetting thoughts and promotes relaxation can be helpful.

Progressive Relaxation Progressive relaxation refers to a method in which people learn to relax systematically, completely, and by choice. To learn the full technique, consult Chapter 18 of this book. The basic idea is to tighten all the muscles in a given area of the body (the arms, for instance) and then voluntarily relax

APPLICATIONS: *Continued*

Table 11–4 Undergraduate Stress Questionnaire

Have any of the following stressful events happened to you at any time during the last two weeks?

If any has, please check the space next to it. If an item has not occurred, then please leave it blank.

______ Death (family member or friend)
______ Death of a pet
______ Working while in school
______ Parents getting a divorce
______ Registration for classes
______ Trying to decide on major

______ Talked with a professor
______ Trying to get into your college
______ Had a class presentation
______ Had projects, research papers due
______ Had a lot of tests
______ It's finals week

______ Applying to graduate school
______ You have a hard upcoming week
______ Lots of deadlines to meet
______ Missed your menstrual period and waiting
______ Had an interview
______ Applying for a job

______ Sat through a boring class
______ Can't understand your professor
______ Did badly on a test
______ Went into a test unprepared
______ Crammed for a test
______ Used a fake I.D.

______ Breaking up with boy/girlfriend
______ Holiday
______ Bad haircut today
______ Victim of a crime
______ Can't concentrate
______ Coping with addictions

______ Found out boy/girlfriend cheated on you
______ Did worse than expected on test
______ Stayed up late writing a paper
______ Problems with your computer
______ Favorite sports team lost
______ Ran out of typewriter ribbon while typing

______ Change of environment (new doctor, dentist, etc.)
______ Bothered by not having family's social support
______ Arguments, conflict of values with friends
______ Had a visit from a relative and entertained them
______ Noise disturbed you while trying to study
______ Maintaining a long distance boy/girlfriend

______ Assignments in all classes due the same day
______ Dealt with incompetence at the registrar's office
______ Someone borrowed something without your permission
______ Exposed to upsetting TV show, book, or movie
______ Problem getting home when drunk
______ Had confrontation with an authority figure

______ Got to class late
______ Parents controlling with money
______ Feel isolated
______ Decision to have sex on your mind
______ No sex in awhile
______ Living with boy/girlfriend

______ Felt some peer pressure
______ Felt need for transportation
______ Couldn't find a parking space
______ Property stolen
______ Car/bike broke down, flat tire, etc.
______ Got a traffic ticket

______ No time to eat
______ Having roommate conflicts
______ Had to ask for money
______ Lack money
______ Checkbook didn't balance
______ You have a hangover

______ Someone you expected to call did not
______ Lost something (especially wallet)
______ Erratic schedule
______ Thoughts about future
______ Dependent on other people
______ No sleep

______ Sick, injury
______ Fought with boy/girlfriend
______ Performed poorly at a task
______ Heard bad news
______ Thought about unfinished work
______ Feel unorganized

______ Someone cut ahead of you in line
______ Job requirements changed
______ Someone broke a promise
______ Someone did a "pet peeve" of yours
______ Can't finish everything you needed to do

(Source: Crandall, Preisler, & Aussprung, 1992.)

Guided imagery Intentional visualization of images that are calming, relaxing, or beneficial in other ways.

them. By first tensing and relaxing each area of the body, you can learn to be highly aware of how muscle tension feels. Then when each area is relaxed, the change is more noticeable and more controllable. In this way it is possible, with practice, to greatly reduce tension. People who have difficulty learning progressive relaxation may find biofeedback helpful.

Guided Imagery Relaxation can also be promoted by visualizing peaceful scenes. Pick several places

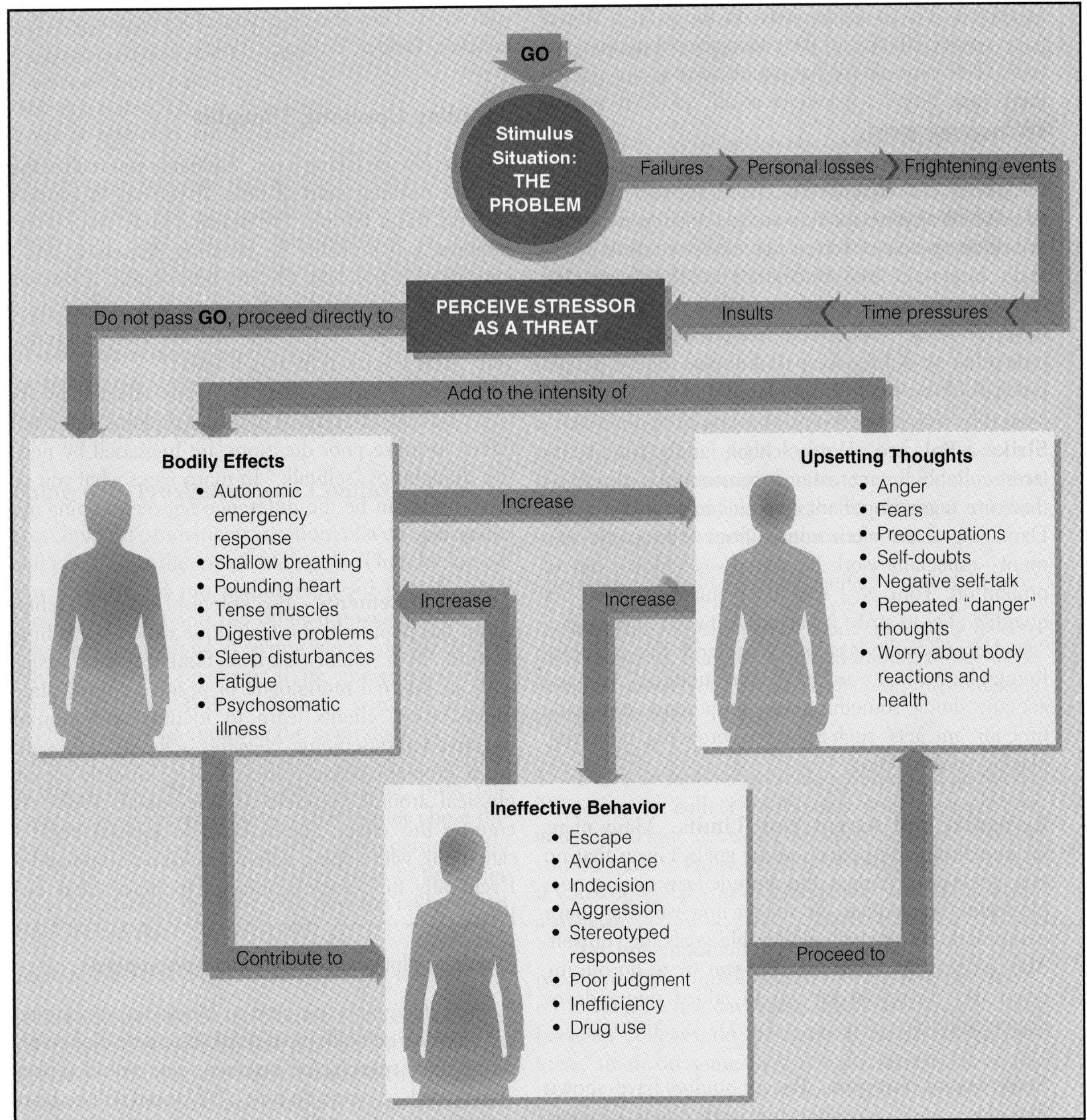

Fig. 11–17 *The stress game. (Adapted from Rosenthal and Rosenthal, 1980.)*

where you feel safe, calm, and at ease. Typical locations might be a beach or lake, the woods, floating on an air mattress in a warm pool, or lying in the sun at a quiet park. To relax, vividly imagine yourself in one of these locations. In the visualized scene, you should be alone and in a comfortable position. It is important to visualize the scene as realistically as possible. Try to feel, taste, smell, hear, and see what you would actually experience in the calming scene. Practice forming such images several times a day for about 5 minutes each time. When your scenes become familiar and detailed they can be used to reduce anxiety and encourage relaxation (Rosenthal, 1993).

Modifying Ineffective Behavior

Stress is often made worse by our response to it. The following suggestions may help you deal with stress more effectively.

Applications: *Continued*

In class you may want to describe some of the frustrations and conflicts you have experienced and how you handled them. Prepare to discuss frustrations and conflicts you have resolved unusually effectively or that you might have handled better. Do you have some additional hints to share with other students?

Learning Check

1. Exercise, meditation, and progressive relaxation are considered effective ways of countering negative self-statements. T or F?
2. Research shows that social support from family and friends has little effect on the health consequences of stress. T or F?
3. One element of stress inoculation is training in the use of positive coping statements. T or F?
4. Stereotyped responding can be particularly troublesome in coping with frustration. T or F?

Critical Thinking

5. Steve always feels extremely pressured when the due date arrives for his major term papers. How could he reduce stress in such instances?

Answers:

1. F 2. F 3. T 4. T 5. The stress associated with doing term papers can be almost completely eliminated by making a long-term assignment into many small daily or weekly assignments. Students who habitually procrastinate are often amazed at how pleasant college work can be once they renounce "brinkmanship."

EXPLORATION

Meditation—The Twenty-Minute Vacation

Meditation refers to a family of mental exercises designed to focus attention in a way that interrupts the typical flow of thoughts, worries, and analysis (Shapiro, 1984; Wilson, 1986). Meditation takes many forms and has many meanings in various cultures. Here we are interested in meditation as a self-control strategy for lowering physical and mental arousal. People who regularly use meditation as a stress reduction technique often report less daily physical arousal and anxiety. Even if meditation is not practiced daily, it may be a useful technique for interrupting worries and fearful thinking (Wilson, 1986).

Receptive Meditation Meditation takes two major forms. In **concentrative meditation,** attention is given to a single focal point, such as an object, a thought, or one's own breathing. In contrast, **receptive meditation** is "open," or expansive. That is, attention is widened to include a nonjudgmental awareness of one's total subjective experience and presence in the world (Walsh, 1984). An example of this type of meditation is losing all self-consciousness while walking in the wilderness with a quiet and receptive mind. To gain insight into receptive meditation, try the following exercise sometime.

> While walking outdoors, silently complete this statement four or five times: Right now I see . . . . Then complete each of the following statements four or five times and proceed to the next one: Right now I hear . . . . Right now I smell . . . . Right now I feel . . . . Each time, become aware of what you see, hear, smell, and feel. Then repeat the process as many times as you like.

At first you will tend to name what you are experiencing. If you can stop doing that and just be intensely aware of your surroundings—without thinking—you will have some idea of what receptive meditation is like. If you can learn to be openly aware without using any words, you will be even closer.

Although it may not seem so, receptive meditation is regarded as more difficult to attain than concentrative meditation (Smith, 1986). For this reason, we will discuss concentrative meditation as a practical self-control method.

Question: How is concentrative meditation done?

Concentrative Meditation The basic idea in concentrative meditation is to sit still and quietly focus on some external object or on a repetitive internal stimulus such as a word or your own breathing (Wilson, 1986). In one experiment, college students were instructed to concentrate on breathing:

> While you are sitting, let your breath become relaxed and natural. Let it set its own pace and depth if you can. Then focus your attention on your own breathing: the movements of your belly, not your nose and throat. Do not allow extraneous thoughts or stimuli to pull your attention

EXPLORATION

> away from your breathing. This may be hard to do at first, but keep directing your attention back to it. Turn everything else aside if it comes up. (Maupin, 1965)

Not all subjects responded to this exercise, but at the end of a 2-week period, those who did reported experiences of deep concentration, pleasant bodily sensations, and extreme detachment from outside worries and distractions.

An alternative approach you may want to try involves the use of a **mantra.** Mantras are smooth, flowing words that are easily repeated. Instead of focusing on breathing, you can silently repeat a mantra. One widely used mantra is the word "om." If you belong to an organized religion your mantra could be a phrase from a familiar prayer. Like breathing, a mantra is basically used as a focus for attention. If other thoughts arise during meditation, one should return attention to the mantra as often as necessary to maintain meditation.

The Relaxation Response A principal claim of many commercial meditation courses is that they offer a mantra tailored to the needs of each individual. But medical researcher Herbert Benson found that the physical benefits of meditation are the same no matter what word is used. These include lowered heart rate, blood pressure, muscle tension, and other signs of stress.

Benson believes that the core of meditation is the **relaxation response.** By this he means an innate physiological pattern that opposes activation of the body's fight-or-flight mechanisms. Benson feels, quite simply, that most of us have forgotten how to relax deeply. Subjects in his experiments have had considerable success in producing the relaxation response by following these instructions:

> Sit quietly in a comfortable position. Close your eyes. Deeply relax all your muscles, beginning at your feet and progressing up to your face. Keep them deeply relaxed.
>
> Breathe through your nose. Become aware of your breathing. As you breathe out, say the word "one" silently to yourself.
>
> Do not worry about whether you are successful in achieving a deep level of relaxation. Maintain a passive attitude and permit relaxation to occur at its own pace. Expect distracting thoughts. When these distracting thoughts occur, ignore them and continue repeating "one." (Adapted from Benson, 1977)

Question: What effects does meditation have, other than producing relaxation?

Effects of Meditation Many extravagant claims have been made about meditation. For example, members of the Transcendental Meditation (TM) movement have stated that 20 minutes of meditation is as restful as a full night's sleep. This, however, is simply not true. One study, for instance, found that merely "resting" for 20 minutes produces the same bodily effects as meditation (Holmes, 1984; Holmes et al., 1983). Long-term meditators have also claimed improvement in memory, alertness, creativity, and intuition. Again, such claims must be regarded as unproven. Most are based on personal testimonials or poorly controlled studies. Contrary to such claims, a study by Warrenburg and Pagano (1983) found no improvement in verbal, musical, or spatial skills that could be linked to TM.

Before you dismiss meditation, however, let's explore a little further. A thorough review of studies on meditation leads to a number of interesting conclusions (Pagano and Warrenburg, 1983).

As already stated, meditation does reliably elicit the relaxation response. The fact that other activities will do the same does not cancel the value of meditation as a way to control relaxation. Also, it is important to remember that relaxation is mental as well as physical. As a stress-control technique, meditation may be a good choice for people who find it difficult to "turn off" upsetting thoughts when they need to relax (Smith, 1986).

Regular meditators consistently report lower levels of day-to-day stress and a greater sense of well-being. This effect appears to be genuine. It cannot be explained as a placebo effect or the result of who chooses to learn meditation. It is interesting to note, however, that similar stress reduction occurs when people set aside time daily to engage in other restful activities. Muscle relaxation, positive day-dreaming, and even leisure reading can bring similar benefits.

There is some evidence that those who meditate regularly react more strongly to stressful stimuli during laboratory testing. However, they recover faster than non-meditators and say they felt less stressed.

As you can see, the effects of meditation are positive, and beneficial, but far from magical. In fact, it must be concluded that many activities will elicit the relaxation response. Benson (1975) believes that the following elements are the key to producing the relaxation response.

1. A quiet environment
2. Decreased muscle tension
3. A mental device (such as a repeated word) that helps shift thoughts away from ordinary, rational concerns
4. A passive attitude toward whether you are "succeeding" at becoming relaxed

Summary To summarize, research suggests that concentrative meditation is only one of several ways to elicit the relaxation response. For many people, sitting quietly and "resting" can be as effective. However, if you are the type of person who finds it difficult to ignore upsetting thoughts, then concentrative meditation might be a better way to promote relaxation. More important than the method you choose, however, is a willingness to set aside time each day to intentionally relax. Meditation and similar techniques provide a valuable, stress-lowering "time-out" from the normal clamor of thoughts and worries—something almost everyone could use in our fast-paced society.

Concentrative meditation Meditation in which attention is focused on a single object or thought.

Receptive meditation Meditation in which attention is widened to include an awareness of one's total subjective experience.

Mantra A word or sound used as the focus of attention in concentrative meditation.

Relaxation response The pattern of physiological responses that occur throughout the body at times of deep relaxation.

EXPLORATION

LEARNING CHECK

1. The focus of attention in concentrative meditation is "open," or expansive. T or F?
2. Mantras are words said silently to oneself to end a session of meditation. T or F?
3. Research conducted by Herbert Benson indicates that careful selection of a mantra is necessary to obtain the physical benefits of meditation. T or F?
4. The most immediate benefit of meditation appears to be its capacity for producing the relaxation response. T or F?

Critical Thinking

5. Meditation tends to interrupt negative self-statements and other upsetting internal "talk." In this sense, the effects of meditation are similar to what technique?

Answers: 1. F 2. F 3. F 4. T 5. Stress inoculation (the use of coping statements).

Chapter Summary

■ ***What is health psychology? How does behavior affect health?***

- **Health psychologists** are interested in behavior that helps maintain and promote health.
- Studies of health and illness have identified a number of **behavioral risk factors** and **health-promoting behaviors.**
- Health psychologists have pioneered efforts to *prevent* the development of unhealthy habits and to improve well-being through **community health campaigns.**

■ ***What is stress? What factors determine its severity?***

- **Stress** occurs when demands are placed on an organism to adjust or adapt.
- Stress is more damaging in situations involving *pressure*, a *lack of control*, *unpredictability* of the stressor, and *intense* or *repeated* emotional shocks.
- Stress is intensified when a situation is perceived as a *threat* and when a person does not feel *competent* to cope with it.
- In work settings, prolonged stress can lead to **burnout.**
- The **primary appraisal** of a situation greatly affects our emotional response to it. Stress reactions, in particular, are related to an appraisal of threat.
- During a **secondary appraisal** some means of coping with a situation is selected. Coping may be either **problem-focused** or **emotion-focused** or both.

■ ***What causes frustration and what are typical reactions to it?***

- **Frustration** is the negative emotional state that occurs when progress toward a goal is blocked. Sources of frustration may be usefully classified as *external* or *personal.*
- External frustrations are based on *delay*, *failure*, *rejection*, *loss*, and other direct blocking of motives. Personal frustration is related to *personal characteristics* over which one has little control.
- Frustrations of all types become more intense as the *strength*, *urgency*, or *importance* of the blocked motive increases.
- Major behavioral reactions to frustration include *persistence*, *more vigorous responding*, *circumvention*, *direct aggression*, *displaced aggression* (including *scapegoating*), and *escape*, or *withdrawal.*

■ ***Are there different types of conflict? How do people react to conflict?***

- **Conflict** occurs when one must choose between contradictory alternatives.
- Five major types of conflict are **approach-approach** (choice between two positive alternatives), **avoidance-avoidance** (both alternatives are negative), **approach-avoidance** (a goal or activity has both positive and negative aspects), **double approach-avoidance** (both alternatives have positive and negative qualities) and **multiple approach-avoidance** (several alternatives each have good and bad qualities).
- Approach-approach conflicts are usually the easiest to resolve.
- Avoidance conflicts are difficult to resolve and are characterized by *inaction*, *indecision*, *freezing*, and a *desire to escape* (called *leaving the field*).
- People usually remain in approach-avoidance conflicts, but fail to resolve them. Approach-avoidance conflicts are associated with *ambivalence* and *par-*

tial approach. Vacillation is probably the most common reaction to double approach-avoidance conflicts.

■ ***What are defense mechanisms?***

- Anxiety, threat, or feelings of inadequacy frequently lead to the use of **defense mechanisms.** These are habitual psychological strategies used to avoid or reduce anxiety.
- A large number of defense mechanisms have been identified, including *compensation, denial, fantasy, intellectualization, isolation, projection, rationalization, reaction formation, regression, repression,* and *sublimation.*

■ ***What do we know about coping with feelings of helplessness and depression?***

- The concept of **learned helplessness** has been used to explain the failure to cope with threatening situations and as a model for understanding **depression. Mastery training** acts as one major antidote to helplessness.
- **Depression** is a major, and surprisingly common, emotional problem. Actions and thoughts that counter feelings of helplessness tend to reduce depression.

■ ***How is stress related to health and disease?***

- Work with the *Social Readjustment Rating Scale* indicates that an accumulation of **life changes** can increase susceptibility to accident or illness. However, immediate psychological and mental health is more closely related to the intensity and severity of daily annoyances, known as **hassles** or **microstressors.**
- Intense or prolonged stress (especially when it is associated with negative emotional response), may cause damage in the form of ulcers and other *psychosomatic* problems. **Psychosomatic** (mind-body) **disorders** have no connection to **hypochondria,** the tendency to imagine that one has some terrible disease.
- During **biofeedback training,** bodily processes are monitored and converted to a signal that indicates what the body is doing. With practice, biofeedback allows alteration of many bodily activities. It shows promise for the alleviation of some psychosomatic illnesses.
- People with **Type A personalities** are competitive, striving, and frequently angry or hostile, and they have a chronic sense of time urgency. These characteristics—especially anger and hostility—combine to double the chances of heart attack.
- People who have traits of the **hardy personality** seem to be resistant to stress, even if they also have Type A traits.
- The body reacts to stress in a series of stages called the **general adaptation syndrome** (G.A.S.).
- The stages of the G.A.S. are **alarm, resistance,** and **exhaustion.** The pattern of bodily reactions and changes in resistance observed in the G.A.S. follows closely the pattern observed in the development of psychosomatic disorders. In addition, stress may lower the body's immunity to disease.

■ ***What are the best strategies for managing stress?***

- A sizable number of coping skills can be applied to manage stress. Most of these focus on one of three areas: *bodily effects, ineffective behavior,* and *upsetting thoughts.*

■ ***Is meditation useful for coping with stress?***

- **Receptive meditation** and **concentrative meditation** are self-control techniques that can be used to reduce stress. Two major benefits of meditation are its ability to interrupt anxious thoughts and its ability to elicit the **relaxation response.**

Questions for Discussion

1. Why do you think the relationship between behavioral risk factors and health is so widely ignored? How important is health to you? How do your acquaintances rationalize their unhealthy behaviors? How do you?
2. How could you reduce conflict or avoid an unfortunate decision in the following situations: choosing a school to attend, choosing a major, deciding about marriage, choosing a job, buying a car?
3. Calculate your scores on the SRRS and USQ. Do they correspond? If your scores are elevated, what could you do to reduce the chances of illness? If they are low, what could you do to put more excitement in your life?! Can you see any relationship between periods of illness you have had and the number of life changes or hassles that preceded them?
4. What do you consider the most prominent sources of stress in our society? What do you think should or could be done to combat these stresses?
5. Explain why you agree or disagree with the following statement (attributed to Professor P. T. Barnumandbailey Circuits): "Television is the opiate of the people. If all the TV tubes in the United States suddenly went blank, the mental health of the nation would crumble because people could no longer escape their problems by watching television."

6. How could you best deal with the following sources of frustration: delays, losses, lack of resources, failure, rejection?
7. Many people report becoming extremely frustrated as they learn to use a computer. Why? In what way can this frustration be explained by the concepts of stress?
8. Acts of racial and religious prejudice have increased in frequency over the last few years, as have attacks on gay and lesbian persons. Do you think that the frustration-aggression hypothesis applies to such behavior? Why or why not?
9. What are the advantages and disadvantages of relying on defense mechanisms to cope with threats and anxiety? Do you think it would be possible to be completely free of defense mechanisms?
10. In what ways do schools, parents, and the government encourage feelings of helplessness? In what ways do they (or could they) add to feelings of confidence, competence, and hope?
11. How might the concept of learned helplessness apply to each of the following: achievement in school, poverty, old-age homes, battered women, child abuse?
12. What are the advantages and disadvantages of being a Type A person or a Type B person? How are these two personalities similar to and different from the "hardy" personality?

Chapter 12

Child Development

CHAPTER PREVIEW

Alien Minds

You may not have noticed. Not everyone has. There are alien creatures among us. More arrive daily. They look a lot like you and me, but they're smaller, and they think differently. Their speech is strange. They ask many questions. It's obvious they are trying to understand how we live. Their goal is to inhabit the planet Earth in our place. Who are these creatures? Where are they from? You need not be alarmed: They come not from outer space, but from inner space. They are the product of life perpetuating life. They are children.

Studying children helps answer the question, How did I become the person I am today? This makes the study of children rewarding, but there is more reason for interest: A child's understanding of the world is qualitatively *different from yours and mine. Entering a child's awareness has much of the intrigue of meeting a person from another culture. It might even be compared to encountering an alien mind. In short, children are extremely interesting creatures. A tremendous amount of psychological research has focused on them.*

Question: What branch of psychology studies children?

The study of children is the heart of **developmental psychology.** *However, you should be aware that developmental psychologists are interested in every stage of life from "the*

IN THIS CHAPTER

Developmental psychology The study of progressive changes in behavior and abilities from conception to death.

Neonate A newborn infant.

Grasping reflex Reflexive grasping of objects placed in the palm.

Rooting reflex Reflexive head turning and nursing, elicited by touching the cheek.

Sucking reflex Rhythmic sucking movements elicited by touching the neonate's mouth.

Moro reflex Arm extension and clasping elicited in the neonate by a loud noise or sudden loss of support.

womb to the tomb." Developmental psychology can be described as the study of progressive changes in behavior and abilities from conception to death. *With a definition like this, it's clear that developmental psychology includes many topics—so many in fact, that some appear in other chapters.*

In this chapter, we will discuss a number of general topics and principles of development, including the far-reaching events in the first years of life. The next chapter covers development viewed over an entire life span. It also gives special attention to problems often encountered at various points in life. Perhaps learning about development will contribute to your own development. Find out by reading more!

Survey Questions

- What can newborn babies do?
- How aware are infants of their surroundings?
- What influence does maturation have on early development?
- How do heredity and environment affect development?
- How important are parenting styles?
- Of what significance is a child's emotional attachment to parents?
- How do children acquire language and thinking abilities?
- How do children develop morals and values?
- What are the effects of a poor early environment?
- What can be done to enhance early development?
- How have sex selection, genetic counseling, and the like, affected parents and children?

The Newborn Baby—The Basic Model Comes with Options

At birth the human **neonate** (NEE-oh-NATE: *neo:* new; *nate:* born) is completely dependent on others and will die if not given care. Newborn babies cannot lift their heads, turn over, or feed themselves. Does this mean they are inert and unfeeling? Definitely not! Neonates can see, hear, smell, taste, and respond to pain and touch. Although their senses are less acute at birth, babies are immediately responsive to their surroundings. Neonates will, in fact, follow a moving object with their eyes and will turn in the direction of sounds. Within *hours* after they are born, babies begin to prefer seeing their mother's face, rather than a stranger's (Walton, Bower, & Bower, 1992). (See ■ Figure 12–1.)

■ **Fig. 12–1** *Newborn babies display a special interest in the human face. A preference for seeing their mother's face develops rapidly and encourages social interactions between mother and baby.*

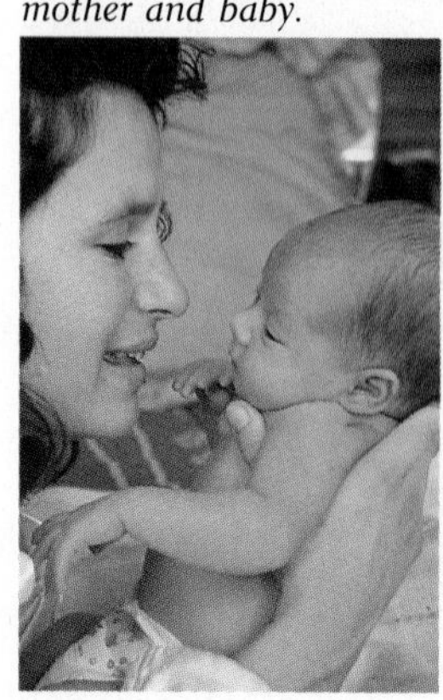

A number of adaptive *reflexes* can be observed in the newborn. If you press an object into a neonate's palm she will grasp it with surprising strength. The **grasping reflex** is so strong that many infants can hang from a raised bar, like little trapeze artists. Very likely, the grasping reflex improves an infant's chances of survival by helping her to avoid falling. Another adaptive reflex can be demonstrated by touching a baby's cheek. Immediately, she will turn toward your finger, as if searching for something.

Question: How is such turning adaptive?

The **rooting reflex,** as this is called, helps infants to find a bottle or breast. Then, when a nipple touches the infant's mouth, the **sucking reflex** helps him obtain needed food. At the same time, food rewards nursing. As a result, nursing rapidly increases in vigor during the first days after birth. Thus, we see that learning begins at once in the newborn.

The **Moro reflex** is also interesting. If a baby's position is changed abruptly, or if the baby is startled by a loud noise, the infant will make movements similar to an embrace. These movements have been compared to the ones used by baby monkeys to cling to their mothers. (It is left to the reader's imagination to decide if there is any connection.)

We are tempted to think of newborn babies as mere bundles of reflexes. But infants can respond in ways that are more subtle than once imagined. For example, Andrew Meltzoff and Keith Moore (1977, 1983) found that babies are born mimics. ■ Figure 12–2 shows Meltzoff as he sticks out his tongue, opens his mouth, and purses his lips at a 20-day-old girl. Will she imitate him? Videotapes made of babies confirmed that they imitate adult facial gestures. As early as 9 months of age, infants can imitate actions a full day after seeing them (Meltzoff, 1988). Such mimicry is obviously an aid to rapid learning in infancy.

Question: How much intelligence does a newborn have?

Child psychologist Jerome Bruner (1984) believes that babies are smarter than most people think. Bruner cites an experiment in which 3- to 8-week-old babies seemed to understand that a person's voice and body are connected. If babies heard their mother's voice coming from where she was standing, they remained calm. If her voice came from a loudspeaker several feet away, the babies became agitated and began to cry. Bruner believes that this and similar experiments show that the human mind is quite active from birth onward (more on this later). Another sign of infant awareness is the fact that newborn babies appear to remember simple speech sounds up to a day after first hearing them (Swain, Zelazo, & Clifton, 1993).

Tests of infant vision offer a further look into the private world of the neonate.

Question: How is it possible to test a baby's vision?

Working with infants always requires imagination, because they cannot talk. To test infant vision, Robert Fantz (1963) invented a device called a **looking chamber** (■ Fig. 12–3a). A child is placed on his or her back inside the chamber, facing a lighted area above. Next, two objects are placed in the chamber. By observing the movements of the infant's eyes and the images they reflect, researchers can tell what the infant is looking at.

Fantz found that 3-day-old babies prefer complex patterns, such as checkerboards and bull's eyes, to simpler colored rectangles. Other psychologists have learned that infants are more excited by circles and

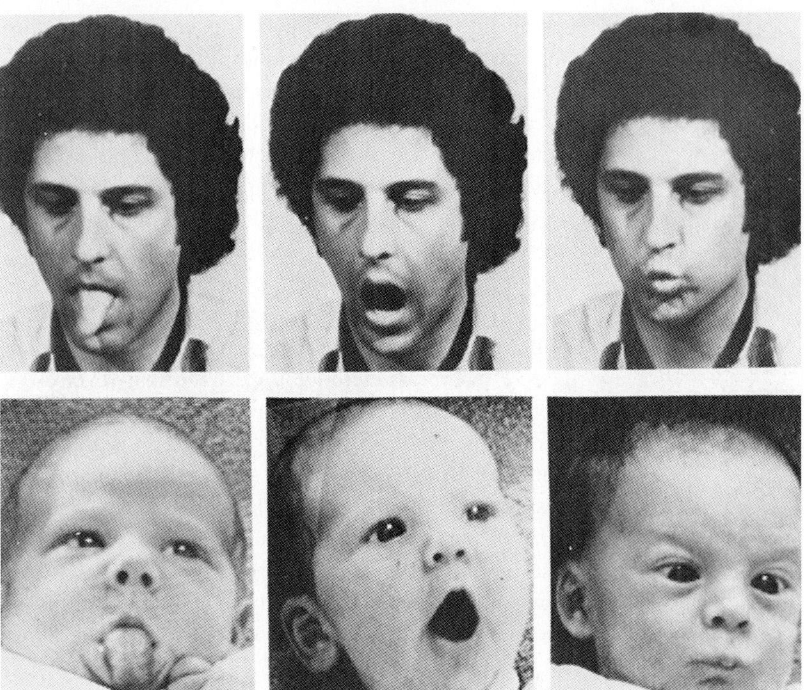

■ **Fig. 12–2** *Infant imitation. In the top row of photos, Andrew Meltzoff makes facial gestures at an infant. The bottom row records the infant's responses. Videotapes of Meltzoff and of tested infants helped ensure objectivity. (Photos courtesy of Andrew N. Meltzoff.)*

■ **Fig. 12–3** (a) *Eye movements and fixation points of infants are observed in Fantz's "looking chamber."* (b) *Thirteen-week-old infants prefer concentric and curved patterns like those on the left to non-concentric and straight-line patterns like those on the right.* (c) *Infants tested in a looking chamber look at the normal face longer than at the scrambled face and at both faces longer than at the design on the right. (Photo courtesy of David Linton. Drawing from "The Origin of Form Perception" by Robert L. Fantz, Copyright © 1961 by Scientific American, Inc. All rights reserved.)*

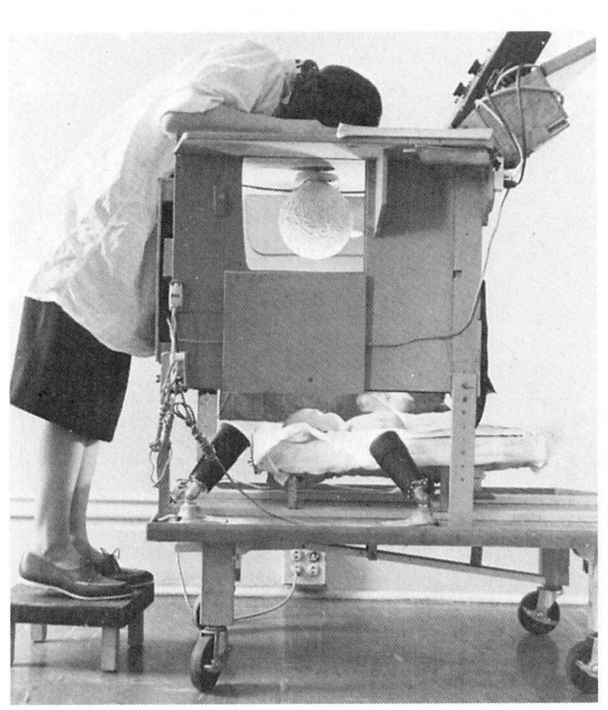

(a)

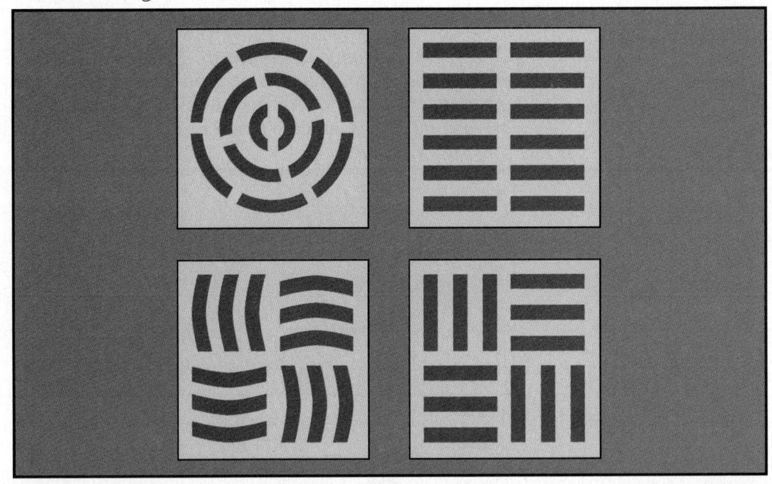

(b)

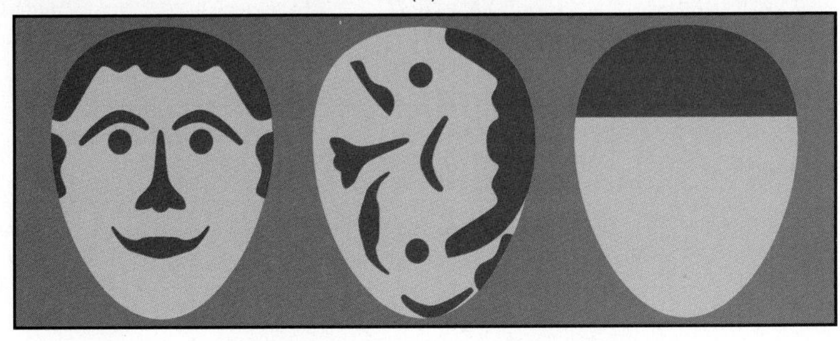

(c)

Looking chamber An apparatus used to test infant perception by observing infant responses to visual stimuli.

Maturation The physical growth and development of the body and nervous system.

General excitement Widespread emotional arousal associated with activation of the autonomic nervous system.

curves and that they will look longer at bright lights (Fig. 12–3b) (Brown, 1990). Within hours after they are born, babies are aware of changes in the position of objects (Slater et al., 1991). Findings such as these demonstrate (as a friend of the author's once put it) that "There really is a person inside that little body."

Of possibly greater interest is the finding that infants will spend more time looking at a human face pattern than at a scrambled face or a colored oval (Fig. 12–3c). When real human faces were used, Fantz found that familiar faces are preferred to unfamiliar faces. However, preference for the familiar reverses at about age 2. At that time, unusual objects begin to hold greater interest for the child. For instance, Jerome Kagan (1971) showed three-dimensional face masks to 2-year-olds. Kagan found that the toddlers were fascinated by a face with eyes on the chin and a nose in the middle of the forehead. He believes the babies' interest came from a need to understand why the scrambled face differed from what they had come to expect.

Maturation

Early development of the abilities we have described closely parallels maturation. **Maturation** refers to physical growth and development of the body—especially the nervous system. Maturation underlies the *orderly sequence* observed in the unfolding of many basic abilities. This is particularly true of motor abilities, such as crawling and walking.

While the *rate* of maturation varies from child to child, the *order* is virtually universal. For instance, the strength and coordination a child needs to sit upright without support appears before that needed for crawling. Therefore, infants the world over typically sit before they crawl (and crawl before they stand, stand before they walk, and so on) (■ Fig. 12–4).

Question: What about my weird cousin Emo who never crawled?

Like cousin Emo, a few children substitute rolling, creeping, or shuffling for crawling. A very few move directly from sitting to standing and walking (Robson, 1984). Even so, an orderly sequence of motor development remains evident. In general, increased muscular control in infants proceeds from *head to toe,* and from the *center* of the body *to the extremities.* Even if cousin Emo flunked crawling, his motor development followed the standard top-down, center-outward pattern.

Early emotional development also follows a pattern closely tied to maturation. Basic **anger, fear,** and **joy**—which appear to be unlearned—take time to develop. General **excitement** is the only emotional response newborn infants clearly express. However, as any parent can tell you, the emotional life of a baby blossoms rapidly. One researcher (Bridges, 1932) observed a large number of babies and found that all the basic human emotions appear before age 2. Bridges found that there is a consistent order in which emotions appear and that the first basic split is between pleasant and unpleasant emotions (■ Fig. 12–5).

■ **Fig. 12–4** *Motor development. Most infants follow an orderly pattern of motor development. Although the order in which children progress is similar, there are large individual differences in the ages at which each ability appears. The ages listed are averages for American children. It is not unusual for many of the skills to appear 1 or 2 months earlier than average or several months later (Frankenberg & Dodds, 1967). Parents should not be alarmed if a child's behavior differs some from the average.*

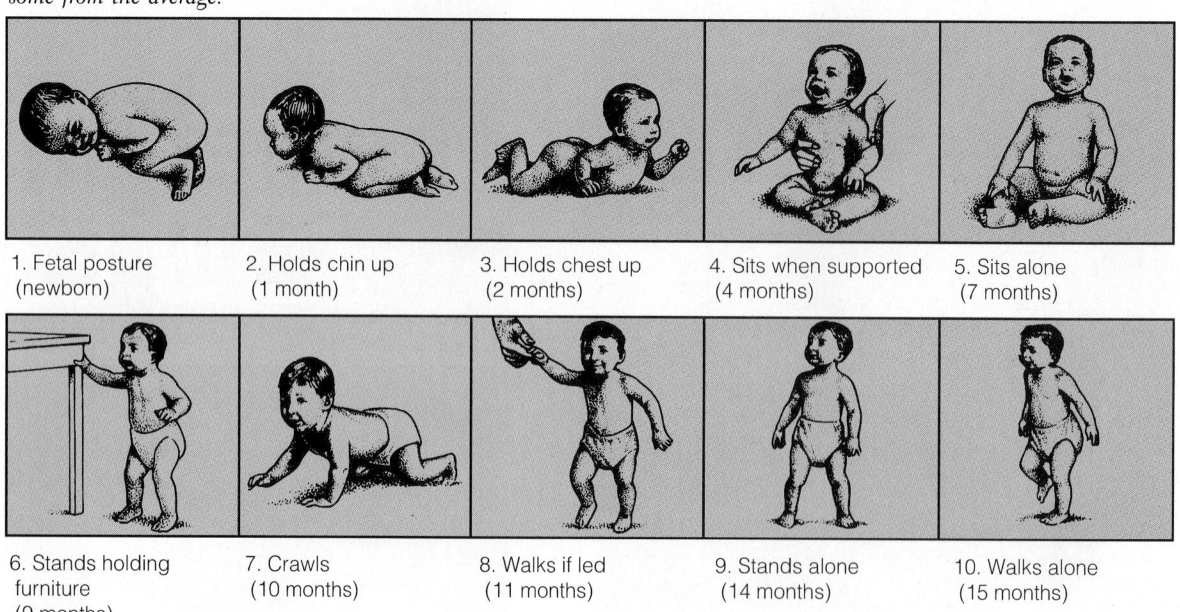

More recent research suggests that by the end of the first year, babies can express happiness, surprise, fear, anger, sadness, disgust, and interest (Saarni, 1982). This important development leads to a fascinating interplay of emotions between infants and adults. For example, by the age of 10 months, infants smile more frequently when another person is nearby (Jones, Collins, & Hong, 1991). A smiling baby, of course, encourages closeness and attention from parents. On the other hand, when new parents see and hear a crying baby, they feel annoyed, irritated, disturbed, or unhappy (Frodi et al., 1978). Such reactions encourage parents to tend to a baby's needs, thus increasing its chances for survival. Babies the world over, it seems, rapidly become capable of letting others know what they like and dislike. (Prove this to yourself sometime by driving a baby buggy.)

Readiness Maturation often creates a condition of **readiness** for learning. The principle of readiness (also known as the **principle of motor primacy**) states that minimum levels of motor, muscular, and physical development must precede the learning of certain skills. It is impossible, for instance, to teach children to walk or to use a toilet before they have matured enough to control the necessary muscles. Parents who try to force children to learn skills for which they are not yet ready invite failure. They also run a risk of needlessly frustrating the child.

Question: Then are there definite ages at which children become ready to learn particular skills?

No. Readiness usually emerges over a period of weeks or months. Training that begins too early will not succeed; training early in a transition period may succeed, but it will be inefficient; and training when a child is maturationally ready produces rapid learning.

Many parents are anxious to see their children progress, and there is always a temptation to try to hurry a child along. However, it is valuable to recognize that much needless grief can be avoided by respecting a child's personal rate of growth. Consider, for instance, the eager parents who toilet train an 18-month-old child in 10 trying weeks of false alarms and "accidents." Had the parents waited until the child was 24 months old, they might have succeeded in just 3 weeks. Parents may control when toilet training starts, but maturation tends to determine when it will be completed (Martin et al., 1984). (Around 30 months is average for completion.) So why fight nature? (The wet look is in.)

Perhaps the most striking aspect of human infants is the dazzling speed with which they are transformed from helpless babies to independent persons. Early growth is extremely rapid. By the third year of life, the child stands, walks, talks, explores, and has a unique personality. At no other time after birth does development proceed more rapidly. During this period, the child's development is shaped by a fascinating interplay between heredity and environment. Before we explore that topic, Table 12–1 summarizes some of the implications of the preceding discussion.

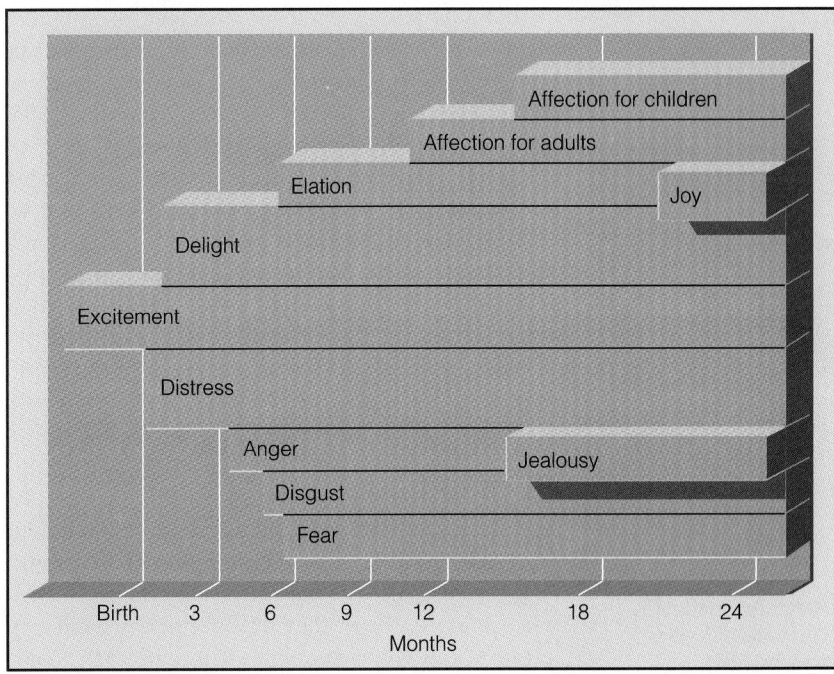

Fig. 12–5 *In the human infant, emotions are rapidly differentiated from an initial capacity for excitement. (After K. M. B. Bridges, 1932. Reprinted by permission of the Society for Research in Child Development, Inc.)*

Table 12–1 The Neonate: Implications for Parents and Caregivers

• From birth onward, infants are responsive to their immediate surroundings and to other people. Mental life and intellectual development also begin immediately. Learning doesn't begin in preschool or kindergarten.
• Maturation proceeds at its own pace and in an orderly sequence. Caregivers should be sensitive to a child's level of development and avoid forcing the pace of learning. The principle of readiness applies to many early skills.
• Even infants under the age of 1 year have feelings and emotional experiences.

Readiness Sufficient maturation for rapid acquisition of a skill.

Principle of motor primacy Principle that motor, muscular, and physical development must precede the learning of certain skills.

Heredity and Environment—The Nurture of Nature

Question: Which has a greater effect on development, heredity or environment?

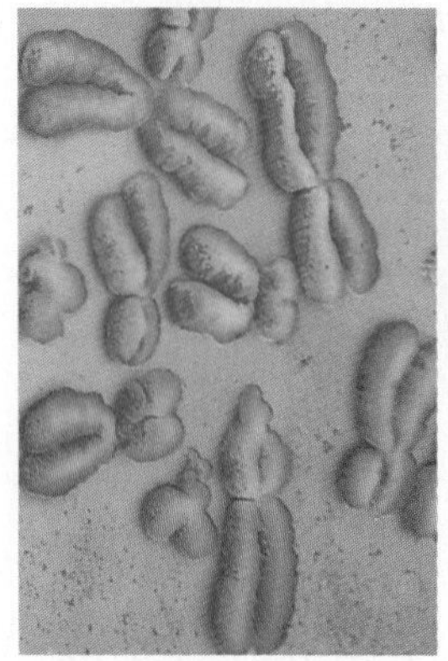

■ **Fig. 12–6** *This image, made with a scanning electron microscope, shows several pairs of human chromosomes. (Colors are artificial.)*

Heredity ("nature") The transmission of physical and psychological characteristics from parents to offspring through genes.

Chromosomes Thread-like "colored bodies" made of DNA in the nucleus of cells.

DNA Deoxyribonucleic acid, a molecular structure that codes genetic information.

Genes Specific areas on a strand of DNA that carry hereditary information.

Polygenic characteristics Personal characteristics that are influenced by a combination of genes.

Dominant gene A gene whose influence will be expressed each time the gene is present.

Recessive gene A gene whose influence will be expressed only when it is paired with a second recessive gene.

For many years psychologists debated—sometimes heatedly—the relative importance of nature versus nurture in determining behavior. The potent effects of heredity certainly cannot be denied. **Heredity** ("**nature**") refers to the transmission of physical and psychological characteristics from parents to offspring through genes. At conception, when a sperm and an ovum (egg) unite, an incredible number of personal features and growth patterns are determined. It is estimated that the genetic information carried in each human cell would fill thousands of 1000-page books—and that's in fine print!

Question: How does heredity operate?

Heredity

The nucleus of every cell in the body contains 46 thread-like structures called **chromosomes** that transmit the coded instructions of heredity (■Fig. 12–6). An exception to this statement is sperm cells and ova, each of which contains only 23 chromosomes. Thus, humans normally receive 23 chromosomes from their mother and 23 from the father. Chromosomes are made up of **DNA,** deoxyribonucleic acid (dee-OX-see-RYE-bo-new-KLEE-ik). DNA is a long, ladder-like chemical molecule that is assembled from smaller molecules (■Fig. 12–7). The order of these molecules, or organic bases, acts as a code for genetic information.

The DNA in each cell contains 300 billion base pairs. That's enough to provide all the instructions needed to make a human—with room left over to spare. **Genes** are small areas of the DNA code. Each gene, which can be up to 30,000 base-pairs long, carries instructions that affect a particular process or personal characteristic. There are 50,000 to 100,000 genes in every human cell (Lowenstein, 1992). In some cases, a single gene is responsible for a particular inherited feature, such as eye color. Most characteristics, however, are **polygenic** (pol-ih-JEN-ik), or determined by many genes working in combination.

Genes may be dominant or recessive. When a gene is **dominant,** the trait it controls will be present every time the gene is present. When a gene is **recessive,** it must be paired with a second recessive gene before its effect will be expressed. An example should make this clearer. We receive one-half of our chromosomes (and genes) from each parent. If you were to get a brown-eye gene from your father and a blue-eye gene from your mother, you would be brown-eyed, because brown-eye genes are dominant.

Question: If brown-eye genes are dominant, how is it that two brown-eyed parents sometimes have a blue-eyed child?

If each parent has two brown-eye genes, the couple's children can only be brown-eyed. But what if each parent has one brown-eye gene and one blue-eye gene? In

■ **Fig. 12–7** (Top left) *The order of the linked molecules (organic bases) that make up the "rungs" on DNA's twisted "molecular ladder" serve as a code for genetic information. The order of the code provides a genetic blueprint that is unique for each individual (except identical twins). The drawing shows only a small section of a DNA strand. An entire strand of DNA is composed of billions of smaller molecules.* (Bottom left) *The nucleus of each cell in the body contains chromosomes made up of tightly wound coils of DNA. (Don't be misled by the drawing: Chromosomes are microscopic in size and the chemical molecules that make up DNA are even smaller.)*

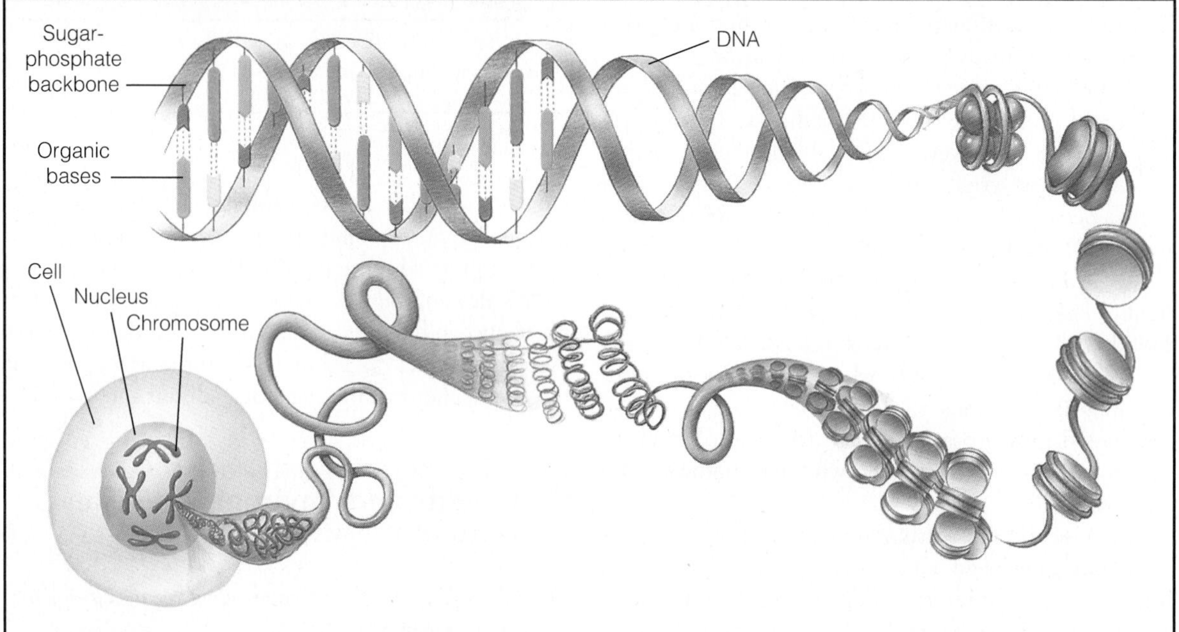

this case the parents would both have brown eyes, but there is 1 chance in 4 that their children will get two blue-eye genes and have blue eyes (■ Fig. 12–8).

Sex is also genetically determined—in this case by two specialized chromosomes. A child who inherits two **X chromosomes** will normally be a female. An X chromosome paired with a **Y chromosome** normally yields a male. The woman's ovum always provides an X chromosome, since she has two X's in her own genetic makeup. In contrast, one-half of the male's sperm carry X chromosomes and the other half Y's. There is evidence that just one gene on the Y chromosome initiates the events that make a male baby. (Gender can be more complex than implied here. See Chapter 19 for more information.)

Whether you received XX or XY chromosomes can be important in ways beyond determining sex. Some traits are **sex-linked,** or carried by recessive genes on the X chromosome. An example is color blindness, which is carried on an X chromosome and given from mother to son. (In a few instances, sex-linked traits are carried on a Y chromosome. However, this is exceedingly rare.)

Nature Hereditary instructions carried by the chromosomes influence development throughout life by affecting the sequence of growth, the timing of puberty, and the course of aging. The broad outlines of the **human growth sequence** are therefore universal. A general pattern of physical development extends from conception to senescence (seh-NESS-ens: aging) and death, as ● Table 12–2 shows. In addition, heredity determines eye color, skin color, and susceptibility to some diseases. It underlies maturation and the orderly sequence of motor development. Heredity also exerts considerable influence over body size and shape, height, intelligence, athletic potential, personality traits, and a host of other details (■ Fig. 12–9). Score 1 for those who favor heredity as the more important factor in development!

Environment

Does the preceding mean that **environment** (nurture) takes a back seat in development? Definitely not. As Aldous Huxley (1965) pointed out, humans today are physically very similar to cave dwellers who lived 30,000 years ago. A bright baby born today could become almost anything—a computer programmer, an engineer, a gangsta rapper, or a biochemist who likes to paint in watercolors, for instance. But an Upper Paleolithic baby could not possibly have grown into

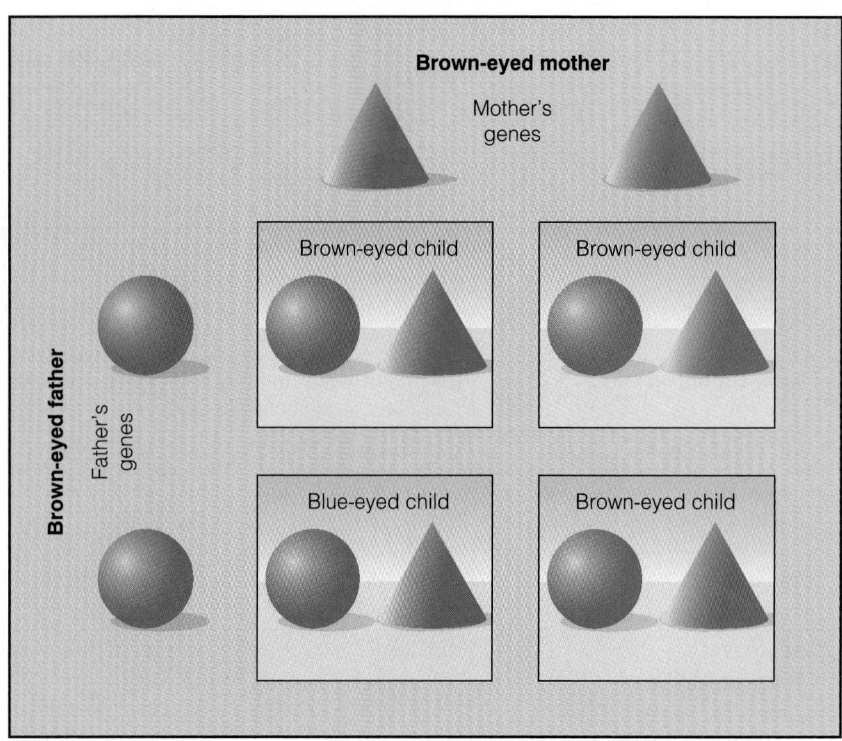

■ **Fig. 12–8** *Gene patterns for children of brown-eyed parents, where each parent has one brown-eye gene and one blue-eye gene. Since the brown-eye gene is dominant, only 1 child in 4 will be blue-eyed.*

■ **Fig. 12–9** *Identical twins. Twins who share identical genes (identical twins) demonstrate the powerful influence of heredity. Even when they are reared apart, identical twins are strikingly alike in motor skills, physical development, and appearance (Horn et al., 1976). At the same time, twins are less alike as adults than they were as children, which shows environmental influences are at work (McCartney, Bernieri, & Harris, 1990).*

X chromosome A female chromosome.

Y chromosome A male chromosome.

Sex-linked trait A trait carried by recessive genes on the X chromosome (or rarely, the Y chromosome).

Human growth sequence The pattern of physical development from conception to death.

Environment ("nurture") The sum total of all external conditions affecting development.

Table 12–2 Human Growth Sequence

Period	Duration	Descriptive Name
Prenatal period	From conception to birth	
Germinal period	First two weeks after conception	Zygote
Embryonic period	2–8 weeks after conception	Embryo
Fetal period	From 8 weeks after conception to birth	Fetus
Neonatal period	From birth to a few weeks after birth	Neonate
Infancy	From a few weeks after birth until child is walking securely; some children walk securely at less than a year, while others may not be able to until age 17–18 months	Infant
Early childhood	From about 15–18 months until about 2–2½ years	Toddler
	From age 2–3 to about age 6	Preschool child
Middle childhood	From about age 6 to about age 12	School-age child
Pubescence	Period of about 2 years before puberty	
Puberty	Point of development at which biological changes of pubescence reach a climax marked by sexual maturity	
Adolescence	From the beginning of pubescence until full social maturity is reached (difficult to fix duration of this period)	Adolescent
Adulthood	From adolescence to death; sometimes subdivided into other periods as shown at left	Adult
Young adulthood (19–25)		
Adulthood (26–40)		
Maturity (41 plus)		
Senescence	No defined limit that would apply to all people; extremely variable; characterized by marked physiological and psychological deterioration	Adult (senile), "old age"

*Note: There is no exact beginning or ending point for the various growth periods. The ages are approximate, and each period may be thought of as blending into the next. (Table courtesy of Tom Bond.)

Temperament The physical foundation of personality, including emotional and perceptual sensitivity, energy levels, typical mood, and so forth.

Easy child A child who is temperamentally relaxed and agreeable.

Difficult child A child who is temperamentally moody and easily angered.

Slow-to-warm-up child A child who is temperamentally restrained, unexpressive, or shy.

anything except a hunter or food gatherer. Score 1 for the environmentalists!

Nature-Nurture Interactions The outcome of this debate is clear: *both* heredity and environment are important. The two are, in fact, inseparable. As a person grows, there is a constant interplay, or *interaction,* between nature and nurture. Heredity shapes development by providing a framework of personal potentials and limitations. These, in turn, are altered by learning, nutrition, disease, culture, and other environmental factors. By themselves, hereditary instructions are meaningless. The unfolding of genetic tendencies is intimately tied to the quality of the environments in which a child lives, learns, and grows (Baker & Clark, 1990; Lipsitt, 1990).

Question: How soon after birth do hereditary differences appear?

Some appear immediately. Newborn babies differ noticeably in activity, irritability, distractibility, and other aspects of **temperament.** (Temperament refers to the physical foundations of personality, such as prevailing mood, sensitivity, and energy levels.) Differences in temperament are significantly influenced by genetics (Braungart et al., 1992). Thus, from birth onward, babies are unique individuals. (See Table 12–3.)

On the basis of temperament, babies can be separated into three major categories. **Easy children** (about 40 percent of those observed) are relaxed and agreeable. **Difficult children** (about 10 percent) are moody, intense, and easily angered. **Slow-to-warm-up children** (about 15 percent) are restrained and unexpressive, or shy. The remaining children do not fit neatly into any single category (Chess & Thomas, 1986). (Perhaps we should call them "generic" children?)

Because of inborn differences in readiness to smile, cry, vocalize, reach out, or pay attention, babies rapidly become *active participants* in their own devel-

Table 12–3 Heredity and Environment: Implications for Parents and Caregivers

• At any given time a child's development reflects the joint effects of heredity and environment. However, caregivers can only influence environment.
• Children vary in temperament. Caregivers should be sensitive to such differences and accept them as natural.
• Parenting is a serious responsibility, especially during the first years of life, which have far-reaching effects.

opment—especially their social development. Growing infants alter parents' behavior at the same time they are changed by it. For example, Amy is an easy baby who smiles frequently and is easily fed. This encourages touching, feeding, and affection from her mother. The mother's responses, in turn, reward Amy and cause more smiling and other positive reactions. A dynamic *relationship* has been created between mother and child.

To summarize, we might say that three factors combine to determine a person's **developmental level** at any stage of life. These are *heredity, environment*, and the individual's *own behavior*, each tightly interwoven with the others.

Developmental level An individual's current state of physical, emotional, and intellectual development.

Learning Check

1. If an infant is startled, it will make movements similar to an embrace. This is known as the
   a. grasping reflex *b.* rooting reflex *c.* Moro reflex *d.* adaptive reflex
2. After age 2, infants tested in a looking chamber show a marked preference for familiar faces and simpler designs. T or F?
3. As a child develops there is a continuous ______________ between the forces of heredity and environment.
4. Which of the following represents a correct sequence?
   a. zygote, fetus, embryo, neonate, infant *b.* zygote, embryo, neonate, fetus, infant
   c. embryo, zygote, fetus, neonate, infant *d.* zygote, embryo, fetus, neonate, infant
5. "Slow-to-warm-up" children can be described as restrained, unexpressive, or shy. T or F?
6. The orderly sequence observed in the unfolding of many basic responses can be attributed to ______________.
7. The principle of motor primacy is also known as ______________.
8. Areas of the DNA molecule called genes are made up of dominant and recessive chromosomes. T or F?
9. If you were going to test newborn infants to see if they prefer their own mother's face to that of a stranger, what precautions would you take? *Critical Thinking*

Answers: 1. c 2. F 3. interaction 4. *d* 5. T 6. maturation 7. readiness 8. F 9. In one study of the preferences of newborns, the hair color and complexion of strangers was matched to that of the mothers. Also, only the mother's or stranger's face was visible during testing. And finally, a scent was used to mask olfactory (smell) cues so that an infant's preference could not be based on the mother's familiar odor (Bushnell, Sai, & Mullin, 1989).

Early Environment—As the Twig Is Bent

Environment obviously begins to modify development immediately after birth, but the prenatal environment is also important. Normally we think of the **intrauterine environment** of the womb as highly protected and stable. In general, it is, but a number of conditions can affect development before birth.

Prenatal Influences

During embryonic and fetal development it is quite possible for the effects of environment to reach the seemingly well-protected interior of the womb. If a mother's health or nutrition is poor, if she contracts certain diseases, such as German measles or syphilis, uses drugs, or is exposed to X-rays or atomic radiation, the fetus may be harmed (Rosenblith, 1992). The resulting damage is referred to as a **congenital problem.** (■ Fig. 12–10). Congenital problems (or "birth defects," as they are sometimes called) are different from **genetic problems,** which are inherited. (You will find more information on genetic problems in this chapter's Exploration.)

■ **Fig. 12–10** *Due to the rapid growth of basic structures, the developing fetus is sensitive to a variety of diseases, drugs, and sources of radiation. This is especially true during the first trimester (3 months) of gestation (pregnancy).*

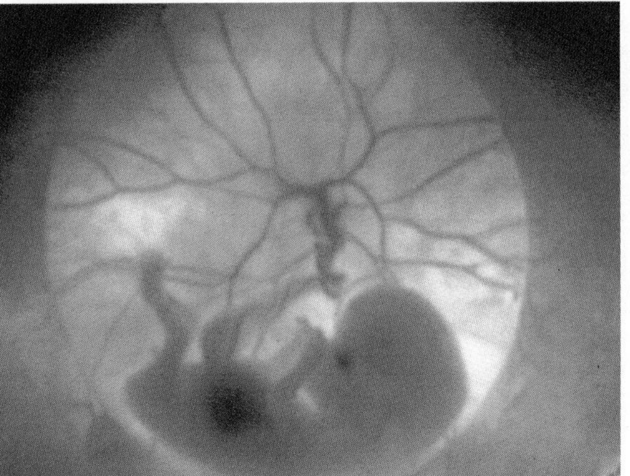

Intrauterine environment The physical and chemical environment within the uterus during prenatal development.

Congenital problems Problems or defects that originate during prenatal development.

Genetic problems Problems caused by defects in the genes or by inherited characteristics.

Fetal alcohol syndrome Birth complications and bodily defects in infants caused by alcohol use by the mother during pregnancy.

Medicated birth The common practice in Western medicine of giving painkilling drugs during labor and birth.

Prepared childbirth Techniques to manage discomfort and facilitate birth with a minimum of painkilling drugs.

Question: How is it possible for the embryo or the fetus to be harmed?

Effects of Drugs As you might know, there is no direct intermixing of blood between a mother and her unborn child. Nevertheless, some substances—especially drugs—do reach the fetus. If the mother is addicted to morphine, heroin, or methadone, the infant may be born with a drug addiction. Just one hit of cocaine taken by a pregnant woman can cause defects in her fetus. Cocaine penetrates the fetus' brain and reduces oxygen flow (Heyser et al., 1992).

At birth, "crack" babies are very excitable and jittery if their mother recently used cocaine (Lester et al., 1991). Otherwise, they are sluggish and depressed. By the time cocaine babies start school, they often suffer from tremors, hyperactivity, listlessness, slowed language learning, and disorganized thinking (Fackelmann, 1991). Many will never be normal.

Most common prescription drugs also reach the fetus. Just a partial listing of troublesome drugs underscores the need for caution in drug use during pregnancy. Potentially damaging substances include general anesthetics, cortisone, tetracycline, excessive amounts of vitamins A, D, B_6, and K, cocaine, some barbiturates, opiates, tranquilizers, steroids, and synthetic sex hormones (Rosenblith, 1992). Even aspirin, a seemingly safe drug, has been linked with lowered infant IQs when taken prenatally (Streissguth et al., 1987). In short, when a pregnant mother takes drugs, her unborn child does too.

■ Fig. 12–11 *Some of the typical features of children suffering from fetal alcohol syndrome include a small non-symmetrical head, a short nose, a flattened area between the eyes, oddly shaped eyes, and a thin upper lip. Many of these features become less noticeable by adolescence. However, mental retardation and other problems commonly follow the FAS child into adulthood. The infant shown here represents a moderate example of FAS.*

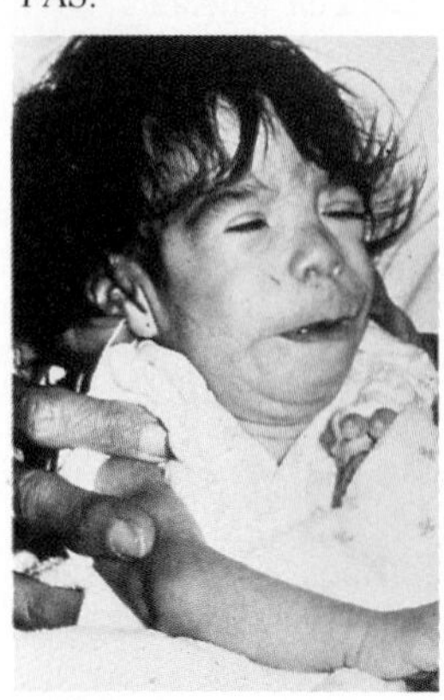

Question: What about alcohol and tobacco?

Repeated heavy drinking by pregnant women causes a pattern known as the **fetal alcohol syndrome (FAS).** Affected infants have low birth weight, bodily defects, facial malformations, and many are mentally retarded. Miscarriages and premature births are also common (■ Fig. 12–11). During pregnancy, frequent drinking of even small amounts of alcohol, or a single "binge" of 5 or more drinks, can cause fetal brain damage. By the time they reach adolescence, FAS children typically have poor problem-solving skills, are mentally retarded, and tend to be impulsive and defiant. Considering the risks, the best advice for pregnant women is to entirely avoid drinking alcohol. The tragedy of FAS is that it is completely preventable (Streissguth, 1992).

Smoking also has an adverse effect on prenatal development. A pregnant woman who smokes 2 packs of cigarettes a day blocks off about 25 percent of the oxygen supply to the fetus. Heavy smokers run a higher risk of miscarrying or giving premature birth to underweight babies (Rosenblith, 1992). The infant death rate immediately before, during, or after birth is 27 percent higher if a woman smokes during pregnancy. Children exposed to smoking before birth score lower in language development and on general mental tests (Fried et al., 1992). Of the many reasons for not smoking, pregnancy appears to be one of the most compelling.

Childbirth

More than ever before, parents can choose how their children will be born. Should it be a conventional hospital birth? Should they try natural childbirth? Should the father be present for the birth? In recent years, researchers have carefully probed the effects of such choices. Let's briefly explore what they have learned.

Conventional Delivery Until recently, **medicated births** in hospital delivery rooms were the rule in Western nations. In such births, the mother is assisted by a physician and given drugs to relieve pain. These drugs range from local analgesics (painkillers) to general anesthetics that cause a loss of consciousness. Increasingly, doctors and parents have come to realize that general anesthesia during birth has major drawbacks. For one thing, drugs dull or block the mother's awareness of birth. They also reduce oxygen flow to the fetus; they increase the likelihood of a forceps delivery (in which the baby is pulled through the birth canal); and they can cause an infant to be born partially anesthetized. For such reasons, babies whose mothers were given heavy doses of anesthetic tend to lag in muscular and neural development.

In the last 5 years there has been a marked move away from the use of general anesthesia during birth. Nevertheless, some form of painkiller is used in 95 percent of all deliveries in the United States and Canada. Certainly, mothers should not feel guilty if they need a painkiller during childbirth. Drugs injected directly into the spinal cord (a *spinal block*) can greatly reduce pain without affecting the child or the mother's alertness. However, where general painkillers are concerned, it appears wise to use as few drugs as possible.

Prepared Childbirth What can parents do to reduce the discomfort of birth while giving their babies the best possible start in life? Many psychologists are convinced that **natural,** or **prepared, childbirth** is the answer. The most widely used approach to natural childbirth is the *Lamaze method* (la-MAHZ), developed by French physician Ferdinand Lamaze.

Couples learn the Lamaze method during pregnancy. To begin, the trainer explains what will happen physically during birth. Women who thoroughly understand what is happening in their bodies tend to have fewer fears and less anxiety. Couples are also taught methods of breathing and muscular control to cut down pain during birth. Another important element is showing the father or a friend how to give emotional support to the mother during childbirth.

Natural childbirth typically shortens labor and reduces pain. In addition, it treats birth as a celebration of life, rather than a medical problem or a disease. Accordingly, parents are more likely to experience birth as a time of great happiness when natural childbirth is used *and* the father is present (Tanzer & Block, 1976).

Question: How important is it for fathers to participate in the birth process?

The emotional intensity of birth magnifies its impact on most parents. A father may form life-long memories at the time of his child's birth that can make a difference in the father's willingness to love and care for the child. Researchers have found that men generally make a better transition to parenthood when they help prepare for childbirth (Grossman et al., 1980).

While participating in the birth is valuable, a father's *attitude* toward his child is probably more important. Fathers who *wanted* to be present during delivery show greater interest in their infants during the first year. They are also more likely to help care for the baby (Grossman & Volkmer, 1984). This is true whether or not the father was actually able to attend the birth.

Many hospitals now have home-like **birthing rooms,** so that fathers can stay at the hospital (■ Fig. 12–12). This allows fathers to participate in the birth and share in caring for the newborn. Even traditional delivery rooms are allowing fathers to be present during birth, either as observers or to coach the mother through labor and childbirth. In some cases, the father cuts the umbilical cord and gives the infant its first bath. Babies are now less often rushed off to a nursery. In many hospitals the baby spends its first night with the parents in the birthing room. Home births, assisted by physicians or licensed midwifes, are also more common. Clearly, such changes are making birth more psychologically rewarding for mother, father, and baby.

Should other aspects of birth and delivery be revised? Highlight 12–1 discusses the pros and cons of "gentle birth."

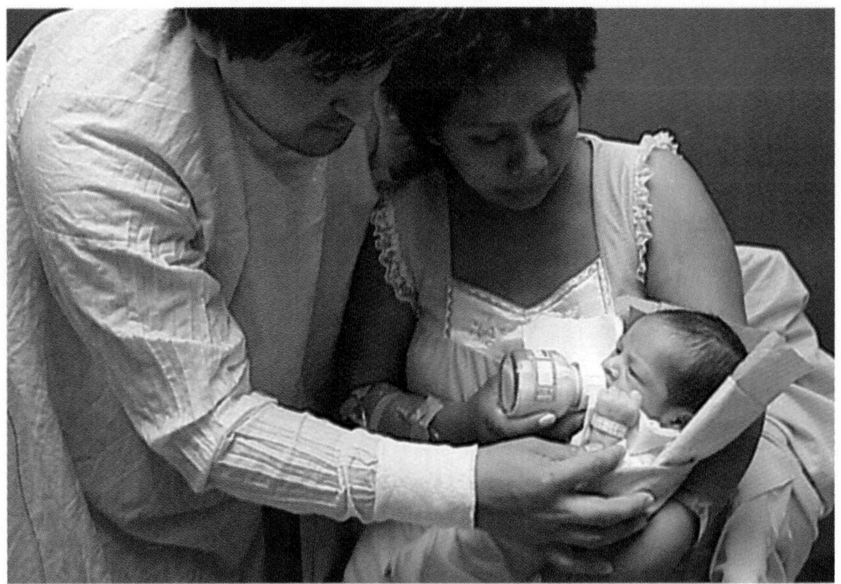

■ **Fig. 12–12** *Changing attitudes toward childbirth have encouraged mothers and fathers to actively prepare for birth and to participate more fully in caring for the newborn.*

Birthing room A room designed to minimize the medical aspects of giving birth.

Gentle birth A method of delivery that purportedly makes birth less stressful for the newborn.

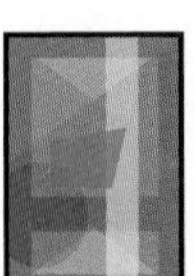

HIGHLIGHT 12–1

Focus on a Controversy

Gentle Birth

From the warm and protected confines of the womb, a baby is forcefully thrust into a cold, noisy world. The new arrival is greeted with glaring lights, booming voices, cutting of the umbilical cord, and weighing on a cold scale. According to French obstetrician Frederick Leboyer (leh-BOY-a), these events make birth a needlessly traumatic experience.

Leboyer (1975) advocates a system of **gentle birth** that he claims is pleasant for both mother and baby. Delivery takes place in a silent, dimly lit room. Immediately after birth, the baby is placed on the mother's abdomen and massaged. After several minutes of soothing, the umbilical cord is cut and the baby is bathed in warm water. Leboyer believes that this approach is superior to conventional birth procedures, which he regards as "violent" and "cruel."

From a medical standpoint, some of Leboyer's methods can be risky. A darkened delivery room, for instance, may delay detection of a "blue baby" or other complications. Still, gentle birth appeals to many parents, and thousands of babies have been delivered by the Leboyer method.

Leboyer claims that gentle births produce children who are happier, healthier, more relaxed, and more emotionally stable. However, evidence in support of this claim is not very convincing. It is true that during the first 15 to 20 minutes after birth, Leboyer babies are more relaxed than other newborns (Oliver & Oliver, 1978). From that point on, however, Leboyer-delivered babies do not differ in any measurable way from conventionally delivered babies (Maziade et al., 1987). Even if

Maternal influences The sum of all effects a mother has on her child.

Caregiving style An identifiable pattern of parental care and interaction with children.

Proactive maternal involvement Sensitive caregiving in which a mother actively provides her child with educational experiences.

Goodness of fit The degree to which parents and children have complementary temperaments.

Parental responsiveness Caregiving based on sensitivity to a child's feelings, needs, rhythms, and signals.

Paternal influences The sum of all effects a father has on his child.

the Leboyer babies did differ, could we conclude that gentle birth is beneficial? What if parents who choose gentle births tend to be more loving or attentive? If this were the case, the later emotional health of their infants might have nothing to do with birth itself.

Undoubtedly, parents should use the method of delivery that makes them most comfortable, and many parents regard gentle birth as a desirable alternative. At this point, however, it appears that gentle births may be done more for parents than for babies!

Maternal and Paternal Influences

In later years a child's environment expands to include the effects of culture, subculture, family, school, television, friends, and peers. However, for the first few years of life, the most important influences come from caregivers. The quality of mothering and fathering is therefore of prime importance.

One revealing study of **maternal influences** began with the selection of children who were unusually competent ("A" children) or who had a low degree of competence ("C" children). As increasingly younger children were observed, it became apparent that A and C patterns were already set by age 3. To learn how this was possible, researchers visited homes and observed children under 3 and their mothers (White & Watts, 1973).

Researchers observed **caregiving styles** that ranged from the "super mother" to the "zoo-keeper mother." Super mothers went out of their way to provide educational experiences for their children and allowed them to initiate some activities. This caregiving style produced an A child, competent in most areas of development. At the other end of the spectrum, zoo-keeper mothers gave their children good physical care, but interacted with them very little. Their child care routines were rigid and highly structured. The result was C children who tended to approach problems inflexibly.

More recent studies mirror the earlier findings. That is, optimal caregiving is characterized by **proactive maternal involvement** (warm, educational interactions between mother and child) (Pettit & Bates, 1989). Proactive mothers talk to their babies more and encourage them to explore their surroundings (Olson, Bates, & Kaskie, 1992). This style of caregiving accelerates mental growth and minimizes behavior problems.

A second major element of optimal caregiving is the **goodness of fit** between parents and children (Chess & Thomas, 1986). For instance, a slow-to-warm-up child with impatient parents will probably have more problems than she would if her parents were easy-going. A similar point is made by a study of 12-year-old children. Those who scored higher in intellectual ability and self-esteem had mothers who were *responsive* to them during childhood (Beckwith, Rodning, & Cohen, 1992). **Parental responsiveness** refers to caregiving that is sensitive to a child's feelings, needs, rhythms, and signals. Effective mothers alter their own behavior to meet their children's changing needs at each stage of growth.

Taken together, such findings support two beliefs long held by developmental psychologists. First, mothering *does* make a difference. Second, early development has lasting effects on a person.

Question: Aren't you overlooking the effects of fathering?

Yes. Fathers also add significantly to an infant's social, emotional, and intellectual growth. In fact, fathers make a unique contribution by interacting with the infant in ways that differ from those typical of mothers. Studies of **paternal influences** have shown that the father's main role tends to be that of a *playmate* for the infant (■ Fig. 12–13).

Fathers typically spend 4 or 5 times as much time playing with their infants as they do in caregiving (Parke & Sawin, 1977). It is true that fathers have become more involved in child care during the last decade. Still, their participation is low compared with the time mothers spend feeding, dressing, grooming, disciplining, teaching, and caring for children (de Luccie & Davis, 1991). Altogether, fathers spend an average of just 26 minutes a day directly interacting with children below the age of 6 (Gottfried & Gottfried, 1988).

It might seem that the father's role as a playmate makes him less important in the child's development. Not so. From birth onward, fathers pay more visual attention to the child than do mothers. They are much more tactile (lifting, tickling, and handling the baby), more physically arousing (engaging in rough-and-tumble play), and more likely to engage in unusual play (imitating baby, for example) (Crawley & Sherrod, 1984). Mothers speak to the infant more, play more conventional games (such as peekaboo), and as previously noted, spend more time in caregiving activities (■ Fig 12–14). Such differences in mothers' and fathers' behavior continue until at least middle childhood (Russell & Russell, 1987).

Overall, fathers are as affectionate, sensitive, and responsive to their children as mothers are. Nevertheless, from the first days of life, infants tend to get very different views of males and females. Females, who offer comfort, nurturance, and verbal stimulation, also tend to be close at hand. Males come and go, and

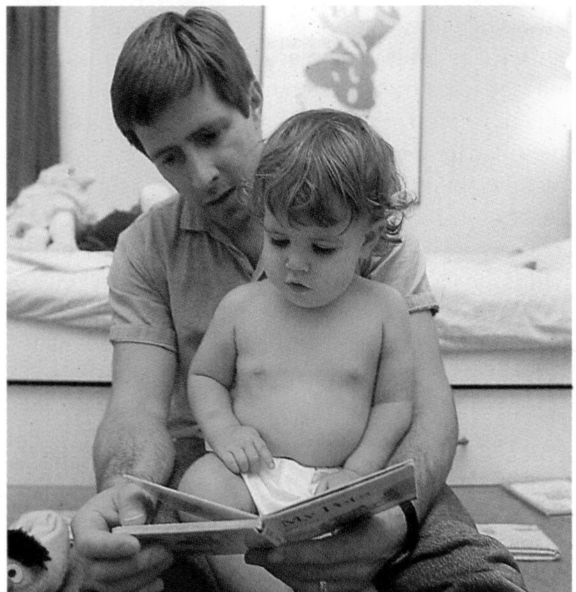

■ **Fig. 12–13** *Fathering typically makes a contribution to early development that differs in emphasis from mothering.*

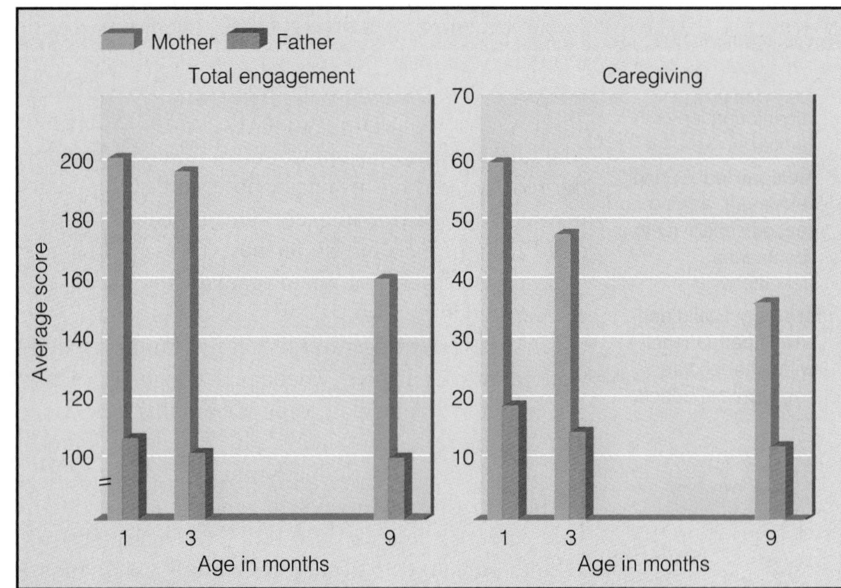

■ **Fig. 12–14** *Mother-infant and father-infant interactions. These graphs show what occurred on routine days in a sample of 72 American homes. The graph on the left records the total amount of contact parents had with their babies, including such actions as talking to, touching, hugging, or smiling at the infant. The graph on the right shows the amount of caregiving (diapering, washing, feeding, and so forth) done by each parent. Note that in both cases mother-infant interactions greatly exceed father-infant interactions. (Adapted from Belsky et al., 1984.)*

when they are present, action, exploration, and risk taking prevail (Herbert & Greenberg, 1983). It's no wonder, then, that maternal and paternal caregiving styles have a major impact on children's sex role development (Siegal, 1987; Silverstein, 1991).

Because children are very adaptable it is tempting to assume that parenting only needs to be "adequate" or just "good enough" for a child to develop normally. It's true, of course, that many children do well with no better than routine care. Nevertheless, excellent parenting tends to optimize children's development. Active, high-quality caregiving is well worth the effort (Baumrind, 1993). (⬬ See Table 12–4.)

⬬ **Table 12–4 Early Environment: Implications for Parents and Caregivers**

• Prenatal development is a time of great vulnerability, especially if a mother takes drugs or abuses alcohol.
• While some methods of birth may have advantages, it is more important that parents are emotionally involved in the process and have a good attitude toward the birth of their child.
• Caregiving styles have major effects on infant development. Optimal development occurs when parents are responsive to their children and actively involved in their progress.

Social development The development of self-awareness, attachment to caregivers, and relationships with other children and adults.

Self-awareness Consciousness of oneself as a person.

Social Development—Baby, I'm Stuck on You

Infants are social creatures from the day they are born. Their ability to imitate adults and their interest in the human face are good examples of their sensitivity to others. Let's explore the origins of social life, especially the child's emotional bonds with parents. Early **social development** lays a foundation for later relationships with parents, siblings, friends, relatives, and schoolmates.

Two major elements of early social development that you should know about are infants' growing self-awareness and their increased awareness of others.

Self-Awareness When you look in a mirror, you recognize the image looking back as your own—except, perhaps, early on Monday mornings. At what age did this sense of recognition first develop? Like many other events in development, **self-awareness** depends on maturation of the nervous system.

Question: How is self-awareness demonstrated in a baby?

BABY BLUES By Rick Kirkman and Jerry Scott

Social referencing Observing others in social situations to obtain information or guidance.

Critical period During development, a period of increased sensitivity to environmental influences.

Imprinting Rapid and relatively permanent learning that occurs during a critical period.

In an experiment that must have been fun to do, mothers of children 9 to 24 months old secretly rubbed a spot of rouge on their child's nose. Each child was then placed in front of a mirror for testing. The question was, "When would the child realize that the red spot was on his or her nose, indicating recognition of the mirror image?" The probability that a child would touch his or her nose was very low at 9 months. However, it jumped dramatically during the second year.

In an even stronger test of self-recognition, infants were shown their own videotaped images on a TV screen. Most infants had to be 15 months old before they could recognize themselves (Lewis & Brooks-Gunn, 1979). Self-awareness, then, closely parallels the human growth sequence. It typically appears sometime after an infant's first birthday (Kagan, 1991). When coupled with an increased awareness of others, self-awareness begins to form the core of social development.

Social Referencing At about the same time that self-awareness develops, infants become increasingly aware of others. Have you ever noticed how adults sometimes glance at the facial expressions of others to decide how to respond to them? **Social referencing** of this sort can also be observed in babies. By 12 months of age, most babies *reference* (glance at) their mothers when placed in an unfamiliar situation (Diekstein & Parke, 1988; Walden & Ogan, 1988).

In one study of social referencing, babies were placed on a visual cliff. (A visual cliff is pictured in Chapter 5, Figure 5–9.) The deep side of the cliff was just high enough so that the babies were tempted to cross it, but did not. (If a visual cliff is very high, babies generally will not cross it, even if called.) Most babies placed on the edge of the cliff repeatedly looked at their mothers. As they did, the mothers made faces at them. (All for science, of course.) When the mothers posed faces of joy or interest, most babies crossed the deep side of the cliff. When they posed fear or anger, few babies crossed (Sorce et al., 1985). Thus, by the end of their first year, infants are aware of the facial expressions of others and seek guidance from them—especially from mother (Hirshberg & Svejda, 1990). Again, we see the roots of an important social skill.

The real core of social development is found in the emotional bonds that babies form with their caregivers. Before we consider this topic directly, let's look at some related animal behavior to see what we can learn from it.

Critical Periods and Imprinting

Question: Why do experiences early in life tend to have such lasting effects?

Part of the answer lies in the existence of critical periods for acquiring particular behaviors. A **critical period** is a time of increased sensitivity to environmental influences (both positive and negative). Events at these times may have a dramatic influence on development long after the period of sensitivity (Bornstein, 1989). For example, the critical period for mastering a second language is before puberty—the earlier the better (Johnson & Newport, 1989).

Often, certain events must occur during a critical period for a person or an animal to develop normally. To illustrate, Konrad Lorenz (1903–1989), an ethologist who studied animal behavior, once became curious about why baby geese follow their mothers. The obvious explanation seemed to be, "It's instinctive," but Lorenz showed otherwise.

Mother Lorenz

Normally, the first large moving object a baby goose sees is its mother. Lorenz hatched geese in an incubator, so the first moving object they saw was Lorenz. From then on, these baby geese followed Lorenz. They even reacted to his call as if he were their mother (■ Fig. 12–15). (Lorenz, 1937)

Imprinting As you can see, "mother-goose" following is not automatic. What is automatic is the tendency to follow a large moving object. Thus, mother-goose following is acquired during a critical period by exposure to a moving object. The rapid and early learning of permanent behavior patterns of this type is called **imprinting.**

■ **Fig. 12–15** *"Mother" Lorenz leads his charges. The goslings have imprinted on Lorenz because he was the first moving object they saw after they hatched.*

In most birds, the critical period for imprinting is very brief. For instance, Hess (1959) found that if ducklings are not allowed to imprint on their mother or some other object within 30 hours after hatching, they never will. (Ducklings have been imprinted on decoys, rubber balls, wooden blocks, and other unlikely objects.) In many animals, imprinting and other events taking place during critical periods have lifelong consequences (Lorenz, 1962).

Revenge of the Jackdaw

Imprinting normally serves to attach a young animal to its mother. It also guides the selection of a mate of the same species at sexual maturity. In another of Lorenz's experiments, a jackdaw (European starling) imprinted on him. When the bird reached sexual maturity, Lorenz became the object of its mating ritual. Part of this ritual involves stuffing worms into the mouth of the intended mate—as a surprised Lorenz learned while asleep on the lawn one day. When Lorenz refused its gift, the jackdaw stuffed a worm in Lorenz's ear. (Showing, perhaps, that it's not nice to fool Mother Nature!)

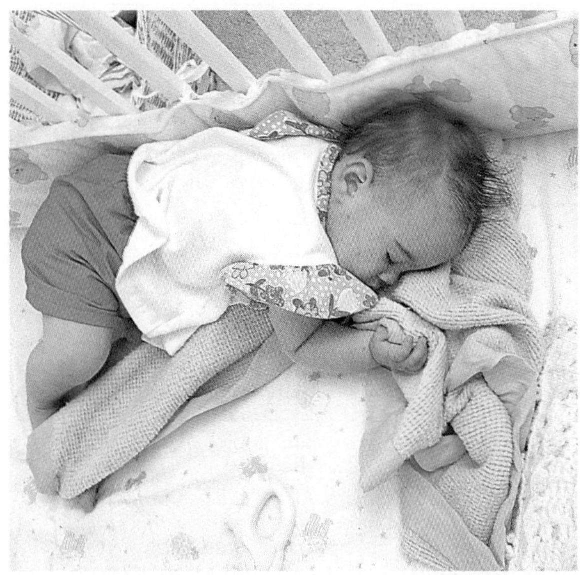

■ **Fig. 12–16** *Most parents are familiar with the storm of crying that sometimes occurs when babies are left alone at bedtime. Bedtime distress is a mild form of separation anxiety. As many parents also know, it is often eased by the presence of "security objects," such as a stuffed animal or favorite blanket. Interestingly, children in cultures where infants and toddlers sleep with their parents show few signs of bedtime distress. Parents in the United States usually want their infants to sleep alone, to promote independence. In many cultures, parents choose to sleep near their infants to promote closeness with them. Either approach is valid (Morelli et al., 1992).*

Attachment

Question: Does imprinting occur in humans?

True cases of imprinting are limited to birds and some other animals (Hess, 1959). However, human infants do form an **emotional attachment** to their *primary caregivers* (usually parents), and there is a critical period (roughly the first year of life) during which this must occur for healthy development. Attachment helps keep babies close to their mothers, who provide safety, stimulation, and a secure "home base" from which a baby can go exploring (Rosenblith, 1992).

A direct sign that an emotional bond has been formed appears when infants are around 8 to 12 months of age. At that time, babies display **separation anxiety** (crying and signs of fear) when their parents leave them alone or leave them with strangers (■ Fig. 12–16).

Psychologist Mary Ainsworth believes that the quality of attachment is revealed by how babies act when their mothers return after a brief separation. Infants who are **securely attached** are upset by the mother's absence and they seek to be near her when she returns. **Insecure-avoidant** infants turn away from their mother when she returns. **Insecure-ambivalent** attachment is revealed when an infant both seeks to be near the returning mother and angrily resists contact with her. Studies of several cultures suggest that these three types of attachment are universal. However, the percentage of children falling in each category differs from culture to culture (Sagi, 1990).

Attachment can have lasting effects. Infants who are securely attached to their parents at age one show more resiliency, curiosity, problem-solving ability, and social competence by the time they reach preschool (Collins & Gunnar, 1990). The key to secure attachment is a mother who is *accepting and sensitive to her baby's signals and rhythms* (Isabella, 1993). Poor attachment occurs when a mother's actions are inappropriate, insufficient, intrusive, overstimulating, or rejecting. An example is the mother who tries to play with a drowsy infant or who ignores the baby when it is looking at her and vocalizing (Isabella & Belsky, 1991).

Question: Does day care for young children interfere with the quality of attachment?

Day Care Authorities generally agree that *high-quality* day care does not have harmful effects on preschool children (Silverstein, 1991). Poor-quality care, however, can be risky (Clarke-Stewart, 1989).

What should parents seeking quality child care look for? It's easy to be swayed by attractive rooms or ample play materials (■ Fig. 12–17). But small group size (12–15 children) and a ratio of 1 caregiver to 3 children (or better) is far more important. Parents should also look for caregivers trained in child development. Ideally, children should be cared for by the same people, day to day. Stable relationships among caregivers and children promote positive social and

Emotional attachment A close emotional bond that infants form with parents, caregivers, or others.

Separation anxiety Distress displayed by infants separated from their parents or caregivers.

Secure attachment A stable and positive emotional bond.

Insecure-avoidant attachment An anxious emotional bond marked by a tendency to avoid reunion with a parent or caregiver.

Insecure-ambivalent attachment An anxious emotional bond marked by a desire to be with a parent or caregiver and resistance to being reunited.

Emotional bonding An especially close emotional bond between infants and their parents, caregivers, or others (another term for attachment).

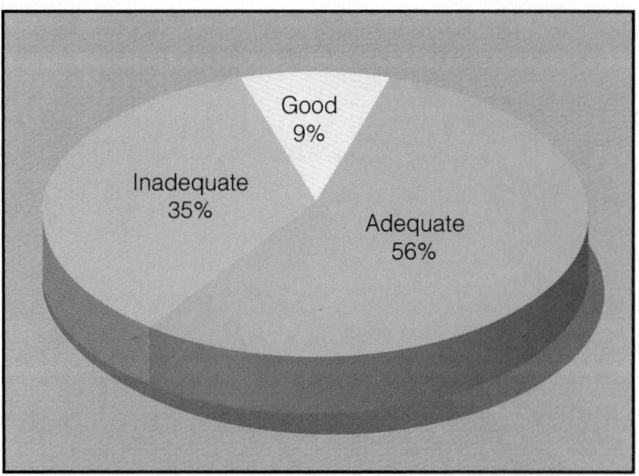

■ Fig. 12–17 *In 1994, the Families Work Institute completed a 5-year study of child care. The study focused on care based in homes other than the child's (rather than day-care centers). In most cases, parents paid for this care, although many of the caregivers were unlicensed. As you can see, child care was "good" in only 9 percent of the homes. In 35 percent of the homes it was rated as inadequate. Wise parents carefully evaluate and monitor the quality of day care their children are receiving (Mehren, 1994).*

mental development (Scarr & Eisenberg, 1993). (Last of all, avoid any child-care center with the words *zoo, menagerie,* or *stockade* in its name.)

When day care for younger children begins to exceed 20 hours a week it can become a problem. Often the child will show some signs of insecurity (Belsky & Rovine, 1988). Insecurity is especially likely if the child is under 3 years of age, if the mother works full-time, if the father helps little in caring for the child, and if the parents' marriage is troubled (Barglow et al., 1987; Scarr & Eisenberg, 1993; Schachere, 1990). On the other hand, good quality care can accelerate the development of language, thinking, and social skills. Many children in day care become more considerate, sociable, intelligent and task oriented. Overall, there are no differences in children with home care versus day care, *if* both are of good quality (Scarr & Eisenberg, 1993).

In recent years a major controversy has raged over whether attachment is influenced by events that occur immediately after birth. For your interest, Highlight 12–2 offers a discussion of "mother-infant bonding."

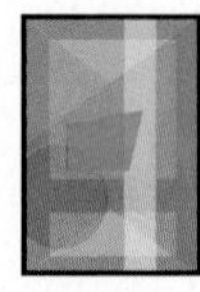

HIGHLIGHT 12–2

Critical Thinking

Mother-Infant Bonding—A Touching Debate

In one hospital ward, new mothers are given traditional contact with their infants: a glimpse after birth and 30-minute visits every 4 hours for feeding. In a second ward, "extended-contact group" mothers are given their babies for 1 hour during the first 3 hours after birth and for an extra 5 hours of contact each afternoon for the first 3 days after delivery. Does extra contact have any effect?

An initial series of studies reported by Marshall Klaus and John Kennell (1982) seemed to suggest that there are lasting benefits to close early contact between a mother and her infant. According to Klaus and Kennell, there is a sensitive period in the first hours after an infant's birth. Therefore, mother-child pairs who spend extra time together form a stronger **emotional bond** to one another. This is especially true, they believe, if skin-to-skin touching is part of early contact.

Klaus and Kennell reported that "bonded" babies are more alert and responsive, as well as healthier and brighter than those denied extra contact. However, the majority of more carefully done studies have failed to support the idea that extended early contact is crucial to the mother-infant bond (Rosenblith, 1992). Critics also point out that adopted children, premature babies, and babies born by cesarean section (surgical birth) all develop normal, affectionate bonds with their mothers. Even Klaus and Kennell now acknowledge that it is unlikely that something as important as emotional attachment would depend *solely* on the first few hours of life (Klaus & Kennell, 1984). Humans are highly adaptable, and there are many opportunities for attachment during the first year of life.

Advocates of bonding continue to believe that early mother-infant contact can be beneficial. Even those experts who doubt that early contact makes a difference agree that allowing mother, father, and infant to be together during the first few hours is humane and natural. So, while most evidence suggests that early contact is *not* necessary, it is undoubtedly a positive, emotionally satisfying experience (Rosenblith, 1992). Ultimately, it is less important *when* secure attachment occurs, than *if* it occurs. In addition, it is valuable to remember that children thrive when they have good relationships with *both* parents (Eyer, 1993).

Motherless Monkeys Research with rhesus monkeys suggests that like imprinting, infant attachments can have lasting effects. Harry Harlow (1966, 1967) showed that baby monkeys separated from their mothers and raised in isolation become troubled adult animals. Among other things, these motherless monkeys never develop normal sexual behaviors, and they make very poor mothers if mated. They are coldly rejecting or indifferent to their babies and may brutalize or injure them. It has been suggested that human parents who abuse, reject, or physically injure their children may be displaying a similar pattern. A sizable percentage of abusive parents were themselves rejected or mistreated as children. Some psychologists also believe that much antisocial behavior can be traced to a lack of attachment in infancy (Magid, 1988). Children with severe attachment problems do not learn to trust and care about others. As a result, many are cruel, angry, and self-destructive.

Meeting a baby's **affectional needs** is every bit as important as meeting more obvious needs for food, water, and physical care. All things considered, one of the most important developments of the first year of life appears to be creation of a bond of trust and affection between the infant and at least one other person (see Chapter 13). Parents are sometimes afraid of "spoiling" a baby with too much attention, but for the first year or two this is nearly impossible. As a matter of fact, a later capacity to experience warm and loving relationships may depend on it. (See ⬬ Table 12–5.)

⬬ **Table 12–5 Social Development: Implications for Parents and Caregivers**

• The quality of a child's relationships with caregivers is a key to healthy development in most areas of competence.
• Secure emotional attachments are fostered by consistent care and by parents who are sensitive to a baby's signals and rhythms.
• High-quality day care is not harmful to preschool children. Poor-quality care, either inside or outside the home, can be harmful.

Affectional needs Emotional needs in general, especially needs for love, attention, and affection.

Cooing Spontaneous repetition of vowel sounds by infants.

LEARNING CHECK

1. The intrauterine environment is so protected that it has little effect on a person's development. T or F?
2. Two important elements of effective mothering are ______________ maternal involvement and parental ______________ to a child's feelings, needs, rhythms, and signals.
3. Patterns of paternal behavior typically differ little from maternal caregiving patterns. T or F?
4. Clear signs of self-awareness or self-recognition are evident in most infants by the time they reach 8 months of age. T or F?
5. Social ______________ of parents' facial expressions is evident in infants by the time they are 1 year old.
6. A duckling can be imprinted after the critical period has passed if special attention is given to its affectional needs. T or F?
7. The development of separation anxiety in an infant corresponds to the formation of an attachment to parents. T or F?
8. Research has shown conclusively that mother-infant contact immediately after birth is essential for optimal development. T or F?
9. In Mary Ainsworth's system for rating the quality of attachment, secure attachment is revealed by a lack of distress when an infant is left alone with a stranger. T or F?

Critical Thinking

10. Attachment quality is usually attributed to the behavior of parents or caregivers. How might infants contribute to the quality of attachment?

Answers: 1. F 2. proactive, responsiveness 3. F 4. F 5. referencing 6. F 7. T 8. F 9. F 10. An infant's behavior patterns, temperament, and emotional style may greatly influence parents' behavior. As a result, infants can affect attachment as much as parents do (Oatley & Jenkins, 1992).

Language Development—Fast-Talking Babies

There's something almost miraculous about a baby's first words. As infants, how did we manage to leap into the world of language? As will soon be apparent, social development provides a foundation for language learning. But before we explore that connection, let's begin with a survey of language development.

Language Acquisition The development of language is closely tied to maturation. As any parent can tell you, babies can cry from birth on. By 1 month of age, the infant can control crying enough to use it as an attention-getting device. At about 1 month, parents can also tell the nature of the infant's needs from the tone of the crying. Around 6 to 8 weeks of age, babies begin **cooing** (the repetition of vowel sounds like "oo" and "ah").

BABY BLUES By Rick Kirkman and Jerry Scott

Babbling The repetition by infants of meaningless language sounds (including both vowel and consonant sounds).

Single-word stage The period in language development when a child first begins to use single words.

Telegraphic speech Two-word sentences that "telegraph" (communicate) a simple idea.

Biological predisposition The presumed biological readiness of humans to learn certain skills, such as how to use language.

Psycholinguist A specialist in the psychology of language and language development.

Signal Any behavior, such as touching, vocalizing, gazing, or smiling, that allows nonverbal interaction and turn-taking between parent and child.

Turn-taking The tendency of parent and child to alternate in the sending and receiving of signals or messages.

By the time a child is 6 months old, the nervous system has matured enough to allow the child to grasp objects, to smile, laugh, sit up, and to **babble.** In the babbling stage, consonant sounds are added to produce a continuous outpouring of repeated language sounds. The influence of environment at this stage is indicated by the fact that babbling increases when parents talk to the child.

At about 1 year of age, the child can stand alone for a short time and can respond to words such as *no* or *hi.* Soon afterward, the first connection between words and objects is formed, and children may address their parents as "Mama" or "Dada." By the time they have reached the age of 1½ to 2 years, children have learned to stand and walk alone. By the same ages, their vocabulary may include from 24 to 200 words. At first there is a **single-word stage,** during which the child says things such as "go," "juice," or "up." Soon after, words are arranged in simple 2-word sentences called **telegraphic speech:** "Want Teddy," "Mama gone." Just before age 2, the child's comprehension and use of words takes a leap forward (Reznick & Goldfield, 1992). From this point on, the child's vocabulary and language skills grow at a phenomenal rate. By first grade, the child can understand around 8000 words and use about 4000.

The Roots of Language

In a fascinating study, researchers Louis Sander and William Condon (1974) filmed newborn infants as the babies listened to various sounds. A later frame-by-frame analysis of the films showed something astonishing: Infants move their arms and legs in synchrony to the rhythms of human speech. Random noise, rhythmic tapping, or disconnected vowel sounds will not produce this "language dance." Only the natural rhythms of speech have this effect.

Why would day-old infants "dance" to speech but not other sounds? One possibility is that language recognition is innate. Linguist Noam Chomsky (1968, 1975) has long claimed that humans have a **biological predisposition** to develop language. According to Chomsky, language organization is inborn, much like a child's ability to coordinate walking. If such inborn language recognition does exist, it may explain why children around the world use a limited number of patterns in their first sentences. Typical patterns include (Mussen et al., 1979):

Identification:	"See kitty."
Non-existence:	"Allgone milk."
Possession:	"My doll."
Agent-Action:	"Mama give."
Negation:	"Not ball."
Question:	"Where doggie?"

Question: Does Chomsky's theory explain why language develops so rapidly?

Perhaps. But many psychologists feel that Chomsky underestimates the importance of learning (Bruner, 1983). **Psycholinguists** (specialists in the psychology of language) have shown that language is not magically "switched on" by adult speech. Imitation of adults and rewards for correctly using words (as when a child asks for a cookie) are an important part of language learning. Also, when a child makes a language error, parents typically repeat the child's sentence, with needed corrections (Bohannon & Stanowicz, 1988). More important is the fact that parents and children begin to communicate long before the child can speak. Months of shared effort precede the child's first word (Miller, 1977). From this point of view, the filmed infants' behavior reflects a readiness to interact *socially* with parents, not innate language recognition. The next section explains why.

Question: How do parents communicate with infants before they can talk?

Early Communication Parents go to a great deal of trouble to get babies to smile and vocalize (■ Fig. 12–18). In doing so, they quickly learn to change their actions to keep the infant's attention, arousal, and activity at optimal levels (Brazelton et al., 1974). A familiar example is the, "I'm-Going-to-Get-You Game." In it, the adult says, "I'm gonna getcha . . . . I'm gonna getcha . . . . I'm gonna getcha . . . . Gotcha!" Through such games, adults and babies come to share similar rhythms and expectations (Stern, 1982). Soon a system of shared **signals** is created. Touching, vocalizing, gazing, and smiling help lay a foundation for later language use. Specifically, these signals establish a pattern of "conversational" **turn-taking** (Bruner, 1983; Snow, 1977).

Mother	Ann
"Oh what a nice little smile!"	(smiles)
"Yes, isn't that nice?"	
"There."	
"There's a nice little smile."	(burps)
"Well, pardon you!"	
"Yes, that's better, isn't it?"	

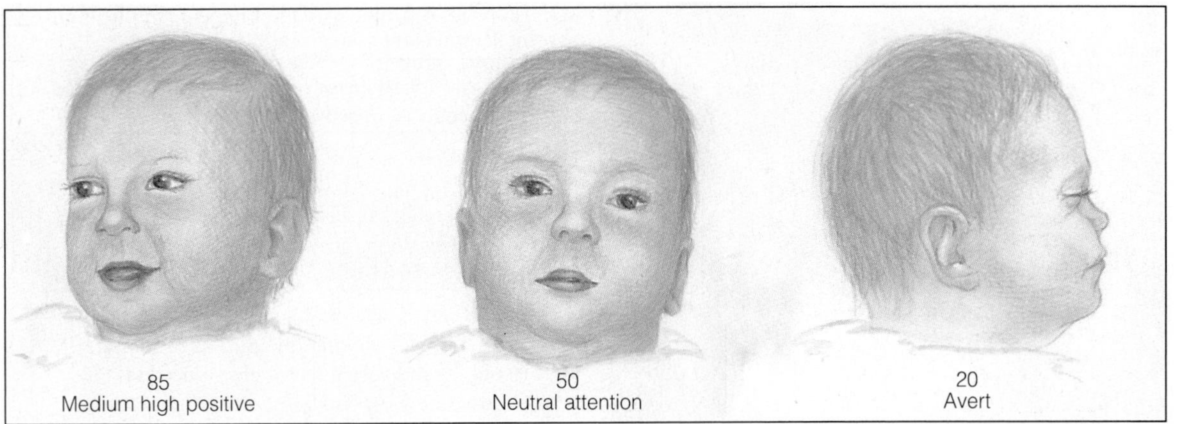

■ **Fig. 12–18** *Infant engagement scale. These samples from a 90-point scale show various levels of infant engagement, or attention. Babies participate in prelanguage "conversations" with parents by giving and withholding attention and by smiling, gazing, or vocalizing. (From Beebe et al., 1982.)*

"Yes." (vocalizes)
"Yes." (smiles)
"What's so funny?"

Although such exchanges may look meaningless, they represent real communication. A baby's vocalizations and attention provide a way of interacting emotionally with parents. Even infants as young as 3 months make more speech-like sounds when an adult engages them in a turn-taking pattern of interaction (Bloom et al., 1987). (For another perspective on turn-taking, see ■ Figure 12–19.) Overall, the more time parents spend interacting with children the faster they learn to talk (Hart & Risley, 1992).

Parentese Parents help children learn language in more ways than they may suspect. One way is through the use of **caretaker speech** (also know as caregiver speech or parentese). When talking to infants, parents around the world raise their tone of voice, use short, simple sentences, and repeat themselves more. They also slow their rate of speaking, and use exaggerated voice inflections: "Did Jenny eat it A-L-L UP?"

Question: What is the purpose of such changes?

Parents are apparently trying to help their children learn language. When a baby is still babbling, parents tend to use long, adult-style sentences. But as soon as the baby says its first word they switch to parentese.

In addition to being simpler, parentese also has a distinct "musical" quality all its own (Fernald & Mazzie, 1991). No matter what language mothers speak, the melodies, pauses, and inflections they use to comfort, praise, or give warning are universal. Psychologist Anne Fernald has found that mothers of all nations talk to their babies with similar rising and falling changes in pitch. For instance, we praise babies with a rising, then falling pitch ("BRA-vo!" "GOOD girl!"). Warnings are delivered in a short, sharp rhythm ("Nein! Nein!" "Basta! Basta!" "Not! Dude!"). To give comfort, parents use low, smooth, drawn-out tones ("Oooh poor baaa-by." "Oooh pobrecito.") A high-pitched, rising melody is used to call attention to objects ("See the pretty BIRDIE?") (Fernald, 1989). (See ■ Figure 12–20.)

Caretaker speech An exaggerated pattern of speech used by adults when talking to infants.

■ **Fig. 12–19** *This graph shows the development of turn-taking in games played by an infant and his mother. For several months Richard responded to games such as peekaboo and "hand-the-toy-back" only when his mother initiated action. At about 9 months, however, he rapidly began to initiate action in the games. Soon, he was the one to take the lead about one half of the time. Learning to take turns and to direct actions toward another person underlie basic language skills. (From Bruner, 1983.)*

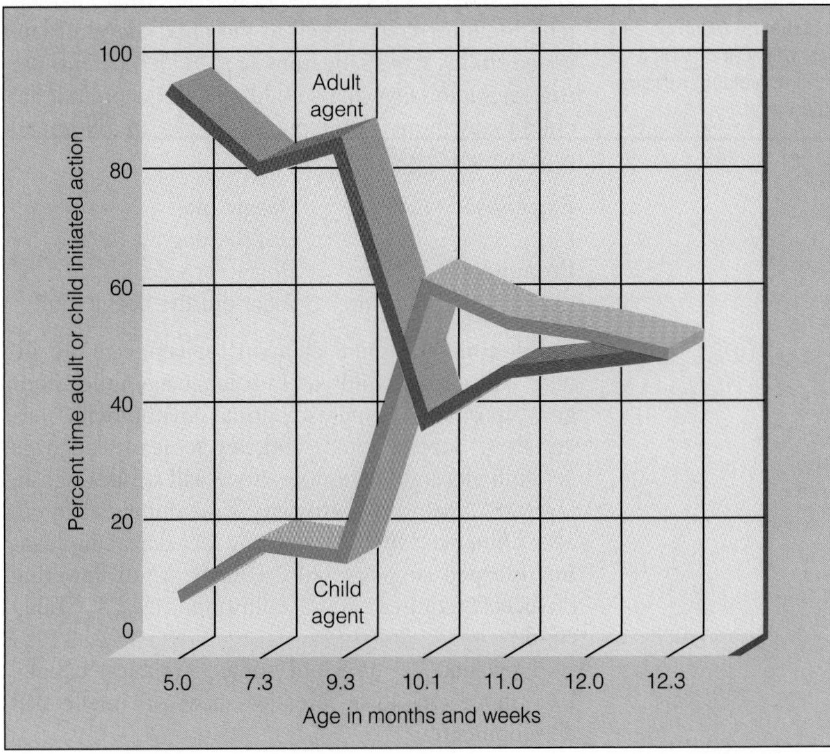

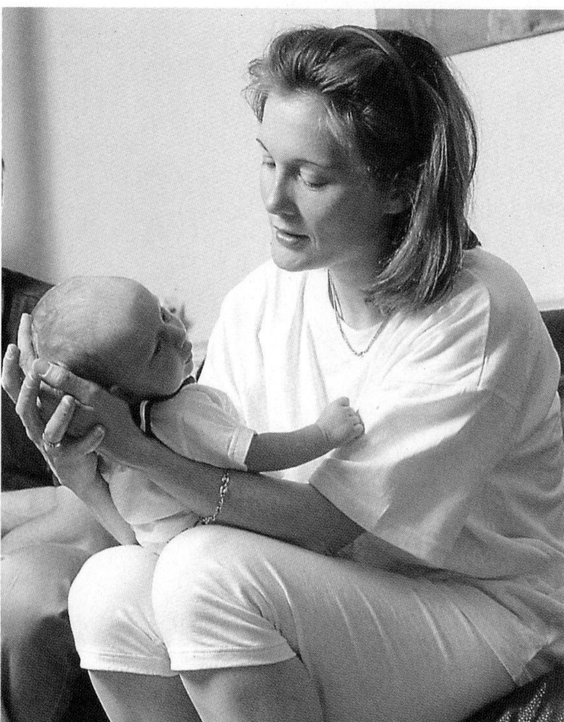

■ Fig. 12–20 *As with caretaker speech, parents use a distinctive style when singing to an infant. Even people who speak another language can tell if a tape-recorded song was sung to an infant or an adult. Likewise, lullabies remain recognizable when electronic filtering removes words (Trehub et al., 1993a, 1993b).*

Transformation The mental ability to change the shape or form of a substance (such as clay or water) and realize that its volume remains the same.

Caretaker speech helps parents get babies' attention, communicate with them, and teach them language. Later, as a child's speaking improves, parents tend to adjust their speech to the child's level of language ability. Especially from age 1½ to 4, parents use strategies to clarify what a child says and to prompt the child to say more. Two typical strategies are (Newman & Newman, 1978):

Expansion:	*Child:*	Doggie bite.
	Parent:	Yes, the dog bit *the toy.*
Prompting:	*Child:*	Doggie briggle.
	Parent:	What did the doggie do?

In summary, some elements of language are innate: All normal children learn language, unless they grow up in an extremely abnormal environment. Nevertheless, our inherited tendency to learn language certainly does not determine if we will speak English, German, Spanish, or Russian. Environmental forces also influence whether a person develops simple or sophisticated language skills. Clearly, a full flowering of speech requires careful cultivation. (See ⬭ Table 12–6.)

Now that we have our subjects (babies) talking, let's move on to a broader view of intellectual development.

⬭ **Table 12–6 Language Development: Implications for Parents and Caregivers**

• The pace of language learning is closely related to maturation and need not be "hurried."
• Non-verbal communication sets the stage for acquiring language. Children gain language ability when parents engage them in exchanges that involve signaling, turn-taking, and non-verbal communication.
• In the early stages of language learning, caregivers can help their children by using simplified grammar and accentuated voice inflections ("parentese"). As children become more verbal, expanding, prompting, and restating can facilitate language learning.

Cognitive Development—How Do Children Learn To Think?

Question: How different is a child's understanding of the world from that of an adult?

Generally speaking, a child's thinking is less abstract than an adult's. Children use fewer generalizations, categories, or principles. They also tend to base their understanding of the world on particular examples, immediate sensations, and objects they can see or touch.

A sign of the concrete nature of thinking in childhood can be found in the fact that before age 6 or 7, children are unable to make **transformations.** If you show a child a short, wide glass full of milk and a tall, narrow glass (also full), the child will tell you that the taller glass contains more milk. Children will tell you this even if you allow them to watch as you pour milk from the short glass into an empty, tall glass. They are not bothered by the fact that the milk appears to be transformed from a smaller to a larger amount (■ Fig. 12–21). They respond only to the fact that *taller* seems to mean *more.* After about age 7, children are no longer fooled by this situation. Perhaps this is why 7 has been called the "age of reason." From age 7 on, we see a definite trend toward more logical, adult-like thought (Flavell, 1992).

Question: Is there any pattern to the growth of intellect in childhood?

According to the Swiss psychologist and philosopher Jean Piaget (1951, 1952) there is.

Piaget's Theory of Cognitive Development

Jean Piaget (Jahn pea-ah-JAY) believed that all children pass through a series of distinct stages in intellec-

■ Fig. 12–21 *Children under age 7 intuitively assume that a volume of liquid increases when it is poured from a short, wide container into a taller, thinner one. This girl has poured one cup of milk into containers of various sizes. If asked which container holds the most milk, she will pick the one where the milk has reached the highest level. Children make such judgments based on the height of the liquid, not its volume.*

■ Fig. 12–22 *Jean Piaget—philosopher, psychologist, and keen observer of children.*

tual development (■ Fig. 12–22). Many of his ideas came from observing his own children as they solved various thought problems. (It is tempting to imagine that Piaget's illustrious career was launched one day when his wife said to him, "Watch the children for a while, will you, Jean?") Piaget's many observations convinced him that intellect grows through processes that he called *assimilation* and *accommodation.*

Assimilation refers to using existing patterns in new situations. Let's say that a plastic hammer is Benjamin's favorite toy. Benjamin holds the hammer properly and loves to pound on blocks with it. For his birthday Benjamin gets an oversized toy wrench. If he uses the wrench for pounding, it has been assimilated to an existing mental structure.

In **accommodation,** existing ideas are modified to fit new requirements. For instance, a younger child might think that a dime is worth less than a (larger) nickel. As the child begins to spend money, he or she will be forced to alter ideas about what "more" and "less" mean. Thus, new situations are assimilated to existing ideas, and new ideas are created to accommodate new experiences.

Piaget's theories have had a profound effect on our thinking about children (Beilin, 1992). The following is a brief summary of what he found.

The Sensorimotor Stage (0–2 Years) In the first 2 years of life, a child's intellectual development is largely *non-verbal.* The child is mainly concerned with learning to coordinate *purposeful* movements with information from the senses. Also important at this time is gradual emergence of the concept of **object permanence** (an understanding that objects that are out of sight still exist). By about age 1½, Piaget said, the child begins to actively pursue disappearing objects. Younger infants, he believed, behave as if objects cease to exist when they are out of sight. By age 2, the child can anticipate the movement of an object behind a screen. For example, when watching an electric train the child looks ahead to the end of a tunnel, rather than staring at the spot where the train disappeared.

In general, developments in this stage indicate that the child's conceptions are becoming more *stable.* Objects cease to appear and disappear magically, and a more orderly and predictable world replaces the confusing and disconnected sensations of infancy.

The Preoperational Stage (2–7 Years) During the preoperational period, the child is developing an ability to think *symbolically* and to use language. But the child's thinking is still very **intuitive.** For example, after lifting a Styrofoam cup, 75 percent of 4- to 6-year-olds say the cup has no weight! Most children judge weight intuitively (by the way an object feels) while they are in the preoperational stage (Smith, Carey, & Wiser, 1985).

During the preoperational period, the child's use of language is not always as sophisticated as it might seem. Children have a tendency to confuse words with the objects they represent. If the child calls a toy block a "car" and you use it to make a "train," the child may

Assimilation The application of existing mental patterns to new situations.

Accommodation The modification of existing mental patterns to fit new demands.

Sensorimotor stage Stage of intellectual development during which sensory input and motor responses become coordinated.

Object permanence Concept that objects continue to exist even when they are hidden from view.

Preoperational stage Period of cognitive development during which children begin to use language and think symbolically, yet remain intuitive and egocentric.

Intuitive thought Thinking that makes little or no use of reasoning and logic.

Moral development The development of values, beliefs, and thinking abilities that guide responsible behavior.

Preconventional moral reasoning Moral thinking based on the consequences of one's choices or actions (punishment, reward, or an exchange of favors).

Conventional moral reasoning Moral thinking based on a desire to please others or to follow accepted rules and values.

Postconventional moral reasoning Moral thinking based on carefully examined and self-chosen moral principles.

In addition to the three major levels, Kohlberg identified six stages of moral development. In time, Kohlberg found it necessary to combine stages 5 and 6 because it proved difficult, in practice, to separate them (Kohlberg, 1981b). He remained firm in his belief, however, that morality develops in preconventional, conventional, and postconventional phases.

Question: Does everyone eventually reach the highest level?

Kohlberg and his associates found that people advance through the stages at different rates and that many people fail to reach the "principled" postconventional stage. In fact, many do not even reach the conventional level. For instance, a survey in England revealed that 11 percent of men and 3 percent of women would commit murder for $1 million if they were assured of getting away with the crime ("They'd kill," 1991). (Also, see ■Figure 12–25.)

The preconventional stages (1 and 2) are most characteristic of young children and delinquents (Nelson, Smith, & Dodd, 1990). Conventional group-oriented morals of stages 3 and 4 are characteristic of older children and most of the adult population. Kohlberg estimated that postconventional morality, representing self-direction and higher principles, is achieved by only about 20 percent of the adult population.

■ Fig. 12–25 *Each of us faces moral dilemmas, both large and small, every day. Dishonesty on taxes, sexual faithfulness, abortion, speeding, found valuables, temptations to lie, honesty in business—these and many other situations raise moral questions. A moral dilemma familiar to most students involves being unprepared for an exam. Sadly, the majority of American children function at the preconventional level of moral development at school: A 1990 poll found that two thirds would cheat to pass an important exam.*

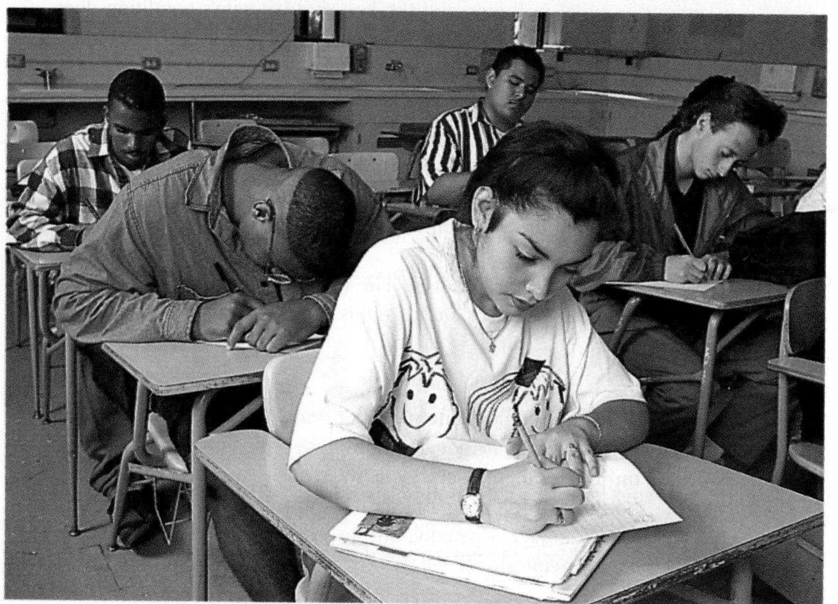

Morality in the Real World To illustrate the importance of moral development, let us compare two very different individuals. First let's apply Kohlberg's analysis to statements attributed to Nazi officer Adolf Eichmann, accused of sharing responsibility for the deaths of millions of Jews in Germany during World War II:

> In actual fact, I was merely a little cog in the machinery that carried out the directives of the German Reich [stage 1]. It was really none of my business [stage 2]. Yet what is there to "admit"? I carried out my order [stage 1]. (Kohlberg, 1969)

Compare this to the words of Mahatma Gandhi, the famous leader who protested British rule of India. Gandhi once addressed a British court:

> I had to either submit to a system which I considered had done irreparable harm to my country, or incur the risk . . . . I am here, therefore, to invite and cheerfully submit to the highest penalty that can be inflicted upon me for what in law is a deliberate crime and what appears to me to be the highest duty of a citizen.

Gandhi, like other great leaders (Lincoln, Martin Luther King), was clearly operating at a postconventional level of morality in his political life.

Moral development is a promising topic for further study. As an example, consider the work of psychologist Carol Gilligan.

Justice or Caring? Gilligan (1982) has pointed out that Kohlberg's system is concerned mainly with the ethics of *justice*. Based on studies of women who faced real-life dilemmas, Gilligan argues that there is also an ethic of *caring* and responsibility to others. As one illustration, Gilligan presented the following story to 11- to 15-year-old American children.

The Porcupine and the Moles

> Seeking refuge from the cold, a porcupine asked to share a cave for the winter with a family of moles. The moles agreed. But because the cave was small, they soon found they were being scratched each time the porcupine moved about. Finally, they asked the porcupine to leave. But the porcupine refused, saying, "If you moles are not satisfied, I suggest that you leave."

Gilligan found that boys who read this story tended to opt for justice in resolving the dilemma: "It's the moles' house. It's a deal. The porcupine leaves." In contrast, girls tended to look for solutions that would keep all parties happy and comfortable, such as "Cover the porcupine with a blanket."

Gilligan's point is that male psychologists have, for the most part, defined moral maturity in terms of jus-

Table 12–9 Moral Development: Implications for Parents and Caregivers

• Children's capacity for moral behavior is based, in part, on their abilities to reason about moral choices. For this reason, younger children tend to make simplified moral choices.
• Achieving justice is a dominant moral standard, but children may benefit from learning other ways of defining moral behavior.
• Parents act as models of moral behavior for their children. Parents can teach moral reasoning by example and by asking their children to reason about moral dilemmas and choices.

tice and autonomy. From this perspective, women's concern with relationships can look like a weakness rather than a strength (Muuss, 1988). (A woman who is concerned about what pleases or helps others would be placed at stage 3 in Kohlberg's system.) But Gilligan believes that caring is also a major element of moral development and she suggests that males may lag in achieving it (Gilligan & Attanucci, 1988).

Question: Does the evidence support Gilligan's position?

Several studies have found little or no difference in men's and women's moral reasoning abilities (Mednick, 1989; Walker, 1989). Indeed, both men and women may use caring *and* justice to make moral decisions (Donenberg & Hoffman, 1988). The choice of whether to use justice or caring as a moral yardstick appears to depend on the *situation* a person faces (Smetana, Killen, & Turiel, 1991). Gilligan does deserve credit, nevertheless, for identifying a second major way of judging morality.

Whatever the outcome of such debates, studying moral development seems highly worthwhile. Many of the problems facing us today—overpopulation, environmental destruction, crime, prejudice—are essentially problems of individual conscience. (See Table 12–9.)

We have now examined development in several major areas. To conclude our discussion, the next section describes the effects of *deprivation* and *enrichment.* These are conditions that can affect nearly all facets of a child's early years.

Deprivation and Enrichment—In Search of Tender Loving Care

News item: "Wild Child Raised by Apes Found in Africa." Over the years there have been several reported discoveries of "feral children." These are children who supposedly have grown up in the care of animals and who act like animals when found. Actually, there is little documented evidence that such children have existed, but we needn't go this far afield for proof of the destructive effects of early **deprivation.**

There are many confirmed cases of children who have spent the first 5 or 6 years of life in closets, attics, and other restricted environments. When discovered, these children are usually mute, severely retarded, and emotionally damaged. Some suffer from **deprivation dwarfism**—stunted growth associated with isolation, rejection, or general deprivation in the home environment (see boxed news excerpt). Special efforts to teach such children to speak and behave normally often meet with limited success. Examples such as these, as well as the earlier discussion of attachment, suggest that in many ways the first 3 years of life are a *relatively critical period* in development.

Deprivation In development, a lack or withholding of normal stimulation, nutrition, comfort, love, and so forth.

Deprivation dwarfism Stunted growth caused by isolation, rejection, or general deprivation.

Hospitalism A pattern of depression observed in institutionalized infants.

"Closet Child" Now with Loving Parents

LONG BEACH (AP)—Becky's story began to unfold when the Sheriff's Department responded to a tip like hundreds of others. They found Becky in urine-soaked clothes, asleep on a hard cot in her parents' bedroom.

"She was almost like an animal," one of the deputies reported.

Her world then was the bedroom and its closet, in which she was kept for untold hours. Now Becky lives in a spacious foster home.

Since Becky's rescue, she has gained 12 pounds and grown 6 inches. But she is still a mite, for she weighed only 24 pounds and stood only 32 inches tall last April.

When she was found, Becky couldn't even crawl; now she walks. Then, she knew only a few words—now she speaks in sentences. She is, except for the hurt in her eyes, like almost any toddler.

But Rebecca is no toddler. She is 9 years old, and her pediatrician says she may never catch up.

Question: What aspects of deprivation are responsible for the damage done?

One of the earliest hints came when psychoanalyst René Spitz (1945) compared two groups of infants. One group was made up of healthy and lively babies in an institution Spitz called the "nursery." Spitz studied a second group of babies in a "foundling home" who suffered from a condition called **hospitalism.**

Perceptual stimulation Varied, patterned, and meaningful sensory input.

This is a pattern of deep depression marked by weeping and sadness and long periods of immobility or mechanical rocking. A lack of normal responsiveness to other humans is also typical of the problem. The foundling home had an unusually high rate of infant deaths. Development of the babies that survived was severely retarded.

Spitz compared conditions at the two institutions and found some striking differences. At the nursery, each baby had a separate attendant. At the foundling home, there were 8 babies to a nurse. In view of this, Spitz considered the "wasting away" of the foundling home babies a result of their lack of dependable "mother figures."

Question: In other words, the babies failed to form an attachment to an adult, right?

Yes. Other studies have shown that lack of attachment is a major element in early deprivation. For example, making living conditions better for a group of children in a Canadian institution failed to reverse their declining mental health. The children improved only when they were placed with caring foster parents or adoptive parents (Flint, 1978).

A second major factor in many cases of deprivation is a lack of **perceptual stimulation.** All of the "wasted" babies that Spitz studied were well cared for physically. However, they were kept in bare rooms in cribs with white sheets hung on the sides. The infants could see only the blank ceiling, and their only contact with others came during a few brief periods each day when they were quickly fed or changed. To put it mildly, there was *nothing happening* for these children: no change, no input, no cuddling, no attention, and most of all, no stimulation. This was deprivation in the fullest sense of the word.

Perceptual, intellectual, and emotional deprivation can occur in any family, at any income level. However, when families must cope with poverty the risk that children will be victims of deprivation is magnified. Highlight 12–5 explores the linkages between poverty and early childhood deprivation.

■ **Fig. 12–26** *Children who grow up in poverty run a high risk of experiencing many forms of deprivation. There is evidence that lasting damage to social, emotional, and cognitive development occurs when children must cope with severe early deprivation.*

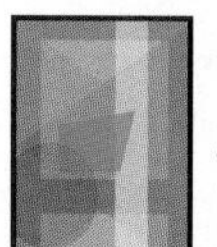

HIGHLIGHT 12–5

A Closer Look At

The Impact of Poverty

Psychologists have long known that poverty is associated with retarded emotional and intellectual development. By the age of 5, children who grow up in poor homes have lower IQs. They are also more fearful, unhappy, and prone to hostile or aggressive behavior. But these observations leave an important question unanswered: Exactly how does poverty contribute to such problems?

Basically, researchers have found that poverty wears down families. Unemployment, decaying neighborhoods, crime, and social disorder all take a toll on parenting (■ Fig. 12–26). Even when parents have the best intentions, poverty can lead to many kinds of deprivation. For example, the longer a family remains poor, the less likely parents are to express love and warmth toward their children. The longer they are poor, the more likely parents are to use harsh discipline. Fighting and conflict are common in poor families. Stimulating language environments are not. Most important, children living in poverty tend to be deprived of learning opportunities, both at home and in inferior schools.

None of these observations suggests that poor parents intentionally deprive their children. Typically, when family income increases, parents use the extra money to enhance their children's lives. How, then, can the odds of success be improved for poor children? According to a major study done by the Carnegie Corporation, the most important steps are:

- Educate parents about caregiving
- Make sure that quality child care is available to working parents
- Promote physical health and safety for all children

■ Get communities involved in supporting young children and their families

Almost everyone knows that good nutrition is important in early childhood. As this discussion suggests, it is equally important to nourish the mind. (Sources: Carnegie Corporation, 1994; Dodge, Pettit, & Bates, 1994; Duncan, Brooks-Gunn, & Klebanov, 1994; Garrett, Ng'andu, & Ferron, 1994; Hashima & Amato, 1994.)

Early Stimulation

Experiments with animals have confirmed the destructive effects of a lack of stimulation in infancy. For example, Harry Harlow separated infant rhesus monkeys from their mothers at birth. The real mothers were replaced with **surrogate** (substitute) **mothers.** These were essentially dummies of approximately the same size and shape as real monkeys. Some of the surrogates were made of cold, unyielding wire, and others were covered with soft terry cloth (■ Fig. 12–27). When the infants were given a choice between the two mothers, they consistently chose to spend most of their time clinging to the cuddly terry-cloth mother. This was true even when a bottle was mounted in the wire mother, making it the source of food.

The "love" and attachment displayed toward the cloth mothers was identical to that shown toward natural mothers. When frightened by rubber snakes, wind-up toys, and other "fear stimuli," the infant monkeys ran to their cloth mothers and clung to them for security (Harlow & Zimmerman, 1958). Harlow concluded that one of the most important dimensions of early stimulation is **contact comfort,** supplied by touching, holding, and stroking an infant (■ Fig. 12–28). Harlow's findings are backed up by human research, as well. For example, researchers have found that prematurely born babies benefit physically and emotionally from affectionate touching and massage by parents (Miller & Holditch-Davis, 1992; Schok & Samuels, 1992; Watt, 1990).

For many psychologists, contact comfort is part of the rationale for advocating breast-feeding of infants. Breast-feeding almost guarantees that a baby will receive an adequate amount of touching and handling. Breast-feeding also aids attachment and early cognitive development (Jensen et al., 1981; Morrow-Tlucak, Haude, & Ernhart, 1988). Even without such advantages, breast-feeding is advisable. For the first few days after giving birth, mothers produce **colostrum** (kuh-LOSS-trum), rather than milk. Colostrum is a fluid rich in proteins that carries antibodies from the mother

Surrogate mother A substitute mother (often an inanimate dummy in animal research).

Contact comfort A pleasant and reassuring feeling infants get from touching something soft and warm, usually the mother.

Colostrum The first milk produced by a woman for a few days after giving birth.

■ **Fig. 12–27** *An infant monkey clings to a cloth-covered surrogate mother. Baby monkeys become attached to the cloth "contact-comfort" mother but not to a similar wire mother. This is true even when the wire mother provides food. (Photo courtesy of Harry Harlow, University of Wisconsin Primate Laboratory.)*

■ **Fig. 12–28** *Extra touching, massage, and human contact is especially beneficial for premature and low-birth-weight infants.*

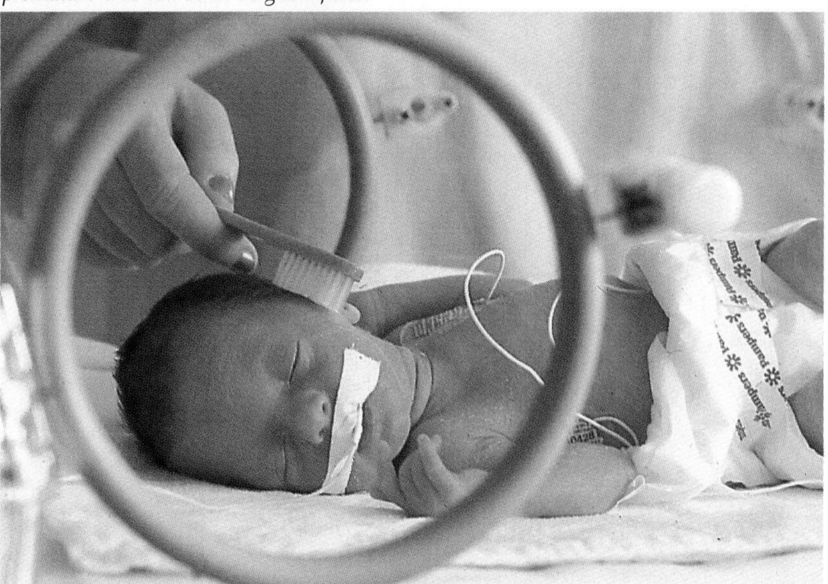

Enriched environment An environment deliberately made more novel, complex, and perceptually stimulating.

Enrichment In development, any attempt to make a child's environment more novel, complex, and perceptually or intellectually stimulating.

Visually directed reaching Coordinated, visually guided reaching for a particular object.

Early childhood education program Programs that provide stimulating intellectual experiences, typically for disadvantaged preschoolers.

to the newborn. These antibodies help prevent certain infectious diseases. Colostrum is also easier for the newborn to digest than cow's milk and many infant formulas.

Question: What about the mother who can't breast-feed or who prefers not to?

The advantages of breast-feeding are not overriding. If a mother is aware of the importance of touching and cuddling, bottle feeding need not be psychologically inferior to breast-feeding. A mother's warmth or coldness, relaxation or tension, and acceptance or rejection are more important than the choice of breast or bottle. As mentioned earlier, being sensitive to a baby's feeding rhythms and needs seems to be the key to promoting healthy infant attachment.

Contact comfort may also underlie the tendency of many children to become attached to inanimate objects, such as blankets or stuffed toys. This does not appear to be a cause for alarm, however. A study of 2- to 3-year-old "blanket-attached" children found that they were no more insecure than others (Passman, 1987). (So, maybe Linus is okay after all.)

Enrichment If too little stimulation limits development, can an abundance of stimulation enhance it? Many attempts to answer this question have made use of **enriched environments.** Enriched environments are deliberately made more novel, complex, and stimulating. Enriched environments for infants may be the "soil" from which brighter children grow. To illustrate, let us begin with an experiment in which rats were raised in an enriched environment (Kretch et al., 1962).

Building Bigger and Better Brains

To begin, infant rats were divided into two groups. One group was raised in *stimulus-poor* conditions. These animals were housed in adequate but unstimulating cages. The cages had gray walls, and they contained nothing to explore or investigate. The second group was housed in a sort of "rat wonderland." The walls of the *stimulus-enriched* environment were decorated with colored patterns, and the cage was filled with platforms, ladders, and cubbyholes to be explored. When the rats reached adulthood, their ability to learn mazes was tested. The stimulated rats dramatically out-performed their deprived relatives. In addition, later tests showed that the stimulated rats had brains that were larger and heavier, with a thicker cortex.

It is a long leap from rats to people, but it is hard to overlook an increase in brain size caused by sensory stimulation. If stimulation can enhance the "intelligence" of a lowly rat, it is reasonable to assume that human infants also benefit from stimulation.

Question: Is there any evidence that this is actually the case?

As might be expected, it is much harder to demonstrate that such things occur in humans. In Chapter 14 you will find a full discussion of the effects of environment on intelligence. For now, let us examine two examples of enrichment applied to humans.

Infants like to reach out and touch things, but normally it takes about 5 months after birth for this skill to develop. In an experiment done at a state hospital, newborn infants were given several kinds of extra stimulation each day for several months (White & Held, 1966). Each child in the stimulus enrichment condition was handled an extra 15 minutes daily. Each was placed in a position that allowed visual exploration outside the crib. White crib sheets were replaced by patterned sheets with colorful animal designs. A collection of bright and colorful objects was hung over each child's crib. As limited as these changes may seem, they caused **visually directed reaching** to occur an average of 6 weeks early. This may not sound like an earth-shaking improvement in adult terms, but to an infant it is a substantial acceleration in development.

The preceding is only one of many experiments showing a positive relationship between stimulation and improvements in various abilities—particularly those that might be labeled "intellectual." One of the most encouraging examples of the benefits of enrichment is Program Head Start. The goal of Head Start is to prepare disadvantaged children for school by providing intellectual stimulation and helping them "learn to learn." Studies of Head Start children show real improvements in their abilities and school performance (Lee, Brooks-Gunn, & Schnur, 1988). This is especially true for the most needy children.

There is little question that **early childhood education** programs enrich the lives of many children (Campbell & Ramey, 1994; Lee, et al., 1990). Programs like Head Start can't work miracles, but they can prepare children for school. They also teach children social and emotional skills that may help them cope better with life (Zigler & Styfco, 1994). For example, as teens, former Head Start participants are less likely to drop out of school, get arrested, or get pregnant, among other things (Zigler & Muenchow, 1992).

Summary Most people recognize that babies need lots of "tender loving care" where their physical needs are concerned. But as the previous discussion shows, a complete definition of tender loving care should include a baby's psychological needs as well. In general, the effects of deprivation and enrichment appear to apply to *all* of the categories of development discussed earlier in this chapter. It would be a good idea to place perceptual and intellectual stimulation, affectionate touching, and personal warmth high on any list of infant needs. (See ● Table 12–10.)

Table 12–10 Deprivation and Enrichment: Implications for Parents and Caregivers

• All of early childhood should be viewed as a relatively critical period in development.
• Infants and young children thrive in enriched, stimulating environments.
• Touch and human contact are important elements of infant development.
• Children need a sense of security, belonging, and support; they need to feel loved.

A Look Ahead The first years of life are a magic and sensitive time. What can parents do to make the most of this period in development? The Applications section that follows gives some practical advice. After that, an Exploration delves into recent advances in genetics and reproductive technologies that are sure to affect our lives.

Learning Check

1. According to Kohlberg, the conventional level of moral development is marked by a reliance on outside authority. T or F?
2. Self-interest and avoiding punishment are elements of postconventional morality. T or F?
3. About 80 percent of all adults function at the postconventional level of moral reasoning. T or F?
4. Gilligan regards gaining a sense of justice as the principal basis of moral development. T or F?
5. Harlow's "motherless monkeys" became attached to the wire surrogate mother if it fed them. T or F?
6. René Spitz attributed hospitalism to an absence of perceptual stimulation. T or F?
7. Bottle feeding prevents a mother from providing an adequate amount of contact comfort for an infant. T or F?
8. Early childhood education programs can be characterized as attempts to enrich the environments of deprived children. T or F?
9. Some of Carol Gilligan's work involved presenting real-life dilemmas concerning abortion to a group of women. Why might any conclusions drawn from such studies be open to question? *Critical Thinking*

Answers: 1. T 2. F 3. F 4. F 5. F 6. F 7. F 8. T 9. To identify differences between men's and women's moral reasoning, men and women must face the same dilemma; Gilligan, therefore, cannot draw firm conclusions about how men might react, based on the dilemma she presented to women (Mednick, 1989).

APPLICATIONS: *Enriching Early Development—A Magic Time of Life*

There are so many expensive playthings in Derek's room that it looks like a display for a toy store. The walls are covered with posters and photographs. Model airplanes, rockets, a pterodactyl, and a miniature solar system dangle from the ceiling. For several hours a day, Derek's mother plays classical music for him—through his own stereo system. Each evening, Derek watches educational videotapes about animals, premath skills, and nuclear physics. Every day, Derek's mother drills him with flash cards in hopes that he will learn to read before any of the neighbor children. Derek is taking swimming lessons at a local pool. Derek is 2½. At present his favorite toy is a fake cellular phone.

Derek's parents obviously mean well. But are they really enhancing his early development? Let's put it this way: By the time he is 5, if Derek's parents ask him to change a light bulb, he will hold it in the socket and wait for the world to revolve around him.

Facilitating Early Development

Understandably, parents want to see their children's potentials develop fully. As discussed earlier in the chapter, proactive parental involvement in a child's progress can be highly beneficial. It is easy, however, to go overboard and overwhelm a child. "Enrichment" that does not match a child's needs is of little value. How can parents strike a balance between enrichment and "pushing" a child early in life? As a start, it helps to have appropriate goals for infancy. Child expert

Statistical child An "average" child defined by combining the characteristics of many children.

Particular child A specific child.

Burton White (1990) believes that for the first year or so of life the three goals for healthy development are:

1. Giving the infant a feeling of being loved and cared for.
2. Encouraging interest in the outside world.
3. Helping the infant develop specific skills.

Let's see how these goals apply to parental behavior. (For an excellent description of early development, and practical advice for effective parenting, consult White's book, *The First Three Years of Life.*)

Attachment Giving an infant a feeling of being loved and cared for helps build secure mother-infant and father-infant bonds. The importance of giving good physical care to a baby is self-evident. Beyond that, parents should touch, hold, and handle their infant frequently. Parents should also attend promptly to a baby's cries as often as possible. Parents sometimes believe that they should let babies "cry it out" to avoid spoiling them.

There will, of course, be times when nothing will console an unhappy, but otherwise healthy baby. But for the first year of life, it is best to respond promptly to a baby's signs of discomfort. Infants are better off in the long run if they are tended to and comforted in a loving way (White, 1990). This helps them feel secure and it strengthens their emotional bonds with parents.

Overindulgence As mentioned earlier, spoiling very young infants is nearly impossible. As children begin to become more mobile and independent, however, overindulgence becomes more of a risk. From about age 2 on, parents are asking for trouble if they do everything, and buy everything they can for the child, no matter what. Another clear sign of overindulgence is giving in to the child's demands, even when they go against your better judgment. Effective parents are very loving and even quite indulgent of their children. What spoils a child is a lack of firm age-appropriate limits and guidelines for acceptable behavior. (Information on setting and maintaining such limits is discussed in the Applications section of Chapter 13.)

The Outside World In the first year of life, parents can help encourage a baby's interest in the world. This is done by seeing that the baby is regularly involved in activities that interest her or him. To do this, parents must pay close attention to the baby's signals about likes and dislikes, as well as what holds the baby's attention. Burton White (1990) recommends using an infant seat to keep the baby near you as you move around the house. That way, the baby gets a change of scene and you get to interact with her more often.

To encourage an infant's exploration of the world, try to minimize the use of restrictive devices. Playpens, jump seats, and gates should not be used for long periods, if at all. Families in which children are developing optimally make little use of such devices. Restricting exploration tends to stifle a child's natural curiosity.

Parents can contribute greatly to intellectual growth through their attitudes toward a child's *investigation* of the world. The child who repeatedly hears, "Don't touch that" (chair, handle, trash, radio, pencil, flower) or "I told you not to" (go up there, play with that, leave this spot, get dirty, and so forth) may become passive and intellectually dulled (Carew et al., 1976). Placing virtually all common objects off-limits for a child is a serious mistake. When children begin to crawl and walk, it makes more sense to "child-proof" a house than to try to strictly enforce rules about what the child can and cannot touch.

Respecting Individual Variation A major element of good child rearing in infancy consists of knowing what the normal pattern of emerging skills is and facilitating their emergence. If an infant lags far behind expected milestones in development, parents should take note and find out why (White, 1990). However, within normal ranges it is valuable to remember that individual differences in maturation rates are the rule.

Aware parents recognize the difference between the **statistical child** and the **particular child.** Developmental norms specifying ages at which particular abilities appear are based on *averages.* There is always a *wide range of normal variation* around each average. Thus, we can expect plateaus, reversals, and periods of rapid advancement in the development of a particular child. This applies not only to the emergence of motor skills, such as crawling and walking, but also to language development and the stages of cognitive development described by Piaget. In all areas of development, a child's uniqueness should be respected. This means resisting the temptation to compare the child with others—particularly in the child's presence. Each child is an individual and should be judged as such.

Enrichment As we have noted, babies need stimulation. By keeping this need in mind, parents can do much to provide varied sensory experience during infancy. A baby should be surrounded by colors, music, people, and things to see, taste, smell, and touch. Babies are not vegetables. It makes perfect sense to take them outside, to hang mobiles over their cribs, to place mirrors nearby, or to rearrange their rooms now and then.

It also makes sense to talk to infants, from birth onward. Try to talk about present events, such as what you are doing, objects the baby is looking at, and parts of the baby's body you are touching. As you interact with a baby, be sure to respond to his or her coos, gurgles, and other vocalizations—not just to crying (White, 1990). Remember, as we noted earlier, the more time babies spend interacting with parents, the faster they develop language and thinking abilities (Hart & Risley, 1992).

Throughout a baby's second year it is very important to watch for signs of hearing loss, which can have a devastating effect on cognitive development. To test for hearing loss, the baby's mother should call to her or him in a normal voice from 6–10 feet away. As she calls repeatedly for about a minute, the baby should turn accurately toward her voice. If the baby does not, or if you have doubts about an infant's hearing, seek professional advice (White, 1990).

Responsiveness Most parents could put far more imagination into enriching an infant's surroundings than they typically do. The presence of stimulating play materials in the home, together with responsive parents, is strongly related to how quickly children progress (Bradley et al., 1989; Luster & Dubow, 1992).

Question: How should a parent decide if enrichment is being overdone?

The answer depends more on the *quality* of enrichment than on its quantity. Remember that the goal in enrichment is to create a world that *responds* to the infant—not one that bombards the infant with stimuli. Elaborately enriched environments are unnecessary and can be upsetting to a baby (White, 1990).

The concept of **responsiveness,** mentioned earlier, applies to toys and objects, as well as to parents' behavior. Toys that respond to a child's actions, such as balls, rattles, mirrors—even a spoon and a pie tin—help speed infant learning. Experiences that allow children to see cause-and-effect results from their own behavior are particularly effective. As psychologist Paul Chance points out, the most expensive toys tend to be the least responsive. The least responsive toy available is probably a $500 color television, while one of the most responsive is a $1 rubber ball (Chance, 1982).

Drawbacks of Forced Teaching Many authorities are concerned about parents who try to push their children's development in a misguided attempt to produce "super babies." It's worth saying again that flooding an infant with stimuli, flash cards, and exercises is not enriching. **Forced teaching** of reading, pre-math skills, gymnastics, swimming, musical skills, and the like, can bore or oppress a child. Such practices, which are sometimes called "hothousing," are like trying to force plants to bloom prematurely (Hyson et al., 1991).

Forced teaching An accelerated pace of learning in young children that is dictated by an adult.

Forced teaching is both expensive and unnecessary (White, 1990). Parents who approach play and learning as if their preschooler were on the fast track for Harvard are filling their own needs at the expense of the child (Alvino et al., 1985). True enrichment is responsive to the child's curiosity and interests. It does not make the child feel pressured to perform. Many of the things Derek's parents did (in the opening vignette) would be perfectly appropriate for an older child, especially when the child's own interests are taken into account. The next section offers some further guidelines for parents.

Piaget Revisited

Piaget's theory suggests that the ideal way to guide intellectual development is to provide experiences that are only slightly novel, unusual, or challenging. Remember, a child's intellect develops mainly through accommodation. As old concepts and thinking habits become obsolete, they are discarded or adapted to fit new demands.

To stretch a child's intellect, demands must be made, but experiences that are too far beyond the familiar may cause frustration and withdrawal. Therefore, gradually expanding beyond a child's current level of comprehension is usually most productive. Effective parents typically follow a sort of *one-step-ahead strategy* when adapting their instruction to their infants' current level of ability (Heckhausen, 1987).

In addition, Piaget's work shows the importance of relating to a child on the right level. If you give a physical explanation when a very young child asks, "Why does the sun come up in the morning?" you may have missed the point. Answering in terms of the child's egocentric viewpoint is often more likely to be meaningful. An answer such as, "So that you will know it's time to get up" is completely satisfactory for a young child. Later, explanations can be made increasingly abstract and accurate.

Question: Are there any guidelines for relating to children at their own level?

In a delightful book entitled *Using Psychology,* psychologist Morris Holland offers some suggestions

APPLICATIONS: *Continued*

about how best to relate to children at different stages of intellectual development. The following points are drawn from his discussion (Holland, 1975).

1. **Sensorimotor stage (0–2).** Active play with a child is most effective at this stage. Encourage explorations in touching, smelling, and manipulating objects. Peekaboo is a good way to establish the permanence of objects.
2. **Preoperational stage (2–7).** Although children are beginning to talk to themselves and to act out solutions to problems, touching and seeing things will continue to be more useful than verbal explanations. Concrete examples will also have more meaning than generalizations. The child should be encouraged to classify things in different ways. Learning the concept of conservation may be aided by demonstrations involving liquids, beads, clay, and other substances.
3. **Concrete operational stage (7–11).** Children in this stage are beginning to use generalizations, but they still require specific examples to grasp many ideas. Expect a degree of inconsistency in the child's ability to apply concepts of time, space, quantity, and volume to new situations.
4. **Formal operations stage (11-adult).** At this point, it becomes more realistic to explain things verbally or symbolically to a child. Helping the child to master general rules and principles now becomes productive. Encourage the child to create hypotheses and to imagine how things could be.

Keeping this general outline in mind should help you adjust to the changing patterns of intellect displayed by developing children.

LEARNING CHECK

1. The idea that the particular child is different from the "statistical child" applies to language development and cognitive skills, but not to motor development. T or F?
2. Parental overindulgence is likely to occur when parents fail to set firm age-appropriate guidelines for their children's behavior. T or F?
3. To promote accommodation, it is best to provide information or experiences only moderately beyond a child's current level of comprehension. T or F?
4. Playing peekaboo is a good way to help the sensorimotor child master the concept of conservation. T or F?
5. A key element of enrichment in infancy and early childhood is the concept of ________________.

Critical Thinking

6. Forced teaching ignores what principle of early maturation and development?

Answers: 1. F 2. T 3. T 4. F 5. responsiveness 6. Readiness.

EXPLORATION

The Brave New World of Genetics and Reproduction

In his famous novel, *Brave New World,* Aldous Huxley described a futuristic society in which "baby factories" produce thousands of duplicate humans to do society's labor. Huxley, writing in the 1930s, envisioned a future in which biological engineering would be used for sinister and totalitarian ends. Now that the future has arrived, we find instead that some of the possibilities Huxley anticipated have made it possible for previously infertile couples to have children. And yet, as is often true, new solutions create new problems. In this Exploration we will briefly describe some recent developments in medicine and genetics that raise interesting social, psychological, and ethical questions.

In the recent past, adoption was the only alternative for couples with untreatable infertility. Now, such couples have an array of new options. Let's investigate two that are of special interest.

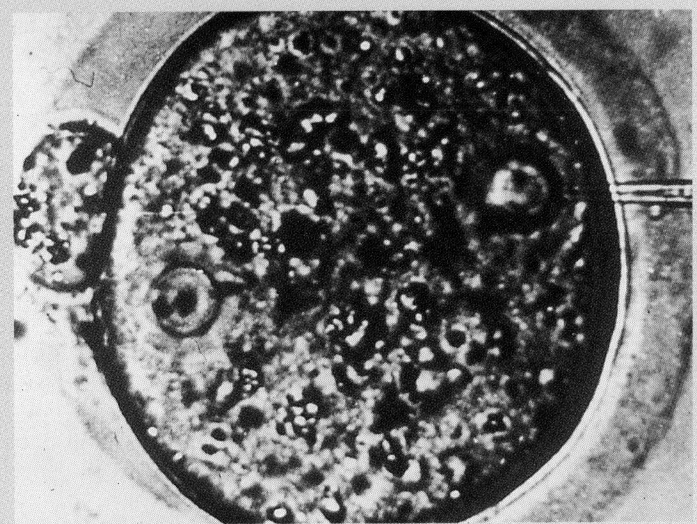

■ Fig. 12–29 *During in vitro fertilization, ova from the woman or a donor are mixed with sperm from the man or a donor. If both the egg and sperm are donated, both nominal parents are genetically unrelated to the "test-tube" baby.*

Artificial Insemination If her husband is sterile, a woman can undergo **artificial insemination.** In this procedure, sperm from an anonymous donor are used to impregnate the woman. Donors are selected so that their eye and hair color, height, and so on, match the husband's as closely as possible. For emotional reasons, some of the husband's sperm are sometimes mixed with the donor sperm so that it is impossible to tell who was actually the father. (Men who are sterile often produce sperm, but their sperm count is too low for them to father a child.)

Test-Tube Babies A technique called **in vitro fertilization** has made it possible for some infertile couples to bear children who share both the mother's and father's genes. To produce a "test-tube" baby, egg cells are surgically collected from the mother's ovary. The egg cells are then placed in a petri dish of nutrients and the father's sperm cells are added (■ Fig. 12–29). (A womb with a view!) After an egg cell is fertilized and begins dividing, it is implanted in the mother's womb, where it develops normally. In a new variation on in vitro fertilization, an unrelated woman may donate an egg cell to the infertile couple. The egg cell is then fertilized with the husband's sperm and implanted in the wife's uterus. Infertile couples who are considering this technique should be warned, however. Even using the latest methods, only 15 percent of in vitro attempts are successful, and the cost ranges from $8000 to $13000.

Questions and Controversies

The procedures outlined here raise a number of practical, emotional, moral, and even religious issues. Many will no doubt occur to the reader. A few that may not are listed here.

Many donors for artificial insemination are used repeatedly. One clinic reported that a single donor fathered 50 babies. What if this donor harbored a genetic disease or defect? What if children fathered by the same donor were to meet and marry? Since they would be half brother and sister, their offspring would run a high risk of having genetic defects. What rules of testing and record keeping should apply to artificial insemination by donor?

Many scientists believe that handling egg cells for in vitro fertilization may increase the risk of deformities in babies. If a child is born with a defect, is the physician responsible? Frequently, more than one egg is fertilized. Should they be donated to another infertile couple? Is letting them die an abortion? Should in vitro fertilization be allowed if the man and woman are not married? If they divorce, who should get "custody" of the ova?

Sex Selection Another recent development that may have an impact on parenthood is the possibility of selecting an infant's sex prior to conception. The procedure involves separating X- and Y-bearing sperm and then artificially fertilizing the egg cell with all male-producing or all female-producing sperm.

Currently, sex selection techniques cannot *guarantee* to produce a child of the desired sex. Sex selection is also relatively expensive (about $500), and some

Artificial insemination Medically engineered impregnation.

In vitro fertilization Fertilization of an ovum outside a woman's body.

EXPLORATION

couples may be discouraged by the need for artificial insemination. A further worry is that two-thirds of all childless American couples say they would prefer to have a boy as a first child.

Question: If large numbers of couples select their children's sex, would there be an excess of male births?

Seventy-three percent of all potential parents who would be willing to use sex-selection technology say they would choose sons (Steinbacher & Gilroy, 1990). If many couples were to make this choice, the male-female population balance would be upset. Birth rate and population growth would slow dramatically once 70 percent of the population became male.

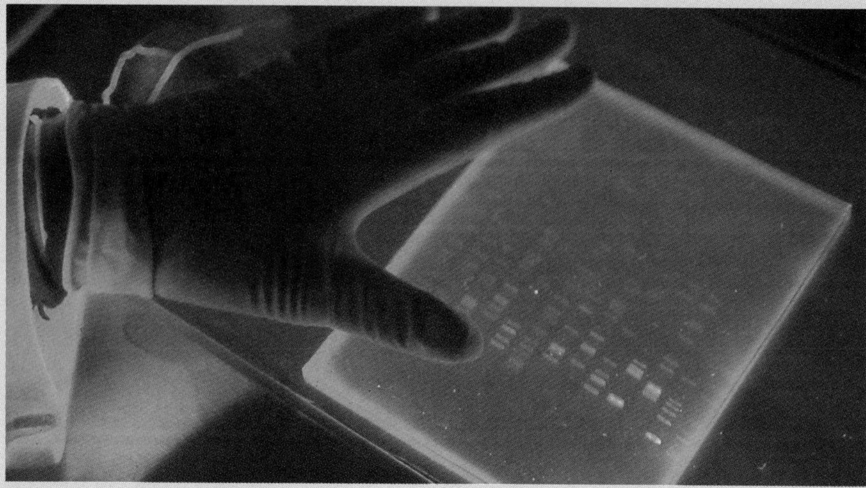

■ **Fig. 12–30** *Strands of DNA can be chemically broken into shorter segments which (after further manipulation) can be displayed for analysis. The pink-glowing pieces of DNA you see here are enlarged many times.*

Genetics and Parenthood

In recent years, having children has also been influenced by an improved understanding of human genetics. Increasingly, it has become possible to combat troubles that "run in the family." It is now possible to identify a large number of genetic disorders, such as sickle-cell anemia, hemophilia, cystic fibrosis, muscular dystrophy, albinism, and some forms of mental retardation.

Scientists are currently hard at work on a giant project to identify, in order, every gene on every human chromosome. The result will be a map of the **human genome** (JEEN-ome), or entire set of genes (■ Fig. 12–30). Having, in essence a "full set of instructions for making a human" will allow advanced identification of genetic diseases and new tests to detect those diseases in people. It will take at least another decade to produce a complete blueprint of all human genes. At that point, doctors, biologists, and you and I will face a host of new ethical and practical dilemmas to resolve.

Genetic Counseling Today, prospective parents who suspect that they may be carriers of genetic disorders may seek **genetic counseling.** By examining the family history of each future parent, and in some cases by directly mapping chromosomes, geneticists can calculate the risk of a genetic disorder (Rowley, 1984).

Question: What can a couple do if the risk of a genetic defect is high?

Knowing the risks, parents can choose not to have a child; or, if the odds are in their favor, they may elect to take the chance. Even when there is a reasonable likelihood of a genetic disorder, some couples elect to have children, but then have a test performed during pregnancy to detect the presence or absence of the genetic defect. Such prenatal testing is done by **amniocentesis** (AM-nee-oh-SEN-tee-sis), which involves taking a sample of amniotic fluid from the mother's womb. This procedure allows determination of fetal sex and the detection of many genetic defects.

Amniocentesis is usually done at about the fifteenth week of pregnancy. An alternate procedure, called **chorionic villus sampling** can be done between 6 and 8 weeks of pregnancy. This technique takes a small piece of the placenta for analysis. Either method allows couples who do not object to abortion to terminate the pregnancy when a serious genetic defect is detected. Parents who consider abortion unacceptable still have the advantage of forewarning so that they may prepare the best possible care for the child (■ Fig. 12–31).

The Future

Recent advances in genetics, the exploding knowledge about how DNA controls heredity, and mapping of the human genome will bring profound changes to the human condition. Let's sample some of the possibilities.

Eugenics It is probably true that domestic plants and animals have been improved more in the past 50 years than in the previous 5000. This improvement has been accomplished primarily through **eugenics** (you-JEN-iks), or selective breeding for desirable characteristics. Some extremists have already proposed that eugenics be applied to humans. But the very idea is loaded with ethical problems. How would we decide what characteristics are desirable? And who would decide who can have children and who cannot? In practice, it is unlikely that widespread human eugenics will ever be practiced. On the other hand, some genetic diseases will almost certainly be "cured." Even without such direct efforts, the steady use of genetic counseling could have a eugenic effect on future generations.

Genetic Engineering It is now becoming possible to remove defective genes and replace them with normal ones. Could such genetic engineering also be used to produce beauty, intelligence, re-

EXPLORATION

■ **Fig. 12–31** *Bree Walker Lampley, a TV celebrity in Los Angeles, has a genetic condition that causes deformity of the hands and feet. Before she became pregnant, she knew she had a 50 percent chance of giving birth to a baby with the same trait. Despite public criticism, she had a baby (who did, in fact, inherit her genetic condition). The social pressures she faced illustrate the dilemmas people who carry genetic defects often face (Rennie, 1994).*

sistance to aging, or superhuman athletic potential? In theory yes, but practically speaking, probably not. Literally thousands of genes affect such qualities, not to mention the effects of environment. For this reason, limited genetic engineering involving one or two genes may soon be used to combat specific diseases such as diabetes or cancer, and inherited disorders. Tampering with genes on a major scale is not likely in the near future. **Cloning,** the production of an entire organism from a single cell, is also likely to remain science fiction (where humans are concerned) for the immediate future.

Gene Cards One authority on genetic engineering and genetic defects predicts that people will one day carry a "gene identity card" based on blood tests made during childhood. These would show what hereditary diseases a person is predisposed to, or which problems may be passed on in childbearing when combined with the gene pattern of a mate (Milunsky, 1992).

Rapid advances in techniques that affect heredity and conception have an important place in the understanding of behavior. And as we have seen, such changes raise a number of important psychological and ethical questions. Some additional questions of interest are provided in the Questions for Discussion that conclude this chapter.

Human genome The entire set of human genes.

Genetic counseling Providing guidance and testing to prospective parents regarding the risks of bearing a child with a genetic disorder.

Amniocentesis Testing of the amniotic fluid from a pregnant woman's womb to identify fetal sex and to detect genetic defects in the fetus.

Chorionic villus sampling Testing of a small piece of the placenta early in pregnancy to detect genetic defects in the fetus.

Eugenics Selective breeding for desirable characteristics.

Cloning The production of an entire organism using the DNA from a single cell.

LEARNING CHECK

1. The procedure known as in vitro fertilization involves fertilizing a woman with donor sperm. T or F?
2. Test-tube babies are produced by fertilizing an egg cell outside of the body. T or F?
3. Current sex selection procedures can consistently produce male offspring, but they cannot guarantee female babies. T or F?
4. Amniocentesis is primarily used to select sex before birth. T or F?
5. The term *eugenics* refers to the production of an entire organism from a single cell. T or F?
6. Many people who should seek genetic screening choose not to be tested. Why do you think people resist testing? ***Critical Thinking***

Answers: 1. F 2. T 3. F 4. F 5. F 6. The most typical reasons given are that: People would rather not know they carry a defect because it would mean their children might be at risk too; they fear being stigmatized; they worry that their health insurance may be affected; and they are concerned that they may be turned down for future employment.

Authoritarian parents Parents who enforce rigid rules and demand strict obedience to authority.

Overly permissive parents Parents who give their children little guidance, allow them too much freedom, or do not hold them responsible for their actions.

Authoritative parents Parents who supply firm and consistent guidance combined with love and affection.

Overprotection Excessively guarding and shielding a child from possible stresses.

Problems of Childhood—Why Parents Get Gray Hair

Can you remember a time in your childhood when your actions led to a disaster or a near disaster? It shouldn't be hard. It's a wonder that many of us survive childhood at all. Where I grew up, digging underground tunnels, wriggling down chimneys, hopping on trains, jumping off houses, crawling through storm drains, making bombs—and worse—were common childhood adventures.

Question: If initiative and industry are important in childhood, what limits should parents place on a child's freedom to explore the world?

CLOSE TO HOME By John McPherson

"All right now, give Mommy the super-glue."

Parenting Styles

An answer is provided by psychologist Diana Baumrind (1980, 1991), who has studied the effects of three major styles of parenting. According to Baumrind, each style tends to have a different effect on children's behavior. See if you recognize the styles she describes.

Authoritarian parents view children as having few rights but adult-like responsibilities. The authoritarian parent tends to demand strict adherence to rigid standards of behavior ("Do it because I say so"). The child is expected to stay out of trouble and to accept without question what the parents regard as right or wrong behavior. The children of such parents typically are obedient and self-controlled. But they also tend to be emotionally stiff, withdrawn, apprehensive, and lacking in curiosity.

Overly permissive parents view children as having few responsibilities but rights similar to adults. Such parents require little responsible behavior from their children ("Do whatever you want"). Rules are not enforced, and the child usually gets his or her way. This tends to produce dependent, immature children who misbehave frequently. Such children are aimless and tend to "run amok."

Baumrind describes **authoritative parents** as those who balance their own rights with those of their children. Such parents are highly effective because they are demanding but not authoritarian. They control their children's behavior, but they are also loving, caring, and responsive ("Do it for this reason"). Effective parents approach discipline in a way that is firm and consistent, not harsh or rigid. In general, they encourage the child to act responsibly. This parenting style produces children who tend to be competent, self-controlled, independent, assertive, and inquiring.

By balancing freedom and restraint, effective parents help children become responsible adults. The consistent, well-explained limits set by authoritative parents teach children how to think and make good decisions on their own (Baumrind, 1991).

As an added guide to parenting, it may help to remember that stress is a normal part of life—even in childhood. Certainly this does not mean that parents should go out of their way to stress a child. However, it does suggest that children need not be completely shielded from stressful stimulation. Overprotection can be as damaging as overly stressing a child or being overly strict or permissive. **Overprotection,** which is sometimes called "smother love," refers to excessively shielding a child from possible stresses.

Most children do a good job of keeping stress at comfortable levels when *they* initiate an activity (Murphy & Moriarty, 1976) (■ Fig. 13–5). At a public swimming pool, for instance, some children can be observed making death-defying leaps from the high dive, while others stick close to the wading area. If no immediate danger is present, it is reasonable to let children get stuck in trees, make themselves dizzy, squabble with neighborhood children, and so forth. Getting into a few scrapes can help prepare a child to cope with later stresses. (Just think, if your author hadn't crawled through a few storm pipes, his adult interest in plumbing the depths of the psyche might have gone down the drain.)

Question: How can you tell if a child is being subjected to too much stress?

■ **Fig. 13–5** *Most children do a good job of keeping stress at comfortable levels when they initiate an activity.*

Normal Childhood Problems

Child specialists Chess, Thomas, and Birch (1976) have listed a number of difficulties experienced at times by almost every child. These can be considered normal reactions to the unavoidable stress of growing up.

1. All children experience occasional **sleep disturbances,** including wakefulness, frightening dreams, or a desire to get into their parents' bed.
2. **Specific fears** of the dark, dogs, school, or a particular room or person are also common.
3. Most children will be **overly timid** at times, allowing themselves to be bullied by other children into giving up toys, a place in line, and the like.
4. Temporary periods of **general dissatisfaction** may occur, when nothing pleases the child.
5. Children also normally display periods of **general negativism** marked by tantrums, refusal to do anything requested, or a tendency to say no on principle.
6. Another normal problem is **clinging,** in which children refuse to leave the sides of their mothers or to do anything on their own.
7. Development does not always advance smoothly. Every child will show occasional **reversals** or **regressions** to more infantile behavior.

An additional problem common to the elementary school years is **sibling rivalry.** It is normal for a certain amount of jealousy, rivalry, and even hostility to develop between brothers and sisters. Some sibling conflict may even be constructive. A limited amount of aggressive give-and-take between siblings provides an opportunity to learn emotional control, self-assertion, and good sportsmanship (Bank & Kahn, 1982). Parents can help keep such conflicts within bounds by not "playing favorites" and by resisting the temptation to compare one child with another. Supportive and affectionate fathering, in particular, seems to minimize conflicts and jealousy among siblings (Rolling & Belsky, 1992).

Parents should also expect some **rebellion** from their children. Most school-age children rebel at times against the rules and limitations of the adult world. For many children, being with other children offers a chance to "let off steam" by doing some of the things the adult world forbids. It is normal for children to be messy, noisy, hostile, or destructive to a moderate degree.

It is important to keep in mind that "normal problems" can signal a more serious disturbance if they worsen or last for long periods. Problems of a more serious nature are identified in the following sections.

General negativism A tendency to respond negatively to almost all situations or requests.

Clinging A problem in which a child literally clings to a parent or refuses to leave the parent's side.

Regression Any return to an earlier, more infantile behavior pattern.

Sibling rivalry Competition among brothers and sisters for attention, dominance, status within the family, and so forth.

Childhood rebellion Open resistance to, or defiance of, adult authority.

Serious Childhood Problems—Off to a Bad Start

By the time he was five, Billy resembled a parent's worst nightmare. Billy threw uncontrollable temper tantrums and never seemed to sleep. He had not learned to talk. He got into closets and tore up his mother's dresses and urinated on her clothes. He smashed furniture and spread soap powder and breakfast food all over the floors. He attacked his mother at every opportunity, once going for her throat with his teeth. He tried to stuff his baby brother in a toy box. When Billy's parents bought him a doll they called by his brother's name, they began finding the doll pushed head down in the toilet bowl.

Billy refused to eat anything but cold, greasy hamburgers from a certain drive-in. To get through a week, his parents were forced to buy the hamburgers by the sack and hide them around the house, so Billy wouldn't eat them all at once. When his parents went out driving they had to detour around drive-ins to prevent Billy from frothing at the mouth and trying to jump out the window (Moser, 1965). Billy, you may note, was not an average five-year-old.

Question: What was his problem?

Billy was an *autistic* child. His problem is rare. Few children get off to as bad a start in life as Billy. Al-

Enuresis An inability to control urination, particularly with regard to bed-wetting.

Encopresis A lack of bowel control; "soiling."

Overeating Eating in excess of one's daily caloric needs.

Anorexia nervosa Active self-starvation or a sustained loss of appetite that has psychological origins.

Pica A craving for unnatural foods or substances such as chalk, ashes, and the like.

Delayed speech Speech that is developmentally delayed; that is, speech that begins well after the normal age for language development.

Stuttering Chronic hesitation or stumbling in speech.

Learning disability Any substantial problem with reading, math, or writing.

Dyslexia An inability to read with understanding.

though severe emotional and behavioral disturbances affect only a minority of children, the number involved is larger than most people realize.

Question: What is the nature of these problems?

Toilet-Training Disturbances

Difficulty sometimes centers on toilet training or bowel and bladder habits. The two most common problems are **enuresis** (EN-you-REE-sis: lack of bladder control) and **encopresis** (EN-coh-PREE-sis: lack of bowel control). Enuresis is more common than encopresis and many times more common among males than females. Both wetting and soiling can be a means of expressing frustration or pent-up hostility.

Parents should not be overly alarmed by some delays in toilet training or by a few "accidents." As mentioned in Chapter 12, 30 months is the average age for completing toilet training. It is not unusual, however, for some children to take 6 months longer (age 3). Even when problems persist, they may be purely physical. Many bed-wetters, for instance, have difficulty because they become extremely relaxed when asleep. These children can be helped by limiting the amount they drink during the evening. They should also use the toilet before going to bed, and they can be rewarded for "dry" nights. Understanding, tact, and sympathy can do much to alleviate mild disturbances. Where more serious problems exist, parents should seek professional help.

Feeding Disturbances

Feeding disturbances take a variety of forms. The disturbed child may vomit or refuse food for no reason or may drastically overeat or undereat. **Overeating** is sometimes encouraged by a parent who feels unloved and compensates by showering the child with "love" in the form of food. Some parents overfeed simply because they consider a fat baby healthy or desirable. Whatever the case, overfed children develop eating habits and conflicts that have lifelong consequences.

As described in Chapter 10, cases of *undereating*, or self-starvation, are called **anorexia nervosa** (AN-or-REX-yah ner-VOH-sah, nervous loss of appetite). The victims of anorexia nervosa are mostly adolescent females. In addition to the causes described in Chapter 10, anorexia may reflect conflicts about maturing sexually. By starving themselves, adolescent girls can limit figure development and prevent menstruation. This delays the time when they must face adult responsibilities. As discussed in Chapter 10, pressures to conform to unrealistic standards of appearance also often contribute to self-starvation (Nagel & Jones, 1992).

Another childhood eating difficulty is called **pica** (PIE-ka). Some children go through a period of intense appetite during which they eat or chew on all sorts of inedible substances. The two most common substances are plaster and chalk. But some children try to eat things like buttons, rubber bands, mud, or paint flakes. The latter can be quite dangerous because some paint contains lead, which is highly poisonous.

Speech Disturbances

The two most common speech problems are **delayed speech** and **stuttering.** A delay in learning to talk can be a serious handicap. An example is Tommy, who at age 5 was still talking in telegraphic speech: "Me go. Outdoor. Mama in car now. Dink Tommy cup" (Van Riper & Emerick, 1984). Delayed speech is sometimes caused by too little intellectual stimulation in early childhood. Other possible causes are parents who discourage the child's attempts to grow up, childhood stresses, mental retardation, and emotional disturbances.

In the past, stuttering was held to be a psychological disturbance, and many parents were made to feel guilty about their children's speech problems. Now, researchers believe that stuttering usually has physical origins. For example, stuttering is 4 times more common in males than in females, and it seems to be at least partially inherited. However, learned fears, anxieties, and speech patterns probably add to the problem as well (Van Riper & Emerick, 1984).

Stuttering is most likely to occur when a person fears that he or she is going to stutter. Thus, parents must be careful not to add to a child's anxiety and frustration by being angry or critical. If a child begins speech therapy before adolescence, there is a chance that stuttering will disappear. In some cases it may even disappear on its own. But if it doesn't disappear, or isn't treated, stuttering can become a lifelong problem.

Learning Disorders

Soon after Gary entered school, he became shy and difficult. Gary's teacher suspected a learning disability, and a specialist confirmed it. **Learning disorders** include problems with reading, math, or writing. A learning disorder is said to exist when a child's school achievement is well below what would be expected for his or her age and level of intelligence (DSM-IV, 1994). Gary's specific problem was **dyslexia** (dis-LEX-yah), an inability to read with understanding. Because of it, he often felt confused and "stupid" in class, although his intelligence was normal.

Approximately 10 to 15 percent of school-age children have some degree of dyslexia. Dyslexia is sometimes called "word blindness." When dyslexic children try to read, they often reverse letters (such as seeing *b* for *d*) and words (*was* and *saw*, for example). Some also try to read from right to left. Dyslexia appears to be caused by a malfunction of language processing areas on the left side of the brain (Hynd & Semrud-Clikeman, 1989). Dyslexia is typically treated by special educational programs that use exercises in hearing, touch, and vision to improve reading comprehension.

Attention-Deficit Hyperactivity Disorder

One of the most significant childhood problems is **attention-deficit hyperactivity disorder (ADHD)** (McKinney, 1989). The ADHD child is constantly in motion and cannot concentrate (■ Fig. 13–6). The child talks rapidly, cannot sit still, rarely finishes work, acts on impulse, and cannot pay attention. As the term ADHD implies, a child's problem may be primarily cognitive (poor attention) or behavioral (hyperactivity) (Silver, 1990). Usually it is both. ADHD affects 3 to 5 percent of all children, 5 times as many boys as girls. Because they are impulsive, inattentive, and defiant, adolescents and young adults who suffer from ADHD have 4 times as many auto accidents as other young drivers (Ehrman, 1993). Unless it is carefully managed, ADHD frequently leads to school drop-outs and lifelong problems with antisocial behavior (Mannuzza et al., 1993).

Question: What causes attention-deficit hyperactivity disorder?

The problem is believed to result from a brain condition present at birth. Specific areas of the brain associated with language, motor control, and attention are smaller than normal in ADHD children. For reasons that remain a mystery, something appears to interfere with normal growth in these brain areas during fetal development (Riccio et al., 1993).

Many parents believe that their children's hyperactive behavior is triggered by eating sugar. However, a recent, very careful test found that sugary diets have no effect at all on the behavior of either normal or hyperactive children. "Sugar highs" in children appear to be nothing more than a popular myth (Wolraich et al., 1994).

Question: How is ADHD treated?

Treatment for ADHD includes drugs, behavioral management approaches, and family counseling (Silver, 1990). Physicians typically use the stimulant drug Ritalin (methylphenidate) to control ADHD. It might seem that stimulants would make hyperactivity worse. But the drugs actually have a calming effect. Most likely, this is because the drugs lengthen the ADHD child's attention span and reduce impulsiveness (Solanto, 1984).

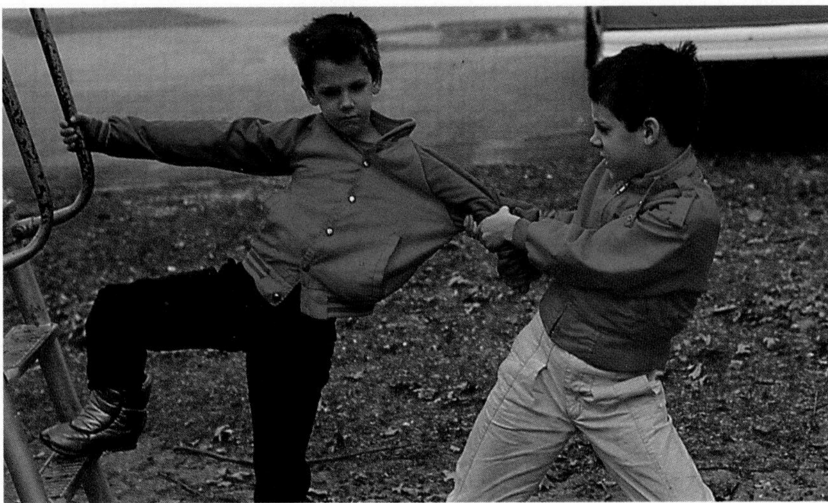

■ **Fig. 13–6** *The ADHD child's inability to hold still and pay attention can seriously disrupt learning.*

Even when it appears to be effective, Ritalin remains controversial. Stimulant drugs can retard physical growth, at least temporarily. Also, many experts believe that some children are wrongly given drugs for ordinary misbehavior, not because they actually suffer from ADHD. Even though 800,000 American children take Ritalin and similar drugs, many questions about their long-term health impact remain unanswered (Rubin, 1990).

Few specialists today would recommend the use of drugs to treat ADHD without also providing therapy for behavioral and emotional problems. For many children, behavior modification is as effective as drug treatment (Carlson et al., 1992). **Behavior modification** is the application of learning principles to change or eliminate maladaptive or abnormal behavior. (See Chapter 18 for more information.) The basic idea is to find times when the ADHD child is calm and paying attention and to reward the child for such behavior. Children are also taught how to monitor their own behavior and how to ignore distractions. When children learn self-control in this way, improvements are more lasting than they are with drug treatment alone (Franks, 1987).

Attention-deficit hyperactivity disorder A behavioral problem characterized by short attention span and restless movement.

Behavior modification Application of learning principles to change or eliminate maladaptive behavior.

Autism A severe disorder involving mutism, sensory spin-outs, sensory blocking, tantrums, unresponsiveness to others, and other difficulties.

Childhood Autism

Childhood **autism** (AW-tiz'm) is a problem that affects 1 in 2500 children, boys 4 times more often than girls. Autism is one of the most severe childhood problems. The autistic child is locked into a private world and appears to have no need for affection or contact with others. Autistic children sometimes do not even seem to know or care who their parents are.

In addition to being extremely isolated, the autistic child may throw gigantic temper tantrums—sometimes including self-destructive behavior such as head

Echolalia A compulsion to repeat everything that is said to them.

Operant shaping Gradually molding responses by rewarding ever-closer approximations to a final desired pattern.

Child abuse Physically or emotionally harming a child; also refers to neglect.

banging. Sadly, many well-meaning parents unintentionally reward such behavior with attention and concern (Edelson, 1984). Many autistic children are mute. If they speak at all, autistic children often infuriatingly parrot back everything said, a response known as **echolalia** (EK-oh-LAY-li-ah). These children also engage in frequent repetitive actions such as rocking, flapping their arms, or waving their fingers in front of their eyes. Additionally, they may show no response to an extremely loud noise (sensory blocking) or they may spend hours watching a water faucet drip (sensory "spin-out") (Rimland, 1978). Finally, autistic persons don't seem to understand what other people are thinking—or even that they do think. This impairment makes the autistic very inept in social situations (Firth, 1993).

Question: Do parents cause autism?

At one time experts blamed parents for autism. It is now recognized that autism is caused by congenital defects in the nervous system. That's why even as babies, autistic children are aloof and do not cuddle or mold to their parents' arms. Brain scans suggest that the defect may lie in the cerebellum, which affects attention and motor activity (Courchesne et al., 1988).

Question: Can anything be done for an autistic child?

Even with help, only about 25 percent of all autistic children approach normalcy and only 2 percent are able to live independently. Nevertheless, almost all autistic children can make progress with proper care. When treatment is begun early, behavior modification has been particularly successful.

Do you remember Billy, the autistic child described earlier? Billy was one of the first patients in a pioneering program designed by psychologist Ivar Lovaas. Billy was selected for the program because of his unusual appetite for hamburgers. Teaching Billy to talk illustrates one aspect of his treatment. It began with his learning to blow out a match—making a sound like "who." Each time he made the "who" sound, Billy was rewarded with a bite of his beloved hamburgers. Next he was rewarded for babbling meaningless sounds. If he accidentally said a word, he was rewarded. After several weeks, he was able to say words such as *ball, milk, mama,* and *me.* By this painstaking process, Billy was eventually taught to talk. Notice that this process is basically an example of **operant shaping,** discussed in Chapter 7.

In a behavior modification program, each of an autistic child's maladaptive behaviors is altered using reward and punishment. In addition to food, therapists have found that sensory stimulation, such as tickling or music, is often very reinforcing for the autistic child (Rincover & Newsom, 1985). And strangely enough, following actions such as head banging and hand biting with punishment can bring a swift end to self-destructive behavior (Haywood et al., 1982). When such efforts are combined with home treatment by parents, considerable progress can be made. A few children, in fact, approach near normal functioning (McEaching, Smith, & Lovaas, 1993).

Autism and other severe childhood problems are a monumental challenge to the ingenuity of psychologists, educators, and parents. However, great strides have been made in the last few years. There is reason to believe that in the future even more help will be available to children who get a bad start in life.

Child Abuse—Cycles of Violence

Sadly, no account of problems in development would be complete without a brief discussion of **child abuse.** Much as we might like to believe otherwise, child abuse is widespread. From 3.5 to 14 percent of all children are physically abused by parents. Even if the lower figure is right, that would mean that 2 million children are physically battered each year in the United States and Canada alone (Browne, 1986). In about one third of all cases of physical abuse, the child is seriously injured. Every year thousands of children are killed by their own parents (Finkelhor & Dziuba-Leatherman, 1994).

Question: What are abusive parents like?

Characteristics of Abusive Parents

Abusive parents are usually young (under 30) and from lower income levels. However, professionals who treat child abuse see parents of all ages and income levels.

Abusive parents often have a high level of stress and frustration in their lives. Typical problems include depression, loneliness, marital discord, unemployment, drug abuse, divorce, family violence, heavy drinking, and work anxieties (Famularo et al., 1992; Giovannoni & Becerra, 1979).

Some parents are aware that they are mistreating a child but are unable to stop. Other abusive parents literally hate their children or are disgusted by them. The child's sloppiness, diapers, crying, or needs are unbearable to the parent. Often these parents expect the child to love them and make them happy. When the child (who is usually under 3 years old) cannot meet such unrealistic demands, the parent reacts with lethal anger. In addition, abusive mothers are more likely to believe that their children are acting *intentionally* to annoy them (Bauer & Twentyman, 1985).

Cycles of Violence The core of much child abuse is a cycle of violence that flows from one generation to the next. Roughly one third of all parents who were abused as children mistreat their own children. A second third do not routinely abuse their children. However, they are likely to do so when stressed (Oliver, 1993). Such parents simply never learned to love, communicate with, or discipline a child. When does the cycle of violence begin? Sad to say, it shows up almost immediately:

Abusive Toddlers

> In a study, abused 1- to 3-year-olds were observed as they interacted with playmates. The question of interest was, How do abused children react when another child is crying or distressed? In almost every instance, abused children responded to distress with fear, threats, or physical assault. (Main & George, 1985)

In short, abused children rapidly become abusive children. Later, many become abusive adults (Oliver, 1993).

Question: How do caring parents who were abused as children differ from abusive parents who continue the cycle of violence?

Adults who are able to break the abusive cycle are more likely to have received emotional support from a non-abusive adult during childhood or to have been in therapy. They also tend to have an emotionally supportive relationship with a mate (Egeland, Jacobvitz, & Sroufe, 1988). Without such support, childhood abuse greatly increases the lifetime risk of emotional problems, substance abuse, and violence (Malinosky-Rummell & Hansen, 1993).

Question: What can be done about child abuse?

Preventing Child Abuse

Many public agencies now have teams to identify battered or neglected children. However, legal "cures" for child abuse are not very satisfying. The courts can take custody of a child, or the parents may voluntarily agree to place the child in a foster home. Foster care can be an improvement, but it may also further traumatize the child. In some cases the child is allowed to remain with the parents, but under court supervision. Even then, there is a chance of further injury, unless the parents get help. Some of the most effective programs teach parents child-care skills and how to manage stress (Wolfe & Wekerle, 1993).

Self-help groups staffed by former child abusers and concerned volunteers are also a major aid to parents. One such group is Parents Anonymous, a national organization of parents determined to help each other stop abusing children. Local groups set up networks of members that parents can call in an abuse crisis or when they feel one coming on. Parents also learn how to curb violent impulses and how to cope with their children. Experts recommend that a parent who is tempted to shake or strike a crying infant should try any of the following (Evans, 1993):

- Leave the room and call a friend.
- Put on some soothing music.
- Take 10 deep breaths and calm yourself; then take 10 more.
- Move to another room and do some exercise.
- Take a shower.
- Sit down, close your eyes, and vividly imagine yourself in a pleasant place.
- If none of the preceding strategies work, seek professional help. (Telephone numbers are listed at the end of this chapter.)

Dangerous Attitudes Another way of preventing child abuse is by changing attitudes. Despite newspaper and TV coverage of the problem, many parents believe it is their "right" to slap or hit their children. A survey of parents found that physical punishment is widely accepted in this country (■ Fig. 13–7). In a

■ Fig. 13–7 *Widespread acceptance of physical punishment creates an atmosphere in which angry parents can easily lose control and abuse their children. Even parents who would never strike a child may fall prey to the "shaken baby syndrome." In such cases, an angry parent violently shakes an infant (often one that won't stop crying). The result can be brain injuries that cause mental retardation, blindness, or even death.*

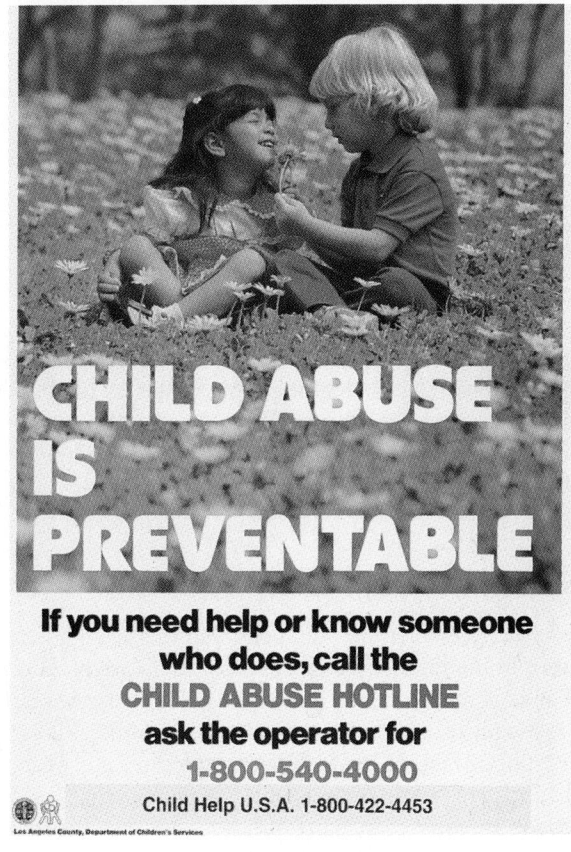

1994 *USA Today* poll, 67 percent of all adults surveyed agreed that, "a good, hard spanking" is sometimes necessary to discipline a child. As a society we seem to say, "Violence is okay if the child isn't injured; if the child is injured, then it's child abuse." Of course, when the child is injured, it's too late to take back the violence. By condoning punishment that borders on abuse, we greatly raise the chances of injury. The best solution to physical abuse, then, may lie in rethinking our attitudes toward physical punishment and toward the rights of children. It is also important to remember that emotional abuse can be just as damaging as physical abuse. Parents inflict long-lasting emotional scars when they persistently humiliate, intimidate, or terrorize their children.

To face the problem squarely, we must realize that the line between acceptable discipline and child abuse is easily blurred. Fortunately, public opinion regarding spanking is starting to shift. Several states have banned spanking in schools. However, child victimization will continue as long as we as a society tolerate it (Finkelhor & Dziuba-Leatherman, 1994).

LEARNING CHECK

See if you can answer these questions before you continue reading.

1. Occasional reversals and regressions to more infantile behavior are sure signs that a significant childhood problem exists. T or F?
2. Sleep disturbances and specific fears can be a sign of significant childhood problems when they are prolonged or exaggerated. T or F?
3. A moderate amount of sibling rivalry is considered normal. T or F?
4. Encopresis is the formal term for lack of bladder control. T or F?
5. The ADHD child is lost in his or her own private world. T or F?
6. According to Diana Baumrind's research, effective parents are authoritarian in their approach to their children's behavior. T or F?
7. Approximately 30 percent of all parents who were abused as children mistreat their own children. T or F?

Critical Thinking

8. Several Scandinavian countries have made it illegal for parents to spank their own children. Does this infringe on the rights of parents?

Answers: 1. F 2. T 3. T 4. F 5. F 6. F 7. T 8. Such laws are based on the view that it should be illegal to physically assault any person, regardless of their age. While parents may believe they have a "right" to spank their children, it can be argued that children need special protection because they are small, powerless, and dependent.

Adolescence The culturally defined period between childhood and adulthood.

Puberty The biologically defined period during which a person matures sexually and becomes capable of reproduction.

Growth spurt An often dramatic acceleration in physical growth that coincides with puberty.

Adolescence—The Best of Times, the Worst of Times

Adolescence is a time of change, exploration, exuberance, and youthful searching. It can also be a time of worry and problems, especially in today's world. It might even be fair to describe adolescence as "the best of times, the worst of times." Just in case you weren't taking notes in junior high, let's survey the challenges of this colorful chapter of life.

Adolescence and Puberty

Adolescence refers to the period during which we move from childhood to acceptance as an adult. This change is recognized in almost all cultures. However, the length of adolescence varies greatly from culture to culture (Siegel, 1982). For example, most 14-year-old girls in North America live at home and go to school. In contrast, many 14-year-old females in rural villages of the Near East are married and have children (Santrock, 1993). In our culture, 14-year-olds are adolescents. In others, they may be adults.

Many people confuse adolescence with puberty. But as you can see, the culturally defined period of adolescence differs from puberty, which is a *biological* event. **Puberty** refers to rapid physical growth, coupled with hormonal changes that bring sexual maturity. Interestingly, the peak **growth spurt** during puberty occurs earlier for girls than for boys (■ Fig. 13–8). This difference accounts for the 1- to 2-year period when girls tend to be taller than boys. (Remember going to dances where the girls towered over the boys?) For girls the onset of puberty typically occurs between 11 and 14 years of age. For most boys the age range is 13 to 16 years (Kaluger & Kaluger, 1984).

Biologically, most people reach reproductive maturity in the early teens. Social and intellectual maturity, however, may still lie years ahead. Young adolescents often make fateful decisions that affect their entire lives, even though they are immature in cognitive development, knowledge, and social experience. The tragically high rates of teenage pregnancies and drug abuse in many western nations are prime examples. The younger an adolescent becomes sexually active, delinquent, or involved with drugs, the more the resulting damage (White & DeBlassie, 1992).

When you were going through puberty, did you ever spend *hours* preparing to attend a party, dance, or other social event? If you did, you weren't alone. Puberty tends to dramatically increase body awareness and concerns about physical appearance. Beyond this, about one half of all boys and one-third of all girls report being dissatisfied with their appearance during early adolescence (Rosenbaum, 1979). In many instances, such feelings are related to the *timing* of puberty. Girls who are temporarily "too tall," boys who are "too small," and both boys and girls who lag in sexual development are likely to be upset about their bodies (Petersen et al., 1991).

Question: How much difference does the timing of puberty make?

Early and Late Maturation Because puberty involves so many rapid changes, it can be stressful for just about anyone. When puberty comes unusually early or late, its impact may be magnified—for both good and bad.

For boys, maturing early is generally beneficial. Typically, it enhances their self-image and gives them an advantage socially and athletically (Petersen, 1987). For such reasons, early-maturing boys tend to be more poised, relaxed, dominant, self-assured, and popular with their peers (Santrock, 1993). Many late-maturing boys are anxious about being behind in development. However, after they catch up they tend to be more eager, talkative, self-assertive, and tolerant of themselves than average maturers.

For girls, the advantages of early maturation are less clear-cut. In elementary school, developmentally advanced girls tend to have *less* prestige among peers. Presumably, this is because they are larger and heavier than their classmates. By junior high, however, early development includes secondary sexual characteristics. This leads to a more positive body image, *greater* peer prestige, and adult approval (Brooks-Gunn & Warren, 1988). In contrast, later-maturing girls have the possible advantage of usually growing taller and thinner than early-maturing girls. Other relevant findings are that early-maturing girls date sooner and are more independent and more active in school; they are also more often in trouble at school (Siegel, 1982).

As you can see, there are costs and benefits associated with both early and late puberty. One added cost of early maturation is that it may force premature identity formation (Siegel, 1982). When a teenager begins to look like an adult, he or she may be treated like an adult. Ideally, this change can encourage greater maturity and independence. But what happens when a person is treated as an adult before he or she is emotionally ready? Then the search for identity may end too soon, leaving the person with a distorted, poorly formed sense of self (see Highlight 13–1).

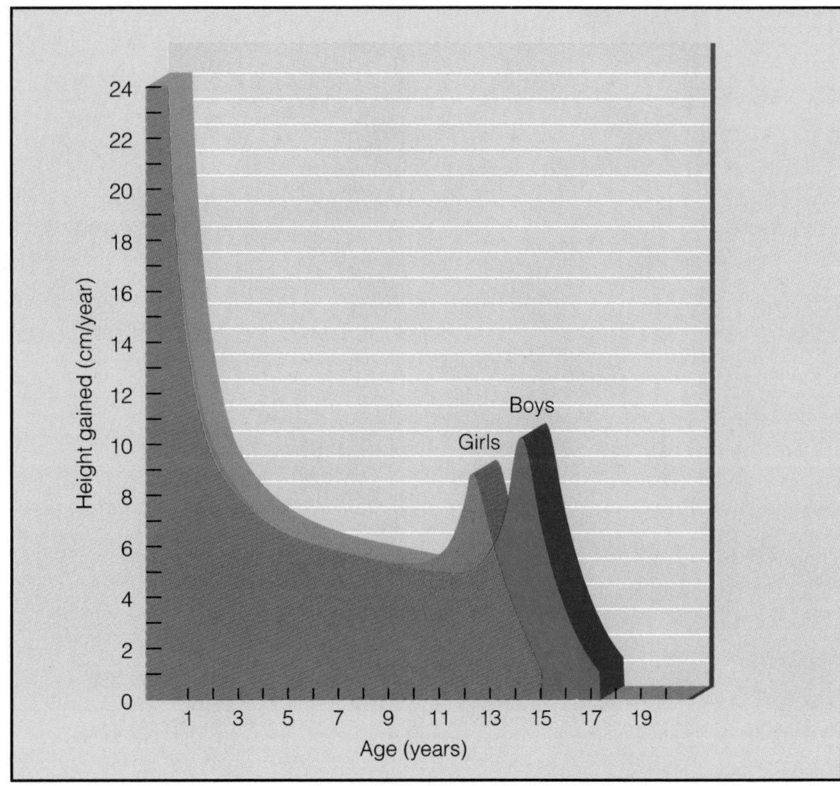

■ **Fig. 13–8** *The typical rate of growth for boys and girls. Notice that growth in early adolescence equals that for ages 1 to 3. Note too the earlier growth spurt for girls.*

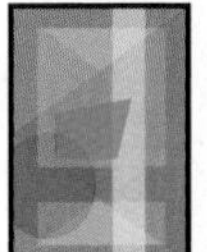

HIGHLIGHT 13–1

Focus on a Controversy

Hurried into Adulthood?

Psychologist David Elkind (1981) believes that many parents are hurrying their children's development. Elkind is concerned about parents who try to raise their babies' IQs, force them to "read" flash cards, or have them swimming and doing gymnastics before they are 3 months old. Such pushing, he believes, partly explains why more children have recently begun to show serious stress symptoms. Moreover, hurried children are turning into hurried teenagers—urged by parents

■ **Fig. 13–9** *Typical clothing worn by young adolescents 40 years ago and today.*

Social markers Visible or tangible signs that indicate a person's social status or role.

Imaginary audience The group of people a person imagines is watching (or will watch) his or her actions.

and the media alike to grow up fast (■Fig. 13–9). Elkind believes that too many teenagers are left without the guidance, direction, and support they need to become healthy adults (Elkind, 1984).

Elkind's main point is that today's teenagers have adulthood thrust on them too soon. Violence, drug abuse, X-rated movies, youth crime, teenage pregnancy, divorce and single parent families, date rape, aimless schools—all this, and more, strikes Elkind as evidence that there is no place for teenagers in today's society.

According to Elkind, the traditional **social markers** of adolescence have all but disappeared. (Markers are signs that tell where a person stands socially—such as a driver's license or a wedding ring.) As an example, Elkind notes that clothing for children and teenagers is increasingly adult-like. Girls especially are urged to wear seductive clothing and revealing swimsuits.

Clearly, Elkind is stating a clinical opinion. It's possible that his view exaggerates the problem somewhat—indeed, much of what he says is debatable. Nevertheless, his portrayal of hurried adolescents as "all grown up with no place to go" is highly thought provoking.

Search for Identity

As discussed earlier, many psychologists regard identity formation as a key task of adolescence. To be sure, problems of identity occur at other times too. But in a very real sense, puberty signals that the time has arrived to begin forming a new, more mature image of oneself. Answering the question, "Who am I?" is also spurred by cognitive development. After adolescents have attained the stage of formal operations, they are better able to ask questions about their place in the world and about morals, values, politics, social relationships, and private thoughts. Then too, being able to think about hypothetical possibilities allows the adolescent to contemplate the future and ask more realistically, "Who will I be?" (Suls, 1989).

David Elkind has noted another interesting pattern in adolescent thought. According to Elkind (1984), many teenagers are preoccupied with **imaginary audiences.** That is, they act like others are as aware of their thoughts and feelings as they are themselves. Sometimes this leads to painful self-consciousness—as in thinking that *everyone* is staring at a bad haircut you just received. The imaginary audience also seems to underlie attention-seeking "performances" involving outlandish dress or behavior. In any case, adolescents become very concerned with controlling the impressions they make on others (Santrock, 1993). For many, being "on stage" in this way helps define the shape of an emerging identity.

Question: What effects do parents have on identity formation?

Parents and Peers The adolescent search for identity frequently leads to increased conflict with parents. This is especially true in early adolescence (Eccles et al., 1993). However, some conflict with parents is probably necessary for growth of a separate identity. A complete lack of conflict may mean that the adolescent is afraid to seek independence.

Actually, adolescents and parents usually agree to a large degree about basic topics such as religion, marriage, and morals. The largest conflicts tend to be over more superficial differences regarding styles of dress, manners, social behavior, and the like. Adolescents naturally desire more freedom, but they do not want their parents to abruptly abandon them. Teenagers do best when they are given gradual increases in personal freedom and more opportunities to make decisions. Problems occur when parents crack down too hard or throw their hands up and surrender control over the adolescent's behavior (Eccles et al., 1993).

In high school were you a jock, preppy, brain, hacker, surfer, cowboy, punk, mod, druggie, warthog, dervish, gargoyle, or aardvark? (Well, okay, I made up the last four—the rest are real.) Increased identifica-

QUALITY TIME
Gail Machlis
I never really knew my father; he was always videotaping me.
© 1993 Chronicle Features
machlis

■ Fig. 13–10 *Membership in friendship groups, cliques, "posses," or "crews" helps adolescents build an identity apart from their relationship to parents. However, over-identification with a clannish group that rejects anyone who looks or acts different can limit personal growth.*

tion with **peer groups** is quite common during adolescence. To an extent, membership in such groups gives a measure of security and a sense of identity apart from the family. Beyond this, group membership provides practice in belonging to a social network. Children tend to see themselves more as members of families and small friendship groups, not as members of society as a whole. Therefore, gaining a broader, member-of-society perspective can be a major step toward adulthood (Hill, 1993) (■ Fig. 13–10).

Question: But aren't groups also limiting?

Yes, they are. Conformity to peer values peaks in early adolescence, but it remains strong at least through high school (Newman, 1982). Throughout this period there is always a danger of allowing group pressure to **foreclose** personal growth (Newman & Newman, 1987). By the end of high school, many adolescents have not yet sufficiently explored various interests, values, vocations, skills, or ideologies on their own (see Highlight 13–2). Perhaps this is why many students view moving on to work or college as a chance to break out of earlier roles—to expand or reshape personal identity. For many who choose college, the effect may be more a matter of placing further changes in identity on hold. By doing so, college students keep open the possibility of changing majors, career plans, personal style, and so on. Typically, commitment to an emerging adult identity grows stronger in later college years (Santrock, 1993).

Peer group A group of people who share similar social status.

HIGHLIGHT 13–2

Cultural Diversity

Minority Youth and the Search for Identity

As they define an adult identity, minority adolescents often face a barrage of prejudice and negative stereotypes from the majority culture (Spencer, 1990). In many ways, society seems to say to them, "You are invisible," "You are bad," or "You are not one of us." This discourages contact with members of the majority culture and limits the "trying on" of various identities and values.

For such reasons, and others as well, minority adolescents run a high risk of adopting a personal identity prematurely (Spencer & Markstron-Adams, 1990). The danger in this is that it severely limits the exploration of various life paths. Too often, these "foreclosed" identities take forms such as gang member, school drop-out, unskilled laborer, unmarried parent, or "second-class citizen."

Minority youth, of course, share the same hopes, dreams, and aspirations as any other social group. What they frequently do not share is the means to attain their goals. As psychologist Margaret Beale Spencer (1990) says, "Broader American culture could be enriched by the talents, creativity, and intelligence of minority youngsters who have been provided the opportunity to reach their potentials." Before that can happen, minority youth need to feel that they have a positive role to play in society. Enhanced group pride, educational opportunities, positive models,

Career development One's entire career path, from choosing an initial occupation through retirement.

Exploration phase The period during which career alternatives are explored.

Establishment phase The period during which a person enters a career and builds competence in it.

Midcareer phase A stable central career phase marked by high competence and full status.

Later career phase The concluding career phase prior to retirement; marked by high status and respect arising from long experience.

Fantasy stage Stage of career exploration in which persons imagine themselves filling unlikely roles.

Tentative stage Stage of career exploration in which planning becomes more realistic, although still broad.

Realistic stage Stage of career exploration in which career options are narrowed and more specific plans are made.

and a more tolerant society could do much to keep a broad range of options open to *all* of today's youth (Blechman, 1992).

The search for identity we have discussed here may be intensified during adolescence, but it does not end there. For example, the process of selecting a career often starts in childhood and continues into young adulthood. In the next section we will take a brief look at this interesting aspect of personal development.

Vocational Choice—Charting a Course in the World of Work

John was always an excellent student, but his real love was sports. Being on the track team was, in fact, the high point of his college career. (About 7 feet high, to be exact. John was a high-jumper.) After he graduated, John was hired by a large accounting firm at an enviable starting salary. Yet within 2 years, John knew he had made a mistake. Accounting left him dissatisfied, restless, and often bored.

In college, John's career choice had seemed highly practical. Now he was miserable. What could he do about it? John decided to take a chance. He quit his job, and after several years of additional education, financial hardship, and personal sacrifice, he accepted his first college coaching position.

Vocational Choice

As John's story illustrates, vocational decisions are neither permanent nor easily undone. Usually, by the time a person has selected a career path, it takes a big effort to change course. Moreover, changing careers can be a major risk. (What if John had discovered that he also disliked coaching?) The reality that John faced is illustrated by a survey in which 44 percent of those polled said that for better or worse, they felt "locked into" their current jobs (Renwick & Lawler, 1979). Clearly, there is value in making good vocational choices, and in making them early, if possible.

Career Development John's abrupt change is somewhat unusual. For most people who enter professions, **career development** tends to flow through four broad phases (■ Fig. 13–11). These are: (1) the **exploration phase,** during which an initial search for career possibilities is made; (2) the **establishment phase,** during which the person finds a job, enters a career, develops competence, and gains status; (3) the **midcareer phase,** which is a time of high productivity and acceptance by co-workers; and (4) the **later career phase,** when the individual serves as a respected expert and often as a mentor (role model and guide) for younger workers (Van Maanen & Schein, 1977).

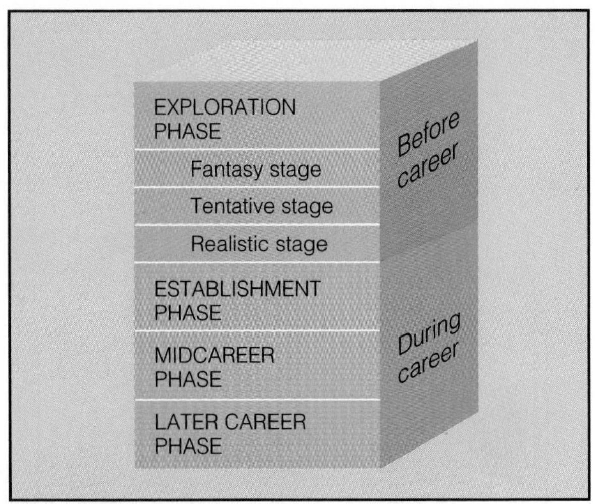

■ **Fig. 13–11** *A model of career development. The exploration phase can be divided into three substages of vocational choice.*

Of the four phases, the one most likely to be of immediate relevance to you is exploration. Let's probe this phase in more depth.

Question: How do most people choose their vocations?

During the exploration phase, most people go through a recognizable series of stages as they choose a vocation (Ginzberg, 1984).

In the **fantasy stage,** children under age 10 simply *imagine* what they want to be when they grow up. The roles they fantasize—such as president, pilot, rock star, rodeo rider, or TV announcer—may be unrealistic, but they do show that children realize that they will need to work someday.

During the **tentative stage** (roughly, ages 10 to 18) adolescents begin to form more realistic, if somewhat general, ideas about what they want to do. However, their plans may shift several times during this period, and they typically remain tentative. Toward the end of high school, many students begin to more fully appreciate the importance of choosing a vocation. They also become aware that there are limits to their options and barriers to certain careers.

After high school, various social and practical pressures lead most people to narrow their range of vocational options. During this **realistic stage,** the first steps are taken to find out what specific jobs are like and to prepare for them. At this time, many college students use course work as a way to discover what they are good at and what holds their interest.

By the early 20s, most people begin to carry out their vocational plans. This involves completing necessary training and landing that important first job.

The preceding description implies that most people carefully choose a vocation or career. Actually, there is evidence that vocational choice is often rather haphazard (Janis & Wheeler, 1978). For example, it is not unusual for students to allow a tentative choice of a major to determine school course work. Soon, they find themselves channeled into a career path—without really having made a clear decision.

Question: How would a person go about improving the quality of his or her vocational choice?

To begin with, it helps to recognize that our attraction to certain jobs or careers is influenced by many factors. Some of the more important influences are socioeconomic status, intelligence, school achievement, family background, gender, and personal interests (Kaplan & Stein, 1984). As much as these factors may influence your own choice, it is also important to realize that you have the potential to succeed in a variety of occupations. This is reflected by the fact that the best single predictor of what job category you will enter is your **vocational aspiration,** which is simply what you tell yourself you would like to do.

The world of work is complex and rapidly changing. In the face of such changes, it is becoming more important to make careful, informed decisions about what kind of work you would like to do. To make sure your vocational choice will be realistic and personally rewarding, you must (1) gain an accurate understanding of various occupations and (2) get a clear picture of your own interests, needs, and goals.

Question: That seems obvious. But how?

Vocational Counseling A good way to improve occupational choice is to consult a **vocational counselor.** These professionals are counseling psychologists who have specialized in the skills and knowledge needed to match people with jobs. A vocational counselor can help you clarify your career goals, and he or she can administer vocational interest and aptitude tests to guide your choice. Many colleges now offer vocational counseling at campus **career centers.** These centers also typically hold a wealth of information about various jobs and careers. Many offer computerized programs that guide students through the initial steps of career decision making (Katz, 1993). (An introductory discussion of careers in psychology appears in Appendix A, near the end of this text.)

If formal guidance is unavailable, you will have to serve as your own "vocational counselor." A good way to start is to consult the *Occupational Outlook Handbook,* available in most libraries. This book, published yearly by the U.S. Department of Labor, provides objective information about the outlook for various occupations. The *Handbook* includes job descriptions, information on training requirements, average earnings, and the number of jobs likely to be available in coming years. A simple look at such facts could prevent many students from pursuing over-populated careers (law, for instance).

To find out what a particular job is really like may require more initiative. In many occupations the nature of the work is not what it seems from the outside. For instance, medical students are often dismayed when they first begin to realize that disease is ugly and that many medical procedures are distasteful. To find out beforehand what an occupation is like, it is advisable to talk to several people in that line of work. Be sure to ask your informants what they dislike about their jobs, as well as what they like. If possible, you might even spend a day observing people in an occupation that interests you.

Beginning a career is only one of the major challenges of adulthood. We'll explore others in a moment. Before you read more, here's a chance to check your progress.

Vocational aspiration The vocation one would like to have.

Vocational counselor A counseling psychologist who helps people match their interests, talents, and goals with available careers.

Career center A counseling facility that offers testing, career guidance, and information on various careers.

Learning Check

1. In most societies, adolescence begins with the onset of puberty and ends with its completion. T or F?
2. Early-maturing boys tend to experience more clear-cut advantages than do early-maturing girls. T or F?
3. According to David Elkind, the traditional markers of adolescence and adulthood have been blurred. T or F?
4. The imaginary audience refers to conformity pressures that adolescents believe adults apply to them. T or F?
5. The establishment phase of career development is a time during which an initial search for career possibilities is made. T or F?
6. Many people go through a ____________________ stage and a ____________________ stage before they become more realistic about choosing a career.
7. The best single predictor of what occupations college students will enter is their IQ scores. T or F?
8. Elkind suggests that many adolescents are "hurried into adulthood." Yet, many young people live at home longer than ever before (often into their early 20s). Does this contradict Elkind's thesis? *Critical Thinking*

Answers: 1. F 2. T 3. T 4. F 5. F 6. fantasy, tentative 7. F 8. Not necessarily. Prolonged dependence on parents appears to be based on economic pressures, not on an extension of adolescent social status.

Transition period Time span during which a person leaves an existing life pattern behind and moves into a new pattern.

Challenges of Adulthood—Charting Life's Ups and Downs

After a "settling down" period somewhere in the 20s, adult development is uniform and uninteresting, right? Wrong! A fairly predictable series of challenges is associated with development from adolescence to old age.

Question: What personality changes and psychological developments can a person look forward to in adulthood?

Further study has added important detail to the events discussed by Erikson. One informative account is based on clinical work by Roger Gould, a psychiatrist interested in adult personality. Gould's research (1975) reveals that common patterns for American adults are as follows.

Ages 16–18: Escape from Dominance Ages 16 to 18 are marked by a struggle to escape from parental dominance. Efforts to do so cause considerable anxiety about the future and conflicts about continuing dependence on parents.

Ages 18–22: Leaving the Family The majority of people break away from their families in their early 20s. Leaving home is usually associated with building new friendships with other adults. These friends serve as substitutes for the family and as allies in the process of breaking ties.

Ages 22–28: Building a Workable Life The trend in the mid-20s is to seek mastery of the real world. Two dominant activities are striving for accomplishment (seeking competence) and reaching out to others. Note that the second activity corresponds to Erikson's emphasis on seeking intimacy at this time. Married couples in this age group tend to place a high value on "togetherness."

Ages 29–34: Crisis of Questions Around the age of 30 many people experience a minor life crisis. The heart of this crisis is a serious questioning of what life is all about. Assurance about previous choices and values tends to waver. Unsettled by these developments, the person actively searches for a style of living that will bring meaning to the second half of life. Marriages are particularly vulnerable during this time of dissatisfaction. Extramarital affairs and divorces are common symptoms of the "crisis of questions."

Ages 35–43: Crisis of Urgency People of ages 35 to 43 are typically beginning to become more aware of the reality of death. Having a limited number of years to live begins to exert pressure on the individual. Intensified attempts are made to succeed at a career or to achieve one's life goals. Generativity, in the form of nurturing, teaching, or serving others, helps alleviate many of the anxieties of this stage.

Ages 43–50: Attaining Stability The urgency of the previous stage gives way to a calmer acceptance of one's fate in the late 40s. The predominant feeling is that the die is cast and that former decisions can be lived with. Those who have families begin to appreciate their children as individuals and ease up on their tendency to extend their own goals to their children's behavior.

Age 50 and Up: Mellowing After age 50 a noticeable mellowing occurs. Emphasis is placed on sharing day-to-day joys and sorrows. There is less concern with glamour, wealth, accomplishment, and abstract goals. Many of the tensions of earlier years give way to a desire to savor life and its small pleasures. (A recent study of typical life goals and concerns at various ages parallels many of the points made by Gould. See Table 13–2.)

Question: Where does the midlife crisis fit in?

A Midlife Crisis?

It is clear that difficulty at the midpoint of life is not universal. Many people thrive during this period and have no special problems. However, psychologist Daniel Levinson carried out an in-depth study of adult lives that shows what a "midlife crisis" looks like if one does occur. Levinson (1978, 1986) identifies 5 periods during adulthood when people typically make major transitions (Table 13–3). A **transition period** ends one life pattern and opens the door to new possibilities (Levinson, 1986). At such times, people address concerns about themselves, their work, and their relationships to others.

Table 13–2 Typical Life Goals and Concerns

	Typical goals are related to:	Typical concerns are related to:
Young adults	Education and family	Relationships and friends
Middle-aged	Children's lives and personal property	Occupational worries
Elderly	Good health, retirement, leisure, community	Health fears

Nurmi, 1992.

Table 13-3 Three Views of Developmental Challenges

Erikson	Gould	Levinson
CHILDHOOD		
Trust/mistrust (1) Autonomy/shame, doubt (1–3) Initiative/guilt (3–5) Industry/inferiority (6–12)		
ADOLESCENCE		
Identity/confusion (12–18)	Escape from dominance (16–18)	Early adulthood transition (17–22)
EARLY ADULTHOOD		
Intimacy/isolation	Leaving the family (18–22) Building a workable life (22–28) Crisis of questions (29–34)	Early adulthood transition (17–22) Age 30 transition (28–33)
MIDDLE ADULTHOOD		
Generativity/self-absorption	Crisis of urgency (35–43) Attaining stability (43–50) Mellowing (50+)	 Midlife transition (40–45) Age 50 transition (50–55)
LATE ADULTHOOD		
		Late adult transition (60–65)
OLD AGE		
Integrity/despair		

Levinson found that most of his subjects (all males) went through a period of instability, anxiety, and change between the ages of 37 and 41 as they approached the midlife transition. (Notice that this corresponds closely to Gould's crisis-of-urgency period.) Levinson believes that most of what he has said about men's lives also applies to women (Levinson, in press). At the very least, both men and women appear to move through repeated cycles of stability and transition in adulthood (Ornstein & Isabella, 1990).

Roughly one half of all the men studied by Levinson defined the midlife period as a sort of "last chance" to achieve their goals. Such goals were often stated as a key event—for example, attaining a supervisory position, achieving a certain income, becoming a full professor, or shop steward, and so forth. For these individuals the midlife period is stressful, but manageable.

A smaller percentage of men experienced a serious midlife decline. Often, this pattern was based on having chosen a dead-end job or lifestyle. In some cases it meant that subjects had achieved material success but they felt that what they were doing was pointless.

In a third pattern, a few hardy individuals appeared to be "breaking out" of a seriously flawed life structure. For them, a decision to "start over" was typically followed by 8 to 10 years of rebuilding.

Thus, it can be seen that the midlife transition, if it occurs at all, can be both a danger and an opportunity. Ideally it is a time of reworking old identities, of achieving long-sought goals, of finding one's own truths, and of preparing for later maturity and aging. It is important to emphasize again, however, that many people's lives differ greatly from the generalized summaries given here. Adult development is complex and each person's path through life is unique.

HIGHLIGHT 13–3

Using Psychology

Making Career Decisions

Question: Why do adults always ask children what they want to be when they grow up?

Answer: Because they're looking for good ideas.

Making career transitions is one of the major challenges of adulthood. One way to improve career decisions is to examine how you approach them. Psychologist Irving Janis and Dan Wheeler (1978) have described how people typically deal with work dilemmas, especially those that lead to a

■ **Fig. 13–17** *Social centers and exercise programs for senior citizens are a direct expression of the benefits predicted by activity theory. Remaining active may also give older persons a feeling of control over their lives. As discussed in Chapter 11, feelings of control contribute to mental and physical well-being.*

jection of the elderly. As Alex Comfort (1976) points out, the concept of "oldness" is often used to expel people from useful work. According to Comfort, retirement is frequently just another name for dismissal and unemployment.

Another facet of ageism is stereotyping of the aged. Popular stereotypes of the "dirty old man," "meddling old woman," "senile old fool," and the like, help perpetuate the myths underlying ageism. Contrast such images to those associated with youthfulness: The young are perceived as fresh, whole, attractive, energetic, active, emerging, appealing, and so forth. Even positive stereotypes can be a problem. If older people are perceived as financially well off, wise, or experienced, it can blind others to the real problems of the elderly (Gatz & Pearson, 1988). The important point, then, is to realize that there is a tremendous diversity among the elderly—ranging from the infirm and senile, to aerobic-dancing grandmothers.

Question: What can be done about ageism?

Countering Myths about Aging

One of the best ways to combat ageism is to counter stereotypes with facts. For example, studies show that in many occupations older workers perform better at jobs requiring *both* speed and skill (Giniger et al., 1983). Gradual slowing with age is a reality. But often, it is countered by experience, skill, or expertise (Schaie, 1988). One study, for example, showed that older typists responded slower on reaction-time tests than younger typists. Nevertheless, there was no difference in the actual typing speeds of younger and older typists (Salthouse, 1987). Rather than basing retirement on a person's age, it would make more sense, perhaps, to base it on job performance.

Taking a broader view, Bernice Neugarten (1971) examined the lives of 200 people between the ages of 70 and 79. Neugarten found that 75 percent of these people were satisfied with their lives after retirement. Similarly, another study found that only 30 percent of retired persons find retirement stressful (Bosse et al., 1991). Neugarten's findings also refuted other myths about aging.

1. Old persons generally do not become isolated and neglected by their families. Most *prefer* to live apart from their children.
2. Old persons are rarely placed in mental hospitals by uncaring children.
3. Old persons who live alone are not necessarily lonely or desolate.
4. Few elderly persons ever show signs of senility or mental decay, and few ever become mentally ill.

In short, most of the elderly studied by Neugarten were integrated, active, and psychologically healthy. As psychologist Carol Ryff (1989) has pointed out, the six criteria of well-being in old age are as follows:

- Self-acceptance
- Positive relations with others
- Autonomy (personal freedom)
- Environmental mastery
- A purpose in life
- Continued personal growth

It is revealing to note that the same list could apply at any age during adulthood.

Enlightened views of aging call for an end to the forced obsolescence of the elderly. As a group, older people represent a valuable source of skill, knowledge, and energy that we can no longer afford to cast aside. As we face the challenges of this planet's uncertain future, we need all the help we can get!

Death and Dying—The Curtain Falls

DEAR ABBY: Do you think about dying much? *(signed)* CURIOUS

DEAR CURIOUS: No, it's the last thing I want to do.

"I'm not afraid of dying. I just don't want to be there when it happens." Woody Allen

Death is a topic of importance to us all. The statistics on death are very convincing: One out of one dies. In spite of this, there tends to be a conspiracy of silence surrounding the topic of death. As a result, most of us

■ Fig. 13–18 *Death may be inevitable, but it can be faced with dignity and, sometimes, even humor. Mel Blanc's famous sign-off, "That's all folks," is engraved on a marble headstone over his grave. Blanc was the voice of Bugs Bunny, Porky Pig, and many other cartoon characters.*

are poorly informed about a process that is as basic as birth.

We have seen in this chapter that it is valuable to understand major trends in the course of development. With this in mind, let us now explore emotional responses to death, the inevitable conclusion of every life (■ Fig. 13–18).

Fears of Death

Fears of death are not so extensive as might be supposed. In a poll of 1500 adults, only about 4 percent showed evidence of directly fearing their own death (Kastenbaum & Aisenberg, 1972). It might seem that as people grow older they would become more fearful of death. However, older persons actually have fewer death fears than younger people. Older people more often fear the *circumstances* of dying, such as pain or helplessness, rather than death itself (Thorson & Powell, 1990). For many people, to die well is no less an accomplishment than to live well (Rinpoche, 1992).

These findings seem to indicate a general lack of death fears, but there is another possibility. It may be more accurate to say that they reflect a deeply ingrained denial of death. The mere fact that death has been something of a taboo subject suggests that underlying fears do exist. The average person's exposure to death consists of the artificial and unrealistic portrayals of death on TV. By the time the average person is 17 years old, he or she will have witnessed roughly 18,000 TV deaths. With few exceptions these will have been *homicides*, not deaths due to illness or aging (Oskamp, 1984).

Reactions to Impending Death

A more direct account of emotional responses to death comes from the work of Elizabeth Kübler-Ross (1975). Kübler-Ross is a **thanatologist** (THAN-ah-TOL-oh-jist: one who studies death) who spent hundreds of hours at the bedsides of the terminally ill. She found that dying persons tend to display several emotional reactions as they prepare for death. Five basic reactions are described here.

Thanatologist A specialist who studies emotional and behavioral reactions to death and dying.

Denial Protecting oneself from an unpleasant reality by refusing to perceive it or believe it.

Depression A state of deep despondency marked by apathy, emotional negativity, and behavioral inhibition.

1. **Denial and isolation.** A typical first reaction to impending death is an attempt to deny its reality and to isolate oneself from information confirming that death is really going to occur. Initially the person may be sure that "It's all a mistake," that lab reports or X-rays have been mixed up, or that a physician is in error. This may proceed to attempts to ignore or avoid any reminder of the situation.
2. **Anger.** Many dying individuals feel anger and ask, "Why me?" As they face the ultimate threat of having everything they value stripped away, their anger can spill over into rage or envy toward those who will continue living. Even good friends may temporarily evoke anger because their health is envied.
3. **Bargaining.** In another common reaction the terminally ill bargain with themselves or with God. The dying person thinks, "Just let me live a little longer and I'll do anything to earn it." Individuals may bargain for time by trying to be "good" ("I'll never smoke again"), by righting past wrongs, or by praying that if they are granted more time they will dedicate themselves to their religion.
4. **Depression.** As death draws near and the person begins to recognize that it cannot be prevented, feelings of futility, exhaustion, and deep depression may set in. The person recognizes that he or she will be separated from friends, loved ones, and the familiar routines of life, and this causes a profound sadness.
5. **Acceptance.** If death is not sudden, many people manage to come to terms with dying and accept it calmly. The person who accepts death is neither happy nor sad, but at peace with the inevitable. Acceptance usually signals that the struggle with death has been resolved. The need to talk about death ends, and silent companionship from others is frequently all that is desired.

Not all terminally ill persons display all these reactions, nor do they always occur in this order. Individual styles of dying vary greatly, according to emotional maturity, religious belief, age, education, the attitudes of relatives, and so forth. Generally, there

Near-death experience A pattern of experiences that may occur when a person is clinically dead and then resuscitated.

does tend to be a movement from initial shock, denial, and anger toward eventual acceptance of the situation. However, some people who seem to have accepted death may die angry and raging against the inevitable. Conversely, the angry fighter may let go of the struggle and die peacefully. In general, one's approach to dying will mirror his or her style of living (DeSpelder & Strickland, 1983).

It is best not to think of Kübler-Ross' list as a fixed series of stages to go through in order. It is an even bigger mistake to assume that someone who does not show all the listed emotional reactions is somehow deviant or immature (Shneidman, 1987). Rather, the list describes typical reactions to impending death. It is also interesting to note that many of the same reactions accompany any major loss, be it divorce, loss of a home due to fire, death of a pet, or loss of a job.

Question: How can I make use of this information?

First, it can help both the dying individual and survivors recognize and cope with periods of depression, anger, denial, and bargaining. Second, it helps to realize that close friends or relatives of the dying person may feel many of the same emotions before or after the person's death because they, too, are facing a loss.

Perhaps the most important thing to recognize is that the dying person may have a need to share feelings with others and to discuss death openly. Too often, the dying person feels isolated and separated from others by the wall of silence erected by doctors, nurses, and family members. Adults tend to "freeze up" with a dying person, saying things such as, "I don't know how to deal with this."

■ **Fig. 13–19** *Visual sensations in the form of a tunnel of light or a spiral can be induced by many conditions other than near-death experiences. Such patterns appear to be related to activity in the visual cortex of the brain—especially those that occur when the brain is deprived of oxygen (Blackmore, 1993).*

Understanding what the dying person is going through may make it easier for you to offer support at this important time. A simple willingness to be with the person and to honestly share his or her feelings can help bring dignity, acceptance, and meaning to death.

Emotional reactions to impending death tell us little about what it is actually like to die. As described in Highlight 13–5, many people have "died" and then lived to tell about it. Let's see what can be learned from their very close encounters with death.

HIGHLIGHT 13–5

Focus on a Controversy

Near-Death Experiences—Back from the Brink

The emergency room doctors work feverishly over a heart attack victim. "I think we've lost him," says one of the doctors. The patient, who appears to have died, hears the doctor's words, then a buzzing sound. From somewhere above, he sees his own lifeless body on the table. Then he enters a dark tunnel and passes into an area of bright light. There, he is met by a "being of light" who shows him a rapid playback of his entire life. At some point he reaches a barrier. He is completely at peace and feels engulfed by love, but he knows he must go back. Suddenly, he is in his body again. One of the doctors exclaims, "Look his heart's beating!" The patient recovers. For the rest of his life, he is profoundly affected by his journey to the threshold of death and back.

The preceding description contains all the core elements of a **near-death experience (NDE).** People who die a "clinical" death and are then resuscitated typically experience all or most of the following: a feeling of separation from their body, entering darkness or a tunnel, seeing a light, entering the light, a life review, feeling at peace.

Many people regard NDEs as spiritual experiences that seem to verify the existence of an afterlife. In contrast, medical explanations attribute NDEs to the physiological reactions of an oxygen-starved brain (■ Fig. 13–19). Indeed, many elements of NDEs can be produced by other conditions, such as hallucinogenic drugs, migraine headaches, general anesthetics, extreme fatigue, high fever, or just falling asleep.

While debate about the meaning of NDEs continues, one thing is certain: Near-death experiences can profoundly change personality and life goals. Many near-death survivors claim that they are no longer motivated by greed, competition, or material success. Instead, they become more concerned about other people and their needs.

There is a degree of comfort in knowing that people who have "died" and lived to tell about it were not frightened or in pain. Beyond that, perhaps we can learn something from such close encounters with death. As many near-death survivors have learned, death can be an excellent yardstick for measuring what is really important in life. (Sources: Blackmore, 1991, 1993; Kellehear, 1993; Moody, 1975; Ring, 1980.)

■ **Fig. 13–20** *As cultural rituals, funerals encourage a release of emotion and provide a sense of closure for survivors, who must come to terms with the death of a loved one.*

Bereavement and Grief

Typically, a period of grief follows **bereavement** (the loss of a friend or relative to death). **Grief** is a natural and normal reaction as survivors adjust to their loss.

Grief tends to follow a predictable pattern (Parkes, 1979; Schulz, 1978). Grief usually begins with a period of **shock** or numbness. For a brief time the bereaved remain in a dazed state in which they may show little emotion. Most find it extremely difficult to accept the reality of their loss. This phase usually ends by the time of the funeral, which unleashes tears and bottled-up feelings of despair (■ Fig. 13–20).

Initial shock is followed by sharp **pangs of grief.** These are episodes of painful yearning for the dead person and, sometimes, anguished outbursts of anger. During this period the wish to have the dead person back is intense. Often, mourners continue to think of the dead person as alive. They may hear his or her voice and see the deceased vividly in dreams. For some time, agitated distress alternates with silent despair, and suffering is acute.

The first powerful reactions of grief gradually give way to weeks or months of **apathy, dejection,** and **depression.** The person faces a new emotional landscape with a large gap that cannot be filled. Life seems to lose much of its meaning, and a sense of futility dominates the person's outlook. The mourner is usually able to resume work or other activities after 2 or 3 weeks. However, insomnia, loss of energy and appetite, and similar signs of depression may continue.

Little by little, the bereaved person accepts what cannot be changed and makes a new beginning. Pangs of grief may still occur, but they are less severe and less frequent. Memories of the dead person, though still painful, now include positive images and nostalgic pleasure. At this point, the person can be said to be moving toward **resolution.** Reaching this point can take many months, or longer.

As was true of approaching death, individual reactions to grief vary considerably. In general, however, a month or two typically passes before the more intense stages of grief have run their course. As you can see, grief allows survivors to discharge their anguish and to prepare to go on living.

Question: Is it true that suppressing grief leads to more problems later?

It has long been assumed that suppressing grief may later lead to more severe and lasting depression. However, there is little evidence to support this idea. A lack of intense grief does not usually predict later problems (Wortman & Silver, 1989). Bereaved persons should work through their grief at their own pace and in their own way—without worrying about whether they are grieving too much or too little. Some additional suggestions for coping with grief follow.

Coping with Grief

- Face the loss directly and do not isolate yourself.
- Discuss your feelings with relatives and friends.
- Do not block out your feelings with drugs or alcohol.
- Allow grief to progress naturally; neither hurry nor suppress it. (Coni et al., 1984)

A Look Ahead The subject of death brings us full circle in the cycle of life. In the upcoming Applications section, we will return to the topic of parenting, a process that deeply links the lives of adults and children. But first, a word from your conscience: It's time for a Learning Check.

Bereavement Period of emotional adjustment that follows the death of a loved one.

Grief An intense emotional state that follows the death of a lover, friend, or relative.

Shock During grief, a period during which a person seems dazed or emotionally numbed.

Pangs of grief Episodes of intense and anguished yearning for a person who has died.

Apathy Indifference, listlessness, and a loss of motivation.

Dejection Demoralization and discouragement.

Depression A state of deep despondency marked by emotional negativity and behavioral inhibition.

Resolution With respect to grief, an acceptance of loss and the need for building a new life.

LEARNING CHECK

Check your comprehension with these questions.

1. Building a workable life tends to be the dominant activity during which age range?
   a. 18–22 *b.* 22–28 *c.* 29–34 *d.* 35–43
2. Levinson's description of the "midlife crisis" corresponds roughly to Gould's
   a. escape from dominance *b.* crisis of questions *c.* crisis of urgency *d.* settling-down period
3. The vigilant style of making career choices is characterized by panic and illogical decisions. T or F?
4. The average male experiences menopause between the ages of 45 and 50. T or F?
5. Many indications of biological aging start to become evident as early as the mid-20s. T or F?
6. An expert on the problems of aging is called a ______________________.
7. The activity theory of optimal aging holds that aging individuals should restrict their activities and withdraw from former community activities. T or F?
8. After age 65, a large proportion of older people show significant signs of senility and most require special care. T or F?
9. In the reaction that Kübler-Ross describes as bargaining, the dying individual asks, "Why me?" T or F?
10. A dazed state of shock or numbness is typical of the first phase of grief. T or F?
11. Most evidence supports the idea that suppressing grief leads to later problems, such as severe depression. T or F?

Critical Thinking

12. Why might you reasonably question Gould's and Levinson's accounts of adult development?

Answers: 1. *b* 2. *c* 3. F 4. F 5. T 6. gerontologist 7. F 8. F 9. F 10. T 11. F 12. As mentioned, Levinson's studies only involved men. Also, both Gould and Levinson may be describing typical patterns of adult development *in Western societies*. It is doubtful that these patterns apply equally well to all cultures.

APPLICATIONS: *Effective Parenting—Raising Healthy Children*

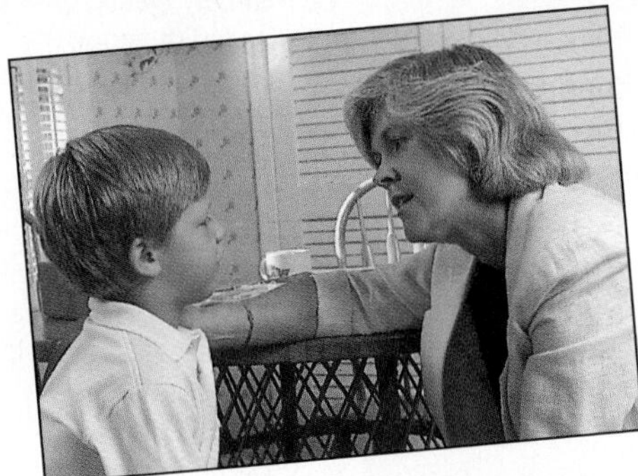

Raising children draws many of the problems of development into a single arena. When parenting is effective, both adult and child benefit. When parents fail to give their children a good start in life, everybody suffers—the child, the parents, and society as a whole. In addition to the skills needed for achievement, effective parents give their children a capacity for love, joy, responsibility, and fulfillment.

Question: What can parents do to promote healthy development in their children?

Earlier we noted that effective parents control their children's behavior in a way that is both fair and loving. Two key ingredients of effective parenting are communication and discipline. In each area, parents can set an example of understanding and acceptance that goes beyond their traditional role as mere dispensers of "dos" and "don'ts."

Rearing Children

No psychologist would deny that love is essential for healthy development, but *discipline* can be equally important. Parents with unmanageable, delinquent, or unhappy children often can honestly claim that they give them lots of love. Yet when parents fail to provide a framework of guidelines for behavior, children become antisocial, aggressive, and insecure. As noted earlier in this chapter, overly permissive parents—those who allow themselves to be dominated or manipulated—create lifelong patterns of self-serving behavior in their children.

Question: Does this mean that discipline should be strict and unbending?

No. Recall that authoritarian parenting also has undesirable effects on children. Families do not need to be run like a military boot camp. Children are no more comfortable with autocratic commands than adults are. As stated before, effective discipline is authoritative yet sensitive. The goal is to socialize a child without destroying the bond of love and trust between parent and child. One 22-year-long study found that children whose parents are critical, harsh, or authoritarian often become self-absorbed adults. They also have a higher than average record of violence and substance abuse (Dubow et al., 1987; Weiss et al., 1992).

Question: How can a balance be maintained?

Consistency Discipline should give children freedom to express their deepest feelings through speech and actions. This does not mean freedom to do entirely as one pleases. It means that the child can move freely within well-defined guidelines for acceptable behavior. Of course, individual parents may choose limits that are more "strict" or less "strict." But this choice is less important than the **consistency** of parental standards. Consistent discipline gives a child a sense of security and stability. Inconsistency makes the child's world seem unreliable and unpredictable.

Question: What does consistency in child management mean in practice?

To illustrate the mistakes that parents often make, let's consider some examples of *inconsistency* (Fontenelle, 1989). The following are mistakes to avoid.

- Saying one thing and doing something else. You tell the child, "Bart, if you don't eat your Brussels sprouts you can't have any dessert." Then you feel guilty and offer him some dessert.
- Making statements you don't mean. "If you don't quiet down I'm going to stop the car and make you walk home."
- Overstating consequences. "Look what you did to the flower bed. You can't ever ride your bike again."
- Changing *no* to *yes*, especially to quiet a nagging child. A good example is the parent who first refuses to buy the child a toy, and later gives in and buys it.
- Not checking to see if the child has actually done something you requested, such as picking up clothes or making a bed.
- Contradicting the rules your spouse has set for the child. Parents need to agree on child discipline and not undermine each other's efforts.
- Not meaning what you say the first time. Children quickly learn how many times they can be warned before they are actually about to be punished.
- Responding differently to the same misbehavior. One day a child is sent to his room for fighting with his sister. The next day the fighting is overlooked.

Random discipline makes children feel angry and confused because they cannot control the consequences of their own behavior. Inconsistency also gives children the message: "Don't believe what I say because I usually don't mean it."

Effects of Child Discipline

Consistent or not, parents tend to base discipline on one or more of the following techniques: power assertion, withdrawal of love, or child management (Coopersmith, 1968; Hoffman, 1977).

Power assertion refers to physical punishment or to a show of force in which parents take away toys or privileges. As an alternative, some parents use **withdrawal of love** by refusing to speak to a child, by threatening to leave, by rejecting the child, or by otherwise acting as if the child is temporarily unlovable. **Management techniques** combine praise, recognition, approval, rules, reasoning, and the like to encourage desirable behavior. Each of these approaches can effectively control a child's behavior, but their side effects differ considerably.

Question: What are the side effects?

Power-oriented techniques—particularly harsh or severe physical punishment—are associated with fear, hatred of parents, and a lack of spontaneity and warmth. Severely punished children also tend to be defiant, rebellious, and aggressive (Patterson, 1982).

Withdrawal of love, which is a major middle-class mode of discipline, produces children who tend to be self-disciplined. We might say that such children have developed a good conscience. They are often described as "model" children or as unusually "good." But as a side effect, they are also frequently anxious, insecure, and dependent on adults for approval.

Management techniques also have their limitations. Most important is the need to carefully adjust them to a child's level of understanding. Younger children may not always see the connection between rules, explanations, and their own behavior. In spite of this limitation, management techniques receive a big plus in an important area of child development. Psychologist Stanley Coopersmith (1968) found a direct connection between parental styles of discipline and a child's **self-esteem.**

Question: What is self-esteem?

Self-Esteem The term self-esteem refers to a quiet confidence that comes from regarding oneself a worthwhile person. High self-esteem is essential for emotional health. Individuals with low self-esteem have a low estimation of their value as people.

Discipline A framework of guidelines for acceptable behavior.

Consistency With respect to child discipline, the maintenance of stable rules of conduct.

Power assertion The use of physical punishment or coercion to enforce child discipline.

Withdrawal of love Withholding affection to enforce child discipline.

Management techniques Combining praise, recognition, approval, rules, and reasoning to enforce child discipline.

Self-esteem Regarding oneself as a worthwhile person; a positive evaluation of oneself.

In direct studies of children, Coopersmith found that low self-esteem is related to the use of physical punishment or withholding of love. High self-esteem, in contrast, was related to management techniques that emphasized clear and consistent discipline coupled with high parental interest and concern for the child. Thus it seems best for parents to minimize physical punishment and to avoid unnecessary withdrawal of love.

Question: Are you saying that physical punishment and withdrawal of love should not be used?

Guidelines for Parents Effective parents use each of the three major types of discipline at one time or another, and each has its place. Coopersmith's findings simply suggest that physical punishment and withdrawal of love should be used with caution. In using these two forms of punishment, parents should observe the following guidelines (also see Chapter 7, Highlight 7–3).

1. Parents should separate disapproval of the act from disapproval of the child. Instead of saying, "I'm going to punish you because *you are bad,*" say, "I'm upset about *what you did.*"
2. State specifically what misbehavior you are punishing. Explain why you have set limits on this kind of conduct.
3. Punishment should never be harsh or injurious to a child. Don't physically punish a child while you are angry. Also remember that giving a child the message "I don't love you right now" can be more painful and damaging than any spanking.
4. Punishment is most effective when it is administered immediately. This statement is especially true for younger children.
5. Spanking and other forms of physical punishment are not particularly effective for children under age 2. The child will only be confused and frightened. Spankings also become less effective after age 5 because they tend to humiliate the child and breed resentment.
6. If you choose to use physical punishment, reserve it for situations that pose an immediate danger to the younger child; for example, when a child runs into the street.
7. Remember too that it is usually more effective to reinforce children when they are being good than it is to punish them for misbehavior.

After age 5, management techniques are the most effective form of discipline, especially techniques that emphasize communication. It is not possible here to discuss all of the methods used by effective parents. Instead, we will focus on several principles that apply broadly to parenting.

Effective Parenting

Parenting experts Don Dinkmeyer and Gary McKay (1989) believe that there are four basic ingredients of a positive parent-child relationship.

- **Mutual respect.** Effective parents try to avoid nagging, hitting, debating, and talking down to their children. They also avoid doing things for their children that children can do for themselves. (Constantly stripping children of opportunities to learn and take responsibility prevents them from becoming independent and from developing self-esteem.)
- **Shared enjoyment.** Some time each day, effective parents spend time with their children, doing something that both the parent and child enjoy.
- **Love.** This goes almost without saying, but many parents assume their children know that they are loved. It is important to communicate your caring by words and by actions such as hugging.
- **Encouragement.** Children who receive frequent encouragement come to believe in themselves. In authoritarian households the child's sense of worth comes from getting rewards and avoiding punishments from powerful parents. Effective parents don't just praise their children for "winning," for "success," or for "good" behavior. They encourage their children by recognizing progress and attempts to improve.

In practice, encouragement means:

- Valuing and accepting children.
- Pointing out positive aspects of a child's behavior.
- Showing faith in children; letting them try things on their own.
- Giving recognition for effort and improvement.
- Showing appreciation for the child's contributions to the family.

Communication between Parents and Children

When clear communication is maintained between parent and child, many discipline problems can be avoided before they develop. Parenting expert Haim Ginott (1965) suggested that it is essential to make a distinction between a child's feelings and a child's behavior. Since children (and parents, too) do not choose how they will feel, it is important to allow free expression of feelings.

Accepting Feelings The child who learns to regard some feelings as "bad," or unacceptable, is being asked to deny a very real part of his or her experience. Ginott encouraged parents to teach their children that all feelings are appropriate; it is only actions that are subject to disapproval. Many parents are unaware of just how often they block communication and the expression of feelings in their children. Consider this typical conversation excerpted from Ginott's book (1965):

Son: I am stupid, and I know it. Look at my grades in school.
Father: You just have to work harder.
Son: I already work harder and it doesn't help. I have no brains.
Father: You are smart, I know.
Son: I am stupid, I know.
Father: (loudly) You are not stupid!
Son: Yes, I am!
Father: You are not stupid. Stupid!

By debating with the child, the father misses the point that his son *feels* stupid. It would be far more helpful for the father to encourage the boy to talk about his feelings.

Question: How could he do that?

He might say, "You really feel that you are not as smart as others, don't you? Do you feel this way often? Are you feeling bad at school?" In this way, the child is given a chance to express his emotions and to feel understood. The father might conclude the conversation by saying, "Look, son, in my eyes you are a fine person. But I understand how you feel. Everyone feels stupid at times."

Encouragement Again, it is valuable to remember that supportive parents encourage their children. In terms of communication, encouragement sounds like this (Dinkmeyer & McKay, 1989):

> "It looks like you enjoyed that."
> "I have confidence in you, you'll make it."
> "It was thoughtful of you to ______________."
> "Thanks. That helped a lot."
> "You really worked hard on that."
> "You're improving. Look at the progress you've made."

I-Messages Communication with a child can also be the basis of effective discipline. Thomas Gordon (1970), a child psychologist who has developed a program called Parent Effectiveness Training (PET), offers a useful suggestion. Gordon believes that parents should send **I-messages** to their children, rather than you-messages.

Question: What's the difference?

You-messages take the form of threats, name-calling, accusing, bossing, lecturing, or analyzing. Generally, you-messages tell children what's "wrong" with them.

An I-message is a form of communication that tells children what effect their behavior had on you. To illustrate the difference, consider this example. After a hard day's work, Susan wants to sit down and rest awhile. She begins to relax with a newspaper when her 5-year-old daughter starts banging loudly on a toy drum. Most parents would respond with a you-message:

> "You go play outside this instant." (bossing)
> "Don't ever make such a racket when someone is reading." (lecturing)
> "You're really pushing it today, aren't you?" (accusing)
> "You're a spoiled brat." (name-calling)
> "You're going to get a spanking!" (threatening)

Gordon suggests sending an I-message such as, "I am very tired, and I would like to read. I feel upset and can't read with so much noise." This forces the child to accept responsibility for the effects of her actions.

To summarize, an I-message states the behavior to which you object. It then clearly tells the child the consequence of his or her behavior and how that makes you feel. Here's a "fill-in-the-blanks" I-message: "When you (state the child's behavior), I feel (state your feelings) because (state the consequences of the child's behavior). For example, "When you go to Jenny's without telling me, I worry that something might have happened to you because I don't know where you are" (Dinkmeyer & McKay, 1989).

Natural and Logical Consequences Children are greatly influenced by the consequences of their actions. Sometimes **natural consequences** arise which tend to discourage misbehavior. For example, the child who refuses to eat dinner will get uncomfortably hungry if snacking is not allowed. A child who throws a temper tantrum may gain nothing but a sore throat and a headache if the tantrum is ignored (Fontenelle, 1989). An alternative to natural consequences are those defined by parents. These are sometimes called **logical consequences** because they should be rational

I-message A message that states the effect someone else's behavior had on you.

Natural consequences The effects that naturally tend to follow a particular behavior.

Logical consequences Reasonable consequences that are defined by parents.

APPLICATIONS: *Continued*

and reasonable. In situations that don't have natural consequences parents must set up logical consequences for the child. For example, a parent might say, "We'll go to the zoo when you've picked up all these toys," or "You can play with your dolls as soon as you've taken your bath," or "You two can settle down or leave the table until you're ready to join us."

The concept of logical, parent-defined consequences can be combined with I-messages to handle many day-to-day instances of misbehavior. The key idea is to use an I-message to set up consequences and then give the child a choice to make: "Michelle, we're trying to watch TV. You may settle down and watch with us or go play elsewhere. You decide which you'd rather do" (Dinkmeyer & McKay, 1989).

Question: How could Susan have dealt with her 5-year-old—the one who was banging on a drum?

A response that combines an I-message with logical consequences would be, "I would like for you to stop banging on that drum; otherwise, please take it outside." If the child continues to bang on the drum inside the house, then she has caused the toy to be put away. If she takes it outside, she has made a decision to play with the drum in a way that respects her mother's wishes. In this way, both parent and child have been allowed to maintain a sense of self-respect and a needless clash has been averted.

After you have stated consequences and let the child decide, be sure to respect the child's choice. If the child repeats the misbehavior, you can let the consequences remain in effect longer. But later, give the child another chance to cooperate. With this, or any other child management technique, remember to be firm, kind, consistent, respectful, and encouraging. And last of all, try every day to live the message you wish to communicate.

LEARNING CHECK

1. According to the text, effective discipline gives children freedom within a structure of consistent and well-defined limits. T or F?
2. Coopersmith found that high self-esteem in childhood is related to discipline based on either management techniques or withdrawal of love. T or F?
3. Spankings and other physical punishment are most effective for children under the age of two. T or F?
4. Authoritarian parents view children as having few rights but many responsibilities. T or F?
5. I-messages are a gentle way of accusing a child of misbehavior. T or F?
6. In situations where natural consequences are unavailable or do not discourage misbehavior, parents should define logical consequences for a child. T or F?

Critical Thinking

7. From the standpoint of learning, why is consistency in child discipline so important?

Answers: 1. T 2. F 3. F 4. T 5. F 6. T 7. Because operant conditioning is based on the consequences that follow responses. In addition to fostering clear communication, consistent consequences shape children's behavior patterns.

EXPLORATION

Approaching Death—New Pathways

In 1967, H. Bedford, a psychology professor from Glendale, California, died at the age of 73. His body was immediately frozen—submerged in liquid nitrogen—making him the first person in the United States to try to cheat death by cryonic suspension (Keeffe, 1977). Mr. Bedford's story is only one indication of changing attitudes toward dying.

For some, death is a sudden tragedy. For others, it is a long-wished-for release. Whatever the case, death—the last phase of life—is something we all must face. It therefore behooves each of us to know

EXPLORATION

something about death. In this section we will add to our earlier discussion of death by considering four departures from traditional approaches to dying. These are the hospice movement, passive euthanasia, active euthanasia, and cryonics.

Hospice

At the beginning of this century most people died at home. Today, in the United States more than 70 percent of all deaths take place outside the home, most often in either a hospital or a nursing home. Just as some people have begun to question traditional funeral practices (embalming, viewing, elaborate and expensive caskets and ceremonies), many are now beginning to question treatment of the terminally ill. Too often, dying persons are isolated, frightened, in pain, and stripped of control over their final days of life. The hospice concept was created to counter this situation.

A **hospice** is a special program for the terminally ill. Hospices may be housed in medical centers or they may combine temporary in-patient care with care at home. Hospice care neither hastens nor postpones death. The goal is to improve the quality of life in the person's final days. The first hospice was created in recognition of dying individuals' needs to be included, to know that someone still cares, to maintain control over their lives, and to have a say in their own dying (Larson, 1990). In operation, the first hospices presented a striking contrast to the grim wards for the terminally ill found in many hospitals.

Question: How is a hospice different?

First, there are lots of people present. A hospice offers support, counseling, guidance, and companionship from volunteers, other patients, staff, clergy, and counselors. Friendship and kindness are expressed toward patients so that when the time comes to die, they know they will be remembered with respect and love.

Second, the atmosphere differs markedly from that of a traditional hospital. A hospice attempts to provide pleasant surroundings, an atmosphere of intentional informality, and a sense of continued living for patients. Unlimited around-the-clock visits are permitted by relatives, friends, children, and even pets. Patients receive constant attention, play games, make day trips, have pre-dinner cocktails if they choose, enjoy entertainment, and visit with volunteers. In short, life goes on for them.

A third aspect of hospice care is the freedom of choice allowed to patients. Patients decide about their own diets, about whether or not they will use painkilling drugs, and about whether or not they want to continue medical care. Patients can also choose freedom from intolerable pain. This is usually achieved by giving drugs, such as morphine, in dosages that relieve pain without making the person groggy (Larson, 1990).

Many communities in the United States now have hospice programs or free-standing hospice facilities. In either case, treatment for the terminally ill has drastically improved. Even traditional hospitals are doing a better job—largely as a result of pioneering efforts in the hospice movement.

A Right to Die?

The "right to die" concept might be better stated as a right to live in peace and comfort until death. Much of the interest in this issue began with the Karen Ann Quinlan case. In 1975 Karen lapsed into a coma after suffering an overdose of drugs and alcohol. After doctors said she would never recover, Karen's parents began a legal fight to turn off the respirator and other devices being used to prolong her life. In 1976 the New Jersey Supreme Court issued a landmark decision giving permission to the parents to order removal of Karen's life-support equipment. Despite the doctors' prediction, Karen continued to live for another 10 years. Karen died in 1985 at the age of 31.

Is there a right to die? Doctors and other medical personnel are legally and morally bound to prolong and preserve life, and in most states relatives and guardians cannot legally give permission for removal of life-supporting equipment. One way out of this dilemma that is gaining support is the **living will.** The intent of a living will is to free the terminally and irreversibly ill from a slow and cruel death, allowing death with dignity. The will is made out when the person is still healthy, and states that, in the event of terminal illness (as diagnosed by two or more doctors), the person does not want to have life sustained by medical machines or heroic measures. A living will is not yet binding in most states, but it does make clear the wishes of terminally ill persons unable to speak for themselves. The following excerpt is from one widely used living will.

A Living Will

> If at such a time the situation should arise in which there is no reasonable expectation of my recovery from extreme physical or mental disability, I direct that I be allowed to die and not be kept alive by medications, artificial means or "heroic measures." I do, however, ask that medication be mercifully administered to me to alleviate suffering even though this may shorten my remaining life. (Reprinted with permission from Concern for Dying, 250 West 57th Street, New York, NY, 10017.)

To make sure your living will is effective you should do the following: Use a form that is recognized by your state's laws. Obtain signatures of the required number of witnesses, preferably non-relatives. Ask your doctor whether he or she will honor your wishes. If so, give your physician a copy of your living will. Give copies of your living will to several close friends and relatives. Periodically review your living will and revise it if necessary.

Euthanasia

The right to die won for Karen Quinlan by her parents may be thought of as **passive euthanasia** (YOU-tha-NAY-zyah), in which death is allowed to occur but is not actively caused. In **active euthanasia,** or "physician assisted suicide," steps would be taken at a patient's request to

Hospice A medical facility or program dedicated to providing optimal care for persons who are dying.

Living will A written declaration stating that a person prefers not to have his or her life artificially prolonged in the event of a terminal illness.

Passive euthanasia Allowing death to occur without trying to prevent it or encourage it.

Active euthanasia Deliberately inducing death.

deliberately hasten death, perhaps by administering drugs that induce death painlessly. Both forms of euthanasia present ethical dilemmas for physicians, who are trained to keep patients alive. On the other hand doctors are also sworn to *humane* treatment. With the second point in mind, proponents of euthanasia believe that it is a basic human right to die with dignity and a minimum of discomfort.

To a degree, passive euthanasia is already practiced in the United States. In the Netherlands, doctors are allowed help patients die, as long as certain safeguards are followed. The patient has to be terminally ill, in pain, mentally competent, and must repeatedly express a wish to die (Shapiro & Bowermaster, 1994). Should active euthanasia ever become legal in the United States and Canada (many people find the idea totally unacceptable), it might also become possible for next of kin to request euthanasia for an incapacitated individual.

There are several arguments against euthanasia. The case of Karen Delahanty of Avon, Connecticut, provides a good starting point. After a head-on automobile accident, Karen entered a coma from which doctors predicted she would never recover. One year later she miraculously regained consciousness. What if euthanasia had been carried out?

Other questions that arise, in addition to unexpected recovery, include: What guarantee is there that the choice of euthanasia would be made freely and without pressure? Would the infirm feel that it is their "duty" to die, to avoid being a burden to families? Can family members be trusted to make a correct decision? Would they feel guilt afterward? What about the medical personnel involved; how would they respond emotionally to "mercy killing"? (Shapiro & Bowermaster, 1994). No doubt you can think of other objections.

Cryonics

To complete our brief sampling of new approaches to death, let's return to cryonics. Cryonics involves freezing a person's body immediately after death. The idea is to keep the person frozen until medical science perfects ways to thaw, restore, and revive the person. Those who have been placed in **cryonic suspension** obviously are gambling that if they are revived, a cure will exist for whatever killed them.

Question: Does freezing actually work?

Cryonic suspension must be viewed as a symbolic attempt to cheat death or perhaps as an emotional hedge against the finality of death. At this point, cryonic suspension is impractical because freezing does serious damage to the body (Vogel, 1988). The ice crystals formed by freezing and unfreezing the human brain would almost surely turn it to mush—wiping out most or all of the memories stored there. If a person frozen at death were ever to be successfully revived, that person would have no identity, and perhaps no understanding of where he or she was or why he or she was there. Such persons would, in most cases, be quite old. (To date, most of the persons who have been frozen have been middle-aged or older.) Even the most optimistic supporters of cryonic suspension admit that there is currently no way to preserve bodies so that their organs will resume functioning when they are thawed (Darwin & Wowk, 1992).

Another problem is the great expense of maintaining cryonic capsules for many years. (Aging LSD guru Tim Leary has arranged to have only his head frozen—he can't afford the whole-body treatment.) And in California (where else?), a case has already surfaced where careless operators of a cryonics service allowed a number of bodies to defrost.

Whereas it is true that for a few pioneering souls there is clearly "ice after death," immortality, it would seem, does not yet fall within the province of technology (Shermer, 1992).

Cryonic suspension Freezing the body or head at death in hopes that future revival will become possible.

Learning Check

1. The goal of a hospice is to freeze persons who have died of diseases that might one day become curable. T or F?
2. In passive euthanasia, death is allowed to occur but is not actively induced. T or F?
3. Cryonic suspension is a type of passive euthanasia. T or F?
4. Active euthanasia is now legal in most states, providing that the terminally ill patient has signed a living will. T or F?

Critical Thinking

5. Which of the emotional reactions to impending death (described earlier) relates most directly to cryonic suspension?

Answers: 1. F 2. T 3. F 4. F 5. A good case can be made for the idea that people seeking cryonic suspension are still *bargaining*: "Just let me live a little longer and I'll do anything to earn it."

Chapter Summary

- ***What are the typical tasks and dilemmas of childhood, adolescence, adulthood, and old age?***

- According to Erikson, each life stage provokes a specific **psychosocial dilemma.** In order of occurrence, these are: *trust versus mistrust, autonomy versus shame and doubt, initiative versus guilt, industry versus inferiority, identity versus role confusion, intimacy versus isolation, generativity versus stagnation,* and *integrity versus despair.*
- In addition to the dilemmas identified by Erikson, we recognize that each **life stage** requires successful mastery of certain **developmental tasks.**

- ***What is the nature of effective parenting?***

- Three major parental styles are **authoritarian, permissive,** and **authoritative** (effective). When judged by its effects on children, authoritative parenting appears to benefit children the most.

- ***What are some of the more serious childhood problems?***

- Few children grow up without experiencing some of the normal problems of childhood, including **negativism, clinging, specific fears, sleep disturbances, general dissatisfaction, regression, sibling rivalry,** and **rebellion.**
- Major areas of difficulty in childhood are *toilet training* (including **enuresis** and **encopresis**); *feeding disturbances,* such as **overeating, anorexia nervosa** (self-starvation), and **pica** (eating non-food substances); *speech disturbances* (**delayed speech, stuttering**); **learning disorders**, including **dyslexia; attention-deficit hyperactivity disorder;** and other problems).
- **Childhood autism** is representative of some of the more severe problems that can occur. Some cases of autism are being treated successfully with **behavior modification.**
- **Child abuse** is a major problem for which few solutions currently exist. Roughly 30 percent of all abused children become abusive adults. Emotional support and therapy appear to help break the cycle of abuse.

- ***In what ways is adolescent development especially challenging?***

- **Adolescence** is a culturally defined social status. **Puberty** is a biological event.
- *Early maturation* is beneficial mostly for boys; its effects are mixed for girls. One danger of early maturation is *premature identity formation.*
- Adolescent **identity formation** is accelerated by cognitive development and influenced by parents and **peer groups.**

- ***How do people select careers for themselves?***

- Four broad periods in **career development** are the **exploration phase,** the **establishment phase,** the **midcareer phase,** and the **later career phase.**
- The exploration phase can be further divided into a **fantasy stage,** a **tentative stage,** and a **realistic stage.**
- **Vocational counseling** can greatly aid career decision making.

- ***What happens psychologically during adulthood?***

- Certain relatively consistent events mark **adult development** in our society. These range from escaping parental dominance in the late teens to a noticeable acceptance of one's lot in life during the 50s.
- Some research indicates that a *midlife crisis* affects many people in the 37–41 age range, but this is by no means universal.
- Adjustment to later middle age is sometimes complicated for women by **menopause** and for men by a **climacteric.**

- ***What are some of the psychological challenges of aging?***

- Both the *number* and *proportion* of older people in the population has grown.
- **Biological aging** begins between 25 and 30, but peak performance in specific pursuits may come at various points throughout life.
- Intellectual declines associated with aging are limited, at least through one's 70s. This is especially true of individuals who remain mentally active.
- **Gerontologists** have proposed two major theories of successful aging. The **disengagement theory** holds that withdrawal from society is necessary and desirable in old age. The **activity theory** counters that optimal adjustment to aging is tied to continuing activity and involvement. There is an element of truth to each, but the activity theory applies to more people.
- **Ageism** refers to prejudice, discrimination, and stereotyping on the basis of age. It affects people of all ages, but is especially damaging to older people. Most ageism is based on stereotypes, myths, and misinformation.

- ***What are typical emotional and psychological reactions to death and bereavement?***

- Typical emotional reactions to impending death are **denial, anger, bargaining, depression,** and **acceptance.**
- **Near-death experiences** frequently result in significant changes in personality, values, and life goals.

- **Bereavement** also brings forth a typical series of reactions, ranging from shock to final acceptance.

■ ***How do effective parents discipline their children?***

- Effective parental discipline tends to emphasize **child management techniques** (especially communication), rather than **power assertion** or **withdrawal of love.**
- Responsibility, mutual respect, consistency, love, encouragement, and clear communication are features of effective parenting. Much misbehavior can be managed by use of **I-messages** and the application of **natural** and **logical consequences.**

■ ***In what ways are attitudes toward death changing?***

- New approaches to death include the **hospice** movement, **living wills,** and **cryonic suspension.**
- A continuing controversy concerns the ethics of **passive euthanasia** and **active euthanasia.**

Questions for Discussion

1. Describe an incident from your own childhood that you consider growth promoting. Describe an incident that set you back or had a negative effect on you. How do these incidents differ?
2. Were you physically punished as a child? What is your attitude toward physical punishment now? Would you use physical punishment on your own children?
3. As an element of discipline, what are the advantages and disadvantages of making a child feel guilty?
4. Anthropologist Margaret Mead has charged, "We have become a society of people who neglect our children, are afraid of our children." Do you agree?
5. Do we need a "children's liberation movement" to establish the civil rights of children? (Keep in mind that few parents show their children the courtesy they show strangers.)
6. Do you know a person who seems to have "flunked" one or more of Erikson's developmental stages? What effect has this had on the person's subsequent development?
7. Perhaps you remember being grouped in elementary school according to your skills in reading, writing, or math. Could such groupings (as well as competitive sports) contribute to feelings of inferiority? Why or why not?
8. Many children are now part of "blended" stepfamilies. How would this affect the development of a child's sense of identity?
9. What cultural factors do you think would affect the length of adolescence? The onset of puberty? The social effects of early and late maturation for males and females?
10. In what ways do parents add to the conflicts of young adults who are seeking independence?
11. How common do you think it is to experience a "midlife crisis"? Would you expect people of other cultures to experience a similar crisis? People born in various decades have very different life experiences. How much do you think this affects patterns of development and the likelihood of problems at midlife?
12. Will the patterns of adult development in the year 2020 be the same as the patterns suggested by Gould? If not, what patterns do you hypothesize? Why?
13. Should passive euthanasia be allowed? Should active euthanasia be allowed? What are the arguments for and against each? Do you think a "living will" is a good idea? Why or why not?
14. If you could choose to remain a particular age which would you choose? Why? What are your attitudes toward aging and death?
15. How general are the emotional reactions to impending death described by Kübler-Ross? Do they describe the reactions before death of people you know who have died?
16. Why do you think dying individuals so often feel isolated? How could the emotional needs of dying persons be better served than they are now in hospitals and nursing homes?

Where to Write for Information

■ **Anorexia Nervosa** National Association of Anorexia Nervosa and Associated Disorders, Box 271, Highland Park, Illinois 60035.

■ **Autism** The National Society for Autistic Children, 101 Richmond St., Huntington, West Virginia 25701; or, Autism Society of America, Suite C1017, 1234 Massachusetts Ave., NW, Washington, D.C., 20005.

■ **Child Abuse** Parents Anonymous, call toll free, (800) 421–0353 to find local chapters or call the National Child Abuse Hot Line, toll free, (800) 422–4453.

■ **Hospice** The National Hospice Organization, 1901 North Ft. Meyer Drive, Arlington, Virginia 22180.

■ **Hyperactivity** Department of Health, Education, and Welfare, Office of the Secretary, Secretary's Committee on Mental Retardation, Washington, D.C. 20201.

■ **Learning Disorders** National Association for Children with Learning Disabilities, 5225 Grace St., Pittsburgh, Pennsylvania 15236.

■ **Living Will** Concern for Dying, 250 West 57th St., New York, New York 10019.

Chapter 14

Intelligence

CHAPTER PREVIEW

What Day Is It?

Ask George in which recent years April 21 fell on a Sunday. Without hesitation he will answer, "1991, 1985, 1974, 1968, 1963, 1957, 1946." Surprisingly, this gives only the slightest hint of his ability. If encouraged, George will go back as far as 1700—with complete accuracy! His calendar calculations cover a range of at least 6000 years: With equal ease he can identify February 15, 2002, as a Friday or August 28, 1591, as a Wednesday.

Question: Is he a genius?

George's abilities are all the more amazing in view of the fact that he is mentally retarded and cannot add, subtract, multiply, or divide even simple numbers (Horwitz et al., 1965). George's strange talent is an example of the savant syndrome, *in which an island of brilliance is found in a sea of retardation. In the savant syndrome, a person of below normal intelligence shows highly developed mental ability in a very limited area, such as mental arithmetic, calendar calculations, art, or music (Treffert, 1988).*

Question: How could George be retarded and have such amazing ability at the same time?

IN THIS CHAPTER

Defining intelligence
Qualities of good tests
Intelligence tests
The concept of IQ
Variations in IQ
The mentally gifted
Mental retardation
Heredity and environment
Applications:
IQ in perspective
Exploration:
The Larry P. case

The striking contrast between George's general retardation and his unusual mental ability is a fitting introduction to the challenge psychologists face in trying to define and measure intelligence. Quite frankly, we are still searching for answers to questions like these: Is intelligence a general trait or a collection of specific skills? Is intelligence determined by the genetic "wheel of fortune" or is it nurtured by environment? Is it possible to construct an intelligence test that is fair to all people? How important is intelligence for "success"? Because our understanding of intelligence is rapidly changing, we cannot hope to give final answers.

For the sake of clarity, this chapter is divided into two parts. First, we will assume that intelligence can be measured, and we will use test results as a way to answer questions about intelligence. Later, we will consider questions that have been raised about intelligence tests and the meaning of their results.

Survey Questions

- How do psychologists define intelligence?
- What are the qualities of a good psychological test?
- What are typical IQ tests like?
- How do IQ scores relate to gender, age, and occupation?
- What does IQ tell us about genius?
- What causes mental retardation?
- How do heredity and environment affect intelligence?
- Are IQ tests fair to all racial and cultural groups?

Intelligence An overall capacity to think rationally, act purposefully, and deal effectively with the environment.

Operational definition The operations (actions or procedures) used to measure a concept.

Defining Intelligence—Intelligence Is . . . You Know, It's . . .

Like so many important concepts in psychology, intelligence cannot be observed directly: It has no mass, occupies no space, and is invisible. Nevertheless, we feel certain it exists. Consider the following two children:

> When she was 14 months old, Anne H. wrote her own name. She taught herself to read at age 2. At age 5, she astounded her kindergarten teacher by walking into class with a stack of encyclopedias—which she proceeded to read. At 10 she breezed through an entire high school algebra course in 12 hours.
>
> At age 10 Billy A. can write his name and can count, but he has trouble with simple addition and subtraction problems and finds multiplication impossible. He has been held back in school twice and is still incapable of doing the work his 8-year-old classmates find easy. His teachers have suggested placing him in a special educational program for slow learners.

Anne is considered a genius; Billy, a slow learner. There seems little doubt that they differ in intelligence.

Question: Wait! Anne's ability is obvious, but how do we know that Billy isn't just lazy?

This dilemma is the same one that **Alfred Binet** faced in 1904. The minister of education in Paris had given Binet the task of finding a way to distinguish slower students from the more capable (or the capable but lazy). In a flash of brilliance, Binet and an associate created a test made up of "intellectual" questions and problems. Next, they learned which questions an average child could answer at each age. Children low in intellectual ability were identified by below-par scores on the test.

Binet's approach gave rise to modern intelligence tests. At the same time, it launched 90 years of debate that has often been heated and at times bitter. Part of the debate is related to the basic difficulty of defining intelligence.

Question: Is there an accepted definition of intelligence?

Defining Intelligence

Most psychologists would probably agree with David Wechsler's general description of **intelligence** as the *global capacity to act purposefully, to think rationally, and to deal effectively with the environment.* To add to the definition, ● Table 14–1 shows results from a survey of 1020 experts on intelligence. At least three quarters of this group agreed that the listed items are important elements of intelligence (Snyderman & Rothman, 1987).

Beyond this, there is so much disagreement that many psychologists simply accept an **operational definition** of intelligence (■ Fig. 14–1). (We define a

Table14–1 Important Elements of Intelligence

Description	Percent of agreement
Abstract thinking or reasoning	99.3
Problem-solving ability	97.7
Capacity to acquire knowledge	96.0
Memory	80.5
Adaptation to one's environment	77.2

(Adapted from Snyderman & Rothman, 1987)

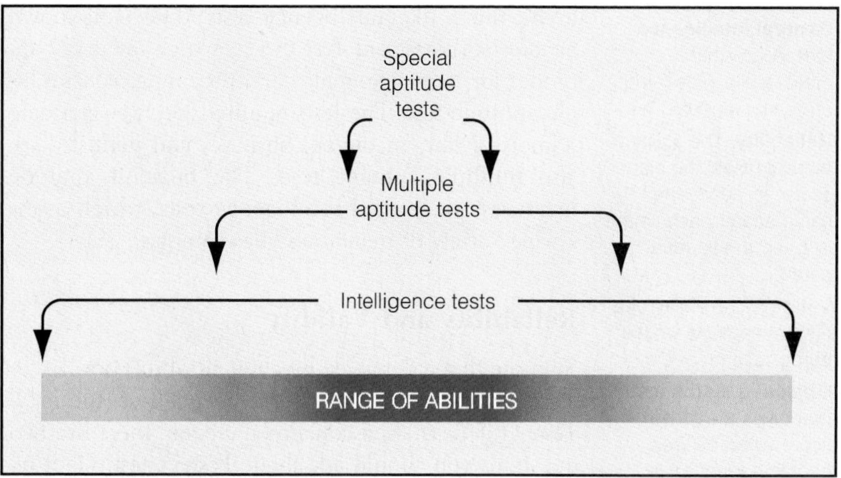

■ **Fig. 14–2** *Special aptitude tests measure a person's potential for achievement in a limited area of ability, such as manual dexterity. Multiple aptitude tests measure potentials in broader areas, such as college work, law, or medicine. Intelligence tests measure a very wide array of aptitudes and mental abilities.*

concept operationally by stating what procedures will be used to measure it.) By selecting test items, a psychologist is saying in a very direct way, "This is what I mean by intelligence." A test that measures memory, reasoning, and verbal fluency offers a very different definition of intelligence than one that measures strength of grip, shoe size, length of the nose, or the person's best Pac-Man score.

Aptitudes As a child, my friend Hedda displayed an aptitude for art. Today, Hedda is a successful graphic artist. How does an aptitude like Hedda's differ from general intelligence? An **aptitude** is a capacity for learning certain abilities. Persons with mechanical, artistic, or musical aptitudes are likely to do well in careers involving mechanics, art, or music, respectively.

Question: Are there tests for aptitudes? How are they different from intelligence tests?

Aptitude tests measure a narrower range of abilities than intelligence tests do (■ Fig. 14–2). For example, **special aptitude tests** predict a person's likelihood of succeeding in a single area, such as clerical work or operating a computer (■ Fig. 14–3). (To learn how psychologists use aptitude tests to select people for employment, see Chapter 22.) **Multiple aptitude tests** measure two or more capacities. Tests of this type tend

Aptitude A capacity for learning certain abilities.

Special aptitude test Test to predict a person's likelihood of succeeding in a particular area of work or skill.

Multiple aptitude test Test that measures two or more aptitudes.

■ **Fig. 14–1** *Modern intelligence tests are widely used to measure cognitive abilities. When properly administered, such tests provide an operational definition of intelligence.*

■ **Fig. 14–3** *Sample questions like those found on tests of mechanical aptitude.*

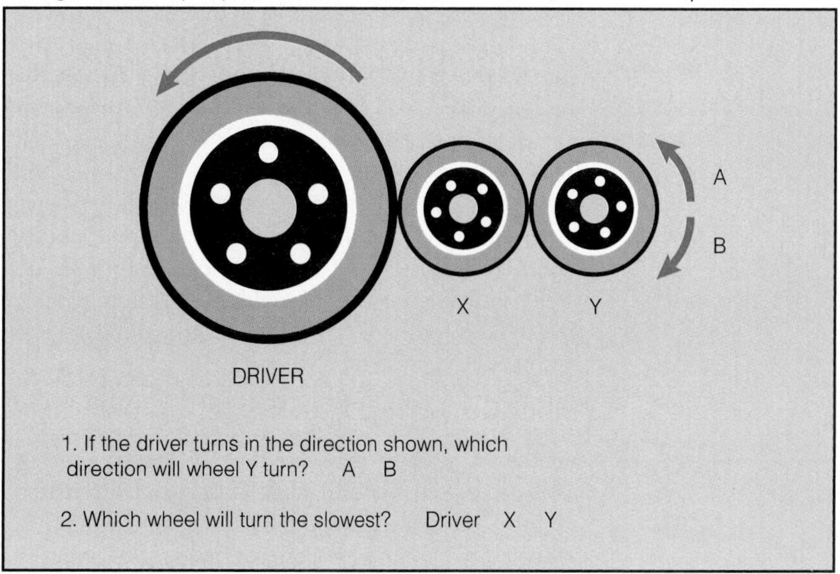

A
B
X
Y
DRIVER
1. If the driver turns in the direction shown, which direction will wheel Y turn? A B
2. Which wheel will turn the slowest? Driver X Y

General intelligence test A test that measures a wide variety of mental abilities.

Reliability The ability of a test to yield the same score, or nearly the same score, each time it is given to the same person.

Validity The ability of a test to measure what it purports to measure.

Objective test A test that gives the same score when different people correct it.

Test standardization Establishing standards for administering a test and interpreting scores.

Norm An average score for a designated group of people.

Stanford-Binet Intelligence Scale A widely used individual test of intelligence; a direct descendant of Alfred Binet's first intelligence test.

Mental age The average mental ability displayed by people of a given age.

to be more like intelligence tests. The well-known *Scholastic Assessment Test* (SAT), which measures aptitudes for language, math, and reasoning, is a multiple aptitude test. The tests required to enter graduate schools of law, medicine, business, and dentistry are also multiple aptitude tests. The broadest aptitude measures are **general intelligence tests,** which assess a wide variety of mental abilities (Anastasi, 1994).

Reliability and Validity

Suppose that a deranged psychologist, Professor Ike Q. Tester, decides to write an intelligence test (the *I. Q. Tester IQ Test*). As a concerned citizen, there are two questions you should ask about Tester's test: "Is it *reliable?*" and "Is it *valid?*"

Question: What does reliability refer to?

If you weigh yourself several times in a row, a reliable bathroom scale gives the same weight each time. Likewise, a **reliable** test must yield the same score, or close to the same score, each time a person takes it. In other words, the scores should be *consistent* and highly correlated. It is easy to see that a test has little value if it is unreliable. Imagine a medical test for pregnancy or breast cancer, for instance, that gives positive and negative responses for the same woman on the same day.

To check the reliability of the *I. Q. Tester IQ Test,* we could administer it to a large group of people. Then each person could be tested again a week later to establish *test-retest reliability.* Reliability is also sometimes measured by comparing the score on one-half of the test items to the score on the other half (*split-half reliability*). If Tester offered two versions of the test, we could correlate scores on one to scores on the other for each person (*equivalent-forms reliability*).

By comparing such scores we find that the Tester Test is quite reliable. In fact, the scores are identical each time the test is given: Everyone scores zero (except Professor Tester, who scores 100 percent and thereby proclaims himself the only human with any intelligence).

Let's concede to Tester that his test is reliable (but for the wrong reasons). A more important question then becomes, Is the test valid? Obviously we have been playing with a silly example. A test has **validity** when it measures what it claims to measure. By no stretch of the imagination could a test of intelligence be valid if the person who wrote it is the only one who can pass it.

Question: How is validity established?

Validity is usually demonstrated by comparing test scores to actual performance. This is called *criterion validity.* A test of legal aptitude, for example, might be validated by comparing scores on the test to grades in law school. If high scores correlate with high grades or some other standard of success, the test may be considered valid. Unfortunately, many tests you will encounter, such as those found in magazines or offered by commercial self-improvement courses, have little or no validity.

Tester's Last Stand Let's return to Professor Tester for a final point. Although he admits that his test has problems, Professor Tester claims that at least it is **objective.** Is he right? Actually, he might be. If the test gives the same score when corrected by different people, it is objective. However, objectivity is not enough to guarantee a fair test. To be useful a psychological test must also be *standardized.*

Test **standardization** refers to two things. First, it means that standard procedures are used in giving the test to all people. That is, the instructions, answer forms, amount of time to work, and so forth, are the same for all test takers. Second, it means finding the **norm,** or average score, made by a large group of people like those for whom the test was designed. Without standardization, it would be unfair to compare the scores of people taking a test on different occasions. And without norms, there would be no way to tell if a score is high, low, or average.

Later in this chapter we will address the question of whether intelligence tests are valid. For now, let's take a practical approach by examining some widely used standardized tests and the meaning of their scores.

Testing Intelligence—The IQ and You

American psychologists quickly saw the value of Binet's test. In 1916, **Lewis Terman** and others at Stanford University revised it for use in the U.S. After more revisions, the **Stanford-Binet Intelligence Scale, Fourth Edition** is still widely used. The first version of the Stanford-Binet assumed that intellectual ability in childhood improves as age increases. Today, the Stanford-Binet (or Binet-4) is still primarily made up of age-ranked questions of increasing difficulty. ⬬ Table 14–2 lists the subtests of the Binet-4.

Intelligence Quotients

The age-ranked questions of the original Stanford-Binet allowed a person's **mental age** to be measured. Mental age is the average mental ability displayed by people of a given age. For example, at ages 8 or 9, very few children can define the word *connection.* At age 10, 10 percent can. At age 13, 60 percent can. In other words, the ability to define *connection* indicates mental ability equal to that of an average 13-year-old and gives a mental age of 13 (on this single item). Table 14–3 is a sample of items that persons of average intelligence can answer at various ages.

Mental age is a good measure of actual ability. But mental age says nothing about whether overall intelligence is *relatively* high or low. To know the meaning of mental age, **chronological age** (age in years) must also be considered. Mental age can then be related to actual age. This yields an **IQ,** or **intelligence quotient.** When the Stanford-Binet was first used in the United States, IQ was defined as mental age (MA) divided by chronological age (CA) and multiplied by 100:

$$\frac{\text{MA}}{\text{CA}} \times 100 = \text{IQ}$$

An advantage of the IQ was that intelligence could be compared among children with different chronological and mental ages. For instance, a 10-year-old child with a mental age of 12 has an IQ of 120:

$$\frac{\text{(MA) } 12}{\text{(CA) } 10} \times 100 = 120 \text{ (IQ)}$$

A second child having a mental age of 12, but with a chronological age of 12 would have an IQ of 100:

$$\frac{\text{(MA) } 12}{\text{(CA) } 12} \times 100 = 100 \text{ (IQ)}$$

The IQ shows that the younger child is brighter than his 12-year-old friend, even though their intellectual skills are actually the same. Notice that IQ equals 100 when MA = CA. An IQ score of 100 is therefore defined as average intelligence.

Question: Then does a person with an IQ score below 100 have below-average intelligence?

Not unless the IQ is far below 100. An IQ of 100 is the *mathematical* average (or mean) for such scores. However, *average intelligence* is usually defined as any score from 90 to 109. The important point is that IQ scores will be over 100 when mental age is higher than age in years (Fig. 14–4), while IQ scores below 100 occur when age in years exceeds mental age. An example of the second situation would be a 15-year-old with an MA of 12:

$$\frac{12}{15} \times 100 = 80 \text{ (IQ)}$$

Table 14–2 Stanford-Binet IV: Ability Areas and Subtests

Verbal Reasoning	
Vocabulary	Name a pictured object or define a word.
Comprehension	Answer questions requiring logic or common sense.
Absurdities	Tell what is wrong with pictures (for example, a bicycle has square wheels).
Verbal relations	Given four words, tell how three are similar.
Quantitative Reasoning	
Quantitative	Use numbered blocks to add and count; solve word problems.
Number series	Given a series of numbers, tell what two numbers would come next. For example, 3, 6, 9, would be followed by 12 and 15.
Equation building	Given a set of numbers and mathematical signs, arrange them to make a true equation. For example, 3, 4, 7, +, = would be arranged as 3 + 4 = 7.
Abstract/Visual Reasoning	
Pattern analysis	Put picture puzzles together; reproduce patterns with blocks.
Copying	Copy arrangements of blocks or draw copies of designs.
Matrices	Complete a matrix of shapes that has one part missing.
Paper folding and cutting	Choose pictures that show how a piece of paper would look if folded or cut.
Short-Term Memory	
Bead memory	Correctly remember the order of beads placed on a stick.
Memory for sentences	Repeat sentences exactly after hearing them once.
Memory for digits	Repeat a series of digits (forward or backward) after hearing them once.
Memory for objects	After seeing several objects, point to the objects in the same order as they were shown.

Deviation IQs The preceding examples are offered to give you insight into the history and meaning of IQ scores. However, it is no longer necessary to calculate IQs for modern tests. Instead, **deviation IQs** are used. A deviation IQ is obtained from a person's *relative standing* among other test takers.

Deviation IQs are based on how far above or below average a person's "raw" score is. (A raw score is the actual number of questions answered correctly. See Appendix B for more information.) Tables are used to convert a person's *relative standing* in his or her age group to an IQ score. For example, a raw score at the 50th percentile (in the middle of the group) equals an IQ of 100. A person who scores at the 84th percentile (above average) gets an IQ score of 116. A raw score at the 16th percentile (below average) equals an IQ of 85. And so forth. This approach avoids certain troublesome errors that occur when IQs are calculated directly (Kamphaus, 1993).

Chronological age Age in years.

Intelligence quotient (IQ) An index of intelligence defined as mental age divided by chronological age and multiplied by 100.

Deviation IQ An IQ obtained statistically from a person's relative standing in his or her age group.

Table 14–3 Sample Items from the Stanford-Binet Intelligence Scale

2 years old	On a large paper doll, points out the hair, mouth, feet, ears, nose, hands, and eyes. When shown a tower built of four blocks, builds one like it.
3 years old	When shown a bridge built of three blocks, builds one like it. When shown a drawing of a circle, copies it with a pencil.
4 years old	Fills in the missing word when asked, "Brother is a boy; sister is a ______." "In daytime it is light; at night it is ______." Answers correctly when asked, "Why do we have houses?" "Why do we have books?"
5 years old	Defines *ball*, *hat*, and *stove*. When shown a drawing of a square, copies it with a pencil.
9 years old	Answers correctly when examiner says, "In an old graveyard in Spain they have discovered a small skull which they believe to be that of Christopher Columbus when he was about 10 years old. What is foolish about that?" Answers correctly when asked, "Tell me the name of a color that rhymes with head." "Tell me a number that rhymes with tree."
Adult	Can describe the difference between laziness and idleness, poverty and misery, character and reputation. Answers correctly when asked, "Which direction would you have to face so your right hand would be toward the north?"

(Terman & Merill, 1960)

Question: How old do children have to be before their IQ scores become stable?

Stability of IQ IQ scores are not very dependable until about age 6 (Schuerger & Witt, 1989). The correlation between IQ scores obtained at age 2 and those obtained at age 18 is only .31. (Recall that a perfect correlation is 1.00, and a correlation of 0.00 occurs when scores are unrelated.) With increasing age, IQs become more reliable. The average change (median change) in IQ on retesting is roughly 5 points in either direction. However, children may show small ups and downs in intelligence test scores as they develop. No typical pattern exists, and in some cases changes in IQ of 15 points or more may take place. Overall, though, changes are usually small after middle childhood (■ Fig. 14–5).

■ **Fig. 14–4** *With a score of 230, Marilyn Mach vos Savant has the highest IQ ever officially recorded. When she was only 7 years and 9 months old, vos Savant could answer questions that the average 13-year-old can answer. At ages 8, 9, and 10, she got perfect scores on the Stanford-Binet scale. Now in her 40s, she is capitalizing on her celebrity by giving lectures and writing books (Lemley, 1986).*

Question: How much does aging affect the IQ?

Since IQ reflects education, maturity, and experience, as well as native intellectual capacity, test scores show a small gradual increase until about age 40 (Eichorn et al., 1981). This trend, of course, is an average. Some people show fairly large gains in IQ, whereas others experience sizable losses. How do the two groups differ? In general, persons who show the largest IQ gains were exposed to stimulating intellectual experiences during early adulthood. Those who decline the most typically suffer from chronic illnesses, drinking problems, or unstimulating lifestyles (Honzik, 1984).

Some studies of IQ have recorded slow declines after middle age, while others indicate little or no change due to aging (Schaie, 1980). As you may recall from Chapter 13, these contradictory results can be explained in this way: When general information or comprehension is emphasized, there is little decline in IQ until advanced age; however, test items requiring speed, rapid insight, or perceptual flexibility show earlier losses and a rapid decline after middle age (Brody, 1992). Overall, age-related losses are small for most healthy, well-educated individuals (Weintraub et al., 1991).

Perhaps the most intriguing link between IQ and aging is the observation that impending death may be signaled by marked changes in brain function. Certain intellectual skills have been shown to decline abruptly about five years before death. This **terminal decline** in IQ can be measured even when a person appears to be in good health (Suedfeld & Piedrahita, 1984).

Question: Is the Stanford-Binet the only intelligence test?

The Wechsler Tests

A widely used alternative to the Stanford-Binet is the **Wechsler Adult Intelligence Scale-Revised,** or **WAIS-R.** This test also has a form for use with children, called the **Wechsler Intelligence Scale for Children-Third Edition (WISC-III).**

The Wechsler tests are similar to the Stanford-Binet, but different in important ways. For one thing, the WAIS-R was specifically designed to test adult intelligence. Of course, the Stanford-Binet may be used to test adults, but it tends to be better suited for children and adolescents. The Wechsler tests yield a single overall IQ, just as the Stanford-Binet does. However, the WAIS and WISC also provide separate scores for **performance** (non-verbal) **intelligence** and **verbal intelligence.** Verbal and non-verbal abilities can be broken down further, to reveal various cognitive strengths and weaknesses. The abilities measured by the Wechsler tests and some sample test items are listed in Table 14–4.

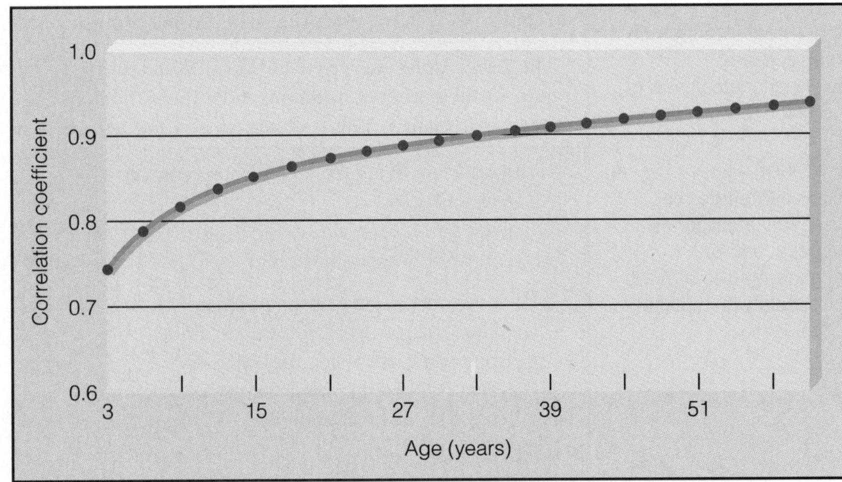

■ Fig. 14–5 *The stability or reliability of IQ scores increases rapidly in early childhood. Scores are very consistent from early adulthood to late middle age. (Source: Schuerger & Witt, 1989.)*

Terminal decline An abrupt decline in measured intelligence about five years before death.

Wechsler Adult Intelligence Scale-Revised (WAIS-R) An adult intelligence test that rates both verbal and performance intelligence.

Wechsler Intelligence Scale for Children-Third Edition (WISC-III) An intelligence test for children that rates both verbal and performance intelligence.

Performance intelligence Intelligence measured by solving puzzles, assembling objects, completing pictures, and other non-verbal tasks.

Verbal intelligence Intelligence measured by answering questions involving vocabulary, general information, arithmetic, and other language- or symbol-oriented tasks.

Table 14–4 Sample Items Similar to Those Used on the WAIS-R

Verbal Subtests	Sample Items
Information	How many wings does a bird have? Who wrote *Paradise Lost*?
Digit span	Repeat from memory a series of digits, such as 3 1 0 6 7 4 2 5, after hearing it once.
General Comprehension	What is the advantage of keeping money in the bank? Why is copper often used in electrical wires?
Arithmetic	Three men divided 18 golf balls equally among themselves. How many golf balls did each man receive? If 2 apples cost 15¢, what will be the cost of a dozen apples?
Similarities	In what way are a lion and a tiger alike? In what way are a saw and a hammer alike?
Vocabulary	This test consists simply of asking, "What is a ____?" or "What does ____ mean?" The words cover a wide range of difficulty or familiarity.
Performance Subtests	**Description of Item**
Picture arrangement	Arrange a series of cartoon panels to make a meaningful story.
Picture completion	What is missing from these pictures?
Block design	Copy designs with blocks (as shown at right).
Object assembly	Put together a jigsaw puzzle.
Digit symbol	Fill in the symbols:

1	2	3	4
X	III	I	0

3	4	1	3	4	2	1	2

(Courtesy of The Psychological Corporation.)

Individual intelligence test A test of intelligence designed to be given to a single individual by a trained specialist.

Group intelligence test Any intelligence test that can be administered to a group of people with minimal supervision.

Table 14–5 Items from the Army Alpha Subtest on "Common Sense"

The *Army Alpha* was given to World War I army recruits in the United States as a way to identify potential officers. In these sample questions, note the curious mixture of folk wisdom, scientific information, and moralism (Kessen & Cahan, 1986). Other parts of the test were more like modern intelligence tests.

1. If plants are dying for lack of rain, you should
   - ☐ water them
   - ☐ ask a florist's advice
   - ☐ put fertilizer around them
2. If the grocer should give you too much money in making change, what is the right thing to do?
   - ☐ buy some candy for him with it
   - ☐ give it to the first poor man you meet
   - ☐ tell him of his mistake
3. If you saw a train approaching a broken track you should
   - ☐ telephone for an ambulance
   - ☐ signal the engineer to stop the train
   - ☐ look for a piece of rail to fit in
4. Some men lose their breath on high mountains because
   - ☐ the wind blows their breath away
   - ☐ the air is too rare
   - ☐ it is always cold there
5. We see no stars at noon because
   - ☐ they have moved to the other side of the earth
   - ☐ they are much fainter than the sun
   - ☐ they are hidden behind the sky

Group Tests

Both the Stanford-Binet and the Wechsler tests are **individual intelligence tests.** Individual tests must be given to a single person by a trained specialist. Other tests of intelligence are designed for use with large groups of people. **Group intelligence tests** are usually given in paper-and-pencil form. Typically, they require test takers to read, to follow instructions, and to solve problems of logic, reasoning, mathematics, or spatial skills. The first group intelligence test was the *Army Alpha*, developed for use in rating World War I military inductees. As you can see in Table 14–5, intelligence testing has come a long way since then.

Scholastic Aptitude Tests If you're wondering if you have ever taken an intelligence test, the answer is probably yes. As mentioned earlier, the *Scholastic Assessment Test* is a multiple aptitude test. So are the *American College Test* (ACT), and the *College Qualification Test* (CQT). Each of these group tests is designed to predict chances for success in college. Because the tests measure a variety of mental aptitudes, each can also be used to estimate general intelligence.

Learning Check

Check your comprehension before you continue reading.

1. The first successful intelligence test was developed by __________ _______________.
2. If we define intelligence by writing a test, we are using
   a. a circular definition *b.* an abstract definition
   c. an operational definition *d.* a chronological definition
3. Place an R or a V after each operation to indicate if it would be used to establish the reliability or the validity of a test.
   a. Compare score on one-half of test items to score on the other half. (   )
   b. Compare scores on test to grades, performance ratings, or other measures. (   )
   c. Compare scores from the test after administering it on two separate occasions. (   )
   d. Compare scores on alternate forms of the test. (   )
4. IQ was originally defined as __________ times 100.
5. The ability to answer general information and comprehension questions shows the most rapid decline during aging. T or F?
6. The WAIS-R is a group intelligence test. T or F?
7. Establishing norms and uniform procedures for administering a test are elements of standardization. T or F?
8. Scores on modern intelligence tests are based on one's deviation IQ (relative standing among test takers) rather than on the ratio between mental age and chronological age. T or F?

9. A person who displays the savant syndrome might score well on a special ________________ test, while scoring very low on an ________________ test.

Critical Thinking

Answers: 1. Alfred Binet 2. c 3. *a.* (R), *b.* (V), *c.* (R), *d.* (R) 4. MA/CA 5. F 6. F 7. T 8. T 9. aptitude, intelligence

Variations in Intelligence—The Numbers Game

Based on scores from a large number of randomly selected people, IQ ranges have been classified as shown in Table 14–6. A look at the percentages reveals a definite pattern. The distribution of IQs approximates a **normal** (bell-shaped) **curve,** in which the majority of scores fall close to the average, with far fewer at the extremes. Figure 14–6 shows this characteristic of measured intelligence.

Question: On the average, do males and females differ in intelligence?

Sex IQ does not give a definite answer to this question because intelligence test items are selected to be equally difficult for both sexes. It seems safe to assume that men and women do not differ in overall intelligence, and no significant IQ difference has been found. However, tests like the WAIS-R allow a comparison of the intellectual strengths and weaknesses of men and women.

For decades, women, as a group, performed better on test items that require verbal ability, vocabulary, and rote learning. Men, in contrast, were best at items that require visualization of spatial relationships and arithmetic reasoning. However, such male-female differences have almost disappeared in recent years among children and young adults. The small differences that still exist appear to be based on a tendency for parents and educators to encourage males, more than females, to learn math and spatial skills (Hyde & Linn, 1988).

Table 14–6 Distribution of Adult IQ Scores on the WAIS-R

IQ	Description	Percent
Above 130	Very superior	2.2
120–129	Superior	6.7
110–119	Bright normal	16.1
90–109	Average	50.0
80–89	Dull normal	16.1
70–79	Borderline	6.7
Below 70	Mentally retarded	2.2

Question: How do IQ scores relate to success in school, jobs, and other endeavors?

IQ and Achievement IQ differences of a few points tell little about intellectual potential. But when a broader range of scores is considered, meaningful differences emerge. The correlation between IQ and school grades is .50—a sizable association. If measured intelligence were the only factor affecting grades, the association might be even higher. However, motivation, special talents, off-campus educational opportunities, and many other factors influence school grades and success.

Interestingly, IQ is not as good a predictor of out-of-school achievements such as art, music, creative writing, dramatics, science, and leadership. Tests related to creativity, such as tests of ideational fluency (imagination) are much more strongly related to such achievements (Wallach, 1985).

As you might expect, there is also a relationship between IQ and job classification. Persons holding white-collar, professional positions average higher IQs than those in blue-collar occupational settings. For example, accountants, lawyers, and engineers average about 125 in IQ. In contrast, miners and farm workers average about 90 (Brody, 1992). It is important to note, however, that there is a range of IQ scores in all occupations. Many people of high intelligence, because of choice or circumstance, can be found in "low-ranking" jobs (Fig. 14–7).

Normal curve A bell-shaped curve with many scores in the middle, tapering to very few extremely high and low scores.

Fig. 14–6 *Distribution of Stanford-Binet Intelligence Test scores for 3184 children. (After Terman & Merrill, 1960.)*

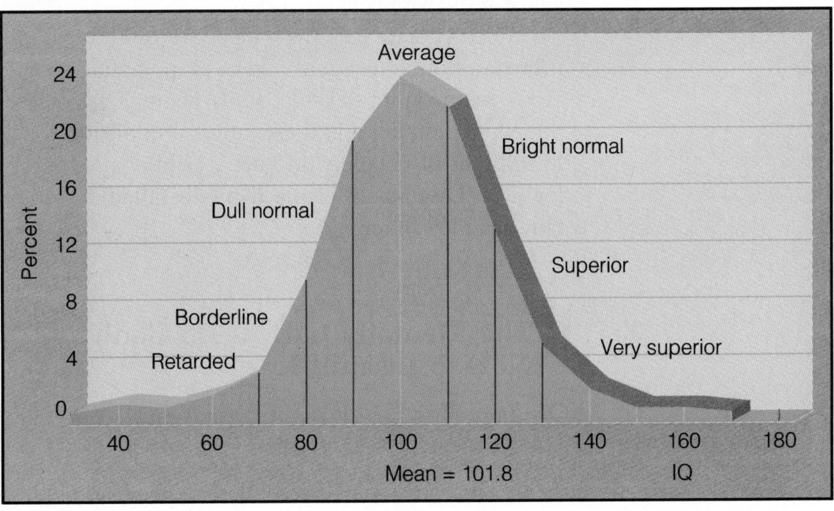

■ Fig. 14–7 *John Kirtley has an IQ score of 174, yet he prefers to do custodial work, feeling that his unusual intellect would be "used" by his employers if he pursued a technical occupation.*

It is tempting to interpret the link between IQ and occupation as evidence that professional jobs require more intelligence. This interpretation is dangerous because IQ tests require the same types of mental gymnastics needed for success in school. Since higher-status jobs often require an academic degree, the apparent connection between IQ and job status may be misleading. Selection procedures for professional jobs appear to be biased in favor of a particular type of intelligence, namely, the kind measured by intelligence tests (McClelland, 1994).

When IQs are extreme—below 70 or above 140—influences on adjustment and one's potential for success become unmistakable. Only about 3 percent of the population fall into these ranges, but this translates to millions of people who have exceptionally high or low IQs. Discussions of the mentally gifted and mentally retarded follow.

The Mentally Gifted—Is Genius Next to Insanity?

Question: How high is the IQ of a genius?

Only about 2 people out of 100 score above 130 on IQ tests. Such people are usually described as "gifted." Less than one half percent of the population scores above 140. These people can certainly be considered gifted or perhaps even "geniuses." However, some psychologists reserve the term *genius* for even higher IQs or for other qualities, such as exceptional creativity or insight (Kamphaus, 1993).

Gifted Children

Are high IQ scores in childhood associated with later ability? To directly answer this question, Lewis Terman selected 1500 children with IQs of 140 or more. Terman followed the development of this gifted group (the "Termites" as he called them) into adulthood. By doing so, Terman countered a number of popular misconceptions about high intelligence (Shurkin, 1992).

Misconception: The gifted tend to be peculiar, socially backward people.
Fact: On the contrary, Terman's gifted subjects were socially well adjusted and showed above-average leadership capacity.
Misconception: "Early ripe means later rot": The gifted tend to fizzle out as adults.
Fact: This is false. When retested as adults, Terman's subjects again scored in the upper IQ ranges.
Misconception: The very bright are usually physically inferior "eggheads" or weaklings.
Fact: This is also a misconception. As a group, the gifted were above average in height, weight, and physical appearance.
Misconception: The highly intelligent person is more susceptible to mental illness ("Genius is next to insanity").
Fact: Terman demonstrated conclusively that the gifted have better than average mental health records, indicating a greater *resistance* to mental illness. However, the very intelligent (IQ of over 180) may have social and behavioral adjustment problems as children (Janos & Robinson, 1985).
Misconception: Intelligence has nothing to do with success, especially in practical matters.
Fact: The later success of Terman's subjects was the most striking finding of the study. Far more of them than average had completed college, earned advanced degrees, and held professional positions. As a group, the gifted had produced dozens of books, thousands of scientific articles, and hundreds of short stories and other publications (Shurkin, 1992; Terman & Oden, 1959).

As noted earlier, IQ scores are not generally good predictors of real-world success. However, when scores are in the gifted range, the likelihood of outstanding achievement does seem to be higher.

Question: Were all of the gifted children superior as adults?

No. Remember that high IQ reveals intellectual *potential* and general mental ability. A high IQ is no guarantee of success or achievement. Some of the gifted had committed crimes, were unemployable, or were poorly adjusted.

Question: How did the more successful subjects differ from the less successful?

Giftedness and Achievement Most had parents who were educated and who valued learning. These parents, it seems, encouraged their children to become avid learners. Successful members of the gifted group also tended to show a high degree of *intellectual determination.* That is, they had a desire to know, to excel, and to persevere (Tomlinson-Keasey & Little, 1990).

As you can see, the most successful gifted persons tend to be *persistent* and *motivated* to learn and succeed. The meaning of such findings is clear: As one educator put it, "No one is paid to sit around being capable of achievement—what you do is always more important than what you should be able to do" (Whimbey, 1980). There are a lot of people walking around with high IQs who have learned and accomplished very little.

Question: How might a parent spot an unusually bright child?

Identifying Gifted Children Early signs of **giftedness** are not always purely "intellectual." The following signs may reveal that a child is gifted:

Giftedness Either the possession of a high IQ or special talents or aptitudes.

- A tendency to seek out and identify with older children and adults
- An ability to absorb information rapidly
- An early fascination with explanations and problem solving
- Talking in complete sentences as early as 2 or 3 years of age
- An unusually good memory
- Precocious talent in art, music, or number skills
- An early interest in books, along with early reading (often by age 3)
- Showing of kindness, understanding, and cooperation toward others (Alvino et al., 1985; Kamphaus, 1993).

Notice that this list contains behavior other than straight "academic" intelligence. Children may be gifted in ways other than having a high IQ (Sternberg & Davidson, 1985). In fact, if artistic talent, mechanical aptitude, musical aptitude, athletic potential, and so on, were considered, 19 out of 20 children could be labeled as having a special "gift" of some sort (■ Fig. 14–8). It may therefore be a mistake to identify giftedness primarily with IQ (Alvino et al., 1985). Such limited definitions of giftedness shortchange children with special talents or potentials (see Highlight 14–1). This is especially true of ethnic minority children, who may be the victims of subtle biases in standardized intelligence tests.

■ **Fig. 14–8** *It is wise to remember that there are many ways in which a child may be gifted. Many schools now offer Gifted and Talented Education programs for students with a variety of special abilities—not just for those who score well on IQ tests.*

General ability factor General mental ability presumed to explain performance on a wide variety of tasks.

Mental retardation The presence of a developmental disability, an IQ score below 70, or a significant impairment of adaptive behavior.

Adaptive behaviors Basic skills and actions considered necessary for self-care and for dealing successfully with the environment.

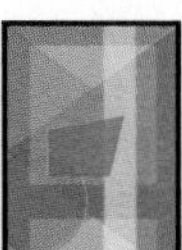

HIGHLIGHT 14–1

Focus on a Controversy

Frames of Mind—Seven Intelligences?

At an elementary school, a student who is two grades behind in reading shows his teacher how to solve a difficult computer programming problem. In a nearby room, one of his classmates, who is poor in math, plays an intricate piece of music on a piano. Both of these children show clear signs of intelligence. And yet, each might score below average on a traditional IQ test. Such observations have convinced many psychologists that it is time to forge new, broader definitions of intelligence. Their basic goal is to better predict "real-world" success—not just the likelihood of success in school (Sternberg, 1992).

One such psychologist is Howard Gardner of Harvard University. Gardner (1985) theorizes that there are actually seven different kinds of intelligence. These include abilities in (1) *language,* (2) *logic and math,* (3) *visual and spatial thinking,* (4) *music,* (5) *bodily-kinesthetic skills* (such as dance or athletics), (6) *intrapersonal skills* (self-knowledge), and (7) *interpersonal skills* (leadership, social abilities).

Most of us are probably strong in only a few types of intelligence. In contrast, geniuses like Albert Einstein seem to be able to use all of the intelligences, as needed, to solve problems.

If Gardner's theory is correct, traditional IQ tests measure only a part of real-world intelligence—namely, linguistic, logical-mathematical, and spatial abilities. A further implication is that our schools may be wasting a lot of human potential. For example, some children might find it easier to learn math or reading if these topics were tied into art, music, dance, drama, and so on.

Not all psychologists agree with Gardner's broader definition of intelligence. His view, in fact, is at odds with studies which suggest that scores on IQ tests mainly reflect an underlying "general intelligence" or **general ability factor** (often referred to as *g*) (Canavan et al., 1986). This *g-factor* is said to explain the high correlations found among scores on various tests of intellectual ability and achievement. Gardner's reply would probably be that such correlations only show how narrowly traditional tests define intelligence. Whether or not he is right, it seems likely that in the future intelligence will not be so strongly equated with IQ.

Being gifted in the sense of having a high IQ is not without its problems, particularly in childhood. The gifted child may become bored in a classroom designed for average children. Boredom can lead to behavioral problems or to clashes with teachers who consider the gifted child a show-off or smart aleck. The extremely bright child may also find classmates less stimulating than older children or adults (Alvino et al., 1985). In recognition of these problems, many school systems now provide special Gifted and Talented Education (GATE) programs and classes for gifted children. Such programs combine classroom enrichment with fast-paced instruction (Horowitz & O'Brien, 1986).

Mental Retardation—A Difference That Makes a Difference

A person with mental abilities far below average is termed **mentally retarded** or **developmentally disabled.** An IQ of approximately 70 or below is regarded as the dividing line for retardation. However, a person's ability to perform **adaptive behaviors** (such as dressing, eating, communicating, shopping, and working) also figures into evaluating retardation (DSM-IV, 1994; Kamphaus, 1993).

Levels of Retardation

Below an IQ of 70, the severity of retardation is classified as shown in Table 14–7. The listed IQ ranges are approximate because IQ scores normally vary a few points. The terms in the right-hand column are listed only to give you a general impression of each IQ range. Unless they are used cautiously, such terms can needlessly limit the educational goals of retarded persons (DSM-IV, 1994).

Question: Are the retarded usually placed in institutions?

No. Total care is only necessary for the **profoundly** retarded. Many of these individuals live within the community in group homes or with their families. The **severely** and **moderately** retarded are capable of mastering basic language skills and routine self-help skills. Many become self-supporting by working in *sheltered workshops* (special simplified work environments). The **mildly** retarded (about 85 percent of all those affected) benefit from carefully structured and supervised education. As adults, these persons, as well as the **borderline retarded,** are capable of living alone and may marry. However, they tend to have difficulties with many of the demands of adult life (Zetlin & Murtaugh, 1990).

It is important to realize that the developmentally disabled have no handicap where feelings are concerned. They are sensitive to rejection and easily hurt by teasing or ridicule. Likewise, they respond warmly to love and acceptance. Professionals working with the retarded emphasize that everyone has a right to self-respect and a place in the community. This is especially important during childhood, when the support of others adds greatly to the retarded person's chances of becoming a well-adjusted member of society (■ Fig. 14–9).

Causes of Retardation

Question: What causes mental retardation?

In 30 to 40 percent of cases, no known biological problem can be identified. In many such cases the degree of retardation is mild, in the 50 to 70 IQ range. Quite often other family members are also mildly retarded. **Familial retardation,** as this is called, occurs mostly in very poor households. In some such homes, nutrition, early stimulation, medical care, intellectual guidance, and emotional support are inadequate. This suggests that familial retardation is based largely on an impoverished environment (Plomin, 1989). Thus, many cases of retardation might be prevented by better nutrition, education, and early childhood enrichment programs. (See Chapter 12.)

Organic Sources of Retardation

About 50 percent of all cases of mental retardation are *organic*, or related to physical disorders, including **birth injuries** (such as a lack of oxygen), **fetal damage** (from disease, infection, or maternal abuse of drugs, especially alcohol or cocaine). Additional causes are **metabolic disorders** (such as cretinism and phenylketonuria, discussed in a moment), and **genetic abnormalities** (DSM-IV, 1994). Severe levels of retardation are likely to be associated with one or more such biological abnormalities. Let's briefly look at several distinctive problems.

Phenylketonuria (PKU) Phenylketonuria (FEN-ul-KEET-uh-NURE-ee-ah) is a genetic disease. It is caused by the lack of an important enzyme, which leads to a buildup of phenylpyruvic acid (a destructive chemical) within the body. PKU is also associated with abnormally low levels of dopamine, an important chemical messenger in the brain. If PKU goes untreated, severe retardation typically occurs by age 3.

PKU is now easily detected in babies by medical testing during the first two weeks of life. PKU can usually be controlled by a special diet low in foods containing the substance (phenylalanine) the child's body can't handle. (Phenylalinine is found in many foods.

● Table 14–7 Levels of Mental Retardation

IQ range	Degree of Retardation	Educational Classification	Required Level of Support
50–55 to 70	Mild	Educable	Intermittent
35–40 to 50–55	Moderate	Trainable	Limited
20–25 to 35–40	Severe	Dependent	Extensive
Below 20–25	Profound	Life support	Pervasive

(DSM-IV, 1994; Hodapp, 1994).

You might be interested to know that it is also found in Aspartame, the artificial sweetener in many diet colas.)

Microcephaly Microcephaly (MY-kro-SEF-ah-lee) means small-headedness. The microcephalic suffers a rare abnormality in which the skull is extremely small or fails to grow. The brain is forced to develop in a limited space, causing severe retardation that usually requires the individual to be placed in an institution. The microcephalic is typically affectionate, well behaved, and easy to work with.

Hydrocephaly Hydrocephaly (HI-dro-SEF-ah-lee: water on the brain) is caused by a buildup of cerebrospinal fluid within brain cavities. Pressure from this fluid can damage the brain and greatly enlarge the head. Hydrocephaly is not uncommon—about 8000 babies are born with the problem each year in the United States. Thanks to new medical procedures, most of these infants will now lead normal lives. Treatment involves surgically implanting a tube that drains

■ Fig. 14–9 *These youngsters are participants in the Special Olympics—an athletic event for the mentally retarded. It is often said of the Special Olympics that "everyone is a winner—participants, coaches, and spectators."*

Familial retardation Mild mental retardation associated with homes that are intellectually, nutritionally, and emotionally impoverished.

Birth injury Any injury or damage that occurs to an infant during delivery.

Fetal damage A congenital problem; that is, damage or injury that occurs to the fetus during prenatal development.

Metabolic disorder Any disorder in metabolism (the rate of energy production and use in the body).

Genetic abnormality Any abnormality in the genes, including missing genes, extra genes, or defective genes.

Phenylketonuria A genetic disease that allows phenylpyruvic acid to accumulate in the body.

Microcephaly A disorder in which the head and brain are abnormally small.

Hydrocephaly A buildup of cerebrospinal fluid within brain cavities.

Cretinism Stunted growth and mental retardation caused by an insufficient supply of thyroid hormone.

Down syndrome A genetic disorder caused by the presence of an extra chromosome; results in mental retardation.

fluid from the brain into the abdomen. If this is done within the first 3 months of life, retardation can usually be avoided.

Cretinism Cretinism (KREET-un-iz-um) is a form of retardation that develops in infancy due to an insufficient supply of thyroid hormone. In some parts of the world, cretinism is caused by too little iodine in the diet (iodine is necessary for normal thyroid function). Widespread use of iodized salt makes this cause of the condition rare in industrialized nations. Cretinism causes stunted physical and intellectual growth that cannot be corrected unless it is detected early. Fortunately, cretinism is easily detected in infancy and may be treated by thyroid hormone replacement.

Down Syndrome The disorder known as Down syndrome causes moderate to severe retardation and a shortened life expectancy (usually around 40 years) in 1 out of 800 babies. Distinctive features of this problem, once referred to as mongolism, are almond-shaped eyes, a slightly protruding tongue, stubby hands, a stocky build, and sometimes a deep crease on the palm of the hand. It is now known that Down children also have an extra chromosome. That is, cells in the child's body have 47 chromosomes, instead of the usual 46. This condition results from flaws in the parents' egg or sperm cells. Thus, while Down syndrome is *genetic*, it is not usually *hereditary* and does not "run in the family."

A very significant factor in Down syndrome is the age of parents at the time of conception. The reproductive cells of older men and women are more prone to errors during cell division, which raises the odds that an extra chromosome will be present. Mothers in their early 20s have about 1 chance in 2000 of giving birth to a Down syndrome baby. At age 40, the odds increase to about 1 in 105. By age 48, the risk reaches 1 in 12. The age of the father is also linked to increased risk. In about 25 percent of cases the father is the source of the extra chromosome (de la Cruz & Muller, 1983).

These rather significant changes in risk should be considered in family planning. There is no "cure" for Down syndrome. However, these children are usually loving and responsive, and they can make progress in a caring environment. Experts working with Down syndrome children emphasize that they can do most of the things that other children can do, only slower. There is evidence that Down children continue to learn and make slow mental progress well into adulthood (Berry et al., 1984). The best hope for Down syndrome victims therefore lies in specially tailored educational programs that enable them to lead fuller lives.

Learning Check

1. The distribution of IQs approximates a ________________ (bell-shaped) curve.
2. The association between IQ and high-status professional jobs proves that such jobs require more intelligence. T or F?
3. Differences in the intellectual strengths of men and women have grown larger in recent years. T or F?
4. Only about 6 percent of the population scores above 140 on IQ tests. T or F?
5. An IQ score below 90 indicates mental retardation. T or F?
6. Many cases of mental retardation without known organic causes appear to be ________________.
7. According to Howard Gardner's theory, the three basic human intelligences are linguistic skills, logic, and spatial skills. T or F?

Match:

8.____ PKU	A.	Too little thyroid hormone
9.____ Microcephaly	B.	Very small brain
10.____ Hydrocephaly	C.	47 chromosomes
11.____ Cretinism	D.	Lack of an important enzyme
12.____ Down Syndrome	E.	Excess of cerebrospinal fluid
	F.	Caused by a lack of oxygen at birth

Critical Thinking

13. Lewis Terman took great interest in the lives of many of the "Termites." He even went so far as to advise them about what kinds of careers they should pursue. What error of observation did Terman make?

Answers

1. normal 2. F 3. F 4. F 5. F 6. familial 7. F 8. D 9. B 10. E 11. A 12. C 13. Terman may have unintentionally altered the behavior of the people he was studying. Although Terman's observations are generally regarded as valid, he did break a basic rule of scientific observation.

Heredity and Environment—Super Rats and Family Trees

Question: Is intelligence inherited?

This seemingly simple question is loaded with controversy. Some psychologists believe that intelligence is strongly affected by heredity. Others feel that environment is dominant. Let's examine some of the evidence for each view.

In a classic study of genetic factors in learning, Tryon (1929) managed to breed separate strains of "maze-bright" and "maze-dull" rats (animals that were extremely "bright" or "stupid" at learning mazes). After several generations of breeding, the slowest "super rat" outperformed the best "dull" rat. This and other studies of **eugenics** (selective breeding for desirable characteristics) suggest that some traits are highly influenced by heredity.

Question: That may be true, but is maze-learning really a measure of intelligence?

No, it isn't. Tryon's study seemed to show that intelligence is inherited, but later researchers found that the "bright" rats were simply more motivated by food and less easily distracted during testing (Whimbey, 1980). When they weren't chasing after rat chow, the "bright" rats were no more intelligent than the supposedly dull rats. Thus, Tryon's study did demonstrate that behavioral characteristics are influenced by heredity, but it was inconclusive concerning intelligence. Because of such problems, animal studies cannot tell us with certainty how heredity and environment affect intelligence. Let's see what human studies reveal.

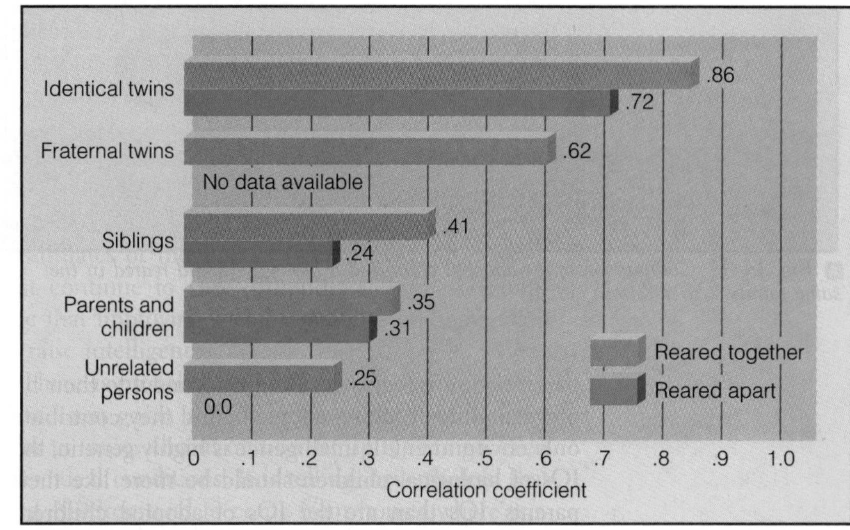

■ **Fig. 14–10** *Approximate correlations between IQ scores for persons with varying degrees of genetic and environmental similarity. Notice that the correlations grow smaller as the degree of genetic similarity declines. Also note that a shared environment increases the correlation in all cases. (Estimates from Bouchard, 1983; Henderson, 1982.)*

Hereditary Influences

Most people are aware that there is a moderate similarity in the intelligence of parents and their children, or between brothers and sisters. As ■ Figure 14–10 shows, the similarity in IQ scores among relatives grows in proportion to their closeness on the family tree.

Question: Does that indicate that intelligence is hereditary?

Not necessarily. Brothers, sisters, and parents share similar environments as well as similar heredity. To separate heredity and environment, we need to make some selected comparisons.

Twin Studies Notice in Figure 14–10 that the IQ scores of fraternal twins are more alike than those of ordinary siblings. **Fraternal twins** come from 2 separate eggs fertilized at the same time. They are no more genetically alike than ordinary siblings. Why then, should the twins' IQ scores be more similar? The reason is environmental: Parents treat twins more alike than ordinary siblings, resulting in a closer match in IQs.

More striking similarities are observed with **identical twins,** who develop from a single egg and have *identical* genes. At the top of Figure 14–10 you can see that identical twins who grow up in the same family have highly correlated IQs. This is what we would expect with identical heredity and highly similar environments. Now, let's consider what happens when identical twins are reared apart. As you can see, the correlation drops, but only from .86 to .72. Psychologists who emphasize genetics believe figures like these show that differences in adult intelligence are roughly 50 percent hereditary (Plomin & Rende, 1991; Weinberg, 1989).

Eugenics Selective breeding for desirable characteristics.

Fraternal twins Twins conceived from two separate eggs.

Identical twins Twins who develop from a single egg and have identical genes.

Question: How do environmentalists interpret the figures?

Environmentalists point out that some separated twins differ by as much as 20 IQ points. In every case where this occurs there are large educational and environmental differences between the twins (Whimbey, 1980). Also, separated twins are almost always placed in homes socially and educationally similar to their biological parents. This fact would tend to inflate apparent genetic effects by making the separated twins' IQs more alike (Kamin, 1981).

Environmental Influences

Strong evidence for an environmental view of intelligence comes from families having one adopted child and one biological child. As ■ Figure 14–11 shows,

and achievement. Strong encouragement of success in school is characteristic of many Asian-American families. Observations such as this emphasize that group differences in average IQ are based on environmental effects, not on heredity (Alva, 1993; Caplan et al., 1992; Yee et al., 1993).

A third argument against Jensen is that he overlooks the point made by the Dove Test. The assumptions, biases, and content of standard IQ tests do not always allow meaningful comparisons between ethnic, cultural, or racial groups (Helms, 1992; Miller-Jones, 1989). As Leon Kamin (1981) says, "The important fact is that we cannot say which sex (or race) might be more intelligent, because we have no way of measuring 'intelligence.' We have only IQ tests." Kamin's point is that the makers of IQ tests decided in advance to use test items that would give men and women equal IQ scores.

It would be just as easy to put together an IQ test that would give blacks and whites in this country equal scores. Differences in IQ scores are not a fact of nature, but a decision by the test makers. This is why whites do better on IQ tests written by whites, and blacks do better on IQ tests devised by blacks. Another example of this fact is an intelligence test made up of 100 words selected from the *Dictionary of Afro-American Slang*. Williams (1975) gave the test to 100 black and 100 white high school students in St. Louis and found that the black group averaged 36 points higher than the white group.

Perhaps the most devastating criticism of Jensen is that his logic is faulty. Consider this example: Corn comes in different varieties selectively bred to grow to a certain height. If we plant tall and short varieties side by side in the same field, we will observe a genetically determined difference in their height at maturity. But what if we take corn (all of the same variety) and plant half in a fertile field and half in poor soil? Again we observe a difference in maximum height, but this time it is clearly a mistake to assume that it is genetically caused.

Only when African-American children are raised in exactly the same surroundings as white children can hereditary factors be clearly assessed. Along this line, one revealing study looked at the fate of African-American children adopted by white families. These children had IQ scores averaging 106, which is comparable to the national average for white children (Scarr-Salapatek & Weinberg, 1975). It is not clear if the black children were actually "brighter" as a result of this experience or if they were just better prepared to take a "white" test. The fact remains, however, that when an equal opportunity for intellectual development can close the IQ gap, then narrow genetic views of IQ differences must be abandoned.

Questioning the Concept of IQ—Beyond the Numbers Game

African Americans are not the only segment of the population with reason to question the validity of intelligence testing and the role of heredity in determining intelligence. The clarifications won by African Americans extend to others as well.

Consider the 9-year-old child confronted with this question on an intelligence test: "Which of the following does not belong with the others? Roller skates, airplane, train, bicycle." If the child fails to answer "airplane," does it reveal a lack of intelligence? It can be argued that an intelligent choice could be based on any of these alternatives: Roller skates are not typically used for transportation; an airplane is the only non-land item; a train can't be steered; a bicycle is the only item with just two wheels. The parents of a child who misses this question may have reason to be angry since educational systems tend to classify children and then make the label stick.

Recent court decisions have led some states to outlaw the use of intelligence tests in public schools (see the Exploration section). Criticism of intelligence testing has also come from the academic community. Harvard University psychologist David McClelland believes that IQ is of little value in predicting real competence to deal effectively with the world. McClelland concedes that IQ predicts school performance, but when he compared a group of college students with straight A's to another group with poor grades, he found no differences in later career success (McClelland, 1973, 1994).

Standardized Testing

In addition to IQ tests, 400 to 500 million standardized multiple-choice tests are given in schools and workplaces around the nation each year. Many, like the *Scholastic Assessment Test*, may determine whether a person is admitted to college. Other tests—for employment, licensing, and certification—directly affect the lives of thousands by qualifying or disqualifying them for jobs.

Widespread reliance on standardized intelligence tests and aptitude tests raises questions about the relative good and harm they do. On the positive side, tests can open opportunities as well as close them. A high test score may allow a disadvantaged youth to enter college, or it may identify a child who is bright but emotionally disturbed. Test scores may also be fairer and more objective than arbitrary judgments made by admissions officers or employment interviewers. Also, tests *do* accurately predict academic performance. The fact that academic performance *does not* predict later success may call for an overhaul of college course work, not an end to testing.

On the negative side, mass testing can occasionally exclude people of obvious ability. In one case, a student who was seventh in his class at Columbia University, and a member of Phi Beta Kappa, was denied entrance to law school because he had low scores on the *Law School Admissions Test.* Other complaints relate to the frequent appearance of bad or ambiguous questions on standardized tests, overuse of class time to prepare students for the tests (instead of teaching general skills), and in the case of intelligence tests, the charge that tests are often biased. Also, most standardized tests demand passive recognition of facts, assessed with a multiple-choice format. They do not, for the most part, test a person's ability to think critically or creatively or to apply knowledge to solve problems (Jones & Appelbaum, 1989).

What should we make of the positive and negative aspects of standardized testing? Robert Glaser says we should remember that tests are "limited tools for limited purposes." Glaser also says that tests are now used primarily to *select* people. In schools they could instead be used to *adapt* instruction to the strengths, weaknesses, and needs of each student—thereby increasing the chances of success.

Conclusion

An application of the preceding discussion to your personal understanding of intelligence can be summarized in this way: Intelligence tests are a two-edged sword; we have learned much from their use, yet they have the potential to do great harm. In the final analysis, it is important to remember—as Howard Gardner has pointed out—that creativity, motivation, physical health, mechanical aptitude, artistic ability, and numerous other qualities not measured by intelligence tests contribute to achievement of life goals. Also remember that IQ is not intelligence. IQ is an index of intelligence (as narrowly defined by a particular test). Change the test and you change the score. An IQ is not some permanent number stamped on the forehead of a child that forever determines potential.

Let us end on an optimistic note. As discussed earlier in Highlight 14–2, some psychologists and educators are seeking ways to teach necessary intellectual skills to all children. In some cases their success has been striking. One experiment divided 40 children from extremely disadvantaged (slum) families into 2 groups. Children in the control group received no extra attention or training. Beginning shortly after birth, the experimental group was given a wide variety of stimulation to develop perceptual, motor, and language abilities. At age 2, the children in the experimental group were placed in small classes with other children and several teachers. Each child received lots of teacher attention and exposure to a broad range of topics and thinking exercises. When tested at age 5, the average IQ for the control group was about 95; the average for the experimentals was 124 (Whimbey, 1980). These results should be encouraging to everyone interested in the fulfillment of human potentials.

LEARNING CHECK

1. The WAIS-R, Binet-4, and Dove Test are all culture-fair intelligence scales. T or F?
2. Jensen's claim that heredity accounts for racial differences in average IQ ignores environmental differences and the cultural bias inherent in standard IQ tests. T or F?
3. IQ scores predict school performance. T or F?
4. IQ is not intelligence; it is one index of intelligence. T or F?
5. Assume that a test of memory for words is translated from English to Spanish. Would the Spanish version of the test be equal in difficulty to the English version? ***Critical Thinking***

Answers: 1. F 2. T 3. T 4. T 5. Probably not, because the Spanish words might be longer or shorter than the same words in English. The Spanish words might also sound more or less alike than words on the original test. Translating an intelligence test into another language can subtly change the meaning and difficulty of test items.

EXPLORATION

The Larry P. Case—"Six-Hour Retardates"

The Case: *Larry P. vs. the California State Superintendent of Education.*

The issue: Larry P. is one of six African-American children who claimed that biased IQ test scores were wrongly used to place them in classes for the educable mentally retarded (EMR).

The Outcome: In a landmark decision, a federal judge ruled that IQ test scores alone can no longer be used for EMR placement.

The ruling has virtually eliminated IQ testing in California schools. Similar rulings in other states have had the same effect (Kamphaus, 1993). The bare facts of the Larry P. case only hint at the interesting issues it raised. Testimony during the trial brought out the following:

For Larry P.: All six youngsters suing the state had scored below 75 on standardized IQ tests. But they scored from 17 to 35 points higher when retested by psychologists who used language and examples the children were familiar with.

For the State: Experts admitted that IQ test questions can be easier for some groups than for others. However, they held that IQ tests accurately predict school performance and are therefore valid.

For Larry P.: Witnesses pointed out that EMR assignments are almost always permanent. They also described the devastating effects of placing a child of normal intelligence in an EMR class. One researcher found that other students commonly refer to EMR students with cruel nicknames. EMR students are not expected to progress beyond the third- to fifth-grade level. Thus, by the time of graduation, a child of normal intelligence would be hopelessly behind other students. After graduation, EMR students find it difficult to get jobs, because they have been labeled "retarded."

For the State: Defense experts claimed that IQ tests help prevent mistakes in EMR assignments—for example, by revealing the true potential of a child who might be considered "slow" by a biased teacher. They also defended the EMR program as an effort to help less able students.

For Larry P.: Roughly twice as many African-American and Latino children are found in EMR classes than would be expected based on the percentage of African Americans and Latinos in the general population. This fact suggests a defect in the tests, not in the children.

Ignorance vs. Stupidity In the end, the judge ruled that IQ tests violate federal anti-discrimination laws. He was convinced, he said, that they are based mainly on verbal tasks that are unfair to children whose home environment does not provide practice in formal English or verbal skills. He further held that "if tests suggest that a young child is probably going to be a poor student, the school cannot, on that basis alone, deny that child the opportunity to develop and improve the academic skills necessary for success in our society."

Supporters of the Larry P. decision believe that it affirms the rights of disadvantaged children, whose ignorance—a lack of knowledge—has been mistaken for stupidity—a lack of intelligence. One such supporter is Jane Mercer, a sociologist who gave key testimony in the case.

Six-hour Retardates Mercer testified that the more a child's family is like the average white Anglo middle-class norm, the better the child scores on IQ tests. Mercer believes that schools often label children retarded when actually the children only lack culturally tied knowledge. Mercer has found that many African American or Latino EMR students show abundant signs of normal intelligence. A child who does poorly in the classroom or on an IQ test may function perfectly well at home and in the community. Mercer refers to such children as "six-hour retardates"—youngsters who are "retarded" only during the school day.

Question: If standardized IQ tests cannot be used to assess student abilities, what can?

SOMPA Mercer and her associate June Lewis think they have an answer. They call it SOMPA, which stands for System of Multicultural Pluralistic Assessment. SOMPA is not a new test. Rather, it's a different way of looking at children.

Question: How does SOMPA differ from standard IQ tests?

SOMPA combines three ways of assessing a child. First, it looks for any medical problems that may be causing low school performance. Next, the child's behavior outside the classroom is evaluated to avoid the mistake of creating a "six-hour retardate" on the basis of a test score. Third, SOMPA assumes that when everything else is held constant (educational advantages at home, especially), the child who has learned the most probably has the most "learning potential." Off-campus environments, however, are not equal. SOMPA therefore assumes that true potential can be masked by a child's cultural background. To avoid this problem, SOMPA compares each child's WISC score with that of children from similar backgrounds.

To show how SOMPA works, Mercer offers an example. Maria Gonzales is 7. She lives with her mother, father and five brothers and sisters in an inner-city barrio. Maria's mother and father both grew up in rural Mexico, where the mother finished fourth grade and the father second grade. Maria's family speaks only Spanish.

The average score for a child like Maria—with a background so different from core Anglo culture—is about 85. Maria's score on the WISC was 114, almost 30 points above this average. Mercer estimates Maria's real learning potential at 133. If her family had been more like the middle-class norm, Maria's score of 114 would have been accepted as accurate. Considering her age and background, Maria's performance on the WISC is truly outstanding. Maria is probably a gifted

EXPLORATION

child whose potential should not be wasted.

More IQ Controversy In 1986, Judge Robert Peckham, who issued the original opinion, reiterated the California IQ test ban. In fact, he added to it, saying "The prohibition on IQ tests goes further and prohibits any use of an IQ test as part of an assessment which could lead to special education placement or services, even if the test is only part of a comprehensive assessment plan" (Landers, 1986). This directive pretty much eliminated any form of IQ tests, even SOMPA, for evaluating African-American children.

Soon after Judge Peckham's ruling, a group of African-American parents filed a suit claiming that the ban on IQ testing discriminated against their children. It was nearly impossible, they pointed out, to use tests to identify learning disabilities or other problems if a child was making poor progress in school. In 1992, Judge Peckham revised his decision again. Children could be tested for learning disabilities, he decided, if their parents requested it. The ban on routine use of IQ tests for placement in EMR classes remains in effect, however (Turkington, 1992).

The State of the Debate

Understandably, the Larry P. decision and those that followed remain controversial. Some psychologists object to the courts making educational decisions. Others point out that they must now resort to non-standard alternative measures. Many of these alternatives are subjective and open to potential abuse. It may become easier, for instance, to rid classrooms of "problem children"—late bloomers, troublemakers, quirky learners—who may not be intellectually deficient, but just need more attention and understanding. Without IQ tests, how can such children be identified?

A typical reply from critics of IQ testing is that an IQ gives little information about the cause of a low score. It therefore tells little about what corrective action should be taken. To improve mental ability, IQ scores are not needed. The purpose of school is to help children learn and develop skills needed in adjusting to life and work (Baumeister, 1987).

In the years since the Larry P. case, studies of traditional intelligence tests continue to show that IQ tests predict school performance quite well (Kamphaus, 1993). Thus, it is fair to ask, Should a child who is intelligent, but educationally disadvantaged, be placed in a class that is too advanced for his or her ability level? Certainly, it is damaging to be falsely labeled "retarded." However, it can also be damaging to place children in classes for which they are unprepared.

What Do You Think? If you were the judge in the Larry P. case, how would you have ruled? If you were a school psychologist, how would you feel about using IQ tests or alternatives such as SOMPA? In your opinion, what role should IQ tests have in a democratic society?

LEARNING CHECK

1. The basic issue of the Larry P. case was whether children's IQs are lowered by placement in EMR classes. T or F?
2. Before the Larry P. case, placement in EMR classes was almost always done on the basis of group IQ test scores. T or F?
3. SOMPA is designed to obtain IQ scores from an assessment of a child's physical health and social functioning. T or F?
4. In the SOMPA system, IQ scores are compared to norms for children of similar cultural and social backgrounds. T or F?
5. According to the latest ruling, IQ tests can be used for educational placement in California EMR programs only when they are part of a comprehensive assessment plan. T or F?
6. Much of the Larry P. case centered on whether IQ tests are accurate measures of intelligence for all children. In other words, the debate revolved around the ____________ of IQ tests. ***Critical Thinking***

Answers: 1. F 2. T 3. F 4. T 5. F 6. validity

Chapter Summary

■ ***How do psychologists define intelligence?***

- **Intelligence** refers to one's general capacity to act purposefully, think rationally, and deal effectively with the environment.
- In practice, intelligence is **operationally defined** by the creation of intelligence tests.
- General intelligence is distinguished from specific **aptitudes. Special aptitude tests** and **multiple aptitude tests** are used to assess a person's capacities for learning various abilities. Aptitude tests measure a narrower range of abilities than **general intelligence tests** do.

■ ***What are the qualities of a good psychological test?***

- To be of any value, a psychological test must be **reliable** (give consistent results). A worthwhile test must also have **validity,** meaning that it measures what it claims to measure.
- Widely used intelligence tests are **objective** (they give the same result when scored by different people) and **standardized** (the same procedures are always used in giving the test, and **norms** have been established so that scores can be interpreted).

■ ***What are typical IQ tests like?***

- The first practical intelligence test was assembled by **Alfred Binet.** A modern version of Binet's test is the **Stanford-Binet Intelligence Scale, Fourth Edition.** A second major intelligence test is the **Wechsler Adult Intelligence Scale-Revised** (WAIS-R). The WAIS-R measures both **verbal** and **performance** intelligence.
- In addition to **individual tests,** intelligence tests have also been produced for use with groups. A **group test** of historical interest is the *Army Alpha.* The SAT, the ACT, and the CQT are group scholastic aptitude tests. Although narrower in scope than IQ tests, they bear some similarities to them.

■ ***How do IQ scores relate to gender, age, and occupation?***

- Intelligence is expressed in terms of an **intelligence quotient** (IQ). IQ is defined as **mental age** (MA) divided by **chronological age** (CA) and then multiplied by 100. An "average" IQ of 100 occurs when mental age equals chronological age.
- Modern IQ tests no longer calculate IQs directly. Instead the final score reported by the test is a **deviation IQ.**
- IQ scores become fairly stable at about age 6, and they become increasingly reliable thereafter. On the average, IQ scores continue to gradually increase until middle age. Later intellectual declines are moderate for most people until their 70s. Shortly before death, a more significant **terminal decline** in intelligence is often observed.
- The distribution of IQ scores approximates a **normal curve.** There are no overall differences between males and females in tested intelligence. However, very small gender differences may result from the intellectual skills our culture encourages males and females to develop.
- IQ is related to school grades and job status. The second association may be somewhat artificial because educational credentials are required for entry into many occupations.

■ ***What does IQ tell us about genius?***

- People with IQs in the **gifted** or "genius" range of above 140 tend to be superior in many respects.
- By criteria other than IQ, a large proportion of children might be considered gifted or talented in one way or another. Intellectually gifted children often have difficulties in average classrooms and benefit from special accelerated programs.

■ ***What causes mental retardation?***

- The terms **mentally retarded** and **developmentally disabled** are applied to those whose IQ falls below 70 or who lack various **adaptive behaviors.**
- Further classifications of retardation are: **mild** (50–55 to 70), **moderate** (35–40 to 50–55), **severe** (20–25 to 35–40), and **profound** (below 20–25). Chances for educational success are related to the degree of retardation.
- About 50 percent of the cases of mental retardation are **organic,** being caused by birth injuries, fetal damage, metabolic disorders, or genetic abnormalities. The remaining cases are of undetermined cause.
- Many cases of subnormal intelligence are thought to be the result of **familial retardation,** a generally low level of educational and intellectual stimulation in the home, coupled with poverty and poor nutrition.
- Five specialized forms of organic retardation are **phenylketonuria** (PKU), **microcephaly, hydrocephaly, cretinism,** and **Down syndrome.**

■ ***How do heredity and environment affect intelligence?***

- Studies of **eugenics** in animals and familial relationships in humans demonstrate that intelligence is partially determined by **heredity.** However, **environment** is also important, as revealed by changes in tested intelligence induced by stimulating environments.

- There is evidence that some elements of intelligence can be taught. Intelligence therefore reflects the combined effects of both heredity and environment in the development of intellectual abilities.

■ ***Are IQ tests fair to all racial and cultural groups?***

- Traditional IQ tests often suffer from a degree of **cultural bias.** For this and other reasons, it is wise to remember that IQ is merely an **index** of intelligence and that intelligence is narrowly defined by most tests.
- The use of standard IQ tests for educational placement of students (especially into special education classes) has been prohibited by law in some states. Whether this is desirable and beneficial to students is currently being debated.

Questions for Discussion

1. In what ways do you think our society encourages the development of different intellectual skills in males and females?
2. Do you know your IQ? Would you like to know it? Why or why not?
3. What advantages or disadvantages would you expect to be associated with knowing your own IQ? With having a teacher know your IQ? With having your parents know your IQ?
4. How might public education be restructured to encourage full intellectual development for all children? How might grading be changed to reflect broader definitions of intelligence?
5. How would you define "gifted"? Why are definitions important? What are the negative consequences of defining intelligence and giftedness at all?
6. How would you feel about the application of eugenics to human reproduction? Can you think of circumstances under which you would or would not consider it acceptable?
7. The debate over the relative importance of heredity and environment in determining intelligence has raged for decades. Why do you think the debate has lasted so long and attracted so much interest? If the heritability of IQ could be known with certainty, what difference would it make?
8. An organization called the Repository for Germinal Choice in Escondido, California, serves as a sperm bank for men, such as noted scholars and professionals, who presumably possess high IQs. Over 150 babies have been produced by artificial insemination from the sperm bank. Do you regard this as wise or unwise, ethical or unethical, foolish or inspired?

Chapter 15

Personality

IN THIS CHAPTER

Defining personality
Key concepts
Trait theories
Psychodynamic theories
Behavioral theories
Humanistic theories
Comparison of theories
Assessing personality
Sudden murderers
Applications:
Understanding shyness
Exploration:
Self-monitoring

CHAPTER PREVIEW

The Hidden Essence

Rural Colorado. The car lurched over the last few yards of brain-jarring ruts. Before us stood an ancient farmhouse, a hulking monument to neglect. Annette was out of the house—hooting and whooping—before we had stopped.

If anyone was suited for a move to the "wilds" of Colorado, it was Annette, the "terror of Tenth Street." Still, it was hard to imagine a more radical change. After separating from her husband, she had traded housewifery in the city for survival in the high country. Survival, by the way, is no exaggeration. Annette was working as a ranch hand and as a lumberjack (lumberjill?), trying to make it alone through some hard winters.

So radical were the changes in Annette's life, I must confess I expected just as radical a change in her. She was, on the contrary, more her "old self" than ever.

Perhaps you have had a similar experience. After several years of separation it is always intriguing to see an old friend. Often you will be struck at first by ways in which the person has changed. Soon, however, you will probably be pleased to discover how superficial such changes really are. Under it all there is a core that ties the semi-stranger before you to the person you once knew. It is exactly this core of consistency that psychologists have in mind when they use the term personality.

The Extra Dimension *Despite our advanced technology, the human dimension still determines success or failure in many situations. Errors in human judgment contributed* *significantly to the* Challenger *spacecraft disaster. Similarly, it is often said that the most dangerous part of an automobile is "the nut at the wheel." Without doubt, personality touches many aspects of our daily lives. Selecting a mate, choosing friends, getting along with co-workers, voting for a president, and numerous other activities raise questions about personality.*

What is personality? How does it differ from temperament, character, or attitudes? Is it possible to measure personality characteristics? These and related questions are the concerns of this chapter.

Survey Questions

- How do psychologists use the term *personality?*
- What core concepts make up the psychology of personality?
- Are some personality traits more basic or important than others?
- How do psychodynamic theories explain personality?
- What do behaviorists emphasize in their approach to personality?
- How do humanistic theories differ from other perspectives?
- How do psychologists measure personality?
- What causes shyness? What can be done about it?
- How does self-monitoring affect behavior?

Do You Have Personality?

"Jim's not handsome, but he has a great personality." "My father's business friends think he's a nice guy, but they should see him at home where his real personality comes out." "It's hard to believe Tanya and Nikki are sisters. They have such opposite personalities."

It's obvious from such statements that we all frequently use the term *personality.* But when asked, many people seem hard pressed to define personality. Most simply end up saying something about "charm," "charisma," or "style." If you use *personality* in such ways, you are giving it a different meaning than psychologists do. To a psychologist it makes little sense to ask, "Do I have personality?" or to proclaim, "She has lots of personality." In psychological terms, everyone has personality.

Question: Then how do psychologists use the term?

Most psychologists regard **personality** as a person's *unique and relatively stable behavior patterns.* In other words, personality refers to the consistency in who you are, have been, and will become. It also refers to the special blend of talents, attitudes, values, hopes, loves, hates, and habits that makes each of us a unique person.

Question: How is that different from the way most people use the term?

Many people confuse personality with **character.** The term *character* implies that a person has been *judged* or *evaluated,* not just described. If, by saying someone has "personality," you mean the person is friendly, outgoing, and attractive, you are really referring to what is considered good character in our culture. But in some cultures it is deemed good for a person to be fierce, warlike, and cruel. So, while everyone in a particular culture has personality, not everyone has character—or at least not good character. (Do you know any good characters?)

Personality is also distinct from **temperament.** As mentioned in Chapter 12, temperament is the "raw material" from which personality is formed. Temperament refers to the hereditary aspects of one's emotional nature: sensitivity, activity levels, prevailing mood, irritability, and adaptability (Kagan, 1989). As you may recall, even newborn babies differ in temperament.

Personality A person's unique and relatively stable behavior patterns.

Character Personal characteristics that have been judged or evaluated; a person's desirable or undesirable qualities.

Temperament The hereditary aspects of personality, including sensitivity, activity levels, prevailing mood, irritability, and adaptability.

Personality trait A behavioral characteristic displayed in most situations.

Psychology Looks at Personality

Psychologists use a large number of concepts to explain personality. It might be wise, therefore, to start with a few key terms. These ideas should help you keep your bearings as you read this chapter.

Traits We use the idea of traits every day in talking about the personalities of friends and acquaintances. For instance, my friend Dan is *sociable, orderly,* and *intelligent.* His sister Andrea is *shy, sensitive,* and *creative.* In general, psychologists think of **traits** as specific *lasting qualities* within a person that are inferred from observed behavior. If you see Dan talking to strangers—first at a supermarket and later at a party—you might deduce that he is "sociable." You might then predict from this trait that he will also be sociable at school or at work. As you can see, we often use traits to predict future behavior from past behavior (Rowe,

Personality type A style of personality defined by a group of related traits.

Introvert A person whose attention is focused inward; a shy, reserved, self-centered person.

Extrovert A person whose attention is directed outward; a bold, sociable, outgoing person.

■ **Fig. 15–1** *Do these men have personality? Do you?*

HIGHLIGHT 15–1

A Closer Look At

Personality—When Is the Plaster Set?

At what age are the major outlines of personality firmly established? When is the "plaster set"? Certainly, it is possible for personality to change dramatically at any age. This is rare, however. Studies show that in your 20s the mold of your personality begins to harden. By age 30, personality has typically become quite stable. After that, major shifts in who you are tend to be unusual. Research suggests that when major changes do occur, they are associated with dramatic life events, such as personal catastrophes or tragedies. After age 30, simply moving to a new city, changing your looks, or finding new friends won't reshape your basic personality. The person you are at age 30 is, for the most part, the person you will be at age 60. (Sources: Costa & McCrae, 1992; Roan, 1992.)

1987) (■ Fig. 15–2). Traits also imply some consistency in behavior. As an example, think about how little the personality traits of your best friends have changed in the last 5 years (Highlight 15–1). It would be strange indeed to feel like you were talking with a different person each time you met a friend or acquaintance.

■ **Fig. 15–2** *Psychologists and employers are especially interested in the personality traits of individuals who hold high-risk, high-stress positions involving public safety, such as police, air traffic controllers, and nuclear power plant employees.*

Types Have you ever asked the question, "What type of person is she (or he)?" before meeting someone new? An interest in personality *types* is quite natural. People who have several traits in common are said to have the same **personality type** (Potkay & Allen, 1986). Informally, it is quite common to speak of personality types. Your own thinking might include the executive type, the athletic type, the motherly type, the Yuppie type, the strong silent type, and so forth. If I asked you to define these informal types, you would probably list a different collection of traits for each one.

Question: How valid is it to speak of personality "types"?

Over the years, psychologists have proposed many ways to categorize personalities into types. Consider the idea, first advanced by Swiss psychiatrist Carl Jung (yoong), that a person is either an **introvert** (shy, self-centered person) or an **extrovert** (bold, outgoing person). These terms are so widely used that you may think of yourself and your friends as being one type or the other. However, the wildest, wittiest, most party-loving "extrovert" you know is introverted at times, and extremely introverted persons are assertive and sociable in some situations. In short, two categories (or even several) are often inadequate to fully describe differences in personality. That's why rating people on a list of traits is often more informative than classifying them into two or three types.

THE FAR SIDE By GARY LARSON

The four basic personality types

Even though types tend to oversimplify personality, they do have value. Most often, types are used as a shorthand way of labeling people who have several key traits in common. You might recall from Chapter 11, for instance, that classifying people as Type A or Type B personalities helps predict their chances of suffering a heart attack. (Type A personalities have these traits: competitive, striving, hostile, and time-urgent.) Similarly, you will read in Chapter 16 about unhealthy personality types such as the paranoid personality, the dependent personality, and the antisocial personality. Each is defined by a specific collection of maladaptive traits.

Self-Concept Another way of understanding personality is to focus on a person's self-concept. The rough outlines of your own self-concept would be revealed by this request: "Please tell us about yourself." In other words, a **self-concept** is a person's *perception* of his or her own personality traits. It consists of all your ideas and feelings about who you are (Potkay & Allen, 1986).

Many psychologists believe that self-concepts have a major impact on behavior. We creatively build our self-concepts out of daily experience. Then we slowly revise them as we have new experiences. Once a stable self-concept exists, it tends to shape our subjective world by guiding what we attend to, remember, and think about (Markus & Nurius, 1986).

An individual's self-concept can greatly affect personal adjustment—especially when the self-concept is *inaccurate* or *inadequate* (Potkay & Allen, 1986). As an example, consider Maryanne, a student who thinks she is stupid, worthless, and a failure, despite having completed three years of college with good grades. With such a negative self-concept, Maryanne will probably be depressed or anxious no matter how well she does. Problems of this type are explored later in this chapter.

Self-concept A person's perception of his or her own personality traits.

Personality theory A system of concepts, assumptions, ideas, and principles used to understand and explain personality.

Trait theorist A psychologist interested in classifying, analyzing, and interrelating traits, to understand and explain personality.

Personality Theories Personality is so complex that we might easily become lost without a guiding framework for understanding it. How do the observations we make about personality fit together? How does personality develop? Why do people become emotionally unhealthy? How can they be helped? To answer such questions, psychologists have created a dazzling array of theories. A **personality theory** is a system of assumptions, ideas, and principles proposed to explain personality (■ Fig. 15–3).

As there are dozens of personality theories, it is possible to introduce only a few of the most influential. Four broad perspectives we will consider are: **trait theories, psychodynamic theories, behavioristic theories,** and **humanistic theories.** Trait theories attempt to learn what traits make up personality and how

■ **Fig. 15–3** *English psychologist Hans Eysenck believes that many personality traits are related to whether you are mainly introverted or extroverted and whether you tend to be emotionally stable or unstable (highly emotional). These characteristics, in turn, are related to four basic types of temperament first recognized by the early Greeks. The types are:* melancholic *(sad, gloomy),* choleric *(hot-tempered, irritable),* phlegmatic *(sluggish, calm), and* sanguine *(cheerful, hopeful). (Adapted from Eysenck, 1981.)*

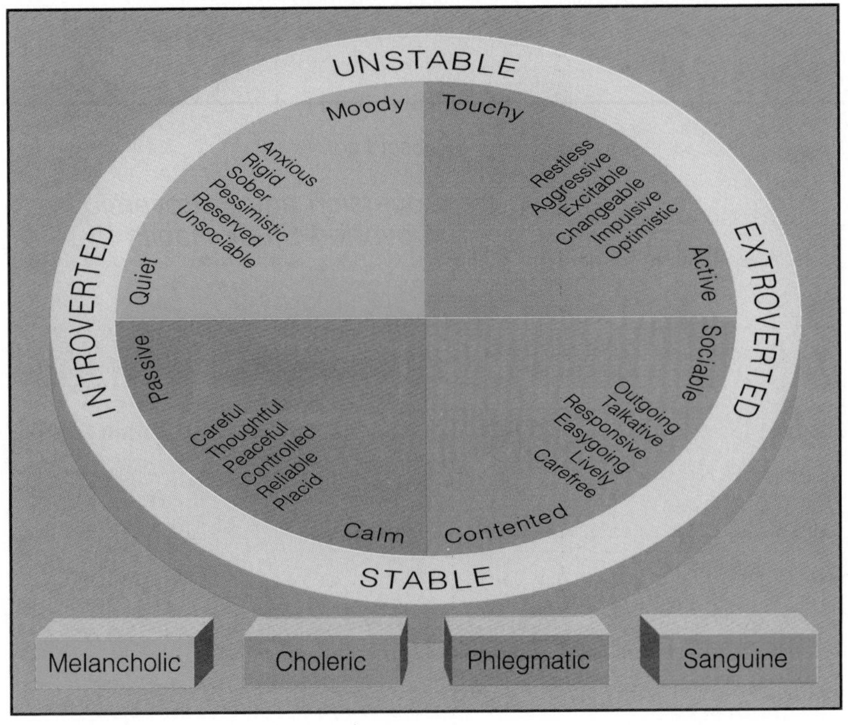

Common traits
Personality traits that are shared by most members of a particular culture.

Individual traits
Personality traits that define a person's unique individual qualities.

they relate to actual behavior. Psychodynamic theories focus on the inner workings of personality, especially internal conflicts and struggles. Behavioristic theories place greater importance on the external environment and on the effects of conditioning and learning. Humanistic theories stress private, subjective experience and personal growth.

The Trait Approach—Describe Yourself in 18,000 Words or Less

Now that you are oriented, let's take a deeper look at personality. How many words can you think of to describe the personality of a close friend? You should have little trouble making a long list: Over 18,000 English words refer to personal characteristics. As we have said, **traits** are *relatively permanent and enduring qualities* that a person shows in most situations. For example, if you are usually optimistic, reserved, and friendly, these qualities might be considered stable traits of your personality.

Question: What if I am sometimes pessimistic, uninhibited, or shy?

The first three qualities are still traits as long as they are most *typical* of your behavior. Let's say Ima Student approaches most situations with optimism, but has a habit of expecting the worst each time she takes a test. If her pessimism is limited to this situation or to a few others, it is still accurate and useful to describe her as an optimistic person. Notice again, in Highlight 15–2, that traits help us predict behavior.

HIGHLIGHT 15–2

A Closer Look At

Introversion and Extroversion—Extroverted Study Habits

As we have noted, separating people into broad types, such as "introvert" or "extrovert," may oversimplify personality. However, introversion/extroversion can also be thought of as a trait. Knowing how you rate on this single dimension of personality would allow us to predict how you will behave in a variety of settings. Where, for example, do you prefer to study in the library? One study found that students scoring high in the trait of extroversion choose study locations that have higher noise levels and provide more chances for socializing (Campbell & Hawley, 1982). In the campus library at Colgate University (where the study was done), you can find extroverted students in the second floor lounge. Or, if you prefer, more introverted students can be found studying in the carrels on the first and third floors!

In general, the trait approach attempts to identify traits that best describe a person. Take a moment to check the traits in Table 15–1 that you feel describe your personality. Are the traits you checked of equal importance? Are some stronger or more basic than others? Do any overlap? For example, if you checked "dominant," did you also check "confident" and "bold"? Answers to these questions would interest a **trait theorist.** To understand personality, trait theorists attempt to classify traits and to discover which are most basic.

Question: Are there different kinds of traits?

Classifying Traits

Psychologist Gordon Allport (1961) identified several kinds of traits. **Common traits** are those shared by most members of a culture. Common traits show how people from a particular nation or culture are similar, or which traits the culture emphasizes. In American culture, for example, competitiveness is a fairly common trait. Among the Hopi of Northern Arizona, it is a relatively rare trait.

Of course, common traits tell us little about individuals. While many people are competitive in American culture, each person may rate high or low in this trait. Usually we are also interested in these unique qualities, or **individual traits.** If the difference between common traits and individual traits is unclear,

Table 15–1 Adjective Checklist

Check the traits you feel are characteristic of your personality. Are some more basic than others?

aggressive	jealous	helpful
organized	sociable	emotional
ambitious	honest	orderly
clever	funny	anxious
confident	religious	conforming
loyal	dominant	good-natured
generous	dull	liberal
calm	accurate	curious
warm	nervous	optimistic
bold	humble	kind
cautious	uninhibited	meek
reliable	visionary	neighborly
sensitive	cheerful	passionate
mature	thoughtful	compulsive
talented	serious	intelligent

consider this analogy: If you were going to buy a pet dog, you would want to know the general characteristics of a particular breed (its common traits). In addition, you would want to know about the "personality" of a specific dog before selecting it (its individual traits).

Allport also made distinctions between **cardinal traits, central traits,** and **secondary traits.** A cardinal trait is so basic that all of a person's activities can be traced to the trait's existence. It is said, for instance, that an overriding factor in the life of Albert Schweitzer was "reverence for every living thing." Likewise, Abraham Lincoln's personality was dominated by the cardinal trait of honesty. According to Allport, few people have cardinal traits.

Question: How do central and secondary traits differ from cardinal traits?

Central Traits Central traits are the basic building blocks of personality. Allport found that a surprisingly small number of central traits are enough to capture the essence of a person. College students asked to describe someone they knew well mentioned an average of only 7 central traits (Allport, 1961).

In contrast, secondary traits are less consistent and less important aspects of a person. For this reason, any number of secondary traits could be listed in a personality description. Your own secondary traits include such things as food preferences, attitudes, political opinions, musical tastes, and so forth. In Allport's terms, a personality description might therefore include the following.

Name: Jane Doe
Age: 22
Cardinal traits: None
Central traits: Possessive, autonomous, artistic, dramatic, self-centered, trusting
Secondary traits: Prefers colorful clothes, likes to work alone, politically liberal, always late (and so forth).

Source Traits A second major approach to the study of traits is illustrated by the work of Raymond B. Cattell (1965). Cattell was dissatisfied with merely classifying traits. Instead, he wanted to reach deeper into personality to learn how traits are organized and interlinked.

Cattell began by studying features that make up the visible areas of personality. He called these **surface traits.** Through the use of questionnaires, direct observation, and life records, Cattell assembled data on the surface traits of a large number of people. He then noted that surface traits often appear in *clusters,* or groups. In fact, some traits appeared together so often that they seemed to represent a single more basic trait. Cattell called such underlying personality characteristics **source traits.**

Question: How do source traits differ from Allport's central traits?

The main difference is that Allport classified traits subjectively, whereas Cattell used a statistical technique called **factor analysis** to reduce surface traits to source traits. Factor analysis uses correlations to identify traits that are interrelated. Using this approach, Cattell developed a list of 16 underlying source traits. He considers this the basic number necessary to describe an individual personality.

Cattell's source traits are measured by a test called the *Sixteen Personality Factor Questionnaire* (often referred to as the 16 PF). Like many tests of its type, the 16 PF can be used to produce a **trait profile.** A trait profile presents a graph of a person's scores for each trait. Trait profiles can be very helpful for obtaining a "picture" of an individual personality or for making comparisons between the personalities of two or more persons (■ Fig. 15–4).

The Big Five Noel is outgoing and friendly, conscientious, emotionally stable, and smart. His brother Joel is introverted, hostile, irresponsible, emotionally unpredictable, and disinterested in ideas (stupid). You

Cardinal trait A personality trait so basic that all of a person's activities relate to it.

Central traits The core traits that characterize an individual personality.

Secondary traits Traits that are inconsistent or relatively superficial.

Surface traits The visible or observable traits of personality.

Source traits Basic underlying traits of personality; each source trait is reflected in a number of surface traits.

Factor analysis A statistical technique used to correlate multiple measurements that reflect some general underlying factor.

Trait profile A graph of the scores obtained on several personality traits.

■ **Fig. 15–4** *The 16 source traits measured by Cattell's 16 PF are listed beside the graph. Scores can be plotted as a profile for an individual or a group. The profiles shown here are group averages for airline pilots, creative artists, and writers. Notice the similarity between artists and writers and the difference between these two groups and pilots. (After Cattell, 1973.)*

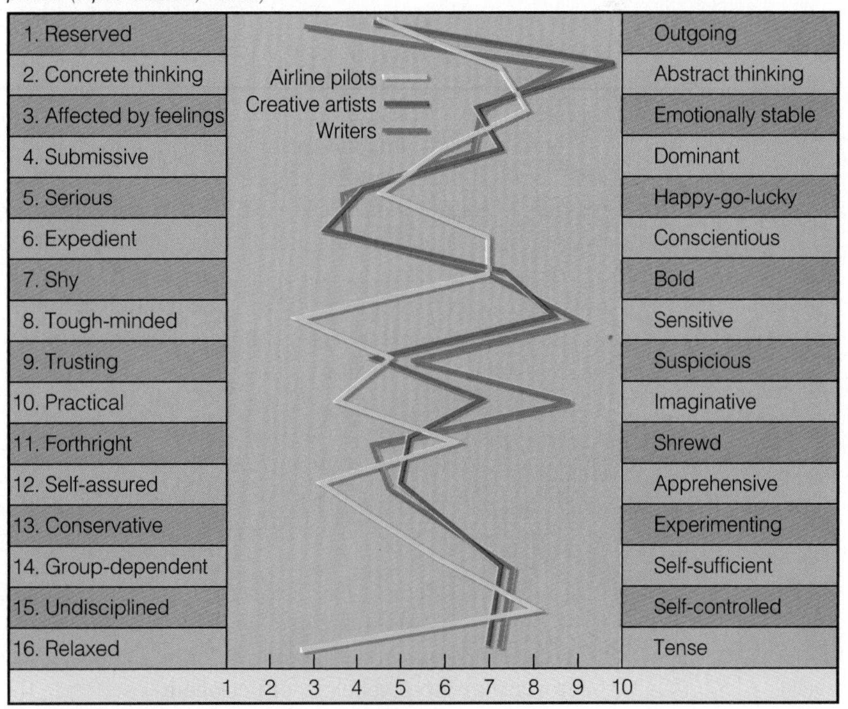

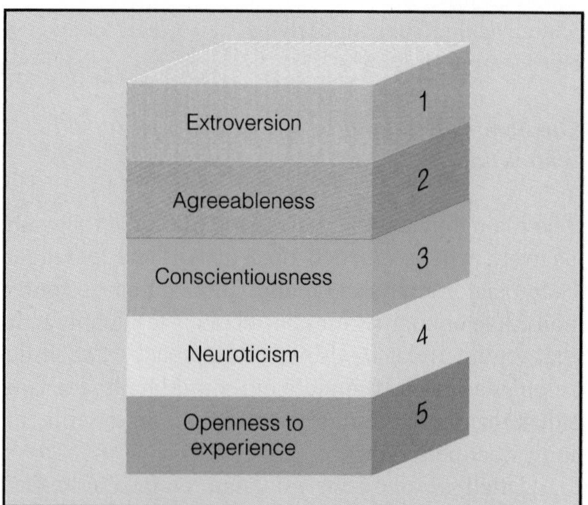

■ **Fig. 15–5** *The Big Five. According to the five-factor model, basic differences in personality can be "boiled down" to the dimensions shown here. The five-factor model answers these essential questions about a person: Is she/he extroverted or introverted? Agreeable or difficult? Conscientious or irresponsible? Emotionally stable or unstable? Smart or unintelligent? These questions cover a large measure of what we might want to know about someone's personality.*

Five-factor model Proposes that the most universal dimensions of personality are extroversion, agreeableness, conscientiousness, neuroticism, and openness to experience.

will be spending a week in a space capsule with either Noel or Joel. Who would you choose? If the answer seems obvious, it may be because we have described Noel and Joel in terms of the **five-factor model** of personality. The "Big Five" factors listed in ■ Figure 15–5 are the result of attempts to further reduce Cattell's 16 factors to just 5 universal dimensions (Digman, 1990; Goldberg, 1993). The Big Five may be the best answer of all to the question, What are the most basic dimensions of personality?

If you would like to compare the personalities of two people, try rating them informally on the 5 dimensions shown in Figure 15–5. For factor 1, *extroversion,* rate how introverted or extroverted each person is. Factor 2, *agreeableness,* refers to how friendly, nurturant, and caring a person is, as opposed to cold, indifferent, self-centered, or spiteful. A person who is *conscientious* (factor 3) is self-disciplined, responsible, and achieving. People low on this factor are irresponsible, careless, and undependable. The fourth factor, *neuroticism,* refers to the presence of negative, upsetting emotions. People who are high in neuroticism tend to be anxious, emotionally "sour," and irritable. Finally, people who rate high on factor 5, *openness to experience,* are intelligent, open to new ideas, and interested in cultural pursuits (Digman, 1990). The beauty of this model is that almost any trait you might name will be related to one of the five factors.

Before you read the next section, take a moment to answer the questions in Highlight 15–3. Doing so will add to your understanding of a long-running controversy in the psychology of personality.

HIGHLIGHT 15–3

Rate Yourself

How Do You View Personality?

The questions that follow may help you gain insight into the assumptions you make about personality. Answer true or false for each statement.

1. My friends' actions are fairly consistent from day to day and in different situations. T or F?
2. Whether a person is honest or dishonest, kind or cruel, a hero or a coward, depends mainly on circumstances. T or F?
3. Most people that I have known for several years have pretty much the same personalities now as they did when I first met them. T or F?
4. The reason that people in some professions (such as teachers, lawyers, or doctors) seem so much alike is because their work requires that they act in particular ways. T or F?
5. One of the first things I would want to know about a potential roommate is what the person's personality is like. T or F?
6. I believe that immediate circumstances usually determine how people act at any given time. T or F?
7. To be comfortable in a particular job, a person's personality must match the nature of the work. T or F?
8. Almost anyone would be polite at a wedding reception; it doesn't matter what kind of personality the person has. T or F?

Now count the number of times you marked true for the odd-numbered items. Do the same for the even-numbered items. If you agreed with most of the odd-numbered items, you tend to view behavior as strongly influenced by personality traits or lasting personal dispositions. If you agreed with most of the even-numbered items, you view behavior as strongly influenced by external situations and circumstances. If the number of times you answered true is nearly equal for odd and even items, you place equal weight on traits and situations as sources of behavior. This is the view now held by many personality psychologists.

Traits, Consistency, and Situations

For many years, psychologists debated this question: Which most affects our behavior, personality traits or external circumstances? There is now little doubt that personality traits remain consistent over long periods of time (Conley, 1984; Costa & McCrae, 1992; Roan,

1992). And yet, *situations* also exert a powerful influence on behavior. For instance, it would be unusual to find someone reading a book at a football game or dancing at a movie. Likewise, few people sleep in roller coasters or tell jokes at funerals. On the other hand, your personality traits may help predict whether you choose to read a book, go to a movie, or attend a football game in the first place. Most psychologists now agree that traits *interact* with situations to determine behavior (Carson, 1989). (This point is expanded later in this chapter.)

To illustrate some **trait-situation interactions,** imagine what would happen if you moved from a church to a classroom to a party to a football game. As the setting changed, your behavior would probably become more loud and boisterous. This change would demonstrate situational effects on behavior. At the same time, your personality traits would also be apparent: If you were quieter than average in class, you would probably be quieter than average in the other settings too (Rorer & Widiger, 1983).

Question: How much does heredity affect personality traits?

Do We Inherit Personality?

Some breeds of dogs have reputations for being friendly, aggressive, intelligent, calm, or emotional. Such differences fall in the realm of **behavioral genetics**—the study of inherited *behavioral* traits. We know that facial features, eye color, body type, and other physical characteristics are inherited. So are many behavioral traits. For instance, selective breeding of animals can lead to striking differences in social behavior, emotionality, learning ability, aggression, activity, and other behaviors (Sprott & Staats, 1975).

Question: To what extent do such findings apply to humans?

Genetic studies of humans rely on comparisons of identical twins and other close relatives (Plomin, DeFries, & McClearn, 1990). Such studies are not as conclusive as work done with animals. Nonetheless, they show that intelligence, some mental disorders, temperament, and other complex qualities are influenced by heredity (Gatz, 1990). (For examples of behavioral genetic research, see Chapters 12, 14, and 17.) In view of findings like these, we also might wonder, Do genes affect personality?

Question: Wouldn't comparing the personalities of identical twins help answer the question?

It would indeed—especially if the twins were separated at birth or soon after.

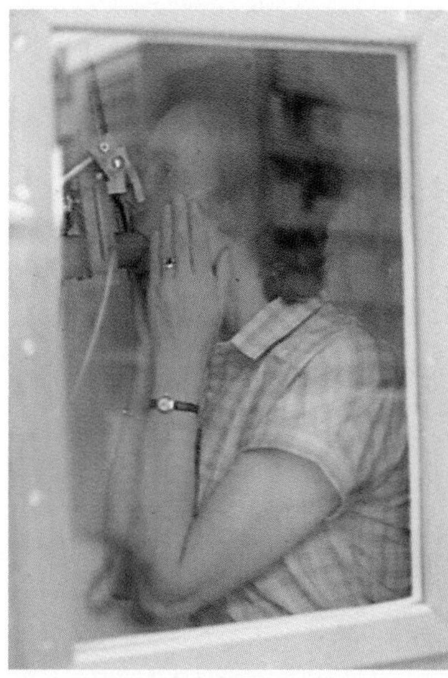

■ **Fig. 15–6** *Reunited identical twins Terry and Margaret undergo lung function tests at the University of Minnesota. Researchers collected a wide range of medical and psychological data for each set of twins.*

Twins and Traits Over the past decade, psychologists at the University of Minnesota have been studying identical twins who grew up in different homes. At the university, reunited twins take a wide range of medical and psychological tests (■ Fig. 15–6). The results of these tests and other studies indicate that identical twins are much alike, even when they are reared apart (Bouchard et al., 1990; Lykken et al., 1992).

Like all identical twins, reunited twins are astonishingly similar in appearance and voice quality. Observers are also struck by how often the twins display identical facial gestures, hand movements, and nervous tics, such as nail biting or finger tapping. Separated twins also tend to share similar talents. If one twin excels at art, music, dance, drama, or athletics, the other is likely to also—despite wide differences in childhood environment (Farber, 1981). However, Highlight 15–4 explains why it's wise to be cautious about some reports of extraordinary similarities in reunited twins.

Trait-situation interaction Expression of a personality trait that is influenced by external settings or circumstances.

Behavioral genetics The study of inherited behavioral traits and tendencies.

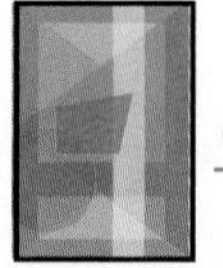

HIGHLIGHT 15–4

Critical Thinking

The Minnesota Twins

Many reunited twins in the Minnesota study displayed similarities far beyond what would be expected on the basis of heredity. A good example is provided by the "Jim twins," James Lewis and James Springer. Both Jims had married and divorced women named Linda. Both had undergone police training. Both had named their first-born sons James Allan. Both drove Chevrolets and vacationed at the same beach each summer. Both listed carpentry and mechanical drawing among their hobbies. Both had built benches around trees in their yards. And so forth (Holden, 1980).

Such coincidences may seem amazing at first. But the astute reader will realize that they have little to do with genetics. Equally "amazing" similarities may also occur for unrelated persons. In fact, one study compared twins with unrelated pairs of students of the same age and sex. The unrelated pairs were almost as alike as the twins with respect to political beliefs, musical interests, religious preferences, jobs held, hobbies, favorite foods, and so on (Wyatt et al., 1984). This is true because people of the same age and sex live in the same historical times and select from a similar range of societal options.

Imagine that you were separated at birth from a twin brother or sister. If you were reunited with your twin today, what would you do? Quite likely, you would spend the next several days comparing every imaginable detail of your lives. Under such circumstances it is virtually certain that you and your twin would compile a long list of similarities. ("Wow! I use the same brand of toothpaste you do!") Yet, two unrelated persons of the same age, sex, and race could probably rival your list—*if* they were as motivated to find similarities.

To summarize, many of the seemingly "astounding" coincidences shared by reunited twins may be a special case of the fallacy of positive instances, described in Chapter 1. Similarities blaze brightly in the memories of reunited twins, while differences are ignored.

Studies of separated twins make it clear that heredity has a sizable effect on each of us. All told, it seems reasonable to conclude that there is a genetic factor in personality (Gatz, 1990). Heredity appears to be responsible for 20 to 45 percent of the variation in some personality traits (Loehlin et al., 1988; Pedersen, et al., 1988; Plomin, 1989). Notice, however, that the same figures imply personality is shaped as much, or more, by environment as it is by heredity (Gatz, 1990). That's why the personalities of separated twins slowly become more and more different the longer they live apart (Baker & Daniels, 1990; McCartney, Bernieri, & Harris, 1990).

In summary, each personality is a unique blend of heredity and environment, biology and culture (Baker & Clark, 1990). We are not—thank goodness—genetically programmed robots whose behavior and personality traits are "wired in" for life.

Learning Check

1. ______________ refers to the hereditary aspects of a person's emotional nature.
2. The term ______________ refers to the presence or absence of desirable personal qualities.
   a. personality *b.* source trait *c.* character *d.* temperament
3. A system that classifies all people as either introverts or extroverts is an example of a ______________ approach to personality.
4. An individual's perception of his or her own personality constitutes that person's ______________.
5. According to Allport, few people have ______________ traits.
6. Central traits are those shared by most members of a culture. T or F?
7. Cattell believes that clusters of ______________ traits reveal the presence of underlying ______________ traits.
8. Cattell's personality questionnaire provides ratings on 16 surface traits. T or F?
9. Which of the following is *not* one of the Big Five personality factors?
   a. submissiveness *b.* agreeableness *c.* extroversion *d.* neuroticism
10. To understand personality it is wise to remember that traits and situations ______________ to determine our behavior.
11. ______________ ______________ is the study of how heredity influences personality, intelligence, and other behavioral traits and patterns.

Critical Thinking

12. How does memory contribute to the formation of an accurate or inaccurate self-image?

Answers: 1. Temperament 2. *c* 3. type 4. self-concept 5. cardinal 6. F 7. surface, source 8. F 9. *a* 10. interact 11. Behavioral genetics 12. As discussed in Chapter 8, memory is highly selective, and long-term memories are often revised or distorted to fit new information. Such properties add to the moldability of self-concepts.

Psychoanalytic Theory—Id Came to Me in a Dream

Psychodynamic theorists are not content with studying personality traits. Instead, they want to probe under the surface of personality—to learn what drives, conflicts, and energies animate us. **Psychoanalytic theory,** the best-known psychodynamic approach, grew out of the work of Sigmund Freud, a Viennese physician. Freud became interested in personality when he realized that many of his patients' problems seemed to lack physical causes. Starting about 1890 and continuing until he died in 1939, Freud evolved a theory of personality that deeply influenced modern thought. Freud's theory is far more complex than a short sketch can show. We will consider only its main features.

Question: How did Freud view personality?

The Structure of Personality

Freud viewed personality as a dynamic system directed by three mental structures, the **id**, the **ego**, and the **superego.** According to Freud, most behavior involves activity of all three systems.

The Id The id is made up of innate biological instincts and urges. It is self-serving, irrational, impulsive, and totally **unconscious.** The id operates on the **pleasure principle.** This means that pleasure-seeking urges of all kinds are freely expressed. If everyone's personality were solely under control of the id, the world would be chaotic beyond belief.

Freud thought of the id as a well of energy for the entire **psyche** (sie-KEY), or personality. This energy, called **libido** (lih-BEE-doe), flows from the **life instincts** (called **Eros**). According to Freud, libido promotes survival, underlies sexual desires, and is expressed whenever we seek pleasure. Freud also described a **death instinct. Thanatos,** as he called it, is responsible for aggressive and destructive urges (■ Fig. 15–7). Freud offered humanity's long history of wars and violence as evidence of such urges. Most id energies, then, are aimed at discharging tensions related to sex and aggression.

■ Fig. 15–7 *Freud considered personality an expression of two conflicting forces, life instincts and the death instinct. Both are symbolized in this drawing by Allan Gilbert. (If you don't immediately see the death symbolism, stand farther from the drawing.)*

The Ego The ego is sometimes described as the "executive," because it directs energies supplied by the id. The id is like a blind king or queen whose power is awesome but who must rely on others to carry out orders. The id can only form mental images of things it desires. The ego wins power to direct behavior by relating the desires of the id to external reality.

Question: Are there other differences between the ego and the id?

Yes. Recall that the id operates on the pleasure principle. The ego, in contrast, is guided by the **reality principle.** That is, the ego delays action until it is practical or appropriate. The ego is the system of thinking, planning, problem solving, and deciding. It is in conscious control of the personality.

Question: What is the role of the superego?

The Superego The superego acts as a judge or censor for the thoughts and actions of the ego. One part of the superego, called the **conscience,** reflects actions

Psychoanalytic theory Freudian theory of personality that emphasizes unconscious forces and internal conflicts.

Id The primitive part of personality, which is unconscious, supplies energy, and demands gratification.

Unconscious Region of the mind that is beyond awareness.

Pleasure principle A desire for immediate satisfaction of wishes, desires, or needs.

Psyche The mind, mental life, and personality as a whole.

Libido In Freudian theory, the force, primarily pleasure oriented, that energizes personality.

Eros Freud's name for the "life instincts."

Thanatos The death instinct postulated by Freud.

Ego The executive part of personality that directs rational behavior.

Reality principle Delaying action (or pleasure) until it is appropriate.

Superego A judge or censor for thoughts and actions.

Conscience The part of the superego that causes guilt when its standards are not met.

Ego ideal The part of the superego representing ideal behavior; a source of pride when its standards are met.

Neurotic anxiety Apprehension felt when the ego struggles to control id impulses.

Moral anxiety Apprehension felt when thoughts, impulses, or actions conflict with the superego's standards.

Unconscious The region of the mind that is beyond awareness, especially impulses and desires not directly known to a person.

Conscious Region of the mind that includes all mental contents a person is aware of at any given moment.

Preconscious An area of the mind containing information that can be voluntarily brought to awareness.

Psychosexual stages The oral, anal, phallic, and genital stages, during which various personality traits are formed.

for which a person has been punished. When standards of the conscience are not met, you are punished internally by *guilt* feelings. A second part of the superego is the **ego ideal.** The ego ideal reflects all behavior one's parents approved of or rewarded. The ego ideal is a source of goals and aspirations. When its standards are met, we feel *pride*. By these processes, the superego acts as an "internalized parent" to bring behavior under control. In Freudian terms, a person with a weak superego will be a delinquent, criminal, or antisocial personality. In contrast, an overly strict or harsh superego may cause inhibition, rigidity, or unbearable guilt.

The Dynamics of Personality

Question: How do the id, ego, and superego interact?

It is important to recognize that Freud did not picture the id, ego, and superego as parts of the brain or as "little people" running the human psyche. In reality, they are separate and conflicting mental processes. Freud theorized a delicate balance of power among the three. For example, the demands of the id for immediate pleasure often clash with the superego's moral restrictions. Perhaps an example will help clarify the role of each part of the personality.

Freud in a Nutshell

Let's say you are sexually attracted to an acquaintance. The id clamors for immediate satisfaction of its sexual desires, but is opposed by the superego (which finds the very thought of sex shocking). The id says, "Go for it!" The superego icily replies, "Never even think that again!" And what does the ego say? The ego says, "I have a plan!"

Of course, this is a drastic simplification, but it does capture the core of Freudian thinking. To reduce tension, the ego could begin actions leading to friendship, romance, courtship, and marriage. If the id is unusually powerful, the ego may give in and attempt a seduction. If the superego prevails, the ego may be forced to *displace* or *sublimate* sexual energies to other activities (sports, music, dancing, push-ups, cold showers). According to Freud, internal struggles and rechanneled energies typify most personality functioning.

Question: Is the ego always caught in the middle?

Basically yes, and the pressures on it can be intense. In addition to meeting the conflicting demands of the id and superego, the overworked ego must deal with external reality. According to Freud, you feel anxiety when your ego is threatened or overwhelmed. Impulses from the id cause **neurotic anxiety** when the ego can barely keep them under control. Threats of punishment from the superego cause **moral anxiety.** Each person develops habitual ways of calming these anxieties, and many resort to using *ego-defense mechanisms* to lessen internal conflicts. (Defense mechanisms are discussed in Chapter 11).

Levels of Awareness A major principle of psychoanalytic theory, and other psychodynamic theories, is that behavior often expresses unconscious (or hidden) internal forces. The **unconscious** contains repressed memories and emotions, plus the instinctual drives of the id. Interestingly, modern scientists have found brain areas that seem to have the kinds of unconscious effects that Freud described. Especially important are areas linked with emotion and memory—such as the hippocampus in the limbic system (Reiser, 1985; Wilson, 1985).

Even though they are beyond awareness, unconscious thoughts, feelings, or urges may slip into behavior in disguised or symbolic form. For example, if you meet someone you would like to know better, you may unconsciously leave a book or a jacket at the person's house to ensure another meeting.

Question: Earlier you said that the id is completely unconscious. Are the actions of the ego and superego unconscious?

At times, yes, but they also operate on two other levels of awareness (■ Fig. 15–8). The **conscious** level includes everything you are aware of at a given moment, including thoughts, perceptions, feelings, and memories. The **preconscious** contains material that can be easily brought to awareness. If you stop to think about a time when you felt angry or rejected, you will be moving this memory from the preconscious to the conscious level of awareness.

The operation of the superego gives another sign of the levels of awareness. At times we consciously try to live up to moral codes or standards. Yet, at other times a person may feel guilty without knowing why. Psychoanalytic theory credits this kind of guilt to unconscious workings of the superego. Freudian psychology holds that truly unconscious events cannot be easily brought to awareness or directly known.

Personality Development

Let's continue with a look at how psychoanalytic theory explains personality development. Freud theorized that the core of personality is formed before age 6 in a series of **psychosexual stages.** His account holds that childhood urges for erotic pleasure have lasting effects on development. Freud's emphasis on infantile sexuality remains controversial. However, Freud used the term *sex* very broadly to refer to several different physical sources of pleasure.

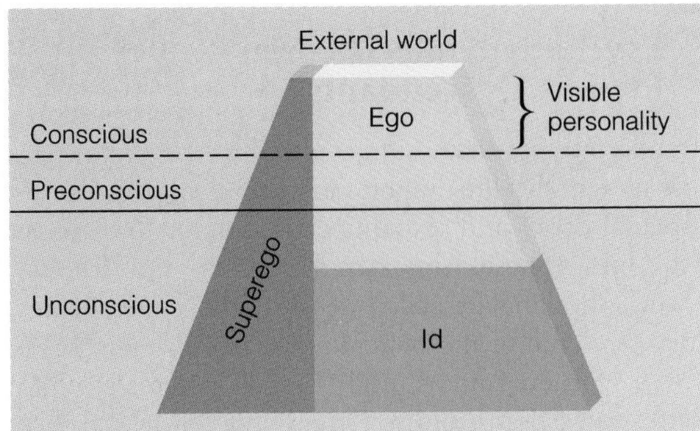

■ **Fig. 15–8** *The approximate relationship between the id, ego, and superego, and the levels of awareness.*

A Freudian Fable? Freud identified four psychosexual stages, the **oral, anal, phallic,** and **genital.** (He also described a period of "latency" between the phallic and genital stages. Latency is explained in a moment.) At each stage, a different part of the body becomes a child's primary **erogenous zone** (an area capable of producing pleasure). Each area then serves as the main source of pleasure, frustration, and self-expression. Freud believed that many adult personality traits can be traced to **fixations** in one or more of the stages.

Question: What is a fixation?

A fixation is an unresolved conflict or emotional hang-up caused by overindulgence or by frustration. As we describe the psychosexual stages you'll see why Freud considered fixations important.

The Oral Stage During the first year of life, most of an infant's pleasure comes from stimulation of the mouth. If a child is overfed or frustrated, oral traits may be created. Some examples of adult expressions of oral needs are gum chewing, nail biting, smoking, kissing, overeating, and alcoholism (■ Fig. 15–9.).

Question: What if there is an oral fixation?

Fixation early in the oral stage produces an **oral-dependent** personality. Oral-dependent persons are gullible (they swallow things easily!), passive, and need lots of attention (they want to be mothered). Frustrations later in the oral stage may cause aggression, often in the form of biting. Fixation here creates an **oral-aggressive** adult who likes to argue ("biting sarcasm" is their forte!), is cynical, and exploits others.

The Anal Stage Between the ages of 1 and 3, the child's attention shifts to the process of elimination. When parents attempt toilet training, the child can gain approval or express rebellion or aggression by "holding on" or by "letting go." Therefore, harsh or lenient toilet training can cause an anal fixation that may lock such responses into personality. Freud described the **anal-retentive** (holding-on) personality as obstinate, stingy, orderly, and compulsively clean. The **anal-expulsive** (letting-go) personality is disorderly, destructive, cruel, or messy.

■ **Fig. 15–9** *Was Freud's ever-present cigar a sign of an oral fixation? Was it a phallic symbol? Was it both? Or was it neither? An inability to say for sure is one of the shortcomings of psychoanalytic theory.*

The Phallic Stage Adult traits of the **phallic personality** are vanity, exhibitionism, sensitive pride, and narcissism (excessive vanity and self-love). Freud theorized that phallic fixations develop between the ages of 3 and 6. At this time, increased sexual interest causes the child to be physically attracted to the parent of the opposite sex. In males this attraction leads to an **Oedipus conflict.** In it, the boy feels rivalry with his father for the affection of the mother. Freud believed that the male child feels threatened by the father (specifically, the boy fears castration). To ease his anxieties, the boy must **identify** with the father. Their rivalry ends when the boy seeks to become more like his father. As he does, he begins to accept the father's values and form a conscience.

Question: What about the female child?

In a parallel to the Oedipus conflict, called the **Electra conflict,** the girl loves her father and competes with her mother. However, according to Freud, the girl identifies with the mother more gradually. This, he said, is less effective in creating a conscience. Freud believed that females already feel castrated. Because of

Erogenous zone Any body area that produces pleasurable sensations.

Fixation A lasting conflict developed as a result of frustration or overindulgence.

Oral stage The period when infants are preoccupied with the mouth as a source of pleasure and means of expression.

Oral-dependent personality A person who wants to passively receive attention, gifts, love, and so forth.

Oral-aggressive personality A person who uses the mouth to express hostility. Also, one who actively exploits others.

Anal stage The psychosexual stage corresponding roughly to the period of toilet training (ages 1 to 3).

Anal-retentive personality A person who is obstinate, stingy, or compulsive, and who generally has difficulty "letting go."

Anal-expulsive personality A disorderly, destructive, cruel, or messy person.

Phallic stage The psychosexual stage (roughly ages 3 to 6) when a child is preoccupied with the genitals as a source of pleasure.

Phallic personality A person who is vain, exhibitionistic, sensitive, and narcissistic.

Oedipus conflict A boy's sexual attraction to his mother, and feelings of rivalry with his father.

Electra conflict A girl's sexual attraction to her father and feelings of rivalry with her mother.

Latency According to Freud, a period in childhood when psychosexual development is more or less interrupted.

Genital stage Period of full psychosexual development, marked by the attainment of mature adult sexuality.

Neo-Freudian A theorist who accepts the broad features of Freud's theory but has revised parts of it.

Basic anxiety A primary form of anxiety that arises from living in a hostile world.

this, they are less driven to identify with their mothers than boys are with their fathers. This particular part of Freudian thought has been thoroughly (and rightfully) rejected by modern feminists. It is probably best understood as a reflection of the male-dominated times in which Freud lived.

Latency According to Freud there is a period of *latency* from age 6 to puberty. Latency is not actually a stage. Rather, it is a quiet time during which psychosexual development is dormant or interrupted. Freud's belief that psychosexual development is "on hold" at this time is hard to accept. Nevertheless, Freud saw latency as a relatively quiet time compared to the stormy first 6 years of life.

The Genital Stage At puberty an upswing in sexual energies activates all the unresolved conflicts of earlier years. This upsurge, according to Freud, is the reason why adolescence can be such a trying time, filled with emotion and turmoil. The genital stage begins at puberty. It is marked, during adolescence, by a growing potential for responsible social-sexual relationships. The genital stage ends with a mature capacity for love and the realization of full adult sexuality.

Critical Comments As bizarre as Freud's developmental theory might seem, it has been influential for several reasons. First, it pioneered the idea that the early years of life help shape adult personality. Second, it identified feeding, toilet training, and infantile sexual experiences as critical events in personality formation. Third, Freud was among the first to propose that development proceeds through a series of stages. (Erik Erikson's psycho*social* stages, described in Chapter 13, are a modern offshoot of Freudian thinking.)

Question: Is the Freudian view of development widely accepted?

Despite his contributions, few psychologists wholeheartedly embrace Freud's theory today. In some cases Freud was clearly wrong. His portrayal of the elementary school years (latency) as free from sexuality and unimportant for personality development is hard to believe. His idea of the role of a stern or threatening father in the development of a strong conscience in males has also been challenged. Studies show that a son is more likely to develop a strong conscience if his father is affectionate and accepting, rather than stern and punishing (Mussen et al., 1969; Sears et al., 1957). Freud also overemphasized sexuality in personality development; other motives and cognitive factors are of equal importance. Many more criticisms could be listed, but the fact remains that there is an element of truth to much of what Freud said.

Psychodynamic Theories—Freud's Descendants

Freud's ideas quickly attracted a brilliant following. Just as rapidly, the importance Freud placed on instinctual drives and sexuality caused many to disagree with him. Those who stayed close to the core of Freud's thinking are called **neo-Freudians** (*neo* means "new"). Some of the better-known neo-Freudians are Karen Horney, Anna Freud (Freud's daughter), Otto Rank, and Erich Fromm. Other early followers broke away more completely from Freud and created their own opposing theories. This group includes people such as Alfred Adler, Harry Sullivan, and Carl Jung.

Question: How did the thinking of these people differ from Freud's ideas?

The full story of other psychodynamic theories must await your first course in personality. For now, let's sample two views. The first embraces most but not all of Freud's theory (Horney). The second involves a carry-over of Freudian ideas into a related but unique theory (Jung).

Karen Horney (1885–1952)

As a neo-Freudian, Karen Horney (HORN-eye) remained faithful to most of Freud's ideas. Yet at the same time, she altered or rejected some ideas and added many of her own. Horney also resisted Freud's more mechanistic, biological, and instinctive ideas. For example, as a woman, Horney rejected Freud's claim that "anatomy is destiny." This view, woven into Freudian psychology, held that males are dominant or superior to females. Horney was among the first to challenge the obvious male bias in Freud's thinking.

Horney also disagreed with Freud about the causes of neurosis. Freud held that neurotic (anxiety-ridden) individuals are struggling with forbidden id drives that they fear they cannot control. Horney's view was that a core of **basic anxiety** occurs when people feel isolated and helpless in a hostile world. These feelings, she believed, are rooted in childhood. Trouble occurs when an individual tries to control basic anxiety by exaggerating a single mode of interacting with others.

Question: What do you mean by "mode of interacting"?

According to Horney, each of us can move **toward** others (by depending on them for love, support, or friendship), we can move **away** from others (by withdrawing, acting like a "loner," or being "strong" and independent), or we can move **against** others (by attacking, competing with, or seeking power over them). Horney believed that emotional health reflects a balance in moving toward, away from, and against others.

In her view, emotional problems tend to lock people into overuse of one of the three modes—an insight that remains valuable today.

Carl Jung (1875–1961)

Carl Jung was a student of Freud's, but the two parted ways as Jung began to develop his own ideas. Like Freud, Jung called the conscious part of the personality the ego. However, he further noted that a **persona,** or "mask" exists between the ego and the outside world. The persona is the "public self" presented to others. It is most apparent when we adopt particular roles or hide our deeper feelings. As mentioned earlier, Jung believed that actions of the ego may reflect attitudes of **introversion** (in which energy is mainly directed inward), or of **extroversion** (in which energy is mainly directed outward).

Question: Was Jung's view of the unconscious the same as Freud's?

Jung used the term **personal unconscious** to refer to what Freud simply called the unconscious. The personal unconscious is a storehouse for experiences, feelings, and memories that cannot be directly brought into awareness. But Jung departed from Freud and also proposed a deeper **collective unconscious** shared by all humans. Jung believed that from the beginning of time, all humans have had experiences with birth, death, power, god figures, mother and father figures, animals, the earth, energy, evil, rebirth, and so on. According to Jung, such universals create **archetypes** (AR-KEH-types: original ideas or patterns).

Archetypes, found in the collective unconscious, are unconscious images that cause us to respond emotionally to *symbols* of birth, death, energy, animals, evil, and the like. Jung believed that he detected symbols of such archetypes in the art, religion, myths, and dreams of every culture and age. Let us say, for instance, that a man dreams of dancing with his sister. To Freud this would probably be a sign of hidden incestuous feelings. To Jung the image of the sister might represent an unexpressed feminine side of the man's personality and the dream might represent the cosmic dance that intertwines "maleness" and "femaleness" in all lives.

Question: Are some archetypes more important than others?

Two particularly important archetypes are the **anima** (female principle) and the **animus** (male principle). In men, the anima is an unconscious, idealized image of women. This image is based, in part, on real experiences with women (the man's mother, sister, friends). However, the experiences men have had with women throughout history form the true core of the anima. The reverse is true of women, who possess an animus or idealized image of men. The anima in males and the animus in females enable us to relate to members of the opposite sex. The anima and animus also make it possible for people to learn to express both "masculine" and "feminine" sides of their personalities.

Jung regarded the **self archetype** as the most important of all. The self archetype represents unity. Its existence causes a gradual movement toward balance, wholeness, and harmony within the personality. Jung felt that we become richer and more completely human when a balance is achieved between the conscious and unconscious, the anima and animus, thinking and feeling, sensing and intuiting, the persona and the ego, introversion and extroversion.

Question: Was Jung talking about self-actualization?

Essentially he was. Jung was the first to use the term *self-actualization* to describe a striving for completion and unity. He believed that the self archetype is symbolized in every culture by **mandalas** (magic circles) of one kind or another (■ Fig. 15–10).

Jung's theory may not be scientific, but clearly he was a man of genius and vision. If you would like to know more about Jung and his ideas, a good starting place is his autobiography, *Memories, Dreams, Reflections.*

Persona The "mask" or public self presented to others.

Personal unconscious A mental storehouse for a single individual's unconscious thoughts.

Collective unconscious A mental storehouse for unconscious ideas and images shared by all humans.

Archetype A universal idea, image, or pattern, found in the collective unconscious.

Anima An archetype representing the female principle.

Animus An archetype representing the male principle.

Self archetype An unconscious image representing unity, wholeness, completion, and balance.

Mandala A circular design representing balance, unity, and completion.

■ **Fig. 15–10** *Jung regarded circular designs as symbols of the self-archetype and representations of unity, balance, and completion within the personality.*

LEARNING CHECK

1. List the three divisions of personality postulated by Freud. ____________
2. Which division is totally unconscious? ____________
3. Which division is responsible for moral anxiety? ____________
4. Freud proposed the existence of a life instinct known as Thanatos. T or F?
5. Freud's view of personality development is based on the concept of ____________ stages.
6. Arrange these stages in the proper order: phallic, anal, genital, oral. ____________
7. Freud considered the anal-retentive personality to be obstinate and stingy. T or F?
8. Karen Horney theorized that people control basic anxiety by moving toward, away from, and ____________ others.
9. Carl Jung's theory states that archetypes, which are found in the personal unconscious, exert an influence on behavior. T or F?

Critical Thinking

10. Many adults would find it embarrassing or humiliating to drink from a baby bottle. Can you explain why?

Answers:

1. id, ego, superego 2. id 3. superego 4. F 5. psychosexual 6. oral, anal, phallic, genital 7. T 8. against 9. F 10. A psychoanalytic theorist would say that it is because the bottle rekindles oral conflicts and feelings of vulnerability and dependence.

Behavioral personality theory Any model of personality that emphasizes observable behavior and learning.

Learning theorist A psychologist interested in the ways that learning shapes and explains personality.

Learning Theories of Personality—Habit I Seen You Before?

Question: How do behaviorists approach personality?

According to some critics, as if people are robots like R2D2 of *Star Wars* fame. Actually, the behaviorist position is not nearly that mechanistic, and its value is well established. The behaviorists have shown repeatedly that children can *learn* things like kindness, hostility, generosity, or destructiveness (Bandura & Walters, 1963; Hoffman, 1975). But what does this have to do with personality? Everything, according to the behavioral viewpoint.

The behaviorist position is that personality is no more (or less) than a collection of learned behavior patterns. Personality, like other learned behavior, is acquired through classical and operant conditioning, observational learning, reinforcement, extinction, generalization, and discrimination (■ Fig. 15–11). When Mother says, "It's not nice to make mud pies with Mommy's blender. If we want to grow up to be a big girl, we won't do it again, will we?" she serves as a model and in other ways shapes her daughter's personality.

■ **Fig. 15–11** *Freud believed that aggressive urges are "instinctual." In contrast, behavioral theories assume that personal characteristics such as aggressiveness are learned. Is this boy's aggression the result of observational learning, harsh punishment, or prior reinforcement?*

Strict **learning theorists** reject the idea that personality is made up of consistent traits. They would assert, for instance, that there is no such thing as a trait of "honesty" (Bandura, 1973; Mischel, 1968).

Question: Certainly some people are honest while others are not. How can honesty not be a trait?

A learning theorist would agree that some of the people you know are honest *more often* than others. But knowing this does not allow us to predict for certain whether a person will be honest in a specific situation. It would not be unusual, for example, to find that a person honored for returning a lost wallet had cheated on a test or broken the speed limit. If you were to ask a learning theorist, "Are you an honest person?" the reply might be, "In what situation?"

A good example of how situations influence behavior is shown in ■ Figure 15–12. The graphs give the results of a role-playing experiment in which college students had to ask a professor for an extension

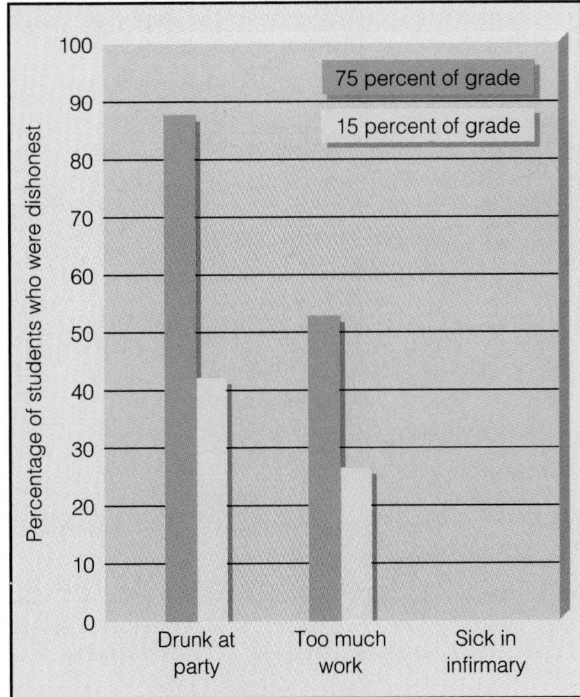

■ **Fig. 15–12** *Honesty is greatly influenced by circumstances. Many students were dishonest when the true reason for wanting an extension on an overdue paper was a poor excuse ("drunk at party"). Fewer were dishonest when the excuse was semi-legitimate ("too much work") and none lied when their excuse was legitimate ("sick in infirmary"). The importance of the paper for a course grade also influenced honesty. (Data from Greene & Saxe, 1990.)*

on an assigned paper. For some students the paper was worth 15 percent of their final grade; for others it was worth 75 percent. Each student was assigned one of three reasons why the paper was late: they had a hangover, had too much work to do, or had the flu. The students were then sent in to plead their cases. As Figure 15–12 shows, most students lied about why their paper was late when they had an illegitimate excuse (a hangover) and the paper was critical to their grade. When their excuse was legitimate (the flu) none lied (Greene & Saxe, 1990).

As you can see, learning theorists are interested in the external causes of our actions. However, this emphasis on **situational determinants** does not entirely remove the person from the picture. Situations always interact with a person's prior learning history to activate behavior.

Situations vary greatly in their impact. Some are especially powerful, whereas others are trivial and have little effect on behavior. The more powerful the situation, the easier it is to see what is meant by situational determinants. For example, each of the following situations would undoubtedly have a strong influence on behavior: an escaped lion walks into the supermarket; you accidentally sit on a lighted cigarette; you find your lover in bed with your best friend. Yet even these situations could provoke very different reactions from different personalities. That's why behavior is always a product of both prior learning and the situations in which people find themselves.

As discussed earlier, trait theorists also believe that situations affect behavior. But in their view, situations interact with *traits*, rather than a person's learning history. So, in essence, learning theorists favor replacing "traits" with "prior learning" to explain behavior.

Question: How do learning theorists view the structure of personality?

Personality = Behavior

The behavioral view of personality can be illustrated with an early theory proposed by John Dollard and Neal Miller (1950). In their view, **habits** make up the structure of personality. As for the dynamics of personality, Dollard and Miller believe that habits are governed by four elements of learning: **drive, cue, response,** and **reward.** A *drive* is any stimulus strong enough to goad a person to action (such as hunger, pain, lust, frustration, fear). *Cues* are signals from the environment that guide *responses* so they are most likely to bring about *reward* or reinforcement.

Question: How does that relate to personality?

An example may clarify this viewpoint. Let's say a child is frustrated by an older brother who takes a toy from her. The child could make any of several responses. She could throw a temper tantrum, hit her brother, tell Mother, and so forth. The response she chooses is guided by available cues and the previous effects of each response. If telling Mother has paid off in the past, and the mother is present, telling again may be her immediate response. If a different set of cues exists (if Mother is absent or if the older brother looks particularly menacing), the girl may select some other response. To an outside observer, the child's actions seem to reflect her personality. To the learning theorist, they are a direct reaction to the combined effects of drive, cue, response, and reward.

Question: Doesn't this analysis leave out a lot?

Yes. Learning theorists first set out to provide a simple, clear model of personality. But in recent years they have had to face a fact that they originally tended to overlook. The fact is: People think. The new breed of behavioral psychologists—who include perception, thinking, expectations, and other mental events in their views—are called **social learning theorists.** (The label *social* is used because they also stress social relationships and modeling.)

Social Learning Theory The "cognitive behaviorism" of social learning theory can be illustrated by

Situational determinants External conditions that strongly influence behavior.

Habit A deeply ingrained, learned pattern of behavior.

Drive Any stimulus (especially an internal stimulus such as hunger) strong enough to goad a person to action.

Cue External stimuli that guide responses, especially by signaling the presence or absence of reinforcement.

Response Any behavior, either observable or internal.

Reward Anything that produces pleasure or satisfaction; a positive reinforcer.

Social learning theory An explanation of personality that combines learning principles, cognition, and the effects of social relationships.

Psychological situation A situation as it is perceived and interpreted by an individual, not as it exists objectively.

Expectancy Anticipation about the effect a response will have, especially regarding reinforcement.

Reinforcement value The subjective value a person attaches to a particular activity or reinforcer.

Self-reinforcement Praising or rewarding oneself for having made a particular response (such as completing a school assignment).

three concepts proposed by Julian Rotter (1975). They are: the psychological situation, expectancy, and reinforcement value. Let's examine each.

Someone trips you. How do you respond? Your response probably depends on whether you think it was planned or an accident. It is not enough to know the setting in which a person responds. We also need to know the person's **psychological situation;** that is, how the person *interprets* or *defines* the situation. Here's another example. Let's say you score low on an exam. Do you consider it a challenge to work harder, a sign that you should drop the class, or an excuse to get drunk? Again, your interpretation is important.

An **expectancy** refers to your anticipation that making a response will lead to reinforcement. To continue the example, if working harder has paid off in the past, it is a likely reaction to a low test score. But to predict your response, we would also have to know if you *expect* your efforts to pay off in the present situation. In fact, expected reinforcement may be more important than actual past reinforcement. And what about the *value* you attach to grades, school success, or personal ability? Rotter's third concept, **reinforcement value,** states that humans attach different values to various activities or rewards. This, too, must be taken into account to understand personality.

One more idea deserves mention here. At times, we all evaluate our actions and may reward ourselves with special privileges or treats when the evaluation is positive (■Fig. 15–13). With this in mind, social learning theory adds the concept of **self-reinforcement** to the behavioristic view. That is, habits of self-praise and self-blame become an important part of personality. In fact, self-reinforcement can be thought of as the behaviorist's counterpart to the superego (Highlight 15–5).

■ **Fig. 15–13** *Through self-reinforcement we reward ourselves for personal achievements and other "good" behavior.*

HIGHLIGHT 15–5

Rate Yourself

Self-Reinforcement—Being Good to Yourself

The following statements, adapted from a scale developed by Elaine Heiby (1983), will add to your understanding of self-reinforcement. Check those that apply to you.

- ☐ I often think positive thoughts about myself.
- ☐ I frequently meet standards that I set for myself.
- ☐ I try not to blame myself when things go wrong.
- ☐ I usually don't get upset when I make mistakes because I learn from them.
- ☐ I can get satisfaction out of what I do even if it's not perfect.
- ☐ When I make mistakes I take time to reassure myself.
- ☐ I don't think talking about what you've done right is too boastful.
- ☐ Praising yourself is healthy and normal.
- ☐ I don't think I have to be upset every time I make a mistake.
- ☐ My feelings of self-confidence and self-esteem stay pretty steady.

People who agree with all or most of the preceding statements tend to have high rates of self-reinforcement. And, as the last item suggests, high rates of self-reinforcement are related to high self-esteem. The reverse is also true: Numerous studies have shown that mildly depressed college students tend to have low rates of self-reinforcement (Heiby, 1983).

It is not known if low self-reinforcement leads to depression, or the reverse. But in any case, learning to be more self-reinforcing appears to lessen depression (Fuchs & Rehm, 1977). From a behavioral viewpoint, there is value in learning to be "good to yourself."

Behavioristic View of Development

Question: How do learning theorists account for personality development?

Many of Freud's major points can be restated in terms of modern learning theory. Miller and Dollard (1950) agree with Freud that the first 6 years are crucial for personality development, but for different reasons. Rather than thinking in terms of psychosexual urges and fixations, they ask, "What makes early learning experiences so lasting in their effects?" Their answer is that childhood is a time of urgent and tearing drives, powerful rewards and punishments, and crushing frustrations. Also important is **social reinforcement** based on the effects of attention and approval from others. These forces combine to shape the core of personality.

Critical Situations Miller and Dollard consider four developmental situations to be of critical importance. These are (1) **feeding,** (2) **toilet** or **cleanliness training,** (3) **sex training,** and (4) learning to express **anger** or **aggression.**

Question: Why are these of special importance?

Feeding serves as an illustration. If children are fed when they cry, they are encouraged to actively manipulate their parents. The child allowed to cry without being fed learns to be passive. Thus, a basic active or passive orientation toward the world may be created by early feeding experiences. Feeding can also affect later social relationships because the child learns to associate people with satisfaction and pleasure or with frustration and discomfort.

Toilet and cleanliness training can be a particularly strong source of emotion for both parents and children. Parents are usually aghast the first time they find a child smearing feces about with gay abandon. Their reaction is often sharp punishment. For the child, the result is frustration and confusion. Many attitudes toward cleanliness, conformity, and bodily functions are formed at such times. Studies also show that severe, punishing, or frustrating toilet training can have undesirable effects on personality development (Sears et al., 1957). Toilet and cleanliness training therefore demand patience and a sense of humor.

Question: What about sex and anger?

When, where, and how a child learns to express anger and aggression are of obvious importance. So too is expression of sexual behavior. Both types of experiences can leave an imprint on personality. Specifically, permissiveness for sexual and aggressive behavior in childhood is linked to adult needs for power (McClelland & Pilon, 1983). This link probably occurs because permitting such behaviors allows children to get pleasure from asserting themselves.

Sex training also involves learning "male" and "female" behaviors—which creates an even broader basis for shaping personality.

Becoming Male or Female From birth onward, children are identified as boys or girls and encouraged to learn sex-appropriate behavior. According to social learning theory, identification and imitation contribute greatly to personality development in general and to sex training in particular. **Identification** refers to the child's emotional attachment to admired adults, especially to those the child depends on for love and care. Identification typically encourages **imitation,** a desire to be like the valued and admired adult (■ Fig. 15–14). Many "male" or "female" traits come from children's conscious or unconscious attempts to imitate the behavior of a same-sex parent with whom they identify.

■ **Fig. 15–14** *Adult personality is influenced by identification with parents.*

Question: If children are around parents of both sexes, why don't they imitate behavior typical of the opposite sex as well as of the same sex?

You may recall from Chapter 7 that Albert Bandura and others have shown that learning takes place vicariously as well as directly (Bandura, 1965). This means that we can learn without direct reward by observing and remembering the actions of others. But the actions we choose to imitate depend on their outcome. For example, boys and girls have equal chances to observe adults and other children acting aggressively. However, girls are less likely than boys to imitate aggressive behavior because they rarely see female aggression rewarded or approved. Thus, many arbitrary "male" and "female" qualities are passed on at the same time sexual identity is learned.

A study of preschool children by Lisa Serbin and Daniel O'Leary (1975) found that teachers are three times more likely to pay attention to boys who are aggressive or disruptive than to girls acting the same way. Boys who hit other students or who broke things typically got loud scoldings and became the center of

Social reinforcement Praise, attention, approval, and/or affection from others.

Critical situations Situations during childhood that are capable of leaving a lasting imprint on personality.

Identification Feeling emotionally connected to a person and seeing oneself as like him or her.

Imitation An attempt to match one's own behavior to another person's behavior.

attention for the whole class. When teachers responded to disruptive girls, they gave brief, soft rebukes that others couldn't hear. Since we know that attention of almost any kind reinforces children's behavior, it is clear that the boys were being encouraged to be active and aggressive. Serbin and O'Leary found that girls got the most attention when they were within arm's reach, more or less clinging to the teacher.

The pattern just described grows stronger throughout elementary school. In all grades, boys are louder, faster, and more boisterous than girls. Day after day, boys receive a disproportionate amount of the teacher's attention (Sadker & Sadker, 1994).

It's easy to see that teachers unwittingly encourage girls to be submissive, dependent, and passive. Similar differences in reinforcement probably explain why males are responsible for much more aggression in society than females are. By age 10, boys expect to get less disapproval from parents for aggression than girls do. This is especially true if the aggression is provoked by another boy (Perry, Perry, & Weiss, 1989). Among adults, rates of murder and assault are consistently higher for men (Deaux, 1985). (The development of sex roles and a male or female identity is discussed further in Chapter 19.)

LEARNING CHECK

1. Learning theorists believe that personality "traits" really are ______ acquired through prior learning. They also emphasize ______ determinants of behavior.
2. Dollard and Miller consider cues the basic structure of personality. T or F?
3. To explain behavior, social learning theorists include mental elements, such as ______ (the anticipation that a response will lead to reinforcement).
4. Self-reinforcement is to behavioristic theory as superego is to psychoanalytic theory. T or F?
5. Which of the following is *not* a "critical situation" in the behaviorist theory of personality development?
   a. feeding *b.* sex training *c.* language training *d.* anger training
6. In addition to basic rewards and punishments, a child's personality is also shaped by ______ reinforcement.
7. Social learning theories of development emphasize the impact of identification and ______.

Critical Thinking

8. Julian Rotter's concept of *reinforcement value* is closely related to a motivational principle discussed in Chapter 10. Can you name it?

Answers: 1. habits, situational 2. F 3. expectancies 4. T 5. c 6. social 7. imitation 8. incentive value

Humanism An approach that focuses on human experience, problems, potentials, and ideals.

Human nature Those traits, qualities, potentials, and behavior patterns most characteristic of the human species.

Free choice The ability to freely make choices that are not controlled by genetics, learning, or unconscious forces.

Subjective experience Reality as it is perceived and interpreted, not as it exists objectively.

Humanistic Theory—Peak Experiences and Personal Growth

Humanism is a reaction to the static quality of trait theories, the pessimism of psychoanalytic theory, and the mechanical nature of learning theory. At its core is a positive image of what it means to be human. Humanists reject the Freudian view of personality as a battleground for biological instincts and unconscious forces. Instead, they view **human nature** as inherently *good* and seek ways to allow our potentials to emerge. Humanists also oppose the mechanical, "thing-like" overtones of the behaviorist viewpoint. We are not, they say, merely a bundle of moldable responses; rather, we are creative beings capable of **free choice.** To a humanist the person you are today is largely the product of all of your previous choices. The humanistic viewpoint also places greater emphasis on immediate **subjective experience,** rather than on prior learning. Humanists believe that there are as many "real worlds" as there are people. To understand behavior we must learn how a person subjectively views the world—what is "real" for her or him.

Question: Who are the major humanistic theorists?

There are many psychologists whose theories fall within the humanistic tradition. Of these, the best known are Carl Rogers (1902–1987) and Abraham Maslow (1908–1970). Since Maslow's idea of self-actualization was introduced in Chapter 1, let's begin with a more detailed look at this facet of his thinking.

Maslow and Self-Actualization

Abraham Maslow became interested in people who were living unusually effective lives. How were they different from the average person? To find an answer, Maslow began by studying the lives of great men and women, such as Albert Einstein, William James, Jane

Adams, Eleanor Roosevelt, Abraham Lincoln, John Muir, and Walt Whitman. From there he moved on to directly study artists, writers, poets, and other creative individuals.

Along the way, Maslow's thinking changed radically. At first he studied only people of obvious creativity or high achievement. However, it eventually became clear that a housewife, carpenter, clerk, or student could live creatively and make full use of his or her potentials. Maslow referred to this tendency as *self-actualization* (Maslow, 1954). (See Highlight 15–6.)

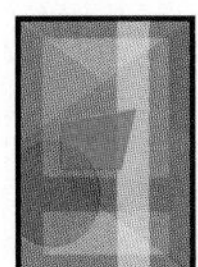

HIGHLIGHT 15–6

A Closer Look At

Self-Actualizers—Lives of the Emotionally Rich

In his studies, Maslow found that **self-actualizers** shared many similarities. Whether famous or unknown, academically distinguished or uneducated, rich or poor, self-actualizers tend to fit the following profile.

1. **Efficient perceptions of reality.** Subjects were able to judge situations correctly and honestly and were very sensitive to the fake and dishonest.
2. **Comfortable acceptance of self, others, nature.** Subjects accepted their own human nature with all its shortcomings. The shortcomings of others and the contradictions of the human condition were also accepted with humor and tolerance.
3. **Spontaneity.** Maslow's subjects extended their creativity into everyday activities. They tended to be unusually alive, engaged, and spontaneous.
4. **Task centering.** Most subjects had a mission to fulfill in life or some task or problem outside of themselves to pursue. Humanitarians such as Albert Schweitzer or Mother Teresa represent this quality.
5. **Autonomy.** Subjects were free from dependence on external authority or other people. They tended to be resourceful and independent.
6. **Continued freshness of appreciation.** The self-actualizer seems to constantly renew appreciation of life's basic goods. A sunset or a flower will be experienced as intensely time after time as it was the first. There is an "innocence of vision," like that of an artist or child.
7. **Fellowship with humanity.** Maslow's subjects felt a deep identification with others and the human situation in general.
8. **Profound interpersonal relationships.** The interpersonal relationships of self-actualizers are marked by deep, loving bonds.
9. **Non-hostile sense of humor.** This refers to the wonderful capacity to laugh at oneself. It also refers to the kind of humor a man like Abraham Lincoln had. Lincoln probably never made a joke that hurt anybody. His wry comments were a gentle prodding at human shortcomings.
10. **Peak experiences.** All of Maslow's subjects reported the frequent occurrence of **peak experiences.** These were marked by feelings of ecstasy, harmony, and deep meaning. Subjects reported feeling at one with the universe, stronger and calmer than ever before, filled with light, beautiful and good, and so forth. In short, self-actualizers feel safe, non-anxious, accepted, loved, loving, and alive.

Self-actualization The process of fully developing personal potentials.

Self-actualizer One who is living creatively and making full use of his or her potentials.

Task centering Focusing on the task at hand, rather than on one's own feelings or needs.

Autonomy A freedom from dependence on external authority or the opinions of others.

Peak experiences Temporary moments of self-actualization.

Question: Maslow's choice of self-actualizing people for study seems pretty subjective. Is it really a fair representation of self-actualization?

Although Maslow tried to investigate self-actualization empirically, his choice of people for study was subjective. Undoubtedly there are many ways to reach full development of personal potential. Maslow's primary contribution was to draw attention to the *possibility* of continued personal growth. Maslow considered self-actualization an ongoing process, not a simple end point to be attained only once.

Question: What steps can be taken to promote self-actualization?

Maslow made few specific recommendations about how to proceed. Nevertheless, a number of helpful suggestions can be gleaned from his writings (Maslow, 1954, 1967, 1971).

Steps toward Self-Actualization There is no magic formula for leading a more creative life. Self-actualization is primarily a *process*, not a goal or an end point. As such, it requires hard work, patience, and commitment. Here are some ways to begin.

1. **Be willing to change.** Begin by asking yourself, "Am I living in a way that is deeply satisfying to me and which truly expresses me?" If not, be prepared to make changes in your life. Indeed, ask yourself this question often and accept the need for continual change.
2. **Take responsibility.** You can become an architect of self by acting as if you are personally responsible for every aspect of your life. Shouldering responsibility in

Fully functioning person A person living in harmony with her or his deepest feelings, impulses, and intuitions.

Self A continuously evolving conception of one's personal identity.

Self-image Total subjective perception of one's body and personality (another term for self-concept).

Symbolization The process of admitting an experience to awareness.

Incongruence State that exists when there is a discrepancy between one's experiences and self-image or between one's self-image and ideal self.

Incongruent person A person who has an inaccurate self-image or whose self-image differs greatly from the ideal self.

this way helps end the habit of blaming others for your own shortcomings.

3. **Examine your motives.** Self-discovery involves an element of risk. If most of your behavior seems to be directed by a desire for safety or security, it may be time to test the limits of these needs. Try to make each life decision a choice for growth, not a response to fear or anxiety.

4. **Experience honestly and directly.** Wishful thinking is another barrier to personal growth. Self-actualizers trust themselves enough to accept all kinds of information without distorting it to fit their fears and desires. Try to see yourself as others do. Be willing to admit, "I was wrong" or, "I failed because I was irresponsible."

5. **Make use of positive experiences.** Maslow considered peak experiences temporary moments of self-actualization. Therefore, you might actively repeat activities that have caused feelings of awe, amazement, exaltation, renewal, reverence, humility, fulfillment, or joy.

6. **Be prepared to be different.** Maslow felt that everyone has a potential for "greatness," but most fear becoming what they might. As part of personal growth, be prepared to trust your own impulses and feelings; don't automatically judge yourself by the standards of others. Accept your uniqueness.

7. **Get involved.** Maslow found with few exceptions that self-actualizers tend to have a mission or "calling" in life. For these people, "work" is not done just to fill deficiency needs, but to satisfy higher yearnings for truth, beauty, brotherhood, and meaning. Get personally involved and committed. Turn your attention to problems outside yourself.

8. **Assess your progress.** Since there is no final point at which one becomes self-actualized, it is important to gauge your progress frequently and to renew your efforts. If you feel bored at school, at a job, or in a relationship, consider it a challenge or an indication that you have not taken responsibility for personal growth. Almost any activity can be used as a chance for self-enhancement if it is approached creatively.

Carl Rogers' Self Theory

Like Freud, Carl Rogers based his theory on clinical experience. Unlike Freud, who portrayed the normal personality as "adjusted" to internal conflict, Rogers saw greater possibility for inner harmony. The **fully functioning person,** he said, is one who has achieved an openness to feelings and experiences and has learned to trust inner urges and intuitions (Rogers, 1961). Rogers believed that this attitude is most likely to occur when a person receives ample amounts of love and acceptance from others.

■ **Fig. 15–15** *Humanists consider self-image a central determinant of behavior and personal adjustment.*

Personality Structure and Dynamics Rogers' theory of personality centers on the concept of the **self,** a flexible and changing perception of personal identity (■ Fig. 15–15). The self is made up of those experiences identified as "I" or "me" that are separated from "not-me" experiences. Much human behavior can be understood as an attempt to maintain consistency between one's **self-image** and one's actions. For example, individuals who think of themselves as kind and considerate will act that way in most situations.

Question: Let's say I know a person who thinks she is kind and considerate, but she really isn't. How does this fit Rogers' theory?

According to Rogers, experiences that match the self-image are **symbolized** (admitted to consciousness) and contribute to gradual changes in the self. Information or feelings inconsistent with the self-image are said to be **incongruent.** It is incongruent, for example, to think of yourself as a considerate person if others frequently mention your rudeness. It is also incongruent to pretend you are kind when you are feeling callous or to say you are not angry when you are seething inside.

Experiences seriously incongruent with the self-image can be threatening, and they are often distorted or denied conscious recognition. Blocking, denying, or distorting experiences prevents the self from changing. This creates a gulf between the self-image and reality. As the self-image grows more unrealistic, the **incongruent person** becomes confused, vulnerable, dissatisfied, or seriously maladjusted (■ Fig. 15–16). (For more information, also see Chapter 16.) Recent studies have confirmed that people who know themselves well tend to like and feel good about themselves (Baumgardner, 1990). Poor self-knowledge is associated with low self-esteem (Campbell, 1990).

When your self-image is consistent with what you really think, feel, do, and experience, you are best able to actualize your potentials. Rogers also considered it essential to have congruence between the self-image and the **ideal self.** The ideal self is similar to Freud's ego ideal. It is an image of the person you would most like to be.

Question: Is it really incongruent not to live up to one's ideal self?

Rogers was aware that we never fully attain our ideals, but the greater the gap between the way you see yourself and the way you would like to be, the greater the tension and anxiety experienced. The Rogerian view of personality can therefore be summarized as a process of maximizing potentials by accepting information about oneself as realistically and honestly as possible. In accord with Rogers' thinking, researchers have found that people with a close match between their self-image and ideal self tend to be socially poised, confident, and resourceful. Those with a poor match tend to be depressed, anxious, insecure, and lacking in social skills (Gough et al., 1983; Scott & O'Hara, 1993). Highlight 15–7 provides another perspective on the ways in which self-image can influence our behavior.

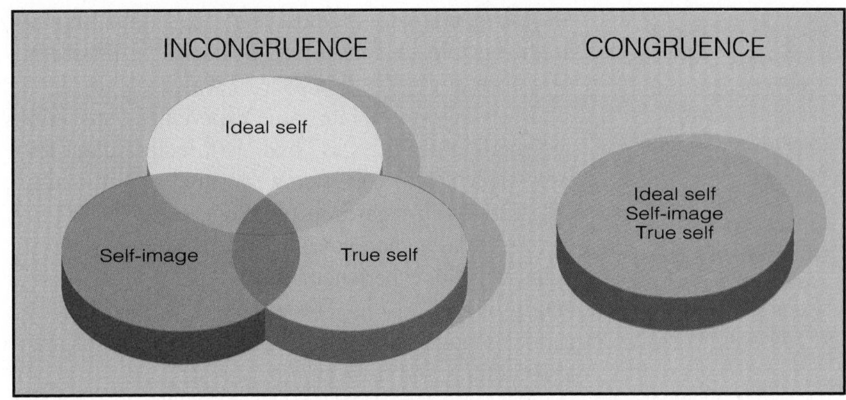

■ **Fig. 15–16** *Incongruence occurs when there is a mismatch between any of these three entities: the ideal self (the person you would like to be), your self-image (the person you think you are), and the true self (the person you actually are). Self-esteem suffers when there is a large difference between one's ideal self and self-image. Anxiety and defensiveness are common when the self-image does not match the true self.*

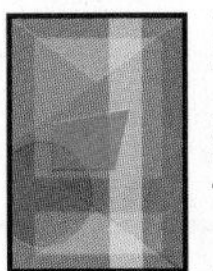

HIGHLIGHT 15–7

Research Frontier

Possible Selves— Trying on a Self for Size

Your ideal self is only one of many personal identities you may have pondered. Psychologists Hazel Markus and Paula Nurius (1986) believe that each of us harbors images of many **possible selves.** These selves include the person we would most like to become (the ideal self), as well as other selves we could become or are afraid of becoming.

Possible selves translate our hopes, fears, fantasies, and goals into specific images of who we *could* be. Thus, a beginning law student might picture herself as a successful attorney; the husband in a troubled marriage might picture himself as a divorcé; and a person on a diet might imagine both slim and grossly obese possible selves. Such self-images tend to direct future behavior. They also give meaning to current behavior and help us evaluate it. For example, the unhappy spouse might be moved by upsetting images of his "divorcé self" to try saving the marriage.

Even day-to-day decisions may be guided by possible selves. Purchasing clothes, a car, cologne, membership in a health club, and the like may be influenced by images of a valued future self. Of course, identities are not all equally possible. As Markus and Nurius point out, almost everyone over age 30 has probably felt the anguish of realizing that some cherished possible selves will never be realized.

Ideal self An idealized image of oneself.

Possible self A collection of beliefs, feelings, and images concerning the person one could become.

Conditions of worth Internal standards used to judge the value of one's thoughts, actions, feelings, or experiences.

Humanistic View of Development

Why do mirrors, photographs, tape recorders, and the reactions of others hold such fascination and threat for most people? Carl Rogers' theory suggests it is because they provide information about one's self. The development of a self-image depends greatly on information from the environment. It begins with a sorting of perceptions and feelings: my body, my toes, my nose, I want, I like, I am, and so on. Soon, it expands to include self-evaluation: I am a good person, I did something bad just now, and so forth.

Question: How does development of the self contribute to later personality functioning?

Rogers believed that positive and negative evaluations by others cause children to develop internal standards of evaluation he called **conditions of worth.** In other words, we learn that some actions win our parents' love and approval whereas others are rejected. More importantly, parents often label many of a child's *feelings* as bad or wrong. For example, a child might be told that it is wrong to feel angry toward a brother or sis-

Positive self-regard Thinking of oneself as a good, lovable, worthwhile person.

Organismic valuing A natural, undistorted, full-body reaction to an experience.

Unconditional positive regard Unshakable love and approval given without qualification.

ter—even when anger is justified. Likewise, a little boy might be told that he must not cry or be afraid, two very normal emotions.

Learning to evaluate some experiences or feelings as "good" and others as "bad" is directly related to a later capacity for self-esteem, positive self-evaluation, or **positive self-regard,** to use Rogers' term. To think of yourself as a good, lovable, worthwhile person, your behavior and experiences must match your internal conditions of worth. The problem is that this can cause incongruence by leading to the denial of many true feelings and experiences.

To put it simply, Rogers regarded many adult adjustment problems as an attempt to live by the standards of others. He believed that congruence and self-actualization are encouraged by replacing conditions of worth with **organismic valuing.** Organismic valuing is a direct, gut-level response to life that avoids the filtering and distortion of incongruence. It involves trusting one's own feelings and perceptions and being one's own "locus of evaluation." Organismic valuing is most likely to develop, Rogers felt, when children (or adults) receive "unconditional positive regard" from others. That is, when they are "prized" as worthwhile human beings, just for being themselves, without any conditions or strings attached.

Learning Check

1. Humanists view human nature as basically good and they emphasize the effects of subjective learning and unconscious choice. T or F?
2. Maslow used the term ________________ to describe the tendency of certain individuals to fully use their talents and potentials.
3. According to Rogers, a close match between the self-image and the ideal self creates a condition called incongruence. T or F?
4. Markus and Nurius describe alternative self-concepts that a person may have as "possible selves." T or F?
5. Rogers' theory considers acceptance of conditions of ________________ a troublesome aspect of development of the self.
6. According to Maslow, a preoccupation with one's own thoughts, feelings, and needs is characteristic of self-actualizing individuals. T or F?
7. Maslow regarded ________________ experiences as times of temporary self-actualization.

Critical Thinking

8. What role would "possible selves" have in the choice of a college major?

Answers: 1. F 2. self-actualization 3. F 4. T 5. worth 6. F 7. peak 8. Career decisions almost always involve, in part, picturing oneself occupying various occupational roles.

Personality Theories—Overview and Comparison

Question: Which personality theory is right?

Each theory has added to our understanding of personality by organizing observations of human behavior. Nevertheless, theories can never be fully proved or disproved. We can only determine if evidence tends to support a theory or to disconfirm it. At the same time that theories are neither true nor false, their implications or predictions may be. The best way to judge a theory, then, is in terms of its *usefulness* for explaining behavior, for stimulating research, and for suggesting ways of treating psychological disorders. Each theory has fared differently in these areas.

Trait Theories Traits are very useful for describing and comparing personalities. Many of the personality tests used by clinical psychologists are based on trait theories. However, trait theories can be criticized for having a circular quality. For example, how do we know that a young man named Delon has the trait of shyness? Because we frequently observe Delon avoiding conversations with others. And why doesn't Delon socialize with others? Because shyness is a trait of his personality. And how do we know he has the trait of shyness? Because we observe that he avoids socializing with others. And so on.

Psychoanalytic Theory By present standards, psychoanalytic theory seems to over-emphasize sexuality and biological instincts. These distortions were corrected somewhat by the neo-Freudians, but problems remain. One of the most telling criticisms of Freudian theory is that it can explain any psychological event *after* it has occurred. But beforehand, it offers little help in predicting future behavior. For this reason, many psychoanalytic concepts are difficult or impossible to test.

Behavioristic Theory Learning theories have provided a good framework for personality research. Of the three major perspectives, the behaviorists have made the best effort to rigorously test and verify their ideas. They have, however, been criticized for understating the impact that temperament, emotion, thinking, and subjective experience have on personality. Social learning theory can be regarded as an attempt to answer some of these criticisms.

Humanistic Theory A great strength of the humanists is the light they have shed on positive dimensions of personality. As Maslow (1968) put it, "Human nature is not nearly as bad as it has been thought to be. It is as if Freud supplied us with the sick half of psychology and we must now fill it out with the healthy half." Despite their contributions, the humanists can be criticized for using imprecise concepts that are difficult to measure or study objectively. Even so, humanistic thought has encouraged many people to seek greater self-awareness and personal growth. Also, humanistic concepts are widely used in counseling and psychotherapy.

In the final analysis, we need all four major perspectives to explain personality. Each perspective provides a sort of lens through which personality can be viewed. In many instances, a balanced picture emerges only when each theory is considered. ⬬ Table 15–2 provides a final overview of the four principal approaches.

Personality Assessment—Psychological Yardsticks

One of the great values of studying personality is the refinement it brings to personality measurement and testing. The results are highly useful in research, industry, education, and clinical work.

Question: How is personality "assessed"?

Psychologists use **interviews, observation, questionnaires,** and **projective tests** to measure personality. Each method is a refinement of more informal ways of judging a person. All forms of personality assessment have limitations (described later). For this reason, they are often used in combination.

At one time or another, you have probably "sized up" a potential date, friend, or employer by engaging in conversation (interview). Perhaps you have asked a friend, "When I am delayed I get angry. Do you?" (questionnaire). Maybe you watch your professors when they are angry or embarrassed to learn what they are "really" like (observation). Or possibly you have noticed that when you say, "I think people feel . . . ," you may be expressing your own feelings (projection). Let's see how psychologists apply each of these approaches to probe personality.

The Interview

A very direct way to learn about personality is to engage a person in conversation. An interview is described as **unstructured** if the conversation is informal

Interview (personality) A face-to-face meeting held for the purpose of gaining information about an individual's personal history, personality traits, current psychological state, and so forth.

Unstructured interview An interview in which conversation is informal and topics are taken up freely as they arise.

⬬ **Table 15–2 Comparison of Four Views of Personality**

	Trait Theories	Psychoanalytic Theory	Behaviorist Theory	Humanist Theory
View of human nature	neutral	negative	neutral	positive
Is behavior free or determined?	determined	determined	determined	free choice
Principal motives	depends on one's traits	sex and aggression	drives of all kinds	self-actualization
Personality structure	traits	id, ego, superego	habits	self
Role of unconscious	minimized	maximized	practically non-existent	minimized
Conception of conscience	traits of honesty, etc.	superego	self-reinforcement punishment history	ideal self, valuing process
Developmental emphasis	combined effects of heredity and environment	psychosexual stages	critical learning situations identification and imitation	development of self-image
Barriers to personal growth	unhealthy traits	unconscious conflicts, fixations	maladaptive habits; unhealthy environment	conditions of worth, incongruence

Structured interview An interview that follows a prearranged plan, usually a series of planned questions.

Halo effect The tendency to generalize a favorable or unfavorable first impression to unrelated details of personality.

Rating scale A list of personality traits or aspects of behavior on which a person is rated.

Behavioral assessment Recording the frequency of various behaviors.

Situational test Simulating real-life conditions so that a person's reactions may be directly observed.

and the interviewee determines what topics are discussed. In a **structured** interview, the interviewer obtains information by asking a series of planned questions.

Question: How are interviews used?

Interviews are used to identify personality disturbances; to select persons for employment, college, or special programs; and to study the dynamics of personality. Interviews also provide information for counseling or therapy. For instance, a counselor might ask a depressed person, "Have you ever contemplated suicide? What were the circumstances?" The counselor might then follow up by asking, "How did you feel about it?" or, "How is what you are now feeling different from what you felt then?"

In addition to providing information, interviews make it possible to observe a person's tone of voice, hand gestures, posture, and facial expressions. Such "body language" cues are important because they may radically alter the message sent, as when a person claims to be "completely calm," but trembles uncontrollably.

Limitations Interviews give rapid insight into personality, but they are subject to certain limitations. For one thing, interviewers can be swayed by preconceptions. A person identified as a "housewife," "college student," "high school athlete," "punk," or "ski bum" may be misjudged because of an interviewer's bias toward a particular lifestyle. Second, an interviewer's own personality may influence the interviewee's behavior. When this occurs, it can accentuate or distort the interviewee's apparent traits. A third problem is that people sometimes try to deceive interviewers. For example, a person accused of a crime might pretend to be mentally disabled to avoid punishment.

A fourth problem is the **halo effect.** The halo effect is a tendency to generalize a favorable or unfavorable impression to unrelated details of personality (■ Fig. 15–17). A person who is likable or physically attractive may be rated more mature, intelligent, or adjusted than he or she actually is. The halo effect is something to keep in mind when interviewing for employment. First impressions do make a difference.

Even with their limitations, interviews are a respected method of personality assessment. In many cases, interviews are an essential step to additional personality testing and to counseling or therapy.

■ Fig. 15–17 *What is your initial impression of the person wearing the black jacket? If you think that she looks friendly, attractive, or neat, your subsequent perceptions might be altered by a positive first impression. Interviewers are often influenced by the halo effect (see text).*

Direct Observation and Rating Scales

Are you fascinated by bus depots, airports, subway stations, or other public places? Many people relish a chance to observe the behavior of others. When used as an assessment procedure, direct observation is a simple extension of this natural interest in "people watching." For instance, a psychologist might arrange to observe a disturbed child playing with other children. Does the child remain withdrawn from others? Does she become hostile or aggressive without warning? By careful observation, the psychologist will identify personality characteristics and clarify the nature of the child's problems.

Question: Wouldn't observation be subject to the same problems of misperception as an interview?

Yes. Misperceptions can be a difficulty. For this reason, **rating scales** are sometimes used (■ Fig. 15–18). Rating scales limit the chance that some traits will be overlooked while others are exaggerated. Perhaps they should be standard procedures for choosing a roommate, spouse, or lover!

An alternative to rating scales is to do a **behavioral assessment.** In this case, observers record how often various *actions* occur, not what traits they think a person has. For example, psychologists working with hospitalized mental patients may find it helpful to record the frequency of patients' aggression, self-care, speech, and unusual behaviors (Alevizos & Callahan, 1977). Behavioral assessments are not strictly limited to visible behavior. They can also be helpful in probing thought processes. In one study, for example, students high in math anxiety were asked to think aloud while doing math problems. Then their thoughts were analyzed to pinpoint the causes of their anxiety (Blackwell et al., 1985).

Situational Testing A specialized form of direct observation is called **situational testing.** Situational tests are based on the premise that the best way to

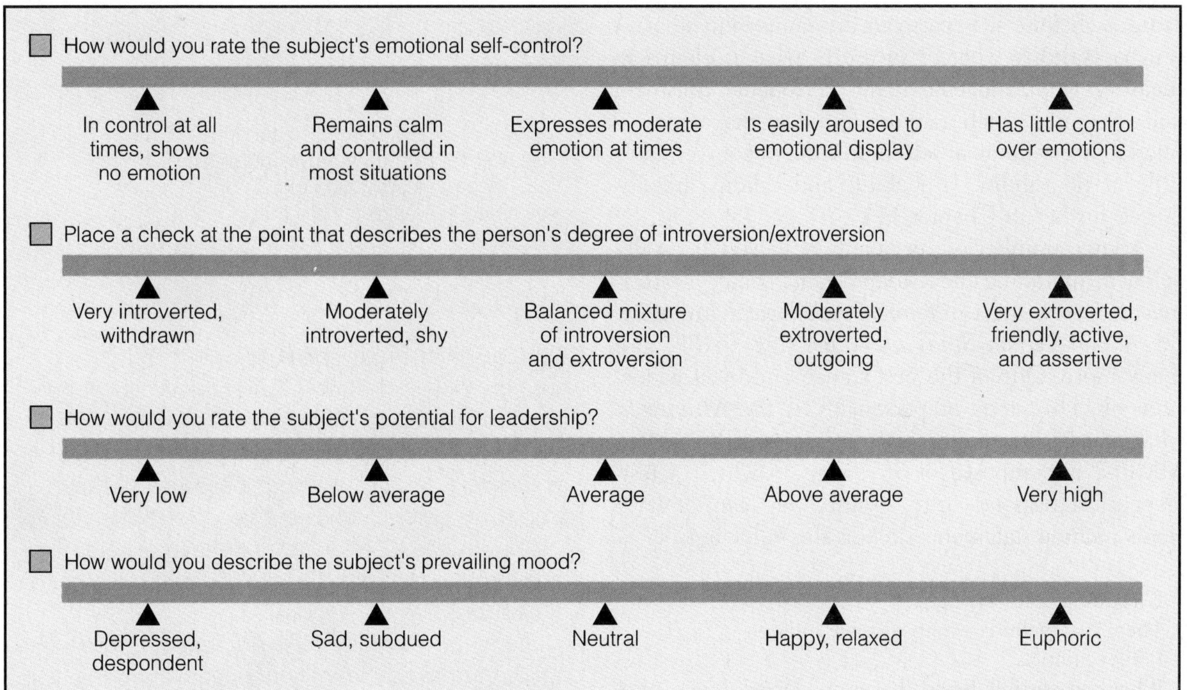

How would you rate the subject's emotional self-control?
In control at all times, shows no emotion
Remains calm and controlled in most situations
Expresses moderate emotion at times
Is easily aroused to emotional display
Has little control over emotions
Place a check at the point that describes the person's degree of introversion/extroversion
Very introverted, withdrawn
Moderately introverted, shy
Balanced mixture of introversion and extroversion
Moderately extroverted, outgoing
Very extroverted, friendly, active, and assertive
How would you rate the subject's potential for leadership?
Very low
Below average
Average
Above average
Very high
How would you describe the subject's prevailing mood?
Depressed, despondent
Sad, subdued
Neutral
Happy, relaxed
Euphoric

■ **Fig. 15–18** *Sample rating scale items. To understand how the scale works, imagine someone you know well. Where would you place check marks on each of the scales to rate that person's characteristics?*

Personality questionnaire A paper-and-pencil test consisting of questions that reveal aspects of personality.

Objective test A test that gives the same score when different people correct it.

Reliability The ability of a test to yield nearly the same score each time it is given to the same person.

learn how a person reacts to certain types of situations is to simulate those situations. Situational tests expose a person to frustration, temptation, pressure, boredom, or other conditions capable of revealing personality characteristics.

Question: How are situational tests done?

An interesting example of situational testing is the judgmental firearms training provided by many police departments (■ Fig. 15–19). At times, police officers must make split-second decisions about using their weapons. A mistake may be fatal. In a "shoot-don't shoot" test, actors play the part of armed criminals. As various high-risk scenes are acted out live or on videotape, officers must decide to shoot or hold fire. A newspaper reporter who once took the test (and failed it) gives this account (Gersh, 1982):

> I judged wrong. I was killed by a man in a closet, a man with a hostage, a woman interrupted when kissing her lover, and a man I thought was cleaning a shotgun. . . . I shot a drunk who reached for a comb, and a teenager who pulled out a black water pistol. Looked real to me.

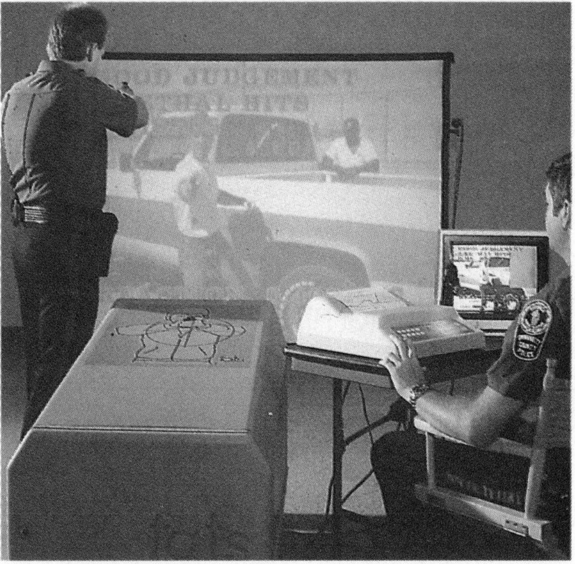

■ **Fig. 15–19** *A police officer undergoes judgmental firearms testing. Variations on this situational test are used by a growing number of police departments. All officers must score a passing grade.*

In addition to the training it provides, situational testing may uncover police cadets who lack the good judgment needed to carry a gun out on the street.

Personality Questionnaires

Most **personality questionnaires** are paper-and-pencil tests requiring people to answer questions about themselves. As measures of personality, questionnaires are more *objective* than interviews or observation. Questions, administration, and scoring are all standardized so that scores are unaffected by the opinions or prejudices of the examiner. However, this is not enough to ensure a test's accuracy. It must also be both *reliable* and *valid.* A test is **reliable** if it yields close to the same

Validity The ability of a test to measure what it purports to measure.

Minnesota Multiphasic Personality Inventory-2 (MMPI-2) One of the best-known and most widely used objective personality questionnaires.

MMPI-2 profile A graphic representation of an individual's scores on each of the primary scales of the MMPI-2.

Validity scales Scales that tell whether test scores should be invalidated for lying, inconsistency, or "faking good."

score each time it is given to the same individual. A test has **validity** when it measures what it claims to measure. Unfortunately, many personality tests you will encounter, such as those found in magazines or offered by commercial self-improvement courses, have little or no validity. (Reliability and validity are discussed further in Chapter 14.)

A large number of personality tests have been developed, including the *Guilford-Zimmerman Temperament Survey*, the *California Psychological Inventory*, the *Allport-Vernon Study of Values*, the *16 PF*, and many more. One of the best-known and most widely used objective tests of personality is the *Minnesota Multiphasic Personality Inventory-2* (MMPI-2). The MMPI-2 is composed of 567 items to which a test-taker must respond "true," "false," or "cannot say." Items include statements such as the following.

Everything tastes the same.
There is something wrong with my mind.
I enjoy animals.
Whenever possible I avoid being in a crowd.
I have never indulged in any unusual sex practices.
Someone has been trying to poison me.
I daydream often.*

Question: How can these items show anything about personality? For instance, what if a person has a cold so that "everything tastes the same"?

Highlight 15–8 offers an answer to this question (and a little bit of fun).

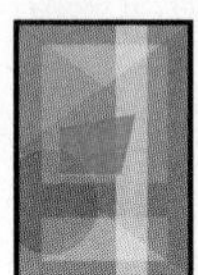

Highlight 15–8

A Closer Look At

Personality Tests—A Roast and a Rationale

Humorist Art Buchwald (1965) once lampooned personality questionnaires by writing his own test. The following is a sample of his items. Answer "Yes," "No," or "Don't bother me, I can't cope!"

I would enjoy the work of a chicken flicker.
My eyes are always cold.
Frantic screams make me nervous.
I believe I smell as good as most people.
Most of the time I go to sleep without saying good-bye.
I use shoe polish to excess.
The sight of blood no longer excites me.

More recently, psychologist Carol Sommer has added the following gems to Buchwald's list.

I salivate at the sight of mittens.
As an infant I had very few hobbies.
Spinach makes me feel alone.
Dirty stories make me think about sex.
I stay in the bathtub until I look like a raisin.
I like to put chameleons on plaid cloth.
I never finish what I

Such questions may seem ridiculous, but they are not very different from the real thing. How, then, do the items on tests such as the MMPI-2 reveal anything about personality? The answer is that a single item tells little about personality. For example, a person who agrees that "Everything tastes the same" might simply have a cold. It is only through *patterns* of response that personality dimensions are revealed.

Items on the MMPI-2 were selected for their ability to correctly identify persons with particular psychiatric problems. For instance, if a series of items is consistently answered in a particular way by depressed persons, it is assumed that others who answer the same way are also prone to depression. As silly as the gag items in the preceding lists may seem, it is possible that some could actually work in a legitimate test. But before an item could become part of a test, it would have to be shown to correlate highly with some trait or dimension of personality.

The MMPI-2 measures 10 major aspects of personality (listed in ● Table 15–3). After the MMPI-2 is scored, results are charted as an **MMPI-2 profile** (■ Fig. 15–20). By comparing a person's profile to scores produced by normal adults, a psychologist can identify various personality disorders. Additional scales are capable of identifying substance abuse, eating disorders, Type A behavior, repression, anger, cynicism, low self-esteem, family problems, inability to function in a job, and other problems of interest to clinicians and employers (Hathaway & McKinley, 1989).

Question: How accurate is the MMPI-2?

The accuracy of the MMPI-2 or any other personality questionnaire rests on the assumption that people are willing to tell the truth about themselves. Because of the importance of this assumption, the MMPI-2 has additional **validity scales** to detect attempts by test takers to "fake good" (make themselves look good) or "fake bad" (make it look like they have problems). Other scales help adjust final scores that are affected by personal defensiveness or by tendencies to exaggerate shortcomings and troubles.

*Reproduced by permission. Copyright 1989, by the University of Minnesota Press.

● Table 15–3 MMPI-2 Basic Clinical Subscales

1. **Hypochondriasis** (HI-po-kon-DRY-uh-sis). Exaggerated concern about one's physical health.
2. **Depression.** Feelings of worthlessness, hopelessness, and pessimism.
3. **Hysteria.** The presence of physical complaints for which no physical basis can be established.
4. **Psychopathic deviate.** Emotional shallowness in relationships and a disregard for social and moral standards.
5. **Masculinity/femininity.** One's degree of traditional "masculine" aggressiveness or "feminine" sensitivity.
6. **Paranoia.** Extreme suspiciousness and feelings of persecution.
7. **Psychasthenia** (sike-as-THEE-nee-ah). The presence of obsessive worries, irrational fears (phobias) and compulsive (ritualistic) actions.
8. **Schizophrenia.** Emotional withdrawal and unusual or bizarre thinking and actions.
9. **Mania.** Emotional excitability, manic moods or behavior, and excessive activity.
10. **Social introversion.** One's tendency to be socially withdrawn.

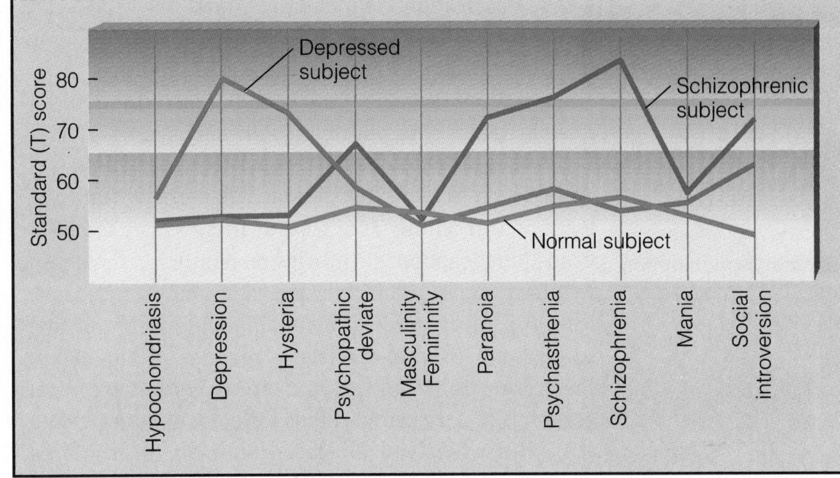

■ **Fig. 15–20** *An MMPI-2 profile showing hypothetical scores indicating normality, depression, and psychosis. High scores begin at 66 and very high scores at 76. An unusually low score (40 and below) may also reveal personality characteristics or problems.*

Unfortunately, the validity scales are not enough to ensure accuracy. If MMPI-2 scores alone are used to classify a person as emotionally disturbed, large numbers of normal people will be incorrectly labeled (Cronbach, 1990). (Highlight 15–9 discusses a related controversy.) Fortunately, such judgments usually take into account information from interviews or other sources.

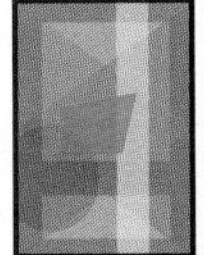

HIGHLIGHT 15–9

Focus on a Controversy

Honesty Tests—Do They Tell the Truth?

Each year, millions of anxious job seekers take paper-and-pencil **honesty tests** given by companies that hope to avoid hiring dishonest workers. Honesty tests (also known as integrity tests) assume that poor attitudes toward various dishonest acts—such as taking office supplies home from work or leaving work early—predispose a person to dishonest behavior. Most of the tests also ask people how honest they think the average person is, and how honest they are in comparison. Surprisingly, many job applicants willingly rate their own honesty as below average. (You have to admire them for being honest about it!) Honesty tests also ask about prior brushes with the law, past acts of theft or deceit, and attitudes toward use of illicit drugs and alcohol.

Question: Is honesty testing valid?

This question is still very much in dispute. Some psychologists believe that the best honesty tests are sufficiently valid to be used for making employment decisions (Ones et al., 1993). Others, however, remain unconvinced. To date, studies have failed to demonstrate that honesty tests can accurately *predict* if a person will be a poor risk on the job (Saxe, 1991). Psychologists are also concerned because honesty tests are often administered by untrained businesspersons. Yet another cause for concern is the fact that 96 percent of test takers who fail are incorrectly labeled as dishonest (Camara & Schneider, 1994).

Some states have banned the use of honesty tests as the sole basis for deciding whether to hire a person. Yet, it's easy to understand why employers want to do whatever they can to reduce theft and dishonesty in the workplace. The pressures to use honesty tests are intense. No doubt, the debate about honesty testing will continue. Honest.

Honesty test A paper-and-pencil test designed to detect attitudes, beliefs, and behavior patterns that predispose a person to dishonest behavior.

Projective Tests of Personality—Inkblots and Hidden Plots

Projective tests take a very different approach to personality than the techniques already discussed. Inter-

Projective tests Psychological tests making use of ambiguous or unstructured stimuli.

Rorschach Inkblot Test A projective test comprised of 10 standardized inkblots.

Thematic Apperception Test (TAT) A projective test consisting of 20 different scenes and life situations about which respondents make up stories.

views, observation, rating scales, and inventories try to directly identify overt, observable traits (Vane & Guarnaccia, 1989). By contrast, projective tests attempt to indirectly uncover deeply hidden or *unconscious* wishes, thoughts, and needs.

As a child you may have delighted in finding faces and objects in cloud formations. Or perhaps you have learned something about your friends' personalities from their reactions to movies or paintings. If so, you will have some insight into the rationale for projective tests. A **projective test** provides *ambiguous stimuli* that subjects are asked to describe or make up stories about. Describing an unambiguous stimulus (a picture of an automobile, for example) tells little about your personality. But when you are faced with an unstructured stimulus or situation, you must organize what you see in terms of your own life experiences. Everyone sees something different in a projective stimulus, and what is perceived can reveal the inner workings of one's personality.

Because projective tests have no right or wrong answers, the ability of subjects to fake or "see through" such tests is greatly reduced (Vane & Guarnaccia, 1989). Moreover, projective tests can be a rich source of information, since responses are not restricted to simple true/false or yes/no answers.

Question: Is the inkblot test a projective technique?

The Rorschach Inkblot Test

The inkblot test, or *Rorschach* (ROR-shock), is one of the oldest and most widely used projective tests. Developed by Swiss psychologist Hermann Rorschach in the 1920s, it consists of 10 standardized inkblots. These vary in color, shading, form, and complexity.

Question: How does the test work?

First, a person is shown each blot and asked to describe what he or she sees in it (■ Fig. 15–21). Later the psychologist may return to a blot, asking the person to identify specific sections of it, to elaborate on previous descriptions, or to give new impressions about what it contains. Obvious differences in content—such as "blood dripping from a dagger" versus "flowers blooming in a field"—are important for identifying personal conflicts and fantasies. But surprisingly, content is considered less important than what parts of the inkblot are used to form an image and how the image is organized. These factors allow psychologists to view the ways in which a person perceives the world and to detect disorders in personality functioning.

The Thematic Apperception Test

Another popular projective test is the *Thematic Apperception Test* (TAT) developed by Harvard psychologist and personality theorist Henry Murray (1893–1988).

Question: How does the TAT differ from the Rorschach?

The TAT consists of 20 sketches depicting various scenes and life situations (■ Fig. 15–22). The person being tested is shown each sketch and is asked to make up a story about the people in it. Later the person is shown each sketch a second or, perhaps, a third time and asked to elaborate on previous stories or to construct new stories for each.

Scoring of the TAT is restricted to analyzing the content of the stories. Interpretations focus on how people feel, how they interact, what events led up to the incidents depicted in the sketch, and how the story will end. The psychologist might also count the number of times the central figure in each story is angry, overlooked, apathetic, jealous, or threatened. For ex-

■ **Fig. 15–21** *Inkblots similar to those used on the Rorschach. What do you see?*

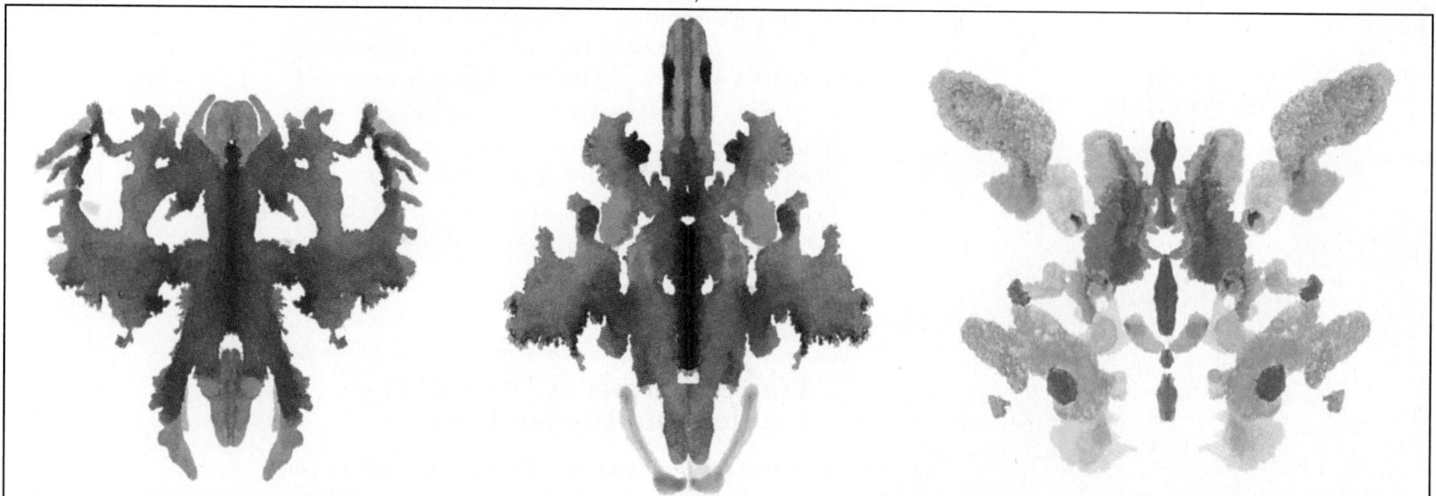

■ **Fig. 15–22** *This is a picture like those used for the Thematic Apperception Test. If you wish to simulate the test, tell a story that explains what led up to the pictured situation, what is happening now, and how the action will end.*

ample, here is a story written by a student to describe Figure 15–22.

> The girl has been seeing this guy her mother doesn't like. The mother is telling her that she better not see him again. The mother says, "He's just like your father." The mother and father are divorced. The mother is smiling because she thinks she is right. But she doesn't really know what the girl wants. The girl is going to see the guy again, anyway.

Question: How accurate are projective tests?

Limitations of Projective Testing Although projective tests have been popular with clinical psychologists, their validity is considered lowest among tests of personality. Objectivity and reliability (consistency) of judgments among different users of the TAT and Rorschach is also low. Note that after the subject interprets an ambiguous stimulus, the scorer must interpret the subject's (sometimes) ambiguous responses. In a sense, the interpretation of a projective test may be a projective test for the scorer!

Despite the drawbacks of projective tests, many psychologists believe they still have value, especially as part of a **battery** (group) of tests and interviews. In the hands of a skillful clinician, projective tests can detect major conflicts and aid in setting goals for therapy. Moreover, since projective tests are unstructured, they may be a better way to get clients to talk about anxiety-provoking topics than direct questions are.

Test battery A group of tests and interviews given to the same individual.

Sudden Murderers—A Research Example

Personality assessments provide us with clues to some of the most perplexing human events. Consider Fred Cowan, a model student in school and described by those who knew him as quiet, gentle, and a man who loved children. Despite his size (6 feet tall, 250 pounds), Fred was described by a co-worker as "someone you could easily push around."

Fred Cowan is representative of a puzzling phenomenon: the sudden murderer—a gentle, quiet, shy, good-natured person who explodes without warning into violence (Lee et al., 1977). Two weeks after he was suspended from his job, Fred returned to work determined to get even with his supervisor. Unable to find the man, he killed four co-workers and a policeman before taking his own life.

Question: Isn't such behavior contrary to the idea of personality traits?

It might seem that sudden murderers are newsworthy simply because they seem to be such unlikely candidates for violence. On the contrary, research conducted by Melvin Lee, Philip Zimbardo, and Minerva Bertholf suggests that sudden murderers explode into violence *because* they are shy, restrained, and inexpressive, not in spite of it. These researchers studied prisoners at a California prison. Ten were inmates whose homicide was an unexpected first offense. Nine were criminals with a record of habitual violence prior to murder. Sixteen were inmates convicted of nonviolent crimes.

Question: Did the inmates differ in personality makeup?

Lee and his associates administered a battery of tests to the inmates. Included were the MMPI, a test measuring shyness, an adjective checklist, and personal interviews with each inmate. As expected, the sudden murderers were passive, shy, and overcontrolled (restrained) individuals. The habitually violent inmates were "masculine" (aggressive), undercontrolled (impulsive), and less likely to view themselves as shy than the average person (Lee et al., 1977).

Interviews and other observations have revealed that quiet, overcontrolled individuals are likely to be especially violent if they ever lose control. Their attacks are usually triggered by a minor irritation or frustration, but the attack reflects years of unexpressed feelings of anger and belittlement. When sudden murderers finally release the strict controls they have maintained on their behavior, a furious and frenzied attack ensues. Usually it is totally out of proportion to the offense against them, and often they have amnesia for some or all of their violent actions.

In comparison, the previously violent murderers showed very different reactions. Although they killed, their violence was moderate—usually only enough to do the necessary damage. Typically, they felt they had been cheated or betrayed and that they were doing what was necessary to remedy the situation or to maintain their manhood (Lee et al., 1977).

A Look Ahead The preceding example illustrates how some of the concepts and techniques discussed in this chapter can be applied to further our understanding. The Applications section that follows should add balance to your view of personality. Following that, the concluding Exploration discusses some interesting ideas about how we define ourselves and present ourselves to others. Don't be shy. Read on!

LEARNING CHECK

1. Planned questions are used in a ________________ interview.
2. The halo effect is the tendency of an interviewer to influence what is said by the interviewee. T or F?
3. Which of the following is considered the most objective measure of personality?
   a. rating scales *b.* personality questionnaires *c.* projective tests *d.* TAT
4. Situational testing allows direct ________________ of personality characteristics.
5. A psychotic person would probably score highest on which MMPI-2 scale?
   a. depression *b.* hysteria *c.* schizophrenia *d.* mania
6. The use of ambiguous stimuli is most characteristic of
   a. interviews *b.* projective tests *c.* personality inventories *d.* direct observation
7. The content of one's responses to the MMPI-2 is considered an indication of unconscious wishes, thoughts, and needs. T or F?
8. Doing a behavioral assessment requires direct observation of the person's actions or a direct report of the person's thoughts. T or F?
9. A surprising finding is that sudden murderers are usually undercontrolled, very masculine, and more impulsive than average. T or F?
10. A test is considered valid if it consistently yields the same score when the same person takes it on different occasions. T or F?

Critical Thinking

11. Projective testing would be of greatest interest to which type of personality theorist?

Answers: 1. structured 2. F 3. *b* 4. observation 5. *c* 6. *b* 7. F 8. T 9. F 10. F 11. Psychodynamic, because projective testing is designed to uncover unconscious thoughts, feelings, and conflicts.

APPLICATIONS: *Barriers and Bridges—Understanding Shyness*

As a personality trait, **shyness** refers to a tendency to avoid others, as well as feelings of social inhibition (uneasiness and strain when socializing) (Buss, 1980). Shy persons fail to make eye contact, retreat when spoken to, speak too quietly, and display little interest or animation in conversations. Do you:

- Find it hard to talk to strangers?
- Lack confidence with people?
- Feel uncomfortable in social situations?
- Feel nervous with people who are not close friends?

If so, you may be part of the 50 *percent* of college students who consider themselves shy (Carducci & Stein, 1988).

Question: What causes shyness?

Elements of Shyness

To begin with, shy persons often lack **social skills.** Many simply have not learned how to meet others or how to start a conversation and keep it going. **Social anxiety** is also a factor in shyness. Almost everyone feels nervous in some social situations (such as meeting an attractive stranger). Typically, this is a reaction to *evaluation fears* (fears of being embarrassed, ridiculed, or rejected, or of seeming inadequate). In general, however, evaluation fears are more frequent or intense for shy persons. A third problem for shy persons is a **self-defeating bias** in their thinking. Specifically, shy persons almost always blame themselves when a social encounter doesn't go well (Girodo, 1978).

Situational Causes of Shyness Shyness is most often triggered by *novel* or *unfamiliar* social situations. A person who does fine with family or close friends may become shy and awkward when meeting a stranger. Shyness is also magnified by formality, by meeting someone of higher status, by being noticeably different from others, or by being the focus of attention (as in giving a speech) (Buss, 1980; Pilkonis, 1977).

Question: Don't most people become cautious and inhibited in such circumstances?

Yes. That's why we need to see how the personalities of shy and non-shy persons differ.

Dynamics of the Shy Personality

There is a tendency to think that shy persons are wrapped up in their own feelings and thoughts. But surprisingly, researchers Jonathan Cheek and Arnold Buss (1979) found no connection between shyness and **private self-consciousness** (attention to inner feelings, thoughts, and fantasies). Instead, they discovered that shyness is linked to **public self-consciousness.**

Persons who rate high in public self-consciousness are intensely aware of themselves as *social objects* (Buss, 1980). They are concerned about what others think of them, and they feel that others are evaluating them. They worry about saying the wrong thing or appearing foolish. In public, they may feel "naked" or as if others can "see through them." Such feelings trigger anxiety or outright fear during social encounters, leading to awkwardness and inhibition (Buss, 1986).

As mentioned, almost everyone feels anxious in at least some social situations. But there is a key difference in the way shy and non-shy persons *label* this anxiety. Shy persons tend to consider their social anxiety a *lasting personality trait.* Shyness, in other words, becomes part of their self-concept. In contrast, non-shy persons believe that *external situations* cause their occasional feelings of shyness. When non-shy persons feel anxiety or "stage fright," they assume that almost anyone would feel as they do under the same circumstances (Zimbardo et al., 1978).

Labeling is important because it affects *self-esteem.* In general, non-shy persons tend to have higher self-esteem than shy persons. This is because non-shy persons give themselves credit for their social successes and they recognize that failures are often due to circumstances. In contrast, shy people blame themselves for social failures and never give themselves credit for successes (Buss, 1980; Girodo, 1978).

Question: What can be done to reduce shyness?

Shy Beliefs

While directing a shyness clinic, psychologist Michel Girodo (1978) observed that shyness is often maintained by unrealistic or self-defeating beliefs. Here's a sample of such beliefs.

1. *If you wait around long enough at a social gathering, something will happen.*
Comment: This is really a cover-up for fear of starting a conversation. For two people to meet, at least one has to make an effort and it might as well be you.

Shyness A tendency to avoid others plus uneasiness and strain when socializing.

Social skills Proficiency at interacting with others.

Social anxiety A feeling of apprehension in the presence of others.

Self-defeating bias A distortion of thinking that impairs behavior.

Private self-consciousness Preoccupation with inner feelings, thoughts, and fantasies.

Public self-consciousness Intense awareness of oneself as a social object.

2. *Other people who are popular are just lucky when it comes to being invited to social events or asked out.* *Comment:* Except for times when a person is formally introduced to someone new, this is false. People who are more active socially typically make an effort to meet and spend time with others. They join clubs, invite others to do things, strike up conversations, and generally leave little to luck.
3. *The odds of meeting someone interested in socializing are always the same, no matter where I am.* *Comment:* This is another excuse for inaction. It pays to seek out situations that have a higher probability of leading to social contact, such as clubs, teams, and school events.
4. *If someone doesn't seem to like you right away, they really don't like you and never will.* *Comment:* This belief leads to much needless shyness. Even when a person doesn't show immediate interest, it doesn't mean the person dislikes you. Liking takes time and opportunity to develop.

Unproductive beliefs like the preceding can be replaced with statements such as the following.

1. I've got to be active in social situations.
2. I can't wait until I'm completely relaxed or comfortable before taking a social risk.
3. I don't need to pretend to be someone I'm not; it just makes me more anxious.
4. I may think other people are harshly evaluating me, but actually I'm being too hard on myself.
5. I can set reasonable goals for expanding my social experience and skills.
6. Even people who are very socially skillful are never successful 100 percent of the time. I shouldn't get so upset when an encounter goes badly. (Adapted from Girodo, 1978)

Social Skills

Learning social skills takes practice. There is nothing "innate" about knowing how to meet people or start a conversation. Social skills can be directly practiced in a variety of ways. It can be helpful, for instance, to get a tape recorder and listen to several of your conversations. You may be surprised by the way you pause, interrupt, miss cues, or seem disinterested. Similarly, it can be useful to look at yourself in a mirror and exaggerate facial expressions of surprise, interest, dislike, pleasure, and so forth. By such methods, most people can learn to put more animation and skill into their self-presentation. (For a discussion of related skills, see the section on self-assertion in Chapter 20.)

Opening Lines If you would like to start a conversation to meet someone new, what's the best way to begin? In a study reported by psychologist Chris Kleinke (1986) 1000 men and women rated typical "opening lines." An analysis of these statements revealed that they fell into three categories: *direct*, *innocuous* (mild or harmless), and *cute-flippant*. The examples that follow illustrate each category (adapted from Kleinke, 1986).

Direct

I feel a little embarrassed about this, but I'd like to meet you.
Since we're both sitting alone, would you care to join me?
That's a very pretty (sweater, jacket, skirt) you have on.

Innocuous

Hi.
Would you watch my books for a minute?
It's beautiful today, isn't it?
Can you give me directions to ____________?

Cute-Flippant

Do you think I deserve a break today?
I play the field, and I think I just hit a home run.
Your place or mine?
I'm easy. Are you?

By a large margin, both men and women preferred opening lines that were direct or innocuous. Cute or flippant statements were least liked, especially by women. The kinds of opening lines so often used by male and female characters in the movies appear to be duds in real life.

Conversation One of the simplest ways to make better conversation is by learning to ask questions. A good series of questions shifts attention to the other person and shows you are interested. Nothing fancy is needed. You can do fine with questions such as, "Where do you (work, study, live)? Do you like (dancing, travel, music)? How long have you (been at this school, worked here, lived here)?" After you've broken the ice, the best questions are often those that are *open ended* (Girodo, 1978):

"What parts of the country have you seen?" (as opposed to: "Have you ever been to Florida?")
"What's it like living on the west side?" (as opposed to: "Do you like living on the west side?")
"What kinds of food do you like?" (as opposed to: "Do you like Chinese cooking?")

It's easy to see why open-ended questions are helpful. In replying to open-ended questions, people often give

APPLICATIONS: *Continued*

"free information" about themselves. This extra information can be used to ask other questions or to lead into other topics of conversation.

This brief sampling of ideas is no substitute for actual practice. Overcoming shyness requires a real effort to learn new skills and test old beliefs and attitudes. It may even require the help of a counselor or therapist. At the very least, a shy person must be willing to take social risks. Breaking down the barriers of shyness will always include some awkward or unsuccessful encounters. Nevertheless, the rewards are powerful: human companionship and personal freedom.

LEARNING CHECK

1. Surveys show that 14 percent of American college students consider themselves shy. T or F?
2. Social anxiety and evaluation fears are seen almost exclusively in shy individuals; the non-shy rarely have such experiences. T or F?
3. Unfamiliar people and situations most often trigger shyness. T or F?
4. Public self-consciousness plus a tendency to label oneself as shy are major characteristics of the shy personality. T or F?
5. Changing personal beliefs and practicing social skills can be helpful in overcoming shyness. T or F?
6. Shyness is a trait of Leshaun's personality. Like most shy people, Leshaun is most likely to feel shy in unfamiliar social settings. Leshaun's shy behavior demonstrates that the expression of traits is governed by what concept? ***Critical Thinking***

Answers: 1. F 2. F 3. T 4. T 5. T 6. trait-situation interactions

EXPLORATION

Self-Monitoring—Which Me Do You See?

As you walk into the room, you face a dilemma that challenges party-goers everywhere: On the left, a conversation is taking place between three similar people—a film lover, an art lover, and a music lover. On the right side of the room, a mixed group has formed, including a member of the peace movement, a military "hawk," and a feminist. Which group do you join? Your answer may depend on whether you are high or low in *self-monitoring* (Snyder & Harkness, 1984).

Self-monitoring refers to how much people *monitor* (observe, regulate, and control) the image of themselves they display to others in public. Some of us are **high self-monitors,** who are very sensitive to situations and expectations. It is as if high self-monitors ask, "Who does this situation want me to be, and how can I be that person?" In contrast, **low self-monitors** are less interested in controlling the impression they make. Such people seek to faithfully express what they really think and feel. It is as if they want to know, "Who am I, and how can I be me in this situation?" (Snyder, 1987).

The Public Self

Self-monitoring has been extensively studied by psychologist Mark Snyder. In general, persons high in self-monitoring take a flexible approach to defining themselves. They are very interested in their public "image." Low self-monitors, on the other hand, try to accurately present their beliefs and principles no matter what the situation is. Snyder believes that the way people define what they regard as "me" has an impact on their lives and behavior.

To return to the party, Snyder and Harkness (1984) found that in similar situations high self-monitors preferred to join clearly defined groups. At the party, for example, they could strike a "cultured" pose if they joined the first group. However, the second group would put them in a difficult position: Any image they projected could offend at least one member of the group. Such group differences had far less impact on low self-monitors. Basically, they chose whichever group had someone with whom they could identify.

Question: How can you tell if you are high or low in self-monitoring?

> **Self-monitoring** Regulation and control of the image one displays to others in public.
>
> **High self-monitor** A person who actively changes the impression he or she makes to fit situations and expectations.
>
> **Low self-monitor** A person who seeks to faithfully express who he or she is, regardless of the situation.

EXPLORATION

High or Low? To measure this characteristic, Snyder developed the *Self-Monitoring Scale.* Although the entire scale cannot be reprinted here, the items that follow are examples of statements that separate highs from lows.

High Self-Monitors

I would probably make a good actor.
I'm not always the person I appear to be.
I guess I put on a show to impress and entertain others.

Low Self-Monitors

I have never been good at games like charades or improvisational acting.
In a group, I am rarely the center of attention.
At a party, I let others keep the jokes and stories going.

If you are still not sure what your self-monitoring style is, the following comparisons may be helpful. Each difference has been verified in studies of self-monitoring (Snyder, 1987).

■ **Highs** are keenly interested in the actions of others and in trying to "read" their motives, attitudes, and traits. Presumably, high self-monitors do this so that they will know how to present themselves to a particular person, such as a date.
■ **Lows** seek to match their public behavior to their private attitudes, feelings, and beliefs. Lows tend to speak their mind no matter who is listening.
■ **Highs** are flexible and adaptable, and they display different behavior from situation to situation.
■ **Lows** change little from situation to situation. They value a match between who they believe they are and what they do. Lows do not want to change opinions to please others or win their favor.
■ **Highs** tend to declare who they are by listing their roles and memberships (student, post office employee, member of the school orchestra, third-ranking player of the tennis team, and so on).
■ **Lows** identify themselves in terms of their beliefs, emotions, values, and personality.
■ **Highs** choose friends who are skilled or knowledgeable in various areas. They also tend to have specific friends for specific activities.
■ **Lows** have friends who tend to all be alike in basic ways. No matter what the activity, they prefer to get together with the same friends.
■ **Highs** are concerned with outer appearances. They choose their clothes, hair style, jewelry, and so forth, to project an image.
■ **Lows** have a wardrobe that is less varied; they do not have to look different as often as high self-monitors do.
■ **Highs** initiate dating based mainly on the date's appearance. (In the personals column their ads are the ones that emphasize appearance.)
■ **Lows** are more interested in a potential date's personality.
■ **Highs** believe it is possible to love two people at the same time.
■ **Lows** believe that there is only one real love for a person.
■ **Highs** prefer jobs where their role is very clearly defined.
■ **Lows** prefer jobs where they can "just be themselves."

Implications As you can see, there are advantages and disadvantages to being either high or low in self-monitoring. In general, high self-monitors are adaptable and present themselves well in social situations. However, they tend to reveal little about their private feelings, beliefs, and intentions. This, plus gaps between their attitudes and actions, may have a negative effect on relationships. The primary drawback to being low in self-monitoring is a tendency to be unresponsive to the demands of different situations. Low self-monitors want to "just be themselves," even when adjustments in self-presentation would make them more effective.

One True Self? Is there a single "true self" that underlies the many roles we play in daily life? Studies of self-monitoring raise questions about the idea that each person has a "true self." High self-monitors, in particular, act as if they have many selves. For these people, controlling the image they impart is a way of life, at parties, in meetings, in classes, and elsewhere. The "public self" of high self-monitors may or may not be backed by a perceived "real me" on the inside. In many cases, it may be better to try to understand the self *in action* by looking at the ways people define themselves. Just as the answer to the question "Who am I?" varies for each person, the answer to the question "Do I have a single true self?" may vary too.

Do you have a single true self? Give the question some thought the next time you go to a party!

LEARNING CHECK

1. Self-monitoring refers to how much people compare their self-image to the image others hold of them. T or F?
2. Low self-monitors tend to ask, "Who does this situation want me to be?" T or F?
3. In social situations, high self-monitors prefer clearly defined groups that do not create self-presentation conflicts. T or F?
4. A low self-monitor would probably agree with the statement, "I usually prefer to wear my most comfortable clothes, no matter what the occasion is." T or F?
5. "Handsome Tom Cruise look-alike seeking slim fashion-model type fox for flights of fancy." This ad would most likely be placed by a person high in self-monitoring. T or F?

Critical Thinking

6. Which of Carl Jung's concepts is most relevant to the behavior of high self-monitors?

Answers: 1. F 2. F 3. T 4. T 5. T 6. persona

Chapter Summary

- ***How do psychologists use the term* personality?**

- **Personality** is made up of one's unique and enduring behavior patterns.
- **Character** is personality evaluated, or the possession of desirable qualities.
- **Temperament** refers to the hereditary and physiological aspects of one's emotional nature.

- ***What core concepts make up the psychology of personality?***

- Personality **traits** are lasting personal qualities that are inferred from behavior.
- Personality **types** group people into categories on the basis of shared traits or similar characteristics.
- Behavior is influenced by **self-concept,** which is a perception of one's own personality traits.
- **Personality theories** combine interrelated assumptions, ideas, and principles to explain personality.

- ***Are some personality traits more basic or important than others?***

- **Trait theories** attempt to specify qualities of personality that are most lasting or characteristic of a person.
- Allport made useful distinctions between **common traits** and **individual traits** and between **cardinal, central,** and **secondary traits.**
- A second trait approach, developed by Cattell, attributes visible **surface traits** to the existence of 16 underlying **source traits.**
- Source traits are measured by the *Sixteen Personality Factor Questionnaire* (16 PF). The outcome of the 16 PF may be graphically presented as a **trait profile.**
- The **five-factor model** of personality reduces traits to 5 universal dimensions of personality.
- Traits appear to **interact** with **situations** to determine behavior.
- **Behavioral genetics** and studies of separated **identical twins** suggest that **heredity** contributes significantly to adult personality traits.

- ***How do psychodynamic theories explain personality?***

- Like other **psychodynamic** approaches, Sigmund Freud's **psychoanalytic theory** emphasizes unconscious forces and conflicts within the personality.
- In Freud's theory, personality is made up of the **id, ego,** and **superego.**
- **Libido,** derived from the life instincts, is the primary energy running the personality. Conflicts within the personality may cause **neurotic anxiety** or **moral anxiety** and motivate use of **ego-defense mechanisms.**
- The personality operates on three levels, the **conscious, preconscious,** and **unconscious.**
- The Freudian view of personality development is based on a series of **psychosexual stages:** the **oral, anal, phallic,** and **genital** stages. **Fixation** at any stage can leave a lasting imprint on personality.

- ***What do behaviorists emphasize in their approach to personality?***

- **Behavioral theories** of personality emphasize learning, conditioning, and immediate effects of the environment.
- **Learning theorists** generally stress the effects of **prior learning** and **situational determinants** of behavior.
- Learning theorists John Dollard and Neal Miller consider **habits** the basic core of personality. Habits express the combined effects of **drive, cue, response,** and **reward.**
- **Social learning theory** adds cognitive elements, such as perception, thinking, and understanding to the behavioral view of personality. Examples of such concepts include the **psychological situation, expectancies,** and **reinforcement value.** Some social learning theorists treat "conscience" as a case of **self-reinforcement.**
- The behavioristic view of personality development holds that **social reinforcement** in four situations is critical. The **critical situations** are **feeding, toilet** or **cleanliness training, sex training,** and **anger** or **aggression training. Identification** and **imitation** are of particular importance in sex training.

- ***How do humanistic theories differ from other perspectives?***

- **Humanistic theory** emphasizes **subjective experience** and needs for **self-actualization.**
- Abraham Maslow's study of **self-actualizers** identified characteristics they share, ranging from efficient perceptions of reality to frequent peak experiences.
- Carl Rogers' theory views the **self** as an entity that emerges from personal experience. Experiences that match the **self-image** are **symbolized** (admitted to consciousness), while those that are **incongruent** are excluded.
- The **incongruent person** has a highly unrealistic self-image and/or a mismatch between the self-image and the ideal self. The **congruent** or **fully functioning** person is flexible and open to experiences and feelings.

- In the development of personality, humanists are primarily interested in the emergence of a **self-image** and in **self-evaluations.**
- As parents apply **conditions of worth** to children's behavior, thoughts, and feelings, children begin to do the same. Internalized conditions of worth then contribute to incongruence and disrupt the **organismic valuing process.**

■ *How do psychologists measure personality?*

- Techniques typically used for **personality assessment** are **interviews, observation, questionnaires,** and **projective tests.**
- **Structured** and **unstructured interviews** provide much information, but they are subject to interviewer bias and misperceptions. The **halo effect** may also lower the accuracy of an interview.
- **Direct observation,** sometimes involving **situational tests, behavioral assessment,** or the use of **rating scales,** allows evaluation of a person's actual behavior.
- **Personality questionnaires,** such as the *Minnesota Multiphasic Personality Inventory-2* (MMPI-2), are **objective** and **reliable,** but their **validity** is open to question.
- **Honesty tests,** which are essentially personality questionnaires, are widely used by businesses to make hiring decisions. Their validity is hotly debated.
- **Projective tests** ask a subject to project thoughts or feelings to an ambiguous stimulus or unstructured situation.
- *The Rorschach,* or inkblot test, is a well-known projective technique. A second is the *Thematic Apperception Test (TAT).*
- The validity and objectivity of projective tests are quite low. Nevertheless, projective techniques are considered useful by many clinicians, particularly as part of a **test battery.**

■ *What causes shyness? What can be done about it?*

- **Shyness** is a mixture of social inhibition and social anxiety. It is marked by heightened **public self-consciousness** and a tendency to regard one's shyness as a lasting trait. Shyness can be lessened by changing *self-defeating beliefs* and by improving *social skills.*

■ *How does self-monitoring affect behavior?*

- People vary in their degree of **self-monitoring** or desire to control the impression they make on others.
- **High self-monitoring** persons try to fit their public image to various situations. **Low self-monitors** are interested in accurately expressing their feelings, beliefs, and values, regardless of the situation.

Questions for Discussion

1. If you could select only three personality traits, which would you consider most basic? Why? Do you think that the "Big Five" personality dimensions embody the core of personality? What, if anything, do they leave out?
2. Do you know anyone who seems to have a cardinal trait? What do you think are the central traits of your personality? Secondary traits?
3. Why do you think that media coverage of reunited twins has exaggerated the role of genetics in human behavior and personality?
4. Can you describe an action you performed recently that seems to represent operation of the id, ego, or superego? How would a behaviorist or a humanist interpret the same event?
5. Can you cite observations that support Freud's scheme of psychosexual stages? What observations contradict the stages?
6. Is "Mr. Clean" an anal-retentive?
7. The film *Close Encounters of the Third Kind* culminates with a visit to Earth by a magnificent round spaceship. The ship opens to reveal child-like creatures who have come to take a chosen few to a new life among the stars. What archetypal symbols are represented by these images? Can you think of other films, works of art, or images that seem to symbolize Jungian archetypes?
8. As a child, with whom did you identify? What effect did this have on your personality? How does imitation differ from identification?
9. Presently, what are the most prominent "possible selves" you visualize? How have these self-images influenced your behavior?
10. Which theory of personality seems to best explain your personality?
11. Have you ever been interviewed or given a personality test? How accurate did you consider the resulting assessment of personality?
12. Do you think that preoccupation with one's public self (high self-monitoring) means that a person has no single "true self"? Or, could it be that the thought "I like to look good to others" is a core element of the person's true self-image?

Chapter 16

Abnormal Behavior: Deviance and Disorder

CHAPTER PREVIEW

Catch-22: A Practical Definition of "Crazy"

"Can't you ground someone who's crazy?"

"Oh, sure, I have to. There's a rule saying I have to ground anyone who's crazy."

"Then why don't you ground me? I'm crazy. Ask Clevinger."

"Clevinger? Where is Clevinger? You find Clevinger and I'll ask him."

"Then ask any of the others. They'll tell you how crazy I am."

"They're crazy."

"Then why don't you ground them?"

"Why don't they ask me to ground them?"

"Because they're crazy, that's why."

"Of course they're crazy," Doc Daneeka replied. "I just told you they're crazy, didn't I? And you can't let crazy people decide whether you're crazy or not, can you?"

Yossarian looked at him soberly and tried another approach.

"Is Orr crazy?"

"He sure is," Doc Daneeka said.

"Can you ground him?"

"I sure can. But first he has to ask me to. That's part of the rule."

IN THIS CHAPTER

Psychopathology
Normal and abnormal behavior
Mental disorders
Personality disorders
Sexual deviance
Adjustment disorders
Anxiety disorders
Dissociative disorders
Somatoform disorders
Theories of maladjustment
Applications:
Dangers of psychiatric labeling
Exploration:
The insanity defense

"Then why doesn't he ask you to?"

"Because he's crazy," Doc Daneeka said. "He has to be crazy to keep flying combat missions after all the close calls he's had. Sure, I can ground Orr. But first he has to ask me to."

"That's all he has to do to be grounded?"

"That's all. Let him ask me."

"And then you can ground him?" Yossarian asked.

"No. Then I can't ground him."

"You mean there's a catch?"

"Sure there's a catch," Doc Daneeka replied. "Catch-22. Anyone who wants to get out of combat duty isn't really crazy."

There was only one catch and that was Catch-22, which specified that a concern for one's own safety in the face of dangers that were real and immediate was the process of a rational mind. Orr was crazy and could be grounded. All he had to do was ask; and as soon as he did, he would no longer be crazy and would have to fly more missions. Orr would be crazy to fly more missions and sane if he didn't, but if he was sane he had to fly them. If he flew them he was crazy and didn't have to; but if he didn't want to he was sane and had to. Yossarian was moved very deeply by the absolute simplicity of this clause of Catch-22 and let out a respectful whistle.

"That's some catch, that Catch-22," he observed.

*"It's the best there is," Doc Daneeka agreed.**

This excerpt from Joseph Heller's novel, Catch 22, *captures the ambiguities presented by the classic question, What is normal? In the 1800s, doctors and non-professionals alike used such terms as "crazy," "insane," "cracked," and "lunatic" quite freely. The "insane" were thought of as bizarre and definitely different from you or me.*

Today our understanding of mental disorders is growing ever more sophisticated. Drawing the line between normal and abnormal can be done only by weighing some complex issues. In this chapter and the next we will summarize major psychological problems and their characteristics.

Survey Questions

- How is normality defined, and what are the major psychological disorders?
- What is a personality disorder?
- What are the most common sexual disorders?
- What problems result when a person suffers high levels of anxiety?
- How do psychologists explain anxiety-based disorders?
- Is psychiatric labeling damaging?
- What role does the concept of insanity play in criminal trials?

Psychopathology The scientific study of mental, emotional, and behavioral disorders; also, abnormal or maladaptive behavior.

Abnormal Behavior—What Is Normal?

William Milligan was accused of being the "university rapist" who attacked four women near Ohio State University. At his trial, psychiatrists testified that Milligan had nine separate personalities. The rapist was apparently "Adelena," a personality identified as an "18-year-old lesbian." Unlike the fictional excerpt from *Catch-22*, William Milligan's *psychopathology* was real.

Psychopathology

A large variety of problems fall into the general category of psychopathology. **Psychopathology** *is the scientific study of mental, emotional, and behavioral disorders.* The term also refers to abnormal or maladaptive behavior itself. Thus, psychopathology may be further defined as an *inability to behave in ways that foster the well-being of the individual and ultimately of society* (■ Fig. 16–1). This definition covers not only obviously maladaptive behavior, such as drug addiction, compulsive gambling, or loss of contact with reality, but also any behavior that interferes with personal growth and self-fulfillment (Carson & Butcher, 1992).

Mental health problems are extensive. William Milligan's severe disorder is but one hint of their prev-

**Catch 22*, Copyright 1955, 1961 by Joseph Heller. Reprinted by permission of Simon and Schuster, Inc., a division of Gulf & Western Corporation.

■ **Fig. 16–1** *The self-portraits shown here were painted by Andy Wilf between 1978 and 1981. During that time, Wilf is said to have increasingly abused drugs and alcohol. This dramatic series of images is a record of his self-destructive descent into a private hell. The third painting shows a shrouded skull—and foretells the artist's fate. Wilf died of a drug overdose early in 1982. Drug abuse is but one of the many psychopathologies, or "problems in living," psychologists seek to alleviate. (Courtesy of Ulrike Kantor, Ulrike Kantor Gallery.)*

alence. Here are the facts on psychopathology in the United States:

- ■ 1 out of every 100 persons will become so severely disturbed as to require hospitalization at some point in his or her lifetime.
- ■ Some 3 to 6 percent of the aged suffer from organic psychoses.
- ■ In any given week, 7 percent of the population is experiencing an anxiety-related disorder.
- ■ 1 out of every 8 school-aged children is seriously maladjusted.
- ■ 10 to 20 percent or more of all adults will suffer a major depression in their lifetime.
- ■ Each year over 2 million persons are admitted or readmitted to out-patient services or psychiatric treatment in general hospitals.

Defining Abnormality "That guy is really wacko, I think his porch lights are dimming." "Yeah, the butter's sliding off his waffle. I'd say he's at least a half-bubble short of level." Informally, it's tempting to make snap judgments about mental health. However, to seriously classify certain behaviors or certain people as psychologically unhealthy raises complex and age-old issues.

Defining normality can be a tricky business. We might begin by saying that psychopathology is characterized by **subjective discomfort.** That is, the unhealthy personality will be marked by unhappiness, anxiety, depression, or other signs of emotional upset.

Question: But couldn't a person be psychotic without feeling subjective discomfort?

Yes. A problem with this definition is that a person's behavior might be quite maladaptive without causing personal discomfort. A psychotic person displaying obviously bizarre and maladjusted behavior might feel "on top of the world." It could be said, also, that a *lack* of discomfort may reveal a problem. If you were to show no signs of grief or depression after the death of a friend or loved one, we might suspect psychopathology. In practice, subjective discomfort accounts for most instances in which people voluntarily seek professional help.

Some psychologists have tried to pin down normality more objectively by using **statistical definitions.** For example, since we know that anxiety is a characteristic of several disorders, we could devise a test to learn how many people show low, medium, or high levels of anxiety. Usually, the results of such a test will form a **normal** (bell-shaped) **curve** (■ Fig. 16–2). (Normal in this case is a statistical concept referring only to the shape of the curve.) Notice that most people score in the center region of such a curve. Those people who deviate from the average by being anxious all the time (high anxiety) might be considered abnormal. Incidentally, a person who never feels anxiety might also be considered abnormal.

Question: Then a statistical definition of abnormality tells us nothing about the meaning of a deviation from the norm?

Right. It is as statistically "abnormal" (unusual) for a person to score above 145 on an IQ test as it is to score below 55, but only in the second case would we consider the score "abnormal" or undesirable (Wakefield, 1992).

Subjective discomfort Personal, private feelings of discomfort or unhappiness.

Statistical abnormality Abnormality defined by an extreme score on some dimension, such as IQ or anxiety.

Normal curve A bell-shaped curve with a large number of scores in the middle, tapering to very few extremely high and low scores.

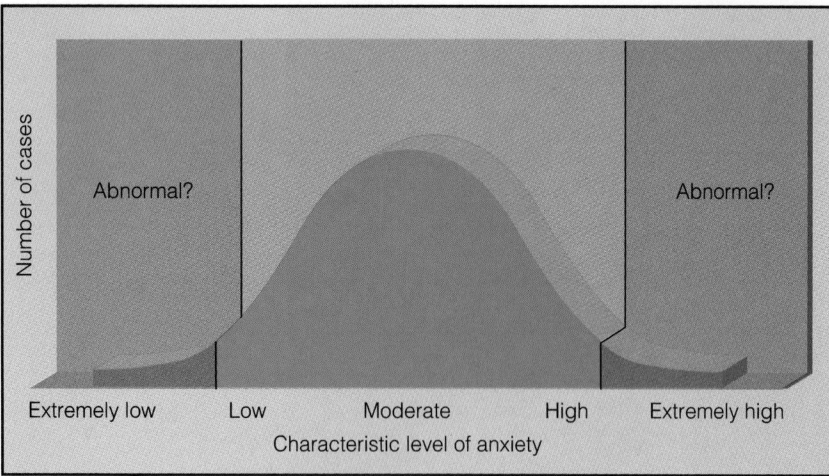

■ **Fig. 16–2** *The number of people displaying a personal characteristic may help define what is statistically abnormal.*

Social non-conformity Failure to conform to societal norms or the usual minimum standards for social conduct.

Situational context The social situation, behavioral setting, or general circumstances in which an action takes place.

Cultural relativity Perceptions and judgments made relative to the values of one's culture.

Another major problem with statistical definitions is the question of *where to draw the line* between normality and abnormality. Most behavioral problems range from mild to severe. To take a new example, we could obtain the average frequency of sexual intercourse for persons of a particular age, sex, and marital status. Obviously, a person who feels driven to seek sexual release dozens of times a day has a problem. But as we move back toward the norm we face the statistical problem of drawing lines. How often must an otherwise normal behavior occur before it becomes abnormal? In short, statistical boundary lines are often somewhat arbitrary (Widiger & Trull, 1991).

Social non-conformity may also serve as a basis for judging normality. Abnormal behavior can sometimes be viewed as a failure in *socialization*. In this case, the individual may not have adopted the usual minimum rules for social conduct or may have learned to engage in socially destructive or self-destructive behavior. This type of non-conformity must be carefully distinguished from that shown by highly creative individuals or by those who have a unique lifestyle (■ Fig. 16–3). Personal eccentricities can be charming and perfectly healthy. It should be noted also that strict adherence to social norms is no guarantee of mental health. In some cases, psychopathology takes the form of rigid conformity.

Before any behavior can be defined as normal or abnormal, we must consider the **situational context** in which it occurs. Is it normal to stand outside and water a lawn? It depends on whether or not it is raining. Is it abnormal for a grown man to remove his pants and expose himself to another man or woman in a place of business? It depends on whether the other person is a bank clerk or a doctor! Almost any imaginable behavior can be considered normal in some context, as the following example indicates.

■ **Fig. 16–3** *Social non-conformity does not automatically indicate psychopathology.*

> In mid-October, 1972, an airplane carrying a rugby team called the Old Christians crashed in the snow-capped Andes of South America. Incredibly, 16 of the 45 people who had been aboard at the time of the crash survived 73 days in deep snow and subfreezing temperatures. They were forced to use extremely grim measures to do so—they ate the bodies of those who had died in the crash. (*Time*, 1973)

Culture is one of the most influential contexts in which any behavior is judged. In some cultures it is considered normal to believe that plants and trees are inhabited by spirits, or to defecate or urinate in public, or to appear naked in public. In our culture each of these behaviors would be considered unusual or abnormal. Cultural differences also affect the diagnosis of mental disorders. There is, in other words, a high degree of **cultural relativity** in perceptions of normality and abnormality. Still, all known cultures classify people as abnormal if they either fail to communicate with others or are consistently unpredictable in their actions. Thus, cultural values and practices affect perceptions of normality in subtle—and not so subtle—ways, as described in Highlight 16–1.

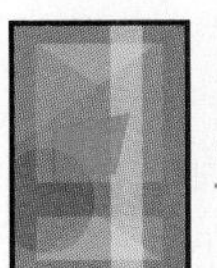

Highlight 16–1

Critical Thinking

The Politics of "Madness"

The year is 1840. You are a slave who has tried repeatedly to escape from a cruel and abusive master. An expert is consulted about your "abnormal" behavior. His conclusion? You are suffering from "drapetomania," a mental "disorder" that causes slaves to run away (Wakefield, 1992).

As this example suggests, psychiatric terms are easily abused. Historically, some have been applied to culturally disapproved behaviors that are not really disorders. For example, all of the following were once considered disorders: "drapetomania," "childhood masturbation disorder," "lack of vaginal orgasm," "self-defeating personality disorder" (applied mainly to women), and "nymphomania" (a woman with a healthy sexual appetite) (Wakefield, 1992).

In judging normality, gender is probably the most common source of bias, because standards tend to be based on males (Tavris, 1993). According to psychologist Marcie Kaplan (1983) and others, women are penalized both for conforming to female stereotypes and for ignoring them. If a woman is independent, aggressive, and unemotional, she may be considered "unhealthy." Yet at the same time, a woman who is vain, emotional, irrational, and dependent on others (all "feminine" traits in our culture) may be classified as a histrionic, or dependent personality.

Perhaps the most easily abused diagnosis women face is "premenstrual dysphoric disorder." This "disorder" is essentially a list of some of the normal changes that precede many women's menstrual periods. If a man experiences similar changes in mood, they are regarded as just "normal ups and downs" (Tavris, 1993). Such differences help illustrate the subtle influence that culture may have on perceptions of disorder and normality.

Question: If abnormality is so hard to define, how are judgments of psychopathology made?

It should be clear at this point that all definitions of abnormality are **relative.** Consider, for example, a woman named Joan who has an intense fear of heights. Joan can't look out the window of a tall building or fly in an airplane. Are her fears a mental disorder? Most likely Joan will *not* be diagnosed as suffering from a phobic disorder (described later) because she lives in a small town without tall buildings and she has no need to fly. To be a problem, Joan's fears must interfere with her normal activities and cause her marked distress (Widiger & Trull, 1991).

In spite of the great difficulty of formally defining abnormality, we know that psychological disturbances occur and that they must be identified. Each of the standards we have discussed helps define abnormality. As Joan's example suggests, an additional core feature of all abnormal behavior is that it is **maladaptive.** Rather than helping a person to cope successfully, abnormal behavior makes it more difficult for the person to meet the demands of day-to-day life. In her particular life circumstances, Joan's fears are not seriously maladaptive. For another person they could be a major problem.

Various levels of functioning—from superior to severely disturbed—are described in ⬬ Table 16–1. Note that the bottom of the scale reads "persistent danger of hurting self or others." Clearly, behavior at this level is maladaptive.

In practice, the judgment that a person needs help usually occurs when the person *does something* (hits a person, hallucinates, stares into space, collects rolls of toilet paper, and so forth) that *annoys* or *gains the attention* of a person in a *position of power* in the person's life (an employer, teacher, parent, spouse, or the person himself or herself). That person then *does something* about it. (A police officer may be called, the person may be urged to see a psychologist, a relative may start commitment proceedings, or the person may voluntarily seek help.)

Maladaptive behavior Behavior that makes it difficult to adapt to the environment and meet the demands of day-to-day life.

Mental disorder A significant impairment in psychological functioning.

Classifying Mental Disorders—Problems by the Book

Psychological problems are grouped into broad categories of maladaptive behavior. The most widely used system of classification is found in the *Diagnostic and Statistical Manual of Mental Disorders* (DSM-IV, 1994). The purpose of the manual is to provide a common language for therapists, researchers, social agencies, and health workers. DSM-IV helps professionals diagnose and classify mental disorders and select appropriate therapies (■ Fig. 16–4).

A **mental disorder** is a significant impairment in psychological functioning (Widiger & Trull, 1991). If you were to glance through DSM-IV, you would find a wide range of disorders described, including those listed in ⬬ Table 16–2. It is not possible here to discuss all of the problems in the table. (However, many are covered in other chapters.) The descriptions that follow will give you an overview of some of the major disorders. Most of these, and some not mentioned here, are discussed in more detail in this chapter and

Psychotic disorder A severe psychological disorder characterized by a retreat from reality, by hallucinations and delusions, and by social withdrawal.

Table 16–1 Levels of Functioning

Scale	Level of Functioning	Examples
100	Superior functioning in a wide range of activities. No symptoms.	Life's problems never seem to get out of hand. Person is sought out by others because of his or her many positive qualities.
90	Absent or minimal symptoms, functioning well in all areas, no more than everyday problems.	Has mild anxiety before exams, occasional arguments with family members.
80	If symptoms are present, they are brief and common reactions to stressors. No more than slight impairment in relationships, work, or school.	Has difficulty concentrating after family arguments, is falling behind in schoolwork.
70	Some mild symptoms, or some difficulty with relationships, work, or school.	Mood is depressed and has mild insomnia. Has been truant at school and has stolen things at home.
60	Moderate symptoms or moderate problems with relationships, work, or school.	Emotions are blunted, speech evasive, occasional panic attacks, no friends, unable to keep a job.
50	Serious symptoms or any serious impairments in relationships, work, or school.	Person has suicidal thoughts, engages in obsessional rituals, shoplifts, has no friends, unable to keep a job.
40	Some impairment in grasp of reality or in communication, plus major impairments in work or school, relationships, judgment, thinking, or mood.	Speech is illogical, obscure, or irrelevant. Person is depressed and avoids friends, neglects family, and is unable to work.
30	Behavior is considerably affected by delusions or hallucinations; or, person is seriously impaired in communication or judgment; or, is unable to function in almost all areas.	Person is sometimes incoherent, acts grossly inappropriately, is preoccupied with suicide, stays in bed all day, has no job, home, or friends.
20	Some danger of hurting self or others; or, occasionally fails to maintain minimal personal hygiene; or, communication is grossly impaired.	Person makes tentative suicide attempts, is frequently violent and manically excited, smears own feces, is either incoherent or mute.
10	Persistent danger of severely hurting self or others; or, persistent inability to maintain minimal personal hygiene; or, serious suicidal acts.	Repeatedly violent, maintains almost no personal hygiene, has made potentially lethal suicide attempts.

(Adapted from *Global Assessment of Functioning Scale,* DSM-IV, 1994.)

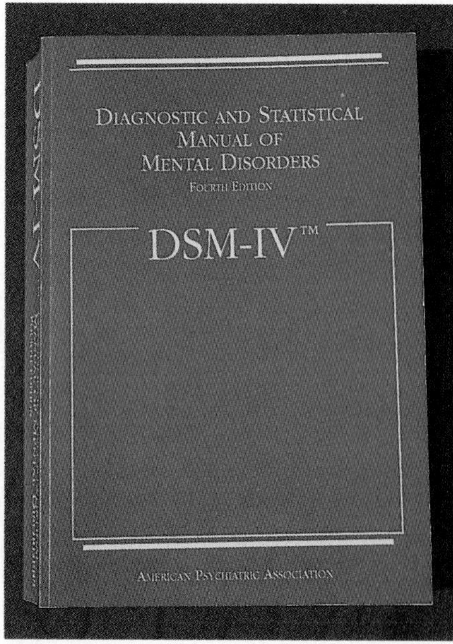

Fig. 16–4 *DSM-IV is not the only system for classifying mental disorders. Nevertheless, most activities in mental health settings—from diagnosis to therapy to billing of insurance companies—are influenced by the DSM. DSM-IV is both a scientific document and a social one. Major disorders are well-documented problems. Some problems, however, have little to do with "mental illness." Instead, they are primarily socially disapproved behaviors.*

the next. Some major risk factors for the development of mental disorders are listed in Table 16–3.

An Overview of Mental Disorders

Psychotic disorders are characterized by a retreat from reality, by hallucinations and delusions, and by social withdrawal. Psychotic disorders are often severe and can lead to hospitalization. The psychotic person can no longer tell what is fantasy or hallucination and what is real. In addition, a major loss of ability to control thoughts and actions usually occurs. Here's what a young college student who became psychotic told his father:

> It's the strangest thing. I hear voices, hundreds of them, telling me that everyone wants me dead. It's like all the radios of the world blaring all the stations at once, and it doesn't stop. It jams my brain. (Weisburd, 1990)

Schizophrenia, delusional disorders, and some severe mood disorders are forms of psychosis. Psychotic

Table 16–2 Major DSM-IV Categories

DISORDERS USUALLY FIRST DIAGNOSED IN INFANCY, CHILDHOOD, OR ADOLESCENCE
- **Mental Retardation**
  - Example: Mild Mental Retardation
- **Learning Disorders**
  - Example: Reading Disorder
- **Motor Skills Disorder**
  - Example: Developmental Coordination Disorder
- **Pervasive Developmental Disorders**
  - Example: Autistic Disorder
- **Disruptive Behavior and Attention-Deficit Disorders**
  - Example: Attention Deficit/Hyperactivity Disorder
- **Feeding and Eating Disorders of Infancy or Early Childhood**
  - Example: Pica
- **Tic Disorders**
  - Example: Transient Tic Disorder
- **Communication Disorders**
  - Example: Stuttering
- **Elimination Disorders**
  - Example: Enuresis
- **Other Disorders of Infancy, Childhood, or Adolescence**
  - Example: Separation Anxiety Disorder

DELIRIUM, DEMENTIA, AMNESTIC, AND OTHER COGNITIVE DISORDERS
- **Delirium**
  - Example: Delirium Due to a General Medical Condition
- **Dementia**
  - Example: Dementia of the Alzheimer's Type
- **Amnestic Disorders** (memory loss)
  - Example: Amnestic Disorder Due to a General Medical Condition
- **Cognitive Disorder Not Otherwise Specified**

MENTAL DISORDERS DUE TO A GENERAL MEDICAL CONDITION NOT ELSEWHERE CLASSIFIED
- **Catatonic Disorder Due to a General Medical Condition**
- **Personality Change Due to a General Medical Condition**
- **Mental Disorder Not Otherwise Specified Due to a General Medical Condition**

SUBSTANCE RELATED DISORDERS
- Example: Cocaine Use Disorder

SCHIZOPHRENIA AND OTHER PSYCHOTIC DISORDERS
- **Schizophrenia**
  - Example: Schizophrenia, Paranoid Type
- **Schizophreniform Disorder**
- **Schizoaffective Disorder**
- **Delusional Disorder**
  - Example: Delusional Disorder, Grandiose Type
- **Brief Psychotic Disorder**
- **Shared Psychotic Disorder (Folie a Deux)**
- **Psychotic Disorder Due to a General Medical Condition**
- **Substance-Induced Psychotic Disorder**
- **Psychotic Disorder Not Otherwise Specified**

MOOD DISORDERS
- **Depressive Disorders**
  - Example: Major Depressive Disorder
- **Bipolar Disorders**
  - Example: Bipolar I Disorder
- **Mood Disorder Due to a General Medical Condition**
- **Substance-Induced Mood Disorder**
- **Mood Disorder Not Otherwise Specified**

ANXIETY DISORDERS
- Example: Panic Disorder

SOMATOFORM DISORDERS
- Example: Conversion Disorder

FACTITIOUS DISORDERS (faked disability or illness)
- Example: Factitious Disorder

DISSOCIATIVE DISORDERS
- Example: Dissociative Identity Disorder

SEXUAL AND GENDER IDENTITY DISORDERS
- **Sexual Dysfunctions**
  - Example: Sexual Arousal Disorder
- **Paraphilias**
  - Example: Voyeurism
- **Sexual Disorder Not Otherwise Specified**
- **Gender Identity Disorders**
  - Example: Gender Identity Disorder

EATING DISORDERS
- Example: Anorexia Nervosa

SLEEP DISORDERS
- **Primary Sleep Disorders**
  - **Dyssomnias**
    - Example: Primary Insomnia
  - **Parasomnias**
    - Example: Sleep Terror Disorder
- **Sleep Disorders Related to Another Mental Disorder**
  - Example: Insomnia related to Post-Traumatic Stress Disorder
- **Other Sleep Disorders**
  - Example: Substance-Induced Sleep Disorder

IMPULSE CONTROL DISORDERS NOT ELSEWHERE CLASSIFIED
- Example: Kleptomania

ADJUSTMENT DISORDERS
- Example: Adjustment Disorder

PERSONALITY DISORDERS
- Example: Antisocial Personality Disorder

Organic mental disorder A mental problem caused by a malfunction of the brain.

Substance related disorder Abuse of or dependence on a mood- or behavior-altering drug.

Mood disorder A major disturbance in mood or emotion.

Anxiety disorder Disruptive feelings of fear, apprehension, or anxiety, or distortions in behavior that are anxiety related.

Somatoform disorder Physical symptoms that mimic disease or injury for which there is no physical cause.

Dissociative disorder Temporary amnesia, multiple personality, or depersonalization.

Personality disorder A maladaptive personality pattern.

Sexual and gender identity disorders Any of a wide range of difficulties with sexual identity, deviant sexual behavior, or sexual adjustment.

Table 16–3 Risk Factors for Mental Disorder

Social conditions: poverty, stressful living conditions, homelessness, social disorganization, overcrowding
Family factors: parents who are immature, mentally disturbed, criminal, or abusive; severe marital strife; extremely poor child discipline; disordered family communication patterns
Psychological factors: low intelligence, learning disorders
Biological factors: genetic defects or inherited vulnerabilities, poor prenatal care, very low birth weight, chronic physical illness or disability, exposure to toxic chemicals or drugs, head injuries

symptoms may also be related to medical problems (such as brain diseases), abuse of drugs, and other conditions (DSM-IV, 1994).

Organic mental disorders are problems caused by brain pathology; that is, by senility, drug damage, diseases of the brain, injuries, the toxic effects of poisons, and so on (■ Fig. 16–5). Organic disorders are often accompanied by severe emotional disturbances, impaired thinking, memory loss, personality changes, and delirium. Psychotic symptoms may also occur (Costello & Costello, 1992).

It could be argued that almost all mental disorders are at least partly biological. For this reason, DSM-IV does not include a separate category for "organic mental disorders." Nevertheless, all of the following problems are closely associated with organic damage: delirium, dementia, amnestic, and other cognitive disorders; mental disorders due to a general medical condition; and substance related disorders.

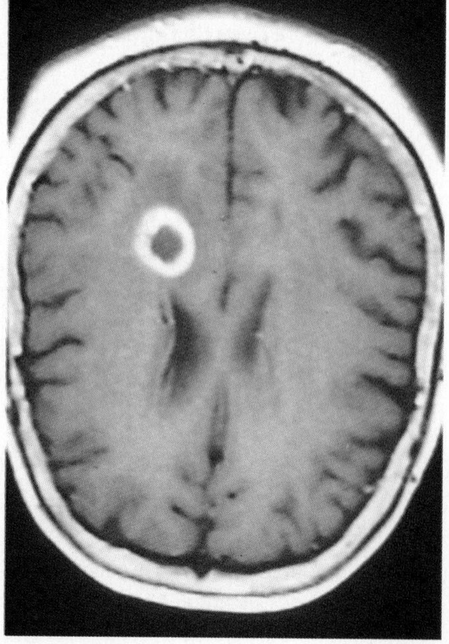

■ **Fig. 16-5** *This MRI scan of a human brain (viewed from the top) reveals a tumor (dark spot). Mental disorders sometimes have organic causes of this sort. However, in many instances no organic damage can be found.*

Substance related disorders are defined as abuse of or dependence on mood- or behavior-altering drugs, such as alcohol, barbiturates, opiates, cocaine, amphetamines, hallucinogens, marijuana, and nicotine. Problems in this category center on damaged functioning at home or on the job, and an inability to stop using the drug. Active drug intoxication or drug withdrawal, delirium, dementia, amnesia, psychosis, emotional problems, sexual problems, and sleep disturbances may also be substance related.

Mood disorders primarily involve disturbances in affect, or emotion. Individuals suffering from mood disorders may be *manic*, meaning agitated, euphoric, and hyperactive, or they may be *depressed*, or both. In any case, extremes of mood are intense or long lasting and depressed individuals run a high risk of suicide. Mood disorders may include psychotic symptoms, and they are sometimes due to medical conditions or drug abuse (DSM-IV, 1994). Mood disorders are discussed in the next chapter.

Anxiety disorders may take the form of *panic* (in which the person suffers sudden unexplainable feelings of total panic), *phobias* (excessive, irrational fears), or *generalized anxiety* (chronic and persistent anxiety). Other anxiety disorders are *post-traumatic stress disorder* (high anxiety that persists long after an extremely distressing event, such as military combat) and *acute stress disorder* (high anxiety that occurs immediately after a highly distressing event, such as an airliner crash). A pattern known as *obsessive-compulsive* behavior is also associated with anxiety (more on this later).

Somatoform disorders (so-MAT-oh-form) are indicated when a person has physical symptoms that mimic physical disease or injury (paralysis, blindness, illness, or chronic pain, for example) for which there is no identifiable cause. The assumption in such cases is that psychological factors underlie the symptoms.

Dissociative disorders include cases of sudden temporary *amnesia* and instances of *multiple personality* like William Milligan displayed. Also included are frightening episodes of *depersonalization*. Depersonalization refers to feelings of being outside one's body, of behaving like a robot, or of being in a dream world.

Personality disorders are deeply ingrained, unhealthy personality patterns. Such patterns are usually apparent by adolescence and continue throughout most of adult life. They include paranoid (overly suspicious), narcissistic (self-loving), dependent, borderline, and antisocial personality types, as well as others.

Sexual and gender identity disorders include *gender identity disorders* (where a person's sexual identity does not match his or her physical gender) and a wide range of deviations in sexual behavior known as *para-*

philias (exhibitionism, fetishism, voyeurism, and so on). Also found in this category are a variety of *sexual dysfunctions* (problems in sexual desire, arousal, or response; see Chapter 19).

Question: Shouldn't neurosis be included in the list of problems?

The term *neurosis* is fading from use because it tends to lump together too many separate problems. Behavior once considered "neurotic" is now classified as an anxiety, somatoform, or dissociative disorder (or in some cases as a mild mood disorder). Even so, you may sometimes hear the term *neurosis* used to loosely refer to problems associated with excessive anxiety.

Question: Is insanity the same as psychosis?

No. Psychosis is a *psychiatric* term that describes a particular type of mental disorder. **Insanity** is a *legal* term. Persons who are declared "insane" are not legally responsible for their actions and can be involuntarily committed to a mental hospital. Legally, insanity is usually established by the testimony of psychologists and psychiatrists who serve as **expert witnesses** in a court of law. In practice, those who are committed are usually judged to be a danger to themselves or to others, or they are severely mentally disabled (Turkheimer & Parry, 1992). (See this chapter's Exploration for further discussion of insanity.)

Question: To what extent are mentally disordered persons a danger to others?

By amazing coincidence, the following Highlight addresses that very question.

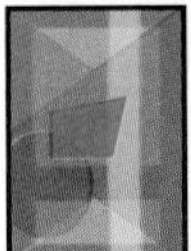

HIGHLIGHT 16–2

Focus on a Controversy

Are the Mentally Ill Prone to Violence?

Jeffrey Dahmer was everyone's worst nightmare brought to life (■ Fig. 16–6). Dahmer drugged his victims, drilled holes in their skulls, sexually molested their lifeless bodies, dismembered them, and ate their body parts, which he stored in a refrigerator.

How accurately does a case like Dahmer's reflect the risk of violence by the mentally ill? Are the mentally ill or formerly mentally ill likely to be violent? Extensive research on this question leads to the following conclusions.

■ Only persons who are *actively psychotic* are more violence prone than non-patients. That is, if a person is experiencing delusions and hallucinations, the risk of violence is elevated. Other mental problems are unrelated to violence.

■ Only persons *currently* experiencing psychotic symptoms are at increased risk for violence. Violent behavior is not related to being a former mental patient or having had psychotic symptoms *in the past.*

Thus, Dahmer's case, like many others in the news, gives a false impression. Even when we consider people who are actively psychotic, we find that the vast majority are not violent. The risk of violence from mental patients is actually many times lower than that posed by persons who have the following attributes: young, male, poor, and intoxicated.

Beliefs about mental disorders are important because they affect laws and personal attitudes toward the mentally ill. People who strongly believe that the mentally ill are prone to violence are typically afraid to have former mental patients as neighbors, co-workers, or friends. But as you can see, only a small minority of the actively mentally ill pose an increased risk. Former mental patients, in particular, are no more likely to be violent than people in general. The overwhelming majority of violent crimes are committed by people who are not mentally ill. (Sources: Monahan, 1991; Teplin, Abram, & McClelland, 1994.)

■ **Fig. 16–6** *Although Jeffrey Dahmer's case is extreme, he is typical of the mentally disordered persons who make the evening news. Most have committed murder or some other heinous crime. This gives the impression that the mentally ill are violent and dangerous. In reality, only a tiny percentage of all mentally disordered persons are more violent than average. (Dahmer was killed in a Wisconsin prison by another inmate in November, 1994.)*

Neurosis An outdated term once used to refer to anxiety disorders, somatoform disorders, dissociative disorders, and some forms of depression.

Insanity Legally, an inability to manage one's affairs or to be aware of the consequences of one's actions.

Expert witness A person recognized by a court of law as being qualified to give expert testimony on a specific topic.

The sections that follow continue our discussion by describing in greater detail some of the problems already mentioned. A full discussion of schizophrenia and other more severe problems is reserved for the next chapter. Before you read further, see if you can answer these questions.

Learning Check

1. Amnesia, multiple personality, and depersonalization are possible problems in
   a. mood disorders *b.* somatoform disorders c. psychosis *d.* dissociative disorders
2. Which among the following is *not* a major psychological problem listed in DSM-IV?
   a. mood disorders *b.* personality disorders *c.* insanity *d.* anxiety disorders
3. A major difference between psychotic disorders and anxiety disorders (or other milder problems) is that in psychosis the individual has lost contact with reality as shown by the presence of ______________ or ______________.
4. In a court of law, sanity is determined by tests administered by court-appointed lawyers. T or F?
5. Statistical definitions of abnormality successfully avoid the limitations of other approaches. T or F?
6. One of the most powerful contexts in which judgments of normality and abnormality are made is
   a. the family *b.* occupational settings c. religious systems *d.* culture

Critical Thinking

7. Brian, a fan of grunge rock, occasionally wears a skirt in public. Does Brian's cross-dressing indicate that he has a mental disorder?

Answers:

1. *d* 2. *c* 3. delusions, hallucinations 4. F 5. F 6. *d* 7. Probably not. Undoubtedly Brian's cross-dressing is socially disapproved by many people. Nevertheless, to be classified as a mental disorder it must cause him to feel disabling shame, guilt, depression, or anxiety. The cultural relativity of behavior like Brian's is revealed by the fact that it is fashionable and acceptable for women to wear men's clothing.

Personality Disorders—Blueprints for Maladjustment

As stated earlier, personality disorders are deeply ingrained maladaptive personality patterns. For example, the paranoid personality is overly suspicious, mistrusting, hypersensitive, guarded, and distrustful of the honesty of others. Narcissistic persons are preoccupied with their own self-importance: They need constant admiration and they are absorbed in fantasies of power, wealth, brilliance, beauty, and love. The dependent personality is marked by an extreme lack of self-confidence; others are allowed to run the person's life, and the person places his or her own needs second to others. In a histrionic personality disorder, the person seeks attention by exaggerating emotion and acting very dramatically. The case described in Highlight 16–3 captures the flavor of a severe personality disorder.

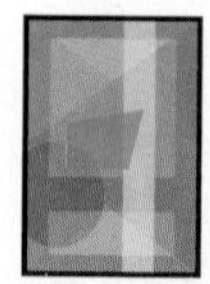

Highlight 16–3

A Closer Look At

Borderline Personality—The Sad Case of Judy

"Get out of here and leave me alone so I can die in peace," Judy screamed at her nurses. Although only 42 years old and normally very attractive, Judy looked old, disheveled, and haggard in the seclusion room of the psychiatric hospital. On one of her arms, long dark red marks mingled with the scars of previous suicide attempts. Judy once bragged that her record was 67 stitches. Today, the nurses had to strap her into restraints to keep her from gouging her eyes out. She was given a sedative and slept for 12 hours. She woke calmly and asked for her therapist—even though this latest incident was ostensibly triggered by his canceling her morning appointment and re-scheduling it for later that afternoon.

Judy has a borderline personality disorder. Although she is capable of working, Judy has repeatedly lost jobs because of her turbulent relationships with others. At times she can be friendly and a real charmer. At other times she is extremely unpredictable, moody, and even suicidal. Being a friend to Judy means accepting a burden that is nearly unbearable at times. The cancellation of an appointment, special dates that are forgotten, a wrong turn of phrase—these and similar small incidents may trigger Judy's anger or, worse yet, a suicide attempt. Judy's only hope lies in intensive, long-term therapy.

Table 16–4 Personality Disorders and Typical Degree of Impairment

Moderate Impairment
Dependent Unhealthy submissiveness and dependence on others (clinging) **Histrionic** Excessive emotion and attention-seeking behavior **Narcissistic** Exaggerated self-importance and desire for constant admiration **Antisocial** Irresponsible and antisocial behavior, such as aggression, deceit, recklessness, and lack of remorse
High Impairment
Obsessive-compulsive Orderliness, perfectionism, and rigid routine **Schizoid** Limited emotion and a lack of interest in close personal relationships with others **Avoidant** Discomfort in social situations, fear of evaluation, timidity
Severe Impairment
Borderline Extremely unstable self-image, relationships, moods, and impulses **Paranoid** A deep distrust and suspiciousness of the motives of others, which are seen as demeaning or threatening **Schizotypal** Social isolation, extremely odd behavior, and disturbed thought patterns, but not actively psychotic

(From DSM-IV, 1994 and Millon, 1981.)

The list of personality disorders is long (Table 16–4), so let us focus on a single frequently misunderstood problem, the antisocial personality.

Question: What are the characteristics of an antisocial personality?

Antisocial Personality

The individual with an **antisocial personality** (sometimes referred to as a *sociopath* or *psychopath*) typically has a long history of conflict with society. Antisocial persons are irresponsible, impulsive, selfish, lacking in judgment and morals, and unable to learn from experience. They are also incapable of deep feelings, including guilt, shame, fear, loyalty, and love. In short, the sociopath is poorly socialized, has a general disregard for the truth, and seems to lack a conscience (DSM-IV, 1994).

Question: Are sociopaths dangerous?

Many sociopaths are delinquents or criminals who may pose a threat to the general public (Fig. 16–7). However, sociopaths are rarely the crazed murderers that have been portrayed on TV and in movies. In fact, many sociopaths create a good first impression and are frequently described as charming. Their lying, self-serving manipulation and lack of dependability only gradually become evident to their "friends." Many successful business persons, entertainers, politicians, and other seemingly normal persons reveal sociopathic leanings by coldly using others for their own ends.

Fig. 16–7 *Studies show that more than 65 percent of all persons with antisocial personalities have been arrested, usually for crimes such as robbery, vandalism, or rape.*

Antisocial personality A person who lacks a conscience, is emotionally shallow, impulsive, selfish, and tends to manipulate others.

Question: What causes sociopathy?

People with antisocial personalities usually have a childhood history of emotional deprivation, neglect, and physical abuse (Pollock et al., 1990). As mentioned in Chapter 13, some psychologists believe that infants who fail to form a healthy emotional attachment to a caregiver may become prone to antisocial behavior (Magid, 1988). Adult sociopaths also display some subtle physical problems. For example, they produce unusual brain-wave patterns suggesting underarousal of the brain. This condition may explain why many sociopaths are thrill seekers. Quite likely, they are searching for stimulation strong enough to overcome their chronic under-arousal and "boredom" (Carson & Butcher, 1992).

In a revealing study, psychopaths were shown extremely grisly and unpleasant photographs. The photos were so upsetting that normal people are visibly star-

Paraphilias Compulsive or destructive deviations in sexual preferences or behavior.

Pedophilia Sex with children, or child molesting.

Fetishism Gaining sexual gratification from inanimate objects; especially, an inability to achieve sexual arousal without the object.

Exhibitionism Deriving sexual pleasure from displaying the genitals (usually), to an unwilling viewer ("flashing").

Voyeurism Deriving sexual pleasure from viewing the genitals of others, usually without their knowledge or permission (peeping).

Transvestic fetishism Achieving sexual arousal by wearing clothing of the opposite sex.

Sexual sadism Gaining sexual pleasure by inflicting pain during the sex act.

Sexual masochism Deriving sexual pleasure from having pain inflicted during the sex act.

Frotteurism Sexually touching or rubbing against a non-consenting person.

tled by them. The psychopaths, however, showed no startle response to the photos (Patrick et al., 1993). (They didn't "bat an eyelash.") Those with antisocial personalities might therefore be described as *emotionally cold*. They simply do not feel normal pangs of conscience, guilt, or anxiety. This coldness seems to account for an unusual ability to calmly lie, cheat, steal, or manipulate others.

Question: Can sociopathy be treated?

Antisocial personality disorders are rarely treated with success. All too often, sociopaths manipulate therapy like any other situation. If it is to their advantage to act "cured," they will do so, but they return to former patterns of behavior at the first opportunity. There is, however, some evidence that antisocial behavior declines somewhat after age 40 (Hare, McPherson, & Forth, 1988).

Sexual Deviance—Trench Coats, Whips, Leathers, and Lace

Sexual deviance implies a departure from socially accepted standards of behavior. By the most strict standards (including the law in some states), any sexual activity other than face-to-face heterosexual intercourse between married adults is "deviant." But public standards are often at odds with behavior found privately acceptable. By private standards, large numbers of people regard oral sex, masturbation, and premarital sex as perfectly normal. None of these behaviors are listed in DSM-IV. Neither is homosexuality, which is a variation in sexual preference, not a sexual disorder. (See the discussion of sexual orientation in Chapter 19 for more information.)

Paraphilias

From a psychological point of view, the mark of true sexual deviations is that they are compulsive and destructive. Typically, they cause guilt, anxiety, or discomfort for one or both participants. Deviations fitting this definition are called **paraphilias (PAIR-eh-FIL-ih-ahs).** The paraphilias cover a wide variety of behaviors, including **pedophilia** (sex with children), **fetishism** (sexual arousal associated with inanimate objects), **exhibitionism** (displaying the genitals to unwilling viewers), **voyeurism** (viewing the genitals of others without their permission), **transvestic fetishism** (achieving sexual arousal by wearing clothing of the opposite sex), **sexual sadism** (deriving sexual pleasure from inflicting pain), **sexual masochism** (desiring pain as part of the sex act), and **frotteurism** (sexually touching or rubbing against a non-consenting person, usually in a public place such as a subway) (DSM-IV, 1994).

Sexual deviance is a highly emotional subject, and many misconceptions exist about it. Two of the most misunderstood problems are exhibitionism and pedophilia. Check your understanding against the information that follows.

Exhibitionism Exhibitionism is a common problem. Roughly 35 percent of all sexual arrests are for "flashing." Exhibitionists are typically male and married, and most come from strict and repressive backgrounds. Exhibitionists have the highest repeat rate among sexual offenders. Most of them feel a deep sense of inadequacy, which produces a compulsive need to prove their "manhood" by frightening women. While exhibitionists are usually harmless, those who approach closer than arm's reach may be dangerous (Sue et al., 1990). In general, a woman confronted by an exhibitionist can assume that his goal is to shock and alarm her. By becoming visibly upset she actually encourages him (Hyde, 1990).

Child Molestation Child molesters, who also are usually males, are often pictured as despicable perverts lurking in dark alleys. In fact, most are married and two thirds are fathers. Many are rigid, passive, puritanical, or religious. In one half to two thirds of all cases of pedophilia, the offender is a friend, acquaintance, or relative of the child. Molesters are also often thought of as child rapists, but most molestations rarely exceed fondling (Sue et al., 1990).

Question: How serious are the effects of a molestation?

The impact varies widely and is affected by how long the abuse lasts and whether genital sexual acts are involved (Freize, 1987). Many authorities believe that a single incident of fondling is unlikely to cause severe emotional harm to a child. For most children the event is frightening, but not a lasting trauma. This is why parents are urged not to overreact to such incidents or to become hysterical. Doing so only further frightens the child (Wilson et al., 1984). This does not mean, however, that parents should ignore hints from a child that a molestation may have occurred. Unfortunately, most sexual abuse tends to involve ongoing incidents (England & Thompson, 1988). Here are some hints of trouble that parents should watch for.

Recognizing Signs of Child Molestation

1. The child fears being seen nude (for instance, during bathing), when such fears were absent before.
2. The child develops physical complaints, such as headaches, stomachaches, and other stress symptoms.
3. The child displays anxiety, fidgeting, shame, or discomfort when any reference to sexual behavior occurs.
4. The child becomes markedly emotional and irritable.

5. The child engages in hazardous risk taking, such as jumping from high places or riding a bicycle dangerously in traffic.
6. The child reveals self-destructive or suicidal thoughts, self-blame.
7. The child shows a loss of self-esteem or self-worth.
(Adapted from Frederick, 1987)

Repeated molestations, those that involve force or threats, and incidents that exceed fondling can leave lasting emotional scars. As adults, many victims of incest or molestation develop sexual phobias. For them, lovemaking may evoke vivid and terrifying memories of the childhood victimization (Frederick, 1987; Jehu, 1984). Serious harm is especially likely to occur if the molester is someone the child deeply trusts. Molestations by parents, close relatives, teachers, youth leaders, and similar persons can be quite damaging (Freize, 1987). In such cases professional counseling is often needed.

Rape

As the preceding discussion suggests, the picture of sexual deviance that most often emerges is one of sexual inhibition and immaturity. Typically, some relatively infantile sexual expression (like exhibitionism or pedophilia) is selected because it is less threatening than normal sexuality. Rapists are a notable exception to this pattern, however. Rapists often inflict more violence on their victims than is necessary to achieve their goal. Many women feel confident that their chances of being raped are low. But the facts tell a different story (Koss, 1993).

The Facts on Rape

- At least 1 woman in 7 will be raped in her lifetime. Because many rapes go unreported, the true figure is probably 1 in 4.
- Approximately 1 college woman in 6 is a victim of rape.
- In 65 to 80 percent of all cases the rapist is a friend or acquaintance of the victim.
- Rape by an acquaintance is as devastating as rape by a stranger.
- Five percent of rapes result in pregnancy.
- Four to 30 percent of rape victims contract sexually transmitted diseases.

Rape is not a sexual disorder. It is a crime. Indeed, most authorities no longer think of rape as a primarily sexual act. Rather, it is an act of brutality or aggression based on the need to debase others. Many rapists are antisocial personalities who impulsively take what they want without concern for the feelings of the victim or guilt about their deed. Others harbor deep-seated resentment or outright hatred of women. However, the problem may reach far deeper, as indicated in Highlight 16–4.

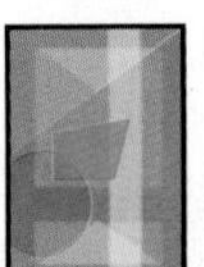

HIGHLIGHT 16–4

A Closer Look At

Sex Role Stereotyping and Rape—Is Ours a Rape-Supportive Culture?

A number of writers have suggested that rape is in some ways related to sex role socialization. That is, many people learn to believe that women should not show direct interest in sex. Men, on the other hand, are taught to take the initiative and to persist in attempts at sexual intimacy—even when the woman says no.

Psychologists James Check and Neil Malamuth believe that such attitudes create a "rape-supportive culture." In their view, rape is only an extreme expression of a system that condones coercive (forced) sexual intimacy. They point out, for instance, that the single most used cry of rapists to their victims is, "You know you want it." And afterward, "There now, you really enjoyed it, didn't you."

To test the hypothesis that stereotyped images contribute to rape, male college students were classified as either high or low in sex role stereotyping. Each student then read one of three stories: The first described voluntary intercourse; the second depicted stranger rape; and the third described acquaintance rape (forced intercourse on a date).

As predicted, college males high in sex role stereotyping were more aroused by the rape stories. Their arousal patterns, in fact, were similar to those found among actual rapists. Moreover, a chilling 44 percent of those tested indicated they would consider rape—especially if they could be sure of not being caught (Check & Malamuth, 1983).

In another study of rape, over half of a sample of adults agreed with the statement, "A woman who goes to the home or apartment of a man on the first date implies she is willing to have sex" (Burt, 1980). In view of such attitudes—and the continuing widespread belief that when a woman says no she means yes—it is little wonder that rape occurs every 6 minutes in the United States. Perhaps the time has come for our culture to make it clear that no means no.

Forcible rape Sexual intercourse carried out against the victim's will, under the threat of force.

Quite often, the rapist's goal is not strictly sexual intercourse; it is to attack, subordinate, humiliate, and degrade the victim. Typical after-effects for the victim include rage, guilt, depression, loss of self-esteem, shame, sexual adjustment problems, and in many cases, a lasting mistrust of male-female relationships (Freize, 1987). The impact is so great that most women continue to report fear, anxiety, and sexual dysfunction a year and a half or more after being raped. Even years later, rape survivors are more likely to suffer from depression, alcohol or drug abuse, and other emotional problems (Koss, 1993).

Any man who doubts the seriousness of rape should imagine himself mistakenly placed in jail, where he is violently raped (sodomized) by other inmates. There is no pleasure in rape for victims of either sex. It is truly a despicable crime.

LEARNING CHECK

1. Which of the following personality disorders is associated with an inflated sense of self-importance and a constant need for attention and admiration?
   a. narcissistic *b.* antisocial *c.* paranoid *d.* manipulative
2. Over one half of all persons with antisocial personalities have been arrested. T or F?
3. Antisocial personality disorders are difficult to treat, but there is typically a decline in antisocial behavior a year or two after adolescence. T or F?
4. The formal term for child molesting is
   a. sadism *b.* pedophilia *c.* frotteurism *d.* fetishism
5. What percentage of arrests for sexual offenses involve exhibitionism? ________________

6. Rape is primarily an act of brutality or aggression, rather than an exclusively sexual act. T or F?

Critical Thinking

7. A number of myths about rape make rape more likely to occur. Can you name some of them?

Answers:

1. *a* 2. T 3. F 4. *b* 5. 35 percent 6. T 7. All of these are myths: A woman who appears alone in public and dresses attractively is "asking for it." When a woman says no she really means yes. Many women who are raped actually enjoy it. If a woman goes home with a man on a first date she is interested in sex. If a woman is sexually active, she is probably lying if she says she was raped. Many more such myths could be listed.

Anxiety Apprehension, dread, or uneasiness similar to fear, but based on an unclear threat.

Anxiety-Based Disorders—When Anxiety Rules

Imagine for a moment the feeling of waiting to take an important test for which you are unprepared; or waiting to give a speech to a large audience of strangers; or being followed by a police car while you are driving. You have almost certainly felt **anxiety** in one of these situations. As you may have noticed, the physical reactions that accompany anxiety are similar to those felt in fear. Anxiety is similar to fear, except that anxiety is a response to an *unclear or ambiguous threat.* For instance, what we commonly call "stage fright" is actually anxiety, because an audience poses no real threat to safety (except, perhaps, at extremely bad talent shows). Compared to anxiety, fear is more focused and intense. Typically it is the result of a specific, identifiable threat (Kleinknecht, 1986). When we are fearful we say to ourselves, "A terrible event is happening and I must take action right now to stop it." When we are anxious we say, "A terrible event may happen. I may not be able to deal with it, but I've got to be ready to try" (Zinbarg et al., 1992).

Disruptive Anxiety

We all occasionally feel anxiety, and at times of great stress, anxiety may be intense. But anxiety that is out of proportion to a situation may reveal a problem. An example is a college student who appeared at the counseling center because he was deathly afraid of examinations. He had already skipped three exams by remaining in bed petrified by fears of failure (Suinn, 1975).

The student showed clear signs of having a disruptive emotional problem, but one that did not involve a loss of contact with reality. As mentioned earlier, such problems were once called neuroses. Now they are classified separately as anxiety disorders, dissociative disorders, and somatoform disorders. In general, these problems involve the following features:

- High levels of anxiety and/or restrictive, self-defeating behavior patterns
- A tendency to use elaborate defense mechanisms or avoidance responses to maintain minimal functioning
- Pervasive feelings of stress, insecurity, inferiority, unhappiness, and dissatisfaction with life
- The person feels threatened, but doesn't do anything about it

In short, affected persons struggle to preserve control, but they remain ineffective and unhappy (Zinbarg et al., 1992).

Question: If fear and anxiety are normal emotions, when do they signal a problem?

A problem exists when anxiety becomes intense or persistent enough to prevent a person from doing what he or she wants or needs to do. Also, persons with anxiety disorders feel that their anxieties are out of control—that they cannot stop worrying. Anxiety, fears, and phobias are probably the most common psychological disturbances today. On any given day, roughly 7 percent of the adult population could be diagnosed as having an anxiety disorder (Landers, 1989).

Question: Do such problems cause a "nervous breakdown"?

Adjustment Disorders Anxiety-based problems seriously disrupt people's lives and almost always cause misery. However, they rarely bring about a total "breakdown." Actually, the term *nervous breakdown* has no formal meaning. Also, "nervous breakdown" seems to imply some sort of disease of the nervous system. But there is nothing physically wrong with the nerves of an anxious or emotionally troubled individual. What many people have in mind when they use the term is properly called an **adjustment disorder.**

Adjustment disorders occur when ordinary life stresses push people beyond their ability to cope effectively. Examples of such stresses are prolonged unemployment, extreme marital strife, and chronic physical illness. The presence of an adjustment disorder is signaled by extreme irritability, sleep disturbances, loss of appetite, physical complaints, and apathy, anxiety, or depression (DSM-IV, 1994). Often, these problems are successfully treated with rest, sedation, supportive counseling, and a chance to "talk through" fears and anxieties.

Question: How is an adjustment disorder different from an anxiety disorder?

The outward symptoms can be similar. However, adjustment disorders typically disappear when life circumstances improve. This shows their link to stressful events.

Anxiety Disorders

In most anxiety disorders, the person's distress seems greatly out of proportion to the situation. Consider, for example, the following description of Ethel B:

> She was never completely relaxed, and complained of vague feelings of restlessness, and a fear that something was "just around the corner." Although she felt that she had to go to work to help pay the family bills, she could not bring herself to start anything new for fear that something terrible would happen on the job. She had experienced a few extreme anxiety attacks during which she felt "like I couldn't breathe, like I was sealed up in a transparent envelope. I thought I was going to have a heart attack. I couldn't stop shaking." (*Suinn, 1975)

Distress like Ethel B's is a key element in anxiety disorders. Many psychologists believe that it also underlies dissociative and somatoform disorders, where maladaptive behavior serves to reduce anxiety and discomfort. To deepen your understanding, let's examine several anxiety-based disorders. (A list of anxiety disorders is provided in Table 16–5.)

Generalized Anxiety Disorder The essential feature of a **generalized anxiety disorder** is at least 6 months of unrealistic or excessive anxiety and worry (DSM-IV, 1994). The discomfort felt in this disorder is sometimes described as **free-floating anxiety,** because the anxiety is related to many different worries. Affected individuals typically complain of sweating, racing heart, clammy hands, dizziness, upset stomach, and rapid breathing. They are also continually preoccupied by worries, which makes them irritable and unable to concentrate (Wilson, 1986).

Question: Was Ethel B's problem a generalized anxiety disorder?

No. The added presence of *anxiety attacks* indicates she suffered from **panic disorder.**

Panic Disorder (without Agoraphobia) In this very disturbing pattern, constant tension, worry, and anxiety occasionally explode into *sudden, unexpected* episodes of intense panic. Victims of a panic attack experience heart palpitations or chest pain, choking or smothering sensations, vertigo, feelings of unreality, trembling, and fears of dying, going crazy, or losing control during the attack. Many believe that they are having a heart attack, are going insane, or are about to die. Needless to say, this pattern leaves a person unhappy and uncomfortable much of the time.

Panic attacks may also occur in other anxiety disorders. What sets a panic disorder apart is that the

Table 16–5 Anxiety Disorders

Anxiety Disorders
Generalized anxiety disorder
Panic disorder
Without Agoraphobia
With Agoraphobia
Agoraphobia (without a history of panic disorder)
Specific phobia
Social phobia
Obsessive-compulsive disorder
Post-traumatic stress disorder
Acute stress disorder

(DSM-IV, 1994.)

*From *Fundamentals of Behavior Pathology* by R. M. Suinn. Copyright © 1975. Reprinted by permission of John Wiley & Sons, Inc. Additional Suinn quotes in this chapter and the next are from the same source.

Adjustment disorder An emotional disturbance caused by on-going stressors within the range of common experience.

Generalized anxiety disorder The person is in a chronic state of tension and worries about work, relationships, ability, or impending disaster.

Free-floating anxiety Anxiety that is very general and pervasive.

Panic disorder (without agoraphobia) The person is in a chronic state of anxiety, and also has brief moments of sudden, intense, unexpected panic.

Panic disorder (with agoraphobia) A chronic state of anxiety and brief moments of sudden panic. The person fears that these panic attacks will occur in public places or unfamiliar situations.

Agoraphobia (without panic) The person fears that something extremely embarrassing will happen to them if they leave the house or enter unfamiliar situations.

Specific phobia An intense, irrational fear of specific objects, activities, or situations.

Social phobia An intense, irrational fear of being observed, evaluated, embarrassed, or humiliated by others in social situations.

panic attacks seem to appear without warning ("out of the blue"), rather than just in certain situations (DSM-IV, 1994).

Panic Disorder (with Agoraphobia) Panic disorders are often accompanied by an intense irrational fear called **agoraphobia** (ah-go-rah-FOBE-ee-ah). Agoraphobics fear that they will have a panic attack in public places or unfamiliar situations. Or more simply, agoraphobia is an intense fear of leaving the house and familiar surroundings. Typically, the agoraphobic person finds ways of avoiding areas of insecurity—such as crowds, open roads, supermarkets, automobiles, and so on (Zane & Milt, 1984). As a result, some agoraphobics are literally house-bound (DSM-IV, 1994).

Agoraphobia Some people suffer from agoraphobia without actually having panic attacks. In such cases they fear that something extremely embarrassing will happen to them. For example, an agoraphobic person may refuse to go outside because she fears having a sudden attack of dizziness, or diarrhea, or shortness of breath. Being outside the home alone, being in a crowd, standing in line, being on a bridge, or in a car, bus, or train can be impossible for an agoraphobic (DSM-IV, 1994).

Specific Phobia As stated earlier, phobias are intense, irrational fears that persist even when there is no real danger (Kleinknecht, 1986). In a **specific phobia,** persistent fears, anxiety, and avoidance are focused on various objects, activities, or situations (■ Fig. 16–8). Persons affected by phobias recognize that their fears are unreasonable and excessive, but they cannot control them.

■ Fig. 16–8 *If you are a person who has a strong fear of snakes (ophidiophobia), merely looking at this picture may be unsettling.*

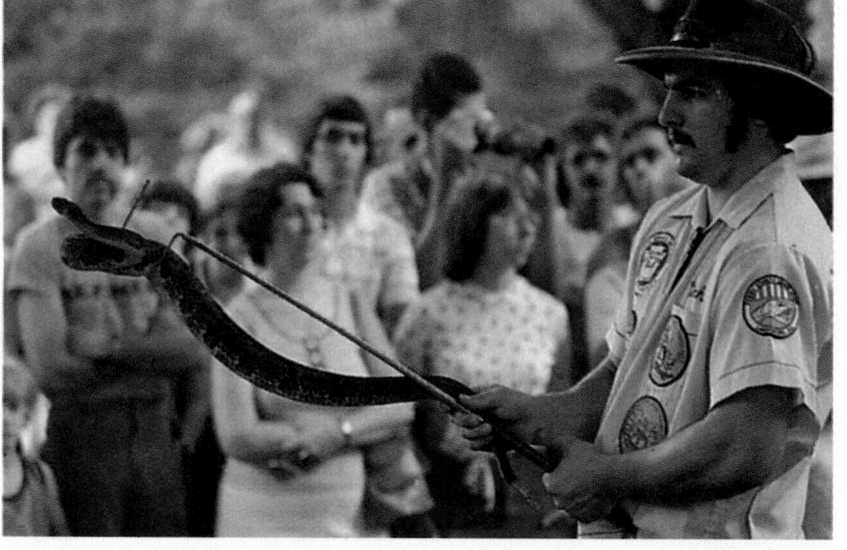

Table 16–6 Common Phobias

Acrophobia—fear of heights
Astraphobia—fear of storms, thunder, lightning
Arachnophobia—fear of spiders
Aviophobia—fear of airplanes
Claustrophobia—fear of closed spaces
Hematophobia—fear of blood
Microphobia—fear of germs
Nyctophobia—fear of darkness
Pathophobia—fear of disease
Pyrophobia—fear of fire
Xenophobia—fear of strangers
Zoophobia—fear of animals

Specific phobias can be classified according to the type of object or situation that is feared. The most common types are listed here.

Animal type—fear of a specific type of animal, such as a dog, spider, or snake
Natural environment type—fear of heights, storms, the ocean, caves, and the like
Blood, injection, injury type—fear of blood, injections, injuries, medical procedures
Situational type—fear of specific situations, such as airplanes, elevators, enclosed spaces
Other type—fear of a wide range of other situations, such as those that may lead to choking, vomiting, or catching an illness

These types, of course, only outline the possibilities. Specific phobias may be attached to nearly any object or situation. Many of the more common specific phobias have been given names, such as those listed in Table 16–6.

Obviously, by combining the appropriate root word with the word *phobia,* any number of unlikely fears can be named. Some are *acarophobia,* a fear of itching; *zemmiphobia,* fear of the great mole rat; *phobosophobia,* fear of fear; *arachibutyrophobia,* fear of peanut butter sticking to the roof of the mouth, and *hippopotomonstrosesquipedaliophobia,* fear of long words!

Almost everyone has a few mild phobias: Fears of heights, closed spaces, or bugs and crawly things are common. A phobic disorder differs from such garden-variety fears in that it produces overwhelming anxiety which may cause vomiting, wild climbing and running, or fainting. For a phobic disorder to exist, the person's fear must disrupt his or her daily life. Phobic persons are so threatened that they will go to almost any length to avoid the feared object or situation.

Social Phobia In a **social phobia,** the person fears social situations in which he or she can be observed, evaluated, embarrassed, or humiliated by others. This

■ Fig. 16–9 *The severe obsessions and compulsions of billionaire Howard Hughes led him to live as a recluse for over 20 years. Hughes had an intense fear of contamination. To avoid infection, he constructed sterile, isolated environments in which his contact with people and objects was strictly limited by complicated rituals. Before handling a spoon, for instance, Hughes had his attendants wrap the handle in tissue paper and seal it with tape. A second piece of tissue was then wrapped around the first before he would touch it (Hodgson & Miller, 1982). A spoon prepared as Hughes required is shown here.*

leads to avoidance of certain social situations, such as eating, writing, using the rest room, or speaking in public. When the situation cannot be avoided, it is endured with intense anxiety or distress. Social phobias greatly impair a person's functioning at work, at school, in social activities, or in personal relationships (DSM-IV, 1994).

Obsessive-Compulsive Disorder **Obsessions** are images or thoughts that intrude into consciousness against a person's will. You have probably experienced a mild obsessional thought in the form of some song or stupid commercial jingle that is repeated over and over in your mind. This may be irritating, but it is certainly not disturbing in any major sense. True obsessions are so disturbing that they cause anxiety or extreme discomfort. The most common obsessions are about violence (such as poisoning one's spouse or stabbing a child), about being "dirty" or "unclean," about whether one has performed some action (such as turning off the stove), and about committing immoral acts (Wilson, 1986).

Obsessions usually give rise to **compulsions.** These are irrational acts a person feels driven to repeat (■ Fig. 16–9). Often, the compulsive act helps control or block out anxiety caused by the obsession. For example, a minister who finds profanities popping into his mind might take up compulsively counting his heartbeat to prevent himself from thinking "dirty" words.

Many people with compulsions can be classified as *checkers* or *cleaners* (Kleinknecht, 1986). Thus, a person who feels guilty or unclean because of a conflict about masturbation might be driven to wash his or her hands hundreds of times a day. And a young mother who repeatedly has an image of a knife plunging into her infant might count all the knives in the house several times a day and check repeatedly to see that they are locked away. Doing this is strongly motivated by a need to reduce her anxieties, at least temporarily.

Of course, not all obsessive-compulsive disorders are so dramatic. Many simply involve extreme orderliness and rigid routine. Compulsive attention to detail and rigid adherence to procedures and rules make the highly anxious person feel more secure by keeping activities totally structured and under control. Notice, too, that when such patterns are long-standing, but less intense, they may be classified as a personality disorder.

Stress Disorders Most anxiety disorders have little connection to the actual degree of threat. A notable exception is found in **acute stress disorder** and **post-traumatic stress disorder (PTSD).** These problems occur when stresses *outside the range of normal human experience* cause a significant emotional disturbance (DSM-IV, 1994). Such reactions frequently follow sudden disasters, such as floods, tornadoes, earthquakes, or serious accidents (■ Fig. 16–10). Research shows that stress disorders also affect many political hostages, combat veterans, prisoners of war, and victims of terrorism, violent crime, and child molestation (Frederick, 1987). It is sad to note that female victims of sexual abuse and assault may be the single largest group experiencing PTSD (Coyne & Downey, 1991).

Symptoms of stress disorders include repeatedly reliving the traumatic event, avoiding stimuli associated with the event, and a numbing of emotions. Also common are insomnia, nightmares, guardedness, an inability to concentrate, irritability, and explosions of anger or aggression. If such reactions last less than a month after a traumatic event, the problem is called an acute stress disorder. If they last more than a month, the person is suffering from post-traumatic stress disorder (DSM-IV, 1994). PTSD may surface long after the stress has passed—as has happened to many veterans of the Vietnam War (Fontana et al., 1992).

Dissociative Disorders

Dissociative reactions are marked by striking episodes of *amnesia*, *fugue*, or *multiple personality*. **Dissociative amnesia** is the inability to recall one's name, address, or past. **Dissociative fugue** (sounds like "fewg") involves fleeing to escape extreme conflict or threat. Dissociations are often triggered by highly traumatic events, as the following case illustrates (Braun, 1986).

Obsessive-compulsive disorder An extreme preoccupation with certain thoughts and compulsive performance of certain behaviors.

Obsession Recurring irrational or disturbing thoughts or mental images that a person cannot avoid.

Compulsion An act an individual feels driven to repeat, often against his or her will.

Acute stress disorder Psychological disturbance lasting up to one month following stresses that would produce anxiety in anyone who experienced them.

Post-traumatic stress disorder Psychological disturbance lasting more than one month following stresses that would produce anxiety in anyone who experienced them.

Dissociative amnesia Loss of memory (partial or complete) for past events and, especially, for personal identity.

Dissociative fugue Fleeing to escape extreme emotional conflict, anxiety, or threat.

Dissociative identity disorder The presence of two or more distinct personalities or personal identities.

Schizophrenia A type of psychosis characterized by withdrawal from reality, delusions, hallucinations, and a "split" between thought and emotion.

Hypochondriasis A preoccupation with fears of having a serious disease. Ordinary physical signs are interpreted as proof that the person has a disease, but no physical disorder can be found.

Somatization disorder Afflicted persons have numerous physical complaints. Typically, they have consulted many doctors, but no organic cause for their distress can be identified.

Pain disorder Pain that has no identifiable physical cause and appears to be of psychological origin.

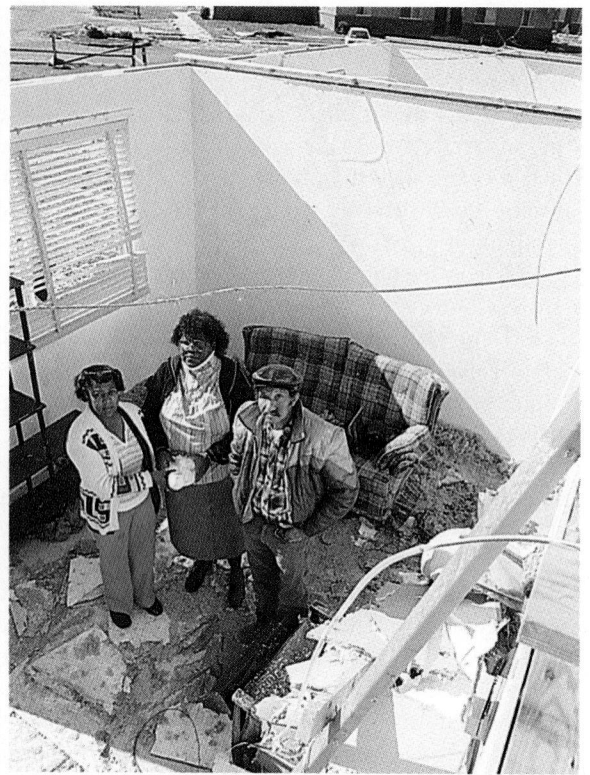

■ **Fig. 16–10** *In the aftermath of natural disasters, some survivors suffer from acute stress reactions. For some, the flare-up of anxiety and distress may occur months or years after the stressful event is over, an example of a post-traumatic stress reaction. For example, during the year following the Exxon Valdez oil spill disaster, 9 percent of residents in affected communities experienced the symptoms of PTSD (Palinkas et al., 1993).*

> An American soldier in the Vietnam war wandered into the countryside and ambushed Vietcong soldiers without any memory of his actions. His fugue and amnesia were triggered when he discovered the dead body of a Vietnamese child he had adopted. Later, in therapy, he was able to remember the incident: "After 15 years in the Army, he was all I had. It's all my fault! It's all my fault! If I had just taken you over to the hooch, you wouldn't be there, man! It's not fair. They ain't gotta kill kids." (Spiegel, 1986)

It can easily be seen that forgetting one's identity and fleeing unpleasant situations can serve as defenses against intolerable anxiety.

Dissociative identity disorder (also called multiple personality disorder) is a relatively rare condition. Persons suffering from this disorder have two or more separate personalities (DSM-IV, 1994). (Note that multiple personality is *not* schizophrenia. Schizophrenia is a form of psychosis, discussed in the next chapter.) One of the most dramatic examples of multiple personality ever recorded is described in the book *Sybil* (Schreiber, 1973). Sybil had 16 different personalities. Each personality had a distinct voice, vocabulary, and posture. One personality could play the piano (not Sybil), but the others could not.

When a personality other than Sybil was in control, Sybil experienced a "time lapse," or memory blackout. Sybil's amnesia and alternate personalities developed during childhood when she was regularly beaten, locked in closets, perversely tortured, sexually abused, and almost killed. Sybil's first dissociations allowed her to escape by creating another person who would suffer torture in her place. Dissociative identity disorders often begin with similar unbearable childhood experiences. A history of childhood trauma, especially sexual abuse, is found in over 95 percent of persons with multiple personalities (Ross et al., 1990).

Therapy for dissociative identity disorders may make use of hypnosis, which allows contact with the various personalities. The goal of therapy is *integration* and *fusion* of the various personalities into a single, balanced entity (Kluft, 1988). Fortunately, multiple personality is far rarer in real life than it is in TV dramas!

Somatoform Disorders

Perhaps you have known someone, particularly someone prone to anxiety, who seems to be practically obsessed by fears of having a serious disease. Usually such individuals are preoccupied with bodily functions, such as their heartbeat or digestion. Minor physical problems, such as a small sore or an occasional cough, convince them that they have cancer or some other disease. Typically, their unwarranted fear of having a disease persists despite the fact that there is no medical basis for their complaints (DSM-IV, 1994).

Question: Are you describing hypochondria?

Yes. In **hypochondriasis** (HI-po-kon-DRY-uh-sis), the person interprets normal sensations and small bodily signs as proof that he or she has a terrible disease. Persons who have a related problem called **somatization disorder** (som-ah-tuh-ZAY-shun) express their anxieties in the form of various bodily complaints such as vomiting or nausea, shortness of breath, difficulty swallowing, or painful menstruation. Typically, they feel ill much of the time and visit doctors repeatedly. Most are taking medicines or other treatments, but no organic cause can be found for their distress (Lipowski, 1988). Similarly, a person suffering from **pain disorder** is disabled by pain that has no identifiable physical basis (DSM-IV, 1994).

A rarer somatoform disorder ("body-form" disorder) is called a *conversion reaction.* In this case, psychologists theorize that severe emotional conflicts are "converted" into symptoms that actually disturb phys-

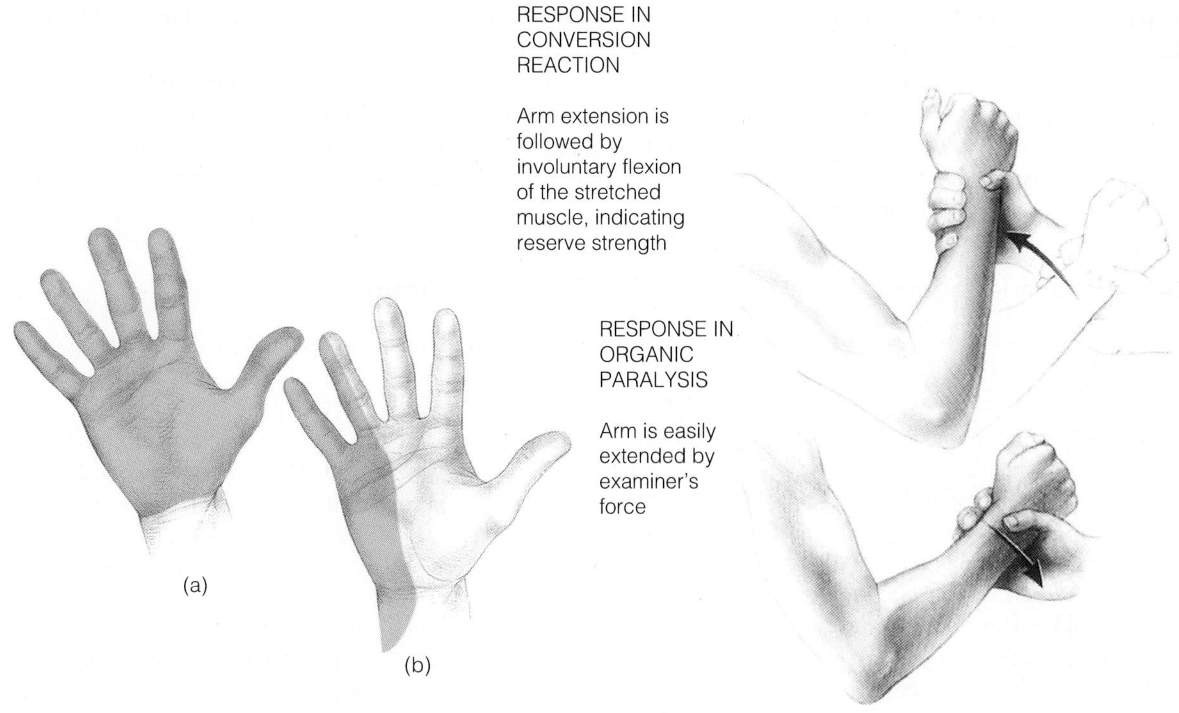

RESPONSE IN CONVERSION REACTION

Arm extension is followed by involuntary flexion of the stretched muscle, indicating reserve strength

RESPONSE IN ORGANIC PARALYSIS

Arm is easily extended by examiner's force

(a)

(b)

Conversion disorder A bodily symptom that mimics a physical disability but is actually caused by anxiety or emotional distress.

■ **Fig. 16–11** (left) *"Glove" anesthesia is a conversion reaction involving loss of feeling in areas of the hand that would be covered by a glove* (a). *If the anesthesia were physically caused, it would follow the pattern shown in* (b). (right) *To test for organic paralysis of the arm, an examiner can suddenly extend the arm, stretching the muscles. A conversion reaction is indicated if the arm pulls back involuntarily. (Adapted from* Weintraub, 1983.)

ical functioning or closely resemble a physical disability. **Conversion disorders** are usually quite dramatic. For instance, a soldier might become deaf or lame or develop "glove anesthesia" just before a battle.

Question: What is "glove anesthesia"?

"Glove anesthesia" is a loss of sensitivity in the areas of the skin that would normally be covered by a glove. Glove anesthesia shows that conversion symptoms often contradict known medical facts. The system of nerves in the hands does not form a glove-like pattern and could not cause the observed symptoms. Conversion reactions are also revealed by a disappearance of symptoms when the victim is asleep, hypnotized, or anesthetized (■ Fig. 16–11). Another sign of a conversion reaction is victims' seeming lack of concern about their sudden disabilities. (Be careful not to confuse somatoform disorders with psychosomatic disorders. As discussed in Chapter 11, psychosomatic disorders are illnesses in which actual physical damage or dysfunction results from emotional reactions to stress.)

The physical symptoms of a conversion disorder usually serve to excuse the person from a threatening situation. In one case a college student who had a minor traffic accident awakened the following morning with a numbness in his legs and found himself unable to move them. A conversion reaction was suspected when it was noted that he did not seem at all disturbed by his inability to walk. This sign is referred to as *la belle indifférence.* Investigation revealed that his parents were pressuring him to stay in school (although he wanted to quit) and that he was not prepared for his final exams. If he failed his exams, he expected to be drafted (Suinn, 1975).

A final note of interest: Conversion disorders probably account for many of the so-called miracle cures attributed to faith healers or medical quacks. Persons with conversion symptoms who firmly believe they are being helped may undergo a "miraculous" cure, but they usually develop new symptoms later.

Three Theories—Pathways to Anxiety and Disorder

Question: What causes the problems described in the preceding discussion?

Because we are both biological and social creatures, it is not surprising that susceptibility to anxiety-based disorders appears to be partly inherited. Studies of parents suffering from panic disorder, for instance, show that an unusually large number (60 percent) of their children are born with a fearful, inhibited temperament (Rosenbaum et al., 1989). Such children are irritable and wary as infants, shy and fearful as toddlers, and by school age they are quiet and cautious introverts. Authorities believe that such children are at high risk for

Psychodynamic Pertaining to internal motives, conflicts, unconscious forces, and other dynamics of mental life.

Humanistic Any system of thought focused on subjective experience and human problems and potentials.

Existential A system of thought that focuses on the elemental problems of existence, such as death, meaning, choice, and responsibility.

Self-image Total subjective perception of oneself; another term for self-concept.

Behavioristic Any approach that emphasizes overt, observable behavior and the effects of learning and conditioning.

Avoidance learning Learning that occurs when making a particular response delays or prevents the onset of a painful or unpleasant stimulus.

Anxiety reduction hypothesis Explains the self-defeating nature of avoidance responses as a result of the reinforcing effects of relief from anxiety.

anxiety problems, such as panic attacks, in adulthood (Rosenbaum et al., 1991).

At least three major psychological perspectives on the causes of dissociative, anxiety, and somatoform disorders can be identified. The perspectives are (1) the *psychodynamic* approach, (2) the *humanistic-existential* approach, and (3) the *behavioral* approach.

Psychodynamic Approach

Freud was the first to propose an explanation for what was then known as neurosis. According to Freud, disturbances like those we have described represent a raging conflict among subparts of the personality—the id, ego, and superego.

Freud particularly emphasized that intense anxiety can be caused by forbidden id impulses for sex or aggression that threaten to break through into behavior. It is as if the person is in a constant state of fear that the ego will be overwhelmed and that the person may do something "crazy" or unacceptable. Also important in the Freudian view is guilt generated by the superego in response to these impulses. Caught in the middle, the ego eventually is overwhelmed. This forces the person to adopt rigid defense mechanisms and misguided, inflexible behavior to prevent a disastrous loss of control.

Humanistic-Existential Approaches

Humanistic psychologist Carl Rogers interpreted emotional disorders as the end product of a faulty **self-image** (Rogers, 1959). Rogers believed that anxious individuals have built up unrealistic mental images of themselves. This leaves them vulnerable to contradictory information. Let's say, for example, that an essential part of a student's self-image is the idea that she is highly intelligent. If the student does poorly in school, she may deny or distort her perceptions of herself and her perceptions of the situation. Rigid use of defense mechanisms, a conversion reaction, anxiety attacks, or similar symptoms may result from threats to one's self-image. These symptoms in turn become new threats that provoke further distortions. We have, in other words, a classic example of a vicious cycle of maladjustment and anxiety that feeds on itself once started.

Some psychologists take a more existential view and stress that unhealthy anxiety reflects a loss of *meaning* in one's life. According to them, we must show *courage* and *responsibility* in our choices if life is to have meaning. Too often, they say, we give in to "existential anxiety" and avoid making life-enhancing choices. Existential anxiety is the anguish that comes from knowing that we are personally responsible for our lives. Hence, we have a crushing need to choose wisely and courageously as we face life's empty and impersonal void.

From the existential view, people who are unhappy and anxious are living in "bad faith." That is, they have collapsed in the face of the awesome responsibility to choose a meaningful existence. In short, they have lost their way in life.

Behavioral Approach

Behaviorists generally assume that the "symptoms" we have discussed are learned, just as other behaviors are. You might recall from Chapter 7, for instance, that phobias can be acquired through classical conditioning. Similarly, anxiety attacks may reflect conditioned emotional responses that are generalized to new situations. As another example, the hypochondriac's "sickness behavior" may be reinforced by the sympathy and attention he or she gets.

One point that all theorists agree on is that disordered behavior is ultimately self-defeating and paradoxical. A paradox is a contradiction. The contradiction in self-defeating behavior is that it makes the person more miserable in the long run, but its immediate effect is to temporarily lower anxiety.

Question: But if the person becomes more miserable in the long run, how does the pattern get started?

The behavioral explanation is that self-defeating behavior begins with avoidance learning (described earlier, in Chapter 7). Here's a quick review of **avoidance learning** to refresh your memory:

> An animal is placed in a special cage. After a few minutes a light comes on, followed a moment later by a painful shock. Quickly, the animal escapes into a second chamber. After a few minutes, a light comes on in this chamber, and the shock is repeated. Soon the animal learns to avoid pain by moving before the shock occurs. Once an animal learns to avoid the shock, it can be turned off altogether. A well-trained animal may avoid the non-existent shock indefinitely.

The same analysis can be applied to disordered human behavior. A behaviorist would say that the powerful reward of *immediate relief* from anxiety keeps self-defeating avoidance behavior alive. This view, known as the **anxiety reduction hypothesis,** seems to explain why the behavior patterns we have discussed often look very "stupid" to outside observers.

There is probably a core of truth to each of the three psychological explanations. For this reason, understanding anxiety-based disorders may be aided by combining parts of all three perspectives. Each viewpoint also suggests a different approach to treatment.

Because there are many possibilities, a full discussion of therapy is found later, in Chapter 18.

A Final Note—You're Okay, Really! It is your author's hope that you will not fall prey to the psychological equivalent of "medical student's disease" after reading this chapter. Medical students, it seems, have a tendency to notice in themselves the symptoms of each dreaded disease they study. As a psychology student you may have noticed what seem to be abnormal tendencies in your own behavior. If so, don't panic. In the majority of instances, this only shows that pathological behavior is an *exaggeration* of normal defenses and reactions, not that your behavior is abnormal.

A Look Ahead Two interesting topics conclude our discussion in this chapter. The upcoming Applications describes a classic experiment that asked the question, If a normal person were placed in a mental hospital, how would he or she be perceived by other patients and by the hospital staff? The answer is fascinating and instructive. After that, an Exploration discusses the validity of pleading "not guilty by reason of insanity" in the courtroom.

Learning Check

See if you can correctly answer the following questions about the anxiety disorders we have discussed.

1. Excessive anxiety over ordinary life stresses is characteristic of which of the following disorders?
   a. free-floating anxiety disorder *b.* agoraphobia *c.* hypochondriasis *d.* adjustment disorder
2. Panic disorder can occur with or without agoraphobia, but agoraphobia cannot occur alone, without the presence of a panic disorder. T or F?
3. Alice has a phobic fear of blood. The formal term for her fear is
   a. nyctophobia *b.* hematophobia *c.* pathophobia *d.* pyrophobia
4. A person who intensely fears eating, writing, or speaking in public suffers from ______________________________ ______________________.
5. "Checkers" and "cleaners" suffer from which disorder?
   a. acarophobia *b.* panic disorder with agoraphobia
   c. generalized anxiety disorder *d.* obsessive-compulsive disorder
6. The symptoms of acute stress disorders last less than one month; post-traumatic stress disorders last more than one month. T or F?
7. Which of the following is *not* a dissociative disorder?
   a. fugue *b.* amnesia *c.* conversion reaction *d.* multiple personality
8. Freud's original psychodynamic explanation of "neurosis" was based on the avoidance learning hypothesis. T or F?
9. The existential explanation of unhealthy anxiety is based on a conflict between subparts of the personality. T or F?
10. Many of the physical complaints associated with anxiety disorders are closely related to activity of what part of the nervous system? ***Critical Thinking***

Answers: 1. *d* 2. F 3. *b* 4. social phobia 5. *d* 6. T 7. *c* 8. F 9. F 10. The autonomic nervous system (ANS), especially the sympathetic branch of the ANS.

APPLICATIONS: *On Being Sane in Insane Places*

Question: Suppose someone were committed to a psychiatric hospital by accident. Would the staff notice? Would the person be able to get out?

David Rosenhan of Stanford University set out to answer these questions and another: How accurately do psychiatric hospitals distinguish between people who are psychotic and those who are healthy?

To find out, Rosenhan and several colleagues had themselves committed (Rosenhan, 1973). Entrance to mental hospitals was gained by faking only one symptom. Rosenhan and the others complained of hearing voices that said "empty," "hollow," and "thud." In 11 out of 12 tries, they were admitted with a diagnosis of "schizophrenia."

Pseudo-Patients

After being admitted, these "pseudo-patients" dropped all pretense of mental illness. Yet, even though they acted completely normal, none of the researchers was ever recognized by hospital *staff* as a phony patient. Other patients were not so easily fooled. It was not unusual for a real patient to say to one of the researchers, "You're not crazy, you're checking up on the hospital!" or, "You're a journalist."

Rosenhan and the others spent from one to seven weeks in hospitals before being discharged. The hospitals ranged from very modern and plush to ancient and shoddy. No matter how good the facilities or how good the hospital's reputation, Rosenhan found some disturbing conditions. Contact between staff and patients was very limited and sometimes marked by fear or hostility. It was found that attendants and staff only spent an average of 11 percent of their time out of the "cage," the glassed-in central compartment in the ward.

It was not unusual for the morning attendants to wake patients with a hostile call of: "Come on, you m__________ f________s, out of bed!" When patients tried to talk with staff, they were often ignored or received strange replies. One pseudo-patient approached a psychiatrist and politely asked when he might get grounds privileges. The doctor's reply was, "Good morning, Dave. How are you today?"

Rosenhan found that therapy other than drugs was very limited. Daily contact of patients with psychiatrists, psychologists, or physicians averaged about 7 minutes. On the other hand, the researchers were given a total of 2100 pills to swallow, an average of 7 pills a day per patient. (Only 2 of the 2100 pills were actually taken, the rest being pocketed or flushed down the toilet.)

Non-Persons Patients tended to be treated as non-persons. A nurse unbuttoned her uniform to adjust her bra in front of a room full of male patients. She was not being sexy; she just didn't consider the patients men. Patients would often be discussed by the staff while the patient was standing nearby. It was as if patients were invisible or pieces of furniture.

A situation that sums up Rosenhan's findings better than any other is his note-taking. Rosenhan began taking notes by carefully jotting things on a small piece of paper hidden in his hand. He learned quickly that hiding was totally unnecessary. He was soon walking around with a clipboard and note pads, recording observations and collecting data.

No one questioned this behavior. Note-taking was simply seen as a symptom of his "illness." As a matter of fact, Rosenhan found that anything he did was ignored. When a staff member manhandled a patient (as happened occasionally), Rosenhan would be right there—taking notes on the whole incident!

Psychiatric Labels

These observations clarify the failure of staff members to detect the fake patients. Because they were seen in the context of a mental ward, and because they had been *labeled* schizophrenic, anything the pseudo-patients did was seen as a symptom of their psychotic "illness."

To return to the original hypothetical question about talking your way out of an accidental commitment, it should be clear that it could be quite futile to say, "Look, this is all a mistake. I'm not crazy. You've got to let me out." The response might very well be, "Have you had these paranoid delusions for long?"

Many mental health professionals found Rosenhan's findings hard to believe. This led to a follow-up study, in which the staff of another hospital was warned that one or more pseudo-patients were going to try to gain admission over the next 3 months. Thus alerted, the staff at this hospital tried to identify fake incoming patients. Among 193 candidates, 41 were labeled fakes by at least one staff member, and 19 more were labeled "suspicious." This only served to confirm Rosenhan's original findings since he never sent any patients—fake or otherwise—to this hospital!

APPLICATIONS: *Continued*

Stigma It is important to note that all of the normal people who served as pseudo-patients in the original studies were discharged as schizophrenics (psychotics) "in remission" (temporarily free of symptoms). In other words, the label that prevented hospital staff from seeing the normality of the researchers stayed with them when they left. Such labels frequently stigmatize their bearers. Psychiatrist Karl Menninger (1964) once commented that:

> A label can blight the life of a person even after his recovery from mental illness. A young doctor I knew suffered for a time from some anxiety and indecision. He consulted a psychiatrist and soon recovered. Unfortunately, a "tentative" diagnosis of schizophrenia got abroad—I don't know how—and the young doctor's professional career was seriously impaired. He was injured, not by mental illness but by a word.

If you doubt that psychiatric labels can be stigmatizing, try to make a list of politicians you know of who have publicly revealed that they have suffered from mental illness. Your list is likely to be *very* short.

Implications Rosenhan's findings carry a cautionary message for professionals and non-professionals alike: Labels can be dangerous. As Stoller (1967) said, "When a person is labeled—neurotic, psychotic, executive, teacher, salesman, psychologist—either by himself or by others, he restricts his behavior to the role and even may rely upon the role for security."

The terms presented in this chapter and the next can, and do, aid communication about human problems. But if used carelessly, they may do great damage. Everyone has felt or acted "crazy" during brief periods of stress or high emotion. A person whose emotional problems extend over a longer period of time is different from you or me only in the severity of his or her difficulty.

It is therefore more productive to label problems than to label people. Think of the difference in impact between saying, "He is experiencing a serious emotional disorder" and saying, "He is a psychotic." Which statement would you choose to have said about yourself?

Even such careful usage of labels can cause difficulties. Some people are relieved to learn that their problem has a name and that it is shared by others. Others, however may be upset to learn that they are considered "mentally ill." The stigma that still clings to this term discourages some people from seeking needed professional help (McReynolds, 1989).

As a final point, it is important to realize that even severely disturbed persons appreciate being treated normally. Rosenhan's research makes it clear that people are not helped by being thrust into the patient role. One former patient's comments clarify this last point:

> After I got back from the hospital, my friends tried to *act* like nothing had changed. But I could tell they weren't being honest. For instance, a friend invited me to dinner and everything went fine until I dropped my fork. Both my friend and his wife jumped up and stared at me like they thought I might explode. I was quite embarrassed.

Remember, no matter how disturbed a person may be, he or she continues to merit respect and compassion.

LEARNING CHECK

1. In the majority of their attempts, Rosenhan's pseudo-patients were admitted to mental hospitals after complaining only that they were hearing voices. T or F?
2. Although they were often detected by professional staff members, the normality of the pseudo-patients was never recognized by other patients. T or F?
3. During a short hospital stay, one pseudo-patient was denied psychiatric drugs even though he requested them. T or F?
4. Rosenhan found that almost anything pseudo-patients said or did was interpreted as a symptom of their "illness." T or F?
5. When they were alerted that a number of pseudo-patients might try to gain entry, hospital staff members were able to more accurately detect the fakes. T or F?
6. The powerful impact of psychiatric labels is related to what perceptual principle (discussed in Chapter 5)? ***Critical Thinking***

Answers: 1. T 2. F 3. F 4. T 5. F 6. perceptual expectancy (set)

EXPLORATION

Psychology and the Law—The "Twinkie Defense"

Mark David Chapman claimed that devils forced him to kill former Beatle John Lennon. In court, his lawyer asserted that Chapman was "not guilty by reason of insanity." However, at mid-trial Chapman decided to plead guilty to second-degree murder. His reason? He said that God had visited him in his cell and told him to confess.

Chapman's case was one of thousands each year that mingle law, psychiatry, psychology, and public opinion. For over 130 years, the **insanity defense** has bedeviled the courts and raised difficult legal, moral, and psychological questions.

Question: What exactly is the insanity defense?

Insanity

The insanity defense entered Western law as the **M'Naghten rule.** In 1843 the English House of Lords ruled on the case of Daniel M'Naghten, a "madman" who attempted to kill a member of Parliament, but murdered another man instead. The court held that a defendant—in this case M'Naghten—must understand the wrongfulness of his or her actions to be held responsible for them. Persons suffering from "mental disease or other defects" that prevent them from knowing right from wrong are "insane." In the U.S. legal system, the taking of life by an insane person is not murder.

Defendants may also claim that they knew their act was wrong, but they had an **irresistible impulse** they could not control. An example is the person who finds his or her spouse in a stranger's arms and kills in a jealous rage. A related defense claims **diminished capacity** to control actions or to know right from wrong. A person who commits a crime while under the influence of drugs might make this plea.

The Twinkie Defense The problems posed by the insanity defense are vividly shown by three legal cases. In Oakland, California, a jury declared Darlin June Cromer sane in the racial killing of a 5-year-old boy. This was the verdict, despite the fact that one psychiatrist testified that Cromer was "the most psychotic person" he'd ever seen. Cromer was sentenced to life in prison.

On the opposite side of the Bay, Dan White admitted killing San Francisco Mayor George Moscone and Supervisor Harvey Milk. However, White's lawyer convinced the jury that White acted with diminished capacity. The defense claimed, among other things, that White was deranged from eating too much "junk food"—an argument that became known as the "Twinkie Defense." (For those unschooled in junk food, a Twinkie is a small sponge cake with a sugary cream filling.)

Testimony in the trial established that White planned the murders beforehand and carefully avoided security guards to reach his victims. White received a 7-year jail sentence. (He was paroled 3 years later.) The verdict so outraged many citizens that a new law in California now bans claims of "diminished capacity". In yet another case, "Vampire Killer" Richard Chase was convicted of killing six people and drinking the blood of some of his victims. Chase was declared sane.

These cases point to the inconsistencies of a system that allows people who appear sane to be judged insane, and apparently insane people to be judged sane.

Question: How is sanity determined?

Expert Testimony The most sensational criminal trials involving insanity have a typical pattern: Defense psychiatrists interview the defendant and then testify that he or she was insane at the time of the crime; prosecution psychiatrists examine the defendant and testify to his or her sanity. After these **expert witnesses** contradict one another's testimony, it's up to the jury to decide who is right.

But more often, this "battle of the experts" never takes place. In 4 out of 5 cases, prosecutors, defense attorneys, medical experts, and judges agree *before* trial that the defendant is mentally ill (Bower, 1984). Thus, if a person really is psychotic, in most cases experts agree fairly readily.

Opinion, Please The preceding brief discussion raises several interesting questions.

1. The states of Montana, Idaho, and Utah have banned the insanity plea, but in most states it remains intact. Several other states now allow only a "guilty, but insane" plea. (Jeffrey Dahmer pleaded "guilty, but insane.") In your opinion, should questions of sanity be considered in criminal trials? Should the insanity defense be allowed?

Before you answer, you should know that pleas of insanity are actually relatively rare, being used in only about 1 out of every 100 court cases. In only about 1 out of 500 of these cases does the insanity defense succeed. Nationally, this amounts to about 150 cases a year in the United States (Silver et al., 1994).

More important, a verdict of innocence by reason of insanity does not set a person free. In most states it requires automatic commitment to a mental hospital. Thereafter, the law places the burden of proof on patients. To be released, they must show that they are no longer a danger to themselves or others. Moreover, in most cases, persons declared "insane" are hospitalized longer than they would have been imprisoned for a criminal conviction. The average hospital stay is about 3 years (Silver et al., 1994). Nevertheless, in some instances, the public may still rightly ask if justice has been served.

2. Should the courts accept pleas of diminished capacity? Before you answer this question, think about the "guilt" of a severely retarded person or someone with a brain tumor who commits a crime.

3. In your opinion, who should decide if a person should be committed? Should it be a judge? A jury? A psychiatrist? A psychologist? Who should decide when an "insane" person can be released? Should a person have the right to refuse treatment? What if the person committed a crime?

Before answering, it may be useful to know that psychiatric predictions of violent behavior are largely inaccurate. Follow-ups of arrests and mental hospital

EXPLORATION

records show that from two thirds to nine tenths of the time, experts are *wrong* in forecasting violence (Loftus & Monahan, 1980). At present, there is no way to accurately predict which individuals are likely to be dangerous to themselves or to others (Teplin, Abram, & McClelland, 1994).

As you can see, there are no easy answers to the preceding questions. Nevertheless, when issues of "madness," personal freedom, criminal responsibility, and justice are raised, everyone has an opinion. What's yours?

Insanity defense Legal plea that says a person who was incapable of knowing right from wrong at the time of a crime is not guilty.

M'Naghten rule A rule in English common law for judging sanity and legal responsibility.

Irresistible impulse An uncontrollable impulse to act.

Diminished capacity Impaired mental competence to control actions or know right from wrong.

Expert witness A person recognized by a court of law as being qualified to give expert testimony on a specific topic.

LEARNING CHECK

1. Daniel M'Naghten was a lawyer who defended a member of the British House of Lords who was accused of murder, but who pleaded insanity. T or F?
2. In a court of law, the insanity defense is based on the premise that persons who are mentally defective cannot be held fully responsible for their actions. T or F?
3. A person who committed a crime while suffering from a mind-altering reaction to a prescription medicine might have some success in claiming innocence due to diminished capacity. T or F?
4. In every state of the United States, insanity can be used as a legal defense as long as expert witnesses are willing to testify that the defendant was insane at the time of the crime. T or F?
5. Psychiatric predictions of future violence are correct only in about one-tenth to one-third of all forecasts. T or F?
6. Many states began to restrict use of the insanity defense after John Hinkley, Jr., who tried to murder President Ronald Reagan, was acquitted by reason of insanity. What does this trend reveal about insanity? *Critical Thinking*

Answers:

1. F 2. T 3. T 4. F 5. T 6. It emphasizes again that insanity is a legal concept, not a psychiatric diagnosis. Laws reflect community standards. When those standards change, lawmakers may seek to alter definitions of legal responsibility.

Chapter Summary

■ ***How is normality defined, and what are the major psychological disorders?***

- Formal definitions of abnormality usually take into account all or most of the following: *subjective discomfort, statistical definitions* (or *norms*), *social nonconformity*, and the *cultural* or *situational context* of behavior.
- Problems exist with each definition in that all are *relative* standards.
- A key element in judgments of disorder is that a person's behavior must be *maladaptive*. In practice, judging normality is a social act influenced by many factors.
- Major categories of **psychopathology** are described in the *Diagnostic and Statistical Manual of Mental Disorders (DSM-IV)*.
- Major problems discussed in this chapter and the next include *psychotic disorders, organic mental disorders, substance related disorders, mood disorders, anxiety disorders, somatoform disorders, dissociative disorders, personality disorders, and sexual or gender identity disorders.*
- Traditionally, the term *neurosis* has been used to describe milder, anxiety related disorders. However, the term is fading from use.
- **Insanity** is a legal term defining whether a person may be held responsible for his or her actions. Sanity is determined in court on the basis of testimony by **expert witnesses.**

■ ***What is a personality disorder?***

- **Personality disorders** are deeply ingrained maladaptive personality patterns.

■ **Fig. 17–6** *This series of paintings by Louis Wain reflects a troubled personality. Wain was a British illustrator who became schizophrenic in middle age. As Wain's psychosis progressed, his cat paintings became highly abstract and fragmented. In many ways, Wain's paintings resemble the perceptual changes caused by psychedelic drugs such as mescaline and LSD. Recent research suggests that psychosis may, in fact, be the result of mind-altering changes in brain chemistry. (Derik Bayes/Courtesy Guttman-Maclay* Life *Picture Service.)*

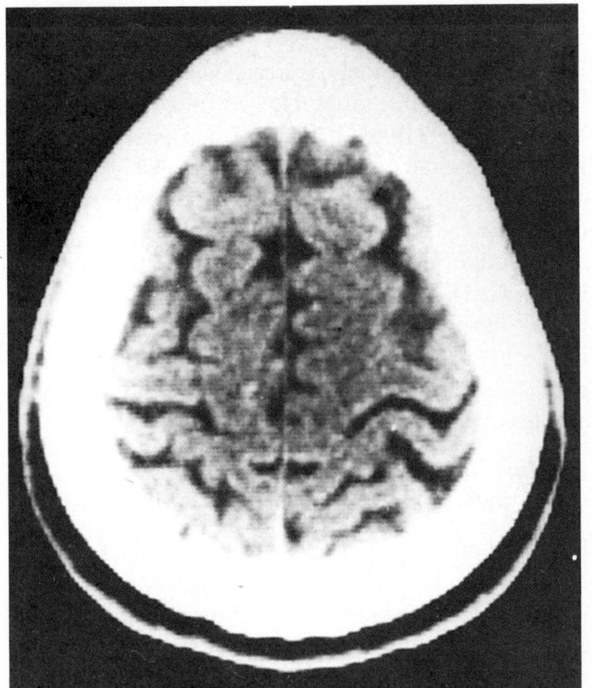

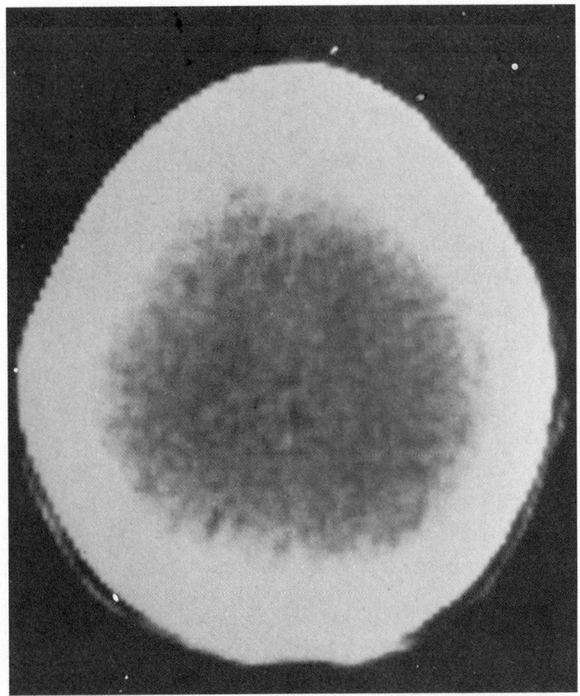

■ **Fig. 17–7** *(left) CT scan of would-be presidential assassin John Hinkley, Jr., taken when he was 25. The X-ray image shows widened fissures in the wrinkled surface of Hinkley's brain. (right) CT scan of a normal 25-year-old's brain. In most young adults the surface folds of the brain are pressed together too tightly to be seen. As a person ages, surface folds of the brain normally become more visible. Pronounced brain fissuring in young adults may be a sign of schizophrenia, chronic alcoholism, or other problems (McKean, 1982).*

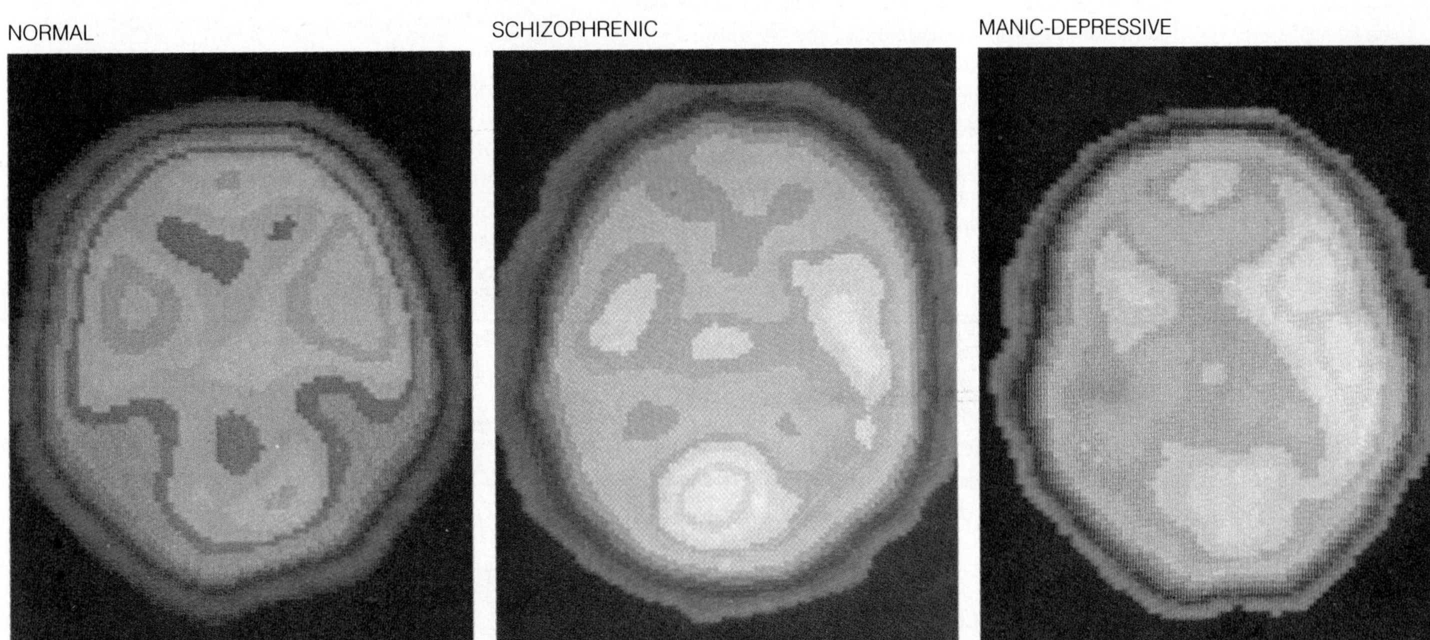

■ **Fig. 17–8** *Positron emission tomography produces PET scans of the human brain. In the scans shown here, red, pink, and orange indicate lower levels of brain activity; white and blue indicate higher activity levels. Notice that activity in the schizophrenic brain is quite low in the frontal lobes (top area of each scan). Activity in the manic-depressive brain is low in the left brain hemisphere and high in the right brain hemisphere. The reverse is more often true of the schizophrenic brain. Researchers are trying to identify consistent patterns like these to aid diagnosis of mental disorders.*

Stress-vulnerability model Attributes psychosis to a combination of environmental stress and inherited susceptibility.

Mood disorder Major disturbances in mood or emotion, such as depression or mania.

Depressive disorders Emotional disorders primarily involving sadness, despondency, and depression.

Bipolar disorders Emotional disorders involving both depression and mania.

Dysthymic disorder Moderate depression that persists for two years or more.

Cyclothymic disorder Moderate manic and depressive behavior that persists for two years or more.

Reactive depression A serious depression that appears to be a reaction to some identifiable event.

Maternity blues A brief and relatively mild state of depression often experienced by mothers 2 or 3 days after giving birth.

Postpartum depression A mild to moderately severe depression that begins within 3 months following childbirth.

enough stress may be pushed to a psychotic break. (Battle-field psychosis is an example.) However, some people inherit a difference in brain chemistry or brain structure that makes them more susceptible, even to normal life stresses.

Thus, the right combination of inherited potential and environmental stress brings about mind-altering changes in brain chemicals. This explanation is called a **stress-vulnerability model.** It seems to apply to other forms of psychopathology as well, such as depression (Fowles, 1992; Gottesman, 1991; Yank et al., 1993).

Ultimately, distinctions between organic and functional psychoses may be dropped, and treatment of major disturbances may become more chemical than psychological. But for now, psychosis remains "a riddle wrapped in a mystery inside an enigma." Let us hope the recent advances that we have so briefly explored are as promising as they appear to be.

Mood Disorders—Peaks and Valleys

Nobody loves you when you're down and out—or so it seems. Psychologists have gradually come to realize that **mood disorders** are among the most serious of all. Two general types of mood disorder are **depressive disorders** and **bipolar disorders.** (See ● Table 17–3.) In depressive disorders, sadness and despondency are exaggerated, prolonged, or unreasonable. Indications of a depressive disorder are dejection, hopelessness, inability to feel pleasure or to take interest in anything, fatigue, sleep and eating disturbances, feelings of worthlessness, an extremely negative self-image, and often, recurrent thoughts of suicide. In bipolar disorders, persons go both "up" and "down" emotionally (DSM-IV, 1994).

In terms of sheer numbers, studies show that in Europe and North America, between 10 and 20 percent of the adult population has had a major depressive episode at some time (DSM-IV, 1994). At any given time, roughly 5 percent of the population is suffering from a mood disorder (Landers, 1989).

● **Table 17–3 DSM-IV Classification of Mood Disorders**

Bipolar Disorders	Depressive Disorders
Cyclothymic disorder	Dysthymic disorder
Bipolar I disorder (mostly manic) Bipolar II disorder (mostly depressed)	Major depressive disorder Single episode Recurrent

(DSM-IV, 1994)

Moderate Mood Disorders

If a person is moderately depressed more days than not for at least 2 years, the problem is called a **dysthymic disorder** (dis-THY-mik). If depression alternates with periods when the person's mood is elevated, expansive, or irritable, the problem is called a **cyclothymic disorder** (SIKE-lo-THY-mik) (DSM-IV, 1994).

In serious cases of depression it becomes impossible for a person to function at work or at school. Sometimes, depressed individuals cannot even feed or clothe themselves. When depression and/or mania is even more severe, the person may become psychotic and lose touch with reality.

Question: How are mood disorders different from milder, more normal feelings of depression?

If a loved one dies or a person suffers a major failure, loss, or setback, a period of mourning or depression is to be expected. Depression at such times represents an emotional adjustment that is completed within a reasonable time.

When someone is continuously or intensely depressed, we must look for causes that go beyond the apparent triggering incident. In many such **reactive depressions,** we find that the person was unprepared to cope with a major loss because of a previous series of disappointments. For example, after his car is stolen and he fails a class, a college student learns that his girlfriend back home has become engaged to someone else. The student stops eating regularly, withdraws from friends, and neglects studying. In other instances, the person is simply emotionally dependent or immature. In any case, the triggering incident for depression is often merely the "last straw" that reveals an underlying emotional disturbance. Let's take a moment to consider a related form of depression that afflicts many women.

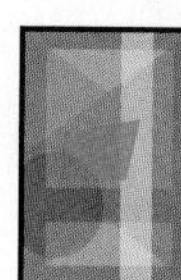

HIGHLIGHT 17–4

A Closer Look At

Postpartum Depression

Two weeks after the birth of her first child, Cheryl realized something was wrong. She could no longer ignore that she was extremely irritable, fatigued, tearful, and depressed. "Shouldn't I be happy?" she wondered. "What's wrong with me?"

Many women are surprised to learn that they face an increased risk of depression after giving birth. The two most common forms of the problem are **maternity blues** and **postpartum depression.** (The term *postpartum* refers to the time period following childbirth.)

An estimated 50 to 80 percent of all women undergo a temporary disturbance in mood that usually lasts from 24 to 48 hours after childbirth. These "third-day maternity blues" are marked by crying, fitful sleep, tension, anger, and irritability. For most women, this reaction is a normal part of adjusting to hormonal changes and childbirth. Their depression is brief and relatively mild. For some women, however, the maternity blues can be the beginning of a more lasting depression. As many as 20 percent (1 in 5) of all women who give birth may develop a mild to moderate depressive disorder. Typical signs of postpartum depression are mood swings, despondency, feelings of inadequacy, and feeling unable to cope with the new baby. Depression of this kind may last anywhere from 2 months to about a year.

Could Cheryl's postpartum depression have been predicted? Perhaps. The risk is increased by high levels of anxiety or depression during pregnancy, by poor marital adjustment, and by negative attitudes toward child rearing. The occurrence of stressful life events before giving birth is also a major factor (Whiften, 1988). Because giving birth and adjusting to parenthood can both be stressful, it may be that such added problems push women toward depression.

Psychologists are still studying the best ways to prevent and treat postpartum depression. Presently, the amount of social support a woman receives seems to be an important part of the problem. That is, women who become depressed are also likely to perceive their husbands as unsupportive. Efforts to educate prospective parents about the risk of postpartum depression and the value of mutual support may prove helpful (Hopkins et al., 1984).

Major Mood Disorders

Major mood disorders are marked by lasting extremes of emotion. About 14 percent of patients admitted to mental hospitals suffer from major mood disorders. Usually, one of the following patterns predominates. In a **bipolar I disorder,** the individual is mostly loud, elated, hyperactive, and energetic, but has also had one or more periods of depression. In a **bipolar II disorder** the person is mostly sad and guilt ridden, but has had one or more manic episodes. The person who only goes "down" emotionally suffers from a **major depressive disorder** (DSM-IV, 1994).

Major mood disorders can be limited primarily to emotional extremes. Quite often, however, persons with major mood disorders also have psychotic symptoms. This combination of mood disorder and a break with reality is called an **affective psychosis.**

Question: How do such problems differ from other types of psychosis?

Affective Psychoses Manic individuals throw themselves into fits of activity characterized by extreme distractibility, rapid shifts in thoughts ("flights of ideas"), constant talking, and restless movement. In advanced stages, manic behavior becomes more and more incoherent, agitated, and out of control. Eating or sleeping may be ignored until manic individuals push themselves into states of total delirium. (This behavior accounts for public images of the "raving maniac.") The following excerpt from a case history illustrates manic-psychotic behavior.

> Her husband had returned home to find her twirling around the living room bizarrely draped in her wedding gown tied with a bath towel and wearing a lamp shade. She gaily greeted him, laughed with an ear-piercing shrillness, and invited him to stay for the exciting "coming-out" party she was giving. Strewn on the table were a thousand handwritten invitations signed with a flourish and addressed to such dignitaries as the president of the United States, the justices of the Supreme Court, the emperor of Japan. She made incessant noises: singing her own ballads, shouting mottoes, which she devised, reciting limericks, making rhyming sounds, and yelling obscenities. (Suinn, 1970)

Depressive reactions show a reverse pattern in which feelings of failure, sinfulness, worthlessness, and total despair are dominant. The person becomes extremely subdued or withdrawn and may be intensely suicidal. Depressive reactions pose a serious threat to survival. Suicide attempted during a psychotic depression is rarely a simple "plea for help." Usually, the person intends to succeed and may give no prior warning (■ Fig. 17–9).

Manic and depressive states often appear to be related in bipolar disorders. That is, when manic behavior occurs, it may still be a reaction to depression. The manic person may seek to escape feelings of worthlessness and depression in an unending rush of activity.

Question: How do major mood disorders differ from dysthymic and cyclothymic disorders?

The major mood disorders usually involve more severe emotional changes. Also, of course, the person's emotional excesses can be accompanied by psychotic delusions and hallucinations. As a further distinction, major mood disorders and affective psychoses more often appear to be **endogenous** (en-DODGE-eh-nus: produced from within) rather than a reaction to external events.

Major mood disorders Disorders marked by lasting extremes of emotion and often including psychotic symptoms.

Bipolar I disorder A mood disorder in which a person is mostly manic (excited, hyperactive, energetic), but has also had one or more periods of depression.

Bipolar II disorder A mood disorder in which a person is mostly depressed (sad, despondent, guilt ridden), but has also had one or more manic episodes.

Major depressive disorder A mood disorder in which the person has suffered one or more intense episodes of depression.

Affective psychosis A general term for any major mood disorder that includes psychotic symptoms.

Endogenous depression Depression produced from within (perhaps by chemical imbalances in the brain), rather than as a reaction to life events.

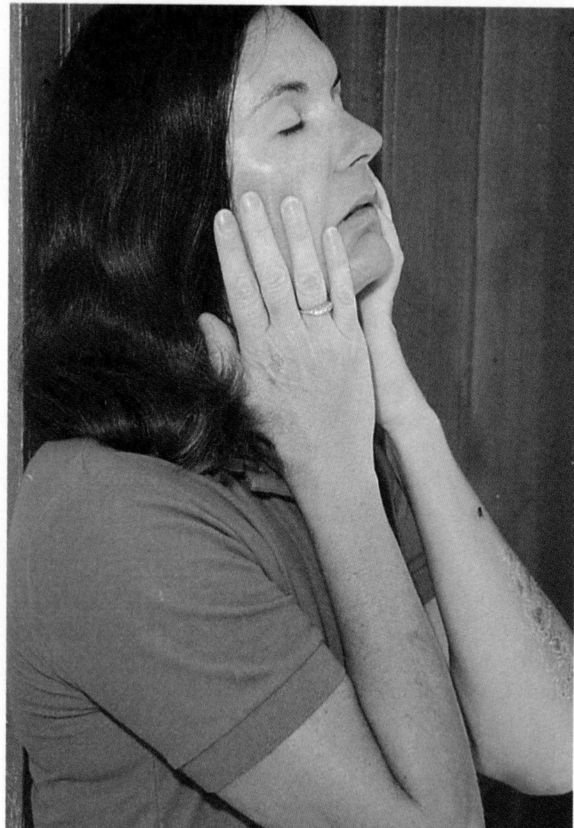

■ **Fig. 17–9** *In a depressive psychosis, suicidal impulses can be intense and despair total.*

Seasonal affective disorder Depression that occurs during fall and winter; presumably related to decreased exposure to sunlight.

The Causes of Mood Disorders

Question: How is depression explained?

Depression and other mood disorders have resisted adequate explanation and treatment. Some scientists are focusing on the biology of mood changes. These researchers are interested in brain chemicals and transmitter substances, especially serotonin, noradrenaline, and dopamine levels (Ricci & Wellman, 1990). Their findings are complex and inconclusive, but progress has been made. For example, the chemical *lithium carbonate* can be effective for treating some cases of depression, particularly those also showing manic behavior (Melia, O'Sullivan, & Barry, 1988).

Other researchers seek psychological explanations. Psychoanalytic theory, for instance, holds that depression is caused by repressed anger that is displaced and turned inward as self-blame and self-hate (Isenberg & Schatzberg, 1976). As discussed in Chapter 11, behavioral theories of depression emphasize learned helplessness (Abramson et al., 1985). Cognitive psychologists believe that self-criticism and negative, distorted, or self-defeating thoughts underlie many cases of depression. (This view is discussed in Chapter 18.) Clearly, life stresses trigger many mood disorders. This is especially true for people who have personality traits and thinking patterns that make them vulnerable to depression (Franche & Dobson, 1992; Gatz, 1990; Miranda, 1992).

Overall, women are twice as likely as men to experience depression. Authorities believe that social and environmental conditions are the main reason for this difference. Factors that contribute to women's greater risk of depression include conflicts between work and parenting, reproductive stresses, the strain of providing emotional support for others, marital strife, sexual and physical abuse, and poverty. Nationwide, poverty is concentrated among women and children. As a result, poor women frequently suffer the stresses associated with single parenthood, loss of control over their lives, poor housing, and dangerous neighborhoods (Russo, 1990).

As you might guess, the fact that major mood disorders appear to be endogenous implies that genetics may be involved, especially in bipolar disorders (Gatz, 1990; Plomin & Rende, 1991). As a case in point, the rate of depression among children of depressed parents is higher even if the children are adopted (Dunner, 1985). If one identical twin is depressed, the other has an 80 percent chance of suffering depression, too. For non-twin siblings the probability is 35 percent. As we have noted, psychological causes are important in many cases of depression. But for major mood disorders, biological factors seem to play a larger role. (For an interesting look at another cause of depression, see Highlight 17–5).

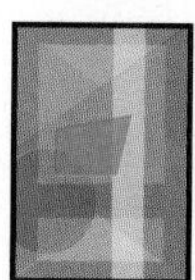

HIGHLIGHT 17–5

Research Frontier

Feeling Sad? It Could Be SAD.

Unless you have experienced a winter of "cabin fever" in the far north, you may be surprised to learn that the rhythms of the seasons underlie some depressions. Researcher Norman Rosenthal has found that some people suffer depression only during the fall and winter months. Almost anyone can get a little depressed when days are short, dark, and cold. But when a person's symptoms are lasting and disabling, the problem is called **seasonal affective disorder (SAD)** (Rosenthal et al., 1984; Smyth, 1991).

Starting in the fall, people with SAD sleep longer but more poorly. During the day they feel tired and drowsy and they tend to overeat. With each passing day they become more sad, anxious, irritable, and socially withdrawn. Although their depressions are usually only moderately severe, many victims of SAD face each winter with

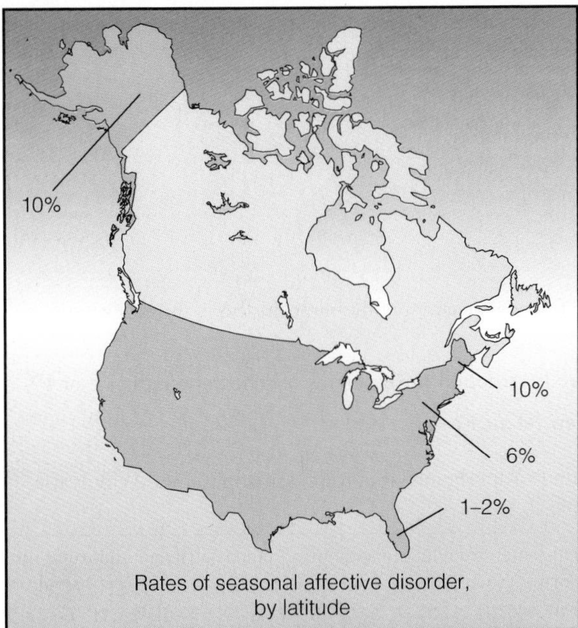

■ **Fig. 17–10** *Seasonal affective disorder appears to be related to reduced exposure to daylight during the winter. SAD affects 1 to 2 percent of Florida's population, about 6 percent of the people living in Maryland and New York City, and nearly 10 percent of the residents of New Hampshire and Alaska (Booker & Hellekson, 1992).*

■ **Fig. 17–11** *An hour or more of bright light a day can dramatically reduce the symptoms of seasonal affective disorder. Treatment is usually necessary from fall through spring. Some people respond best to artificial light in the early morning that creates a false "dawn" two hours earlier than normal (Avery et al., 1993).*

a sense of foreboding. SAD affects 4 times more women than men, and most victims show signs of suffering from a bipolar disorder. SAD is especially prevalent in northern latitudes, where days are very short during the winter (Booker & Hellekson, 1992) (■ Fig. 17–10).

The mechanisms underlying SAD are still a mystery. Some experts believe seasonal depressions are related to the release of more melatonin during the winter. This hormone is secreted by the pineal gland to regulate the body's response to changing light conditions. What is known is that many SAD patients can be helped by extra doses of bright light (■ Fig. 17–11). This treatment, which is called **phototherapy,** involves exposing SAD patients to one or more hours of very bright fluorescent light each day. Phototherapy relieves depression within 3 to 7 days for 80 percent of those treated (Hellekson & Rosenthal, 1987). For many SAD sufferers a hearty dose of light appears to be the next best thing to vacationing in the tropics.

Phototherapy A treatment for seasonal affective disorder that involves daily exposure to bright light.

While we await the outcome of attempts to understand and treat depression, a problem remains: Thousands of depressed people commit suicide each year. What can be done about it? Later in this chapter, the Applications section will provide some answers.

Learning Check

Match the following:

______ 1. Schizotypal personality
______ 2. Disorganized schizophrenia
______ 3. Catatonic schizophrenia
______ 4. Paranoid schizophrenia
______ 5. Major mood disorders

A. Manic or depressive behavior
B. Mutism, odd postures, immobility
C. Non-psychotic disorder
D. Silliness, bizarre behavior, personality disintegration
E. Delusions of grandeur or persecution
F. Anxiety attacks, irrational fears

6. Major mood disorders, especially bipolar disorders, often appear to be endogenous. T or F?

7. Learned helplessness is emphasized by ______________ theories of depression.
   a. humanistic *b.* biological *c.* behavioristic *d.* psychoanalytic

8. The drug lithium carbonate has been shown to be an effective treatment for schizophrenia. T or F?

9. Environmental explanations of schizophrenia emphasize emotional trauma and
   a. manic parents *b.* schizoaffective interactions
   c. psychedelic interactions *d.* disturbed family relationships

10. The ______________ ______________ of a schizophrenic person runs a 46 percent chance of also becoming psychotic.

11. Enlarged surface fissures and ventricles, as revealed by CT scans, are frequently found in the brains of chronic schizophrenics. T or F?

12. Abnormally high numbers of noradrenaline receptors have been found in the brains of schizophrenics. T or F?

13. The acronym SAD stands for schizotypal affective disorder. T or F?

Critical Thinking

14. Enlarged surface fissures and ventricles are frequently found in the brains of chronic schizophrenics. Why is it a mistake to conclude that such features cause schizophrenia?

Answers: 1. C 2. D 3. B 4. E 5. A 6. T 7. *c* 8. F 9. *d* 10. identical twin 11. T 12. F, (dopamine receptors) 13. F 14. Because correlation does not confirm causation. Structural brain abnormalities are merely *correlated* with schizophrenia. They could be additional symptoms, rather than causes, of the disorder.

Treatment—Medical Approaches

Psychotherapy Any psychological treatment for behavioral or emotional problems.

Somatic therapy Any bodily therapy, such as drug therapy, electroconvulsive therapy, or psychosurgery.

Chemotherapy Use of psychoactive drugs or chemicals to treat mental or emotional disturbances.

Question: Is psychosis incurable? If a person's symptoms temporarily disappear, can an unexpected relapse occur?

An organic psychosis cannot be "cured" in the usual sense, but it may be controlled with drugs and other techniques. With functional psychoses the outlook is still rather negative, but many people do recover (■ Fig. 17–12). It is wrong to fear "former mental patients" or to exclude them from work, friendships, and other social situations. A psychotic episode does not inevitably lead to lifelong dysfunction. Too often, however, it leads to unnecessary rejection based on groundless fears. As we noted in Chapter 16, only persons who are *actively psychotic* have an elevated chance of being violent. Even this group is responsible for only a tiny percentage of all the violent incidents in any given community (Monahan, 1992).

■ **Fig. 17–12** *At least 1 schizophrenic patient in 4 had completely recovered 10 years after being diagnosed. Three out of 4 had improved. New treatments for schizophrenia and other major mental disorders may improve these odds. (Source: FDA Consumer, 1993.)*

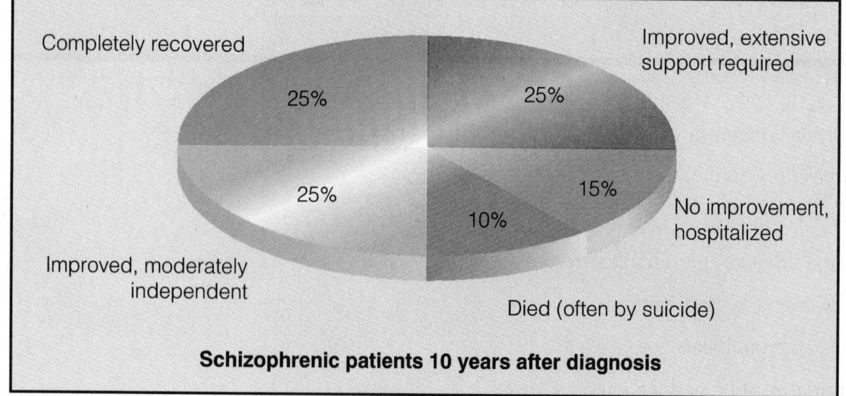

Question: What can be done about psychosis?

Two basic forms of treatment exist. The first, called **psychotherapy,** can be described as two people talking about one person's problems. Psychotherapy is a special relationship between a psychologist and a person in trouble. Psychotherapy may be applied to anything from a brief crisis to a full-scale psychosis. However, psychologists tend *not* to treat patients with major depressive disorders, schizophrenia, or similarly severe conditions. Major mental disorders are more often treated medically (Knesper, et al., 1989). Because approaches vary greatly, a complete discussion of psychotherapy is found in the next chapter.

A second major approach to treatment is **somatic** (bodily) **therapy.** The main somatic treatments are *chemotherapy*, *electroconvulsive therapy*, and *psychosurgery*. Somatic therapy is often done in the context of psychiatric *hospitalization.* All the somatic approaches have a medical slant and they are mostly used to treat psychoses and major mood disorders.

Drugs

The atmosphere in mental hospitals changed radically in the mid-1950s with the widespread adoption of chemotherapy (CHEM-oh-therapy). **Chemotherapy** is the use of drugs or chemical substances to alleviate the symptoms of emotional disturbance. Drugs may relieve the anxiety attacks and other discomforts of nonpsychotic disorders. More often, however, they are used to combat psychosis and major mood disorders.

Question: What types of drugs are used in chemotherapy?

The three major classes of drugs are *minor tranquilizers, major tranquilizers (antipsychotics),* and *antidepressants.* **Minor tranquilizers** calm anxious or agitated persons; **antidepressants** improve the mood of depressed individuals; and **antipsychotics** control hallucinations and other symptoms of psychosis.

Question: Are drugs a valid approach to treatment?

Drugs have shortened hospital stays and greatly improved the chances for recovery from psychiatric disorders. Because of drug therapy, it has become possible for many individuals to return to the community, where they can be treated on an "out-patient" basis.

Few experts would argue for a return to the conditions that existed before chemotherapy became available. But there are some drawbacks. First of all, drugs generally do not *cure* mental illness—they only relieve symptoms. If a patient stops taking his or her medication, the symptoms may return. Nevertheless, relief from symptoms may allow patients to benefit more fully from psychotherapy and other attempts to help them.

Limitations of Drug Therapy Many psychiatric drugs have adverse side effects. For example, 10 percent of patients taking major tranquilizers for long periods develop **tardive dyskinesia** (TAR-div dis-cah-NEE-zyah). This neurological condition is marked by rhythmic facial and mouth movements, such as chewing, sucking, or smacking the lips. Unusual movements of the arms (such as "fly-catching" motions) and other restless movements are also common (Rosenthal, 1993).

Perhaps the most valid criticism of chemotherapy is the simple observation that it is easily overused. Only about 50 percent of the victims of disabling mental illness are helped by drugs, but nearly all receive them. Apparently, there is a great temptation to reach for the prescription pad. Many observers agree that too many drugs are being given to too many people. Researcher David Rosenhan (whose work was described in the Applications section of Chapter 16) believes that drugs often are not merely given at therapeutic levels. Rather, they are sometimes used to keep patients docile and easy to manage. Many critics believe that the locks that came off the doors of old-style institutions have been replaced at times by "chemical locks" or "chemical straitjackets." Another problem is that the ease with which drugs can be given may discourage the use of psychotherapy. This and related controversies are explored further in Highlight 17–6.

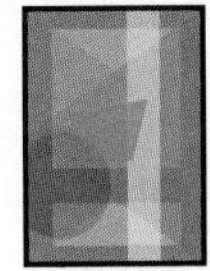

HIGHLIGHT 17–6

Focus on a Controversy

Psychiatric "Wonder Drugs"

New psychiatric drugs are often hailed as medical "miracles." However, all drugs involve a tradeoff between benefits and risks. For example, the new drug Clozaril (clozapine) can relieve the symptoms of schizophrenia in some previously "hopeless" cases. But Clozaril is nearly as dangerous as it is helpful: 2 out of 100 patients taking the drug suffer from a potentially fatal blood disease. Because of this risk, all patients must have a blood test once a week. Those whose white blood cell count drops below normal must immediately stop taking the drug or they will die. Is the risk worth it? Many experts think it is, because chronic schizophrenia robs people of almost everything that makes life worth living.

It's possible, of course, that newer drugs will improve the risk-benefit ratio in the treatment of schizophrenia. For example, the recently approved drug Risperdal (risperidone) appears to be as effective as Clozaril, without the lethal risk. It also shows no signs of causing tardive dyskinesia.

Prozac (fluoxetine) is another drug that has raised hopes for improved treatment. Prozac, a new antidepressant, is used primarily to treat mood disorders. Prozac is popular because it causes fewer side effects than other antidepressants. Soon after it was introduced, however, claims began to surface that people using Prozac tended to become suicidal. The verdict today? The risk of suicide is actually *lower* for patients taking Prozac than those taking a placebo (Tollefson et al., 1993).

While the suicide controversy has cooled, another is still blazing. Psychiatrist Peter Kramer (1993) has charged that Prozac alters the personalities of people who take it. In some cases, he believes, Prozac may be used to transform people into improved, but unnatural, versions of themselves. (Kramer calls this effect "cosmetic psychopharmacology.") Defenders of Prozac and similar drugs respond that what Kramer has observed is just the natural response to correcting a biochemical imbalance. Instead of becoming someone they're not, they say, patients feel more

Minor tranquilizers Drugs (such as Valium) that produce relaxation or reduce anxiety.

Antidepressants Mood elevating drugs.

Antipsychotics Drugs that, in addition to having tranquilizing effects, also tend to reduce hallucinations and delusional thinking.

Tardive dyskinesia A neurological disorder associated with excessive use of antipsychotic drugs.

Electroconvulsive therapy (ECT) A treatment for depression, consisting of an electric current passed through the brain, which induces a convulsion.

Psychosurgery Any surgical alteration of the brain that changes behavior or emotional response.

Prefrontal lobotomy An antiquated surgery in which portions of the frontal lobes were destroyed or disconnected from other brain areas.

like themselves than they have in years (Metzner, 1994).

Criticisms like Kramer's remain open to debate. What isn't disputed is that even the best new drugs are not cure-alls. They help for some people and for some problems, but not for all. It is noteworthy that for serious mental disorders a combination of medication and psychotherapy almost always works better than drugs alone. Drugs can be therapeutic, but they are seldom "miraculous." (Additional sources: Kemper, 1991; Maugh, 1992.)

In the long run, concern over side effects and the overuse of drugs may bring about a better balance between chemotherapy and psychotherapy. But where psychosis and mood disorders are concerned, drugs will undoubtedly remain a major mode of treatment.

Shock

Electroconvulsive therapy (ECT) is a rather drastic medical treatment for depression. In the usual ECT session, a 150-volt electrical current is passed through the brain for slightly less than a second (■ Fig. 17–13). The current triggers a convulsion and causes the patient to lose consciousness for a short time. Muscle relaxants and sedative drugs are given before ECT to soften its impact. Treatments are given in a series of 6 to 8 sessions spread over 3 to 4 weeks.

■ Fig. 17–13 *In electroconvulsive therapy, electrodes are attached to the head, and a brief electrical current is passed through the brain. ECT is used in the treatment of severe depression.*

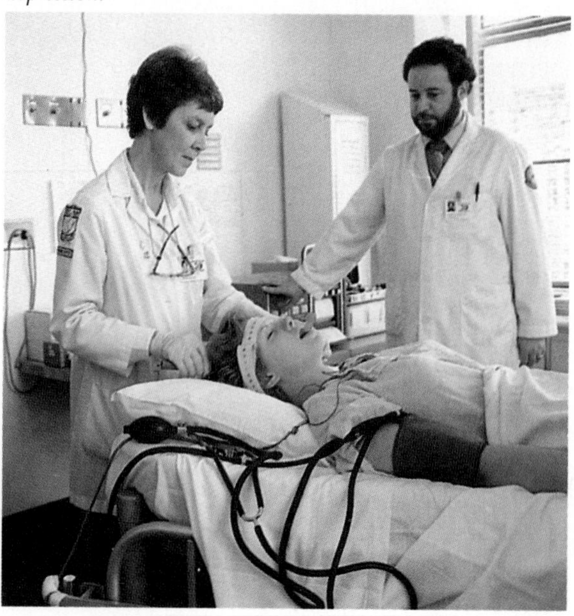

Question: How does shock help?

Actually, it is the seizure activity that is believed to be helpful. Proponents of ECT claim that shock-induced seizures alter the biochemical balance in the brain, bringing an end to severe depression and suicidal behavior (Swartz, 1993). Others have charged that ECT works only by confusing patients so they can't remember why they were depressed (Kohn, 1988).

The ECT Debate Many people consider ECT a distasteful procedure, and not all professionals support its use. In fact, experts continue to debate the value of ECT and the seriousness of its side effects. Critics claim that ECT causes permanent memory losses and occasional brain damage. Proponents of ECT argue that detailed brain scans show no evidence of damage (Kohn, 1988). Also, it has been reported that if electrodes are applied to only one side of the head, memory loss is greatly reduced (Rosenberg & Pettinati, 1984). However, ECT done in this way may not end depression (Sackheim et al., 1987).

Those who support ECT view it as being like any other medical treatment: It involves calculated risks (Weiner, 1984). As is true of chemotherapy, the major problem with ECT seems to lie in overuse and misuse. Some patients have had hundreds of shock treatments and have suffered damage in the process.

What, then, can be said about ECT? Most experts seem to agree on the following: (1) At best, ECT produces only temporary improvement—it gets the patient out of a bad spot, but it must be combined with other treatments; (2) ECT does cause permanent memory losses in many patients; and (3) ECT should be used only as a last resort after drug therapy has failed (Kohn, 1988). All told, ECT is considered by many to be a valid treatment for selected cases of depression—especially when it rapidly ends wildly self-destructive or suicidal behavior (Endler & Persad, in press; Isaac & Armat, 1990).

Psychosurgery

The most extreme biological treatment is **psychosurgery,** a general term applied to any surgical alteration of the brain. The best-known psychosurgery is the *lobotomy.* In the **prefrontal lobotomy** and related techniques, the frontal lobes are surgically disconnected from other areas of the brain. The original goal of this procedure was to calm persons who had not responded to any other type of treatment.

When the lobotomy was first introduced in the 1940s, there were enthusiastic claims for its success. But later studies suggested that some patients were calmed, some showed no noticeable change, and some became "vegetables." Lobotomies also produced a high rate of undesirable side effects, such as seizures, extreme lack of emotional response, and even stupor (Valenstein, 1980). As such problems became apparent, the lobotomy was abandoned.

Question: To what extent is psychosurgery used now?

Psychosurgery is still considered a valid treatment by many neurosurgeons. However, most now use sophisticated **deep lesioning** techniques. In this approach, small target areas are destroyed in the brain's interior. The appeal of deep lesioning is that it can have fairly specific effects. For instance, a patient with uncontrollable aggressive impulses may be calmed by psychosurgery (Valenstein, 1980).

It is worth remembering that all forms of psychosurgery are *irreversible*. A drug can be given or taken away. You can't take back psychosurgery. Many critics argue that psychosurgery should be banned altogether. Others continue to report success with psychosurgical procedures. All things considered, it is perhaps most accurate, even after decades of use, to describe psychosurgery as an experimental technique.

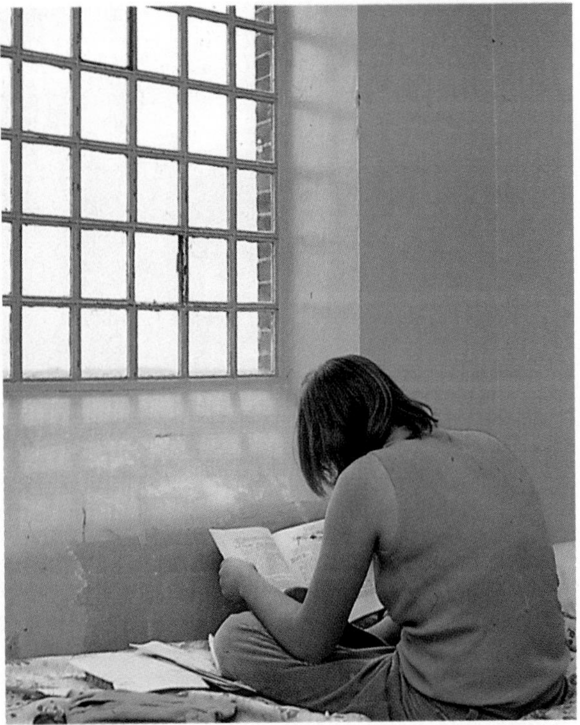

■ Fig. 17–14
Depending on the quality of the institution, hospitalization may be a refuge or a brutalizing experience. Many state "asylums" or mental hospitals are antiquated and in need of drastic improvement.

Hospitalization

Somatic therapy, psychotherapy, and other techniques may require a special setting or special control for a period of time. Traditionally, this has meant a trip to a psychiatric hospital or state institution. **Hospitalization** by itself is a form of treatment. Staying in a psychiatric ward removes patients from situations that may be provoking or maintaining their problems. At its best, the hospital is a sanctuary—a controlled environment in which diagnosis, support, refuge, and psychotherapy are provided (Bachrach, 1984). At worst, an institution can be a brutalizing experience that leaves a person less prepared to face the world than before (■ Fig. 17–14).

Hospitals are ideally used as a last resort after other forms of treatment within the community have been exhausted. Most psychiatric patients do as well with short-term hospitalization as they do with longer periods. For this reason, the average stay in psychiatric hospitals is now just 20 days, rather than 3 to 4 months, as it was 20 years ago.

A new emphasis in psychiatric treatment is called **partial hospitalization.** Patients in these programs no longer reside in institutions. Even for the acutely disturbed, over-night hospital stays are becoming less common. For example, some patients spend their days in the hospital, but go home at night. Others attend therapy sessions during the evening, after work. A major advantage of partial hospitalization is that patients can go home and practice what they've been learning. Gradually, the number of hours patients spend at the hospital is reduced. Eventually, most people return to normal life.

Deinstitutionalization In the last 30 years the population in large mental hospitals has dropped by two-thirds, a process called **deinstitutionalization.** This reduction was based, in part, on a desire to improve the odds that hospitalization would be helpful. Many long-term patients become so "institutionalized" that they have difficulty returning to the community. Traditionally, long-term hospitalization can lead to dependency, isolation, and continued emotional disturbance (Chamberlin & Rogers, 1990).

Question: How successful have such policies been?

In truth, their success has been limited. Many states welcomed a reduction in mental hospital populations as a way to save money. The upsetting result has been that many chronic patients were discharged to a lonely existence in hostile communities without adequate care. Many former patients have joined the ranks of the homeless (Rossi, 1990). Others are repeatedly jailed for minor crimes such as trespassing, vagrancy, and disturbing the peace (Shadish, et al., 1989). In short, patients who moved from hospitalization to unemployment, homelessness, and social isolation all too often are jailed or rehospitalized for further treatment (Rossi, 1990; Turkheimer & Parry, 1992).

Large mental hospitals may no longer be warehouses for society's unwanted, but many former patients are no better off in bleak nursing homes,

Deep lesioning Use of an electrode (electrified wire) to destroy small areas deep within the brain.

Mental hospitalization Confinement to a protected environment that provides therapy for mental, emotional, and behavioral problems.

Partial hospitalization Treatment in which patients spend only part of their time at the hospital.

Deinstitutionalization Reduced use of full-time commitment to mental institutions to treat mental disorders.

Half-way house A community-based facility for individuals making the transition from an institution (mental hospital, prison, and so forth) to independent living.

Community mental health center A facility offering a wide range of mental health services, such as prevention, counseling, consultation, and crisis intervention.

Paraprofessional An individual who works in a near-professional capacity under the supervision of a more highly trained person.

■ Fig. 17–15 *A well-run half-way house can be a humane and cost-effective way to ease former mental patients back into the community (Coursey, Ward-Alexander, & Katz, 1990).*

single-room hotels, board-and-care homes, jails, or shelters (Isaac & Armat, 1990). Ironically, high-quality care is available in almost every community. As much as anything, a simple lack of sufficient funding prevents large numbers of people from getting the help they need.

It would help greatly if better rehabilitation programs were offered after hospital treatment (Anthony, Cohen, & Kennard, 1990). One such approach is the use of **half-way houses,** which can ease a patient's return to the community. Half-way houses are short-term group living facilities (■ Fig. 17–15). Typically, they offer patients supervision and support, without being as restrictive and medically-slanted as hospitals. They also keep people near their families. Most important, half-way houses can reduce a person's chances of being readmitted to a hospital (Coursey, Ward-Alexander, & Katz, 1990).

Community Mental Health Programs

The creation of community mental health centers has been a bright spot in the area of mental health care. **Community mental health centers** attempt to shift emphasis away from hospitalization and seek new answers to mental health problems. Typically, they provide short-term treatment, out-patient care, and special crisis or emergency services (Spielberger & Stenmark, 1985).

If it is like most, the primary aim of the mental health center in your community is to directly aid troubled citizens. The second goal of mental health centers is *prevention.* Consultation, education, and crisis intervention are used to end or prevent problems before they become serious. Also, some centers attempt to raise the general level of mental health in target areas by combating problems such as unemployment, delinquency, and drug abuse (Levine et al., 1993).

Question: How have community mental health centers fared in meeting their goals?

In practice, they have concentrated much more on providing clinical services than they have on prevention. This situation appears to be primarily the result of wavering government support (translation: money). Overall, community mental health centers have succeeded in making mental health services more accessible than ever before. Many of their programs are made possible by **paraprofessionals,** individuals who work under the supervision of more highly trained staff. Some paraprofessionals are ex-addicts, ex-alcoholics, or ex-patients who have "been there." Many more are persons (paid or volunteer) who have skills in tutoring, crafts, or counseling or who are simply warm, understanding, and skilled at communication. There is a severe shortage of people working in mental health care. The contributions of paraprofessionals will undoubtedly continue to grow. A career as a paraprofessional should not be overlooked by students planning to work in the field of mental health (see Appendix A).

A Look Ahead By the time you finish reading this page, someone in the United States will have attempted suicide. Suicide is a disturbing and widely misunderstood problem. In the Applications section we will examine what is known about suicide and how it can sometimes be prevented. The Exploration section concludes with a provocative discussion of how our society handles "crazy" behavior.

LEARNING CHECK

1. The use of chemotherapy has required longer hospital stays since drugs can only be given under hospital supervision. T or F?
2. ECT is a modern form of chemotherapy. T or F?

3. Electroconvulsive therapy is used mainly as a treatment for depression. T or F?

4. Tardive dyskinesia is a possible complication in long-term use of
   a. major tranquilizers *b.* energizers *c.* minor tranquilizers *d.* ECT

5. Currently, the frontal lobotomy is the most widely used form of psychosurgery. T or F?

6. Psychosurgery can be reversed if it is unsuccessful. T or F?

7. Whenever possible, the community mental health movement emphasizes prevention of mental health problems. T or F?

8. Research indicates that relatively short periods of psychiatric hospitalization are as beneficial as long-term hospital stays. T or F?

9. The residents of Berkeley, California, once voted on a referendum to ban the use of ECT within city limits. Do you think that the use of certain psychiatric treatments should be controlled by law? ***Critical Thinking***

Answers: 1. F 2. F 3. T 4. *a* 5. F 6. F 7. T 8. T 9. The question of who can prescribe drugs, do surgery, and administer ECT is controlled by law. However, psychiatrists strongly object to residents, city councils, or government agencies making *medical* decisions.

APPLICATIONS: *Suicide—Lives on the Brink*

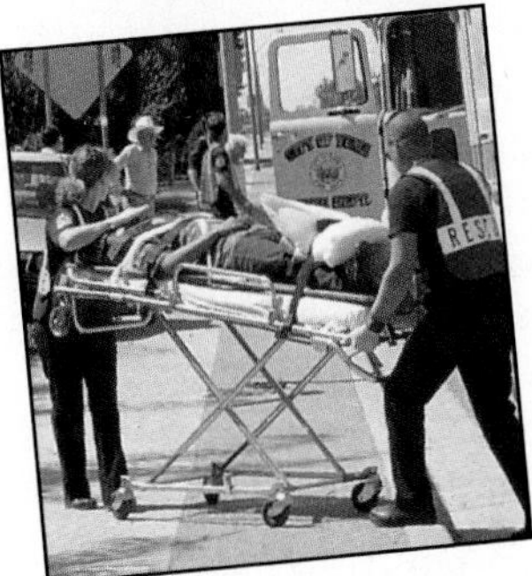

"Suicide: A permanent solution to a temporary problem."

Suicide ranks as the seventh cause of death in the United States. Roughly 1 person out of 100 attempts suicide during his or her lifetime. Sooner or later you are likely to be affected by the suicide attempt of a friend, relative, neighbor, or co-worker. Check your knowledge of suicide patterns against the following information.

Question: What factors affect suicide rates?

Season Suicide rates vary greatly, but some general patterns emerge. Contrary to popular belief, suicide rates are lower than average between Thanksgiving and Christmas (Phillips & Wills, 1987). On the other hand, more suicides take place at New Year's than during any other 24-hour period. A "Monday effect" also exists, with higher suicide rates occurring on the first day of the week. This pattern applies mainly to men, especially those between the ages of 41 and 65. It probably reflects the fact that traditional "breadwinners" can be especially depressed as they begin another work week—or another week of looking for a job (McCleary et al., 1991).

Sex Men have the questionable honor of being better at suicide than women. Three times as many men as women *complete* suicide, but women make more attempts. More men than women die by suicide because they typically use a gun or an equally fatal method (Garland & Zigler, 1993). Women most often attempt a drug overdose—a method that leaves greater chance of help arriving before death occurs. Sadly, women are beginning to use more lethal methods than in the past (Rogers, 1990). This, combined with a higher rate of attempts, may soon place women and men at equal risk of death by suicide.

Age Age is also a factor in suicide. Suicide rates gradually rise during adolescence. They then sharply increase during young adulthood (ages 20–24). From then until age 84 the rate continues to gradually rise with advancing age (Shneidman, 1987). As a result, more than half of all suicides are committed by individuals over 45 years old. However, there has been a steady increase in the total number of suicides by adolescents and young adults (Parachini, 1986). Part of this increase comes from the ranks of college students, where suicide is the leading cause of death. Contrary to popular belief, the most dangerous time for student suicide is the first 6 weeks of a semester, not during final exams.

School is a factor in some suicides, but only in the sense that suicidal students were not living up to their own extremely high standards. Many were good students. Other important factors in student suicide are chronic health problems (real or imagined) and interpersonal difficulties (some suicides are rejected lovers, but others are simply withdrawn and friendless people).

Of special concern to psychologists is the recent dramatic increase in adolescent suicides. At present,

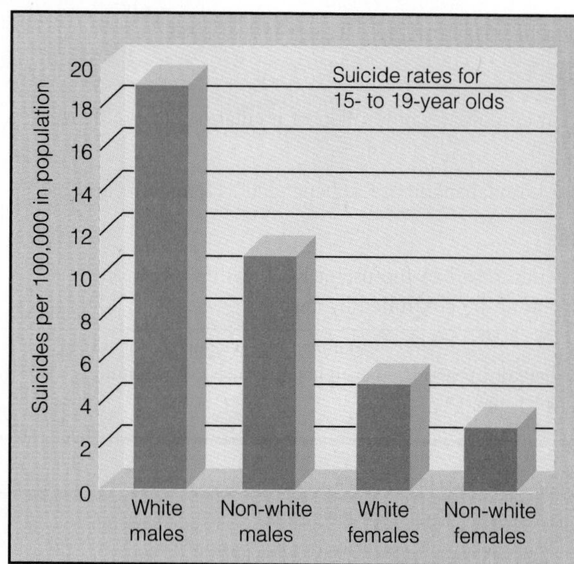

■ **Fig. 17–16** *Adolescent suicide rates vary for different racial and ethnic groups. Higher rates occur among whites than among non-whites. White male adolescents run the highest risk of suicide. Considering gender alone, it is apparent that more male than female adolescents commit suicide. This is the same as the pattern observed for adults.*

about 1 million teenagers attempt suicide each year in the United States and 7000 of those die (Cimons, 1991). This total—about 19 deaths per day—is triple the suicide rate reported 20 years ago (Garland & Zigler, 1993). Also distressing is the fact that an increasing number of youths employ such highly lethal methods as shooting themselves to commit suicide (■ Fig. 17–16).

Income Some professions, such as medicine and psychiatry, have higher than average suicide rates. Overall, however, suicide is quite democratic. It is equally a problem of the rich and the poor.

Marital Status An additional factor in suicide is marital status. Marriage (when successful) may be the best natural guard against suicidal impulses. The highest suicide rates are found among the divorced, the next highest rates occur among the widowed, lower rates are recorded for single persons, and married individuals have the lowest rates of all.

Question: Why do people try to kill themselves?

Immediate Causes of Suicide

Suicides typically combine three emotions: despair, guilt, and anger. In other words, the person wants to die (escape), wants to be killed (punished), and wants to hurt (or punish) others. Where do such feelings come from? Usually they are preceded by a history of interpersonal troubles with family, in-laws, or a lover or spouse. Often there are drinking problems, sexual adjustment problems, or job difficulties. (The highest risk for suicide involves this combination: Older divorced white male, physically ill, substance abuser, living alone.) ● Table 17–4 lists the major risk factors for suicide.

● **Table 17–4 Major Risk Factors for Suicide**

- Drug or alcohol abuse
- A prior suicide attempt
- Depression or other mood disorder
- Hopelessness
- Antisocial or aggressive behavior
- Family history of suicidal behavior
- Shame, humiliation, failure, or rejection
- Availability of a firearm

(Garland & Zigler, 1993)

A combination of factors such as these lead to severe depression and a preoccupation with death as the "answer" to the person's suffering. There is usually a break in communication with others that causes the person to feel isolated and misunderstood. Self-image becomes very negative. The person feels worthless and helpless and wants to die. Severe feelings of *hopelessness* are a warning that the risk of suicide is very high (Beck et al., 1990).

A long history of such conditions is not always necessary to produce a wish to die. People who attempt suicide are not necessarily "mentally ill." Anyone may temporarily reach a state of depression severe enough to attempt suicide. Most dangerous for the average person are times of divorce, separation, failure, and bereavement. Each can create what seems like an intolerable situation and can motivate an intense desire for escape.

The causes of increased adolescent suicide remain unclear. As with adults, there is often a backdrop of problems with drugs, depression, school, peers, family, divorced parents, or the breakup of a romance. To make matters worse, most adolescents who attempt suicide are socially isolated and poor at solving problems in their personal relationships (Cole et al., 1992; Sadowski & Kelley, 1993).

Some experts suggest that many cases of adolescent suicide result from unrealistic expectations. For example, parents may create feelings of despair by pressuring their children to meet impossibly high standards. Even without parental pressure, teenagers may expect the impossible of themselves in school, sports, romance, or progress toward a future career. Extremely high expectations and an unusual degree of sensitivity to hurt and disappointment can bring self-esteem to rock bottom over even the smallest "failure" (Cole et al., 1992; Mack, 1986). Again, the outcome is feelings of helplessness, hopelessness, and a desire to escape.

Preventing Suicide

Question: Is it true that people who talk about or threaten suicide are rarely the ones who try it?

No. This is one of the major fallacies about suicide. Of every 10 potential suicides, 8 give warning beforehand. A person who threatens suicide should be taken seriously—even one who seems to be "crying wolf." (See ■ Figure 17–17). A potential suicide may say nothing more than, "I feel sometimes like I'd be better off dead." Warnings may also come indirectly. If a friend gives you a favorite ring and says, "Here, I won't be needing this anymore," or comments, "I guess I won't get my watch fixed—it doesn't matter anyway," it may be a plea for help. The warning signs listed in ● Table 17–5, especially if observed in combination, can signal an impending suicide attempt (Larson, 1990).

Question: Is it true that suicide can't be prevented, that the person will find a way to do it anyway?

No. The decision to attempt suicide usually comes when a person is alone, depressed, and unable to view matters objectively. You *should* intervene if someone seems to be threatening suicide.

It is estimated that about two thirds of all suicide attempts fall in the "to be" category. That is, they are made by people who do not really want to die. Almost a third more are characterized by a "to be or not to be" attitude. These people are *ambivalent* or undecided about dying.

Only about 3 to 5 percent of cases represent individuals who definitely want to die. Most people, therefore, are relieved when someone comes to their aid. Remember that suicide is almost always a cry for help and that you *can* help. As suicide expert Edwin Shneidman (1987) puts it, "Suicidal behavior is often a form of communication, a cry for help born out of pain, with clues and messages of suffering and anguish and pleas for response."

● Table 17–5 Warning Signs of Potential Suicide

- Withdrawal from contact with others
- Sudden swings in mood
- Recent occurrence of life crisis or emotional shock
- Personality change
- Gift giving of prized possessions
- Depression
- Aggression and/or risk taking
- Preoccupation with death
- Direct threats to commit suicide

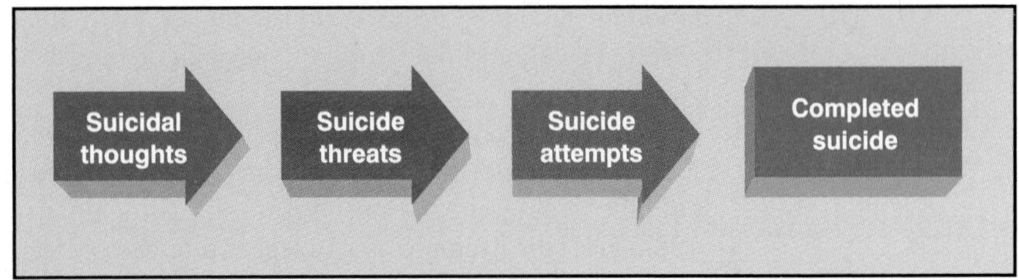

■ **Fig. 17–17** *Suicidal behavior usually progresses from suicidal thoughts, to threats, to attempts. A person is unlikely to make an attempt without first making threats. Thus, suicide threats should be taken seriously (Garland & Zigler, 1993).*

Question: What is the best thing to do if someone hints they are thinking about suicide?

How To Help

It helps to know some of the common characteristics of suicidal thoughts and feelings. Suicide expert Edwin Shneidman (1987) has identified several.

1. **Escape.** Everyone at times feels like running away from an upsetting situation. Running away from home, quitting school, abandoning a marriage—these are all departures. Suicide, of course, is the ultimate escape. It helps when suicidal persons see that the natural wish for escape doesn't have to be expressed by ending it all.
2. **Unbearable psychological pain.** Emotional pain is what the suicidal person is seeking to escape. A goal of anyone hoping to prevent suicide should be to reduce the pain in any way possible. Ask the person, "Where does it hurt?"
3. **Frustrated psychological needs.** Often, suicide can be prevented if a distraught person's frustrated needs can be identified and eased. Is the person deeply frustrated in his or her search for love, achievement, trust, security, or friendship?
4. **Constriction of options.** The suicidal person feels helpless and decides that death is the *only* solution. The person has narrowed all his or her options solely to death. The rescuer's goal, then, is to help broaden the suicidal person's perspective. Even when all the choices are unpleasant, suicidal persons can usually be made to see that their *least unpleasant option* is better than death.

Knowing these patterns will give some guidance in talking to a suicidal person. In addition, your most important task may be to establish *rapport* with the person. You should offer support, acceptance, and legitimate caring.

Remember that a suicidal person feels misunderstood. You should therefore try to accept and understand the feelings the person is expressing. Shneidman (1987) gives the example of a college senior who made straight A's for three and one-half years and then received a B. The student became deeply depressed and was determined to kill himself. His friends pointed out that he still had a 3.98 grade average. But by talking about grades they missed the point. The student's problem was the loss of his perfect record. It would be better to say, "I understand your desire to keep your perfect average. That grade must seem devastating." Acceptance should also extend to the idea of suicide itself. It is completely acceptable to ask, "Are you thinking of suicide?"

Establishing communication with suicidal persons may be enough to carry them through a difficult time. You may also find it helpful to get day-by-day commitments from them to meet for lunch, share a ride, and the like. Let the person know you *expect* her or him to be there. Such commitments, even though small, can be enough to tip the scales when a person is alone and thinking about suicide.

Don't end your efforts too soon. One of the most dangerous times for suicide is when a person suddenly seems to get better after a severe depression. Many experts agree that this often means that the person has finally made the decision to end it all. The improvement in mood is deceptive because it comes from an anticipation that suffering is at an end.

Crisis Intervention There are over 300 centers for suicide prevention in the United States, and most sizable cities have mental health crisis intervention teams. Both services have staff trained to talk with suicidal persons over the phone. Give a person who seems to be suicidal the number of one of these services. Urge the person to call you or the other number if he or she becomes frightened or impulsive. Or better yet, help the person make an appointment to get psychological treatment (Garland & Zigler, 1993).

The preceding applies mainly to persons who are having mild suicidal thoughts. If a person actually threatens suicide, you must act more quickly. Ask how the person plans to carry out the suicide. A person who has a *concrete, workable plan*, and the means to carry it out, should be asked to accompany you to the emergency ward of a hospital.

If a person seems on the verge of attempting suicide, don't worry about overreacting. Call the police, crisis intervention, or a rescue unit. Needless to say, you should call immediately if a person is in the act of attempting suicide or if a drug has already been taken. The majority of suicide attempts come at temporary low points in a person's life and may never be repeated. Get involved—you may save a life!

Suicide: A Summary of Facts

The following is a list of useful facts to know about suicide.

1. More men than women commit suicide; but women make more attempts.
2. College students are most likely to attempt suicide during the first part of the school quarter or semester.
3. Many people temporarily become depressed enough to contemplate suicide. Those who would attempt suicide are not all psychotic or suffering from lasting mental illness.
4. Suicide strikes both the rich and the poor.
5. A person who is suicidal once may never again become suicidal. Preventing suicide is well worth the effort.
6. Most potentially suicidal persons give warning.
7. People who talk about suicide *do* often attempt it.
8. The majority of people (two thirds) who attempt suicide do not really want to die, and most of the remainder are ambivalent about dying.
9. A *sudden* improvement in mood after a suicidal depression can mean that the person has decided to carry out a suicide attempt.
10. Four major characteristics of the suicidal state are (1) psychological pain, (2) frustrated needs, (3) a desire to escape, and (4) constricted options.
11. Suicide can often be prevented by the efforts of family, friends, and mental health professionals.

Learning Check

1. More women use guns in their suicide attempts than do men. T or F?
2. While the overall suicide rate has remained about the same, there has been a decrease in adolescent suicides. T or F?
3. Suicide is equally a problem of the rich and the poor. T or F?

APPLICATIONS: *Continued*

4. The highest suicide rates are found among divorced males. T or F?
5. The majority (two-thirds) of suicide attempts fall in the "to be" category. T or F?
6. What two major risk factors contributed to the 1994 suicide of Kurt Cobain, lead singer for the rock group Nirvana? ***Critical Thinking***

Answers: 1. F 2. F 3. T 4. T 5. T 6. Drug or alcohol abuse and availability of a firearm.

EXPLORATION

Who Is "Crazy" and What Should Be Done about It?

The best-known critic of traditional psychiatric treatment for "mental illness" is psychiatrist Thomas Szasz (pronounced saz). Szasz (1966, 1983, 1987) believes that mental illness is a myth. Szasz charges that traditional medical concepts of diseases have been wrongly applied to emotional problems. The *medical model,* as it is called, treats such problems as "diseases" with "symptoms" that can be "cured."

Szasz believes that brain diseases eventually may be found, but that they are not empirically demonstrated as yet. He thus regards "mental illness" as just an idea used when trying to deal with disturbing behavior. If "mental patients" starve themselves, attack members of their families, commit arson or theft, kill themselves, or kill prominent persons, what does psychiatry do? It pardons them (says they are not responsible for their actions) and imprisons them (commits them to a mental hospital for "treatment"). Or, it says they are sane, responsible, and guilty of a crime. In this case they are imprisoned in jail. Szasz believes that labels such as *psychosis* are used mainly to transform people from being responsible for their actions to being non-responsible "patients" who need pity and therapy.

Another of Szasz's points is that "mental illness" and all its categories are merely descriptions of the unlimited variety of human behavior. The labels used to classify mental illness do not explain anything. They are merely applied to behaviors that violate social or psychiatric norms. Thus, the concept of mental illness is used to deal with persons whose behavior creates a *social disturbance* or violates social rules. If a person acts in a way that "offends" society and a law exists against such acts, the person may be jailed. If no law exists, the person may be "treated." In this sense, the distinction between madness and badness, or mental illness and criminality, is a *moral judgment,* not a medical reality.

In light of such thinking, Szasz and a number of other experts prefer to view emotional disturbances as "problems in living." This view makes the goal of therapy "change" rather than "cure" and changes "patients" to "clients." It has also led Szasz to question the handling of the civil rights of psychiatric "patients." Szasz estimates that 90 percent of all patients in mental hospitals are there involuntarily. He sees this as a serious mistake. To commit people because they *might* be dangerous to themselves is indefensible by Szasz's standards.

According to Szasz, the only legitimate reason for depriving a person of freedom is for being "dangerous to others," but then only if the person has broken the law by committing violence or by threatening to do so. Szasz considers the vast majority of "disturbed" persons as no more dangerous than a randomly selected group of citizens. He therefore rejects involuntary commitment as "punishment without trial, imprisonment without limit, and stigmatization without hope of redress."

Point and Counterpoint Szasz does not assert that bizarre behavior is normal. His position is merely that it cannot be explained or sensibly treated using a strict medical model. Szasz's critics reply that advances in neuroscience increasingly call his ideas into question. Certainly, a brain damaged by disease, accident, or drugs can lead to illness, including mental or emotional illness. Szasz's reply is that clearly demonstrated brain abnormalities still apply to only a small percentage of all cases of psychopathology.

It is undoubtedly a mistake to assume that the arguments raised by Szasz justify abandoning the tremendous advances in mental health care found in current approaches. All societies have classified some of their members into categories analogous to our term "mentally ill." The social problems created by "crazy" behavior will not vanish by changing the words used to describe it. Szasz does, however, raise serious questions about civil rights and involuntary commitment.

Recently, several states have made it easier to force the mentally ill into hospitals (Shogren, 1994). Forced treatment might appear to be humane in some instances. But as a final bit of food for thought, consider the following incident, recorded by a reporter visiting a large state mental hospital.

EXPLORATION

A thin man, old and dry, stopped the guide and said, "When the hell you gonna get me a suit and let me outa here? How about it? . . . ." The guide said something indefinite and the man walked away, nodding. This was the section for killers, I had been told, so I asked what the thin man had done. "He painted a horse." "He what?" "He painted a horse." "What's wrong with that?" "It was in a field. A live horse. He was drunk and somebody bet him he couldn't make a horse look like a zebra, I think, so he painted it and they put him here. For being drunk probably." "How long has he been in?" "Thirty-seven years. By the time they got around to letting him out he really was crazy . . . . For his own good we just can't let him go out of here."*

*Bruce Jackson, "Our prisons are criminal," *New York Times Magazine,* September 22, 1973, pp. 54–57.

On what basis should we as a society involuntarily commit people? How often would ending involuntary commitment mean freedom to wander lost and neglected on the streets, without family, friends, or hope? Is it better to force mentally ill persons off the streets and into hospitals? What do you think is the right way to deal with "crazy" behavior?

LEARNING CHECK

1. Szasz has argued that it is inappropriate to apply a medical or disease model to what he terms "problems in living." T or F?
2. Szasz points out that most people in mental hospitals are there voluntarily. T or F?
3. Psychosis is the only disorder that Szasz recognizes as a legitimate mental disease. T or F?

Critical Thinking

4. The new trend that favors forcing the chronically mentally ill off the streets and into hospitals is a reversal of an earlier trend. Can you name the former pattern?

Answers: 1. T 2. F 3. F 4. Deinstitutionalization

Chapter Summary

■ ***What are the general characteristics of psychosis?***

- **Psychosis** is a break in contact with reality that is marked by **delusions, hallucinations, sensory changes, disturbed emotions and communication,** and in some cases, **personality disintegration.**
- Psychotic symptoms tend to be most prominent during short *episodes* of increased disturbance.
- A **brief reactive psychosis** may follow extremely stressful life events.
- An **organic psychosis** is based on known injuries or diseases of the brain. Other problems of unknown origin are termed **functional psychoses.**
- Three common causes of organic psychosis are *untreated syphilis* **(general paresis),** *poisoning,* and **senile dementia** (especially **Alzheimer's disease**).

■ ***How do delusional disorders differ from other forms of psychosis?***

- A diagnosis of **delusional disorder** is almost totally based on the presence of delusions of grandeur, persecution, infidelity, romantic attraction, or physical disease.
- The most common delusional disorder is **paranoid psychosis.** Because they often have intense and irrational delusions of persecution, paranoids may be violent if they believe they are threatened.

■ ***What forms does schizophrenia take?***

- **Schizophrenia** is the most frequently occurring psychosis. It is distinguished by a split between thought and emotion, and by delusions, hallucinations, and communication difficulties.
- Schizophrenia should not be confused with multiple personality disorder or with **schizotypal personality disorder,** which involves gradual withdrawal into isolation from others and odd, apathetic behavior.
- **Disorganized schizophrenia** is marked by extreme personality disintegration and silly, bizarre, or obscene behavior. Social impairment is usually extreme.
- **Catatonic schizophrenia** is associated with *stupor, mutism,* and odd postures. Sometimes violent and agitated behavior also occurs.
- In **paranoid schizophrenia** (the most common subtype), outlandish delusions of grandeur and persecution are coupled with psychotic symptoms and personality breakdown.

- **Undifferentiated schizophrenia** is the term used to indicate a lack of clear-cut patterns of disturbance.

■ ***What causes schizophrenia?***

- Current explanations of schizophrenia emphasize a combination of *environmental stress, inherited susceptibility*, and *biochemical abnormalities* in the body or brain.
- A number of environmental factors appear to increase the risk of developing schizophrenia. These include viral infection during the mother's pregnancy, birth complications, early **psychological trauma,** and a **disturbed family environment,** especially one marked by **deviant communication.**
- Studies of twins and other close relatives strongly support *heredity* as a major factor in schizophrenia. Recent biochemical studies have focused on abnormalities in brain transmitter substances, especially **dopamine** and its receptor sites.
- Additional abnormalities in brain structure or activity have been detected in schizophrenic brains by the use of **CT scans, MRI scans,** and **PET scans.**
- The dominant explanation of schizophrenia is the **stress-vulnerability model.**

■ ***What are mood disorders? What causes depression?***

- **Mood disorders** primarily involve disturbances of mood or emotion, producing *manic* (agitated, elated, hyperactive) or *depressive* (sad, apathetic, suicidal) states.
- Long-lasting, though relatively moderate, depression is called a **dysthymic disorder.** Chronic, though moderate, swings in mood between depression and elation are called a **cyclothymic disorder. Reactive depressions** are often triggered by external events; however, they are more intense or prolonged than normal.
- **Major mood disorders** involve extremes of mood or emotion. **Bipolar disorders** combine mania and depression.
- In a **bipolar I disorder** the person is mostly manic, but has had at least one major depression. In a **bipolar II disorder** the person is mostly depressed, but has had at least one manic episode.
- The problem known as **major depressive disorder** involves extreme sadness and despondency, but no evidence of mania.
- When a major mood disorder is accompanied by psychotic symptoms, it is called an **affective psychosis.**
- **Postpartum depression** is a mild to moderate depressive disorder that affects many women after they give birth. Postpartum depression is more serious than the more common **maternity blues.**
- **Seasonal affective disorder (SAD),** which occurs during the winter months is another common form of depression. SAD is typically treated with **phototherapy.**
- *Biological, psychoanalytic, cognitive,* and *behavioral* theories of depression have been proposed. Heredity is clearly a factor in susceptibility to mood disorders. Research on the causes and treatment of depression continues.

■ ***How are major mental disorders treated?***

- Three **somatic** approaches to treatment of psychosis are **chemotherapy** (use of drugs), **electroconvulsive therapy (ECT)** (brain shock for the treatment of depression), and **psychosurgery** (surgical alteration of the brain). All three techniques are capable of producing serious side effects, and all are controversial to a degree because of questions about effectiveness and side effects.
- **Hospitalization** is often associated with the administration of somatic therapy, and it is also considered a form of treatment.
- Prolonged hospitalization has been discouraged by **deinstitutionalization** and by **partial-hospitalization** policies. As long as community care remains poor however, repeated hospitalization is likely.
- A development in mental health care that seeks to avoid or minimize hospitalization is the creation of **community mental health centers.** Community mental health centers also have as their goal the prevention of mental health problems through education, consultation, and **crisis intervention.**

■ ***Why do people commit suicide? Can suicide be prevented?***

- Suicide is statistically related to such factors as age, sex, and marital status. However, in individual cases the potential for suicide is best identified by a *desire to escape, unbearable psychological pain, frustrated psychological needs,* and a *constriction of options.*
- Suicide can often be prevented by the efforts of family, friends, and mental health professionals.

■ ***What does it mean to be "crazy"? What should be done about it?***

- Thomas Szasz has raised challenging questions about the nature of abnormal behavior and its relationship to personal responsibility and civil rights.
- Public policies concerning treatment of the chronically mentally ill continue to evolve as authorities try to strike a balance between providing help and taking away personal freedoms.

Questions for Discussion

1. What positive and negative roles do mental institutions and private psychiatric hospitals play in society?
2. Is Szasz justified in his appraisal of mental institutions as simply prisons by another name?
3. Do you think Szasz is unrealistically romantic in his approach to mental illness, or is he the wave of the future?
4. A social critic once charged that, "The psychiatrist unfailingly recognizes the madman by his excited behavior on being incarcerated." Do you agree or disagree?
5. Under what circumstances would you consider it reasonable for a stranger to be involuntarily committed? A friend? A close relative? Yourself?
6. In your opinion how could a person experiencing a severe "problem in living" be most effectively helped?
7. Should a mental patient have the right to refuse medication? To demand legal counsel and alternative medical opinions? To refuse to work in a mental hospital or to choose the work that will be done? To communicate by phone, letter, or in person with anyone at any time? To keep personal property (including drugs, matches, pocketknives, and other potentially harmful materials? To request an alternative to legal commitment to a mental hospital? To be represented by an independent "advocate" who is not on the hospital staff?
8. In view of what you know about the causes of psychosis, how valid do you consider the medical model of mental illness? What are the advantages and disadvantages of such a model? What are the advantages and disadvantages of a psychological model?
9. If the genetic component is large in major problems such as schizophrenia and mood disorders, should we try genetically to identify individuals at risk when no sure treatments are available? Should people who are close relatives of affected persons receive special counseling?
10. It may soon become possible to tell before birth if a fetus carries genes for early-onset Alzheimer's disease. If familial Alzheimer's is detected, should the parents be told?
11. The parents of John Hinkley (who attempted to assassinate President Reagan) have complained that "The comedian Robin Williams has great fun making sick jokes about 'crazies' like our son John, but does he joke about muscular dystrophy or cancer? Of course not." Do you agree or disagree with the point they are making?
12. In 1991 a book containing detailed instructions about how to commit suicide was published. The book, entitled *Final Exit*, was an instant best-seller. Why do you think the book was so popular? Do you think it is ethical to make suicide instructions readily available to the public? Is suicide, or assisting the suicide of another person, ever ethical? When and why?

Chapter 18

Therapies

CHAPTER PREVIEW

Quiet Terror on a Spring Afternoon

The warm California sun was shining brightly. Outside my office window an assortment of small birds sang to a beautiful spring day. I could hear them between Susan's frightened sobs.

As a psychologist, I see many students with personal problems. Still, I was somewhat surprised to see Susan at my office door. Her excellent work in class and her healthy, casual appearance left me unprepared for her first words. "I feel like I'm losing my mind," she said. "Can I talk to you?"

In the next hour, Susan sketched the features of her own personal hell. Her calm exterior hid a world of overwhelming fear, anxiety, and depression. She had lost several part-time jobs because at each one she began to fear her co-workers and the customers so much that she could barely bring herself to speak to them. Her social phobia led to absenteeism and embarrassing interchanges with customers. At each job she held it was only a matter of time until she got fired.

At school Susan felt "different" and was sure that other students could tell she was "weird." Several disastrous romances had left her terrified of men. Lately she had become so depressed that she had begun to think frequently of suicide. At times she became so terrified for no apparent reason that her heart pounded wildly and she felt that she was about to lose control of herself completely.

IN THIS CHAPTER

Susan's visit to my office was an important turning point. Emotional conflicts had made her existence a living nightmare. At a time when she was becoming her own worst enemy, Susan realized that she needed the help and support of another person. In Susan's case, that person was a talented psychologist to whom I referred her. By combining various forms of psychotherapy, the psychologist was able to help Susan come to grips with her emotions and return a healthy balance to her personality.

This chapter discusses psychological methods used to alleviate problems like Susan's. First, we will describe therapies that emphasize the value of gaining insight *into personal problems. Later, we will focus on* behavior therapies *and* cognitive therapies, *which are used to directly change troublesome actions and thoughts.*

Survey Questions

- How do psychotherapies differ?
- How did modern therapies originate?
- Is Freudian psychoanalysis still used?
- What are the major humanistic therapies?
- What is aversion therapy?
- How is behavior therapy used to treat phobias, fears, and anxieties?
- What role does reinforcement play in behavior therapy?
- Can therapy change thoughts and emotions?
- Can psychotherapy be done with groups of people?
- What do various therapies have in common?
- How are behavioral principles applied to everyday problems?
- How would a person go about finding professional help?
- Do cultural differences affect counseling and psychotherapy?

Psychotherapy Any psychological technique used to facilitate positive changes in a person's personality, behavior, or adjustment.

Psychotherapy—Getting Better by the Hour

Humpty-Dumpty sat on a wall.
Humpty-Dumpty had a great fall.
All the King's horses and all the King's men,
Couldn't put Humpty together again.

In our age of stress, conflict, and anxiety, who will put you together again, and how will they do it? Actually, the odds are good that you will *not* experience a life-impairing emotional problem like Susan's, but if you did, what kind of help is available? In most cases, the answer is some form of *psychotherapy.*

Question: What is psychotherapy?

Psychotherapy is any psychological technique used to facilitate positive changes in a person's personality, behavior, or adjustment. The psychotherapist has many approaches to choose from: psychoanalysis, desensitization, Gestalt therapy, logotherapy, client-centered therapy, reality therapy, behavior therapy—to name but a few.

Due to an explosive growth in the number of therapies, some confusion may exist about how they differ. To begin, it is helpful to recognize that psychotherapies vary widely in emphasis, as described in Highlight 18–1. For this reason, the best approach may differ for a particular person or problem.

HIGHLIGHT 18–1

A Closer Look At

Dimensions of Therapy

The term *psychotherapy* most often refers to verbal interaction between trained mental health professionals and their clients. Many therapists also use learning principles to directly alter troublesome behaviors, as described later in this chapter.

The terms listed here describe basic aspects of various therapies. Notice that more than one term may apply to a particular therapy. For example, it would be possible to have a directive, action-oriented group therapy or a non-directive, individual, insight-oriented therapy.

- **Individual therapy** A therapy involving only one client and one therapist.
- **Group therapy** A therapy session in which several clients participate at the same time.

■ **Insight therapy** Any psychotherapy whose goal is to lead clients to a deeper understanding of their thoughts, emotions, and behavior.

■ **Action therapy** Any therapy designed to bring about direct changes in troublesome thoughts, habits, feelings, or behaviors, without seeking insight into their origins or meanings.

■ **Directive therapy** Any approach in which the therapist provides strong guidance.

■ **Non-directive therapy** A style of therapy in which clients assume responsibility for solving their own problems; the therapist assists, but does not guide or give advice.

■ **Time-limited therapy** Any therapy begun with the expectation that it will last only a certain limited number of sessions.

■ **Supportive therapy** An approach in which the therapist's goal is to offer support, rather than to promote personal change. A person trying to get through an emotional crisis or one who wants to solve day-to-day problems may benefit from supportive therapy.

Myths Popular accounts tend to depict psychotherapy as a complete personal transformation—a sort of "major overhaul" of the psyche. But this ignores the realities of solving human problems. Therapy is *not* equally effective for all problems. Chances of improvement are fairly good for phobias, low self-esteem, some sexual problems, and marital conflicts. More complex problems, however, can be difficult to treat. Also, contrary to what many people think, therapy usually does not bring about dramatic changes in behavior or an end to personal problems. For many people, the major benefit is that therapy provides comfort, support, and a way to make constructive changes (Zilbergeld, 1983).

In short, it is often unrealistic to expect psychotherapy to undo a person's entire past history. Yet even when problems are severe, therapy may help a person gain a new perspective or learn behaviors to better cope with life (Carson & Butcher, 1992). Psychotherapy can be hard work for both client and therapist. But when it succeeds, there are few activities more rewarding.

As a final point, you should note that psychotherapy is not always undertaken to solve a psychological problem or crisis. Therapy can also encourage personal growth and enrichment for people who are already functioning effectively (Buck, 1990). Table 18–1 lists some widely accepted elements of positive mental health that therapists seek to restore or promote (Bergin, 1991).

Table 18–1 Elements of Positive Mental Health

- Personal autonomy and independence
- A sense of identity
- Feelings of personal worth
- Skilled in interpersonal communication
- Sensitivity, nurturance, and trust
- Genuine and honest with self and others
- Self-control and personal responsibility
- Committed and loving in personal relationships
- Capacity to forgive others and oneself
- Personal values and a purpose in life
- Self-awareness and motivation for personal growth
- Adaptive coping strategies for managing stresses and crises
- Fulfillment and satisfaction in work
- Good habits of physical health

(Adapted from Bergin, 1991.)

Origins of Therapy—Bored Skulls and Hysteria on the Couch

The history of treatment for psychological problems gives ample reason for appreciating modern therapies. Archaeological findings dating to the Stone Age suggest that most primitive approaches were marked by fear and superstitious belief in demons, witchcraft, and magic. One of the more dramatic "cures" practiced by primitive "therapists" was a process called **trepanning** (treh-PAN-ing; also sometimes spelled *trephining*). A hole was bored, chipped, or bashed into the skull of the patient, presumably to relieve pressure or release evil spirits (■ Fig. 18–1). Actually, trepanning may have simply been an excuse to kill people who were unusual, since many of the "patients" didn't survive the "treatment."

During the Middle Ages, treatment for the mentally ill in Europe focused on **demonology.** Abnormal behavior was attributed to supernatural forces such as possession by the devil or the curses of witches and wizards. As a treatment, **exorcism** was used to drive out the evil. For the fortunate, exorcism was a religious ritual. More often, it took the form of physical torture to make the body an inhospitable place for the devil to reside (■ Fig. 18–2).

One explanation for the rise of demonology may lie in a condition called **ergotism** (AIR-got-ism). In the Middle Ages, rye fields were often infested with ergot fungus. Ergot, we now know, is a natural source of LSD and other mind-altering chemicals. Eating bread made from tainted grain can cause symptoms that might easily be interpreted as possession, bewitchment, or madness. Pinching sensations, convulsions, muscle twitches, facial spasms, delirium, and visual hallucinations are all common reactions to ergot poisoning (Kety, 1979; Matossian, 1982). Thus, many of

Trepanning In modern usage, any surgical procedure in which a hole is bored in the skull; historically, the chipping or boring of holes in the skull to "treat" mental disturbance.

Demonology In medieval Europe, the study of demons and the treatment of persons "possessed" by demons.

Exorcism In medieval Europe, the practice of expelling or driving off an "evil spirit," especially one residing in a person who is "possessed."

Ergotism A pattern of psychotic-like symptoms that accompanies poisoning by ergot fungus.

■ **Fig. 18–1** *Primitive "treatment" for mental disorders sometimes took the form of boring a hole in the skull. This example shows signs of healing, which means the patient survived the treatment. Many didn't.*

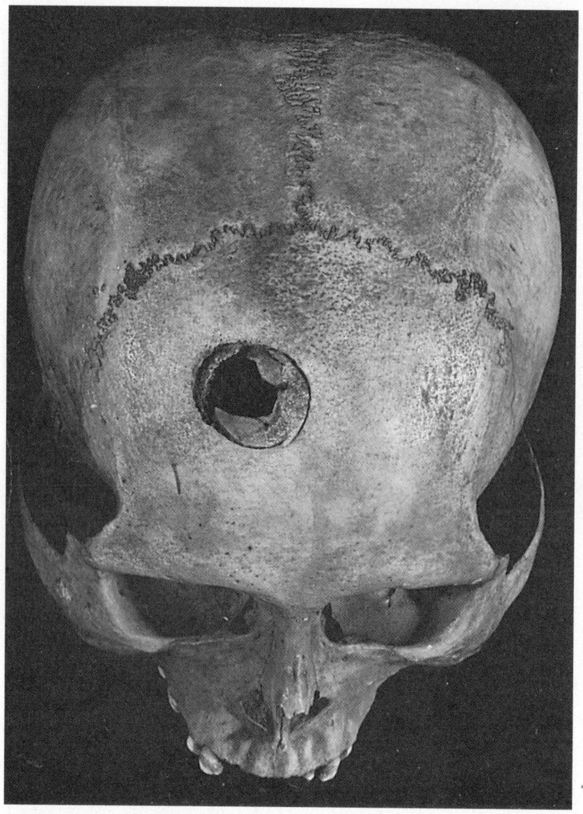

the "patients" of demonology may have been doubly victimized (■ Fig. 18–3).

The idea that the emotionally disturbed are "mentally ill" and that they should be treated compassionately emerged after 1793. This was the year **Philippe Pinel** changed the Bicêtre Asylum in Paris from a squalid "madhouse" into a mental hospital by personally unchaining the inmates. Although over 200 years have passed since Pinel began humane treatment for the emotionally disturbed, the process of improving conditions in psychiatric hospitals and of changing public attitudes toward psychotherapy continues today.

Increased acceptance of the value of psychotherapy is a positive sign, but public attitudes toward the disturbed still tend to be colored by suspicion and fear. Perhaps as more people take part in psychotherapy as a growth experience, it will become more widely understood.

Question: When was psychotherapy developed?

The first true psychotherapy was developed around the turn of the century by Sigmund Freud. As a physician in Vienna, Freud was intrigued by the cases of **hysteria** he encountered (physical symptoms such as paralysis or numbness without known physical cause). As you

■ **Fig. 18–2** (left) *Many early asylums were no more than prisons with inmates held in chains.* (right) *One late nineteenth-century "treatment" was based on swinging the patient in a harness—presumably to calm the patient's nerves.*

■ Fig. 18–3 (top) *Supernatural explanations attributed abnormal behavior to the work of the devil or "possession" by demons, like the one pictured.* (bottom) *Actually, many cases of "possession" in medieval Europe and "bewitchment" in colonial New England may be explained by the psychedelic effects of ergot fungus. Two ears of rye infested with the fungus (dark areas) are shown here.*

may recall, such problems are now called *somatoform disorders* (see Chapter 16). Slowly, Freud became convinced that the symptoms of hysteria were only the tip of the iceberg and that deeply hidden unconscious conflicts (frequently sexual in nature) were to blame. Based on this insight, Freud went on to develop his own form of therapy. Since **psychoanalysis,** as Freud called his technique, is the "granddaddy" of most modern psychotherapies, let us examine it in some detail.

Psychoanalysis—Expedition into the Unconscious

Question: Isn't psychoanalysis the therapy where the patient lies on a couch?

Freud's patients usually reclined on a couch during therapy, while Freud sat out of sight taking notes and offering interpretations. This arrangement was selected

■ Fig. 18–4 *Pioneering psychotherapist Sigmund Freud in his office.*

to encourage relaxation and a free flow of thoughts and images from the unconscious (■ Fig. 18–4). It is the least important characteristic of psychoanalysis and many modern analysts have abandoned it.

Question: How did Freud treat emotional problems?

Freud's theory stressed that repressed memories, motives, and conflicts—particularly those stemming from instinctual drives for sex and aggression—were the cause of neurosis. Although unconscious and repressed, these factors remain active in the personality, forcing the person to develop rigid ego-defense mechanisms and to devote excessive amounts of time and energy to compulsive and self-defeating behavior. Freud relied on four basic techniques to uncover the unconscious roots of neurosis (Freud, 1949). These are **free association, dream analysis, analysis of resistance,** and **analysis of transference.**

Free Association During psychoanalysis, the patient must say whatever comes to mind without regard for whether it makes sense or is painful or embarrassing. Thoughts are allowed to move freely from one association to the next.

Dream Analysis The purpose of free association is to lower defenses so that unconscious material may emerge. Freud also considered dreams an unusually good way to tap the unconscious. Freud referred to dreams as "the royal road to the unconscious" because he felt that forbidden desires and unconscious feelings are more freely expressed in dreams. He distinguished

Hysteria Wild emotional excitability associated with apparent physical disabilities (numbness, blindness, and the like) that have no known physical cause.

Psychoanalysis Freudian therapy that emphasizes the discovery of unconscious conflicts.

Free association Having a client say anything that comes to mind, regardless of how unimportant it may seem.

Manifest dream content The surface, "visible" content of a dream.

Latent dream content The hidden or symbolic meaning of a dream, as revealed by dream interpretation.

Dream symbols Images in dreams whose personal or emotional meanings differ from their literal meanings.

Resistance Blocking that occurs during free association; topics the client resists thinking or talking about.

Transference The tendency to direct feelings toward a therapist that match feelings the client had for important persons in his or her past.

Short-term dynamic therapy Modern psychodynamic therapy designed to produce insights within a shorter time than traditional psychoanalysis.

Spontaneous remission The disappearance of a psychological disturbance without the aid of therapy.

Waiting-list control group People who receive no treatment in tests of the effectiveness of psychotherapy.

between the **manifest** (obvious, visible) **content** and the **latent** (hidden) **content** of dreams.

To appreciate fully the unconscious message of a dream, Freud sought to reveal its latent meaning by interpreting **dream symbols.** Let's say a young husband reports a dream in which he pulls a pistol from his waistband and aims at a target while his wife watches. The pistol repeatedly fails to discharge, and the man's wife laughs at him. Freud might see this as an indication of repressed feelings of sexual impotence, with the gun serving as a disguised image of the penis.

Analysis of Resistance When free associating or describing dreams, the patient may *resist* talking about or thinking about certain topics. Such **resistances** are said to reveal particularly important unconscious conflicts. As the analyst becomes aware of resistances, he or she brings them to the patient's awareness so they can be dealt with realistically.

Analysis of Transference The individual undergoing psychoanalysis may transfer feelings to the therapist that relate to important past relationships with others. At times the patient may act as if the analyst were a rejecting father, an unloving or overprotective mother, or a former lover. **Transference** is considered a prime opportunity to help the patient undergo an emotional re-education. As the patient re-experiences repressed emotions, the therapist can help the patient recognize and understand them. Troubled individuals often provoke anger, rejection, boredom, criticism, and other negative reactions from others. Effective therapists learn to avoid reacting as others do, and playing the patient's habitual "games." This, too, contributes to therapeutic change (Strupp, 1989).

Question: Is psychoanalysis still used?

Psychoanalysis Today Traditional psychoanalysis called for 3 to 5 therapy sessions a week, often for many years. Because of the huge amount of time and money this requires, psychoanalysts have become relatively rare. Today, most therapists who use psychoanalytic theory have switched to doing **short-term dynamic therapy.** In this approach, therapists rely on direct interviewing to more rapidly uncover unconscious conflicts (Davanloo, 1980). They also seek to actively provoke emotional reactions that lower defenses and provide insights. By such means, the length of therapy has been shortened considerably (Eckert, 1993; Trujillo, 1986).

The development of newer, more streamlined dynamic therapies is in part due to questions about the effectiveness of traditional psychoanalysis. One critic, H. J. Eysenck (1967), went so far as to suggest that psychoanalysis simply takes so long that there is a **spontaneous remission** of symptoms (improvement due to the mere passage of time). How might we tell if a particular therapy, or the passage of time is responsible for a person's improvement? Typically, some individuals are randomly assigned for treatment, while others are placed on a waiting list. If members of this **waiting-list control group** improve at the same rate as those in therapy, the therapy may be of little value.

How seriously should the possibility of spontaneous remission be taken? It is true that problems ranging from hyperactivity to anxiety improve with the passage of time. However, researchers have confirmed that psychoanalysis is usually better than no treatment at all (Bergin & Suinn, 1975). Also, therapists are continuing to refine psychoanalysis in ways that are making it more effective (Weiss, 1990).

The value of Eysenck's critique and of others that followed is that they encouraged psychologists to try new ideas and techniques. Researchers began to ask: "When psychoanalysis works, why does it work? What procedures are essential, and which are unnecessary?" Based on intuition, personal philosophy, clinical experience, and the personality theory they find most acceptable, modern therapists have given surprisingly varied answers to these questions. Upcoming sections will acquaint you with some of the therapies currently in use.

LEARNING CHECK

See if you can answer the following questions. If you miss any, review the previous sections.

Match:

____ 1. Directive therapies	**A.** Change behavior
____ 2. Action therapies	**B.** Place responsibility on client
____ 3. Insight therapies	**C.** The client is guided strongly
____ 4. Non-directive therapies	**D.** Seek understanding

5. Pinel is famous for his use of exorcism. T or F?

6. Freud developed trepanning. T or F?

7. In psychoanalysis, an emotional attachment to the therapist by the patient is called
a. free association *b.* manifest association *c.* resistance *d.* transference

8. Waiting-list control groups help separate the effects of therapy from improvement related to the mere passage of time. What other type of control group might be needed to learn if therapy is truly beneficial? ***Critical Thinking***

Answers: 1. C 2. A 3. D 4. B 5. F 6. F 7. d 8. Placebo therapy is sometimes used to assess the benefits of real therapy. Placebo therapy superficially resembles the real thing, but lacks key elements that are thought to be therapeutic.

Humanistic Therapies—Restoring Human Potential

The goal of traditional psychoanalysis is adjustment. Freud was actually quite conservative in his claims: Any of his patients, he said, could expect only to change their "hysterical misery into common unhappiness"! The humanistic therapies outlined in upcoming sections are generally more optimistic. Most assume that it is possible for people to live rich and rewarding lives and to make full use of their potential. Psychotherapy is seen as a means of giving natural tendencies toward mental health a chance to emerge.

Question: What is client-centered therapy? How is it different from psychoanalysis?

Client-Centered Therapy

Psychoanalysts delve into childhood, dreams, and the unconscious. Psychologist Carl Rogers (1902–1987) found it more productive to explore *conscious* thoughts and feelings (■ Fig. 18–5). The psychoanalyst tends to take a position of authority from which he or she offers interpretations of what is "wrong" with the patient or of what dreams or childhood experiences "mean." Rogers believed that what is right or valuable for the therapist may not be right and valuable for the client. (Rogers preferred the term *client* to *patient* because "patient" implies a person is "sick" and needs to be "cured.") **Client-centered therapy** (also called person-centered therapy) is *non-directive.* The client is the center of a process of personal growth. He or she determines what will be discussed during each session.

■ **Fig. 18–5** *Psychotherapist Carl Rogers, who originated client-centered therapy.*

Client-centered therapy A non-directive therapy based on gaining insights from conscious thoughts and feelings; emphasizes accepting one's true self.

Unconditional positive regard Unshakable personal acceptance of another person.

Empathy A capacity for taking another's point of view; the ability to feel what another is feeling.

Authenticity The ability of a therapist to be genuine and honest regarding his or her feelings.

Reflection The process of rephrasing or repeating thoughts and feelings so clients can hear what they are saying about themselves.

Question: If the client runs things, what does the therapist do?

The therapist's job is to create an "atmosphere of growth" by maintaining four basic conditions.

Health-Promoting Conditions First, the therapist offers the client **unconditional positive regard.** In other words, the client is accepted *totally.* The therapist refuses to react with shock, dismay, or disapproval to anything the client says or feels. Total acceptance by the therapist is the first step to self-acceptance by the client.

Second, the therapist attempts to achieve genuine **empathy** for the client by trying to see the world through the client's eyes and by trying to feel some part of what he or she is feeling.

As a third essential condition, the therapist strives to be **authentic** in his or her relationship with clients. The therapist must not hide behind a professional role. Rogers believed that phony fronts and facades destroy the growth atmosphere sought in client-centered therapy.

Fourth, the therapist does not make interpretations, propose solutions, or offer advice. Instead, the therapist **reflects** the client's thoughts and feelings. By repeating or restating what the client has said, or by telling the client what emotion he or she seems to be displaying, the therapist serves as a psychological "mirror." In this way, clients learn to see themselves more clearly and realistically. Rogers believed that a person armed with a realistic self-image and with a new level of self-acceptance will gradually discover solutions to life problems. His faith in the capacity for emotional health is movingly expressed in Highlight 18–2.

Existential therapy An insight therapy that focuses on the problems of existence, such as death, meaning, choice, and responsibility; emphasizes making courageous life choices.

Free will The presumed ability of humans to freely make choices not determined by heredity, past conditioning, or other dictates.

Death, freedom, isolation, meaninglessness The universal challenges of existence, including: an awareness of one's mortality; the responsibility that comes with freedom to choose; the fact that each person is ultimately isolated and alone in his or her private world; and the reality that meaning must be created in life.

Logotherapy A form of existential therapy that emphasizes the need to find and maintain meaning in one's life.

Confrontation In existential therapy, confronting clients with their own values and with the need to take responsibility for the quality of their existence.

Gestalt A German word meaning form, pattern, or whole.

Gestalt therapy Focuses on immediate awareness to help clients rebuild thinking, feeling, and acting into connected wholes; emphasizes the integration of fragmented experiences.

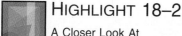

HIGHLIGHT 18–2

A Closer Look At

Carl Rogers and Personal Growth

Like other humanistic psychologists, Carl Rogers (1980) believed deeply that there is a natural human urge to seek health and self-growth. Rogers' belief is vividly expressed by the following words:

> I remember that in my boyhood the bin in which we stored our winter's supply of potatoes was in the basement, several feet below a small window. The conditions were unfavorable, but pale white sprouts . . . would grow two or three feet in length as they reached toward the light of the distant window. The sprouts were, in their bizarre, futile growth, a sort of desperate expression of the directional tendency I have been describing. . . . In dealing with clients whose lives have been terribly warped, in working with men and women on the back wards of state hospitals, I often think of those potato sprouts. . . . The clue to understanding their behavior is that they are striving, in the only ways that they perceive as available to them, to move toward growth, toward becoming. To healthy persons, the results may seem bizarre and futile but they are life's desperate attempt to become itself. This potent constructive tendency is an underlying basis of the person-centered approach.

Existential Therapy

According to the existentialists, "being in the world" (existence) creates deep and unavoidable conflicts. Each of us, they say, must deal with the realities of death. We must face the fact that each person creates his or her private world by making choices. We must overcome the isolation of living on a vast and indifferent planet. We must confront depressing feelings of meaninglessness.

Question: What do these concerns have to do with psychotherapy?

Like client-centered therapy, **existential therapy** tries to promote self-knowledge and self-actualization. However, there are important differences. Client-centered therapy seeks to uncover a "true self" hidden behind an artificial screen of defenses. In contrast, existential therapy emphasizes the idea of **free will.** That is, through *choices* one can *become* the person he or she wants to be.

Existential therapy attempts to restore meaning and vitality to life so that the individual has the *courage* to make rewarding and socially constructive choices. Typically, existential therapy focuses on the "ultimate concerns" of human existence. These include the inescapable givens of **death, freedom, isolation,** and **meaninglessness** (Yalom, 1980).

Question: What does an existential therapist do?

One example of existential therapy is Victor Frankl's **logotherapy.**

Frankl (1955) developed his approach on the basis of experiences in a Nazi concentration camp. In the camp Frankl observed the breakdown of countless prisoners as they were stripped of all hope and human dignity. Frankl felt that those who survived with their sanity did so because they had managed to hang on to a sense of *meaning* (logos). In some cases this was nothing more than the ultimate human freedom—the freedom to choose one's own attitude in any set of circumstances.

Like most existential therapists, Frankl used a flexible approach centered around **confrontation.** The person is challenged to examine the quality of his or her existence and choices and to *encounter* the unique, intense, here-and-now interaction of two human beings. When existential therapy is successful, it brings about a reappraisal of what's important in life. Indeed, some clients experience an emotional rebirth not unlike that seen in people who have survived a close brush with death. Logotherapy is regarded as successful when clients regain a strong sense of purpose and meaning in life (Dyck, 1987).

Gestalt Therapy

Gestalt therapy, which is most often associated with Frederick (Fritz) Perls (1969), is built around the idea that perception, or *awareness,* becomes disjointed and incomplete in the maladjusted individual. The Gestalt approach is more directive than either client-centered therapy or existential therapy and it places a special emphasis on immediate experience.

Question: What does Gestalt mean?

The German word **Gestalt** means "whole," or "complete." The Gestalt therapist seeks to help the individual rebuild thinking, feeling, and acting into connected wholes. This is achieved by expanding personal awareness, by accepting responsibility for one's thoughts, feelings, and actions, and by filling in gaps in experience.

Question: What do you mean by gaps in experience?

Gestalt therapists believe that we often shy away from expressing or "owning" upsetting feelings. This creates a gap in self-awareness that may become a barrier to personal growth. For example, a person who feels anger after the death of a parent might go for years without expressing it. This and similar threatening gaps may block emotional health.

Working either one-to-one or in a group setting, the Gestalt therapist encourages the individual to become more aware of his or her immediate experience. Rather than discussing *why* he or she feels guilt, anger, fear, or boredom, the client is encouraged to have these feelings in the "here and now" and to become fully aware of them. The therapist helps promote awareness by drawing attention to the client's posture, voice, and eye or hand movements. The client may also be asked to exaggerate a vague feeling until it becomes clear. Gestalt therapists believe that expressing such feelings allows people to "take care of unfinished business" and break through emotional impasses.

In all his writings, Perls' basic message comes through clearly: Emotional health comes from knowing what you *want* to do, not dwelling on what you *should* do, *ought* to do, or *should want* to do. Another way of stating this idea is that emotional health comes from taking full responsibility for one's feelings and actions. For example, it means changing "I can't" to "I won't," or "I must" to "I choose to."

Question: How does Gestalt therapy help people discover their real wants?

Above all else, Gestalt therapy emphasizes *present* experience. Clients are urged to stop intellectualizing and talking *about* feelings. Instead they learn to: live now; live here; stop imagining; experience the real; stop unnecessary thinking; taste and see; express rather than explain, justify, or judge; give in to unpleasantness and pain just as to pleasure; surrender to being as you are (Naranjo, 1970).

LEARNING CHECK

See if you can answer the following questions.

Match:

______ 1. Client-centered therapy — A. Meaning
______ 2. Gestalt therapy — B. Unconditional positive regard
______ 3. Existential therapy — C. Gaps in awareness
______ 4. Logotherapy — D. Choice and becoming

5. The Gestalt therapist tries to *reflect* a client's thoughts and feelings. T or F?

6. Client-centered therapy is directive. T or F?

7. Confrontation and encounter are concepts of existential therapy. T or F?

8. How might using the term *patient* affect the relationship between a person seeking help and a therapist? ***Critical Thinking***

Answers: 1. B 2. C 3. D 4. A 5. F 6. F 7. T 8. The terms *doctor* and *patient* imply a large gap in status and authority between a person and his or her therapist. Client-centered therapy attempts to narrow this gap by making the person the final authority concerning solutions to his or her problems.

Behavior Therapy—Healing by Learning

Five times a day, for several days, Brooks Workman stopped what she was doing and vividly imagined opening a soft-drink can. She then pictured herself bringing the can to her mouth and placing her lips on it. Just as she was about to drink, hordes of roaches poured out of the can and scurried into her mouth—writhing, twitching, and wiggling their feelers (Williams & Long, 1991).

Question: Why would anyone imagine such a thing?

Brooks Workman's behavior is not as strange as it sounds. Her goal was self-control: Brooks felt that she was drinking too many colas and she wanted to cut down. The method she chose (called *covert sensitization*) is a form of **behavior therapy** (Cautela & Kearney, 1986). Behavioral approaches include behavior modification, aversion therapy, systematic desensitization, token economies, and other techniques. In each instance, learning principles are employed to make constructive changes in behavior.

Behavior therapy The use of learning principles to make constructive changes in behavior.

Behavior therapists believe that insight, or deep understanding of one's problems, is often unnecessary for improvement. Instead, behavior therapists try to directly alter troublesome thoughts and actions. Brooks Workman didn't need to probe into her past or her emotions and conflicts; she simply wanted to break her habit of drinking too many colas. Even when serious problems are at stake, techniques like the one she used have proved valuable.

Question: In general, how does behavior therapy work?

Behavior modification The direct application of classical and operant conditioning to change human behavior.

Classical conditioning A basic form of learning in which existing (reflex) responses become associated with new stimuli.

Conditioned aversion A learned dislike or conditioned negative emotional response to some stimulus.

Aversion therapy Suppression of a response by associating it with aversive (painful or uncomfortable) stimuli.

Rapid smoking Prolonged smoking at a forced pace; used to produce an aversion to smoking.

Behavior therapy is based on one basic assumption: People have *learned* to be the way they are. Consequently, if they have learned responses that cause problems, then they can change them or *relearn* more appropriate responses. Broadly speaking, **behavior modification** refers to any attempt to use the learning principles of *classical* (*respondent*) *conditioning* and *operant conditioning* to change human behavior.

Question: How does classical conditioning work? I'm not sure I remember.

Classical conditioning was described in Chapter 7. Here is a brief review of conditioning principles:

> A neutral stimulus is followed by an *unconditioned stimulus (US)* that consistently produces an unlearned reaction, called the *unconditioned response (UR)*. Eventually the previously neutral stimulus begins to produce this response directly. The response is then called a *conditioned response (CR)*, and the stimulus becomes a *conditioned stimulus (CS)*. Thus, for a child the sight of a hypodermic needle (CS) is followed by an injection (US), which causes anxiety or fear (UR). Eventually the sight of a hypodermic (the conditioned stimulus) may produce anxiety or fear (a conditioned response) *before* the child gets an injection.

Question: What does classical conditioning have to do with behavior modification?

Classical conditioning can be used to associate discomfort with a bad habit. Psychologists call discomfort used in this way an *aversion*. An aversion may be used to combat an undesirable habit, as in the case of the woman who wanted to drink fewer colas. When more powerful versions of this approach are used, it is called *aversion therapy*.

Aversion Therapy—A Little Pain Goes a Long Way

Imagine that you are eating an apple. Suddenly you discover that you just bit a large green worm in half. You vomit. Months pass before you can eat an apple again without feeling ill. You now have a *conditioned aversion* to apples.

Question: How is a conditioned aversion used in therapy?

In **aversion therapy,** an individual learns to associate a strong aversion (or negative emotional response) to an undesirable habit such as smoking, drinking, or gambling. Aversion therapy has been used to cure hiccups, sneezing, stuttering, vomiting, bed-wetting, marijuana smoking, compulsive hair-pulling, and alcoholism. It is also used in the treatment of fetishism, transvestism, and other "maladaptive" sexual behaviors. (To learn how aversion therapy can help people quit smoking, see Highlight 18–3). There is little doubt that aversive conditioning is an everyday occurrence. For example, not many physicians who treat lung cancer are smokers nor do many emergency room doctors drive without using their seat belts (Rosenthal & Steffek, 1991).

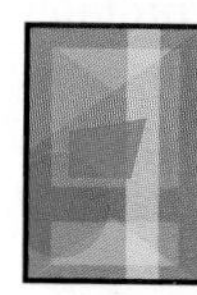

HIGHLIGHT 18–3
Using Psychology

Puffing Up an Aversion

The fact that nicotine is toxic makes it easy to create an aversion to smoking. Behavior therapists have found that electric shock, nauseating drugs, and similar aversive stimuli are not required to make smokers uncomfortable. All that is needed is for the smoker to smoke—rapidly and for a long time.

Rapid smoking is the most widely used aversion therapy for smoking (Lichtenstein, 1982). In this method, clients are told to smoke continuously, taking a puff every 6 to 8 seconds. Rapid smoking continues until the smoker is miserable and can stand it no more. By then, most people are thinking, "I never want to see another cigarette for the rest of my life."

Studies suggest that rapid smoking is one of the most effective behavior therapies for smoking (Tiffany et al., 1986). Nevertheless, anyone tempted to try rapid smoking should realize that it is very unpleasant. Without the help of a therapist, most people quit too soon for the procedure to succeed. (An alternative method that is more practical is described in the Applications section of this chapter.)

The most basic problem with rapid smoking—as with other stop-smoking methods—is that about one half of those who quit smoking begin again. During at least the first year after quitting, there is no "safe point" after which relapse becomes less likely (Swan & Denk, 1987).

Because the "evil weed" calls so strongly to former smokers, support from a stop-smoking group or a close, caring person can make a big difference. Former smokers who get encouragement from others are much more likely to stay smoke free (Gruder et al., 1993). Those whose social groups include many smokers are more likely to begin smoking again (Mermelstein, 1986).

An excellent example of aversion therapy is provided by the work of Roger Vogler and his associates (1977). Vogler works with alcoholics who are unable to stop drinking. For many clients, aversion therapy is a last chance. They have often been threatened with desertion by relatives and friends, have lost their jobs, and have tried Alcoholics Anonymous, psychotherapy, detoxification, vitamin therapy, and even Antabuse therapy. (Antabuse is a drug that causes an alcoholic to become violently nauseated after he or she drinks.) Here is a typical aversion procedure:

> While drinking an alcoholic beverage, painful (although non-injurious) electric shocks are delivered to the client's hand. From the client's point of view, the shocks are unpredictable; he or she never knows for sure when one is due. Most of the time, however, the shocks come as the client is beginning to take a drink of alcohol (■ Fig. 18–6).

This *response-contingent* (or response-connected) shock obviously takes the pleasure out of drinking. Shocks also cause the alcohol abuser to develop a conditioned aversion to drinking. Normally, misery caused by alcohol abuse comes long after the act of drinking—too late to have much effect. But if we can link the sight and smell of alcohol with *immediate* discomfort, then drinking will begin to make the individual very uncomfortable.

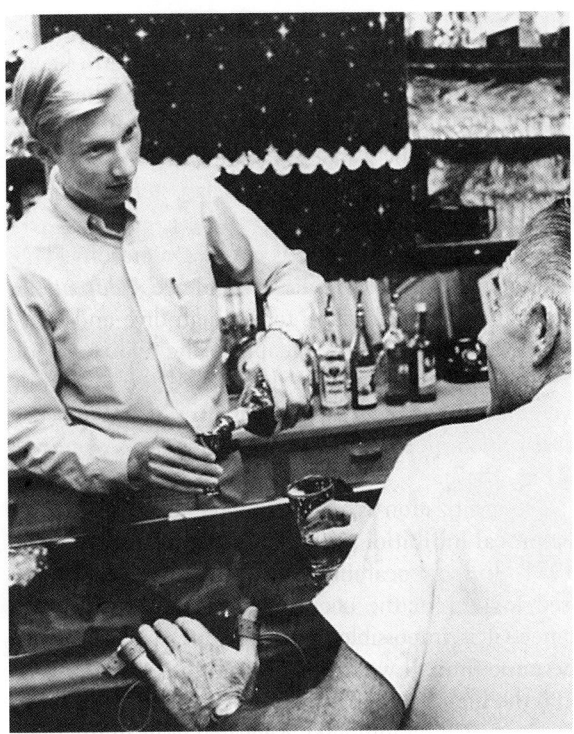

■ **Fig. 18–6** *Aversion therapy for drinking. The sights, smells, and tastes of drinking are associated with unpleasant electric shocks applied to the hand.*

Question: But can't the person tell when it is "safe" to drink and when it is not?

Transfer, or *generalization*, of aversion conditioning to the "real world" is a problem. With this in mind, Vogler constructed in his office a vivid re-creation of a "friendly neighborhood tavern," complete with a bar, tables, soft lights, music, and a bartender. Also provided are a "living room," a "bedroom," and a "kitchen." Clients undergo aversion therapy in a setting as much like the normal site of their drinking as possible, and carryover of the aversion training is improved.

Actually, aversion therapy is used as a last resort, even for problems as serious as alcohol abuse. Vogler and his associates also train alcoholics to discriminate blood alcohol levels (so clients can tell how drunk they are). They teach alcoholics alternatives to drinking and offer education programs on alcohol abuse as well as general counseling (Vogler et al., 1977). They have also added an interesting twist to their aversion therapy: Alcohol abusers are videotaped as they go from sober to drunk. Later, they watch the videotaped drinking bout and see themselves with slurred speech, dropping cigarette ashes in their drinks and saying stupid and belligerent things. Most react with shame and embarrassment when they see the tapes. Apparently, few people have any idea how unattractive they are when drunk.

To add to the effect, the bartender is trained to provoke clients into becoming argumentative and obnoxious. Presumably, this is not too hard to do by the time the client is saying, "I am 'masshhhed' " (Vils, 1976). In the videotape self-confrontation held later, grossly drunken behaviors are replayed until the client says, "Okay, okay, I've seen enough." Seeing themselves as obnoxious drunks adds to the aversion people feel for drinking, and it increases their determination to quit.

Response contingent Applying reinforcement, punishment, or other consequences only when a certain response is made.

Generalization Transfer of a learned response from one stimulus situation to other similar situations.

Question: I'm not sure I'm comfortable with the idea of treating humans this way.

People are often disturbed (shocked?) by such methods. It must be emphasized that clients usually volunteer for aversion therapy because it helps them overcome a destructive habit. Indeed, commercial aversion programs for overeating, smoking, and alcohol abuse have attracted large numbers of willing customers. And more importantly, aversion therapy can be justified by its long-term benefits. As behaviorist Donald Baer put it, "A small number of brief, painful experiences is a reasonable exchange for the interminable pain of a lifelong maladjustment" (Baer, 1971).

Desensitization—Who's Afraid of a Big, Bad Hierarchy?

Assume that you are a swimming instructor who wants to help a child overcome fear of the high diving board. How might you proceed? Directly forcing a terrified

5. What two principles underlie systematic desensitization? ______________ and ______________

6. When desensitization is carried out through the use of live or filmed models, it is called
a. cognitive therapy *b.* flooding *c.* covert desensitization *d.* vicarious desensitization

7. The three basic steps in systematic desensitization are: Construct a hierarchy, flood the person with anxiety, and imagine relaxation. T or F?

Critical Thinking

8. If alcoholics who take Antabuse become ill after drinking alcohol, why don't they develop an aversion to drinking?

Answers:

1. classical (or respondent), operant 2. *c* 3. response 4. T 5. adaptation, reciprocal inhibition 6. *d* 7. F 8. Their discomfort is delayed enough to prevent it from being closely associated with drinking. Fortunately, there are safer, better ways to do aversion therapy.

Operant conditioning Learning based on the consequences of making a response.

Extinction A gradual decrease in the frequency of a non-reinforced response.

Time out Removing a person from a situation in which rewards for maladaptive behavior are available, in order to produce extinction; also, withholding social reinforcers (attention, approval) when undesirable responses are made.

Operant Principles—All the World Is a Skinner Box?

Question: Aversion therapy and desensitization are forms of behavior modification based on classical conditioning. Where does operant conditioning fit in?

The principles of operant conditioning were developed by B. F. Skinner and other psychologists mostly through laboratory research with animals. The operant principles most frequently used by behavior therapists to deal with *human* behavior are:

1. **Positive reinforcement.** An action that is followed by reward will occur more frequently. If children whine and get attention, they will whine more frequently. If you get A's in your psychology class, you may become a psychology major.
2. **Non-reinforcement.** An action that is not followed by reward will occur less frequently.
3. **Extinction.** If a response is not followed by reward after it has been repeated many times, it will go away. After winning three times, you pull the handle on a slot machine 30 times more without a payoff. What do you do? You go away. So does the response of handle pulling (for that particular machine, at any rate).
4. **Punishment.** If a response is followed by discomfort or an undesirable effect, the response will be suppressed (but not necessarily extinguished).
5. **Shaping.** Shaping means rewarding actions that are closer and closer approximations to a desired response. If a response is complicated, it may never occur and thus may never be rewarded. If I want to reward a retarded child for saying "ball," I may begin by rewarding the child for saying anything that starts with a *b* sound.
6. **Stimulus control.** Responses tend to come under the control of the situation in which they occur. If I set my clock 10 minutes fast, I can get to work on time in the morning. My departure is under the stimulus control of the clock, even though I know it is fast.
7. **Time out.** A time-out procedure usually involves removing the individual from a situation in which reinforcement occurs. Time out prevents reward from following an undesirable response; it is a variation of non-reinforcement. For example, children who fight with each other can be sent to separate rooms and allowed out only when they are able to behave more calmly (Olson & Roberts, 1987). (For a more thorough review of operant principles, return to Chapter 7.)

As simple as these principles may seem, they have been used very effectively by behavior modification specialists to overcome difficulties in work, home, school, and industrial settings. Let's see how.

Non-Reinforcement and Extinction—Time Out in the Attention Game

An extremely overweight mental patient had a persistent and disturbing habit: She stole food from other patients. No one could persuade her to stop stealing or to diet. For the sake of her health, a behavior therapist assigned her a special table in the ward dining room. If she approached any other table, she was immediately removed from the dining room. Since her attempts to steal food went unrewarded, they rapidly disappeared. Additionally, any attempt to steal from others usually resulted in the patient's missing her own meal (Ayllon, 1963).

Question: What operant principles did the therapist in this example use?

The therapist used *non-reward* to produce *extinction.* The most frequently occurring human behaviors lead to some form of reward. An undesirable response can be eliminated by *identifying* and *removing* the rewards that maintain it. But people don't always do things for food, money, or other obvious rewards. Most of the rewards maintaining human behavior are more subtle.

Attention, *approval*, and *concern* are common yet powerful reinforcers for humans (■ Fig. 18–9).

For instance, in a classroom we often find that misbehaving children are surrounded by others who giggle and pay attention to them. If seating is rearranged so that the disruptive children are surrounded by less responsive students, misbehavior decreases. Attention from a teacher (even scolding) can also be a reinforcer. An experiment showed that when teachers paid extra attention to classroom misbehavior, it increased. It increased even when the attention took the form of saying things such as "Sit down!" When misbehaving children were *ignored* and attention was given to children who were *not* misbehaving, misbehavior decreased (Madsen et al., 1968).

Question: How are non-reward and extinction applied in therapy?

Non-reward and extinction can eliminate many problem behaviors, especially in schools, hospitals, and institutions. Often, difficulties center around a limited number of particularly disturbing responses. A typical strategy used in institutions is called *time out*. Time out means refusing to reward maladaptive responses, usually by refusing to play the *attention* game. Another form of time out is to remove an individual immediately from the setting in which an undesirable response occurs, so that the response will not be rewarded. For example:

> Fourteen-year-old Josh periodically appeared in the nude in the activity room of a training center for disturbed juveniles. This behavior always generated a great deal of attention from staff and other patients. Usually Josh was returned to his room and confined there. During this "confinement," he often missed doing his usual chores. As an experiment he was placed on time out. The next time he appeared nude, counselors and other staff members greeted him normally and then ignored him. Attention from other patients rapidly subsided. Sheepishly he returned to his room and dressed.

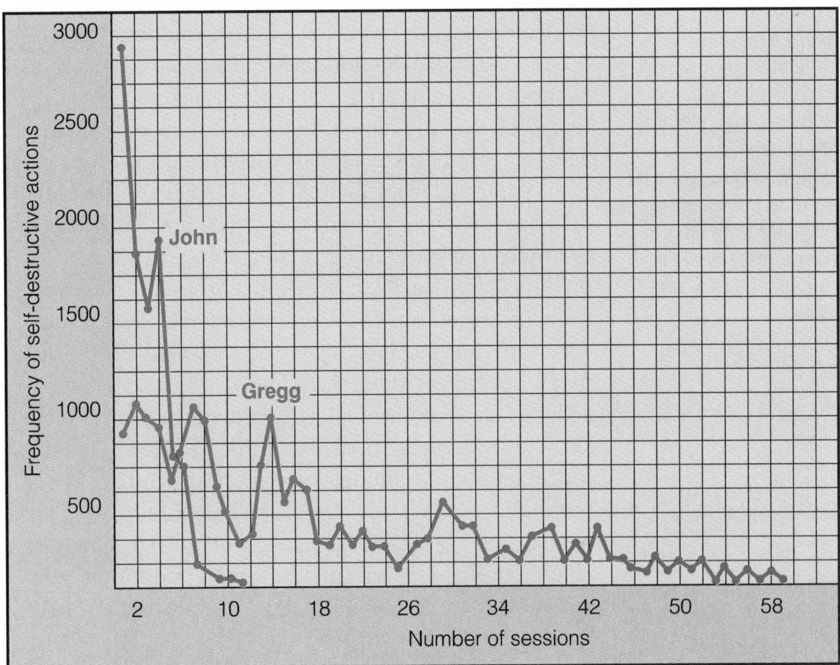

■ **Fig. 18–9** *This graph shows extinction of self-destructive behavior in two autistic boys. Before extinction began, the boys received attention and concern from adults for injuring themselves. During extinction, self-damaging behavior was ignored. (Adapted from Lovaas & Simons, 1969.)*

Reinforcement and Token Economies—The Target Is Health

This section might be called "Throwing a Lifeline to the Unreachable." A distressing problem faced when dealing with the severely disturbed is how to "break through" to a patient who cannot, or will not, communicate. Mental patients sometimes spend years in hospitals without noticeable improvement.

Question: What can be done in such circumstances?

An approach that has been widely used is based on *tokens*. **Tokens** are *symbolic* rewards that can be exchanged for real rewards. (As you may recall from Chapter 7, tokens are secondary reinforcers.)

Tokens may be printed slips of paper, plastic "poker" chips, check marks, points, or gold stars. Whatever form they take, tokens serve as rewards because they may be exchanged for candy, food, cigarettes, recreation, or other privileges, such as private time with a therapist, outings, or using the stereo. Tokens are being used in mental hospitals, halfway houses for drug addicts, schools for the retarded, programs for delinquents, and ordinary classrooms. Their use is usually associated with dramatic improvements in behavior and overall adjustment (Sullivan & O'Leary, 1990).

By using tokens, a therapist can *immediately* reward a positive response. This allows a therapist to use operant shaping to influence behavior directly instead of vaguely urging patients to "get themselves together." For maximum impact, the therapist selects specific **target behaviors** for improvement and then reinforces them with tokens. For example, a mute mental patient might first be given a token each time he or she says a word. Next, tokens may be given for speaking a complete sentence. Later, the patient could gradually be required to speak more often, then to answer questions, and eventually to carry on a short conversation in order to receive tokens. In this way, patients who have not spoken more than a few words for months or years have been returned to the world of normal communication.

Tokens Symbolic rewards, or secondary reinforcers (such as plastic chips, gold stars, or points) that can be exchanged for real reinforcers.

Target behaviors Specific actions or other behaviors (such as speech) that a therapist seeks to modify.

Token economy A therapeutic program in which desirable behaviors are reinforced with tokens.

Cognitive therapy The use of learning principles and other methods to change maladaptive thoughts, beliefs, and feelings.

Full-scale use of tokens in an institutional setting produces a **token economy** (Kazdin, 1988). In a token economy, patients are rewarded with tokens for a wide range of socially desirable or productive activities. They must *pay* tokens for privileges and for engaging in problem behavior (■ Fig. 18–10). For example, tokens are given to patients who get out of bed, dress themselves, take required medication, arrive for meals on time, and the like. Work at constructive activity, such as gardening, cooking, or custodial duties, may also earn tokens. Patients must *exchange* tokens for meals and for private rooms, movies, passes, off-ward activities, and other privileges. Patients are *charged* tokens for staying in bed, disrobing in public, talking to themselves, fighting, crying, and similar target behaviors.

The effect of a token economy can be a radical change in patients' overall adjustment and morale. Patients have an incentive to change and they are held responsible for maladaptive habits and actions. Many "hopelessly" retarded, mentally ill, and delinquent people have been returned to a productive life by means of token economies.

Question: Wouldn't there be a problem with generalization of improvements brought about by a token economy?

Yes. Lack of generalization can again be a problem. To minimize this, patients are praised and given *social* recognition when they receive tokens. Each time a token is given, the therapist says something like, "That was very good," or "You're doing so well."

By the time they are ready to leave the program, patients may be earning tokens on a weekly basis for maintaining sane, responsible, and productive behavior (Binder, 1976). Typically, the most effective token economies are those that gradually switch from tokens to *social rewards* such as recognition and approval (Lieberman et al., 1976). Such rewards are what patients will receive when they return to family, friends, and community.

Cognitive Therapy—Think Positive!

Question: How would a behavior therapist treat a problem like depression? None of the techniques described seem to apply.

As we have discussed, behavior therapists usually try to change troublesome actions. However, in recent years a new breed of therapist has appeared. **Cognitive therapists,** as they are called, are interested in thoughts, as well as visible behavior. Rather than looking only at

■ **Fig. 18–10** *Shown here is a token used in one token economy system; also pictured is a list of credit values for various activities. Tokens may be exchanged for items or for privileges listed on the board. (After photographs by Robert P. Liberman.)*

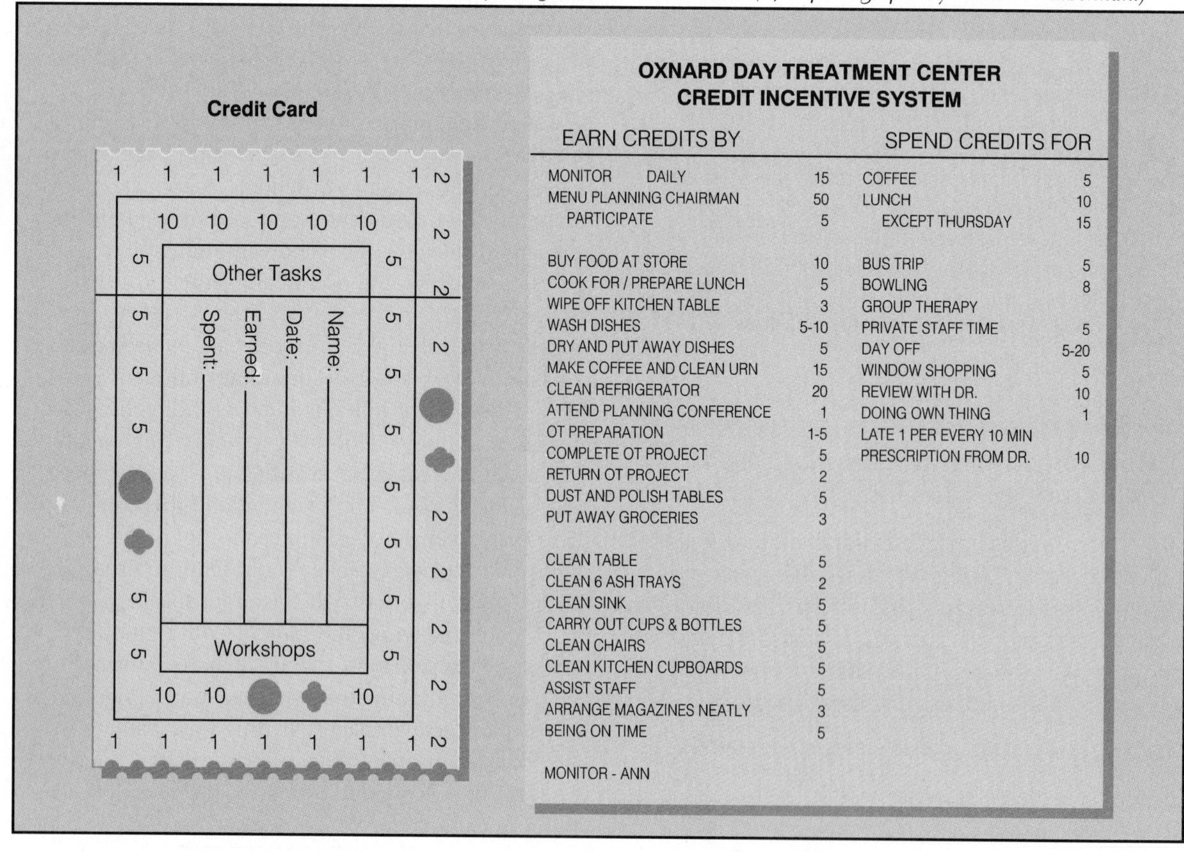

OXNARD DAY TREATMENT CENTER
CREDIT INCENTIVE SYSTEM

EARN CREDITS BY		SPEND CREDITS FOR	
MONITOR DAILY	15	COFFEE	5
MENU PLANNING CHAIRMAN	50	LUNCH	10
PARTICIPATE	5	EXCEPT THURSDAY	15
BUY FOOD AT STORE	10	BUS TRIP	5
COOK FOR / PREPARE LUNCH	5	BOWLING	8
WIPE OFF KITCHEN TABLE	3	GROUP THERAPY	
WASH DISHES	5-10	PRIVATE STAFF TIME	5
DRY AND PUT AWAY DISHES	5	DAY OFF	5-20
MAKE COFFEE AND CLEAN URN	15	WINDOW SHOPPING	5
CLEAN REFRIGERATOR	20	REVIEW WITH DR.	10
ATTEND PLANNING CONFERENCE	1	DOING OWN THING	1
OT PREPARATION	1-5	LATE 1 PER EVERY 10 MIN	
COMPLETE OT PROJECT	5	PRESCRIPTION FROM DR.	10
RETURN OT PROJECT	2		
DUST AND POLISH TABLES	5		
PUT AWAY GROCERIES	3		
CLEAN TABLE	5		
CLEAN 6 ASH TRAYS	2		
CLEAN SINK	5		
CARRY OUT CUPS & BOTTLES	5		
CLEAN CHAIRS	5		
CLEAN KITCHEN CUPBOARDS	5		
ASSIST STAFF	5		
ARRANGE MAGAZINES NEATLY	3		
BEING ON TIME	5		

MONITOR - ANN

actions, cognitive therapists try to learn what people think, believe, and feel. They then help clients change *thinking patterns* that lead to troublesome emotions or behaviors (Beck & Weishaar, 1989).

Cognitive Therapy for Depression

Cognitive therapy has been especially effective for treating depression. As you may recall from Chapter 11, Aaron Beck (1991) believes that negative, self-defeating thoughts underlie depression. According to Beck, depressed persons see themselves, the world, and the future in negative terms. Beck (1985, 1991) believes this occurs because of several major distortions in thinking. The first is **selective perception:** If five good things happen during the day and three bad things, the depressed person will focus only on the bad. **Overgeneralization** is a second thinking error underlying depression. An example would be considering yourself a total failure, or completely worthless, if you were to lose a job or fail one class. To complete the picture, Beck says that depressed persons tend to *magnify* the importance of undesirable events, and they engage in **all-or-nothing thinking** (seeing each event as completely good or bad, right or wrong, successful or a failure) (Beck, 1985).

Question: What do cognitive therapists do to alter such patterns?

Cognitive therapists make a step-by-step effort to correct negative thoughts that lead to depression or similar problems. At first, clients are taught to recognize and keep track of their own thoughts. The client and therapist then look for ideas and beliefs that cause depression, anger, avoidance, and so forth. For example, here's how a therapist might challenge all-or-nothing thinking (Burns & Persons, 1982):

> **Patient:** I'm feeling even more depressed. No one wants to hire me, and I can't even clean up my apartment. I feel completely incompetent!
> **Therapist:** I see. The fact that you are unemployed and have a messy apartment proves that you are completely incompetent?
> **Patient:** Well . . . I can see that doesn't add up.

Next, clients are asked to gather information to test their beliefs. For instance, a depressed person might list his or her activities for a week. The list is then used to challenge all-or-nothing thoughts, such as "I had a terrible week" or "I'm a complete failure." With more coaching, clients learn to alter thoughts in ways that improve their moods, actions, and relationships.

Cognitive therapy is as effective as drugs for treating many cases of depression. More important, people who have adopted new thinking patterns are less likely to become depressed again—a benefit that drugs can't impart (Evans et al., 1992; Hollon et al., 1992).

In an alternate approach, cognitive therapists look for an *absence* of effective coping skills and thought patterns, not for the *presence* of self-defeating thinking (Meichenbaum, 1977). The aim is to teach clients how to cope with anger, depression, shyness, stress, and similar problems. Stress inoculation, which was described in Chapter 11, is a good example of this approach.

Cognitive therapy is a promising and rapidly expanding specialty. Before we leave the topic, let's explore one more widely used form of cognitive therapy.

Rational-Emotive Therapy

According to Albert Ellis (1973; 1993), the basic idea of **rational-emotive therapy (RET)** is as easy as ABC. Ellis assumes that people become unhappy and develop self-defeating habits because of unrealistic or faulty *beliefs.*

Question: How are beliefs important?

Ellis analyzes problems in this way: The letter A stands for an **activating experience,** which the person assumes to be the cause of C, an emotional **consequence.** For instance, a person who is rejected (the activating experience) feels depressed, threatened, or hurt (the consequence). Rational-emotive therapy shows the client that the true cause of difficulty is what comes between A and C: In between is B, the client's irrational and unrealistic **beliefs.** In this example, the unrealistic belief leading to unnecessary suffering is: "I must be loved and approved by almost everyone at all times" (Highlight 18–5). RET holds that events cannot *cause* us to have feelings. We feel as we do because of our beliefs and expectations (Kottler & Brown, 1992).

Highlight 18–5

Using Psychology

Ten Irrational Beliefs—Which Do You Hold?

1. I must be loved and approved by almost every significant person in my life or it's awful and I'm worthless.
Example: "One of my roommates doesn't seem to like me. I must be a total zero."
2. I should be completely competent and achieving in all ways to be a worthwhile person.
Example: "I don't understand my chemistry class. I guess I really am a stupid person."

Selective perception Perceiving only certain stimuli among a larger array of possibilities.

Overgeneralization Blowing a single event out of proportion by relating it to other unrelated situations.

All-or-nothing thinking Classifying objects or events as absolutely right or wrong, good or bad, acceptable or unacceptable.

Rational-emotive therapy (RET) Attempts to change or remove irrational beliefs that cause emotional problems.

Activating experience In RET, any personal experience that appears to evoke a response, especially an emotional response.

Emotional consequence In RET, a person's emotional reaction to any given situation.

Belief In RET, a conviction or assumption that affects emotional reactions to various experiences.

Irrational assumption An unrealistic or self-defeating belief that leads to emotional upsets and maladaptive behavior.

3. Certain people I must deal with are thoroughly bad and should be severely blamed and punished for it.
Example: "The old man next door is such a pain. I'm going to play my stereo even louder the next time he complains."
4. It is awful and upsetting when things are not the way I would very much like them to be.
Example: "I should have gotten a B in that class. The teacher is unfair."
5. My unhappiness is always caused by external events; I cannot control my emotional reactions.
Example: "You make me feel awful. I would be happy if it weren't for you."
6. If something unpleasant might happen, I should keep dwelling on it.
Example: "I'll never forget the time my boss insulted me. I think about it every day at work."
7. It is easier to avoid difficulties and responsibilities than to face them.
Example: "I don't know why my wife seems angry. Maybe it will just pass by if I ignore it."
8. I should depend on others who are stronger than I am.
Example: "I couldn't survive if he left me."
9. Because something once strongly affected my life, it will do so indefinitely.
Example: "My girlfriend dumped me during my junior year in college. I don't know if I can ever trust a woman again."
10. There is always a perfect solution to human problems and it is awful if this solution is not found.
Example: "I'm so depressed about politics in this country. It all seems hopeless."

(Adapted from Rohsenow & Smith, 1982.)

Ellis (1979, 1987) believes that most irrational beliefs come from three core ideas, each of which is unrealistic:

1. I *must* perform well and be approved of by significant others. If I don't, then it is awful, I cannot stand it, and I am a rotten person.
2. You *must* treat me fairly. When you don't, it is horrible, and I cannot bear it.
3. Conditions *must* be the way I want them to be. It is terrible when they are not, and I cannot stand living in such an awful world.

It's easy to see that such beliefs can lead to much grief and needless suffering in a less than perfect world. Rational-emotive therapists are very directive in their attempts to change a client's irrational beliefs and "self-talk." The therapist may directly attack clients' logic, challenge their thinking, confront them with evidence contrary to their beliefs, and even assign "homework" for the clients. Here, for instance, are some examples of statements that dispute irrational beliefs (after Kottler & Brown, 1992):

- "Where is the evidence that you are a loser just because you didn't do well this one time?"
- "Who said the world should be fair? That's your rule."
- "What are you telling yourself to make yourself feel so upset?"
- "Is it really terrible that things aren't working out as you would like? Or is it just inconvenient?"

RET has been criticized by some as superficial and argumentative, but Ellis' basic insight has considerable merit. Many of us would probably do well to give up our irrational beliefs. Improved self-acceptance and a better tolerance of daily annoyances are the benefits of doing so (Ellis, 1987).

The value of cognitive approaches is further illustrated by three techniques (*covert sensitization, thought stopping,* and *covert reinforcement*) described in the Applications section that concludes this chapter. A little later you can see what you think of them.

Learning Check

1. Behavior modification programs aimed at extinction of an undesirable behavior typically make use of what operant principles?
   a. punishment and stimulus control
   b. punishment and shaping
   c. non-reinforcement and time out
   d. stimulus control and time out
2. Attention can be a powerful ______________________ for humans.
3. Token economies depend on the time-out procedure. T or F?
4. Tokens basically allow the operant shaping of desired responses or "target behaviors." T or F?
5. According to Beck, selective perception, overgeneralization, and ______________________ thinking are cognitive habits that underlie depression.

6. RET teaches people to change the antecedents of irrational behavior. T or F?

7. In Aaron Beck's terms, a belief such as "I must perform well or I am a rotten person" involves two thinking errors. These are: ***Critical Thinking***

Answers 1. c 2. reinforcer 3. F 4. T 5. all-or-nothing 6. F 7. Overgeneralization and all-or-nothing thinking.

Group Therapy—People Who Need People

Question: Is group therapy just individual therapy with more than one person?

Most of the psychotherapies we have discussed can be adapted for use in groups (Shaffer & Galinsky, 1989). Psychologists first tried working with groups as a practical response to the need for more therapists than were available. To their surprise, group therapy not only worked, it also offered some special advantages (■Fig. 18–11).

In **group therapy,** a person can *act out* or directly experience problems. Doing so often produces insights that might not occur from merely talking about problems. In addition, other group members with similar problems can offer support and useful input. Groups also help form a bridge between therapy and real-life problems by providing a situation that is more realistic than the protected atmosphere of individual therapy. For reasons such as these, a number of specialized groups and techniques have emerged. Because they range from Alcoholics Anonymous to Marriage Encounter, we will sample only a few representative approaches.

Psychodrama

One of the first group approaches was developed by Jacob L. Moreno (1953), who called his technique **psychodrama.** In psychodrama, an individual **role-plays** (acts out) dramatic incidents resembling those that cause problems in real life. For example, Don, a disturbed teenager, might act out a typical family fight, with the therapist playing his father and with other patients playing his mother, brothers, and sisters. It was Moreno's belief that insights and the emotional relearning from these enactments transfer to real-life situations. Therapists using psychodrama often find **role reversals** especially helpful (Leveton, 1977). For instance, Don would be asked to role-play his father or mother, to better understand their feelings. A related method is the **mirror technique,** in which Don might briefly join the audience and watch as another group member plays his role. This allows the teenager to see himself as others do (Shaffer & Galinsky, 1989).

Family Therapy

Family relationships are the source of great pleasure, and all too often, of great pain for many people. In **family therapy,** husband, wife, and children work as a group to resolve the problems of each family member. Family therapy tends to be brief and focused on specific problems, such as frequent fights or a depressed teenager (Berman, 1982). Over the last 10 years, family therapy has become one of the most frequently used approaches to therapy (Sayette & Mayne, 1990).

Family therapists believe that problems are rarely limited to a single family member: A problem for one

Group therapy Psychotherapy conducted with a group of people.

Psychodrama A therapy in which clients act out personal conflicts and feelings in the presence of others who play supporting roles.

Role-playing The dramatic enactment or reenactment of significant life events.

Role reversal Taking the role of another person to learn how one's own behavior appears to others.

Mirror technique Observing another person reenact one's own behavior, like a character in a play; designed to help persons to see themselves more clearly.

Family therapy Technique in which all family members participate, both individually and as a group, to change destructive relationships and communication patterns.

■**Fig. 18–11** *A group therapy session. Group members offer mutual support while sharing problems and insights.*

Family system The family as an entire unit, including all its members, their relationships, and their typical patterns of behavior.

Sensitivity group A group experience designed to increase self-awareness and sensitivity to others.

Encounter group A group experience based on intensely honest expressions of feelings and reactions of participants to one another.

Large-group awareness training Any of a number of programs (many of them commercialized) that claim to increase self-awareness and facilitate constructive personal change.

Therapy placebo effect Improvement caused not by the actual process of therapy but by a client's expectation that therapy will help.

is considered a problem for all. That is, families often contribute to and maintain maladaptive behavior. If changes are not made in the **family system,** changes in any single family member may not last. Thus, family members work together to improve communication, to change destructive patterns, and to see themselves and each other in new ways. This helps them reshape distorted perceptions and interactions directly, with the very persons with whom they have troubled relationships (Goldfried, Greenberg, & Marmar, 1990).

Question: Does the therapist work with the whole family at once?

The family therapist treats the family as a unit, but may not meet with the entire family at each session. If a family crisis is at hand, the therapist may first try to identify the most resourceful family members, who can help solve the immediate problem. The therapist and family members may then work on resolving more basic conflicts and on improving family relationships. In some instances, family therapists look beyond the present family to previous generations. Understanding a troubled marriage, for example, may be aided by identifying conflicts that have carried over from each spouse's parents or even grandparents.

Group Awareness Training

During the 1960s and 1970s, the human potential movement led many people to become interested in personal growth experiences. Often, their interest was expressed by participation in sensitivity training or encounter groups.

Question: What is the difference between sensitivity groups and encounter groups?

Sensitivity groups tend to be less confrontive than encounter groups. Participants in sensitivity groups take part in exercises that gently enlarge awareness of oneself and others. For example, in a "trust walk," participants expand their confidence in others by allowing themselves to be led about while blindfolded.

In **encounter groups** more intense emotion and communication may take place. Here, the emphasis is on tearing down defenses and false fronts through discussion that can be brutally honest. Because there is a danger of hostile confrontation and psychological damage, encounter group participation is safest when members are carefully screened and when a trained leader guides the group. Encounter group "casualties" are rare, but they do occur (Shaffer & Galinsky, 1989).

In business settings, psychologists still use the basic principles of sensitivity and encounter groups—truth, self-awareness, and self-determination—to improve employee relationships. Specially designed encounter groups for married couples are also widely held (Schutz, 1986). However, in the last decade there has been a shift away from public participation in sensitivity and encounter groups. Instead, hundreds of thousands of people have taken part in various forms of **large-group awareness training** (Finkelstein et al., 1982). Lifespring, Actualizations, est, the Forum, and similar commercial programs are well-known examples. Like the smaller groups that preceded them, large-group trainings combine psychological exercises, confrontation, new viewpoints, and group dynamics to promote personal change.

Question: Are sensitivity, encounter, and awareness groups really psychotherapies?

Judging from the glowing testimonials given by many participants, such groups must fill some need not met by society or traditional psychotherapy. However, there is, at present, little evidence that these experiences are truly therapeutic (Finkelstein et al., 1982). Many of the claimed benefits may simply result from a kind of **therapy placebo effect** related to positive expectations, a break in daily routine, and an excuse to act differently. The importance of such factors is easily illustrated: Participants in a weekend "retreat" that featured nothing more than volleyball, charades, and ballroom dancing also reported enhanced mental health (McCardel & Murray, 1974)! Kurt Back (1972) may have summarized it best when he said, "Encounter groups may comfort, but they do not cure anything." For some the experience is positive, for some negative, and for many it is merely a diversion.

A danger you should be aware of in some large-group training programs is that participants may be verbally attacked by a "trainer" as part of the "educational" process. For some people, such attacks *create* an emotional crisis that did not exist before. Unwary participants then resolve this crisis by converting to the organization that promotes the training (Cushman, 1989). Also, a recent study detected only small short-term benefits and no long-term benefits after participants completed one well-known program (Fisher et al., 1989). Don't expect your life to be transformed by a large-group experience.

For better or worse, the largest group therapy of all may be on your radio, as discussed in Highlight 18–6.

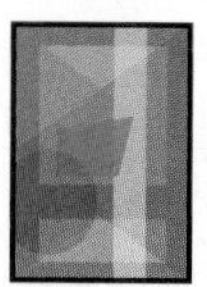

HIGHLIGHT 18–6

Focus on a Controversy

"Psych Jockeys" and Telephone Counselors

By now, you have probably heard a phone-in radio psychologist. On a typical program, callers describe problems arising from child abuse, loneliness, love affairs, phobias, sexual adjustment, or depression. The radio psychologist then offers reassurance, advice, or suggestions for getting help.

Talk-radio psychology may seem harmless, but it raises some important questions. For instance, is it reasonable to give advice without knowing anything about a person's background? Might the advice do harm? What good can a psychologist do in three minutes?

In defense of themselves, radio psychologists point out that listeners may learn solutions to their own problems by hearing others talk. Many also stress that their work is educational, not therapeutic. Certainly for some callers a radio psychologist may be the only person willing to listen to their problems.

The real issue seems to be the question of when advice becomes therapy. The American Psychological Association has taken the position that media psychologists should discuss only problems of a general nature, instead of actually counseling a person. For example, if a caller complains about insomnia, the radio psychologist should talk about insomnia in general, not probe the caller's personal life (Schommer, 1984).

By giving information, advice, and social support, radio psychologists probably do help some listeners (Levy, 1989). Even so, a good guide for anyone tempted to call a radio psychologist might be "let the consumer beware."

The same advice applies to telephone therapists. These "counselors" can be reached through 900-number services for $3 to $4 per minute. To date, there is no evidence that telephone counseling is effective. Successful face-to-face therapy is based on a continuing *relationship* between two people. In telephone therapy, a lack of visual cues and limited personal contact seriously undermines the prospect for success ("Report," 1994).

It's important to note that legitimate therapists occasionally use the phone to calm, console, or advise clients between therapy sessions. Also, use of the telephone for suicide hot lines and crisis counseling is well established. However, where commercial telephone therapists are concerned, consumers might well ask themselves, How much confidence would I place in a physician who would make a diagnosis over the phone? Many telephone "therapists" may be nothing more than untrained operators (Newman, 1994).

Psychotherapy—An Overview

Question: How effective is psychotherapy?

Judging the outcome of therapy is tricky. Nevertheless, there is evidence that therapy is beneficial. A recent analysis of hundreds of studies showed a strong pattern of positive effects for psychotherapy and behavioral treatments (Lipsey & Wilson, 1993). These findings, of course, are based on averages: For some people therapy was tremendously helpful; for others it was unsuccessful; overall it was effective for more people than not. Speaking more subjectively, one real success—in which a person's life is lastingly changed for the better—can be worth the frustration of several cases in which little progress is made.

It is common to think of therapy as a long, slow process. But this is not always the case. Research reveals that most people can expect improvement in a reasonably brief time. An analysis of over 2400 patients found that about 50 percent felt better after only 8 therapy sessions. After 26 sessions, roughly 75 percent had improved (Howard et al., 1986) (■ Fig. 18–12). The typical "dose" of therapy is one hourly session per week. This means that the majority of patients had improved after 6 months of therapy, and half felt better in just 2 months. Keep in mind that people often suffer for several years before seeking help. In view of this, such rapid improvement is impressive.

Question: What do psychotherapies have in common?

■ **Fig. 18–12** *The dose-improvement relationship in psychotherapy. This graph shows the percentage of patients who improved after varying numbers of therapy sessions. Notice that the most rapid improvement took place during the first 6 months of once-a-week sessions. (From Howard et al., 1986.)*

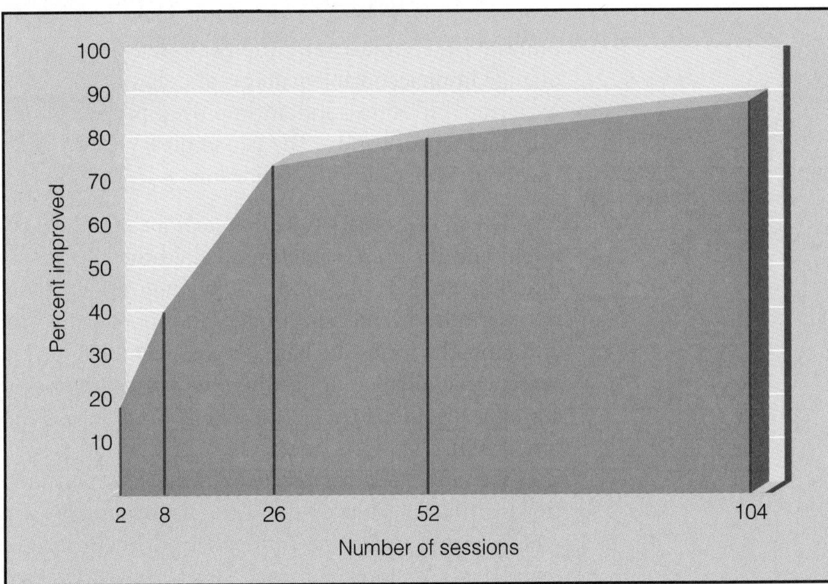

Table 18–2 Comparison of Psychotherapies

	Insight or Action?	Directive or Non-Directive?	Individual or Group?	Therapy's Strength*
Psychoanalysis	Insight	Directive	Individual	Searching honesty
Short-term dynamic therapy	Insight	Directive	Individual	Productive use of conflict
Client-centered therapy	Insight	Non-directive	Individual	Acceptance, empathy
Existential therapy	Insight	Both	Individual	Personal empowerment
Gestalt therapy	Insight	Directive	Both	Focus on immediate awareness
Behavior therapy	Action	Directive	Both	Observable changes in behavior
Cognitive therapy	Action	Directive	Individual	Constructive guidance
Rational-emotive therapy	Action	Directive	Individual	Clarity of thinking and goals
Psychodrama	Insight	Directive	Group	Constructive reenactments
Family therapy	Both	Directive	Group	Shared responsibility for problems

*This column based in part on Andrews (1989).

Core Features of Psychotherapy

The therapies we have sampled are but a few of the approaches in use. The number of different therapies could easily exceed 200 today. The examples cited in this chapter were selected because they represent some of the basic variations in philosophy or techniques and because they offer ideas that may be of immediate use to you. For a summary of major differences among psychotherapies, see Table 18–2. To add to your understanding, let us briefly summarize what all of the techniques have in common.

All the psychotherapies we have discussed include some combination of the following goals: insight, resolution of conflicts, an improved sense of self, a change in unacceptable patterns of behavior, better interpersonal relations, and an improved picture of oneself and the world. To accomplish these goals, psychotherapies offer the following.

1. Therapy provides a *caring relationship* between client and therapist, sometimes called the *therapeutic alliance* (Stiles et al., 1986). *Emotional rapport* based on warmth, friendship, understanding, acceptance, and empathy forms the basis for this relationship. The therapeutic alliance unites the client and therapist in working together to solve the client's problems (Gaston, 1990).
2. Therapy offers a *protected setting* in which emotional *catharsis* (release) can take place. Therapy provides a sanctuary in which the client is free to express fears, anxieties, and personal secrets without fear of rejection or loss of confidentiality (Weiss, 1990).
3. All therapies to some extent offer an *explanation* or *rationale* for the suffering the client has experienced, and they propose a line of action that if followed will end this suffering.
4. Therapy also provides clients with a *new perspective* about themselves and their situation and a chance to practice *new behaviors* (Crencavage & Norcross, 1990; Stiles et al., 1986).

Because therapies have much in common, a majority of psychologists in the United States have become **eclectic** in their work (Jensen, Bergin, & Greaves, 1990). Eclectic therapists use whatever methods best fit a particular problem. In addition, some seek to combine the best elements of various therapies into more general systems (Patterson, 1989).

If you recall that our discussion began with trepanning and demonology, it is clear that psychotherapy has come a long way. Still, the search for ways to improve psychotherapy remains an urgent challenge for those who devote their lives to helping others.

Basic Counseling Skills

A number of general helping skills can be distilled from the various approaches to therapy. These suggest several points to keep in mind when you would like to comfort a person in distress, such as a troubled friend or relative. (Also, see Table 18–3.)

Active Listening People frequently talk "at" each other without really listening. A person with problems

Table 18–3 Helping Behaviors

To help another person gain insight into a personal problem it is valuable to keep the following comparison in mind.

Behaviors that Help	Behaviors that Hinder
Active listening	Probing painful topics
Acceptance	Judging/moralizing
Reflecting feelings	Criticism
Open-ended questioning	Threats
Supportive statements	Rejection
Respect	Ridicule/sarcasm
Patience	Impatience
Genuineness	Placing blame
Paraphrasing	Opinionated statements

(Adapted from Kottler & Brown, 1992.)

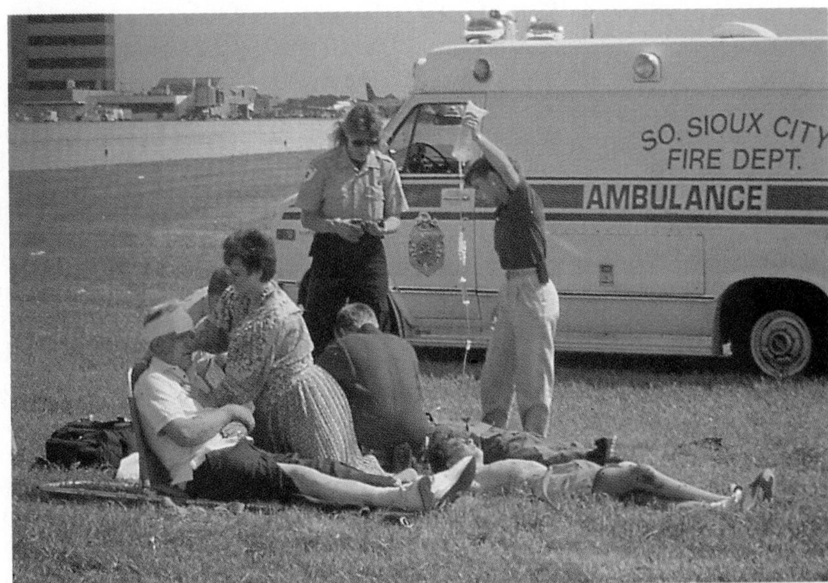

Fig. 18–13 *Teams of psychologists and counselors are often assembled to provide support to victims of major accidents and natural disasters. Because their work is stressful and often heart-wrenching, relief workers also benefit from on-site counseling. Expressing emotions and talking about feelings are major elements of disaster counseling.*

needs to be heard. Make a sincere effort to listen to and understand the person. Try to accept the person's message without judging it or immediately leaping to conclusions (Kottler & Brown, 1992). Let the person know you are listening, with eye contact, posture, your tone of voice, and your replies (Ivey & Galvin, 1984).

Clarify the Problem People who have a clear idea of what is wrong in their lives are in a better position to discover solutions. Try to understand the problem from the person's point of view. As you do, check your understanding often. For example, you might ask, "Are you saying that you feel depressed just at school? Or in general?" Remember, a problem well defined is often half solved.

Focus on Feelings Feelings are neither right nor wrong. By focusing on feelings you can avoid making the person defensive. Passing judgment on what is said prevents the free outpouring of emotion that is the basis for catharsis (Fig. 18–13). For example, a friend confides that he has failed a test. Perhaps you know that he studies very little. If you say, "Maybe if you studied a little more you would do better," he will probably become defensive or hostile. Much more can be accomplished by saying, "You must feel very frustrated" or simply, "How do you feel about it?" (Ivey & Galvin, 1984).

Avoid Giving Advice Many people mistakenly think that they must solve others' problems for them. Remember that your goal is to provide understanding and support, not solutions (Egan, 1984). Of course, it is reasonable to give advice when you are asked for it, but beware of the trap of the "Why don't you . . .? Yes, but . . ." game. According to psychotherapist Eric Berne (1964), this "game" follows a pattern: Someone says, "I have this problem." You say, "Why don't you do thus and so?" The person replies, "Yes, but . . ." and then gives several reasons why your suggestion won't work. If you make a new suggestion, the reply will once again be, "Yes, but . . ." because the person either knows more about his or her personal situation than you do or because he or she has reasons for avoiding your advice. The student described earlier knows he needs to study. His problem is to understand why he doesn't *want* to study.

Accept the Person's Frame of Reference W. I. Thomas said, "Things perceived as real are real in their effect." Try to resist the temptation to contradict the person with your point of view. Since we all live in different psychological worlds, there is no "correct" view of a life situation. A person who feels that his or her point of view is understood feels freer to examine it objectively and to question it. (Accepting and understanding the perspective of another person can be especially difficult when cultural differences exist. See this chapter's Exploration for more information.)

Reflect Thoughts and Feelings One of the best things you can do when offering support to another person is to give feedback by simply restating what is said. This is also a good way to encourage a person to talk. If your friend seems to be at a loss for words, *restate* or *paraphrase* his or her last sentence. Here's an example.

Friend: I'm really down about school. I can't get interested in any of my classes. I flunked my Spanish test, and somebody stole my notebook for psychology.
You: You're really upset about school, aren't you?
Friend: Yeah, and my parents are hassling me about my grades again.

You: You're feeling pressured by your parents?
Friend: Yeah, damn.
You: It must make you angry to be pressured by them.

As simple as this sounds, it is very helpful to someone trying to sort out feelings. Try it. If nothing else, you'll develop a reputation as a fantastic conversationalist!

Silence Studies show that counselors tend to wait longer before responding than do people in everyday conversations. Pauses of 5 seconds or more are not unusual, and interrupting is rare. Listening patiently lets the person feel unhurried and encourages her or him to speak freely (Goodman, 1984).

Questions Because your goal is to encourage free expression, *open questions* tend to be the most helpful (Goodman, 1984). A *closed question* is one that can be answered yes or no. Open questions call for an open-ended reply (see Chapter 15). Say, for example, that a friend tells you, "I feel like my boss has it in for me at work." A closed question would be, "Oh yeah? So, are you going to quit?" Open questions, such as, "Do you want to tell me about it?" or "How do you feel about it?" are more likely to be helpful.

Maintain Confidentiality Your efforts to help will be wasted if you fail to respect the privacy of someone who has confided in you. Put yourself in the person's place. Don't gossip.

These guidelines are not an invitation to play "junior therapist." Professional therapists are trained to approach serious problems with skills far exceeding those described here. However, the points made help define the qualities of a therapeutic relationship. They also emphasize that each of us can supply two of the greatest mental health resources available at any cost: friendship and honest communication.

A Look Ahead In the Applications section that follows we will return briefly to behavioral approaches. There you will find a number of useful techniques that you may be able to apply to your own behavior. You'll also find a discussion of when to seek professional help, and how to go about doing it. Here's your author's professional advice: This is an Applications you won't want to skip reading.

Learning Check

1. In psychodrama, people attempt to form meaningful wholes out of disjointed thoughts, feelings, and actions. T or F?
2. Most large-group awareness trainings make use of Gestalt therapy. T or F?
3. There are no dangers in participating in an encounter group. T or F?
4. Which therapy places great emphasis on role-playing?
   a. psychodrama *b.* awareness training *c.* family therapy *d.* encounter groups
5. According to the APA, media psychologists should educate, they should not do therapy on the air. T or F?
6. Emotional ______________________ (release) in a protected setting is an element of most psychotherapies.
7. To aid a troubled friend, you should focus on facts rather than feelings, and you should critically evaluate what the person is saying to help him or her grasp reality. T or F?
8. One danger of giving advice is the tendency for the interchange to slip into the "Yes, but" game. T or F?

Critical Thinking

9. In your opinion, do psychologists have a duty to protect others who may be harmed by their clients? For example, if a patient has homicidal fantasies about his ex-wife, should she be informed?

Answers

1. F 2. F 3. F 4. *a* 5. T 6. catharsis 7. F 8. T 9. According to the law, there is a duty to protect others where a therapist could, with little effort, prevent serious harm. However, this duty can conflict with a client's rights to confidentiality and with client-therapist trust. Therapists often must make difficult choices in such situations.

APPLICATIONS: *Self Management and Seeking Professional Help*

"Throw out the snake oil, ladies and gentlemen, and throw away your troubles. Doctor B. Havior Modification is here to put an end to all human suffering."

True? Well, not quite. Behavior therapy is not a cure-all. Its use is often quite complicated and requires a great deal of experience and expertise. Also, there are times when therapists regard insight therapy as more appropriate than behavior therapy. Still, behavior therapy offers a straightforward solution to many problems.

It would be a serious mistake to presume that you could effectively apply the principles of behavior therapy to major personal problems. As mentioned elsewhere in this book, professional help is available and should be sought when a significant problem exists. For lesser difficulties there is a good chance that you might succeed in modest attempts to apply the principles of behavior therapy to yourself. Let us see how this might be done.

Covert Reward and Punishment—Boosting Your "Willpower"

"Have you ever decided to quit smoking cigarettes, watching television too much, eating too much, drinking too much, or driving too fast?"

"Well, one of those applies. I have decided several times to quit smoking."

"When have you decided?"

"Usually after I am reminded of how dangerous smoking is—like when I heard that my uncle had died of lung cancer. He smoked constantly."

"If you have decided to quit 'several times' I assume you haven't succeeded."

"No, the usual pattern is for me to become upset about smoking and then to cut down for a day or two."

"You forget the disturbing image of your uncle's death, or whatever, and start smoking again."

"Yes, I suppose if I had an uncle die every day or so, I might actually quit!"

The use of electric shock to condition an aversion seems remote from everyday problems. Even naturally aversive actions are difficult to apply to personal behavior. As mentioned earlier, for instance, rapid smoking is difficult for most smokers to carry out on their own. And what about a problem like overeating? It would be difficult indeed to eat enough to create a lasting aversion to overeating. (Although it is sometimes tempting to try.)

In view of such limitations, psychologists have developed an alternative procedure that can be used to curb smoking, overeating, and other habits (Cautela & Bennett, 1981; Cautela & Kearney, 1986).

Covert sensitization Use of aversive imagery to reduce the occurrence of an undesired response.

Covert Sensitization Obtain six 3 X 5 cards and on each write a brief description of a scene related to the habit you wish to control. The scene should be so *disturbing* or *disgusting* that thinking about it would temporarily make you very uncomfortable about indulging in the habit. For smoking, the cards might read:

- I am in a doctor's office. The doctor looks at some reports and tells me I have lung cancer. He says a lung will have to be removed and sets a date for the operation.
- I am in bed under an oxygen tent. My chest feels caved in. There is a tube in my throat. I can barely breathe.
- I wake up in the morning and smoke a cigarette. I begin coughing up blood.
- Other cards would continue along the same line.

For overeating the cards might read:

- I am at the beach. I get up to go for a swim and I overhear people whispering to each other, "Isn't that fat disgusting?"
- I am at a store buying clothes. I try on several things that are too small. The only things that fit look like rumpled sacks. Salespeople are staring at me.

And so forth.

The trick, of course, is to get yourself to imagine or picture vividly each of these disturbing scenes *several times* a day. Imagining the scenes can be accomplished by placing them under *stimulus control*. Simply choose something you do *frequently* each day (such as getting a cup of coffee or getting up from your chair). Next make a rule. Before you can get a cup of coffee or get up from your chair, or whatever you have selected as a cue, you must take out your cards and *vividly picture* yourself engaging in the action you wish to curb (eating or smoking, for example). Then *vividly picture* the scene described on the top card. Imagine the scene for 30 seconds.

After visualizing the top card, move it to the bottom so the cards are rotated. Make up new cards each week. The scenes can be made much more upsetting

Thought stopping Use of aversive stimuli to interrupt or prevent upsetting thoughts.

Covert reinforcement Using positive imagery to reinforce desired behavior.

than the samples given here. The samples are toned down to keep you from being "grossed out."

Covert sensitization can also be used directly in situations that test your self-control. A person trying to lose weight, for instance, might be able to turn down a tempting dessert in this way: The person should look at the dessert and visualize maggots crawling all over it. If this image is made as vivid and nauseating as possible, losing your appetite is almost a certainty. If you want to apply this technique to other situations, be aware that vomiting scenes are especially effective. Covert sensitization may sound as if you are "playing games with yourself," but it can be a great help if you want to cut down on a bad habit (Cautela & Kearney, 1986). Try it!

Thought Stopping As discussed earlier, behavior therapists have begun to realize that thoughts, like visible responses, can also cause trouble. Think of times when you have repeatedly "put yourself down" mentally or when you have been preoccupied by needless worries, fears, or other negative and upsetting thoughts. If you would like to gain control over such thoughts, recent experiments show how it can be done.

The simplest thought-stopping technique makes use of mild punishment to suppress upsetting mental images and internal "talk." Simply place a large, flat rubber band around your wrist. As you go through the day apply this rule: Each time you catch yourself thinking the upsetting image or thought, pull the rubber band away from your wrist and snap it. You need not make this terribly painful. Its value lies in drawing your attention to how often you form negative thoughts and in interrupting the flow of thoughts. Strong punishment is not required.

Question: It seems like this procedure might be abandoned rapidly. Is there an alternative?

A second thought-stopping procedure requires only that you interrupt upsetting thoughts each time they occur. Begin by setting aside time each day during which you will deliberately think the unwanted thought. As you begin to form the thought, shout "stop!" aloud, with conviction. (Obviously, you should choose a private spot for this part of the procedure!)

Repeat the thought-stopping procedure 10 to 20 times for the first two or three days. Then switch to shouting "stop!" covertly (to yourself) rather than aloud. Thereafter, thought stopping can be carried out throughout the day, whenever upsetting thoughts occur (adapted from Williams & Long, 1991). After several days of practice, you should be able to stop unwanted thoughts whenever they occur.

Covert Reinforcement Earlier we discussed how punishing images can be linked to undesirable responses, such as smoking or overeating, to decrease their occurrence. Many people also find it helpful to covertly *reinforce* desired actions. For example, suppose your target behavior is, once again, not eating dessert. If this were the case, you could do the following (Cautela & Bennett, 1981; Cautela & Kearney, 1986):

> Imagine that you are standing at the dessert table with your friends. As dessert is passed, you politely refuse and feel good about staying on your diet.

These images would then be followed by imagining a pleasant, reinforcing scene:

> Imagine that you are your ideal weight. You look really slim in your favorite color and style. Someone you like says to you, "Gee, you've lost weight. I've never seen you look so good."

For many people, of course, actual direct reinforcement (as described in the Chapter 7 Applications) is the most powerful way to alter behavior. Nevertheless, covert or "visualized" reinforcement can have similar effects. To make use of covert reinforcement, choose one or more target behaviors and rehearse them mentally. Then follow each rehearsal with a vivid rewarding image.

Self-Directed Desensitization—Overcoming Common Fears

You have prepared for two weeks to give a speech in a large class. As your turn approaches, your hands begin to tremble and perspire. Your heart pounds and you find it difficult to breathe. You say to your body, "Relax!" What happens? Nothing!

Relaxation The key to desensitization is relaxation. To inhibit fear, one must *learn* to relax. Here is a method for achieving deep-muscle relaxation.

> Tense the muscles in your right arm until they tremble. Hold them tight for about five seconds and then let go. Allow your hand and arm to go limp and to relax completely. Repeat the procedure. Releasing tension two or three times will allow you to feel whether or not your arm muscles have relaxed. Repeat the tension-release procedure with your left arm. Compare it with your right arm. Repeat until the left arm is equally relaxed.

Apply the tension-release technique to your right leg; to your left leg; to your abdomen; to your chest and shoulders. Clench and release your chin, neck, and throat. Wrinkle and release your forehead and scalp. Tighten and release your mouth and face muscles. As a last step, curl your toes and tense your feet. Then release.

Practice relaxation with the tension-release method until you can achieve complete relaxation quickly (5 to 10 minutes).

After you have practiced relaxation once a day for a week or two, you will begin to be able to tell when your body (or a group of muscles) is tense. Also, you will begin to be able to relax on command. As an alternative, you might want to try imagining a very safe, pleasant, and relaxing scene. Some people find such images as relaxing as the tension-release method (Rosenthal, 1993). Once you have learned to relax, the next step is to identify the fear you would like to control and construct a *hierarchy*.

Procedure for Constructing a Hierarchy Make a list of situations (related to the fear) that make you anxious. Try to list at least 10 situations. Some should be very frightening and others only mildly frightening. Write a short description of each situation on a separate 3 X 5 card. Place the cards in order from the least disturbing situation to the most disturbing. Here is a sample hierarchy for a student afraid of public speaking:

1. Being given an assignment to speak in class
2. Thinking about the topic and the date the speech must be given
3. Writing the speech; thinking about delivering the speech
4. Watching other students speak in class the week before the speech date
5. Rehearsing the speech alone; pretending to give it to the class
6. Delivering the speech to my roommate; pretending my roommate is the teacher
7. Reviewing the speech on the day it is to be presented
8. Entering the classroom; waiting and thinking about the speech
9. Being called; standing up; facing the audience
10. Delivering the speech

Using the Hierarchy When you have mastered the relaxation exercises and have the hierarchy constructed, set aside time each day to work on reducing your fear. Begin by performing the relaxation exercises. When you are completely relaxed, visualize the scene on the first card (the least frightening scene). If you can *vividly* picture and imagine yourself in the first situation twice *without a noticeable increase in muscle tension*, proceed to the next card. Also, as you progress, relax yourself between cards.

Each day, stop when you reach a card that you cannot visualize without tension after making three attempts. Each day, begin one or two cards before the one on which you stopped the previous day. Continue to work with the cards until you can visualize the last situation without experiencing tension (techniques are based on Wolpe, 1974).

Don't be discouraged if you are unable to relax completely while imagining the upsetting scenes. Research shows that in many instances your fear will still lessen after repeated exposure to the feared situations (Kleinknecht, 1986).

By using this approach you should be able to reduce the fear or anxiety associated with things such as public speaking, entering darkened rooms, asking questions in large classes, heights, talking to members of the opposite sex, and taking tests. Even if you are not always able to reduce a fear, you will have learned to place relaxation under voluntary control. This alone is valuable because controlling unnecessary tension can increase energy and efficiency.

Seeking Professional Help—When, Where, and How?

Question: How would I know if I should seek professional help at some point in my life?

Although there is no simple answer to this question, the following guidelines may be helpful.

1. If your level of psychological discomfort (unhappiness, anxiety, or depression, for example) becomes comparable to a level of physical discomfort that would cause you to see a doctor or dentist, you should consider seeing a psychologist or a psychiatrist.
2. Another sign that should influence your decision is the occurrence of significant changes in observable behavior such as the quality of your work (including schoolwork), your rate of absenteeism, your use of drugs (including alcohol), or your relationships with others who are important to you.
3. Perhaps you have at some time urged a friend or relative to seek professional help and were then dismayed because they refused to recognize the extent of their problem. If *you* find friends or relatives making a similar suggestion, recognize that they may be seeing things more objectively than you.

Table 18–4 Reasons for Consulting a Mental Health Professional

Reason	Percent
Depression	21.2
Marital problems	16.8
Child-rearing problems	9.7
Difficulty in social relationships	5.3
Difficulty in work relationships	5.3
Suicidal thoughts	5.3
Alcohol/drug dependence	3.5
Desire to quit smoking	2.6
Obsession about something	2.6
Sexual dysfunction	2.6
Weight loss/eating disorders	1.8
Spousal/partner abuse	1.8
Hallucinations/hearing voices	1.8
Other	19.5

Note: Respondents could list more than one reason.
(Adapted from Murstein & Fontaine, 1993.)

4. If you have persistent or disturbing suicidal thoughts or impulses, you should seek help immediately.

Table 18–4 lists the reasons most often given by people who voluntarily sought help from a mental health professional.

Locating a Therapist

Question: If I wanted to talk to a therapist, how would I find one?

1. *The yellow pages.* Psychologists are listed in the telephone book under "Psychologist" or in some cases under "Counseling Services." Psychiatrists are generally listed as a subheading under "Physicians." Counselors are usually found under the heading "Marriage and Family Counselors." These listings will usually put you in touch with individuals in private practice.
2. *Community or county mental health centers.* Most counties and many cities in the United States now offer public mental health services. (These are listed in the phone book.) Public mental health centers usually provide counseling and therapy services directly and can make referrals to private therapists.
3. *Mental health associations.* Many cities have mental health associations organized by concerned citizens. Groups such as these usually keep listings of qualified therapists and of other services and programs in the community.
4. *Colleges and universities.* If you are a student, don't overlook counseling services offered by a student health center or special student counseling facilities.
5. *Newspaper advertisements.* Some psychologists advertise their services in newspapers. Also, low-cost "outreach" clinics occasionally try to make their presence known to the public by advertising. In either case, you should carefully inquire into a therapist's training and qualifications. Without the benefit of a referral from a trusted person, it is wise to be cautious.
6. *Crisis hotlines.* The typical crisis hotline is a telephone service staffed by community volunteers. These people are trained to provide information concerning a wide range of mental health problems. They also have lists of organizations, services, and other resources in the community to which they can refer you for help.

Table 18–5 summarizes all of the sources for psychotherapy, counseling, and referrals we have discussed, as well as some additional possibilities.

Question: How would I know what kind of a therapist to see? How would I pick one?

Options The choice between a psychiatrist and a psychologist is somewhat arbitrary. Both are trained to do psychotherapy. While a psychiatrist can administer somatic therapy and prescribe drugs, a psychologist can work in conjunction with a physician if such services are needed.

Fees for psychiatrists are usually higher, averaging about $100 an hour. Psychologists average about $85 an hour. Counselors and social workers typically charge about $70 per hour. Group therapy averages only $40 because the therapist's fee is divided among several people (Engler & Goleman, 1992).

Table 18–5 Mental Health Resources

- Family doctors
- Mental health specialists, such as psychiatrists, psychologists, social workers, or mental health counselors
- Health maintenance organizations
- Community mental health centers
- Hospital psychiatry departments and outpatient clinics
- University- or medical school-affiliated programs
- State hospital outpatient clinics
- Family service/social agencies
- Private clinics and facilities
- Employee assistance programs
- Local medical, psychiatric, or psychological societies

Source: National Institute of Mental Health

With fees in mind, your decision may be influenced by whether you have health insurance that will cover the expense. If fees are a problem, keep in mind that many individual therapists charge on a sliding scale, or ability-to-pay basis, and that community mental health centers almost always charge on a sliding scale.

Some communities and college campuses have counseling services staffed by sympathetic **paraprofessionals** or **peer counselors.** These services are free or very low cost. There is a natural tendency, perhaps, to doubt the abilities of paraprofessionals. However, many studies have shown that paraprofessional counselors are often as effective as professionals (Christensen & Jacobson, 1994).

Also, don't overlook **self-help groups,** which can add valuable support to professional treatment. Members of a self-help group typically share a particular type of problem, such as eating disorders or coping with an alcoholic parent. Self-help groups offer members mutual support and a chance to discuss problems. In many instances helping others also serves as therapy for those who give help (Levine, Toro, & Perkins, 1993). For some problems, self-help groups may be the best choice of all (Christensen & Jacobson, 1994).

Question: What about self-help books?

Large numbers of people turn to self-help books each year. At their best, self-help books can provide valuable information and advice. At their worst, self-help books are like a fast-food version of psychotherapy: They are quick and inexpensive, but low in nutritional value (Marx et al., 1992).

Some self-help books simply promise too much or make personal change sound too easy. Such books can lead readers to unfairly blame themselves for conditions over which they have little control. A person who is already feeling overwhelmed might end up feeling utterly hopeless if he or she can't follow the advice given in a self-help book. (Gambrill, 1992).

About one-third of all therapists at least occasionally recommend self-help books to their clients. This practice, which is called **bibliotherapy** (book-therapy), suggests that certain books do have value. Bibliotherapy is typically used to support traditional therapy. People who read self-help books on their own run a risk of getting bad advice or actually being harmed by what they read (Gambrill, 1992; Marx et al., 1992).

In summary, if the problem is not too serious, and you read with a healthy dose of skepticism, some self-help books can actually be helpful. Table 18–6 lists the 10 books given the most favorable ratings by therapists in a recent survey (Marx et al., 1992).

Table 18–6 Favorably Rated Self-Help Books

What Color Is Your Parachute (Bolles, 1987)
On Death and Dying (Kübler-Ross, 1969)
Passages (Sheehy, 1977)
Parent Effectiveness Training (Gordon, 1970)
Adult Children of Alcoholics (Woititz, 1983)
The Relaxation Response (Benson, 1975)
When I Say No I Feel Guilty (Smith, 1975)
When Bad Things Happen To Good People (Kushner, 1981)
Women Who Love Too Much (Norwood, 1985)
The Road Less Traveled (Peck, 1980)

Marx et al., 1992

Qualifications You can usually get information about the training and qualifications of a therapist simply by asking. A reputable therapist will be glad to reveal his or her background. If you have any doubts, credentials may be checked and other helpful information can be obtained from local branches of any of the following organizations. You can also write to the addresses listed here.

American Family Therapy Association
2020 Pennsylvania Ave. N.W., Suite 273
Washington, DC 20006

American Psychiatric Association
1400 K Street N.W.
Washington, DC 20005

American Psychological Association
750 1st Street, N.E.
Washington, DC 20002

American Association of Humanistic Psychology
7 Hartwood Dr.
Amherst, NY 14226

Canadian Psychiatric Association
200–237 Argyle
Ottawa, ONT K2P1B8

National Mental Health Association
1021 Prince St.
Alexandria, VA 22314

The question of how to pick a particular therapist remains. The best way is to start with one short consultation with a respected psychiatrist or psychologist or with a counselor at a mental health center. This will allow the person you consult to evaluate the nature of your difficulty and recommend an appropriate type of therapy or a therapist who is likely to be helpful. As an alternative you might ask the person teaching this course for a referral.

Paraprofessional An individual who works in a near-professional capacity under the supervision of a more highly trained person.

Peer counselor A non-professional person who has learned basic counseling skills.

Self-help group A group of people who share a particular type of problem and provide mutual support to one another.

Bibliotherapy Use of books to impart helpful information, either alone or as an adjunct to other forms of therapy.

Table 18–7 Psychotherapy Danger Signals

- Sexual advances by therapist
- Therapist makes repeated verbal threats or is physically aggressive
- Therapist is excessively blaming, belittling, hostile, or controlling
- Therapist makes excessive small talk; talks repeatedly about his/her own problems
- Therapist encourages prolonged dependence on him/her
- Therapist demands absolute trust or tells client not to discuss therapy with anyone else

Question: How would I know whether or not to quit or ignore a therapist?

Evaluating a Therapist A balanced look at psychotherapies suggests that all *techniques* are about equally successful (Omer & London, 1988; Stiles et al., 1986). However, all *therapists* are not equally successful. Far more important than the approach used are the therapist's personal qualities (Luborsky et al., 1986). The most consistently successful therapists are those who are willing to use whatever method seems most helpful for a client. They are also marked by personal characteristics of warmth, integrity, sincerity, and empathy (Patterson, 1989; Strupp, 1989).

It is perhaps most accurate to say that at this stage of development, psychotherapy is an art, not a science. The *relationship* between a client and therapist is the therapist's most basic tool (Strupp, 1989). This is why you must trust and easily relate to a therapist for therapy to be effective. (See Table 18–7.) Clients who like their therapist are generally more successful in therapy (Gomes-Schwartz et al., 1978; Talley et al., 1990). An especially important part of the therapeutic alliance is agreement about the goals of therapy. It is therefore a good idea to think about what you would like to accomplish by entering therapy. Write down your goals and discuss them with your therapist during the first session (Goldfried et al., 1990). Your first meeting with a therapist should also answer all of the following questions (Somberg et al., 1993):

- Will the information I reveal in therapy remain completely confidential?
- What risks do I face if I begin therapy?
- How long do you expect treatment to last?
- What form of treatment do you expect to use?
- Are there alternatives to therapy that might help me as much or more?

It's always tempting to avoid facing up to personal problems. With this in mind, you should give a therapist a fair chance and not give up too easily. But don't hesitate to change therapists or to terminate therapy if you lose confidence in the therapist or if you don't relate well to the therapist as a person.

Learning Check

1. Covert sensitization and thought stopping combine aversion therapy and cognitive therapy. T or F?
2. Like covert aversion conditioning, covert reinforcement of desired responses is also possible. T or F?
3. Exercises that bring about deep-muscle relaxation are an essential element in covert sensitization. T or F?
4. Items in a desensitization hierarchy should be placed in order from the least disturbing to the most disturbing. T or F?
5. The first step in desensitization is to place the visualization of disturbing images under stimulus control. T or F?
6. Persistent emotional discomfort is a clear sign that professional psychological counseling should be sought. T or F?
7. Community mental health centers rarely offer counseling or therapy themselves; they only do referrals. T or F?
8. In many instances, a therapist's personal qualities have more of an effect on the outcome of therapy than does the type of therapy used. T or F?

Critical Thinking

9. Would it be acceptable for a therapist to urge a client to break all ties with a troublesome family member?

Answers: 1. T 2. T 3. F 4. T 5. F 6. T 7. F 8. T 9. Such decisions must be made by clients themselves. Therapists can help clients evaluate important decisions and feelings about significant persons in their lives. However, actively urging a client to sever a relationship borders on unethical behavior.

EXPLORATION

Cultural Issues in Counseling and Psychotherapy

Western nations are rapidly moving toward cultural pluralism. A pluralistic society combines the traditions of many racial and ethnic groups in a rich and varied tapestry. Our own multicultural society increasingly calls for therapists who can work with clients from varied cultural backgrounds (Lee, 1991b). Consider the following case history:

David Chan

David Chan, a 21-year-old college student majoring in engineering, was failing his classes and suffering from headaches, indigestion, and insomnia. A medical doctor could find no physical cause for David's illness, so he sought counseling. During his first session David seemed depressed and anxious. He responded to questions with short, polite, but impersonal statements that revealed little about his feelings. After several more sessions, the counselor was able to see that David did not like engineering and felt pressured by his parents to go into this field. The counselor felt that David was too dependent on his parents and unable to express his anger towards them. To help him vent his feelings, the counselor used a Gestalt technique called the "empty chair." The counselor asked David to imagine that his parents were seated in two chairs placed opposite him. After much prompting, David was able to express his true feelings toward his parents. However, in the following counseling sessions, David seemed more withdrawn and guilt-ridden than ever (Sue & Sue, 1991).

David's counselor had a long history of success with other clients. What went wrong in his work with David? The fault lies in subtle cultural differences between the counselor, who is an Anglo-American, and David, a Chinese American.

David's cultural heritage emphasizes moderation, self-discipline, patience, humility, and above all, respect for one's parents. David's counselor has been trained to value independence, openness, and free expression of personal thoughts and feelings. Because he used his own experience as a guide, the counselor misunderstood David's restrained answers to questions, which merely reflect David's deference to authority. The counselor's use of the empty chair technique also appears to have been a mistake. "Honor thy parents" is a very basic Chinese-American value. Asking David to "talk back" to his parents actually made his conflicts worse. For David, a less direct, more culturally aware approach might have been more helpful (Sue & Sue, 1991).

Traditional theories of counseling and psychotherapy tend to emphasize values like those listed in Table 18–1. However, these values are not shared by all cultures or ethnic groups. For example, American culture strongly emphasizes competition and individualism, whereas others stress cooperation and group effort. What is considered healthy or ideal in one culture can be undesirable in another. In David's case, the behavior that his counselor saw as overly passive is actually a preferred way of interacting in Chinese-American culture. In short, therapists and counselors are learning that they need to use strategies and techniques that are consistent with the life experiences and cultural values of their clients (Lee, 1991b).

Cultural Barriers

Counseling and psychotherapy rely on honest and direct communication. Yet, when a client and therapist come from different cultural backgrounds, misunderstandings are common (Axelson, 1985). Cultural groups vary greatly in their beliefs, values, religious convictions, lifestyles, sexual attitudes, family structures, and preferred languages. The culturally aware therapist must be very careful to not make false assumptions about a client's personal history, values, goals for therapy, or expectations (Sue & Zane, 1987).

Psychologists Derald Sue and David Sue (1990) believe there are four main **cultural barriers** to effective counseling. These include differences in language, social class, cultural values, and non-verbal communication. Non-verbal communication provides a good example of how even small cultural differences can lead to misunderstandings. In most Native American cultures, one of the ways you show respect is by not making eye contact. This is why American Indians who enter therapy may spend much of their time looking at their feet or at the ground. To look a therapist in the eye is to challenge his or her authority and be disrespectful. But if the therapist doesn't understand Native American culture, the client's behavior looks like a textbook case of poor self-esteem. In light of such misunderstandings, it's not surprising that over half of all Native Americans do not return after a first therapy session with non-native therapists (Heinrich, Corbine, & Thomas, 1990).

Culturally Skilled Counselors

A **culturally skilled counselor** is a therapist who has the awareness, knowledge, and skills necessary to intervene successfully in the lives of clients from diverse cultural backgrounds. Counselors, of course, need to be aware of issues faced by almost everyone, such as problems with personal relationships, education and achievement, work and career, parenting, and personal growth. In addition, the culturally skilled counselor must know about the special conflicts and problems typical of members of various racial or ethnic groups (Lee & Richardson, 1991).

A major step toward competence as a culturally skilled counselor is to become more aware of one's own cultural values and biases. Whatever a counselor's own ethnocultural background, he or she must try to avoid thinking of clients in terms of stereotypes. The therapist must also affirm that minority cultural beliefs and values are different, but not inferior to his or her own (Heinrich, Corbine, & Thomas, 1990). He or she needs to gain knowl-

Cultural barriers Differences in language, social class, cultural values, and non-verbal communication that impede social interaction.

Culturally skilled counselor A therapist who has the awareness, knowledge, and skills necessary to treat clients from diverse cultural backgrounds.

EXPLORATION

edge about the history and culture of diverse groups of people, often by direct experience in the community (Lee, 1991b). This allows the culturally skilled counselor to use appropriate methods and choose appropriate goals (Sue & Sue, 1990).

Contrary to what our discussion may imply, cross-cultural counseling can be quite successful. Cultural barriers are transcended on a regular basis by counselors who can achieve empathy with their clients. This is aided by being able to mentally take the role of the client (Scott & Borodovsky, 1990).

Question: What do you mean by "mentally take the role of the client"?

Multicultural counselors attempt to put themselves in their clients' shoes by making sure they understand the client's sense of ethnic identity, degree of acculturation, family influences, sex-role socialization, religious or spiritual beliefs, and immigration experiences (Lee, 1991a). The more the counselor's and client's backgrounds differ, the more important it is for such factors to guide therapy.

If a therapist is knowledgeable enough, it can also be valuable to incorporate cultural beliefs and healing practices into therapy. Many ethnic groups make little distinction between religious and secular life. As a consequence, spiritual beliefs may greatly influence everyday life and personal adjustment. For this reason, therapists sometimes work with clergy or tribal healers to bridge the gap between cultures (Heinrich, Corbine, & Thomas, 1990; Richardson, 1991).

In summary, the culturally skilled counselor must be able to do all of the following (Lee, 1991b):

- Establish rapport with a person from a different cultural background
- Adapt traditional theories and techniques to meet the needs of clients from non-European ethnic or racial groups
- Be sensitive to cultural differences without resorting to stereotypes
- Treat members of racial or ethnic communities as individuals
- Be aware of a client's ethnic identity and degree of acculturation to the majority society
- Use existing helping resources within a cultural group to support efforts to resolve problems

Conclusion Multicultural awareness has helped broaden our ideas about mental health and optimal development. Furthermore, the lessons learned in cross-cultural counseling draw attention to other differences that may have an impact on therapy. Effective therapists need to be sensitive not only to racial and ethnic differences, but also to differences related to age, sexual orientation, religious beliefs, handicaps, and other such dimensions ("Guidelines," 1993). It is also worth remembering that cultural barriers apply to communication in all areas of life, not just therapy. While such differences can be challenging, they are also frequently enriching.

LEARNING CHECK

1. As the case history of David Chan shows, it is almost impossible for counseling or psychotherapy to succeed when the cultural backgrounds of a client and therapist are very different. T or F?
2. A major difference in social class between a client and a therapist, such as urban poor versus upper middle-class, is considered less of a barrier than differences in non-verbal communication. T or F?
3. The culturally skilled counselor must be highly aware of his or her own cultural background, as well as that of clients. T or F?
4. Although Marsha cannot really know what it is like to leave a war-torn nation and emigrate to a strange country, she has talked extensively with members of the Vietnamese-American community and feels great empathy for them. Marsha has met a key requirement for effective cross-cultural counseling of Vietnamese immigrants. T or F?

Critical Thinking

5. The essence of culturally skilled counseling could be summarized as an awareness of the social and cultural ________________ in which people live.

Answers: 1. F 2. F 3. T 4. T 5. contexts

Chapter Summary

■ ***How do psychotherapies differ?***

- **Psychotherapies** may be classified as **insight, action, directive, non-directive,** or **supportive** therapies, and combinations of these. Therapies may be conducted either *individually* or in *groups*, and they may be *time limited.*

■ ***How did modern therapies originate?***

- Primitive approaches to mental illness were often based on superstition. **Trepanning** involved boring a hole in the skull. **Demonology** attributed mental disturbance to supernatural forces and prescribed **exorcism** as the cure. In some instances, the actual cause of bizarre behavior may have been **ergot poisoning.** More humane treatment began in 1793 with the work of *Philippe Pinel* in Paris.

■ ***Is Freudian psychoanalysis still used?***

- Freud's **psychoanalysis** was the first formal psychotherapy. Psychoanalysis seeks a release of repressed thoughts and emotions from the unconscious. The psychoanalyst uses **free association, dream analysis,** and analysis of **resistance** and **transference** to reveal health-producing insights.
- Some critics have argued that traditional psychoanalysis has received credit for *spontaneous remissions* of symptoms. However, psychoanalysis has been shown to be better than no treatment at all. Also, **short-term dynamic therapy** (which relies on psychoanalytic theory but is brief and focused) is as effective as other major therapies.

■ ***What are the major humanistic therapies?***

- **Client-centered** (or **person-centered**) **therapy** is non-directive and is dedicated to creating an atmosphere of growth. *Unconditional positive regard, empathy, authenticity,* and *reflection* are combined to give the client a chance to solve his or her own problems.
- **Existential therapies,** such as Frankl's **logotherapy,** focus on the end result of the choices one makes in life. Clients are encouraged through *confrontation* and *encounter* to exercise *free will* and to take responsibility for their choices.
- **Gestalt therapy** emphasizes immediate awareness of thoughts and feelings. Its goal is to rebuild thinking, feeling, and acting into *connected wholes* and to help clients break through emotional blocks.

■ ***What is aversion therapy?***

- **Behavior therapists** use various **behavior modification** techniques that apply learning principles to change human behavior.
- In **aversion therapy,** classical conditioning is used to associate maladaptive behavior (such as smoking or drinking) with pain or other aversive events in order to inhibit undesirable responses.

■ ***How is behavior therapy used to treat phobias, fears, and anxieties?***

- Classical conditioning also underlies **systematic desensitization,** a technique used to overcome fears and anxieties. In desensitization, gradual **adaptation** and **reciprocal inhibition** break the link between fear and particular situations.
- Typical steps in desensitization are: Construct a **fear hierarchy;** learn to produce total relaxation; and perform items on the hierarchy (from least to most disturbing).
- Desensitization may be carried out with real settings or it may be done by *vividly imagining* the fear hierarchy. Desensitization is also effective when it is administered **vicariously;** that is, when clients watch **models** perform the feared responses.
- A new technique called **eye-movement desensitization** shows promise as a treatment for traumatic memories and stress disorders.

■ ***What role does reinforcement play in behavior therapy?***

- Behavior modification also makes use of operant principles, such as **positive reinforcement, nonreinforcement, extinction, punishment, shaping, stimulus control,** and **time out.** These principles are used to extinguish undesirable responses and to promote constructive behavior.
- Non-reward can extinguish troublesome behaviors. Often this is done by simply *identifying* and *eliminating* reinforcers, particularly *attention* and *approval.*
- To apply positive reinforcement and operant shaping, symbolic rewards known as **tokens** are often used. Tokens allow *immediate reinforcement* of selected **target behaviors.**
- Full-scale use of tokens in an institutional setting produces a **token economy.** Toward the end of a token economy program, patients are shifted to **social rewards** such as recognition and approval.

■ ***Can therapy change thoughts and emotions?***

- **Cognitive therapy** emphasizes changing thought patterns that underlie emotional or behavioral problems. Its goals are to correct distorted thinking and/or teach improved coping skills.
- In a variation of cognitive therapy called **rational-emotive therapy** (RET), clients learn to recognize and challenge their own **irrational beliefs.**

■ ***Can psychotherapy be done with groups of people?***

- **Group therapy** may be a simple extension of individual methods or it may be based on techniques developed specifically for groups.
- In **psychodrama,** individuals enact roles and incidents resembling their real-life problems. In **family therapy,** the family group is treated as a unit.
- Although they are not literally psychotherapies, **sensitivity** and **encounter groups** attempt to encourage positive personality change. In recent years, commercially offered **large-group awareness trainings** have become popular. However, the therapeutic benefits of such programs are questionable.

■ ***What do various therapies have in common?***

- To alleviate personal problems, all psychotherapies offer a *caring relationship*, *emotional rapport*, a *protected setting*, *catharsis*, *explanations* for the client's problems, a *new perspective*, and a chance to practice *new behaviors*.
- Many **basic counseling skills** underlie a variety of therapies. These include *listening actively*, helping to *clarify the problem*, *focusing on feelings*, avoiding the giving of *unwanted advice*, accepting the person's *perspective*, *reflecting* thoughts and feelings, being *patient* during silences, using *open questions* when possible, and maintaining *confidentiality*.

■ ***How are behavioral principles applied to everyday problems?***

- Cognitive techniques can be an aid to managing personal behavior. In **covert sensitization**, aversive images are used to discourage unwanted behavior. **Thought stopping** uses mild punishment to prevent upsetting thoughts. **Covert reinforcement** is a way to encourage desired responses by mental rehearsal. *Desensitization* pairs relaxation with a hierarchy of upsetting images in order to lessen fears.

■ ***How would a person go about finding professional help?***

- Sources of psychological help exist in most communities. A competent and reputable therapist can usually be located through public sources of information or a *referral*.
- Practical considerations such as cost and qualifications enter into choosing a therapist. However, the therapist's personal characteristics are of equal importance.

■ ***Do cultural differences affect counseling and psychotherapy?***

- Many **cultural barriers** to effective counseling and therapy have been identified. Aware therapists are beginning to seek out the knowledge and skills needed to intervene successfully in the lives of clients from diverse cultural backgrounds.
- The **culturally skilled counselor** must be able to establish rapport with a person from a different cultural background and adapt traditional theories and techniques to meet the needs of clients from non-European ethnic or racial groups.

Questions for Discussion

1. What preconceptions did you have about psychotherapy? Has your understanding of therapy changed? Has your attitude changed?
2. If you were going to become a therapist, would you be more inclined to master the skills of a psychodynamic therapy, insight therapy, behavior therapy, or cognitive therapy? Why?
3. What similarities do you think Carl Rogers would have seen in the role of being a "good therapist" and the role of being a "good parent"?
4. Do you think it would be right for a therapist to allow a person to make suicide an "existential choice" or an expression of "free will"?
5. Based on the techniques described, would you cooperate with a therapist who wanted to use behavior therapy? Are there some techniques you find acceptable and others not?
6. Describe a time when you helped someone resolve a personal problem. Describe a time when you were unsuccessful in helping. What factors seemed to make a difference?
7. In your opinion, are radio psychologists engaged in education or therapy? Is talk-show psychology ethical? What about telephone therapy? What value is there for listeners and callers in talking with a radio psychologist?
8. Select a bad habit you would like to break or a positive behavior you would like to encourage, and explain how you might use a behavioral or cognitive technique to alter your behavior.
9. What psychological services are available in your area? Would you know how to find or make use of them? What concerns would affect your decision to seek help?
10. Computers have been programmed to simulate psychotherapy. Which style of therapy would you expect a computer program to most closely duplicate? If a computer were programmed to provide help for a limited problem such as test anxiety, would you find computer therapy acceptable?
11. It has been said that, to a degree, all counseling and therapy relationships are cross-cultural in nature. Do you agree or disagree?

Chapter 19

Gender and Sexuality

CHAPTER PREVIEW

That Magic Word

Sex\seks n 1. One of the two divisions of organisms formed on the distinction of male and female.

"Sex" has many meanings: reproduction, gender, sexual identity, intimacy, and much more. Of the various meanings, the simplest would seem to be the reference to gender. What, really, could be simpler? Males are males and females are females, right? Wrong. Even something as basic as gender is complicated and many sided.

Gender *The complexity of gender is illustrated by the attempt of Dr. Renée Richards to enter a women's tennis tournament. Dr. Richards is a transsexual. Formerly she was Dr. Richard Raskin, an ophthalmologist. As a man, Richard Raskin was a modestly successful tennis player. After a sex-change operation, Dr. Richards tried to launch a new tennis career as a woman. Understandably, other women players protested. Officials finally decided to use a genetic sex test to determine if Dr. Richards could compete. She, in turn, protested this test. Genetically she would still be considered male, but psychologically she is female—she has female genitals, and she functions socially as a female (Hyde, 1990). Is Dr. Richards, then, male or female?*

IN THIS CHAPTER

You might view the case of Renée Richards as an unfair example because transsexuals seek to alter natural gender. For most people, the various indicators of gender are in agreement. Nevertheless, it is not unusual to find occasional ambiguities among the dimensions of a person's "sex." Contrary to common belief, gender is not a simple either-or classification. In the first part of this chapter, we will consider some basic dimensions of "maleness" and "femaleness." An essential question we will address is, How does one become male or female?

Sexual Behavior *Each of us is by nature a sexual creature. This inescapable reality springs from the basic biology of reproduction. With this reality in mind, later sections of this chapter discuss sexual behavior, sexual arousal and response, sexual problems, and attitudes toward sexuality. These are topics you may feel you already know a lot about. Therefore, before reading further, you may find it interesting to see if you can correctly answer the* Human Sexuality Quiz. *Answers follow the quiz. The reasons for the answers can be found in this chapter.*

Human Sexuality Quiz *Indicate which of the statements are true and which are false.*

1. Women are generally incapable of multiple orgasm.
2. More than half of all cases of erection problems in males are psychologically caused.
3. Frequent nocturnal emissions ("wet dreams") in males indicate the existence of a sexual disorder.
4. Male sexual potency and female pleasure in intercourse are closely related to penis size.
5. Of the various sexual dysfunctions, premature ejaculation is one of the easiest to treat.
6. In recent years, medical advances have brought about a decline in the overall occurrence of sexually transmitted diseases.
7. For women, masturbation typically involves stimulation of the clitoris.
8. Sterilization in both men and women usually abolishes the sex drive.
9. Women have two kinds of orgasm, vaginal and clitoral.
10. The "sexual revolution" has brought about greater changes in women's sexual behavior than men's.
11. Men are more physically aroused by explicit erotic stimuli (such as pornographic films) than women are.
12. Maximum sexual responsiveness generally occurs at a later age for women than it does for men.

Answers: 1. F 2. T 3. F 4. F 5. T 6. F 7. T 8. F 9. F 10. T 11. F 12. T

Survey Questions

- What are the basic dimensions of gender?
- How does one's sense of maleness or femaleness develop?
- What is psychological androgyny (and is it contagious)?
- What are the most typical patterns of human sexual behavior?
- To what extent do males and females differ in sexual response?
- Have recent changes in attitudes affected sexual behavior?
- What impacts have sexually transmitted diseases had on sexual behavior?
- What are the most common sexual adjustment problems? How are they treated?
- What is the role of touching in personal relationships?

Gender Development—Circle One: XX or XY?

It has been said that the one thing you will never forget about a person is that person's sex. Considering the number of activities, relationships, conflicts, and choices influenced by gender, it is no wonder that we pay close attention to it. Let's begin with a few basic questions: What does it mean to be male or female? What are the dimensions of gender? How do gender and sex role differences develop?

Male or Female?

Traditionally, the basic physical differences between males and females have been divided into *primary* and *secondary* sexual characteristics. **Primary sexual characteristics** refer to the sexual and reproductive organs themselves: the penis, testes, and scrotum in males and the vagina, ovaries, and uterus in females (■ Figs. 19–1 and ■ 19–2). As described in Chapter 13, **secondary sexual characteristics** appear at puberty in response to hormonal signals from the pituitary gland. In females, secondary sexual characteristics involve development of the breasts, broadening of the hips, and other changes in body shape. Males develop facial and body hair, and the voice deepens. These changes signal readiness for reproduction. Reproductive maturity is especially evident in the female **menarche** (MEN-ar-kee: the onset of menstruation). Soon after menarche, monthly **ovulation** begins. Ovulation refers to the release of ova (eggs) from the ovaries. From the first ovulation until **menopause** (the end of regular monthly fertility cycles), women can bear children.

Question: What causes the development of sex differences?

Sex Hormones In general terms, both primary and secondary sexual characteristics are related to the action of sex hormones in the body. (*Hormones* are chemical substances secreted by glands of the endocrine system.) The **gonads** (or sex glands) affect sexual development and behavior by secreting **estrogens** (female hormones) and **androgens** (male hormones). The gonads in the male are the testes; female gonads are the ovaries. The adrenal glands (located above the kidneys) also supply sex hormones in both males and females. At puberty, adrenal secretions add to the development of secondary sexual characteristics.

Interestingly, all individuals normally produce both estrogens and androgens. It is the proportion of these hormones that influences sex differences. In fact, the development of male or female anatomy is largely due to the presence or absence—before birth—of **testosterone** (one of the androgens) (Breedlove, 1994).

Question: Then is biological sex determined by the sex hormones?

Primary sexual characteristics Gender as defined by the genitals and internal reproductive organs.

Secondary sexual characteristics Sexual features such as the breasts, body shape, and facial hair.

Menarche The onset of menstruation.

Ovulation The release of an ovum (egg cell) by the ovaries.

Menopause An end to regular monthly menstrual periods.

Gonads The primary sex glands; the testes in males and ovaries in females.

Estrogen Any of a number of female sex hormones.

Androgen Any of a number of male sex hormones.

Testosterone Male sex hormone, secreted mainly by the testes.

■ **Fig. 19–1** *Cutaway view of internal and external male reproductive structures.*

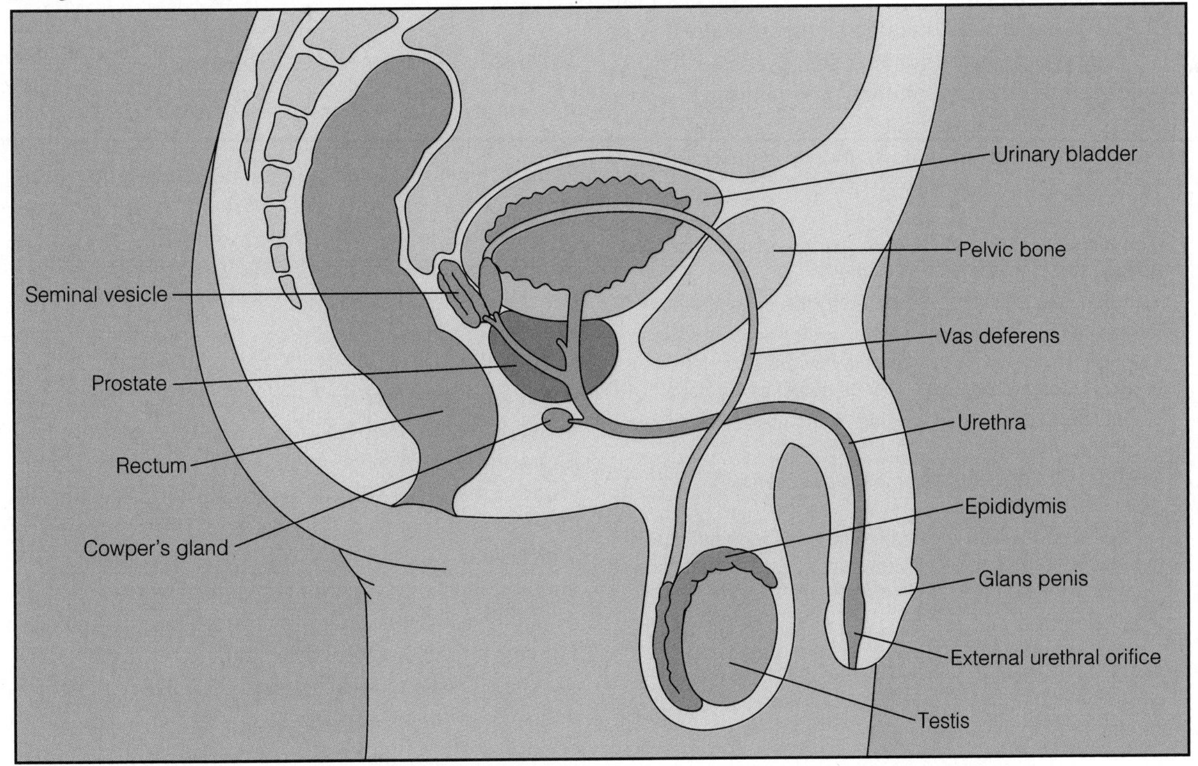

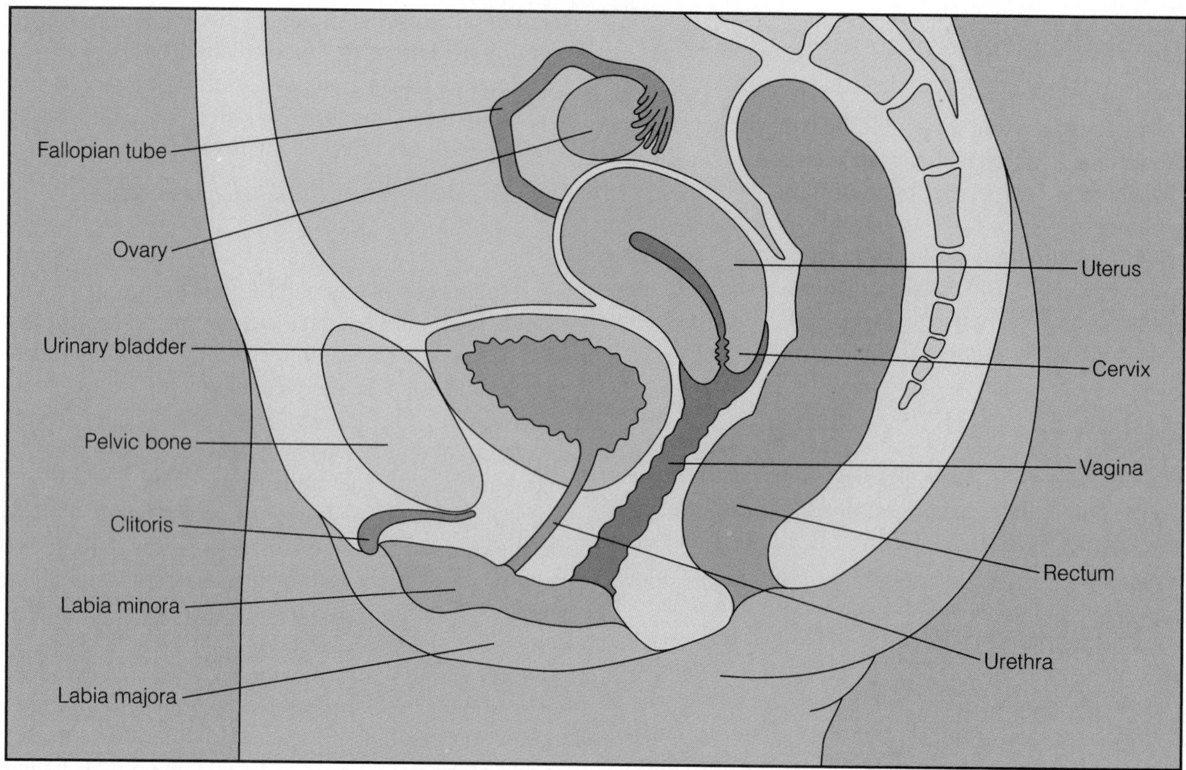

■ Fig. 19–2 *Cutaway view of internal and external female reproductive structures.*

Not entirely. As suggested by our discussion in the Chapter Preview, gender cannot be reduced to a single dimension.

Dimensions of Gender At the very least, any evaluation of gender must include (1) **genetic sex** (XX or XY chromosomes), (2) **gonadal sex** (ovaries or testes), (3) **hormonal sex** (predominance of androgens or estrogens), (4) **genital sex** (clitoris and vagina in females, penis and scrotum in males), and (5) **gender identity** (one's personal sense of maleness or femaleness). To see why gender must be defined along several dimensions, let's follow the sequence of events involved in becoming male or female.

Genetic sex Gender as indicated by the presence of *XX* (female) or *XY* (male) chromosomes.

Gonadal sex Gender as indicated by the presence of ovaries (female) or testes (male).

Hormonal sex Gender as indicated by a preponderance of estrogens (female) or androgens (male) in the body.

Genital sex Gender as indicated by the presence of male or female genitals.

Gender identity One's personal, private sense of maleness or femaleness.

***X* chromosome** The female chromosome contributed by the mother; produces a female when paired with another *X* chromosome, and a male when paired with a *Y* chromosome.

***Y* chromosome** The male chromosome contributed by the father; produces a male when paired with an *X* chromosome. Fathers may give either an *X* or a *Y* chromosome to their offspring.

Prenatal Gender Development

Becoming male or female starts simply enough. Genetic sex is determined at the instant of conception: Two **X chromosomes** initiate development of a female; an X chromosome plus a **Y chromosome** produces a male. Genetic sex remains the same throughout life. But it alone does not determine gender. We must also consider hormonal effects before birth.

For the first 6 weeks of prenatal growth, there is no difference between a genetically male and a genetically female embryo. However, if a Y chromosome is present, testes develop in the embryo and supply testosterone. This stimulates growth of the penis and other male structures (■ Fig. 19–3). In the absence of testosterone, the embryo will develop female reproductive organs and genitals, regardless of genetic sex (Breedlove, 1994). It might be said, then, that nature's primary impulse is to make a female.

Development of the embryo usually matches genetic sex, but not always. A genetic male will fail to develop male genitals if too little testosterone is formed

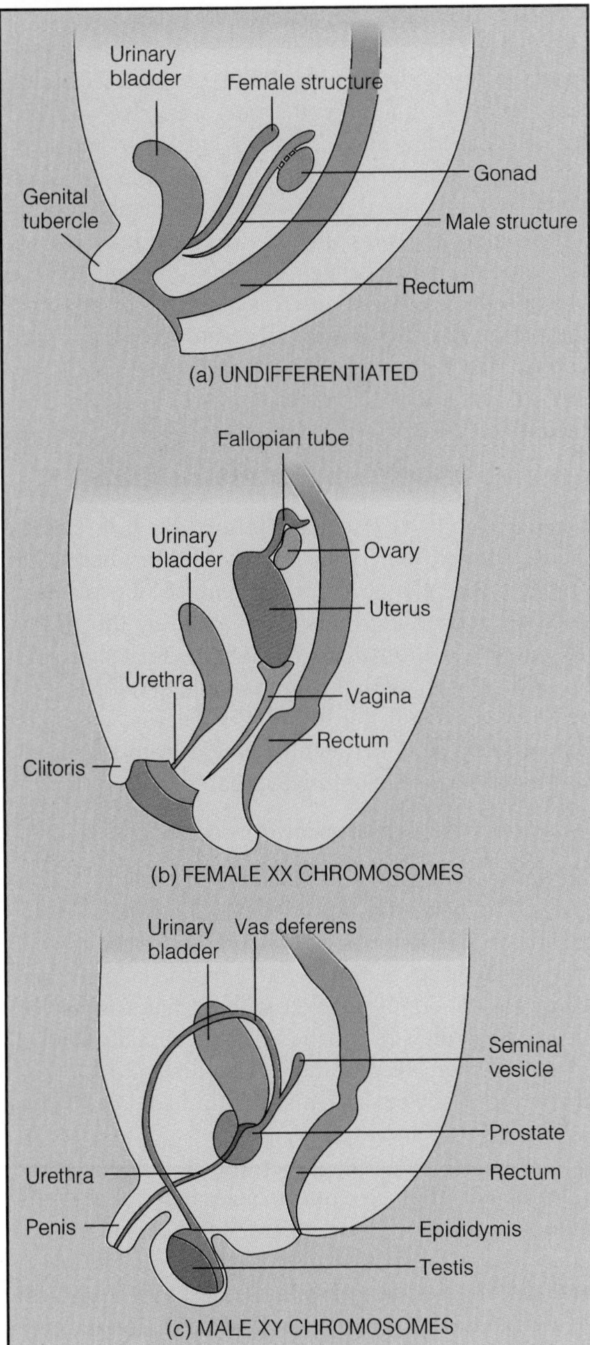

■ **Fig. 19–3** *Prenatal development of the reproductive organs. Early development of ovaries or testes affects hormonal balance and alters sexual anatomy.* (a) *At first the sex organs are the same in the human male and female.* (b) *When androgens are absent, female structures develop.* (c) *Male sex organs are produced when androgens are present.*

during prenatal growth. Even if testosterone is present, an inherited *androgen insensitivity* may exist, again resulting in female development (Breedlove, 1994).

Similarly, androgens must be either at low levels or absent for an XX embryo to develop as a female. Thus, for both genetic males and females, hormonal problems before birth may result in **hermaphroditism** (her-MAF-ro-dite-ism). This term refers to defects in sexual development that result in dual or ambiguous sexual anatomy. For instance, a developing female may be masculinized by *progestin* (a drug given to prevent miscarriage) or by the *androgenital syndrome* (an-dro-JEN-ih-tal). In the androgenital syndrome, the child's body produces estrogen, but a genetic abnormality causes the adrenal glands to release too much androgen. In such cases a female child may be born with male genitals.

Question: Would such a child be reared as a male?

Some are. Usually, however, the condition is detected and corrected by surgery. If necessary, extra estrogen may be given after birth.

Origins of Male-Female Differences Some researchers believe that in addition to guiding physical development, the interplay of sex hormones before birth may also "sex-type" the brain (Breedlove, 1994; Money, 1987). Changes in the brain are then thought to alter later chances of developing masculine or feminine characteristics.

Question: Does that mean there is a physical basis for male and female traits?

In animals, clear links exist between prenatal hormones and the later emergence of male or female behaviors. For humans, however, the evidence suggests that most sex-linked behavior is learned (Caplan et al., 1985, 1987; Hare-Mustin & Marecek, 1988). Be that as it may, some researchers believe that prenatal exposure to androgens or estrogens at least exerts a subtle **biological biasing effect** on later psychosexual development in humans.

Question: Is there any evidence for that?

Consider females who have been exposed to androgens before birth. After birth, their hormone balance shifts to female and they are raised as girls. Does prenatal exposure to male hormones have any masculinizing effect on their psychological development? Medical psychologist John Money has observed that during childhood, such girls are typically "tomboys" who prefer the company of boys to girls. However, this masculinization does not persist into adulthood. After adolescence, the girls' tomboyism usually gives way to traditional interests in marriage and motherhood (Money, 1987; Money & Mathews, 1982). Cases like these seem to show that both prenatal hormones and later social factors contribute to adult sexual identity.

At the risk of getting mired in the "battle of the sexes," let's consider one more idea. Some researchers believe that biology underlies male-female differences in thinking abilities. Women, they contend, are more often "left-brained," and men, "right-brained." The

Androgen insensitivity An inherited disorder in which male embryos fail to develop male genitals because of an unresponsiveness to testosterone.

Hermaphroditism The condition of having genitals suggestive of both sexes; ambiguous genital sexuality.

Androgenital syndrome An inherited disorder that causes the adrenal glands to produce excess androgens, sometimes masculinizing developing females before birth.

Biological biasing effect Hypothesized effect that prenatal exposure to male or female hormones has on development of the body, nervous system, and later behavior patterns.

Sex role socialization The process of learning behaviors considered appropriate for one's gender in a given culture.

Sex roles Separate patterns of traits, mannerisms, interests, and behaviors that are regarded as "male" and "female" by one's culture.

left brain, you may recall, is largely responsible for language and rote learning. The right brain is superior at spatial reasoning. Thus, some psychologists believe that biological differences explain why men (as a group) do slightly better on spatial tasks and math and why women are slightly better at language skills. Others, however, strongly reject this theory. To them, such claims are based on shaky evidence and sexist thinking (Caplan et al., 1985; Hellige, 1990). The most telling evidence on this point may be the fact that differences between male and female scores on the *Scholastic Assessment Test* are rapidly declining (Feingold, 1988). The same applies to tests of math ability (Hyde, Gennema, & Lamon, 1990). These observations are probably explained by the growing similarity of male and female interests, experiences, and educational goals.

The one thing that is certain in the gender debate is that males and females are more alike than they are different (Maccoby & Jacklin, 1974; Tavris, 1992). It is important to realize that any differences that may exist are small and based on *averages* (■ Fig. 19–4). Many women are better than men at math and many men are better than women at verbal skills. Scores for men and women overlap so much that it is impossible to predict if any one individual will be good or bad at math or language simply from knowing his or her gender (Sapolsky, 1987). There is no biological basis for the unequal treatment women have often faced at work, school, and elsewhere (Hyde & Linn, 1988). The important differences between men and women are not in our genes or hormones. Instead, most male-female differences can be traced to social differences in power and opportunities and differences in the ways that men and women are treated in society (Tavris, 1992).

■ Fig. 19–4 *Recorded differences in various abilities that exist between men and women are based on averages. For example, if we were to record the number of men and women who have low, medium, or high scores on tests of language ability, we might obtain graphs like those shown. For other abilities, men would have a higher average. However, such average differences are typically small. As a result, the overlap in male-female abilities is very large (Breedlove, 1994).*

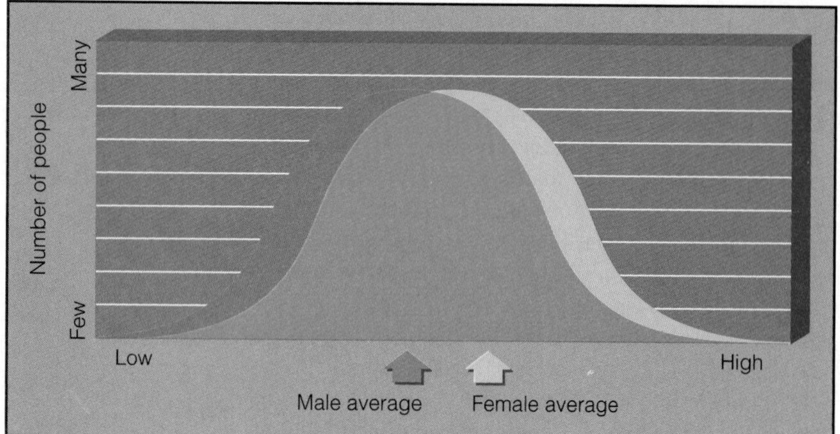

Gender Identity Your personal, private sense of maleness or femaleness, which is referred to as *gender identity*, can be distinguished from *sex roles*. Sex roles are observable traits, mannerisms, interests, and behaviors defined by one's culture as "male" or "female."

Gender identity is a *learned* self-perception. This point is emphasized by cases of hermaphroditism. What happens if we compare two individuals having the same degree of gender ambiguity, one raised as a boy and the other as a girl? Usually, we will find that the person raised as a girl will regard herself as a girl and act like a girl. Likewise, the individual raised as a boy will act like a boy and identify himself as a boy (Money, 1987).

Question: At what age is gender identity acquired?

Gender identity is essentially formed by 3 or 4 years of age (Money, 1977). Accordingly, children born with ambiguous gender have few problems as long as a final decision concerning their sex is made by the age of 18 months. If the parents consistently treat the child as only a boy or a girl, the child should develop a clear sense of gender. If the decision is delayed, the child may develop a gender identity at odds with his or her biological sex, or a confused sexual identity.

Question: How is gender identity acquired?

Obviously, it begins with *labeling* ("It's a boy," "It's a girl"). The powerful impact of labeling is revealed by an interesting study. In an experiment, people were shown videotapes of 4 male and 4 female babies. Each baby was randomly labeled with a male or female name. Regardless of a baby's real sex, infants labeled male were perceived as more masculine and stronger than those labeled as female (Burnham, & Harris, 1992).

Labeling is important because it influences **sex role socialization.** Sex role socialization refers to the countless subtle pressures exerted by parents, peers, and cultural forces that urge boys to "act like boys" and girls to "act like girls." In the next section we will investigate sex roles and sex role socialization in more detail.

Sex Roles and Socialization

Sex roles are probably as important as chromosomal, genital, or hormonal sex in their influence on adult sexual behavior. A **sex role** is the favored pattern of behavior expected of individuals on the basis of their gender. In our culture, boys are usually encouraged to be strong, fast, aggressive, dominant, achieving, and otherwise "male." Females have typically been expected to be sensitive, intuitive, passive, emotional, and "naturally" interested in household chores and child rearing. All cultures define sex roles. As Highlight 19–1 points out, this often leads to stereotyped thinking about males and females.

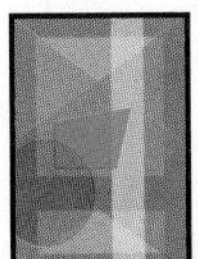

HIGHLIGHT 19–1

Cultural Diversity

Sex Role Stereotypes

Question: How many men does it take to change a light bulb?
Answer: None. Real men aren't afraid of the dark.

This joke pokes fun at North American stereotypes of manhood. Despite much progress in the last 20 years, **sex role stereotypes** continue to have a major impact on men and women in Western societies. Sex role stereotypes are widely held beliefs about what men and women are actually like. *Sex roles* tend to dictate how men and women should act. In contrast, *sex role stereotypes* are over-simplified assumptions about the nature of men and women. In essence, sex role stereotypes treat learned sex roles as if they were real gender differences.

Are women suited to be fighter pilots, corporate presidents, military commanders, or race car drivers? A person with strong sex role stereotypes might say, "No, because women are not sufficiently aggressive, dominant, or mechanically inclined for such roles." Yet, today we know that women have performed successfully in virtually all realms of human endeavor. Nevertheless, sex role stereotypes persist. The United States has never had a woman President, and it wasn't until 1984 that a woman was even nominated as a Vice-Presidential candidate.

In many occupational roles women continue to score "firsts" of the kind just mentioned. Nonetheless, sex role stereotypes are a major obstacle where employment is concerned. Unequal pay for comparable work and experience is a major problem for women (Frieze, Olson, & Good, 1990). Even on college campuses, female faculty members lag behind males in pay and promotions. For many jobs your chances of being hired could be reduced by your gender, be it male or female (Click, Zion, & Nelson, 1988). Like all stereotypes, those based on sex roles ignore the wonderful diversity of humanity and human potential.

"The committee on women's rights will now come to order."
Huck/Punch/London

Sex role stereotypes Over-simplified and widely held beliefs about the basic characteristics of men and women.

The "naturalness" of sex roles becomes questionable when different cultures are compared. For example, Ethel Albert (1963) identified numerous cultures in which women do the heavy work because men are considered too weak for it. In Russia, roughly 75 percent of all medical doctors are women, and women make up a large portion of the work force. Many more examples could be cited, but perhaps one of the most interesting is anthropologist Margaret Mead's (1935) observations of the Tchambuli people of New Guinea.

Sex roles for the Tchambuli are a nearly perfect reversal of American stereotypes. Tchambuli women do the fishing and manufacturing and are expected to control the power and economic life of the community. Women also take the initiative in courting and sexual relations. Tchambuli men, on the other hand, are expected to be dependent, flirtatious, and concerned with their appearance. Art, games, and theatrics occupy most of the Tchambuli males' time, and males are particularly fond of adorning themselves with flowers and jewelry.

As the Tchambuli demonstrate, activities regarded as "appropriate" for males and females vary in different cultures (■ Fig. 19–5). The arbitrary nature of sex roles is also apparent. A man is no less a man if he cooks, sews, or cares for children. A woman is no less a woman if she excels in sports, succeeds in business, or works as an auto mechanic. Still, adult personality and gender identity are closely tied to cultural definitions of "masculinity" and "femininity."

An interesting side effect of sex role socialization is the imprint it leaves on activities having nothing to do with gender. There is considerable evidence, for example, that boys are more aggressive than girls and that girls have more emotional empathy than boys do (Block, 1979; Maccoby & Jacklin, 1974).

Question: How are such differences created?

Sex Role Socialization Learning sex roles begins immediately after birth. Baby girls are held more gently and treated more tenderly than boys. Both parents play more roughly with their sons than with their daughters (who are presumed to be more "delicate").

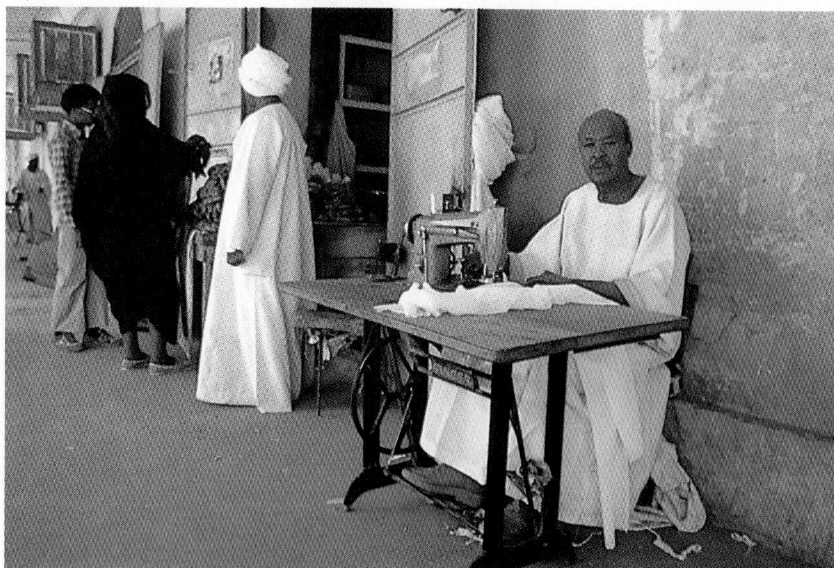

■ Fig. 19–5 *Behaviors that are considered typical and appropriate for each sex (sex roles) vary a great deal from culture to culture. Undoubtedly some cultures magnify sex differences more than others (Breedlove, 1994).*

Instrumental behavior Behavior directed toward the achievement of some goal; behavior that is instrumental in producing some effect.

Expressive behavior Behavior that expresses or communicates emotion.

Later, boys are allowed to roam over a wider area without special permission. They are also expected to run errands earlier than girls. Daughters are told that they are pretty and that "nice girls don't fight." Boys are told to be strong and that "boys don't cry." Sons are more often urged to control emotions than are daughters, and parents tolerate aggression toward other children more in boys than in girls.

The toys purchased for boys and girls are strongly sex-typed: dolls for girls; trucks and guns for boys. Fathers, especially, tend to encourage their children to play with "appropriate" sex-typed toys (Bradley & Gobbart, 1989) (Fig. 19–6). By the time children reach kindergarten they have learned to think that doctors, fire fighters, and pilots are men and that nurses, secretaries, and hairdressers are women (Blaske, 1984). And why not? The work force in North America is still highly segregated by sex, and children learn from what they observe. Stereotyped sex roles are even the norm in children's picture books (McDonald, 1989)!

■ Fig. 19–6 *One study found that even the parents of two-year-olds strongly encourage their toddlers to play with "sex-appropriate" toys. Parents' non-verbal responses to toys were consistently more positive when a toy matched stereotypes for the child's gender (Caldera, Huston, & O'Brien, 1989).*

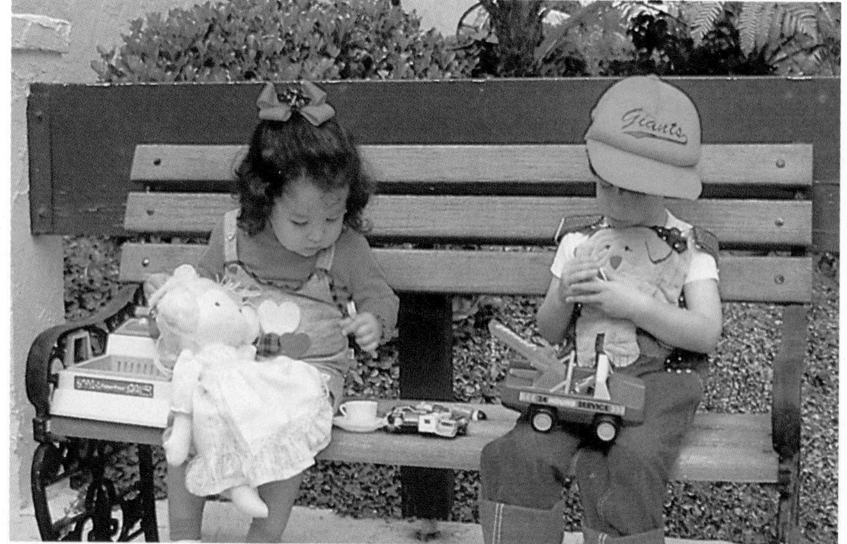

Overall, parents tend to encourage their sons to engage in **instrumental** (goal-directed) **behaviors,** to control their emotions, and to prepare for the world of work. Daughters, on the other hand, are encouraged in **expressive** (emotion-oriented) **behaviors** and, to a lesser degree, are socialized for motherhood.

As they are growing up, children tend to segregate themselves into same-sex groups. During much of childhood, this limits conflicts between male and female patterns of behavior. However, as children move into adolescence they begin to spend more time with members of the opposite sex. This brings the dominant, competitive style of boys into conflict with the nurturant, expressive style of girls, often placing girls at a disadvantage (Maccoby, 1990).

When told that they respond differently to boys and girls, parents often explain that it is because there are "natural" differences between the sexes (Wilson et al., 1984). But what comes first, "natural differences" or the expectations that create them? In our culture, "male" seems—for many—to be defined as "not female." That is, parents often have a vague fear of expressive and emotional behavior in male children, because to them it seems to imply effeminacy (Wilson et al., 1984). Many parents who would not be troubled if their daughters engaged in "masculine" play might be upset if their sons played with dolls or imitated "female" mannerisms.

To summarize, sex role socialization in our society prepares children for an adult world in which men are expected to be instrumental, conquering, controlling, and unemotional and in which women are expected to be expressive, emotional, passive, and dependent. Thus, sex role socialization prepares us to be highly competent in some respects and handicapped in others. Of course, many people find traditional sex roles perfectly comfortable. It seems evident, however, that just about everyone will benefit when the more stereotyped and burdensome aspects of sex roles are set aside. The next section explains why.

Androgyny—Are You Masculine, Feminine, or Androgynous?

Are you aggressive, ambitious, analytical, assertive, athletic, competitive, decisive, dominant, forceful, independent, individualistic, self-reliant, and willing to take risks? If so, you are quite "masculine." Are you affectionate, cheerful, childlike, compassionate, flatterable, gentle, gullible, loyal, sensitive, shy, soft-spoken, sympathetic, tender, understanding, warm, and yielding? If so, then you are quite "feminine."

Question: What if I have traits from both lists?

Then you may be **androgynous** (an-DROJ-ih-nus). The two lists just given are from the work of psychologist Sandra Bem. Using lists of various traits, Bem constructed the *Bem Sex Role Inventory (BSRI),* a list of 20 "masculine" traits (self-reliant, assertive, and so forth), 20 "feminine" traits (affectionate, gentle), and 20 neutral traits (truthful, friendly). Next, Bem and her associates gave the BSRI to thousands of people, asking them to say whether or not each trait applied to them. Of those surveyed, 50 percent fell into traditional masculine or feminine categories; 15 percent scored higher on traits of the opposite gender; and 35 percent were androgynous, getting high scores on both the masculine and feminine items.

■ **Fig. 19–7** *Androgynous individuals adapt easily to both traditionally "masculine" and "feminine" situations.*

Question: You haven't said yet what it means to be androgynous. Is it having both male and female traits?

Psychological Androgyny The word **androgyny** (an-DROJ-ih-nee) literally means "man-woman." Androgyny sounds as if it might have something to do with androids, asexuality, or sex-change operations, but it actually refers to having both masculine and feminine traits.

Bem's interest in androgyny stems from her belief that our complex society requires flexibility with respect to sex roles. She believes that it is right, and more than ever necessary, for men to be gentle, compassionate, sensitive, and yielding and for women to be forceful, self-reliant, independent, and ambitious—*as the situation requires.* In short, Bem feels that more people should be androgynous (■ Fig. 19–7).

Adaptability In an interesting series of experiments, Bem and her associates tried to show that androgynous individuals are more adaptable and less hindered by sex roles or images of what is appropriate "masculine" or "feminine" behavior. For example, in one experiment Bem gave people the choice of performing either a "masculine" activity (oil a hinge, nail boards together, and so forth) or a "feminine" activity (prepare a baby bottle, wind yarn into a ball, and so on). Masculine men and feminine women consistently chose sex-appropriate activities, even when the opposite choice paid more!

Bem's conclusion from a number of studies is that rigid sex roles can seriously restrict behavior, especially for men (Bem, 1974, 1975a, 1975b, 1981). She believes that masculine males have great difficulty expressing warmth, playfulness, and concern—even when these qualities are appropriate. Masculine men, it seems, tend to view such traits as unacceptably "feminine." Masculine men also find it hard to accept emotional support from others, especially from women (Ashton & Fuehrer, 1993). Problems faced by highly feminine women are the reverse of those faced by masculine men. Such women have trouble being independent and assertive, even when these qualities are desirable.

Psychological androgyny The presence of both "masculine" and "feminine" traits in a single person (as masculinity and femininity are defined within one's culture).

Bem Sex Role Inventory (BSRI) A list of 60 personal traits including "masculine," "feminine," and "neutral" traits; used to rate one's degree of androgyny.

In the years since Bem's first studies, androgyny has been variously supported, attacked, and debated. Now, as the dust begins to settle, the picture looks like this:

- Having "masculine" traits primarily means that a person is independent and assertive. Scoring high in "masculinity," therefore, is related to high self-esteem and to success in many situations (Long, 1989).
- Having "feminine" traits primarily means that a person is nurturant and interpersonally oriented. People who score high in "femininity," therefore, tend to experience greater social closeness with others and more happiness in marriage.

In sum, there are advantages to possessing both "masculine" and "feminine" traits, whatever one's gender may be (Ickes, 1993; Spence, 1984). In general, androgynous persons are more flexible when it comes to coping with difficult situations (Jurma & Powell, 1994;

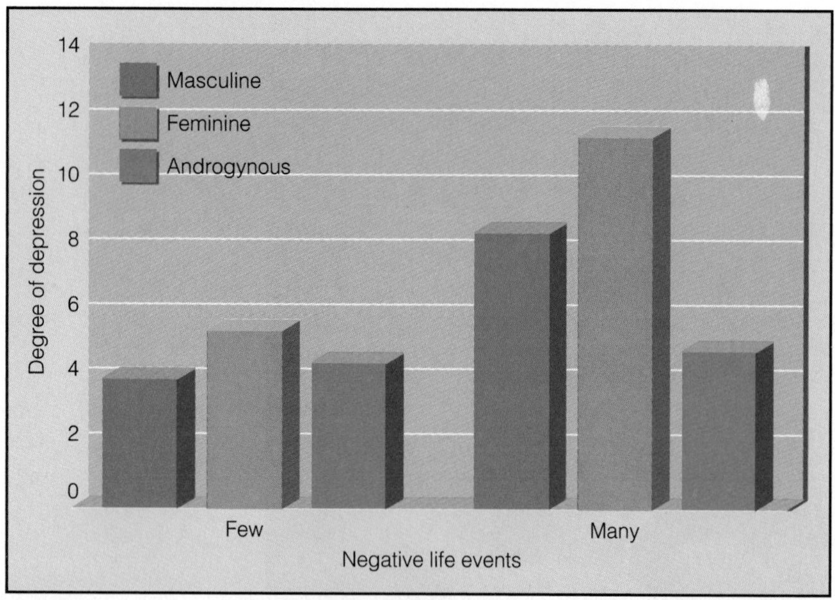

■ **Fig. 19–8** *Another indication of the possible benefits of androgyny is found in a study of reactions to stress. When confronted with an onslaught of negative events, strongly masculine or feminine persons become more depressed than androgynous individuals do (adapted from Roos & Cohen, 1987).*

Spangenberg & Lategan, 1993). (See ■ Figure 19–8.) As they grow older, men and women who are androgynous tend to be more satisfied with their lives. Apparently, this is because androgynous persons can use both instrumental and emotionally expressive capacities to enhance their lives and relationships (Dean-Church & Gilroy, 1993).

It is worth saying again that many people remain comfortable with traditional views of masculinity and femininity. Nevertheless, researchers have done much to show that "masculine" traits and "feminine" traits can exist in the same person and that androgyny can be a highly adaptive balance.

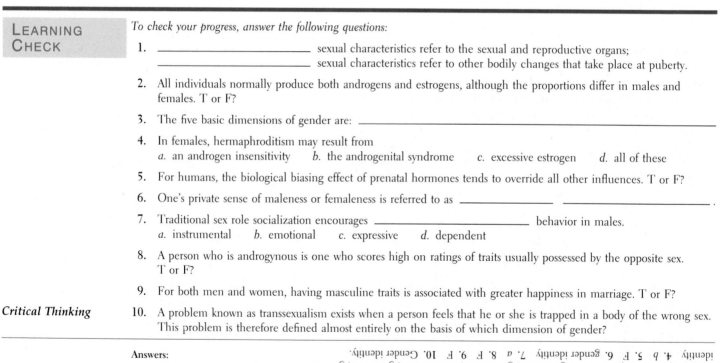

Learning Check

To check your progress, answer the following questions:

1. ______________ sexual characteristics refer to the sexual and reproductive organs; ______________ sexual characteristics refer to other bodily changes that take place at puberty.
2. All individuals normally produce both androgens and estrogens, although the proportions differ in males and females. T or F?
3. The five basic dimensions of gender are: ______________
4. In females, hermaphroditism may result from
   a. an androgen insensitivity *b.* the androgenital syndrome *c.* excessive estrogen *d.* all of these
5. For humans, the biological biasing effect of prenatal hormones tends to override all other influences. T or F?
6. One's private sense of maleness or femaleness is referred to as ______________ ______________.
7. Traditional sex role socialization encourages ______________ behavior in males.
   a. instrumental *b.* emotional *c.* expressive *d.* dependent
8. A person who is androgynous is one who scores high on ratings of traits usually possessed by the opposite sex. T or F?
9. For both men and women, having masculine traits is associated with greater happiness in marriage. T or F?

Critical Thinking

10. A problem known as transsexualism exists when a person feels that he or she is trapped in a body of the wrong sex. This problem is therefore defined almost entirely on the basis of which dimension of gender?

Answers:

1. Primary, secondary 2. T 3. genetic sex, gonadal sex, hormonal sex, genital sex, gender identity 4. *b* 5. F 6. gender identity 7. *a* 8. F 9. F 10. Gender identity.

Sexual Behavior—Mapping the Erogenous Zone

Question: When does sexual behavior first appear in humans?

A capacity for sexual arousal is apparent at birth or soon after. Sexual researcher Alfred Kinsey verified instances of *orgasm* (sexual climax) in boys as young as 5 months old and girls as young as 4 months (Kinsey et al., 1948, 1953). Kinsey also found that children aged 2 to 5 years spontaneously touch and exhibit their genitals.

Sexual behavior continues in various forms throughout childhood and adolescence. But as a child matures, cultural norms place greater restrictions on sexual activities. Still, 50 percent of males and 25 percent of females report having engaged in preadolescent sex play. In adulthood, norms continue to shape sexual activity along socially approved lines. In our culture, sex between children, incest (sex between close relatives), prostitution, and extramarital sex all tend to be discouraged.

As was the case with sex role behavior, it can be seen that such restrictions are somewhat arbitrary. Comparing various cultures shows that less restriction is usually accompanied by more sexual activity of all kinds. Apart from cultural norms, it can be said that any sexual act engaged in by consenting adults is "normal" if it does not hurt anyone.

Sexual Arousal Sexual arousal in humans is complex. It may, of course, be produced by direct stimulation of the body's **erogenous zones** (eh-ROJ-eh-nus: productive of pleasure or erotic desire). Human erogenous zones include the genitals, mouth, breasts, ears, anus, and to a lesser degree, the surface of the entire body. It is clear, however, that more than physical contact is involved: A urological or gynecological examination rarely results in any sexual arousal. Human sexual arousal obviously includes a large cognitive element (see Highlight 19–2). Indeed, arousal may be triggered by mere thoughts or images.

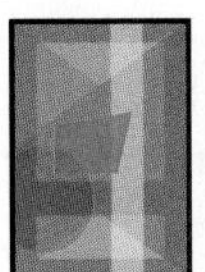

HIGHLIGHT 19–2

A Closer Look At

Sexual Scripts

In a restaurant we commonly expect certain things to occur. It could even be said that each of us has a restaurant "script" that defines a plot, dialogue, and actions that should take place. Researcher John Gagnon (1977) believes that, similarly, we learn a variety of **sexual scripts** that guide our behavior.

Sexual scripts determine when and where we are likely to express sexual feelings, and with whom. They provide a "plot" for the order of events in lovemaking, and they outline "approved" actions, motives, and outcomes.

When two people follow markedly different scripts, misunderstandings are almost sure to occur. Consider, for instance, what happens when a woman acting out a "friendly-first-date" script is paired with a man following a "seduction" script: The result is often anger, hurt feelings, or worse. Even newlyweds may find that their sexual "agendas" differ. In such cases, considerable "rewriting" of scripts is often needed for sexual compatibility.

However you may feel about the reality of sexual scripts, one implication of this line of thought seems inescapable: For humans the mind (or brain) is the ultimate erogenous zone (Knox, 1984).

Erogenous zones Areas of the body that produce pleasure and/or provoke erotic desire.

Sexual script An unspoken mental plan that defines a "plot," dialogue, and actions expected to take place in a sexual encounter.

Sex drive The strength of one's motivation to engage in sexual behavior.

Question: Are men more easily sexually aroused than women?

Apparently not. To answer the question, one study used medical recording devices to measure sexual arousal in males and females as they listened to erotic tape recordings. It was found that the erotic material was equally arousing for both sexes (Heiman, 1977). This and similar findings suggest that women are no less *physically* aroused by erotic stimuli than are men. However, compared with men, women more often have a negative *emotional* response to explicit pictures of sex. That is, women more often report feeling upset and disgusted by these stimuli (Hoyenga & Hoyenga, 1984).

If the capacity for sexual arousal is measured by frequency of orgasm (brought about by masturbation or intercourse), the peak of male sexual activity is at age 18. Kinsey's studies (done in the early 1950s) placed the peak of female sexual activity at about 30 years of age. However, in recent years women have participated more fully in sexual activities, and at an earlier age (Janus & Janus, 1993). The peak rate of female sexual activity still appears to occur later than that of males. However, male and female sexual behavior is rapidly becoming more alike (Oliver & Hyde, 1993). ■ Figure 19–9 shows the results of a recent major survey of sexual behavior among American adults. As you can see, the frequency of sexual intercourse is very similar for men and women (Laumann et al., 1994).

Question: What causes differences in sex drive?

Sex Drive Attitudes toward sex, sexual experience, and recency of sexual release are all obviously important, but physical factors may also play a role. In males the strength of the sex drive is related to the amount of androgens secreted by the testes. When the supply of androgens dramatically increases at puberty, sex drive increases too.

Surprisingly, the "male" hormones, or androgens, may also affect female sex drive. In addition to estro-

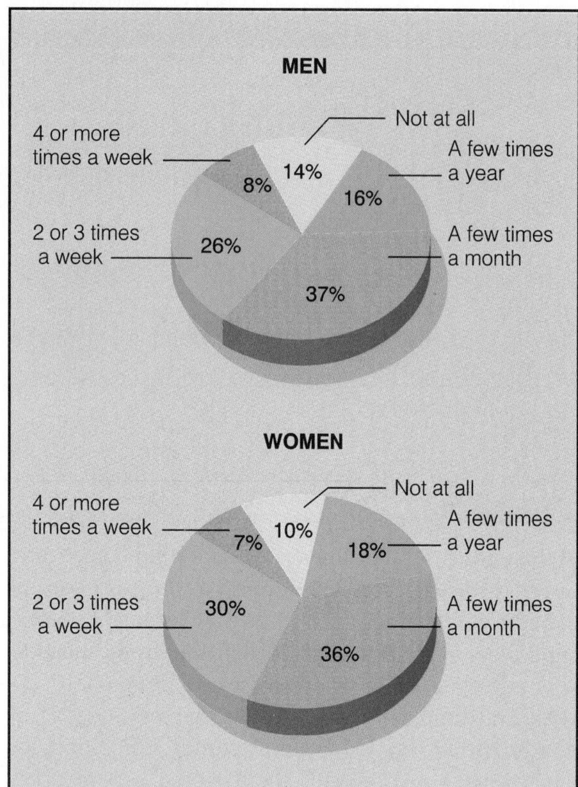

■ **Fig. 19–9** *These graphs show the frequency of sexual intercourse for American adults. To generalize, about one third of the people surveyed have sex twice a week or more, one third a few times a month, and one-third a few times a year or not at all. The overall average is about once a week (Laumann et al., 1994).*

Nocturnal orgasm An orgasm that occurs spontaneously during sleep or dreaming.

Castration Surgical removal of the testicles. Castration differs from sterilization, a procedure (such as vasectomy or tubal ligation) that merely makes a man or woman infertile.

Masturbation Production of sexual pleasure or orgasm by manipulation of the genitals other than by intercourse.

gen, a woman's body produces small amounts of androgens. Evidence suggests that these androgens may increase the sex drive in women just as they do in men. One study found that frequency of intercourse for married women was highest when their androgen levels were at a peak (Persky et al., 1978). Furthermore, when women are given androgens for medical reasons, some report increased sexual desire (Carlson, 1991). Some women also report variations in arousal at various times during their monthly cycles. If such a relationship does exist, its effects are probably small, since women may engage in sexual activity at any time during their monthly cycles (including during menstruation).

Question: Are nocturnal emissions ("wet dreams") an indication of an unusually strong sex drive? Do they ever indicate sexual disorders? Do both men and women experience nocturnal orgasms?

According to Kinsey's studies, about 85 percent of males and 35 percent of females have had sexual dreams that resulted in orgasm. These incidents typically begin during adolescence and may continue throughout adulthood. Kinsey found some reduction in the number of men who have nocturnal orgasms after marriage, but no change among women. Nocturnal orgasm may best be considered a completely normal (if relatively infrequent) form of sexual release.

Question: Does alcohol stimulate the sex drive?

In general, no. Alcohol is a *depressant*. As such, it may, in small doses, stimulate erotic desire by lowering inhibitions. This effect no doubt accounts for alcohol's reputation as an aid to seduction. (Humorist Ogden Nash once summarized this bit of folklore by saying, "Candy is dandy, but liquor is quicker.") However, in larger doses alcohol suppresses orgasm in women and erection in men. Increasing levels of drunkenness cause a progressive *decrease* in sexual desire, arousal, pleasure, and performance (Crowe & George, 1989).

Question: Does removal of the testes or ovaries abolish the sex drive? Also, what happens to the sex drive in old age?

In lower animals, castration (surgical removal of the testicles) or removal of the ovaries usually completely abolishes sexual activity in *inexperienced* animals. Sexually experienced animals (particularly higher animals such as monkeys) may show little immediate change in sexual behavior after castration. In humans, the effects of male and female castration vary. Initially, some individuals show a decline in sex drive, while others experience no change. This is why castration of sex offenders is unlikely to be effective in curbing their behavior. However, after several years have passed, almost all subjects do report a decrease in sex drive.

The preceding observations have nothing to do with the effects of *sterilization*. The vast majority of men and women who choose surgically based birth control (such as a vasectomy or a tubal ligation) experience no loss of sex drive. If anything, they may become more sexually active when pregnancy is no longer a concern.

A natural decline in sex drive typically accompanies aging and reduced sex hormone output (Smith, 1990). (See ■Figure 19–10.) However, sexual activity does not come to an unavoidable end. In some cases, men and women in their 90s have continued active sex lives. The crucial factor for an extended sex life appears to be regularity and opportunity. ("Use it or lose it.") Individuals who fairly regularly engage in intercourse have little difficulty in later years. Many people in their 70s, 80s, and 90s report that sex is at least as gratifying as ever (Janus & Janus, 1993).

Masturbation One of the most basic human sexual behaviors is masturbation. **Masturbation** may be defined as deliberate self-stimulation that causes sexual pleasure or orgasm. Rhythmic self-stimulation has been observed in infants under 1 year of age. In adulthood, masturbation in the male usually takes the form of stroking or other manipulation of the penis. Female masturbation most often centers on stimulation of the clitoris or the areas immediately surrounding it. Some questions commonly asked about masturbation follow.

Question: In adulthood, do more men masturbate than women?

Yes. Of the women who took part in a recent national survey, 89 percent reported that they had masturbated at some time. Of the males, 95 percent reported that they had masturbated. (Some cynics add, "And the other 5 percent lied!") As ■ Figure 19–11 shows, masturbation is a regular feature of the sex lives of many people (Janus & Janus, 1993).

Question: What purpose does masturbation serve?

Through masturbation, people discover what is pleasing sexually and what their natural rhythms and preferences are. Masturbation is therefore an important part of the psychosexual development of most adolescents. Among other things, it provides a healthy substitute for sexual intercourse at a time when sexual activity is discouraged and young people are maturing emotionally (Strong & DeVault, 1994).

Question: Is it immature for masturbation to continue after marriage?

If it is, there are a large number of "immature" people around! Morton Hunt found that approximately 70 percent of married men and women masturbate at least occasionally. Generally speaking, masturbation is a valid sexual activity at any age, and it may continue after marriage without posing any threat to a relationship. Contrary to popular myths, people are not compelled to masturbate because they lack a sexual partner. Actually, the people who are most sexually active are also the ones who masturbate the most. Masturbation is just "one more item on the menu" for people with active sex lives (Laumann et al., 1994).

Question: Is there any way in which masturbation can cause harm?

Fifty years ago, a child might have been told that masturbation would cause insanity, acne, sterility, or other such nonsense. "Self-abuse," as it was often called, has enjoyed a long and unfortunate history of religious and medical condemnation. The contemporary view is that masturbation is a normal and acceptable sexual behavior. Enlightened parents are well aware of this fact. Still, many children are punished or made to feel guilty for touching their genitals. This practice is unfortunate since there is no harm caused by masturbation itself. Typically, the only negative effects of masturbation are the fear, guilt, or anxiety that occur when an individual has learned negative attitudes toward it.

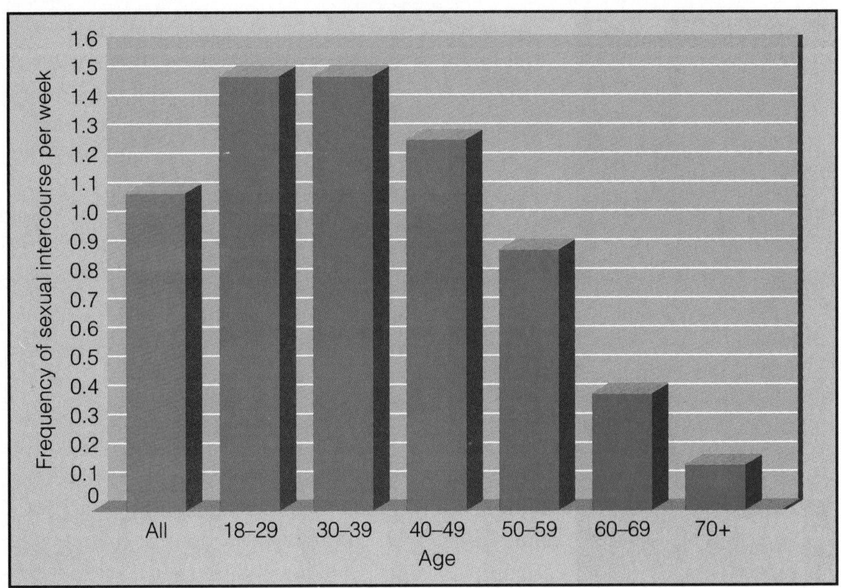

■ **Fig. 19–10** *Average frequency of sexual intercourse per week for adults in the United States. Average intervals for intercourse decline from once every 4–5 days in young adulthood, to once every 16 days in the 60s. Remember that averages such as these are lowered by the inclusion of people who are abstinent or who do not have sexual partners (such as many widowed persons). However, the age declines noted here also show up for people who are married, ranging from an average rate of intercourse of twice a week for couples under 30 to once every three weeks for those over 70. This suggests that the average frequency of intercourse does decline with advancing age (Smith, 1990).*

Sexual Orientation—Who Do You Love?

Sexual behavior and romantic relationships are strongly influenced by a person's sexual orientation. **Sexual orientation** refers to one's degree of emotional and erotic attraction to members of the same gender, opposite gender, or both genders. A person who is **heterosexual** is romantically and erotically attracted to

Sexual orientation One's degree of emotional and erotic attraction to members of the same gender, opposite gender, or both genders.

Heterosexual A person romantically and erotically attracted to members of the opposite sex.

■ **Fig. 19–11** *Percentage of men and women who masturbate. (Data from Janus and Janus, 1993.)*

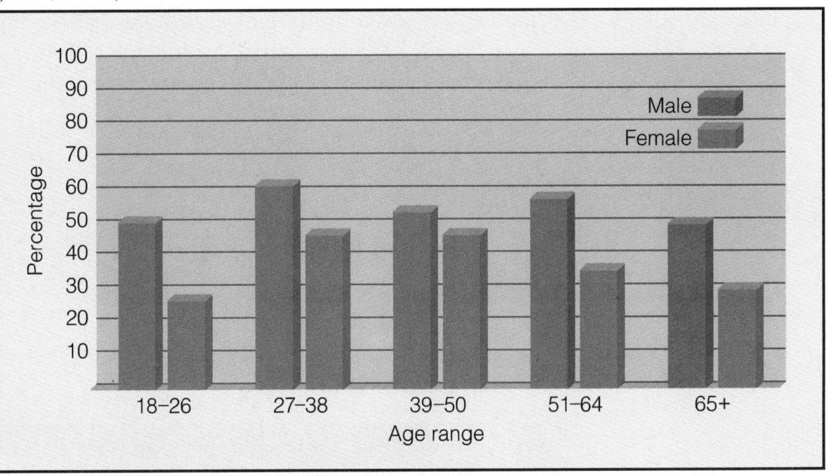

Homosexual A person romantically and erotically attracted to same-sex persons.

Bisexual A person romantically and erotically attracted to both men and women.

members of the opposite sex. Those who are **homosexual** are attracted to persons whose gender matches their own. An individual who is **bisexual** is attracted to both men and women. In short, sexual orientation answers these questions: Who are you attracted to? Who do you have erotic fantasies about? Do you love men, or women, or both? (Garnets & Kimmel, 1991; Seligman, 1994).

Sexual orientation is a very deep part of personal identity. Starting with their earliest erotic feelings, most people remember being attracted to either the opposite sex or the same sex. The chances are practically nil of an exclusively heterosexual or homosexual person being "converted" from one orientation to the other. If you are heterosexual, you are probably certain that nothing could ever make you have homoerotic feelings. If so, then you know how homosexual persons feel about the prospects for changing *their* sexual orientation (Seligman, 1994).

Question: But what about people who have had both heterosexual and homosexual relationships?

Many such instances involve homosexual persons who temporarily date or marry members of the opposite sex because of pressures to fit into a predominantly heterosexual society. When these people realize they are being untrue to themselves, their personal identity and relationships may shift accordingly. Other apparent shifts in orientation probably involve people who are fundamentally bisexual. Overall, sexual orientation is a very stable personal characteristic (Garnets & Kimmel, 1991).

Question: What determines a person's sexual orientation?

Research suggests that a combination of hereditary, biological, social, and psychological influences combine to produce one's sexual orientation (Marmor, 1985; Money, 1987). As one author summarizes, "Like much of human behavior, a combination of biological and social factors are most likely involved in the development of sexuality" (Gladue, 1987).

Highlight 19–3 summarizes some interesting recent findings about the origins of sexual orientation.

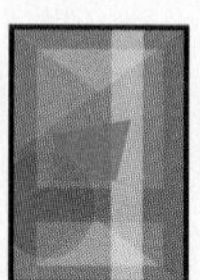

HIGHLIGHT 19–3

Research Frontier

Genes, the Brain, and Sexual Orientation

Why are some people attracted to members of the opposite sex while others prefer members of the same sex? New evidence suggests that sexual orientation is at least partly hereditary. One recent study found that if one identical twin is homosexual or bisexual, there is a 50 percent chance that the other twin is too. This and related findings leads some researchers to estimate that sexual orientation is from 30 to 70 percent genetic (Bailey et al., 1993; Bailey & Pillard, 1991).

How could genes affect sexual orientation? Possibly, heredity shapes areas of the brain that orchestrate sexual behavior. Support for this idea comes from the work of neurobiologist Simon LeVay. He and other scientists have shown that various brain structures do indeed differ in heterosexuals and homosexuals (LeVay, 1993). Other research suggests that sexual orientation is influenced by a gene or genes found on the X chromosome. Thus, genetic tendencies for homosexuality may be passed from mothers to their children (Hamer et al., 1993).

Many people mistakenly believe that homosexuality is caused by a hormone imbalance. However, it is *highly unlikely* that hormone levels *cause* variations in sexual orientation. Hormone levels of most gay men and lesbians are within the normal range (Gladue, 1987). It is also a mistake to think that parenting makes children homosexual. There is little difference between the development of children with gay or lesbian parents and those who have heterosexual parents (Patterson, 1992).

All of these findings tend to discredit myths about parental behavior making children homosexual or claims that homosexuality is merely a preference. While learning contributes to one's sexual orientation, it appears that nature strongly prepares people to be either homosexual or heterosexual (LeVay, 1993).

Homosexuality

As the preceding discussion implies, homosexuality is part of the normal range of variations in sexual orientation (Garnets & Kimmel, 1991). Gay men, lesbians, and bisexuals encounter hostility because they are members of a minority group, not because there is anything inherently wrong with them (Seligman, 1994). Based on a recent national survey, it is estimated that about 7 percent of all adults regard themselves as homosexual or bisexual (see ● Table 19–1). Among men, 1 in 25 is homosexual. Among women, 1 in 50 is a lesbian. About 1 person in 25 is bisexual. These percentages are small, but they indicate that roughly 7 persons out of every 100 in the United States are bisexual or homosexual (Janus & Janus, 1993).

Table 19–1 Sexual Orientation among Adults

	Men	Women
Heterosexual	91%	95%
Homosexual	4%	2%
Bisexual	5%	3%

(Janus & Janus, 1993)

When evaluating homosexuality, it is important to remember that cultural standards for sexual behavior vary greatly. A survey of 76 cultures found that almost two thirds accept some form of homosexuality (Weinberg & Williams, 1974). About 25 percent of all males and 20 percent of all females have had at least one homosexual experience. Historically, homosexuality has been a part of human sexuality since the dawn of time.

In contrast to heterosexuals, homosexual persons tend to discover their sexual orientation at a fairly late date—often not until early adolescence. Very likely, this is because they are surrounded by powerful cultural images that contradict their natural feelings. It is probably difficult for most heterosexual persons to imagine how stressful it is to deny something as basic as one's sexual orientation. Yet, understandably, homosexual persons may be reluctant to accept or acknowledge their sexual orientation. Doing so risks rejection by family, friends, and others (Krivascka, Savin-Williams, & Slater, 1992).

Testing consistently shows no differences in personality or adjustment between heterosexuals and homosexuals (Bell et al., 1981; Marmor, 1980). Emotional adjustment, then, appears to be independent of sexual preference (Siegelman, 1987). For these and other reasons, homosexuality is not considered a sexual disorder (DSM-IV, 1994). Sexual orientation is not related to a person's ability to function in society, work constructively, maintain mental health, care for children, or form caring relationships (Seligman, 1994).

The problems faced by gay men and lesbians tend to be related to rejection by family, discrimination in employment and housing, and the undercurrents of **homophobia** and **heterosexism** in American society. (*Homophobia* refers to prejudice, fear, and dislike aimed at homosexuals. *Heterosexism* is the belief that heterosexuality is better or more natural than homosexuality.)

Homophobia A powerful fear of homosexuality.

Heterosexism The belief that heterosexuality is better or more natural than homosexuality.

Ninety-two percent of gay males and 81 percent of lesbian women have at one time or another suffered verbal abuse—or worse—because of their sexual orientation (Herek, 1989). Much of this rejection is based on false stereotypes about gay and lesbian people. The following points are a partial reply to such stereotypes (Melton, 1989). Gay and lesbian people:

- Do not try to convert others to homosexuality.
- Do not molest children.
- Are not mentally ill.
- Do not hate persons of the opposite sex.
- Do not, as parents, make their own children gay.
- Do frequently have long-term, caring, monogamous relationships.
- Are no less able to contribute to society than heterosexuals.

Homosexual persons are found in all walks of life, at all social and economic levels, and in all cultural groups. As a group they are as diverse in terms of race, ethnicity, age, parenthood, relationships, careers, health, education, politics, and sexual behavior as the heterosexual community (Garnets & Kimmel, 1991). Perhaps as more people come to see gay and lesbian people in terms of their humanity, rather than their sexuality, the prejudices they have faced will wane.

Learning Check

1. A capacity for sexual arousal is apparent at birth or soon after. T or F?
2. Areas of the body that produce erotic pleasure are called ________________ zones.
3. When exposed to erotic stimuli, men and women vary in their most common emotional reactions, but there appears to be no difference in their levels of physical arousal. T or F?
4. There is some evidence to suggest that sexual activity and sex drives peak later for males than they do for females. T or F?
5. It is possible (and normal) for sexual activity to continue to ages of 80 or 90. T or F?
6. More males than females report that they masturbate. T or F?
7. Masturbation can cause physical harm, according to the latest research reports. T or F?
8. Whether a person has erotic fantasies about men or women is a strong indicator of his or her sexual orientation. T or F?
9. Research suggests that homosexuality is closely related to hormonal imbalances found in roughly 7 percent of all adults. T or F?

Critical Thinking

10. Why do you think that fidelity in marriage is strongly encouraged by law and custom?

Answers:

1. T 2. erogenous 3. T 4. F 5. T 6. T 7. F 8. T 9. F 10. Through marriage laws and customs, human societies tend to foster enduring bonds between sexual partners to help ensure that children are cared for and not just produced (Ainsworth, 1989).

Excitement phase The first phase of sexual response, indicated by initial signs of sexual arousal.

Plateau phase The second phase of sexual response during which physical arousal is further heightened.

Orgasm A climax and release of sexual excitement.

Resolution The fourth phase of sexual response, involving a return to lower levels of sexual tension and arousal.

Ejaculation The release of sperm and seminal fluid by the male at the time of orgasm.

Refractory period A short time period after orgasm during which males are unable to again reach orgasm.

Human Sexual Response—Sexual Interactions

Objective information about human sexual response was greatly expanded by the pioneering work of gynecologist William Masters and psychologist Virginia Johnson (1966, 1970). In a series of experiments, interviews, and controlled observations, Masters and Johnson directly studied sexual intercourse and masturbation in nearly 700 males and females. The information they obtained has significantly improved our understanding of human sexuality.

According to Masters and Johnson, sexual response in both males and females can be divided into four phases, (1) **excitement,** (2) **plateau,** (3) **orgasm,** and (4) **resolution** (■ Fig. 19–12 and ■ Fig. 19–13). These responses are the same for people of all sexual orientations (Garnets & Kimmel, 1991).

Male Response Sexual arousal in the male is signaled by erection of the penis during the excitement phase. There is also a rise in heart rate, increased blood flow to the genitals, enlargement of the testicles, erection of the nipples, and numerous other bodily changes. If sexual stimulation ends, the excitement phase will gradually subside. Continued stimulation moves the individual into the plateau phase, in which physical changes and subjective feelings of arousal become more intense. An end to sexual arousal during this phase will be resolved more slowly and may produce considerable frustration.

Further stimulation during the plateau phase brings about a reflex release of tension resulting in sexual climax, or orgasm. In the mature male, orgasm is usually accompanied by **ejaculation** (release of seminal fluid). Afterward, it is followed by a short **refractory period** during which a second orgasm is impossible. (Many men cannot even be stimulated to erection until the refractory phase has passed.) Only rarely is the male refractory period immediately followed by a second orgasm. Orgasm is usually followed by *resolution,* a return to lower levels of sexual tension and arousal.

■ Fig. 19–12 *Male sexual response cycle. The green line shows that sexual arousal rises through the excitement phase and levels off for a time during the plateau phase. Arousal peaks during orgasm and then returns to pre-excitement levels. During the refractory period, immediately after orgasm, a second sexual climax is typically impossible. However, after the refractory period has passed, there may be a return to the plateau phase, followed by a second orgasm (dotted line). (Reproduced by permission from Frank A. Beach [ed.],* Sex and Behavior, *NY: John Wiley & Sons, Inc., 1965.)*

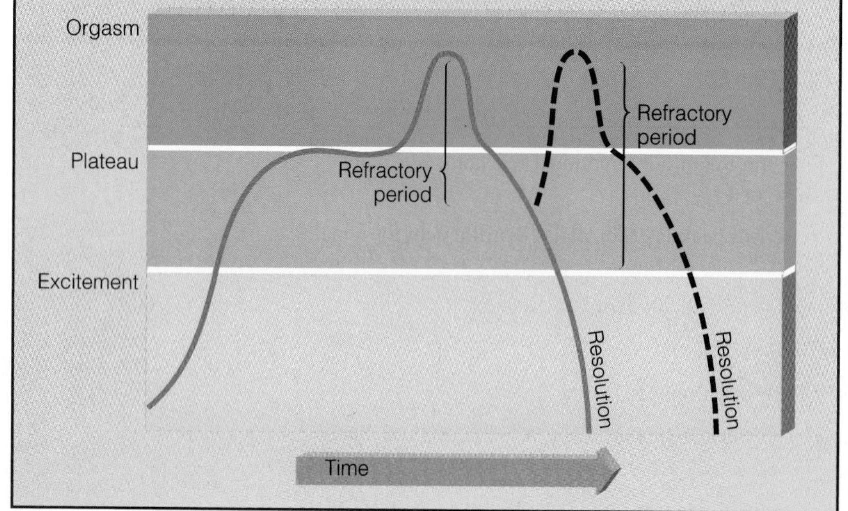

Female Response Although the timing and intensity of the phases vary from person to person, the basic pattern of response for women is the same as that for men. During the excitement phase of arousal, a complex pattern of changes takes place to prepare the vagina for intercourse. These changes correspond to erection in the male. Also (as in the male) the nipples become erect, pulse rate rises, and the skin may become flushed. Most women go through a plateau stage comparable to that in the male, although a few follow a pattern of response that essentially skips the plateau (see Fig. 19–13).

During orgasm, from 3 to 10 muscular contractions of the vagina, uterus, and related structures serve to discharge sexual tension. In a few women, a small amount of fluid is released from the urethra during orgasm. However, vaginal lubrication produced during the earlier stages of arousal probably more often accounts for the perceptions of women who believe they have ejaculated. Both orgasm and resolution in the female usually last longer than they do in the male. After orgasm, about 15 percent of all women return to the plateau phase and may have one or more additional orgasms before resolution.

Before the work of Masters and Johnson, there was considerable debate about whether a difference exists between female orgasm associated with the vagina and orgasm derived from stimulation of the clitoris. Sigmund Freud had said in his writings that a clitoral orgasm was an "immature" form of female response.

Since the clitoris is the female structure comparable to the penis, Freud believed that women whose orgasms centered on the clitoris had not fully accepted their femininity.

Masters and Johnson exploded the Freudian myth by showing that there is no difference in physical response no matter what form of stimulation produces orgasm. As a matter of fact, the inner two thirds of the vagina is relatively insensitive to touch. Most sensations during intercourse, therefore, come from stimulation of the clitoris and other external structures.

It now seems apparent that sensations from many sources are fused together into the total experience of orgasm and that, for the majority of women, one of the more important sources of these sensations is the clitoris. When women in one study were asked to express a preference for vaginal or clitoral stimulation, most said they would rather not choose, but if forced to choose, two thirds preferred clitoral sensations (Fisher, 1973). Similarly, researcher Shere Hite conducted an unscientific yet thought-provoking survey of 3000 women. Among these women, only 26 percent reported regularly reaching orgasm during intercourse without separate massaging of the clitoris (Hite, 1976). To downgrade the "clitoral orgasm" ignores the basic physiology of female sexual response.

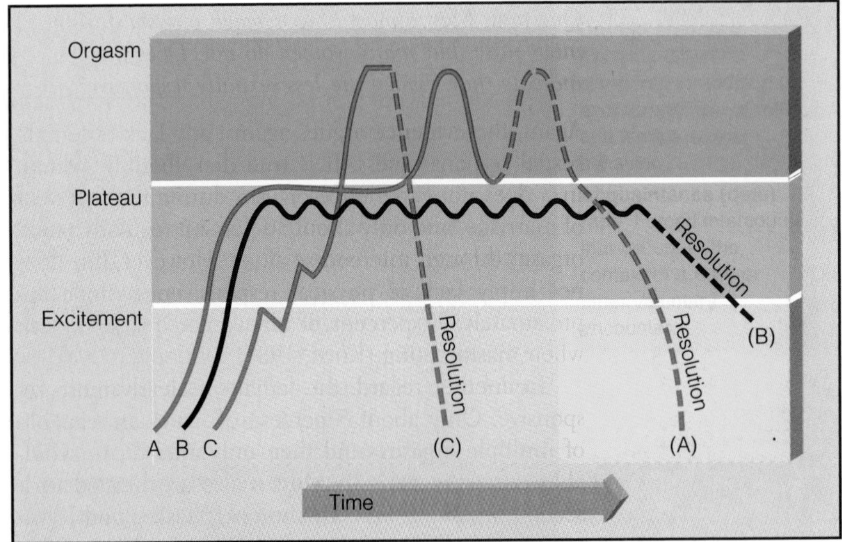

■ **Fig. 19–13** *Female sexual response cycle. In pattern A, arousal rises from excitement, through the plateau phase, and peaks in orgasm. Resolution may be immediate, or it may first include a return to the plateau phase and a second orgasm (dotted line). In pattern B, arousal is sustained at the plateau phase and slowly resolved without sexual climax. Pattern C shows a fairly rapid rise in arousal to orgasm. Little time is spent in the plateau phase and resolution is fairly rapid. (Reproduced by permission from Frank A. Beach [ed.],* Sex and Behavior, *NY: John Wiley & Sons, Inc., 1965.)*

Male and Female Responses Compared

The research of Masters and Johnson indicates that similarities between male and female sexual responses outweigh the differences. However, differences that do exist may have an effect on sexual adjustment. For example, it was found that women typically go through the sexual phases more slowly than men do. During lovemaking, from 10 to 20 minutes is often required for a woman to go from excitement to orgasm.* Males may experience all four stages in as little as 4 minutes. These differences should be kept in mind by couples seeking sexual compatibility.

Question: Does that mean that a couple should try to time lovemaking to promote simultaneous orgasm?

At one time the concept of simultaneous orgasm (both partners reaching sexual climax at the same time) was considered the ideal "goal" of lovemaking. More recently, it has been rejected as an artificial concern that may reduce sexual enjoyment. It is more advisable to aim for the satisfaction of both partners through some combination of intercourse and manual stimulation than it is to self-consciously inhibit spontaneity, communication, and pleasure. A recent national survey found that the vast majority of American adults no longer feel that simultaneous orgasm is necessary for satisfying lovemaking (Janus & Janus, 1993).

Question: Does slower response mean that women are less sexual than men?

Definitely not. During masturbation, 70 percent of females reach orgasm in 4 minutes or less. This finding casts serious doubts on the idea that female response is actually slower. Slower female response during intercourse probably occurs because stimulation to the clitoris is less direct. It might be said that the male simply provides too little stimulation for more rapid female response, not that the female is in any way inferior.

Question: Does penis size affect female response?

Masters and Johnson found that the vagina adjusts to the size of the penis and that subjective feelings of pleasure and intensity of orgasm are not related to penis size. They also found that while individual differences exist in flaccid penis size, there tends to be much less variation in size during erection. This is why erection has been referred to as the "great equalizer." Contrary to popular belief, there is no relationship between penis size and male sexual potency.

* There is much variation, however. In a study of 1000 married women, it was found that 50 percent of them reached orgasm if intercourse lasted 1 to 11 minutes; if intercourse lasted 15 minutes or more, the rate increased to 66 percent. Twenty-five percent of the wives said that orgasm occurred within 1 minute of the start of intercourse (Brewer, 1981). (Note that these times refer only to intercourse, not to an entire arousal sequence.)

cludes extinction of conditioned muscle spasms by progressive relaxation of the vagina, desensitization of fears of intercourse, and masturbation or manual stimulation to associate pleasure with sexual approach by the woman's partner. Hypnosis has also been used successfully in some cases (Kaplan, 1974).

Summary Solving sexual problems can be difficult. The problems described here are rarely solved without professional help (a possible exception is premature ejaculation). If a serious sexual difficulty is not resolved in a reasonable amount of time, the aid of an appropriately trained psychologist, physician, or counselor should be sought. The longer the problem is ignored, the more difficult it is to solve. But professional help is available.

Relationships and Sexual Adjustment

Question: What can be done to improve sexual adjustment?

Often, it is best to view sexual adjustment within the broader context of a relationship. Conflict and unresolved anger in other areas frequently take their toll in sexual adjustment, and mutually satisfying relationships tend to carry over into sexual relations. Sex is not a performance or a skill to be mastered like playing tennis. It is a form of communication within a relationship. Couples with strong and caring relationships can probably survive most sexual problems. A couple with a satisfactory sex life but a poor relationship rarely lasts.

Sex researchers and therapists Masters and Johnson (1970) have discussed how sexual partners can best approach disagreements about each other's sexual needs and wishes. When disagreements arise over issues such as frequency of lovemaking, who initiates lovemaking, or what behavior is appropriate, Masters and Johnson believe that the rule should be, "Each partner must accept the other as the final authority on his or her own feelings."

Partners are urged to give feedback about their feelings by following what therapists call the "touch and ask" rule: Touching and caressing should often be followed by questions such as, "Does that feel good?" "Do you like that?" and so forth (Knox, 1984). When problems do arise, partners are urged to be *responsive* to each other's needs at an *emotional* level and to recognize that all sexual problems are *mutual*. "Failures" should always be shared without placing blame. Masters and Johnson believe that it is particularly important to avoid the "numbers game." That is, couples should avoid being influenced by statistics on the average frequency of lovemaking, by stereotypes about sexual potency, and by the superhuman sexual exploits portrayed in movies and magazines.

Question: Are there any other guidelines for maintaining a healthy emotional relationship?

Intimacy and Communication

A study that compared happily married couples with unhappily married couples found that, in almost every regard, the happily married couples showed superior *communication* skills. Three patterns that are almost always related to serious long-term problems in relationships are defensiveness (including whining), stubbornness, and refusal to talk with your partner (the "big freeze") (Gottman & Krokoff, 1989). Many couples find that communication is facilitated by observing the following guidelines.

Avoid "Gunnysacking" Persistent feelings, whether positive or negative, need to be expressed. Gunnysacking refers to saving up feelings and complaints. These are then "dumped" during an argument or are used as ammunition in a fight. Gunnysacking is very destructive to a relationship.

Be Open about Feelings Happy couples not only talk more, they convey more personal feelings and show greater sensitivity to their partners' feelings. As one expert put it, "In a healthy relationship, each partner feels free to express his likes, dislikes, wants, wishes, feelings, impulses, and the other person feels free to react with like honesty to these. In such a relationship, there will be tears, laughter, sensuality, irritation, anger, fear, baby-like behavior, and so on" (Jourard, 1963).

Don't Attack the Other Person's Character Whenever possible, expressions of negative feelings should be given as statements of one's own feelings, not as statements of blame. It is far more constructive to say, "It makes me angry when you leave things around the house" than it is to say, "You're a slob!" Remember too, that if you use the words "always" or "never," you are probably mounting a character attack.

Don't Try to "Win" a Fight Constructive fights are aimed at resolving shared differences, not at establishing who is right or wrong, superior or inferior.

Recognize That Anger Is Appropriate Constructive and destructive fights are not distinguished by whether or not anger is expressed. A fight is a fight, and anger is appropriate. As is the case with any other emotion in a relationship, anger should be expressed. However, constructive expression of anger requires that couples fight fair by sticking to the real issues and not "hitting below the belt." Resorting to threats, such as announcing "This relationship is over," is especially damaging.

Try to See Things through Your Partner's Eyes Marital harmony is closely related to the ability to put yourself in another person's place (Long & Andrews, 1990). When a conflict arises, always pause and try to take your partner's perspective. Seeing things through your partner's eyes can be a good reminder that no one is ever totally right or wrong in a personal dispute.

Don't Be a "Mind-Reader" The preceding suggestion should not be taken as an invitation to engage in "mind-reading." Assuming that you know what your partner is thinking or feeling can muddle or block communication. Hostile or accusatory mind-reading, like the following examples, can be very disruptive: "You're just looking for an excuse to criticize me, aren't you?" "You don't really want my mother to visit, or you wouldn't say that." Rather than *telling* your partner what he or she thinks, *ask* her or him.

To add to these guidelines, Bryan Strong and Christine DeVault (1994) suggest that if you really want to mess up a relationship, you can almost totally avoid intimacy and communication by doing the following.

Ten Ways to Avoid Intimacy

1. Don't talk about anything meaningful, especially about feelings.
2. Never show your feelings; remain as expressionless as possible.
3. Always be pleasant and pretend everything is okay even if you are upset or dissatisfied.
4. Always win, never compromise.
5. Always keep busy; that way you can avoid intimacy and make your partner feel unimportant in your life.
6. Always be right; don't let on that you are human.
7. Never argue or you may have to reveal differences and make changes.
8. Make your partner guess what you want. That way, you can tell your partner that he or she doesn't really understand or love you.
9. Always take care of your own needs first.
10. Keep the television set on. Wouldn't you rather be watching TV than talking with your partner?

Remember, to encourage intimacy, wise couples *avoid* the practices in the preceding list.

As a last point, it is worth restating that sexual adjustment and loving relationships are interdependent. As one observer put it, when sex goes well, it's 15 percent of a relationship, and when it goes badly it's 85 percent (Knox, 1984). As a shared pleasure, a form of intimacy, a means of communication, and a haven from everyday tensions, a positive sexual relationship can do much to enhance a couple's mutual understanding and caring. Likewise, an honest, equitable, and affectionate out-of-bed relationship contributes greatly to sexual satisfaction (Hatfield et al., 1982).

LEARNING CHECK

1. Males suffering from primary erectile dysfunction have never been able to have or maintain an erection. T or F?
2. According to the latest figures, most erectile disorders are caused by physical problems. T or F?
3. Sensate focus is the most common treatment for premature ejaculation. T or F?
4. Premature ejaculation is considered the rarest of the male sexual adjustment problems. T or F?
5. As it is for male sexual arousal disorder, the sensate focus technique is a primary treatment mode for female sexual arousal disorder. T or F?
6. Vaginismus, which appears to be a phobic response to sexual intercourse, can also cause dyspareunia. T or F?
7. Masters and Johnson urge sexual partners to recognize that all sexual problems are mutual and not just one partner's problem. T or F?
8. The term *gunnysacking* refers to the constructive practice of hiding anger until it is appropriate to express it. T or F?
9. Who would you expect to have the most frequent sex and the most satisfying sex, married couples or single persons? ***Critical Thinking***

Answers: 1. T 2. F 3. F 4. F 5. T 6. T 7. T 8. F 9. Contrary to mass media portrayals of sexy singles, married couples have the most sex and are most likely to have orgasms when they do (Laumann et al., 1994). Greater opportunity, plus familiarity with a partner's needs and preferences probably account for these findings.

EXPLORATION

Touching—Does It Always Have Sexual Implications?

The whole thing began because Sidney Jourard is a people watcher. One day, sitting in a coffeehouse in San Juan, Puerto Rico, where he was a Peace Corps consultant, he wondered how many times the couple at the next table would touch each other in 1 hour. During the next 2 years, he did the same thing in London and Paris while studying at London's Tavistock Clinic. When he went to Gainesville, Florida, to teach psychology at the University of Florida, he checked out an American couple for the 1 hour. The two people at the Gainesville table touched each other 2 times in 1 hour. In Paris the touch total for 1 hour was 110. In San Juan, 180. And in London? In London, the two people touched each other not at all.

From this information you must draw your own conclusions. Jourard—back at Gainesville, Florida, teaching, being a therapist, and practicing hatha yoga—refused to. But his interest led him to make further surveys.

He gave booklets to his Gainesville students, 54 males and 84 females. Each booklet contained four diagrams of the body divided into 24 zones, the idea lifted (he says with a straight face) from a butcher's meat chart. He then asked his students to report, anonymously of course, which area of their bodies had been touched by mother, father, best-friend-same-sex, and best-friend-opposite-sex. Furthermore, each student was asked to show which zones he or she had touched on these four persons. Time range: within the last year. The charts in Figure 19–15 show the result. Here Jourard will draw conclusions about "body accessibility."

■ **Fig. 19–15** *Results of Jourard's study of interpersonal touch. Figures shown are the percentages of young adults touched in each body area, during a 1-year period, by the persons listed. Touching patterns are highly influenced by culture. People in other countries touch much more, or less, than is customary in the United States. (After Jourard, 1966.) Also, touching patterns change over time. More recent studies of touching show significant increases in women's reports of being touched in the area from the thighs to the shoulders by an opposite sex friend. Men show similar increases in being touched in the pelvic area and upper torso by an opposite sex friend. These trends seem to reflect a liberalization of intimate touching in love and dating relationships (Thayer, 1988).*

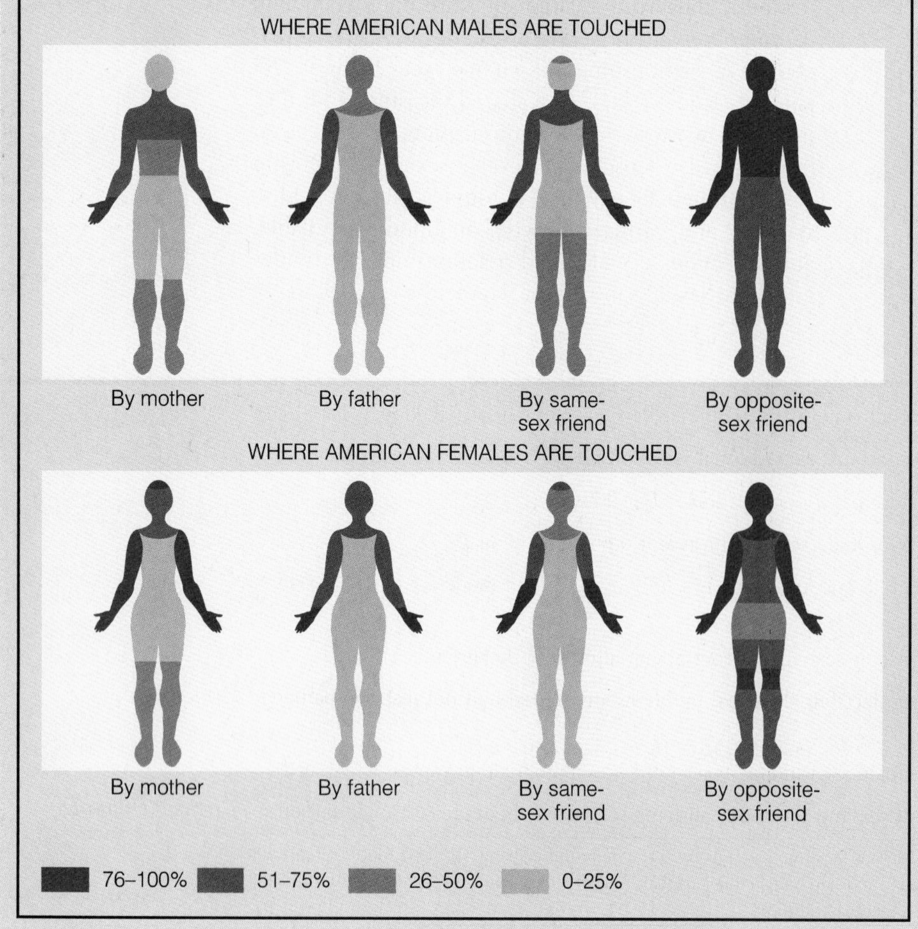

"If you're out of love," says the professor, "you're out of touch."

"There isn't a great deal of body contact going on outside the strictly sexual context. It's almost as if all possible meanings of a touch are eliminated except the caress with the sexually arousing intent. . . . Most regions of a young adult's body remain untouched unless one has a close friend of the opposite sex, and that depends on the relationship going on between them."

One of our touch taboos, then, is that we equate touch with sexuality. Therefore, unless the relationship is sexual, *mustn't touch.*

Jourard goes on to say that in family physical contact, the daughters are "the favored ones." A girl's parents touch her more than they would if she were a boy. Right up into her 20s. Parents stop touching boys about the time they reach what used to be called the Age of Reason—when one can commit sin. Furthermore, a girl's mother is allowed, or allows herself (having herself once been a favored one), to give frequent touches to a girl's hair. One-half of the parents get to touch her on the lips, and half manage a literal pat on the back. But—taboo, taboo—only 13 percent of the girls received a paternal pat on the bottom, and none of the girls touched or were touched by their fath-

EXPLORATION

ers in the genital area. (Not quite the case with regard to male students and Mamma.)

Outside the best-friend-opposite-sex category, very little touching goes on, but when it does happen between lovers, the professor says, "There is a virtual deluge of physical contact all over the body. . . . I suspect that the transformation from virginity or even preorgasmic existence to the experience of having a sexual climax is so radical as to be equivalent to a kind of rebirth."

For Jourard, in our maddeningly crowded world, touch may be our salvation. "I think that body contact has the function of confirming one's bodily being," he says. Yet, how can one learn to touch lovingly if one is not permitted to touch and be touched when young? To touch and be touched at times other than when making love?

"It's a blunted way of life," Jourard says. "People need physical contact to increase awareness and sensitivity to the body. But, instead, we use our relationship with others as a means to increase our status and social position. We are afraid to let others get close because then we are trapped. . . . The price we pay for this estrangement is loneliness." (The preceding article was written by H. E. F. Donohue, 1968.)

LEARNING CHECK

1. In his first casual observations, Jourard noted the highest rates of touching in
   a. Florida   *b.* France   *c.* Puerto Rico   *d.* England
2. Within the family, boys are typically touched more by parents than girls are. T or F?
3. Jourard recorded the highest rates of touching by
   a. mothers   *b.* fathers   *c.* same-sex friends   *d.* opposite-sex friends
4. In North American culture, the hands are the most accepted areas of the body for touching by others. T or F?
5. If a man touches a woman on the arm or shoulder while talking to her at work, has he sexually harassed her? ***Critical Thinking***

Answers: 1. *c* 2. F 3. *d* 4. T 5. It depends on her wishes: Even touching that involves "public" areas of the body can be harassing if it is an unwanted intrusion on personal privacy.

Chapter Summary

■ ***What are the basic dimensions of gender?***

- Physical differences between males and females can be divided into **primary sexual characteristics** (genital and reproductive organs) and **secondary sexual characteristics** (other bodily features).
- Reproductive maturity in females is signaled by **menarche** (the onset of menstruation). The development of both primary and secondary sexual characteristics is influenced by **androgens** (male sex hormones) and **estrogens** (female sex hormones).
- Gender can be broken down into **genetic sex, gonadal sex, hormonal sex, genital sex,** and **gender identity.**
- Gender development begins with genetic sex (XX or XY chromosomes). It is then influenced by prenatal hormonal influences. **Androgen insensitivity,** exposure to *progestin,* the **androgenital syndrome,** and similar problems can cause problems in the formation of the genitals. Resulting gender ambiguities are called **hermaphroditism.**
- Many researchers believe that prenatal hormones can exert a **biological biasing effect** that combines with **social factors** present after birth to influence psychosexual development. On most psychological dimensions, men and women are more alike than they are different.

■ ***How does one's sense of maleness or femaleness develop?***

- Social factors are especially apparent in learned **gender identity** and the effect of **sex roles** and **sex role socialization** on behavior.
- Sex roles contribute to the development of **sex role stereotypes** that often distort perceptions about the kinds of occupations for which men and women are suited.
- Gender identity, which is based to a large extent on labeling, usually becomes stable by age 3 or 4 years. Sex role socialization in particular seems to account for most observed male/female differences. Parents tend especially to encourage boys in **instrumental behaviors** and girls in **expressive behaviors.**

■ ***What is psychological androgyny (and is it contagious)?***

- Research conducted by Sandra Bem and others indicates that roughly one third of all persons are **androgynous.** Approximately 50 percent are traditionally masculine or feminine.
- Psychological androgyny (possessing both masculine and feminine traits) appears related to greater adaptability or flexibility in behavior.

■ ***What are the most typical patterns of human sexual behavior?***

- Sexual behavior is quite "natural," being apparent soon after birth and expressed in various ways throughout life. "Normal" sexual behavior is defined differently by various cultures. There appears to be little difference in sexual responsiveness between males and females.
- There is some evidence that the sex drive peaks at a later age for females than it does for males, although this difference is diminishing. Sex drive in both males and females may be related to bodily levels of androgens.
- **Nocturnal orgasms** are a normal, but relatively minor, form of sexual release. **Castration** may or may not influence sex drive in humans. **Sterilization** does not alter sex drive.
- There is a gradual decline in the frequency of sexual intercourse with increasing age. However, many elderly persons remain sexually active and great variations exist at all ages.
- **Masturbation** is a normal and completely acceptable behavior practiced by a large percentage of the population. For many, masturbation is an important part of sexual self-discovery. It is valid in marriage and normally has no harmful effects.
- **Sexual orientation** refers to one's degree of emotional and erotic attraction to members of the same gender, opposite gender, or both genders. A person may be **heterosexual, homosexual,** or **bisexual.**
- A combination of hereditary, biological, social, and psychological influences combine to produce one's sexual orientation.
- As a group, homosexual men and women do not differ psychologically from heterosexuals.

■ ***To what extent do males and females differ in sexual response?***

- Human sexual response can be divided into four phases: (1) **excitement;** (2) **plateau;** (3) **orgasm;** and (4) **resolution.** Both males and females may go through all four stages in 4 or 5 minutes. But during lovemaking, most females typically take longer than this, averaging from 10 to 20 minutes.
- Males experience a **refractory period** after orgasm and only 5 percent of men are multi-orgasmic. Fifteen percent of women are consistently multi-orgasmic, and at least 48 percent are capable of multiple orgasm.
- There do not appear to be any differences between "vaginal orgasms" and "clitoral orgasms" in the female. Mutual orgasm has been abandoned by most sex counselors as the ideal in lovemaking.

■ ***Have recent changes in attitudes affected sexual behavior?***

- Attitudes toward sexual behavior, especially the behavior of others, have been significantly liberalized, but actual changes in sexual behavior have been more gradual.
- Another change has been earlier and more frequent sexual activity among adolescents and young adults. Also evident are a greater acceptance of female sexuality and a narrowing of differences in male and female patterns of sexual behavior.
- **Acquaintance rape** and rape-supportive myths and attitudes remain major problems.

■ ***What impact have sexually transmitted diseases had on sexual behavior?***

- During the last 20 years there has been a steady increase in the incidence of **sexually transmitted diseases.** This increase, coupled with the emergence of **acquired immune deficiency syndrome,** has had a sizable impact on patterns of sexual behavior, including increased awareness of high-risk behaviors and some curtailment of risk taking.

■ ***What are the most common sexual adjustment problems? How are they treated?***

- The principal problems in sexual adjustment are **desire disorders, arousal disorders, orgasm disorders,** and **sexual pain disorders.**
- Behavioral methods and counseling techniques have been developed to alleviate each problem. However, most sexual adjustment problems are

closely linked to the general health of a couple's *relationship*. For this reason, *communication skills* that foster and maintain intimacy are the key to successful relationships.

■ ***What is the role of touching in personal relationships?***

- Patterns of touching vary from culture to culture, and they depend on the nature of the relationship between two people. Touch can therefore have a variety of meanings, most of which are non-sexual.

Questions for Discussion

1. Do your patterns of touching and being touched correspond to those found by Jourard?
2. In what ways does sexual contact differ from non-sexual touching? Do you feel, as Jourard did, that people should touch more? Why or why not?
3. Would you be jealous if your spouse or lover were touched (in a non-sexual way) by a person of the same sex? Opposite sex?
4. Do you think the sexual revolution has increased touching by encouraging openness or decreased it by defining more casual touching as potentially sexual?
5. In recent years there has been a dramatic increase in child molestation trials involving day-care workers. Some teachers and child-care workers complain that they are now afraid to touch or hug children. Is this new reticence to touch an over-due correction or a saddening loss?
6. Imagine that you were born as a member of the opposite sex. In what ways would your life so far have been different? (Consider relationships, self-image, clothing, recreation, interests, career plans, and so forth.)
7. In your opinion, what are the advantages and disadvantages of distinctly different male/female sex roles?
8. Mentally change your male friends to females and your female friends to males. Can you separate the "human being" or "core person" from your friends' normal gender identities and sex roles? What effect does this have on your perception of others?
9. Female sexual behavior appears to be changing more rapidly than male behavior. To what do you attribute the different rate of change?
10. Recall your own education about sexuality. In what ways and at what age would you recommend that children learn about sex?
11. The American teen pregnancy rate is alarmingly high. What do you think is the cause? What should be done to change this trend?
12. How should a couple go about deciding whether they are ready for a sexual relationship? What can be done to reduce the frequency of STDs?
13. How could vaginismus be the result of classical conditioning? How is the treatment similar to systematic desensitization?
14. You work in the critical care unit of a hospital and are assigned to an AIDS patient. Should you be worried about contracting the disease? Why or why not?

Chapter 20

Social Behavior

IN THIS CHAPTER

Group membership
Personal space
Attribution theory
Needs for affiliation
Interpersonal attraction
Conformity
Social power
Obedience
Compliance
Applications:
Self-assertion
Exploration:
Social traps

CHAPTER PREVIEW

The Social Animal

To live alone, one must be either an animal or a god.
Aristotle

No man is an Iland, intire of itselfe.
John Donne

Your assignment is this: You have been given a written message and the name, address, and occupation of the person who should receive it. This "target person" lives over 1500 miles away in a city you have never visited. You are allowed to move the message through the mail, but you may send it only to a first-name acquaintance. That person, in turn, must mail the message only to one of his or her first-name acquaintances. The message is to be moved in this manner until it reaches the target person, whom the previous person must know by name.

Sound impossible? Social psychologist Stanley Milgram and his associates asked a number of people to try moving a message in this way. Amazingly, about 1 message in 5 made it. Even more amazing was the number of people needed to complete a chain between two strangers separated by half a continent. The average number of "links" required was about 7 people (Korte & Milgram, 1970; Milgram, 1967)!

Question: How is that possible?

Actually, the 7-link average is not as astounding as it might seem. Each of us is enmeshed in a complex network of social relationships, and each person's network overlaps with many others. If you know hundreds of people, and each of them knows hundreds more, a chain of 7 people can create millions of possible interconnections. Undeniably, humans are social animals.

***Social psychology** is the scientific study of how individuals behave, think, and feel in social situations (that is, in the presence, actual or implied, of others) (Baron & Byrne, 1990). Every day, there is a fascinating interplay between our own behavior and that of people around us. Social behavior has been the target of an immense amount of psychological study—too much, in fact, for us to cover in detail. Therefore, this chapter and the next are social psychology "samplers." It is hoped that you will find the topics interesting and thought provoking.*

Survey Questions

- How does group membership affect individual behavior?
- What unspoken rules govern the use of personal space?
- How do we perceive the motives of others, and the causes of our own behavior?
- Why do people affiliate?
- What factors influence interpersonal attraction?
- What have social psychologists learned about conformity, social power, obedience, and compliance?
- How does self-assertion differ from aggression?
- What is a social trap?

Humans in a Social Context—People, People, Everywhere

We are born into an organized society. Established values, expectations, and behavior patterns are present when we arrive. So too is **culture,** an ongoing pattern of life that is passed from one generation to the next. Some readily visible aspects of culture are language, marriage customs, concepts of ownership, and sex roles.

Roles The groups to which you belong form your most immediate day-to-day social environment. Each person is a member of many groups: the family, teams, church groups, work groups, and so on. Some groups are formal and organized. Others are informal and loosely defined. All groups influence the behavior of their members. In each group we occupy a *position* in the *structure* of the group. **Social roles** are patterns of behavior expected of persons in various social positions. For instance, expectations exist for playing each of the following roles: mother, teacher, employer, student. Some roles are **ascribed,** meaning they are not under the individual's control: male or female, son, adolescent, inmate. **Achieved** roles are those attained voluntarily or by special effort: spouse, teacher, scientist, band leader (■Fig. 20–1).

Question: What effect does role-playing have on behavior?

Roles allow us to anticipate the behavior of others. When a person is acting as a physician, mother, clerk, or police officer, we expect certain behaviors. In general, roles are quite useful because they streamline many of our daily interactions with others. However, roles have a negative side too. It is not unusual for a person to occupy two or more conflicting roles. Getting caught in a **role conflict** can be quite uncomfortable or frustrating. Consider, for example, the traffic court judge whose son is brought before her with a violation, or the teacher who must flunk a close friend's daughter.

The impact of roles is dramatically illustrated by an experiment conducted by psychologist Philip Zimbardo and his students at Stanford University. In this experiment, normal, healthy, male college students were paid to serve as "inmates" and "guards" in a simulated prison (Zimbardo et al., 1973).

On the second day of their "imprisonment," the prisoners staged a number of disturbances, but their rebellion was quickly suppressed by the guards. Over the next few days the guards behaved with increasing brutality and the prisoners became more traumatized, passive, and dehumanized. Four prisoners had to be

Social psychology The scientific study of how individuals behave, think, and feel in social situations.

Culture An ongoing pattern of life, characterizing a society at a given point in history.

Social role Expected behavior patterns associated with particular social positions (such as daughter, worker, student).

Ascribed role A role that is assigned to a person; a role one has no choice about playing.

Achieved role A role that is assumed voluntarily.

Role conflict Trying to occupy two or more roles that make conflicting demands on behavior.

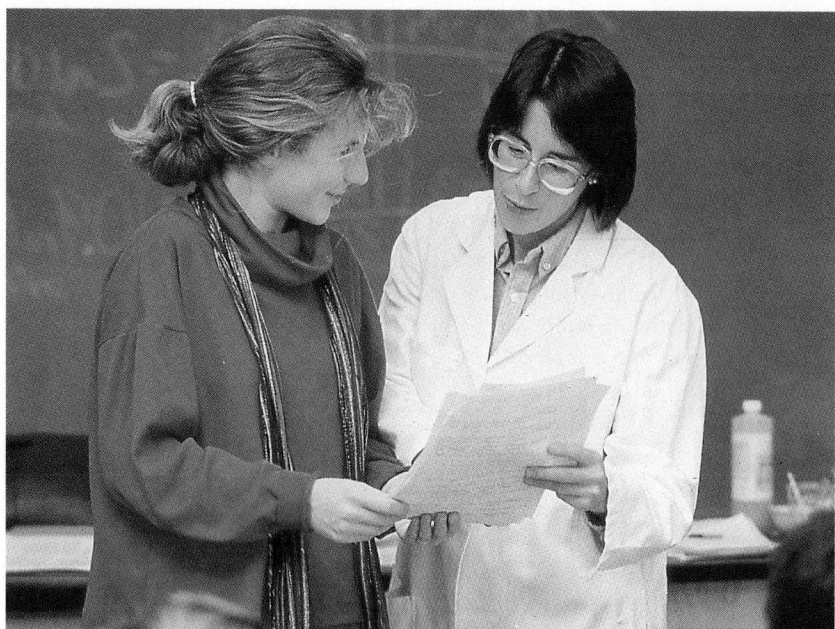

■ **Fig. 20–1** *Roles have a powerful impact on social behavior. What kinds of behavior do you expect from your teachers? What behaviors do they expect from you? What happens if either of you fails to match the other's expectations?*

Status An individual's position in a social structure, especially with respect to power, privilege, or importance.

Group structure The network of roles, communication pathways, and power in a group.

Group cohesiveness The degree of attraction among group members or their commitment to remaining in the group.

released in the first 4 days because of reactions such as hysterical crying, confusion, and severe depression. Each day, the guards tormented the prisoners with more frequent commands, insults, and demeaning tasks. After 6 days the experiment was halted.

What had happened? Zimbardo's interpretation is that the roles—prisoner and guard—assigned to participants were so powerful that in just a matter of days the experiment had become "reality" for those involved. Afterward, many of the guards found it hard to believe their own behavior. As one recalls, "I was surprised at myself. I made them call each other names and clean toilets out with their bare hands. I practically considered the prisoners cattle" (Zimbardo, 1973). It would seem that the source of many destructive human relationships can be found in destructive roles.

Status Position in a group also determines one's **status.** In most groups, higher status is associated with special privileges and respect. Status can operate very subtly to influence behavior in many situations. For example, in one interesting experiment, researchers left dimes in phone booths. When subjects entered the booths they were approached by a researcher who said, "Excuse me, I think I left a dime in this phone booth a few minutes ago. Did you find it?" Seventy-seven percent of the people returned the money when the researcher was well dressed, but only 38 percent returned it to poorly dressed researchers (Bickman, 1974). Perhaps the better treatment given "higher status" individuals in this example explains some of the modern preoccupation with status symbols. Highlight 20–1 discusses another subtle dimension of status.

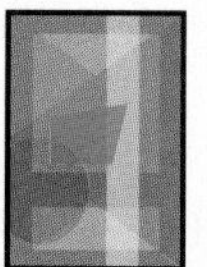

HIGHLIGHT 20–1

A Closer Look At

Touch and Status

Pause for a moment and think about who you touch during a typical day. Do you think that social status affects your patterns of touching and being touched by others?

It would be surprising if touching weren't affected by status. Touch is one of the most basic forms of communication. Its message can be one of warmth, friendship, caring, nurturance, or sexual interest (see Chapter 19). In addition, touching is a "privilege" of power and high status. Older persons, for instance, are more likely to touch younger persons than the reverse. Likewise, people of high socioeconomic status are more likely to touch those of lower status. Of course, such differences tend to disappear when people greet or take leave of one another. At such times, touching (a hug, a kiss, or a handshake) follows highly ritualized patterns.

In public or impersonal settings there is one more difference in touching that is related to status. Men, by virtue of their higher status and greater power in society, are more likely to touch women than women are to touch men (Major, Schmidlin, & Williams, 1990). This difference is highly visible in most work settings: Picture a male boss touching his female secretary on the shoulder or arm to get her attention; she, in turn, never touches him. While women have moved toward equal status with men, patterns of social touching suggest that subtle inequalities in power and dominance persist.

Question: Are there other dimensions of group membership?

Structure and Cohesion Groups are made up of people who are in some way interrelated. Two very important dimensions of any group are its *structure* and *cohesiveness.* **Group structure** is the organization of roles, communication pathways, and power in the group. Organized groups such as an army or an athletic team have a high degree of structure. Informal friendship groups may or may not be highly structured. **Group cohesiveness** is basically an indication of the degree of attraction among group members. Members of cohesive groups literally tend to stick together: They are more likely to stand or sit close together and focus attention on one another. They also show more signs of mutual affection and their behavior tends to be closely coordinated (Levine & Moreland, 1990). Cohesiveness is the basis for much of the power that groups exert over their members. Therapy groups, businesses, sports teams, and the like, often actively seek to strengthen group cohesion.

Norms A very important aspect of the functioning of any group is its norms. **Norms** are standards of conduct for appropriate behavior in various situations. If you have the slightest doubt about the existence of powerful group norms, Stanley Milgram once suggested this test: Board a crowded bus, find a seat, and begin singing loudly in your fullest voice. Milgram's guess was that not more than 1 person in 100 could actually carry out these instructions.

The impact of norms on behavior was recently illustrated in an experiment on littering. The question was, Does the amount of trash already discarded in an area affect the likelihood that people will add to the litter? As subjects walked into a public parking garage, they were given a handbill. As you can see in ■ Figure 20–2, the more litter there was in the garage, the more likely people were to drop their handbill on the floor. Apparently, seeing that others had already littered implied a lax norm about whether littering is acceptable. The moral? The cleaner a public area is kept, the less it will need to be cleaned (Cialdini, Reno, & Kallgren, 1990).

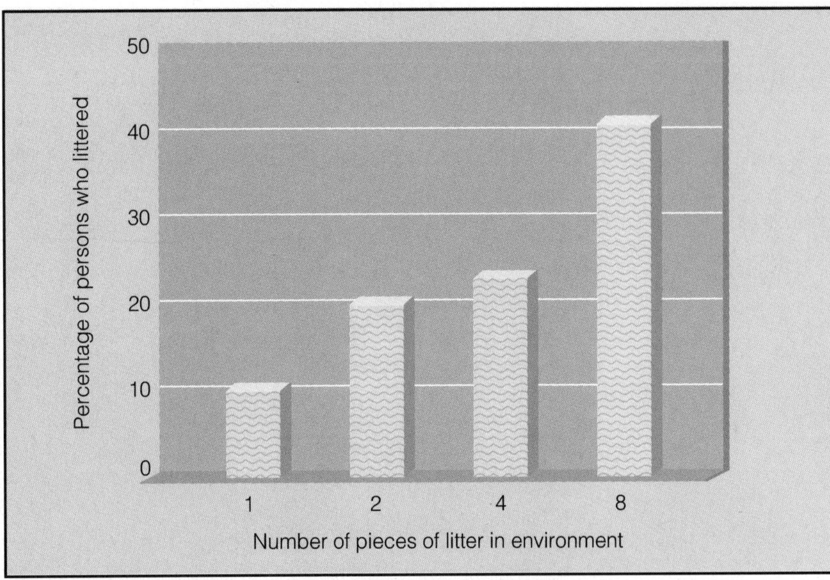

■ **Fig. 20–2** *Results of an experiment on norms concerning littering. The prior existence of litter in a public setting implies that littering is acceptable. This encourages others to "trash" the area. (From Cialdini, Reno, & Kallgren, 1990.)*

Question: How are norms formed?

One early study of how group norms are formed made use of a striking illusion called the **autokinetic effect.** In a completely darkened room, a stationary pinpoint of light will appear to drift or move about. (The light is therefore "autokinetic," or "self-moving.") Muzafer Sherif (1906–1988) found that estimates of how far the light moves vary widely from person to person. However, when two or more people give estimates at the same time, their judgments rapidly converge. A similar convergence of attitudes, beliefs, and behavior takes place among members of most groups.

Norms are often based on our *perceptions* of what others think and do. For example, a majority of college students believe that they are more troubled about excessive drinking than the average student is. Apparently, many students are fooled by a false norm that they help create by not speaking up. If disapproving students outnumber "party animals," campus norms for acceptable drinking should be more conservative than they typically are (Prentice & Miller, 1993).

A good example of the influence that norms have on behavior is found in the unspoken rules governing the use of *personal space.* Since personal space is an intriguing topic in its own right, let's take a moment to examine it.

Norm An accepted (but often unspoken) standard of conduct for appropriate behavior.

Autokinetic effect The apparent movement of a stationary pinpoint of light displayed in a darkened room.

Personal space An area surrounding the body that is regarded as private and subject to personal control.

Proxemics Systematic study of the human use of space, particularly in social settings.

Personal Space—Invisible Boundaries

An interesting aspect of social behavior is the effort people expend to regulate the space around their bodies. Each person has an invisible "spatial envelope" that defines his or her **personal space** and extends "I" or "me" boundaries past the skin.

Question: What effect does personal space have on behavior?

Maintaining and regulating personal space directly affects many social interactions. There are norms covering the interpersonal distance considered appropriate for formal business, casual conversation, waiting in line with strangers, and other situations. The study of rules for the personal use of space is called **proxemics** (Hall, 1974) (■ Fig. 20–3).

The existence of personal space and the nature of proxemics can be demonstrated by "invading" the space of another person. The next time you are talking with an acquaintance, move closer and watch the reaction. Most people show immediate signs of discomfort and step back to re-establish their original distance. Those who hold their ground will turn to the side, look away, or position an arm in front of themselves as a kind of barrier to intrusion. If you persistently edge toward your subjects, you should find it easy to move them several feet from their original positions. The

■ **Fig. 20–3** *The use of space in public places is governed by unspoken norms, or "rules," about what is appropriate.*

Intimate distance The most private space immediately surrounding the body (up to about 18 inches from the skin).

Personal distance The distance maintained when interacting with close friends (about 18 inches to 4 feet from the body).

Social distance Distance at which impersonal interaction takes place (about 4 to 12 feet from the body).

Public distance Distance at which formal interactions occur (about 12 feet or more from the body).

existence of spatial norms may explain why people who feel offended by another person sometimes say, "Get out of my face."

Question: Would this technique work with a good friend?

Possibly not. Conventions governing comfortable or acceptable distances vary according to relationships as well as activities. Hall (1966) identified four basic zones, intimate, personal, social, and public distance (■ Fig. 20–4). The distances listed here apply to face-to-face interactions in North American culture. Norms for personal distance vary greatly from culture to culture. In many Middle Eastern countries, for instance, people hold their faces only inches apart when conversing. In Western Europe, the English sit closer together when talking than the French do. The Dutch, on the other hand, sit farther apart than the French do (Remland, Jones, & Brinkman, 1991). In many parts of the world, merely crossing a border results in a noticeable change in spatial norms.

■ **Fig. 20–4** *Typical spatial zones (in feet) for face-to-face interactions in North America. Often, we must stand within intimate distance of others in crowds, buses, subways, elevators, and other public places. At such times, privacy is maintained by avoiding eye contact, by standing shoulder to shoulder or back to back, and by positioning a purse, bag, package, or coat as a barrier to spatial intrusions.*

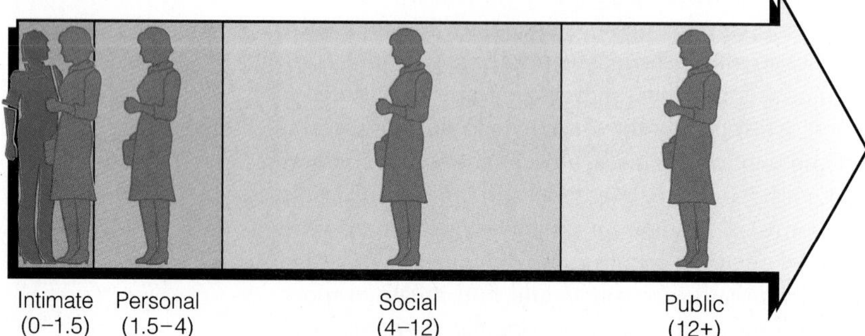

1. **Intimate distance.** For the majority of American adults, the most private and exclusive space extends about 18 inches out from the skin. Entry within this space (face to face) is reserved for special people or special circumstances. Lovemaking, comforting others, and cuddling children all take place within this space.
2. **Personal distance.** This is the distance maintained in comfortable interaction with friends. It extends from about 1½ to 4 feet from the body. Personal distance basically keeps people within "arm's reach" of each other.
3. **Social distance.** Impersonal business and casual social gatherings take place in a range of about 4 to 12 feet. This distance eliminates most touching, and it formalizes conversation by requiring greater voice projection. "Important people" in many business offices use the imposing width of their desks to maintain social distance.
4. **Public distance.** When people are separated by more than 12 feet, interactions take on a decidedly formal quality. At this distance people look "flat" and the voice must be raised. Formal speeches, lectures, business meetings, and the like, are conducted at public distance.

Because spatial behavior is very consistent, you can learn much about your relationship to others by observing the distance you comfortably hold between yourselves. Watch for this dimension in your daily social activities. But be aware of cultural differences, too. Otherwise, you might misread another person's spatial behavior. People of different nationalities often have different norms for personal space. When they do, both are likely to be uncomfortable when talking, as one tries to move closer and the other keeps moving back. This can lead to misunderstandings in which one person feels that the other is being too familiar, while the other feels rejected.

We have now explored some basic facts of social life and a striking example of group norms. In the next section we will consider a kind of impromptu detective work that we engage in as we try to guess the motives of others and the causes of their actions. Let's see how this is done.

Social Perception—Behind the Mask

As much as we might like to think otherwise, it is probably impossible to completely know another person. In fact, in many instances we must form impressions of people from only the smallest shreds of evidence. How do we form such impressions? How do they affect our behavior? Many of the answers lie in **attribution,** the process of making inferences about behavior. (Attribution was also discussed briefly in Chapter 10.) To learn how we fill in the "person behind the mask," let's explore the making of attributions.

Attribution Theory

Two people enter a restaurant and order different meals. Nell tastes her food, then salts it. Bert salts his food before tasting it. How would you explain their behavior? In Nell's case, you might assume that the *food* needed salt. If so, you have attributed her actions to an **external** cause. With Bert, you might be more inclined to conclude that he must really *like* salt. If so, you would be saying that the cause of his behavior is **internal** (McGee & Snyder, 1975).

Question: What effects do such interpretations have?

It is difficult to fully understand social behavior without considering internal and external attributions. For instance, let's say that Jim, who is in one of your classes, seems to avoid you. You see Jim at a market. Do you say hello to him? It could depend on how you have explained Jim's actions to yourself (Wegner & Vallacher, 1977). Have you assumed his avoidance is caused by shyness? Coincidence? Dislike?

Question: How do people make such judgments?

Making Attributions Two factors that greatly influence attribution are the **consistency** and **distinctiveness** of a person's behavior (Kelly, 1967). If Jim has consistently avoided you, it is clear that he was not just in a bad mood on each occasion, so coincidence is ruled out. Still, Jim's avoidance could mean he is shy, not that he dislikes you. This is why distinctiveness is also important. If Jim seems to avoid others too, you may conclude that he is shy. If his avoidance is consistently and distinctively linked with you, you will probably assume that he dislikes you. You could be wrong, of course, but your behavior toward Jim will change just the same.

To infer causes, we typically take into account the behavior of the **actor,** the **object** of the action, and the **setting** in which the action occurs (Kelly, 1967). Imagine for example, that someone compliments your taste in clothes. If you are at a picnic, you may attribute this compliment to what you are wearing (the "object"), unless, of course, you're wearing your worst "grubbies." If you are, you may simply assume that the person (or "actor") is friendly, or tactful. However, if you are at a clothing store and a salesperson compliments you, you will probably attribute it to the setting—not to what you are wearing or to the salesperson's true feelings. In making attributions we are very sensitive to **situational demands.** When a person is quiet and polite in church or at a funeral, it tells us little about the individual's motives. The situation demands such behavior.

When situational demands are quite strong, we tend to **discount** claims that a person's actions are internally caused (also see Highlight 20–2). For example, you have probably discounted the sincerity of professional athletes who endorse shaving creams, hair tonics, deodorants, and the like. Obviously, the athletes' endorsements are well explained by the large

Attribution The process of making inferences about the causes of one's own behavior, and that of others.

External cause A cause of behavior that is assumed to lie outside a person.

Internal cause A cause of behavior assumed to lie within a person—for instance, a need, preference, or personality trait.

Consistency When making attributions, noticing that a behavior changes very little on different occasions.

Distinctiveness When making attributions, noticing that a behavior occurs only under specific circumstances.

Actor In making attributions, the person whose behavior is being interpreted.

Object In making attributions, the aim, motive, or target of an action.

Setting In making attributions, the social and/or physical environment in which an action occurs.

Situational demands Unstated expectations that define desirable or appropriate behavior in various settings and social situations.

Discounting Downgrading internal explanations of behavior when a person's actions appear to have strong external causes.

Consensus The degree to which people respond alike. In making attributions, consensus implies that responses are externally caused.

Self-handicapping Arranging to perform under conditions that usually impair performance, so as to have an excuse for a poor showing.

Fundamental attributional error The tendency to attribute the behavior of others to internal causes (personality, likes, and so forth) while attributing one's own behavior to external causes (situations and circumstances).

sums of money they receive. It's not necessary to assume they actually *like* the potions they sell.

Consensus (or agreement) is another factor affecting attribution. A consensus in the behavior of a number of people implies that the behavior has an external cause. If millions of people go to see a particular movie, we tend to say *the movie* is good. If someone you know goes to see a movie six times, when others are staying away in droves, the tendency is to assume that *the person* likes "that type of movie."

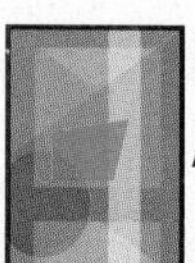

HIGHLIGHT 20–2

A Closer Look At

Self-Handicapping—Smoke Screen for Failure

Have you ever known someone who got drunk before taking an exam? Why would a person risk failure in this way? Often, the reason lies in an interesting effect called **self-handicapping.**

Steven Berglas (1986) has done studies showing that self-handicapping occurs when a person does not feel very confident about succeeding. To protect a fragile self-image, people sometimes arrange to be evaluated while "handicapped." That way, they can attribute failure to the handicap. And what if they succeed? Well, so much the better. Their self-image then gets a boost because they succeeded under conditions that everyone knows hinder performance. In other words, self-handicappers try to arrange a no-lose situation in which their positive image of themselves is protected no matter what the outcome (Murray & Warden, 1992).

There are many ways to arrange self-handicapping. In Chapter 1, for example, we discussed how procrastination on school assignments may actually be an attempt to protect one's self-image (Ferrari, 1991). Of the many ways to self-handicap, however, drinking alcohol is among the most popular—and dangerous. In the eyes of many, alcohol reduces personal responsibility for performance. Therefore, a person who is drunk can attribute failure to being "loaded," while accepting success if it occurs.

A person who gets drunk at times when he or she will be evaluated should be aware that this represents self-handicapping. Examples include being drunk for school exams, job interviews, or an important first date. Those who cope with anxiety in this way run a high risk of developing a pattern of alcohol abuse.

Any time you set up reasonable excuses for a poor performance, you are self-handicapping. Most of us have used self-handicapping at times when we faced a difficult challenge and were doubtful about success. Life would be harsh if we didn't sometimes give ourselves a break from accepting total responsibility for success or failure. Self-handicapping, therefore, becomes a problem when it turns into a habit, rather than a way of coping with life's toughest demands (Kleinke, 1986). So, watch out for self-handicapping, but don't be too hard on yourself.

Actor and Observer Let's say that at the last five parties you have attended, you've seen a woman named Pam. Based on this, you assume that Pam is very outgoing and likes to socialize. You see Pam at yet another gathering and mention that she seems to like parties. She says, "Actually, I hate these parties, but I get invited to play my tuba at them. My music teacher says I need to practice in front of an audience, so I keep attending these dumb events. Want to hear a Sousa march?"

We seldom know the real reasons for others' actions. That's why we tend to infer causes from *circumstances*. However, in doing so, we often make mistakes of the type just described. The most common error is to attribute the actions of *others* to *internal causes*, while attributing our *own* behavior to situations (*external causes*) (Jones & Nisbett, 1971; Kelly, 1971). This mistake is made so often that it is called the **fundamental attributional error** (Ross, 1977).

Psychologists have found that we consistently attribute the behavior of others to their wants, motives, and personality traits. In contrast, we tend to find external explanations for our own behavior. No doubt you chose *your* major in school because of what it has to offer. Other students choose *their* majors because of the kind of people they are (Wegner & Vallacher, 1977). Other people who don't leave tips in restaurants are cheapskates. If you don't leave a tip it's because the service was bad. And, of course, other people are always late because they are irresponsible. I am late because I have a good reason.

Implications As you can see, attribution theory attempts to summarize how we think about ourselves and others (■Fig. 20–5). It also tries to identify some of the consistent errors or biases in our interpretations. In addition to providing a better understanding of behavior, attribution theory has helped identify some practical problems. Let's conclude with a brief example.

Ye Old Double Standard Attribution research has uncovered an interesting double standard for men and

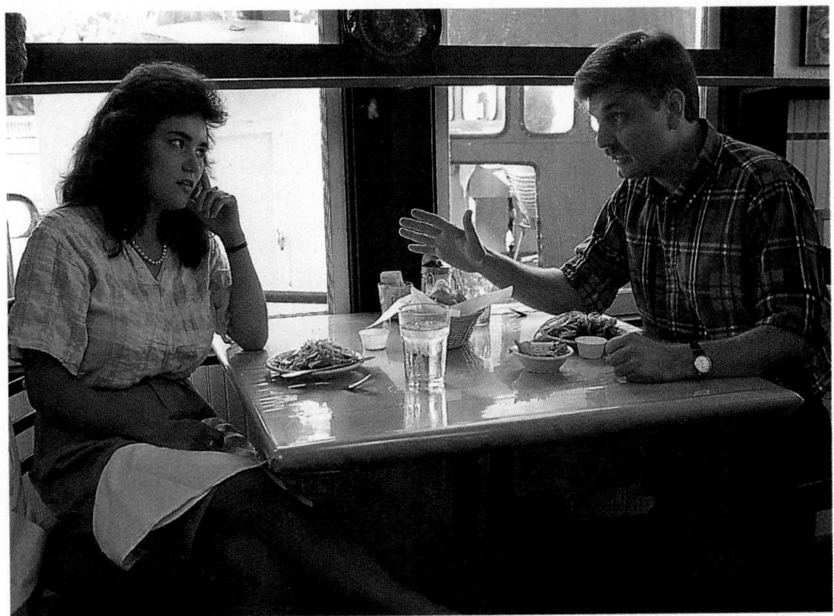

■ **Fig. 20–5** *Distressed couples tend to attribute their partners' actions to the worst possible motives, such as bad intentions or selfishness. Thus, attributional styles may lead to serious conflicts in marriage and other relationships (Holtzworth-Munroe & Hutchinson, 1993; Noller & Ruzzene, 1991).*

women. In a study by Kay Deaux and Tim Emswiller (1974), men and women overheard a male or female perform extremely well on a perception task. Subjects were then asked to rate whether the test taker's success was due to his or her ability, to luck, or to some combination of the two. Both men and women attributed male success mainly to skill and women's performances mainly to luck! This was true even though male and female performances were identical. Another more recent study found that as early as *kindergarten*, boys tend to take credit for successes. Girls, in contrast, tend to discount their own performances ("put themselves down") (Burgner & Hewstone, 1993). Throughout life, such attributions no doubt dog the heels of many talented and successful women.

LEARNING CHECK

1. *Male*, *female*, and *adolescent* are examples of ______________ roles.
2. Status refers to a set of expected behaviors associated with a social position. T or F?
3. Research has shown that the number of first-name acquaintances needed to interconnect two widely separated strangers averages about 7 people. T or F?
4. The Stanford prison experiment demonstrated the powerful influence of the autokinetic effect on behavior. T or F?
5. Social psychology is the study of how people behave in ______________.
6. If two people position themselves 5 feet apart while conversing, they are separated by a gap referred to as ______________ distance.
7. When situational demands are strong, we tend to attribute a person's actions to internal causes. T or F?
8. The fundamental attributional error is to attribute the actions of others to internal causes, while attributing our own behavior to external causes. T or F?
9. The Stanford prison experiment also illustrates a major concept of personality theory (Chapter 15), especially social learning theory. Can you name it? *Critical Thinking*

Answers: 1. ascribed 2. F 3. T 4. F 5. social situations or the presence of others 6. social 7. F 8. T 9. It is the idea that behavior is often strongly influenced by situations rather than by personal traits.

The Need for Affiliation—Come Together

Question: Why do people choose to associate with others?

We have already observed that the **need to affiliate** appears to be a basic human characteristic. But why? Probably because affiliation helps meet needs for approval, support, friendship, and information. We also seek company to alleviate fear or anxiety. An experiment in which college women were threatened with painful electric shock serves as an illustration.

Need to affiliate The desire to associate with other people.

Zilstein's Shock Shop

A man introduced as Dr. Gregor Zilstein ominously explained to arriving subjects, "We would like to give each of you a series of electric shocks . . . these shocks will

Social comparison Making judgments about ourselves through comparison with others.

Downward comparison Comparing yourself with a person who ranks lower than you on some dimension.

Upward comparison Comparing yourself with a person who ranks higher than you on some dimension.

Interpersonal attraction Social attraction to another person.

Physical proximity One's actual physical nearness to others in terms of housing, work, school, and so forth.

hurt, they will be painful." In the room was a frightening electrical device that seemed to verify Zilstein's plans. While waiting to be shocked, each subject was given a choice of waiting alone or with other subjects. Women frightened in this way more often chose to wait with others than did subjects told that the shock would be a mild tickle or tingle (Schachter, 1959).

Apparently, the frightened women found it comforting or reassuring to be with others. The tempting conclusion is that "misery loves company." But this is not completely accurate.

In a later experiment, women expecting to be shocked were given the option of waiting with other shock subjects, with women waiting to see their advisors, or alone. Most subjects chose to wait with other future "victims." In short, misery seems to love miserable company! In general, we tend to seek the company of people in circumstances similar to our own.

Question: Is there a reason for that?

Yes. Other people provide information for evaluating one's own reactions. When a situation is threatening or unfamiliar, or when a person is in doubt, *social comparisons* serve as a guide for behavior (Banaji & Prentice, 1994).

Social Comparison Theory

In some cases objective standards for self-evaluation exist. If I want to know how tall I am, I simply get out a tape measure. But how do I know if I am a good athlete, guitarist, worker, parent, or friend? How do I know if my views on politics, religion, or grunge rock are unusual or widely shared? The only yardstick available for such evaluations is provided by comparing myself to others.

Eminent social psychologist Leon Festinger (1919–1989) was among the first to point out that group membership fills needs for **social comparison.** When there are no objective standards, we must turn to others to evaluate our actions, feelings, opinions, or abilities. When students gather to compare notes after a classroom exam, they satisfy needs for social comparison.

Festinger (1954) emphasized that social comparisons are not made randomly or on some ultimate scale. To illustrate, let's say we ask a student named Wendy if she is a good tennis player. If Wendy compares herself to a professional, the answer will be no. But this tells little about her relative ability. In Wendy's group of tennis partners, she might be considered an excellent player. Useful personal evaluation requires comparison with people of similar backgrounds, abilities, and circumstances (Miller, Turnbull, & McFarland, 1988). On a fair scale of comparison, Wendy knows she is good and takes pride in her tennis skills. In the same way, thinking of yourself as successful, talented, responsible, or fairly paid depends entirely on whom you compare yourself with.

In addition to providing information, social comparisons may, at times, be made in ways that reflect a desire for self-protection or self-enhancement. If you feel threatened, you may make a **downward comparison** with someone less fortunate than yourself (Banaji & Prentice, 1994). For example, if you have a part-time job and your employer cuts your hours, you may comfort yourself by thinking about a friend who just lost a job.

Question: What about upward comparisons? Do they occur, too?

As Wendy's tennis playing suggests, comparing yourself with people of much higher ability will probably just make you feel bad (Wheeler and Miyake, 1992). However, **upward comparisons** are sometimes used for self-improvement. One way that Wendy can learn to improve her tennis skills is to compare herself with players who are only a little better than she is (Banaji & Prentice, 1994).

In general, social comparison theory holds that desires for self-evaluation, self-protection, and self-enhancement provide motives for associating with others. In doing so, they influence which groups we join.

Question: Don't people also affiliate out of attraction for one another?

They do, of course. The next section tells why.

Interpersonal Attraction—Social Magnetism?

"Birds of a feather flock together." "Familiarity breeds contempt." "Opposites attract." "Absence makes the heart grow fonder." Interest in what attracts people to one another has spawned an extensive folklore about what factors are important. This is understandable, since **interpersonal attraction** is the basis for most voluntary social relationships.

Question: What attracts people to each other?

Several factors determine with whom you are likely to become friends. A brief discussion of each follows.

Physical Proximity It may be difficult to admit, but our friends (and even lovers) are selected more on the basis of opportunity than we might like to believe. Nearness plays a powerful role in making friends. In a study of friendship patterns in a campus married-student housing complex, it was found that the closer people lived to each other, the more likely they were to be friends (Festinger et al., 1950). People in love like to think they have found the "one and only" per-

■ Fig. 20–6 *What attracts people to each other? Proximity and frequency of contact have a surprisingly large impact.*

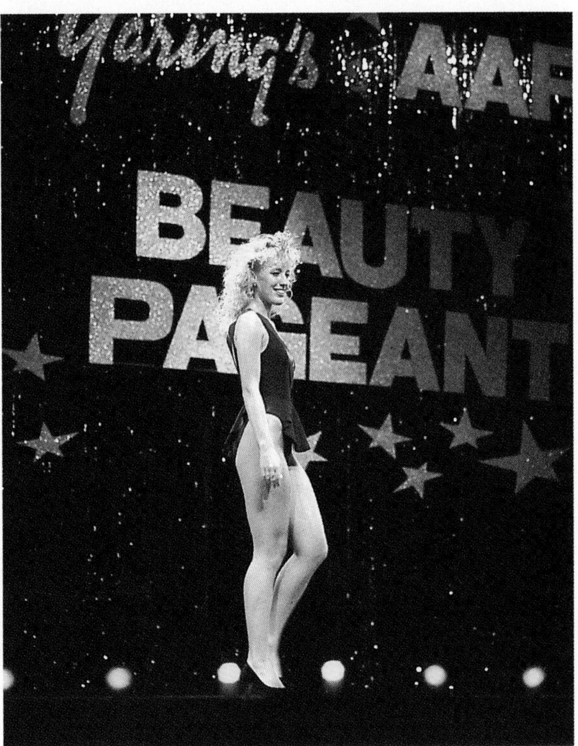

■ Fig. 20–7 *Physical beauty can be socially advantageous because of the widespread belief that "what is beautiful is good." However, physical beauty is generally unrelated to actual personal traits and talents.*

son in the universe for them. In reality, they have probably found the one and only person in a 5-mile radius—or at least within driving distance (Buss, 1985)!

A main reason for proximity's effect is that it increases the *frequency of contact* between people. A variety of experiments show that we are generally attracted to people with whom we have had frequent contact (Saegert et al., 1973). In other words, there does seem to be a "boy-next-door" or "girl-next-door" effect in romantic attraction, and a "folks-next-door" effect in friendship (■ Fig. 20–6).

Physical Attractiveness As might be expected, beautiful people are consistently rated more appealing than those of average appearance. This is due, in part, to the **halo effect** (see Chapter 15), in which we assume that attractive people are also likable, intelligent, warm, witty, mentally healthy and socially skilled (Feingold, 1992a). Basically, we tend to assume that "what is beautiful is good" (■ Fig. 20–7). However, there are limits to the traits we associate with beauty. For instance, we do not expect beautiful people to be more honest or concerned about others (Johnson, 1991)! And in reality, physical attractiveness has almost no connection to intelligence, talents, or abilities (Feingold, 1992a).

Being physically attractive can be an advantage for both males and females. Good-looking people are less lonely, less socially anxious, more popular, more socially skilled, and more sexually experienced than unattractive people (Feingold, 1992a). Where romance is concerned, physical attractiveness has more influence on a woman's fate than on a man's (Feingold, 1990). For instance, there is a strong relationship between physical beauty in women and their frequency of dating. For men, looks are unrelated to dating frequency. Among older married couples there is a tendency for attractive women to be paired with highly educated men with high incomes. For men, however, there is little relationship between attractiveness and the achievement of status (Udry & Eckland, 1984).

If you view this state of affairs as rather shallow and sexist, it may be reassuring to know that beauty is a factor mainly in initial acquaintance. Later, more substantial personal qualities become important (Berscheid 1994). It takes more than appearance to make a lasting relationship. Even first impressions are less affected by beauty if we are given information about a person that helps us see her or him as an individual (Johnson, 1991).

Physical attractiveness A person's degree of physical beauty, as defined by his or her culture.

Halo effect The tendency to generalize a favorable first impression to unrelated personal characteristics.

Competence The degree of general ability or proficiency a person displays.

Competence We are also attracted to those who are talented or competent, but there is an interesting twist to this, as revealed in the following example.

Clever but Clumsy

In an experiment on attraction, college students listened to one of four tapes of a supposed candidate for the "College Quiz Bowl." On two of the tapes the person

Similarity The extent to which two people are alike in background, age, interests, attitudes, beliefs, and so forth.

Homogamy Marriage of two people who are similar to one another.

Self-disclosure The process of revealing private thoughts, feelings, and one's personal history to others.

Reciprocity A reciprocal interchange or return in kind.

Overdisclosure Self-disclosure that exceeds what is appropriate for a particular relationship or social situation.

was represented as highly intelligent; on the other two he was depicted as average in ability. One of the "intelligent" and one of the "average" tapes included an incident in which the candidate clumsily spilled coffee on himself. Those listening to the tapes rated as *most* attractive the superior candidate who blundered, and as *least* attractive the student who was average and clumsy. The superior but clumsy student was more attractive than the student who was only superior. (Aronson, 1969)

The upshot of this experiment seems to be that we like people who are competent but imperfect—which makes them more "human."

Similarity Take a moment to mentally list as many of your friends as you can. What do they have in common (other than the joy of knowing you)? It is highly likely that most are close to you in age and of the same sex and race as you. There will be exceptions, of course. However, similarity on these three dimensions is the general rule for friendships.

One of the most consistent findings about interpersonal attraction is that people with similar backgrounds, interests, attitudes, beliefs, and personalities are attracted to each other (Carli, Ganley, & Pierce-Otay, 1991). This is probably at least partially due to the reinforcing value of seeing our beliefs and attitudes affirmed by others. It shows we are "right" and reveals that they are clever people as well! We even tend to like people more if they are in the same mood as we are, be it good or bad (Locke & Horowitz, 1990).

Does similarity also influence mate selection? Highlight 20–3 provides an answer.

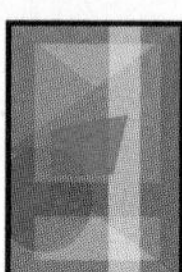

HIGHLIGHT 20–3

A Closer Look At

Selecting a Mate—Reflections in a Social Mirror

Ninety percent of all people in Western societies marry at some point. What, beyond attraction, determines how people pair up? The answer is that we tend to marry someone who is like us in almost every way, a pattern called **homogamy** (huh-MOG-ah-me) (Caspi & Herbener, 1990).

A variety of studies show that people who marry are highly similar in age, education, race, religion, and ethnic background. In addition, the correlation of attitudes and opinions for married couples is .5. For mental abilities it is .4, and for socioeconomic status, height, weight, and eye color it is .3. In general, you are far more likely to choose someone similar to yourself as a mate than someone very different. This is probably a good thing, because personality traits tend to be closely matched for husbands and wives in marriages that are most stable (Kim, Martin, & Martin, 1989). Conversely, the risk of eventual separation or divorce is highest among couples with sizable differences in age and education (Tzeng, 1992).

A second question of interest concerns what traits people look for in a mate. In the United States, both men and women agree that the following are the first six most important qualities: kindness and understanding, intelligence, exciting personality, good health, adaptability, and physical attractiveness.

Despite such agreement, men and women do differ on some rankings. Men, for instance, rank physical attractiveness as the third most important feature, whereas women rank it sixth. A second major difference concerns good earning capacity: Men rank it eleventh; women rank it eighth. Apparently, for most people, romance is leavened with a dash of practicality. Even so, kindness and understanding are ranked first by almost everyone. (Source: Buss, 1985)

Question: How do people who are not yet friends learn if they are similar?

Self-Disclosure Getting to know others requires a willingness to talk about more than just the weather, sports, or nuclear physics. At some point you must begin to share private thoughts and feelings and reveal more of your true self. Engaging in such **self-disclosure** is a major step toward friendship. Self-disclosure refers to the process of letting yourself be known to others. The ability to reveal your thoughts and feelings to others is a basic skill for developing close relationships. Lack of self-disclosure is frequently associated with anxiety, unhappiness, and loneliness (Meleshko, & Alden, 1993; Mikulincer & Nachshon, 1991).

Experimental work confirms that we more often reveal ourselves to persons we like than to those we find less attractive (Chaiken & Derlega, 1974). Disclosing oneself to others also requires a degree of trust. Many people play it safe, or "close to the vest," with people they do not know well. Indeed, there are definite norms about when self-disclosure is acceptable and when it is not. Moderate self-disclosure leads to **reciprocity** (a return in kind) (Huston & Levinger, 1978). **Overdisclosure,** however, gives rise to suspicion and reduced attraction (Rubin, 1975). (Imagine standing in line at a market and having the person in front of you say, "Lately I've been thinking about how I really feel about myself. I think that I'm pretty well adjusted, but I occasionally have some questions about my sexual adequacy.")

When self-disclosure proceeds at a moderate pace, it is accompanied by growing trust and intimacy. When it is too rapid or inappropriate, we are likely to "back off" and wonder about the person's motives. Thus, as friends talk, they influence each other in ways that gradually deepen the level of liking, trust, and self-disclosure (Miller, 1990). Likewise, satisfaction in romantic relationships is associated with high levels of emotional self-disclosure (Vera & Betz, 1992).

Social Exchange Theory As relationships progress, quite often they can be understood in terms of maximizing rewards while minimizing "costs" in any **social exchange.** When a relationship ceases to be attractive, people often say, "I'm not getting anything out of it any more." Actually they probably are, but their costs—in terms of effort, irritation, or lowered self-esteem—have exceeded their rewards. According to social exchange theory, we unconsciously weigh such rewards and costs. For a relationship to last, it must be *profitable* (its rewards must exceed its costs) for both parties. For instance, John and Ruthie have been dating for two years. While they still have fun at times, they also frequently argue and bicker. If the friction in their relationship gets much stronger, it will exceed the rewards of staying together. When that happens they will probably split up.

Actually, just being profitable is not the whole story. It is more accurate to say that a relationship needs to be profitable *enough.* Generally, the balance between rewards and costs in a relationship is judged in comparison with what we have come to expect from past experience. The personal standard used to evaluate rewards and costs is called the **comparison level.** The comparison level is high for a person who has had a history of satisfying and rewarding relationships. It is lower for someone whose relationships have been unsatisfying. Thus, the decision to continue a relationship is affected by your personal comparison level. That is, a lonely person, or one whose friendships have been marginal, might stay in a relationship that you would consider unacceptable.

Love Scale
1. If ________________ were feeling bad, my first duty would be to cheer him (her) up.
2. I feel that I can confide in ________________ about virtually everything.
3. I find it easy to ignore ________________'s faults.
Liking Scale
1. When I am with ________________, we are almost always in the same mood.
2. I think that ________________ is unusually well adjusted.
3. I would highly recommend ________________ for a responsible job.

■ **Fig. 20–8** *Sample love-scale and liking-scale items. Each scale consists of 13 items similar to those shown. Scores on these scales correspond to other indications of love and liking. (Reprinted by permission of Zick Rubin.)*

Loving and Liking—Dating, Rating, Mating

Question: Does romantic attraction differ from interpersonal attraction?

In an earlier discussion we treated love as an emotion (see Chapter 10) and pointed out that passionate or **romantic love** is marked by heightened arousal. We also discussed various types of love that result from combinations of intimacy, passion, and commitment. To get another angle on love, psychologist Zick Rubin (1973) chose to think of it as an attitude held by one person toward another. This allowed him to develop "liking" and "love" scales to measure each "attitude" (see ■ Fig. 20–8). Next, he asked dating couples to complete each scale twice; once with their date in mind and once for a close friend of the same sex.

Question: What were the results?

Scores for love of partner and love of friend differed more than those for **liking** (⬬ Table 20–1). In other words, dating couples liked *and* loved their partners, but mostly liked their friends. Women, however, were a little more "loving" of their friends than were men. Does this reflect real differences in the strength of male friendships and female friendships? Maybe not, since it is more acceptable in our culture for women to express love for one another than it is for men. Nevertheless, a recent study confirmed that dating

Social exchange theory Theory stating that rewards must exceed costs for relationships to endure.

Social exchange An interchange in which attention, affection, help, approval, or other valued entities are exchanged.

Comparison level A personal standard used to evaluate rewards and costs in a social exchange.

Romantic love Love that is associated with high levels of interpersonal attraction, heightened arousal, and mutual absorption.

Liking A relationship based on intimacy, but lacking passion and commitment.

⬬ **Table 20–1 Average Love and Liking Scores for Date and Same-Sex Close Friend**

Attitude toward dating partner		
	Love score	Liking score
Women	89.5	88.5
Men	89.4	84.7
Attitude toward close friend		
	Love score	Liking score
Women	65.3	80.5
Men	55.0	79.1

(Source: Rubin, 1970)

Mutual absorption With regard to romantic love, the nearly exclusive attention lovers give to one another.

Secure attachment A stable and positive emotional bond.

Avoidant attachment An emotional bond marked by a tendency to resist commitment to others.

Ambivalent attachment An emotional bond marked by conflicting feelings of affection, anger, and emotional turmoil.

couples feel a mixture of love and friendship for their partners. In fact, 44 percent of a group of dating persons named their romantic partner as their closest friend (Hendrick & Hendrick, 1993).

Another way in which love and friendship differ is the degree of mutual absorption. Romantic love, in contrast to simple liking, usually involves deep **mutual absorption** of the lovers. In other words, lovers (unlike friends) attend almost exclusively to one another. It's not surprising then, that couples scoring high on Rubin's love scale spend more time gazing into each other's eyes than do couples who score low on the scale. As the song says, "Millions of people go by, but they all disappear from view—'cause I only have eyes for you."

Love and Attachment

Sheela has been dating Paul for over a year. Although they have had some rough spots, Sheela is comfortable, secure, and trusting in her love for Paul. Charlene, in contrast, has had a long series of unhappy romances with men. She is basically a loner who has difficulty trusting others. Like Sheela, Eduardo has been dating the same person for a year. However, his relationship with Helen has been stormy and troubled. Eduardo is strongly attracted to Helen. Yet, he is also in a constant state of anxiety over whether she really loves him.

Sheela, Charlene, and Eduardo might be surprised to learn that the roots of their romantic relationships may lie in childhood. There is growing evidence that early attachments to caregivers (see Chapter 12) can have a lasting impact on how we relate to others (Shaver & Hazan, 1993). For example, recent studies of dating couples have identified secure, avoidant, and ambivalent attachment patterns similar to those seen in early child development (Mikulincer & Nachshon, 1991).

A **secure** attachment style like Sheela's is marked by caring, intimacy, supportiveness, and understanding in love relationships. Secure persons regard themselves as friendly, good natured, and likable and they think of others as generally well intentioned, reliable, and trustworthy. People with a secure attachment style find it relatively easy to get close to others. They are comfortable depending on others and having others depend on them. In general, they don't worry too much about being abandoned or about having someone become too emotionally close to them.

Charlene's **avoidant** attachment style reflects a fear of intimacy and a tendency to pull back when things don't go well in a relationship. The avoidant person is suspicious, aloof, and skeptical about love. He or she tends to see others as either unreliable or overly eager to commit to a relationship. As a result, avoidant persons find it hard to completely trust and depend on others. Avoidant persons get nervous when anyone gets too close emotionally. Basically, they want to avoid intimacy.

Persons like Eduardo have an **ambivalent** attachment style, marked by mixed emotions about relationships. Conflicting feelings of affection, anger, emotional turmoil, physical attraction, and doubt leave them in an unsettled, ambivalent state. Often, ambivalent persons regard themselves as misunderstood and unappreciated. They tend to see their friends and lovers as unreliable and unable or unwilling to commit themselves to lasting relationships. Ambivalent persons worry that their romantic partners don't really love them or may leave them. While they want to be extremely close to their partners, they are also preoccupied with doubts about the partner's dependability and trustworthiness.

Question: How could emotional attachments early in life affect adult relationships?

It appears that we use early attachment experiences to build mental models about affectionate relationships. Later, we use these models as a sort of blueprint for forming, maintaining, and breaking bonds of love and affection (Simpson, 1990). Thus, the quality of childhood bonds to parents or other caregivers may hold a key to understanding how we approach romantic relationships (Shaver & Hazen, 1993). Maybe it's no accident that persons who are romantically available are often described as "unattached."

It is fascinating to think that our relationships may be influenced by events early in childhood. Could the source of adult mating patterns reach even farther back? The next section explores that possibility.

Evolution and Mate Selection

Many psychologists have come to believe that evolution left an imprint on men and women that influences everything from sexual attraction and infidelity to jealousy and divorce. According to David Buss, the key to understanding human mating patterns is not found just in learning, socialization, attachment, or culture. Rather, we must also understand how evolved behavior patterns guide our choices (Buss, 1994).

In a study of 37 cultures on 6 continents, Buss found the following patterns: Compared with women, men are more interested in casual sex; they prefer younger, more physically attractive partners; and they get more jealous over real or imagined sexual infidelities than they do over a loss of emotional commitment. Compared with men, women prefer slightly older partners who appear to be industrious, higher in status, or economically successful; women are more upset by a partner who becomes emotionally involved with someone else, rather than one who is sexually unfaithful (Buss, 1994; Buss et al., 1992).

Why do such differences exist? Buss and other researchers believe that **evolutionary psychology** explains many human mating patterns. Mating preferences, they say, evolved in response to the differing reproductive challenges faced by men and women (■ Fig. 20–9).

As a rule, women must invest more time and energy in reproduction and nurturing the young than men do. Consequently, women evolved an interest in whether their partners will stay with them and whether their mates have the resources to provide for their children.

In contrast, the reproductive success of men depends on their mates' fertility. Men, therefore, tend to look for health and youth in a prospective mate, as signs of suitability for reproduction. This preference, perhaps, is why some older men abandon their first wives in favor of young, beautiful "trophy wives." Evolutionary theory further explains that the male emphasis on mates' sexual fidelity is based on concerns about the paternity of offspring. From a biological perspective, men do not benefit from investing resources in children they did not sire (Buss, 1994).

A sizable body of evidence supports the evolutionary view of mating preferences. However, it is important to remember that evolved mating tendencies are subtle at best and easily overruled by other factors. Indeed, some mating patterns may simply reflect the fact that men still tend to control the power and resources in most societies (Feingold, 1992a). Most important of all, remember that when either men or women choose mates, kindness and intelligence still rate highest. They are love's greatest allies.

■ **Fig. 20–9** *According to evolutionary psychologists, women tend to be concerned with whether mates will devote time and resources to a relationship. Men place more emphasis on physical attractiveness and sexual fidelity.*

Evolutionary psychology Study of the evolutionary origins of human behavior patterns.

LEARNING CHECK

Before you read more, check your comprehension with the following questions.

1. Women threatened with electric shock in an experiment generally chose to wait alone or with other women not taking part in the experiment. T or F?
2. The need to affiliate is related to interest in social comparison. T or F?
3. Social comparisons are made pretty much at random. T or F?
4. Interpersonal attraction is increased by all but one of the following. (Which does not fit?)
   a. physical proximity *b.* competence *c.* similarity *d.* social costs
5. High levels of self-disclosure are reciprocated in most social encounters. T or F?
6. Women rate their friends higher on the love scale than do men. T or F?
7. The most striking finding about marriage patterns is that most people choose mates whose personalities are quite unlike their own. T or F?
8. Both ambivalent and avoidant attachment patterns are associated with difficulties in trusting a romantic partner. T or F?
9. Compared with men, women tend to be more upset by sexual infidelity than by a loss of emotional commitment on the part of their mates. T or F?
10. How have contemporary communications networks altered the effects of proximity on interpersonal attraction? ***Critical Thinking***

Answers:

1. F 2. T 3. F 4. *d* 5. F 6. T 7. F 8. T 9. F 10. It is now possible to interact with another person by telephone, fax, short-wave radio, modem, or similar means. This makes actual *physical* proximity less crucial in interpersonal attraction, because frequent contact is possible even at great distances.

Social influence Changes in a person's behavior induced by the presence or actions of others.

Conformity Bringing one's behavior into agreement or harmony with norms or with the behavior of others in a group.

Social Influence—Follow the Leader

One of the most heavily researched topics in social psychology concerns the effects of **social influence.** When people interact, they almost always affect one another's behavior. Let's probe the ways in which such influence takes place.

Imagine a traffic signal brightly flashing the word WAIT. As you and a number of other pedestrians wait for it to change, a well-dressed man in a suit crosses against the light. How many people follow him? Do you think the answer would be different if the man were dressed in a denim shirt, patched pants, and scuffed shoes? This street-corner setting was used in an early experiment on social influence. As you might have guessed, more people followed the well-dressed man than the one dressed in shabby clothes (Lefkowitz et al., 1955).

In another sidewalk experiment, various numbers of people were assembled on a busy New York City street. On cue they all looked at a sixth-floor window across the street. A camera recorded the number of passersby who also stopped to stare. The larger the influencing group, the more people were swayed to join in staring at the window (Milgram et al., 1969).

Question: Are there different kinds of social influence?

Social influence ranges from simple suggestion to intensive indoctrination (brainwashing). Everyday behavior is probably most influenced by group pressures for conformity. Conformity situations develop when individuals become aware of differences between themselves and group actions, norms, or values (Baron & Byrne, 1990). Let us consider this important dimension of social life in more detail.

Conformity

When John first started working at the Fleegle Flange Factory, he found it easy to process 300 flanges an hour, while those around him averaged only 200. Other workers told him to slow down and take it easy. "I get bored," he said and continued to do 300 flanges an hour. At first John had been welcomed, but now conversations broke up when he approached and other workers laughed at him or ignored him when he spoke. Although he never made a conscious decision to conform, in another week John's output had slowed to 200 flanges an hour.

As mentioned earlier, all groups have unspoken shared rules of conduct called *norms.* The broadest norms, defined by society as a whole, establish "normal" or acceptable behavior in most situations. Comparing hairstyles, habits of speech, dress, eating habits, and social customs in two or more cultures makes it clear that we all conform to social norms. In fact, a degree of uniformity is necessary if we are to interact comfortably. Imagine being totally unable to anticipate the actions of others. In stores, schools, and homes this would be frustrating and disturbing. On the highways it would be lethal.

Perhaps the most basic of all group norms is, as John discovered, "Thou shalt conform!" (Suedfeld, 1966). This is equally true for the Hell's Angels, the Daughters of the American Revolution, a street-corner gang, or the board of directors of a large corporation. Groups of all kinds exert considerable pressures toward uniformity on their members. Like it or not, everyday life is filled with instances of **conformity** (■ Fig. 20–10).

Question: How strong are group pressures for conformity?

The Asch Experiment One of the better known experiments on conformity was staged by Solomon Asch in the early 1950s. Asch's experiment is best appreciated by placing yourself in the position of a subject. Assume that you are seated at a table with six other students. Your task is actually quite simple. On

■ **Fig. 20–10** *Conformity is a subtle dimension of daily life. Notice the similarities in clothing and hairstyles among these couples.*

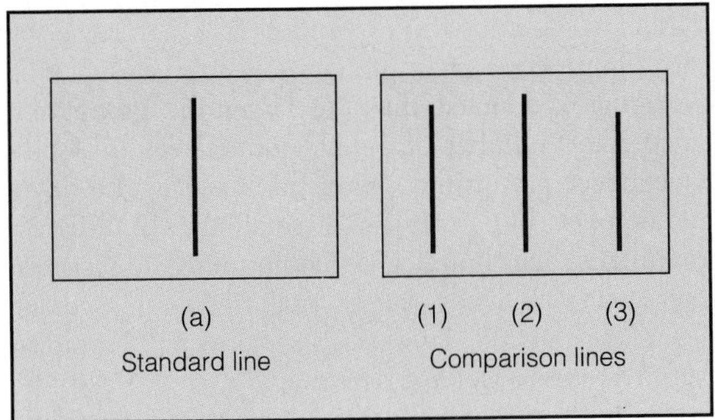

■ Fig. 20–11 *Stimuli used in Solomon Asch's conformity experiments.*

each trial you are asked to select from among three lines the one that matches a standard line (■ Fig. 20–11).

As the testing begins, each subject announces an answer for the first card. When your turn comes, you find yourself in complete agreement with the others. "This isn't hard at all," you say to yourself. For several more trials your answers correspond to those of the group. Then comes a shock. All six people announce that line 1 matches the standard, and you were about to say line 2 matches. Suddenly you feel alone and upset. You nervously look at the lines again as the room falls silent. Everyone seems to be staring at you as the experimenter awaits your answer. Do you yield to the group?

In this experiment the other "students" were all accomplices coached to give the wrong answer on about a third of the trials. Few real subjects suspected trickery; hence, the group pressure created was very realistic (Asch, 1956).

Question: How many people yielded to group pressure?

Subjects conformed to the group on about one third of the critical trials. Of those tested, 75 percent yielded at least once. The significance of these results is underscored by the fact that the other subjects tested alone erred in less than 1 percent of their judgments. Those who yielded to group pressures were clearly denying what their eyes told them.

Question: Are some people more susceptible to group pressures than others?

A variety of experiments have shown that people with high needs for structure or certainty are more likely to be influenced. People who are anxious, low in self-confidence, or concerned with the opinions or approval of others are also more susceptible. Certain situations also encourage conformity, sometimes with disastrous results. Highlight 20–4 offers a prime example.

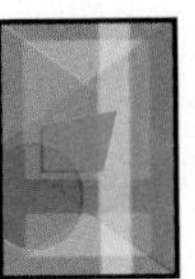

HIGHLIGHT 20–4

Critical Thinking

Groupthink—Agreement at Any Cost

What happens when people in positions of power fall prey to pressures for conformity? To find out, Yale psychologist Irving Janis (1918–1990) analyzed a collection of disastrous decisions made by government officials. His conclusion? Many such fiascoes are the result of **groupthink**—a compulsion by decision makers to maintain each other's approval, even at the cost of critical thinking (Janis, 1989). Groupthink has been blamed for many embarrassments, such as John F. Kennedy's backing of the Bay of Pigs invasion in Cuba or Ronald Reagan's Iran-Contra scandal. It also seems to have contributed to the *Challenger* space shuttle disaster.

The core of groupthink is misguided group loyalty that prevents members from "rocking the boat" or questioning weak arguments and sloppy thinking. In other words, groupthink is more likely to occur when group members emphasize their emotional bonds, rather than the task at hand. The resulting conformity pressures and self-censorship cause members to believe that greater agreement and unanimity exists than actually does (Bernthal & Insko, 1993; Turner et al., 1992).

To prevent groupthink, group leaders should take the following steps:

- Define each group member's role as that of critical evaluator.
- Avoid stating any personal preferences in the beginning.
- State the problem factually, without bias.
- Invite a group member or outside person to play devil's advocate.
- Make it clear to group members that they will be held accountable for their decisions (Kroon et al., 1992).

In addition, Janis suggested that there should be a "second-chance" meeting to re-evaluate important decisions. That is, each decision should be reached twice. In an age clouded by the threat of nuclear war and similar disasters, even stronger solutions to the problem of groupthink would be welcome. Perhaps we should form a group to think about it?!

Groupthink A compulsion by members of decision-making groups to maintain agreement, even at the cost of critical thinking.

Group sanctions Rewards and punishments (such as approval or disapproval) administered by groups to enforce conformity among members.

Unanimity Being unanimous or of one mind; agreement.

Social power The capacity to control, alter, or influence the behavior of another person.

Reward power Social power based on the capacity to reward a person for acting as desired.

Coercive power Social power based on the ability to punish others.

Question: How do groups enforce norms?

Group Factors in Conformity In most of our experiences with groups, we have been rewarded with acceptance and approval for conformity and threatened with rejection or ridicule for non-conformity. These reactions are called **group sanctions.** Negative sanctions (or punishments) for non-conformity range from laughter, staring, or social disapproval to complete rejection or formal ostracism. This is illustrated by later experiments in which Asch made up groups of 6 real subjects and 1 trained dissenter. When "Mr. Odd" announced his wrong answers, he was greeted with derisive laughter and sidelong glances. Such treatment helps explain why we are especially likely to conform when we are concerned about whether our views are right or wrong (Alicke & Doherty, 1992).

Question: Wouldn't the effectiveness of group sanctions depend on the importance of the group?

Yes. The more important group membership is to a person, the more he or she will be influenced by other group members. That's why the Asch experiments are impressive. Since these were only temporary groups, sanctions were informal and rejection had no lasting importance, and yet the power of the group was evident.

Question: What other factors, besides importance of the group, affect the degree of conformity?

Earlier we described an experiment in which passersby were influenced by a group of people staring at a building. We noted that the larger the group, the greater the number of people influenced. In Asch's face-to-face groups the size of the majority also made a difference, but a surprisingly small one. In other experiments, the number of conforming subjects increased dramatically as the majority was increased from 2 to 3 people. However, a majority of 3 produced about as much yielding as a majority of 8. Next time you want to talk someone into (or out of) something, take two friends along and see what a difference it makes! (Sometimes it helps if the two are large and mean-looking.)

Even more important than the size of the majority is its **unanimity.** Having at least one person in your corner can greatly reduce pressures to conform. When Asch provided subjects with an ally (who also opposed the majority by giving the correct answer), conformity was lessened. In terms of numbers, a unanimous majority of 3 is more powerful than a majority of 8 with 1 dissenting. Perhaps this accounts for the rich diversity of human attitudes, beliefs, opinions, and lifestyles. If you can find at least one other person who sees things as you do (no matter how weird), you can be relatively secure in your opposition to other viewpoints.

LEARNING CHECK

1. The effect one person's behavior has on another is called __________ __________.
2. Conformity is a normal aspect of social life. T or F?
3. Subjects in Solomon Asch's conformity study yielded on about 75 percent of the critical trials. T or F?
4. Non-conformity is punished by negative group __________.
5. Janis used the term __________ to describe a compulsion among decision-making groups to maintain an illusion of unanimity.

Critical Thinking

6. Would it be possible to be completely non-conforming (that is, to not conform to *some* group norm)?

Answers: 1. social influence 2. T 3. F 4. sanctions 5. groupthink 6. A person who did not follow at least *some* norms concerning normal social behavior would very likely be perceived as extremely bizarre, disturbed, or psychotic.

Social Power—Who Can Do What to Whom?

Here's something to think about: Whereas *strength* is a quality possessed by individuals, *power* is always social—it arises when people come together and disappears when they disperse. In trying to understand the ways in which people are able to influence each other, it is helpful to distinguish among five types of **social power** (Raven, 1974).

Reward power lies in the ability to reward a person for complying with desired behavior. Teachers try to exert reward power over their students through the use of grades. Employers command reward power by their control of wages and bonuses.

Coercive power is based on the ability to punish a person for failure to comply. Coercive power is the basis for most statute law, in that fines or imprisonment are used to control behavior.

Legitimate power comes from acceptance of a person as an agent of an established social order. For example, elected leaders and supervisors have legitimate power. So does a teacher in the classroom, but outside the classroom that power would have to come from another source.

Referent power is based on respect for or identification with a person or a group. The person "refers to" the source of referent power for direction. Referent power is responsible for much of the conformity observed in groups.

Expert power is based on recognition that another person has knowledge or expertise necessary for achieving a goal. Allowing teachers or experts to guide behavior because you believe in their ability to produce desirable results is an example. Physicians, lawyers, psychologists, and plumbers have expert power.

A person who has power in one situation may have very little in another. In those situations where a person has power, he or she is described as an *authority*. In the next section we will investigate *obedience*. Obedience is a special type of conformity to the demands of an authority.

Obedience—Would You Electrocute a Stranger?

The question is this: If ordered to do so, would you shock a man with a known heart condition who is screaming and asking to be released? Certainly we can assume that few people would do so. Or can we? In Nazi Germany, obedient soldiers (once average citizens) helped slaughter over 9 million people in concentration camps. Another example of the same phenomenon was an infamous incident during the Vietnam War when Lt. William Calley led a bloody massacre of helpless civilians at a village called My Lai. Do such inhumane acts reflect deep character flaws? Are they the acts of heartless psychopaths or crazed killers? Or are they simply the result of obedience to authority? What are the limits of such obedience? These are questions that puzzled social psychologist Stanley Milgram (1965) when he began a provocative series of studies on **obedience.**

Question: How did Milgram study obedience?

As was true of the Asch experiments, Milgram's research is best appreciated by imagining yourself as a subject. Place yourself in the following situation.

Legitimate power Social power based on a person's position as an agent of an accepted social order.

Referent power Social power gained when one is used as a point of reference by others.

Expert power Social power derived from possession of knowledge or expertise.

Obedience Conformity to the demands of an authority.

Milgram's Obedience Studies

Imagine answering a newspaper ad to take part in a "learning" experiment at Yale University. When you arrive, a coin is flipped and a second subject, a pleasant-looking man in his 50s, is designated the "learner." By chance you have become the "teacher."

Your task is to read a list of word pairs to be memorized by the learner. You are to punish him with an electric shock each time he makes a mistake. The learner is taken to an adjacent room and you watch as he is seated in an "electric chair" apparatus and electrodes are attached to his wrists. You are then escorted to your position in front of a "shock generator." On this device is a row of 30 switches labeled from 15 to 450 volts and accompanied by descriptions ranging from "Slight Shock" to "Extreme Intensity Shock" and finally "Danger Severe Shock." Your instructions are to administer a shock each time the learner makes a mistake. You are to begin with 15 volts and then move one switch (15 volts) higher for each additional mistake (■ Fig. 20–12).

The experiment begins, and the learner soon makes his first error. You flip a switch. More mistakes. Rapidly you reach the 75-volt level. The learner moans after each shock. At 100 volts he complains he has a heart condition. At 150 volts he says he no longer

■ **Fig. 20–12** *Scenes from Stanley Milgram's study of obedience: the "shock generator," strapping a "learner" into his chair, and a "teacher" being told to administer a severe shock to the learner.*

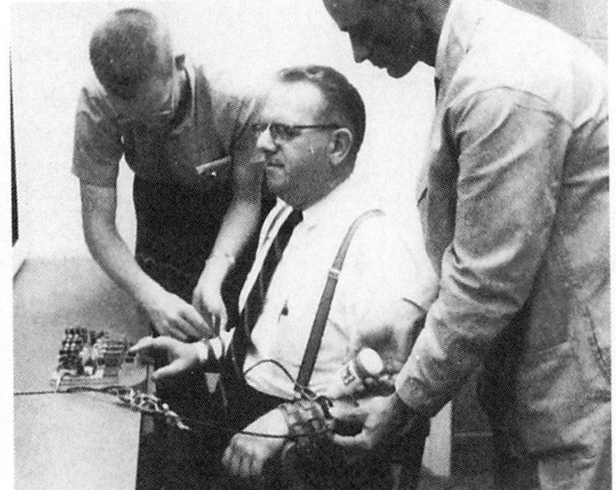

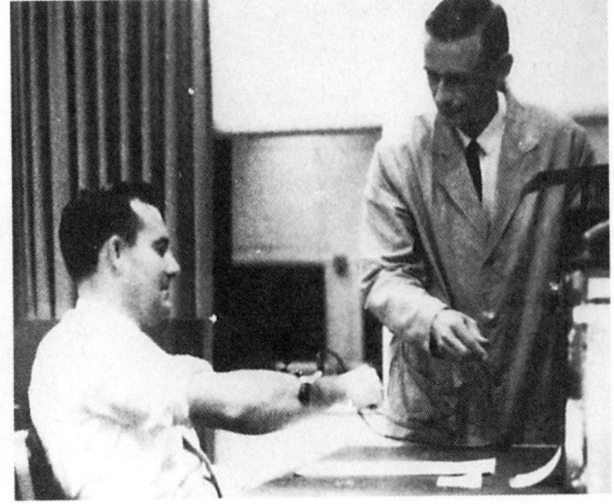

wants to continue and demands release. At 300 volts he screams and says he can no longer give answers.

At some point during the experiment, you begin to protest to the experimenter. "That man has a heart condition," you say; "I'm not going to kill that man." The experimenter says, "Please continue." Another shock and another scream from the learner and you say, "You mean I've got to keep going up the scale? No, sir. I'm not going to give him 450 volts!" The experimenter says, "The experiment requires that you continue." For a time the learner refuses to answer any more questions and screams with each shock (Milgram, 1965). Then he falls chillingly silent for the remainder of the experiment.

Question: I can't believe many people would do this. What happened?

Milgram also doubted that many people would obey his orders, and when he polled a group of psychiatrists before the experiment, they predicted that less than 1 percent of those tested would obey. The astounding fact is that 65 percent of those tested obeyed completely by going all the way to the 450-volt level. Virtually no one stopped short of 300 volts ("Severe Shock") (■ Fig. 20–13).

Question: Was the learner injured?

The time has come to reveal that the "learner" was actually an actor who turned a tape recorder on and off in the shock room. No shocks were ever administered, but the dilemma for the "teacher" was quite real. Subjects protested, sweated, trembled, stuttered, bit their lips, and laughed nervously. Clearly they were disturbed by what they were doing, but most obeyed the experimenter's orders. (The ethical questions raised by this experiment are discussed in the Exploration for Chapter 2.)

Question: Why did so many people obey?

Milgram's Follow-Up Some have suggested that the prestige of Yale University contributed to subjects' willingness to obey. Could subjects have assumed that the professor running the experiment would not really allow anyone to be hurt? To investigate this possibility, the experiment was rerun in a shabby office building in nearby Bridgeport, Connecticut. There was nothing in either the location or the experimenter's appearance to inspire confidence. Under these conditions fewer people obeyed (48 percent), but the reduction was minor.

Milgram was quite disturbed by the willingness of people to knuckle under to authority and to senselessly shock someone. In later experiments, he tried in various ways to reduce obedience. He found that distance between the teacher and the learner was of importance. When subjects were in the *same room* as the learner, only 40 percent were fully obedient. When they were *face to face* with the learner and required to force his hand down on a simulated "shock plate," only 30 percent obeyed (■ Fig. 20–14). *Distance* from the authority also had an effect. When the experimenter delivered his orders over the phone, only 22 percent obeyed. You may doubt that Milgram's study of obedience applies to you. If so, take a moment to read Highlight 20–5.

■ **Fig. 20–13** *Results of Milgram's obedience experiment. Only a minority of subjects refused to provide shocks, even at the most extreme intensities. The first substantial drop in obedience occurred at the 300-volt level (Milgram, 1963).*

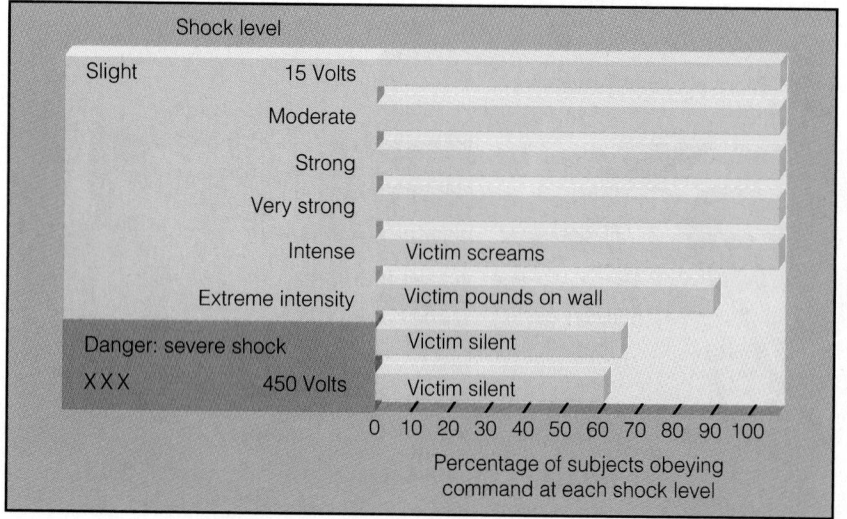

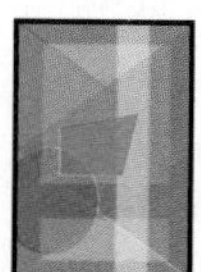

HIGHLIGHT 20–5

Critical Thinking

Quack Like a Duck

The demonstration described here has become a favorite of many psychology teachers (Halonen, 1986). Imagine your response to the following events. On the first day of class, your professor begins to establish the basic rules of behavior for the course. Seats are assigned and you must move to a new location. You are told not to talk during class. Your professor tells you that you must have permission to leave early. You are told to bring your textbook to class at all times.

Up to this point you might have no problem with your professor's orders. Then the demands become less reasonable. The professor says, "Use only a pencil for taking notes. Borrow one if you must." "Take off your watch." "Keep both hands on your desk top at all times." "All students who are freshmen stand at the back of the class." The demonstration is capped by orders that you cannot follow without looking silly: "Stick two fingers up your nose and quack like a duck."

Where do you think you would draw the line in obeying such orders? In reality, you might find yourself obeying a legitimate authority long after that person's demands had become unreasonable. What would happen, though, if a few students resisted orders given early in the sequence? Would that help free others to disobey? For an answer, let's return to some final remarks on Milgram's experiment.

Implications Milgram's research raises nagging questions about our willingness to commit antisocial or inhumane acts commanded by a "legitimate authority." The excuse so often given by war criminals—"I was only following orders"—takes on new meaning in this light. Milgram suggested that when directions come from an authority, people rationalize that they are not personally responsible for their actions (■ Fig. 20–15). Others have pointed out that "crimes of obedience" may be committed by ordinary people responding to normal social psychological processes. In locales as diverse as Vietnam, Rwanda, Bosnia, South Africa, Nicaragua, Sri Lanka, and Laos the tragic result has been "sanctioned massacres" of chilling proportions (Kelman & Hamilton, 1989).

Question: Aren't you taking an overly dim view of obedience?

Obedience to authority is obviously necessary and desirable in many circumstances. Just the same, it is probably true, as C. P. Snow (1961) has observed, "When you think of the long and gloomy history of man, you will find more hideous crimes have been committed in the name of obedience than in the name of rebellion." With this in mind, let us end this discussion on a more positive note. In one of his experiments, Milgram found that group support can greatly reduce destructive obedience. When real subjects saw two other "teachers" (both actors) resist orders and walk out of the experiment, only 10 percent continued to obey. Thus, a personal act of courage or moral fortitude by one or two members of a group may free others to disobey misguided or unjust authority.

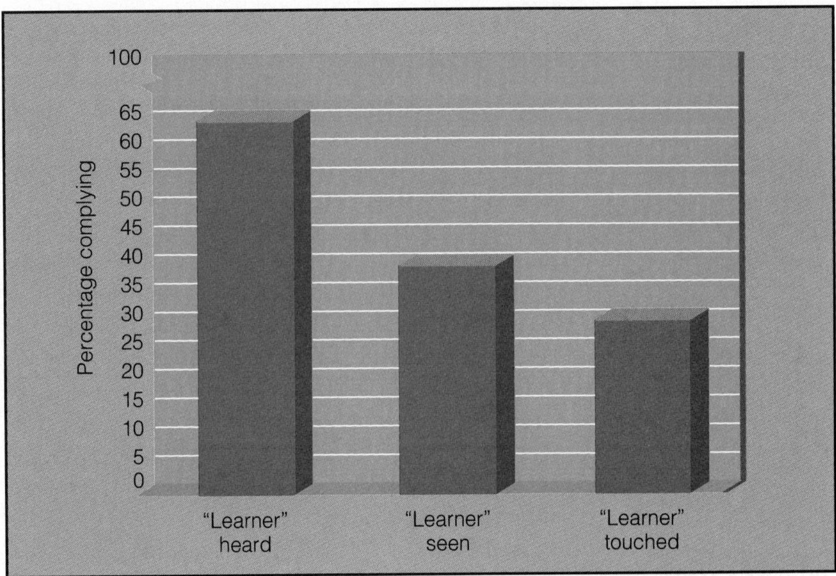

■ **Fig. 20–14** *Physical distance from the "learner" had a significant effect on the percentage of subjects obeying orders.*

Compliance—A Foot in the Door

In *conformity* situations the pressure to "get in line" is usually indirect. When an authority commands *obedience* the pressure is direct and difficult to resist. There is a third interesting possibility. The term **compliance** has been used to describe situations in which a person with little or no authority makes a direct request to another person (Deaux, Dane, & Wrightsman, 1993).

Compliance Bending to the requests of a person who has little or no authority or other form of social power.

Pressures to comply are quite common. For example, a stranger might ask you to yield a phone booth so he can make a call, a saleswoman might suggest that you buy a more expensive watch than you had planned on, or a co-worker might ask you for 50 cents to buy a cup of coffee.

■ **Fig. 20–15** *Obedience to authority is often necessary and reasonable; however, it can also be destructive.*

Foot-in-the-door effect The tendency for a person who has first complied with a small request to be more likely later to fulfill a larger request.

Door-in-the-face effect The tendency for a person who has refused a major request to subsequently be more likely to comply with a minor request.

Low-ball technique A strategy in which commitment is gained first to reasonable or desirable terms, which are then made less reasonable or desirable.

Question: What determines whether a person will comply with a request?

Many factors could be listed, but three stand out as especially interesting. Let's briefly consider each.

The Foot-in-the-Door Effect People who sell door-to-door have long recognized that once they get a foot in the door, a sale is almost a sure thing. To state the **foot-in-the-door principle** more formally, a person who first agrees to a small request is later more likely to comply with a larger demand (Dillard, 1991). Evidence suggests, for instance, that if someone asked you to put a large, ugly sign in your front yard to promote safe driving, you would refuse. If, however, you had first agreed to put a small sign in your window, you would later be much more likely to allow the big sign to be placed in your yard (Freedman & Fraser, 1966).

Apparently, the foot-in-the-door effect is based on observing one's own behavior. Seeing yourself agree to a small request helps convince you that you didn't mind doing what was asked. After that, you are more likely to comply with a larger request (Dillard, 1991).

The Door-in-the-Face Effect Let's say that a neighbor comes to your door and asks you to feed his dogs, water his plants, and mow his yard while he is out of town for a month. This is quite a major request—one that most people would probably turn down. Feeling only slightly guilty, you tell your neighbor that you're sorry but you can't help him. Now, what if the same neighbor returns the next day and asks you if you would at least pick up his mail while he is gone. Chances are very good that you would honor this request, even if you might have resisted it otherwise.

Psychologist Robert Cialdini and his associates coined the term **door-in-the-face effect** to describe the reverse of the foot-in-the-door effect (Cialdini et al., 1975). On some occasions the best way to get a person to agree to a small request is to first make a major request. After the person has turned down the major request ("slammed the door in your face"), he or she may be more willing to agree to a lesser demand. This strategy works because a person who follows a large request with a smaller one seems to be making a concession. Because the person appears to have given up something, many people feel that they must repay them by giving in to the smaller request (Dillard, 1991).

The Low-Ball Technique Anyone who has purchased an automobile will recognize a third way of inducing compliance. Automobile dealers are notorious for convincing customers to buy a car by offering "low-ball" prices that undercut the competition. The dealer first gets the customer to agree to buy at an attractively low price. Then, once the customer is committed, various techniques are used to bump the price up before the sale is concluded (see Highlight 20–6).

The **low-ball technique** consists of getting a person committed to act and then making the terms of acting less desirable. Here's another example: A fellow student asks to borrow $25 for a day. This seems reasonable and you agree. However, once you have given your classmate the money, he explains that it would be easier to repay you after payday, in two weeks. If you agree, you've succumbed to the low-ball technique. Here's another example, one that doesn't involve money: Let's say you ask someone to give you a ride to school in the morning. Only after the person has agreed do you tell her that you have to be there at 6 A.M.

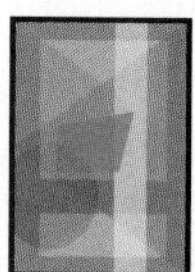

HIGHLIGHT 20–6
Using Psychology

How to Drive a Hard Bargain

Your local car lot is a good place to see compliance take place. Automobile salespersons play the compliance game daily and get very good at it. If you understand what they are up to, you will have a far better chance of resisting their tactics.

A Foot in the Door The salesperson offers you a test drive. If you accept, you will have made a small commitment of time to a particular car and to the salesperson. The salesperson will then ask you to go to an office and fill out some papers, "just to see what kind of a price" he or she can offer. If you go along, you will be further committed.

The Low-Ball Technique To get things under way the salesperson will offer you a very good price for your trade-in or will ask you to make an offer on the new car, "any offer, no matter how low." The salesperson will then ask if you will buy the car if she or he can sell it for the price you state. If you say yes, you have virtually bought the car. Most people find it very difficult to walk away once bargaining has reached this stage.

The Hook Is Set Once buyers are "hooked" by a low-ball offer, the salesperson goes to the manager to have the sale "approved." On returning, the salesperson will tell you with great disappointment that the dealership would lose money on the deal. "Couldn't you just take a little less for the trade-in or pay a little more for the car?" the salesperson will ask. At this point many people hesitate and grumble, but most give in and accept some "compromise" price or trade-in amount.

Milking the Sale By the time you strike a deal, you can be sure that the price you accept will give the dealership the minimum profit it requires on all sales—and probably much more. To add insult to injury, the salesperson will then try to increase the profit by convincing you to add various options to your car—extra mirrors, a stereo system, cruise control, and so forth. All of these items cost less from independent suppliers, so many people pay hundreds of dollars too much for them alone.

Evening the Odds To combat all of the preceding, get a final "best offer" in writing. Then walk out. Go to another dealer and see if the salesperson will better the price, in writing. When he or she does, return to the first dealership and negotiate for an even better price. Then decide where to buy.

Passive Compliance

Complying with requests is a normal part of daily social life. At times, however, a willingness to comply can exceed what is reasonable. Researcher Thomas Moriarty (1975) has demonstrated excessive, **passive compliance** under realistic conditions. Moriarty became interested in the "little murders" of daily life—the personal insults, rebuffs, and sacrifices of dignity that have become so common. Moriarty observed that many people will put up with almost anything to avoid a confrontation. He decided to put this passive, "no-hassle" attitude to experimental test.

In one experiment, two subjects (one actually an accomplice) were given a difficult test in a very small room. The subjects were seated back to back and left alone to work. As soon as the experimenter left, the phony subject turned on a portable cassette player at full volume. Real subjects who failed to complain were treated to a 17-minute blast of nerve-wracking rock music. The accomplice was instructed to turn the music off only after a third request. In this particular experiment, 80 percent of the subjects said nothing, although they glared, covered their ears, stopped work, and so forth. An interview later showed that most were angry or annoyed, but were afraid to tell the other "subject" to be quiet.

Passive compliance Passively bending to unreasonable demands or circumstances.

Question: Could it be that people failed to complain because they didn't want to disrupt the testing?

Yes, it is possible that the passivity observed in this study is unique to the experimental setting. However, when Moriarty and his students staged loud conversations behind theater patrons or people studying in a library, very few protested. In other naturalistic experiments, people were accosted in phone booths. The experimenter explained that he had left a ring in the booth and asked if the subject had found it. When the subject said no, the experimenter demanded that the subject empty his pockets. Most did.

In these and similar situations, people passively accepted having their personal rights trampled, even when objecting presented no threat to their safety. Overly passive women, in particular, tend to be ripe targets for exploitation, especially by men (Richards, Rollerson, & Phillips, 1991). Have we become "a nation of willing victims?" Certainly, we hope not. Nevertheless, researchers such as Milgram and Moriarty have identified a significant social problem. We will address the problem again in the Applications section of this chapter.

A Look Ahead In the upcoming Applications, we will return to the problem of passive behavior to learn how to better handle difficult social situations. Then, in the Exploration, we will examine the nature of social traps. A social trap is a situation in which individuals blindly act in ways that do collective harm.

Learning Check

1. An ability to punish others for failure to obey is the basis for
   a. referent power *b.* legitimate power *c.* expert power *d.* coercive power
2. The term *compliance* refers to situations in which a person complies with commands made by a person who has authority. T or F?
3. Obedience in Milgram's experiments was related to
   a. distance between learner and teacher *b.* distance between experimenter and teacher
   c. obedience of other teachers *d.* all of these
4. Obedience is conformity to the commands of an ________________.
5. By repeating his obedience experiment in a downtown office building, Milgram demonstrated that the prestige of Yale University was the main reason for subjects' willingness to obey in the original experiment. T or F?
6. The research of Thomas Moriarty and others has highlighted the problem of ________________ ________________, rather than obedience to authority.

Critical Thinking

7. Modern warfare allows killing to take place impersonally and at a distance. How does this relate to Milgram's experiments?

Answers: 1. *d* 2. F 3. *d* 4. authority 5. F 6. passive compliance 7. There is a big difference between killing someone in hand-to-hand combat and killing someone by lining up images on a video screen. Milgram's research suggests that it is easier for a person to follow orders to kill another human when the victim is at a distance and removed from personal contact.

APPLICATIONS: *Assertiveness Training—Standing Up for Your Rights*

Most of us have been rewarded, first as children and later as adults, for compliant, obedient, or "good" behavior. Perhaps this is why so many people find it difficult to assert themselves. Or perhaps non-assertion is related to anxiety about "making a scene" or feeling disliked by others. Whatever the causes, some people suffer tremendous anguish in any situation requiring poise, self-confidence, or self-assertion. Have you ever done any of the following?

- Hesitated to question an error on a restaurant bill because you were afraid of making a scene?
- Backed out of asking for a raise or a change in working conditions?
- Said yes when you wanted to say no?
- Been afraid to question a grade that seemed unfair?

Assertiveness training Instruction in how to be self-assertive.

Self-assertion A direct, honest expression of feelings and desires.

Aggression Hurting another person or achieving one's goals at the expense of another person.

Overlearning Learning or practice that continues after initial mastery of a skill.

If you have ever had difficulty asserting yourself in similar situations, behavior therapist Joseph Wolpe has a solution for you: a technique called **assertiveness training.**

Question: What is done in assertiveness training?

Assertiveness training is a very direct procedure. By using group exercises, videotapes, mirrors, and staged conflicts, the instructor teaches assertive behavior. People learn to practice honesty, disagreeing, questioning authority, and assertive postures and gestures. As their self-confidence improves, non-assertive clients are taken on "field trips" to shops and restaurants where they practice what they have learned.

Non-assertion requiring therapy is unusual. Nevertheless, many people become tense or upset in at least some situations in which they must stand up for their rights. For this reason, many people have found the techniques and exercises of assertiveness training helpful. If you have ever eaten a carbonized steak when you ordered it rare, or stood in silent rage as a clerk ignored you, the following discussion will be of interest.

Self-Assertion

The first step in assertiveness training is to convince yourself of three basic rights: You have the right to refuse, to request, and to right a wrong. **Self-assertion** involves standing up for these rights by speaking out in your own behalf.

Question: Is self-assertion just getting things your own way?

Not at all. A basic distinction can be made between *self-assertion* and *aggressive* behavior. Assertion is a direct, honest expression of feelings and desires. It is not exclusively self-serving. People who are non-assertive are usually patient to a fault. Sometimes their pent-up anger explodes with unexpected fury, which can be very destructive to relationships. In contrast to assertive behavior, aggression does not take into account the feelings or rights of others. Aggression is an attempt to get one's own way no matter what. Assertion techniques emphasize firmness, not attack (● Table 20–2).

Assertiveness Training The basic idea in assertiveness training is that each assertive action is practiced until it can be repeated even under stress. For example, let's say it really angers you when a store clerk waits on several people who arrived after you did. To improve your assertiveness in this situation, you would begin by *rehearsing* the dialogue, posture, and gestures you would use to confront the clerk or the other customer. Working in front of a mirror can be very helpful. If possible, you should *role-play* the scene with a friend. Be sure to have your friend take the part of a really aggressive or irresponsible clerk, as well as a cooperative one. Rehearsal and role-playing should also be used when you expect a possible confrontation with someone—for example, if you are going to ask for a raise, challenge a grade, or confront a landlord.

Question: Is that all there is to it?

No. Another important principle is **overlearning.** When you rehearse or role play assertive behavior, it is essential to continue practice until your responses

APPLICATIONS: *Continued*

Table 20–2 Comparison of Assertive, Aggressive, and Non-assertive Behavior

	Actor	Receiver of behavior
Non-assertive behavior	Self-denying inhibited, hurt, and anxious; lets others make choices; goals not achieved	Feels sympathy, guilt, or contempt for actor; achieves goals at actor's expense
Aggressive behavior	Achieves goals at others' expense; expresses feelings, but hurts others; chooses for others or puts them down	Feels hurt, defensive, humiliated, or taken advantage of; does not meet own needs
Assertive behavior	Self-enhancing; acts in own best interests; expresses feelings; respects rights of others; goals usually achieved, self-respect maintained	Needs respected and feelings expressed; may achieve goal; self-worth maintained

become almost automatic. This helps prevent you from getting flustered in the actual situation.

One more technique you may find useful is the **broken record.** A good way to prevent assertion from becoming aggression is to simply restate your request as many times and in as many ways as necessary. As an illustration, let's say you are returning a pair of shoes to a store. After two wearings the shoes fell apart, but you bought them two months ago and no longer have a receipt. The broken record could sound something like this:

Customer: I would like to have these shoes replaced.
Clerk: Do you have a receipt?
Customer: No, but I bought them here, and since they are defective, I would like to have you replace them.
Clerk: I can't do that without a receipt.
Customer: I understand that, but I want them replaced.
Clerk: Well, if you'll come back this afternoon and talk to the manager.
Customer: I've brought these shoes in because they are defective.
Clerk: Well, I'm not authorized to replace them.
Customer: Yes, well, if you'll replace these, I'll be on my way.

Notice that the customer did not attack the clerk or create an angry confrontation. Simple persistence is often all that is necessary for successful self-assertion.

Question: How would I respond assertively to a put-down?

Responding assertively to verbal aggression (a "put-down") is a real challenge. The tendency is to respond aggressively, which usually makes things worse. A good way to respond to a put-down uses the following steps. (1) If you are wrong, admit it; (2) acknowledge the person's feelings; (3) assert yourself about the other person's aggression; (4) briskly end the interchange.

Psychologists Robert Alberti and Michael Emmons (1986) offer an example of how to use the four steps. Let's say you accidentally bump into someone. The person responds angrily, "Damn it! Why don't you watch where you're going! You fool, you could have hurt me!" A good response would be to say, "I'm sorry I bumped you. I didn't do it intentionally. It's obvious you're upset, but I don't like your calling me names, or yelling. I can get your point without that."

Now, what if someone insults you indirectly ("I love your taste in clothes, it's so 'folksy' ")? Alberti and Emmons suggest you ask for a clarification ("What are you trying to say?"). This will force the person to take responsibility for the aggression. It can also provide an opportunity to change the way the person interacts with you: "If you really don't like what I'm wearing, I'd like to know it. I'm not always sure I like the things I buy, and I value your opinion."

To summarize, self-assertion does not supply instant poise, confidence, or self-assurance. However, it is a way of combating anxieties associated with life in an impersonal and sometimes intimidating society. If you are interested in more information, you can consult a book entitled *Your Perfect Right* by Alberti and Emmons (1986).

Broken record A self-assertion technique involving repeating a request until it is acknowledged.

LEARNING CHECK

1. In assertiveness training, people learn techniques for getting their way in social situations and angry interchanges. T or F?
2. Non-assertive behavior causes hurt, anxiety, and self-denial in the actor, and sympathy, guilt, or contempt in the receiver. T or F?

APPLICATIONS: *Continued*

3. Overlearning should be avoided when rehearsing assertive behaviors. T or F?

4. The "broken record" must be avoided, because it is a basic non-assertive behavior. T or F?

Critical Thinking

5. When practicing self-assertion, do you think it would be better to improvise your own responses or imitate those of a person skilled in self-assertion?

Answers:

1. F 2. T 3. F 4. F 5. A recent study found that imitating an assertive model is more effective than improvising your own responses (Kipper, 1992). If you know an assertive and self-assured person, you can learn a lot by watching how they handle difficult situations.

EXPLORATION

Social Traps—The Tragedy of the Commons

You are in a packed theater in an older building. Halfway through the feature movie (*Bambi Meets Godzilla*) you begin to smell smoke. The screen goes dark. You try to stay calm as you shuffle toward a distant exit sign. Suddenly someone screams. You lunge for the door. Instantly, you are caught in a crush of people. The crowd jams together so tightly that only a few people can squeeze through the door. If the fire moves swiftly, many lives will be lost.

This situation—panic during a fire—is a classic example of a *social trap*. Each person in a theater who runs toward the exits has acted in his or her immediate self-interest. Yet if *everyone* bolts at once the chances that anyone will survive may be very low.

Social Traps

Question: What exactly is a social trap?

A **social trap** is any social situation that rewards actions that have undesired effects in the long run (Cross & Guyer, 1980). On an individual level, it is quite common for people to be "trapped" by immediate rewards that are followed by delayed costs or suffering. For instance, many people are enticed into drinking too much at parties because their pleasure is immediate and their discomfort (a hangover) comes later. Many people go into debt because they get the immediate reward of owning desirable goods; only later do they suffer when a staggering credit card bill arrives. For the immediate pleasures of intimacy, many teenagers later pay the price of pregnancy, forced marriage, early divorce, curtailed education, and so on.

Behavioral traps that involve groups of people, or social traps, as we have called them, are especially interesting. In a social trap no one individual intentionally acts against the group interest, but if many people act alike, collective harm is done. For example, each person who leaves work at 5 P.M. in a congested city expects to gain by getting home earlier. Yet if everyone leaves at 5:00, the resulting traffic jam ensures that everyone will, in fact, arrive home late and emotionally frazzled. The problem could be solved if some people would wait a half hour or more before leaving. However, no one does this because immediate self-interest encourages a "fast getaway."

A related example is the fact that many large cities now have rapid transit systems that are underused by their citizens. Each person decides that it is more convenient to own and drive a separate car (in order to run errands and so on). However, we see again that individual behavior affects the welfare of others. Because everyone wants to drive for "convenience," driving becomes inconvenient: The mass of cars in most cities causes irritating traffic snarls and a lack of parking spaces. Each car owner has been drawn into a trap.

The Tragedy of the Commons

Social traps are especially damaging when we are enticed into overuse of scarce resources. This is exactly what happened a few years ago to crab fishermen in Alaska.

Initially, crabs were plentiful and fishermen were few. Each fisherman was therefore able to make large, lucrative catches. To raise their profits, fishermen began to add second, third, and fourth boats to their operations. For a while this did, in fact, increase individual profits. But as the size of the fishing fleet continued to grow, the number of crabs available to be caught by any boat decreased.

Eventually, so many crabs were caught that their rate of reproduction slowed. As a result, crab fishermen began to go bankrupt in large numbers. Individually their actions made sense. But collectively the group suffered greatly.

Ecologist Garrett Hardin (1968; 1985) calls situations like the one just described the **tragedy of the commons.** Tragedies of this sort often occur when people share a scarce resource. Each person acts in his or her self-interest, which causes the resource to be used up so that everyone suffers. More familiar examples of this dilemma are the lack of individual incentives to conserve gasoline, water, or electricity. Whenever one's personal comfort or convenience is involved, it is highly tempting to "let others worry about it." Yet in the long run everyone stands to lose.

EXPLORATION

Social Problems

Many major social problems can be thought of as social traps. In most cases of environmental pollution, for instance, there are immediate benefits for polluting and major long-term costs. If one person pollutes a river or trashes the roadside, it has little noticeable effect. But as many people do the same, problems that affect everyone quickly mount. As another example, consider the farmer who applies pesticides to a crop to save it from insect damage. The farmer benefits immediately. However, if other farmers follow suit, the local water system may be permanently damaged.

Traps also exist at the international level. Countries continue to add to their nuclear stockpiles in order to be more "secure." Yet, doing so may eventually increase the chances of a final nuclear holocaust. It's no wonder that people who study international conflicts often come away shaking their heads and wondering, "How did we get into this mess?"

Question: What can be done to avoid social traps?

Escaping Traps In some situations it might be possible to dismantle social traps by rearranging rewards and costs. For example, many companies are tempted to pollute because it saves them money and increases profits. To reverse the situation, a pollution tax could be levied so that it would cost more, not less, for a business to pollute. As another example, we could reward lower individual consumption of resources. Some power companies have already experimented with a meter that charges lower rates for using power at "off-peak" periods (also see Chapter 22).

There is evidence that in real social traps, people are more likely to restrain themselves when they believe others will too (Messick et al., 1983). Otherwise they are likely to think, "Why should I be a sucker? I don't think anyone else is going to conserve" (fuel, electricity, water, paper, crabs, or whatever).

Other problems may be harder to solve. What, for instance, can be done about truck drivers who cause dangerous traffic jams because they will not pull over on narrow roads? How can littering be discouraged or prevented? How would you make car-pooling or using public transportation the first choice for most people? Or how could people simply be encouraged to stagger their departure times to and from work? All of these and more are social traps that need springing. It is important that we not fall into the trap of ignoring them.

> **Social trap** A social situation that tends to provide immediate rewards for actions that will have undesired effects in the long run.
>
> **Tragedy of the commons** A social trap in which individuals, each acting in his or her immediate self-interest, overuse a scarce group resource.

LEARNING CHECK

1. A social trap is any situation in which undesired actions are rewarded in the long run. T or F?
2. Individuals in a social trap act in ways that appear to be rational, but that create problems for the group as a whole. T or F?
3. The tragedy of the commons occurs when individuals use a shared resource too quickly because they get immediate rewards for doing so. T or F?
4. Rearranging individual rewards and costs is one way to dismantle social traps. T or F?
5. What social trap accompanies most major holidays? *Critical Thinking*

Answers: 1. F 2. T 3. T 4. T 5. Travel nightmares are the rule as people jam trains, planes, and highways on major holidays.

Chapter Summary

- ***How does group membership affect individual behavior?***

- Humans are social animals enmeshed in a complex network of social relationships. **Social psychology** studies how individuals behave, think, and feel in social situations.
- **Culture** provides a broad social context for our behavior. One's *position* in groups defines a variety of **roles** to be played.
- **Social roles,** which may be *achieved* or *ascribed*, are particular behavior patterns associated with social positions. When two or more contradictory roles are held, **role conflict** may occur. The Stanford prison experiment showed that destructive roles may override individual motives for behavior.
- Positions within groups typically carry higher or lower levels of **status.** High status is associated with special privileges and respect.
- **Group structure** refers to the organization of roles,

communication pathways, and power within a group. **Group cohesiveness** is basically the degree of attraction among group members.

- **Norms** are standards of conduct enforced (formally or informally) by groups. The **autokinetic effect** has been used to demonstrate that norms rapidly form even in temporary groups.

■ ***What unspoken rules govern the use of personal space?***

- The study of personal space is called **proxemics.** Four basic spatial zones around each person's body are **intimate distance** (0–18 inches), **personal distance** (1½–4 feet), **social distance** (4–12 feet), and **public distance** (12 feet or more).

■ ***How do we perceive the motives of others, and the causes of our own behavior?***

- **Attribution theory** is concerned with how we make inferences about behavior. A variety of factors affect attribution, including **consistency, distinctiveness, situational demands,** and **consensus.**
- The **fundamental attributional error** is to ascribe the actions of others to internal causes, while attributing one's own behavior to external causes.
- **Self-handicapping** involves arranging excuses for poor performance. This is done to protect one's self-image or self-esteem.

■ ***Why do people affiliate?***

- The **need to affiliate** is tied to additional needs for approval, support, friendship, and information. Additionally, research indicates that affiliation is related to reducing anxiety and uncertainty.
- **Social comparison theory** holds that we affiliate to evaluate our actions, feelings, and abilities. Social comparisons are also made for purposes of self-protection and self-enhancement.

■ ***What factors influence interpersonal attraction?***

- **Interpersonal attraction** is increased by **physical proximity** (nearness), **frequent contact, physical attractiveness, competence,** and **similarity.** A large degree of similarity on many dimensions is characteristic of *mate selection.*
- **Self-disclosure** occurs more when two people like one another. Self-disclosure follows a **reciprocity norm:** Low levels of self-disclosure are met with low levels in return, whereas moderate self-disclosure elicits more personal replies. However, **overdisclosure** tends to inhibit self-disclosure by others.
- According to **social exchange theory,** we tend to maintain relationships that are *profitable;* that is, those for which perceived rewards exceed perceived costs.
- **Romantic love** has been studied as a special kind of attitude. Love can be distinguished from liking by the use of attitude scales. Dating couples like *and* love their partners but only like their friends. Love is also associated with greater *mutual absorption* between people.
- Adult love relationships tend to mirror patterns of **emotional attachment** observed in infancy and early childhood. **Secure, avoidant,** and **ambivalent** patterns can be defined on the basis of how a person approaches romantic and affectionate relationships with others.
- **Evolutionary psychology** attributes human mating patterns to the differing reproductive challenges faced by men and women since the dawn of time.

■ ***What have social psychologists learned about conformity, social power, obedience, and compliance?***

- In general, **social influence** refers to alterations in behavior brought about by the behavior of others. **Conformity** to group pressure is a familiar example of social influence.
- Virtually everyone conforms to a variety of broad social and cultural norms. **Conformity pressures** also exist within smaller groups. The famous Asch experiments demonstrated that various **group sanctions** encourage conformity.
- **Groupthink** refers to compulsive conformity in group decision making. Victims of groupthink seek to maintain each other's approval, even at the cost of critical thinking.
- Social influence is also related to five types of **social power: reward power, coercive power, legitimate power, referent power,** and **expert power.**
- **Obedience** to authority has been investigated in a variety of experiments, particularly those by Milgram. Obedience in Milgram's studies decreased when the victim was in the same room, when the victim and subject were face to face, when the authority figure was absent, and when others refused to obey.
- **Compliance** with direct requests is another means by which behavior is influenced. Three strategies for inducing compliance are the **foot-in-the-door technique,** the **door-in-the-face approach,** and the **low-ball technique.**
- Recent research suggests that in addition to excessive obedience to authority, many people show a surprising **passive compliance** to unreasonable requests.

■ ***How does self-assertion differ from aggression?***

- **Self-assertion,** as opposed to **aggression,** involves clearly stating one's wants and needs to others. Learning to be assertive is accomplished by *role playing, rehearsing* assertive actions, *overlearning,* and use of specific techniques, such as the *"broken record."*

■ *What is a social trap?*

● A **social trap** is a social situation in which immediately rewarded actions have undesired effects in the long run. One prominent social trap occurs when limited public resources are overused, a problem called the **tragedy of the commons.**

Questions for Discussion

1. How do you explain the behavior of the guards in Zimbardo's prison study? What could be done to prevent this from happening in real prisons? Can you name other situations in which roles encourage undesirable behavior?
2. How do people maintain a sense of privacy or distance from strangers when they are in crowded situations that force them close together?
3. Many students hesitate to ask questions in class. How would a student explain this behavior? How would an instructor explain the behavior? How do these explanations relate to attribution theory?
4. Think of your closest friends. Which theory best explains your relationships: social comparison, social exchange, or the general factors underlying interpersonal attraction?
5. Why do you think that people sometimes underdisclose to a friend or spouse and overdisclose to strangers?
6. Using yourself (or someone you know well) as an example, what parallels can you see between early childhood attachments and adult affectionate relationships?
7. Would it be possible to be completely nonconforming (that is, to not conform to *some* group norm)?
8. How serious, in your estimation, are problems of conformity, obedience, and passive compliance?
9. Can you think of a personal experience in which you were subjected to group pressures similar to those in the Asch experiment? How did you feel? Did you yield?
10. In view of the Milgram obedience experiment, do you think the civil disobedience of the civil rights and anti-war movements was justified? Why or why not?
11. Is "blind obedience" ever necessary? Explain.
12. If you were placed in charge of an important decision-making group, what would you do to minimize groupthink? Do you think that some types of committees or groups are especially prone to groupthink? How serious a problem do you think groupthink is in the government? In the military? In business? In schools? In community groups?
13. Reread the experiments performed on passive compliance. What would have been an assertive response to the situations described? An aggressive response?
14. What social traps can you identify in day-to-day experience? What could be done to change them?
15. Garrett Hardin believes that it is a mistake to send food to countries wracked by famine. According to Hardin, this only allows the population of such countries to expand so that a later, larger disaster becomes inevitable. In your opinion, is it more or less humane to supply food under such circumstances?

Chapter 21

Attitudes, Culture, and Human Relations

IN THIS CHAPTER

Attitudes
Persuasion
Cognitive dissonance
Brainwashing and cults
Prejudice
Group conflict
Aggression
Helping others
Applications:
Living with diversity
Exploration:
Sociobiology

CHAPTER PREVIEW

Doomsday for the Seekers

Hardly a year passes, it seems, without a doomsday group of one kind or another making the news. In one classic example of such groups, a woman named Mrs. Keech claimed she was receiving messages from beings on a planet called Clarion. The beings told Mrs. Keech that they had detected a fault in the earth's crust that would submerge North America, causing an unimaginable natural disaster. The date of this event would be December 21. However, Mrs. Keech and her band of followers, who called themselves the Seekers, had no fear: On December 20 they expected to be met at midnight by a flying saucer and taken to safety in outer space.

The night of December 20 arrived, and the Seekers gathered at Mrs. Keech's house. Many had given up jobs and possessions to prepare for departure. Expectations were high and commitment was total. But as the night wore on, midnight passed and the world continued to exist. It was a bitter and embarrassing disappointment for the Seekers.

Question: Did the group break up then?

The story now takes an amazing twist—one that intrigued social psychologists. Instead of breaking up, the Seekers became more *convinced than ever before that they had been right. At about 5* A.M. *Mrs. Keech announced that she had received a message explaining that the Seekers had saved the world.*

Before the night of December 20, the Seekers had been uninterested in convincing other people that the world was coming to an end. Now they called newspapers, magazines, and radio stations to explain what had happened and to convince others of their accomplishment.

How do we explain this strange turn in the behavior of Mrs. Keech's doomsday group? An answer may lie in the concept of cognitive dissonance. *Cognitive dissonance also helps to explain many aspects of attitude change. Watch for a discussion of cognitive dissonance later in this chapter.*

Survey Questions

- What are attitudes? How are they acquired?
- How are attitudes measured and changed?
- Under what conditions is persuasion most effective?
- What is cognitive dissonance? What does it have to do with attitudes and behavior?
- Is brainwashing actually possible? How are people converted to cult membership?
- What causes prejudice and intergroup conflict? What can be done about these problems?
- How do psychologists explain human aggression?
- Why are bystanders so often unwilling to help in an emergency?
- What can be done to lower prejudice and promote social harmony?
- How does the theory of sociobiology try to explain social behavior?

Attitudes—Belief + Emotion + Action

What is your attitude toward birth control, environmental groups, higher education, imported automobiles, psychology? The answers have far-reaching effects on your behavior. The effects of attitudes are intimately woven into our actions and views of the world. Our tastes, friendships, votes, preferences, and goals are all touched by attitudes.

Question: What specifically is an attitude?

An **attitude** is a mixture of belief and emotion that predisposes a person to respond to other people, objects, or institutions in a positive or negative way. Attitudes summarize past experience and *predict* or direct future actions. For example, an approach known as the **misdirected letter technique** demonstrates that actions are closely connected to attitudes.

The Luck of the Irish

During a period of civil violence in Ireland, attitudes held toward the Irish were measured in a sample of English households. Later, wrongly addressed letters were sent to the same households. Each letter had either an English name or an Irish name on it. The question was: Would the "Irish" letters be returned to the Post Office or thrown away? As predicted, letters were more often thrown away by people living in households where anti-Irish attitudes had been measured earlier (Howitt et al., 1977).

"Your attitude is showing," is sometimes said. This statement seems simple, but actually there are three ways in which attitudes are expressed. Most attitudes have a **belief component,** an **emotional component,** and an **action component.** Consider, for example, your attitude toward gun control. You will have beliefs about whether or not gun control would affect rates of crime or violence. You will have emotional responses to guns, finding them either attractive and desirable or threatening and destructive. And, you will have a tendency to seek out or to avoid gun ownership. The action component of your attitude will probably also include support of organizations that urge or oppose gun control. As you can see, attitudes orient us to the social world. In doing so, they prepare us to act in certain ways (Olson & Zanna, 1993).

Question: How do people acquire attitudes?

Attitude Formation

Attitudes are acquired in several basic ways. Sometimes, attitudes come from **direct contact** with the object of the attitude—such as opposing pollution when

Attitude A learned tendency to respond to people, objects, or institutions in a positive or negative way.

Misdirected letter technique A way of measuring attitudes toward a group; letters addressed to the group are sent to households and the number forwarded is counted.

Belief component What a person thinks or believes about the object of an attitude.

Emotional component One's feelings toward the object of an attitude.

Action component How one tends to act toward the object of an attitude.

Direct contact In forming attitudes, the effects of direct experience with the object of the attitude.

■ Fig. 21–1 *Attitudes are an important dimension of social behavior. They are often rooted in reference groups.*

Interaction with others In forming attitudes, the influence of discussions with others who hold particular attitudes.

Child rearing In forming attitudes, the effects of parental values, beliefs, and practices.

Group membership As a factor in forming attitudes, social influences associated with belonging to various groups.

Mass media Collectively, all media that reach very large audiences (magazines, for instance, are a medium of mass communication).

Mean world view Viewing the world and other people as dangerous and threatening.

Chance conditioning Conditioning that takes place by chance or coincidence.

a nearby factory ruins your favorite river. Attitudes are also learned through **interaction with others** holding the same attitude. If three of your friends are volunteers at a local recycling center, and you talk with them about their beliefs, you will probably come to favor recycling too. Attitudes are also acquired through the effects of **child rearing.** For example, if both parents belong to the same political party, chances are 2 out of 3 that the child will belong to that party as an adult.

In the previous chapter we discussed group forces that operate to bring about conformity. There is little doubt that many of the attitudes we hold are influenced by **group membership** (■ Fig. 21–1). In one classic study, for example, groups were formed to discuss the case of a juvenile delinquent. Most participants believed that what the boy needed was love, kindness, and friendship. To test group pressures on attitudes, a person who advocated severe punishment was added to each group.

Question: How did group members react to the "deviate"?

At first they directed almost all of their comments to him. But when the deviate stuck to his position, an interesting thing happened. Soon, he was almost completely excluded from conversation. And later, the deviate was strongly rejected in ratings made by other group members (Schachter, 1951). Group pressures for conformity and the difficulty of holding deviant attitudes can be clearly seen in this outcome.

Attitudes are also influenced by the **mass media.** As Marshall McLuhan put it, we are "massaged" by the media, meaning we are threatened, urged, cajoled, persuaded, and otherwise influenced. Ninety-nine percent of American and Canadian homes have a television set, which is on an average of over 7 hours a day. As we noted in Chapter 7, the values and information thus channeled into homes exert a powerful influence on how people perceive, think about, and react to their world. For instance, frequent television viewers overestimate their chances of being involved in a violent incident (Roberts & Bachen, 1981). Heavy viewers are also less likely to feel that most people can be trusted (Gerbner & Gross, 1976). Taken together, such findings suggest that the heavy dose of violence on television may lead viewers to develop a **"mean" world view** (Heath & Petraitis, 1987).

Some attitudes are inadvertently formed by **chance conditioning** (Olson & Zanna, 1993). Let's say, for instance, that you have had three encounters in your lifetime with psychologists. If by chance all three were negative, you might take an unduly dim view of psychology and psychologists. In the same way, people often develop strong attitudes toward cities, restaurants, or parts of the country on the basis of one or two unusually good or bad experiences with each. Highlight 21–1 provides a recent example of how conditioning may contribute to attitude formation.

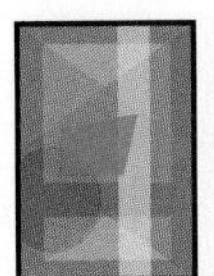

HIGHLIGHT 21–1

Research Frontier

Rock Music Videos and Antisocial Attitudes

Many rock music videos are filled with images of rebellion, violence, drunkenness, sexual promiscuity, and degradation of women. Rock videos almost always show such behavior in a positive light, making it seem desirable and commonplace. Does this affect viewers' attitudes toward antisocial behavior? To find out, Christine and Ranald Hansen (1990) staged an experiment in which college students watched three rock videos that were high in antisocial content, or three neutral music videos. Afterward, subjects "accidentally" saw one of two "job applicants" (who were actually accomplices in the experiment) make an obscene gesture with his hand. Later, each subject was asked to rate how likable the job applicants were and if they should be hired.

As you might expect, subjects who had only watched neutral videos liked the antisocial job applicant less and gave him low ratings.

Question: What about the students who had watched antisocial videos? Were their attitudes influenced?

Clearly they were. Subjects who had just seen a barrage of antisocial images rated the "job applicant" who made the obscene gesture just as highly as the one who didn't.

As the Hansens point out, music elicits positive emotional responses. What if these good feelings are repeatedly associated with antisocial themes? Quite likely, classical conditioning will strengthen positive attitudes toward antisocial behavior (Hansen & Hansen, 1990).

Question: Why are some attitudes acted on, while others are not?

To answer this question, let's consider an example. Assume that a person agrees that automobiles add to air pollution, and strongly objects to smog. Why would the person continue to drive to work every day? Probably it is because the *immediate consequences* of our actions weigh heavily on the choices we make. No matter what the person's attitude, it is difficult to resist the immediate convenience of driving. Also important is our expectation of how *others will evaluate* our actions. By taking this factor into account, researchers have been able to predict family planning choices, alcohol use by adolescents, re-enlistment in the National Guard, voting on a nuclear power plant initiative, and so forth (Cialdini et al., 1981). Finally, we must not overlook the effect that long-standing *habits* have on action (Triandis, 1977). Say a "male chauvinist" boss vows to change his sexist attitudes toward female employees. Two months later it would not be unusual for his behavior to show the effects of habit rather than his intention to change.

In short, there are often large differences between attitudes and behavior—particularly between privately held attitudes and public behavior. However, barriers to action typically fall when a person holds an attitude with **conviction.** To have *conviction* means that an attitude is of central importance to a person. The issues about which you have conviction are those that you feel strongly about (emotionally), that you believe are important, that you frequently think about and discuss, and that you feel knowledgeable about (Abelson, 1988). Attitudes that are held with passionate conviction often lead to major changes in personal behavior (Olson & Zanna, 1993).

Question: Can attitudes be measured?

Attitude Measurement

There are a number of approaches to the measurement of attitudes. In some cases, individuals are simply asked in a straightforward way to express attitudes toward a particular issue. For example, a person might be asked in an **open-ended interview,** "What are your thoughts about freedom of speech on college campuses?" The second approach, which has been very useful as a measure of attitudes toward groups, uses a **social distance scale.** Social distance indicates the degree to which one person would be willing to have contact with another person. That is, the individual is asked to state his or her willingness to admit members of a particular group to various levels of social closeness. These levels range from "would exclude from my country" to "would admit to marriage in my family."

The use of **attitude scales** is one of the most common methods of measurement. Attitude scales consist of statements expressing various possible views on an issue. For example, "Socialized medicine would destroy the quality of health care in this country" or "This country needs a national health care program." People are asked to agree or disagree with each item on a 5-point scale by ranking it from "strongly agree" to "strongly disagree." By computing scores on all items, a person can be rated for overall acceptance or rejection of a particular issue. When used in public polls, attitude scales have provided much useful information about the feelings of large segments of the population.

Conviction Beliefs that are important to a person and that evoke strong emotion.

Open-ended interview An interview in which persons are allowed to freely state their views.

Social distance scale A rating of the degree to which a person would be willing to have contact with a member of another group.

Attitude scale A collection of attitudinal statements with which respondents indicate agreement or disagreement.

Reference group Any group that an individual identifies with and uses as a standard for social comparison.

Persuasion A deliberate attempt to change attitudes or beliefs with information and arguments.

Communicator In persuasion, the person presenting arguments or information.

Message In persuasion, the content of a communicator's arguments or presentation.

Audience The person or group toward whom a persuasive message is directed.

Attitude Change—Why the "Seekers" Went Public

Although attitudes are relatively stable, they are subject to change. Some attitude change can be understood in terms of the concept of **reference groups.** A reference group is a group whose values and attitudes a person regards as relevant to his or her own. It is not necessary to be in face-to-face contact with others for them to serve as a reference group. It depends instead on whom you identify with or care about.

In the 1930s Theodore Newcomb studied real-life attitude change among students at Bennington College. Most students came from conservative homes, but Bennington was a very liberal school. Newcomb found that most students shifted significantly toward more liberal attitudes during their 4 years at Bennington. Those who did not change kept parents and hometown friends as their primary reference group. This is typified by one student's statement, "I decided I'd rather stick to my father's ideas." Those who did change identified primarily with the campus community. Notice that all students could count the college and their families as *membership* groups. However, one group or the other tended to become their point of reference.

Question: What about advertising and other direct attempts to change attitudes? Are they effective?

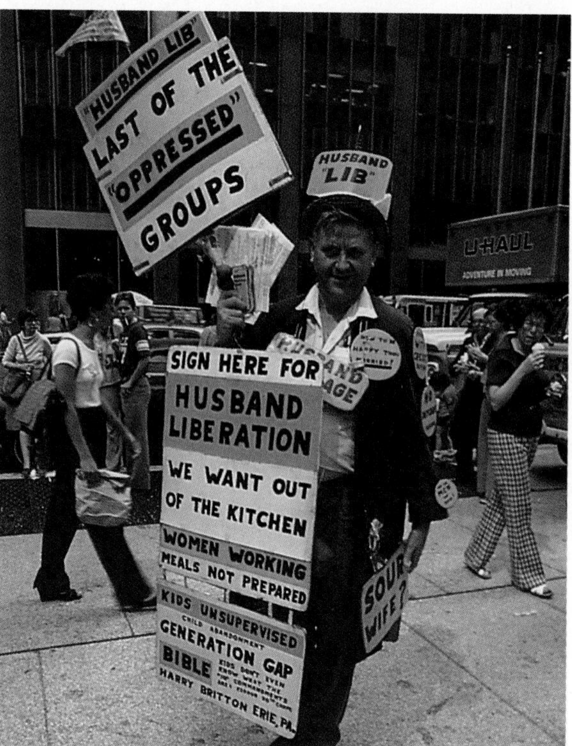

■ **Fig. 21–2** *Persuasion. Would you be likely to be swayed by this person's message? Successful persuasion is related to characteristics of the communicator, the message, and the audience.*

Persuasion

Businesses, politicians, and others who seek to persuade us obviously believe that attitude change can be induced. Over $10 billion is spent yearly on television advertising in the United States alone. **Persuasion** refers to any deliberate attempt to change attitudes by imparting information. Persuasion can range from the daily blitz of media commercials to personal discussion among friends. In most cases, the success or failure of attempted persuasion can be understood if we consider characteristics of the **communicator,** the **message,** and the **audience** (■ Fig. 21–2).

Let's say you have a chance to promote an issue important to you (for or against nuclear power, for instance) at a community gathering. Whom should you choose to make the presentation, and how should that person present it? Research on persuasion suggests that attitude change is encouraged when the following conditions are met.

1. The communicator is likable, expressive, trustworthy, an expert on the topic, and similar to the audience in some respect.
2. The message appeals to emotions, particularly to fear or anxiety.
3. The message also provides a clear course of action that will, if followed, reduce fear or produce personally desirable results.
4. The message states clear-cut conclusions.
5. The message is backed up by facts and statistics.
6. Both sides of the argument are presented in the case of a well-informed audience.
7. Only one side of the argument is presented in the case of a poorly informed audience.
8. The persuader appears to have nothing to gain if the audience accepts the message.
9. The message is repeated as frequently as possible (Aronson, 1992; Eagly & Chaiken, 1992; Johnson, 1991).

You should have little difficulty seeing how these principles are applied in the selling of everything from underarm deodorants to presidents.

Role-Playing We all know from personal observation that emotional experiences can dramatically alter attitudes. The person who gives up drinking after nearly dying in an automobile accident caused by drunkenness serves as an example. To actively bring about such attitude change, psychologists have experimented with creating similar experiences through role-playing.

Janis and Mann (1965) asked women who were known smokers to play the role of cancer patients. A doctor told each of the women that he had some bad news: She had lung cancer and would have to undergo immediate surgery. The women played out the part by asking questions about the surgery, if it might fail, and so on. Women in the role-playing group drastically reduced their smoking. Those who listened to a tape recording of similar information showed little change.

Question: Why should role-playing have more effect than hearing the same information?

Cognitive Dissonance Theory Certainly emotional impact and realism have some effect, but part of the explanation also lies in the concept of **cognitive dissonance.**

Cognitions are thoughts. Dissonance means clashing. The influential theory of cognitive dissonance (Festinger, 1957) states that contradicting or clashing thoughts cause discomfort. That is, we have a need for *consistency* in our thoughts, perceptions, and images of ourselves (Thibodeau & Aronson, 1992).

What happens if people act in ways that are inconsistent with their attitudes or self-images? Typically, the contradiction makes them uncomfortable. Such discomfort can motivate people to bring their thoughts or attitudes into agreement with their actions. For example, smokers are told on every pack that cigarettes endanger their lives. They light up and smoke. How do they resolve the tension between this information and their actions? They could quit smoking, but it may be easier to convince themselves that smoking is not really so dangerous. To do this, many smokers seek examples of people who have lived long lives as heavy smokers and they associate with other smokers who support their choice. Many smokers also avoid information concerning the link between smoking and cancer. Cognitive dissonance theory also suggests that people tend to reject new information that contradicts ideas they already hold, in a sort of "don't bother me with the facts, my mind is made up" strategy.

Now recall Mrs. Keech and her doomsday group. Why did their belief in Mrs. Keech's messages *increase* after the world failed to end? Why did they suddenly become interested in convincing others that their beliefs were correct? Cognitive dissonance theory explains that after publicly committing themselves to their beliefs, they had a strong need to maintain their stand. In effect, convincing others served as a way of adding proof that they were right.

Cognitive dissonance also underlies attempts to convince *ourselves* that we've done the right thing. Here's an example you may recognize: As romantic partners become better acquainted, they sooner or later begin to notice things they don't like about each other. How do they reduce the cognitive dissonance and doubts caused by their partners' shortcomings? A recent study found that we tend to create stories that change our partners' faults into virtues: he seems cheap, but he's really frugal; she seems egotistical, but she's really self-confident; he's not stubborn, he just has integrity; she's not undependable, she's a free spirit; and so on (Murray & Holmes, 1993).

Question: Acting contrary to one's attitudes doesn't always bring about change. How does cognitive dissonance account for that?

The amount of **reward,** or **justification,** for acting contrary to one's attitudes and beliefs can influence the amount of dissonance created. In a now classic study, college students performed an extremely boring task that consisted of turning wooden pegs on a board for an extended time. Afterward, they were asked to help lure others into the experiment by pretending it was interesting and enjoyable. Students paid $20 for lying to others did not change their own negative opinion of the task. Those who were paid only $1 later rated the experience as actually being pleasant and interesting. In other words, those paid $20 experienced no dissonance. These students could reassure themselves that anybody would tell a little white lie for $20. Those paid $1 were faced with the conflicting thought, "I lied, but I had no good reason to do it." Rather than admit to themselves that they had lied, these students changed their attitude toward what they had done (Festinger & Carlsmith, 1959) (■ Fig. 21–3).

Other studies indicate that we are especially likely to experience dissonance when we cause an event to occur that we would rather hadn't occurred (Cooper & Fazio, 1984). Let's say, for example, that you agree to help a friend move to a new apartment. The big day arrives and you feel like staying in bed. Actually,

Cognitive dissonance An uncomfortable clash between self-image, thoughts, beliefs, attitudes, or perceptions and one's behavior.

Justification In cognitive dissonance theory, the degree to which one's actions are justified by rewards or other circumstances.

■ **Fig. 21–3** *Summary of the Festinger and Carlsmith (1959) study from the viewpoint of a person experiencing cognitive dissonance.*

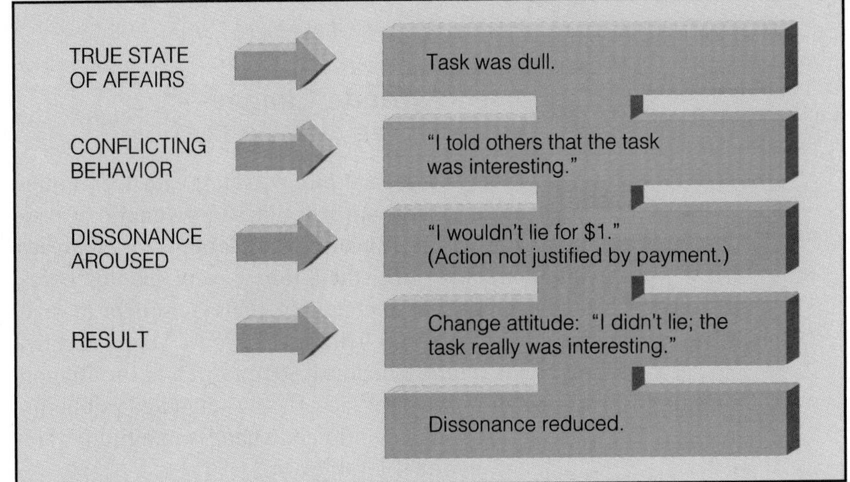
TRUE STATE OF AFFAIRS
Task was dull.
CONFLICTING BEHAVIOR
"I told others that the task was interesting."
DISSONANCE AROUSED
"I wouldn't lie for $1."
(Action not justified by payment.)
RESULT
Change attitude: "I didn't lie; the task really was interesting."
Dissonance reduced.

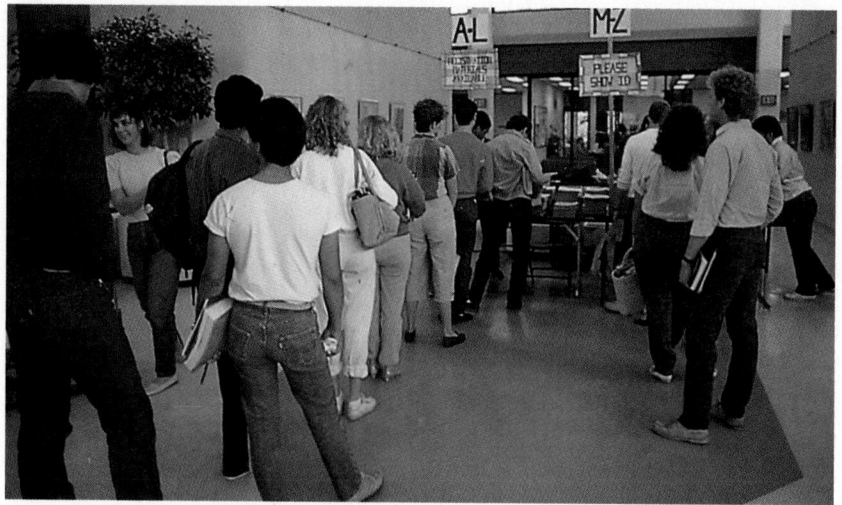

■ **Fig. 21–4** *Making choices often causes dissonance. This is especially true if the rejected alternative is perceived as better than the one selected. To minimize such dissonance, we tend to emphasize positive aspects of what we choose, while downgrading other alternatives. Thus, college students are more likely to think their courses will be good after they have registered than they did before making a commitment (Rosenfeld et al., 1983).*

you wish you hadn't promised to help. To reduce dissonance, you may convince yourself that the work will actually be "sort of fun" or that your friend really deserves the help. We often make such adjustments in attitudes to minimize cognitive dissonance (■ Fig. 21–4).

LEARNING CHECK

1. Attitudes have three parts, a ________ component, an ________ component, and an ________ component.
2. Which of the following is associated with attitude formation?
   a. group membership *b.* mass media *c.* chance conditioning *d.* child rearing *e.* all of the preceding *f.* *a* and *d* only
3. Because of the immediate consequences of actions, behavior contrary to one's stated attitudes is often enacted. T or F?
4. Items such as "would exclude from my country" or "would admit to marriage in my family" are found in which attitude measure?
   a. a reference group scale *b.* a social distance scale *c.* an attitude scale *d.* an open-ended interview
5. In presenting a persuasive message, it is best to give both sides of the argument if the audience is already well informed on the topic. T or F?
6. Much attitude change is related to a desire to avoid clashing or contradictory thoughts, an idea summarized by ________ ________ theory.

Critical Thinking

7. Students entering a college gym are asked to sign a banner promoting water conservation. Later, the students shower at the gym. What effect would you expect signing the banner to have on how long students stay in the showers?

Answers: 1. belief, emotional, action 2. *e* 3. T 4. *b* 5. T 6. cognitive dissonance 7. Cognitive dissonance theory predicts that students who sign the banner will take shorter showers, to be consistent with their publicly expressed support of water conservation. This is exactly the result observed in a study done by social psychologist Elliot Aronson.

Brainwashing Engineered or forced attitude change involving a captive audience.

Forced Attitude Change—Brainwashing and Cults

Many people associate *brainwashing* with techniques used by the Communist Chinese on American prisoners during the Korean War. Through various types of "thought reform," the Chinese were able to coerce approximately 16 percent of these prisoners to sign false confessions (Schein et al., 1957). More recently, the mass murder/suicide at Jonestown and the Branch Davidian tragedy at Waco, Texas, rekindled public interest in the subject of forced changes in attitudes, beliefs, and personal loyalties.

Question: What is brainwashing? How does it differ from other persuasive techniques?

As we have noted, advertisers, politicians, educators, religious organizations, and others actively seek to alter attitudes and opinions. To an extent, their persuasive efforts resemble brainwashing, but there is an important difference: **Brainwashing** requires a *captive* audience. If you are offended by a television commercial, you can tune it out. Prisoners in the POW camps in Korea (and later in Vietnam) were completely at the mercy of their captors. James McConnell noted that complete control over the environment allows a degree of psychological manipulation that would be impossible in a normal setting.

Question: How does captivity facilitate persuasion?

Brainwashing

McConnell identified three techniques used in brainwashing: (1) The target person is isolated from other people who would support his or her original attitudes; (2) the target is made completely dependent on his or her captors for satisfaction of needs; and (3) the indoctrinating agent is in a position to reward the target for changes in attitude or behavior.

Brainwashing typically begins with an attempt to make the target person feel completely helpless. Physical and psychological abuse, lack of sleep, humiliation, and isolation serve to **unfreeze** former values and beliefs. **Change** comes about when exhaustion, pressure, and fear become unbearable. At this point, prisoners reach the breaking point and sign a false confession or cooperate to gain relief. When they do, they are suddenly rewarded with praise, privileges, food, or rest. Continued coupling of hope and fear with additional pressures to conform then serves to **refreeze** new attitudes (Schein et al., 1961).

Question: How permanent are changes caused by brainwashing?

In most cases, the dramatic shift in attitudes brought about by brainwashing is temporary. Most "converted" prisoners who returned to the United States after the Korean War eventually reverted to their original beliefs and repudiated their indoctrinators.

Cults

Exhorted by their leader, some 900 members of the Reverend Jim Jones' People's Temple picked up paper cups and drank purple Kool-Aid laced with the deadly poison cyanide. Psychologically, the mass suicide at Jonestown in 1978 is not so incredible as it might seem. The inhabitants of Jonestown were isolated in the jungles of Guyana, intimidated by guards and lulled with sedatives. They were also cut off from friends and relatives and totally accustomed to obeying rigid rules of conduct, which primed them for Jones' final "loyalty test." Of greater psychological interest is the question of how people reach such a state of commitment and dependency.

Question: Why do people join groups such as the People's Temple?

The People's Temple was a classic example of a cult. A **cult** is a group in which the leader's personality is more important than the beliefs he or she preaches. Cult members give their allegiance to this person and follow his or her dictates almost without question (■ Fig. 21–5). Psychologist Margaret Singer (1979) has studied and aided hundreds of former cult members. Her interviews reveal that in recruiting new members, cults use a powerful blend of guilt, manipulation, isolation, deception, fear, and escalating commitment. In this respect, cults employ high-pressure indoctrination techniques not unlike those used in brainwashing (Isser, 1991).

■ **Fig. 21–5** *In April 1993, David Koresh and members of his Branch Davidian group perished in an inferno at their Waco, Texas, compound. Authorities believe the fire was set by a cult member, under the direction of Koresh. Like Jim Jones did years before in Jonestown, Koresh took nearly total control of his followers' lives. He told them what to eat, dictated sexual mores, and directed the paddling of errant followers. Followers were persuaded to surrender money, property, and even their children and wives. Like Jones, Koresh also took mistresses and had children out of wedlock. Like other cult leaders, Jones and Koresh demanded absolute loyalty and obedience, with tragic results (Reiterman, 1993).*

Recruitment Some of those interviewed by Singer were suffering from marked psychological distress

Unfreezing In brainwashing, a loosening of convictions about former values, attitudes, and beliefs.

Change In brainwashing, the point at which a person begins to repudiate former attitudes and beliefs.

Refreezing In brainwashing, the process of rewarding and strengthening new attitudes and beliefs.

Cult A group that professes great devotion to some person, and follows that person almost without question; cult members are typically victimized by their leaders in various ways.

Prejudice A negative emotional attitude held against members of a particular group of people.

Racism Racial prejudice that has become institutionalized (that is, it is reflected in government policy, schools, and so forth) and that is enforced by the existing social power structure.

Sexism Institutionalized prejudice against members of either sex, based solely on their gender.

Ageism An institutionalized tendency to discriminate on the basis of age; prejudice based on age.

Discrimination Treating members of various social groups differently in circumstances where their rights or treatment should be identical.

when they joined a cult. Most, however, were simply undergoing a period of mild depression, indecision, or alienation from family and friends. Cult members try to catch potential converts at a time of need—especially when a sense of belonging will be attractive to the convert. For instance, many converts were approached just after a romance had broken up, or when they were struggling with exams, were trying to choose a major, or were simply at loose ends and "on the street." Another dangerous time is when young adults are having difficulty becoming independent from their family (Sirkin, 1990). At such times, people are easily persuaded that joining the group is all they must do to be happy again (Schwartz, 1991).

Question: How is conversion achieved?

Conversion Often it begins with intense displays of affection and understanding ("love bombing"). Next comes isolation from non-cult members and drills, discipline, and rituals (all night meditation or continuous chanting, for instance) to wear down physical and emotional resistance, as well as to generate commitment. In short, cults tend to appeal to recruits' emotions, while discouraging critical thinking (Galanti, 1993).

At first, recruits make small commitments (to stay after a meeting, for example). Then, large commitments are encouraged (to stay an extra day, to call in sick at work, and so forth). Making a major commitment is usually the final step. The new devotee signs over a bank account or property to the group, takes up residence with the group, and so forth. Such major public commitments create a powerful cognitive dissonance effect in which it becomes virtually impossible for converts to admit that they have made a mistake.

Once in the group, members are cut off from family and friends (former reference groups), and the cult can control the flow and interpretation of information to them. Members are isolated physically (by continuous activity) and psychologically from their former value systems and social structures. Conversion is complete when they come to think of themselves more as group members than as individuals. At that point obedience is nearly total (Schwartz, 1991).

Question: Why do people stay in cults?

Most former members mention guilt and fear as the main reasons for not leaving when they wished they could. Most had been reduced to child-like dependency on the group for meeting all their daily needs (Singer, 1979). After they leave the group, many former cult members suffer from anxiety, panic attacks, and emotional disturbances much like post-traumatic stress syndrome (West, 1993).

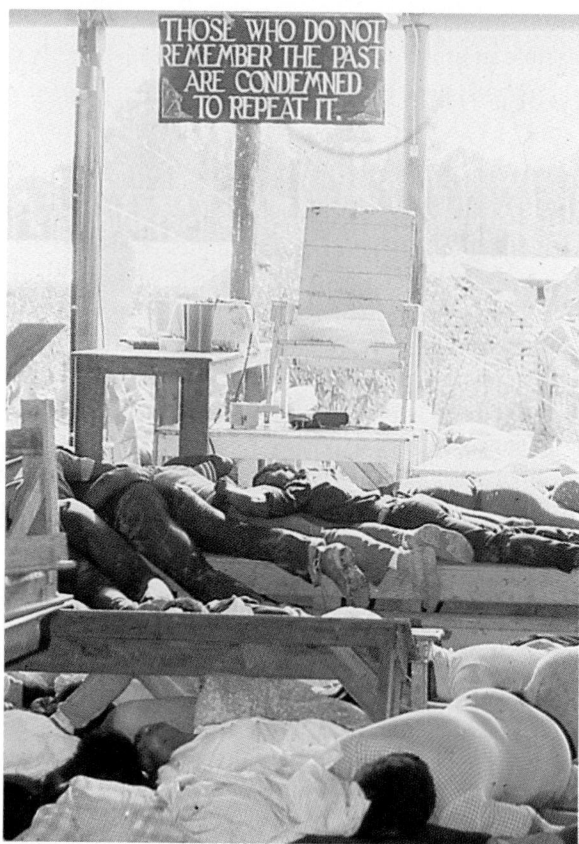

■ **Fig. 21–6** *Aftermath of the mass suicide at Jonestown. How do cult-like groups recruit new devotees? (See text.)*

Behind the "throne" from which Jim Jones ruled Jonestown was a sign bearing these words: "Those who do not remember the past are condemned to repeat it" (■ Fig. 21–6). If we are to take the Reverend Jones at his word, then we should remember that cults are but one example of the danger of trading independence for security. Cults are merely the most visible sign of how we all can be influenced by sophisticated psychological coercion and by our need for approval from others.

Prejudice—Attitudes That Injure

Prejudice is a negative attitude or prejudgment tinged with unreasonable suspicion, fear, or hatred. Often prejudice is institutionalized and backed by social power structures. In such cases it is referred to as **racism, sexism,** or **ageism,** depending on the group affected. Since sexism and ageism were discussed in earlier chapters, let's focus on racial prejudice and racism. Both racial prejudice and institutionalized racism may lead to *discrimination.* **Discrimination** refers to behavior that prevents individuals from doing things they might reasonably expect to be able to do, such as buying a house, riding a bus, or attending a high-quality school.

Discrimination is often deeply woven into society. One remarkable study, for instance, involved 15 college students who had received no traffic citations in the previous year. Each student attached a bumper sticker for a well-known, militant black organization to his or her car (Heussenstamm, 1971). During the next 17 days the group received a total of 33 traffic citations! The power relationship between the white establishment and black militants (at least as interpreted by individual police officers) is clear.

Question: How do prejudices develop?

Becoming Prejudiced

One major theory suggests that prejudice is a form of **scapegoating.** Scapegoating, you may recall, is a type of displaced aggression in which hostilities triggered by frustration are redirected to "safe" targets. One interesting test of this hypothesis was conducted at a summer camp for young men. Subjects were given a difficult test they were sure to fail. Additionally, completing the test caused them to miss a trip to the theater (normally the high point of their weekly entertainment). Attitudes toward Mexicans and Japanese were measured before the test and after the men had failed the test and missed the entertainment. Subjects in this study consistently rated members of these two groups lower after being frustrated (Miller & Bugelski, 1970).

At times, the development of prejudice (like other attitudes) can be traced to direct experiences with members of the rejected group. A child who is repeatedly bullied by members of a particular racial or ethnic group may develop resentment that forms the core of a lifelong dislike for all members of the group. The tragedy in such cases is that once dislike is established, it prevents accepting additional, more positive experiences that could reverse the damage.

Gordon Allport (1958) concluded that there are two important sources of prejudice. **Personal prejudice** occurs when members of another racial or ethnic group represent a threat to the individual's security or comfort. For example, members of another group may be viewed as competitors for jobs. **Group prejudice** occurs simply through a person's adherence to *group norms*. In other words, you may have no personal reason for disliking out-group members, but your friends, acquaintances, or co-workers expect it of you.

The Prejudiced Personality Other research suggests that prejudice at times is a general personality characteristic.

Question: Do you mean some people are more prone to prejudice than others?

Apparently, some are. Theodore Adorno and his associates (1950) carefully probed what they called the **authoritarian personality** (ah-thor-ih-TARE-ee-un). These researchers started out by studying anti-Semitism as a means of understanding the social climate that existed in Germany during World War II. In the process, they found that people who are prejudiced against one group tend to be prejudiced against *all* out-groups.

Question: What are the characteristics of the prejudice-prone personality?

The authoritarian personality has a collection of personal attitudes and values marked by rigidity, inhibition, and over-simplification. Authoritarians tend to be very **ethnocentric.** That is, they use their own national, ethnic, or religious group as a basis for judging all other groups and they consider their own group superior to others. In addition to rejecting out-groups, authoritarians are overwhelmingly concerned with power, authority, and obedience. To measure these qualities, the *F scale* was created (the *F* stands for "fascism"). This attitude scale is made up of statements such as the ones that follow—to which the authoritarian readily agrees (Adorno et al., 1950).

Authoritarian Beliefs

- Obedience and respect for authority are the most important virtues children should learn.
- People can be divided into two distinct classes: the weak and the strong.
- If people would talk less and work more, everybody would be better off.
- What this country needs most, more than laws and political programs, is a few courageous, tireless, devoted leaders, in whom the people can put their faith.
- Nobody ever learns anything really important except through suffering.
- Every person should have complete faith in some supernatural power whose decisions are obeyed without question.
- Certain religious sects that refuse to salute the flag should be forced to conform to such patriotic action or else be abolished.

As children, authoritarians were usually severely punished. Most learned to fear authority (and to covet it) at an early age. In general, people are more likely to express authoritarian beliefs when they feel threatened (Doty, Peterson, & Winter, 1991). An example would be calling for more severe punishment in the schools when the economy is bad and job insecurities are high. Authoritarians are not happy people.

It should be readily apparent from the list of authoritarian beliefs that the F scale is slanted toward politically conservative authoritarians. To be fair, psychologist Milton Rokeach (1918–1988) noted that rigid and authoritarian personalities can be found at

Scapegoating Blaming a person or a group for the actions of others or for conditions not of their making.

Displaced aggression Redirecting aggression to a target other than the actual source of one's frustration.

Personal prejudice Prejudicial attitudes held toward persons who are perceived as a direct threat to one's own interests.

Group prejudice Prejudice held out of conformity to group views.

Authoritarian personality A personality pattern characterized by rigidity, inhibition, prejudice, and excessive concern with power, authority, and obedience.

Ethnocentrism Placing one's own group or race at the center—that is, tending to reject all other groups but one's own.

Dogmatism An unwarranted positiveness or certainty in matters of belief or opinion.

both ends of the political spectrum. Rokeach (1960), therefore, preferred to describe rigid and intolerant thinking as **dogmatism.** (Dogmatism is an unwarranted positiveness or certainty in matters of belief or opinion.) Dogmatic persons find it difficult to change their beliefs, even when the evidence contradicts them (Davies, 1993).

Even if we discount the obvious bigotry of the dogmatic or authoritarian personality, racial prejudice runs deep in many nations. To illustrate, one experiment showed that liberal, white, male college students were more willing to give shocks (under laboratory conditions) to a black victim than to a white victim (Shulman, 1974). We will probe deeper into the roots of such prejudiced behavior in an upcoming discussion, but first let's stop for a Learning Check.

Learning Check

1. Brainwashing differs from other persuasive attempts in that brainwashing requires a ______________________ .
2. Which statement about brainwashing is *false?*
   a. The target person is isolated from others.
   b. Attitude changes brought about by brainwashing are usually permanent.
   c. The first step is unfreezing former values and beliefs.
   d. Cooperation with the indoctrinating agent is rewarded.
3. Margaret Singer found that most former cult members had experienced a major psychological disturbance just prior to joining the cult. T or F?
4. Which of the following is *not* a technique typically used by cults to recruit new members?
   a. "love bombing" and isolation
   b. drills and rituals to wear down resistance
   c. physical intimidation and veiled threats
   d. a succession of smaller to larger commitments
5. The authoritarian person tends to regard his or her own group as superior and the basis for judging all other groups, a quality referred to as ______________________ .

Critical Thinking

6. In criminal trials, defense lawyers sometimes try to identify and eliminate prospective jurors who have authoritarian personality traits. Can you guess why?

Answers:

1. captive audience 2. *b* 3. F 4. *c* 5. ethnocentrism 6. Because authoritarians tend to believe that punishment is effective. They are therefore more likely to vote for conviction.

Social stereotypes Oversimplified images of the traits of individuals who belong to a particular social group.

Intergroup Conflict—The Roots of Prejudice

An unfortunate by-product of group membership is that it often limits contact with people in other groups. Additionally, groups themselves may come into conflict. Both events tend to foster unpleasant feelings and prejudices toward the out-group. The bloody clash of opposing forces in Ireland, South Africa, and Hometown, U.S.A. are reminders that intergroup conflict is a widespread problem of modern life. Daily we read of jarring clashes between nations, communities, races, and political, religious, or ethnic groups. In many cases, intergroup conflict is accompanied by *stereotyped* images of out-group members and by bitter prejudice.

Question: What exactly do you mean by a stereotype?

Social stereotypes are oversimplified images of people who fall into a particular category. There is a good chance that you have stereotyped images of some of the following categories: redneck, politician, show-off, do-gooder, juvenile delinquent, business executive, housewife, snob, playboy, teenager, slob, spoiled brat, billionaire. Stereotypes have a powerful effect on how we treat others (Andersen, Klatzky, & Murray, 1990). In general, the top three categories on which most stereotypes are based are gender, age, and race (Fiske, 1993a).

Stereotypes tend to simplify people into "us" and "them" categories. Actually, aside from the fact that they always oversimplify, stereotypes may be either *positive* or *negative.* ● Table 21–1 shows stereotyped images of various national and ethnic groups and their changes over a 34-year period (■ Fig. 21–7). Notice that many of the qualities listed are desirable. Note too, that while the overall trend was a decrease in negative stereotypes, belief in the existence of some negative traits increased.

Even though stereotypes sometimes include positive traits, they are mainly used to maintain control over other people. When a person is stereotyped, the easiest thing for her or him to do is to abide by others' expectations—even if the expectations are demeaning. That's why no one likes to be stereotyped. Being forced into a small, distorted social "box" by stereotyping is limiting and insulting. Stereotypes rob people of their individuality. Without stereotypes there would be far less hate, prejudice, exclusion, and conflict (Fiske, 1993b).

Table 21–1 University Students' Characterization of Ethnic Groups, 1933 and 1967

Trait	Percent Checking Trait 1933	Percent Checking Trait 1967	Trait	Percent Checking Trait 1933	Percent Checking Trait 1967	Trait	Percent Checking Trait 1933	Percent Checking Trait 1967
Americans			**Italians**			**Jews**		
Industrious	48	23	Artistic	53	30	Shrewd	79	30
Intelligent	47	20	Impulsive	44	28	Mercenary	49	15
Materialistic	33	67	Musical	32	9	Grasping	34	17
Progressive	27	17	Imaginative	30	7	Intelligent	29	37
Germans			**Irish**			**Blacks**		
Scientific	78	47	Pugnacious	45	13	Superstitious	84	13
Stolid	44	9	Witty	38	7	Lazy	75	26
Methodical	31	21	Honest	32	17	Ignorant	38	11
Efficient	16	46	Nationalistic	21	41	Religious	24	8

(Source: M. Karlins, T. L. Coffman, and G. Walters, "On the fading of social stereotypes: Studies in three generations of college students," *Journal of Personality and Social Psychology* 13 (1969): 1–16.)

In the years since 1967, there have been further declines in negative stereotypes, but also some recent reversals. Some observers believe that racial and ethnic prejudice is on the upswing. But often, today's racism takes the form of **symbolic prejudice** (also called "modern prejudice") (Brewer & Kramer, 1985). That is, many people realize that crude and obvious racism is socially unacceptable. However, this may not stop them from expressing prejudice in disguised forms when they state their opinions on issues such as affirmative action programs, busing, immigration, crime, and so on. In effect, modern racists find ways to rationalize their prejudice so that it seems to be based on issues other than raw racism.

Symbolic prejudice Prejudice that is expressed in disguised fashion.

Stereotypes held by the prejudiced tend to be unusually irrational. When given a list of negative statements about other groups, prejudiced individuals agree with most of them. Particularly revealing is the fact that they often agree with conflicting statements. Thus, a prejudiced person may say that Jews are both "pushy" and "standoffish" or that African Americans are both "ignorant" and "sly." In one study, prejudiced subjects even expressed negative attitudes toward two non-existent groups, the "Piraneans" and the "Danirians." Note, too, that when a prejudiced person meets a pleasant or likable member of a rejected group, the out-group member tends to be perceived as "an exception to the rule," not as evidence against the stereotype. Even when such "exceptional" experiences begin to accumulate, a prejudiced person may not change his or her stereotyped belief (Fiske, 1993a).

Fig. 21–7 *Racial and ethnic pride are gradually replacing stereotypes and discrimination, but the problem of prejudice is far from solved.*

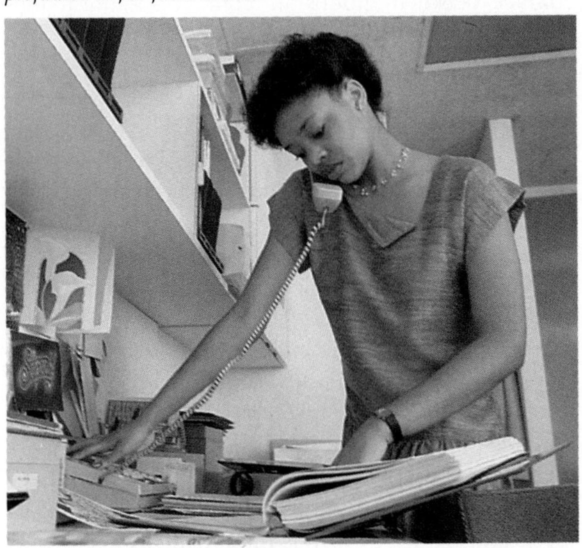

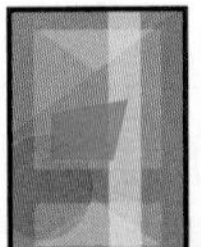

HIGHLIGHT 21–2

Cultural Diversity

Enemy Images

"Huns, Krauts, Japs." If you've watched many vintage war movies you've probably heard these ugly and hateful terms. During World War II, as in all wars, public images of "the enemy" were monstrous and dehumanizing. Even today, in the absence of active hostilities, enemy images tend to depict our national rivals as evil or less than human. For example, media images of Russians have long depicted them as inhumane, vicious torturers who enjoy murder and inflicting pain. In the movie *Rambo,* for instance, two Russian soldiers are shown enjoying themselves as they torture Sylvester Stallone with electric shock and hot

Status inequalities Differences in the power, prestige, or privileges of two or more persons or groups.

Equal-status contact Social interaction that occurs on an equal footing, without obvious differences in power or status.

knives (Silverstein, 1989). (Given a chance, some movie critics might join in.)

In times of war, dehumanizing images are used to make it seem that a nation's enemies *deserve* hatred and even death. Undoubtedly, for many soldiers, such images provide a degree of emotional insulation that makes it easier to harm another human. Yet during times of peace, such images can lead to dangerous misperceptions of the motives and actions of other nations. Especially dangerous is the tendency to exaggerate the threat posed by "enemy" nations. For example, a study found that college students thought that actions (both good and bad) supposedly performed by the former Soviet Union were based on sinister motives; when the same actions were attributed to the U.S., students assumed the motives were positive (Silverstein, 1989). It will be interesting to see if the recent restructuring of the Soviet Union changes such biases.

In many ways, ethnic jokes, racial stereotypes, degrading names, out-group slurs, and the like are small-scale examples of the damage that "enemy" images can do. Clashes ranging from those between street gangs, to those between nations, are fueled, in part, by dehumanizing images of "the enemy."

Question: How do stereotypes and intergroup tensions develop?

Two experiments, both in unlikely settings and both using children as subjects, offer some insight into these problems.

Experiments in Prejudice

What is it like to be discriminated against? Those who have never experienced discrimination probably can't imagine it. In a unique experiment, elementary school teacher Jane Elliot sought to give her pupils direct experience with prejudice.

On the first day of the experiment, Elliot announced that brown-eyed children were to sit in the back of the room and that they could not use the drinking fountain. Blue-eyed children were given extra recess time and got to leave first for lunch. At lunch, brown-eyed children were prevented from taking second helpings because they would "just waste it." Brown-eyed and blue-eyed children were kept from mingling, and the blue-eyed children were told they were "cleaner" and "smarter" (Peters, 1971).

At first, Elliot had to maintain these imposed conditions of prejudice. She also made an effort to constantly criticize and belittle the brown-eyed children. To her surprise, the blue-eyed children rapidly joined in and were soon outdoing her in the viciousness of their attacks. The blue-eyed children began to feel superior, and the brown-eyed children felt just plain awful. Fights broke out. Test scores of the brown-eyed children fell.

Question: How lasting were the effects of this experiment?

The effects were short lived, because two days later the roles of the children were reversed. Before long, the same destructive effects occurred again, but this time in reverse. The implications of this experiment are unmistakable. In less than one day it was possible to get children to hate each other because of **status inequalities** and eye color. (Status inequalities are differences in the power, prestige, or privileges of two or more persons or groups.) Certainly the effects of a lifetime of real racial or ethnic prejudice are infinitely more powerful and destructive.

Question: What can be done to combat prejudice?

Equal-Status Contact Progress has been made through attempts to educate the general public about the lack of justification for prejudice. Changing the belief component of an attitude has long been known to be one of the most direct means of changing the entire attitude. Thus, when people are made aware that minority group members share the same goals, ambitions, feelings, and frustrations as they do, intergroup relations may be improved.

However, this is not the whole answer. As we noted earlier, there is often a wide difference between attitudes and actual behavior. Until non-prejudiced behavior is engineered, changes can be quite superficial. Several lines of thought (including cognitive dissonance theory) suggest that more frequent **equal-status contact** between groups in conflict should reduce prejudice and stereotypes (Olson & Zanna, 1993).

Question: But does it?

Much evidence suggests that it does. For example, in one early study white women who lived in integrated and segregated housing projects were compared for changes in attitude toward their African-American neighbors. Women in the integrated project showed a favorable shift in attitudes toward members of the other racial group. Those in the segregated project showed no change or actually became more prejudiced than before (Deutsch & Collins, 1951). In other studies, mixed-race groups have been formed at work, in the laboratory, and at schools. The conclusion from such research is that personal contact with a disliked group will induce friendly interracial behavior, respect, and liking. However, these benefits occur only when personal contact is on an equal footing (Cook, 1985).

To test the importance of equal-status contact directly, Gerald Clore and his associates set up a unique summer camp for children. The camp was directed by one white male, one white female, one black male, and one black female. Each campsite had three black and three white campers and one black and one white counselor. Thus, blacks and whites were equally divided in number, power, privileges, and duties. Did the experience make a difference? Apparently it did: Testing showed that the children had significantly more positive attitudes toward opposite-race children after the camp than they did before (Clore, 1976).

Superordinate Goals Let us now consider a revealing study of intergroup conflict and its reduction. Muzafer Sherif and his associates did an ingenious experiment, also at a summer camp, with 11-year-old boys. When the boys arrived at camp, they were split into two groups and housed in separate cabins. At first the groups were kept apart to build up in-group friendships. During this time, cooperative games and activities were used to develop group pride and identification. Soon each group had a flag, and a name (the "Rattlers" and the "Eagles"), and had staked out its own territory. At this point the two groups were placed in competition with each other. After a number of clashes, disliking between the two groups bordered on hatred. Outright hostility erupted as the boys baited each other, started fights, and raided each other's cabins (Sherif et al., 1961).

Question: Were they allowed to go home hating each other?

As an experiment in reducing intergroup conflict, and to prevent the boys from remaining enemies, various strategies were tried to reduce tensions. Holding meetings between leaders from each group did nothing. Just getting the groups together also did little. When the groups were invited to eat together, the event became a free-for-all.

Finally, emergencies that required cooperation among members of both groups were staged at the camp. For example, the water supply was damaged in a way so that all the boys had to work together to repair it. Creation of this and other **superordinate goals** helped restore peace between the two groups. As members were forced to cooperate, hostilities subsided (see Highlight 21–3). Cooperation and shared goals seem to help reduce conflict by encouraging people in opposing groups to see themselves as members of a single, larger group (Gaertner et al., 1990). Superordinate goals, in other words, have a "we're all in the same boat" effect on perceptions of group membership (Olson & Zanna, 1993).

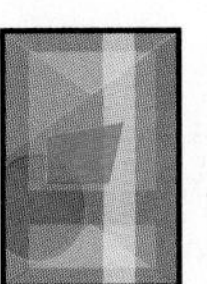

HIGHLIGHT 21–3

A Closer Look At

Superordinate Goals—Finding Common Ground

A superordinate goal exceeds or overrides other lesser goals. Where group conflict is concerned, superordinate goals are those that unite groups in pursuit of a common goal. Can such shared goals exist on a global scale? One example might be a desire to avoid nuclear holocaust. Politically, this goal may be far from universal. But its superordinate quality is increasingly evident. Scientists now project that if *any* country suffers a nuclear attack, all other countries would suffer a terrifying "nuclear winter." In effect, almost everyone, friend and foe alike, would share the same fate (Sagan & Turco, 1990).

Nuclear winter refers to a devastating drop in global temperature that would follow the fire storms, dust, and smoke of a nuclear strike. The probable result would be global crop failure, famine, and death on a large scale. Even if there were no counter-attack, a hostile country could pay dearly for its aggression (Turco et al., 1983).

It is probably fair to say that nations need to find more commonalties and shared goals. It's true that the former Soviet Union has become less of a threat to world peace. But at the same time, other "unstable" nations are moving rapidly toward nuclear weapons capability. In view of the implications of nuclear winter, perhaps finding a way to reduce the threat of nuclear warfare will prove to be a superordinate goal. Another that comes quickly to mind is the need to preserve the natural environment on a global scale.

Superordinate goal A goal that exceeds or overrides all others; a goal that renders other goals relatively less important.

"Jigsaw" Classrooms Contrary to the hopes of many, integrating public schools often has little positive effect on racial prejudice. In fact, prejudice may be made worse, and the self-esteem of minority students frequently decreases (Aronson, 1992).

Question: If integrated schools provide equal-status contact, shouldn't prejudice be reduced?

Theoretically, yes. But in practice, minority group children often enter newly integrated schools unprepared to compete on an equal footing. Elliot Aronson and his colleagues argue that the competitive nature of schools almost guarantees that children will *not* learn to like and understand each other. In the typical classroom, children compete fiercely for the approval of the teacher. Successful students learn to feel supe-

Mutual interdependence A condition in which two or more persons must depend on one another to meet each person's needs or goals.

Jigsaw classroom A method of reducing prejudice; each student receives only part of the information needed to complete a project or prepare for a test.

Aggression Any action carried out with the intention of harming another person.

Ethologist A person who studies the natural behavior patterns of animals.

rior and often hold unsuccessful students in contempt. This is a high-stakes game in which only a few can win. It is clearly not a good way to reduce prejudice.

With the preceding in mind, Aronson pioneered a way to apply the concept of superordinate goals to ordinary classrooms. According to Aronson, such goals are effective because they make people **mutually interdependent.** Each person's needs are linked to those of others in the group, and cooperation is encouraged (Deutsch, 1993).

Question: How has this idea been applied?

Aronson has successfully created **"jigsaw" classrooms** that emphasize cooperation rather than competition. The term *jigsaw* refers to the pieces of a jigsaw puzzle. In Aronson's method, each child is given a "piece" of the information needed to prepare for a test (■ Fig. 21–8).

In a typical session, children are divided into groups of 5 or 6 and given a topic to study for a later exam. Each child is given his or her "piece" of information and asked to learn it. For example, one child might have information on Thomas Edison's invention of the light bulb; another, facts about his invention of the long-playing phonograph record; and a third, information on Edison's childhood. After the children have learned their individual parts, they teach them to others in the group. Even the most competitive children quickly realize that they cannot do well without the aid of everyone in the group. Each child makes a unique and essential contribution, so the children learn to listen to, and respect, each other.

■ Fig. 21–8 *In a "jigsaw" classroom, children help each other prepare for tests. As they teach each other what they know, the children learn to cooperate and to respect the unique strengths of each individual.*

Does the jigsaw method work? Compared to children in traditional classrooms, children in jigsaw groups were less prejudiced, they liked their classmates more, they had more positive attitudes toward school, their grades improved, and their self-esteem increased (Aronson et al., 1979; Webb & Farivar, 1994). Incidentally, brighter students are not sacrificed by this method. High achievers working in cooperative groups never do worse than when learning alone, and often they do better (Johnson & Johnson, 1987). Such results are quite encouraging. As Kenneth Clark (1965) has said, "Racial prejudice . . . debases all human beings—those who are its victims, those who victimize, and in quite subtle ways, those who are merely accessories."

Aggression—The World's Most Dangerous Animal

For a time, the City Zoo of Los Angeles, California, had on display two examples of the world's most dangerous animal—the only animal capable of destroying the earth and all other animal species. Perhaps you have already guessed which animal it was. In the cage were two college students, representing the species *Homo sapiens!*

The human capacity for **aggression** seems staggering. It has been estimated that during the 125-year period ending with World War II, 58 million humans were killed by other humans (an average of nearly 1 person per minute). Murder now ranks as a major cause of death in the United States. One American kills another every 23 minutes—making the United States one of the world's most violent nations (Meredith, 1984). It is estimated that more than 1.4 million American children are subjected to physical abuse by parents each year. Over 25 percent of all married American men and women have physically attacked their spouse (O'Leary et al., 1989). War, homicide, riots, family violence, assassination, rape, assault, forcible robbery, and other violent acts offer further testimony to the realities of human aggression (■ Fig. 21–9).

Question: What causes aggression?

The complexity of aggression has given rise to a number of potential explanations for its occurrence. Brief descriptions of some of the major possibilities follow.

Instincts

Some theorists argue that as humans, we are naturally aggressive, having inherited a "killer instinct" from our animal ancestors. **Ethologists** theorize that aggression is a biologically rooted behavior observed in all ani-

■ Fig. 21–9 *Ritualized human aggression. Violent and aggressive behavior is so commonplace it may be viewed as entertainment. How "natural" is aggressive behavior?*

mals, including humans. Noted ethologist Konrad Lorenz (1966, 1974) also believed that humans lack certain innate patterns that inhibit aggression in other animal species. For example, in a dispute over territory or dominance, two wolves may growl, lunge, bare their teeth, and fiercely threaten each other. In most instances, though, neither is killed or even wounded. One wolf, recognizing the dominance of the other, will typically bare its throat in a gesture of submission. The dominant wolf could kill in an instant, but it is inhibited by the submissive gesture. In contrast, human confrontations of equal intensity almost always end in injury or homicide.

The idea that humans are "naturally" aggressive has an intuitive appeal, but many psychologists question it. Many of Lorenz's "explanations" of aggression are little more than loose comparisons between human and animal behavior. Just labeling a behavior as "instinctive" does little to explain it. More important, we are left with the question of why some individuals or human groups (the Arapesh, the Senoi, the Navajo, the Eskimo, and others) show little hostility or aggression. And, thankfully, the vast majority of humans *do not* kill or harm others.

Biology

Despite problems with the instinctive view, there is evidence that a biological basis for aggression may exist. Physiological studies have shown that there are brain areas capable of triggering or ending aggressive behavior (see Chapter 3). Also, researchers have found a relationship between aggression and such physical factors as hypoglycemia (low blood sugar), allergy, and specific brain injuries and disorders. None of these conditions, however, can be considered a direct *cause* of aggression. Instead, they probably lower the threshold for aggression, making hostile behavior more likely to occur (Baron & Richardson, 1994).

The effects of alcohol and other drugs provide another indication of the role of the brain and biology in violence and aggression. A variety of studies show that alcohol is involved in large percentages of murders and violent crimes (Collins, 1981; Lagerspetz, 1981). Like the conditions already noted, intoxicating drugs seem to lower inhibitions to act aggressively—often with tragic results (Bushman & Cooper, 1990).

To summarize, the fact that we are biologically *capable* of aggression does not mean that aggression is inevitable or "part of human nature." In 1986, a group of 20 eminent scientists gathered to examine the evidence and hammer out a statement on this issue. They concluded that, "Biology does not condemn humanity to war . . . . Violence is neither in our evolutionary legacy nor in our genes. The same species that invented war is capable of inventing peace" (Scott & Ginsburg, 1994; UNESCO, 1990). Humans are fully capable of learning to inhibit their use of violence (Lore & Schultz, 1993).

Frustration-aggression hypothesis States that frustration tends to lead to aggression.

Frustration

Step on a dog's tail and you may get nipped. Frustrate a human and you may get insulted (■ Fig. 21–10). The **frustration-aggression hypothesis** states that frustration is closely associated with aggression (Dollard et

■ Fig. 21–10 *Some freeway shootings may be a reaction to the frustration of traffic congestion. The fact that automobiles provide anonymity, or a loss of personal identity, may also encourage aggressive actions that would not otherwise occur.*

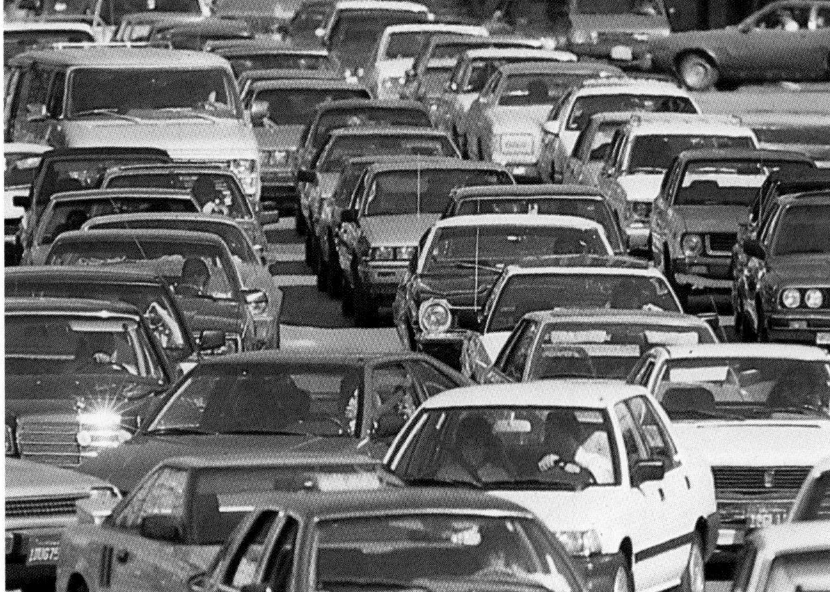

Aversive stimulus Any stimulus that produces discomfort or displeasure.

Aggression cues Stimuli or signals that are associated with aggression and that tend to elicit it.

Weapons effect The observation that weapons serve as strong cues for aggressive behavior.

Social learning theory Combines learning principles with cognitive processes, socialization, and modeling, to explain behavior.

al., 1939). At several points in earlier chapters we have considered examples of the link between frustration and aggression.

Question: Does frustration always produce aggression?

Although the connection is strong, a moment's thought will show that frustration does not *always* lead to aggression. Frustration, for instance, may lead to stereotyped responding or perhaps to a state of "learned helplessness" (see Chapter 11). Also, aggression can occur in the absence of frustration. This possibility is illustrated by sports spectators who start fights, throw bottles, tear down goal posts, and so forth, after their team has *won.*

Aversive Stimuli Frustration probably encourages aggression because it is aversive (uncomfortable). Various **aversive stimuli,** such as insults, high temperatures, pain, and even disgusting scenes or odors can heighten hostility and aggression (Anderson, 1989; Berkowitz, 1990) (■ Fig. 21–11). Such stimuli probably raise overall arousal levels so that we become more sensitive to **aggression cues** (Berkowitz, 1982; Carlson, Marcus-Newhall, & Miller, 1990). They also tend to activate ideas, memories, and expressions associated with anger and aggression (Berkowitz, 1990).

Question: What do you mean by "aggression cues"?

Some cues, or signals, for aggression are internal (angry thoughts, for instance). Many are external: Certain words, actions, and gestures of others are strongly associated with aggressive response. A raised middle finger, for instance, is an almost universal invitation to aggression in North America.

Even inanimate objects may serve as cues for aggression. In one classic experiment, subjects gave shocks to another person in a laboratory. Before doing so, they were ridiculed and shocked by the other person. Just before subjects got a chance to "return the favor," they saw either a couple of badminton rackets or a shotgun and a revolver on a table in the testing room. In either case, the experimenter explained that someone had left the objects there, and he casually moved them aside. Subjects who glimpsed the guns gave stronger shocks to the person who had angered them than did subjects who saw the sports equipment (Berkowitz, 1968). The implication of this **weapons effect** seems to be that the symbols and trappings of aggression encourage aggression. A prime example is the fact that murders are almost 3 times more likely to occur in homes where guns are kept. Nearly 80 percent of the victims in such homes are killed by a family member or acquaintance. Only 4 percent are murdered by strangers (Kellermann et al., 1993).

■ **Fig. 21–11** *Personal discomfort caused by aversive (unpleasant) stimuli can make aggressive behavior more likely. For example, studies of crime rates show that the incidence of highly aggressive behavior, such as murder, rape, and assault, rises as the air temperature goes from warm to hot to sweltering (Anderson, 1989). The results you see here further confirm the heat-aggression link. The graph shows that there is a strong association between the temperatures at major league baseball games and the number of batters hit by a pitch during those games. When the temperature goes over 90°, watch out for that fastball! (Reifman, Larrick, & Fein, 1991.)*

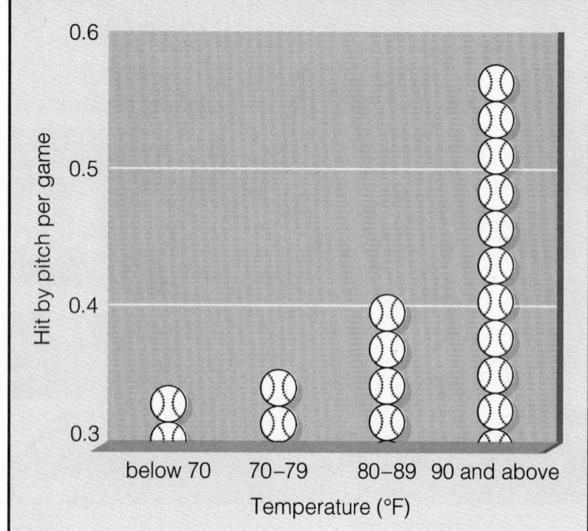

Social Learning

One of the most widely accepted explanations of aggression is also the simplest. **Social learning theory** holds that we learn to be aggressive by observing aggression in others (Bandura, 1973). According to this view, there is no instinctive human programming for fist fighting, pipe-bombing, knife wielding, gun loading, 95-mile-an-hour "bean balls," or other elements of violent or aggressive behavior. Hence, aggression must be learned. This, quite likely, is why being physically abused as a child is strongly related to violent behavior in adulthood (Marshall & Rose, 1988).

Social learning theorists predict that individuals growing up in non-aggressive cultures will themselves be non-aggressive. Those raised in a culture with aggressive models and heroes will learn aggressive responses. Considered in such terms, it is no wonder that America has become one of the most violent of all countries. It is estimated that a violent crime occurs every 54 seconds in the United States. Approximately 40 percent of the population owns firearms. Nationally, 70 percent agree that "When a boy is growing up, it is very important for him to have a few fist fights." Eighteen percent of the population admit to having slapped or kicked another person (Stark & McEvoy, 1970). Children and adults are treated to an almost nonstop parade of aggressive models (in the media as well as in actual behavior—see Highlight 21–4). We are, without a doubt, an aggressive culture.

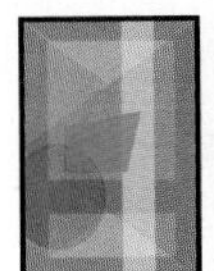

HIGHLIGHT 21–4

Focus on a Controversy

Aggression and Pornography—Is There a Link?

The debate on the effects of pornography is heating up again. Until recently, most evidence suggested that viewing pornography has no major adverse effects. This conclusion appears to remain valid for stimuli that can be described as merely erotic or sexual in content. However, in the last 10 years there has been a dramatic increase in the number of aggressive-pornographic stimuli appearing in the mass media. **Aggressive pornography** refers to depictions in which violence, threats, or obvious power differences are used to force someone (usually a woman) to engage in sex.

The principal finding of studies on aggressive-pornographic stimuli is that they do increase aggression by males against females. In a summary of various experiments, researchers Neil Malamuth and Ed Donnerstein (1982) concluded that "exposure to mass media stimuli that have violent *and* sexual content increases the audience's aggressive-sexual fantasies, beliefs in rape myths, and aggressive behavior." Donnerstein and Daniel Linz (1986) further conclude that it is media *violence* that is most damaging. As they put it, "Violent images, rather than sexual ones, are most responsible for people's attitudes about women and rape." The problem, then, extends far beyond X-rated films and books. Mainstream movies, magazines, music videos (like those mentioned earlier), and television programs are equally to blame for reinforcing the myth that women find force or aggression pleasurable (Linz, Donnerstein, & Penrod, 1988).

The World According to TV Did you know that the world is populated primarily by males, professionals, whites, and members of the middle class? Did you know that women make up only 28 percent of the population; that one half of all women are teenagers or in their early 20s; that more than one third are unemployed or have no purpose beyond offering emotional support to men or serving as objects of sexual desire? That minorities are generally service workers, criminals, victims, or students? That over one half of all villains have accents? That most victims are single women, young boys, or non-whites? If you watch much TV, these are the impressions you get daily on the tube (Carlson, 1986; Charren & Sandler, 1983).

It is clear that TV reality does not match the real world. Every day, TV provides an endless stream of bad models, especially concerning violence. In the United States there are about 188 hours of violent programs per week. Eighty-one percent of all programs contain violence, averaging 5.2 aggressive acts per hour (Huesmann & Eron, 1986). More than half of all music videos contain violence, and more than three fourths of these violent videos include sexual imagery (Brown, 1986). TV law officers more often than not contribute to violence, rather than prevent it. Murder, robbery, kidnapping, and assault make up 85 percent of TV crimes. In real life, they total about 5 percent. On TV, law officers resolve the majority of criminal investigations with violent acts (Carlson, 1986).

Aggressive pornography Media depictions of sexual violence or of forced participation in sexual activity.

Disinhibition The removal of inhibition; results in acting out behavior that normally would be restrained.

Desensitization A reduction in emotional sensitivity to a stimulus.

Question: How does TV violence affect children?

As Albert Bandura showed in his studies of imitation (Chapter 7), children may learn new aggressive actions by watching violent or aggressive behavior, or they may learn that violence is "okay." Either way, they are more likely to act aggressively. It is important to remember that younger children do not grasp the nuances of TV plots. A child may simply remember that when good guys were bothered in some way by others, they aggressed. Heroes on TV are as violent as the villains, and they usually receive praise for their violence. TV dramas tend to give the message that violence leads to success and popularity.

In addition to teaching new antisocial actions, television may **disinhibit** dangerous impulses that viewers already have. For example, many TV programs give the message that violence is normal, acceptable behavior. For some people, this message can lower inhibitions against acting out hostile feelings (Berkowitz, 1984).

Another effect of TV violence is that it tends to lower sensitivity to violent acts. As anyone who has seen a street fight or a mugging can tell you, TV violence is sanitized and unrealistic. The real thing is gross, ugly, and gut wrenching. Even when it is graphic, TV violence is viewed in the relaxed and familiar setting of the home. For at least some viewers, this combination diminishes emotional reactions to violent scenes. When Victor Cline and his associates showed a bloody fight film to a group of boys, they found that heavy TV viewers (averaging 42 hours a week) showed much less emotion than those who watched little or no TV (Cline et al., 1972). Television, it seems, can cause a **desensitization** to violence.

Preventing Aggression

Question: What can be done about aggression?

Social learning theory implies that "aggression begets aggression." In other words, watching a prize fight,

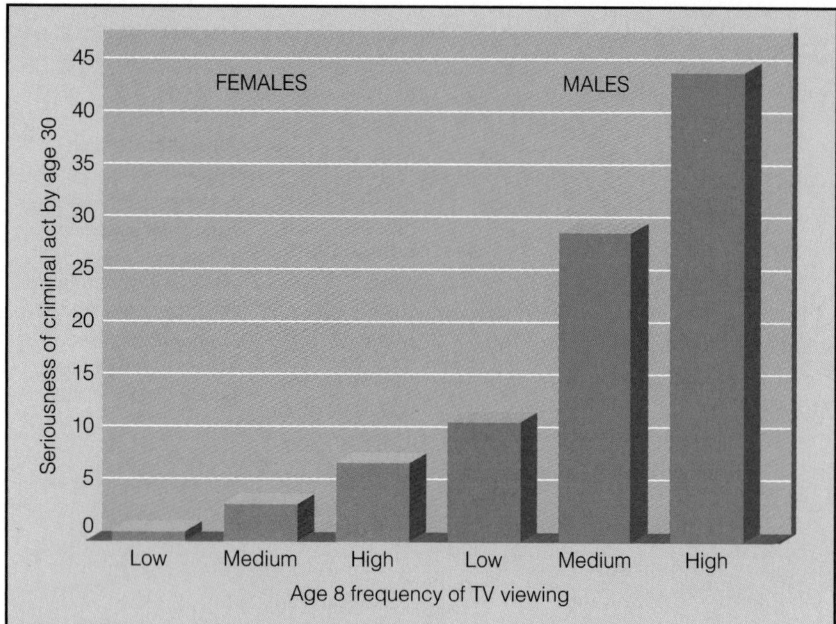

■ **Fig. 21–12** *Although TV violence does not cause aggression, it can encourage it. The likelihood of committing criminal acts by age 30 is related to the amount of TV watching a person did when he or she was a child (Eron, 1987). (Graph copyright 1987 by the American Psychological Association, Inc. Reprinted by permission of the author.)*

sporting event, or violent television program may increase aggression, rather than drain off aggressive urges. A case in point is provided by psychologist Leonard Eron, who spent 22 years following over 600 children into adulthood. Eron (1987) observes, "Among the most influential models for children were those observed on television. One of the best predictors of how aggressive a young man would be at age 19 was the violence of the television programs he preferred when he was 8 years old" (■ Fig. 21–12). According to Eron, children learn aggressive strategies and actions from TV violence (also see Chapter 8). Because of this, they are more prone to aggression when they face frustrating situations or cues. Others have found that viewers who watch violent videotapes have more aggressive thoughts. As we have noted, violent thoughts often precede violent actions (Bushman & Geen, 1990). Thus, the spiral of aggression might be broken if we did not so often portray it, reward it, and glorify it (Lore & Schultz, 1993). (See Highlight 21–5.)

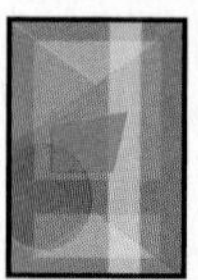

Highlight 21–5

Using Psychology

Buffering Television's Impact

Other than pulling the plug, what can parents do about television's negative effects on children?

Actually, quite a lot. Children typically model parents' TV viewing habits, and they are guided by parents' reactions to programs. Parents can make a big difference if they do the following (Eron, 1986; Huesmann, 1986; Schneider, 1987).

Parents as TV Guides

1. Limit total viewing time so that television does not dominate your child's view of the world. If necessary, set schedules for when watching TV is allowed.

2. Closely monitor what your child does watch. Change channels or turn off the TV if you object to a program. Be prepared to offer games and activities that stimulate your child's imagination and creativity.

3. Actively seek programs your child will enjoy, especially those that model positive behavior and social attitudes.

4. Watch television with your child so that you can counter what is shown. Help your child distinguish between reality and TV fantasies. Reply to distortions and stereotypes as they appear on screen.

5. Discuss the social conflicts and violent solutions shown on television. Ask your child in what ways the situations are unrealistic and why the violence shown would not work in the real world. Encourage the child to propose more mature, realistic, and positive responses to situations.

6. Show by your own disapproval that violent TV heroes are not the ones to emulate. Remember, children who identify with TV characters are more likely to be influenced by televised aggression.

By following these guidelines you can help children learn to enjoy television without being overly influenced by programs and advertisers.

Question: Couldn't TV's impact also be used constructively?

TV as a Positive Model There is no denying TV's tremendous power to inform and to entertain. When these features are combined, as they were in specials such as *Roots* or *Holocaust*, the effect can be quite constructive. Perhaps the best examples of TV as a positive social force are the educational programs "Barney and Friends," "Sesame Street," and "Mr. Rogers' Neighborhood." Over 150 research reports have dealt with the impact of these programs. An overwhelming majority of these evaluations are positive (■ Fig. 21–13). Clearly, television can teach children while holding their interest and attention.

■ **Fig. 21–13** *A recent study by Jerome and Dorothy Singer found that preschoolers who watch "Barney and Friends" show improved cognitive skills and knowledge—such as knowing colors and shapes, numbers, vocabulary, good manners, and facts about nature and health (deGroot, 1994).*

As a model for positive attitudes and responses, TV could be used to promote helping, cooperation, charity, and brotherhood in the same way that it has tended to stereotype and encourage aggression. Over 200 studies have now shown that **prosocial behavior** on TV increases prosocial behavior by viewers (Hearold, 1987). To illustrate, children in one experiment watched a TV program that emphasized helping (a "Lassie" episode). Later, these children were more willing than others to help a puppy in distress even when it meant skipping a chance to win prizes (Rubinstein et al., 1974).

Anger Control On a personal level, some psychologists have succeeded in teaching people to control their anger and aggressive impulses. The key to **anger control** is the fact that people who respond calmly to upsetting situations tend to see them as *problems to be solved.* Therefore, to limit anger, people are taught to:

1. Define the problem as precisely as possible.
2. Make a list of possible solutions.
3. Rank the likely success of each solution.
4. Choose a solution and try it.
5. Assess how successful the solution was, and make adjustments if necessary.

Taking these steps has helped many people to lessen tendencies toward child abuse, family violence, and other destructive outbursts (Meichenbaum et al., 1982).

Beyond this, the question remains, How shall we tame the world's most dangerous animal? There is no easy answer. Only a challenge of pressing importance. The solution will undoubtedly involve the best efforts of thinkers and researchers from many disciplines.

For the more immediate future, it is clear that we need more people who are willing to engage in helpful, altruistic, *prosocial* behavior. In the next section we will examine some of the forces that operate to prevent people from helping others. Also discussed are a few glimmerings about how to encourage prosocial behavior.

Prosocial behavior Behavior toward others that is helpful, constructive, or altruistic.

Anger control Personal strategies for reducing or curbing anger.

Bystander apathy Unwillingness of bystanders to offer help during emergencies or to become involved in others' problems.

Prosocial Behavior—Helping Others

Late one night, tenants of a Queens, New York, apartment building watched and listened in horror as a young woman named Kitty Genovese was murdered on the sidewalk outside. From the safety of their rooms, no fewer than 38 people heard the agonized screams as her assailant stabbed her, was frightened off, and returned to stab her again.

Kitty Genovese's murder took over 30 minutes, but none of her neighbors tried to help. None even called the police until after the attack had ended. Perhaps it is understandable that no one wanted to get involved. After all, it could have been a violent lovers' quarrel. Or helping might have meant risking personal injury. But what prevented these people from at least calling the police?

Question: Isn't this an example of the alienation of city life?

News reports treated this incident as evidence of a breakdown in social ties caused by the impersonality of the city. While it is true that urban living can be dehumanizing, this does not fully explain such instances of **bystander apathy.** According to psychologists Bibb Latané and John Darley (1968), failure to help is related to the number of people present. Over the years many studies have shown that the *more* potential helpers present, the *lower* the chances that help will be given (Latané et al., 1981).

Question: Why would people be less willing to help when others are present?

In Kitty Genovese's case, the answer is that everyone thought *someone else* would help. The dynamics of this effect can be illustrated in this way: Suppose that two motorists have stalled at roadside, one on a sparsely traveled country road and the other on a busy freeway. Who gets help first?

APPLICATIONS: *Continued*

Cultural Awareness

Living comfortably in a multicultural society means getting to know a little about other groups. Getting acquainted with a person whose cultural background is different from your own can be a wonderful learning experience. No one culture has all the answers or the best ways of doing things. Multicultural populations enrich a community's food, music, arts, and philosophy. Likewise, learning about different racial, cultural, and ethnic groups can be personally rewarding.

The importance of cultural awareness often lies in subtleties and details. For example, in large American cities, many small stores are owned by Korean immigrants. Some of these Korean-American merchants have been criticized for being cold and hostile to their customers. Refusing to place change directly in customers' hands, for instance, helped trigger an African-American boycott of Korean grocers in New York City in 1991. The core of the problem was a lack of cultural awareness on both sides.

In America, if you walk into a store, you expect the clerk to be courteous to you. One way of showing politeness is by smiling. But in the Confucian-steeped Korean culture, a smile is reserved for family members and close friends. If a Korean, or Korean American has no reason to smile, he or she just doesn't smile. There's a Korean saying: "If you smile a lot, you're silly." Expressions such as "thank you" and "excuse me" are also used sparingly and strangers rarely touch each other—not even to return change in a business transaction.

Here's another example of how ignorance of cultural practices can lead to needless friction and misunderstanding: An African-American woman who wanted to ease racial tensions took a freshly baked pie to her neighbors across the way, who were Orthodox Jews. At the front door the woman extended her hand, not knowing that Orthodox Jews don't shake women's hands. Once she was inside, she picked up a kitchen knife to cut the pie, not knowing the couple kept a kosher household and used different knives for different foods. The woman's well-intentioned attempt at neighborliness ended in an argument! Knowing a little more about each other's cultures could have prevented both of the conflicts just described.

LEARNING CHECK

1. Multiculturalism refers to the belief that various subcultures and ethnic groups should be blended into a single emergent culture. T or F?
2. Patricia Devine found that many people who hold non-prejudiced beliefs still have prejudiced thoughts and feelings in the presence of minority group individuals. T or F?
3. Individuating information tends to be a good antidote for stereotypes. T or F?
4. Just-world beliefs are the primary cause of social competition. T or F?

Critical Thinking

5. Why is it valuable to learn the terms by which members of various groups prefer to be addressed (for example, Mexican-American, Latino [or Latina], Hispanic, or Chicano [Chicana])?

Answers: 1. F 2. T 3. T 4. F 5. Because labels might have negative meanings that are not apparent to persons outside the group. People who are culturally aware allow others to define their own identities, rather than imposing labels on them.

EXPLORATION

Sociobiology—Do Genes Guide Social Behavior?

A small band of men moves cautiously through a rubble-strewn battlefield. Without warning, a grenade sails overhead and lands at their feet. There is no time for escape. Instinctively, one of the men dives at the grenade, covers it with his own body, and shields his comrades from certain death. Scenes such as this have occurred in almost every modern war. How are such altruistic actions explained?

EXPLORATION

Sociobiology According to a viewpoint called **sociobiology,** many human social behaviors have roots in heredity. Sociobiologists, such as Harvard zoologist Edward Wilson, believe that competition, war, territoriality, aggression, sibling rivalry, conformity, male-female differences, fear of strangers, altruism, and many other behaviors are "in our genes."

The core idea in sociobiology is that social behavior evolves in ways that maximize fitness for survival. For instance, animals who compete successfully for food, territory, mates, and so forth, are more likely to survive and reproduce. Thus, competitiveness gradually becomes a trait of following generations. Sociobiologists believe that many human traits evolved through similar patterns of natural selection.

Applying the concept of natural selection to explain human nature may make sense for some behaviors. But how do sociobiologists explain altruistic actions like the selfless heroism of the soldier described earlier? The answer is intriguing. Sociobiologists point out that altruistic suicides can be observed in many animal species. For example, if a honeybee stings an intruder to protect its hive, the bee will die. How could such behavior evolve if altruistic bees never get a chance to reproduce and pass on their genes? Sociobiologists reply that altruistic actions help improve chances that an animal's *kin* will survive.

Each individual shares some genes in common with close family members. So, while the altruistic individual's genes may not be passed on directly, they are perpetuated by close kin. In human terms, sociobiologists argue that a person might sacrifice his or her own chance of survival to ensure the survival of a number of close relatives. Of course, heroic soldiers are typically unrelated to their comrades. Nevertheless, a soldier may act for the good of the group because altruism has been "bred into" humans during eons of evolution.

Biological Determinism Sociobiology deserves credit for offering a fresh perspective on human behavior. In fact, sociobiology produces some fascinating images when it is taken to its logical extremes: It is almost as if genes are at the helms of great hulking machines (our bodies) that they use for protection and self-preservation. Sociobiology seems to say that genes manipulate our behavior to ensure *their* survival (or at least the survival of duplicate genes in the bodies of our relatives).

Sociobiology's major strength is that it helps relate human behavior to biology. Its major weakness is that it probably overstates its case. The degree of biological determinism assumed by sociobiologists is so extreme that even most biologists question it.

Critique Thinking about the biological foundations of human behavior is always interesting. However, the conclusions drawn by sociobiologists are highly questionable (Lerner & von Eye, 1992). Evolution and natural selection, for instance, may have favored development of the human brain, rather than of specific behavioral traits. Humans equipped with large brains are resourceful, adaptable, and flexible. Intelligence, in fact, would seem to have much more to do with our survival than strict genetic programming does. Likewise, development during each person's own lifetime provides a powerful explanation for most behavior patterns (Lerner & von Eye, 1992).

Many critics of sociobiology point out that evolution progresses too slowly to account for many behavioral adaptations. The spread of ideas, traditions, and cultural patterns is much more rapid. To return to our earlier example, altruism may indeed be a necessity for a society to endure. However, selfless acts need not be coded into our nature by genes; they may be explained equally well by learning.

The danger inherent in sociobiology is that it can be used to support the social status quo. By defining human nature as relatively fixed and (in the short run) unchanging, sociobiology discourages attempts to change current cultural practices. Edward Wilson has said, for instance, that since males are typically more aggressive than females, "Even with identical education and equal access to all professions, men are more likely to continue to play a disproportionate role in political life, business, and science." If you are a female, that should make you angry. If you are a male, it should make you angry on behalf of your mother, sisters, daughters, wife, lover, or female friends.

Conclusion In the realm of ideas it's also a matter of survival of the fittest. To many observers it appears that sociobiology will have to evolve greatly if it is going to survive. In the meantime, the sociobiology debate should prove interesting. (Sources: Blaustein, 1983; Gould, 1976; Kamin, 1985; Kitchner, 1985; Lerner & von Eye, 1992; Lumsden & Wilson, 1983; Snowdon, 1983; Wilson, 1975)

Sociobiology Theory that social behavior evolved in ways that maximize fitness for survival of the species.

Biological determinism Belief that behavior is controlled by biological processes, such as heredity or evolution.

LEARNING CHECK

1. The core idea of sociobiology is that social behavior evolved in ways that maximize individual fitness for survival. T or F?
2. Sociobiologists believe that altruistic behavior evolved because individual sacrifice improved chances that immediate family members and close kin would survive. T or F?
3. The majority of biologists endorse sociobiological explanations of behavior. T or F?

EXPLORATION

4. Critics of sociobiology point out that natural selection among humans might have favored enlargement of the brain and behavioral flexibility—not selection of specific behavioral traits. T or F?

Critical Thinking

5. Sociobiology is highly controversial because it takes an extreme position in an age-old debate that also applies to human development, intelligence, and personality. What is the debate and what is sociobiology's position?

Answers: 1. F 2. T 3. F 4. T 5. The nature-nurture debate. Sociobiology places an extreme emphasis on nature (inborn behavioral tendencies).

Chapter Summary

■ ***What are attitudes? How are they acquired?***

- **Attitudes** are learned dispositions made up of a **belief component,** an **emotional component,** and an **action component.**
- Attitudes may be formed by *direct contact, interaction* with others, *child-rearing practices,* and *group pressures. Peer group influences,* the *mass media,* and *chance conditioning* also appear to be important in attitude formation.

■ ***How are attitudes measured and changed?***

- Attitudes are typically measured by use of techniques such as **open-ended interviews, social distance scales,** and **attitude scales.** Attitudes expressed in these ways do not always correspond to actual behavior.
- Attitude change is related to **reference group** membership, to *deliberate* **persuasion,** and to significant personal experiences (which may be engineered through *role-playing*).

■ ***Under what conditions is persuasion most effective?***

- Effective persuasion occurs when characteristics of the **communicator,** the **message,** and the **audience** are well matched. In general, a likable and believable communicator who repeats a credible message that arouses emotion in the audience and states clear-cut conclusions will be persuasive.

■ ***What is cognitive dissonance? What does it have to do with attitudes and behavior?***

- The maintenance and change of attitudes is closely related to needs for consistency in thoughts and actions. **Cognitive dissonance theory** explains the dynamics of such needs.
- Cognitive dissonance occurs when there is a clash between thoughts or between thoughts and actions. The amount of reward or justification for one's actions influences whether dissonance occurs. We are motivated to reduce dissonance when it occurs, often by changing beliefs or attitudes.

■ ***Is brainwashing actually possible? How are people converted to cult membership?***

- **Brainwashing** is a form of forced attitude change. It depends on control of the target person's total environment. Three steps in brainwashing are **unfreezing, changing,** and **refreezing** attitudes and beliefs.
- Many cults recruit new members with high-pressure indoctrination techniques resembling brainwashing. Such groups attempt to catch people when they are vulnerable. Then they combine *isolation,* displays of *affection, discipline and rituals, intimidation,* and *escalating commitment* to bring about conversion.

■ ***What causes prejudice and intergroup conflict? What can be done about these problems?***

- **Prejudice** is a negative attitude held toward members of various out-groups. One theory attributes prejudice to **scapegoating.** A second account says that prejudices may be held for personal reasons (**personal prejudice**) or simply through adherence to group norms (**group prejudice**).
- Prejudiced individuals tend to have an **authoritarian** or **dogmatic personality,** characterized by rigidity, inhibition, intolerance, over-simplification, and **ethnocentrism.**
- Intergroup conflict gives rise to hostility and the formation of **social stereotypes. Status inequalities** tend to build prejudices. **Equal-status contact** tends to reduce it.
- Psychologists have emphasized the concept of **superordinate goals** as a key to reducing intergroup

conflict, be it racial, religious, ethnic, or national. On a smaller scale, **jigsaw classrooms** (which encourage cooperation through **mutual interdependence**) have been shown to be an effective way of combating prejudice.

■ ***How do psychologists explain human aggression?***

- **Aggression** and violence are serious social problems and the subject of much current research. **Ethological explanations** of aggression attribute it to inherited instincts. **Biological explanations** emphasize brain mechanisms and physical factors related to thresholds for aggression.
- According to the **frustration-aggression hypothesis,** frustration and aggression are closely linked. Frustration is only one of many **aversive stimuli** that can arouse a person and make aggression more likely. Aggression is especially likely to occur when **aggression cues** are present.
- **Social learning theory** has focused attention on the role of **aggressive models** in the development of aggressive behavior.

■ ***Why are bystanders so often unwilling to help in an emergency?***

- Four decision points that must be passed before a person gives help are: **noticing, defining** an emergency, **taking responsibility,** and **selecting** a course of action. Helping is less likely at each point when other potential helpers are present.
- Helping is encouraged by general arousal, **empathic arousal,** being in a good mood, low effort or risk, and perceived similarity between the victim and the helper. For several reasons, giving help tends to encourage others to help too.

■ ***What can be done to lower prejudice and promote social harmony?***

- **Multiculturalism** is an attempt to give equal status to different ethnic, racial, and cultural groups.
- Greater tolerance can be encouraged by neutralizing stereotypes with **individuating information;** by looking for **commonalties** with others; and by avoiding the effects of **just-world beliefs, self-fulfilling prophecies,** and **social competition.**
- **Cultural awareness** is a key element in promoting greater social harmony.

■ ***How does the theory of sociobiology try to explain social behavior?***

- **Sociobiology** attempts to explain human social behavior by relating it to natural selection and human evolution. Although some elements of the theory are difficult to defend, sociobiology has prompted a healthy debate about the biological origins of human behavior.

Questions for Discussion

1. Choose an issue you feel strongly about. State your attitudes concerning the issue. How did you come to hold your present attitudes? What types of experiences or variables influenced you?
2. How has the anti-smoking campaign of the American Cancer Society made use of cognitive dissonance to discourage smoking?
3. In what ways do magazine and television advertisements apply the principles of persuasion? (Consider the communicator, the message, and the audience.)
4. If you were asked to establish a program to end conflict between students attending two rival high schools, what steps would you take?
5. What do you think are the superordinate goals facing the nation and the world? (To be truly superordinate a goal would have to be seen as valid by nearly everyone.) Do such goals exist? How could such a goal be converted into greater intergroup cooperation?
6. Studies of capital punishment show that it has either no effect on deterring homicides, or that there is a slight *decline* after it is abolished. How would a social learning theorist explain this decline? If capital punishment does not deter homicides, do you think it can be justified for other reasons? If so, what, in your opinion, are they?
7. Describe a situation in which you did or did not offer help to someone who was, or might have been, in need. What influenced your decision? In view of what you know about helping behavior, can you explain why rape or assault victims are advised to shout "Fire!"?
8. Kenneth Clark has said, "Prejudice is a way that human beings have of betraying the fragility of their egos." What do you think Clark meant? Do you agree?
9. The view that humans are instinctively aggressive "naked apes" has been quite popular. To what do you attribute this popularity? Do you consider humans naturally aggressive? What evidence can you give for or against this view?
10. Sociobiologists have been accused of making a basic error by assuming that human nature is revealed by the behavior of citizens in modern societies. What do you think are the basic, universal characteristics of human nature?

Chapter 22

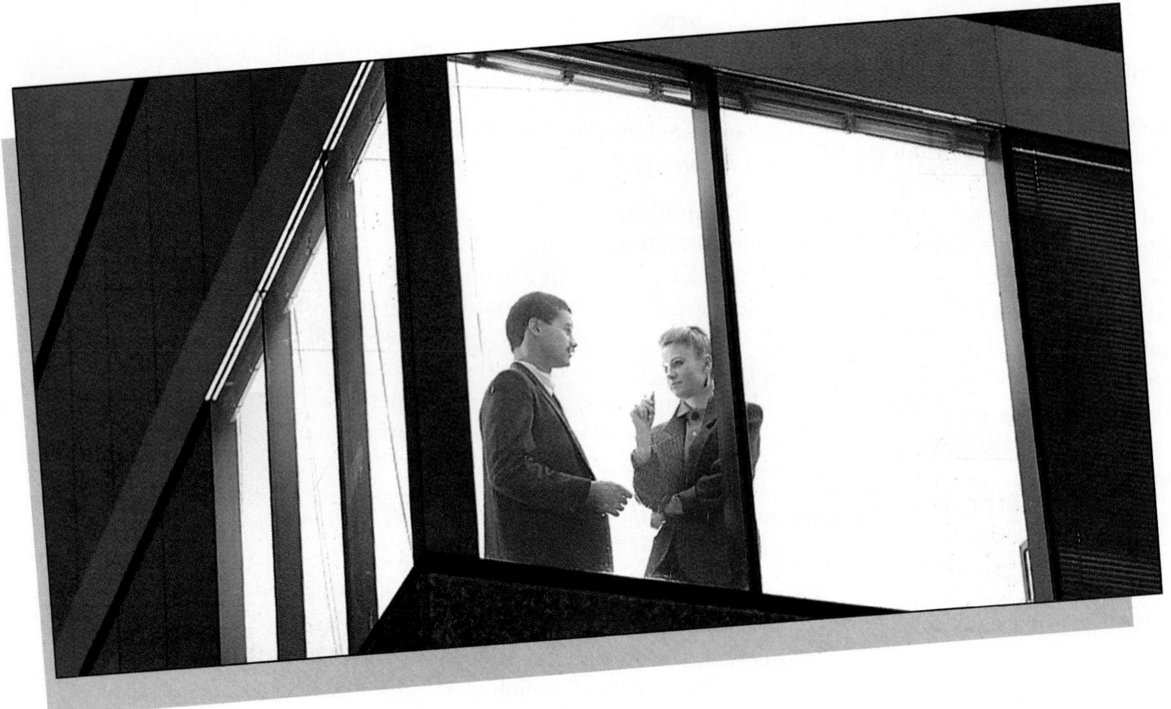

Applied Psychology

IN THIS CHAPTER

Industrial psychology
Engineering psychology
Organizational psychology
Environmental psychology
Educational psychology
Consumer psychology
Law and psychology
Sports psychology
Applications:
Communication at work
Exploration:
Space psychology

CHAPTER PREVIEW

Bird Brains

Imagine yourself lost at sea in a tiny rubber raft, the victim of a boating accident. After 10 hours adrift, you begin to lose all hope of being found. Then, seemingly out of nowhere, a Coast Guard helicopter swoops in and lifts you from the waves. Gratefully, you thank your rescuers. But with a laugh, they insist the real credit belongs to three "bird brains."

Sound far-fetched? In preliminary tests, pigeons—who are sharp-eyed and nearly immune to boredom—have been taught to aid search-and-rescue crews. The pigeons are first conditioned in Skinner boxes to peck images of red or yellow rafts, life vests, and life preservers. During rescues, they ride in a chamber under a helicopter, where their pecking is monitored electronically. A buzzer in the cockpit, activated by the pecking, guides pilots to the target (Japenga, 1982; Stark, 1981).

***Applied psychology** refers to the use of psychological principles and research methods to solve practical problems, such as finding victims lost at sea. Increasingly, psychology is being used to enhance the quality of life and improve human performance. And, as we will soon see, the ocean is not the only place where applied psychology can make a life-or-death difference.*

The Towering Inferno *All too often, fires in high-rise buildings lead to needless deaths. Using the elevators, for instance, can be fatal. During a fire, they act as chimneys for smoke and poisonous fumes (Keating & Loftus, 1981).*

Question: How can psychology improve the odds for survival?

In the confusion following a fire alarm, many people ignore posted instructions for safe escape. To remedy the situation, psychologists Jack Keating and Elizabeth Loftus created an unusual, life-saving "fire alarm." The best alarm, they found, is a voice *that tells people exactly what to do. After much research, they designed the following message to be broadcast during fires.*

> Female voice: "*May I have your attention, please. May I have your attention, please.*"
> Male voice: "*There has been a fire reported on the 20th floor. While this report is being verified, the building manager would like you to proceed to the stairways and walk down to the 18th floor. Please do not use the elevators, as they may be needed. Please do not use the elevators, but proceed to the stairways.*" *(Loftus, 1979)*

As simple as this message seems, it contains certain key elements: (1) Research has shown that switching from a female to a male voice (or the reverse) is very attention-getting; *(2) during emergencies, people like to feel that some* authority *is in control (the "building manager" in this case); (3) the crucial reminder to avoid the elevators is* repeated, so *it will be remembered.*

Sea rescues and escaping from fires may be dramatic examples of applying psychology, but they are far from unusual. In fields as diverse as industry, sports, law, and medicine, psychology is being applied to our lives. Let's see how.

Survey Questions

- What are the major areas of applied psychology?
- How is psychology applied in business, engineering, and industry?
- What have psychologists learned about the effects of our physical and social environments?
- How does psychology apply to education, consumer behavior, law, and sports?
- What can be done to improve communication in work settings?
- How is psychology being applied in space missions?

Introduction to Applied Psychology

Question: What are the major areas of applied psychology?

The largest areas are clinical and counseling psychology (see Chapter 1). A closely related specialty is **community psychology.** Instead of focusing on individuals (as clinical and counseling psychologists do), community psychologists treat whole neighborhoods or communities as their "clients" (Conyne & Clack, 1981). (Community psychologists have BIG offices!) Typically, community psychologists emphasize prevention, education, and consultation to promote community mental health. Often, they target drug abuse, child neglect, unemployment, prejudice, and similar problems for solution. Such efforts help prevent mental health problems before they begin (Grubb, 1988).

Beyond the clinical areas in psychology, the list of applications grows large. In this chapter we will cover the psychology of work, environmental behavior, education, consumer behavior, law, and sports. To begin, let's see how psychology is applied in business and industry.

Applied psychology The use of psychological principles and research methods to solve practical problems.

Community psychology Use of community resources to promote mental health and treat or prevent mental health problems.

Industrial/Organizational Psychology—Psychology at Work

Do you consider work a blessing? Or a curse? Or do you simply agree that it is "better to wear out than to rust out"? Whatever your attitude, the simple fact is

Table 22–1 Topics of Special Interest to Industrial/Organizational Psychologists

Absenteeism	Pay schedules
Decision making	Personnel selection
Design of organizations	Personnel training
Employee stress	Productivity
Employee turnover	Promotion
Interviewing	Task analysis
Job enrichment	Task design
Job satisfaction	Work behavior
Labor relations	Work environment
Machine design	Worker evaluations
Management styles	Work motivation
Minority workers	

Industrial/organizational psychology A field that focuses on the psychology of work and on behavior within organizations.

Flexitime A work schedule that allows flexible starting and quitting times.

Engineering psychology (human factors engineering) A specialty concerned with the design of machines and work environments so that they are compatible with human perceptual and physical capacities.

Display Any dial, screen, light, or other device used to provide information about a machine's activity to a human operator.

Control Any knob, handle, button, lever, or other device used to alter the activity of a machine.

Natural design Human factors engineering that makes use of perceptual signals that are understood by people without any need to learn them.

Feedback Information on the effects a response has had that is returned to the person performing the response.

that most adults work for a living. From the 1920s until the present, **industrial/organizational psychologists** have studied the problems people face at work. Very likely, their efforts will affect how you are selected for a job and tested, trained, or evaluated for promotions. A psychologist may even help design the machines you use at work, or the work environment itself.

Industrial/organizational psychologists are employed mostly by government, industry, and businesses. Typically, they work in three major areas. These are (1) testing and placement (personnel psychology), (2) human relations at work, and (3) industrial engineering (the design of machines and work environments) (Landy & Trumbo, 1985). To get a fuller flavor of what I-O psychologists do, look at Table 22–1. As you can see, their interests are quite varied. As a further illustration, Highlight 22–1 gives an interesting sample of I-O research.

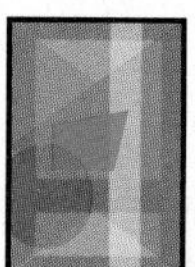

HIGHLIGHT 22–1

Using Psychology

Flexitime

If you've ever worked "9 to 5" you know that traditional time schedules can be confining. They also doom many workers to a daily battle with rush-hour traffic. To improve worker morale, industrial psychologists sometimes recommend the use of flexible working hours, or **flexitime.** The basic idea of flexitime is that starting and quitting times are flexible, as long as employees are present during a core work period (Owen, 1976). For example, employees might be allowed to arrive between 7:30 A.M. and 10:30 A.M. and to depart between 3:30 P.M. and 6:30 P.M.

Is flexitime really an improvement? Studies of two groups of clerical workers suggest that in many cases it is. After a switch to flexitime, a number of benefits were observed, including more job satisfaction, better work-group relations, better relations with supervisors, and less absenteeism (Narayan & Nath, 1982; Orpen, 1981). Perhaps it is better, when possible, to bend hours instead of people.

Question: You mentioned that industrial psychologists sometimes help design machines. What does a "shrink for machines" do?!

Engineering Psychology

However helpful a machine may be in theory, it is of little value until it can be operated by humans. A pocket calculator that is difficult to handle might just as well be a paperweight. An automobile design that blocks large areas of the driver's vision could be deadly. To adapt machines for human use, the **engineering psychologist** (or **human factors engineer**) must make them *compatible* with our sensory and motor capacities (Neff, 1985; Wickens & Kramer, 1985). For example, **displays** must be easy to perceive, **controls** must be easy to use, and the tendency to make errors must be minimized (Fig. 22–1). Many of the machines we rely on each day were designed, in part, by human factors engineers. Some familiar examples include push-button telephones, "user-friendly" computers, home appliances, cameras, airplane controls, and traffic signals. More elaborate machines, such as the United States space shuttle, stretch human capacities to their limits—and require *extensive* human factors engineering.

Donald Norman (1988) refers to effective human factors engineering as **natural design.** Effective design makes use of signals that are naturally understood by people without any need to learn them. An example of natural design is the row of vertical buttons in elevators. The pattern of the buttons mimics the layout of the floors. This is simple, natural, and clear. In contrast, Norman tells about a friend who became trapped for a few moments by a double set of glass doors at the front of a public building. None of the doors had visible handles or hinges, and the poor man tried repeatedly to push on the wrong (hinged) side of the doors. An effective natural design would have included a visible plate, handle, or hinge to signal where to push.

Another major point that Norman emphasizes will be familiar to you from Chapter 7. Effective design provides clear **feedback.** That is, in good design each control produces an immediate and obvious effect.

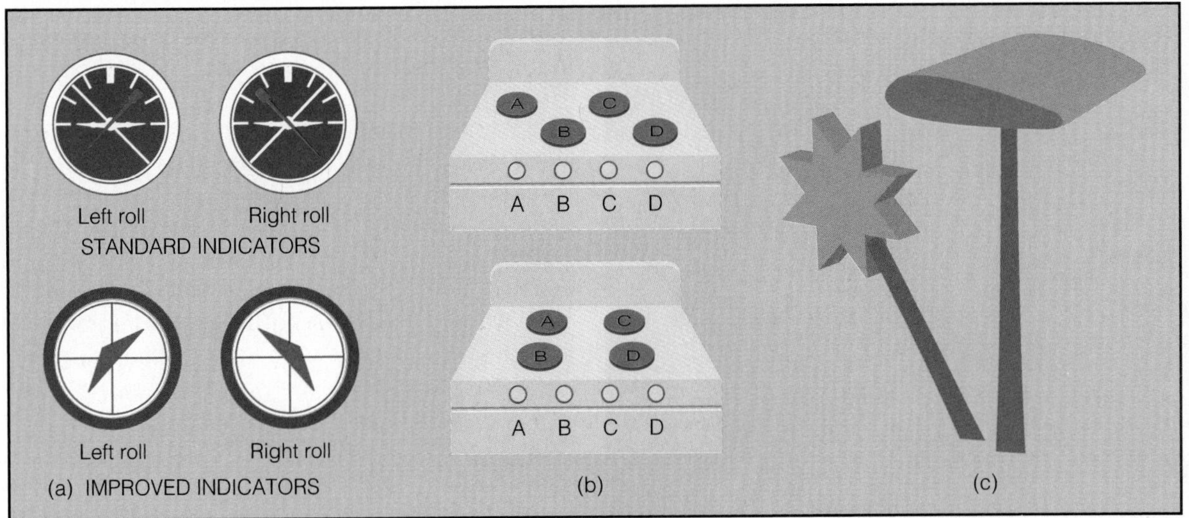

■ **Fig. 22–1** *Human factors engineering.* (a) *Early roll indicators in airplanes were perceptually confusing and difficult to read (top). Improved displays are clear even to non-pilots. Which would you prefer if you were flying an airplane in heavy fog?* (b) *Even on a stove, the placement of controls is important. During simulated emergencies, subjects made no errors in reaching for the controls on the top stove. In contrast, they erred 38 percent of the time with the bottom arrangement (Chapanis & Lindenbaum, 1959).* (c) *Sometimes the shape of a control is used to indicate its function, so as to discourage errors. For example, the left control might be used to engage and disengage the gears of an industrial machine, whereas the right control might operate the landing flaps on an airplane. (The shapes are exaggerated here.)*

The audible click designed into many computer keyboards is a good example. As Norman points out, the "human error" cited as the cause of many accidents and disasters often misses the real culprit: poor design.

Personnel Psychology

The mark of maturity, Sigmund Freud said, is a capacity for love and work. While most people gladly embrace love, many would just as soon forget work. Yet the fact is, employed adults spend an average of over 2000 hours a year at their jobs. With so much time at stake, understanding the world of work is clearly a "survival skill."

At present, the odds are 9 out of 10 that you are, or will be, employed in business or industry. Thus, nearly everyone who holds a job is sooner or later placed under the "psychological microscope" of personnel selection. Clearly, there is value in knowing how selection for hiring and promotion is done.

Question: How do personnel psychologists make employee selections?

Job Analysis Personnel selection begins with a **job analysis** to find out exactly what workers do and what skills or knowledge they need to succeed in a job (Landy, Shankster, & Kohler, 1994). A job analysis may be done by interviewing expert workers or supervisors, by giving them questionnaires, by directly observing work, or by identifying **critical incidents.** Critical incidents are situations that an employee *must* be able to cope with if he or she is going to succeed in a particular job. The ability to deal calmly with a mechanical emergency, for example, is a critical incident for an airline pilot. Once job requirements are known, psychologists can state what skills, aptitudes, and interests are needed (■ Fig. 22–2).

Selection Procedures After desirable skills and traits are identified, the next step is to learn which job applicants have them. Today, the methods most often used for evaluating job candidates include collecting *biodata,* conducting *interviews,* giving *standardized psychological tests,* and the *assessment center* approach. Let's see what each entails.

As simple as it may seem, one good way to predict job success is to collect **biodata** (detailed biographical information) from applicants. The idea behind biodata is that past behavior is a good predictor of future behavior. By learning in detail about a person's life, it is often possible to say whether the person is suited for a particular type of work. Some of the most useful items of biodata include past athletic interests, academic achievements, scientific interests, extracurricular activities, religious activities, social popularity, friction with brothers and sisters, attitudes toward school, and parents' socioeconomic status (Eberhardt & Muchinsky, 1982). Such facts tell quite a lot about personality, interests, and abilities. In addition to earlier experiences, a person's recent life activities also help predict job success (Schmidt, Ones, & Hunter, 1992).

The traditional **personal interview** is still one of the most popular ways to select people for jobs or pro-

Personnel psychology Branch of industrial/organizational psychology concerned with testing, selection, placement, and promotion of employees.

Job analysis A detailed description of the skills, knowledge, and activities required by a particular job.

Critical incidents Situations that arise in a job, with which a competent worker must be able to cope.

Biodata Detailed biographical information about a job applicant.

Personal interview Formal or informal questioning of job applicants to learn their qualifications and to gain an impression of their personalities.

■ **Fig. 22–2** *Analyzing complex skills has also been valuable to the U.S. Air Force. When million-dollar aircraft and the lives of pilots are at stake, it makes good sense to do as much training and research as possible on the ground. Air force psychologists use flight simulators like the one pictured here to analyze the complex skills needed to fly jet fighters. Skills can then be taught without risk on the ground. The General Electric simulator shown here uses a computer to generate full-color images that respond realistically to a pilot's use of the controls. (Photograph supplied courtesy of General Electric Company.)*

Halo effect The tendency of an interviewer to extend a favorable or unfavorable impression to unrelated aspects of an individual's personality.

Vocational interest test A paper-and-pencil test that assesses a person's interests and matches them to interests found among successful workers in various occupations.

Aptitude test A test that rates a person's potential to learn skills required by various occupations.

motions (Schmitt & Robertson, 1990). However, as we discussed in Chapter 15, interviews are subject to the *halo effect* and similar problems. That's why psychologists continue to study factors that affect interviews, with an eye on improving their value (see Highlight 22–2) (Harris, 1989). Even with their limitations, interviews are a valid and effective way of predicting how people will perform on the job (Landy, Shankster, & Kohler, 1994).

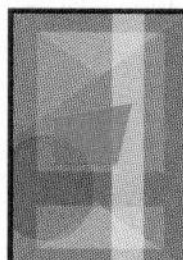

HIGHLIGHT 22–2

A Closer Look At

The Sweet Smell of Success? Not Always.

Each year, clothing and cosmetics manufacturers spend huge sums to convince us that their products make us more attractive. Actually, such claims are somewhat justified. You might recall from Chapter 15, for instance, that physically attractive people are often given more positive evaluations in interviews—even on traits that have no connection with appearance. Presumably, this might also apply to the effects of wearing a pleasant perfume or cologne. But does it? In an interesting study, *female* interviewers did, in fact, give higher ratings to job applicants who wore pleasant scents. But *males*, in contrast, gave *lower* ratings to persons who wore perfume or cologne (Baron, 1983).

Psychologist Robert Baron, who did this experiment, speculates that the male interviewers were more aware of the scents and resented the implied attempt to influence their ratings. Whatever the case, one thing is clear: If possible, you should learn an interviewer's sex beforehand—if you want to avoid making a flagrant, fragrant error, that is. In general, a direct effort to make a good impression—such as emphasizing your positive traits and past successes—is most effective (Gilmore & Ferris, 1989).

Question: What kinds of tests do personnel psychologists use?

In addition to general intelligence and personality tests (described in Chapters 14 and 15), personnel psychologists often use **vocational interest tests.** Tests such as the *Kuder Occupational Interest Survey* and the *Strong-Campbell Interest Inventory* probe interests with items like the following:

I would prefer to
a. visit a museum
b. read a good book
c. take a walk outdoors

Interest inventories typically reflect the six major themes shown in ⬬ Table 22–2. If you take an interest test and your choices match those of people who are successful in a given occupation, it is assumed that you, too, would be comfortable doing the work they do.

Aptitude tests are another mainstay of personnel psychology. Such tests rate a person's potential to learn tasks or skills used in various occupations. Tests exist for clerical, verbal, mechanical, artistic, legal, and medical aptitudes, plus many others. For example, tests of clerical aptitude emphasize the capacity to do

⬬ **Table 22–2 Vocational Interest Themes**

Theme	Sample College Major	Sample Occupation
Realistic	Agriculture	Mechanic
Investigative	Physics	Chemist
Artistic	Music	Writer
Social	Education	Counselor
Enterprising	Business	Sales
Conventional	Economics	Clerk

(Holland, 1985; Snow, 1986.)

rapid, precise, and accurate office work. One section of a clerical aptitude test might therefore ask a person to mark all identical numbers and names in a long list of pairs like those shown here. (Also see ■ Fig. 22–3.)

49837266	49832766
Global Widgets, Inc.	Global Wigets, Inc.
874583725	874583725
Sevanden Corp.	Sevanden Corp.
Perlee Publishing	Perlee Puhlishing

Paper-and-pencil tests sometimes seem far removed from the day-to-day challenges of work. In recent years, psychologists have tried to make employment testing more interesting and relevant. For example, Patricia Dyer and other psychologists are developing **multi-media computerized tests.** These tests use computers to present realistic work situations—in living color and stereo sound. As potential employees watch typical work scenes unfold, the action freezes on various problems. The applicant is then asked what he or she would do in that situation. In addition to screening job applicants, multi-media presentations can be used to improve the job skills of current employees. It won't be long before multi-media tests are widely used (DeAngelis, 1994).

After college, chances are good that you will encounter the **assessment center** approach to personnel selection (Landy, Shankster, & Kohler, 1994). Assessment centers are set up by many large organizations to do in-depth evaluations of job candidates. This approach has become so popular that the list of businesses using it—Ford, IBM, Kodak, Exxon, Sears, Bell Telephone, and thousands of others—reads like a corporate *Who's Who.*

Question: How do assessment centers differ from the selection methods already described?

Assessment centers are primarily used to fill management and executive positions. Applicants are first tested and interviewed at an assessment center. Then they are observed and evaluated in simulated work situations. For example, in one exercise, applicants are given an **in-basket test.** This test consists of a basket full of memos, requests, and problems typical of those faced by executives. Each applicant is asked to quickly read all of the materials and to take appropriate action. In another, more stressful test, applicants take part in a **leaderless group discussion** in which they try to solve a realistic business problem. While the group grapples with the problem, "clerks" bring in price changes, notices about delayed supplies, and so forth. By observing applicants, it is possible to evaluate leadership skills and to see how job candidates cope with stress.

Question: How well does this approach work?

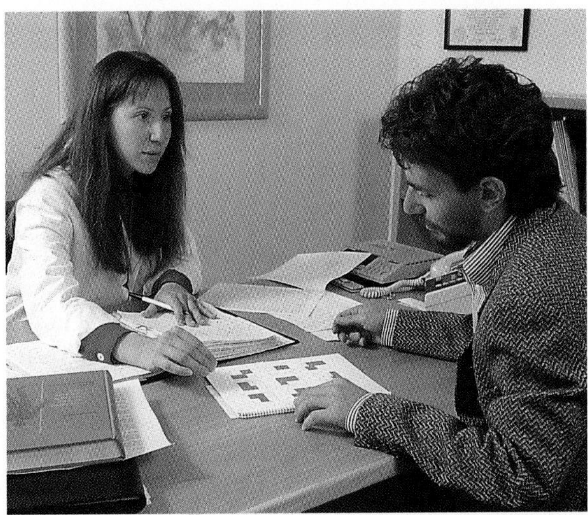

■ **Fig. 22–3** *Aptitude tests are used to select job candidates and to advise people about what types of work they are likely to be good at.*

Assessment centers have had considerable success in predicting performance in a variety of jobs, careers, and advanced positions (Borman et al., 1983; Landy, Shankster, & Kohler, 1994). One study of women, for instance, found that assessment center predictions of management potential were closely related to career progress 7 years later (Ritchie & Moses, 1983). On the basis of long-range studies, it appears that future success is most clearly predicted by oral communication skills, leadership, energy, resistance to stress, tolerance for uncertainty, need for advancement, and planning skills (Ritchie & Moses, 1983).

As you will soon learn, psychologists working in business do far more than match people with jobs. Let's see how they contribute to management and the quality of work.

Multi-media computerized test A test that uses a computer to present life-like situations; test takers react to problems posed by the situations.

Assessment center A program set up within an organization to conduct in-depth evaluations of job candidates.

In-basket test A testing procedure that simulates the individual decision-making challenges that executives face.

Leaderless group discussion A test of leadership that simulates group decision making and problem solving.

Scientific management (Theory X) An approach to managing employees that emphasizes work efficiency.

Theories of Management and Job Satisfaction

At 7 A.M. each morning at a major manufacturing plant, more than 400 assembly line workers, supervisors, and top executives begin their work day talking, joking, and exercising together, all to the beat of amplified music. To say the least, these are unusual working conditions. To understand the rationale behind them, let's consider two basic theories of employee management.

Theory X and Theory Y One of the earliest attempts to improve worker efficiency was made in 1923 by Frederick Taylor, an engineer. To speed up production, Taylor standardized work routines and stressed careful planning, control, and orderliness. Today, modern versions of Taylor's approach are called **scientific management** (also known as **Theory X,** for reasons explained shortly). Scientific management uses time-and-motion studies, task analysis, job specialization, assembly lines, pay schedules, and the like, to increase productivity.

Question: It sounds like scientific management treats people as if they were machines. Is that true?

To some extent it is. Managers who follow Theory X tend to assume that workers must be goaded or guided into being productive. Many psychologists working in business, of course, are concerned with improving **work efficiency** (defined as maximum output at lowest cost). As a result, they alter conditions they believe will affect workers (such as time schedules, work quotas, bonuses, and so on). Some might even occasionally wish that people would act like well-oiled machines. However, most recognize that **psychological efficiency** is just as important as work efficiency. In addition to achieving high productivity, businesses that prosper must be able to retain workers, minimize absenteeism, sustain good morale and labor relations, and so forth. Management that ignores or mishandles the human element can be devastatingly costly.

The term *Theory* X was coined by psychologist Douglas McGregor (1960) as a way to distinguish scientific management from a newer management style. McGregor dubbed this newer approach, which emphasizes human relations at work, **Theory Y.**

Question: How is this approach different?

Theory Y managers assume that workers enjoy autonomy and are willing to accept responsibility. They also assume that worker needs and goals can be meshed with the company's goals, and that people are not naturally passive or lazy. In short, Theory Y assumes that people are industrious, creative, and rewarded by challenging work. It appears that given the proper conditions of freedom and responsibility, many people *will* work hard to gain competence and use their talents fully.

Many features of Theory Y are illustrated by the Honda plant at Marysville, Ohio. As you may already know, the automobile industry has a long history of labor-management clashes and worker discontent. In fact, outright sabotage by assembly line workers is not uncommon. To avoid such problems, Honda initiated a series of simple, seemingly successful measures. They include the following practices.

- Regardless of their position, all employees wear identical white uniforms. This allows workers and supervisors to interact on a more equal footing and builds feelings of teamwork.
- To further minimize status differences, all employees hold the title *associate.*
- Private offices, separate dining halls, and reserved parking spaces for executives were abolished.
- Employees work alongside company executives, to whom they have easy access.
- Every employee has a say in, and responsibility for, quality control and safety.
- Departmental meetings are held daily. At this time, announcements are discussed, decisions are made, and thoughts are freely shared (Abrams, 1983).

Two elements that make Theory Y methods effective are *participative management* and *management by objectives.* In **participative management,** employees at all levels are directly involved in decision making (■ Fig. 22–4). By taking part in decisions that affect them, employees like those at the Honda factory come to see work as a cooperative effort—not as something imposed on them by an egotistical boss. The benefits include greater productivity, greater job satisfaction, and less job-related stress (Jackson, 1983).

■ **Fig. 22–4** *Participative mahagement techniques encourage employees at all levels to become involved in decision making. Quite often this arrangement leads to greater job satisfaction.*

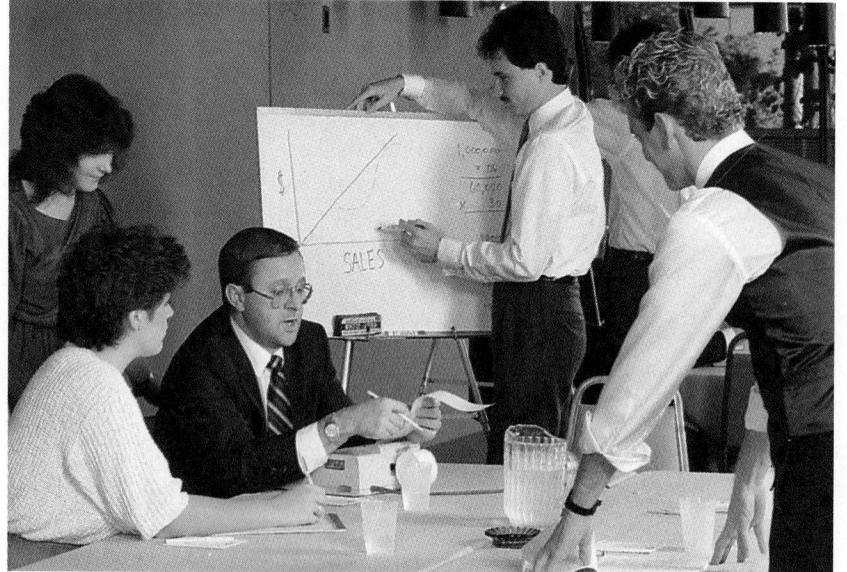

Work efficiency Maximum output (productivity) at lowest cost.

Psychological efficiency Maintenance of good morale, labor relations, employee satisfaction, and similar aspects of work behavior.

Theory Y A management style that emphasizes human relations at work and that views people as industrious, responsible, and interested in challenging work.

Participative management An approach to management that allows employees at all levels to participate in decision making.

Question: What does "management by objectives" refer to?

In **management by objectives,** workers are given specific goals to meet, so they can tell if they are doing a good job. Typical objectives include reaching a certain sales total, making a certain number of items, or reducing waste by a specific percentage. In any case, workers are free to choose (within limits) how they will achieve their goals. As a result, they feel a greater sense of independence and personal responsibility for their work.

How can workers below the management level be involved more in their work? One popular answer is by the creation of **quality circles.** These are voluntary discussion groups that meet regularly, with or without supervision. Members of quality circles try to find ways to solve business problems or to improve efficiency (Jewell, 1990). Usually such groups do not have the power to put their suggestions into practice directly. But good ideas speak for themselves and many are adopted by management. Quality circles have many limitations. Nevertheless, studies verify that greater involvement can lead to better performance and job satisfaction (Buch & Spangler, 1990; Marks, 1986).

Job Satisfaction It often makes perfect sense to apply Theory X methods to work. However, doing so without taking worker needs into account can be a case of winning the battle while losing the war. That is, immediate productivity may be enhanced while job satisfaction is lowered. And when job satisfaction is low, absenteeism skyrockets, morale falls, and there is a high rate of employee turnover (leading to higher training costs and inefficiency). Understandably, many of the methods used by enlightened Theory Y managers ultimately improve **job satisfaction.**

Question: Under what conditions is job satisfaction highest?

Basically, job satisfaction comes from a good fit between work and a person's interests, abilities, needs, and expectations. What, then, do workers consider important? In the early 1970s, American workers were asked to rate the importance of 25 aspects of work. Their first 8 choices were as follows (*Work in America*, 1973):

1. Interesting work
2. Enough help and equipment to get the job done
3. Enough information to get the job done
4. Enough authority to get the job done
5. Good pay
6. Opportunity to develop special abilities
7. Job security
8. Seeing the results of one's work

A second survey in the early 1980s again found that satisfying, rewarding work ranked first in worker preference. However, high income rose to second place (Weaver & Mathews, 1987). Some observers worry that a swing toward greater materialism has occurred in the last 10 to 15 years. Even if this is true, intrinsically interesting work still tops the list. To summarize much research, we can say that job satisfaction is highest when workers are (1) allowed ordinary social contacts with others; (2) given opportunities to use their own judgment and intelligence; (3) recognized for doing well; (4) given a chance to apply their skills; (5) given relative freedom from close supervision; and (6) given opportunities for promotion and advancement.

Job Enrichment For years, the trend in business and industry was to make work more streamlined and efficient and to tie better pay to better work. There is now ample evidence that incentives such as bonuses, earned time off, and profit sharing can increase productivity (Horn, 1987). However, in recent years far too many jobs have become routine, repetitive, boring, and unfulfilling. To combat the discontent this can breed, many psychologists recommend a strategy called **job enrichment.** Job enrichment has been used with great success by large corporations such as IBM, Maytag, Western Electric, Chrysler, and Polaroid. It usually leads to lower production costs, increased job satisfaction, reduced boredom, and less absenteeism.

Question: How is job enrichment done?

Job enrichment applies many of the principles we have discussed. Usually it involves removing some of the controls and restrictions on employees, giving them greater freedom, choice, and authority. In some cases, employees also switch to doing a complete cycle of work. That is, they complete an entire item or project, instead of doing an isolated part of a larger process. Whenever possible, workers are given feedback about their work or progress. This feedback comes to them directly, instead of to a supervisor.

Merely assigning a person more tasks is usually not enriching. Overloaded workers just feel stressed and they tend to make more errors. True job enrichment increases workers' *knowledge.* That is, workers are encouraged to learn a broad range of skills and information related to their occupations (Campion & McClelland, 1993). In short, most people seem to enjoy being good at what they do.

Although we have only scratched the surface of industrial/organizational psychology, it is time to move on for a look at another applied area of great personal relevance. Before we begin, here's a Learning Check on the preceding discussion.

Management by objectives A management technique in which employees are given specific goals to meet in their work.

Quality circle A discussion group in which employees voluntarily seek to solve business problems.

Job satisfaction The degree to which a person is comfortable with or satisfied with his or her work.

Job enrichment Making a job more personally rewarding, interesting, or intrinsically motivating; typically involves increasing worker knowledge.

Learning Check

1. To gain attention for an emergency announcement, it is better to switch from a male voice to a female voice than it is to do the reverse. T or F?
2. An important element of engineering psychology is making ________ and ________ compatible with human use. This is often best accomplished through ________ design.
3. Identifying critical work incidents is sometimes included in a thorough ________ ________.
4. Detailed biographical information about a job applicant is referred to as ________.
5. The Strong-Campbell Inventory is a typical aptitude test. T or F?
6. A leaderless group discussion is most closely associated with which approach to employee selection?
   a. aptitude testing *b.* personal interviews *c.* job analysis *d.* assessment center
7. Theory X, or scientific management, is concerned primarily with improving ________ ________.
8. Participative management is often a feature of businesses that adhere to Theory Y. T or F?
9. For the majority of workers, job satisfaction is almost exclusively related to the amount of pay received. T or F?
10. Job enrichment is a direct expression of scientific management principles. T or F?

Critical Thinking

11. Job enrichment basically increases what type of motivation?

Answers:
1. F 2. displays, controls, natural 3. job analysis 4. biodata 5. F 6. *d* 7. work efficiency 8. T 9. F 10. F
11. Intrinsic motivation.

Environmental psychology The formal study of how environments affect behavior.

Physical environments Natural settings, such as forests and beaches, as well as environments built by humans, such as buildings, ships, cities.

Social environment An environment defined by a group of people and their activities or interrelationships (such as a parade, revival meeting, or sports event).

Behavioral setting A smaller area within an environment whose use is well defined, such as a bus depot, waiting room, or lounge.

Environmental Psychology—Life in the Big City

If cities were drivers, some would get lots of speeding tickets. Others would spend most of their time in the slow lane, watching the scenery go by. Informally, you may have noticed that the pace of life varies from city to city. Psychologist Robert Levine and his students decided to measure the overall tempo of 36 American cities to see how they compare.

To rate a city's pace, Levine looked at four indicators: walking speed, working speed, talking speed, and the percentage of men and women wearing watches. The results? The three fastest cities were Boston, Buffalo, and New York—all in the Northeast. The three slowest cities were in the South and West: Shreveport, Sacramento, and Los Angeles. No surprises here. But Levine's other findings are surprising. Levine and his team also found that there is a correlation between the pace of life and heart disease. Just as there are Type A personalities (heart attack-prone personalities, see Chapter 11), there also seem to be Type A cities. Very likely, Type A people are attracted to fast-paced Type A cities—where they then do their best to keep the pace (Levine, 1990).

The work of Robert Levine, and psychologists like him, falls into an area known as **environmental psychology,** a specialty concerned with how environments influence our behavior. Environmental psychologists are interested in both **physical environments** (natural or constructed) and **social environments** (such as a dance, business meeting, or party) (Gifford, 1987). They also give special attention to **behavioral settings** (for example, an office, locker room, church, casino, or classroom) (Schoggen, 1989). As you have no doubt noticed, various environments and behavioral settings tend to "demand" certain actions (■ Fig. 22–5). Consider, for example, the difference between a library and a campus center lounge. In which would a conversation be more likely to occur?

Other major interests of environmental psychologists are personal space, territorial behavior (see Highlight 22–3), stressful environments, architectural design, environmental protection, and many related topics (● Table 22–3).

● **Table 22–3 Topics of Special Interest to Environmental Psychologists**

Architectural design	Noise
Behavioral settings	Personal space
Cognitive maps	Personality and environment
Constructed environments	Pollution
Crowding	Privacy
Energy conservation	Proxemics
Environmental stressors	Resource management
Heat	Territoriality
Human ecology	Urban planning
Littering	Vandalism
Natural environment	

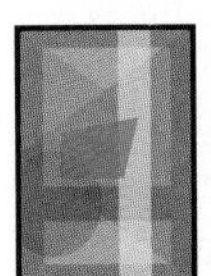

HIGHLIGHT 22–3

A Closer Look At

Territoriality

In Chapter 20 we noted that powerful norms govern the use of the space immediately surrounding each person's body. As we move farther from the body, it becomes apparent that personal space also extends to adjacent areas that we claim as our "territory." For example, in the library, **territorial behavior** might include protecting your space with a coat, handbag, book, or other personal belonging. "Saving a place" at a theater or a beach also demonstrates the tendency to identify a space as "ours."

Respect for the temporary ownership of space is widespread. It is not unusual for a person to "take over" an entire table or study room by looking annoyed when others intrude. Your own personal territory may include your room, specific seats in many of your classes, or a particular table in the cafeteria or library that "belongs" to you and your friends.

Researchers have found that the more attached you are to an area, the more likely you are to signal your "ownership" with obvious **territorial markers,** such as decorations, plants, photographs, posters, or even graffiti. College dorms and business offices are prime places to observe this type of territorial marking. Interestingly, burglars are less likely to break into houses that have lots of obvious territorial cues, such as fences (even if small), parked cars, lawn furniture, exterior lights, and security signs (Brown & Bentley, 1993). (A highly territorial bulldog may help, too.)

■ **Fig. 22–5** *Various behavioral settings place strong demands on people to act in expected ways.*

Environmental Influences A major finding of environmental research is that much of our behavior is controlled, in part, by specific types of environments (Gifford, 1987). For example, many shopping malls and department stores are designed like mazes. Their twisting pathways encourage shoppers to linger and wander while looking at merchandise. Likewise, many college classrooms clearly define a speaker-audience relationship. Discussion among students tends to be discouraged by seats that are bolted to the floor, facing an authority at the front of the room (Wong, Somer, & Cook, 1992). Even public bathrooms influence behavior. Since the seating is limited, few people hold meetings there!

Psychologists have also found that a variety of environmental factors influence the amount of vandalism that occurs in public places. On the basis of psychological research, many architects now "harden" and "de-opportunize" public settings to discourage vandalism and graffiti (Wise, 1982). Some such efforts limit opportunities for vandalism (doorless toilet stalls, tiled walls). Others weaken the lure of likely targets. (Strangely enough, a raised flower bed around signs helps protect them because people resist trampling the flowers to get to the sign.)

Given the personal impact that environments have, it is important to know how we are affected by stressful or unhealthy environments—a topic we will consider next.

Territorial behavior Any behavior that tends to define a space as one's own or that protects it from intruders.

Territorial markers Objects and other signals whose placement indicates to others the "ownership" or control of a particular area.

Density The number of people in a given space or, inversely, the amount of space available to each person.

Crowding A subjective feeling of being overstimulated by a loss of privacy or by the nearness of others (especially when social contact with them is unavoidable).

Stressful Environments

Everyone has his or her own list of complaints about large cities. Traffic congestion, pollution, crime, and impersonality are urban problems that immediately come to mind. To this list psychologists have added crowding, noise, and over-stimulation as major sources of urban stress. Recent psychological research has begun to clarify the impact of each of these conditions on human functioning.

Crowding Over-population ranks as one of the most serious problems facing the world today. The world's population is now over 5.5 billion. World population doubled in the period from 1950 to 1987. It will double again in the next 39 years (Erlich & Erlich, 1990) (■ Fig. 22–6). Each day, the world population grows by 250,000 (a quarter of a million) people (United Nations Population Fund, 1993).

Nowhere are the effects of over-population more evident than in the teeming cities of many underdeveloped nations. Closer to home, the jammed buses, subways, and living quarters of our own large cities are ample testimony to the stresses of crowding.

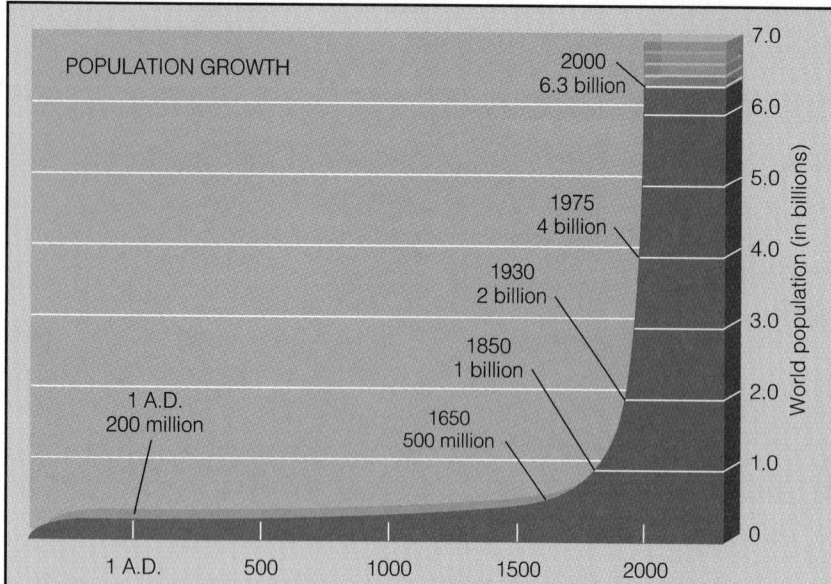

■ **Fig. 22–6** *Population growth has slowed slightly in recent years, but world population still threatens to double again in less than 40 years (graph source: Population Institute). Over-population and rapid population growth are closely connected with environmental damage, international tensions, and rapid depletion of non-renewable resources. Some demographers predict that if population growth is not limited voluntarily before it reaches 10 billion, it will be limited by widespread food shortages, disease, infant mortality, and early death (Erlich & Erlich, 1990).*

Question: Is there any way to assess the effect crowding has on people?

One approach is to study the effects of overcrowding among animals. Although the results of animal experiments cannot be considered conclusive for humans, they point to some disturbing effects.

Question: For example?

In an interesting experiment, John Calhoun (1962) let a group of laboratory rats breed without limit in a confined space. Calhoun provided plenty of food, water, and nesting material for the rats. All that the rats lacked was space. At its peak, the colony numbered 80 rats. Yet, it was housed in a cage designed to comfortably hold about 50. Overcrowding in the cage was heightened by the actions of the two most dominant males. These rascals staked out private territory at opposite ends of the cage, gathered harems of 8 to 10 females, and prospered. Their actions forced the remaining rats into a small, severely crowded middle area.

Question: What effect did crowding have on the animals?

A high rate of pathological behavior developed in both males and females. Females gave up nest building and caring for their young. Pregnancies decreased, and infant mortality ran extremely high. Many of the animals became indiscriminately aggressive and went on rampaging attacks against others. Abnormal sexual behavior was rampant, with some animals displaying hypersexuality and others total sexual passivity. Many of the animals died, apparently from stress-caused diseases. The link between these problems and overcrowding is unmistakable.

Question: But does that apply to humans?

Many of the same pathological behaviors can be observed in crowded inner-city ghettos. It is therefore tempting to assume that violence, social disorganization, and declining birthrates as seen in these areas are directly related to crowding. However, the connection has not been so clearly demonstrated with humans. People living in the inner city suffer disadvantages in nutrition, education, income, and health care. These, more than crowding, may deserve the blame (Freedman, 1975). In fact, most laboratory studies using human subjects have failed to produce any serious ill effects by crowding people into small places. Most likely, this is because *crowding* is a psychological condition that is separate from **density** (the number of people in a given space).

Question: How does crowding differ from density?

Crowding refers to *subjective* feelings of being overstimulated by social inputs or by a loss of privacy. Whether high density is experienced as crowding may depend on relationships among those involved (■ Fig. 22–7). In an elevator, subway, or prison, high densities may be uncomfortable. In contrast, a musical concert, party, or reunion may be most pleasant at high density

■ **Fig. 22–7** *Woodstock '94. High densities do not automatically produce feelings of crowding. The nature of the situation and the relationship between crowd members are also important.*

levels. Thus, physical crowding may interact with situations to intensify existing stresses or pleasures (Schaeffer et al., 1988). When crowding causes a *loss of control* over one's immediate social environment, stress is likely to result (Geen & Bushman, 1989; Lepore, Evans, & Schneider, 1992).

Increased stress probably explains why death rates increase among prison inmates and mental hospital patients who live in crowded conditions. Even milder instances of crowding can have a negative impact. People who live in crowded conditions often become guarded and withdrawn from others (Evans & Lepore, 1993).

Overload One unmistakable result of high densities and crowding is a condition that psychologist Stanley Milgram called **attentional overload.** Large cities tend to bombard residents with continuous sensory stimulation, information, and contact with others. The resulting sensory and cognitive overload can be quite stressful. Highlight 22–4 describes one dimension of this sensory assault.

HIGHLIGHT 22–4

A Closer Look At

The High Cost of Noise

How serious are the effects of daily exposure to noise? A study of children attending schools near Los Angeles International Airport suggests that constant noise can be quite damaging. Children from the noisy schools were compared with similar students attending schools farther from the airport (Cohen et al., 1980). These comparison students were from families of comparable social and economic makeup. Testing showed that children attending the noisy schools had higher blood pressure than those from the quieter schools. They were more likely to give up attempts to solve a difficult puzzle. And they were poorer at proofreading a printed paragraph—a task that requires close attention and concentration.

The greater tendency of the noisy-school children to give up or become distracted is a serious handicap. It may even reveal a state of "learned helplessness" (described in Chapter 11) caused by daily, uncontrollable blasts of sound. Even if such damage proves to be temporary, it is clear that **noise pollution** is a major source of environmental stress.

Milgram (1970) believed that city dwellers learn to prevent attentional overload by engaging only in brief, superficial social contacts, by ignoring non-essential events, and by fending off others with cold and unfriendly expressions. In short, many city dwellers find that a degree of callousness is essential for survival.

Question: Is there any evidence that such strategies are actually adopted?

A fascinating study suggests they are. In several large American cities and smaller nearby towns, a young child stood on a busy street corner and asked passing strangers for help, saying, "I'm lost. Can you call my house?" About 72 percent of those approached in small towns offered to help. Only about 46 percent of those who were asked for help in the cities gave aid. In some cities (Boston and Philadelphia) only about one third were willing to help (Takooshian et al., 1977). A more recent analysis of 65 studies confirmed that country people are more likely to help than city people (Steblay, 1987). Thus, a blunting of sensitivity to the needs of others may be one of the more serious costs of urban stresses and crowding.

Attentional overload A stressful condition caused when sensory stimulation, information, and social contacts make excessive demands on attention.

Noise pollution Stressful and intrusive noise; usually artificially generated by machinery, but also including noises made by animals and humans.

Toxic Environments Human activities drastically change the natural environment. We burn fossil fuels, destroy forests, use chemical products, strip, clear, and farm the land. In doing so, we alter natural cycles, animal populations, and the very face of the earth. The long-range impact of such activities is already becoming evident through global warming, the extinction of plants and animals, a hole in the ozone layer, and polluted land, air, water, and oceans (Stern, 1992) (■ Fig. 22–8).

■ **Fig. 22–8** *As astronomer Carl Sagan once said, "When you look closely, you find so many things going wrong with the environment, you are forced to reassess the hypothesis of intelligent life on earth."*

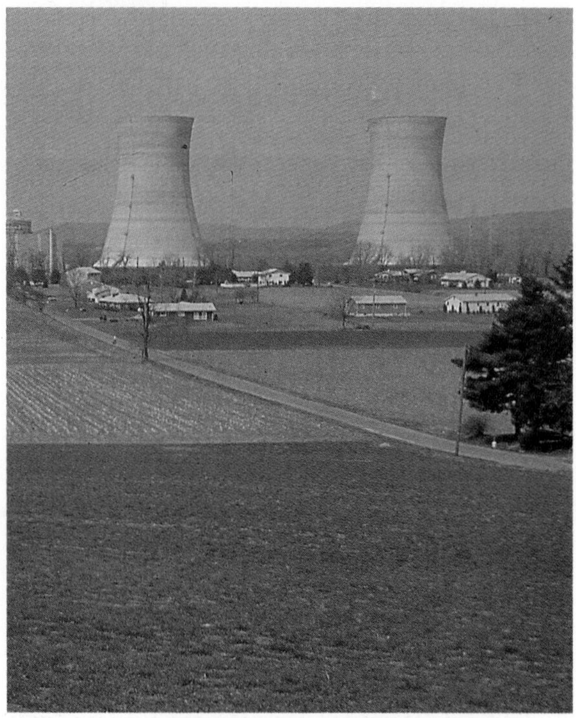

■ **Fig. 22–9** *People tend to have prolonged emotional responses to technological disasters. Long after an accidental release of radioactivity by the Three Mile Island Nuclear Power Plant, nearby residents continued to feel stressed and apprehensive (Baum & Fleming, 1993).*

Environmental assessment Measurement and analysis of the effects an environment has on the behavior of people within that environment.

Cognitive map A mental image of an area (building, city, country) that guides movement from one location to another.

Architectural psychology Study of the effects buildings have on behavior and the design of buildings using behavioral principles.

On a smaller scale there is plenty of evidence that unchecked environmental damage will be costly to our children and descendants. For example, studies show that exposure to toxic hazards, such as radiation, pesticides, and industrial chemicals leads to an elevated risk of physical and mental disease (Baum & Fleming, 1993) (■ Fig. 22–9).

How can people be encouraged to help preserve the environment? Psychological research has shown that it is best to combine several strategies. Persuasion and education can be used to get individuals and businesses to voluntarily reduce activities that damage the environment. Effective appeals may be based on self-interest (cost savings), the collective good (protecting one's own children and future generations), or simply a personal desire to take better care of the planet. Changing the consequences of wasteful energy use, polluting, and the like can also alter behavior. For example, energy taxes can be used to increase the cost of using fossil fuels; rebates can be offered for installing insulation or buying energy-efficient appliances; and tax breaks can be given to companies that take steps to preserve the environment (Dwyer et al., 1993; Kempton, Darley, & Stern, 1992).

Environmental Problem Solving

While overcrowding and pollution rank high on the list of environmental stresses, they are only two of the many challenges that press for attention. To conclude, let's sample some of the solutions that psychologists have provided for environmental problems.

Problem The way people think about the environment greatly affects their behavior. Mental "maps" of various areas, for instance, often guide actions and alter decisions. A case in point is a study done in Philadelphia. There, researchers found that an existing school bus route contributed to truancy. The problem was that many of its stops were at corners where children were afraid of being attacked and beaten (Conyne & Clack, 1981).

Solution By doing an **environmental assessment,** psychologists develop a picture of environments as they are perceived by the people using them. An assessment often includes such things as charting areas of highest use in buildings, using attitude scales to measure reactions to various settings (such as schools, businesses, and parks) and even having people draw a version of their cognitive map of a building, campus, or city (Stokols, 1978).

In the case of the school children, residents of the neighborhood were asked to rate how much stress they felt when walking in various areas. The result was a contour map (somewhat like a high- and low-pressure weather map) that showed the areas of highest perceived stress. This "stress map" was then used to reroute school buses to "low-pressure" areas.

Problem Anyone who has ever lived in a college dorm knows that at times a dorm hall can be quite a "zoo." Most architects aim to create buildings in which people will be comfortable, happy, and healthy. But sometimes they miss the mark with human behavior. In one well-known experiment, Baum and Valins (1977) found that students housed in long, narrow, corridor-design dormitories often feel crowded and stressed. The crowded students tended to withdraw from others and even made more trips to the campus health center than students living in less crowded buildings.

Solution **Architectural psychology** is a specialty of growing importance for designing buildings. By studying the effects of existing buildings, psychologists are often able to suggest design changes that solve or avoid problems. For example, Baum and Valins (1979) studied two basic dorm arrangements. One dorm had a long corridor with one central bathroom. As a result, residents were constantly forced into contact with one another. The other dorm had rooms clustered in threes. Each of these suites shared a small bathroom. Even though the amount of space available to each student was the same in both dorms, students in the

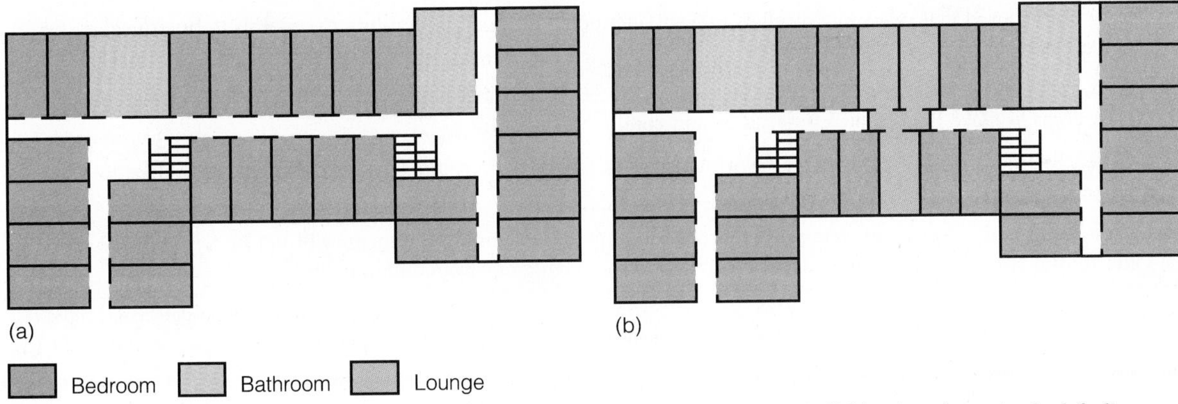

■ **Fig. 22–10** *An architectural solution for crowding. Psychologists divided a dorm hall like that shown in the left diagram (a) into two shorter halls separated by unlocked doors and a lounge area (b). This simple change minimized unwanted social contacts and greatly reduced feelings of crowding among dorm residents. (Adapted from Baum & Davis, 1980.)*

long-corridor dorm reported feeling more crowded. They also made fewer friends in their dorm and showed greater signs of withdrawing from social contact.

Question: What sort of solution does this suggest?

A later study showed that small architectural changes can greatly reduce stress in high-density living conditions. Baum and Davis (1980) compared students living in a long-corridor dorm housing 40 students to those living in an altered long-corridor dorm. In the altered dorm, Baum and Davis divided the hallway in half with unlocked doors and made three center bedrooms into a lounge area (■ Fig. 22–10). At the end of the term, students living in the divided dorm reported less stress from crowding. They also formed more friendships and were more open to social contacts. In comparison, students in the long-corridor dorm felt more crowded, stressed, and unfriendly, and they kept their doors shut much more frequently—presumably because they "vahnted to be alone." Similar improvements have been made by altering the interior design of businesses, schools, apartment buildings, mental hospitals, and prisons.

Problem The rapid worldwide consumption of natural resources is one of the most devastating of all social problems. Industrialized nations, in particular, are consuming world resources at an alarming rate. The United States and Canada, for instance, have a little over 5 percent of the world's population. Yet we consume 25 to 30 percent of all the fossil fuels and raw materials used annually. In the face of projected shortages and squandered resources, what can be done to encourage conservation on a personal level?

Solution Try as you might to reduce your use of energy (electricity, for instance), you would probably find it difficult to do. A major problem is that *feedback* about energy use (the monthly bill) arrives long after the temptation to turn up the heat or to leave lights on (see Chapter 7). Psychologists aware of this problem have shown that lower energy bills result from simply giving families daily feedback about their use of gas or electricity (Seligman & Darley, 1978).

Programs that give monetary rewards for energy conservation are even more effective (Cone & Hayes, 1980.) This is especially true for "master-metered" apartment complexes. In such apartments, families do not receive individual bills for their utilities. Consequently, they have no reason to save gas and electricity. Often, they consume about 25 percent more energy than they would in an individually metered apartment (McClelland & Cook, 1980). At this rate of waste, apartment owners can split any savings (from reduced consumption) with their tenants—and still be ahead.

Conclusion We have had room here only to hint at the creative and highly useful work being done in environmental psychology. While many environmental problems remain, it is encouraging to see that behavioral solutions exist for at least some of them. Surely, creating and maintaining healthy environments is one of the major challenges facing coming generations (Stokols, 1992).

LEARNING CHECK

1. Although male rats in Calhoun's crowded animal colony became quite pathological, female rats continued to behave in a relatively normal fashion. T or F?
2. To clearly understand behavior, it is necessary to make a distinction between crowding and ________ (the number of people in a given space).

3. Milgram believed that many city dwellers prevent attentional overload by limiting themselves to superficial social contacts. T or F?

4. Performing an environmental ____________________ might be a good prelude to redesigning college classrooms to make them more comfortable and conducive to learning.

5. So far, the most successful approach for bringing about energy conservation is to add monetary penalties to monthly bills for excessive consumption. T or F?

Critical Thinking

6. Many of the most damaging changes to the environment being caused by humans will not be felt until sometime in the future. How does this complicate the problem of preserving environmental quality?

Answers: 1. F 2. density 3. T 4. assessment 5. F 6. A delay of consequences (rewards, benefits, costs, and punishers) tends to reduce their impact on immediate behavior.

Educational psychology The field that seeks to understand how people learn and how teachers instruct.

Teaching strategy A plan for effective teaching.

A Panorama of Applied Psychology

We have discussed work and the environment at some length because both have major effects on our lives. To provide a fuller account of the diversity of applied psychology, let's conclude by briefly sampling some additional topics of interest.

Educational Psychology

You have just been asked to teach a class of fourth-graders for a day. What will you do? (Assume that bribery, showing them films, and a field trip to a video arcade are out.) If you ever do try teaching, you might be surprised at how challenging it can be. Effective teachers must understand processes involved in learning, instruction, classroom dynamics, and testing. Fortunately, teachers (and their students) have benefited greatly from the work of educational psychologists (see Highlight 22–5). Specifically, **educational psychology** seeks to understand how people learn and how teachers instruct (Thornburg, 1984) (■ Fig. 22–11).

■ Fig. 22–11 *Educational psychologists are interested in enhancing learning and improving teaching.*

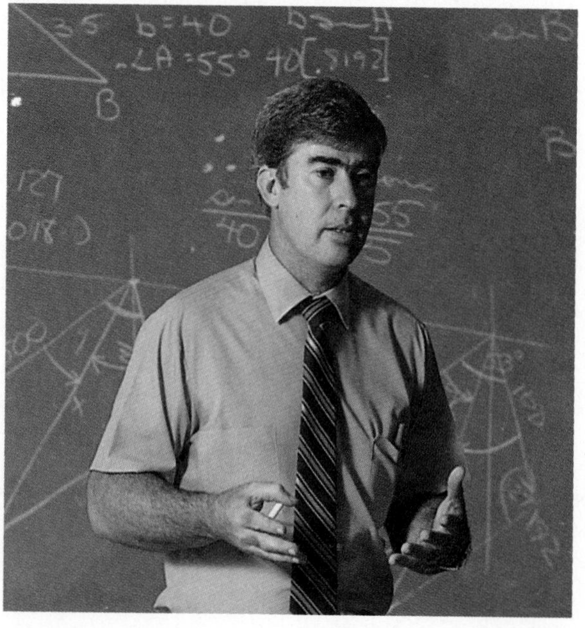

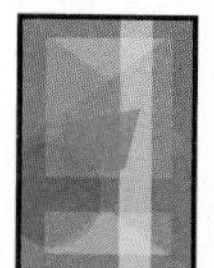

HIGHLIGHT 22–5

Using Psychology

Elements of a Teaching Strategy

Whether it's "breaking in" a new co-worker, instructing a friend in a hobby, or helping a child learn to read, the fact is, we all teach at times. The next time you are asked to share your knowledge, how will you do it? One good way to become more effective is to use a specific **teaching strategy.** The example that follows was designed for classroom use, but it applies to many other situations as well (adapted from Thornburg, 1984).

Step 1: Learner preparation. Begin by gaining the learner's attention, and focus interest on the topic at hand.

Step 2: Stimulus presentation. Present instructional stimuli (information, examples, and illustrations) deliberately and clearly.

Step 3: Learner response. Allow time for the learner to respond to the information presented (by repeating correct responses or asking questions, for example).

Step 4: Reinforcement. Give positive reinforcement (praise, encouragement) and feedback ("Yes, that's right," "No, this way," and so on) to strengthen correct responses.

Step 5: Evaluation. Test or assess the learner's progress so that both you and the learner can make adjustments when needed.

Step 6: Spaced review. Periodic review is an important step in teaching because it helps strengthen responses to key stimuli.

Table 22–4 Topics of Special Interest to Educational Psychologists

Aptitude testing	Language learning
Classroom management	Learning theory
Classroom motivation	Moral development
Classroom organization	Student adjustment
Concept learning	Student attitudes
Curriculum development	Student needs
Disabled students	Teacher attitudes
Exceptional students	Teaching strategies
Gifted students	Teaching styles
Individualized instruction	Test writing
Intellectual development	Transfer of learning
Intelligence testing	

Table 22–5 Topics of Special Interest to Consumer Psychologists

Attitude change	Marketing research
Brand loyalty	Marketing strategies
Brand recognition	Mass media effects
Buying habits	Opinion leaders
Consumer attitudes	Opinion polling
Consumer complaints	Package design
Consumer needs	Product image
Consumer protection	Promotional schemes
Consumer values	Shopping behavior
Effects of advertising	Subcultural markets
Family decision making	

What are the best ways to teach? Is there an optimal teaching style for different age groups, topics, or individuals? These and many related questions lie at the heart of educational psychology (Table 22–4). In addition to studying such questions, educational psychologists design aptitude and achievement tests, evaluate educational programs, and participate in teacher training at colleges and universities.

Question: As a student, I've encountered many different teaching styles. Do different styles affect classroom learning?

There is little doubt that teachers can greatly affect student interest, motivation, and creativity. But what styles have what effects? To answer this question, psychologists have compared a number of teaching styles. Two of the most basic are direct instruction and open teaching.

In **direct instruction,** factual information is presented by lecture, demonstration, and rote practice. In **open teaching,** active teacher-student discussion is emphasized (Peterson, 1979). And now, the winner: As it turns out, both approaches have certain advantages. Students of direct instruction do slightly better on achievement tests than students in open classrooms (Thornburg, 1984). However, students of open teaching do somewhat better on tests of abstract thinking, creativity, and problem solving. They also tend to be more independent, curious, and positive in their attitudes toward school (Peterson, 1979). At present, it looks as if a balance of teaching styles goes hand in hand with a balanced education.

Although we have viewed only a small sample of educational research, its value for improving teaching and learning should be apparent. In the next section we will consider how psychology is applied in a very different context—the highly competitive world of consumer affairs.

Consumer Psychology

Whether it's buying a car, toothpaste, a record, or lunch, we are all consumers. **Consumer psychology** is an applied field that focuses on why consumers act as they do (Robertson & Kassarjian, 1991) (Table 22–5). Consumer psychology is a rapidly growing specialty, especially as it is applied to business and advertising.

Many people give little thought to why they buy what they do. But in fact, **consumer behavior** can be separated into several steps. These include deciding to spend, selecting a brand, shopping, making the purchase, and evaluating the product in use (Robertson & Kassarjian, 1991). At each step, advertising, packaging, and a host of other factors affect our behavior. To pinpoint such factors, a type of public opinion polling called **marketing research** is often done.

In marketing research, people in a representative sample are asked to give their personal impressions of products, services, and advertising. In this way, researchers have learned, among other things, that powerful, widely held **brand images** often develop. A case in point is the images many people have of automobiles, such as: Mercedes-Benz (high status), Corvette (power and sportiness), Buick (conservatism), and so forth (Robertson & Kassarjian, 1991). Brand images often direct buying behavior and help explain why many people purchase products for their labels as much as for their performance.

In addition to marketing research, consumer psychologists do laboratory testing of products (see Highlight 22–6). They also try to match products to consumer needs. They test public acceptance of new products, brand names,* and packaging. And they

* The importance of product names is illustrated by the difficulty Chevrolet had in initial attempts to market its *Nova* model in South America. Until the name was changed, consumers shunned the car. The problem? In Spanish, *no va* means "doesn't go"!

Direct instruction Presentation of factual information by lecture, demonstration, and rote practice.

Open teaching Instruction based on active teacher-student discussion.

Consumer psychology Specialty area that seeks to understand consumer behavior and apply psychology to advertising, marketing, and product testing.

Consumer behavior All of the actions involved in deciding to spend, selecting a brand, shopping, making the purchase, and evaluating a product in use.

Marketing research A type of public opinion polling used to assess consumer views of products, services, and advertising.

Brand image The image that consumers have of various products, especially with regard to their personal or emotional meanings.

Consumerism Formal attempts to enhance consumer knowledge, rights, and welfare.

Psychology of law Study of the psychological and behavioral dimensions of the legal system.

Mock jury A group that realistically simulates a courtroom jury.

design various strategies to change buying habits (through the use of TV commercials, printed advertisements, premiums, contests, promotional schemes, and the like).

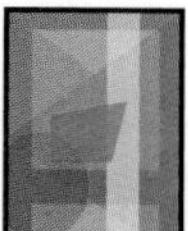

Highlight 22–6

Critical Thinking

Name that Beer

It is quite common for products to be promoted as "superior," "the best," "unmistakably different," and the like. How well do such claims hold up? In one recent test, three nationally advertised brands of beer were compared. The results are typical of many similar tests: When consumers sampled beer under controlled conditions—where taste was the only cue available—there was no evidence of any noticeable difference in brands (Fowler, 1982).

Although beer lovers would probably disagree, it appears that the labels could be interchanged on many major brands and no one would notice the difference. It is minimal differences of this sort that spur massive, image-conscious advertising campaigns.

Question: It sounds like consumer psychology is concerned with getting people to buy things they don't need. Is that the case?

It is true that many consumer psychologists use their knowledge to increase sales. However, not all consumer psychology is profit-oriented. For instance, principles of consumer behavior may be used to encourage the conservation of gasoline, water, or electricity. Also, many consumer psychologists are interested in protecting and enhancing consumer welfare by persuading people to act in their own best interest. Advertising campaigns concerning auto seat belt use, highway safety, drug abuse prevention, and the like, all draw on an understanding of consumer behavior (Olander, 1990).

As a final example, it was consumer psychologists who documented the large number of commercials on "kid vid" (children's television programs). Each year the average child sees over 20,000 commercials—most of which are for highly sugared cereals and overpriced toys. Related research showed that children under age 6 are easily victimized because they often cannot distinguish commercials from the program itself (Oskamp, 1984). Another example of how children may be victimized is the fact that 6-year-olds are nearly as familiar with the cigarette mascot "Old Joe Camel" as they are with Mickey Mouse (Fischer et al., 1991). Such findings have helped advance the cause of **consumerism** (attempts to enhance consumer knowledge, rights, and welfare) for both children and adults.

Psychology and Law

One of the best places to see psychology in action is the local courthouse. Jury trials are often fascinating studies in human behavior. Does the defendant's appearance affect the jury's decision? Do the personality characteristics or attitudes of jurors influence how they vote? These and many more questions have been investigated in recent years by psychologists interested in law (Davis, 1989) (see Table 22–6).

Jury Behavior When a case goes to trial, jurors must listen to days or weeks of testimony and then decide guilt or innocence. How do they reach their decision? Psychologists use **mock juries** made up of volunteers to probe such behavior. Some mock juries are simply given written evidence and arguments to read before making a decision. Others are shown videotaped trials staged by actors. Either way, studying the behavior of mock juries helps us understand what determines how real jurors vote.

Some of the findings of jury research are unsettling. Studies show that jurors are rarely able to put aside their biases, attitudes, and values while making a decision (Watson et al., 1984). For example, jurors are less likely to find attractive defendants guilty (on the basis of the same evidence) than unattractive defendants (Perlman & Cozby, 1983). There is an interesting twist, however. If it appears that being attractive helped a person commit a crime, it can work against her or him in court (Tedeschi et al., 1985). An example would be a handsome man on trial for swindling money from an unmarried middle-aged woman.

A second major problem is that jurors are not very good at separating evidence from other information,

Table 22–6 Topics of Special Interest in the Psychology of Law

Arbitration	Juror attitudes
Attitudes toward law	Jury decisions
Bail setting	Jury selection
Capital punishment	Mediation
Conflict resolution	Memory
Criminal personality	Parole board decisions
Diversion programs	Police selection
Effects of parole	Police stress
Expert testimony	Police training
Eyewitness testimony	Polygraph accuracy
Forensic hypnosis	Sentencing decisions
Insanity plea	White-collar crime

such as their perceptions of the defendant, attorneys, witnesses, and what they think the judge wants. When jurors are told to ignore information that slips out in court, they find it hard to do so. Often, their final verdict is influenced by inadmissible evidence, such as mention of a defendant's prior conviction (Watson et al., 1984). A related problem occurs when jurors take into account the severity of the punishment a defendant faces (Sales & Hafemeister, 1985). Jurors are not supposed to let this affect their verdict, but many do.

A third area of difficulty arises because jurors usually cannot suspend judgment until all the evidence is in. Typically, jurors form an opinion early in the trial. It then becomes hard for them to fairly judge evidence that contradicts their opinion.

Problems like these are troubling in a legal system that prides itself on fairness. However, all is not lost. Each of the factors discussed has much less effect as a crime becomes more severe or the evidence becomes more clear-cut (Tedeschi et al., 1985). Although it is far from perfect, the jury system works reasonably well in most cases.

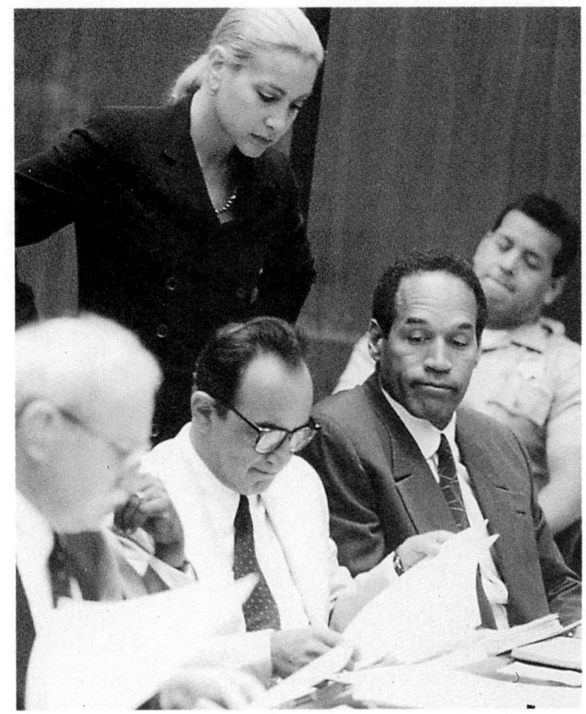

■ **Fig. 22–12** *The behavior of juries and jurors has been extensively studied. The findings of such studies are applied by psychologists who act as advisors to attorneys during the jury selection process. Jury selection in the O. J. Simpson murder trial took two months, as defense and prosecution lawyers struggled for the advantage in jury makeup.*

Jury Selection Before a trial begins, opposing attorneys are allowed to disqualify potential jurors who may be biased. For example, a person who knows anyone connected with the trial can be excluded. Beyond this, however, attorneys try to use jury selection to remove people who may cause trouble for them. For instance, jurors who believe in rape myths (that a woman may "ask for it" by her actions or style of dress, for example) are less likely to convict an accused rapist (Watson et al., 1984).

Only a limited number of potential jurors can be excused. As a result, many attorneys are now asking psychologists for help in identifying people who will favor or harm their efforts (■ Fig. 22–12). Several techniques are typically used. As a first step, *demographic information* is frequently collected for each juror. Much can be guessed by knowing a juror's age, sex, race, occupation, education, political affiliation, religion, and socioeconomic status. Most of this information is available from public records.

To supplement demographic information, a *community survey* may be done to find out how local citizens feel about the case. The assumption is that jurors probably have attitudes similar to people with backgrounds like their own. Although talking with potential jurors outside the courtroom is not permitted, other information networks are available. If possible, a psychologist may interview relatives, acquaintances, neighbors, and co-workers of potential jurors.

Back in court, psychologists also often watch for *authoritarian personality* traits in potential jurors (see Chapter 21). (Authoritarians tend to believe that punishment is effective, and they are more likely to vote for conviction.) At the same time, the psychologist typically observes potential jurors' *non-verbal behavior*. The idea is to try to learn from body language which side the person favors (Sales & Hafemeister, 1985).

Many of these techniques were used some years ago in the defense of automaker John DeLorean. As you may recall, DeLorean was charged with setting up a $25 million cocaine deal. Before the trial, DeLorean's attorneys had a national survey done to see if he would have a better chance if the trial were held away from Los Angeles. As it turned out, the public attitude was the same all over the country: Everyone thought DeLorean was guilty. (He was eventually acquitted.)

Cases like DeLorean's, the Menendez brothers', William Kennedy Smith's, and O. J. Simpson's raise troubling ethical questions. In each case, wealthy clients had the advantage of psychological jury selection—something most people cannot afford. Attorneys, of course, can't be blamed for trying to improve their odds of winning a case. And since both sides help select jurors, the net effect in most instances is probably a more balanced jury (Sales & Hafemeister, 1985). At its worst, jury analysis leads to unjust verdicts. At its best, it helps to identify and remove only people who would be highly biased.

Sports psychology Study of the psychological and behavioral dimensions of sports performance.

Task analysis Breaking complex skills into their subparts.

Jury research is perhaps the most direct link between psychology and law, but there are others. Psychologists evaluate people for sanity hearings, do counseling in prisons, advise lawmakers on public policy, help train police cadets, and more (Sales & Hafemeister, 1985). In the future, it is quite likely that psychology will have a growing impact on law and the courts.

Sports Psychology

Question: What does psychology have to do with sports?

As almost all serious athletes soon learn, peak performance requires more than physical training. Mental and emotional "conditioning" are also important. Recognizing this fact, many teams, both professional and amateur, now include psychologists on their staffs (Greenspan, 1983). On any given day, a sports psychologist might teach an athlete how to relax, how to ignore distractions, or how to cope with emotions. The sports psychologist might also provide personal counseling for performance-lowering stresses and conflicts (Neff, 1990). Other psychologists are interested in studying factors that affect athletic achievement, such as skill learning, the personality profiles of champion athletes, the effects of spectators, and related topics (● Table 22–7). In short, **sports psychologists** seek to understand and improve sports performance and to enhance the benefits of participating in sports (■ Fig. 22–13).

Because sports have strong positive or negative effects on participants, they often provide valuable information on human behavior in general. For example, a study of Little League baseball found that children's self-esteem improved significantly after a season of play (Hawkins & Gruber, 1982). In other work, psychologists have learned that such benefits are most likely to occur when competition, rejection, criticism, and the "one-winner mentality" are minimized.

● **Table 22–7 Topics of Special Interest to Sports Psychologists**

Achievement motivation	Hypnosis
Athletic personality	Mental practice
Athletic task analysis	Motor learning
Coaching styles	Peak performance
Competition	Positive visualization
Control of attention	Self-regulation
Coping strategies	Skill acquisition
Emotions and performance	Social facilitation
Exercise and mental health	Stress reduction
Goal setting	Team cooperation
Group (team) dynamics	Training procedures

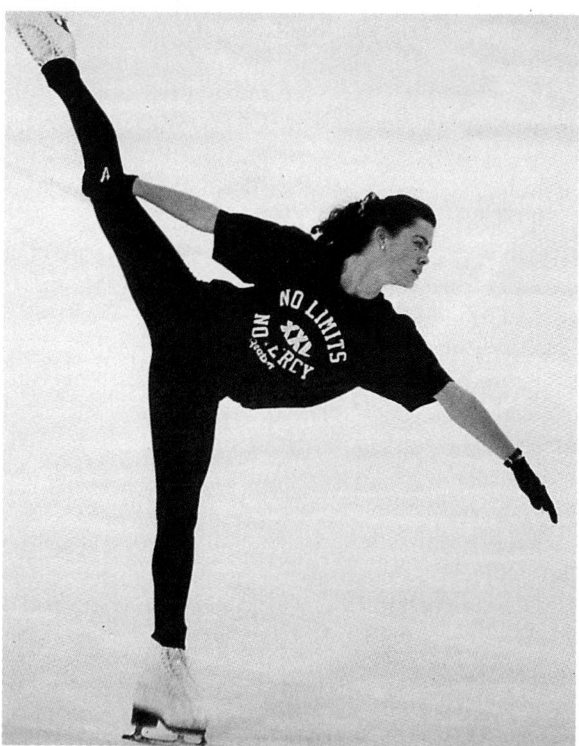

■ **Fig. 22–13** *Sports psychologists have played a significant role in helping prepare athletes for peak performance in the Olympic Games. Stress management, attention regulation, mental imagery, motivation, self-confidence, and many other psychological factors greatly affect athletic performance.*

When working with children in sports, it is also important to emphasize fair play, intrinsic rewards, self-control of emotions, independence, and self-reliance (Orlick, 1975).

Adults, of course, may also benefit from sports. For many, the payoffs are stress reduction, a better self-image, and improved general health. Researchers have reported, for instance, that distance running is associated with lower levels of tension, anxiety, fatigue, and depression than is found in the non-running population (Gondola & Tuckman, 1982).

Before the advent of sports psychology, it was debatable whether athletes improved because of "homespun" coaching methods, or in spite of them. For example, in early studies of volleyball and gymnastics, it became clear that people teaching these sports had very little knowledge of crucial, underlying skills (Salmela, 1974, 1975).

Question: How has psychology helped?

An ability to do detailed studies of complex skills has been one of the major contributions. In a psychological **task analysis,** sports skills are broken into subparts, so that key elements can be identified and taught (see

Highlight 22–7). Such methods are an extension of techniques first used for job analyses, as described earlier.

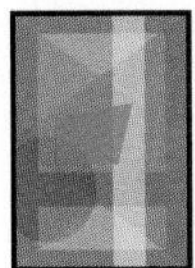

HIGHLIGHT 22–7

Using Psychology

Taking the Pulse of a Bull's-Eye

It doesn't take much to be off target in the Olympic sport of marksmanship. The object is to hit a bull's-eye the size of a dime at the end of a 165-foot-long shooting range. Nevertheless, an average of 50 bull's-eyes out of 60 shots is not unusual in international competition (prone position).

What does it take—beyond keen eyes and steady hands—to achieve such accuracy? The answer is surprising. Sports psychologists have found that top marksmen consistently squeeze the trigger *between* heartbeats (■ Fig. 22–14). Apparently the tiny tremor induced by a heartbeat is enough to send the shot astray (Pelton, 1983). Without careful psychological study, it is doubtful that this element of marksmanship would have been identified. Now that its importance is known, competitors have begun to use various techniques—from relaxation training to biofeedback—to steady and control their heartbeat. In the future, the best marksmen may be those who set their sights on mastering their hearts.

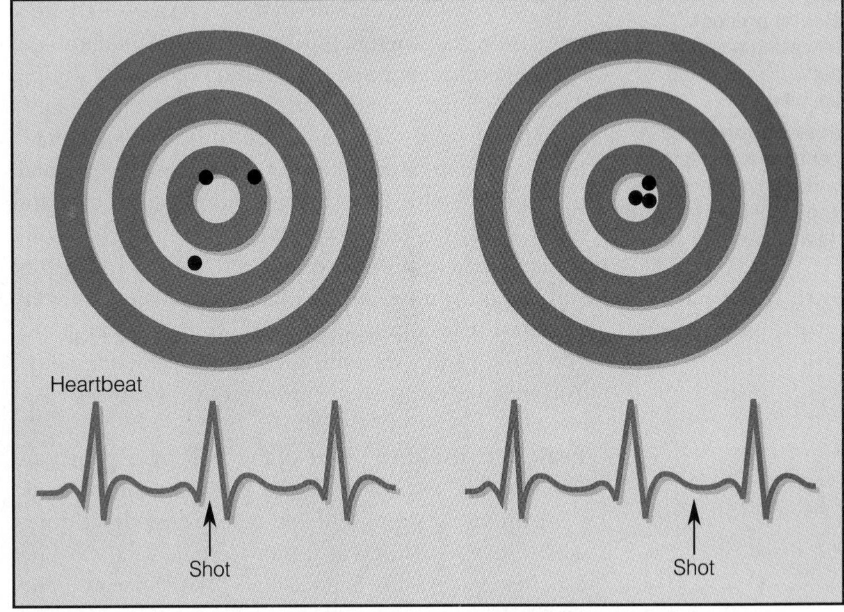

■ **Fig. 22–14** *The target on the left shows what happens when a marksman fires during the heart's contraction. Higher scores, as shown by the three shots on the right, are more likely when shots are made between heartbeats. (Adapted from Pelton, 1983.)*

Motor Skills Sports psychologists are very interested in how we learn motor skills. A **motor skill** is a series of actions molded into a smooth and efficient performance. Typing, walking, pole-vaulting, shooting baskets, playing golf, driving a car, writing, and skiing are all motor skills.

A basketball player may never make exactly the same shot twice in a game. This makes it almost impossible to practice every shot that might occur. How, then, do athletes become skillful? Typically, athletic performances involve learning **motor programs.** Motor programs are mental plans or models of what a skilled movement should be like. Motor programs allow an athlete—or a person simply walking across a room—to perform complex movements that fit changing conditions. If, for example, you have learned a "bike-riding" motor program, you can easily ride bicycles of different sizes and types on a large variety of surfaces.

Throughout life you will face the challenge of learning new motor skills. How can psychology make your learning more effective? Studies of sports skills suggest that you should keep the following points in mind for optimal skill learning (Drowatzky, 1975; Gagne & Fleishman, 1959; Klausmeir, 1975; Meichenbaum, 1977; Singer, 1978):

Motor skill A series of actions molded into a smooth and efficient performance.

Motor program A mental plan or model that guides skilled movement.

1. Begin by observing and imitating a *skilled model.* Modeling provides a good mental picture of the skill. At this point, try simply to grasp a visual image of the skilled movement.
2. Learn *verbal rules* to back up motor learning. Such rules are usually most helpful in the early phases of skill learning. When first learning cross-country skiing, for example, it is helpful to say, "left arm, right foot, right arm, left foot." Later, as a skill becomes more automated, internal speech may actually get in the way.
3. Practice should be as *lifelike* as possible so that artificial cues and responses do not become a part of the skill. A competitive diver should practice on the board, not on a trampoline. If you want to learn to ski try to practice on snow, not straw.
4. Get *feedback* from a mirror, videotape, coach, or observer. Whenever póssible, get someone experienced in the skill to direct attention to *correct responses* when they occur.
5. When possible, it is better to practice *natural units* rather than breaking the task into artificial parts. When learning to type, it is better to start with real words rather than nonsense syllables.
6. Learn to *evaluate* and *analyze* your own performance. Remember, you are trying to learn a motor program, not just train your muscles. Motor skills are actually very mental.

Mental practice Imagining a skilled performance to aid learning.

Peak performance A performance during which physical, mental, and emotional states are harmonious and optimal.

The last point leads to one more suggestion. Research has shown that merely thinking about or imagining a skilled performance can aid learning (Hinshaw, 1991). This technique, called **mental practice,** seems to help by refining motor programs. Of course, mental practice is not better than actual practice. However, mental practice is better than no practice at all. Thus, for many skills, it is best to combine mental practice with actual practice (Romero & Silvestri, 1990). The better you are at forming mental images, the more mental rehearsal will help (Isaac, 1992). When you begin to get really good at a skill, give mental practice a try. You may be surprised at how effective it can be.

Peak Performance One of the most interesting topics in sports psychology is the phenomenon of **peak performance.** Many athletes report episodes during which they felt almost as if they were in a trance. The experience has also been called "flow" because the athlete becomes one with his or her performance and flows with it. At such times, athletes experience intense concentration, detachment from surroundings, a lack of fatigue and pain, a subjective slowing of time, and feelings of unusual power and control (Browne & Mahoney, 1984). It is at just such times that "personal bests" tend to occur.

A curious aspect of flow is that it cannot be forced to happen. In fact if a person stops to think about it, the flow state goes away. Psychologists are now seeking to identify conditions that facilitate peak performance and the unusual mental state that usually accompanies it. Promising work is being done to train athletes to use physical relaxation, guided imagery, mental rehearsal, self-hypnosis, and the like, to attain peak performance.

At present, sports psychology is a very young field, and still much more an art than a science. Nevertheless, interest in the field is rapidly expanding.

A Look Ahead Although we have sampled several major areas of applied psychology, they are by no means the only applied specialties. Others that immediately come to mind are school psychology, military psychology, health psychology (discussed in Chapter 11) and space psychology (a skyrocketing field that is really looking up—see this chapter's Exploration). Before we explore the "final frontier," the Applications section returns to the work environment with some advice on how to be an effective communicator.

Learning Check

Match the term on the left with one or more related topics or concepts from the list on the right.

____ 1. Educational psychology	**A.** non-verbal ratings	**F.** brand image
____ 2. Consumer psychology	**B.** teaching strategies	**G.** styles of instruction
____ 3. Psychology of law	**C.** peak performance	**H.** community campaigns
____ 4. Sports psychology	**D.** marketing research	**I.** task analysis
	E. eyewitnesses	

5. Compared to direct instruction, open teaching produces better scores on achievement tests. T or F?
6. Which of the following is *not* commonly used by psychologists to aid jury selection?
   a. mock testimony *b.* information networks *c.* community surveys *d.* demographic data
7. Mental models, called ____________ ____________, appear to underlie well-learned motor skills.
8. Learning verbal rules to back up motor learning is usually most helpful in the early stages of acquiring a skill. T or F?

Critical Thinking

9. To maximize performance at competitions, sports psychologists recommend that athletes have set routines that they follow during the hours leading up to a contest. How would such routines help?

Answers: 1. B, G 2. D, F 3. A, E 4. C, I 5. F 6. *a* 7. motor programs 8. T 9. As discussed in Chapter 11, stress is reduced when a person feels in control of a situation. Following a routine helps athletes maintain a sense of order and control so that they are not over aroused when the time comes to perform.

APPLICATIONS: *Improving Communication at Work*

Just a minute, I want to expand on the confusion. This is where I'm assuming we're just going to throw it up for air. I mean, let's tie all this up in loose ends.

The bottom line is we've got to round-file this puppy ASAP before it goes belly-up. Stan says we're talking mouth-breather here. Copy Monica, Steve, and the bean-counters with your input and let's circle the wagons in the AM.

I was just, like, totally embarrassed, I mean, like abso-double-lutely, totally incinerated, you know? I mean, to the max. I'm all, "I'm just totally sorry Mr. Thompson." And he's all, "If this is the way you do business, I'm not interested."

Each of the people just quoted probably intended to express his or her ideas clearly. As you can see, however, their efforts are less than a model of clarity.

Getting the Message Across Effective communication is crucial in many work settings. When communication is muddled, important messages may get lost. Feelings can be crushed. Trust may be damaged. Poor decisions are made. Almost always, group effectiveness is impaired.

Clearly, people who work together depend on good communication. Service-oriented work with customers, and ethno-cultural diversity in the work force also put a premium on communication skills. For such reasons, getting a job, keeping it, and excelling in your work all depend on knowing how to communicate clearly with others (Goldstein & Gilliam, 1990).

Effective Communication

To improve your communication skills, or to keep them sharp, remember the following points.

1. **State your ideas clearly and decisively.** News reporters learn to be precise about the "who, what, when, where, how, and why" of events. At work, the same list is a good guide when you are making a request, giving instructions, or answering a question. Rather than saying, "I need someone to give me a hand sometime with some stuff," it would be better to say, "Blake, would you please meet me in the storeroom in 5 minutes? I need help lifting a box." Notice that the second request answers all of these questions: Who? Blake. What? Could you help me? How? By lifting a box. When? In 5 minutes. Where? In the storeroom. Why? It takes two people.

As you speak, avoid overuse of ambiguous words and phrases ("wiggle words") such as, *I guess, I think, kinda, sort of, around, some, about, you know,* and *like.* Here's an example: "Basically, I sort of feel like we should kinda pause. I mean, and, let's see, maybe reconsider, you know, rethink some of this stuff." It would be better to say: "I believe we should revise our plans immediately." Ambiguous messages leave others in doubt as to your true thoughts and wishes.

Also try not to overuse intensifiers (*very, really, absolutely, extra, super, awesome, ultimate, completely* and so on). Super extra frequent use of such awesome words really causes them to completely lose their ultimate effectiveness.

2. **Eschew the meretricious utilization of polysyllabic locutions. (Don't overuse big words.)** Overuse of obscure vocabulary is often a sign of insecurity. Big words may make you sound important, but they can also blur your message. Which of the following two statements is clearer? "Pulchritude possesses solely cutaneous profundity." Or, "Beauty is only skin deep"?

Trendy, overused "buzz words" or phrases should also be avoided. Often they are just a way of *sounding like* you are saying something: "Personally, I feel we've got to be more synergistically proactive and start networking in a programmatic fashion if we want to avoid being negatively impacted by future megatrends in the client-purveyor interface." Translation: "I don't have any worthwhile thoughts on the topic."

3. **Avoid excessive use of jargon or slang.** Most professions have their own specialized terminology. Here's an example of some printers' jargon: "TR the last two lines but STET the leading." (Reverse the order of the last two lines but don't change the spacing between them.) Jargon can provide a quick, shorthand way of expressing ideas. However, jargon and technical lingo should be avoided unless you are sure that others are familiar with it. Otherwise, people may misunderstand you or feel left out. Using slang can have the same effect as jargon. Slang that excludes people from a conversation makes them feel belittled. (The second quotation at the beginning of this Application is full of slang.)

4. **Avoid loaded words.** Words that have strong emotional meanings (loaded words) can have unintended effects on listeners. For example, the observation "What a stupid-looking tie," implies that anyone

who likes the tie is stupid. In the same way, saying "I think the supervisor's new schedule is a *dumb* idea" brands anyone who agrees with the schedule as foolish. Good decision making and problem solving require an atmosphere in which people feel that their ideas are respected, even when they disagree.

5. **Use people's names.** Work relationships go more smoothly when you learn names and use them. An impersonal request such as, "Hey you, could you make 5 copies of this for me?" is not likely to promote future cooperation. Of course, whether you use a first or last name will depend on how formal your relationship to a person is. In any case, learning names is well worth the effort. (The Applications in Chapter 8 tells how to improve your memory for names.)

6. **Be polite and respectful.** Being polite is important, but don't be artificially servile or stilted. Overuse of expressions such as *sir, madame, with your permission, if you would be ever so kind,* and so on, can actually be insulting. True politeness puts others at ease. Phony politeness makes people feel that they are being made fun of, or manipulated, or that you are faking it to win approval. Being polite can be difficult when tempers flare. If you have a dispute with someone at work, remember to use the techniques of self-assertion described in Chapter 20.

In addition to *what* you say, *how* you say it can be important. Psychologist Chris Kleinke (1986) has noted several speech cues that communicate self-confidence and add credibility to your message.

7. **Use an expressive tone of voice.** People who know a subject well or who believe in their point of view usually speak with an expressive, animated tone of voice. Speaking energetically, with good voice inflection, typically adds to one's credibility. Don't, however, use a higher pitched voice, as this suggests nervousness.

8. **Speak fluently.** Before you speak, try to collect your thoughts so that you can get right to the point. Stammering, repeating yourself, frequent pauses, and overuse of "ahs," "uhms," and "you knows," implies incompetence or nervousness.

9. **Speak quickly.** A brisk rate of speech tends to be persuasive because it implies knowledge, competence, enthusiasm, and confidence. It also helps hold your listener's attention.

10. **Make use of non-verbal cues.** Remember that non-verbal cues, such as facial expressions and hand gestures, can help accentuate your message and structure it for listeners. In Western cultures, making eye contact while speaking is a particularly important non-verbal cue. In a group, don't talk to the ceiling, or to just one person. Try to make eye contact with each person in the group. That way, each feels included and knows that your message is meant for her or him. Another advantage of eye contact is that it lets you watch for feedback from listeners, whose reactions can guide your communication efforts.

Be aware that your behavior sends messages, too. Actions can parallel, amplify, contradict, or undermine what you are saying. For example, being late for a meeting tells others that they are not very important to you. Likewise, your manner of dress, personal grooming—even the way you decorate your personal work space—all send messages. Think about the message you want to send and be sensitive to non-verbal channels of information.

Being a Good Listener

Effective communication is a two-way street. In addition to expressing yourself clearly you must also be a good listener. We have already discussed good classroom listening habits (Chapter 1) and listening in counseling situations (Chapter 18). Here are some additional pointers that apply to work settings.

1. **Make an honest effort to pay attention.** Stop what you are doing, actively give the speaker your attention, and resist distractions. Communicate your interest by posture and body position. Make eye contact with the speaker to show your interest.

2. **Try to identify the speaker's purpose.** Is he or she informing, requesting, discussing, persuading, correcting, digressing, or entertaining? Listen for main themes rather than isolated facts. A good listener will be able to answer the question: What is this person's central message? Thus, as you listen, pretend that you will have to summarize the speaker's message for someone else.

3. **Suspend evaluation.** As you listen, try to keep an open mind. Avoid hasty judging, disagreeing, rejecting, or criticizing. There will be time later to think about what was said. After you have heard an entire message, evaluate the information it contains and decide how to use it. Then reply or take action.

4. **Check your understanding.** Let the other person talk, but occasionally acknowledge and confirm what he or she is saying. Restate important parts of the message in your own words to make sure you understand it. Ask questions and clarify points you don't understand. Don't let doubts or ambiguities go unresolved.

APPLICATIONS: *Continued*

5. **Pay attention to non-verbal messages.** Listeners must also be aware of the information provided by gestures, facial expressions, eye contact, touching, body positioning, and voice qualities such as volume, rate, pitch, emphasis, hesitations, and silences. Good listeners are also good observers.
6. **Accept responsibility for effective communication.** As a listener, it is up to you to actively search for meaning and value in what is said. You can facilitate communication as much by being a good listener as you can by being an effective speaker.

The art of effective communication is well worth cultivating. The points made here are basic, but they can go a long way toward ensuring your success at work—like, totally, abso-double-lutely, you know what I mean?

(Sources: Hartgrove-Freile, 1990; Hellriegel, Slocum, & Woodman, 1986; Jewell, 1989; Kleinke, 1986; Timm, & Peterson, 1990.)

LEARNING CHECK

1. The sentence, "Copy Monica, Steve, and the bean-counters with your input and let's circle the wagons in the A.M.," shows the danger of using loaded words. T or F?
2. "You've got to REM out some of the TSRs in your AUTOEXEC.BAT file and reboot if you want that software to run." For a beginning computer user, the problem with this message is its overuse of ______________ .
3. An expressive, higher-pitched tone of voice tends to be more persuasive and credible. T or F?
4. Paying attention to non-verbal messages is an element of effective communication for both speakers and listeners. T or F?
5. From the perspective of social psychology, effective communication is likely to increase what dimension of group membership? ***Critical Thinking***

Answers: 1. F 2. jargon 3. F 4. T 5. Group cohesion.

EXPLORATION

Space Psychology—Life on the High Frontier

The first human outpost in space is drawing nearer. By the year 2000 the United States hopes to orbit a continuously inhabited space station (Sobel, 1994). Many engineering problems must be solved before a permanent space habitat becomes a reality. Yet the real challenge may lie in the psychological adjustments needed for men and women to live in space (■ Fig. 22–15).

The Challenge of Living Aloft

Life in the "mini-world" of a space station won't be easy, physically or mentally. For months at a time, space station residents will be restricted to tiny living quarters with little privacy. During an interplanetary trip, explorers would be confined for nearly 2 years.

No doubt the first long-term space residents will find life in orbit stressful. Even small disagreements can lead to tense clashes when people must live in cramped quarters. Living aloft would be similar to spending several months among a group of strangers in a small room from which you cannot escape.

In addition to confinement, long-term space inhabitants will face other trying conditions. These include restricted movement, separation from loved ones, isolation from recreation and hobbies, sensory monotony, noise, and many other stresses. It's no wonder that some astronauts reported restlessness, depression, and boredom after spending months aboard Skylab, a small space station orbited in the early 1970s.

Space Strike America's third Skylab crew spent a highly productive three and one-half months in space. The crew—Edward Gibson, Gerald Carr, and William Pogue—also staged the world's first "space strike." Along with the pesky irritations of confined living, the crew felt pressured by an 18-hour-per-day work schedule. After 6 weeks the crew had fallen far behind in chores and experiments. The first signs of trouble surfaced at that time: Carr told Mission Control, "There's nothing worse than having to gobble your meal in order to get some

EXPLORATION

■ **Fig. 22–15** *The permanently manned space station* Freedom *will be assembled in orbit by space shuttle crews beginning around the turn of the century.* Freedom *will provide the United States and its partners—Canada, Japan, and nine European nations—with a habitat in which men and women will live and work in space for extended periods of time. Solving the behavioral problems of living in space will be an important step toward human exploration of the solar system. (Art by Stan Jones, courtesy of NASA, Johnson Space Center.)*

task done that really should have been scheduled some other time, so please loosen up!" In a sudden burst of defiance, the astronauts went on strike and did exactly as they pleased. Gibson went to the solar console. Carr and Pogue sat in the wardroom, looked out the window, and took photographs.

Obviously, no one on earth was going to fly up and punish the astronauts for skipping their chores. The crisis was finally resolved when the crew was given more time to do experiments and fewer tasks to complete. Although the Skylab-3 strike was brief, it shows how important the human element will be in space.

Space Habitats

Clearly, space habitats must be designed with human behavior in mind. What will it take to make a congenial space station—one capable of sustaining emotional well-being and efficient performance? To begin, the *social* environment or "micro-society" on a space station will need to operate as smoothly as possible. For this reason, many problems may be avoided by carefully selecting and training future space residents *before* they go aloft.

It also would be wise to identify—and ease—stressors in space living quarters. To this end, psychologists have pinpointed several key areas of concern. Much has been learned by studying people confined to submarines, missile silos, Antarctic stations, simulated space stations on earth, and the like. Let's sample some expected problems and possible solutions.

General Environment Design of a space station as a living environment must take many human factors into account. For instance, researchers have learned that astronauts prefer rooms with clearly defined "up" and "down"—even in the weightlessness of space. Provisions must be made for regular exercise and full-body showers. As trivial as it might seem, a lack of showers was a major complaint among subjects in earlier confinement experiments.

Inside a space station there should be some flexibility in the use of living and work areas. Behavior patterns change over time, and control of one's environment helps lower stress. At the same time, people need stability. Psychologists have found, for instance, that eating becomes an important high point in monotonous environments. Eating at least one meal together each day can help keep a crew working as a social unit.

Sleep cycles will need to be carefully controlled in space to avoid disrupting bodily rhythms. In earlier space missions astronauts had difficulty sleeping while the remainder of the crew continued to work and talk. Problems with sleep will be worsened by the constant noise on a space station. Fans, pumps, switches, lights, and the like constantly click, hum, or throb on a spacecraft. At best, a space station will be at least as noisy as the typical office. At first, such noise is annoying. After weeks or months, it can become a serious stressor. Researchers are experimenting with various earmuffs, eyeshades, and sleeping arrangements to alleviate such difficulties.

Privacy Psychologists are helping engineers design space habitats that meet human needs for privacy. However, privacy will have to be based mainly on temporarily blocking out visual and auditory contact with others. In the first permanent space stations, there will be too little room for separate quarters.

Forced togetherness is stressful mainly because temporary retreat from contact with the group is difficult or impossible. Thus, control over the amount of contact one has with others is more important than having a private room. Designers do recognize, however, the need to define private territories. It will be important to identify small areas that can be personalized and "owned" by each individual. Desks, lockers, sleep stations, and the like, could fill this need if they are not shared with others.

Sensory Restriction Sensory monotony will be a problem in space, even with the magnificent vistas of earth below. (How many times would you have to see the North American continent before you lost interest?)

Researchers are developing stimulus environments that will use music, videotapes, and other diversions to combat monotony and boredom. Again, they are trying to provide choice and control for workers. Studies of confined living make it clear that one person's symphony is another's grating noise. Where music is concerned, individual earphones may be all that is required.

Most people in restricted environments find that they prefer non-interactive pastimes such as reading, listening to music, looking out windows, writing, and watching films or television. As much as anything, this preference may show again the need for privacy. A person can psychologically withdraw from the group by reading or listening to music. A good selection of passive entertainments looks like a must for any space station. Interestingly, Russian astronauts, who make much use of music, have also reacted with delight to grab bags containing unexpected toys or novelties.

Social Isolation Separation from family, friends, and one's home community is

EXPLORATION

a major stressor. However, the ability to talk regularly with family via two-way televised meetings should help ease feelings of social isolation. Some psychologists also believe that there should be a psychological support group on earth with whom a space station crew would talk to prevent emotional problems. In short, the best antidote for social isolation will probably be abundant opportunities to communicate with associates and loved ones on earth. Experienced astronauts and cosmonauts particularly endorse contact with loved ones as a positive influence on their performance in space (Kelly & Kanas, 1993).

Conflict Resolution and Mental Health Many studies of long-term isolation show steady declines in motivation. Most inhabitants intend to use their free time for creative pursuits. But in reality they end up marking time and many become apathetic. Judging from submarine missions and Antarctic bases, as many as 5 percent of space inhabitants may experience some psychological disturbance. Most often the problem will be depression. However, in rare instances people have become paranoid, psychotic, suicidal, or uncontrollably aggressive. As stated earlier, the risk of such problems may be minimized by carefully selecting personnel. Even so, it will be important to teach crew members basic counseling skills for solving conflicts.

Life on Spaceship Earth Why is the idea of living in space so fascinating? Perhaps it is because human strengths and weaknesses will be magnified in the miniature world of a space station. As psychologist Yvonne Clearwater (1985) says:

> The space station represents the first glimmerings of recognition that some of the toughest challenges in space—as on earth—concern human behavior, not technology . . . . Ironically, the farther we go from earth and the longer we stay away, the more we will need to know about ourselves. Scientists working on the space effort believe that psychological factors will become increasingly important for the success or failure of future space missions.

It is curiously fitting that the dazzling technology of space travel has highlighted the inevitable importance of human behavior. Here on earth, as in space, we cannot count on technology alone to solve problems. The threat of nuclear war, social conflict, crime, prejudice, overpopulation, environmental damage, famine, homicide, economic disaster—these and most other major problems facing us are behavioral (Kirk & Picard, in press). Will spaceship earth endure? It's a psychological question.

Conclusion Work, leisure, family, community, and environment all contribute to the quality of our lives. And as we have seen throughout this text, psychology has much to offer in each of these areas. It is my sincere hope that you have found enough relevance and value in this book to kindle a lifelong interest in psychology. Psychology's future looks exciting. What role will it play in your life?

(Sources: Chaikin, 1985; Clearwater, 1985; Connors, Harrison, & Akins, 1985; Engle & Lott, 1980; Joyce, 1984; Sobel, 1994.)

LEARNING CHECK

1. The Skylab-3 space strike was caused mainly by dissatisfaction with the poor quality of meals in space. T or F?
2. Researchers have learned that astronauts have no preference for living quarters with clearly defined "up" and "down" orientations. T or F?
3. Research shows that needs for privacy can be met by providing ways to temporarily withdraw from social contact with a group, even when physical withdrawal is impossible. T or F?
4. Most people in restricted environments prefer group pastimes, such as playing card games, skits, or group singing. T or F?
5. On a spacecraft, how would blocking visual and auditory contact with others affect crowding? ***Critical Thinking***

Answers: 1. F 2. F 3. T 4. F 5. While density would remain high, the sense of crowding would be reduced because crew members would feel that they have some control over their immediate social environment.

Chapter Summary

- ■ ***What are the major areas of applied psychology?***

- **Applied psychology** refers to the use of psychological principles and research methods to solve practical problems.
- Major applied specialties include the following areas of psychology: clinical and counseling, community, industrial/organizational, engineering, environmental, educational, consumer, legal, sports psychology, and related areas.

- ■ ***How is psychology applied in business, engineering, and industry?***

- **Industrial/organizational psychologists** are interested in the problems people face at work. Typically they specialize in **personnel psychology, human relations** at work, and/or **engineering psychology** (the design of machines and work environments for human use).
- Personnel psychologists try to match people with jobs by combining **job analysis** with a variety of selection procedures. These include gathering **biodata, interviewing,** giving **standardized psychological tests** (**interest inventories, aptitude tests,** and **computerized tests**), and using **assessment centers.**
- Two basic approaches to business and industrial management are **scientific management** (**Theory X**) and **human relations** approaches (**Theory Y**). Theory X is most concerned with *work efficiency*, whereas, Theory Y emphasizes *psychological efficiency*.
- **Job satisfaction** is not directly related to productivity, but it is linked to absenteeism, morale, employee turnover, and other factors that affect overall business efficiency. Job satisfaction is usually enhanced by Theory Y oriented **job enrichment.**

- ■ ***What have psychologists learned about the effects of our physical and social environments?***

- **Environmental psychologists** are interested in the effects of **behavioral settings, physical** or *social environments*, and human **territoriality,** among many other major topics.
- Over-population is a major world problem, often reflected at an individual level in crowding.
- Animal experiments indicate that excessive crowding can be unhealthy. However, human research shows that psychological feelings of **crowding** do not always correspond to **density** (the number of people in a given space).
- One major consequence of crowding is **attentional overload.**
- A large number of practical problems—from *noise pollution* to architectural design—have come under the scrutiny of environmental psychologists. In many cases, effective behavioral solutions to such problems have been found, often as a result of first doing a careful **environmental assessment.**

- ■ ***How does psychology apply to education, consumer behavior, law, and sports?***

- **Educational psychologists** seek to understand how people learn and teachers instruct. They are particularly interested in **teaching styles,** such as *direct instruction* and *open teaching,* and *teaching strategies.*
- **Consumer psychologists** study *consumer behavior* and serve as consultants to businesses and advertising agencies. Consumer psychologists often do **marketing research** to aid the promotion of various products. Some also do research that helps advance the cause of **consumerism** and consumer welfare.
- The **psychology of law** includes studies of courtroom behavior and other topics that pertain to the legal system. Psychologists also serve various consulting and counseling roles in legal, law enforcement, and criminal justice settings. Studies of **jury behavior** show that jury decisions are often far from objective.
- **Sports psychologists** seek to enhance sports performance and the benefits of sports participation. A careful **task analysis** of sports skills is one of the major tools for improving coaching and performance.
- A **motor skill** is a nonverbal response chain assembled into a smooth performance. Motor skills are guided by internal mental models called **motor programs.**

- ■ ***What can be done to improve communication in work settings?***

- State your message clearly and precisely. Try to avoid overuse of obscure vocabulary, jargon, slang, and loaded words. Learn and use people's names. Be polite, but not servile. Be expressive when you speak. Pay attention to non-verbal cues and the messages they send.
- To be a good listener, actively pay attention, identify the speaker's purpose and core message, suspend evaluation while listening, check your understanding, and make note of non-verbal information.

- ■ ***How is psychology being applied in space missions?***

- **Space psychologists** study the many behavioral challenges that accompany space flight and life in restricted environments.
- Space habitats must be designed with special attention to environmental stressors, privacy, social isolation, conflict resolution, and the maintenance of mental health.

Questions for Discussion

1. In your opinion, what are the advantages and disadvantages of flexitime?
2. If you were selecting a person for a job, how would you try to ensure that the person's skills and interests matched those required by the position?
3. How is an aptitude test different from an interest inventory?
4. How would you attempt to show that a specific personnel selection technique is both valid and reliable?
5. Under what economic and interpersonal conditions would Theory X management be most successful in encouraging productivity? Under what conditions would Theory Y be most successful?
6. What are the advantages and disadvantages of participatory management? Of management by objectives? Of quality circles?
7. Why do you think people tend to "mark their territories"? Under what conditions is such marking most important?
8. What can a person do in a densely packed environment to reduce feelings of crowding?
9. Should extra money be spent constructing buildings that accommodate the needs of people—or should people learn how to satisfy their own needs within cheaper, more energy-efficient buildings?
10. What kinds of incentives and reinforcers would motivate people to work harder to preserve their environment? Why haven't attempts to encourage recycling and energy conservation been more successful?

Appendix A
Careers in Psychology

Let's say that you have taken the first step toward a career in psychology: Your introductory course has convinced you that you want to learn more about human behavior. The next step is to learn more about careers in psychology—something you can begin doing right here.

First Questions Are you suited to a career in psychology? What kinds of jobs are available to persons with associate, bachelor's, master's, or doctoral degrees in psychology? What is the employment outlook for psychology and related fields? These are questions to ask if you are thinking about majoring in psychology. Although this appendix can only provide preliminary answers, it should help you get started. First, let's see if you are on the right track at all:

- Do you have a strong interest in human behavior?
- Are you emotionally stable?
- Do you have good communication skills?
- Do you find theories and ideas challenging and stimulating?
- Do your friends regard you as especially sensitive to the feelings of others?
- Have you read popular books on psychology and found them interesting?
- Do you like science, math, problem solving, or figuring out how things work?
- Have discussions in this text matched some of your own insights about human behavior?
- Do you enjoy working with other people?

If you answered yes to most of these questions, a career in psychology or a related field may be a good choice for you.

Majoring in Psychology

As a quick survey of your classmates might show, the majority of students studying introductory psychology are not psychology majors. More surprising is the fact that about half of all undergraduate psychology majors do not plan to work as psychologists. Nearly 50 percent of all psychology majors seek full-time jobs immediately after they graduate (Woods & Wilkinson, 1987). Many of today's psychology majors recognize that a psychology degree does not limit them to a career in psychology. Learning psychology can provide a general knowledge of behavior that aids success in various occupations.

If you think you would like to major in psychology, but are not interested in graduate training, here are some points to consider:

- Few workers hold one job forever, or even remain in a single line of work for life.

- The nature of work is likely to change greatly in your lifetime, and adaptability will be important.
- A broad education that develops many skills makes a person more vocationally adaptable.
- It is a major myth that every job requires a precise set of skills. Apart from highly technical or specialized jobs, many positions can be filled by persons with differing combinations of skills.
- Specific undergraduate programs do not exist for many mental health professions, making psychology a good undergraduate major leading to later specialized training.
- Job recruiters look primarily for general competence in verbal and written communication, plus social skills and facility in meeting the public.

General Skills For reasons like those listed here, a general education in psychology can lead to a variety of interesting jobs and professions. Even a brief list of "marketable" abilities provided by a psychology degree would include the following: clear, analytic thinking; objectivity and keen observation; an ability to handle data, recognize patterns, and draw conclusions; ability to plan and organize complex activities; ability to communicate clearly, both verbally and in writing; the capacity to comprehend abstract principles and the subtleties of human behavior; ability to critically evaluate evidence; interpersonal skills; and general knowledge relevant to success in many settings.

Again, the point is that even if you do not plan to work as a psychologist, psychology can be a practical undergraduate major.

Education and Options

If you do decide to major in psychology, it is important to be aware of the level of training required for various jobs. While opportunities exist for those with an A.A. or B.A. degree in psychology, many of the most rewarding positions require further education. The discussion that follows should give you some idea of the options at each level.

Associate Degree Level Training in psychology at the associate degree level tends to yield fewer choices than those available to graduates with bachelor's degrees or more advanced training. Even so, all of the jobs listed here are open to persons with a 2-year, A.A. degree.

child care worker
human services worker
mental health assistant
nursing home attendant
playground supervisor
preschool aide
psychiatric technician
public survey worker
recreation aide
rehabilitation aide
senior citizen aide
teacher's aide
ward attendant
youth supervisor

The jobs listed here are only a sample of what is available. People with associate degrees in psychology are qualified to do interviewing, to give and score specific psychological tests, and to communicate the needs of clients to psychologists and other professionals. In general, a person with an associate degree can expect to work directly with clients, but under the supervision of more highly trained professionals.

In some communities, there are specific training programs for students interested in working as psychiatric (or psychological) technicians at hospitals or clinics. Often, a year or two of training can lead directly to a job in a local mental health facility. In some cases, provisions have been made for "psych-tech" trainees to combine classroom study with on-the-job training.

Bachelor's Degree As already mentioned, a bachelor's degree in psychology can be considered preparation for a variety of jobs or occupations. An undergraduate psychology major is also a good prelude to advanced training in several related professions. And, of course, a bachelor's degree is the first step toward a master's or doctoral degree in psychology.

Most of the jobs listed here are available to persons with bachelor's degrees in psychology. Some, however, require additional training (becoming a high school teacher, for example). Also, you would be most competitive for many of these jobs if you were to combine a psychology major with a minor in another area, such as business (Carducci et al., 1987). In other cases, it would be better to make psychology your minor, in combination with a major in a related area (law enforcement and nursing are examples).

advertising agent
art therapist
assistant youth coordinator
biofeedback technician
business management trainee
caseworker
child development specialist
child welfare agent
college admissions representative
counselor aide
crisis intervention team member
customer relations specialist
director of day-care center
drug counselor
educational salesperson
employment counselor
employment interviewer
family services worker
geriatric technician
group home coordinator
high school psychology teacher
human relations director
job analyst
labor relations specialist
management consultant
marketing researcher
music therapist
occupational therapist
patient service representative
personnel worker
probation/parole officer
psychiatric nurse
public health assistant
public relations specialist
recreational therapist

research assistant
sales representative
social worker
special education teacher
statistical assistant
veterans' advisor

Again, these are only some of the possibilities. As the diversity of the list suggests, it is important to remain flexible when pursuing a psychology major. Plan your education so that you are exposed to psychology's many areas of knowledge, and avoid specializing too soon. To further broaden your employment options, consider taking classes in computer programming, mathematics, statistics, accounting, finance, business, marketing, advertising, education, technical writing, or law enforcement.

Master's Level A master's degree in psychology usually requires from 1 to 2 years of graduate-level training beyond the bachelor's degree. The master's degree usually requires completion of a research thesis and/or a certain number of hours of supervised practical experience in an applied setting.

At present, the most popular master's-level specialty is counseling psychology. Undoubtedly, this is because a master's degree in counseling is one of the most direct routes to a career as a mental health professional. Those with a master's degree in counseling psychology may further specialize in marriage and family counseling, vocational or educational counseling, child counseling, or rehabilitation counseling—to name only major possibilities.

Many counselors are self-employed, but some work for human service agencies, at mental health clinics, and occasionally for the military or large businesses. Recently, counselors have begun to move into new areas, such as hospices, child abuse clinics, rape counseling centers, and stress clinics.

Other master's-level specialties, such as human factors engineering, school psychology, psychometrics, clinical psychology, industrial psychology, and general psychology, are also offered. But recently, employment opportunities have become limited for new master's-level psychologists. When positions open in such areas, they are most often filled by doctoral-level psychologists. (However, master's-level psychologists with prior work experience often are competitive for such positions.) On the other hand, a master's degree could make you more competitive for all of the bachelor's-level jobs listed earlier. It might also help you qualify for higher pay. If you are interested in teaching, a master's degree would qualify you to teach at a community college. For such reasons, a master's degree in psychology remains valuable, even in areas other than counseling.

Doctoral Level Earning a doctorate in psychology requires commitment. (That's personal commitment, not commitment to a mental hospital—although some doctoral candidates might disagree!) It usually takes at least 3 years of education beyond a bachelor's degree to attain a doctorate (Ph.D., Psy.D., or Ed.D.). More often, a doctorate takes 4 or more years to complete, and some specialties, such as clinical and counseling psychology, require at least 1 more year of internship. (An internship is a closely supervised, on-the-job training experience for professionals entering the field.)

How do the three doctoral degrees differ? The answer may help you decide which would be most appropriate for you if you want to become a psychologist. A Ph.D. is a research degree. As such, it requires completion of a dissertation (an original research contribution to the field).

Psychologists holding Ph.D. degrees are active in all areas of psychology, including clinical psychology. However, some psychologists who primarily want to work as therapists now earn a Psy.D. degree (Doctor of Psychology) instead of a Ph.D. This newly created degree allows students in clinical psychology to gain practical experience as a psychotherapist rather than doing a dissertation. The Ed.D. (Doctor of Education) is also typically more applied in orientation than the Ph.D. The Ed.D. is usually awarded after completion of an advanced series of courses focused on the psychology of learning and education.

It is also worth mentioning that in most states a doctoral degree alone does not automatically allow a person to practice psychology. To be legally licensed or certified as a psychologist, a person usually must have a doctorate in psychology, plus at least 1 year of internship, and he or she must pass written and oral state licensing exams. As you can see, becoming a psychologist is a major achievement, reflecting the attainment of a high level of knowledge.

Understandably, doctoral-level psychologists have the widest range of work choices. These include settings such as colleges and universities, clinics, rehabilitation centers, government agencies, businesses, industry, the military, and private practice. Also, as you can see in ● Table A–1, psychologists holding doctoral degrees average several thousand dollars per year greater income in most professional positions.

If you wish to pursue a doctorate in psychology, it is not absolutely necessary to make plans now for attending graduate school—but it helps! Getting admitted to a doctoral program in psychology is as difficult as getting into medical school. The sooner you know what kind of program you would like to enter, the better your chances will be of meeting all of its requirements. To learn more, consult the book *Graduate Study in Psychology*, published by the American Psychological Association. This book is loaded with information to help you plan your graduate education. Be sure to read that book's Appendix D, which gives practical, step-by-step information on how to get ac-

Table A–1 Average Income for American Psychologists

Area	Master's	Doctorate
College faculty		
Assistant professor	24,000*	33,000*
Associate professor	29,000*	41,000*
Full professor	35,000*	56,000*
Educational administration	42,000	42,000
Clinical psychology	28,000	40,000
Counseling psychology	26,000	34,000
Research	34,000	38,000
School psychology	28,000*	29,000*
Applied (I/O) psychology	38,000	48,000

*For 9- to 10-month academic year.
Data for Master's faculty from Goodstein, 1986; Data for Doctoral faculty from APA 1990–91 Survey of Graduate Departments of Psychology; remaining data from Stapp & Fulcher, 1983, are projections based on a 6 percent average increase since last assessment. All figures are rounded to nearest thousand U.S. dollars.

Table A–2 Important Factors Influencing Employment and Admission to Graduate School

Business Employment
1. Personality/self-presentation
2. Grades in major subject
3. Non-college jobs held
Graduate School
1. Number of difficult courses taken
2. Breadth of courses taken
3. Samples of writing ability
4. Overall grade point average
5. Letters of recommendation
6. Publications, honors, awards

Source: Milton et al., 1986.

cepted to graduate school. (An address for APA publications is given at the end of this discussion.)

Table A–2 shows why there is value in deciding early if you intend to seek employment or if you plan to enter graduate school (Milton et al., 1986). The table gives the results of a national survey of college faculty members and people in business involved in hiring college graduates. As you can see, business people and faculty members differ greatly in what they believe is most important when considering students for employment or admission. Personality and an ability to present oneself effectively are highly valued in the business world. Public speaking ability, interviewing skills, writing skills, and job experience—all these should be high on your list of priorities if you plan to seek immediate employment when you graduate. Notice too, that grades do count. The list for graduate school admission in Table A–2 speaks for itself.

Employment Outlook

The good news is that overall, jobs for people with psychology degrees are expected to increase faster than average in coming years. However, professional-level jobs (master's and doctorate) will account for a relatively small percentage of total new positions. With projections for a decline in college enrollments, academic positions will be in especially short supply. Even in industrial, clinical, and other applied areas, there will be much competition for positions. However, this should not deter a person who is strongly interested in psychology from pursuing a doctoral-level career. It simply means that it is wise to take steps to make yourself highly employable. These include (1) attending an APA accredited graduate school; (2) gaining work experience while in school (by working as a research assistant, teaching assistant, or even as a volunteer, if necessary); and (3) specializing in additional skills that are in demand, such as computer programming, prevention, consumer protection, therapy for special populations (such as the mentally retarded), and research in heavily funded areas (such as drug abuse research) (Schneider, 1991).

Best Bets At all degree levels, applied areas are probably the best bet for employment in the near future. The prospects remain reasonably good for clinical and counseling psychologists, industrial/organizational psychologists, and clinical or psychiatric social workers. Health psychology and health-related jobs also look good, especially anything associated with senior citizens, as the "grandparent boom" continues. Two of the fastest growing jobs for the next decade are projected to be employment interviewers and occupational therapists. Both positions are open to holders of bachelor's and master's degrees.

For further information on careers in psychology, talk with your psychology teacher or visit the campus career center if your school has one. Additional sources of information follow shortly.

The Future In addition to the jobs discussed here, there are a number of emerging specialties that are likely to grow rapidly. It shouldn't be long before job titles such as the following become more common: shyness counselor, thanatologist, retirement counselor, jury selection specialist, weight control counselor, stress reduction counselor, executive recruiter, and sleep disorders therapist. In short, psychology should remain a stimulating and innovative field as the demand for psychological skills and services continues to grow. Perhaps psychology holds a future for you.

Additional Sources of Information

American Psychological Association. *Careers in psychology.* (Address: 750 1st Street, N.E., Washington, DC, 20002. One copy of this pamphlet will be sent free, on request.)

American Psychological Association. *Career encounters in psychology*, 1991. (Videotape: Address given above.)

American Psychological Association. *Getting In: A step-by-step plan for gaining admission to graduate school in psychology*, 1993. (Address given above.)

American Psychological Association. *Graduate study in psychology* (revised annually). Washington, DC: 1992, with 1993 Addendum. (Address given above.)

American Psychological Association. *Psychology and You*, 1986. (Address given above. One copy of this pamphlet will be sent free, on request.)

Keith-Spiegel, P. *The complete guide to graduate school admission: Psychology and related fields.* Hillsdale, NJ: Erlbaum, 1990.

Purdy, J. E., Reinehr, R. C., & Swartz, J. D. Graduate admissions criteria of leading psychology departments. *American Psychologist, 44*, 960–961, 1989.

Woods, P. J. (Ed.), with C. S. Wilkinson. *Is psychology the major for you? Planning for your undergraduate years.* Washington, DC: American Psychological Association, 1987.

Appendix B

Statistics*

Statistics from "Heads" to "Tails"

Let's say a friend of yours invites you to try your hand at a "game of chance." He offers to flip a coin and pay you a dollar if the coin comes up heads. If the coin shows tails, you must pay him a dollar. He flips the coin: tails—you pay him a dollar. He flips it again: tails. Again: tails. And again: tails. And again: tails.

At this point you are faced with a choice. Should you continue the game in an attempt to recoup your losses? Or should you assume that the coin is biased and quit before you really get "skinned"? Taking out a pocket calculator (and the statistics book you carry with you at all times), you compute the odds of obtaining 5 tails in a row from an unbiased coin. The probability is 0.031 (roughly 3 times out of 100).

If the coin really is honest, 5 consecutive tails is a rare event. Wisely, you decide that the coin is probably biased and refuse to play again. (Unless, of course, your "friend" is willing to take "tails" for the next 5 tosses!)

Perhaps a decision could have been made in this hypothetical example without using statistics. But notice how much clearer the situation becomes when it is expressed statistically.

*Portions of this appendix were contributed by Danniel Downey, Ph.D.

Statistics in Psychology Psychologists try to extract and summarize useful information from the observations they make. To do so, they use two major types of statistics. The first type, called **descriptive statistics,** summarizes or "boils down" numbers so they become more meaningful and easier to communicate to others. The second type, known as **inferential statistics,** is used for decision making, for generalizing from small samples, and for drawing conclusions. As was the case in the coin-flipping example, psychologists must often base decisions on limited data. Such decisions are much easier to make with the help of inferential statistics.

Descriptive Statistics

Statistics bring greater clarity and precision to psychological thought and research. To see how, let's begin by considering three basic types of descriptive statistics: **graphical statistics,** measures of **central tendency,** and measures of **variability.**

Graphical Statistics Table B–1 shows simulated scores on a test of hypnotic susceptibility given to 100 college students. With such disorganized data, it is hard to form an overall "picture" of the differences in hypnotic susceptibility. But by using a **frequency distribution,** large amounts of information can be

Table B–1 Raw Scores of Hypnotic Susceptibility

55	86	52	17	61	57	84	51	16	64
22	56	25	38	35	24	54	26	37	38
52	42	59	26	21	55	40	59	25	57
91	27	38	53	19	93	25	39	52	56
66	14	18	63	59	68	12	19	62	45
47	98	88	72	50	49	96	89	71	66
50	44	71	57	90	53	41	72	56	93
57	38	55	49	87	59	36	56	48	70
33	69	50	50	60	35	67	51	50	52
11	73	46	16	67	13	71	47	25	77

Table B–2 Frequency Distribution of Hypnotic Susceptibility Scores

Class Interval	Number of Persons in Class
0–19	10
20–39	20
40–59	40
60–79	20
80–99	10

neatly organized and summarized. A frequency distribution is made by breaking down the entire range of possible scores into *classes* of equal size. Next, the number of scores falling into each class is recorded. In Table B–2, the raw data from Table B–1 have been condensed into a frequency distribution. Notice how much clearer the pattern of scores for the entire group becomes.

Frequency distributions are often shown *graphically* to make them more "visual." **Histograms,** as these graphs are called, are made by labeling class intervals on the *abscissa* (horizontal line) and frequencies (the number of scores in each class) on the *ordinate* (vertical line). Next, bars are drawn for each class interval; the height of each bar is determined by the number of scores in each class (Fig. B–1). An alternate way of graphing scores is the more familiar **frequency polygon** (Fig. B–2). Here, points are placed at the center of each class interval to indicate the number of scores. Then the dots are connected by straight lines.

Measures of Central Tendency Notice in Table B–2 that more scores fall in the range 40–59 than elsewhere. How can we show this fact? A measure of **central tendency** is simply a number describing a "typical score" around which other scores fall. A familiar measure of central tendency is the mean, or "average." But as we shall see in a moment, there are other types of "averages" that can be used. To illustrate each we need an example: Table B–3 shows the raw data

Fig. B–1 *Frequency histogram of hypnotic susceptibility scores contained in Table B–2.*

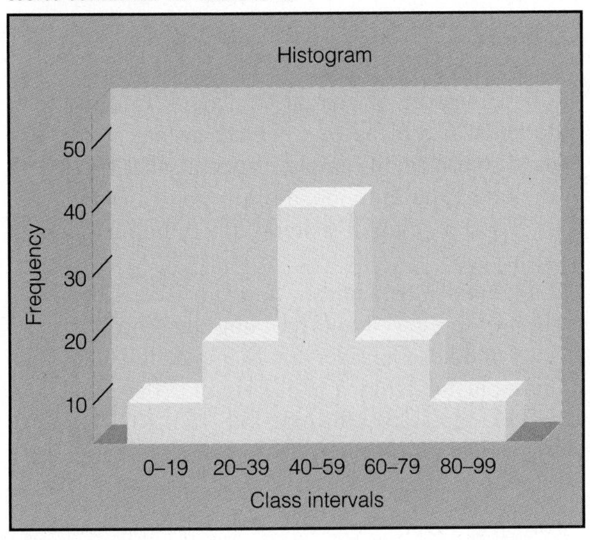

Fig. B–2 *Frequency polygon of hypnotic susceptibility scores contained in Table B–2.*

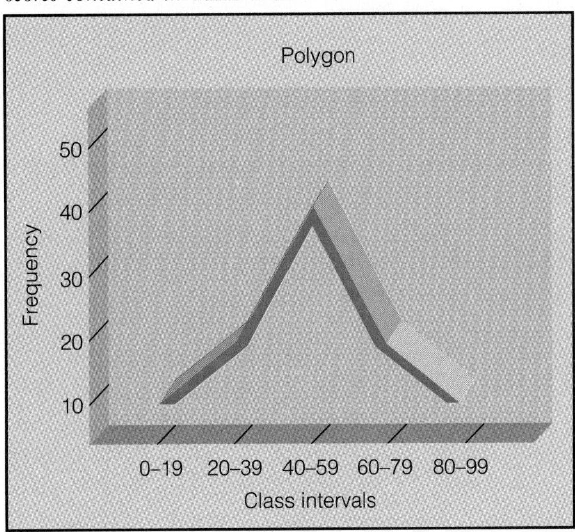

Table B–3 Raw Scores on a Memory Test for Subjects Taking Rememberine or a Placebo

Subject	Group 1 Rememberine	Group 2 Placebo
1	65	54
2	67	60
3	73	63
4	65	33
5	58	56
6	55	60
7	70	60
8	69	31
9	60	62
10	68	61
Sum	650	540
Mean	65	54
Median	66	60

$$\text{Mean} = \frac{\Sigma X}{N} \text{ or } \frac{\text{Sum of all scores, X}}{\text{number of scores}}$$

$$\text{Mean Group 1} = \frac{65 + 67 + 73 + 65 + 58 + 55 + 70 + 69 + 60 + 68}{10}$$

$$= \frac{650}{10} = 65$$

$$\text{Mean Group 2} = \frac{54 + 60 + 63 + 33 + 56 + 60 + 60 + 31 + 62 + 61}{10}$$

$$= \frac{540}{10} = 54$$

Median = the middle score or the mean of the two middle scores*

Median Group 1 = 55 58 60 65 [65 67] 68 69 70 73

$$= \frac{65 + 67}{2} = 66$$

Median Group 2 = 31 33 54 56 [60 60] 60 61 62 63

$$= \frac{60 + 60}{2} = 60$$

☐ indicates middle score(s).

for an imaginary experiment in which two groups of subjects were given a test of memory. Assume that one group was given a drug that might improve memory (let's call the drug Rememberine). The second group received a placebo. Is there a difference in memory scores between the two groups? It's difficult to tell without computing an average.

As one type of "average," the **mean** is calculated by adding all the scores for each group and then dividing by the total number of scores. Notice in Table B–3 that the means reveal a difference between the two groups.

The mean is sensitive to extremely high or low scores in a distribution. For this reason it is not always the best measure of central tendency. (Imagine how distorted it would be to calculate average yearly incomes from a small sample of people that happened to include a multimillionaire.) In such cases the *middle score* in a group of scores—called the **median**—is used instead.

The median is found by arranging scores from the highest to the lowest and selecting the score that falls in the middle. Consider for example, the following weights obtained from a small class of college students: 105, 111, 123, 126, 148, 151, 154, 162, 182. The median for the group is 148, the middle score. Of course, if there is an even number of scores, there will be no "middle score." This problem is handled by averaging the two scores that "share" the middle spot. This procedure yields a single number to serve as the median (see bottom panel of Table B–3).

A final measure of central tendency is the **mode.** The mode is simply the most frequently occurring score in a group of scores. If you were to take the time to count the scores in Table B–3, you would find that the mode of Group 1 is 65, and the mode of Group 2 is 60. The mode is usually easy to obtain. However, the mode can be an unreliable measure, especially in a small group of scores. The mode's advantage is that it gives the score actually obtained by the greatest number of people.

Measures of Variability Let's say a researcher discovers two drugs that lower anxiety in agitated patients. However, let's also assume that one drug consistently lowers anxiety by moderate amounts, whereas the second sometimes lowers it by large amounts, sometimes has no effect, or may even increase anxiety in some patients. Overall, there is no difference in the *average* (mean) amount of anxiety reduction. Even so, an important difference exists between the two drugs. As this example shows, it is not enough to simply know the average score in a distribution. Usually, we would also like to know if scores are grouped closely together or scattered widely.

Measures of **variability** provide a single number that tells how "spread out" scores are. When the scores are widely spread, this number gets larger. When they are close together it gets smaller. If you look again at the example in Table B–3, you will notice that the scores within each group vary widely. How can we show this fact?

The simplest way would be to use the **range,** which is the difference between the highest and lowest scores. In Group 1 of our experiment, the highest score is 73, and the lowest is 55; thus, the range is 18 (73 − 55 = 18). In Group 2, the highest score is 63, and the lowest is 31; this makes the range 32. Scores in Group 2 are more spread out than those in Group 1.

A better measure of variability is the **standard deviation.** To obtain the standard deviation, we find the deviation (or difference) of each score from the mean and then square it (multiply it by itself). These squared deviations are then added and averaged (the total is divided by the number of deviations). Taking the square root of this average yields the standard deviation (● Table B–4). Notice again that the variability for Group 1 (5.4) is smaller than that for Group 2 (where the standard deviation is 11.3).

● Table B–4 Computation of the Standard Deviation

Score − Mean	Deviation (d)	Deviation Squared (d^2)
Group 1 Mean = 65		
65 − 65 =	0	0
67 − 65 =	2	4
73 − 65 =	8	64
65 − 65 =	0	0
58 − 65 =	−7	49
55 − 65 =	−10	100
70 − 65 =	5	25
69 − 65 =	4	16
60 − 65 =	−5	25
68 − 65 =	3	9
		292

$$SD = \sqrt{\frac{\text{sum of } d^2}{n}} = \sqrt{\frac{292}{10}} = \sqrt{29.2} = 5.4$$

Score − Mean	Deviation (d)	Deviation Squared (d^2)
Group 2 Mean = 54		
54 − 54 =	0	0
60 − 54 =	6	36
63 − 54 =	9	81
33 − 54 =	−21	441
56 − 54 =	2	4
60 − 54 =	6	36
60 − 54 =	6	36
31 − 54 =	−23	529
62 − 54 =	8	64
61 − 54 =	7	49
		1276

$$SD = \sqrt{\frac{\text{sum of } d^2}{n}} = \sqrt{\frac{1276}{10}} = \sqrt{127.6} = 11.3$$

Standard Scores A particular advantage of the standard deviation is that it can be used to "standardize" scores in a way that gives them greater meaning. For example, John and Susan both took psychology midterms, but in different classes. John earned a score of 118, and Susan scored 110. Who did better? It is impossible to tell without knowing what the average score was on each test, and whether John and Susan scored at the top, middle, or bottom of their classes. We would like to have one number that gives all this information. A number that does this is the **z-score.**

To convert original scores to z-scores, we subtract the mean from the score. The resulting number is then divided by the standard deviation for that group of scores. To illustrate, Susan had a score of 110 in a class with a mean of 100 and a standard deviation of 10. Therefore, her z-score is +1.0 (● Table B–5). John's score of 118 came from a class having a mean of 100 and a standard deviation of 18; thus his z-score is also +1.0 (see Table B–5). Originally it looked as if John did better on his midterm than Susan did. But we now see that relatively speaking, their scores were equivalent. Compared to other students, each was an equal distance above average.

Table B–5 Computation of a z-Score

$$z = \frac{X - \bar{X}}{SD} \text{ or } \frac{\text{score} - \text{mean}}{\text{standard deviation}}$$

$$\text{Susan: } z = \frac{110 - 100}{10} = \frac{+10}{10} = +1.0$$

$$\text{John: } z = \frac{118 - 100}{18} = \frac{+18}{18} = +1.0$$

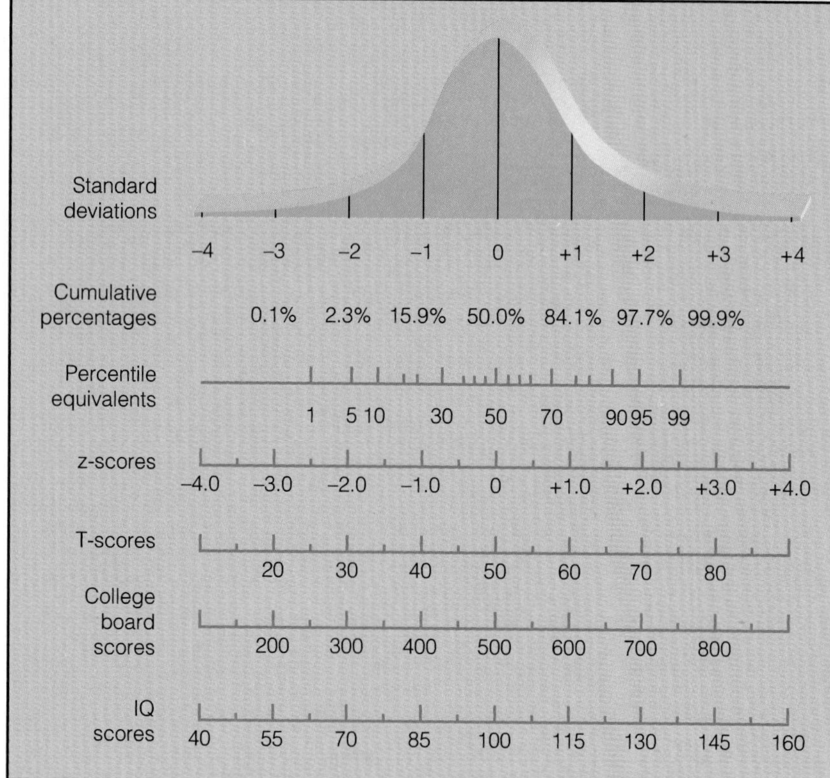

Fig. B–3 *The normal curve. The normal curve is an idealized mathematical model. However, many measurements in psychology closely approximate a normal curve. The scales you see here show the relationship of standard deviations, z-scores, and other measures to the curve.*

Table B–6 Area Under the Normal Curve as a Percentage of Total Area for a Variety of z-Scores

z-Score	Percentage of Area to the Left of This Value	Percentage of Area to the Right of This Value
−3.0 SD	00.1	99.9
−2.5 SD	00.6	99.4
−2.0 SD	02.3	97.7
−1.5 SD	06.7	93.3
−1.0 SD	15.9	84.1
−0.5 SD	30.9	69.1
0.0 SD	50.0	50.0
+0.5 SD	69.1	30.9
+1.0 SD	84.1	15.9
+1.5 SD	93.3	06.7
+2.0 SD	97.7	02.3
+2.5 SD	99.4	00.6
+3.0 SD	99.9	00.1

The Normal Curve

When chance events are recorded, we find that some outcomes have a high probability and occur very often; others have a low probability and occur infrequently; still others have little probability and occur rarely. As a result, the distribution (or tally) of chance events typically resembles a **normal curve** (Fig. B–3). Most psychological traits or events are determined by the action of a large number of factors. Therefore, like chance events, measures of psychological variables tend to roughly match a normal curve. For example, direct measurement has shown such characteristics as height, memory span, and intelligence to be distributed approximately along a normal curve. In other words, many people have average height, memory ability, and intelligence. However, as we move above or below average, fewer and fewer people are found.

It is very fortunate that so many psychological variables tend to form a normal curve, because much is known about the curve. One valuable property concerns the relationship between the standard deviation and the normal curve. Specifically, the standard deviation measures off set proportions of the curve above and below the mean. For example, in Figure B–4, notice that roughly 68 percent of all cases (IQ scores, memory scores, heights, or whatever) fall between one standard deviation above and below the mean (±1 SD); 95 percent of all cases fall between ±2 SD; and 99 percent of the cases can be found between ±3 SD from the mean.

Table B–6 gives a more complete account of the relationship between z-scores and the percentage of cases found in a particular area of the normal curve. Notice for example, that 93.3 percent of all cases fall below a z-score of +1.5. A z-score of 1.5 on a test (no matter what the original, or "raw," score was) would be a good performance, since roughly 93 percent of all scores fall below this mark. Relationships between the standard deviation (or z-scores) and the normal curve do not change. This makes it possible to com-

Fig. B–4 *Relationship between the standard deviation and the normal curve.*

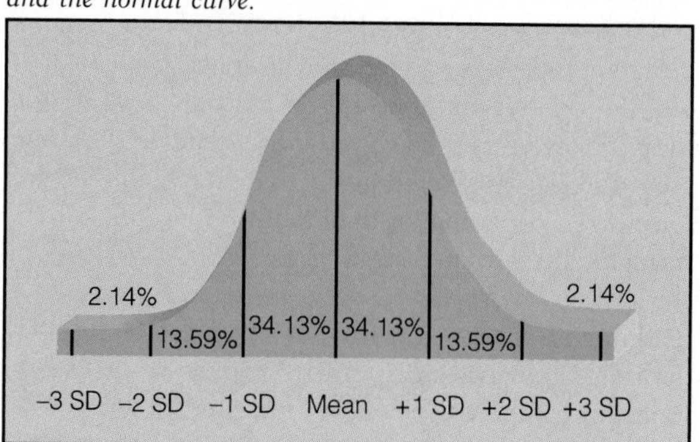

pare various tests or groups of scores if they come from distributions that are approximately normal.

Inferential Statistics

Let's say that a researcher studies the effects of a new therapy on a small group of depressed individuals. Is he or she interested only in these particular individuals? Usually not, since except in rare instances, psychologists seek to discover general laws of behavior that apply widely to humans and animals. Undoubtedly the researcher would like to know if the therapy holds any promise for all depressed people. As stated earlier, **inferential statistics** are techniques that allow us to make inferences. That is, they allow us to generalize from the behavior of small groups of subjects to that of the larger groups they represent.

Samples and Populations In any scientific study, we would like to observe the entire set, or **population,** of subjects, objects, or events of interest. However, this is usually impossible or impractical. Observing all Catholics, all cancer patients, or all mothers-in-law could be both impractical (since all are large populations) and impossible (since people change denominations, may be unaware of having cancer, and change their status as relatives). In such cases, **samples** (smaller cross sections of a population) are selected, and observations of the sample are used to draw conclusions about the entire population.

For any sample to be meaningful, it must be **representative.** That is, the sample group must truly reflect the membership and characteristics of the larger population. In our earlier hypothetical study of a memory drug, it would be essential for the sample of 20 people to be representative of the general population. A very important aspect of representative samples is that their members are chosen at **random.** In other words, each member of the population must have an equal chance of being included in the sample.

Significant Differences In our imaginary drug experiment, we found that the average memory score was higher for the group given the drug than it was for persons who didn't take the drug (the placebo group). Certainly this result is interesting, but could it have occurred by chance? If two groups were repeatedly tested (with neither receiving any drug), their average memory scores would sometimes differ. How much must two means differ before we can consider the difference "real" (not due to chance)?

Notice that the question is similar to one discussed earlier: How many tails in a row must we obtain when flipping a coin before we can conclude that the coin is biased? In the case of the coin, we noted that obtaining 5 tails in a row is a rare event. Thus, it became reasonable to assume that the coin was biased. Of course, it is possible to get 5 tails in a row when flipping an honest coin. But since this outcome is unlikely, we have good reason to suspect that something other than chance (a loaded coin, for instance) caused the results. Similar reasoning is used in tests of statistical significance.

Tests of **statistical significance** provide an estimate of how often experimental results could have occurred by chance alone. The results of a significance test are stated as a probability. This probability gives the odds that the observed difference was due to chance. In psychology, any experimental result that could have occurred by chance 5 times (or less) out of 100 (in other words, a probability of .05 or less) is considered *significant.* In our memory experiment, the probability is .025 ($p = .025$) that the group means would differ as they do by chance alone. This allows us to conclude with reasonable certainty that the drug actually did improve memory scores.

Correlation

Many of the statements that psychologists make about behavior do not result from the use of experimental methods. Rather, they come from keen observations and measures of existing phenomena. A psychologist might note, for example, that the higher a couple's socioeconomic and educational status, the smaller the number of children they are likely to have. Or that grades in high school are related to how well a person is likely to do in college. Or even that as rainfall levels increase within a given metropolitan area, crime rates decline. In these instances, we are dealing with the fact that two variables are **co-relating** (varying together in some orderly fashion).

The simplest way of visualizing a correlation is to construct a **scatter diagram.** In a scatter diagram, two measures (grades in high school and grades in college, for instance) are obtained. One measure is indicated by the X axis and the second by the Y axis. The scatter diagram plots the intersection (crossing) of each pair of measurements as a single point. Many such measurement pairs give pictures like those shown in ■ Figure B–5.

Figure B–5 also shows scatter diagrams of three basic kinds of relationships between variables (or measures). Graphs A, B, and C show **positive relationships** of varying strength. As you can see, in a positive relationship, increases in the X measure (or score) are matched by increases on the Y measure (or score). An example would be finding that higher IQ scores (X) are associated with higher college grades (Y). A **zero correlation** (or relationship) is pictured in graph D.

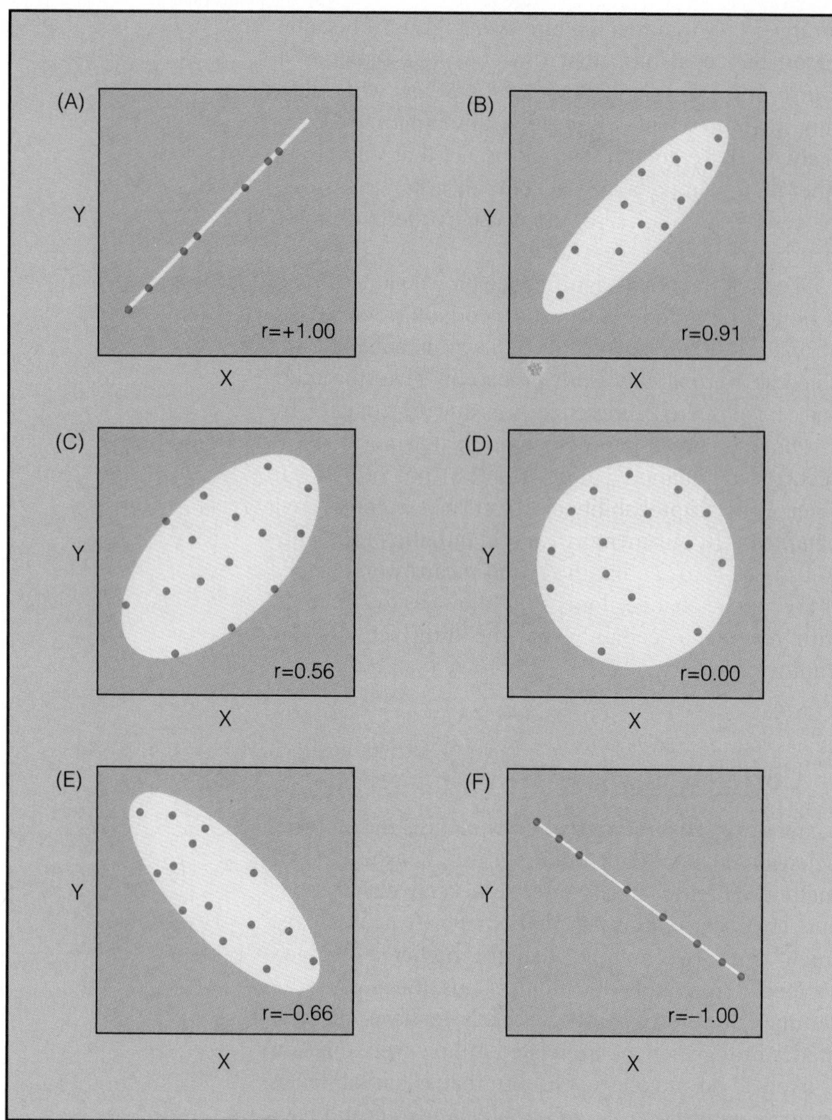

■ **Fig. B–5** *Scatter diagrams showing various degrees of relationship for a positive, zero, and negative correlation. (Adapted from Pagano, 1981.)*

This might be the result of comparing subjects' hat sizes (X) to their college grades (Y). Graphs E and F both show a **negative relationship** (or correlation). Notice that as values of one measure increase, those of the second become smaller. An example might be the relationship between amount of alcohol consumed and scores on a test of coordination: Higher alcohol levels are correlated with lower coordination scores.

Correlations can also be expressed as a **coefficient of correlation.** This coefficient is simply a number falling somewhere between +1.00 and −1.00. If the number is zero or close to zero, it indicates a weak or nonexistent relationship. If the correlation is +1.00, a **perfect positive relationship** exists; if it is −1.00, a **perfect negative relationship** has been discovered. The most commonly used correlation coefficient is called the Pearson *r*. Calculation of the Pearson *r* is relatively simple, as shown in ⬬ Table B–7. (The numbers shown are hypothetical.)

As stated in Chapter 2, correlations in psychology are rarely perfect. Most fall somewhere between zero and plus or minus 1. The closer the correlation coefficient is to +1.00 or −1.00, the stronger the relationship. An interesting example of some typical correlations is provided by a study that compared the IQs of adopted children with the IQs of their biological mothers. At age 4, the children's IQs correlated .28 with their mothers' IQs. By age 7 the correlation was .35. And by age 13 it had grown to .38.

Correlations often provide highly useful information. For instance, it is valuable to know that there is a correlation between cigarette smoking and lung cancer rates. Another example is the fact that higher consumption of alcohol during pregnancy is correlated with lower birth weight and a higher rate of birth defects. There is a correlation between the number of recent life stresses experienced and the likelihood of emotional disturbance. Many more examples could be cited, but the point is, correlations help us to identify relationships that are worth knowing.

Correlations are particularly valuable for making **predictions.** If we know that two measures are correlated, and we know a person's score on one measure, we can predict his or her score on the other. For example, most colleges have formulas that use multiple correlations to decide which applicants have the best chances for success. Usually the formula includes such predictors as high school GPA, teacher ratings, extracurricular activities, and scores on the *Scholastic Assessment Test* (SAT) or some similar test. Although no single predictor is perfectly correlated with success in college, together the various predictors correlate highly and provide a useful technique for screening applicants.

There is an interesting "trick" you can do with correlations that you may find useful. It works like this: If you *square* the correlation coefficient (multiply *r* by itself), you will get a number telling the **percent of variance** accounted for by the correlation. For example, the correlation between IQ scores and college grade point average is .5. Multiplying .5 times .5 gives .25, or 25 percent. This means that 25 percent of the variation in college grades is accounted for by knowing IQ scores. In other words, with a correlation of .5, college grades are "squeezed" into an oval like the one shown in graph C, Figure B–5. IQ scores take away some of the possible variation in corresponding grade point averages. If there were no correlation between IQ and grades, grades would be completely free to vary, as shown in Figure B–5, graph D.

Along the same line, a correlation of +1.00 or −1.00 means that 100 percent of the variation in the Y measure is accounted for by knowing the X measure:

If you know a person's X score, you can tell exactly what the Y score is. An example that comes close to this state of affairs is the high correlation (.86) between the IQs of identical twins. In any group of identical twins, 74 percent of the variation in the "Y" twins' IQs is accounted for by knowing the IQs of their siblings (the "X's").

Correlation and Causation It is very important to recognize that finding a correlation between two measures does not automatically mean that one causes the other: *Correlation does not demonstrate causation.* When a correlation exists, the best we can say is that two variables are related. Of course, this does not mean that it is impossible for two correlated variables to have a cause-and-effect relationship. Rather, it means that we cannot *conclude*, solely on the basis of correlation, that a causal link exists. To gain greater confidence that a cause-and-effect relationship exists, an experiment must be performed (see Chapter 1).

Often, two correlated measures are related as a result of the influence of a third variable. For example, we might observe that the more hours students devote to studying, the better their grades. Although it is tempting to conclude that more studying produces (causes) better grades, it is possible (indeed, it is probable) that grades and the amount of study time are both related to the amount of motivation or interest a student has.

The difference between cause-and-effect data and data that reveal a relationship of unknown origin is one that should not be forgotten. Since we rarely run experiments in daily life, the information on which we act is largely correlational. This should make us more humble and more tentative in the confidence with which we make pronouncements about human behavior.

Table B–7 IQ and Grade Point Average for Computing Pearson *r*

Student No.	IQ X	Grade Point Average Y	X Score Squared X^2	Y Score Squared Y^2	X Times Y XY
1	110	1.0	12,100	1.00	110.0
2	112	1.6	12,544	2.56	179.2
3	118	1.2	13,924	1.44	141.6
4	119	2.1	14,161	4.41	249.9
5	122	2.6	14,884	6.76	317.2
6	125	1.8	15,625	3.24	225.0
7	127	2.6	16,124	6.76	330.2
8	130	2.0	16,900	4.00	260.0
9	132	3.2	17,424	10.24	422.4
10	134	2.6	17,956	6.76	348.4
11	136	3.0	18,496	9.00	408.0
12	138	3.6	19,044	12.96	496.8
Total	1503	27.3	189,187	69.13	3488.7

$$r = \frac{\Sigma XY - \dfrac{(\Sigma X)(\Sigma Y)}{N}}{\sqrt{\left[\Sigma X^2 - \dfrac{(\Sigma X)^2}{N}\right]\left[\Sigma Y^2 - \dfrac{(\Sigma Y)^2}{N}\right]}}$$

$$= \frac{3488.7 - \dfrac{1503(27.3)}{12}}{\sqrt{\left[189{,}187 - \dfrac{(1503)^2}{12}\right]\left[69.13 - \dfrac{(27.3)^2}{12}\right]}}$$

$$= \frac{69.375}{81.088} = 0.856 = 0.86$$

(Adapted from Pagano, 1981.)

Glossary

Ablation Surgical removal of tissue.
Absolute threshold The minimum amount of physical energy necessary to produce a sensation.
Accommodation (perceptual) Changes in the shape of the lens of the eye that serve to focus objects at varying distances.
Accommodation (Piaget) The modification of existing mental patterns to fit new demands.
Acculturative stress Stress caused by the many changes and adaptations required when a person moves to a foreign culture.
Acetylcholine The neurotransmitter released by neurons to activate muscles.
Achieved role A role that is assumed voluntarily.
Achievement motivation A need for success or the attainment of excellence.
Acquisition The period in conditioning during which a response is reinforced.
Action component That part of an attitude consisting of how one tends to act toward the object of the attitude.
Action potential The nerve impulse, which is a rapid change in electrical charge across the cell membrane.
Activation As reflected in facial expressions, the degree of arousal experienced by the person making the expression.
Activation-synthesis hypothesis Theory that relates dream content to motor commands in the brain, which are made, but not carried out during sleep.
Active euthanasia Deliberately inducing death.
Activity theory Theory of aging stating that the best adjustment to aging occurs for individuals who remain active mentally, socially, and physically.
Actor In making attributions, the person whose behavior is being interpreted.
Acuity That aspect of visual perception having to do with the sharpness or resolution of images.
Acupuncture The Chinese medical art of relieving pain and treating illness by inserting thin needles at various points on the body.
Acute stress disorder Psychological disturbance lasting up to one month following stresses, such as natural disasters or military combat, that would produce anxiety in anyone who experienced them.
Adaptation level An internal or mental "average" or "medium" point that is used to judge amounts.
Adaptive behaviors (emotion) Actions that aid humans and animals in their attempts to survive and adapt to changing conditions.
Adaptive behaviors (retardation) Basic skills and actions considered necessary for self-care and for dealing successfully with the environment.
Addiction Development of physical dependence on a drug such that craving and physical discomfort (withdrawal symptoms) occur in its absence.
Adjustment disorder Emotional disturbance caused by stressors within the range of common experience; stress is ongoing and produces anxiety and physical symptoms.
Adolescence The socially defined period between childhood and adulthood.
Adrenal glands Endocrine glands whose hormones arouse the body, regulate salt balance, adjust the body to stress, and affect sexual functioning.
Adrenaline A hormone produced by the adrenal glands that tends, in general, to arouse the body.
Affect Pertaining to emotion or feelings.
Affectional needs One's emotional needs in general but, especially, needs for love, attention, and affection.
Affective psychosis A general term for any major mood disorder that includes psychotic symptoms.
Afterimage A visual sensation that persists after a stimulus is removed.
Ageism Discrimination or prejudice based on a person's age.
Aggression Any action carried out with the intent of harming another person.
Aggression cues Stimuli or signals that are associated with aggression and tend to elicit it.
Agnosia A disturbance in the ability to perceive the meaning of stimuli, such as words, objects, or pictures.
Agoraphobia (without panic) Persons fear that something extremely embarrassing will happen to them if they leave the house or enter unfamiliar situations.
Alarm reaction First stage of the G.A.S., during which bodily resources are mobilized to cope with a stressor.
Alcohol Common name for ethyl alcohol, the intoxicating element in fermented and distilled liquors.
All-or-nothing thinking Classifying objects or events as absolutely right or wrong, good or bad, acceptable or unacceptable, and so forth.
Altered state of consciousness A condition of awareness distinctly different in quality or pattern from waking consciousness.
Alzheimer's disease An age-related disease characterized by memory loss, mental confusion, and in its later stages, by a nearly total loss of mental abilities.
Ambiguous stimuli Patterns that allow more than one perceptual organization.
Ambivalence Mixed positive and negative feelings or simultaneous attraction and repulsion.
Ambivalent attachment An emotional bond marked by conflicting feelings of affection, anger, and emotional turmoil.
American Sign Language A language system of hand gestures used by deaf and hearing-impaired persons.
Ames room An intentionally distorted room that

interrupts perceptual constancies.

Amnesia Loss of memory (partial or complete) for past events and, especially, loss of memory for one's identity.

Amniocentesis Testing of the amniotic fluid from a pregnant woman's womb to identify fetal sex and to detect genetic defects in the fetus.

Amphetamine psychosis A severe disruption of psychological functioning caused by abuse of amphetamines.

Amphetamines A class of synthetic drugs having stimulant effects on the nervous system.

Anagrams Test A test of creativity in which subjects try to make as many new words as possible from the letters in a given word.

Anal stage In Freud's theory, the psychosexual stage corresponding roughly to the period of toilet training (age 1 to 3) and characterized by a preoccupation with the process of elimination.

Androgen Any of a number of male sex hormones, especially testosterone.

Androgen insensitivity An inherited disorder in which male embryos fail to develop male genitals because of an unresponsiveness to testosterone.

Androgenital syndrome An inherited disorder that causes the adrenal glands to produce excess androgens, sometimes masculinizing developing females before birth.

Androgyny The presence of both "masculine" and "feminine" traits in a single person (as masculinity and femininity are traditionally defined within one's culture).

Animal model In research, an animal whose behavior is used to discover principles that may apply to human behavior.

Anorexia nervosa Active self-starvation or a sustained loss of appetite that has psychological origins.

Anosmia Loss or impairment of the sense of smell.

Antecedents Events that precede a response.

Anterograde amnesia Loss of the ability to form or retrieve memories for events that occur after an injury or trauma.

Anthropomorphic fallacy The error of attributing human thoughts, feelings, or motives to animals.

Anti-depressant A mood-elevating drug.

Antipsychotic A drug that, in addition to having tranquilizing effects, also tends to reduce hallucinations and delusional thinking.

Antisocial personality A person who seems to lack a conscience, is emotionally shallow, impulsive, selfish, and tends to manipulate others; also referred to as a sociopath or psychopath.

Anxiety Apprehension, dread, or uneasiness similar to fear but based on an unclear threat.

Anxiety disorder A disorder characterized by disruptive feelings of fear, apprehension, or anxiety or by distortions in behavior that are anxiety related.

Anxiety reduction hypothesis An explanation of the self-defeating nature of many avoidance responses that emphasizes the immediate reinforcing effects of relief from anxiety.

Aphasia A speech disturbance resulting from damage to language areas on the temporal lobes of the brain.

Apparent distance hypothesis An explanation of the moon illusion stating that the horizon seems more distant than the night sky because there are more depth cues near the horizon.

Applied psychology The use of psychological principles and research methods to solve practical problems.

Applied research Scientific study undertaken to solve immediate practical problems.

Approach-approach conflict A condition in which a person or animal must choose between two positive, or desirable, alternatives.

Approach-avoidance conflict An unpleasant condition in which a person or animal is simultaneously attracted to and repelled by the same goal.

Aptitude A capacity for learning certain abilities.

Aptitude test A test that rates a person's potential to learn skills required by various occupations.

Archetype A universal idea, image, or pattern, found in the collective unconscious.

Architectural psychology Study of the effects buildings have on behavior and the design of buildings using behavioral principles.

Arousal The overall level of excitation or activation in a person or animal.

Arousal theory A theory of motivation that assumes people prefer to maintain "ideal," or comfortable, levels of arousal.

Artificial insemination Medically engineered impregnation.

Artificial intelligence Any artificial system (often a computer program) that is capable of human-like problem solving or skilled responding.

Ascribed role A role that is assigned to a person; a role one has no choice about playing.

Assertiveness training Instruction in how to be self-assertive.

Assessment Evaluation or measurement.

Assessment center A program set up within an organization to conduct in-depth evaluations of job candidates.

Assimilation In Piaget's theory, the application of existing mental patterns to new situations (that is, the new situation is assimilated to existing mental schemes).

Association cortex All areas of the cerebral cortex that are not specifically sensory or motor in function.

Astigmatism Defects in the cornea, lens, or eye that cause some areas of vision to be out of focus.

Astrology False system based on the belief that human behavior is influenced by the position of stars and planets.

Attention Orienting toward or focusing on some stimulus.

Attention-deficit hyperactivity disorder A behavioral problem characterized by short attention span and restless movement.

Attentional overload A stressful condition caused when sensory stimulation, information, and social contacts make excessive demands on attention.

Attitude A learned tendency to respond to people, objects, or institutions in a positive or negative way.

Attitude scale A collection of attitude statements with which respondents indicate agreement or disagreement.

Attribution The process of making inferences about the causes of one's own behavior, and that of others. In emotion, the process of attributing perceived arousal to a particular source.

Auditory area Sites on the temporal lobes where auditory information registers.

Auditory ossicles The three small bones that link the eardrum to the inner ear.

Authenticity In Carl Rogers' terms, the ability of a therapist to be genuine and honest regarding his or her feelings.

Authoritarian parents Parents who enforce rigid rules and demand strict obedience to authority.

Authoritarian personality A personality pattern characterized by rigidity, inhibition, prejudice, and an excessive concern with power, authority, and obedience.

Authoritative parents Parents who supply firm and consistent guidance combined with love and affection.

Autism A severe disorder of childhood involving mutism, sensory spin-outs, sensory blocking, tantrums, unresponsiveness to others, and other difficulties.

Autokinetic effect The apparent movement of a stationary pinpoint of light displayed in a darkened room.

Autonomic nervous system The neural system that connects the brain with the internal organs and glands.

Autonomy A freedom from dependence on external authority or the opinions of others.

Aversion therapy Suppression of an undesirable response by associating it with aversive (painful or uncomfortable) stimuli.

Aversive stimulus Any stimulus that produces discomfort or displeasure.

Avoidance learning Learning that occurs when making a particular response delays or prevents the onset of a painful or unpleasant stimulus.

Avoidance-avoidance conflict An unpleasant condition requiring a choice between two negative, or mutually undesirable, alternatives.

Avoidant attachment An emotional bond marked by a tendency to resist commitment to others.

Axon A thin fiber that conducts information away from the cell body of a neuron.

Babbling The repetition by infants of meaningless language sounds (including both vowel and consonant sounds).

Bait shyness An unwillingness or hesitation on the part of animals to eat a particular food; often caused by the presence of a taste aversion.

Barbiturate One of a large group of sedative drugs.

Barnum effect The tendency to consider a personal description accurate if it is stated in very general terms.

Base rate The basic rate at which an event occurs over time; the basic probability of an event.

Baseline A record of the initial frequency of a target behavior.

Basic (or "pure") research Scientific study undertaken without concern for immediate practical application.

Basic needs The first four levels of needs in Maslow's hierarchy; lower needs tend to be more potent than higher needs.
Basic research Scientific inquiry done to advance basic knowledge, not to solve a practical problem.
Basic suggestion effect The tendency of hypnotized persons to carry out suggested actions as if they were involuntary.
Behavior modification The application of learning principles to change human behavior, especially maladaptive behavior.
Behavior therapy The use of learning principles to make constructive changes in behavior.
Behavioral assessment Recording the frequency of various behaviors.
Behavioral genetics The study of inherited behavioral traits and tendencies.
Behavioral medicine The study of behavioral factors associated with physical illness and its treatment.
Behavioral personality theory Any model of personality that emphasizes observable behavior, stimuli and responses, and the impact of learning.
Behavioral risk factors Behaviors that increase the chances of disease or injury or that shorten life expectancy.
Behavioral setting A smaller area within an environment whose use is well defined, such as a bus depot, waiting room, or lounge.
Behaviorism The study of overt, observable behavior.
Bem Sex Role Inventory (BSRI) A list of 60 personal traits including "masculine," "feminine," and "neutral" traits; used to rate one's degree of androgyny.
Bereavement Period of emotional adjustment that follows the death of a loved one.
Beta-endorphin A natural chemical produced by the pituitary gland that is similar in structure and pain-killing effect to opiate drugs such as morphine.
Biased sample A sample that does not accurately reflect the population from which it was drawn.
Bibliotherapy Use of books to impart helpful information, either alone or as an adjunct to other forms of therapy.
Binocular depth cues Depth cues that function only when both eyes are used.
Biochemical abnormality A disturbance of the body's chemical systems, especially in brain chemicals or neurotransmitters.
Biodata Detailed biographical information about a job applicant.
Biofeedback Information about bodily activities that aids voluntary regulation of bodily states.
Biological aging Physiological changes that accompany increasing age and alter a variety of physical and psychological functions.
Biological biasing effect Hypothesized effect that prenatal exposure to male or female hormones has on development of the body, nervous system, and later behavior patterns.
Biological constraints Biological limits on what an animal or person can easily learn.
Biological determinism Belief that behavior is controlled by biological processes, such as heredity or evolution.
Biological predisposition The presumed biological readiness of humans to learn certain skills, such as how to use language.
Biological rhythm Any cycle of biological activity, such as sleep and waking cycles or changes in body temperature.
Biopsychologist A psychologist who studies the relationship between behavior and biological processes, especially activity in the nervous system.
Biopsychology The study of biological processes as they relate to behavior.
Bipolar disorders Emotional disorders involving both depression and extremely elevated or manic moods and behavior.
Bipolar I disorder A mood disorder in which a person is mostly manic (excited, hyperactive, energetic), but has also had one or more periods of depression.
Bipolar II disorder A mood disorder in which a person is mostly depressed (sad, despondent, guilt ridden), but has also had one or more manic episodes.
Birth injury Any injury or damage that occurs to an infant during delivery.
Birthing room A room designed to minimize the medical aspects of giving birth.
Bisexual A person romantically and erotically attracted to both men and women.
Blind spot A portion of the retina lacking visual receptors (the point where the optic nerve leaves the eye).
Bottom-up processing Organizing perceptions by beginning with low-level features.
Brain dominance The language-producing cerebral hemisphere.
Brainstem The lowest portions of the brain, including the cerebellum, medulla, and reticular formation.
Brainstorming Method of creative thinking that separates the production and evaluation of ideas.
Brainwashing Engineered or forced attitude change involving a captive audience.
Branching program A computer program that gives learners corrective information and exercises based on the nature of their errors.
Brand image The image that consumers have of various products, especially with regard to their personal or emotional meanings.
Brief reactive psychosis A sudden, brief psychotic break that follows the occurrence of an extremely stressful event.
Brightness The intensity of light reflected from or emanating from a surface.
Brightness constancy The apparent (or relative) brightness of various objects remains the same as long as each object is illuminated by the same amount of light.
Broca's area A language area related to grammar and pronunciation.
Bulimia nervosa Excessive eating (gorging) usually followed by self-induced vomiting and/or taking laxatives.
Burnout A job-related condition of mental, physical, and emotional exhaustion.

Caffeine A natural drug with stimulant properties; found in coffee and tea and added to artificial beverages and medicines.
Caffeinism Excessive consumption of caffeine, leading to dependence and a variety of physical and psychological complaints.
Camouflage Designs that break up figure-ground organization, making objects more difficult to see.
Cannabis sativa The hemp plant, from whose leaves and flowers marijuana and hashish are derived.
Cannon-Bard theory According to this theory, emotional feelings and bodily arousal occur simultaneously and both begin with activity in the thalamus.
Cardinal trait A personality trait so basic or powerful that all or most of a person's activities spring from existence of the trait.
Career center A counseling facility that offers testing, career guidance, and information on various careers.
Career development One's entire career path, from choosing an initial vocation through retirement.
Caregiving styles Identifiable patterns of parental caretaking and interaction with children.
Caretaker speech An exaggerated pattern of speech used by adults when talking to infants.
Case study An intensive investigation of the behavior of a single person.
Castration Surgical removal of the testicles. Castration differs from sterilization, a procedure (such as vasectomy or tubal ligation) that merely makes a man or woman infertile.
Cataplexy A sudden temporary paralysis of the muscles.
Catatonic episode Period of extreme stupor, immobility, and unresponsiveness.
Catatonic schizophrenia Schizophrenia marked by stupor, rigidity, unresponsiveness, posturing, mutism, and, sometimes, agitated, purposeless behavior.
Causation The act of causing some effect.
Central nervous system The brain and spinal cord.
Central traits The core traits that characterize an individual personality.
Cerebellum A cauliflower-shaped projection at the base of the brain that controls posture and coordination.
Cerebral cortex The layer of tissue that forms the outer layer and surface of the cerebrum; the cerebral cortex is responsible for basic sensory and motor functions as well as higher mental processes in humans.
Cerebral hemispheres The right and left halves of the cerebrum.
Cerebrum The two large hemispheres that cover the upper part of the brain.
Character Personal characteristics that have been judged or evaluated; a person's desirable or undesirable qualities.
Chemical senses Senses, such as smell and taste, that respond to chemical molecules.
Chemotherapy Use of psychoactive drugs to treat mental or emotional disturbances.
Chorionic villus sampling Testing of a small piece of the placenta early in pregnancy to detect genetic defects in the fetus.
Chromosomes Thread-like structures ("colored bodies") in the nucleus of each cell that are made

up of DNA which carries the genes. Normal human cells have 23 pairs of chromosomes (46 total).

Chronological age A person's age in years.

Circadian rhythms Cyclical changes in bodily function and arousal that vary on a schedule approximating one 24-hour day.

Clairvoyance The purported ability to perceive events at a distance or through physical barriers.

Classical conditioning A basic form of learning in which existing reflex responses come to be elicited by new stimuli (also known as respondent conditioning).

Client-centered therapy A non-directive therapy based on drawing insights from conscious thoughts and feelings; emphasizes accepting one's true self.

Climacteric A time in late middle age when males experience a significant change in health, vigor, or appearance; roughly analogous to menopause in women.

Clinging A problem in which a child literally clings to a parent or refuses to leave the parent's side.

Clinical psychologist A specialist who treats or does research on psychological problems.

Clinical study An intensive investigation of the behavior of a single person, especially one suffering from some injury, disease, or disorder.

Cloning The production of an entire organism using the DNA from a single cell.

Closure Gestalt term for the perceptual tendency to complete figures by "closing" or ignoring small gaps.

Cocaine A crystalline drug derived from coca leaves; used as a central nervous system stimulant and local anesthetic.

Cochlea The snail-shaped organ that makes up the inner ear.

Coefficient of correlation A statistical index ranging from −1.00 to +1.00 that indicates the direction and degree of correlation.

Coercive power Social power based on the ability to punish others.

Cognition The process of thinking, knowing, or mentally processing information.

Cognitive behavior therapy The use of learning principles to change maladaptive thoughts, beliefs, and feelings that underlie emotional and behavioral problems.

Cognitive behaviorism An approach that combines behavioral principles with cognition (perception, thinking, anticipation) to explain behavior.

Cognitive dissonance An uncomfortable clash between self-image, thoughts, beliefs, attitudes, or perceptions and one's behavior.

Cognitive learning Higher-level learning involving thinking, knowing, understanding, and anticipation.

Cognitive map A mental image of an area (building, city, country) that guides movement from one location to another.

Cognitive psychology The study of human thinking, knowing, understanding, and information processing.

Cognitive therapy The use of learning principles and other methods to change maladaptive thoughts, beliefs, and feelings.

Collective unconscious A mental storehouse for unconscious ideas and images shared by all humans.

Color blindness A total inability to perceive colors.

Color weakness An inability to fully distinguish some colors from others.

Colostrum The first milk produced by a woman for a few days after giving birth. Colostrum is rich in antibodies to disease.

Commitment In a relationship, the degree to which you feel bound to another person.

Common traits Personality traits that are shared by most members of a particular culture.

Communicator In persuasion, the person presenting arguments or information.

Community health campaign A community-wide education program that provides information about factors that affect health and what to do about them.

Community mental health center A facility offering a wide range of mental health services, such as prevention, counseling, consultation, and crisis intervention.

Community psychology Use of community resources to promote mental health and treat or prevent mental health problems.

Companionate love Intimacy and commitment without passion.

Comparative psychology The study and comparison of the behavior of different species, especially animals.

Compensation Counteracting a real or imagined weakness by emphasizing desirable traits or by seeking to excel in other areas.

Competence As a factor in interpersonal attraction, the degree of general ability or proficiency a person displays.

Compliance Bending to the requests of a person who has little or no authority or other form of social power.

Compulsion An act an individual feels driven to repeat, often against his or her will.

Computer simulations Computer programs that mimic some aspect of human thinking, decision making, or problem solving.

Computer-assisted instruction (CAI) Learning aided by computer-presented information and exercises.

Concentrative meditation Mental exercise based on focusing attention on a single target of contemplation.

Concept A generalized idea representing a class of related objects or events.

Concept formation The process of classifying information into meaningful categories by direct experience, rule learning, or exposure to prototypes (idealized models).

Conceptual rule A formal rule by which one may decide if an object or event is an example of a particular concept.

Concrete operational stage Period of cognitive development during which children become able to use the concepts of time, space, volume, and number, but in ways that remain simplified and concrete.

Condensation Combining several people, objects, or events into a single dream image.

Conditional statement A statement that contains a qualification, often of the *if-then* form.

Conditioned aversion A learned dislike or conditioned negative emotional response to some stimulus.

Conditioned emotional response An emotional response that has been linked to a previously non-emotional stimulus by classical conditioning.

Conditioned response A reflex response linked to a new stimulus through learning.

Conditioned stimulus A previously neutral stimulus that acquires the capacity to evoke a response by being paired with an unconditioned stimulus.

Conditioning chamber An apparatus designed for the study of operant conditioning in animals; a Skinner box.

Conditions of worth Internal standards used to judge the value of one's thoughts, actions, feelings, or experiences.

Conduction deafness Poor transfer of sounds from the eardrum to the inner ear.

Cones Visual receptors for colors and daylight visual acuity.

Conflict A stressful condition that occurs when a person must choose between incompatible or contradictory alternatives.

Conformity Bringing one's behavior into agreement or harmony with norms or with the behavior of others in a group.

Confrontation In existential therapy, the process of confronting clients with their own values and with the need to take responsibility for the quality of their existence.

Congenital problems Problems or defects that originate during prenatal development.

Conjunctive concept A concept defined by the presence of two or more specific features. (For example, to qualify as an example of the concept an object must be both red *and* triangular.)

Connector neuron A nerve cell that serves as a link between two others.

Connotative meaning The subjective, personal, or emotional meaning of a word or concept.

Conscience In Freudian theory, the part of the superego that causes guilt when its standards are not met.

Conscious Region of the mind that includes all mental contents (thoughts, images, feelings, memories, and so on) a person is aware of at any given moment.

Consciousness A person's experience of mental awareness, including current sensations, perceptions, memories, and feelings.

Consensus The degree to which people respond alike. In making attributions, consensus implies that responses are externally caused.

Consequences Effects that follow a response.

Consequences Test A test of creativity based on listing the consequences that would follow a basic change in the world.

Conservation In Piaget's theory, mastery of the concept that the volume of matter remains unchanged (is conserved) even when the shape or appearance of objects changes.

Consistency When making attributions, noticing that a behavior changes very little on different occasions.

Consolidation Process by which relatively permanent memories are formed in the brain.

Constructive processing Reorganizing memories on the basis of logic, inference, or the addition of new information.

Consumer behavior All of the actions involved in deciding to spend, selecting a brand, shopping, making the purchase, and evaluating a product in use.

Consumer psychology Specialty area that focuses on understanding consumer behavior and applying psychology to advertising, marketing, product testing, and the like.

Consumerism Formal attempts to enhance consumer knowledge, rights, and welfare.

Consummate love A loving relationship that combines passion, commitment, and intimacy.

Contact comfort A pleasant and reassuring feeling human and animal infants get from touching or clinging to something soft and warm, usually the mother.

Context Information surrounding a stimulus that gives meaning to the stimulus; with regard to behavior, the social situation, behavioral setting, or other surrounding circumstances in which an action takes place.

Continuous reinforcement A schedule of reinforcement in which every correct response is followed by a reinforcer.

Control (experimental) Eliminating, identifying, or equalizing all factors in an experiment that could affect the outcome.

Control (human factors) Any knob, handle, button, lever, or other device used to alter the activity of a machine.

Control (stress) With regard to stress, the ability to exert some influence over one's circumstances.

Control group In an experiment, subjects exposed to all conditions *except* the independent variable.

Control questions In a polygraph exam, questions that almost always provoke anxiety, thus providing a baseline of emotional responsiveness.

Conventional moral reasoning Moral thinking based on a desire to please others or to follow accepted rules and values.

Convergence The simultaneous turning inward of the two eyes as they focus on nearby objects.

Convergent thought Thinking directed toward discovery of a single established correct answer; conventional thinking.

Conversion disorder A symptom or disability that appears to be physical but that actually results from anxiety, stress, or emotional conflict.

Cooing Spontaneous repetition of vowel sounds by infants.

Coping statements Reassuring, self-enhancing statements that are used to stop self-critical thinking.

Corpus callosum The large bundle of fibers connecting the right and left cerebral hemispheres.

Correlation An orderly relationship between two events, measures, or variables.

Correlational study A non-experimental study designed to measure the degree of relationship (if any) between two or more events, measures, or variables.

Corticalization An increase in the relative size of the cerebral cortex.

Counseling psychologist A specialist who treats milder emotional and behavioral disturbances.

Counselor An adviser who helps people solve problems with marriage, career, schoolwork, or the like.

Counterirritation Using mild pain to block more intense or long-lasting pain.

Courtesy bias The tendency to give "polite" answers so as not to hurt an interviewer's feelings.

Covert behavior A response that is internal or hidden from view.

Covert reinforcement Using positive imagery to reinforce desired behavior.

Covert sensitization Use of aversive imagery to reduce the occurrence of an undesired response.

Cranial nerve One of 12 major nerves that leave the brain without passing through the spinal cord.

Created image A mental image that has been assembled or invented rather than simply remembered.

Cretinism Stunted growth and mental retardation caused by an insufficient supply of thyroid hormone.

Critical incidents Situations that arise in a job, with which a competent worker must be able to cope.

Critical period During development, a period of increased sensitivity to environmental influences. Also, a time during which certain events must take place for normal development to occur.

Critical situations Situations during childhood that are capable of leaving a lasting imprint on personality.

Critical thinking An ability to evaluate, compare, analyze, critique, and synthesize information.

Cross-cultural psychologist A psychologist who studies the ways in which culture affects human behavior.

Crowding A subjective feeling of being overstimulated by a loss of privacy or by the nearness of others (especially when social contact with them is unavoidable).

Cryonic suspension Freezing the body or head at death in hopes that future revival will become possible.

Crystalized abilities Abilities that a person has intentionally mastered; accumulated knowledge and skills.

CT scan Computed tomography scan; a computer-enhanced X-ray image of the brain.

Cue External stimuli or signs that guide responses, especially those that signal the likely presence or absence of reinforcement.

Cult A group that professes great devotion to some person, idea, or thing.

Cultural psychologist A psychologist who studies the ways in which culture affects human behavior.

Cultural relativity Perceptions and judgments made relative to the values of one's culture.

Cultural values The values attached to various objects and activities by people in a given culture.

Culture An ongoing pattern of life, characterizing a society at a particular stage in its development or at a given point in history.

Culture-fair test A test (such as an intelligence test) designed to minimize the importance of skills and knowledge that may be more common in some cultures than in others.

Curare A drug that competes with acetylcholine, causing paralysis.

Curiosity drive A hypothesized drive assumed to underlie a wide range of investigative and stimulus-seeking behaviors.

Curve of forgetting A graph that shows the amount of memorized information remembered after varying lengths of time.

Curvilinear relationship A relationship that forms a curved line when graphed.

Cyclothymic disorder Moderate manic and depressive behavior that persists for two years or more.

Dark adaptation The process by which the eye adapts to low illumination and becomes more light-sensitive, principally by a shift to rod vision.

Data Observed facts or evidence (*data:* plural; *datum:* singular).

Data reduction system Any system that selects, analyzes, or condenses information.

Daydream A vivid waking fantasy.

Declarative memory That part of long-term memory containing factual information.

Deductive thought Thought that applies a general set of rules to specific situations; for example, using the laws of gravity to predict the behavior of a single falling object.

Deep lesioning Use of an electrode (electrified wire) to destroy small areas deep within the brain.

Deep sleep Stage 4 sleep; the deepest form of normal sleep.

Defense mechanisms Habitual and often unconscious psychological strategies used to avoid or reduce anxiety.

Deinstitutionalization Reduced use of full-time commitment to mental institutions to treat mental disorders.

Delayed speech Speech that is developmentally delayed; that is, speech that begins well after the normal age for language development has passed.

Delta waves Large, slow brain waves that occur in deeper sleep (stage 3 and stage 4).

Delusion A false belief held against all contrary evidence.

Delusional disorder A psychosis marked by severe delusions of grandeur, jealousy, persecution, or similar preoccupations.

Demonology In medieval Europe, the study of demons and the treatment of persons "possessed" by demons.

Dendrites Fibers projecting from nerve cells that receive information from other neurons and carry it to the cell body.

Denial Protecting oneself from an unpleasant reality by refusing to perceive it or believe it.

Denotative meaning The exact, dictionary definition of a word or concept; its objective meaning.

Density The number of people in a given space or, inversely, the amount of space available to each person.

Dependent variable In an experiment, the condition (usually a behavior) that reflects the effects of the independent variable.

Depressant A substance that decreases activity in the body and nervous system.
Depression A state of deep despondency marked by apathy, emotional negativity, and behavioral inhibition.
Depressive disorders Emotional disorders primarily involving sadness, despondency, and depression.
Deprivation In development, the loss or withholding of normal stimulation, nutrition, comfort, love, and so forth; a condition of lacking.
Deprivation dwarfism Stunted growth caused by isolation, rejection, or general deprivation.
Depth cues Perceptual features that impart information about distance and three-dimensional space.
Depth perception The ability to see three-dimensional space and to accurately estimate distances.
Desensitization Reducing fear or anxiety by repeatedly exposing a person to emotional stimuli while the person is deeply relaxed.
Determinism The doctrine that all behavior has prior causes.
Detoxification To remove poison or the effects of poison; in the treatment of alcoholism, the withdrawal of the patient from alcohol.
Developmental level An individual's current state of physical, emotional, and intellectual development.
Developmental milestone A significant turning point or marker in personal development.
Developmental psychologist A psychologist who studies the course of human growth and development.
Developmental psychology The study of progressive changes in behavior and abilities from conception to death.
Developmental task Any skill that must be mastered, or personal change that must take place, for optimal development at a particular life stage.
Deviant communication Patterns of communication that cause guilt, anxiety, confusion, anger, conflict, and emotional turmoil.
Deviation IQ An IQ obtained statistically from a person's relative standing in his or her age group.
Diet The types and amounts of food and drink regularly consumed over a period of time.
Difference threshold The smallest change in stimulus intensity that can be detected by an observer.
Digit-span test A test of attention and short-term memory in which a string of digits is recalled.
Diminished capacity Impaired mental competence to control actions or know right from wrong.
Direct instruction Presentation of factual information by lecture, demonstration, and rote practice.
Direct observation (personality) Any observation of a person's behavior in a natural or prearranged situation undertaken to form an impression of his or her personality.
Discounting Downgrading internal explanations of behavior when a person's actions appear to have strong external causes.
Discovery learning Learning based on insight or understanding rather than on mechanical application of rules.
Discrimination Treating members of various social groups differently in circumstances where their rights or treatment should be identical.
Discriminative stimuli Stimuli that precede rewarded and non-rewarded responses in operant conditioning and that come to exert some control over whether the response is made.
Disease-prone personality A personality style associated with poor health; marked by persistent negative emotions, including anxiety, depression, and hostility.
Disengagement theory of aging States that it is normal and desirable for the aged to withdraw from roles they held earlier.
Dishabituation A reversal of habituation.
Disinhibition The removal of inhibition, resulting in the acting out of behavior that normally would be restrained.
Disjunctive concept A concept defined by the presence of at least one of several possible features. (For example, to qualify an object must be either blue *or* circular.)
Disorganized schizophrenia Schizophrenia marked by incoherence, disorganized behavior, bizarre thinking, and flat or grossly inappropriate emotions.
Displaced aggression Redirecting aggression to a target other than the actual source of one's frustration.
Display Any dial, screen, light, or other device used to provide information about a machine's activity to a human operator.
Dissection Separation of tissues into their parts.
Dissociative amnesia Loss of memory (partial or complete) for past events and, especially, loss of memory for one's personal identity.
Dissociative disorder Temporary amnesia, multiple personality, or depersonalization.
Dissociative fugue Fleeing to escape extreme emotional conflict, anxiety, or threat.
Dissociative identity disorder The presence of two or more distinct personalities or personal identities (multiple personality).
Distinctiveness As a basis for making causal attributions, noticing that a behavior occurs only under a specific (distinct) set of circumstances.
Distractors False items included with a correct item to form a test of recognition memory (for example, the wrong answers on a multiple-choice test).
Disuse Theory that memory traces weaken when memories are not periodically used or retrieved.
Divergent thought Thinking that produces many ideas or alternatives; a major element in original or creative thought.
Divided attention Allotting mental space or effort to various tasks or parts of a task.
DNA Deoxyribonucleic acid; a twisted, ladder-like molecular structure containing the chemical code for genetic information.
Dogmatism An unwarranted positiveness or certainty in matters of belief or opinion.
Dominant gene A gene whose influence will be expressed each time the gene is present.
Door-in-the-face effect The tendency for a person who has refused a major request to subsequently be more likely to comply with a minor request.
Dopamine An important transmitter substance found in the brain, especially in the limbic system, an area associated with emotional response.
Double approach-avoidance conflict An unpleasant state in which one is simultaneously attracted to, and repelled by each of two alternatives.
Double standard Applying different standards for judging the appropriateness of male and female sexual behavior.
Double-blind experiment A test in which neither subjects nor experimenters know which subjects are in the experimental group.
Down syndrome A genetic disorder caused by the presence of an extra chromosome; results in mental retardation.
Dream symbols Images in dreams that serve as visible signs of hidden ideas, desires, impulses, emotions, relationships, and so forth.
Drill and practice A basic computer-assisted learning format, typically consisting of questions and answers.
Drive The psychological expression of a motive, for example, hunger, thirst, or a drive for success.
Drug interaction A combined effect of two drugs that exceeds the addition of one drug's effects to the other.
Drug tolerance A reduction in the body's response to a drug.
Dyslexia An inability to read with understanding, often caused by a tendency to misread letters (by seeing their mirror images, for instance).
Dyspareunia Genital pain before, during, or after sexual intercourse.
Dysthymic disorder A moderate level of depression that has persisted for two years or more but has not included periods of severe depression.

Early childhood education program Programs that provide stimulating intellectual experiences, typically for disadvantaged preschoolers.
Easy child A child who is temperamentally relaxed and agreeable.
Echo A brief continuation of sensory activity in the auditory system after a sound is heard.
Echolalia A compulsion, sometimes observed in autistic children, to repeat everything that is said.
Eclectic Selected from many sources.
Educational psychology The study of learning, teaching, and related topics.
Educational simulations Computer programs that simulate real-world settings or situations to promote learning.
Effective parents Parents who supply firm and consistent guidance combined with love and affection.
Effector cells Cells in muscles and glands specialized for the production of responses.
Ego In Freudian theory, the executive part of personality that directs rational, realistic behavior.
Ego ideal In Freudian theory, the part of the superego representing ideal behavior; a source of pride when its standards are met.
Egocentric thought Thought that is self-centered and fails to consider the viewpoints of others.
Eidetic imagery The ability to retain a "projected" mental image long enough to use it as a

source of information.
Ejaculation The release of sperm and seminal fluid by the male at the time of orgasm.
Elaborative rehearsal Rehearsal that links new information with existing memories and knowledge.
Electra conflict Freudian concept referring to a girl's sexual attraction to her father and resultant feelings of rivalry with her mother.
Electrical stimulation of the brain (ESB) Direct electrical stimulation and action of brain tissue.
Electroconvulsive therapy (ECT) A medical treatment for severe depression, consisting of an electric shock passed directly through the brain, which produces a convulsion.
Electrode Any wire, needle, or metal plate used to electrically stimulate nerve tissue or to record its activity.
Electroencephalograph (EEG) A device designed to detect, amplify, and record electrical activity in the brain.
Electromagnetic spectrum The full range of electrical and magnetic wavelengths, including X-rays, radio waves, light waves, and so forth.
Emblems Gestures that have widely understood meanings within a particular culture.
Emotion A state characterized by physiological arousal, subjective feelings, changes in facial expression, and adaptive behaviors.
Emotion-focused coping Managing or controlling one's emotional reaction to a stressful or threatening situation.
Emotional appraisal Evaluating the personal meaning of a situation; specific emotions are assumed to result from various appraisals, such as an appraisal of threat leading to anxiety.
Emotional attachment A close emotional bond that infants form with their parents, caregivers, or others.
Emotional bonding An especially close emotional bond between infants and their parents, caregivers, or others (another term for attachment).
Emotional component One's feelings toward the object of an attitude.
Emotional expression Any behavior that gives an outward sign of emotion, especially those signs that communicate emotional states to others.
Emotional feelings The private, subjective experience of having an emotion.
Emotional tone The underlying emotional state an individual is experiencing at any given moment.
Empathy A capacity for taking another's point of view; the ability to feel what another is feeling.
Empirical evidence Facts or information gained by direct observation or experience.
Empty love A relationship based almost entirely on commitment.
Encoding Changing information into a form that allows it to be stored in memory and manipulated in thought.
Encoding failure Failure to store sufficient information to form a useful memory.
Encopresis A lack of bowel control; "soiling."
Encounter group A group experience based on intensely honest expressions of feelings and reactions of participants to one another.
Endocrine system Glands whose secretions pass directly into the bloodstream or lymph system.
Endogenous depression Depression that appears to be produced from within (perhaps by chemical imbalances in the brain), rather than as a reaction to life events.
Endorphins A class of chemicals produced by the pituitary gland that are similar in structure and pain-killing effect to opiate drugs such as morphine.
Energizers Mood-elevating drugs.
Engineering psychology A specialty concerned with the design of machines and work environments so that they are compatible with human perceptual and physical capacities.
Engram Hypothesized physical changes that take place in the brain as it stores information; a memory trace.
Enkephalins Opiate-like brain chemicals that regulate reactions to pain and stress.
Enriched environment An environment deliberately made more novel, complex, and perceptually stimulating.
Enrichment In development, any attempt to make a child's environment more novel, complex, and perceptually or intellectually stimulating.
Enuresis An inability to control urination, particularly with regard to bed-wetting.
Environment ("nurture") The sum total of all external conditions affecting development.
Environmental assessment Measurement and analysis of the effects an environment has on the behavior of people within that environment.
Environmental psychology The formal study of how environments affect behavior.
Episodic drive A drive that occurs in distinct episodes associated with particular conditions (for example, pain avoidance, sexual motivation).
Episodic memory A subpart of declarative memory that records personal experiences that are linked with specific times and places.
Equal-status contact Social interaction that occurs on an equal footing, without obvious differences in power or status.
Ergotism A pattern of psychotic-like symptoms that accompanies poisoning by ergot fungus.
Erogenous zone Any body area that produces pleasurable sensations.
Eros Freud's name for the "life instincts" postulated by his theory.
Escape Reducing discomfort by leaving frustrating situations or by psychologically withdrawing from them.
Escape learning Learning to make a response in order to end an aversive (painful or uncomfortable) stimulus.
Establishment phase The period during which a person enters a career and builds competence in it.
Estrogen Any of a number of female sex hormones.
Estrus Changes in the reproductive organs and sexual drives of animals that create a desire for mating, particularly used to refer to females in heat.
Ethnocentrism Placing one's own group or race at the center—that is, tending to reject all other groups but one's own.
Ethologist A person who studies the natural behavior patterns of animals.
Eugenics Selective breeding for desirable characteristics.
Evolutionary psychology Study of the evolutionary origins of human behavior patterns.
Excitement General emotional arousal associated with activation of the autonomic nervous system.
Excitement phase The first phase of sexual response, indicated by initial signs of sexual arousal.
Exhibitionism Deriving sexual pleasure from displaying the genitals (usually), to an unwilling viewer ("flashing").
Existential therapy An insight therapy that focuses on the problems of existence, such as death, meaning, choice, and responsibility; emphasizes making courageous life choices.
Exorcism In medieval Europe, the practice of expelling or driving off an "evil spirit," especially one residing in the body of a person who is "possessed."
Expectancy An anticipation concerning future events or relationships.
Experiment A formal trial undertaken to confirm or disconfirm a fact or principle.
Experimental group In a controlled experiment, the group of subjects exposed to the independent variable or experimental manipulation.
Experimental psychologist One who scientifically studies human and animal behavior.
Experimental self-observation Wilhelm Wundt's technique of combining trained introspection with objective measurement.
Experimental subjects Humans or animals whose behavior is investigated in an experiment.
Experimenter effect Changes in subjects' behavior caused by the unintended influence of an experimenter's actions.
Expert power Social power derived from possession of knowledge or expertise.
Expert systems Computer programs designed to respond as a human expert would; programs based on the knowledge and rules that underlie human expertise in specific topics.
Expert witness A person recognized by a court of law as being qualified to give expert testimony on a specific topic.
Explicit memory A memory that a person is aware of having; a memory that is consciously retrieved.
Exploration drive Drive to investigate unfamiliar areas of the environment.
Exploration phase The period during which career alternatives are explored.
Expressive behavior Behavior that expresses or communicates emotion.
External cause A cause of behavior that is assumed to lie outside a person.
External eating cue Any external stimulus that tends to encourage hunger or to elicit eating.
External frustration A negative emotional state caused by events or conditions that hinder satisfaction of a motive or that block progress toward a goal.
Extinction A gradual decrease in the frequency of a non-reinforced response.
Extracellular thirst Thirst caused by a reduction in the volume of fluids found between body cells.
Extraneous variable In an experiment, any condition prevented from influencing the outcome.
Extrasensory perception The purported ability

to perceive events in ways that cannot be explained by known capacities of the sensory organs.

Extrinsic motivation Motivation based on obvious external rewards, obligations, or similar factors.

Extrovert A person whose attention is directed outward; a bold, sociable, outgoing person.

Eye-movement desensitization A reduction in fear or anxiety that occurs when a person holds upsetting thoughts in mind while rapidly moving the eyes from side to side.

Facial agnosia An inability to recognize familiar faces.

Facial blend A facial gesture that mixes parts of two or more basic facial expressions.

Facial feedback hypothesis Explanation that says facial expressions generate feelings that help define what emotion a person is feeling.

Fact memory That part of long-term memory containing factual information (declarative memory).

Factor analysis A statistical technique used to correlate multiple measurements. Measurements that form "clusters" of correlations are assumed to reflect some general underlying factor.

Fallacy of positive instances The tendency to remember or notice information which fits one's expectations, while forgetting discrepancies.

False positive An erroneous sense of recognition.

Familial retardation Mild mental retardation associated with homes that are intellectually, nutritionally, and emotionally impoverished.

Family system The family as an entire unit, including all its members, their relationships, and their typical patterns of behavior.

Family therapy Technique in which all family members participate, both individually and as a group, to change destructive relationships and communication patterns.

Fantasy A product of the imagination determined mainly by one's motives or feelings. Fantasy may be used as an escape mechanism.

Fantasy stage Stage of career exploration in which persons imagine themselves filling unlikely roles.

Fatuous love A relationship based on commitment and passion that lacks intimacy.

Feature detector A sensory system highly attuned to a specific stimulus pattern.

Feedback Information on the effects a response has had that is returned to the person performing the response (also known as knowledge of results).

Feeding system Areas on each side of the hypothalamus that initiate eating when stimulated.

Feeling of knowing The ability to predict beforehand whether one will be able to remember something.

Female orgasmic disorder An inability to reach orgasm during intercourse.

Female sexual arousal disorder A lack of physical arousal to sexual stimulation.

Fetal alcohol syndrome A pattern of birth complications and bodily defects in infants caused by consumption of alcohol by the mother during pregnancy.

Fetal damage A congenital problem; that is, damage or injury that occurs to the fetus during prenatal development.

Fetishism Gaining sexual gratification from inanimate objects; especially, an inability to achieve sexual arousal without the object.

Field experiment An experiment conducted in a natural setting.

Figure-ground organization A basic perceptual organization in which part of a stimulus appears to stand out as an object (figure) against a less prominent background (ground).

Five-factor model A model proposing that the five most universal dimensions of personality are extroversion, agreeableness, conscientiousness, neuroticism, and openness to experience.

Fixation (cognition) The tendency to repeat wrong solutions or faulty responses, especially as a result of becoming blind to alternatives.

Fixation (Freudian) In Freudian theory, lasting conflicts developed during a particular psychosexual stage as a result of frustration or over-indulgence.

Fixed action pattern (FAP) An instinctual chain of movements found in almost all members of a species.

Fixed interval schedule A pattern in which a reinforcer is given only when a correct response is made after a set amount of time has passed since the last reinforced response. Responses made before the time interval has ended are not reinforced.

Fixed ratio schedule A pattern in which a set number of correct responses must be made to get a reinforcer. For example, a reinforcer is given for every 4 correct responses.

Flashbulb memories Memories created at times of high emotion that seem especially vivid.

Flat affect An extreme lack of emotion.

Flexitime A work schedule that allows flexible starting and quitting times, centered around a core work period.

Fluency In tests of creativity, fluency refers to the total number of solutions produced.

Fluid abilities Innate abilities based on perceptual, motor, or intellectual speed and flexibility; abilities that are not based on prior intentional learning.

Foot-in-the-door effect The tendency for a person who has first complied with a small request to be more likely later to fulfill a larger request.

Forcible rape Sexual intercourse carried out against the victim's will, under the threat of force.

Forebrain The highest brain areas, including the hypothalamus, thalamus, corpus callosum, and cerebrum.

Formal operations stage Period of cognitive development marked by a capacity for abstract, theoretical, and hypothetical thinking.

Fovea A small depression at the center of the retina containing only cones and providing the greatest sharpness of vision.

Frame of reference A mental or emotional perspective used for evaluating events.

Framing In thought, the terms in which a problem is stated or the way that it is structured.

Fraternal twins Twins conceived from two separate eggs. Fraternal twins are no more alike genetically than other siblings.

Free association In psychoanalysis, the technique of having a client say anything that comes to mind, regardless of how embarrassing or unimportant it may seem.

Free choice The ability to freely make choices that are not controlled by genetics, learning, or unconscious forces.

Free will The doctrine that human beings are capable of freely making choices.

Free-floating anxiety Anxiety that is very general and pervasive.

Frequency theory Holds that, in hearing, the cochlea converts tones up to about 4000 hertz into nerve impulses that match the frequency of each tone.

Frontal lobes Areas at the top front of the cerebral cortex that include sites associated with the control of movement, the processing of smell, and higher mental functions.

Frontal lobotomy The destruction of brain tissue in frontal areas of the brain.

Frotteurism Sexually touching or rubbing against a non-consenting person.

Frustration An internal emotional state resulting from interference with satisfaction of a motive or blocking of goal-directed behavior.

Frustration-aggression hypothesis Hypothesis stating that frustration tends to lead to aggression.

Fugue Taking flight to escape extreme emotional conflict, anxiety, or threat.

Fully functioning person Carl Rogers' term for persons living in harmony with their deepest feelings, impulses, and intuitions.

Functional fixedness A rigidity in problem solving caused by an inability to see new uses for familiar objects.

Functional MRI An MRI scan that records brain activity.

Functional psychosis A psychosis of unknown origin or one presumed to be caused by psychological factors.

Functional solution A detailed, practical, and workable solution.

Functionalism School of psychology concerned with how behavior and mental abilities help people adapt to their environments.

Fundamental attributional error The tendency to attribute the behavior of others to internal causes (personality, likes, and so forth) while attributing one's own behavior to external causes (situations and circumstances).

Galvanic skin response (GSR) A change in the electrical resistance (or inversely, the conductance) of the skin, due to activity in the sweat glands associated with arousal or anxiety.

Gate control theory Proposes that pain messages pass through neural "gates" in the spinal cord.

Gender bias A tendency for researchers to base conclusions solely on subjects of one gender (usually males).

Gender identity One's personal, private sense of maleness or femaleness.

General adaptation syndrome (G.A.S.) A series of bodily reactions to prolonged stress, occurring in three stages: alarm, resistance, and exhaustion.

General intelligence test A test that measures a wide variety of mental abilities.
General negativism A tendency to respond negatively to almost all situations or social interactions.
General paresis A disease that occurs when syphilis attacks the brain; can cause an organic psychosis.
General solution A solution that states the requirements for success, but not in enough detail for further action.
Generalization Transfer of a learned response from one stimulus situation to other similar situations.
Generalized anxiety disorder The person is in a chronic state of tension and worries about work, relationships, ability, or impending disaster.
Generalized reinforcer A secondary reinforcer that has become independent of direct association with primary reinforcers.
Genes Specific areas on a strand of DNA that carry hereditary information affecting various personal characteristics.
Genetic abnormality Any abnormality in the genes, including missing genes, extra genes, or defective genes.
Genetic sex Gender as indicated by the presence of XX (female) or XY (male) chromosomes.
Genital sex Gender as indicated by the presence of male or female genitals.
Genital stage In Freud's theory, the culmination of personality development, marked, among other things, by the attainment of mature adult sexuality.
Gerontologist One who scientifically studies aging and its effects.
Gestalt A German word meaning form, pattern, or whole.
Gestalt psychology The school of psychology emphasizing the study of thinking, learning, and perception in whole units, not by analysis into parts.
Gestalt therapy An approach that focuses on immediate experience and awareness to help clients rebuild thinking, feeling, and acting into connected wholes; emphasizes the integration of fragmented experiences.
Giantism Excessive bodily growth caused by too much growth hormone.
Giftedness Either the possession of a high IQ or special talents or aptitudes.
Goal The target or objective of a motivated and directed chain of behaviors.
Gonadal sex Gender as indicated by the presence of ovaries (female) or testes (male).
Gonads The primary sex glands—the testes in males and ovaries in females.
Grammar A set of rules for combining language units into meaningful speech or writing.
Graphology False system based on the belief that handwriting can reveal personality traits.
Grasping reflex A neonatal reflex consisting of grasping objects placed in the palms.
Gray matter Areas in the nervous system that have a grayish color due to a high concentration of nerve cell bodies.
Grief An intense emotional state that follows the death of a lover, friend, or relative.
Group cohesiveness The degree of attraction among group members or their degree of commitment to remaining in the group.
Group intelligence test Any intelligence test that can be administered to a group of people with minimal supervision.
Group prejudice Prejudice held out of conformity to group views.
Group sanctions Rewards and punishments (such as approval or disapproval) administered by groups to enforce a degree of conformity among members.
Group structure The network of roles, communication pathways, and power in a group.
Group therapy Psychotherapy conducted with a group of people.
Groupthink A compulsion by members of decision-making groups to maintain agreement, even at the cost of critical thinking.
Growth needs In Maslow's hierarchy, the higher level needs associated with self-actualization (needs that contribute to personal growth and full development of personal potential).
Growth spurt An often dramatic acceleration in physical growth that coincides with puberty.
Guided imagery Intentional visualization of images that are calming, relaxing, or beneficial in other ways.
Gustation The sense of taste.

Habit A deeply ingrained, learned pattern of behavior.
Habituation A decrease in perceptual response to a repeated stimulus.
Hair cells Receptor cells within the cochlea that transduce vibrations into nerve impulses.
Half-way house A community-based facility for individuals making the transition from an institution (mental hospital, prison, and so forth) to independent living.
Hallucination An imaginary sensation—such as seeing, hearing, or smelling something that does not exist in the external world.
Hallucinogen Any substance that alters or distorts sensory impressions.
Halo effect The tendency of an interviewer to extend a favorable or unfavorable impression to unrelated aspects of an individual's personality.
Handedness A preference for the right or left hand in most activities.
Hardy personality A personality style associated with superior stress resistance.
Hassle Any distressing, day-to-day annoyance; also called a microstressor.
Health psychology Study of the ways in which psychological principles can be used to maintain and promote health.
Heredity ("nature") The transmission of physical and psychological characteristics from parents to offspring through genes.
Hermaphroditism The condition of having genitals suggestive of both sexes; ambiguous genital sexuality.
Hertz One cycle (or vibration) per second.
Heterosexism The belief that heterosexuality is better or more natural than homosexuality.
Heterosexual A person romantically and erotically attracted to members of the opposite sex.
Heuristic Any strategy or technique that aids problem solving, especially by limiting the number of possible solutions to be tried.
Heuristic Any strategy or technique that aids problem solving, especially by limiting the number of possible solutions to be tried.
Hidden observer A detached part of the hypnotized person's awareness that silently observes events.
Hierarchy A rank-ordered series of higher and lower amounts, levels, degrees, or steps.
Hierarchy of needs A rank ordering of needs based on their presumed strength or potency.
High self-monitors Persons who try to adapt their public image to the demands of various situations by managing the impression they make on others.
Higher-order conditioning Classical conditioning in which a conditioned stimulus is used to reinforce further learning; that is, a CS is used as if it were a US.
Hippocampus A structure in the brain associated with the regulation of emotions and the transfer of information from short-term memory to long-term memory.
Homeostasis A steady state of bodily equilibrium normally maintained automatically by various physiological mechanisms.
Homogamy Marriage of two people who are similar to one another.
Homophobia A powerful fear of homosexuality.
Homosexual A person romantically and erotically attracted to same-sex persons.
Honesty test A paper-and-pencil test designed to detect attitudes, beliefs, and behavior patterns that predispose a person to engage in dishonest behavior.
Hormonal sex Gender as indicated by a preponderance of estrogens (female) or androgens (male) in the body.
Hormone A glandular secretion that affects bodily functions or behavior.
Hospice A medical facility or program dedicated to providing optimal care for persons who are dying.
Hospitalism A pattern of deep depression observed in institutionalized infants marked by weeping and sadness and a lack of normal responsiveness to other humans.
Hue Classification of colors into basic categories of red, orange, yellow, green, blue, indigo, and violet.
Human genome The entire set of human genes.
Human growth sequence The general pattern of physical development from conception to death.
Human immunodeficiency virus (HIV) The sexually transmitted virus that disables the immune system and causes AIDS.
Human nature Those traits, qualities, potentials, and behavior patterns most characteristic of the human species.
Humanism An approach to psychology that focuses on human experience, problems, potentials, and ideals.
Hydrocephaly A buildup of cerebrospinal fluid within brain cavities.

Hyperactivity A behavioral state characterized by short attention span, restless movement, and impaired learning capacity.
Hyperopia Difficulty focusing nearby objects (farsightedness).
Hypersomnia Extreme daytime sleepiness.
Hyperthyroidism Faster metabolism and excitability caused by an overactive thyroid gland.
Hypnic jerk A reflex muscle twitch throughout the body that often occurs as one is falling asleep.
Hypnogogic images Vivid mental images that may occur just as one enters stage 1 sleep; although somewhat dream-like, the images are usually not associated with REMs.
Hypnosis An altered state of consciousness characterized by narrowed attention and increased suggestibility.
Hypnotic susceptibility scale Any test designed to assess an individual's capacity for becoming hypnotized.
Hypoactive sexual desire A persistent loss of sexual motivation.
Hypochondriac A person who is excessively preoccupied with minor bodily problems or who complains about illnesses that appear to be imaginary.
Hypochondriasis A preoccupation with minor bodily problems and the presence of illnesses that appear to be imaginary.
Hypoglycemia Below-normal blood sugar level.
Hypopituitary dwarfism Shortness and smallness caused by too little growth hormone.
Hypothalamus A small area at the base of the brain that regulates many aspects of motivation and emotion, especially hunger, thirst, and sexual behavior.
Hypothesis The predicted outcome of an experiment or an educated guess about the relationship between variables.
Hypothetical possibilities Suppositions, guesses, or projections.
Hypothyroidism Slower metabolism and sluggishness caused by an underactive thyroid gland.
Hysteria Wild emotional excitability sometimes associated with the development of apparent physical disabilities (numbness, blindness, and the like) without known physical cause.

Icon A mental image or representation.
Id According to Freud, the most primitive part of personality, which remains unconscious, supplies energy to other parts of the psyche, and demands immediate gratification.
Ideal self An idealized image of oneself (the person one would like to be).
Identical twins Twins who develop from the same egg and who, therefore, have identical genes.
Identification Incorporating the goals and values of another person into one's own behavior; feeling emotionally connected to a person and wanting to be like him or her.
Illogical thought Thought that is intuitive, invalid, or haphazard.
Illusion A misleading or distorted perception.
Illusory figure An implied shape that is not actually bounded by an edge or an outline.
Illustrators Gestures used while speaking to illustrate what one is saying.
Image Most often, a mental representation that has picture-like qualities; an icon.
Imaginary audience The group of people a person imagines is watching (or will watch) his or her actions.
Imitation An attempt to match one's own behavior to another person's behavior.
Immune system System that mobilizes bodily defenses (such as white blood cells) against invading microbes and other disease agents.
Implicit memory A memory that a person does not know exists; a memory that is retrieved unconsciously.
Impossible figure A stimulus pattern that cannot be organized into a stable perception.
Impotence An outdated term for male erectile disorder.
Imprinting A rapid and relatively permanent type of learning that occurs during a limited time period early in life.
In vitro fertilization Fertilization of an ovum outside a woman's body.
In-basket test A testing procedure that simulates the individual decision-making challenges that executives face.
Incentive value The value a goal holds for a person or animal above and beyond the goal's ability to fill a need.
Incest Sexual contact with a close relative or family member.
Incongruence State that exists when there is a discrepancy between one's experiences and self-image or between one's self-image and ideal self.
Incongruent person A person who has an inaccurate self-image or a person whose self-image differs greatly from the ideal self.
Independent variable In an experiment, the condition being investigated as a possible cause of some change in behavior. The values that this variable takes do not depend on any other condition; they are chosen by the experimenter.
Individual intelligence test A test of intelligence designed for administration to a single individual by a trained specialist.
Individual traits Personality traits that comprise a person's unique individual qualities.
Individuating information Information that helps define a person as an individual, rather than as a member of a group or social category.
Inductive thought A type of thinking in which a general rule or principle is inferred from a series of specific examples; for instance, inferring the laws of gravity by observing many falling objects.
Industrial-organizational psychology The psychology of work and organizations, especially with respect to personnel selection, human relations, and management.
Infatuation Passionate attraction to another person in the absence of intimacy and commitment.
Information bits Meaningful units of information, such as numbers, letters, words, or phrases.
Information chunks Information bits grouped into larger units.
Innate behavior Inborn, unlearned behavior.
Insanity Legally, a mental disability shown by an inability to manage one's affairs or to be aware of the consequences of one's actions.
Insecure-ambivalent attachment An anxious emotional bond marked by a desire to be with a parent or caregiver and resistance to being reunited.
Insecure-avoidant attachment An anxious emotional bond marked by a tendency to avoid reunion with a parent or caregiver.
Insight A sudden mental reorganization of a problem that causes the solution to seem self-evident.
Insomnia Difficulty in getting to sleep or staying asleep.
Instinctive drift The tendency of learned responses to shift toward innate response patterns.
Instructional games Educational computer programs designed to resemble games in order to motivate learning.
Instrumental behavior Behavior directed toward the achievement of some goal; behavior that is instrumental in producing some effect.
Intelligence An overall capacity to think rationally, act purposefully, and deal effectively with the environment.
Intelligence quotient (IQ) An index of intelligence defined as a person's mental age divided by his or her chronological age and multiplied by 100.
Interference The tendency for new memories to impair retrieval of older memories, and the reverse.
Internal cause A cause of behavior that is assumed to lie within a person—for instance, a need, preference, or personality trait.
Internal representation Any image, concept, precept, symbol, or process used to mentally represent information during thought.
Interpersonal attraction Social attraction to another person.
Interview (personality) A face-to-face meeting held for the purpose of gaining information about an individual's personal history, personality traits, current psychological state, and so forth.
Intimacy The presence of affection, sharing, communication, and mutual support in a relationship.
Intimate distance The most private space immediately surrounding the body (about 18 inches from the skin).
Intra-cranial stimulation Direct electrical stimulation and activation of brain tissue.
Intracellular thirst Thirst triggered when fluid is drawn out of cells due to an increased concentration of salts and minerals outside the cell.
Intrauterine environment The physical and chemical environment within the uterus during prenatal development.
Intrinsic motivation Motivation that comes from personal enjoyment of an activity, rather than from external rewards.
Introspection To look within; to examine one's own thoughts, feelings, or sensations.
Introvert A person whose attention is focused inward; a shy, reserved, self-centered person.
Intuitive thought Quick, impulsive thinking that makes little or no use of formal reasoning and logic.
Inverted U function A curve, roughly in the shape of an upside-down U, that relates the quality of performance to levels of arousal.
Ion An electrically-charged molecule.
Ion channels Channels through the axon membrane.

Iris Colored circular muscle of the eye that opens and closes to admit more or less light into the eye.
Irrelevant questions In a polygraph exam, neutral, non-threatening, or non-emotional questions.
Ishihara test A test for color blindness and color weakness.

James-Lange theory According to this theory, emotional feelings follow bodily arousal and come from awareness of such arousal.
Jigsaw classroom A method of reducing prejudice in which each student receives a different part of a body of information needed to complete a project or prepare for a test.
Job analysis A detailed description of the skills, knowledge, and activities required by a particular job.
Job enrichment A deliberate attempt to make a job more personally rewarding, interesting, or intrinsically motivating.
Job satisfaction The degree to which a person is comfortable with or satisfied with his or her work.
Just noticeable difference The amount of increase or decrease in a stimulus that can be reliably detected as a change in amount, value, or intensity.
Just-world beliefs Belief that people generally get what they deserve.
Justification In cognitive dissonance theory, the degree to which one's actions are justified by rewards or other circumstances.

Keyword method As an aid to memory, using a familiar word or image to link two items.
Kinesics Study of the meaning of body movements, posture, hand gestures, and facial expressions, commonly called body language.
Kinesthetic imagery Images created by produced, remembered, or imagined muscular sensations.
Kinesthetic senses The senses of body movement and positioning.
Knowledge of results During learning, feedback or information provided about the correctness of responses or other aspects of performance.

Language A collection of words or symbols and rules for combining them which allows them to be used for thinking and communication.
Large-group awareness training Any of a number of programs (many of them commercialized) that claim to increase self-awareness and facilitate constructive personal change.
Latency (Freudian) According to Freud, a period in childhood when psychosexual development is more or less interrupted.
Latency (response) The amount of time that passes between the presentation of a stimulus and the occurrence of a response.
Latent dream content The hidden or symbolic meaning of a dream, as revealed by dream interpretation and analysis.
Latent learning Learning that occurs without obvious reinforcement and that remains unexpressed until reinforcement is provided.
Later career phase The concluding career phase prior to retirement; marked by high status and respect arising from long experience.
Lateralization Specialization in the abilities of the brain hemispheres.
Law of effect Responses that lead to desirable effects are repeated; those that produce undesirable results are not.
Leaderless group discussion A test of leadership that simulates group decision making and problem solving.
Learned helplessness A learned inability to overcome obstacles or to avoid punishment. A learned state of passivity and inaction in the face of aversive stimuli.
Learning Any relatively permanent change in behavior that can be attributed to experience but not to fatigue, malnutrition, injury, and so forth.
Learning disability Any substantial problem with reading, math, or writing.
Learning psychologist A psychologist who studies how learning occurs.
Learning theorist A psychologist interested in the ways that learning shapes and explains personality.
Legitimate power Social power based on a person's position as an agent of an accepted social order.
Lesbianism Female homosexuality.
Lexigram A geometric shape used as a symbol for a word.
Libido In Freudian theory, the force, primarily pleasure-oriented, that energizes the subparts of personality.
Life change units (LCUs) Numerical values assigned to each life event on the Social Readjustment Rating Scale and used to predict the likelihood of illness.
Life expectancy The average number of years a person of a given sex, race, and nationality can expect to live.
Life stages Widely recognized periods of life corresponding to various ages and broad phases of development.
Light sleep Stage 1 sleep, marked by small irregular brain waves and some alpha waves.
Liking A relationship based on intimacy, but lacking passion and commitment.
Limbic system A system of interconnected structures in the forebrain that are closely associated with emotional response.
Limen A threshold or a limit.
Linear relationship A relationship that forms a straight line when graphed.
Lithium carbonate A drug used to lessen mood swings in persons suffering from some types of affective disorders.
Living will A written declaration stating that a person prefers not to have his or her life artificially prolonged in the event of a terminal illness.
Lobes (cerebral cortex) Areas on the cortex bordered by major fissures or associated with particular functions.
Localization of function The principle stating that sensations are determined by the area of the brain that is activated.
Lock and key theory The theory of olfaction which holds that odors are related to the shapes of chemical molecules.
Logical thought Drawing conclusions on the basis of formal principles of reasoning.
Logotherapy A form of existential therapy that emphasizes the need to find and maintain meaning in one's life.
Long-term memory (LTM) The memory system used for relatively permanent storage of meaningful information.
Looking chamber An experimental apparatus used to test infant perception by presenting visual stimuli and observing infant responses.
Loudness The intensity of a sound; determined by the amplitude of sound waves.
Low self-monitor A person who seeks to faithfully express who he or she is, regardless of the situation.
Low-ball technique A strategy in which commitment is gained first to reasonable or desirable terms, which are then made less reasonable or desirable.
Lucid dream A dream in which the dreamer feels awake and capable of normal thought and action.

M'Naghten rule A rule in English common law for judging sanity and legal responsibility.
Maintenance rehearsal Silently repeating or mentally reviewing information to hold it in short-term memory.
Major depressive disorder A mood disorder in which the person has suffered one or more intense episodes of depression.
Major mood disorders Disorders marked by lasting extremes of mood or emotion and often accompanied by psychotic symptoms.
Major tranquilizers (antipsychotics) Drugs that, in addition to having tranquilizing effects, also tend to reduce hallucinations and delusional thinking.
Maladaptive behavior Behavior that makes it more difficult for a person to adapt to his or her environment and meet the demands of day-to-day life.
Male erectile disorder An inability to maintain an erection for sexual intercourse.
Male orgasmic disorder An inability to reach orgasm during intercourse.
Management by objectives A management technique in which employees are given specific goals to meet in their work.
Mandala A circular design representing balance, unity, and completion.
Manic Extremely excited, hyperactive, or irritable.
Manifest dream content The surface, "visible" content of a dream; dream images as they are remembered by the dreamer.
Manipulation drive Drive to investigate objects by touching and handling them.
Mantra A word or sound used as the focus of attention in concentrative meditation.
Marijuana The leaves and flowers of the hemp plant, *Cannabis sativa.*
Marketing research A type of public opinion polling used to assess consumer views of products, services, and advertising.
Masochism Deriving sexual arousal or pleasure from having pain inflicted during the sex act.
Mass media Collectively, all media that reach

very large audiences (magazines, for instance, are a medium of mass communication).
Massed practice A practice schedule in which studying continues for long periods, without interruption.
Mastery training Reinforcement of responses that lead to mastery of a threat or control over one's environment.
Masturbation Production of sexual pleasure or orgasm by manipulation of the genitals other than by intercourse.
Maternal influences The aggregate of all psychological effects mothers have on their children.
Maternity blues A brief and relatively mild state of depression often experienced by mothers 2 or 3 days after giving birth.
Maturation The physical growth and development of the body and nervous system.
Maximum life span The biologically determined maximum number of years humans could live under optimal conditions.
Mean world view Viewing the world and other people as dangerous and threatening.
Means-ends analysis An analysis of how to reduce the difference between the present state of affairs and a desired goal.
Mechanical solution A problem solution achieved by trial and error or by a fixed procedure based on learned rules.
Medicated birth The common practice in Western medicine of giving painkilling drugs during labor and birth.
Meditation A mental technique for quieting the mind and body.
Medulla The enlarged stalk at the base of the brain that connects to the spinal cord and controls vital life functions.
Melatonin A hormone produced by the pineal gland in response to cycles of light and dark.
Memory The mental system for receiving, storing, organizing, altering, and recovering information.
Memory cue Any stimulus associated with a particular memory. The presence of such cues usually enhances memory retrieval.
Memory decay The fading or weakening of memories assumed to occur when memory traces become weaker.
Memory structure The pattern of associations among bits of information stored in memory.
Memory traces Hypothesized physical changes that take place in the brain as it stores information; engrams.
Menarche The onset of menstruation; a woman's first menstrual period.
Menopause An end to regular monthly menstrual periods.
Mental age The average mental ability displayed by people of a given age.
Mental disorder A significant impairment in psychological functioning.
Mental hospitalization Confinement to a protected environment that provides various forms of therapy for mental, emotional, and behavioral problems.
Mental retardation The presence of a developmental disability, a formal IQ score below 70, or a significant impairment of adaptive behavior.
Mental rotation The ability to change the position of an image in mental space in order to examine it from a new perspective.
Mesmerize To hypnotize.
Meta-needs In Maslow's hierarchy, those needs above and beyond the ordinary; needs associated with impulses for self-actualization.
Metabolic disorder Any disorder in metabolism (the rate of energy production and use in the body).
Metabolic rate The rate at which energy is consumed by bodily activity.
Micro-electrode An electrode small enough to record the activity of a single neuron.
Microcephaly A disorder in which the head and brain are abnormally small.
Micromovements Tiny, nearly imperceptible movements associated with changes in muscular tension and activity.
Microsleep A momentary shift in brain wave patterns to those of sleep.
Midbrain The area of the brain consisting of structures linking the forebrain and the brainstem.
Midcareer phase A stable central career phase marked by high competence and full status.
Mild punishment Punishment that has a relatively weak effect, especially punishment that only temporarily slows responding.
Minimal brain dysfunction (MBD) A hypothesized explanation for hyperactivity, involving a lag in brain development or low-level damage to the brain.
Minnesota Multiphasic Personality Inventory-2 (MMPI-2) The latest version of one of the best known and most widely used objective personality questionnaires.
Minor tranquilizers Drugs (such as Valium) that produce relaxation or reduce anxiety.
Mirror technique Observing another person reenact one's own behavior, like a character in a play; designed to help persons to see themselves more clearly.
Misdirected letter technique A way of measuring attitudes toward a group; letters addressed to the group are sent to households and the number forwarded is counted.
MMPI-2 profile A graphic representation of an individual's scores on each of the primary scales of the MMPI-2.
Mnemonic A memory system or aid.
Mock jury A group that realistically simulates a courtroom jury.
Model (learning) A person (either live or filmed) who serves as an example for observational learning or vicarious conditioning.
Model (scientific) In research, an animal whose behavior is used to derive principles that may apply to human behavior.
Modeling Any process in which information is imparted by example, before direct practice is allowed.
Monocular depth cues Depth cues that can be sensed with one eye.
Mood A low intensity, long-lasting emotional state.
Mood disorder A major disturbance in mood or emotion, such as depression or mania.
Moon illusion The apparent change in size that occurs as the moon moves from the horizon (large moon) to overhead (small moon).
Moral anxiety Apprehension felt when one's thoughts, impulses, or actions conflict with standards enforced by the superego.
Moral development The development of values, beliefs, and thinking abilities that act as a guide regarding what is acceptable behavior.
Moro reflex Neonatal reflex evoked by sudden loss of support or the sounding of a loud noise; in response, the arms are extended and then brought toward each other.
Morphemes The smallest meaningful units in a language, such as syllables or words.
Motivation Mechanisms within an organism that initiate, sustain, and direct activities.
Motor cortex An area on the top of the brain directly associated with control of voluntary movements.
Motor neuron A nerve cell that carries motor commands from the central nervous system to muscles and glands.
Motor program A mental plan or model that guides skilled movement.
Motor skill A series of actions molded into a smooth and efficient performance.
MRI scan Magnetic resonance imaging; a computer-enhanced three-dimensional representation of the brain or body, based on the body's response to a magnetic field.
Müller-Lyer illusion A stimulus consisting of two parallel lines tipped with inward or outward pointing Vs. Although they are of equal length, one of the lines appears longer than the other.
Multiculturalism Giving equal status, recognition, and acceptance to different ethnic, racial, and cultural groups.
Multiple approach-avoidance conflict Being simultaneously attracted to and repelled by each of several alternatives.
Multiple aptitude test Test that measures two or more aptitudes.
Multiple personality A form of dissociative disorder in which a person develops two or more distinct personalities.
Muscular imagery Any mental representation based on produced, remembered, or imagined muscular sensations; for instance, the images produced when one imagines hammering a nail.
Muscular responses Visible movement of the muscles or unseen changes in their tension, which creates kinesthetic sensations.
Mutual absorption With regard to romantic love, the almost exclusive attention lovers give to one another.
Mutual interdependence A condition in which two or more persons must depend on one another to meet each person's needs or goals.
Myelin A fatty layer coating some axons that increases the rate at which nerve impulses travel along the axon.
Myoclonus Restless spasms of the leg muscles that disturb sleep.
Myopia A visual defect that makes it difficult to focus distant objects (nearsightedness).

Narcolepsy A serious sleep disturbance in which the individual suffers uncontrollable sleep attacks.
Natural clinical test An accident or other natural event that provides psychological data.
Natural design Human factors engineering that makes use of perceptual signals that are understood by people without any need to learn them.
Natural selection Darwin's theory that evolution favors those plants and animals best suited to their living conditions.
Natural setting The environment in which an organism typically lives.
Naturalistic observation Observation and recording of naturally occurring behavior that is not manipulated experimentally.
Near-death experience A pattern of experiences that may occur when a person is clinically dead and then resuscitated.
Need An internal deficiency that may energize behavior.
Need for achievement (nAch) The desire to excel or meet some internalized standard of excellence.
Need for power The desire to have social impact and control over others.
Need to affiliate The desire to associate with other people.
Negative after-potential A drop in electrical charge below the resting potential.
Negative attention seeking A pattern, seen especially in children, in which misbehavior is used to gain attention.
Negative instance In concept learning, an object or event that does not belong to the concept class.
Negative reinforcement Occurs when a response is followed with an end to discomfort or with the removal of a negative state of affairs.
Negative relationship A relationship in which increases in one measure correspond to decreases in the other.
Negative self-statements Self-critical thoughts that increase anxiety and lower performance.
Negative transfer Mastery of one task conflicts with learning or performing another.
Neglect Ignoring one side of vision or of the body after damage to a brain hemisphere.
Neo-Freudian A personality theorist who accepts the broad features of Freud's theory but has revised the theory to fit his or her own concepts.
Neonate A newborn infant during the first weeks following birth.
Nerve A bundle of neuron fibers supported by connective tissue; nerves can be seen with the unaided eye; neuron fibers are microscopic projections from single cells.
Nerve deafness Deafness caused by damage to the hair cells or auditory nerve.
Network model A model of memory that views it as an organized system of linked information.
Neurilemma A layer of living cells that encases the axons of many neurons.
Neurons Individual nerve cells.
Neuropeptides Brain chemicals that regulate the activity of neurons, thereby influencing memory, emotion, pain, hunger and other behavior.
Neurosis An outdated term once used to refer, as a group, to anxiety disorders, somatoform disorders, dissociative disorders, and some forms of depression.
Neurotic anxiety Apprehension felt when the ego must struggle to maintain control over id impulses.
Neurotransmitter Any of a number of chemical substances secreted by neurons that alter activity in other neurons.
Neutral stimulus A stimulus that fails to elicit a response.
Nicotine A potent stimulant drug found primarily in tobacco; nicotine is a known carcinogen.
Night blindness A visual defect in which daylight vision is normal, but blindness occurs under conditions of low illumination.
Night terror A very frightening NREM sleep episode.
Nightmare An upsetting dream.
Nocturnal orgasm An orgasm that occurs spontaneously during sleep or dreaming.
Noise pollution Stressful and intrusive noise; usually artificially generated by machinery, but also including noises made by animals and humans.
Non-homeostatic drive A drive that is relatively independent of physical deprivation cycles or bodily need states.
Non-love An absence of intimacy, passion, and commitment in a relationship.
Non-reinforcement Withholding reinforcement after selected responses (in other words, extinction training).
Nonsense syllables Invented three-letter words used to test learning and memory.
Noradrenaline A hormone produced by the adrenal glands that tends to arouse the body; noradrenaline is associated with anger.
Norm (social) An accepted (but often unspoken) standard of conduct for appropriate behavior.
Norm (testing) An average score for a designated group of people.
Normal curve A bell-shaped curve with a large number of scores in the middle, tapering to very few extremely high and low scores.
NREM sleep Non-rapid eye movement sleep characteristic of stages 2, 3, and 4, and largely dream-free.
Nystagmus Any involuntary vibration, oscillation, or movement of the eye.

Obedience Conformity to the demands of an authority.
Object In making attributions, the aim, motive, or target of an action.
Object permanence Concept, gained in infancy, that objects continue to exist even when they are hidden from view.
Objective test A test that gives the same score when different people correct it.
Observation Directly gathering data by recording facts or events.
Observational learning Learning achieved by watching and imitating the actions of another or noting the consequences of those actions.
Observer bias The tendency of an observer to distort observations or perceptions to match his or her expectations.
Observer effect Changes in a person's behavior brought about by an awareness of being observed.
Obsession Recurring irrational or disturbing thoughts or mental images a person cannot prevent.
Obsessive-compulsive disorder An extreme, unavoidable preoccupation with certain thoughts and compulsive performance of certain behaviors.
Occipital lobes Portion at the back of the cerebral cortex that includes areas where vision registers in the brain.
Oedipus conflict Freudian concept referring to a boy's sexual attraction to his mother, and feelings of rivalry with his father.
Olfaction The sense of smell.
Olfactory area Sites on the frontal lobes where information on smell registers.
Open teaching Instruction based on active teacher-student discussion.
Open-ended interview An interview in which persons are allowed to freely state their views.
Operant conditioning Learning based on the consequences of responding.
Operant extinction The weakening or disappearance of a non-reinforced operant response.
Operant reinforcer Any event that reliably increases the probability or frequency of responses it follows.
Operant shaping Gradually molding responses by rewarding ever-closer approximations to a final desired pattern.
Operant stimulus discrimination The tendency to make a response when stimuli previously associated with reward are present and to withhold the response when stimuli associated with nonreward are present.
Operant stimulus generalization The tendency to respond to stimuli similar to those present when an operant response was acquired.
Operational definition Defining a scientific concept by stating the specific actions or procedures used to measure it. For example, "hunger" might be defined as "the number of hours of food deprivation."
Opponent-process theory (motivation) States that strong emotions tend to be followed by an opposite emotional state; also the strength of both emotional states changes over time.
Opponent-process theory (sensation) The theory of color vision stating that three coding systems (red or green, yellow or blue, black or white) are used by the visual system to analyze color information.
Oral stage In Freud's theory, the period early in life when infants are preoccupied with the mouth as a source of pleasure and means of expression.
Organ of Corti Center part of the cochlea, containing hair cells, canals, and membranes.
Organic mental disorder A mental or emotional problem caused by malfunction of the brain.
Organic psychosis A psychosis caused by a known brain injury or disease.
Organismic valuing Placing value on an experience on the basis of how one responds to it as an entire organism; judgment made directly on the basis of one's perceptions and feelings.

Pseudo-psychology Any false and unscientific system of beliefs and practices that is offered as an explanation of behavior.
Psi phenomena Events that seem to lie outside the realm of accepted scientific laws.
Psyche The mind, mental life, and personality as a whole.
Psychiatric social worker A professional who applies social science principles to help patients in clinics and hospitals.
Psychiatrist A medical doctor who specializes in treating mental disorders.
Psychoactive drug A substance capable of altering attention, memory, judgment, time sense, self-control, mood, or perception.
Psychoanalysis A Freudian approach to psychotherapy emphasizing the exploration of unconscious conflicts.
Psychoanalyst A mental health professional (usually a medical doctor) trained to practice psychoanalysis.
Psychoanalytic theory Freudian theory of personality that emphasizes unconscious forces and internal conflicts in its explanations of behavior.
Psychobiology A viewpoint that seeks to explain behavior through biological processes, such as activity in the brain and nervous system, genetics, the endocrine system, and evolution.
Psychodrama A therapy in which clients act out personal conflicts and feelings in the presence of others who play supporting roles.
Psychodynamic theory Any theory of behavior that emphasizes internal conflicts, motives, and unconscious forces.
Psychokinesis The purported ability to mentally alter or influence objects or events.
Psycholinguist A specialist in the psychology of language and language development.
Psychological androgyny The presence of both "masculine" and "feminine" traits in a single person (as masculinity and femininity are defined within one's culture).
Psychological dependence Drug dependence that is based primarily on emotional or psychological needs.
Psychological efficiency Maintenance of good morale, labor relations, employee satisfaction, and similar aspects of work behavior.
Psychological situation A situation as it is perceived and interpreted by an individual, not as it exists objectively.
Psychological trauma A psychological injury or shock, such as that caused by violence, abuse, neglect, separation, and so forth.
Psychologist An individual highly trained in the methods, factual knowledge and theories of psychology.
Psychology The scientific study of human and animal behavior.
Psychometrics Mental measurement or testing.
Psychoneuroimmunology Study of the links among behavior, disease, and the immune system.
Psychopath An individual who appears to make no distinctions between right and wrong and who feels no guilt about destructive or antisocial behavior.
Psychopathology The scientific study of mental, emotional, and behavioral disorders; also, abnormal or maladaptive behavior.
Psychophysics The study of the relationship between physical stimuli and the sensations they evoke in a human observer.
Psychosexual stages In Freud's theory of personality development, the oral, anal, phallic, and genital stages, during which various personality traits are formed.
Psychosis A severe psychological disorder characterized by a retreat from reality, hallucinations and delusions, disturbed emotions, and social withdrawal.
Psychosocial dilemma A conflict, between personal impulses and the social world, that affects development.
Psychosomatic disorder Illness in which psychological factors contribute to bodily damage or to damaging changes in bodily functioning.
Psychosurgery Any surgical alteration of the brain designed to bring about desirable behavioral or emotional changes.
Psychotherapist Anyone who does psychological therapy. Persons who call themselves psychotherapists are not always psychologists.
Psychotherapy Any form of psychological treatment for behavioral or emotional problems.
Psychotic disorder A severe psychological disorder characterized by a retreat from reality, by hallucinations and delusions, and by social withdrawal.
Puberty The biologically defined period during which a person matures sexually and becomes capable of reproduction.
Public distance Distance at which formal interactions, such as giving a speech, occur (about 12 feet or more from the body).
Punisher Any event that decreases the probability or frequency of responses it follows.
Punishment Occurs when a response is followed with pain or an otherwise negative event or when a response is followed with the removal of a positive reinforcer (response cost).
Pupil The dark spot at the front of the eye through which light passes.

Quality circle A discussion group in which employees voluntarily seek to solve business problems.

Racism Racial prejudice that has become institutionalized (that is, it is reflected in government policy, schools, and so forth) and that is enforced by the existing social power structure.
Random assignment The use of chance (for example, flipping a coin) to assign subjects to experimental and control groups.
Random search strategy Trying possible solutions to a problem in a more or less random order.
Rapid eye movements (REMs) Swift eye movements during sleep.
Rapid smoking Forced cigarette smoking designed to make smoking aversive and unappealing.
Rating scale A list of various personality traits or aspects of behavior on which a person is rated, during or after observation of the person's behavior.
Rational-emotive therapy (RET) An approach that attempts to change or remove irrational beliefs that cause emotional problems.
Rationalization Justifying one's own behavior by giving reasonable and "rational" but false reasons for it.
Reaction formation Preventing dangerous or threatening impulses from being expressed by exaggerating opposite behavior.
Reactive depression A serious depression that appears to be a reaction to some identifiable event.
Readiness Sufficient maturation for rapid acquisition of a skill.
Realistic stage Stage of career exploration in which career options are narrowed and more specific plans are made.
Reality principle The principle by which the ego functions, involving delaying action (or pleasure) until it is appropriate.
Reality testing Obtaining additional information to check on the accuracy of perceptions.
Recall To supply or reproduce memorized information with a minimum of external cues.
Receptive meditation Meditation in which attention is widened to include an awareness of one's total subjective experience.
Receptor sites Areas on the surface of neurons and other cells that are sensitive to neurotransmitters or hormones.
Recessive gene A gene whose influence will only be expressed when it is paired with a second recessive gene (it cannot be expressed when paired with a dominant gene).
Reciprocal inhibition Principle that one emotional state can block another, such as joy preventing fear, or anxiety inhibiting pleasure.
Reciprocity A reciprocal interchange or return in kind.
Recitation As a memory aid, repeating aloud information one wishes to retain.
Recoding Reorganizing or otherwise transforming information to facilitate storage in memory.
Recognition Memory in which previously learned material is correctly identified as that which was seen before.
Redintegration The process of reconstructing an entire complex memory after observing or remembering only a part of it.
Reference group Any group that an individual identifies with and uses as a standard for social comparison.
Referent power Social power gained when one is used as a point of reference by others.
Referred pain Pain that is felt in one part of body, but comes from another.
Reflection In client-centered therapy, the process of rephrasing or repeating thoughts and feelings so that clients become aware of what they are saying about themselves.
Reflex An innate, automatic response to a stimulus; for example, an eye blink, knee jerk, or dilation of the pupil.
Reflex arc The simplest behavior pattern, involving only three neurons; leads from a stimulus to an automatic response, such as an eye blink or knee jerk.
Refractory period A short time period after orgasm during which males are unable to again reach orgasm.
Refreezing In brainwashing, the process of re-

warding and strengthening new attitudes and beliefs.

Refusal skills training Training that teaches youngsters how to resist influences to begin smoking (can also be applied to other drugs, such as alcohol or cocaine).

Regression Any return to an earlier, more infantile behavior pattern.

Rehearsal Silently repeating or mentally reviewing information to hold it in short-term memory or aid its long-term storage.

Reinforcement Any event that brings about learning or increases the probability that a particular response will occur.

Reinforcement value The subjective value a person attaches to a particular activity or reinforcer.

Relational concept A concept defined by the relationship between features of an object or between an object and its surroundings (for example, "greater than," "lopsided").

Relaxation response The pattern of physiological changes that occurs in the body at times of relaxation.

Relearning Learning again something that was previously learned. Used to measure one's memory of prior learning.

Relevant questions In a polygraph exam, questions to which only a guilty person should react.

Reliability The ability of a test to yield the same score, or nearly the same score, each time it is given to the same person.

REM behavior disorder A failure of normal muscle paralysis, leading to violent actions during REM sleep.

REM rebound The occurrence of extra amounts of rapid eye movement sleep in a person who has been deprived of REM sleep.

REM sleep Sleep marked by rapid eye movements, a return to stage 1 EEG patterns; usually associated with dreaming.

Replicate To reproduce or repeat.

Representative sample A small, randomly selected part of a larger population that accurately reflects characteristics of the whole population.

Representativeness hueristic A tendency to select wrong answers because they seem to match pre-existing mental categories.

Repression Unconsciously pushing out or barring from awareness unwanted memories.

Research method A systematic approach to answering scientific questions.

Resistance Blocking that occurs in psychoanalysis during free association; topics the client resists thinking or talking about.

Resolution (grief) With respect to grief, an acceptance of loss and the need for building a new life.

Resolution (sexual) The fourth phase of sexual response, involving a return to lower levels of sexual tension and arousal.

Respondent conditioning Another term for classical conditioning.

Respondent reinforcement In classical conditioning, reinforcement that occurs when the unconditioned stimulus closely follows the conditioned stimulus.

Response Any muscular action, glandular activity, or other identifiable behavior.

Response chaining The assembly of a series of responses into a chain of actions leading to reinforcement.

Response cost Punishment that occurs when a response leads to the removal of a positive reinforcer.

Response cost Removal of a positive reinforcer after a response is made.

Response-contingent Applying reinforcement, punishment, or other consequences only when a certain response is made.

REST Restricted Environmental Stimulation Therapy.

Resting potential The electrical charge that exists between the inside and outside of a neuron at rest.

Retardation Mental capacity significantly below average; traditionally defined as an IQ score below 70.

Reticular activating system (RAS) A part of the reticular formation that activates the cerebral cortex.

Reticular formation A network of fibers within the medulla associated with attention, alertness, and activation of higher brain areas.

Retina The light-sensitive layer of cells at the back of the eye.

Retinal Part of the chemical compound that makes up rhodopsin (also known as retinene).

Retinal disparity Small discrepancies in the images falling on each retina caused by separation of the eyes.

Retrieval Recovering information from memory.

Retroactive interference The tendency for new memories to interfere with the retrieval of old memories.

Retrograde amnesia Loss of memory for events that preceded a head injury or other amnesia-causing event.

Reversibility of thought Recognition that relationships involving equality or identity can be reversed (for example, if A = B, then B = A).

Reversible figure A stimulus pattern that allows perceivers to reverse figure-ground organization.

Reward Anything that produces pleasure or satisfaction; a positive reinforcer.

Reward power Social power based on the capacity to reward a person for acting as desired.

Rhodopsin The photosensitive pigment in the rods.

Rods Visual receptors that are responsive to dim light but produce only black and white sensations.

Role conflict An upsetting condition that exists when a person tries to occupy two or more roles that make conflicting demands on behavior.

Role model A person who serves as a positive example of desirable behavior.

Role playing The dramatic enactment or re-enactment of significant life events.

Role reversal Taking the role of another person to learn how one's own behavior appears from the other person's perspective.

Romantic love A combination of intimacy and passion that does not include much commitment.

Rooting reflex Neonatal reflex elicited by a light touch to the cheek, causing the infant to turn toward the object and attempt to nurse.

Rorschach Inkblot Test A projective test comprised of 10 standardized inkblots that are described by the person taking the test.

Run of luck A statistically unusual outcome (as in getting 5 heads in a row when flipping a coin) that could still occur by chance alone.

Sadism Deriving erotic satisfaction by the infliction of pain on another; more broadly, love of cruelty.

Sample A subset or portion of a population.

Satiety system Areas on the bottom middle of the hypothalamus that terminate eating.

Saturation That quality of colors related to their being very pure, from a narrow area of the spectrum, or free from mixture with other colors.

Savings score The amount of time saved (expressed as a percentage) when relearning information.

Scapegoating Selecting a person or group of people to take the blame for conditions not of their making; habitual redirection of aggression toward some person or group.

Schedule of reinforcement A rule or plan for determining which responses will be reinforced.

Schizophrenia A psychosis characterized by delusions, hallucinations, apathy, and a "split" between thought and emotion.

Schizotypal personality A non-psychotic personality disorder involving withdrawal, social isolation, and odd behavior, but no break with reality.

Scientific Conducted strictly according to the principles of evidence used in the natural sciences.

Scientific management (Theory X) An approach to managing employees that emphasizes work efficiency.

Scientific method Testing the truth of a proposition by careful measurement and controlled observation.

Scientific observation Orderly observation designed to answer questions about the world.

Scientist-practitioner model Training of clinical psychologists to do both research and therapy.

Seasonal affective disorder Depression that occurs during fall and winter; presumably related to decreased exposure to sunlight.

Secondary appraisal Deciding how to cope with a threat or challenge.

Secondary elaboration Making a dream more logical and complete while remembering it.

Secondary motives Motives based on learned psychological needs.

Secondary reinforcer A learned reinforcer; often one that gains reinforcing properties by association with a primary reinforcer.

Secondary sexual characteristics Sexual features other than the genitals and reproductive organs—such as the breasts, body shape, and facial hair.

Secondary traits Personality traits that are inconsistent or relatively superficial.

Secure attachment A stable and positive emotional bond.

Sedative A substance that calms, tranquilizes, or induces sleep by depressing activity in the nervous system.

Selective attention Voluntarily focusing on a se-

lected portion of sensory input, most likely by rerouting messages within the brain.
Selective combination In problem solving, the ability to connect seemingly unrelated items of information.
Selective comparison The ability to relate a present problem to similar problems solved in the past or to prior experience.
Selective encoding The mental ability to select relevant information while ignoring useless or distracting information.
Selective perception Perceiving only certain stimuli among a larger array of possibilities.
Self A continuously evolving conception of one's personal identity.
Self archetype An unconscious image representing, unity, wholeness, completion, and balance.
Self-actualization The on-going process of fully developing one's personal potential.
Self-assertion A direct, honest expression of feelings and desires.
Self-awareness Consciousness of oneself as a person.
Self-concept Personal perception of one's own personality traits; a collection of beliefs, ideas, and feelings about one's own identity.
Self-disclosure The process of revealing private thoughts, feelings, and personal history to others.
Self-esteem Regarding oneself as a worthwhile person; a positive evaluation of oneself.
Self-evaluation Positive and negative feelings held toward oneself.
Self-fulfilling prophecy A prediction that prompts people to act in ways that make the prediction come true.
Self-handicapping Arranging to perform under conditions that usually lower performance, so as to have an excuse available for a poor showing.
Self-help group A group of people who share a particular type of problem and provide mutual support to one another.
Self-hypnosis A state of hypnosis attained without the aid of a hypnotist; autosuggestion.
Self-image Total subjective perception of one's body and personality (another term for self-concept).
Self-instruction Use of silent questions and instructions to structure learning.
Self-monitoring Regulation and control of the image one displays to others in public.
Self-recording Self-management based on keeping records of response frequencies.
Self-regulated learning Active, self-guided learning.
Self-reinforcement Praising or rewarding oneself for having made a particular response (such as completing a school assignment).
Self-selection feeding Free choice concerning the foods eaten.
Self-testing Answering self-administered questions.
Semantic differential A measure of connotative meaning obtained by rating words or concepts on several dimensions.
Semantic memory A subpart of declarative memory that records impersonal knowledge about the world.
Semantics The study of meanings in language.
Semicircular canals Fluid-filled vestibular canals; the sensory organs for balance.
Senile dementia Serious mental impairment in old age caused by physical deterioration of the brain.
Sensate focus Form of therapy that directs a couple's attention to natural sensations of sexual pleasure.
Sensation The immediate response in the brain caused by excitation of a sensory organ.
Sensation and perception psychologist A psychologist with expert knowledge on the sense organs and the processes involved in perception.
Sensation seeking A personality characteristic of persons who prefer high levels of stimulation.
Sensitivity group A group experience designed to increase self-awareness and sensitivity to others.
Sensorimotor stage Stage of intellectual development during which sensory input and motor responses become coordinated.
Sensory adaptation A decrease in sensory response to an unchanging stimulus.
Sensory analysis The capacity of sensory systems to separate incoming information into important elements.
Sensory coding Various codes used by the sense organs to transmit information to the brain.
Sensory conflict theory Attributes motion sickness to mismatched information from vision, the vestibular system, and kinesthesis.
Sensory deprivation Any major reduction in the amount or variety of sensory stimulation.
Sensory gating Alteration of incoming sensory messages in the spinal cord, before they reach the brain.
Sensory memory The first stage of memory, which holds an explicit and literal record of incoming information for two seconds or less.
Sensory neuron A nerve cell that carries information from the senses toward the central nervous system.
Separation anxiety Distress displayed by infants when they are separated from their parents or principal caregivers.
Serial position effect The tendency for the greatest number of memory errors to occur in the middle portion of an ordered list.
Set A predisposition to respond in a certain way.
Set point A theoretical proportion of body fat that tends to be maintained by changes in hunger and eating.
Setting In making attributions, the social and/or physical environment in which an action occurs.
Severe punishment Intense punishment; by definition, punishment capable of suppressing a response for long periods.
Sex drive The strength of one's motivation to engage in sexual behavior.
Sex role socialization The process of learning behaviors considered appropriate for one's gender in a given culture.
Sex role stereotypes Over-simplified and widely held beliefs about the basic characteristics of men and women.
Sex roles Separate patterns of traits, mannerisms, interests, and behaviors that are regarded as "male" and "female" by one's culture.
Sex-linked trait Traits other than gender that are influenced by genes carried on an X or a Y chromosome.
Sexism Institutionalized prejudice against members of either sex, based solely on their gender.
Sexual and gender identity disorders Any of a wide range of difficulties with sexual identity, deviant sexual behavior, or sexual adjustment.
Sexual aversion Fear, anxiety, or disgust about engaging in sex.
Sexual disorder Any of a wide range of difficulties with sexual identity, sexual behavior, or sexual adjustment.
Sexual masochism Deriving sexual pleasure from having pain inflicted during the sex act.
Sexual orientation One's degree of emotional and erotic attraction to members of the same gender, opposite gender, or both genders.
Sexual sadism Gaining sexual pleasure by inflicting pain during the sex act.
Sexual script An unspoken mental plan that defines a "plot," dialogue, and actions expected to take place in a sexual encounter.
Sexually transmitted disease A disease that is typically passed from one person to the next by intimate physical contact; a venereal disease.
Shape constancy The perceived shape of objects is unaltered by changes in the shape of their images on the retina.
Shaping Gradually molding responses to a final desired pattern.
Short-term dynamic therapy Modern psychodynamic therapy designed to produce insights within a shorter time than traditional psychoanalysis.
Short-term memory (STM) The memory system used to hold small amounts of information for relatively brief time periods.
Shyness A tendency to avoid others plus uneasiness and strain when socializing.
Sibling rivalry Competition among brothers and sisters for attention, dominance, status within the family, and so forth.
Signal In early language development, any behavior, such as touching, vocalizing, gazing, or smiling, that allows non-verbal interaction and turn-taking between parent and child.
Similarity In interpersonal attraction, the extent to which two people are alike in background, age, interests, attitudes, beliefs, and so forth.
Single-blind experiment An arrangement in which subjects remain unaware of whether they are in the experimental group or the control group.
Single-word stage In language development, the period during which a child first begins to use single words.
Situational context The social situation, behavioral setting, or general circumstances in which an action takes place.
Situational demands Unstated expectations that define desirable or appropriate behavior in various settings and social situations.
Situational determinants External conditions that strongly influence behavior.
Situational test Simulating real-life conditions so that a person's reactions may be directly observed.
Size constancy The perceived size of objects remains unchanged despite changes in the size of the

images they cast on the retina.

Size-distance invariance The strict relationship that exists between the distance an object lies from the eyes and the size of its image.

Skin receptors Sensory organs for touch, pressure, pain, cold, and warmth.

Skin senses The senses of touch, pressure, pain, heat, and cold.

Sleep apnea Repeated interruption of breathing during sleep.

Sleep deprivation Being deprived of desired or needed amounts of sleep.

Sleep patterns The order and duration of daily sleep and waking periods.

Sleep spindles Distinctive bursts of brain-wave activity that indicate a person is asleep.

Sleep stages Various levels of sleep depth identified by brain wave patterns and behavioral changes.

Sleep-deprivation psychosis A major disruption of mental and emotional functioning brought about by lack of sleep.

Sleeptalking Speaking while asleep.

Slow-to-warm-up child A child who is temperamentally restrained, unexpressive, or shy.

Social comparison Making judgments about ourselves through comparison with others.

Social development The development of self-awareness, attachment to caregivers, and relationships with other children and adults.

Social distance Distance at which impersonal interaction takes place (about 4 to 12 feet from the body).

Social distance scale An attitude measure that asks people to rate the degree to which they would be willing to have contact with a member of another group.

Social environment An environment defined by a group of people and their activities or interrelationships (such as a parade, revival meeting, or sports event).

Social exchange Any exchange between two people of attention, information, affection, favors, or the like.

Social exchange theory Theory stating that rewards must exceed costs for relationships to endure.

Social influence Changes in a person's behavior induced by the presence or actions of others.

Social learning theory An approach that combines learning principles with cognitive processes (perception, thinking, anticipation), plus the effects of observational learning, to explain behavior.

Social markers Visible or tangible signs that indicate a person's social status or role.

Social motives Learned motives acquired as part of growing up in a particular society or culture.

Social non-conformity Failure to conform to societal norms or the usual minimum standards for social conduct.

Social phobia An intense, irrational fear of being observed, evaluated, embarrassed, or humiliated by others in social situations, such as eating, writing, blushing, or speaking in public.

Social power The capacity to control, alter, or influence the behavior of another person.

Social psychology The study of human social behavior (behavior that is influenced by one's relationship with others).

Social Readjustment Rating Scale (SRRS) A scale that rates the impact of various life events on the likelihood of illness.

Social referencing Observing others in social situations to obtain information or guidance.

Social reinforcement Praise, attention, approval, and/or affection from others.

Social role Expected behavior patterns associated with particular social positions (such as daughter, worker, student).

Social stereotypes Oversimplified images of the traits of individuals who belong to a particular social group.

Social support Close, positive relationships with other people.

Social trap A social situation that tends to provide immediate rewards for actions that will have undesired effects in the long run.

Socialization The process of learning to live in a particular culture by adopting socially acceptable values and behavior.

Sociobiology Theory that social behavior evolved in ways that maximize fitness for survival of the species.

Sociopath Another name for the psychopath or antisocial personality.

Soma The main body of a neuron or other cell.

Somatic pain Pain from the skin, muscles, joints, and tendons.

Somatic system The system of nerves linking the spinal cord with the body and sense organs.

Somatic therapy Any bodily therapy, such as drug therapy, electroconvulsive therapy, or psychosurgery.

Somatization disorder Afflicted persons have numerous physical complaints. Typically, they have consulted many doctors, but no organic cause for their distress can be identified.

Somatoform disorder The presence of physical symptoms that mimic disease or injury for which there is no identifiable physical cause.

Somatoform pain Pain that has no identifiable physical cause and appears to be of psychological origin.

Somatosensory area The part of the parietal lobes that serves as a receiving area for bodily sensations.

Somesthetic sense Pertaining to sensations produced by the skin, muscles, joints, viscera, and organs of balance.

Somnambulist One who sleepwalks.

Sound wave A cyclic compression of air molecules.

Source traits Basic underlying traits of personality; each source trait is reflected in a larger number of surface traits.

Space adaptation syndrome Motion sickness caused by weightlessness.

Spaced practice A practice schedule that alternates study periods with brief rests. (Massed practice, in comparison, continues for long periods, without interruption.)

Spatial neglect A tendency to ignore the left or right side of one's body and the left or right side of visual space after damage to one of the brain hemispheres.

Special aptitude test Test to predict a person's likelihood of succeeding in a particular area of work or skill.

Species-specific behavior Behavior patterns that occur with little variation in almost all members of a species.

Species-typical behavior Behavior patterns that are typical of a species, but not automatic.

Specific phobia An intense, irrational fear of specific objects, activities, or situations.

Spinal nerve One of 62 major nerves that channel sensory and motor information in and out of the spinal cord.

Split-brain operation A surgical technique in which the corpus callosum is cut, functionally disconnecting the two cerebral hemispheres.

Spontaneous recovery The reappearance of a learned response after its apparent extinction.

Spontaneous remission The disappearance of a psychological disturbance without the aid of therapy.

Sports psychology Study of the psychological and behavioral dimensions of sports performance.

SQ3R method A reading method based on these steps: survey, question, read, recite, and review.

Squeeze technique Method for inhibiting ejaculation by compressing the tip of the penis.

Stage ESP The simulation of ESP for the purpose of entertainment.

Stage hypnosis Use of hypnosis to entertain; often, merely a simulation of hypnosis.

Stage of exhaustion Third stage of the G.A.S., at which time the body's resources are exhausted and serious health consequences occur.

Stage of resistance Second stage of the G.A.S., during which bodily adjustments to stress stabilize but at a high physical cost.

Staining Chemically treating tissues to make their details more visible.

Stanford-Binet Intelligence Scale A widely used individual test of intelligence; a direct descendant of Alfred Binet's first intelligence test.

State-dependent learning Memory influenced by one's bodily state at the time of learning and at the time of retrieval. Improved memory occurs when the bodily states match.

Statistical abnormality Abnormality defined on the basis of an extreme score on some measure or dimension, such as IQ or anxiety.

Statistical significance Experimental results that would rarely occur by chance alone.

Status An individual's position in a group or social structure, especially with respect to power, privilege, importance, and so forth.

Status inequalities Differences in the power, prestige, or privileges of two or more persons or groups.

Stereocilia Bristle-like structures on hair cells.

Stereoscopic vision Perception of space and depth caused chiefly by the fact that the eyes receive different images.

Stereotype An inaccurate, rigid, and oversimplified image of members of a social group, especially an outgroup.

Stereotyped response A rigid, repetitive, and non-productive response made mechanically and without regard for its appropriateness.

Stimulant A substance that produces a temporary

increase of activity in the body and nervous system.
Stimulation deafness Deafness resulting from damage caused by exposure to excessively loud sounds.
Stimulus Any physical energy sensed by an organism.
Stimulus control The tendency of stimuli present when an operant response is acquired to subsequently control when and where the response is made.
Stimulus discrimination The learned ability to detect differences in stimuli, often produced by reinforcing responses to one stimulus but not another.
Stimulus generalization The tendency to respond to stimuli similar to, but not identical to, a conditioned stimulus.
Stimulus motives Innate needs for stimulation and information.
Stress The condition that occurs when a challenge or a threat forces a person to adjust or adapt to the environment.
Stress inoculation Use of positive coping statements to control fear and anxiety.
Stress management The application of behavioral strategies to reduce stress and improve coping skills.
Stress reaction The physical response to stress, consisting mainly of bodily changes related to autonomic nervous system arousal.
Stressor A specific condition or event in the environment that challenges or threatens a person.
Stroboscopic movement Illusion of movement in which an object is shown in a rapidly changing series of positions.
Structuralism The school of thought in psychology concerned with analyzing sensations and personal experience into basic elements.
Structured interview An interview that follows a prearranged plan, usually defined by asking a series of planned questions.
Stuttering Chronic hesitation or stumbling in speech.
Subcortex All brain structures below the cerebral cortex.
Subjective discomfort Personal, private feelings of discomfort or unhappiness.
Subjective experience Reality as it is perceived and interpreted, not as it exists objectively; personal, private, non-objective experience.
Sublimation Working off frustrated desires or unacceptable impulses in substitute activities that are constructive or accepted by society.
Subliminal perception Perception of a stimulus presented below the threshold for conscious recognition.
Substance related disorder Abuse of or dependence on a mood- or behavior-altering drug.
Successive approximations A series of steps that change behavior to a desired response pattern.
Sucking reflex Rhythmic sucking movements elicited by touching the neonate's mouth.
Sudden infant death syndrome The sudden, unexplained death of an apparently healthy infant.
Superego In Freudian theory, an internalization of parental values and societal standards.
Superordinate goal A goal that exceeds or overrides all others; a goal that renders other goals relatively less important.
Superstitious behavior In conditioning, a behavior repeated because it seems to produce reinforcement, even though it is actually unnecessary.
Support group A group formed to provide emotional support for its members through discussion of shared stresses and concerns.
Suppression A conscious effort to not think of something or to keep it from awareness.
Surface traits The visible or observable traits of one's personality.
Surrogate mother A substitute mother (often an inanimate dummy in animal research).
Survey method The use of public polling techniques to answer psychological questions.
Syllogism A format for analyzing logical arguments.
Symbolic prejudice Prejudice that is expressed in disguised fashion.
Symbolization In Carl Rogers' theory, the process of admitting an experience to awareness.
Sympathetic system A branch of the autonomic system responsible for arousing and activating the body at times of stress.
Synapse The microscopic space, between an axon terminal and another neuron, over which neurotransmitters pass.
Synesthesia Experiencing one sense in terms normally associated with another sense; for example, "seeing" sounds as colors.
Syntax Rules for ordering words when forming sentences.
Systematic desensitization A guided reduction in fear, anxiety, or aversion.

Tardive dyskinesia A neurological disorder associated with excessive use of major tranquilizers.
Target behaviors Actions or other behaviors (such as speech) that a behavior therapist seeks to modify.
Task centering Focusing on the task at hand, rather than on one's own feelings or needs.
Taste aversion An active dislike for a particular food; frequently created when the food is associated with illness or discomfort.
Taste bud The receptor organ for taste.
Telegraphic speech In language development, the formation of simple two-word sentences that "telegraph" (communicate) a simple idea.
Telepathy The purported ability to directly know another person's thoughts.
Temperament The physical foundation of personality, including emotional and perceptual sensitivity, energy levels, typical mood, and so forth.
Temporal lobes Areas on each side of the cerebral cortex that include the sites where hearing registers in the brain.
Temporary threshold shift A temporary decrease in sensitivity to sound.
Tentative stage Stage of career exploration in which planning becomes more realistic, although still broad.
Terminal decline An abrupt decline in measured intelligence about five years before death.
Territorial behavior Any behavior that tends to define a space as one's own or that protects it from intruders.
Territorial markers Objects and other signals whose placement indicates to others the "ownership" of a particular area.
Test anxiety High levels of arousal and worry that seriously impair test performance.
Test battery A group of tests and interviews given to the same individual.
Test standardization Establishing standards for administering a test and interpreting scores.
Testosterone Male sex hormone, secreted mainly by the testes and responsible for the development of male sexual characteristics.
Thalamus A structure at the center of the brain that relays sensory information to the cerebral cortex.
Thanatologist A specialist who studies emotional and behavioral reactions to death and dying.
Thanatos The death instinct postulated by Freud.
THC Tetrahydrocannabinol, the main active chemical in marijuana.
Thematic Apperception Test (TAT) A projective test consisting of 20 different scenes and life situations about which respondents make up stories.
Theory A system designed to interrelate concepts and facts in a way that summarizes existing data and predicts future observations.
Theory Y A management style that emphasizes human relations at work and that views people as industrious, responsible, and interested in challenging work.
Therapy placebo effect Improvement caused not by the actual process of therapy but by a client's expectation that therapy will help.
Thought stopping Use of aversive stimuli to interrupt or prevent upsetting thoughts.
Threat An event or situation perceived as potentially harmful to one's well-being.
Thyroid gland Endocrine gland whose hormones help regulate metabolism (the production and expenditure of energy within the body).
Time out Removing a person from a situation in which rewards for maladaptive behavior are available, in order to produce extinction; also, the withholding of social reinforcers (attention, approval) when undesirable responses are made.
Tinnitus A ringing or buzzing sensation in the ears not caused by an external stimulus.
Tip-of-the-tongue state The experience of feeling that a memory is available, while being unable to retrieve it.
Token economy A therapeutic program in which desirable behaviors are reinforced with tokens that can be exchanged for goods, services, activities, and privileges.
Token reinforcer A tangible secondary reinforcer such as money, gold stars, poker chips, and the like.
Tokens Symbolic rewards, or secondary reinforcers (such as plastic chips, gold stars, or points) that can be exchanged for real reinforcers.
Top-down processing Applying higher-level knowledge to rapidly organize sensory information into a meaningful perception.
Tragedy of the commons A social trap in which individuals, each acting in his or her immediate self-interest, overuse a scarce group resource.
Trait profile A graphic representation of the ratings obtained by an individual (or sometimes a

group) on each of several personality traits.
Trait theorist A psychologist who is interested in classifying, analyzing, and interrelating traits, and in discovering their origins, to understand and explain personality.
Trait-situation interaction Variations in behavior that occur when the expression of a trait is influenced by settings or circumstances.
Traits (personality) Relatively permanent and enduring qualities of behavior that a person displays in most situations.
Transducer A device that converts energy from one system into energy in another.
Transference In psychoanalysis, the tendency of a client to transfer to the therapist feelings that correspond to those the client had for important persons in his or her past.
Transformation In Piaget's theory, the mental ability to change the shape or form of a substance (such as clay or water) and to perceive that its volume remains the same.
Transformation rules Rules by which a simple declarative sentence may be changed to other voices or forms (past tense, passive voice, and so forth).
Transition period Time-span during which a person leaves an existing life pattern behind and moves into a new pattern.
Transvestic fetishism Achieving sexual arousal by wearing clothing of the opposite sex.
Trepanning In modern usage, any surgical procedure in which a hole is bored in the skull; historically, the chipping or boring of holes in the skull to "treat" mental disturbance.
Triangular theory of love Theory that love is composed of three elements: intimacy, passion, and commitment; different types of love are defined by the presence or absence of each element.
Trichromatic theory The theory of color vision based on the assumption that there are three types of cones, with peak sensitivity to red, green, or blue.
Tryptophan A sleep promoting amino acid.
Tunnel vision Vision restricted to the center of the visual field.
Turn-taking In early language development, the tendency of parent and child to alternate in the sending and receiving of signals or messages.
Two-factor learning Learning that involves both classical conditioning and operant conditioning.
Tympanic membrane The eardrum.
Type A personality A personality type with an elevated risk of heart disease; characterized by time urgency, anger, and hostility.
Type B personality All personality types other than Type A; a low cardiac-risk personality.

Unconditional positive regard Unshakable love and approval given without qualification.
Unconditioned response An innate reflex response elicited by an unconditioned stimulus.
Unconditioned stimulus A stimulus innately capable of eliciting a response.
Unconscious Region of the mind that is beyond awareness, especially impulses and desires not directly known to a person.
Undifferentiated schizophrenia Schizophrenia lacking the specific features of catatonic, disorganized, or paranoid types.
Unfreezing In brainwashing, a loosening of convictions about former values, attitudes, and beliefs.
Unipolar disorder A mood disorder in which a person experiences extended periods of deep depression but has no history of ever having been manic.
Unstructured interview An interview in which conversation is informal and topics are taken up freely as they arise.
Unusual Uses Test A test of creativity in which subjects try to think of new uses for a common object.

Vacillation Wavering in intention or feelings.
Vaginismus Muscle spasms of the vagina that prevent intercourse or cause pain.
Validity The ability of a test to measure what it purports to measure.
Validity scales Scales that tell whether test scores should be invalidated for lying, inconsistency, or "faking good."
Variable Any condition that changes or can be made to change; a measure, event, or state that may vary.
Variable interval schedule A schedule in which a reinforcer is given for the first correct response made after a varied amount of time has passed (measured from the previous reinforced response). Responses made before the time interval has ended are not reinforced.
Variable ratio schedule A pattern in which a varied number of correct responses must be made to get a reinforcer. For example, a reinforcer is given after 3 to 7 correct responses; the actual number changes randomly.
Verbal intelligence Intelligence measured by answering questions involving vocabulary, general information, arithmetic, and other language- or symbol-oriented tasks.
Vestibular senses The senses of balance, body position, and acceleration.
Vicarious classical conditioning Classical conditioning brought about by observing another person react to a particular stimulus.
Vicarious desensitization A reduction in fear or anxiety that takes place vicariously ("second hand") when a client watches models perform the feared behavior.
Virilism The development of male sexual characteristics in a female.
Visceral pain Pain originating in the internal organs.
Visible spectrum That portion of the electromagnetic spectrum to which the eyes are sensitive.
Visual acuity The clarity or sharpness of visual perception.
Visual cliff An apparatus that looks like the edge of an elevated platform or cliff; used to test for depth perception in infants and baby animals.
Visual pigment A chemical found in the rods and cones that is sensitive to light.
Visually directed reaching Coordinated, visually guided reaching for a particular object.
Vocational counselor A counseling psychologist who helps people match their interests, talents, and goals with available careers.
Vocational interest test A paper-and-pencil test that assesses a person's interests and matches them to interests found among successful workers in various occupations.
Volume transmission The spread of neuropeptides into groups of neurons, affecting their behavior.
Vomeronasal organ A sensory organ sensitive to pheromones.
Voyeurism Deriving sexual pleasure from viewing the genitals of others, usually without their knowledge or permission (peeping).

Waiting-list control group A group of people who receive no treatment in experiments designed to test the effectiveness of psychotherapy.
Waking consciousness A state of normal, alert awareness.
Warning system Pain based on large nerve fibers; warns that bodily damage may be occurring.
Weapons effect The observation that weapons serve as strong cues for aggressive behavior; also, the tendency for eyewitnesses to focus almost entirely on an assailant's weapon.
Weber's law States that the just noticeable difference is a constant proportion of the original stimulus intensity; actually applies most accurately to stimuli in the mid-range of intensities.
Wechsler Adult Intelligence Scale-Revised (WAIS-R) A widely used adult intelligence test that rates both verbal and performance intelligence.
Wechsler Intelligence Scale for Children-Third Edition (WISC-III) A widely used intelligence test for children that rates both verbal and performance intelligence.
Weight cycling Repeated swings between losing and gaining weight.
Wellness A positive state of good health; more than the absence of disease.
Wernicke's area An area related to language comprehension.
White matter Portions of the nervous system that appear white due to the presence of myelin.
Whole learning Studying an entire package of information (such as a complete poem) at once.
Wish fulfillment Freudian belief that the content of many dreams reflects unfulfilled desires that cannot be consciously expressed.
Withdrawal of love Withholding affection to enforce child discipline.
Withdrawal symptoms Physical illness and discomfort that accompany the withdrawal of an addictive drug.
Work efficiency Maximum output (productivity) at lowest cost.
Working memory Another name for short-term memory, especially as it is used for thinking and problem solving.

X chromosome The female chromosome contributed by the mother; produces a female when paired with another X chromosome, and a male when paired with a Y chromosome.

Y chromosome The male chromosome contributed by the father; produces a male when paired with an X chromosome. Fathers may give either an X or a Y chromosome to their offspring.

Yerkes-Dodson law A qualification of the inverted U function that states the relationships among arousal, task complexity, and performance.

Zener cards A deck of 25 cards bearing various symbols and used in early parapsychological research.

References

Abe, K., Amatomi, M., & Oda, N. (1984). Sleepwalking and recurrent sleeptalking in children of childhood sleepwalkers. *American Journal of Psychiatry, 141,* 800–801.

Ableson, R. P. (1988). Conviction. *American Psychologist.* 43(4), 267–275.

Abrahamson, D. J., Barlow, D. H., & Abrahamson, L. S. (1989). Differential effects of performance demand and distraction on sexually functional and dysfunctional males. *Journal of Abnormal Psychology,* 98(3), 241–247.

Abrams, A. (1983). Honda Ohio plant transplants Japan methods, harmony. *Los Angeles Times,* Jan. 7, IV, 1–2.

Abramson, L. Y., Seligman, M. E. P., & Teasdale, J. D. (1985) Learned helplessness in humans: Critique and reformulation. In J. C. Coyne (Ed.) *Essential papers on depression.* New York: New York University Press, 259–301.

Abramson, R. (1993). EPA officially links passive smoke, cancer. *Los Angeles Times,* Jan. 8, A27.

Adams, J. (1986). *Conceptual blockbusting.* New York: Norton.

Adelmann, P. K. & Zajonc, R. B. (1989). Facial efference and the experience of emotion. *Annual Review of Psychology, 40,* 249–280.

Ader, R. & Cohen, N., (1993). Psychoneuroimmunology: Conditioning and stress. In L. W. Porter and M. R. Rosenzweig (Eds.), *Annual Review of Psychology, 44,* 53–85.

Adler, T. (1992). Are hormone's benefits real—or a tall tale? *APA Monitor,* Dec., 42, 43.

Adorno, T. W., Frenkel-Brunswik, E., Levinson, D. J., & Sanford, R. N. (1950). *The authoritarian personality.* New York: Harper.

Agnati, L. F., Bjelke, B., & Fuxe, K. (1992). Volume transmission in the brain. *American Scientist,* 80(Jul-Aug), 362–373

Ahles, T. A., Blanchard, E. B, & Leventhal, H. (1983). Cognitive control of pain: Attention to the sensory aspects of the cold pressor stimulus. *Cognitive Therapy and Research,* 7, 159–178.

Ainsworth, M. D. (1989). Attachments beyond infancy. *American Psychologist, 44*(4), 709–716.

Akerstedt, T. (1990). Psychological and psychophysiological effects of shift work. *Scandinavian Journal of Work, Environment & Health, 16*(Suppl. 1), 67–73.

Akerstedt, T., Hume, K., Minors, D., & Waterhouse, J. (1993). Regulation of sleep and naps on an irregular schedule. *Sleep, 16*(8), 736–743.

Albert, E. M. (1963). The roles of women: Question of values. In Farber & Wilson (Eds.), *The potential of women.* New York: McGraw-Hill.

Alberti, R., & Emmons, M. (1986). *Your perfect right.* San Luis Obispo, CA: Impact.

Alberto, P. A. & Troutman, A. C. (1990). *Applied behavior analysis for teachers.* Columbus, OH: Merrill.

Alcock, J. E. (1990). *Science and supernature: A critical appraisal of parapsychology.* Buffalo, NY: Prometheus.

Alessi, S. M. & Trollip, S. R. (1985). *Computer-based instruction.* New York: Prentice-Hall.

Alevizos, P. N., & Callahan, E. J. (1977). Assessment of psychotic behavior. In A. R. Ciminero, K. S. Calhoun, & H. E. Adams (Eds.), *Handbook of behavioral assessment,* New York: Wiley.

Alicke, M. D. & Doherty, K. (1992). Social disagreement and conformity. *Journal of Social Behavior & Personality, 7(1),* 125–137.

Allen, B. (1979). Winged victory of "Gossamer Albatross." *National Geographic, 156,* 642–651.

Allgeier, E. R. & Allgeier, A. R. (1991). *Sexual interactions.* Lexington, MA: Heath.

Alloy, L. B., Peterson, C., Abramson, L. Y., & Seligman, M. E. (1984). Attributional style and the generality of learned helplessness. *Journal of Personality & Social Psychology, 46,* 681–687.

Allport, G. W. (1958). *The nature of prejudice.* Garden City, NY: Anchor Books, Doubleday.

Allport, G. W. (1961). *Pattern and growth in personality.* New York: Holt, Rinehart, and Winston.

Alva, S. A. (1993). Differential patterns of achievement among Asian-American adolescents. *Journal of Youth and Adolescence,* 22(4), 407–423.

Alvino, J., and the Editors of Gifted Children Monthly. (1985). *Parents' guide to raising a gifted child.* Boston, Little, Brown.

Amabile, T. M. (1983). *The social psychology of creativity.* New York: Springer-Verlag.

Amar, P. B. (1993). Biofeedback and applied psychophysiology at the crossroads. *Biofeedback & Self Regulation,* 18(4), 201–209.

Ambady, N. & Rosenthal, R. (1993). Half a minute: Predicting teacher evaluations from thin slices of non-verbal behavior and physical attractiveness. *Journal of Personality & Social Psychology, 64*(3), 431–441.

Anastasi, A. (1994). Aptitude testing. *Encyclopedia of Human Behavior, Vol. 1.* San Diego, CA: Academic Press.

Andersen, S. M., Klatzky, R. L., & Murray, J. (1990). Traits and social stereotypes: Efficiency differences in social processing. *Journal of Personality & Social Psychology,* 59(2), 192–201.

Anderson, B. L., Kiecolt-Glaser, J. K., & Glaser, R. (1994). A biobehavioral model of cancer stress and disease course. *American Psychologist, 49*(5), 389–404.

Anderson, C. A. (1989). Temperature and aggression. *Psychological Bulletin, 106,* 74–96.

Anderson, J. R. (1990). *Cognitive psychology.* New York: Freeman.

Anderson, J. R. (1993). Problem solving and learning. *American Psychologist, 48*(1), 35–44.

Anderson, K. J. (1990). Arousal and the inverted-U hypothesis. *Psychological Bulletin, 107*(1), 96–100.

Andreasen, N. C., Glaum, M., Swayze, V. W.,

O'Leary, D. S. et al. (1993). Intelligence and brain structure in normal individuals. *American Journal of Psychiatry, 150*(1), 130–143.

Andrews, J. D. (1989). Integrating visions of reality. *American Psychologist, 44*(5), 803–817.

Animal rights: CSICOP takes a new direction, (1990). *Skeptical Inquirer, 15,* 4–5.

Annett, M. & Manning, M. (1990). Arithmetic and laterality. *Neuropsychologia,* 28(1), 61–69.

Anthony, W. A., Cohen, M., & Kennard, W. (1990). Understanding the current facts and principles of mental health systems planning. *American Psychologist,* 45(11), 1249–1252.

Arendt, J. (1994). Clinical perspectives for melatonin and its agonists. *Biological Psychiatry,* 35(1), 1–2.

Aronoff, J., Barclay, A. M., & Stevenson, L. A. (1988). The recognition of threatening facial stimuli. *Journal of Personality & Social Psychology, 54*(4), 647–655.

Aronson, E. (1969). Some antecedents of interpersonal attraction. In W. J. Arnold & D. Levine (Eds.). *Nebraska Symposium on Motivation,* Lincoln: University of Nebraska Press.

Aronson, E. (1992). *The Social Animal.* San Francisco: W. H. Freeman.

Aronson, E. with Blaney, N., Sikes, J., Stephan, C., & Snapp, M. (1979). Busing and racial tension: The jigsaw route to learning and liking. In V. J. Derlega & L. H. Janda (Eds.). *Personal adjustment, selected readings,* Glenview, IL: Scott, Foresman.

Asarnow, J. R., Goldstein, M. J., & Ben-Meir, S. (1988). Parental communication deviance in childhood onset schizophrenia spectrum and depressive disorders. *Journal of Child Psychology & Psychiatry & Allied Disciplines.* 29(6), 825–838.

Asch, S. E. (1956). Studies of independence and conformity: A minority of one against a unanimous majority. *Psychological Monographs,* 70(416).

Ash, D. W. & Holding, D. H. (1990). Backward versus forward chaining in the acquisition of a keyboard skill. *Human Factors,* 32(2), 139–146.

Ashton, W. A. & Fuehrer, A. (1993). Effects of gender and gender role identification of participant and type of social support resource on support seeking. *Sex Roles,* 28(7–8), 461–476.

Aslin, R. N. & Smith, L. B. (1988). Perceptual development. *Annual Review of Psychology,* 39, 435–473.

Astronomical Society of the Pacific. (1983). *Astrology and astronomy,* San Francisco.

Athenasiou, R., Shaver, P., & Tavris, C. (1970). Sex. *Psychology Today,* 4(2), 37–52.

Avery, D. H., Bolte, M. A., Dager, S. R., et al. (1993). Dawn simulation of winter depression. *American Journal of Psychiatry, 150*(1), 113–117.

Axelson, J. A. (1985). *Counseling and development in a multicultural society.* Monterey, CA: Brooks/Cole.

Ayllon, T. (1963). Intensive treatment of psychotic behavior by stimulus satiation and food reinforcement. *Behavior Research and Therapy, 1,* 53–61.

Ayllon, T., & Azrin, N. H. (1965). The measurement and reinforcement of behavior of psychotics. *Journal of the Experimental Analysis of Behavior,* 8, 357–383.

Azrin, N. H., Hutchinson, R. R., & McLaughlin, R. (1965). The opportunity for aggression as an operant reinforcer during aversive stimulation. *Journal of Experimental Analysis of Behavior,* 8, 171–180.

Bachman, J. G., & Johnson, L. D. (1979). The freshmen. *Psychology Today, 13,* 78–87.

Bachrach, L. L. (1984). Asylum and chronically ill psychiatric patients. *American Journal of Psychiatry, 141,* 975–978.

Back, K. W. (1972). The group can comfort but it can't cure. *Psychology Today,* 6(7), 28–35.

Baddeley, A. (1990). *Human memory.* Needham Heights, MA: Allyn and Bacon.

Baer, D. M. (1971). Let's take another look at punishment. *Psychology Today,* Oct.

Baer, J. M. (1988). Long-term effects of creativity training with middle school students. *Journal of Early Adolescence,* 8(2), 183–193.

Bahrick, H. P. (1984). Semantic memory content in permastore: Fifty years of memory for Spanish learned in school. *Journal of Experimental Psychology: General, 113*(1), 1–37.

Bailey, J. M. & Pillard, R. C. (1991). A genetic study of male sexual orientation. *Archives of General Psychiatry, 48(12),* 1089–1096.

Bailey, J. M., Pillard, R. C., Neale, M. C., & Agyei, Y. (1993). Heritable factors influence sexual orientation in women. *Archives of General Psychiatry, 50*(3), 217–223.

Bailey, M. B. & Bailey, R. E. (1993). "Misbehavior": A case history. *American Psychologist,* Nov., 1157–1158.

Baillargeon, R. (1991). Reasoning about the height and location of a hidden object in 4.5- and 6.5-month-old infants. *Cognition,* 38(1), 13–42.

Baillargeon, R. & DeVos, J. (1992). Object permanence in young infants: Further evidence. *Child Development, 62(6),* 1227–1246.

Baillargeon, R., De Vos, J., & Graber, M. (1989). Location memory in 8-month-old infants in a non-serach AB task. *Cognitive Development,* 4, 345–367.

Bak, M., Girvin, J. P., Hambrecht, F. T., Kufta, C. V., Loeb, G. E., Schmidt, E. M. (1990). Visual sensations produced by intracortical microstimulation of the human occipital cortex. *Medical and Biological Engineering and Computing, 28(3),* 257–259.

Baker, L. A. & Clark, R. (1990). Genetic origins of behavior: Implications for counselors. *Journal of Counseling & Development,* 68(6), 597–600.

Baker, L. A. & Daniels, D. (1990). Nonshared environmental influences and personality differences in adult twins. *Journal of Personality & Social Psychology,* 58(1), 103–110.

Baker, R. A. (1992). *Hidden memories.* Buffalo, NY: Prometheus Books.

Baldwin, E. (1993). The case for animal research in psychology. *Journal of Social Issues, 49*(1), 121–131.

Bales, J. "Poll: Members give APA high marks." *APA Monitor,* March, 1991, 7.

Ball, G. G., & Grinker, J. A. (1981). Overeating and obesity. In S. J. Mule (Ed.), *Behavior in Excess,* 194–220. New York: Free Press.

Baltes, P. B. (1987). Theoretical propositions of life-span developmental psychology: On the dynamics between growth and decline. *Developmental Psychology,* 23(5), 611–626.

Banaji, M. R. & Prentice, D. A. (1994). The self in social contexts. *Annual Review of Psychology, 45,* 297–332.

Bandura, A. (1965). Vicarious processes: A case of no-trial learning. In L. Berkowitz (Ed.), *Advances in experimental social psychology, Vol. 2,* 1–55. New York: Academic Press.

Bandura, A. (1971). *Social learning theory.* New York: General Learning Press.

Bandura, A. (1973). *Aggression: A social learning analysis.* Englewood Cliffs, NJ: Prentice-Hall.

Bandura, A. (1986). *Social foundations of thought and action: A social cognitive theory.* Englewood Cliffs, NJ: Prentice-Hall.

Bandura, A., & Rosenthal, T. L. (1966). Vicarious classical conditioning as a function of arousal level. *Journal of Personality & Social Psychology,* 3, 54–62.

Bandura, A., & Walters, R. (1959). *Adolescent aggression.* New York: Ronald.

Bandura, A., & Walters, R. (1963). Aggression. In H. W. Stevenson (Ed.), *Child psychology.* Chicago: University of Chicago Press.

Bandura, A., & Walters, R. (1963). *Social learning and personality development.* New York: Holt.

Bandura, A., Blanchard, E. B., Ritter, B. (1969). Relative efficacy of desensitization and modeling approaches for inducing behavioral, affective, and attitudinal changes. *Journal of Personality & Social Psychology, 13(3),* 173–199.

Bandura, A., Ross, D., & Ross, S. A. (1963). Vicarious reinforcement and imitative learning. *Journal of Abnormal and Social Psychology,* 67, 601–607.

Bank, S. P., & Kahn, M. D. (1982). *The sibling bond.* New York: Basic Books.

Barber, T. X. (1970). *Suggested ("hypnotic") behavior: The trance paradigm versus an alternative paradigm.* Harding, Mass. Medfield Foundation, Report No. 103.

Barglow, P. Vaughn, B. E., & Monitor, N. (1987). *Child Development,* 58(4), 945–954.

Barker, E. A. (1993). Evaluating graphology. *Skeptical Inquirer,* 17(Spring), 312–315.

Baron, J. (1993). Why teach thinking? *Applied Psychology: An International Review,* 42(3), 191–214.

Baron, R. A. (1983). "Sweet smell of success"? The impact of pleasant artificial scents on evaluations of job applicants. *Journal of Applied Psychology,* 68, 709–713.

Baron, R. A. & Byrne, D. (1990). *Social psychology.* Boston: Allyn & Bacon.

Baron, R. A. & Richardson, D. R. (1994). *Human aggression.* New York: Plenum.

Barowsky, E. I., Moskowitz, J., & Zweig, J. B. (1990). Biofeedback for disorders of initiating and maintaining sleep. *Annals of the New York Academy of Sciences, 602,* 97–103.

Barr, H. M. & Streissguth, A. P. (1991). Caffeine use during pregnancy and child outcome: A 7-year prospective study. *Neurotoxicological Teratology, 13(4),* 441–448.

Barrett, D. (1993). The "committee of sleep": A study of dream incubation for problem solving. *Dreaming,* 3(2), 115–122.

Barrett, R. J. (1985). Behavioral approaches to individual differences in substance abuse. In Galizio, M. & Maisto, S. A. (Eds.), *Determinants of substance abuse treatment: Biological, psychological, and environmental factors.* New York: Plenum.

Barron, F. (1958). The psychology of imagination. *Scientific American, 199*(3), 150–170.

Barsalou, L. W. (1992). *Cognitive psychology.* Hillsdale, NJ: Lawrence Erlbaum.

Bartlett, J. C. & Searcy, J. (1993). Inversion and configuration of faces. *Cognitive Psychology, 25*(3), 281–316.

Bartz, W. (1990). The basics of critical thought. Personal communication.

Bashore, T. R. & Rapp, P. E. (1993). Are there alternatives to traditional polygraph procedures? *Psychological Bulletin, 113*(1), 3–22.

Batson, C. D. (1990). How social an animal? The human capacity for caring. *American Psychologist,* 45(3), 336–346.

Bauer, W. D., & Twentyman, C. T. (1985). Abusing, neglectful, and comparison mothers' response to child-related and non-child-related stressors. *Journal of Consulting and Clinical Psychology,* 53, 335–343.

Baum, A. & Fleming, I. (1993). Implications of psychological research on stress and technological accidents. *American Psychologist,* 48(6), 665–672.

Baum, A., & Davis, G. E. (1980). Reducing the stress of high-density living: An architectural intervention. *Journal of Personality & Social Psychology,* 38, 471–481.

Baum, A., & Valins, S. (1979). Architectural mediation of residential density and control: Crowding and the regulation of social contact. *Advances in Experimental and Social Psychology, 12,* 131–175.

Baum, A., & Valins, S. (Eds.). (1977). *Human response to crowding: Studies of the effects of residential group size.* Hillsdale, NJ: Erlbaum.

Baumeister, A. A. (1987). Mental retardation: Some conceptions and dilemmas. *American Psychologist,* 42(2), 796–800.

Baumgardner, A. H. (1990). To know oneself is to like oneself: Self-certainty and self—affect. *Journal of Personality & Social Psychology,* 58(6), 1062–1072.

Baumrind, D. (1980, July). New directions in socialization research. *American Psychologist,* 35, 639–652.

Baumrind, D. (1991). The influence of parenting style on adolescent competence and substance use. *Journal of Early Adolescence, 11*(1), 56–95.

Baumrind, D. (1993). The average expectable environment is not good enough. *Child Development,* 64(5), 1299–1317.

Beach, F. A. (1975). Behavioral endocrinology: An emerging discipline. *American Scientist,* 63, 178–187.

Beck, A. T. (1985). Cognitive therapy of depression: New perspectives. In P. Clayton (Ed.), *Depression.* New York: Raven.

Beck, A. T. (1991). Cognitive therapy. *American Psychologist, 46*(4), 368–375.

Beck, A. T. & Weishaar, M. E. (1989). Cognitive Therapy. R. J. Corsini & D. Wedding (Eds.), *Current psychotherapies.* Itasca, IL: Peacock.

Beck, A. T., & Greenberg, R. L. (1974). *Coping with depression.* Institute For Rational Living.

Beck, A. T., & Young, J. E. (1978). College blues. *Psychology Today,* Sept., 80–92.

Beck, A. T., Brown, C., Berchick, R. J., Stewart, B. L. et al. (1990). Relationship between hopelessness and ultimate suicide. *American Journal of Psychiatry,* 147(2), 190–195.

Beckwith, L., Rodning, C., & Cohen, S. (1992). Preterm children at early adolescence and continuity and discontinuity in maternal responsiveness from infancy. *Child Development, 63(5),* 1198–1208.

Beebe, B., Gerstman, L., Carson, B., Dolins, M., Zigman, A., Rosensweig, H., Faughey K., & Korman, M. (1982). Rhythmic communication in the mother-infant dyad. In M. Davis (Ed.), *Interaction rhythms, periodicity in communicative behavior.* New York: Human Sciences Press.

Beecher, H. K. (1959). *Measurement of subjective responses: Quantitative effects of drugs.* New York: Oxford University Press.

Begg, I. M., Needham, D. R., & Bookbinder, M. (1993). Do backward messages unconsciously affect listeners? No. *Canadian Journal of Experimental Psychology,* 47(1), 1–14.

Beidler, L. M. (1963). Dynamics of taste cells. In Y. Zotterman (Ed.), *Olfaction and taste,* Vol. 1. New York: Macmillan.

Beilin, H. (1992). Piaget's enduring contribution to developmental psychology. *Developmental Psychology, 28(2),* 191–204.

Bell, A. P., Weinberg, M. S., & Hammersmith, S. K. (1981). *Sexual preference.* Indiana University Press.

Bellezza, F. S., Six, L. S., & Phillips, D. S. (1992). A mnemonic for remembering long strings of digits. *Bulletin of the Psychonomic Society, 30(4),* 271–274.

Belloc, N. B. (1973). Relationship of physical health practices and mortality. *Preventive Medicine,* 2, 67–81.

Belloc, N. B. & Breslow, L. (1972). Relationship of physical health status and healthy practices. *Preventive Medicine,* 1, 409–421.

Belsky, J. & Rovine, M. J. (1988). Nonmaternal care in the first year of life and the security of infant-parent attachment. *Child Development,* 59(1), 157–167.

Belsky, J., Gilstrap, B., & Rovine, M. (1984). The Pennsylvania infant and family development project, I: Stability and change in mother-infant and father-infant interactions in a family setting at one, three, and nine months. *Child Development,* 55, 692–705.

Bem, S. L. (1974). The measurement of psychological androgyny. *Journal of Consulting and Clinical Psychology,* 42, 155–162.

Bem, S. L. (1975a). Sex-role adaptability: One consequence of psychological androgyny. *Journal of Personality & Social Psychology, 31,* 634–643.

Bem, S. L. (1975b). Androgyny vs. the tight little lives of fluffy women and chesty men. *Psychology Today,* Sept., 58–62.

Bem, S. L. (1981). Gender schema theory. A cognitive account of sex typing. *Psychological Review,* 88, 354–364.

Ben-Shakhar, G., Bar-Hillel, M., Bilu, Y., Ben-Abba, E., & Flug, A. (1986). Can graphology predict occupational success? Two empirical studies and some methodological ruminations. *Journal of Applied Psychology,* 71,4, 645–653.

Benbow, C. P. (1986). Physiological correlates of extreme intellectual precocity. *Neuropsychologia,* 24(5), 719–725.

Beneke, W. M., & Harris, M. B. (1972). Teaching self-control of study behavior. *Behavior Research and Therapy, 10,* 35–41.

Bennett, W., & Gurin, J. (1982). *The dieter's dilemma.* New York: Basic.

Benoit, S. C. & Thomas, R. L. (1992). The influence of expectancy in subliminal perception experiments. *Journal of General Psychology,* 119(4), 335–341.

Benson, H. (1975). *The relaxation response.* New York: Morrow.

Benson, H. (1977). Systematic hypertension and the relaxation response. *The New England Journal of Medicine,* 296, 1152–1156.

Benton, A. L. (1980, Feb.). The neuropsychology of facial recognition. *American Psychologist,* 35, 176–186.

Benwall, R. P. (1990). The illusion of reality. *Psychological Bulletin,* 107(1), 82–95.

Bergin, A. E. (1991). Values and religious issues in psychotherapy and mental health. *American Psychologist, 46,* (4), 394–403.

Bergin, A., & Suinn, R. M. (1975). Individual psychotherapy and behavior therapy. *Annual Review of Psychology,* 26, 509–556.

Berglas, S. (1986). A typology of self-handicapping alcohol abusers. In Saks, M. J. & Saxe, L. (Eds.), *Advances in applied social psychology, Vol.* 3. Hillsdale, NJ: Erlbaum.

Berkowitz, L. (1968). The frustration-aggression hypothesis revisited. In L. Berkowitz (Ed.), *Roots of aggression: A re-examination of the frustration-aggression hypothesis.* New York: Atherton.

Berkowitz, L. (1982). Aversive conditions as stimuli to aggression. In L. Berkowitz (Ed.), *Advances in experimental social psychology, vol 15.* New York: Academic.

Berkowitz, L. (1984). Some effects of thoughts on anti- and prosocial influences of media events: A cognitive-neoassociation analysis. *Psychological Bulletin,* 95, 410–427.

Berkowitz, L. (1988). Frustrations, appraisals, and aversively stimulated aggression. *Aggressive Behavior, 14*(1), 3–11.

Berkowitz, L. (1990). On the formation and regulation of anger and aggression. *American Psychologist,* 45(4), 494–503.

Berlyne, D. (1966). Curiosity and exploration. *Science, 153,* 25–33.

Berman, L. H. (1982). Family therapy. In L. E. Abt, & I. R. Stuart (Eds.), *The newer therapies: A sourcebook.* New York: Van Nostrand, Reinhold.

Berne, E. (1964). *Games people play.* New York: Grove.

Bernthal, P. R. & Insko, C. A. (1993). Cohesiveness without groupthink: The interactive effects of social and task cohesion. *Group & Organization Management, 18(1),* 66–87.

Berry, J. W. (1990). The psychology of acculturation. In R. A. Dienstbier and J. J. Berman (Eds.). *Nebraska Symposium on Motivation 1989: Cross-*

cultural perspectives, 37, Lincoln: Univsersity of Nebraska Press.

Berry, P., Groeneweg, G., Gibson, D., & Brown, R. I. (1984). Mental development of adults with Down syndrome. *American Journal of Mental Deficiency, 89*, 252–256.

Bersheid, E. (1994). Interpersonal relations. *Annual Review of Psychology, 45*, 79–129.

Bersheid, E. & Walster, E. (1974b). A little bit about love. In T. L. Huston (Ed.), *Foundations of interpersonal attraction*. New York: Academic.

Bertsch, G. J. (1976). Punishment of consummatory and instrumental behavior: A review. *Psychological Record, 26*, 13–31.

Best, J. B. (1992). *Cognitive psychology*. St. Paul, MN: West.

Betancur, C., Velez, A., Cabanieu, G., le Moal, M. et al. (1990). Association between left-handedness and allergy: A reappraisal. *Neuropsychologia, 28*(2), 223–227.

Bettelheim, B. (1960). *The informed heart*. New York: Free Press.

Beyerstein, B. (1985). The myth of alpha consciousness. *The Skeptical Inquirer, 10*, 42–59.

Beyerstein, B. L. & Beyerstein, D. F. (1992). *The write stuff: Evaluations of graphology*. Buffalo, NY: Prometheus.

Beyerstein, B. L. (1990). Brainscams: Neuromythologies of the New Age. Special Issue: Unvalidated, fringe, and fraudulent treatment of mental disorders. *International Journal of Mental Health, 19*(3), 27–36.

Biblow, E. (1973). Imaginative play and the control of aggressive behavior. In J. L. Singer (Ed.), *The child's world of make-believe: Experimental studies of imaginative play*. New York: Academic.

Bickman, L. (1974). Clothes make the person. *Psychology Today*, April.

Bierley, C., McSweeney, F. K., & Vannieuwerk, R. (1985). Classical conditioning of preferences for stimuli. *Journal of Consumer Research, 12*, 316–323.

Binder, V. (1976). Behavior modification: Operant approaches to therapy. In V. Binder, A. Binder, & B. Rimland (Eds.), *Modern therapies*. Englewood Cliffs, NJ: Prentice-Hall.

Birch, J. & McKeever, L. M. (1993). Survey of the accuracy of new pseudoisochromatic plates. *Ophthalmic & Physiological Optics, 13*(1), 35–40.

Birnbaum, I. M., Parker, E. S., Hartley J. T., & Nobel, E. P. (1978). Alcohol and memory: Retrieval processes. *Journal of Verbal Learning and Verbal Behavior, 17*, 325–335.

Blackmore, S. (1989). What do we really think? A survey of parapsychologists and sceptics. *Journal of the Society for Psychical Research, 55*(814), 251–262.

Blackmore, S. (1991). Lucid dreaming. *Skeptical Inquirer, 15*, 362–370.

Blackmore, S. (1991). Near-death experiences: In or out of the body? *Skeptical Inquirer, 16*(Fall), 34–45.

Blackmore, S. (1993). *Dying to live*. Buffalo, NY: Prometheus.

Blackwell, R. T., Galassi, J. P., Galassi, M. D., & Watson, T. E. (1985). Are cognitive assessments equal? A comparison of think aloud and thought listing. *Cognitive Therapy and Research, 9*, 399–413.

Blake, J. (1989). *Family size and achievement*. Berkeley: University of California Press.

Blanck, P. D., Bellack, A. S., Rosnow, R. L., et al. (1992). Scientific rewards and conflicts of ethical choices in human subjects research. *American Psychologist, 47*(7), 959–965.

Blane, H. T. (1988). Prevention issues with children of alcoholics. *British Journal of Addiction, 83*(7), 793–798.

Blaske, D. M. (1984). Occupational sex-typing by kindergarten and fourth-grade children. *Psychological Reports, 54*, 795–801.

Blaustein, A. R. (1983). The situation of sociobiology. *Science, 220*, 188–189.

Blechman, E. U. (1992). Mentors for high-risk minority youths. *Journal of Clinical Child Psychology, 2*(2), 160–169.

Block, J. (1979). Socialization influence of personality development in males and females. American Psychological Association Master Lecture, Convention of the American Psychological Association, New York City, Sept., 1979.

Block, R. I. & Ghoneim, M. M. (1993). Effects of chronic marijuana use on human cognition. *Psychopharmacology, 110*(1–2), 219–228.

Bloom, B. (1985). *Developing talent in young people*. New York: Ballantine.

Bloom, K., Russell, A., & Wassenberg, K. (1987). Turn taking affects the quality of infant vocalizations. *Journal of Child Language, 14*(2), 211–227.

Blumenthal, A. L. (1979). The founding father we never knew. *Contemporary Psychology, 24*, 547–550.

Bohan, J. S. (1990). Social constructionism and contextual history: An expanded approach to the history of psychology. *Teaching of Psychology*, 17(2), 82–89.

Bohannon, J. N. & Stanowicz, L. B. (1988). The issue of negative evidence: Adult responses to children's language errors. *Developmental Psychology, 24*(5), 684–689.

Boker, J. R. (1974). Immediate and delayed retention effects of interspersing questions in written instructional passages. *Journal of Educational Psychology, 66*, 96–98.

Bolles, R. C. (1979). *Learning theory*. New York: Holt, Rinehart & Winston.

Bonnet, M. H., & Moore, S. E. (1982). The threshold of sleep: Perception of sleep as a function of time asleep and auditory threshold. *Sleep*, 5(3), 267–276.

Booker, J. M. & Hellekson, C. J. (1992). Prevelance of seasonal affective disorder in Alaska. *American Journal of Psychiatry*, 149(9), 1176–1182.

Bootzin, R. (1973). *Stimulus control of insomnia*. Paper presented at the meeting of the American Psychological Association, Aug., 1973, Montreal.

Borman, W. C., Eaton, N. K., Bryan, J. D., & Rosse, R. S. (1983). Validity of army recruiter behavioral assessment. Does the assessor make a difference? *Journal of Applied Psychology, 68*, 415–419.

Bornstein, M. H. (1989). Sensitive periods in development: Structural characteristics and causal interpretations. *Psychological Bulletin, 105*(2), 179–197.

Borrie, R. A., & Suedfeld, P. (1980). Restricted environmental stimulation therapy in a weight reduction program. *Journal of Behavioral Medicine*, 3, 147–161.

Bosse, R., Aldwin, C. M., Levenson, M. R., & Workman-Daniels, K. (1991). How stressful is retirement? *Journal of Gerontology, 46*(1), 9–14.

Botvin, G. J. & Botvin, E. M. (1992). Adolescent tobacco, alcohol, and drug abuse. *Journal of Developmental & Behavioral Pediatrics, 13(4)*, 290–301.

Bouchard, T. J., Lykken, D. T., McGue, M., Segal, N. L., & Tellegen, A. (1990). Sources of human psychological differences: The Minnesota study of twin reared apart. *Science, 250*, 223–228.

Bouchard, T. J., Jr. (1983). Twins—Nature's twice-told tale. *Yearbook of science and the future*, 66–81. Chicago: Encyclopedia Britannica.

Bower, B. (1984). Not popular by reason of insanity. *Science News, l26*(14), 218–219.

Bower, B. (1990). Gone but not forgotten. *Science News*, 138(Nov. 17), 312–314.

Bower, G. H. (1973). How to . . . uh . . . remember. *Psychology Today*, Oct., 63–70.

Bower, G. H. (1981). Mood and memory. *American Psychologist, 36*, 129–148.

Bower, G. H., & Clark, M. C. (1969). Narrative stories as mediators for serial learning. *Psychonomic Science, 14*, 181–182.

Bower, G. H., & Springston, F. (1970). Pauses as recoding points in letter series. *Journal of Experimental Psychology, 83*, 421–430.

Boysen, S. T. & Berntson, G. G. (1989). Numerical competence in a chimpanzee (Pan troglodytes). *Journal of Comparative Psychology, 103*(1), 23–31.

Bradley, B. S. & Gobbart, S. K. (1989). Determinants of gender-typed play in toddlers. *Journal of Genetic Psychology, 150*(4), 453–455.

Bradley, R. H., Caldwell, B. M., Rock, S. L., Ramey, C. T. et al. (1989). Home environment and cognitive development in the first 3 years of life: A collaborative study involving six sites and three ethnic groups in North America. *Developmental Psychology, 25*(2), 217–235.

Braginsky, B. M., & Braginsky, D. D. (1967). Schizophrenic patients in the psychiatric interview: An experimental study of their effectiveness at manipulation. *Journal of Consulting Psychology, 31*, 543–547.

Brandstadter, J., Wentura, D., & Greve, W. (1993). Adaptive resources of the aging self. *International Journal of Behavioral Development, 16*(2), 323–349.

Bransford, J. & Stein, B. S. (1984). *The IDEAL problem solver*. New York: Freeman.

Bransford, J. D., & McCarrell, N. S. (1977). A sketch of cognitive approach to comprehension: Some thoughts about understanding what it means to comprehend. In P. N. Johnson-Laird & P. C. Wason (Eds.), *Thinking: Readings in cognitive science*. Cambridge: Cambridge University Press.

Bransford, J., Sherwood, R., Vye, N., & Rieser, J. (1986). Teaching thinking and problem solving. *American Psychologist, 41*(10), 1078–1089.

Braun, B. G. (1986). Issues in the psychotherapy of

multiple personality disorder. In B. G. Braun (Ed.). *Treatment of multiple personality disorder.* Washington, DC: American Psychiatric Press.

Braungart, J. M., Plomin, R., DeFries, J. C., & Fulker, D. W. (1992). Genetic influence on tester-rated infant temperament as assessed by Bayley's Infant Behavior Record. *Developmental Psychology, 28*(1), 40–47.

Brazelton, T. B., Koslowski, B., & Main, M. (1974). The origins of reciprocity: The early mother-infant interaction. In M. Lewis, & L. A. Rosenblum, (Eds.), *The effect of the infant on its caregiver.* New York: Wiley-Interscience.

Brecher, E. M. (1975a). Marijuana: The health questions. *Consumer Reports, 40,* 143–149.

Brecher, E. M., & the Editors of *Consumer Reports.* (1972). *Licit and illicit drugs.* Boston: Little, Brown.

Breedlove, S. M. (1994). Sexual differentiation of the human nervous system. *Annual Review of Psychology, 45,* 389–418.

Breland, K., & Breland, M. (1961). The misbehavior of organisms. *American Psychologist, 16,* 681–684.

Bresler, D. E., & Trubo, R. (1979). *Free yourself from pain.* New York: Simon & Schuster.

Breslow, L. & Enstrom, J. E. (1980). Persistence of health habits and their relationship to mortality. *Preventive Medicine,* 9, 469–483.

Brewer, J. S. (1981). Duration of intromission and female orgasm rates. *Medical Aspects of Human Sexuality,* 15(4), 70–71.

Brewer, M. B. & Kramer, R. K. (1985). The psychology of intergroup attitudes and behavior. *Annual Review of Psychology,* 36, 219–243.

Bridges, K. M. B. (1932). Emotional development in early infancy. *Child Development,* 3, 324–334.

Britton, B. K. & Tesser, A. (1991). Effects of time-management practices on college grades. *Journal of Educational Psychology, 83(3),* 405–410.

Brockhaus, A. & Elger, C. E. (1990). Hypalgesic efficacy of acupuncture on experimental pain in man: Comparison of laser acupuncture and needle acupuncture. *Pain,* 43(2), 181–185.

Brody, N. (1992). *Intelligence.* San Diego, CA: Academic Press.

Brooks-Gunn, J. & Warren, M. P. (1988). The psychological significance of secondary sexual characteristics in nine- to eleven-year-old girls. *Child Development,* 59(4), 1061–1069.

Brown, A. M. (1990). Development of visual sensitivity to light and color vision in human infants: A critical review. *Vision Research,* 30(8), 1159–1188.

Brown, A. S. (1974). Satisfying relationships for elderly and their patterns of disengagement. *Gerontologist, 14,* 258–262.

Brown, B. (1980). Perspectives on social stress. In H. Selye (Ed.), *Selye's guide to stress research, Vol. 1.* New York: Van Nostrand Reinhold.

Brown, B. B. & Bentley, D. L. (1993). Residential burglers judge risk. *Journal of Environmental Psychology,* 13(1), 51–61.

Brown, J. D. (1986). Sex in the media. *Planned Parenthood Review,* Winter, 4–7.

Brown, R. T. (1991). Helping students confront and deal with stress and procrastination. *Journal of College Student Psychotherapy, 6(2),* 87–102.

Brown, R., & McNeill, D. (1966). The "tip of the tongue" phenomenon. *Journal of Verbal Learning and Verbal Behavior,* 5, 325–337.

Brown, S. A., Goldman, M. S., & Christiansen, B. A. (1985). Do alcohol expectancies mediate drinking patterns of adults? *Journal of Consulting and Clinical Psychology,* 53(4), 512–519.

Browne, A. (1986). Assault and homicide at home: When battered women kill. In Saks, M. J. & Saxe, L. (Eds.), *Advances in applied social psychology, Vol.* 3. Hillsdale, NJ: Erlbaum.

Browne, M. A., & Mahoney, M. J. (1984). Sport psychology. *Annual Review of Psychology,* 35, 605–625.

Brownell, K. (1988). Yo-yo dieting. *Psychology Today,* Jan., 20–23.

Brownell, K. D. (1982). Obesity: Understanding and treating a serious, prevalent, and refractory disorder. *Journal of Consulting and Clinical Psychology,* 50, 820–840.

Brownell, K. D., Greenwood, M. R. C., Stellar, E. & Shrager, E. E. (1986). The effects of repeated cycles of weight loss and regain in rats. *Physiology and Behavior,* 38, 459–464.

Brugger, P., Landis, T., Regard, M. (1990). A "sheep-goat" effect in repetition avoidance: Extrasensory perception as an effect of subjective probability? *British Journal of Psychology,* 81(4), 455–468.

Bruner, J. (1983). *Child's Talk.* New York: Norton.

Bruner, J. S., & Postman, L. (1949). On the perception of incongruity: A paradigm. *Journal of Personality, 18,* 206–223.

Bryan, J. H., & Test, M. A. (1967). Models and helping. Naturalistic studies in aiding behavior. *Journal of Personality & Social Psychology,* 6, 400–407.

Bryan, J. H., & Walbek, N. H. (1970). Preaching and practicing generosity: Children's actions and reactions. *Child Development, 41,* 329–353.

Buch, K. & Spangler, R. (1990). The effects of quality circles on performance and promotions. *Human Relations,* 43(6), 573–582.

Buchwald, A. (1965). Psyching out. *The Washington Post,* June 20.

Buck, L. & Axel, R. (1991). A novel multigene family may encode odorant receptors. *Cell, 65(1),* 175–187.

Buck, L. A. (1990). Abnormality, normality and health. *Psychotherapy,* 27(2), 187–194.

Buckalew, L. W., & Buckalew, P. B. (1983). Behavioral management of exceptional children using video games as reward. *Perceptual Motor Skills,* 56, 580.

Buckhout, R. (1974). Eyewitness testimony. *Scientific American, 231,* 23–31.

Bunge, M. (1984). What is pseudoscience? *The Skeptical Inquirer,* 9, 36–46.

Burgner, D. & Hewstone, M. (1993). Young children's causal attributions for success and failure. *British Journal of Developmental Psychology,* 11(2), 125–129.

Burka, J. B., & Yuen, L. M. (1983). *Procrastination.* Menlo Park, CA: Addison-Wesley.

Burnham, D. K. & Harris, M. (1992). Effects of real gender and labeled gender on adults' perceptions of infants. *Journal of Genetic Psychology,* 153(2), 165–183.

Burns, D. D., & Persons, J. (1982). Hope and hopelessness: A cognitive approach. In L. E. Abt, & I. R. Stuart (Eds.), *The newer therapies: A sourcebook.* New York: Van Nostrand Reinhold.

Burt, M. R. (1980). Cultural myths and supports for rape. *Journal of Personality & Social Psychology,* 38, 217–230.

Burtt, H. E. (1941). An experimental study of early childhood memory: Final report. *Journal of General Psychology,* 58, 435–439.

Bushman, B. J. & Cooper, H. M. (1990). Effects of alcohol on human aggression. *Psychological Bulletin,* 107(3), 341–354.

Bushman, B. J. & Geen, R. G. (1990). Role of cognitive-emotional mediators and individual differences in the effects of media violence on aggression. *Journal of Personality & Social Psychology,* 58(1), 156–163.

Bushnell, L. W., Sai, F. & Mullin, L. T. (1989). Neonatal recognition of the mother's face. *British Journal of Developmental Psychology,* 7(1), 3–15.

Buss, A. H. (1980). *Self-consciousness and social anxiety.* San Francisco: Freeman.

Buss, A. H. (1986). A theory of shyness. In Jones, W. H., Cheek, J. M., & Briggs, S. R., *Shyness: Perspectives on research and treatment.* New York: Plenum.

Buss, D. M. (1985). Human mate selection. *American Scientist,* 73, 47–51.

Buss, D. M. (1994). *The evolution of desire.* New York: Basic.

Buss, D. M., Larsen, R. J., Western, D., & Semmelroth, J. (1992). Sex differences in jealousy. *Psychological Science,* 3, 251–255.

Butler, R. (1954). Curiosity in monkeys. *Scientific American,* 190(18), 70–75.

Butler, R., & Harlow, H. F. (1954). Persistence of visual exploration in monkeys. *Journal of Comparative Physiological Psychology,* 47, 258–263.

Buyer, L. S. (1988). Creative problem solving: A comparison of performance under different instructions. *Journal of Creative Behavior,* 22(1), 55–61.

Byck, R. (1987). Cocaine use and research: Three histories. In Fisher, S., Raskin, A. & Uhlenhuth, E. H. (Eds.), *Cocaine: Clinical and behavioral aspects.* New York: Oxford University Press.

Byrd, K. R. (1994). The narrative reconstructions of incest survivors. *American Psychologist,* 49(5), 439–440.

Cabanac, M.. & Duclaux, P. (1970). Obesity: Absence of satiety aversion to sucrose. *Science, 168,* 496–497.

Caldera, Y. M., Huston, A. C. & O'Brien, M. (1989). Social interactions and play patterns of parents and toddlers with feminine, masculine, and neutral toys. *Child Development,* 60(1), 70–76.

Calhoun, J. B. (1962). A "behavioral sink." In E. L. Bliss (Ed.), *Roots of behavior.* New York: Harper & Row.

Calvert, S. L. & Cocking, R. R. (1992). Health promotion through mass media. *Journal of Applied Developmental Psychology, 13(2),* 143–149.

Camara, W. J. & Schneider, D. L. (1994). Integrity tests. *American Psychologist,* 49(2), 112–119.

Campbell, F. A. & Ramey, C. T. (1994). Effects of

early intervention on intellectual and academic achievement. *Child Development*, 65(April), 684–698.

Campbell, J. B., & Hawley, C. W. (1982). Study habits and Eysenck's theory of extraversion-introversion. *Journal of Research in Personality*, *16*, 139–146.

Campbell, J. D. (1990). Self-esteem and clarity of the self-concept. *Journal of Personality & Social Psychology*, 59(3), 538–549.

Campion, M. A. & McClelland, C. L. (1993). Follow-up and extension of interdisciplinary costs and benefits of enlarged jobs. *Journal of Applied Psychology*, 78(3), 339–351.

Campos, J. J., Hiatt, S., Ramsay, D., Henderson, C., & Svejda, M. (1978). The emergence of fear on the visual cliff. In M. Lewis, & L. A. Rosenblum (Eds.), *The development of affect*, 149–182. New York: Plenum Press.

Canavan, A. G., Dunn, G., & McMillan, T. M. (1986). Principal components of the WAIS-R. *British Journal of Clinical Psychology*, 25(2), 81–85.

Canavan, D. (1989). Fear of success. In R. C. Curtis (Ed.). *Self-defeating behaviors.* New York: Plenum.

Cannon, T. D., Mednick, S. A., Parnas, J., et al. (1993). Developmental brain abnormalities in the offspring of schizophrenic mothers. *Archives of General Psychiatry*, 50(7), 551–564.

Cannon, W. B. (1932). *The wisdom of the body*. New York: Norton.

Cannon, W. B. (1934). Hunger and thirst. In C. Murchinson (Ed.), *Handbook of general experimental psychology*, Worcester, MA: Clark University Press.

Cannon, W. B., & Washburn, A. L. (1912). An exploration of hunger. *American Journal of Physiology*, 29, 441–454.

Caplan, N., Choy, M. H., & Whitmore, J. K. (1992). Indochinese refugee families and academic achievement. *Scientific American*, Feb., 36–42.

Caplan, P. J., MacPherson, G. M., & Tobin, P. (1985). Do sex-related differences in spatial abilities exist? A multilevel critique with new data. *American Psychologist, 40*, 786–799.

Capner, M. & Caltabiano, M. L. (1993). Factors affecting the progression towards burnout. *Psychological Reports*, 73(2), 555–561.

Capron, C. & Duyme, M. (1992). Assessment of effects of socio-economic status on IQ in a full cross-fostering study. *Nature*, *340*, 552–554.

Carducci, B. J. & Stein, N. D. (1988). *The personal and situational pervasiveness of shyness in college students: A nine-year comparison.* Paper presented at the meeting of the Southeastern Psychological Association, New Orleans, April, 1988.

Carducci, B. J., Deeds, W. C., Jones, J. W., Moretti, D. M., Reed, J. G., Saal, F. E., & Wheat, J. E. (1987). Preparing undergraduate psychology students for careers in business. *Teaching of Psychology, 14*, 16–20.

Carew, J. V., Chan, I., & Halfor, C. (1976). *Observing intelligence in young children: Eight case studies.* Englewood Cliffs, NJ: Prentice-Hall.

Carey, J. C., Stanley, D. A., Biggers, J. (1988). Peak alert time and rapport between residence hall roommates. *Journal of College Student Development*, 29(3), 239–243.

Carey, S. (1986). Cognitive science and science education. *American Psychologist, 41*(10), 1123–1130.

Carli, L. L., Ganley, R., & Pierce-Otay, A. (1991). Similarity and satisfaction in roommate relationships. *Personality & Social Psychology Bulletin, 17*(4), 419–426.

Carlson, C. L., Pelhan, W. E., Milich, R., & Dixon, J. (1992). Single and combined effects of methylphenidate and behavior therapy on the classroom performance of children with attention-deficit hyperactivity disorder. *Journal of Abnormal Child Psychology*, 20(2), 213–232.

Carlson, J. M. (1986). *Prime time law enforcement.* New York: Praeger.

Carlson, M., Marcus-Hewhall, A., & Miller, N. (1990). Effects of situational aggression cues: A quantitative review. *Journal of Personality & Social Psychology*, 58(4), 622–633.

Carlson, N. R. (1991). *Physiology of behavior (4th ed.).* Boston: Allyn & Bacon.

Carmen, R., & Adams, W. R. (1985). *Study skills: A student's guide for survival.* New York: Wiley.

Carnegie Corporation of New York. 1994. *Starting points: Meeting the needs of our youngest children.* New York: The Carnegie Corporation.

Carson, R. A. (1989). Personality. *Annual Review of Psychology, 40*, 227–248.

Carson, R. C. & Butcher, J. N. (1992) *Abnormal psychology and modern life.* Evanston, IL: HarperCollins.

Carter, W. E. (Ed.) (1980). *Cannabis in Costa Rica: A study of chronic marihuana use.* Philadelphia: Institute for the Study of Human Issues.

Cartwright, R. & Lamberg, L. (1992). *Crisis dreaming.* New York: HarperCollins.

Caspi, A. & Herbener, E. S. (1990). Continuity and change: Associative marriage and the consistency of personality in adulthood. *Journal of Personality & Social Psychology*, 58(2), 250–258.

Cattell, R. B. (1965). *The scientific analysis of personality.* Baltimore: Penguin.

Cattell, R. B. (1973). Personality pinned down. *Psychology Today*, July, 40–46.

Cautela, J. R. & Kearney, A. J. (1986). *The covert conditioning handbook.* New York: Springer

Cautela, J. R., & Bennett, A. K. (1981). Covert conditioning. In R. J. Corsini (Ed.), *Handbook of innovative psychotherapies*, 189–204. New York: Wiley.

Ceci, S. J. (1991). How much does schooling influence general intelligence and its cognitive components? *Developmental Psychology*, 27(5), 703–722.

Chaikin, A. (1985). The loneliness of the long-distance astronaut. *Discover*, Feb., 20–31.

Chaikin, A. L., & Derlega, V. J. (1974). *Self-disclosure.* Morristown, NJ: General Learning Press.

Chamberlain, K. & Zika, S. (1990). The minor events approach to stress: Support for the use of daily hassles. *British Journal of Psychology, 81*(4), 469–481.

Chamberlin, J. & Rogers, J. A. (1990). Planning a community-based mental health system. *American Psychologist, 45*(11), 1241–1244.

Chance, P. (1982). Your child's self-esteem. *Parents*, Jan.

Chapanis, A., & Lindenbaum, L. E. (1959). A reaction time study of four control-display linkages. *Human Factors, 1*, 1–7.

Charren, P. & Sandler, M. W. (1983). *Changing channels.* Reading, MA: Addison-Wesley.

Chase, M. H. & Morales, F. R. (1990). The atonia and myoclonia of active (REM) sleep. *Annual Review of Psychology, 41*, 557–584.

Cheadle, A., Psaty, B. M., Diehr, P., Koepsell, T., et al. (1992–93). An empirical exploration of a conceptual model for community-based health-promotion. *International Quarterly of Community Health Education*, 13(4), 329–363.

Check, J. V. P., & Malamuth, N. M. (1983). Sex role stereotyping and reactions to depictions of stranger versus acquaintance rape. *Journal of Personality & Social Psychology*, 45, 344–356.

Cheek, J. & Buss, A. H. (1979). Scales of shyness, sociability and self-esteem and correlations among them. Unpublished research, University of Texas. (Cited by Buss, 1980).

Chesney, M. A., & Rosenman, R. H. (Eds.). (1985). *Anger and hostility in cardiovascular and behavioral disorders.* Washington, DC: Hemisphere.

Chess, S. & Thomas, A. (1986). *Know your child.* New York: Basic.

Chess, S., Thomas, A. & Birch, H. G. (1976). *Your child is a person: A psychological approach to parenthood without guilt.* New York: Penguin.

Chiras, D. D. (1991). *Human biology.* St. Paul: West.

Chollar, S. (1989). Dreamchasers, *Psychology Today*, April, 60–61.

Chomsky, N. (1975). *Reflections on language.* New York: Pantheon.

Chomsky, N. (1986). *Knowledge of language.* New York: Praeger.

Christensen, A. & Jacobson, N. S. (1994). Who (or what) can do psychotherapy. *Psychological Science*, 5(1), 8–14.

Christian, A. G. & McDonald, J. L. (1987). Smokeless tobacco country: From nicotine dependency to oral problems and cancer. *Aviation, Space, & Environmental Medicine*, 58(2), 97–104.

Christiansen, B.A., Smith, G. T., Roehling, P. V., & Goldman, M. S. (1989). Using alcohol expectancies to predict adolescent drinking behavior after one year. *Journal of Consulting & Clinical Psychology*, 57(1), 93–99.

Cialdini, R. B., Petty, R. E., & Cacippo, T. J. (1981). Attitude and attitude change. *Annual Review of Psychology*, 32, 357–404.

Cialdini, R. B., Reno, R. R., & Kallgren, C. A. (1990). A focus theory of normative conduct: Recycling the concept of norms to reduce littering in public places. *Journal of Personality & Social Psychology*, 58(6), 1015–1026.

Cialdini, R. B., Vincent, J. E., Lewis, S. K., Catalan, J., Wheeler, D., & Darby, B. L. (1975). A reciprocal concessions procedure for inducing compliance. The door-in-the-face technique. *Journal of Personality & Social Psychology, 21*, 206–215.

Cimons, M. (1991). Study shows a million teen suicide attempts. *The Los Angeles Times*, Sept. 20, A26.

Cimons, M. (1993). Sex seen as source of most new AIDS cases in women. *The Los Angeles Times*, July 23, A23.

Cipolli, C., Bolzani, R., Cornoldi, C., de Beni, R. et al. (1993). Bizarreness effect in dream recall. *Sleep, 16*(2), 163–170.

Clair, J. M., Karp, D. A., & Yoels, W. C. (1994). *Experiencing the life cycle*. Springfield, IL: Charles C Thomas.

Clark, K. B. (1965). *Dark ghetto*. New York: Harper & Row.

Clark, M. S. & Reis, H. T. (1988). Interpersonal processes in close relationships. *Annual Review of Psychology*, 39, 609–672.

Clark, M. S. & Williamson, G. M. (1989). Moods and social judgments. In H. Wagner & A. Manstead (Eds.) *Handbook of Social Psychophysiology*. New York: Wiley.

Clark, R. D. (1990). The impact of AIDS on gender differences in willingness to engage in casual sex. *Journal of Applied Social Psychology*, 20(9, Pt 2), 771–782.

Clarke-Stewart, A. (1989). Infant day care: Malignant or maligned? *American Psychologist, 44*, 266–273.

Clearwater, Y. (1985). A human place in outer space. *Psychology Today*, July, 34–43.

Click, P., Zion, C. & Nelson, C. (1988). What mediates sex discrimination in hiring decisions? *Journal of Personality & Social Psychology*, 55(2), 178–186.

Cline, V. B., Croft, R. G., & Courrier, S. (1972). Desensitization of children to television violence. *Journal of Personality & Social Psychology*, 27, 360–365.

Clore, G. L. (1976). Interpersonal attraction: An overview. In *Contemporary topics in social psychology*. Morristown, NJ: General Learning Press.

Coates, W., Lehle, D. & Cottington, E. (1989). Trauma and the full moon: A waning theory. *Annals of Emergency Medicine, 18*, 763–765,

Cohen, D. (1974). *Intelligence*. New York: M. Evans.

Cohen, N. L., Waltzman, S. B., & Fisher, S. G. (1993). A prospective, randomized study of cochlear implants. *New England Journal of Medicine, 328(4)*, 233–237.

Cohen, S. & Lichtenstein, E. (1990). Partner behaviors that support quitting smoking. *Journal of Consulting & Clinical Psychology*, 58(3), 304–309.

Cohen, S., Evans, G. W., Krantz, D. S., & Stokols, D. (1981). Cardiovascular and behavioral effects of community noise. *American Scientist*, 69, 528–535.

Cohen, S., Tyrrell, D. A., & Smith, A. P. (1993). Negative life events, perceived stress, negative affect, and susceptibility to the common cold. *Journal of Personality and Social Psychology*, 64(1), 131–140.

Cole, D. E., Protinsky, H. O., & Cross, L. H. (1992). An empirical investigation of adolescent suicidal ideation. *Adolescence*, 27(108), 813–818.

Collins, A. M., & Quillian, M. R. (1969). Retrieval time from semantic memory. *Journal of Verbal Learning and Verbal Behavior*, 8, 240–247.

Collins, J. J. (1981). Alcohol use and criminal behavior: An empirical, theoretical, and methodological overview. In J. J. Collins (Ed.), *Drinking and crime: Perspectives on the relationship between alcohol consumption and criminal behavior*. New York: Guilford.

Collins, W. A. & Gunnar, M. R. (1990). Social and personality development. *Annual Review of Psychology, 41*, 387–416.

Comfort, A. (1976). *A good age*. New York: Crown.

Cone, J. D., & Hayes, S. C. (1980). *Environmental problems/behavioral solutions*. Monterey, CA: Brooks/Cole.

Coni, N., Davison, W., & Webster, S. (1984). *Ageing*. Oxford: Oxford University Press.

Conley, J. J. (1984). Longitudinal consistency of adult personality: Self-reported psychological characteristics across 45 years. *Journal of Personality & Social Psychology, 47*, 1325–1333.

Connolly, J. A., Doyle, A. B. & Reznick, E. (1988). Social pretend play and social interaction in preschoolers. *Journal of Applied Developmental Psychology*, 9(3), 301–313.

Connors, M. M., Harrison, A. A., & Akins, F. R. (1985). *Living Aloft*. Washington, DC: National Aeronautics and Space Administration.

Conway, M. A., Cohen, G., & Stanhope, N. (1992). Very long-term memory for knowledge acquired at school and university. *Applied Cognitive Psychology*, 6(6), 467–482.

Conyne, R. K., & Clack, R. J. (1981). *Environmental assessment and design*. New York: Praeger.

Cook, S. W. (1985). Experimenting on social issues. *American Psychologist, 40*, 452–460.

Cooper, J., & Fazio, R. H. (1984). A new look at dissonance theory. *Advances in Experimental Social Psychology, 17*, 229–226.

Coopersmith, S. (1968). Studies in self-esteem. *Scientific American, 218*, 96–106.

Corballis, M. C. (1980, March). Laterality and myth. *American Psychologist*, 35, 284–295.

Coren, S. (1992). The left-hander syndrome. New York: Free Press.

Coren, S. & Aks, D. J. (1990). Moon illusion in pictures: A multimechanism approach. *Journal of Experimental Psychology: Human Perception & Performance*, 16(2), 365–380.

Coren, S. & Halpern, D. F. (1991). Left-handedness: A marker for decreased survival fitness. *Psychological Bulletin*, 109(1), 90–106.

Cornsweet, T. N. (1970). *Visual perception*. New York: Academic.

Corteen, R. S. & Williams, T. M. (1986). Television and reading skills. In T. M. Williams (Ed.), *The impact of television: A natural experiment in three communities*. Orlando, FL: Academic.

Costa, P. T. & McCrae, R. R. (1992). Multiple uses for longitudinal personality data. *European Journal of Personality, 6(2)*, 85–102.

Costello, T. W. & Costello, J. T. (1992). *Abnormal psychology*. New York: HarperCollins.

Courchesne, E., Yeung-Courchesne, R., Press, G. A., Hesselink, J. R. et al., (1988). Hypoplasia of cerebellar vermal lobules VI and VII in autism. *New England Journal of Medicine*, 318(21), 1349–1354.

Coursey, R. D., Ward-Alexander, L., & Katz, B. (1990). Cost-effectiveness of providing insurance benefits for posthospital psychiatric halfway house stays. *American Psychologist*, 45(10), 1118–1126.

Cowles, J. T. (1937). Food tokens as incentives for learning by chimpanzees. *Comparative Psychology*, Monograph, *14*(5, Whole No. 71).

Cox, F. D. (1993). *Human intimacy*. St. Paul, MN: West.

Coyne, J. C. & Downey, G. (1991). Social factors and psychopathology. In M. R. Rosenzweig and L. W. Porter (Eds.), *Annual Review of Psychology*, 42, 401–425.

Craig, K. (1978). Social modeling influences on pain. In R. A. Sternbach (Ed.), *The psychology of pain*. New York: Raven.

Craik, F. I. M. (1970). The fate of primary items in free recall. *Journal of Verbal Learning and Verbal Behavior*, 9, 143–148.

Crandall, C. S., Preisler, J. J., & Aussprung, J. (1992). Measuring life event stress in the lives of college students: The Undergraduate Stress Questionnaire (USQ). *Journal of Behavioral Medicine*, 15(6), 627–662.

Crawford, H. J., Brown, A., & Moon, C. E. (1993). Sustained attentional and distractional abilities: Differences between low and highly hypnotizable persons. *Journal of Abnormal Psychology*, 102(4), 534–543.

Crawley, S. B., & Sherrod, K. B. (1984). Parent-infant play during the first year of life. *Infant Behavior & Development*, 7, 65–75.

Cregler, L.L., & Mark, H. (1985). Medical Complications of Cocaine Abuse. *New England Journal of Medicine*, 315(23), 1495–1500.

Crencavage, L. M. & Norcross, J. C. (1990). Where are the commonalities among the therapeutic common factors? *Professional Psychology: Research & Practice*, 21(5), 372–378.

Croll, C. (1986). Personal communication.

Cronbach, L. (1990). *Essentials of psychological testing*. New York: Harper & Row.

Cross, J. G., & Guyer, M. J. (1980). *Social traps*. Ann Arbor: The University of Michigan Press.

Crowe, L. C. & George, W. H. (1989). Alcohol and human sexuality: Review and integration. *Psychological Bulletin*, 105(3), 374–386.

Crowe, R. A. (1990). Astrology and the scientific method. *Psychological Reports*, 67, 163–191.

Culver, B., & Ianna, P. (1979). *The gemini syndrome*. Tucson, AZ: Pachart Publishing.

Cumming, E., & Henry, W. E. (1961). *Growing old: The process of disengagement*. New York: Basic.

Cushman, P. (1989). Iron fists/velvet gloves: A study of a mass marathon psychology training. *Psychotherapy*, 26(1), 23.

Cutting, J. E. (1987). Rigidity in cinema seen from the front row, side aisle. *Journal of Experimental Psychology Human Perception and Performance*, 13(3), 323–334.

Cytowic, R. E. (1993). *The man who tasted shapes*. Putnam's Sons.

Czeisler, C. A., Kronauer, R. E., Allan, J. S., et al., (1989). Bright light induction of strong (Type O) resetting of the human circadian pacemaker. *Science*, *244*(June), 1328–1333.

Czeisler, C. A., Richardson, G. S., Zimmerman, J. C., Moore-Ede, M. C., & Weitzman, E. D. (1981). Entrainment of human circadian rhythms by light-dark cycles: A reassessment. *Photochemistry, Photobiology*, 34, 239–247.

Daniel, T. L., & Esser, J. K. (1980). Intrinsic motivation as influenced by rewards, task interest, and task structure. *Journal of Applied Psychology, 65*, 566–573.

Dannemiller, J. L., & Braun, A. (1988). The perception of chromatic figure/ground relationships in 5-month-olds. *Infant Behavior and Development, 11*(1), 31–42.

Darley, J. M. & Latane, B. (1968). Bystander intervention in emergencies: Diffusion of responsibility. *Journal of Personality & Social Psychology, 8*, 377–383.

Darling, C. A., Davidson, J. K., Passarello, L. C. (1992). The mystique of first intercourse among college youth: The role of partners, contraceptive practices, and psychological reactions. *Journal of Youth & Adolescence, 21(1)*, 97–117.

Darwin, C. (1872). *The expression of emotion in man and animals.* Chicago: The University of Chicago Press.

Darwin, M. & Wowk, B. (1992). Cryonics: Reaching for tomorrow. *Skeptic, 1*(2), 32–43.

Davanloo, H. (1980). *Short-term dynamic psychotherapy.* New York: Jason Aronson.

David, H., Borgeat, F., & Saucier, J. (1990). The relation between tachystoscopic pictures and neurotic postpartum depression. *Pre- & Peri-Natal Psychology Journal, 4*(3), 219–227.

Davies, M. F. (1993). Dogmatism and the persistence of discredited beliefs. *Personality & Social Psychology Bulletin, 19*(6), 692–699.

Davis, D. M. (1928). Self-selection of diet by newly weaned infants. *American Journal of Diseases of Children, 36*, 651–679.

Davis, J. H. (1989). Psychology and law: The last 15 years. *Journal of Applied Social Psychology, 19*(3, Pt. 1), 199–230.

Davis, J. R., Vanderploeg, J. M., Santy, P. A., Jennings, R. T., et al. (1988). Space motion sickness during 24 flights of the Space Shuttle. *Aviation, Space, & Environmental Medicine, 59*(12), 1185–1189.

Davis, M. H. & Harvey, J. C. (1992). Declines in major league batting performance as a function of game pressure. *Journal of Applied Social Psychology, 22*(9), 714–735.

Dawson, M. E. (1990). Where does the truth lie? A review of the polygraph test: Lies, truth, and science. *Psychophysiology, 27*(1), 120–121.

De Benedittis, G., Lorenzetti, A., & Pieri, A. (1990). The role of stressful life events in the onset of chronic primary headache. *Pain, 40(1)*, 65–75.

De La Cruz, F. F., & Muller, J. Z. (1983). Facts about Down syndrome. *Children Today, 12*(6), 2–7.

de Luccie, M. F. & Davis, A. J. (1991). Father-child relationships from the preschool years through mid-adolescence. *Journal of Genetic Psychology, 152(2)*, 225–238.

De Toffol, B., Autret, A., Gaymard, B., & Degiovanni, E. (1992). Influence of lateral gaze on electroencephalographic spectral power. *Electroencephalography and Clinical Neurophysiology*, 82, 432–437.

Dean-Church, L. & Gilroy, F. D. (1993). Relation of sex-role orientation to life satisfaction in a healthy elderly sample. *Journal of Social Behavior & Personality, 8*(1), 133–140.

DeAngelis, T. (1994). New tests allow takers to tackle real-life problems. *APA Monitor,* June, p. 14.

Deaux, K. (1985). Sex and gender. *Annual Review of Psychology, 36*, 49–81.

Deaux, K., & Emswiller, T. (1974). Explanation of successful performance on sex-linked tasks: What is skill for the male is luck for the female. *Journal of Personality & Social Psychology, 29*, 80–85.

Deaux, K., Dane, F., & Wrightsman, L. S. (1993). *Social psychology in the '90s.* Monterey: Brooks/Cole.

DeBell, C. S. & Harless, D. K. (1992). B. F. Skinner: Myth and misperception. *Teaching of Psychology, 19(2)*, 68–73.

DeBono, E. (1970). *Lateral Thinking: Creativity step by step.* New York: Harper & Row.

DeBuono, B. A., Zinner, S. H., Daamen, M., & McCormack, W. M. (1990). Sexual behavior of college women in 1975, 1986, and 1989. *New England Journal of Medicine*, 322(12), 821–825.

Deese, J., & Hulse, S. J. (1967). *The psychology of learning (3rd. ed.).* New York: McGraw-Hill.

Deffenbacher, J. L. & Suinn, R. M. (1988). Systematic desensitization and the reduction of anxiety. *Counseling Psychologist, 16*(1), 9–30.

DeGood, D. E. (1975). Cognitive factors in vascular stress responses. *Psychophysiology, 12*, 399–401.

Degreef, G., Ashtari, M., Bogerts, B., et al. (1992). Volumes of ventricular system subdivisions measured from magnetic resonance images in first-episode schizophrenic patients. *Archives of General Psychiatry, 49*(7), 531–537.

deGroot, G. (1994). Psychologists explain Barney's power. *APA Monitor*, June, 4.

Dement, W. (1960). The effect of dream deprivation. *Science, 131*, 1705–1707.

Dement, W. (1972). *Some must watch while some must sleep.* Stanford, CA: Stanford Alumni Association.

Denmark, F. L. (1994). Engendering psychology. *American Psychologist, 49*(4), 329–334.

Denning, P. J. (1987). Computer models of AIDS epidemiology. *American Scientist, 75*, 347–352.

Denning, P. J. (1988). Blindness in designing intelligent systems. *American Scientist, 76*, 118–120.

Dennis, A. R. & Valacich, J. S. (1993). Computer brainstorms: More heads are better than one. *Journal of Applied Psychology, 78*(4), 531–537.

Denollet, J. (1993). Biobehavioral research on coronary heart disease. *Journal of Behavioral Medicine, 16*(2), 115–141.

Deregowski, J. B. (1972, Nov.). Pictorial perception and culture. *Scientific American*, 82–88.

DeSpelder, L. A., & Strickland, A. L. (1983). *The last dance.* Palo Alto, CA: Mayfield.

Deutsch, D. (1978). Pitch memory: An advantage for the left-handed. *Science, 199*, 559–560.

Deutsch, M. (1993). Educating for a peaceful world. *American Psychologist, 48*(5), 510–517.

Deutsch, M., & Collins, M. E. (1951). *Interracial housing.* Minneapolis: University of Minnesota Press.

Devine, D. P. & Spanos, N. P. (1990). Effectiveness of maximally different cognitive strategies and expectancy in attenuation of reported pain. *Journal of Personality & Social Psychology, 58*(4), 672–678.

Devine, P. G. (1990). Stereotypes and prejudice: Their automatic and controlled components. *Journal of Personality & Social Psychology, 56*(1), 5–18.

Devine, P. G., Monteith, M. J., Zuerink, J. R., & Elliot, A. J. (1991). Prejudice with and without compunction. *Journal of Personality & Social Psychology, 60*(6), 817–830.

Dickinson, D. J. & O'Connell, D. Q. (1990). Effect of quality and quantity of study on student grades. *Journal of Educational Research, 83(4)*, 227–231.

Diekstein, S. & Parke, R. D. (1988). Social referencing in infancy: A glance at fathers and marriage. *Child Development, 59*(2), 506–511.

Digman, J. M. (1990). Personality structure: Emergence of the five-factor model. *Annual Review of Psychology*, 41, 417–440.

Dillard, J. P. (1991). The current status of research on sequential-request compliance techniques. *Personality & Social Psychology Bulletin, 17*(3), 283–288.

Dinkmeyer, D. & McKay, G. D. (1989). *The parent's handbook.* Circle Pines, MN: American Guidance Service.

Dixon, J. (1975). Jeanne Dixon strikes back at scientists who knock astrology. *National Star*, Sept. 30, 5.

Dodge, K. A., Pettit, G. S., & Bates, J. E. (1994). Socialization mediators of the relation between socioeconomic status and child conduct problems. *Child Development, 65*(April), 649–665.

Dollard, J., & Miller, N. E. (1950). *Personality and psychotherapy: An analysis in terms of learning, thinking and culture.* New York: McGraw-Hill.

Dollard, J., et al. (1939). *Frustration and aggression.* New Haven: Yale University Press.

Donenberg, G. R. & Hoffman, L. W. (1988). Gender differences in moral development. *Sex Roles, 18*(11–12), 701–717.

Donnerstein, E. I., & Linz, D. G. (1986). The question of pornography. *Psychology Today*, Dec., 56–59.

Donohue, H. E. F. (1968). *Where should you touch?* New York: Hearst.

Dooling, D. J., & Lachman, R. (1971). Effects of comprehension on retention of prose. *Journal of Experimental Psychology, 88*, 216–222.

Dossett, D. L., & Hulvershorn, P. (1983). Increasing technical training efficiency: Peer training via computer-assisted instruction. *Journal of Applied Psychology, 68*, 552–558.

Doty, R. M., Peterson, B. E., & Winter, D. G. (1991). *Journal of Personality & Social Psychology, 61*(4), 629–640.

Dovidio, J. F. (1984). Helping behavior and altruism: An empirical and conceptual overview. In L. Berkowitz (Ed.), *Advances in experimental social psychology, Vol. 17.* New York: Academic.

Dovido, J. F., Allen, J. L., & Schroeder, D. A. (1990). Specificity of empathy-induced helping: Evidence for altruistic motivation. *Journal of Personality & Social Psychology, 59*(2), 249–260.

Drake, R. A. & Ulrich, G. (1992). *Acta Psychologica, 79*(3), 219–226.

Drake, R. A. (1994). Personal communication.

Drake, R. A., & Seligman, M. E. P. (1989). Self-serving biases in causal attributions as a function of altered activation asymmetry. *International Journal of Neuroscience, 45*, 199–204.

Dreyfus, H. L. & Dreyfus, S. E. (1986). Mind over machine. New York: Macmillian/The Free Press.

Driskell, J. L., & Kelly, E. L. A. (1980). A guided notetaking and study skills system for use with university freshmen predicted to fail. *Journal of Reading, 1*, 4–5.

Drowatzky, J. N. (1975). *Motor learning: Principles and practices.* Minneapolis, MN: Burgess.

DSM-IV: Diagnostic and statistical manual of mental disorders (4th ed.). American Psychiatric Association. Washington, D.C., 1994.

Dubbert, P. M. (1992). Exercise in behavioral medicine. *Journal of Consulting and Clinical Psychology, 60*(4), 613–618.

Dubow, E. F., Huesmann, L. R., & Eron, L. D. (1987). Childhood correlates of adult ego development. *Child Development, 58(3)*, 859–869.

Dubreuil, D. L., Endler, N. S., & Spanos, N. P. (1988). Distraction and redefinition in the reduction of low and high intensity experimentally-induced pain. *Imagination, Cognition and Personality*, 7(2), 155–164.

Dujardin, K., Guerrien, A., & Leconte, P. (1990). Sleep, brain activation and cognition. *Physiology & Behavior*, 47(6), 1271–1278.

Duncan, G. S., Brooks-Gunn, J., & Klebanov, P. K. (1994). Economic deprivation and early childhood development. *Child Development*, 65(April), 296–318.

Duncker, K. (1945). On problem solving. *Psychological Monographs*, 58(270).

Dunkle, T. (1982). The sound of silence. *Science* 82, 30–33.

Dunner, D. L. (1985). Recent genetic studies of bipolar and unipolar depression. In J. C. Coyne (Ed.) *Essential papers on depression.* New York: New York University Press.

Dutton, D. G., & Aron, A. P. (1974). Some evidence for heightened sexual attraction under conditions of high anxiety. *Journal of Personality & Social Psychology*, 30, 510–517.

Dwyer, W. O., Leeming, F. C., Cobern, M. K., Porter, B. E., et al. (1993). Critical review of behavioral interventions to preserve the environment. *Environment and Behavior*, 25(3), 275–321.

Dyck, M. J. (1987). Assessing logotherapeutic constructs: Conceptual and psychometric status of Purpose in Life and Seeking of Noetic Goals tests. *Clinical Psychology*, 7(4), 439–447.

Dyer, F. J. (1993). Clinical presentation of the lead-poisoned child on mental ability tests. *Journal of Clinical Psychology*, 49(1), 94–101.

Dywan, J., & Bowers, K. S. (1983). The use of hypnosis to enhance recall. *Science*, 222, 184–185.

Eagly, A. H. & Chaiken, S. (1992). *The psychology of attitudes.* San Diego, CA: Harcourt Brace Jovanovich.

Ebbinghaus, H. (1885). *Memory: A contribution to experimental psychology.* Translated by H. A. Ruger, & C. E. Bussenius, 1913. New York: New York Teacher's College, Columbia University.

Eberhardt, B. J., & Muchinsky, P. M. (1982). An empirical investigation of the factor stability of Owens' biographical questionnaire. *Journal of Applied Psychology*, 67, 138–145.

Eccles, J. S., Midgley, C., Wigfield, A., Buchanan, C. M., Reuman, K. D., Flanagan, C., & Mac Iver, D. (1993). Development during adolescence. *American Psychologist, 48*, 90–101.

Eckhert, P. (1993). Acceleration of change: Catalysts in brief therapy. *Clinical Psychology Review, 13*(3), 241–253.

Edelson, S. M. (1984). Implications of sensory stimulation in self-destructive behavior. *American Journal of Mental Deficiency*, 89, 140–145.

Edinger, J. D., Marsh, G. R., McCall, W. V., Erwin, C. W. et al. (1990). Daytime functioning and nighttime sleep before, during, and after a 146-hour tennis match. *Sleep, 13*(6), 526–532.

Egan, G. (1984). Skilled helping: A problem-management framework for helper training. In D. Larson (Ed.), *Teaching psychological skills*, 133–150. Monterey, CA: Brooks/Cole.

Egeland, B., Jacobvitz, D., & Sroufe, L. A. (1988). Breaking the cycle of abuse. *Child Development*, 59(4), 1080–1088.

Ehrman, J. (1993). Auto accidents, injuries, greater for young adults with attention deficit disorder. *NIH Healthline*, Oct./Nov.

Eich, E., Rachman, S., & Lopatka, C. (1990). Affect, pain, and autobiographical memory. *Journal of Abnormal Psychology*, 99(2) 174–178.

Eichorn, D. H., Hunt, J. V., & Honzik, M. P. (1981). Experience, personality, and IQ: Adolescence to middle age. In D. H. Eichorn, J. A. Clausen, N. Haan, M. P. Honzik, & P. H. Mussen (Eds.), *Present and past in middle life.* New York: Academic.

Einspieler, C., Widder, J., Holzer, A., & Kenner, T. (1988). The predictive value of behavioural risk factors for sudden infant death. *Early Human Development*, 18(2–3), 101–109.

Eisenberg, N. (1991). Meta-analytic contributions to the literature on prosocial behavior. *Personality & Social Psychology Bulletin*, 17(3), 273–282.

Eisenberg, N. & Miller, P. A. (1987). The relation of empathy to prosocial and related behaviors. *Psychological Bulletin, 101*(1), 91–119.

Ekman, P. (1986). *Telling Lies.* New York: Berkley.

Ekman, P. (1992). Facial expression of emotion. *Psychological Science*, 3, 34–38.

Ekman, P. (1993). Facial expression and emotion. *American Psychologist, 48(4)*, 384–392.

Ekman, P. & O'Sullivan, M. (1991). Who can catch a liar? *American Psychologist*, 46(9), 913–920.

Ekman, P., Friesen, W. V., & Bear, J. (1984). The international language of gestures. *Psychology Today*, May, 64–69.

Ekman, P., Levenson, R. W., & Friesen, W. V. (1983). Autonomic nervous system activity distinguishes among emotions. *Science*, 221, 1208–1210.

Elaad, E. & Ben-Shakhar, G. (1991). Effects of mental countermeasures on psychophysiological detection in the guilty knowledge test. *International Journal of Psychophysiology, 11*(2), 99–108.

Elkind, D. (1981). *The hurried child.* Reading, MA: Addison-Wesley.

Elkind, D. (1984). *All grown up & no place to go.* Reading, MA: Addison-Wesley.

Ellis, A. (1973). The no cop-out therapy. *Psychology Today*, 7 (Feb.), 56–60, 62.

Ellis, A. (1979). The practice of rational-emotive therapy. In A. Ellis, & J. Whiteley (Eds.) *Theoretical and empirical foundations of rational-emotive therapy.* Monterey, CA: Brooks/Cole.

Ellis, A. (1987). A sadly neglected cognitive component in depression. *Cognitive Therapy & Research, 11*(1), 121–145.

Ellis, A. (1993). Reflections on rational-emotive therapy. *Journal of Consulting & Clinical Psychology, 61*(2), 199–201.

Ellis, H. C. & Hunt, R. R. (1983). *Fundamentals of human memory and cognition.* Dubuque, IA: William C Brown.

Ellison, G. (1992). Continuous amphetamine and cocaine have similar neurotoxic effects in lateral habenular nucleus and fasciculus retroflexus. *Brain Research, 598(1–2)*, 353–356.

Endler, N. S. & Persad, E. (in press). *Electroconvulsive therapy.* Hans Huber.

Engel, G. (1977, Nov.). Emotional stress and sudden death. *Psychology Today*, 144.

Engelsman, E. L. (1989). Dutch policy on the management of drug-related problems. *British Journal of Addictions, 84*(2), 211–218.

England, L. W. & Thompson, C. L. (1988). Counseling child sexual abuse victims: Myths and realities. *Journal of Counseling & Development*, 66(8), 370–373.

Engle, E., & Lott, A. S. (1980). *Man in flight.* Annapolis, MD: Leeward.

Engler, J. & Goleman, D. (1992). *The consumer's guide to psychotherapy.* New York: Simon & Schuster.

Eppley, K. R., Abrams, A. I., & Shear, J. (1989). Differential effects of relaxation techniques on trait anxiety: A meta-analysis. *Journal of Clinical Psychology*, 45(6), 957–974.

Epstein, R., Langa, R. P., & Skinner, B. F. (1981). "Self-awareness" in the pigeon. *Science, 212*, 695–696.

Erdelyi, M. H., & Appelbaum, A. G., (1973). Cognitive masking: The disruptive effect of an emotional stimulus upon the perception of contiguous neutral items. *Bulletin of the Psychonomic Society, 1*, 59–61.

Ericsson, K. A. & Charness, N. (1994). Expert performance. *American Psychologist*, 49(8), 725–747.

Ericsson, K. A., & Chase, W. G. (1982). Exceptional memory. *American Scientist, 70*, 607–615.

Erikson, E. H. (1963). *Childhood and society.* New York: Norton.

Erlich, P. R. & Erlich, A. H. (1990). The population explosion. *The Amicus Journal*, Winter, 18–29.

Eron, L. D. (1986). Interventions to mitigate the psychological effects of media violence on aggressive behavior. *Journal of Social Issues*, 42(3), 155–169.

Eron, L. D. (1987). The development of aggressive behavior from the perspective of a developing behaviorism. *American Psychologist, 42*, 435–442.

Ethical principles of psychologists and code of conduct (1992). The American Psychological Association. *American Psychologist*, 47(12), 1597–1611.

Evans, G. W. & Lepore, S. J. (1993). Household crowding and social support. *Journal of Personality & Social Psychology*, 65(2), 308–316.

Evans, M. D., Hollon, S. D., DeRubeis, R. J., et al. (1992). *Archives of General Psychiatry, 49*(10),

802–808.
Evans, S. (1993). Keeping cool when the baby won't stop crying. *The Los Angeles Times*, Jan. 25, E-2.
Eyer, D. (1993). *Mother-infant bonding: A scientific fiction.* New Haven, CT: Yale University Press.
Eysenck, H. J. (1967). New ways in psychotherapy. *Psychology Today*, June, 40.
Eysenck, H. J. (Ed.). (1981). *A model for personality.* New York: Springer-Verlag.
Eysenck, M. W. & Keane, M. T. (1990). *Cognitive psychology.* Hove, East Sussex, U.K.: Erlbaum.

Fackelmann, K. A. (1991). The maternal cocaine connection. *Science News, 140(10)*, 152–153.
Fackelmann, K. A. (1993). Marijuana and the brain. *Science News, 143(2)*, 88–89, 94.
Famularo, R., Kinscherff, R., & Fenton, T. (1992). Psychiatric diagnoses of abusive mothers. *Journal of Nervous & Mental Disease, 180*,(10), 658–661.
Fantz, R. L. (1961). The origin of form perception. *Scientific American*, May, 71.
Fantz, R. L. (1963). Pattern vision in newborn infants. *Science, 140*, 296–297.
Farah, M. J. (1988). Is visual imagery really visual? Overlooked evidence from neuropsychology. *Psychological Review*, 95(3), 307–317.
Farah, M. J.; Weisberg, L. L.; Monheit, M. A.; & Peronnet, F. (1989). Brain activity underlying mental imagery. *Journal of Cognitive Neuroscience, 1*(4), 302–316.
Farber, S. L. (1981). *Identical twins reared apart.* New York: Basic.
Farquhar, J. W., Fortmann, S. P., Maccoby, N., Wood, P. D. et al. (1984). The Stanford Five City Project: An overview. In J. D. Matarazzo, S. M. Weiss, J. A. Herd, N. E. Miller, & S. M. Weiss (Eds.). *Behavioral health: A handbook of health enhancement and disease prevention.* New York: Wiley.
Farrimond, T. (1990). Effect of alcohol on visual constancy values and possible relation to driving performance. *Perceptual & Motor Skills, 70*(1), 291–295.
Fath, J. L., Mitchell, C. M., & Govindaraj, T. (1990). An ICAI architecture for troubleshooting in complex, dynamic systems. *IEEE Transactions on Systems, Man, & Cybernetics, 20*(3), 537–558.
Fehr, L. (1976). J. Piaget and S. Claus: Psychology makes strange bedfellows. *Psychological Reports*, 39, 740–742.
Feingold, A. (1988). Cognitive gender differences are disappearing. *American Psychologist*, 43(2), 95–103.
Feingold, A. (1990). Gender differences in effects of physical attractiveness on romantic attraction. *Journal of Personality & Social Psychology*, 59(5), 981–993.
Feingold, A. (1992a). Gender differences in mate selection preferences. *Psychological Bulletin, 111*, 304–341.
Feingold, A. (1992b). Good-looking people are not what we think. *Psychological Bulletin, 111(2)*, 304–341.
Feldman, R. S. & Quenzer, L. F. (1984). *Fundamentals of neuropsychopharmacology.* Sunderland, MA: Sinauer Associates.
Fernald, A. & Mazzie, C. (1991). Prosody and focus in speech to infants and adults. *Developmental Psychology, 27(2)*, 209–221.
Fernald, A. (1989). Intonation and communicative intent in mothers' speech to infants: Is the melody the message? *Child Development, 60(6)*, 1497–1510.
Fernandez, E. & Turk, D. C. (1989). The utility of cognitive coping strategies for altering pain perception. *Pain, 38(2)*, 123–135.
Ferrari, J. R. (1991). Self-handicapping by procrastinators: Protecting self-esteem, social-esteem, or both? *Journal of Research in Personality, 25(3)*, 245–261.
Ferrari, J. R. (1992). Procrastinators and perfect behavior. *Journal of Research in Personality, 26(1)*, 75–84.
Ferster, C. B., Nurnberger, J. I., & Levitt, E. B. (1962). The control of eating. *Journal of Mathematics, 1*, 87–109.
Festinger, L. (1954). A theory of social comparison processes. *Human Relations, 7*, 117–140.
Festinger, L. (1957). *A theory of cognitive dissonance.* Stanford, CA: Stanford University Press.
Festinger, L., & Carlsmith, J. M. (1959). Cognitive consequences of forced compliance. *Journal of Abnormal and Social Psychology*, 58, 203–210.
Festinger, L., Schachter, S., & Back, K. (1950). *Social pressures in informal groups: A study of a housing project.* New York: Harper.
Feuerstein, M., Labbé, E. E., & Kuczmierczyk, A. R. (1986). *Health psychology: A psychobiological perspective.* New York: Plenum.
Feuerstein, R., Rand, Y., & Hoffman, M. B. (1980). *Instrumental enrichment: An intervention program for cognitive modifiability.* Baltimore: University Park.
Finke, R. (1990). *Creative imagery.* Hillsdale, NJ: Erlbaum.
Finkelhor, D. & Dziuba-Leatherman, J. (1994). Victimization of children. *American Psychologist*, 49(3), 173–183.
Finkelstein, P., Wenegrat, B., & Yalom, I. (1982). Large group awareness training. *Annual Review of Psychology*, 33, 515–539.
Firth, U. (1993). Autism. *Scientific American*, June, 108–114.
Fischer, P. M., Schwartz, M. P., Richards, J. W., Goldstein, A. O., & Rojas, T. H. (1991). Brand logo recognition by children aged 3 to 6 years. Mickey Mouse and Old Joe the Camel. *Journal of the American Medical Association*, 266(22), 3145–3148.
Fisher, C. B. & Fyrberg, D. (1994). Participant partners. *American Psycholgist*, 49(5), 417–427.
Fisher, J. D., Silver, R. C., Chinsky, J. M., Goff B. et al. (1989). Psychological effects of participation in a large group awareness training. *Journal of Consulting & Clinical Psychology*, 57(6), 747–755.
Fisher, K. (1984, Dec.). Berkeley study finds stress is value-laden. *APA Monitor*, 26, 30.
Fisher, K. (1986, March). Animal research: Few alternatives seen for behavioral studies. *APA Monitor*, 16–17.
Fisher, R. P. & Geiselman, R. E. (1987). Enhancing eyewitness memory with the cognitive interview. In M. M. Grunegerg, P. E. Morris, & R. N. Sykes (Eds.), *Practical aspects of memory: Current research and issues.* Chinchester, U.K.: Wiley.
Fisher, S. (1973). *The female orgasm.* New York: Basic.
Fiske, S. T., (1993a). Social cognition and social perception. In L. W. Porter and M. R. Rosenzweig (Eds.), *Annual Review of Psychology, 44*, 155–194.
Fiske, S. T., (1993b). Controlling other people. *American Psychologist*, 48(6), 621–628.
Fitzgerald, L. F., & Osipow, S. H. (1986). An occupational analysis of counseling psychology. *American Psychologist, 41*, 535–544.
Flannery, R. B. & Wieman, D. (1989). Social support, life stress, and psychological distress: An empirical assessment. *Journal of Clinical Psychology*, 45(6), 867–872.
Flaum, M. L., Arndt, S., & Andreasen, N. C. (1990). The role of gender in studies of ventricle enlargement in schizophrenia. *American Journal of Psychiatry*, 147(10), 1327–1332.
Flavell, J. H. (1992). Cognitive development: Past, present, and future. *Developmental Psychology, 28(6)*, 998–1005.
Fleming, J. (1974). Field report: The state of the apes. *Psychology Today*, Jan., 46.
Flint, B. M. (1978). *New hope for deprived children.* Toronto: University of Toronto Press.
Flor, H. & Birbaumer, N. (1993). Comparison of the efficacy of electromyographic biofeedback, cognitive-behavioral therapy, and conservative medical interventions in the treatment of chronic musculoskeletal pain. *Journal of Consulting & Clinical Psychology, 61*(4), 653–658.
Flynn, J. R. (1987). Massive IQ gains in 14 nations: What IQ tests really measure. *Psychological Bulletin, 101*(2), 171–191.
Fontana, A., Rosenheck, R., & Brett, E. (1992). War zone traumas and postraumatic stress disorder symptomatology. *Journal of Nervous & Mental Disease, 180*(12), 748–755.
Fontenelle, D. H. (1989). *How to live with your children.* Tucson, AZ: Fisher Books.
Foos, P., & Clark, M. C. (1984). *Human learning*, 2(3).
Foreyt, J. P. (1987a). Behavioral medicine. In Wilson, G. T., Franks, C.M., Kendall, P. C. & Foreyt, J. P. *Review of behavior therapy: Theory and practice, Vol. II.* New York: Guilford.
Foreyt, J. P. (1987b). The addictive disorders. In Wilson, G. T., Franks, C. M., Kendall, P. C. & Foreyt, J. P. *Review of behavior therapy: Theory and practice, Vol. II.* New York: Guilford.
Forgays, D. G. & Belinson, M. J. (1986). Is flotation isolation a relaxing environment? *Journal of Environmental Psychology*, 6(1), 19–34.
Foss, R. D. (1986). Using social psychology to increase altruistic behavior: Will it help? In Saks, M. J. & Saxe, L. (Eds.), *Advances in applied social psychology, Vol.* 3. Hillsdale, NJ: Erlbaum.
Foster, G., & Ysseldyke, J. (1976). Expectancy and halo effects as a result of artificially induced teacher bias. *Contemporary Educational Psychology, 1*, 37–45.
Foulkes, D., & Schmidt, M. (1983). Temporal sequence and unit composition in dream reports

from different stages of sleep. *Sleep, 6*(3), 265–280.

Fouts, R., Fouts, D., & Schoenfield, D. (1984). Sign language conversational interaction between chimpanzees. *Sign Language Studies, 42*, 1–12.

Fowler, R. D. (1991). Running Commentary, *APA Monitor*, April, p. 3.

Fowles, D. C. (1992). Schizophrenia: Diathesis-stress revisited. *Annual Review of Psychology, 43*, 303–336.

Fox, P., & Oakes, W. (1984). Learned helplessness: Non-contingent reinforcement in video game performance produces a decrement in performance on a lexical decision task. *Bulletin of the Psychonomic Society*, 22, 113–166.

Franche, R. & Dobson, K. S. (1992). Self-criticism and interpersonal dependency as vulnerability factors to depression. *Cognitive Therapy & Research, 16*(4), 419–435.

Frankenburg, W. K., & Dodds, J. B. (1967). The Denver Developmental Screening Test. *The Journal of Pediatrics, 1*, 181–191.

Frankl, V. (1955). *The doctor and the soul.* New York: Knopf.

Franklin, D. (1984). Growing up short. *Science News, 125*(6), 92–94.

Franklin, D. (1984, Oct. 20). Crafting sound from silence. *Science News, 126*, 252–254.

Franklin, N. & Tversky, B. (1990). Searching imagined environments. *Journal of Experimental Psychology: General, 119*(1), 63–76.

Franks, C. M. (1987). Behavior therapy with children and adolescents. In Wilson, G. T., Franks, C. M., Kendall, P. C. & Foreyt, J. P. *Review of behavior therapy: Theory and practice, Vol. II.* New York: Guilford.

Frederick, C. J. (1987) Psychic trauma in victims of crime and terrorism. In VandenBos, G. R. & Bryant, B. K. (Eds.) *Cataclysms, crises, and catastrophes: Psychology in action.* Washington, DC: American Psychological Association.

Freedman, D. H. (1993). In the realm of the chemical. *Discover*, June, 69–76.

Freedman, J. L. (1975). *Crowding and behavior.* San Francisco: Freeman.

Freedman, J. L. (1984). Effect of television violence on aggressiveness. *Psychological Bulletin, 96*, 227–246.

Freedman, J. L., & Fraser, S. C. (1966). Compliance without pressure: The foot-in-the-door technique. *Journal of Personality & Social Psychology, 4*, 195–202.

Freeman, W. J. (1991). The physiology of perception. *Scientific American*, Feb., 78–85.

Freiberg, P. (1990). Women and AIDS. *APA Monitor*, Feb., 30.

Freize, I. H. (1987). The female victim. In VandenBos, G. R. & Bryant, B. K. (Eds.) *Cataclysms, crises, and catastrophes: Psychology in action.* Washington, DC: American Psychological Association.

French, C. C., Fowler, M., McCarthy, K. & Peers, D. (1991). A Test of the Barnum Effect, *Skeptical Inquirer*, 15(4), 66–72.

Freud, S. (1900). *The interpretation of dreams.* London: Hogarth.

Freud, S. (1949). *An outline of psychoanalysis.* New York: Norton.

Fried, P. A., O'Connell, C. M., & Walkinson, B. (1992). 60- and 72-month follow-up of children prenatally exposed to marijuana, cigarettes, and alcohol. *Journal of Developmental & Behavioral Pediatrics, 13*(6), 383–391.

Friedman, H. S. & Booth-Kewley, S. (1987). The "disease-prone personality." *American Psychologist, 42*(6), 539–555.

Friedman, M., & Rosenman, R. (1983). *Type A behavior and your heart.* New York: Knopf.

Friedman, M., Thoresen, C. E., Gill, J. J., Powell, et al. (1984). Alteration of Type A behavior and reduction in cardiac recurrences in postmyocardial infarction patients. *American Heart Journal, 108*(2), 237–248.

Frieze, I. H., Olson, J. E., & Good, D. C. (1990). Perceived and actual discrimination in the salaries of male and female managers. *Journal of Applied Social Psychology, 20*(1), 46–67.

Frodi, A. N., Lamb, M. E., Leavitt, L. A., Donovan, W. L., Neff, C. & Sherry, D. (1978). Fathers' and mothers' responses to the faces and cries of normal and premature infants. *Developmental Psychology, 14*, 190–198.

Fuchs, C., & Rehm, L. (1977). A self-control behavior therapy program for depression. *Journal of Consulting and Clinical Psychology, 45*, 206–215.

Fuggle, P. W., Tokar, S., Grant, D. B., & Smith, I. (1992). Rising IQ scores in British children. *Journal of Applied Psychology & Psychiatry & Allied Disciplines*, 33(7), 1241–1247.

Fulgosi, A., & Guilford, J. P. (1968). Short-term incubation in divergent production. *American Journal of Psychology*, 7, 1016–1023.

Fuller, B. (1969). *Utopia or oblivion: The prospects for humanity.* New York: Bantam Matrix.

Fulton, R. (1979). Death and dying in a changing world. *Santa Barbara News Press*, Jan. 21.

Furumoto, L., & Scarborough, E. (1986). Placing women in the history of psychology. *American Psychologist, 41*, 35–42.

Gaertner, S. L., Mann, J. A., Dovido, J. E., et al. (1990). How does cooperation reduce intergroup bias? *Journal of Personality & Social Psychology*, 59(4), 692–704.

Gagne, R. M., & Fleishman, E. A. (1959). *Psychology and human performance.* New York: Holt, Rinehart & Winston.

Gagnon, J. H. (1977). *Human sexualities.* Glenview, IL: Scott, Foresman.

Galanter, E. (1962). Contemporary psychophysics. In *New directions in psychology, Vol. I*, 87–156. New York: Holt, Rinehart & Winston.

Galanti, G. (1993). Cult conversion, deprogramming, and the triune brain. *Cultic Studies Journal, 10*(1), 45–52.

Gallup, G. H. Jr., & Newport, F. (1991). Belief in paranormal phenomena among adult Americans. *Skeptical Inquirer, 15*, 137–146.

Galston, A. W., & Slayman, C. L. (1983). Plant sensitivity and sensation. In G. O Abell & B. Singer (Eds.), *Science and the paranormal* (40–55). New York: Scribner's.

Gambrill, E. (1992). Self-help books. *Skeptical Inquirer, 16*(Summer), 389–399.

Gander, P. H., Myhre, G., Graeber, R. C., et al. (1989). Adjustment of sleep and the circadian temperature rhythm after flights across nine time zones. *Aviation, Space, & Environmental Medicine*, 60(8), 733–743.

Gannon, L. (1993). Menopausal symptoms as consequences of dysrhythmia. *Journal of Behavioral Medicine, 16*(4), 387–402.

Garcia, J., Hankins, W. G., & Rusiniak, K. W. (1974). Behavioral regulation of the milieu interne in man and rat. *Science, 185*, 824–831.

Gardner, H. (1985). *Frames of mind.* New York: Basic.

Gardner, M. (1966). Dermo-optical perception: A peek down the nose. *Science, 151*, 654–657.

Gardner, M. (1993). The false memory syndrome. *Skeptical Inquirer, 17(4)*, 370–375.

Gardner, R. A., & Gardner, B. T. (1969). Teaching sign language to a chimpanzee. *Science, 165*, 664–672.

Garland, A. F. & Zigler, E. (1993). Adolescent suicide prevention. *American Psychologist, 48(2)*, 169–182.

Garnets, L. & Kimmel, D. (1991). Lesbian and gay male dimensions in the psychological study of human diversity. *Psychological perspectives on human diversity in America.* Washington, D.C.: American Psychological Association.

Garrett, P., Ng'andu, N., & Ferron, J. (1994). Poverty experiences of young children and the quality of their home environments. *Child Development*, 65(April), 331–345.

Garside, B. (1993). Physicians Mutual Aid Group. *Health & Social Work, 18*(4), 259–267.

Gaston, L. (1990). The concept of the alliance and its role in psychotherapy. *Psychotherapy*, 27(2), 143–153.

Gates, A. I. (1958). Recitation as a factor in memorizing. In J. Deese (Ed.), *The psychology of learning.* New York: McGraw-Hill.

Gatz, M. (1990). Interpreting behavioral genetic results. *Journal of Counseling & Development*, 68(Jul-Aug), 601–605.

Gatz, M. & Pearson, C. G. (1988). Agesim revised and the provision of psychological services. *American Psychologist*, 43(3), 184–188.

Gauthier, J., Cote, G., & French, D. (1994). The role of home practice in the thermal biofeedback treatment of migraine headache. *Journal of Consulting & Clinical Psychology*, 62(1), 180–184.

Gawin, F. H. (1991). Cocaine addiction: Psychology and neurophysiology. *Science, 251*(5000), 1580–1586.

Gazzaniga, M. S. (1970). *The bisected brain.* New York: Plenum.

Gazzaniga, M. S. (1988). *Mind matters.* Boston: Houghton Mifflin.

Geen, R. G. & Bushman, B. J. (1989). The arousing effects of social presence. In H. Wagner & A. Manstead (Eds.), *Handbook of social psychophysiology.* New York: Wiley.

Geiger, M. A. (1991) Changing multiple-choice answers: Do students accurately perceive their performance? *Journal of Experimental Education*, 59(3), 250–257.

Geiselman, R. E., Fisher, R. P., MacKinnon, D. P., & Holland, H. L. (1986). Eyewitness memory en-

hancement with the cognitive interview. *American Journal of Psychology*, 99, 385–401.
Geldard, F. A. (1972). *The human senses.* New York: Wiley.
Gerbner, G., & Gross, L. (1976). Living with television: The violent profile. *Journal of Communication, 26,* 173–199.
Gersh, R. D. (1982). Learning when not to shoot. *Santa Barbara News Press,* June 20.
Geschwind, N. (1975). The apraxias: neural mechanisms of disorders of learned movement. *American Scientist, 63,* 188–195.
Geschwind, N. (1979). Specializations of the human brain. *Scientific American, 241,* 180–199.
Gesteland, R. C. (1986). Speculations on receptor cells as analyzers and filters. *Experientia, 42,* 287–291.
Gevins, A. (1989). Dynamic functional topography of cognitive tasks. *Brain Topography,* 2(1–2), 37–56.
Gevins, A. S., Bressler, S. L., Cutillo, B. A., Illes, J. et al. (1990). Effects of prolonged mental work on functional brain topography. *Electroencephalography & Clinical Neurophysiology,* 76(4) 339–350.
Gibson, E. J., & Walk, R. D. (1960). The "visual cliff." *Scientific American,* 202(4), 67–71.
Gibson, H. B. & Heap, M. (1991). *Hypnosis in therapy.* Hillsdale, NJ: Erlbaum.
Gifford, R. (1987). *Environmental psychology.* Boston: Allyn & Bacon.
Gilbert, A. N. & Wysocki, C. J. (1987). The smell survey results. *National Geographic,* Oct., 514–524.
Gill, S. T. (1991). Carrying the war into the never-never land of psi. *Skeptical Inquirer,* 15(1), 269–273.
Gillam, B. (1980). Geometrical illusions. *American Psychologist, 242,* 102–111.
Gilligan, C. (1982). *In a different voice.* Cambridge, MA: Harvard University Press.
Gilligan, C. & Attanucci, J. (1988). Two moral orientations: Gender differences and similarities. *Merrill-Palmer Quarterly,* 34(3), 223–237.
Gilmore, D. C. & Ferris, G. R. (1989). The effects of applicant impression management tactics on interviewer judgments. *Journal of Management,* 15(4), 557–564.
Giniger, S., Dispenzieri, A., & Eisenberg, J. (1983). Age, experience, and performance on speed and skill jobs in an applied setting. *Journal of Applied Psychology, 68,* 469–475.
Ginott, H. G. (1965). *Between parent and child: New solutions to old problems.* New York: Macmillan.
Ginsburg, G. S. & Bornstein, P. (1993). Family factors related to children's intrinsic/extrinsic motivational orientation and academic performance. *Child Development,* 64(5), 1461–1474.
Ginzberg, E. (1984). Career development. In D. Brown & L. Brooks (Eds.), *Career choice and development.* San Francisco: Josey-Bass.
Giovannoni, J. M., & Becerra, R. M. (1979). *Defining child abuse.* New York: Free Press.
Girodo, M. (1978). *Shy? (You don't have to be!).* New York: Pocket Books.
Gladue, B. A. (1987) Psychobiological contributions. In L. Diamant (Ed.) *Male and female homosexuality: Psychological approaches.* Washington, DC: Hemisphere.
Glass, A. L., Holyoak, K. J., & Santa, J. L. (1979). *Cognition.* Reading, MA: Addison-Wesley.
Globus, G. (1987). *Dream life, wake life: The human condition through dreams.* Albany, NY: State University of New York Press.
Glovinsky, P. B., Spielman, A. J., Carroll, P., Weinstein, L. et al. (1990). Sleepiness and REM sleep recurrence: The effects of Stage 2 and REM sleep awakenings. *Psychophysiology,* 27(5), 552–559.
Gold, P. E. (1987). Sweet Memories. *American Scientist, 75,* (Mar-Apr), 151–155.
Gold, S. N., Hughes, D., & Hohnecker, L. (1994). Degrees of repression of sexual abuse memories. *American Psychologist,* 49(5), 441–442.
Goldberg, L. R. (1993). The structure of phenotypic personality traits. *American Psychologist, 48(1),* 26–34.
Goldfried, M. R., Greenberg, L. S., & Marmar, C. (1990). Individual psychotherapy: Process and outcome. *Annual Review of Psychology, 41,* 659–688.
Goldiamond, I. (1971). Self-control procedures in personal behavior problems. In M. S. Gazzaniga, & E. P. Lovejoy (Eds.), *Good reading in psychology.* Englewood Cliffs, NJ: Prentice-Hall.
Goldstein, E. B. (1989). *Sensation and perception.* Belmont, CA: Wadsworth.
Goldstein, I. L. & Gilliam, P. (1990). Training system issues in the year 2000. *American Psychologist,* 45(2), 134–143.
Goldstein, M. J. (1985). *The UCLA family project.* Presented at NIMH High-Risk Consortium, San Francisco. Cited by Mirsky & Duncan, 1986.
Goleman, D. (1989). Afternoon nap natural. *New York Times.*
Goleman, D. (1991). Mental Images. *Psychology updates.* New York: HarperCollins.
Gomberg, E. L. (1993). Women and alcohol: Use and abuse. *Journal of Nervous and Mental Disease,* 18(4), 211–219.
Gomes-Schwartz, B., Hadley, S. W., & Strupp, H. H. (1978). Individual psychotherapy and behavior therapy. *Annual Review of Psychology, 29,* 435–471.
Gondola, J. C., & Tuckman, B. W. (1982). Psychological mood state in "average" marathon runners. *Perceptual and Motor Skills, 55,* 1295–1300.
Goodall, J. (1990). *Through a window: My thirty years with the chimpanzees of the Gombe.* Boston: Houghton Mifflin.
Goodglass, H. (1980). Disorders of naming following brain injury. *American Scientist, 68,* 647–655.
Goodman, G. (1984). SASHA tapes: Expanding options for help-intended communication. In D. Larson (Ed.), *Teaching psychological skills.* Monterey, CA: Brooks/Cole.
Goodstein, L. D. (1986). 1985–86 faculty salary survey. *APA Monitor,* March, 37.
Gordon, T. (1970). *P.E.T. parent effectiveness training: A tested new way to raise children.* New York: Peter H. Wyden.
Goss, S., Hall, C., Buckolz, E., & Fishburne, G. (1986). Imagery ability and the acquisition and retention of movements. *Memory & Cognition,* 14(6), 469–477.
Gottesman, I. I. (1991). *Schizophrenia genesis: The origins of madness.*
Gottesman, I. I., & Shields, J. (1982). *The schizophrenic puzzle.* New York: Cambridge University Press.
Gottfried, A. E. & Gottfried, A. W. (1988). *Maternal employment and children's development.* New York: Plenum.
Gottman, J. M. & Krokoff, L. J. (1989). Marital interaction and satisfaction: A longitudinal view. *Journal of Consulting & Clinical Psychology,* 57(1), 47–52.
Gough, H. G., Fioravanti, M., & Lazzari, R. (1983). Some implications of self versus ideal-self congruence on the revised adjective check list. *Journal of Personality & Social Psychology, 44,* 1214–1220.
Gould, R. (1975). Growth toward self-tolerance. *Psychology Today,* Feb.
Gould, S. J. (1976). Biological potential vs. biological determinism. *Natural History,* 85(5).
Grady, D. (1986). Don't get jittery over caffeine. *Discover,* July, 73–79.
Graham, S. (1992). Most of the subjects were White and middle class. *American Psychologist, 47,* 629–639.
Green, J. A., & Shellenberger, R. D. (1986). Biofeedback research and the ghost in the box: A reply to Roberts. *American Psychologist,* Sept., 1003–1005.
Green, K. C. (1989). A profile of undergraduates in the sciences. *American Scientist, 77,* 475–478.
Greene, A. S. & Saxe, L. (1990). *Tall tales told to teachers.* Unpublished manuscript. Brandeis University.
Greene, D., & Lepper, M. R. (1974). How to turn play into work. *Psychology Toady,* Sept., 49.
Greenfield, P. M. & Savage-Rumbaugh, E. S. (1993). Comparing communicative competence in child and chimp: The pragmatics of repetition. *Journal of Child Language,* 20(1), 1–26.
Greenspan, E. (1983). Conditioning athlete's minds. *New York Times Magazine,* Aug. 28, 32–34.
Greenwald, A.G., Spangenberg, E. R., Pratkanis, A. R., & Eskenazi, J. (1991). Double-blind tests of subliminal self-help audiotapes. *Psychological Science,* 2(2), 119–122.
Gregory, R. L. (1990). *Eye and brain: The psychology of seeing.* Princeton, NJ: Princeton University Press.
Griffin, D. R. (1992). *Animal minds.* Chicago: University of Chicago Press.
Grobstein, P., & Chow, K. L. (1975). Perceptive field development and individual experience. *Science, 190,* 352–358.
Gross, T. F. (1990) General test and state anxiety in real examinations: State is not test anxiety. *Educational Research Quarterly, 14(3),* 11–20.
Grossman, F. K., Eichler, L. S., & Winicoff, S. A. (1980). *Pregnancy, Birth and Parenthood.* San Francisco,: Jossey-Bass.
Grossmann, K. E., & Volkmer, H. (1984). Fathers' presence during birth of their infants and paternal involvement. *International Journal of Behavioral Development, 7,* 157–165.
Grover, S. C. (1983). *The cognitive basis of the intellect: A response to Jensen's "Bias in mental testing."* Calgary, Alberta: University of Calgary.

Grubb, H. J. (1988). The role of community psychology in the community. *Journal of Clinical Psychology, 44*(4), 606–610.

Gruder, C. L., Mermelstein, R. J., Kirkendol, S., et al. (1993). Effects of social support and relapse prevention training as adjuncts to a televised smoking-cessation intervention. *Journal of Consulting & Clinical Psychology, 61*(1), 113–120.

Guidelines for providers of psychological services to ethnic, linguistic, and culturally diverse populations. 1993. *American Psychologist, 48*(1), 45–48.

Guilford, J. P. (1950). Creativity. *American Psychologist, 5,* 444–454.

Guilleminault, C., Passouant, P., & Dement, W. C. (1976). *Narcolepsy.* New York: Spectrum.

Gustavson, C. R., & Garcia, J. (1974). Pulling a gag on the wily coyote. *Psychology Today,* May, 68–72.

Gutek, B. A. (1981). Experiences of sexual harassment: Results from a representative survey. Paper presented at symposium of the annual convention, American Psychological Association, August, 1981, Los Angeles, California.

Haber, R. N. (1969). Eidetic images; With biographical sketches. *Scientific American, 220*
(12), 36–44.

Haber, R. N. (1970, May). How we remember what we see. *Scientific American,* 104–112.

Haber, R. N. (1980). How we perceive depth from flat pictures. *American Scientist, 68,* 370–380.

Haier, R. J., Siegel, B. V., Nuechterlein, K. H., Hazlett, et al. (1988). Cortical glucose metabolic rate correlates of abstract reasoning and attention studied with positron emission tomography. *Intelligence, 12,* 199–217.

Hale, B. D. (1982). The effects of internal and external imagery on muscular and ocular concomitants. *Journal of Sport Psychology,* 4(4), 379–387.

Hales, D. (1980). *The complete book of sleep.* Reading, MA: Addison-Wesley.

Hall, C. (1966). *The meaning of dreams.* New York: McGraw-Hill.

Hall, C. (1974). What people dream about. In R. L. Woods, & H. B. Greenhouse (Eds.), *The new world of dreams: An anthology.* New York: Macmillan.

Hall, C., Domhoff, G. W., Blick, K. A., & Weesner, K. E. (1982). The dreams of college men and women in 1950 and 1980: A comparison of dream contents and sex differences. *Sleep,* 5(2), 188–194.

Hall, E. T. (1966). *The hidden dimension.* Garden City, NY: Doubleday.

Hall, E. T. (1974). *Handbook for proxemic research.* Washington, DC: Social Anthropology and Visual Communication.

Halonen, J. S. (1986). *Teaching critical thinking in psychology.* Milwaukee, WI: Alverno Productions.

Hamer D. H., Hu, S., Magnuson, V. L., Hu, N., & Pattatucci, A. M. (1993). A linkage between DNA markers on the X chromosome and male sexual orientation. *Science, 16:261(5119),* 291–292.

Hammer, S., & Hazleton, L. (1984). Cocaine and the chemical brain. *Science Digest,* 92, 58–61, 100–103.

Hansel, C. E. M. (1980). *ESP and parapsychology: A critical reevaluation.* Buffalo, NY: Prometheus.

Hansen, C. H. & Hansen, R. D. (1990). Rock music videos and antisocial behavior. *Basic and Applied Social Psychology, 11*(4), 357–369.

Harder, D. W., Strauss, J. S., Greenwald, D. F., Kokes, R. F., et al. (1989). Life events and psychopathology severity. *Journal of Clinical Psychology,* 45(2), 202–209.

Hardin, G. (1968). The tragedy of the commons. *Science, 162,* 1243–1248.

Hardin, G. (1985) *Filters against folly.* New York: Viking.

Hare, R. D., McPherson, L. M., & Forth, A. E. (1988). Male psychopaths and their criminal careers. *Journal of Consulting & Clinical Psychology,* 56(5), 710–714.

Hare-Mustin, R. T. & Marecek, J. (1988). The meaning of difference. *American Psychologist,* 43(6), 455–464.

Harlow, H. F. (1966). Learning to love. *American Scientist, 54,* 244–272.

Harlow, H. F. (1967). The young monkeys. *Psychology Today,* 1(5), 40–74.

Harlow, H. F., & Harlow, M. K. (1962). Social deprivation in monkeys. *Scientific American, 207,* 136–146.

Harlow, H. F., & Zimmerman, R. R. (1958). The development of affectional responses in infant monkeys. *Proceedings of the American Philosophical Society, 102,* 501–509.

Harlow, J. M. (1868). Recovery from the passage of an iron bar through the head. *Massachusetts Medical Society,* 2, 327.

Harris, L. J. (1993a). Do left-handers die sooner than right-handers? *Psychological Bulletin, 114*(2), 203–234.

Harris, L. J. (1993b). "Left-handedness and life span": Reply to Halpern and Coren. *Psychological Bulletin, 114*(2), 242–247.

Harris, M. M. (1989). Reconsidering the employment interview. *Personnel Psychology,* 42(4), 691–726.

Harrison, G. P. & Katz, D. L. (1987) Letter. *The Lancet, 1,* 863.

Harrison, L. F. & Williams, T. M. (1986). Television and cognitive development. In T. M. Williams (Ed.), *The impact of television: A natural experiment in three communities.* Orlando, FL: Academic.

Harrison, R. H. & Newirth, J. (1990). The effect of sensory deprivation and ego strength on a measure of autistic thinking. *Journal of Personality Assessment,* 54(3–4), 694–703.

Harsch, N. & Neisser, U. (1989). *Substantial and irreversible errors in flashbulb memories of the* Challenger *explosion.* Poster presented at the meeting of the Psychonomic Society, November, 1989, Atlanta, GA.

Hart, B. & Risley, T. R. (1992). American parenting of language-learning children: Persisting differences in family-child interactions observed in natural home environments. *Developmental Psychology, 28(6),* 1096–1105.

Hartgrove-Freile, J. (1990). *Organizations, communication, and culture.* St. Paul, MN: West.

Hartmann, E. L. (1973). *The functions of sleep.* New Haven: Yale University Press.

Hartmann, E. L. (1981). The functions of sleep and memory processing. In W. Fishbein (Ed.) *Sleep, dreams and memory.* New York: SP Medical & Scientific Books.

Hashima, P. Y. & Amato, P. R. (1994). Poverty, social support, and parental behavior. *Child Development,* 65(April), 394–403.

Hatfield, E., Greenberger, D., Traupmann, J., & Lambert, P. (1982). Equity and sexual satisfaction in recently married couples. *Journal of Sex Research, 18,* 18–32.

Hathaway, S. R. & McKinley, J. C. (1989). *MMPI-2: Manual for administration and scoring.* Minneapolis, MN: University of Minnesota Press.

Hauri, P. & Linde, S. (1990). No more sleepless nights. New York: Wiley.

Havighurst, R. J. (1961). Successful aging. *Gerontologist, 1,* 8–13.

Havighurst, R. J. (1979). *Developmental tasks and education.* New York: David McKay.

Hawkins, D. B., & Gruber, J. J. (1982). Little league baseball and players' self-esteem. *Perceptual and Motor Skills,* 55, 1335–1340.

Hayes, C. (1951). *The ape in our house.* New York: Harper & Row.

Hayes, J. R. (1978). *Cognitive psychology: Thinking and creating.* Homewood, IL: Dorsey.

Haywood, H. C., Meyers, C. E., & Switzby, H. N. (1982). Mental retardation. *Annual Review of Psychology,* 33, 309–342.

Hearold, S. L. (1987). Meta-analysis of the effects of television on social behavior. In G. Comstock (Ed.), *Public communication and behavior: Volume 1.* NY: Academic.

Heath, L. & Petraitis, J. (1987). Television viewing and fear of crime: Where is the mean world? *Basic & Applied Social Psychology,* 8(1–2), 97–123.

Heath, L., Bresolin, L. B., & Rinaldi, R. C. (1989). Effects of media violence on children: A review of the literature. *Archives of General Psychiatry,* 46(4), 376–379.

Hebb, D. O. (1949). *Organization of behavior.* New York: Wiley.

Hebb, D. O. (1966). *A textbook of psychology.* Philadelphia: Saunders.

Hebb, D. O. (1974). What psychology is about. *American Psychologist,* 29, 71–79.

Hecht, M. L., Marston, P. J., & Larkey, L. K. (1994). Love ways and relationship quality in heterosexual relationships. *Journal of Social & Personal Relationships, 11*(1), 25–43.

Heckhausen, J. (1987). Balancing for weaknesses and challenging developmental potential. *Developmental Psychology,* 23(6), 762–770.

Heiby, E. M. (1983). Assessment of frequency of self-reinforcement. *Journal of Personality & Social Psychology, 44,* 1304–1307.

Heiman, J. R. (1977). A psychophysiological exploration of sexual arousal patterns in females and males. *Psychophysiology, 14*(3), 266–274.

Heinrich, R. K., Corbine, J. L., & Thomas, K. R. (1990). Counseling Native Americans. *Journal of Counseling and Development,* 69(Nov.-Dec.), 128–133.

Heinrichs, R. W. (1993). Schizophrenia and the brain. *American Psychologist,* 48(3), 221–233.

Held, R. (1971). Plasticity in sensory-motor systems.

In *Contemporary psychology*. San Francisco: Freeman.
Hellekson, C. & Rosenthal, N. (1987). New light on seasonal mood changes. *The Harvard Medical School Mental Health Letter*, 3(10), 4–6.
Heller, J. (1961). *Catch 22*. New York: Simon & Schuster.
Hellige, J. B. (1990). Hemispheric asymmetry. *Annual Review of Psychology*, *41*, 55–60.
Hellriegel, D., Slocum, J. W., & Woodman, R. W. (1986). *Organizational behavior.* St. Paul, MN: West.
Helms, J. E. (1992). Why is there no study of cultural equivalence in standardized ability testing? *American Psychologist*, 47(9), 1083–1101.
Helson, H. (1964). *Adaptation-level theory*. New York: Harper & Row.
Henderson, N. D. (1982). Human behavior genetics. *Annual Review of Psychology*, 33, 403–440.
Hendrick, S. S. & Hendrick, C. (1993). Lovers as friends. *Journal of Social & Personal Relationships*, *10*(3), 459–466.
Heppenheimer, T. A. (1990). Shedding light on inner workings of the brain. *Los Angeles Times*, Feb. 26, B3.
Hepper, P. G. (1990). Origins of fetal handedness. *Nature*, 347(6292), 431.
Herbert, W., & Greenberg, J. (1983, Sept. 10). Behavior: Sex roles remain. *Science News*, *124*, 172.
Herbert. T. B. & Cohen, S. (1993). Depression and immunity. *Psychological Bulletin*, *113*(3), 472–486.
Herek, G. M. (1989). Hate crimes against lesbians and gay men. *American Psychologist*, *44*(6), 948–955.
Herman, J. L. (1992). *Trauma and recovery*, New York: Basic Books.
Heron; W. (1957). The pathology of boredom. *Scientific American*, *196*, 52–56.
Herrnstein, R. J. (1979). Acquisition, generalization, and discrimination reversal of a natural concept. *Journal of Experimental Psychology: Animal Behavior Processes*, *5*, 116–129.
Herrnstein, R. J., Nickerson, R. S., de Sanchez, M., & Swets, J. (1986). Teaching thinking skills. *American Psychologist*, *41*(11), 1279–1289.
Herron, J. (1980). *Neuropsychology of left-handedness.* New York: Academic.
Hershey, J. M.; Kopplin, D. A.; Cornell, J. E. (1991). Doctors of Psychology: Their career experiences and attitudes toward degree and training. *Professional Psychology: Research & Practice, 22(5)*, 351–356.
Herzog, H. A. (1990). Discussing animal rights and animal research in the classroom. *Teaching of Psychology*, *17*(2), 90–94.
Herzog, H. A., Jr. (1991) Conflicts of interests: Kittens and boa constrictors, pets and research. *American Psychologist*, *46*(3), 246–247.
Hess, E. H. (1959). Imprinting. *Science*, *130*, 133–141.
Hess, E. H. (1975a). *The tell-tale eye: How your eyes reveal hidden thoughts and emotions.* New York: Van Nostrand Reinhold.
Hess, E. H. (1975b). The role of pupil size in communication. *Scientific American*, Nov., 110–119.
Heussenstamm, F. K. (1971). Bumper stickers and the cops. *Transaction*, *8*, 32–33.
Heyser, C. J., Spear, N. E., & Spear, L. P. (1992). Effects of prenatal exposure to cocaine on conditional discrimination learning in adult rats. *Behavioral Neuroscience*, *106*(5), 837–845.
Higbee, K. L., Clawson, C., DeLano, L., & Campbell, S. (1990). Using the link mnemonic to remember errands. *Psychological Record*, *40*(3), 429–436.
High-risk sex less common. (1987). *APA Monitor*, Aug., 16.
Hilgard, E. R. (1968). *The experience of hypnosis.* New York: Harcourt Brace Jovanovich.
Hilgard, E. R. (1977). *Divided consciousness.* New York: Wiley.
Hilgard, E. R. (1978). Hypnosis and Pain. In R. A. Sternbach (Ed.), *The psychology of pain.* New York: Raven.
Hilgard, E. R., & Hilgard J. R. (1983). *Hypnosis in the relief of pain.* Los Altos, CA: Kaufmann.
Hill, L. (1990). Effort and reward in college: A replication of some puzzling findings. *Journal of Social Behavior & Personality*, *5(4)*, 151–161.
Hill, P. (1993). Recent advances in selected aspects of adolescent development. *Journal of Child Psychology & Psychiatry & Allied Disciplines*, *34*(1), 69–99.
Hinshaw, K. E. (1991). The effects of mental practice on motor skill performance. *Imagination, Cognition & Personality*, *11*(1), 3–35.
Hirschman, R. S. & Leventhal, H. (1989). *Journal of Applied Social Psychology*, *19*(7) 559–583.
Hirshberg, L. M. & Svejda, M. (1990). When infants look to their parents. *Child Development*, *61*(4), 1175–1186.
Hirt, M. & Pithers, W. (1991). Selective attention and levels of coding in schizophrenia. *British Journal of Clinical Psychology*, 30(2), 139–149.
Hite, S. (1976). *The Hite report.* New York: Macmillan.
HIV and AIDS: Are You At Risk? (1991). Atlanta, GA: United States Centers for Disease Control.
Hobson, J. A. (1988). *The dreaming brain.* New York: Basic.
Hobson, J. A. & Stickgold, R. (1994). Dreaming: A neurocognitive approach. *Consciousness & Cognition*, 3(1), 1–15.
Hobson, J. A., & McCarley, R. W. (1977). The brain as a dream state generator: An activation-synthesis hypothesis of the dream process. *American Journal of Psychiatry*, *134*, 1335–1348.
Hodapp, R. M. (1994). Mental retardation. *Encyclopedia of human behavior,* Vol. 3, 175–185.
Hodgson, R., & Miller, P. (1982). *Selfwatching.* New York: Facts on File.
Hoffman, M. L. (1975). Altruistic behavior and the parent-child relationship. *Journal of Personality & Social Psychology*, 31, 937–943.
Hoffman, M. L. (1977). Moral internalization: Current theory and research. In L. Berkowitz (Ed.), *Advances in experimental and social psychology*, Vol. 10. New York: Academic Press.
Hogben, D. & Lawson, M. J. (1992). Superiority of the keyword method for backward recall in vocabulary acquisition. *Psychological Reports*, *71(3, Pt 1)*, 880–882.
Holden, C. (1980). Twins reunited. *Science 80*, Nov., 55–59.
Holland, J. (1985). *Making vocational choices: A theory of careers.* Englewood Cliffs, NJ: Prentice-Hall.
Holland, M. K. (1975, 1985). *Using psychology: Principles of behavior and your life.* Boston: Little, Brown.
Hollon, S. D., DeRubeis, R. J., Evans, M. D., et al. (1992). Cognitive therapy and pharmacology for depression. *Archives of General Psychiatry*, *49*(10), 774–781.
Holmes, D. S. (1984). Meditation and somatic arousal reduction: A review of the experimental evidence. *American Psychologist*, 39(1), 1–10.
Holmes, D. S., Solomon, S., Cappo, B. M., & Greenberg, J. L. (1983). Effects of transcendental meditation versus resting on physiological and subjective arousal. *Journal of Personality & Social Psychology*, *44*, 1245–1252.
Holmes, T., & Masuda, M. (1972). Psychosomatic syndrome. *Psychology Today*, April, 71.
Holtzworth-Munroe, A. & Hutchinson, G. (1993). Attributing negative intent to wife behavior. *Journal of Abnormal Psychology*, *102*(2), 206–211.
Holyoak, K. J. (1990). Problem solving. Holyoak, K. J. (1990). Problem solving. In D. N. Osherson & E. E. Smith, *Thinking*, Cambridge, MA: The MIT Press.
Honzik, M. P. (1984). Life-span development. *Annual Review of Psychology*, 35, 309–331.
Hopkins, J., Marcus, M., & Campbell, S. B. (1984). Postpartum depression: A critical review. *Psychological Bulletin*, 95, 498–515.
Hopson, J. L. (1986). The unraveling of insomnia. *Psychology Today*, June, 43–49.
Horn, J. C. (1987). Bigger pay for better work. *Psychology Today*, July, 54–57.
Horn, J. C. & Meer, J. (1987). The vintage years. *Psychology Today*, May, 76–93ff.
Horn, J. M., Loehlin, J. C., & Willerman, L. (1979). Intellectual resemblance among adoptive and biological relatives: The Texas adoption project. *Behavior Genetics*, 9, 177–207.
Horn, J. M., Plomine, R., & Rosenman, R. (1976). Heritability of personality traits in adult male twins. *Behavior Genetics*, *6*, 17–30.
Horne, J. A., & Staff, L. H. E. (1983). Exercise and sleep: Body-heating effects. *Sleep*, *6*, 36–46.
Horowitz, F. D. & O'Brien, M. (1986). Gifted and talented children. *American Psychologist*, *41*(10), 1147–1152.
Horvath, A. 0. & Goheen, M. D. (1990). Factors mediating the success of defiance- and compliance-based interventions. *Journal of Counseling Psychology*, 37(4), 363–371.
Horwitz, W. A., Kestenbaum, C., Person, E., & Jarvik, L. (1965). Identical twin "Idiot savants" calendar calculators. *The American Journal of Psychiatry*, *121*, 1075–1079.
Hosch, H. M., & Cooper, D. S. (1982). Victimization as a determinant of eyewitness accuracy. *Journal of Applied Psychology*, 67, 649–652.
Houston, J. P. (1985). *Motivation.* New York: Macmillan.
Howard, A., Pion, G. M., Gottfredson, G. D., Flattau, P. E., et al. (1986). The changing face of American psychology. *American Psychologist*, *41*, 1311–1327.
Howard, K. I., Kopta, S. M., Krause, M. S., & Orlinsky, D. E. (1986). The dose-effect relationship in

psychotherapy. *American Psychologist, 41,* 159–164.

Howitt, D., Craven, G., Iveson, C., Kremer, J., McCabe, J., & Rolph, T. (1977). The misdirected letter. *British Journal of Social and Clinical Psychology, 16,* 285–286.

Hoyenga, K. B., & Hoyenga, K. T. (1984). *Motivational explanations of behavior.* Monterey, CA: Brooks/Cole.

Hsia, Y., & Graham, C. H. (1965). Color blindness. In C. H. Graham (Ed.), *Vision and visual perception.* New York: Wiley.

Hsiung, P. (1990). Expansion of field of view via wide angle imaging. Unpublished document.

Hubel, D. H. (1979a). The brain. *Scientific American, 241*(Sept.), 45–53.

Hubel, D. H. (1979 b). The visual cortex of normal and deprived monkeys. *American Scientist, 67,* 532–543.

Hubel, D. H., & Wiesel, T. N. (1979). Brain mechanisms of vision. *Scientific American, 241,* 150–162.

Huesmann, L. R. (1986). Psychological processes promoting the relation between exposure to media violence and aggressive behavior by the viewer. *Journal of Social Issues,* 42(3), 125–139.

Huesmann, L. R. & Eron, L. D. (1986). The development of aggression in American children as a consequence of television violence viewing. In L. R. Huesmann & L. D. Eron (Eds.), *Television and the aggressive child: A cross-national comparison.* Hillsdale, NJ: Erlbaum.

Huesmann, L. R., Eron, L., Klein, L., Brice, P., & Fischer, P. (1983). Mitigating the imitation of aggressive behaviors by changing children's attitudes about media violence. *Journal of Personality & Social Psychology, 44,* 899–910.

Hugdahl, K., & Karker, A. C. (1981). Biological vs. experimental factors in phobic conditioning. *Behavior Research and Therapy, 19,* 109–115.

Hughes, J. R. (1992). Tobacco withdrawal in self-quitters. *Journal of Consulting & Clinical Psychology, 60*(5), 689–697.

Hughes, J. R., Higgins, S. T., Bickel, W. K., Hunt, W. K., et al. (1991). Caffeine self-administration, withdrawal, and adverse effects among coffee drinkers. *Archives of General Psychiatry, 48*(7), 611–617.

Hunt, M. (1982). *The universe within.* New York: Simon & Schuster.

Hurd, P., Johnson, C. A., Pechacek, T., Bast, L. P., Jacobs, D. R., & Luepker, R. V. (1980). Prevention of smoking in seventh grade students. *Journal of Behavioral Medicine,* 3, 15–28.

Hurley, D. (1989). The search for cocaine's methadone. *Psychology Today,* July/Aug., 59–60.

Huston, T. L., & Levinger, G. (1978). Interpersonal attraction and relationships. *Annual Review of Psychology, 29,* 115–156.

Hutchison, M. (1984). *The book of floating.* New York: Quill.

Huxley, A. (1965). Human potentialities. In R. E. Farson (Ed.), *Science and human affairs.* Palo Alto, CA: Science and Behavior Books.

Hyde, J. S. (1990). *Understanding human sexuality.* New York: McGraw-Hill.

Hyde, J. S. & Linn, M. C. (1988). Gender differences in verbal ability: A meta-analysis. *Psychological Bulletin, 104*(1), 53–69.

Hyde, J. S., Gennema, E., & Lamon, S. (1990). Gender differences in mathematics performance: A meta-analysis. *Psychological Bulletin,* 107(2), 139–155.

Hyland, M. E. (1989). There is no motive to avoid success: The compromise explanation for success-avoiding behavior. *Journal of Personality,* 57(3), 665–693.

Hyman, R. (1989). *The elusive quarry: A scientific appraisal of psychical research.* Buffalo, NY: Prometheus.

Hynd, G. W. & Semrud-Clikeman, M. (1989). Dyslexia and brain morphology. *Psychological Bulletin, 106*(3), 447–482.

Hyson, M. G., Hirsh-Pasek, K., Rescorla, L., Cone, J. et al. (1991). Ingredients of parental "pressure" in early childhood. *Journal of Applied Developmental Psychology, 12(3),* 347–365.

Iaccino, J. F. & Sowa, S. J. (1989). Bizarre imagery in paired-associate learning: An effective mnemonic aid with mixed context, delayed testing, and self-paced conditions. *Perceptual & Motor Skills, 68*(1), 307–316.

Iavecchia, J. H., Iavecchia, H. P. & Roscoe, S. N. (1983). The moon illusion revisited. *Aviation, Space, and Environmental Medicine,* 54, 39–46.

Ickes, W. (1993). Traditional gender roles: Do they make, then break, our relationships? *Journal of Social Issues, 49*(3), 71–86.

Infante-Rivard, C., Fernandez, A., Gauthier, R., David, M., & Rivard, G. E. (1993). Fetal loss associated with caffeine intake before and during pregnancy. *Journal of the American Medical Association, 270*(24), 2940–2943.

Institute of Medicine. (1990). *Broadening the base of treatment for alcohol problems.* Washington, D.C.: National Academy Press.

Isaac, A. R. (1992). Mental practice: Does it work in the field? *Sport Psychologist,* 6(2), 192–198.

Isaac, R. J. & Armat, V. C. (1990). *Madness in the streets: How psychiatry & the law abandoned the mentally ill.* New York: Free Press.

Isabella, R. A. (1993). Origins of attachment. *Child Development,* 64(2), 605–621.

Isabella, R. A. & Belsky, J. (1991). Interactional synchrony and the origins of infant-mother attachment. *Child Development,* 62, 373–384.

Isenberg, P. L., & Schatzberg, A. F. (1976). Psychoanalytic contribution to a theory of depression. In J. O. Cole, A. F. Schatzberg, & S. H. Frazier (Eds.), *Depression: Biology, psychodynamics, and treatment.* New York: Plenum.

Isner, J. M., Estes, N. A. M, Thompson, P. D., Costanzo-Nordin, M. R. et al., (1986). Acute cardiac events temporally related to cocaine abuse. *New England Journal of Medicine,* 315(23), 1438–1443.

Isser, N. (1991). Why cultic groups develop and flourish. *Cultic Studies Journal,* 8(2), 104–121.

Ivey, A. E., & Galvin, M. (1984). Microcounseling: A metamodel for counseling, therapy, business, and medical interviews. In D. Larson (Ed.), *Teaching psychological skills.* Monterey, CA: Brooks/Cole.

Izard, C. E. (1977). *Human emotions.* New York: Plenum.

Izard, C. E. (1990). Facial expressions and the regulation of emotions. *Journal of Personality & Social Psychology,* 58(3), 487–498.

Jackson, B. (1973). Our prisons are criminal. *New York Times Magazine,* Sept. 22, 54, 57.

Jackson, R. J. (1994). A multimodal method for assessing and treating airsickness. *International Journal of Aviation Psychology,* 4(1), 85–96.

Jackson, S. E. (1983). Participation in decision making as a strategy for reducing job-related strain. *Journal of Applied Psychology, 68,* 3–19.

Jacobs, G. D., Benson, H., & Friedman, R. (1993). Home-based central nervous system assessment of multi-factor behavioral intervention for chronic sleep-onset insomnia. *Behavior Therapy,* 24(1), 159–174.

Jacobsen, P. B., Bovbjerg, D. H., Schwartz, M. D., et al., (1993). Formation of food aversions in cancer patients receiving repeated infusions of chemotherapy. *Behavior Research & Therapy,* 31(8), 739–748.

Jacobson, L. E. (1932). The electrophysiology of mental activities. *American Journal of Psychology, 44,* 677–694.

Jahn, R. G. (1982). The persistent paradox of psychic phenomena. *Proceedings of the IEEE,* 70(2), 136–166.

Janis, I. L. (1989). *Crucial decisions.* New York: Free Press.

Janis, I. L., & Mann, L. (1965). Effectiveness of emotional role-playing in modifying smoking habits and attitudes. *Journal of Experimental Research in Personality, 1,* 84–90.

Janis, I. L., & Wheeler, D. (1978). Thinking clearly about career choices. *Psychology Today, 11,* 66–78.

Janos, P. M. & Robinson, N. M. (1985). Psychosocial development in intellectually gifted children. In F. D. Horowitz & M. O'Brien (Eds.), *The gifted and talented: Developmental perspectives.* Washington, DC: American Psychological Association.

Janus, S. S. & Janus, C. L. (1993). *The Janus report.* New York: Wiley.

Japenga, A. (1982). The birds that hunt people. *Los Angeles Times,* May 19 Part V, 1,2.

Jarvik, E. M. (1964). Ciba found. In H. Steinberg et al., *Symposium of animal pharmacology drug action.*

Jehu, D. (1984) Sexual inadequacy. In K. Howells (Ed.), *The psychology of sexual diversity.* Oxford, U.K.: Basil Blackwell.

Jellinik, E. M. (1960). *The disease concept of alcoholism.* New Haven: Hill House.

Jenkins, J. G., & Dallenbach, K. M. (1924). Oblivescence during sleep and waking. *American Journal of Psychology,* 35, 605–612.

Jensen, A. R. (1969). How much can we boost IQ and scholastic achievement? *Harvard Educational Review,* 39(1), 1–123.

Jensen, A. R. (1992). Understanding g in terms of information processing. *Educational Psychology Review,* 4(3), 271–308.

Jensen, J. P., Bergin, A. E., & Greaves, D. W. (1990). The meaning of eclecticism: New survey and analysis of components. *Professional Psychology: Research & Practice, 21*(2), 124–130.

Jensen, M. D., Benson, R. C., & Bobak, I. M. (1981). *Maternity care. The nurse and the family.* St. Louis: Mosby.

Jerabek, I. & Standing, L. (1992). Imagined test situations produce contextual memory enhancement. *Perceptual & Motor Skills, 75(2),* 400.

Jewell, L. N. (1989). *Psychology and effective behavior.* St. Paul, MN: West.

Jewell, L. N. (1990). *Contemporary industrial/organizational psychology.* St. Paul, MN: West.

Johnson, B. T. (1991). Insights about attitudes: Meta-analytic perspectives. *Personality & Social Psychology Bulletin, 17*(3), 289–299.

Johnson, D. W. & Johnson, R. T. (1987). *Learning together and alone: Cooperative, competitive, and individualistic learning.* Englewood Cliffs, NJ: Prentice-Hall.

Johnson, J. S. & Newport, E. L. (1989). Critical period effects in second language learning: The influence of maturational state on the acquisition of English as a second language. *Cognitive Psychology, 21*(1), 60–99.

Johnson, M. K. & Hasher, L. (1987). Human learning and memory. *Annual Review of Psychology,* 38, 631–668.

Johnson, P. C., Jr. (1984). Space medicine. *American Scientist, 72,* 495–498.

Johnson, S. M., & White, G. (1971). Self-observation as an agent of behavioral change. *Behavior Therapy,* 2, 488–497.

Johnston, W. A. & Dark, V. J. (1986). Selective attention. *Annual Review of Psychology,* 37, 43–75.

Jones, E. E., & Nisbett, R. E. (1971). The actor and observer: Divergent perceptions of the causes of behavior. In E. E. Jones, D. E. Kanouse, H. H. Kelley, R. E. Nisbett, S. Valins, & B. Weiner (Eds.). *Attribution: Perceiving the causes of behavior.* Morristown, NJ: General Learning Press.

Jones, L. V. & Appelbaum, M. L. (1989). Psychometric methods. *Annual Review of Psychology, 40,* 23–43.

Jones, S. S., Collins, K., & Hong, H. W. (1991). An audience effect on smile production in 10-month-old infants. *Psychological Science, 2,* 45–49.

Jones, W. R., & Ellis, N. R. (1962). Inhibitory potential in rotary pursuit acquisition. *Journal of Experimental Psychology, 63,* 534–537.

Jourard, S. M. (1963). *Personal adjustment.* New York: Macmillan.

Jourard, S. M. (1966). An exploratory study of body-accessibility. *British Journal of Social and Clinical Psychology,* 5, 221-231.

Jourard, S. M. (1974). *Healthy personality.* New York: Macmillan.

Joy, L. A., Kimball, M. M., & Zabrack, M. L. (1986). Television and aggressive behavior. In T. M. Williams (Ed.), *The impact of television: A natural experiment involving three towns.* New York: Academic.

Joyce, C. (1984). Space travel is no joyride. *Psychology Today,* May, 30–37.

Judson, A. I., & Cofer, C. N. (1956). Reasoning as an associative process: I. "Direction" in a simple verbal problem. *Psychological Reports,* 2, 469–476.

Julesz, B. (1971). *Foundations of cyclopean perception.* Chicago: University of Chicago Press.

Julesz, B. (1975). Experiments in the visual perception of texture. *Scientific American, 232*(April), 34–43.

Julien, R. M. (1988). *A primer of drug action.* San Francisco: Freeman.

Jurma, W. E. & Powell, M. L. (1994). Perceived gender roles of managers and effective conflict management. *Psychological Reports, 74*(1), 104–106.

Jussim, L. and Eccles, J. S. (1992). Teacher expectations. *Journal of Personality & Social Psychology, 63*(6), 947–961.

Kagan, J. (1971). *Change and continuity in infancy.* New York: Wiley.

Kagan, J. (1989). Temperamental contributions to social behavior. *American Psychologist, 44*(4), 668–674.

Kagan, J. (1991). The theoretical utility of constructs for self. *Developmental Review, 11(3),* 244–250.

Kagan, J., & Klein, R. E. (1973). Cross-cultural perspectives on early development. *American Psychologist, 28,* 947–961.

Kahneman, D., & Tversky, A. (1972). Subjective probability: A judgment of representativeness. *Cognitive Psychology,* 3, 430–454.

Kahneman, D., & Tversky, A. (1973). On the psychology of prediction. *Psychological Review, 80,* 237–251.

Kahneman, D., Slovic, P., & Tversky, A. (1982). *Judgment under uncertainty: Heuristics and biases.* Cambridge: Cambridge University Press.

Kakigi, R., Matsuda, Y., & Kuroda, Y. (1993). Effects of movement-related cortical activities on pain-related somatosensory evoked potentials. *Acta Neurologica Scandinavica, 88*(5), 376–380.

Kaluger, G., & Kaluger, M. F. (1984). *Human development.* St. Louis: Times Mirror/Mosby.

Kamin, L. J. (1981). *The intelligence controversy.* New York: Wiley.

Kamin, L. J. (1985). Genes and behavior: The missing link. *Psychology Today,* Oct., 76–78.

Kamiya, J. (1968). Conscious control of brain waves. *Psychology Today 1,* 57–66.

Kamphaus, R. W. (1993). *Clinical assessment of children's intelligence.* Needham Heights, MA: Allyn and Bacon.

Kandel, E. R. (1976). *Cellular basis of behavior: An introduction to behavioral neurobiology.* San Francisco: Freeman.

Kaplan, H. S. (1974). *The new sex therapy.* New York: Brunner/Mazel.

Kaplan, M. (1983). The issue of sex bias in DSM-III: Comments on the articles by Spitzer, Williams, and Kass. *American Psychologist,* 38, 802–803.

Kaplan, P. S., & Stein, J. (1984). *Psychology of adjustment.* Belmont, CA: Wadsworth.

Kapleau, P. (1966). *The three pillars of Zen.* New York: Harper & Row.

Kasamatsu, A., & Hirai, T. (1966). An electroencephalographic study of Zen meditation (Zazen). *Folia Psychiatria et Neurologia Japonica, 20,* 315–336. Reprinted in Tart, (1975), *Altered states of consciousness.*

Kasser, T. & Ryan, R. M. (1993). A dark side of the American dream: Correlates of financial success as a central life aspiration. *Journal of Personality & Social Psychology, 65*(2), 410–422.

Kassin, S. M., Ellsworth, P. C., & Smith, V. L. (1989). The "general acceptance" of psychological research on eyewitness testimony a survey of the experts. *American Psychologist, 44,* 1089–1098.

Kastenbaum, R., & Aisenberg R. (1972). *The psychology of death.* New York: Springer.

Katahn, M. (1984). *Beyond diet.* New York: Norton.

Katahn, M. & McMinn, M. R. (1990). Obesity: A biobehavioral point of view. *Annals of the New York Academy of Sciences, 602,* 189–204.

Katz, M. R. (1993). *Computer-assisted career decision making.* Educational Testing Service.

Katzman, R. (1988). Research directions in Alzheimer's Disease: Advances and opportunities. In M. K. Aronson (Ed.), *Understanding Alzheimer's Disease.* New York: Scribner's.

Kaufman, L. & Rock, I. (1989). The moon illusion thirty years later. In Hershenson, M. (Ed.), *The moon illusion.* Hillsdale, NJ: Erlbaum.

Kazdin, A. E. (1975). *Behavior modification in applied settings.* Homewood, IL: Dorsey Press.

Kazdin, A. E. (1988). The token economy: A decade later. In G. Davey & C. Cullen (Eds.), *Human operant conditioning and behavior modification.* New York: Wiley.

Kearney, M. (1984). A comparison of motivation to avoid success in males and females. *Journal of Clinical Psychology, 40,* 1005–1007.

Keating, J. P., & Loftus, E. F. (1981). The logic of fire escape. *Psychology Today,* June, 14–19.

Keefe, F. J. (1982). Behavioral assessment and treatment of chronic pain: Current status and future directions. *Journal of Consulting and Clinical Psychology, 50,* 896–911.

Keeffe, P. (1977). Ice after death. *Novus,* Sept., 29–33.

Kellehear, A. (1993). Culture, biology, and the near-death experience. *Journal of Nervous & Mental Disease, 181*(3), 148–156.

Kellermann, A. L., Rivara, F. P., Rushforth, N. B., Banton, J. G. et al. (1993). Gun ownership as a risk factor for homicide in the home. *New England Journal of Medicine,* 329(15), 1084–1091.

Kelley, H. H. (1950). The warm-cold variable in first impressions of persons. *Journal of Personality, 18,* 431–439.

Kelley, H. H. (1967). Attribution in social psychology. *Nebraska Symposium on Motivation, 15,* 192–238.

Kelley, H. H. (1971). *Attribution in social interaction.* Morristown, NJ: General Learning Press.

Kelly, A. D. & Kanas, N. (1993). Communication between space crews and ground personnel. *Aviation, Space, & Environmental Medicine, 64*(9, Sect. 1), 795–800.

Kelly, I. W. & Saklofske, D. H. (1994).. Psychology and pseudoscience. *Encyclopedia of human behavior,* 3, 611–618.

Kelly, I. W., Culver, R., & Loptson, P. J. (1989). Astrology and science: An examination of the evidence. In S. K. Biswas et al. (Eds.), *Cosmosperspectives.* Cambridge: Cambridge University Press.

Kelly, T. H., Foltin, R. W., Emurian, C. S., & Fischman, M. W. (1990). Multidimensional behavioral effects of marijuana. *Progress in Neuro-*

psychopharmacology & Biological Psychiatry, 14(6), 885–902.

Kelman, H. C., & Hamilton, V. L. (1989). *Crimes of obedience.* New Haven, CT: Yale University Press.

Kemper, E. (1991). *Antidepressants update.* United States Food and Drug Administration, Paper T91-64.

Kempton, W., Darley, J. M., & Stern, P. C. (1992). Psychological research for the new energy problems. *American Psychologist, 47*(10), 1213–1232.

Kendall-Tackett, K. A. & Simon, A. F. (1992). A comparison of the abuse experiences of male and female adults molested as children. *Journal of Family Violence,* 7(1), 57–62.

Kendrick, D. T. & MacFarlane, S. W. (1986). Ambient temperature and horn honking: A field study of the heat/aggression relationship. *Environment and Behavior,* 18(2), 1986, 179–191.

Kennedy, J. M. (1983). What can we learn about pictures from the blind? *American Scientist, 71,* 19–26.

Kennell, J. H., & Klaus, M. H. (1984). Mother-infant bonding: Weighing the evidence. *Developmental Review, 4,* 275–282.

Kessen, W. & Cahan, E. D. (1986). A century of psychology: From subject to object to agent. *American Scientist, 74,* 640–649.

Kety, S. S. (1979, Sept.). Disorders of the human brain. *Scientific American, 241,* 202–214.

Keys, A., Brozek, J., Henschel, A., Mickelson, O., & Taylor, H. L. (1950). *The biology of human starvation.* Minneapolis: University of Minnesota Press.

Kiecolt-Glaser, J. K. & Glaser, R. (1992). Psychoneuroimmunology: Can psychological interventions modulate immunity? *Journal of Consulting & Clinical Psychology,* 60(4), 569–575.

Kiecolt-Glaser, J. K. & Glaser, R. (1988). Psychological influences on immunity: Implications for AIDS. *American Psychologist,* 43(11), 892–898.

Kiewra, K. A.; DuBois, N. F.; Christian, D.; McShane, A.; et al. (1991). Note-taking functions and techniques. *Journal of Educational Psychology, 83(2),* 240–245.

Kihlstrom, J. F. (1985). Hypnosis. *Annual Review of Psychology 36,* (385–418).

Kim, A., Martin, D., & Martin, M. (1989). Effects of personality on marital satisfaction. *Family Therapy, 16*(3), 243–248.

Kimball, M. M. (1986). Television and sex-role attitudes. In T. M. Williams (Ed.), *The impact of television: A natural experiment in three communities.* Orlando, FL: Academic.

Kimble, D. P. (1990). Functional effects of neural grafting in the mammalian central nervous system. *Psychological Bulletin, 108*(3), 462–479.

Kimble, G. A. (1961). *Hilgard and Marquis' conditioning and learning.* New York: Appleton-Century-Crofts.

Kimble, G. A. (1989). Psychology from the standpoint of a generalist. *American Psychologist, 44*(3), 491–499.

Kimmel, D. C. (1988). Ageism, psychology, and public policy. *American Psychologist, 43*(3), 175–178.

Kimmel, D. C. (1990). *Adulthood and aging.* New York: Wiley & Sons.

King, A. (1992). Comparison of self-questioning, summarizing, and notetaking-review as strategies for learning from lectures. *American Educational Research Journal, 29(2),* 303–323.

King, H. E. (1961). Psychological effects of excitation in the limbic system. In D. E. Sheer (Ed.). *Electrical stimulation of the brain.* Austin: University of Texas Press.

Kinsey, A., Pomeroy, W., & Martin, C. (1948). *Sexual behavior in the human male.* Philadelphia: Saunders.

Kinsey, A., Pomeroy, W., & Martin, C. (1953). *Sexual behavior in the human female.* Philadelphia: Saunders.

Kipnis, D. (1987). Psychology and behavioral technology. *American Psychologist, 42,* 30–36.

Kipper, D. A. (1992). The effect of two kinds of role playing on self-evaluation of improved assertiveness. *Journal of Clinical Psychology, 48*(2), 246–250.

Kirsch, I., Mobayed, C. P., Council, J. R., & Kenny, D. (1992). Expert judgments of hypnosis from subjective state reports. *Journal of Abnormal Psychology, 101*(4), 657–662.

Kitcher, P. (1985). *Vaulting ambition: Sociobiology and the quest for human nature.* Cambridge, MA: MIT Press.

Klaus, M. H., & Kennell, J. H. (1982). *Parent-infant bonding.* St. Louis: Mosby.

Klausmeir, H. J., & Goodwin, W. (1975). *Learning and human abilities.* New York: Harper & Row.

Kleinke, C. L. (1978). *Self-perception: The psychology of personal awareness.* San Francisco: Freeman.

Kleinke, C. L. (1986). *Meeting and understanding people.* New York: Freeman.

Kleinknecht, R. A. (1986). *The anxious self: Diagnosis and treatment of fears and phobias.* New York: Human Sciences Press.

Klinger, E. (1990). *Daydreaming.* Los Angeles, CA: J. P. Tarcher.

Kluft, R. P. (1988). The postunification treatment of multiple personality disorder. *American Journal of Psychotherapy,* 42(2), 212–228.

Knapp, M. L. (1978). *Nonverbal communication in human interaction.* New York: Holt, Rinehart and Winston.

Knesper, D. J., Belcher, B. E., & Cross, J. G. (1989). A market analysis comparing the practices of psychiatrists and psychologists. *Archives of General Psychiatry,* 46(4), 305–314.

Knox, D. (1984). *Human sexuality.* St. Paul, MN: West.

Kogan, N. (1990). Personality and Aging. In J. E. Birren & Warner Schaie (Eds.), *Handbook of the psychology of aging.* San Diego, CA: Academic.

Kohlberg, L. (1969). The cognitive-developmental approach to socialization. In A. Goslin (Ed.), *Handbook of socialization theory and research.* Chicago: Rand McNally.

Kohlberg, L. (1981a). *Essays on moral development. Vol. I. The philosophy of moral development.* San Francisco: Harper.

Kohlberg, L. (1981b). *The meaning and measurement of moral development.* Worcester, MA: Clark University Press.

Kohler, I. (1962). Experiments with goggles. *Scientific American,* Offprint No. 465, 62–72.

Kohler, W. (1925). *The mentality of apes.* New York: Harcourt Brace Jovanovich.

Kohn, A. (1987). Art for art's sake. *Psychology Today,* Sept., 52–57.

Kohn, A. (1988). Shock therapy makes a comeback. *Los Angeles Times,* March 21, 1988, Part II, 5.

Kolb, B. (1989). Brain development, plasticity, and behavior. *American Psychologist, 44*(9), 1203–1212.

Koocher, G. P. (1977). Bathroom behavior and human dignity. *Journal of Personality and Social Psychology,* 35, 120–121.

Koop, C. E. (1988a). *The health consequences of smoking: Addiction.* United States Surgeon General's Report. Washington DC: United States Government Printing Office.

Koop, C. E. (1988b). *Understanding AIDS.* HHS Publication No. (CDC) HHS-88-8404. U.S. Department of Health and Human Services, Rockville, MD.

Korte, C., & Milgram, S. (1970). Acquaintance networks between racial groups. *Journal of Personality & Social Psychology, 15,* 101–108.

Koss, M. P. (1993). Rape. *American Psychologist,* 48(10), 1062–1069.

Koss, M., Gidycz, C. A., & Wisniewski, N. (1987). The scope of rape: Incidence and prevalence of sexual aggression and victimization in a national sample of higher education students. *Journal of Consulting and Clinical Psychology,* 55(2), 162–170.

Kosslyn, S. M. (1975). Information representation in visual images. *Cognitive Psychology,* 7, 341–370.

Kosslyn, S. M. (1983). *Ghosts in the mind's machine.* New York: Norton.

Kosslyn, S. M. (1985). Stalking the mental image. *Psychology Today,* May, 23–28.

Kosslyn, S. M. (1990). Mental imagery. In D. N. Osherson, S. M. Kosslyn, & J. M. Hollerbach (Eds.), *Visual cognition and action.* Cambridge, MA: The MIT Press.

Kosslyn, S. M., Ball, T. M., & Reiser, B. J. (1978). Visual images preserve metric spatial information: Evidence from studies of image scanning. *Journal of Experimental Psychology: Human Perception and Performance, 4,* 47–60.

Kosslyn, S. M.; Seger, C.; Pani, J. R.; & Hillger, L. A. (1990). When is imagery used in everyday life? A diary study. *Journal of Mental Imagery, 14*(3-4), 131–152.

Kottler, J. A., & Brown, R. W. (1992). *Introduction to therapeutic counseling.* Monterey, CA: Brooks/Cole.

Koukkou, M., & Lehmann, D. (1968). EEG and Memory storage in sleep experiments with humans. *Electroencephalography and Clinical Neurophysiology,* 25, 455–462.

Krakow, B. & Neidhardt, J. (1992). *Conquering bad dreams and nightmares.* Berkley Books.

Kramer, P. D. (1993). *Listening to Prozac.* New York: Viking.

Krech, D., Rosenzweig, M. R., & Bennett, E. L. (1962). Relations between brain chemistry and problem solving among rats raised in enriched and impoverished environments. *Journal of Comparative and Physiological Psychology,* 55, 801–807.

Kring, A. M., Kerr, S. L., Smith, D. A., & Neale,

J. M. (1993). Flat affect in schizophrenia does not reflect diminished subjective experience of emotion. *Journal of Abnormal Psychology, 102*(4), 507–517.

Krivascka, J. J., Savin-Williams, R. C., & Slater, B. R. (1992, Nov. 8). *Background paper for the resolution on lesbian, gay, and bisexual youths in the schools.*

Kroll, N. E. A., Schepeler, E. M. & Angin, K. T. (1986). Bizarre imagery: The misremembered mnemonic. *Journal of Experimental Psychology: Learning, Memory, and Cognition, 12*, 42–53.

Kroon, M. B., Van Kreveld, D., & Rabbie, J. M. (1992). Group versus individual decision making: Effects of accountability and gender on groupthink. *Small Group Research, 23(4)*, 427–458.

Krosnick, J. A., Betz, A. L., Jussim, L. J., & Lynn, A. R. (1992). Subliminal conditioning of attitudes. *Personality & Social Psychology Bulletin, 18*(2), 152–162.

Kruger, L., & Liebeskind, J. C. (eds.). (1984). *Advances in pain research and therapy.* New York: Raven Press.

Kubey, R., & Csikszentmihalyi, M. (1990). *Television and the quality of life.* Hillsdale, NJ: Erlbaum.

Kubler-Ross, E. (1975). *Death: The final stage of growth.* Englewood Cliffs, NJ: Prentice-Hall.

Kuhn, D. (1993). Thinking as an epistemological enterprise. *Applied Psychology: An International Review, 42*(3), 226–228.

Kulik, J. A., Bangert-Drowns, R. L., & Kulik, C. C. (1984). Effectiveness of coaching for aptitude tests. *Psychological Bulletin, 95*, 179–188.

Kulik, J. A., Kulik, C. C., & Cohen, P. A. (1980). Effectiveness of computer-based college teaching: A meta-analysis of findings. *Review of Educational Research, 50*, 525–544.

Kunkel, M. A. (1993). A teaching demonstration involving perceived lunar size. *Teaching of Psychology, 20*(3), 178–180.

Kunzendorf, R. G. (1989). After-images of eidetic images: A developmental study. *Journal of Mental Imagery, 13*(1), 55–62.

La Berge, S. P. (1981). Lucid dreaming: Directing the action as it happens. *Psychology Today*, Jan., 48–57.

La Berge, S.P. (1985). *Lucid dreaming.* Los Angeles: Tarcher.

Labbe, R., Firl, A., Jr., Mufson, E. J., & Stein, D. G. (1983). Fetal brain transplants: Reduction of cognitive deficits in rats with frontal cortex lesions. *Science, 221*, 470–472.

Labov, W. (1973). The boundaries of words and their meanings. In C. J. N. Bailey & R. W. Shuy (Eds.) *New Ways of analyzing variation in English.* Washington, DC: Georgetown University Press.

Lackner, J. R. & DiZio, P. (1993). Multisensory, cognitive, and motor influences on human spatial orientation in weightlessness. *Journal of Vestibular Research, 3*(3), 361–372.

Lacks, P. & Morin, C. M. (1992). Recent advances in the assessment and treatment of insomnia. *Journal of Clinical and Consulting Psychology, 60*(4), 586–594.

Lagerspetz, K. (1981). Combining aggression studies in infra-humans and man. In P. F. Brian & D. Benton (Eds.), *Multidisciplinary approaches to aggression research.* New York: Elsevier/North-Holland.

Laing, R. D. (1967). *The politics of experience.* New York: Pantheon.

Laing, R. D. (1970). *The divided self.* New York: Pantheon.

Laird, J. D. (1974). Self-attribution of emotion: The effects of expressive behavior on the quality of emotional experience. *Journal of Personality & Social Psychology, 29*, 475–486.

Laird, J. D. (1984). The real role of facial response in the experience of emotion. *Journal of Personality & Social Psychology, 47*, 909–917.

Lambert, W. E. (1987). The effects of bilingual and bicultural experiences on children's attitudes and social perspectives. In P. Homel, M. Palij, & D. Aaronson (Eds.), *Childhood bilingualism.* Hillsdale, NJ: Erlbaum.

Landers, S. (1989). In U.S., mental disorders affect 15 percent of adults. *The APA Monitor*, Jan., p. 16.

Landers, S. (1986). Judge reiterates I.Q. test ban. *APA Monitor*, Dec., 18.

Landy, F. J., Shankster, L. J., & Kohler, S. S. (1994). Personnel selection and placement. *Annual Review of Psychology, 45*, 261–296.

Langer, E. J., & Abelson, R. P. (1974). A patient by any other name: Clinician group difference in labeling bias. *Journal of Consulting and Clinical Psychology, 42*(1), 4–9.

Langer, E. J., & Piper, A. I. (1987). Prevention of mindblindness. *Journal of Personality & Social Psychology, 53*, 280–287.

Lanzetta, J. T. & Englis, B. G. (1989). Expectations of cooperation and competition and their effects on observers' vicarious emotional responses. *Journal of Personality & Social Psychology, 56*(4), 543–554.

Larkin, K. T., Manuck, S. B., & Kasprowicz, A. L. (1990). The effect of feedback-assisted reduction in heart rate reactivity on videogame performance. *Biofeedback & Self Regulation, 15*(4), 285–303.

Larsen, R. J. & Kasimatis, M. (1990). Individual differences in entrainment of mood to the weekly calendar. *Journal of Personality & Social Psychology, 58*(1), 164–171.

Larson, D. E. (Ed.) (1990). *Mayo Clinic family healthbook.* New York: Morrow.

Latane, L., Nida, S. A., & Wilson, D. W. (1981). The effects of group size on helping behavior. In J. P. Rushton & R. M. Sorrentino (Eds.), *Altruism and helping behavior: Social, personality and developmental perspectives.* Hillsdale, NJ: Erlbaum.

Laumann, E., Michael, R., Michaels, S., & Gagnon, J. (1994). The social organization of sexuality. Chicago: University of Chicago Press.

Laurence, J., & Perry, C. (1983). Hypnotically created memory among highly hypnotizable subjects. *Science, 222*, 523–524.

Lazarus, A. H. (1964). The treatment of chronic frigidity by systematic desensitization. In H. J. Eysenck (Ed.). *Experiments in behavior therapy.* New York: Pergamon.

Lazarus, R. S. (1981a). Little hassles can be hazardous to health. *Psychology Today*, July, 12–14.

Lazarus, R. S. (1991a). Progress on a cognitive-motivational-relational theory of emotion. *American Psychologist, 46*(8), 819–834.

Lazarus, R. S. (1991b). Cognition and motivation in emotion. *American Psychologist, 46*(4), 352–367.

Lazarus, R. S., & Folkman, S. (1984). *Stress, appraisal, and coping.* New York: Springer.

Lazarus, R. S., (1993). From psychological stress to the emotions: A history of changing outlooks. In L. W. Porter and M. R. Rosenzweig (Eds.), *Annual Review of Psychology, 44*, 1–21.

Lazarus, R. S., DeLongis, A., Folkman, S., & Gruen, R. (1985). Stress and adaptational outcomes. *American Psychologist, 40*, 770–779.

Leboyer, F. (1975). *Birth without violence.* New York: Knopf.

Lee, C. C. (1991a). Cultural dynamics. In C. C. Lee & B. L. Richardson (Eds.), *Multicultural issues in counseling.* Alexandria, VA: American Association for Counseling and Development.

Lee, C. C. (1991b). New approaches to diversity. In C. C. Lee & B. L. Richardson (Eds.), *Multicultural issues in counseling.* Alexandria, VA: American Association for Counseling and Development.

Lee, C. C. & Richardson, B. L. (1991). Promise and pitfalls of multicultural counseling. In C. C. Lee & B. L. Richardson (Eds.), *Multicultural issues in counseling.* Alexandria, VA: American Association for Counseling and Development.

Lee, M., Zimbardo, P. G., & Bertholf, M. (1977). Shy murderers. *Psychology Today*, Nov.

Lee, R. T. & Ashforth, B. E. (1990). On the meaning of Maslach's three dimensions of burnout. *Journal of Applied Psychology, 75*(6), 743–747.

Lee, T. D. & Carnahan, H. (1990). When to provide knowledge of results during motor learning: Scheduling effects. *Human Performance, 3*(2), 87–105.

Lee, T., & Seeman, P. (1980). Elevation of brain neuroleptic/dopamine receptors in schizophrenia. *American Journal of Psychiatry, 137*, 191–197.

Lee, V. E., Brooks-Gunn, J. & Schnur, E. (1988). Does Head Start work? A 1-year follow-up comparison of disadvantaged children attending Head Start, no preschool, and other preschool programs. *Developmental Psychology, 24*(2), 210–222.

Lee, V. E., Brooks-Gunn, J., Schnur, E., & Liaw, F. (1990). Are Head Start effects sustained? *Child Development, 61*(2), 495–507.

Leeper, R. W. (1935). A study of a neglected portion of the field of learning: The development of sensory organization. *Pedagogical Seminary and Journal of Genetic Psychology, 46*, 41–75.

Lefkowitz, M., Blake, R. R., & Mouton, J. S. (1955). Status factors in pedestrian violation of traffic signals. *Journal of Abnormal and Social Psychology, 51*, 704–706.

Lemley, B. (1986). I'm not a nerd. *Parade Magazine*, June, 22, 8–9.

Lenzenweger, M. F., Cornblatt, B. A., & Putnick, M. (1991). Schizotypy and sustained attention. *Journal of Abnormal Psychology, 100*(1), 84–89.

Lepore, S. J., Evans, G. W., & Schneider, M. L. (1992). Role of control and social support in explaining the stress of hassles and crowding. *Environment & Behavior, 24*(6), 795–811.

Lepper, M. R. (1985). Microcomputers in education. *American Psychologist, 40*, 1–18.

Lerner, R. M. & von Eye, A. (1992). Sociobiology and human development: Arguments and evidence. *Hu-man Development*, 35(1), 12–33.

Lester, B. M., Corwin, M. L., Sepkoski, C., Seifer, R. et al. (1991). Neurobehavioral syndromes in cocaine-exposed newborn infants. *Child Development, 62(4)*, 694–705.

Lester, D. (1990). Biorhythms and the timing of death. *Skeptical Inquirer, 14*(4), 410–411.

Lett, J. (1990). A field guide to critical thinking. *Skeptical Inquirer, 14*(Winter), 153–160.

Lettvin, J. Y. (1961). Two remarks on the visual system of the frog. In W. Rosenblith (Ed.), *Sensory communication*. Cambridge, MA: MIT Press.

LeVay, S. (1993). *The sexual brain*. Cambridge, MA: The MIT Press.

Leventhal, E. A., Leventhal, H., Shacham, S., & Easterling, D. V. (1989). Active coping reduces reports of pain from childbirth. *Journal of Consulting & Clinical Psychology*, 57(3), 365–371.

Leveton, E. (1977). *Psychodrama for the timid clinician*. New York: Springer.

Levin, S., Yurgelun-Todd, D., & Craft, S. (1989). Contributions of clinical neuropsychology to the study of schizophrenia. *Journal of Abnormal Psychology*, 98(4), 341–356.

Levine, J. M. & Moreland, R. L. (1990). Progress in small group research. *Annual Review of Psychology, 41*, 485–634.

Levine, M., Toro, P. A., & Perkins, D. V., (1993). Social and community interventions. In L. W. Porter and M. R. Rosenzweig (Eds.), *Annual Review of Psychology, 44*, 525–558.

Levine, R. V. (1990). The pace of life. *American Scientist*, 78(Sept.-Oct.), 450–458.

Levinger, G. (1986). Editor's Page. *Journal of Social Issues*, 42(3).

Levinson, D. J. (1986). A conception of adult development. *American Psychologist, 41*(1), 3–13.

Levinson, D. J. (in press). *Seasons of woman's life*. New York: Knopf.

Levis, D. J. (1989). The case for a return to a two-factor theory of avoidance: The failure of non-fear interpretations. In S. B Klein & R. R. Mower (Eds.), *Contemporary learning theories*. Hillsdale, NJ: Erlbaum.

Levy, D. A. (1989). Social support and the media: Analysis of responses by radio psychology talk show hosts. *Professional Psychology: Research & Practice*, 20(2), 73–78.

Levy, J., & Reid, M. (1976). Cerebral organization. *Science*, 337–339.

Lewin, R. (1974). The brain through a cat's eyes. *Saturday Review/World*, Oct. 5.

Lewis, M., & Brooks-Gunn, J. (1979). *Social cognition and the acquisition of self*. New York: Plenum.

Lichtenstein, E. (1982). The smoking problem: A behavioral perspective. *Journal of Consulting and Clinical Psychology*, 50, 804–819.

Lieberman, D. A. (1979). Behaviorism and the mind: A (limited) call for a return to introspection. *American Psychologist*, 34, 319–333.

Lieberman, R. P., Fearn, C. H., Derisi, W., Roberts, J., & Carmona, M. (1976). The credit-incentive system: Motivating the participation of patients in a day hospital. *British Journal of Clinical Psychology, 15*.

Lilly, J. C. (1972). *The center of the cyclone*. New York: Julian Press.

Lindsley, J. G., Hartmann, E. L., & Mitchell, W. (1983). Selectivity in response to L-tryptophan among insomniac subjects: A preliminary report. *Sleep*, 6(3), 247–256.

Lindvall, O., Brundin, P., Widner, H., Rehncrona, S., Gustavii, B., et al. (1990). Grafts of fetal dopamine neurons survive and improve motor function in Parkinson's disease. *Science*, 247(4942) 574–577.

Linton, M. (1979). I remember it well. *Psychology Today*, July, 81–86.

Linz, D. G., Donnerstein, E., & Penrod, S. (1988). Effects of long-term exposure to violent and sexually degrading depictions of women. *Journal of Personality & Social Psychology*, 55(5), 758–768.

Lipman, J. J., Miller, B. E., Mays, K. S., Miller, M. N. et al. (1990). Peak B-endorphin concentration in cerebrospinal fluid: Reduced in chronic pain patients and increased during the placebo response. *Psychopharmacology, 102*(1), 112–116.

Lipowski, Z. J. (1988). Somatization: The concept and its clinical application. *American Journal of Psychiatry, 145*(11), 1358–1368.

Lipsey, M. W. & Wilson, D. B. (1993). The efficacy of psychological, educational, and behavioral treatment. *American Psychologist*, 48(12), 1181–1209.

Lipsitt, L. (1990). Nurture is what affects whether or not the genes get to "play out." *The APA Monitor*, Dec., 13.

Lissner, L., Odell, P. M., D'Agostino, R. B. et al. (1991). Variability of body weight and health outcomes in the Farmington population. *The New England Journal of Medicine*, 324(26), 1839–1844.

Lisspers, J. & Ost, L. (1990). Long-term follow-up of migraine treatment: Do the effects remain up to six years? *Behaviour Research & Therapy*, 28(4), 313–322.

Locke, K. D. & Horowitz, L. M. (1990). Satisfaction in interpersonal interactions as a function of similarity in level of dysphoria. *Journal of Personality & Social Psychology*, 58(5), 823–831.

Loehlin, J. C., Willerman, L., & Horn, J. M. (1988). Human behavior genetics. *Annual Review of Psychology*, 39, 101–133.

Loftus, E. (1977). Shifting human color memory. *Memory & Cognition*, 5, 696–699.

Loftus, E. (1979). Words that could save your life. *Psychology Today*, Nov., 102, 105–106.

Loftus, E. (1980). *Memory*. Reading MA: Addison-Wesley.

Loftus, E. (1993). Psychologists in the eyewitness world. *American Psychologist, 48(5)*, 550–552.

Loftus, E. (1993). The reality of repressed memories. *American Psychologist, 48(5)*, 518–537.

Loftus, E. & Ketcham, K. (1991). *Witness for the defense*. New York: St. Martin's Press.

Loftus, E. F. (1994). The repressed memory controversy. *American Psychologist*, 49(5), 443–444.

Loftus, E., & Loftus, G. (1980). On the permanence of stored information in the human brain. *American Psychologist*, 35, 409–420.

Loftus, E., & Monahan, J. (1980). Trial by data: Psychological research as legal evidence. *American Psychologist*, 35, 270–283.

Loftus, E., & Palmer, J. C. (1974). Reconstruction of automobile destruction: An example of interaction between language and memory. *Journal of Verbal Learning and Verbal Behavior*, 13, 585–589.

Loftus, G. R. & Mackworth, N. H. (1978). Cognitive determinants of fixation location during picture viewing. *Journal of Experimental Psychology: Human Perception and Performance*, 4, 565–572.

Long, D. M. (1991). Fifteen years of transcutaneous electrical stimulation for pain control. *Stereotactic & Functional Neurosurgery, 56(1)*, 2–19.

Long, E. C. & Andrews, D. W. (1990). Perspective taking as a predictor of marital adjustment. *Journal of Personality & Social Psychology*, 59(1), 126–131.

Long, V. 0. (1989). Relation of masculinity to self-esteem and self-acceptance in male professionals, college students, and clients. *Journal of Counseling Psychology*, 36(1), 84–87.

Lord, L. (1985). Morality. *U.S. News & World Report*, December 9, 52–59.

Lore, R. K. & Schultz, L. A. (1993). Control of human aggression. *American Psychologist, 48(1)*, 16–25.

Lorenz, K. (1937). Imprinting. *The Auk, 54*, 245–273.

Lorenz, K. (1962). *King Solomon's ring*. New York: Time.

Lorenz, K. (1966). *On aggression*. Translated by M. Kerr-Wilson. New York: Harcourt Brace Jovanovich.

Lorenz, K. (1974). *The eight deadly sins of civilized man*. Translated by M. Kerr-Wilson. New York: Harcourt Brace Jovanovich.

Lovaas, O., & Simmons, J. (1969). Manipulation of self-destruction in three retarded children. *Journal of Applied Behavior Analysis*, 2, 143–157.

Lowenstein, J. M. (1992). Whose genome is it, anyway? *Discover*, May, 28–31.

Luborsky, L., Crits-Christoph, P., McLellan, A. T. Woody, G. et al. (1986). Do therapists vary much in their success? *American Journal of Orothopsychiatry*, 56(4), 501–512.

Lucas, F. & Sclafani, A. (1990). Hyperphagia in rats produced by a mixture of fat and sugar. *Physiology & Behavior*, 47(1), 51–55.

Luce, G. G. (1965). *Current research on sleep and dreams*. Health Service Publication, No. 1389 U.S. Department of Health, Education and Welfare.

Lumsden, C., & Wilson, E. O. (1983). *Promethean fire*. Cambridge, MA: Harvard University Press.

Luria, A. R. (1968). *The mind of a mnemonist*. New York: Basic.

Luster, T. & Dubow, E. (1991). Home environment and maternal intelligence as predictors of verbal intelligence. *Merrill-Palmer Quarterly*, 38(2) 151–175.

Lykken, D. T. (1974). Psychology and the lie detector industry. *American Psychologist*, 29, 725–739.

Lykken, D. T. (1981). *A tremor in the blood, use and abuses of the lie detector*. New York McGraw-Hill.

Lykken, D. T., McGue, M., Tellegen, A., & Bouchar, T. J. (1992). Emergenesis. *American Psychologist, 47*, 1565–1567.

Lynch, G., & Baudry, M. (1984). The biochemistry of memory: A new and specific hypothesis. *Science, 224*, 1057–1163.

Maccoby, E. E. (1990). Gender and relationships: A developmental account. *American Psychologist*, 45(4), 513–520.

Maccoby, E. E., & Jacklin, C. N. (1974). *The psychology of sex differences.* Stanford, CA: Stanford University Press.

MacCoun, R. J. (1993). Drugs and the law: A psychological analysis of drug prohibition. *Psychological Bulletin, 113*(3), 497–512.

Mack, J. E. (1986). Adolescent suicide: An architectural model. In G. L. Klerman (Ed.), *Suicide and depression among adolescents and young adults.* Washington, DC: American Psychiatric Press.

MacKinnon, D. W. (1968). Selecting students with creative potential. In P. Heist (Ed.), *The creative college student: An unmet challenge.* San Francisco: Jossey-Bass.

Macy, P. (1990). Research with animals and the new zeitgeist. *American Psychologist*, Nov., 1269.

Maddi, S. R. & Kobasa, S. C. (1984). *The hardy executive: Health under stress.* Homewood, IL: The Dorsey Press.

Madigan, S. & O'Hara, R. (1992). Short-term memory at the turn of the century. *American Psychologist, 47(2)*, 170–174.

Madsen, C. H.,Jr., Becher, W. C., Thomas, D. R., Koser, L., & Plager, E. (1968). An analysis of the reinforcing function of "sit down" commands. In R. K. Parker (Ed.), *Readings in educational psychology.* Boston: Allyn & Bacon.

Magid, K. (1988). *High risk: Children without a conscience.* New York: Bantam.

Maier, N. R. F. (1949). *Frustration.* New York: McGraw-Hill.

Main, M., & George, C. (1985). Responses of abused and disadvantaged toddlers to distress and agemates: A study in day care. *Developmental Psychology, 21*, 407–412.

Major, B., Schmidlin, A. M., & Williams, L. (1990). *Journal of Personality & Social Psychology*, 58(4), 634–643.

Malamuth, N. M., & Donnerstein, E. (1982). The effects of aggressive-pornographic mass media stimuli. In L. Berkowitz (Ed.), *Advances in Experimental Social Psychology, 15*, 103–136. New York: Academic.

Malinosky-Rummell, R. & Hansen, D. R. (1993). Long-term consequences of childhood physical abuse. *Psychological Bulletin, 114*(1), 68–79.

Man tells how rod ran through head, (1981). *Los Angeles Times*, Sept. 24, A3.

Mandler, J. M. (1990). A new perspective on cognitive development in infancy. *American Scientist*, 78(3), 236–243.

Mannuzza, S., Klein, R. G., Bessler, A., et al. (1993). Adult outcome of hyperactive boys. *Archives of General Psychiatry*, 50(7), 565–576.

Manton K. G. & Stallard, E. (1991). Cross-sectional estimates of active life expectancy for the U.S. elderly and oldest-old populations. *Journal of Gerontology, 46(3)*, 170–182.

Mantyla, T. (1986). Optimizing cue effectiveness: Recall of 600 incidentally learned words. *Journal of Experimental Psychology: Learning, Memory, and Cognition*, 12(1), 66–71.

Markman, E. M. & Seibert, J. (1976). Classes and collections: Internal organization and resulting holistic properties. *Cognitive Psychology*, 561–577.

Marks, D. F. (1990). Comprehensive commentary, insightful criticism. *Skeptical Inquirer, 14*(3), 413–418.

Marks, D.,F. & Kammann, R. (1979). *The psychology of the psychic.* Buffalo, NY: Prometheus.

Marks, M. T. (1986). The question of quality circles. *Psychology Today*, March, 36–46*ff.*

Markus, H., & Nurius, P. (1986). Possible selves. *American Psychologist, 41*, 954–969.

Marlatt, G. A., & Gordon, J. R. (Eds.). (1985). *Relapse prevention: Maintenance strategies in the treatment of addictive behaviors.* New York: Guilford.

Marlatt, G. A., Baer, J. S., Dononovan, D. M., & Kivlahan, D. R. (1988). Addictive behaviors: Etiology and treatment. *Annual Review of Psychology*, 39, 223–252.

Marmor, J. (1985). Homosexuality: Nature vs nurture. *The Harvard Medical School Mental Health Letter*, 2(4), 5–6.

Marmor, J. (ed.) (1980). *Homosexual behavior: A modern reappraisal.* New York: Basic.

Marques, P., Bradley, J., Shappee, J., & Marques, C. (1982). *Bienestar: Health, well-being and lifestyle choices for Pinal County.* Project West Pinal, University of Arizona Health Sciences Center.

Marsh, C. (1977). A framework for describing subjective states of consciousness. In N. E. Zinberg (Ed.), *Altered states of consciousness*, 121–144. New York: Free Press.

Marshall, L. L. & Rose, P. (1988). Family of origin violence and courtship abuse. *Journal of Counseling and Development*, 66(9), 414–418.

Martin, J. A., King, D. R., Maccoby, E. E., & Jacklin, C. N. (1984). Secular trends and individual differences in toilet-training progress. *Journal of Pediatric Psychology*, 9, 457–467.

Martin, R. J., White, B. D., & Hulsey, M. G. (1991). The regulation of body weight. *American Scientist, 79(Nov-Dec)*, 528–541.

Marx, J. A., Gyorky, Z. K., Royalty, G. M., & Stern, T. E. (1992). Use of self-help books in psychotherapy. *Professional Psychology: Research & Practice*, 23(4), 300–305.

Maslach, C. (1982). *Burnout: The cost of caring.* Englewood Cliffs, NJ: Prentice-Hall.

Maslow, A. H. (1954). *Motivation and personality.* New York: Harper.

Maslow, A. H. (1967). Self-actualization and beyond. In J. F. T. Bugental (Ed.), *Challenges of humanistic psychology.* New York: McGraw-Hill.

Maslow, A. H. (1969). *The psychology of science.* Chicago: Henry Regnery.

Maslow, A. H. (1970). *Motivation and personality.* New York: Harper & Row.

Maslow, A. H. (1971). *The farther reaches of human nature.* New York: Viking.

Maslow, A. H. (1968). *Toward a psychology of being.* New York: Van Nostrand.

Masters, W. H., & Johnson, V. E. (1966). *Human sexual response.* Boston: Little, Brown.

Masters, W. H., & Johnson, V. E. (1970). *The pleasure bond: A new look at sexuality and commitment.* Boston: Little, Brown.

Matarazzo, J. D. (1984). Behavioral immunogens and pathogens in health and illness. In B. L. Hammonds & C. J. Scheirer (Eds.), *Psychology and health.* Washington, DC: American Psychological Association, 5–43.

Matheny, A. P., Jr., Wilson, R. S., & Nuss, S. M. (1984). Toddler Temperament: Stability across settings and over ages. *Child Development, 55*, 1200–1211.

Matillo, G. M., Nesbitt, K. M., & Boyatzis, C. J. (in press). Effects of "The Mighty Morphin Power Rangers" on children's aggression with peers.

Matossian, M. K. (1982). Ergot and the Salem witchcraft affair. *American Scientist, 70*, 355–357.

Matson, J. L., Sevin, J. A., Fridley D., & Love, S. R. (1990). Increasing spontaneous language in three autistic children. *Journal of Applied Behavior Analysis*, 23(2), 227–223.

Matsuda, L. A., Lolait, S. J., Brownstein, M. J., Young, A. C., & Bonner, T. I. (1990). Structure of a cannabinoid receptor and functional expression of the cloned cDNA. *Nature, 346*(6284), 561–564.

Matthews, D. B. (1990). A comparison of burnout in selected occupational fields. *Career Development Quarterly*, 38(3), 230–239.

Matthews, K. A., Wing, R. R., Kulkr, L. H., et al. (1990). Influences of natural menopause on psychological characteristics and symptoms of middle-aged healthy women. *Journal of Consulting & Clinical Psychology*, 58(3), 345–351.

Maugh, T. H. (1988). Researcher uses bits, bytes and Bach for program of note. *Los Angeles Times*, August 20, Part I, 30.

Maugh, T. H. (1990). A new look at order of birth. *The Los Angeles Times*, Feb. 26, B3.

Maugh, T. H. (1992). Chemical abnormalities linked to schizophrenia. *Los Angeles Times*, July 9, A3, A22.

Maupin, E. W. (1965). Individual differences in response to a Zen meditation exercise. *Journal of Consulting Psychology, 29*, 139–145.

Mayer, R. E. (1992). *Thinking, problem solving, and cognition.* New York: Freeman.

Maziade, M., Boudreault, M., Cote, R., & Thivierge, J. (1987). Influence of gentle birth delivery procedures and other perinatal circumstances on infant temperament. *Annual Progress in Child Psychiatry & Child Development*, 291–295.

Mazurski, E. J., Bond, N. W., Siddle, D. A., & Lovibond, P. F. (1993). Classical conditioning of autonomic and affective responses to fear-relevant and fear-irrelevant stimuli. *Australian Journal of Psychology*, 45(3), 69–73.

McBurney, D. H. & Collings, V. B. (1984). *Introduction to sensation/perception*, 2nd ed. Englewood Cliffs, NJ: Prentice-Hall.

McCabe, M. P. (1992). A program for the treatment of inhibited sexual desire in males. *Psychotherapy*, 29(2), 288–296.

McCann, S. L. & Stewin, L. L. (1988). Worry, anxiety, and preferred length of sleep. *Journal of Genetic Psychology, 149*(3), 413–418.

McCardel, J., & Murray, E. J. (1974). Nonspecific factors in weekend encounter groups. *Journal of Consulting Psychology, 42*, 337–345.

McCartney, K., Bernieri, F., & Harris, M. J. (1990). Growing up and growing apart: A developmental meta-analysis of twin studies. *Psychological Bulletin, 107*(2), 226–237.

McCaul, K. D. & Malott, J. M. (1984). Distraction and coping with pain. *Psychological Bulletin, 95*, 516–533.

McCauley, E., & Ehrhardt, A. A. (1976). Female sexual response: Hormonal and behavioral interactions. *Primary Care*, 3, 455.

McCleary, R., Chew, K. S., Hellsten, J. J., & Flynn-Bransford, M. (1991). Age- and sex-specific cycles in United States suicides, 1973 to 1985. *American Journal of Public Health, 81*(11), 1494–1497.

McClelland, D. C. (1958). Risk taking in children with high and low need for achievement. In J. W. Atkinson (Ed.), *Motives in fantasy action and society.* New York: Van Nostrand.

McClelland, D. C. (1961). *The achieving society.* New York: Van Nostrand.

McClelland, D. C. (1965). Achievement and entrepreneurship. *Journal of Personality & Social Psychology, 1*, 389–393.

McClelland, D. C. (1973). Testing for competence rather than "intelligence." *American Psychologist*, 28, 1–14.

McClelland, D. C. (1975). *Power: the inner experience.* New York: Irvington.

McClelland, D. C. (1994). The knowledge-testing-educational complex strikes back. *American Psychologist*, 49(1), 66–69.

McClelland, D. C. & Pilon, D. A. (1983). Sources of adult motives in patterns of parent behavior in early childhood. *Journal of Personality & Social Psychology, 44*, 564–574.

McClelland, L., & Cook, S. W. (1980). Promoting energy conservation in master-metered apartments through group financial incentives. *Journal of Applied and Social Psychology, 10*, 20–31.

McConnell, J. V. (1989). Reinvention of subliminal perception. *The Skeptical Inquirer, 13*, 427–428.

McCrae, R. R. (1987). Creativity, divergent thinking, and openness to experience. *Journal of Personality & Social Psychology*, 52(6), 1258–1265.

McDaniel, M. A. & Schlager, M. S. (1990). Discovery learning and transfer of problem-solving skills. *Cognition & Instruction*, 7(2), 129–159.

McDonald, S. M. (1989). Sex bias in the representation of male and female characters in children's picture books. *Journal of Genetic Psychology, 150*(4), 389–401.

McEachin, J. J., Smith, T., & Lovaas, O. I. (1993). Long-term outcome for children with autism who received early intensive behavioral treatment. *American Journal of Mental Retardation*, 97(4), 359–372.

McFadden, D., & Wightman, F. L. (1983). Audition. *Annual Review of Psychology*, 34, 95–128.

McGaugh, J. L. (1983). Hormonal influences on memory. *Annual Review of Psychology*, 34, 297–323.

McGee, M. G., & Snyder, M. (1975). Attribution and behavior: Two field studies. *Journal of Personality & Social Psychology*, 32, 185–190.

McGinnies, E. (1949). Emotionality and perceptual defense. *Psychological Review*, 56, 244–251.

McGinnis, J. M. & Foege, W. H. (1993). Actual causes of death in the United States. *Journal of the American Medical Association*, 270(18), 2207–2212.

McGrady, A. (1994). Effects of group relaxation training and thermal biofeedback on blood pressure and related physiological and psychological variables in essential hypertension. *Biofeedback & Self Regulation*, 19(1), 51–66.

McGregor, D. (1960). *The human side of enterprise.* New York: McGraw-Hill.

McKean, K. (1982a). A picture of Hinckley's brain. *Discover*, 3, Aug., 78–80.

McKean, K. (1982b). Anatomy of an air crash. *Discover*, Dec., 19–21.

McKean, K. (1984). The fine art of reading voters' minds. *Discover*, May, 66–69.

McKean, K. (1985,). Of two minds: Selling the right brain. *Discover*, April, 30–40.

McKinney, J. D. (1989). Longitudinal research on the behavioral characteristics of children with learning disabilities. *Journal of Learning Disabilities*, 22(3), 141–150, 165.

McKinzie, S. J., Williamson, D. A., & Cubic, B. A. (1993). Stable and reactive body image distortions in bulimia nervosa. *Behavior Therapy*, 24(2), 195–207.

McLatchie, B. H., Lomp, K. G. (1988). Alcoholics Anonymous affiliation and treatment outcome among a clinical sample of problem drinkers. *American Journal of Drug and Alcohol Abuse, 14*(3), 309–324.

McLennan, J. (1992). "University blues": Depression among tertiary students during an academic year. British Journal of Guidance & Counselling, 20(2), 186–192.

McManus, I. C., Sik, G., Cole, D. R., Muellon, A. F., et al. (1988). The development of handedness in children. *British Journal of Developmental Psychology*, 6(3), 257–273.

McMullan, W. E., & Stocking, J. R. (1978). Conceptualizing creativity in three dimensions. *The Journal of Creative Behavior*, 12, 161–167.

McMurdo, M. E. & Gaskell, A. (1991). Dark adaptation and falls in the elderly. *Gerontology*, 37(4), 221–224.

McReynolds, P. (1989). Diagnosis And Clinical Assessment: Current Status and Major Issues. *Annual Review of Psychology*, 40, 83–108.

Mead, M. (1935). *Sex and temperament in three primitive societies.* New York: Morrow.

Medin, D. L. & Ross, B. H. (1992). *Cognitive psychology.* Fort Worth: Harcourt Brace Jovanovich.

Mednick, M. T. (1989). On the politics of psychological constructs: Stop the bandwagon, I want to get off. *American Psychologist*, 44,(8), 1118–1123.

Mehrabian, A. (1969). Significance of posture and position in the communication of attitude and status relationships. *Psychological Bulletin*, 71, 359–372.

Mehren, E. (1994). Study finds most child care lacking. *The Los Angeles Times*, April 8, E-5.

Meichenbaum, D. (1977). *Cognitive behavior modification: An integrative approach.* New York: Plenum.

Meichenbaum, D., Henshaw, D., & Himel, N. (1982). Coping with stress as a problem-solving process. In H. W. Krohne & L. Laux (Eds.), *Achievement, stress, and anxiety.* New York: Hemisphere.

Meier, R. P. (1991). Language acquisition by deaf children. *American Scientist*, 79(1), 60–70.

Melara, R. D., DeWitt-Rickards, T. S., & O'Brien, T. P. (1989). Enhancing lineup identification accuracy: Two codes are better than one. *Journal of Applied Psychology*, 74(5), 706–713.

Meleshko, K. G. & Alden, L. E. (1993). Anxiety and self-disclosure. *Journal of Personality & Social Psychology*,64(6), 1000–1009.

Melia, P., O'Sullivan, D., & Barry, D. (1988). Lithium and rapid-cycling affective disorder. *Irish Journal of Psychological Medicine*, 5(2), 79–83.

Melton, G. B. (1989). Public policy and private prejudice. *American Psychologist*, 44(6), 933–940.

Melton, R. F. (1978). Resolution of conflicting claims concerning the effect of behavioral objectives on student learning. *Review of Educational Research*, 48, 291–302.

Meltzoff A. N. (1988a). Imitation of televised models by infants. *Child Development*, 59(5), 1221–1229.

Meltzoff, A. N. (1988b). Infant imitation and memory: Nine-month-olds in immediate and deferred tests. *Child Development*, 59(1), 217–225.

Meltzoff, A. N. & Moore, M. K. (1983). Newborn infants imitate adult facial gestures. *Child Development*, 54, 702–709.

Meltzoff, A., & Moore, M. K. (1977). Imitation of facial and manual gestures by human neonates. *Science*, Oct., 75–78.

Melzack, R. (1974). Shutting the gate on pain. *Science Year: The World Book science annual.* Palo Alto, CA: Field.

Melzack, R. (1984). The myth of painless childbirth. *Pain, 19*, 321–337.

Melzack, R. & Dennis, S. G. (1978). Neurophysical foundations of pain. In R. A. Sternbach (Ed.), *The psychology of pain.* New York: Raven.

Melzack, R. & Wall, P. D. (1983). *The challenge of pain.* New York: Basic.

Menninger, K. (1964). Psychiatrists use dangerous words. *Saturday Evening Post*, April 25.

Menzies, R. G. & Clarke, J. C. (1993). A comparison of *in vivo* and vicarious exposure in the treatment of childhood water phobia. *Behaviour Research and Therapy*, 31(1), 9–15.

Meredith, N. (1984). The murder epidemic. *Science 84*, Dec., 43–48.

Merikle, P. M. & Skanes, H. E. (1992). Subliminal self-help audiotapes: A search for placebo effects. *Journal of Applied Psychology*, 77(5), 772–776.

Mermelstein, R. (1986). Social support and smoking cessation and maintenance. *Journal of Consulting & Clinical Psychology*, 54(4), 447–453.

Merritt, J. M., Stickgold, R., Pace-Schott, E., Williams, J. et al. (1994). Emotion profiles in the dreams of men and women. *Consciousness & Cognition*, 3(1), 46–60.

Mesquita, B. & Frijda, N. H. (1992). Cultural variations in emotions. *Psychological Bulletin, 112*(2), 179–204.

Messerer, J., Hunt, E., Meyers, G., & Lerner, J. (1984). Feuerstein's instrumental enrichment: A new approach for activating intellectual potential in learning disabled youth. *Journal of Learning Disabilities, 17*, 322–325.

Messick, D. M. & Mackie, D. M. (1989). Intergroup relations. *Annual Review of Psychology, 40*, 45–81.

Messick, D. M., Wilke, H., Brewer, M., Kramer, R. M., Zemke, P. E., & Lui, L. (1983). Individual adaptations and structural change as solutions to social dilemmas. *Journal of Personality & Social Psychology, 44*, 294–309.

Metcalfe, J. (1986). Premonitions of insight predict impending error. *Journal of Experimental Psychology: Learning, Memory, and Cognition, 12*, 623–634.

Metzner, B. S., Rajecki, D. W., & Lauer, J. B. (1994). New majors and the feminization of psychology. *Teaching of Psychology, 21*(1), 5–11.

Metzner, R. J. (1994). Prozac is medicine, not a miracle. *The Los Angeles Times*, March 14, B-7.

Meyer, A. J., Nash, J. D., McAlister, A. L., Maccoby, N., & Farquhar, J. W. (1980). Skills training in a cardiovascular health education campaign. *Journal of Consulting and Clinical Psychology, 48*, 129–142.

Meyer, R. G. & Youngjohn, J. R. (1991). Effects of feedback and validity expectancy on responses in a lie detector interview. *Forensic Reports, 4(3)*, 235–244.

Michotte, A. (1963). *The perception of causality*. New York: Methuen/Basic.

Middlemist, R. D., Knowles, E. S., & Matter, C. F. (1976). Personal space invasions in the lavatory: Suggestive evidence for arousal. *Journal of Personality and Social Psychology, 33*, 541–546.

Mikulincer, M. & Nachshon, O. (1991). Attachment styles and patterns of self-disclosure. *Journal of Personality & Social Psychology, 61*(2), 321–331.

Mikulincer, M., Babkoff, H., Caspy, T., & Sing, H. C. (1989). The effects of 72 hours of sleep loss on psychological variables. *British Journal of Psychology, 80*(2), 145–162.

Milgram, S. (1963). Behavioral study of obedience. *Journal of Abnormal and Social Psychology, 67*, 371–378.

Milgram, S. (1965). Some conditions of obedience and disobedience to authority. *Human Relations, 18*, 57–76.

Milgram, S. (1967). The small-world problem. *Psychology Today*, May, 61–67.

Milgram, S. (1970). The experience of living in the cities: A psychological analysis. *Science, 167*, 1461–1468.

Milgram, S. (1974). *Obedience to authority: An experimental view.* New York: Harper & Row.

Milgram, S., Bickman, L., & Berkowitz, L. (1969). Note on the drawing power of crowds of different size. *Journal of Personality & Social Psychology, 13*, 79–82.

Miller, D. B. & Holditch-Davis, D. (1992). Interactions of parents and nurses with high-risk preterm infants. *Research in Nursing & Health, 15(3)*, 187–197.

Miller, D. T., Turnbull, W., & McFarland, C. (1988). Particularistic and universalistic evaluation in the social comparison process. *Journal of Personality & Social Psychology, 55*(6), 908–917.

Miller, G. (1956). The magical number seven, plus or minus two: Some limits on our capacity for processing information. *Psychological Review, 63*, 81–87.

Miller, G. (1977). *Spontaneous apprentices: children and language*. The Seabury Press.

Miller, L. C. (1990). Intimacy and liking: Mutual influence and the role of unique relationships. *Journal of Personality & Social Psychology, 59*(1), 50–60.

Miller, L. K. (1976). The design of better communities through the application of behavioral principles. In W. E. Craighead, A. E. Kazdin, & M. J. Mahone (Eds.), *Behavior modification: Principles, issues, and applications.* Boston: Houghton-Mifflin.

Miller, L., & Milner, B. (1985). Cognitive risk-taking after frontal or temporal lobectomy-mII. The synthesis of phonemic and semantic information. *Neuropsychologia, 23*, 371–379.

Miller, N. E. (1944). Experimental studies of conflict. In J. McV. Hunt (Ed.), *Personality and the behavior disorders*, Vol. I, 431–465. New York: Ronald Press.

Miller, N. E. (1983). Behavioral medicine: Symbiosis between laboratory and clinic. *Annual Review of Psychology, 34*, 1–31.

Miller, N. E. (1985a). Rx: Biofeedback. *Psychology Today, 19*, 54–59.

Miller, N. E. (1985b). The value of behavioral research on animals. *American Psychologist, 40*, 423–440.

Miller, N. E., & Bugelski. R. (1970). The influence of frustration imposed by the in-group on attitudes expressed toward out-groups. In R. I. Evans, & R. M. Rozelle (Eds.), *Social psychology in life.* Boston: Allyn & Bacon.

Miller, T. Q., Turner, C. W., Tindale, R. S., Posavac, E. J. et al. (1991). Reasons for the trend toward null findings in research on Type A behavior. *Psychological Bulletin, 110(3)*, 469–485.

Miller-Jones, D. (1989). Culture and testing. *American Psychologist, 44*(2), 360–366.

Millon, T. (1981) *Disorders of personality: DSM-III: Axis II.* New York: Wiley.

Milner, B. (1965). Memory disturbance after bilateral hippocampal lesions. In P. Milner, & S. Glickman (Eds.). *Cognitive processes and the brain*, 97–111. Princeton, NJ: Van Nostrand.

Milton, O., Pollio, H., & Eison, J. (1986). *Making sense of college grades: Why the grading system does not work and what can be done about it.* San Francisco, CA: Josey-Bass.

Milunsky, A. (1992). *Heredity and your family's health.* Boston: Houghton Mifflin.

Mintz L. B. & Betz, N. E. (1988). Prevalence and correlates of eating disordered behaviors among undergraduate women. *Journal of Counseling Psychology*, 35(4), 463–471.

Miranda, J. (1992). Dysfunctional thinking is activated by stressful life events. *Cognitive Therapy & Research, 16*(4), 473–483.

Mirsky, A. F. & Duncan, C. C. (1986). Etiology and expression of schizophrenia. *Annual Review of Psychology*, 37, 291–319.

Mischel, W. (1968). *Personality and assessment*. New York: Wiley.

Mitchell, D. (1987). Firewalking cults: Nothing but hot air. *Laser*, Feb., 7–8.

Mitchell, D. B. (1989). How many memory systems? Evidence from aging. *Journal of Experimental Psychology Learning, Memory, and Cognition, 15*(1), 31–49.

Mogg, K., Bradley, B. P., Williams, R., & Mathews, A. (1993). Subliminal processing of emotional information in anxiety and depression. *Journal of Abnormal Psychology, 102*(2), 304–311.

Monahan, J. (1991). Mental disorder and violent behavior. *American Psychologist, 47*(4), 511–521.

Money, J. (1977). Human hermaphroditism. In F. A. Beach (Ed.). *Human sexuality in four perspectives.* Baltimore: Johns Hopkins University Press.

Money, J. (1987). Sin, sickness, or status? *American Psychologist, 42*(4), 384–399.

Money, J., & Mathews, D. (1982). Prenatal exposure to virilizing progestins: An adult follow-up study of twelve women. *Archives of Sexual Behavior, 11*, 73–83.

Monfort, M., Martin, S. A., & Frederickson, W. (1990). Information-processing differences and laterality of students from different colleges and disciplines. *Perceptual & Motor Skills, 70*(1), 163–172.

Monmaney, T. (1987). Are we led by the nose? *Discover*, Sept., 48–56.

Monti-Bloch, L. & Grosser, B. I. (1991). Effect of putative pheromones on the electrical activity of the human vomeronasal organ and olfactory epithelium. *Journal of Steroid Biochemistry and Molecular Biology*, 39(4B), 573–582.

Moody, R. (1975). *Life after life.* Covinda, GA: Mockingbird.

Moore, D. C. (1981). Anorexia nervosa. In S. J. Mule (Ed.), *Behavior in excess.* New York: Free Press.

Moore-Ede, M. C., Sulzman, F. M., & Fuller, C. A. (1982). *The clocks that time us.* Cambridge, MA: Harvard University Press.

Moos, R. H. & Swindle, R. W. (1990). Stressful life circumstances: Concepts and measures. Special Issue: II-IV. Advances in measuring life stress. *Stress Medicine*, 6(3), 171–178.

Morain, D. (1988). In figuring, she plays it by the numbers. *Los Angeles Times*, March 1, Part I, 3.

Morelli, G. A., Rogoff, B., Oppenheim, D., Goldsmith, D. (1992). Cultural variation in infants' sleeping arrangements. *Developmental Psychology, 28(4)*, 604–613.

Moreno, J. L. (1953). *Who shall survive?* New York: Beacon.

Morgan, M. J., Hole, G. J., & Glennerster, A. (1990). Biases and sensitivities in geometrical illusions. Special Issue: Optics, physiology and vision. *Vision Research*, 30(11), 1793–1810.

Moriarty, T. (1975). A nation of willing victims. *Psychology Today*, April, 43–50.

Moritz, A. P., & Zamchech, N. (1946). Sudden and unexpected deaths of young soldiers. *American Medical Association Archives of Pathology, 42*, 459–494.

Morrow-Tlucak, M., Haude, R. H., Ernhart, C. B. (1988). Breastfeeding and cognitive development in the first 2 years of life. *Social Science and Medicine*, 26(6), 635–639.

Moser, D. (1965). The nightmare of life with Billy. *Life*, May 7.

Moss, K. (1989). Performing the light-switch task in lucid dreams: A case study. *Journal of Mental Imagery*, 13(2), 135–137.

Moss, S., & Butler, D. C. (1978). The scientific credibility of ESP. *Perceptual and Motor Skills, 46.*

Moyer, R. S., & Bayer, R. H. (1976). Mental comparison and the symbolic distance effect. *Cognitive Psychology*, 8, 228–246.

Mshelia, A. Y. & Lapidus, L. B. (1990). Depth picture perception in relation to cognitive style and training in non-Western children. *Journal of Cross-Cultural Psychology*, 21(4), 414–433.

Mueller, J. H., & Thompson, W. B. (1984). Test anxiety and distinctiveness of personal information. In H. M. Van Der Ploeg, R. Schwarzer, & C. D. Spielberger (Eds.), *Advances in test anxiety research*, Vol. 3. Hillsdale, NJ: Erlbaum.

Mullington, J. & Broughton, R. (1993). Scheduled naps in the management of daytime sleepiness in narcolepsy-cataplexy. *Sleep*, 16(5) 444–456.

Murphy, L. B., & Moriarty, A. E. (1976). *Vulnerability, coping and growth.* New Haven: Yale University Press.

Murphy, S. T. & Zajonc, R. B. (1992). Affect, cognition, and awareness. *Journal of Personality & Social Psychology*, 64(5), 723–739.

Murray, C. B. & Warden, M. R. (1992). Implications of self-handicapping strategies for academic achievement. *Journal of Social Psychology*, 132(1), 23–37.

Murray, F. S. (1980). Estimation of performance levels by students in introductory psychology. *Teaching of Psychology*, 7, 61–62.

Murray, R. M., Jones, P. B.. O'Callaghan, E., Takei, Noriyoshi, et al. (1992). Genes, viruses and neurodevelopmental schizophrenia. *Journal of Psychiatric Research*, 26(4), 225–235.

Murray, S. L. & Holmes, J. G. (1993). Seeing virtues in faults. *Journal of Personality & Social Psychology*, 65(4), 707–722.

Murray-Smith, D., Kinoshita, S., & McConkey, K. M. (1990). Hypnotic memory and retrieval cues. *British Journal of Experimental and Clinical Hypnosis*, 7(1), 1–8.

Murrell, J., Farlow, M., Ghetti, B., & Benson, M. D. (1991). A mutation in the amyloid precursor protein associated with hereditary Alzheimer's disease. *Science*, 254(5028), 97–98.

Murstein, B. I. & Fontaine, P. A. (1993). The public's knowledge about psychologists and other mental health professionals. *American Psychologist*, 48(7), 839–845.

Mussen, P. H., Conger, J. J., & Kagan, J. (1969). *Child development and personality.* New York: Harper & Row.

Mussen, P. H., Conger, J. J., Kagan, J., & Geiwitz, J. (1979). *Psychological development: A life span approach.* New York: Harper & Row.

Muth, K. D., Glynn, S. M., Britton, B. K., & Craves, M. F. (1988). Thinking out loud while studying text: Rehearsing key ideas. *Journal of Educational Psychology*, 80(3), 315–318.

Muuss, R. E. (1988). Carol Gilligan's theory of sex differences in the development of moral reasoning during adolescence. *Adolescence*, 23(89), 229–243.

Naeye, R. L. (1994). The brain at work. *Discover*, July, 30–31.

Nagel, K. L. & Jones, K. H. (1992). Predisposition factors in anorexia nervosa. *Adolescence*, 27(106), 381–386.

Nagel, K. L. & Jones, K. H. (1992). Sociological factors in the development of eating disorders. *Adolescence, 27(105)*, 107–113.

Naitoh, P., Kelly, T. L., & Englund, C. E. (1989). *Health effects of sleep deprivation.* U.S. Naval Health Research Center Report, No. 89–46.

Naranjo, C. (1970). Present-centeredness: Technique, prescription, and ideal. In J. Fagan, & I. L. Shepherd (Eds), *What is Gestalt therapy?* New York: Harper & Row.

Narayanan, V. K., & Nath, R. (1982). A field test of some attitudinal and behavioral consequences of flexitime. *Journal of Applied Psychology*, 67, 214–218.

Nathans, J., Thomas, P. Piantandia, R. L., Eddy, T. B., Shows, D. S. & Hogness, D. S. (1986). Molecular genetics of inherited variations in human color vision. *Science*, 232, 203–210.

National Commission on Marihuana and Drug Abuse, R. P. Shafer, Chairman. (1973). *Drug use in America: The problem in perspective.* Washington, DC: U.S. Government Printing Office.

National Institute of Mental Health. (1982). Television and behavior: Ten years of scientific progress and implications for the eighties. Washington, DC: U.S. Government Printing Office.

National Institute on Drug Abuse (NIDA) (1976). *Marihuana and health.* Princeton, NJ: Response Analysis Corporation.

Naveh-Benjamin, M. (1990) The acquisition and retention of knowledge: Exploring mutual benefits to memory research and the educational setting. *Applied Cognitive Psychology, 4(4)*, 295–320.

Needles, D. J. & Abramson, L. Y. (1990). Positive life events, attributional style, and hopefulness: Testing a model of recovery from depression. *Journal of Abnormal Psychology*, 99(2), 156–165.

Neff, F. (1990). Delivering sport psychology services to a professional sport organization. *Sport Psychologist*, 4(4), 378–385.

Neff, W. S. (1985). *Work and human behavior.* Chicago: Aldine.

Nelson, J. R., Smith, D. J., & Dodd, J. (1990). The moral reasoning of juvenile delinquents. *Journal of Abnormal Child Psychology*, 18(3), 231–239.

Nelson, R., & Crutchfield, R. S. (1970). Mathematicians: The creative researcher and the average Ph.D. *Journal of Consulting and Clinical Psychology*, 34, 250–257.

Nelson, T. O. (1987). Predictive accuracy of the feeling of knowing across different tasks and across different subject populations and individuals. In M. M. Grunegerg, P. E. Morris, & R. N. Sykes (Eds.), *Practical aspects of memory: Current research and issues.* Chinchester, U.K.: Wiley.

Neter, E., & Ben-Shakhar, G. (1989). The predictive validity of graphological inferences: A meta-analytic approach. *Personality and Individual Differences*, 10(7), 737–745.

Neufeld, R. W. (1970). The effect of experimentally altered cognitive appraisal on pain tolerance. *Psychonomic Science*, 20(2), 106–107.

Neugarten, B. (1971). Grow old along with me! The best is yet to be. *Psychology Today*, Dec., 45.

Newell, A. & Simon, H. A. (1972). *Human problem solving.* Englewood Cliffs, NJ: Prentice-Hall.

Newman, B. M. & Newman, P. R. (1987). The impact of high school on social development. *Adolescence*, 22(87), 525–534.

Newman, P. R. (1982). The peer group. In B. B. Wolman, G. Stricker, S. J. Ellman, P. Keith-Spiegel, & D. S. Palermo, (Eds.), *Handbook of developmental psychology.* Englewood Cliffs, NJ: Prentice-Hall.

Newman, R. (1994). Electronic therapy raises issues, risks. *APA Monitor*, Aug., 25.

Nickerson, R. S., & Adams, M. J. (1979). Long-term memory for a common object. *Cognitive Psychology*, 11, 287–307.

Nicogossian, A. E., & Parker, J. F. (1982). *Space physiology and medicine.* NASA.

Nicol, S. E., & Gottesman, I. I. (1983). Clues to the genetics and neurobiology of schizophrenia. *American Scientist*, 71, 398–404.

Niedenthal, P. M. (1990). Implicit perception of affective information. *Journal of Experimental Social Psychology*, 26(6), 505–527.

Nixon, M. (1990). Professional training in psychology. *American Psychologist*, 45(11), 1257–1262.

Njeri, I. (1991). Beyond the melting pot. *Los Angeles Times*, Jan. 13, E-1, E-8.

Noel, J. G., Forsyth, D. R., & Kelley, K. N. (1987). Improving the performance of failing students by overcoming their self-serving attributional biases. *Basic and Applied Social Psychology*, 8(1–2), 151–162.

Noller, P. & Ruzzene, M. (1991). Communication in marriage. In G. J. O. Fletcher & F. D. Fincham (Eds.), *Cognition and close relationships.* Hillsdale, NJ: Erlbaum.

Norman, D. A. (1988) *The psychology of everyday things.* New York: Basic.

Norris, P. A. (1986) On the status of biofeedback and clinical practice. *American Psychologist*, Sept., 1009–1010.

Nurmi, J. (1992). Age differences in adult life goals, and their temporal extension. *International Journal of Behavioral Development*, *80,(4), 487–508.*

Nurnberger, J. I., & Zimmerman, J. (1970). Applied analysis of human behaviors: An alternative to conventional motivational inferences and unconscious determination in therapeutic programming. *Behavior Therapy*, 1, 59–69.

O'Brien, R. M., Figlerski, R. W., Howard, S. R., & Caggiano, J. (1981). The effects of multi-year, guaranteed contracts on the performance of pitchers in major league baseball. Paper presented at the annual meeting of the American Psychological Association, Los Angeles, Aug. 1981.

O'Leary, K. D., Barling, J., Arias, I., Rosenbaum, A. et al. (1989). Prevalence and stability of physical aggression between spouses: A longitudinal analysis. *Journal of Consulting & Clinical Psychology*, 57(2), 263–268.

O'Malley, M. N., & Andrews, L. (1983). The effect of mood and incentives on helping: Are there some things money can't buy? *Motivation and Emotion*, 7, 179.

O'Sullivan, J. J. & Quevillon, R. P. (1992). 40 years later: Is the Boulder model still alive? *American Psychologist*, *47(1)*, 67–70.

Oatley, K. & Jenkins, J. M. (1992). Human emotions: Function and dysfunction. In M. R. Rosenzweig and L. W. Porter (Eds.), *Annual Review of Psychology*, *45*, 55–85.

Ohman, A. & Soares, J. J. (1993). On the automatic nature of phobic fear. *Journal of Abnormal Psychology*, *102*(1), 121–132.

Ohzawa, I., DeAngelis, G. C., & Freeman, R. D. (1990). Stereoscopic depth discrimination in the visual cortex: Neurons ideally suited as disparity detectors. *Science*, *249*(4972), 1037–1041.

Olander, F. (1990). Consumer psychology: Not necessarily a manipulative science. *Applied Psychology: An International Review*, 39(1), 105–126.

Olds, J. (1977). *Drives and reinforcements: Behavioral studies of hypothalamic functions.* New York: Raven Press.

Olds, J., & Milner, P. (1954). Positive reinforcement produced by electrical stimulation of septal area and other regions of rat brain. *Journal of Comparative and Physiological Psychology*, *47*, 419–427.

Olds, M. E., & Fobes, J. L. (1981). The central basis of motivation: Intracranial self-stimulation studies. *Annual Review of Psychology*, 32, 523–574.

Oliver, C. M., & Oliver, G. M. (1978). Gentle birth: Its safety and its effect on neonatal behavior. *Journal of Obstetrical, Gynecological and Neonatal Nursing.*

Oliver, J. E. (1993). Intergenerational transmission of child abuse. *American Journal of Psychiatry*, *150*(9), 1315–1324.

Oliver, M. B. & Hyde, J. S. (1993). Gender differences in sexuality. *Psychological Bulletin*, *114*(1), 29–51.

Oliwenstein, L. (1993). The gene with two faces. *Discover*, May, 26.

Ollendick, T. H. & King, N. J. (1991). Origins of childhood fears. *Behaviour Research & Therapy*, 29(2), 117–123.

Olmstead, B. (1983). More heavy drinking in colleges. *Los Angeles Times*, Feb. 17.

Olson, J. M. & Zanna, M. P., (1993). Attitudes and attitude change. In L. W. Porter and M. R. Rosenzweig (Eds.), *Annual Review of Psychology*, *44*, 117–154.

Olson, R. L. & Roberts, M. W. (1987). Alternative treatments for sibling aggression. *Behavior Therapy*, *18*(3), 243–250.

Olson, S. L., Bates, J. E., & Kaskie, B. (1992). Caregiver-infant interaction antecedents of children's school-age cognitive ability. *Merrill-Palmer Quarterly*, *38(3)*, 309–330.

Omer, H. & London, P. (1988). Metamorphosis in psychotherapy: End of the systems era. *Psychotherapy*, *25*(2), 171–180.

Ones, D., Viswesvaran, C., & Schmidt, F. L. (1993). Comprehensive meta-analysis of integrity test validities. *Journal of Applied Psychology*, *78*(4), 679–703.

Orlick, T. D. (1975). The sports environment: A capacity to enhance—a capacity to destroy. In B. S. Rushall (Ed.), *The status of psychomotor learning and sport psychology research.* Dartmouth, Nova Scotia: Sport Science Associates.

Orlock, C. (1993). *Inner time.* New York: Birch Lane Press.

Ornstein, R. & Ehrlich, P. (1989). *New world new mind.* New York: Simon & Schuster.

Ornstein, R. E. (1972). *The psychology of consciousness.* San Francisco: Freeman.

Ornstein, S. & Isabella, L. (1990). Age vs stage models of career attitudes of women: A partial replication and extension. *Journal of Vocational Behavior*, *36*, 1–19.

Orpen, C. (1981). Effect of flexible working hours on employee satisfaction and performance: A field experiment. *Journal of Applied Psychology*, *66*, 113–115.

Osgood, C. E. (1952). The nature and measurement of meaning. *Psychological Bulletin*, *49*, 197–237.

Oskamp, S. (1984). *Applied social psychology.* Englewood Cliffs, NJ: Prentice-Hall.

Oster, G. (1984). Muscle sounds. *Scientific American*, 250(3), 108–114.

Overholser, J. C. (1988). Applied psychological hypnosis: Management of problematic situations. *Professional Psychology: Research & Practice*, *19*(4), 409–415.

Overmier, J. B., & Seligman, M. E. P. (1967). Effects of inescapable shock upon subsequent escape and avoidance learning. *Journal of Comparative and Physiological Psychology*, *63*, 23–33.

Overton, D. A. (1985). Contextual stimulus effects of drugs and internal states. In P. D. Balsam, & A. Tomie (Eds.), *Context and learning*, 357–384. Hillsdale, NJ: Erlbaum.

Owen, J. D. (1976). Flextime: Some problems and solutions. *Industrial and Labor Relations Review*, *29*, 152–160.

Oyama, T. & Ichikawa, S. (1990). Some experimental studies on imagery in Japan. *Journal of Mental Imagery*, *14*(3–4), 185–195.

Pagano, R. R. (1981). *Understanding statistics.* St. Paul, MN: West.

Pagano, R. R., & Warrenburg, S. (1983) Meditation. In R J. Davidson, G. E. Schwartz, & D. Shapiro (Eds.), *Consciousness and self-regulation* (153–210). New York: Plenum.

Paivio, A. (1969). Mental imagery in associative learning and memory *Psychological Review*, *76*, 241–263.

Palfai, T. & Jankiewicz, H. (1991). *Drugs and human behavior.* Dubuque, IA: Wm. C. Brown.

Palinkas, L. A., Petterson, J. S., Russell, J., & Downs, M. A. (1993). Community patterns of psychiatric disorders after the Exxon Valdez oil spill. *American Journal of Psychiatry*, *150*(10), 1517–1523.

Palkovitz, R. J., & Lore, R. K. (1980). Note taking and note review: Why students fail questions based on lecture material. *Teaching of Psychology*, 7, 159–160.

Palmer, S. E. (1992). Common region: A new principle of perceptual grouping. *Cognitive Psychology*, *24*(3), 436–447.

Pandina, R. J., Johnson, V., Labouvie, E. W., & White, H. R. (1990). The relationship between alcohol and marijuana use and competence in adolescence. *Journal Of Health & Social Policy*, *1*(3), 89–108, 1990.

Pappenheimer, J. R. (1976). The sleep factor. *Scientific American*, Aug.

Parachini, A. (1986). '84 youth suicides a blip in 7-year drop, report says. *Los Angeles Times*, Nov. 19, V, 1,6.

Park, D. C., Smith, A. D., & Cavanaugh, J. C. (1990). Metamemories of memory researchers. *Memory & Cognition*, *18*(3), 321–327.

Parke, R. D., & Sawin, D. B. (1977). Fathering: It's a major role. *Psychology Today*, Nov.

Parkes, C. M. (1979). Grief: *The painful reaction to the loss of a loved one.* Monograph, University of California, San Diego.

Parks, T. E. (1984). Illusory figures: A (mostly) theoretical review. *Psychological Bulletin*, *95*, 282–300.

Parnes, S. J. (1967). *Creative behavior workbook.* New York: Scribner's.

Pasachoff, J. (1981). *Contemporary astronomy.* New York: Holt, Rinehart & Winston.

Passman, R. H. (1987). Attachments to inanimate objects: Are children who have security blankets insecure? *Journal of Consulting and Clinical Psychology*, 55(6), 825–830.

Patrick, C. J. & Iacono, W. G. (1989). Psychopathy, threat, and polygraph test accuracy. *Journal of Applied Psychology*, *74*(2), 347–355.

Patrick, C. J., Bradley, M. M., & Lang, P. J. (1993). Emotion in the criminal psychopath: Startle reflex modulation. *Journal of Abnormal Psychology*, *102*(1), 82–92.

Patten, B. M. (1990). The history of memory arts. *Neurology*, *40*(2), 346–352.

Patterson, C. H. (1989). Foundations for a systematic eclectic psychotherapy. *Psychotherapy*, *26*(4), 427–435.

Patterson, C. J. (1992). Children of lesbian and gay parents. *Child Development*, *63*(5), 1025–1042.

Patterson, E. W., Myers, G., & Gallant, D. M. (1988). Patterns of substance use on a college campus: A 14-year comparison study. *American Journal of Drug and Alcohol Abuse*, *14*(2), 237–246.

Patterson, G. R. (1982). *Coercive family process.* Eugene, OR: Castilia Press.

Patton, R. W., Corry, J. M., Gettman, L. R., & Graf, J. S. (1986). *Implementing health/fitness programs.* Champaign, IL: Human Kinetics.

Pavlov, I. P. (1927). *Conditioned reflexes.* Translated by G. V. Anrep. New York: Dover.

Pedersen, N. L., Plomin, R., McClearn, G. E., & Friberg, L. (1988). Neuroticism, extraversion, and related traits in adult twins reared apart and reared together. *Journal of Personality & Social Psychology*, 55(6), 950–957.

Pelton, T. (1983). The shootists. *Science 83*, *4*(4), 84–86.

Penfield, W. (1957). Brain's record of past a continuous movie film. *Science News Letter*, April 27, 265.

Penfield, W. (1958). *The excitable cortex in conscious man.* Springfield, IL: Charles C Thomas.

Pennebaker, J. W., Colder, M., & Sharp, L. L. (1990). Accelerating the coping process. *Journal of Personality & Social Psychology,* 58(3), 528–537.

Pennisi, E. (1992). Valentine bind. *Science News, 141* (Feb. 15), 110–111.

Perin, C. T. (1943). A quantitative investigation of the delay of reinforcement gradient. *Journal of Experimental Psychology,* 32, 37–51.

Perkins, K. A. (1993). Weight gain following smoking cessation. *Journal of Consulting & Clinical Psychology, 61*(5), 768–777.

Perlman, D. & Coxby, P. C. (1983). *Social psychology.* NY: Holt, Rinehart & Winston.

Perls, F. (1969). *Gestalt therapy verbatim.* Lafayette, CA: Real People.

Perry, D. G., Perry, L. C., & Weiss, R. J. (1989). Sex differences in the consequences that children anticipate for aggression. *Developmental Psvchology,* 25(2), 312–319.

Persky, H., Lief, H. I., Straus, D., Miller, W. R., & O'Brien, C. P. (1978). Plasma testosterone level and sexual behavior of couples. *Archives of Sexual Behavior,* 7, 157–173.

Peters, W. A. (1971). *A class divided.* Garden City, NY: Doubleday.

Petersen, A. C. (1987). Those gangly years. *Psychology Today,* Sept., 28–34.

Petersen, A. C., Kennedy, R. E. & Sullivan, P. (1991). Coping with adolescence. In M. E. Colten & S. Gore, Eds., *Adolescent Stress.* New York: Aldine de Gruyter.

Petersen, S. E., Fox, P. T., Posner, M. I., Mintun, M. et al. (1988). Positron emission tomographic studies of the cortical anatomy of single-word processing. *Nature, 331*(6157), 585–589.

Peterson, L. R., & Peterson, M. J. (1959). Short-term retention of individual verbal items. *Journal of Experimental Psychology,* 58, 193–198.

Peterson, P. L. (1979). Direct instruction: Effective for what and for whom? *Educational Leadership,* 37, 46–48.

Peterson, S. E. (1992). The cognitive functions of underlining as a study technique. *Reading Research & Instruction, 31(2),* 49–56.

Petitto, L. A. & Marentette, P. F. (1991). Babbling in the manual mode: Evidence for the ontogeny of language. *Science, 251*(March 22), 1493–1496.

Petrie, K., Dawson, A. G., Thompson, L., & Brook, R. (1993). A double-blind trial of melatonin as a treatment for jet lag in international cabin crew. *Biological Psychiatry,* 33(7), 526–530.

Pettit, G. S. & Bates, J. E. (1989). Family interaction patterns and children's behavior problems from infancy to 4 years. *Developmental Psychology,* 25(3), 413–420.

Pfost, K. S. & Fiore, M. (1990). Pursuit of nontraditional occupations: Fear of success or fear of not being chosen? *Sex Roles,* 23(1–2), 15–24.

Phillips, D. P. & Wills, J. S. (1987). A Drop in Suicides around major national holidays. *Suicide and Life-Threatening Behavior, 17,* 1–12.

Phillips, J. L. (1969). *Origins of intellect: Piaget's theory.* San Francisco: Freeman.

Piaget, J. (1951, original French, 1945). *The psychology of intelligence.* New York: Norton.

Piaget, J. (1952). *The origins of intelligence in children.* New York: International University Press.

Piccione, C., Hilgard, E. R., & Zimbardo, P. G. (1989). On the degree of stability of measured hypnotizability over a 25-year period. *Journal of Personality & Social Psychology,* 56(2), 289–295.

Pierce, J. P. (1991). Progress and problems in international public health efforts to reduce tobacco usage. *Annual Review of Public Health,* 12, 383–400.

Pierrel, R., & Sherman, J. G. (1963). Train your pet the Barnabus way. *Brown Alumni Monthly,* Feb.

Piliavin, I. M., Rodin, J., & Piliavin, J. A. (1969). Good samaritanism: An underground phenomenon? *Journal of Personality & Social Psychology, 13,* 289–299.

Pilkonis, P. A. (1977). The behavioral consequences of shyness. *Journal of Personality,* 45, 596–611.

Pilowsky, L. S., Kerwin, R. W., & Murray, R. M. (1993). Schizophrenia: A neurodevelopmental perspective. *Neuropsychopharmacology,* 9(1), 83–91.

Pines, M. (1980). The sinister hand. *Science 80,* Dec., 26–27.

Pion, G. M. (1991). Psychologists wanted: Employment trends over the last decade. In R. R. Kilburg (Ed.), *How to manage your career in psychology.* Washington, DC: American Psychological Association.

Pittman, T. & Heller, J. F. (1987). Social motivation. *Annual Review of Psychology,* 38, 461–489.

Playboy, (1969). *16*(2), 46.

Plomin, R. (1989). Environment and genes: Determinants of behavior. *American Psychologist, 44*(2), 105–111.

Plomin, R. & Rende, R. (1991). Human behavioral genetics. In M. R. Rosenzweig and L. W. Porter (Eds.), *Annual Review of Psychology,* 42, 161–190.

Plomin, R., DeFries, J. C., & McClearn, G. E. (1990). *Behavioral genetics.* San Francisco: Freeman.

Plutchik, R. (1980). *Emotion.* New York: Harper & Row.

Plutchik, R. (1990). Emotions in psychotherapy: A psychoevolutionary perspective. In R. Plutchik & H. Kellerman (Eds.) *Emotion.* San Diego, CA: Academic Press.

Pogatchnik, S. (1990). Kids' TV gets more violent, study finds. *The Los Angeles Times,* Jan. 26, F, 1, 27.

Pollock, V. E., Briere, J., Schneider, L., Knop, J. et al. (1990). Childhood antecedents of antisocial behavior. *American Journal of Psychiatry, 147*(10), 1290–1293.

Potashkin, B. D. & Beckles, N. (1990). Relative efficacy of Ritalin and biofeedback treatments in the management of hyperactivity. *Biofeedback & Self-Regulation, 15*(4), 305–315.

Potkay, C. R., & Allen, B. P. (1986). *Personality: Theory, research, and applications.* Monterey, CA: Brooks/Cole.

Poulin, J. & Walter, C. (1993). Social worker burnout. *Social Work Research & Abstracts,* 29(4), 5–11.

Premack, A. J., & Premack, D. (1972). Teaching language to an ape. *Scientific American,* Oct., 92–99.

Premack, D. (1965). Reinforcement theory. In D. Levine (Ed.), *Nebraska symposium on motivation.* Lincoln: University of Nebraska Press.

Premack, D. (1970). The education of S*A*R*A*H. *Psychology Today,* Sept., 54–58.

Premack, D. (1983). Animal cognition. *Annual Review of Psychology, 34,* 351–362.

Premack, D., & Premack, A. J. (1983). *The mind of an ape.* New York: Norton.

Prentice, D. A. & Miller, D. T. (1993). Pluralistic ignorance of alcohol use on campus. *Journal of Personality and Social Psychology,* 64(2), 243–256.

Pressley, M. (1987). Are Key-word method effects limited to slow presentation rates? An empirically based reply to Hall and Fuson (1986). *Journal of Educational Psychology,* 79(3), 333–335.

Pressley, M., Symons, S., McDaniel, M., A., Snyder, B., et al. (1988). Elaborative interrogation facilitates acquisition of confusing facts. *Journal of Educational Psychology, 80*(3), 268–278.

Pritchard, R. M. (1961). A collimator stabilizing system. *Quarterly Journal of Experimental Psychology, 13,* 181–183.

Pursch, J. A. (1983). Cocaine can give you the business. *Los Angeles Times,* June 12, Part VII, 12.

Rader, P. E., & Hicks, R. A. (1987). Jet lag desynchronization and self assessment of business related performance. Paper presented at the Western Psychological Association meeting in Long Beach, CA, April, 1987.

Radetsky, P. (1992). Straight sex and AIDS vaccines. *Discover, Jan.,* 52–53.

Rafaeli, A., & Klimoski, R. J. (1983). Predicting sales success through handwriting analysis: An evaluation of the effects of training and handwriting sample content. *Journal of Applied Psychology,* 68, 212–217.

Rahe, R. H. (1972). Subjects' recent life changes and their near-future illness reports. *Annals of Clinical Research, 4,* 250–265.

Ramachandran, V. S. (1992a). Filling in gaps in perception. *Current directions in psychological science 1*(6), 199–205.

Ramachandran, V. S. (1992b). Blind spots. *Scientific American,* May, 86–91.

Ramsey, P. H., Ramsey, P. P., & Barnes, M. J. (1987). Effects of student confidence and item difficulty on test score gains due to answer changing. *Teaching of Psychology, 14*(4), 206–209.

Randi, J. (1980). *Flim-flam!* New York: Lippincott & Crowell.

Randi, J. (1983). Science and the chimera. In G. O. Abell & B. Singer (Eds.), *Science and the paranormal.* New York: Scribner's.

Raven, B. H. (1974). The analysis of power and power preference. In J. T. Tebeschi (Ed.), *Prospectus on social power.* Chicago: Aldine.

Raymond, C. (1991). Pioneering research challenges accepted notions concerning the cognitive abilities of infants. *The Chronicle of Higher Education,* Jan. 23, A5–7.

Reed, J. D. & Bruce, D. (1982). Longitudinal tracking of difficult memory retrievals. *Cognitive Psychology, 14,* 280–300.

Reed, S. K. (1992). *Cognition: Theory and applications (3ed).* Pacific Grove, CA: Brooks/Cole.

Reif A. E. (1981). The causes of cancer. *American Scientist,* 69, 437–447.

Reifman, A. S., Larrick, R. P., & Fein, S. (1991). Temper and temperature on the diamond: The heat-aggression relationship in major league baseball. *Personality & Social Psychology Bulletin, 17*(5), 580–585.

Reiser, M. (1985). *Mind, brain, body: Toward a convergence of psychoanalysis.* New York: Basic.

Reiterman, T. (1993). Parallel roads led to Jonestown, Waco. *The Los Angeles Times,* April 23, A-24.

Remland, M. S., Jones, T. S., & Brinkman, H. (1991). Proxemic and haptic behavior in three European countries. *Journal of Nonverbal Behavior, 15*(4), 215–232.

Rennie, J. (1994). Grading the gene tests. *Scientific American,* June, 88–97.

Renwick, P. A., & Lawler, E. E. (1979). What you really want from your job. *Psychology Today, 11*(12), 53–65.

Report of the Ethics Committee, 1993. (1994). *American Psychologist, 49*(7), 659–666.

Rescorla, R. A. (1987). A Pavlovian analysis of goal-directed behavior. *American Psychologist, 42,* 119–126.

Rescorla, R. A. (1988). Pavlovian conditioning: It's not what you think it is. *American Psychologist,* 43:3, 151–160.

Research versus animal rights: Is there a middle ground?, (1989). A. Newman, *American Scientist,* 77(March-April), 135–137.

Reybowski, J. (1982). Social motivation. *Annual Review of Psychology,* 33, 123–154.

Reznick, J. S. & Goldfield, B. A. (1992). Rapid change in lexical development in comprehension and production. *Developmental Psychology,* 28(3), 406–413.

Rhine, J. B. (1953). *New world of the mind.* New York: Sloane.

Rhine, J. B. (1974). Security versus deception in parapsychology. *Journal of Parapsychology,* 38, 99–121.

Rhine, J. B. (1977). History of experimental studies. In B. B. Wolman (Ed.). *Handbook of parapsychology.* New York: Van Nostrand Reinhold.

Rhodewalt, F. & Zone, J. B. (1989). Appraisal of life change, depression, and illness in hardy and nonhardy women. *Journal of Personality & Social Psychology, 56*(1), 81–88.

Ricci, L. C. & Wellman, M. W. (1990). Monamines: Biochemical markers of suicide? *Journal of Clinical Psychology, 46*(1), 106–116.

Riccio, C. A., Hynd, G. W., Cohen, M. J., et al. (1993). Neurological basis of attention deficit hyperactivity disorder. *Exceptional Children, 60*(2), 118–124.

Rice, K. M., Blanchard, E. B., & Purcell, M. (1993). Biofeedback treatments of generalized anxiety disorder. *Biofeedback & Self-Regulation, 18*(2), 93–105.

Richards, L., Rollerson, B., & Phillips, J. (1991). Perceptions of submissiveness: Implications for victimization. *Journal of Psychology, 125(4),* 407–411.

Richardson, B. L. (1991). Utilizing the resources of the African-American church. In C. C. Lee & B. L. Richardson (Eds.), *Multicultural issues in counseling.* Alexandria, VA: American Association for Counseling and Development.

Richardson, P. H. & Vincent, C. A. (1986). Acupuncture for the treatment of pain: A review of evaluative research. *Pain, 24*(1), 15–40.

Ricketts, M. S., & Galloway, R. E. (1984). Effects of three different one-hour single-session treatments for test anxiety. *Psychological Reports, 54,* 113–119.

Riefer, D. M., & Rouder, J. N. (1992). A multinomial modeling analysis of the mnemonic benefits of bizarre imagery. *Memory & Cognition, 20(6),* 601–611.

Rimland, B. (1978). Inside the mind of the autistic savant. *Psychology Today, 12,* 68–80.

Rincover, A. & Newsom, C. D. (1985). The relative motivational properties of sensory and edible reinforcers in teaching autistic children. *Journal of Applied Behavior Analysis, 18(3),* 237–248.

Ring, K. (1980). *Life at death.* New York: Coward, McCann & Geoghegan.

Rinpoche, S. (1992). *The Tibetian way of living and dying.* San Francisco: Harper.

Ritchie, R. J., & Moses, J. L. (1983). Assessment center correlates of women's advancement into middle management: A 7-year longitudinal analysis. *Journal of Applied Psychology, 68,* 227–231.

Roan, S. (1992). Forever set in your ways at 30? *Los Angeles Times,* Sept. 1, E-1, E-2.

Roan, S. (1993). Growth-drug debate: What is too short? *Los Angeles Times,* Feb. 2, E-1, 8.

Roberts, D. F., & Bachen, C. M. (1981). Mass communication effects. *Annual Review of Psychology,* 32, 307–356.

Roberts, R. (1989). Passenger fear of flying: Behavioural treatment with extensive *in-vivo* exposure and group support. *Aviation, Space, & Environmental Medicine, 60*(4), 342–348.

Robertson, T. S. & Kassarjian, H. H. (Eds.), (1991). *Handbook of consumer behavior.* Engelwood Cliffs, NJ: Prentice-Hall.

Robinson, F. P. (1970). *Effective study, 4th ed.* New York: Harper & Row.

Robson, P. (1984). Prewalking locomotor movements and their use in predicting standing and walking. *Child Care, Health & Development, 10,* 317–330.

Rock, I., & Kaufman, L. (1962). The moon illusion II. *Science, 136,* 1023–1031.

Rodin, J. (1978). Stimulus-bound behavior and biological self-regulation: Feeding, obesity, and external control. In G. E. Schwartz, & D. Shapiro (Eds.), *Consciousness and self-regulation.* New York: Plenum.

Rodin, J. (1981). Current status of the internal-external hypothesis for obesity: What went wrong? *American Psychologist, 36,* 361–372.

Roediger, H. L. (1990). Implicit Memory. *American Psychologist, 45*(9), 1043–1056.

Rogers, C. R. (1959). A theory of therapy, personality, and interpersonal relationships, as developed in the client-centered framework. In S. Koch (Ed.), *Psychology: A study of a science,* Vol.3. New York: McGraw-Hill.

Rogers, C. R. (1961). *On becoming a person: A therapist's view of psychotherapy.* Boston: Houghton Mifflin.

Rogers, C. R. (1980). *A way of being.* Boston: Houghton Mifflin.

Rogers, J. M. (1971). Drug abuse—Just what the doctor ordered. *Psychology Today,* Sept., 16–24.

Rogers, J. R. (1990). Female suicide. *Journal of Counseling & Development,* 69(6), 37–38.

Rogler, L. H., Cortes, D. E., & Malgady, R. G. (1991). Acculturation and mental health status among Hispanics. *American Psychologist, 46*(6), 585–597.

Rohsenow, D. J., & Smith R. E. (1982). Irrational beliefs as predictors of negative affective states. *Motivation and Emotion, 6,* 299–301.

Rokeach, M. (1960). *The open and closed mind.* New York: Basic.

Rolling, B. L. & Belsky, J. (1992). The contribution of mother-child and father-child relation-ships to the quality of sibling interaction: A longitudinal study. *Child Development, 63(5),* 1209–1222.

Romero, K. & Silvestri, L. (1990). The role of mental practice in the acquisition and performance of motor skills. *Journal of Instructional Psychology,* 17(4), 218–221.

Ronnett, G. V., Hester, L. D., Nye, J. S., Connors, K., & Snyder, S. H. (1990). Human cortical neuronal cell line: Establishment from a patient with unilateral megalencephaly. *Science,* 248(4955), 603–605.

Roos, P. E. & Cohen, L. H. (1987). Sex roles and social support as moderators of life stress adjustment. *Journal of Personality & Social Psychology,* 52, 576–585).

Rorer, L. G., & Widiger, T. A. (1983). Personality structure and assessment. *Annual Review of Psychology, 34,* 431–463.

Rosch, E. (1977). Classification of real-world objects: Origins and representations in cognition. In P. N. Johnson-Laird, & P. C. Wason (Eds.). *Thinking: Reading in cognitive science.* Cambridge: Cambridge University Press.

Roscoe, S. N. (1985). Bigness is in the eye of the beholder. *Human Factors,* 27(6), 615–636.

Rose, K. J. (1984). How animals think. *Science Digest,* 89(Feb.), 59–61.

Rosen, J. C., & Leitenberg, H. (1982). Bulimia nervosa: Treatment with exposure and response prevention. *Behavior Therapy, 13,* 117–124.

Rosen, L. A., Booth, S. R., Bender, M. E., McGrath, M. L., et al. (1988). Effects of sugar (sucrose) on children's behavior. *Journal of Consulting & Clinical Psychology, 56*(4), 583–589.

Rosenbaum, J. F., Biederman, J., Gersten, M., Hirshfeld, D. R. et al. (1989). Behavioral inhibition in children of parents with panic disorder and agoraphobia: A controlled study. *Annual Progress in Child Psychiatry & Child Development,* 294–315.

Rosenbaum, J. F., Biederman, J., Hirshfeld, D. R., Bolduc, E. A. et al. (1991). Further evidence of an association between behavioral inhibition and anxiety disorders. *Journal of Psychiatric Research,* 25(1–2), 49–65.

Rosenbaum, M. B. (1979). The changing body image of the adolescent girl. In M. Sugar (Ed.), *Female adolescent development.* New York: Brunner/ Mazel.

Rosenberg, J., & Pettinati, H. M. (1984). Differential memory complaints after bilateral and unilateral ECT. *American Journal of Psychiatry, 14,* 1071–1074.

Rosenblith, J. F. (1992). *In the beginning.* Newbury

Park: Sage.

Rosenfeld, P., Giacalone, R. A., & Tedeschi, J. T. (1983). Cognitive dissonance vs. impression management. *Journal of Social Psychology, 120,* 203–211.

Rosenhan, D. L. (1973). On being sane in insane places. *Science, 179,* 250–258.

Rosenman, R. H., Brand, R. J., Jenkins, C. D., Friedman, M., Straus, R., & Wurm, M. (1975). Coronary heart disease in the Western Collaborative Group Study: Final follow-up experience of 8 1/2 years. *Journal of the American Medical Association,* 233, 872–877.

Rosenstiel, T. B. (1991). Americans praise media but still back censorship, postwar poll says. *Los Angeles Times,* March 25, A-9.

Rosenthal, D. (1963). *The Genain quadruplets.* New York: Basic.

Rosenthal, D., & Quinn, O. W. (1977). Quadruplet hallucinations: Phenotypic variations of a schizophrenic genotype. *Archives of General Psychiatry,* 34(7), 817–827.

Rosenthal, N. E., Sack, D. A., Gillin, J. C., Levy, A. J., et al. (1984). Seasonal affective disorder. *Archives of General Psychiatry, 41*(72), 72–80.

Rosenthal, R. (1965). *Clever Hans: A case study of scientific method. Introduction to Clever Hans: (The horse of Mr. Von Osten),* O. Pfungst. New York: Holt, Rinehart & Winston.

Rosenthal, R. (1973). The Pygmalion effect lives. *Psychology Today,* Sept., 56–63.

Rosenthal, R. (1976). *Experimenter effects in behavioral research.* New York: Appleton-Century-Crofts.

Rosenthal, T. L. (1993). To soothe the savage breast. *Behavior Research & Therapy, 31(5),* 439–462.

Rosenthal, T. L. & Steffek, B. D. (1990). Modeling methods. In F. H. Kanfer & A. P. Goldsteing (Eds.), *Helping people change.* Elmsford, NY: Pergamon.

Rosenthal, T. L. & Steffek, B. D. (1991). Modeling methods. In, F. H. Kanfer & A. P. Goldstein (Eds.), *Helping people change.* Elmsford, NY: Pergamon.

Rosenthal, T. L., & Rosenthal, R. (1980). The vicious cycle of stress reaction. Copyright, Renate and Ted Rosenthal, Stress Management Clinic, Department of Psychiatry, University of Tennessee College of Medicine, Memphis, Tennessee.

Rosenthal, T. L., & Zimmerman, B. J. (1978). *Social learning and cognition.* New York: Academic.

Ross, C. A., Miller, S. D., Reagor, P., Bjornson, L. et al. (1990). Structured interview data on 102 cases of multiple personality disorder from four centers. *American Journal of Psychiatry, 147*(5), 596–601.

Ross, J. (1976). The resources of binocular perception. *Scientific American,* March, 80–86.

Ross, L. (1977). The intuitive psychologist and his shortcomings: Distortions in the attribution process. In L. Berkowitz (Ed.), *Advances in experimental social psychology.* New York: Academic.

Ross, M., Karniol, R., & Rothstein, M. (1976). Reward contingency and intrinsic motivation in children. *Journal of Personality & Social Psychology,* 33, 442–447.

Rossi, P. H. (1990). The old homeless and the new homeless in historical perspective. *American Psychologist, 45*(8), 954–959.

Rothblum, E. D., Solomon, L. J., & Murakami, J. (1986). Affective, cognitive, and behavioral differences between high and low procrastinators. *Journal of Consulting Psychology,* 33(4), 387–394.

Rotter, J. B., & Hochreich, D. J. (1975). *Personality.* Glenview, IL: Scott, Foresman.

Rotton, J. & Kelly, I. W. (1985). Much ado about the full moon: A meta-analysis of lunar-lunacy research. *Psychological Bulletin,* 97, 286–306.

Rowe, D. C. (1987). Resolving the person-situation debate. *American Psychologist,* 42, 218–227.

Rowley, P. T. (1984). Genetic screening: Marvel or menace? *Science,* 225, 138–144.

Rubenstein, C. (1983). The modern art of courtly love. *Psychology Today,* July.

Rubenstein, C. & Tavris, C. (1987). Special survey results: 2600 women reveal the secrets of intimacy. *Redbook, 159,* 147–149*ff.*

Rubin, D. C. (1985). The subtle deceiver: Recalling our past. *Psychology Today,* Sept., 38–46.

Rubin, J. (1990). Drugs for Treating Behavior Problems: How Safe Are They? *American Psychologist,* 45(8), 985–86.

Rubin, V., & Comitas, L. (Eds.). (1975). *Ganja in Jamaica.* The Hague: Mouton.

Rubin, Z. (1970a). Jokers wild in the lab. *Psychology Today,* Dec.

Rubin, Z. (1970b). Measurement of romantic love. *Journal of Personality & Social Psychology, 16,* 265–273.

Rubin, Z. (1973). *Liking and loving: An invitation to social psychology.* New York: Holt.

Rubin, Z. (1975). Disclosing oneself to a stranger: Reciprocity and its limits. *Journal of Experimental and Social Psychology, 11,* 233–260.

Rubinstein, E. A., Liebert, R. M, Neale, J. M., & Poulos, R. W. (1974). *Assessing television's influence on children's prosocial behavior.* New York: Brookdale International Institute.

Ruch, F. L. & Zimbardo, P. G. (1971). *Psychology and life.* Glenview, IL: Scott, Foresman.

Ruffin, C. L. (1993). Stress and health: Little hassles vs. major life events. *Australian Psychologist,* 28(3), 201–208.

Rumbaugh, D. M., Hopkins, W. D., Washburn, D. A., & Savage-Rumbaugh, E. S. (1989). Lana chimpanzee learns to count by "numath": A summary of a videotaped experimental report. *Psychological Record,* 39(4), 459–470.

Rushton, N. A. H. (1975). Visual pigments and color blindness. *Scientific American,* March, 64–74.

Russell, G. & Russell, A. (1987). Mother-child and father-child relationships in middle childhood. *Child Development,* 58(6), 1573–1585.

Russell, T. G., Rowe, W., & Smouse, A. D. (1991). Subliminal self-help tapes and academic achievement: An evaluation. *Journal of Counseling and Development, 69(Mar-Apr),* 359–362.

Russo, N. F. (1990). Forging research priorities for women's mental health. *American Psychologist,* 45(3), 368–373.

Ryff, C. D. (1989). Beyond Ponce de Leon and life satisfaction: New directions in quest of successful ageing. *International Journal of Behavioral Development, 12*(1), 35–55.

Saarni, C. (1982). Social and affective functions of nonverbal behavior: Developmental concerns. In R. S. Feldman (Ed.), *Development of nonverbal behavior in children,* 123–148. New York: Springer-Verlag.

Sackheim, H. A., Decina, P., Kanzler, M., & Kerr, B. (1987). Effects of electrode placement on the efficacy of titrated, low-dose ECT. *American Journal of Psychiatry, 144*(11), 1449–1455.

Sacks, O. (1990). *Seeing voices.* New York: Harper Perennial.

Sadker, M. & Sadker, D. (1994). Failing at fairness: How America's schools cheat girls. New York: Scribner's.

Sadock, V. A. (1987). Adolescent sexuality. *The Harvard Medical School Mental Health Letter,* 3(9), 6.

Sadowski, C. & Kelley, M. L. (1993). Social problem solving in suicidal adolescents. *Journal of Consulting and Clinical Psychology, 61*(1), 121–127.

Saegert, S., Swap, W., & Zajonc, R. B. (1973). Exposure, context, and interpersonal attraction. *Journal of Personality & Social Psychology,* 25, 234–242.

Sagan, C. & Turco, R. (1990). Too many weapons in the world. *Parade Magazine,* Feb. 4, 10–13.

Sagi, A. (1990). Attachment theory and research from a cross-cultural perspective. *Human Development,* 33(1), 10–22.

Sales, B. D. & Hafemeister, T. L. (1985). Law and psychology. In Altmeir, E. M. & Meyer, M. E. (Eds.), *Applied specialties in psychology.* NY: Random House.

Salive, M. E., Guralnik, J. M., & Glynn, R. J. (1993). Left-handedness and mortality. *American Journal of Public Health, 83(2),* 265–267.

Salmela, J. H. (1974). An information processing approach to volleyball. *C.V.A. Technical Journal, 1,* 49–62.

Salmela, J. H. (1975). Psycho-motor task demands of artistic gymnastics. In J. H. Salmela (Ed.), *The advanced study of gymnastics: A textbook.* Sundby.

Salmoni, A. W., Schmidt, R. A., & Walter, C. B. (1984). Knowledge of results and motor learning: A review and critical reappraisal. *Psychological Bulletin,* 95, 355–386.

Salovey, P. & Singer, J. A. (1989). Mood congruency effects in recall of childhood versus recent memories. *Journal of Social Behavior & Personality,* 4(2), 99–120.

Salthouse, T. A. (1987). Age, experience, and compensation. In C. Schooler & K. W. Schaie (Eds.), *Cognitive functioning and social structure over the life course,* 142–150. New York: Ablex.

Sampson, E. E. (1993). Identity politics. *American Psychologist, 48*(12), 1219–1230.

Sancho, A. M. & Hewitt, J. (1990). Questioning fear of success. *Psychological Reports,* 67(3, Pt 1), 803–806.

Sanders, G. S., & Simmons, W. L. (1983). Use of hypnosis to enhance eyewitness accuracy: Does it work? *Journal of Applied Psychology, 68,* 70–77.

Santrock, J. W. (1993). *Adolescence.* Dubuque, IA: Brown.

Sapolsky, R. M. (1987). The case of the falling nightwatchmen. *Discover,* July, 42–45.

Sarason, I. G. (1981). Test anxiety, stress, and social support. *Journal of Personality,* 49, 101–114.

Savage-Rumbaugh, E. S., Murphy, J., Sevcik, R. A., Brakke, K. E. et al. (1993). Language comprehension in ape and child. *Monographs of the Society for Research in Child Development, 58*(3–4), v-221.

Savage-Rumbaugh, E. S., Rumbaugh, D. M., Premack, D., & Woodruff, G. (1979). Chimpanzee problem comprehension: Insufficient evidence. *Science, 206*(4423), 1201–1202.

Savage-Rumbaugh, S., Sevcik, R. A., Brakke, K. E., Rumbaugh, D. M. et al. (1990). Symbols: Their communicative use, comprehension, and combination by bonobos (Pan paniscus). *Advances in Infancy Research, 6,* 221–278.

Saxe, L. (1991). Lying. *American Psychologist, 46*(4), 409–415.

Saxe, L., Dougherty, D., & Cross, T. (1985). The validity of polygraph testing. *American Psychologist, 40,* 355–366.

Sayette, M. A. & Mayne, T. J. (1990). Survey of current clinical and research trends in clinical psychology. *American Psychologist, 45*(11), 1263–1266.

Scarr, S. & Eisenberg, M., (1993). Child care research: Issues, perspectives, and results. In L. W. Porter and M. R. Rosenzweig (Eds.), *Annual Review of Psychology, 44,* 613–644.

Scarr, S., & Weinberg, R. A. (1983). The Minnesota adoption studies: Genetic differences and malleability. *Child Development, 54,* 260–267.

Scarr-Salapatek, S., & Weinberg, R. A. (1975). When black children grow up in white homes. *Psychology Today,* Dec.

Schachere, K. (1990). Attachment between working mothers and their infants. *American Journal of Orthopsychiatry, 60*(1), 19–34.

Schachter, S. (1959). *Psychology of affiliation.* Stanford, CA: Stanford University Press.

Schachter, S. (1978). Pharmacological and psychological determinants of smoking. In R. E. Thornton (Ed.), *Smoking behavior.* Edinburgh, U.K.: Churchill Livingston.

Schachter, S., & Rodin, J. (1974). *Obese humans and rats.* Potomac, MD: Earlbaum.

Schachter, S., & Wheeler, L. (1962). Epinephrine, chlorpromazine and amusement. *Journal of Abnormal and Social Psychology, 65,* 121–128.

Schaeffer, M. A., Baum, A., Paulus, P. B., & Gaes, G. C. (1988). Architecturally mediated effects of social density in prison. *Environment & Behavior, 20*(1), 3–19.

Schaie, K. W. (1988). Ageism in psychological research. *American Psychologist,* 43(3), 179–183.

Schaie, K. W. (1994). The course of adult intellectual development. *American Psychologist, 49*(4), 304–313.

Schaller, S. (1991). *A man without words.* New York: Summit.

Schein, E. H., Hill, W. F., Lubin, A., & Williams, H. L. (1957). Distinguishing characteristics of collaborators and resistors among American prisoners of war. *Journal of Abnormal and Social Psychology, 55,* 197–201.

Schein, E. H., Schneier, I., & Barker, C. H. (1961). *Coercive persuasion.* New York: Norton.

Schiavi, R. C., Schreiner-Engle, P., Mandeli, J., Schanzer, H. et al. (1990). Healthy aging and male sexual function. *American Journal of Psychiatry, 147*(6), 766–771.

Schlesier-Stropp, B. (1984). Bulimia: A review of the literature. *Psychological Bulletin,* 38, 247–257.

Schlosberg, H. (1954). Three dimensions of emotion. *Psychological Review, 61,* 81–88.

Schmeidler, G. R. (1977). Methods for controlled research on ESP and PK. In B. B. Wolman (Ed.), *Handbook of parapsychology.* New York: Van Nostrand Reinhold.

Schmid, R. E. (1988). Number of unmarried couples tops 2.3 million. *Santa Barbara News-Press,* May 14, A-9.

Schmidt, F. L., Ones, D. S., & Hunter, J. E. (1992). Personnel selection. *Annual Review of Psychology, 43,* 627–670.

Schmitt, N. & Robertson, I. (1990). Personnel selecton. *Annual Review of Psychology, 41,* 289–319.

Schneider, C. (1987). *Children's television: The art, the business, and how it works.* Chicago: NTC Business Books.

Schneider, H. G. & Shugar, G. J. (1990). Audience and feedback effects in computer learning. *Computers in Human Behavior, 6*(4), 315–321.

Schneider, S. F. (1991). No fluoride in our future. *Professional Psychology: Research & Practice, 22(6),* 456–460.

Schnell, L. & Schwab, M. E. (1990). Axonal regeneration in the rat spinal cord produced by an antibody against myelin-associated neurite growth inhibitors. *Nature, 343*(6255), 269–272.

Schoggen, P. (1989). *Behavior settings.* Stanford, CA: Stanford Universtiy Press.

Schok, K. & Samuels, C. A. (1992). Neonatal bathing and massage intention with fathers, behavioural effects 12 weeks after birth of the first baby. *International Journal of Behavioral Development, 15(1),* 67–81.

Schommer, N. (1984). Shrinks on the air. *Discover,* Oct., 68–70.

Schooler, C., Flora, J. A., & Farquhar, J. W. (1993). Moving toward synergy: Media supplementation in the Stanford Five-City Project. *Communication Research, 20*(4), 587–610.

Schooler, J. W. & Engstler-Schooler, T. Y. (1990). Verbal overshadowing of visual memories: Some things are better left unsaid. *Cognitive Psychology, 22*(1), 36–71.

Schotte, D. E., Cools, J., & McNally, R. J. (1990). Film-induced negative affect triggers overeating in restrained eaters. *Journal of Abnormal Psychology, 99*(3), 317–320.

Schreiber, F. R. (1973). *Sybil.* Chicago: Regency.

Schuele, J. G., & Wiesenfeld, A. R. (1983). Autonomic response to self-critical thought. *Cognitive Therapy and Research, 7,* 189–194.

Schuerger, J. M. & Witt, A. C. (1989). The temporal stability of individually tested intelligence. *Journal of Clinical Psychology, 45*(2), 294–302.

Schulz, R. (1978). *The psychology of death, dying and bereavement.* Reading, MA: Addison-Wesley.

Schunk, D. H. (1990). Goal setting and self-efficacy during self-regulated learning. Special Issue: Self-regulated learning and academic achievement. *Educational Psychologist, 25*(1), 71–86.

Schutte, N. S., Malouff, J. M., Post-Corden, J. C., & Rodasta, A. L. (1988). Effects of playing videogames on children's aggressive and other behaviors. *Journal of Applied Social Psychology, 18*(5), 454–460.

Schutz, W. (1986). Encounter groups. In Kutash, I. L. & Wolf, A. (Eds.), *Psychotherapist's casebook.* San Francisco: Jossey-Bass.

Schwartz, B. (1989). *Psychology of learning & behavior.* New York: Norton.

Schwartz, L. L. (1991). The historical dimension of cultic techniques of persuasion and control. *Cultic Studies Journal, 8(1),* 37–45.

Scientists take stand for animal research, (1989). S. Landers, *APA Monitor,* April, 1, 4.

Sclafani, A., & Springer, D. (1976). Dietary obesity in adult rats: Similarities to hypothalamic and human obesity syndromes. *Psychology and Behavior, 17,* 461–471.

Scott, J. P. & Ginsburg, B. E. (1994). The Seville statement on violence revisited. *American Psychologist, 49*(10), 849–850.

Scott, L. & O'Hara, M. W. (1993). Self-discrepancies in clinically anxious and depressed university students. *Journal of Abnormal Psychology, 102*(2), 282–287.

Scott, N. E. & Borodovsky, L. G. (1990). Effective use of cultural role taking. *Professional Psychology: Research & Practice, 21*(3), 167–170.

Sears, R. R., Maccoby, E. E., & Levin, H. (1957). *Patterns of child rearing.* Evanston, IL: Row, Peterson.

Seidel, W. F., Roth, T., Roehrs, T., Zorick, F., & Dement, W. C. (1984). Treatment of a 12-hour shift of sleep schedule with benzodiazepines. *Science, 224,* 1262–1264.

Seligman, C., & Darley, J. M. (1977). Feedback as a means of decreasing residential energy consumption. *Journal of Applied Psychology, 62,* 363–368.

Seligman, M. E. P. (1972a). For helplessness: Can we immunize the weak? In *Readings in psychology today* (2nd ed.). Del Mar, CA: CRM.

Seligman, M. E. P. (1972b) Phobias and preparedness. In M. E. P. Seligman & J. L. Hager (Eds.), *Biological boundaries of learning.* New York: Appleton-Century-Crofts.

Seligman, M. E. P. (1974). Submissive death: Giving up on life. *Psychology Today, 7,* 80–85.

Seligman, M. E. P. (1989). *Helplessness.* New York: Freeman.

Seligman, M. E. P. (1994). *What you can change and what you can't.* New York: Knopf.

Selkoe, D. J. (1991). Amyloid protein and Alzheimer's disease. *Scientific American,* Nov., 68–78.

Selye, H. (1956, 1976). *The stress of life.* New York: Knopf.

Selye, H. (1976). *Stress in health and disease.* Boston: Butterworth.

Senden, M. V. (1960). *Space and sight.* Translated by P. Heath. Glencoe, IL: Free Press.

Serbin, L. A., & O'Leary, K. D. (1975). How nursery schools teach girls to shut up. *Psychology Today,* Dec., 57–58, 102–103.

Seventy-five percent with AIDS virus are reported infected through heterosexual sex. (1991). *Los Angeles Times,* A-4.

Shadish, W. R., Lurigio, A. L., & Lewis, D. A. (1989). After deinstitutionalization: The present and future of mental health long-term care policy. *Jour-*

nal of Social Issues, 45(3), 1–15.

Shaffer, J. B. & Galinsky, M. D. (1989). *Models of group therapy.* Englewood Cliffs, NJ: Prentice Hall.

Shaffer, L. F. (1947). Fear and courage in aerial combat. *Journal of Consulting Psychology, 11,* 137–143.

Shapiro, D. H. (1984). Overview: Clinical and physiological comparison of meditation with other self-control strategies. In Shapiro, D. H. & Walsh, R. N. (Eds.), *Meditation: Classic and contemporary perspectives.* New York: Aldine.

Shapiro, F. (1989a). Efficacy of the Eye Movement Desensitization procedure in the treatment of traumatic memories. *Journal of Traumatic Stress,* 2(2), 199–223.

Shapiro, F. (1989b). Eye movement desensitization: A new treatment for post-traumatic stress disorder. *Journal of Behavior Therapy & Experimental Psychiatry, 20*(3), 211–217.

Shapiro, F. (1991). Eye movement desensitization and reprocessing procedure. *The Behavior Therapist, 14,* 133–136.

Shapiro, J. P. & Bowermaster, D. (1994). The Case of Dr. Kevorkian Obscures Critical Issues—and Dangers. *US News & World Report,* April 25, on-line edition.

Shatz, M. (1986). Students' guessing strategies: Do they work? *Psychological Reports,* 57(3), 1167–1168.

Shaver, P. R. & Hazen, C. (1993). Adult romantic attachment. In D. Perlman & W. H. Jones (Eds.), *Advances in personal relationships, 4.* London: Kingsley.

Shaw, G. A., & Belmore, S. M. (1983). The relationship between imagery and creativity. *Imagination, Cognition and Personality,* 2, 115–123.

Shedler, J. & Block, J. (1990). Adolescent drug use and psychological health: A longitudinal inquiry. *American Psychologist, 45*(5), 612–630.

Sheehan, P. W., Statham, D. (1989). Hypnosis, the timing of its introduction, and acceptance of misleading information. *Journal of Abnormal Psychology,* 98(2), 170–176.

Sheehy, G. (1976). *Passages: Predictable crises from adult life.* New York: Dutton.

Shepard, R. N. (1975). Form, formation, and transformation of internal representations. In R. L. Solso (Ed.), *Information processing and cognition: The Loyola Symposium.* Hillsdale, NJ: Erlbaum.

Sherif, M., Harvey, O. J., White, B. J., Hood, W. R., & Sherif, C. W. (1961). *Intergroup conflict and cooperation: The Robbers Cave experiment.* University of Oklahoma, Institute of Group Relations.

Shermer, M. (1992). A skeptical look at cryonic suspension. *Skeptic,* 1(2), 50–51.

Shields, P. L. & Rovee-Collier, C. (1992). Long-term memory for context-specific category information at six months. *Child Development, 63(2),* 245–259.

Shiffrin, R. M. (1970). Forgetting: Trace erosion or retrieval failure? *Science, 168,* 1601–1603.

Shiffrin, R. M., & Cook, J. R. (1978). Short-term forgetting of item and order information. *Journal of Verbal Learning and Verbal Behavior, 17,* 189–218.

Shneidman, E. (1987). At the point of no return. *Psychology Today,* March, 54–58.

Shneidman, E. S. (1987). Psychological approaches to suicide. In VandenBos, G. R. & Bryant, B. K. (Eds.), *Cataclysms, crises, and catastrophes: Psychology in action.* Washington, DC: American Psychological Association.

Shogren, E. (1994). Treatment against their will. *The Los Angeles Times,* Aug. 18, A-1, A-14, A-15.

Shore, L. A. (1990). Skepticism in light of scientific literacy. *Skeptical Inquirer, 15,* Fall, 3–4.

Shulman, G. I. (1974). Race, sex and violence: A laboratory test of the sexual threat of the black male hypothesis. *American Journal of Sociology,* 79, 1260–1277.

Shurkin, J. N. (1992). *Terman's kids.* Boston, MA: Little, Brown.

Shweder, R. A. & Sullivan, M. A., (1993). Cultural psychology: Who needs it? In L. W. Porter and M. R. Rosenzweig (Eds.), *Annual Review of Psychology, 44,* 497–523.

Sieber, J. E. & Saks, M. J., (1989). A census of subject pool characteristics and policies. *American Psychologist, 44*(7), 1053–1061

Siegal, M. (1987). Are sons and daughters treated more differently by fathers than by mothers? *Developmental Review,* 7(3), 183–209.

Siegel, J. M., Nienhuis, R., Fahringer, H. M. et al. (1991). Neuronal activity in narcolepsy: Identification of cataplexy related cells in the medial medulla. *Science, 252*(5010), 1315–1318.

Siegel, O. (1982). Personality development in adolescence. In B. B. Wolman, G. Stricker, S. J. Ellman, P. Keith-Spiegel, & D. S. Palermo (Eds), *Handbook of developmental psychology.* Englewood Cliffs, NJ: Prentice Hall.

Siegel, S., Hearst, E., George, N., & O'Neal, E. (1968). Generalization gradients obtained from individual subjects following classical conditioning. *Journal of Experimental Psychology, 78,* 171–174.

Siegelman, M. (1987) Kinsey and others: Empirical input. In L. Diamant (Ed.) *Male and female homosexuality: Psychological approaches.* Washington, DC: Hemisphere.

Siegler, R. S. (1989). Mechanisms of cognitive development. *Annual Review of Psychology,* 40, 353–379.

Silva, C. E. & Kirsch, I. (1992). Interpretive sets, expectancy, fantasy proneness, and dissociation as predictors of hypnotic response. *Journal of Personality & Social Psychology, 63(5),* 847–856.

Silver, E., Cirincione, C., & Steadman, H. J. (1994). Demythologizing inaccurate perceptions of the insanity defense. *Law & Human Behavior, 18*(1), 63–70.

Silver, L. B. (1990). Attention deficit-hyperactivity disorder: Is it a learning disability or a related disorder? *Journal of Learning Disabilities,* 23(7), 394–397.

Silverman, K., Evans, S. M., Strain, E. C., & Griffiths, R. R. (1992). Withdrawal syndrome after the double-blind cessation of caffeine consumption. *New England Journal of Medicine,* 327(16), 1109–1114.

Silverstein, B. (1989). Enemy images. *American Psychologist, 44*(6), 903–913.

Silverstein, L. B. (1991). Transforming the debate about child care and maternal employment. *American Psychologist, 46(1),* 1025–1032.

Simonton, D. K. (1988). Age and outstanding achievement: What do we know after a century of research? *Psychological Bulletin, 104*(2), 251–267.

Simpson, J. A. (1990). Influence of attachment styles on romantic relationships. *Journal of Personality & Social Psychology,* 59(5), 971–980.

Singer, J. L. (1974). Daydreaming and the stream of thought. *American Scientist, 62,* 417–425.

Singer, M. T. (1979). Coming out of the cults. *Psychology Today,* Jan., 72–82.

Singer, R. N. (1978). Motor skills and learning strategies. In H. F. O'Neil, Jr (Ed.), *Learning strategies.* New York: Academic.

Sirkin, M. I. (1990). Cult involvement: A systems approach to assessment and treatment. *Psychotherapy,* 27(1), 116–123.

Skeels, H. M. (1966). Adult status of children with contrasting early life experiences. *Monograph of the Society for Research in Child Development,* 31(3).

Skinner, B. F. (1938). *The behavior of organisms.* Englewood Cliffs, NJ: Prentice-Hall.

Skinner, B. F. (1971). *Beyond freedom and dignity.* New York: Bantam.

Skinner, B. F. (1990) Can psychology be a science of mind? *American Psychologist,* 45(11), 1206–1210.

Slater, A., Mattock, A., & Brown, E. (1990). Size constancy at birth: Newborn infants' responses to retinal and real size. *Journal of Experimental Child Psychology,* 49(2), 314–322.

Slater, A., Mattock, A., Brown, E., & Bremner, J. G. (1991). Form perception at birth: Cohen and Younger (1984) revisited. *Journal of Experimental Child Psychology, 51(3),* 395–406.

Smetana, J. G., Killen, M., & Turiel, E. (1991). Children's reasoning about interpersonal and moral conflicts. *Child Development, 62(3),* 629–644.

Smith, A., & Sugar, O. (1975). Development of above normal language and intelligence 21 years after left hemispherectomy. *Neurology,* 25, 813–818.

Smith, C. & Lapp, L. (1991). Increases in number of REMs and REM density in humans following an intensive learning period. *Sleep, 14*(4), 325–330.

Smith, C., Carey, S., & Wiser, M. (1985). On differentiation: A case study of the developement of the concepts of size, weight, and density. *Cognition, 21*(3), 177–237.

Smith, E. E. (1989). Concepts and induction. In M. I. Posner (Ed.), *Foundations of cognitive science,* Cambridge, MA: The MIT Press.

Smith, J. C. (1986). Meditation, biofeedback, and the relaxation controversy: A cognitive-behavioral perspective. *American Psychologist,* Sept., 1007–1009.

Smith, T. W. (1990). *Adult sexual behavior in 1989: Number of partners, frequency, and risk.* Paper presented to the American Association for the Advancement of Science, February, 1990, New Orleans.

Smith, V. L. & Ellsworth, P. C. (1987) The social psychology of eyewitness accuracy: Misleading questions and communicator expertise. *Journal of*

Applied Social Psychology, 72(2), 294–300.
Smith, V. L., Kassin, S. M., & Ellsworth, P. C. (1989). Eyewitness accuracy and confidence: Within- versus between-subjects correlations. *Journal of Applied Psychology*, 74(2), 356–359.
Smyth, A. (1991). *Seasonal affective disorder.* New York: HarperCollins.
Snow, C. E. (1977). The development of conversation between mothers and babies. *Journal of Child Language*, *4*, 1–22.
Snow, C. P. (1961). Either-or. *Progressive*, Feb., 24.
Snow, R. E. (1986). Individual differences and the design of educational programs. *American Psychologist*, *41*, 1029–1039.
Snowdon, C. T. (1983). Ethology, comparative psychology, and animal behavior. *Annual Review of Psychology*, 34, 63–94.
Snyder, C. R., & Shenkel, R. J. (1975). P. T. Barnum effect. *Psychology Today*, 8, 52–54.
Snyder, M. (1987). *Public appearances and private realities.* New York: Freeman.
Snyder, M. & Harkness, A. R. (1984). *E = f(p): The impact of personality on choice of situation.* Paper presented at the annual meeting of the Midwestern Psychological Association, Chicago.
Snyder, M. & Smith, D. (1985). *Self-monitoring and depression: Precipitating events and copying strategies.* Paper presented at the annual meeting of the Midwestern Psychological Association, Chicago.
Snyder, S. H., & Childers, S. R. (1979). Opiate receptors and opioid peptides. *Annual Review of Neuroscience*, *2*, 35–64.
Snyderman, M. & Rothman, S. (1987). Survey of expert opinion on intelligence and aptitude testing. *American Psychologist*, *42*(2), 137–144.
Sobel,˙ D. (1994). Space—1993. *Discover*, Jan., 56–57.
Solanto, M. V. (1984). Neuropharmacological basis of stimulant drug action in attention deficit disorder with hyperactivity: A review and synthesis. *Psychological Bulletin*, 95, 387–409.
Solomon, R. C., & Wynne, L. C. (1953). Traumatic avoidance learning: Acquisition in normal dogs. *Psychological Monographs*, 67(4, Whole No. 354).
Solomon, R. L. (1980). The opponent-process theory of acquired motivation. *American Psychologist*, Aug., 691–721.
Somberg, D. R., Stone, G., & Claiborn, C. D. (1993). Informed consent: Therapist's beliefs and practices. *Professional Psychology: Research & Practice*, 24(2), 153–159.
Sommer, R. (1977). Toward a psychology of natural behavior. *APA Monitor*, Jan.
Sorce, J. F., Emde, R. N., Campos, J. J., & Klinnert, M. D. (1985). Maternal emotional signaling: Its effect on the visual cliff behavior of 1-year-olds. *Developmental Psychology*, *21*, 195–200.
Spangenberg, J. J. & Lategan, T. P. (1993). Coping, androgyny, and attributional style. *South African Journal of Psychology*, 23(4), 195–203.
Spanos, N. P. (1990). Hypnosis, demonic possession, and multiple personality. In C. A. Ward (Ed.), *Altered states of consciousness and mental health.* Newbury Park, CA: Sage.
Spence, J. T. (1984). Masculinity, femininity, and gender-related traits. In B. A. Maker, & W. B. Maker (Eds.), *Progress in experimental personality research: Normal personality processes* (Vol. 13). New York: Academic.
Spencer, M. B. (1990). Development of minority children. *Child Development*, *61*, 267–269.
Spencer, M. B., & Markstrom-Adams, C. (1990). Identity processes among racial and ethnic minority children in America. *Child Development*, *61*, 290–310.
Sperry, R. W. (1956). The eye and the brain. *Scientific American*, Offprint No. 465, 48–52.
Sperry, R. W. (1968). Hemisphere deconnection and unity in conscious awareness. *American Psychologist*, 23, 723–733.
Spiegel, D. (1986). Dissociation, double binds, and posttraumatic stress in multiple personality disorder. In B. G. Braun (Ed.), *Treatment of multiple personality disorder.* Washington, DC: American Psychiatric Press.
Spielberger, C.D. & Stenmark, D.E. (1985). Community psychology. In Altmaier, E.M. & Meyer, M.E. (Eds.), *Applied specialties in psychology.* New York: Random House.
Spitz, R. A. (1945). Hospitalism: An inquiry into the genesis of psychiatric conditions in early childhood. In *The psychoanalytic study of the child* (Vol. I), 53–74. New York: International University Press.
Sprafka, J. M., Folsom, A. R., Burke, G. L. et al. (1990). Type A behavior and its association with cardiovascular disease prevalence in Blacks and Whites: The Minnesota Heart Survey. *Journal of Behavioral Medicine*, *13*(1), 1–13.
Springer, S. P. & Deutsch, G. (1989). *Left brain, right brain.* New York: Freeman.
Sprott, R. L., & Staats, J. (1975). Behavioral studies using genetically-defined mice—A bibliography. *Behavior Genetics*, 5, 27–82.
Squire, L. R. (1992). Memory and the hippocampus: A synthesis from findings with rats, monkeys, and humans. *Psychological Review*, *99(2)*, 195–231.
Squire, L. R., Knowlton, B., & Musen, G., (1993). The structure and organization of memory. In L. W. Porter and M. R. Rosenzweig (Eds.), *Annual Review of Psychology*, *44*, 453–495.
Squire, L. R., Zola-Morgan, S. (1988). Memory: Brain systems and behavior. *Trends in Neurosciences*, *11*(4), 170–175.
Stalheim-Smith, A. & Fitch, G. K. (1993). *Understanding human anatomy and physiology.* St. Paul, MN: West.
Stanovich, K. E. (1992). *How to think straight about psychology*, 3e. New York: HarperCollins.
Stapp, J., & Fulcher, R. (1983). *Salaries in psychology.* Washington DC: American Psychological Association.
Stark, E. (1981). Pigeon patrol. *Science 81*, Sept., 85–86.
Stark, R., & McEvoy, J. (1970). Middle-class violence. *Psychology Today*, Nov.
Staum, M. J. & Brotons, M. (1992). The influence of auditory subliminals on behavior. *Journal of Music Therapy*, 29(3), 130–185.
Steblay, N. M. (1987). Helping behavior in rural and urban environments: A meta-analysis. *Psychological Bulletin*, *102*(3), 346–356.
Steblay, N. M. (1992). A meta-analytic review of the weapon focus effect. *Law and Human Behavior*, *16*, 413–424.
Steele, C. M. & Josephs, R. A. (1990). Alcohol myopia. *American Psychologist*, *45*(8), 921–933.
Stefanis, C., Dornbush, R. L., & Fink, M. (1977). *Hashish: A study of long-term use.* New York: Raven.
Stein, M. I. (1974). *Stimulating creativity* (Vol. 1). New York: Academic.
Stein, M., Miller, A. H., & Trestman, R. L. (1990). Depression and the immune system. In R. Ader, N. Cohen, & D. L. Felten (Eds.), *Psychoneuroimmunology II.* New York: Academic Press.
Steinbacher, R. & Gilroy, F. (1990). Sex selection technology: A prediction of its use and effect. *Journal of Psychology, 124(3)*, 283–288.
Steinberg, L. D., Catalano, R., & Dooley, P. (1981). Economic antecedents of child abuse and neglect. *Child Development*, 52, 975–985.
Stensaas, L. J., Lavker, R. M., Monti-Bloch, L., Grosser, B. I., & Berliner, D. L. (1991). Ultrastructure of the human vomeronasal organ. *Journal of Steroid Biochemistry and Molecular Biology*, 39(4B), 553–560.
Stepper, S. & Strack, F. (1993). Proprioceptive determinants of emotional and non-emotional feelings. *Journal of Personality & Social Psychology*, *64*,(2), 211–220.
Steriade, M. & McCarley, R. W. (1990). Brainstem control of wakefulness and sleep. NY: Plenum.
Sterman, M. B. (1977). Effects of sensorimotor EEG feedback training on sleep and clinical manifestations of epilepsy. In J. Beatty, & H. Legewie (Eds.), *Biofeedback and behavior.* New York: Plenum.
Stern, D. (1982). Some interactive functions of rhythm changes between mother and infant. In M. Davis (Ed.), *Interaction rhythms, periodicity in communicative behavior.* New York: Human Sciences Press.
Stern, P. C. (1992). Psychological dimensions of global environmental change. In M. R. Rosenzweig and L. W. Porter (Eds.), *Annual Review of Psychology*, *43*, 269–302.
Stern, R. M., Hu, S., Anderson, R. B., Leibowitz, H. W. et al. (1990). The effects of fixation and restricted visual field on vection-induced motion sickness. *Aviation, Space, & Environmental Medicine*, *61*(8), 712–715.
Stern, W. C. (1981). REM sleep and behavioral plasticity: Evidence for involvement of brain catecholamines. In W. Fishbein (Ed.), *Sleep, dreams and memory* (99–109). New York: SP Medical and Scientific Books.
Sternberg, R. J. (1986). A triangular theory of love. *Psychological Review*, 93, 119–135.
Sternberg, R. J. (1987). Liking versus loving: A comparative evaluation of theories. *Psychological Bulletin*, *102*(3), 331–345.
Sternberg, R. J. (1988). *The triangle of love.* New York: Basic.
Sternberg, R. J. (1992). Ability tests, measurements, and markets. *Journal of Educational Psychology*, *84*(2), 134–140.
Sternberg, R. J. & Barnes, M. (1986). Real and ideal others in romantic relationships: Is four a crowd? *Journal of Personality & Social Psychology*, *49*, 1586–1608.

Sternberg, R. J. & Davidson, J. D. (1985). Cognitive development in the gifted and talented. In F. D. Horowitz & M. O'Brien (Eds.), *The gifted and talented: Developmental perspectives,* Washington, DC: American Psychological Association, 37–74.

Sternberg, R. J., & Davidson, J. D. (1982). The mind of the puzzler. *Psychology Today,* June.

Sternberg, R. J., & Grajek, S. (1984). The nature of love. *Journal of Personality & Social Psychology,* 47, 312–329.

Stevens, C. F. (1979). The neuron. *Scientific American, 241*(3), 54–65.

Stiles, W. B., Shapiro, D. A., & Elliott, R. (1986). Are all psychotherapies equivalent? *American Psychologist, 41,* 165–180.

Stokols, D. (1978). Environmental psychology. *Annual Review of Psychology,* 29, 253–295.

Stokols, D. (1992). Establishing and maintaining healthy environments. *American Psychologist, 47(1),* 6–22.

Stoller, F. H. (1967). The long weekend. *Psychology Today, l*(7), 28–33.

Story, M. & Brown, J. E. (1987). Do young children instinctively know what to eat? *The New England Journal of Medicine, 316,* 103–106.

Strack. F., Martin, L. L., & Stepper, S. (1988). Inhibiting and facilitating conditions of facial expressions: A non-obtrusive test of the facial feedback hypothesis. *Journal of Personality & Social Psychology, 54,* 768–777.

Strange, J. R. (1965). *Abnormal psychology.* New York: McGraw-Hill.

Streissguth, A. P. (1992). Fetal alcohol syndrome: Early and long-term consequences. *NIDA Research Monograph, 119,* 126–30.

Streissguth, A. P., Barr, H. M., Sampson, P. D., Darby, B. L. et al. (1989). IQ at age 4 in relation to maternal alcohol use and smoking during pregnancy. *Developmental Psychology, 25*(1), 3–11.

Streissguth, A.P., Treder, R. P., Barr, H. M., Shepard, T. H., Bleyer, W. A.., Sampson, P. D., & Martin, D. C. (1987). Aspirin and acetaminophen use by pregnant women and subsequent child IQ and attention decrements. *Teratology,* 35(2), 211–219.

Strickler, E. M. & Verbalis, J. G. (1988). Hormones and behavior: The biology of thirst and sodium appetite. *American Scientist,* May-June, 261–267.

Strong, B. & DeVault, C. (1994). *Understanding our sexuality.* St. Paul, MN: West.

Strongman, K. T. (1987). *The psychology of emotion.* New York: Wiley.

Strupp, H. H. (1989). Psychotherapy: Can the practitioner learn from the researcher? *American Psychologist, 44*(4), 717–724

Stunkard, A. (1980). *Obesity.* Philadelphia: Saunders.

Stunkard, A. J., Sorenson, T. I. A., Hanis, C., Teasdale, T. et al. (1986). An adoption study of human obesity. *New England Journal of Medicine, 314,* 193–198.

Sue, D. & Sue, D. W. (1991). Counseling strategies for Chinese Americans. In C. C. Lee & B. L. Richardson (Eds.), *Multicultural issues in counseling.* Alexandria, VA: American Association for Counseling and Development.

Sue, D. W. & Sue, D. (1990). *Counseling the culturally different: Theory and practice.* New York: Wiley.

Sue, D., Sue, D. W., & Sue, S. (1990). *Understanding abnormal behavior.* Boston: Houghton Mifflin.

Sue, S. & Zane, N. (1987). The role of culture and cultural techniques in psychotherapy. *American Psychologist, 42,* 37–45.

Suedfeld, P. (1966). *Social processes.* Dubuque, IA: Brown.

Suedfeld, P. (1980). *Restricted environmental stimulation: Research and clinical applications.* New York: Wiley-Interscience.

Suedfeld, P., & Piedrahita, L. E. (1984). Intimations of mortality: Integrative simplification as a precursor of death. *Journal of Personality and Social Psychology,* 47, 848–852.

Suedfeld, P., Metcalfe, J., & Bluck, S. (1987). Enhancement of scientific creativity by flotation REST (restricted environmental stimulation technique). *Journal of Environmental Psychology,* 7(3), 219–231.

Suinn, R. M. (1970). *Fundamentals of behavior pathology.* New York: Wiley.

Suinn, R. M. (1975). *Fundamentals of behavior pathology* (2nd ed.). New York: Wiley.

Suinn, R. M. (1982). Intervention with Type A behaviors. *Journal of Consulting and Clinical Psychology,* 50, 933–949.

Sullivan, M. A. & O'Leary, S. G. (1990). Maintenance following reward and cost token programs. *Behavior Therapy, 21*(1), 139–149.

Suls, J. (1989). Self-awareness and self-identity in adolescence. In J. Worell & F. Danner, Eds. *The adolescent as decision-maker.* New York: Academic.

Sulzman, F. M. (1983). Primate circadian rhythms. *BioScience,* 33(7), 445–450.

Swain, I. U., Zelazo, P. R., & Clifton, R. K. (1993). Newborn infants' memory for speech sounds retained over 24 hours. *Developmental Psychology,* 29(2), 312–323.

Swan, G. E. & Denk, C. E. (1987). Dynamic models for the maintenance of smoking cessation: Event history analysis of late relapse. *Journal of Behavioral Medicine, 10*(6), 527–554.

Swart, L. C. & Morgan, C. L. (1992). Effects of subliminal backward-recorded messages on attitudes. *Perceptual & Motor Skills, 75*(3, Pt 2), 1107–1113.

Swartz, C. M. (1993). ECT or programmed seizures? *American Journal of Psychiatry, 150*(8), 1274–1275.

Swets, J., Bjork, R. A., Cook, T. D., Davison, G. C. et al. (1988). *Enhancing human performance: Issues, theories, and techniques.* Washington, DC: National Academy Press of the United States National Research Council.

Szasz, T. S. (1966). Mental illness is a myth. *The New York Times Magazine,* June 12.

Szasz, T. S. (1983). *Thomas Szasz: Primary values and major contentions.* Buffalo, NY: Prometheus.

Szasz, T. S. (1987). *Insanity: The idea and its consequences.* New York: Wiley.

Taeuber, C. M. (1993). *Sixty-five plus in America.* Washington, DC: United States Bureau of Census.

Takei, N., Sham, P., O'Callaghan, E., Murray, G. K., et al. (1994). Prenatal exposure to influenza and the development of schizophrenia. *American Journal of Psychiatry, 151*(1), 117–119.

Takooshian, H., Haber, S., & Lucido, D. J. (1977). Who wouldn't help a lost child? You, maybe. *Psychology Today,* Feb., 67.

Talley, P. F., Strupp, H. H., & Morey, L. C. (1990). Matchmaking in psychotherapy: Patient-therapist dimensions and their impact on outcome. *Journal of Consulting & Clinical Psychology,* 58(2), 182–188.

Tannenbaum, S. I., & Yukl, G. (1992). Training and development in work organizations. In M. R. Rosenzweig and L. W. Porter (Eds.), *Annual Review of Psychology, 43,* 399–441.

Tanner, J. M. (1973). Growing up. *Scientific American,* Sept., 34–43.

Tanzer, D., & Block, J. L. (1976). *Why natural childbirth?* New York: Schocken.

Tardif, T. Z. & Sternberg, R. J. (1988). What do we know about creativity? In R. J. Sternberg (Ed.), *The nature of creativity.* Cambridge University Press.

Tart, C. T. (1975). *States of consciousness.* New York: Dutton.

Tart, C. T. (1986). Consciousness, altered states, and worlds of experience. *Journal of Transpersonal Psychology, 18*(2), 159–170.

Tashkin, D. P., Simmons, M., & Clark, V. (1988). Effect of habitual smoking of marijuana alone and with tobacco on nonspecific airways hyperreactivity. *Journal of Psychoactive Drugs, 20(1),* 21–25.

Tavris, C. (1992). *The mismeasure of woman.* New York: Touchstone/Simon & Schuster.

Tavris, C. (1993). Beware the incest-survivor machine. *New York Times Book Review,* (Jan. 3), 1, 16–17.

Taylor, C. W. (1978). How many types of giftedness can your program tolerate? *The Journal of Creative Behavior, 12,* 39–51.

Taylor, S. E. (1990). Health Psychology. *American Psychologist, 45*(1), 40–5O.

Taylor, T. E. (1983, March 17). Learning studies of higher cognitive levels in short-term sensory isolation environment. Paper delivered at First International Conference on REST and Self-regulation, Denver, Colorado.

Tedeschi, J. T., Lindskold, S., & Rosenfeld, P. (1985). *Introduction to social psychology.* St. Paul: West Publishing.

Teen sex: Not for love. (1989). *Psychology Today,* May, 10.

Teplin, L. A., Abram, K. M., & McClelland. (1994). Does psychiatric disorder predict violent crime among released jail detainees? *American Psychologist, 49*(4), 335–342.

Terman, L. M., & Merrill, M. A. (1937, revised, 1960). *Stanford-Binet Intelligence Scale.* Boston: Houghton Mifflin.

Terman, L. M., & Oden, M. (1959). *The gifted group in mid-life. Vol. 5, Genetic studies of genius.* Stanford, CA: Stanford University Press.

Terr, L. C. (1991). Childhood traumas. *American Journal of Psychiatry, 148*(1), 10–20.

Terrace, H. S. (1985). In the beginning was the "name." *American Psychologist, 40,* 1011–1028.

Thatcher, R. W., Walker, R. A., & Giudice, S. (1987). Human cerebral hemispheres develop at different rates and ages. *Science, 236,* 1110–1113.

Thayer, S. (1988). Close encounters. *Psychology Today*, March, 31–36.

The mind in motion, by G. Montgomery, (1989). *Discover*, March, 58–68.

They'd kill for $1 million. (1991). *The Los Angeles Times*, July 1, A-8.

Thibodeau, R. & Aronson, E. (1992). Taking a closer look: Reasserting the role of self-concept in dissonance theory. *Personality and Social Psychology Bulletin*, *18*(5), 591–602.

Thies, C. F. & Register, C. A. (1993). Decriminalization of marijuana and the demand for alcohol, marijuana and cocaine. *Social Science Journal*, *30*(4), 385–399.

Thigpen, C. H., & Cleckley, H. M. (1957). *The three faces of Eve*. New York: McGraw-Hill.

Thoman, E. B., Davis, D. H., Graham, S., Scholz, J. P. et al. (1988). Infants at risk for sudden infant death syndrome (SIDS): Differential prediction for three siblings of SIDS infants. *Journal of Behavioral Medicine*, *11*(6), 565–583.

Thompson, C. P., Cowan, T. M., & Frieman, J. (1993). *Memory search by a menorist*. Hillsdale, NJ: Lawrence Erlbaum.

Thompson, R. F. (1985). *The brain*. New York: Freeman.

Thompson, R. F. (1991). Are memory traces localized or distributed? *Neuropsychologia*, *29*(6), 571–582.

Thornburg, H. D. (1984). *Introduction to educational psychology*. St. Paul: West.

Thorson, J. A. & Powell, F. C. (1990). Meanings of death and intrinsic religiosity. *Journal of Clinical Psychology*, *46*(4), 379–391.

Tierny, J. (1987). Stitches: Good news; Better health liked to sin, sloth. *Hippocrates*. Sept./Oct., 30–35.

Tiffany, S. T., Martin, E. M., & Baker, T. B. (1986). Treatments for cigarette smoking: An evaluation of the contributions of aversion and counseling procedures. *Behavior Research & Therapy*, *24*(4), 437–452.

Time, (1973, Jan. 8).

Timm, P. R. & Peterson, B. D. (1990). *People at work*. St. Paul, MN: West.

Tollefson, G. D., Fawcett, J. Winokur, G. Beasley, C., et al. (1993). Evaluation of suicidality during pharmacologic treatment of mood and nonmood disorders. *Annals of Clinical Psychiatry*, *5*(4), 209–224.

Tolman, E. C., & Honzik, C. H. (1930). Introduction and removal of reward and maze performance in rats. *University of California Publications in Psychology*, *4*, 257–275.

Tolman, E. C., Ritchie, B. F., & Kalish, D. (1946). Studies in spatial learning: II. Place learning versus response learning. *Journal of Experimental Psychology*, *36*, 221–229.

Tomlinson-Keasey, C. & Little, T. D. (1990). Predicting educational attainment, occupational achievement, intellectual skill, and personal adjustment among gifted men and women. *Journal of Educational Psychology*, *82*(3), 442–455.

Torrance, M., Thomas, Glyn V., & Robinson, E. J. (1991). Strategies for answering examination essay questions: Is it helpful to write a plan? *British Journal of Educational Psychology*, *61(1)*, 46–54.

Torrey, E. F. (1988). *Surviving schizophrenia: A family manual*. New York: Harper & Row.

Treffert, D. A. (1988). The idiot savant: A review of the syndrome. *American Journal of Psychiatry*, *145*(5), 563–572.

Trehub, S. E., Unyk, A. M., & Trainor, L. J. (1993a). Adults identify infant-directed music across cultures. *Infant Behavior & Development*, *16*(2), 193–211.

Trehub, S. E., Unyk, A. M., & Trainor, L. J. (1993b). Maternal singing in cross-cultural perspective. *Infant Behavior & Development*, *16*(3), 285–295.

Tresemer, D. W. (1977). *Fear of success: An intriguing set of questions*. New York: Plenum.

Triandis, H. C. (1977). *Interpersonal behavior*. Monterey, CA: Brooks/Cole.

Tronick, E., Morelli, G. A., & Ivey, P. K. (1992). The Efe forager infant and toddler's pattern of social relationships. *Developmental Psychology*, *28*(4), 568–577.

Trotter, R. J. (1986). The three faces of love. *Psychology Today*, Sept. 44–54.

Troutt-Ervin, E. D. (1990). Application of keyword mnemonics to learning terminology in the college classroom. *Journal of Experimental Education*, *59*(1), 31–41.

Truax, S. R. (1983). Active search, mediation, and the manipulation of cue dimensions: Emotion attribution in the false feedback paradigm. *Motivation and Emotion*, *7*, 41–60.

Trujillo, M. (1986). Short-term dynamic psychotherapy. In Kutash, I. L. & Wolf, A. (Eds.), *Psychotherapist's casebook*. San Francisco: Jossey-Bass.

Tryon, R. C. (1929). The genetics of learning ability in rats. *University of California Publications in Psychology*, *4*, pp. 71–89.

Tucker, P. & Aron, A. (1993). Passionate love and marital satisfaction at key transition points in the family life cycle. *Journal of Social & Clinical Psychology*, *12*(2), 135–147.

Tulving, E. (1989). Remembering and knowing the past. *American Scientist*, *77*,(4), 361–367.

Turco, R. P., Toon, O. B., Ackerman, T. P. Pollack, J. B., & Sagan, C. (1983). Nuclear winter: Global consequences of multiple nuclear explosions. *Science*, *222*, 1, 283–292.

Turkheimer, E. & Parry, C. D. H. (1992). Why the gap? *American Psychologist*, *47(5)*, 646–655.

Turkington, C. (1986). Pot and the immune system. *APA Monitor*, Aug., 22.

Turkington, C. (1992). Ruling opens door—a crack—to IQ testing some black kids. *APA Monitor*, Dec., 28–29.

Turnbull, C. M. (1961). Some observations regarding the experiences and behavior of the Bambuti Pygmies. *American Journal of Psychology*, *74*, 304–308.

Turner, M. E., Pratkanis, A. R., Probasco, P., & Leve, C. (1992). Threat, cohesion, and group effectiveness: Testing a social identity maintenance perspective on groupthink. *Journal of Personality & Social Psychology*, *63*(5), 781–796.

Tversky, A., & Kahneman, D. (1981). The framing of decisions and the psychology of choice. *Science*, *211*, 453–458.

Tversky, A., & Kahneman, D. (1982). Judgments of and by representativeness. In D. Kahneman, P. Slovic, & A. Tversky, *Judgment under uncertainty: Heuristics and biases*. Cambridge: Cambridge University Press.

Tyler, L. E. (1992). Counseling psychology: Why? *Professional Psychology: Research & Practice*. *23*(5), 342–344.

Tzeng, M. (1992). The effects of socioeconomic heterogamy and changes on marital dissolution for first marriages. *Journal of Marriage and Family*, *54*, 609–619.

Udry, J. R., & Eckland, B. K. (1984). Benefits of being attractive: Differential payoffs for men and women. *Psychological Reports*, *54*, 47–56.

Udry, J. R., & Morris, N. M. (1977). Human sexual behavior at different stages of the menstrual cycle. *Journal of Reproduction and Fertility*, *51*, 419.

Ulett, G. A. (1992). 3000 years of acupuncture: From metaphysics to neurophysiology. *Integrative Psychiatry*, *8*(2), 91–100.

Ulrich, R. E., Stachnik, T. J., & Stainton, N. R. (1963). Student acceptance of generalized personality interpretations. *Psychological Reports*, *131*, 831–834.

Underwood, B. J. (1957). Interference and forgetting. *Psychological Review*, *64*, 49–60.

UNESCO, (1990). The Seville statement on violence. *American Psychologist*, *45*(10), 1167–1168.

United Nations Population Fund. (1993). *Population issues: Briefing kit*. New York: Author.

Valenstein, E. S. (1980). Extent of psychosurgery worldwide. In E. S. Valenstein (Ed.), *The psychosurgery debate*. San Francisco: Freeman.

Valins, S. (1966). Cognitive effects of false heart-rate feedback. *Journal of Personality & Social Psychology*, *4*, 400–408.

Valins, S. (1967). Emotionality and information concerning internal reactions. *Journal of Personality & Social Psychology*, *6*, 458–463.

Van Lawick-Goodall, J. (1971). *In the shadow of man*. New York: Houghton Mifflin.

Van Maanen, J., & Schein, E. H. (1977). Career development. In J. R. Hackman, & J. L. Suttle (Eds.). *Improving life at work*. Santa Monica, CA.: Goodyear.

Van Riper, C. & Emerick, L. (1984). *Speech correction: An introduction to speech pathology and audiology*. Englewood Cliffs, NJ: Prentice-Hall.

VandenBos, G. R. & Bryant, B. K. (1987). Preface. In VandenBos, G. R. & Bryant, B. K. (Eds.), *Cataclysms, crises, and catastrophes: Psychology in action*. Washington, DC: American Psychological Association.

Ventura J., Nuechterlein, K. H., Lukow, D., & Hardesty, J. P. (1989). A prospective study of stressful life events and schizophrenic relapse. *Journal of Abnormal Psychology*, *98*(4), 407–411.

Vera, E. & Betz, N. E. (1992). Relationships of self-regard and affective self-disclosure to relationship satisfaction in college students. *Journal of College Student Development*, *33*(5), 422–430.

Vernoy, M. W. (1989). Simultaneous adaptation to size, distance, and curvature underwater. *Human Factors*, *31*(1), 77–85.

Viegener, B. J., Perri, M. G., Nezu, A. M. et al. (1990). Effects of an intermittent, low-fat, low-calorie diet in the behavioral treatment of obesity. *Behavior Therapy*, *21*(4), 499–509.

Vils, U. (1976). Alcoholism: Tempest in a shot glass. *Los Angeles Times*, Feb. 26.

Vogel, S. (1988). Cold storage. *Discover*, Feb., 52–54.

Vogler, R. E., & Bartz, W. R. (1982). *The better way to drink.* New York: Simon and Schuster.

Vogler, R. E., & Bartz, W. R. (1992). *Teenagers and alcohol.* Philadelphia: Charles Press.

Vogler, R. E., Weissbach, T. A., Compton, J. V., & Martin, G. T. (1977). Integrated behavior change techniques for problem drinkers in the community. *Journal of Consulting and Clinical Psychology, 45*, 267–279.

Vokey, J. R. & Read, J. D. (1985). Subliminal messages: Between the Devil and the media. *American Psychologist, 40* (11), 1231–1239.

Volpicelli, J. R., Ulm, R. R., Altenor, A., & Seligman, M. E. P. (1983). Learned mastery in the rat. *Learning and Motivation, 14*, 204–222.

Von Baumgarten, R., Benson, A., Berthoz, A., Brandt, T. et al. (1984). Spatial orientation in weightlessness and readaptation to earth's gravity. *Science, 225*, 205–225.

Wade, S. E. & Trathen, W. (1989). Effect of self-selected study methods on learning. *Journal of Educational Psychology, 81*(1), 40–47.

Waid, W. M., & Orne, M. T. (1982). The physiological detection of deception. *American Scientist*, 70(July/Aug.), 402–409.

Wakefield, J. C. (1992). The concept of mental disorder. *American Psychologist, 47(3)*, 373–388.

Walden, T. A. & Ogan, T. A. (1988). The development of social referencing. *Child Development*, 59(5), 1230–1240.

Waldvogel, J. A. (1990). The bird's eye view. *American Scientist*, 78(4), 342–353.

Walker, L. J. (1989). A longitudinal study of moral reasoning. *Child Development, 60*(1), 157–166.

Wallach, M. A. (1985). Creativity testing and giftedness. In F. D. Horowitz & M. O'Brien (Eds.), *The gifted and talented: Developmental perspectives*, Washington, DC: American Psychological Association, 99–123.

Wallach, M. A., & Kogan, N. (1965). *Modes of thinking in young children.* New York: Holt.

Walsh, R. (1984). An evolutionary model of meditation research. In Shapiro, D. H. & Walsh, R. N. (Eds.), *Meditation: Classic and contemporary perspectives.* New York: Aldine.

Walster, E. (1971). Passionate Love. In B. I. Murstein (Ed.). *Theories of attraction and love.* New York: Springer.

Walster, E., & Walster, G. W. (1978). *A new look at love.* Reading, MA: Addison-Wesley.

Walton, C. E., Bower, M. L., & Bower, T. G. (1992). Recognition of familiar faces by newborns. *Infant Behavior & Development, 15(2)*, 265–269.

Ward, C. A. (1989). The cross-cultural study of altered states of consciousness and mental health. In C. A. Ward (Ed.), *Altered states of consciousness and mental health.* Newbury Park, CA: Sage.

Ward, P. B., Catts, S. V., Fox, A. M., Michie, P. T. et al. (1991). Auditory selective attention and event-related potentials in schizophrenia. *British Journal of Psychiatry, 158*, 534–539.

Warrenburg, S., & Pagano, R. (1983). Meditation and hemispheric specialization: Absorbed attention in long-term adherence. *Imagination, Cognition and Personality*, 2, 211–229.

Watkins, J. G. (1989). Hypnotic hypermnesia and forensic hypnosis: A cross-examination. *American Journal of Clinical Hypnosis*, 32(2), 71–83.

Watson, D. L., & Tharp, R. G. (1993). *Self-directed behavior: Self-modification for personal adjustment, 4th ed.* Monterey, CA: Brooks/Cole.

Watson, D. L., deBortali-Tregerthan, G., & Frank, J. (1984). *Social Psychology: Science and application.* Glenview, IL: Scott, Foresman.

Watson, J. B. (1913). Psychology as the behaviorist views it. *Psychological Review, 20*, 158–177.

Watt, J. (1990). Interaction, intervention, and development in small-for-gestational-age infants. *Infant Behavior & Development, 13(3)*, 273–286.

Weaver, C. A. (1993). Do you need a "flash" to form a flashbulb memory? *Journal of Experimental Psychology: General, 122*(1), 39–46.

Weaver, C. N. & Matthews, M. D. (1987). What white males want from their jobs: Ten years later. *Personnel*, 4(9), 62–65.

Webb, N. M. & Farivar, S. (1994). Promoting helping behavior in cooperative small groups in middle school mathematics. *American Educational Research Journal*, 31(2), 369–395.

Webb, W. (1975). *Sleep the gentle tyrant.* Englewood Cliffs, NJ: Prentice-Hall.

Webb, W. (1978). Sleep and dreams, Part I. *Annual Review of Psychology, 29*, 223–252.

Wegner, D. M., & Vallacher, R. R. (1977). *Implicit psychology.* New York: Oxford University Press.

Weinberg, M. S., & Williams, C. J. (1974). *Male homosexuals.* New York: Oxford University Press.

Weinberg, R. A. (1989). Intelligence and IQ. *American Psychologist, 44*(2), 98–104.

Weinberger, M., Hiner, S. L., & Tierney, W. M. (1987). In support of hassles as a measure of stress in predicting health outcomes. *Journal of Behavioral Medicine, 10*(1), 19–31.

Weiner, R. D. (1984). Convulsive therapy: 50 years later. *American Journal of Psychiatry, 14*, 1078–1079.

Weintraub, M. I. (1983). *Hysterical conversion reactions.* New York: SP Medical & Scientific Books.

Weisburd, D. E. (1990). Planning a community-based mental health system: Perspective of a family member. *American Psychologist, 45*(11), 1245–1248.

Weisenberg, R. W. (1986). *Creativity.* New York: W. H. Freeman.

Weisfeld, G. E., & Beresford, J. M. (1982). Erectness of posture as an indicator of dominance or success in humans. *Motivation and Emotion, 6*, 113–131.

Weiss, B., Dodge, K. A., Bates, J. E., & Pettit, G. S. (1992). Some consequences of early harsh discipline. *Child Development, 63*(6), 1321–1335.

Weiss, J. (1990). Unconscious mental functioning. *Scientific American*, March, 103–109.

Weiss, J. M. (1972). Psychological factors in stress and disease. *Scientific American, 26*, 104–113.

Weiss, R. (1989). Bypassing the ban. *Science News, 138*, 378–379.

Weiss, R. (1990). Shadows of thoughts revealed. *Science News, 138*(19), 297.

Weiten, W. (1988). Pressure as a form of stress and its relationship to psychological symptomatology. *Journal of Social & Clinical Psychology, 6*(1), 127–139.

Weitzenhoffer, A. M., & Hilgard, E. R. (1959). *Stanford Hypnotic susceptibility Scales Forms A and B.* Palo Alto, CA: Consulting Psychologists Press.

Wells, G. L. (1993). What do we know about eyewitness identification? *American Psychologist, 48(5)*, 553–571.

Wells, G. L., Rydell, S. M., & Seelau, E. P. (1993). The selection of distractors for eyewitness lineups. *Journal of Applied Psychology, 78*(5), 835–844.

Wertheimer, M. (1959). *Productive thinking.* New York: Harper & Row.

West, L. J. (1993). A psychiatric overview of cult-related phenomena. *Journal of the American Academy of Psychoanalysis, 21(1)*, 1–19.

West, T. G. (1991). *In the mind's eye.* Buffalo, NY: Prometheus.

Wetzler, H. P. & Ursano, R. J. (1988). A positive association between physical health practices and psychological well-being. *Journal of Nervous & Mental Disease, 176*(5), 280–283.

Wexley, K. N. (1984). Personnel training. *Annual Review of Psychology*, 35, 519–551.

Wheeler, L. & Miyake, K. (1992). Social comparison in everyday life. *Journal of Personality & Social Psychology, 62(5)*, 760–773.

Wheeler, R. J. & Frank, M. A. (1988). Identification of stress buffers. *Behavioral Medicine, 14*(2), 78–89.

Whiften, V. E. (1988). Vulnerability to postpartum depression. *Journal of Abnormal Psychology, 97*(4), 467–474.

Whimbey, A., with Whimbey, L. S. (1980). *Intelligence can be taught.* New York: Dutton.

Whitbourne, S. K. (1986). *Adult development.* New York: Praeger.

White, B. L. (1990). *The first three years of life.* New York: Prentice-Hall.

White, B. L., & Held, R. (1966). Plasticity of sensorimotor development in the human infant. In J. F. Rosenblith, & W. Allinsmith (Eds.). *The causes of behavior Vol. I.* Boston: Allyn & Bacon.

White, B. L., & Watts, J. C. (1973). *Experience and environment Vol. I.* Englewood Cliffs, NJ: Prentice-Hall.

White, S. D. & DeBlassie, R. R. (1992). Adolescent sexual behavior. *Adolescence, 27(105)*, 183–191.

Whitehead, W. E. (1992). Behavioral medicine approaches to gastrointestinal disorders. *Journal of Consulting and Clinical Psychology, 60*(4), 605–612.

Whitley, B. E. (1993). Reliability and aspects of the construct validity of Sternberg's Triangular Love Scale. *Journal of Social & Personal Relationships, 10*(3), 475–480.

Wickens, C. D., & Kramer, A. (1985). Engineering psychology. *Annual Review of Psychology, 36*, 307–348.

Widiger, T. A. & Trull, T. J. (1991). Diagnosis and clinical assessment. In M. R. Rosenzweig and L. W. Porter (Eds.), *Annual Review of Psychology*, 42, 109–133.

Wiebe, D. J. (1991). Hardiness and stress moderation. *Journal of Personality & Social Psychology, 60*(1),

89–99.

Wilhelm, J. L. (1976). *The search for superman.* New York: Simon & Schuster.

Williams, B. A. (1984). U.S. approves implants to aid the totally deaf. *Santa Barbara News Press,* Nov. 30, part C, 6.

Williams, C. L. & Berry, J. W. (1991). Primary prevention of acculturative stress among refugees. *American Psychologist, 46*(6), 632–641.

Williams, R. (1989). The trusting heart: Great news about Type A behavior. New York: Random House.

Williams, R. L. (1975). The Bitch-100: A culture-specific test. *Journal of Afro-American Issues,* 3, 103–116.

Williams, R. L., & Long, J. D. (1991). *Toward a self-managed life style.* Boston: Houghton Mifflin.

Williams, R. L., et al. (1964). Sleep patterns in young adults: An EEG study. *Electroencephalography and Clinical Neurophysiology,* 376–381.

Williamson, A. M. & Sanderson, J. W. (1986). Changing the speed of shift rotations: A field study. *Ergonomics,* 29(9), 1085–1095.

Williamson, D. A., Davis, C. J., Goreczny, A. J., & Blouin, D. C. (1989). Body-image disturbances in bulimia nervosa: Influences of actual body size. *Journal of Abnormal Psychology,* 98(1), 97–99.

Willinger, M., Hoffman, H. J., & Hartford, R. B. (1994). Infant sleep position and risk for sudden infant death syndrome. *Pediatrics,* 93(5), 814–819.

Wilson, E. O. (1975). Human decency is animal. *New York Times Magazine,* Oct. 12.

Wilson, R. R. (1986). *Don't panic: Taking control of anxiety attacks.* New York: Harper & Row.

Wilson, S., Strong, B., Clarke, L. M., & Thomas, J. (1984). *Human sexuality.* St. Paul, MN: West.

Wilson, W. H. (1989). Reassessment of state hospital patients diagnosed with schizophrenia. *Journal of Neuropsychiatry & Clinical Neurosciences,* 1(4), 394–397.

Winget, C., & Kramer, M. (1979). *Dimensions of dreams.* Gainesville: University Presses of Florida.

Winson, J. (1990). The meaning of dreams. *Scientific American,* Nov., 86–96.

Wise, E. H., & Haynes, S. N. (1983). Cognitive treatment of test anxiety: Rational restructuring versus attentional training. *Cognitive Therapy and Research, 7,* 69–78.

Wise, J. (1982). A gentle deterrent to vandalism. *Psychology Today,* Sept., 31–38.

Wise, R. A. & Rompre, P. P. (1989). Brain dopamine and reward. *Annual Review of Psychology, 40,* 191–225.

Witherspoon, W. (1994). Disorder consumed her life. *Los Angeles Times,* July 28, C:1.

Woehr, D. J. & Cavell, T. A. (1993). Self-report measures of ability, effort, and nonacademic activity as predictors of introductory psychology test scores. *Teaching of Psychology,* 20(3), 156–160.

Wolfe, D. A. & Wekerle, C. (1993). Treatment strategies for child physical abuse and neglect. *Clinical Psychology Review,* 13(6), 473–500.

Wolfe, J. B. (1936). Effectiveness of token rewards for chimpanzees. *Comparative Psychology Monographs,* 12(5), Whole No. 60.

Woloshyn, V. E., Willoughby, T., Wood, E., & Pressley, M. (1990). Elaborative interrogation facilitates adult learning of factual paragraphs. *Journal of Educational Psychology, 82(3),* 513–524.

Wolpe, J. (1974). *The practice of behavior therapy (2nd ed.).* New York: Pergamon.

Wolpin, M., Marston, A., Randolph, C., & Clothier, A. (1992). Individual difference correlates of reported lucid dreaming frequency and control. *Journal of Mental Imagery,* 16(3–4), 231–236.

Wolraich, M. L., Lindgren, S. D., Stumbo, P. J., Stegink, L. D., Appelbaum, M. I., & Kiritsy, M. C. (1994). Effects of diets high in sucrose or aspartame on the behavior and cognitive performance of children. *New England Journal of Medicine,* 330(5), 301–307.

Wong, C. Y., Sommer, R., & Cook, E. J. (1992). The soft classroom 17 years later. *Journal of Environmental Psychology,* 12(4), 337–343.

Wood, J. M. & Bootzin, R. R. (1990). The prevalence of nightmares and their independence from anxiety. *Journal of Abnormal Psychology,* 99(1), 64–68.

Wood, J. M., Bootzin, R. R., Kihlstrom, J. F., & Schacter, D. L. (1992). Implicit and explicit memory for verbal information presented during sleep. *Psychological Science,* 3(4), 236–239.

Woodmansee, J. J. (1970). The pupil response as a measure of social attitudes. In G. F. Summers (Ed.), *Attitude measurement.* Chicago: Rand McNally.

Woods, P. J. (Ed.) with C. S. Wilkinson. (1987). *Is psychology the major for you? Planning for your undergraduate years.* Washington, DC: American Psychological Association.

Work In America. (1973). Special Task Force, Department of Health, Education and Welfare. Cambridge, MA: MIT Press.

Wortman, C. B. & Silver, R. C. (1989). The myths of coping with loss. *Journal of Consulting & Clinical Psychology,* 57(3), 349–357.

Wright, D. B. (1993). Recall of the Hillsborough disaster over time: Systematic biases of "flashbulb" memories. *Applied Cognitive Psychology,* 7(2), 129–138.

Wright, K. (1994). The sniff of legend. *Discover,* April, 60–67.

Wursig, B. (1979). Dolphins. *Scientific American,* 240 (3), 136–148.

Wyatt, J. W., Posey, A., Welker, W., & Seamonds, C. (1984). Natural levels of similarities between identical twins and between unrelated people. *The Skeptical Inquirer,* 9, 62–66.

Yalom, I. D. (1980). *Existential psychotherapy.* New York: Basic.

Yank, G. R., Bentley, K. J., & Hargrove, D. S. (1993). The vulnerability-stress model of schizophrenia. *American Journal of Orthopsychiatry,* 63(1), 55–69.

Yardley, L. (1992). Motion sickness and perception. *British Journal of Psychology,* 83(4), 449–471.

Yee, A. H., Fairchild, H. H., Weizmann, F., & Wyatt, G. E. (1993). Addressing psychology's problems with race. *American Psychologist,* 48(11), 1132–1140.

Yoshida, M. (1993). Three-dimensional electrophysiological atlas created by computer mapping of clinical responses elicited on stimulation of human subcortical structures. *Stereotactic & Functional Neurosurgery,* 60(1–3), 127–134.

Yuille, J. C. & Tollestrup, P. A. (1990). Some effects of alcohol on eyewitness memory. *Journal of Applied Psychology,* 75(3), 268–273.

Zajonc, R. B. (1975). Dumber by the dozen. *Psychology Today,* Jan., 37–43.

Zane, M. D., & Milt, H. (1984). *Your phobia.* Washington, DC: American Psychiatric Press.

Zellner, D. A., Harner, D. E., & Adler, R. L. (1989). Effects of eating abnormalities and gender on perceptions of desirable body shape. *Journal of Abnormal Psychology,* 98(1), 93–96.

Zetlin, A. & Murtaugh, M. (1990). Whatever happened to those with borderline IQs? *American Journal on Mental Retardation,* 94(5), 463–469.

Zigler, E. & Muenchow, S. (1992). *Head Start: The inside story of America's most successful educational experience.* New York: Basic.

Zigler, E. & Styfco, S. J. (1994). Head start. *American Psychologist,* 49(2), 127–132.

Zilbergeld, B. (1983). *The shrinking of America: Myths of psychological change.* Boston: Little Brown.

Zimbardo, P. G., Haney, C., & Banks, W. C. (1973). A pirandellian prison. *The New York Times Magazine,* April 8.

Zimbardo, P. G., Pilkonis, P. A., & Norwood, R. M. (1978). The social disease called shyness. In *Annual editions, personality and adjustment 78/79.* Guilford CT: Dushkin.

Zimmer, C. (1993). Making senses. *Discover,* June, 79–85.

Zimmerman, B. J. (1990). Self-regulated learning and academic achievement: An overview. *Educational Psychologist,* 25(1), 3–17.

Zimmerman, S. & Zimmerman, A. M. (1990). Genetic effects of marijuana. *International Journal of Addictions,* 25(1A), 19–33.

Zinbarg, R. E., Barlow, D. H., Brown, T. A. & Hertz, R. M. (1992). Cognitive-behavioral approaches to the nature and treatment of anxiety disorders. In M. R. Rosenzweig and L. W. Porter (Eds.), *Annual Review of Psychology, 43,* 235- 267.

Zinberg, N. E. (1976). The war over marijuana. *Psychology Today,* Dec., 92–98.

Zoller, C. L., Workman, J. S., & Kroll, N. E. (1989). The bizarre mnemonic: The effect of retention interval and mode of presentation. *Bulletin of the Psychonomic Society,* 27(3), 215–218.

Zubek, J. (1969). Sensory and perceptual-motor processes. In J. Zubek (Ed.). *Sensory deprivation: Fifteen years of research.* New York: Appleton-Century-Crofts.

Zuckerman, M. (1990). The psychophysiology of sensation seeking. *Journal of Personality,* 58(1), 313–345.

Zuckerman, M., & Allison, S. (1976). An objective measure of fear of success: Construction and validation. *Journal of Personality, 40,* 422–430.

Zuckerman, M., Eysenck, S., & Eysenck, H. J. (1978). Sensation seeking in England and America: Cross-cultural, age, and sex comparisons. *Journal of Consulting and Clinical Psychology, 46,* 139–149.

Index

Acknowledgments

Chapter 1 © Richard Mackson, FPG International; **Fig. 1.1** (left) © Jay Fries, The Image Bank, (center) Custom Medical Stock Photo, (right) © Enrico Ferorelli; **Fig. 1.3** (top left) © Bob Daemmrich, Stock Boston, Inc., (top right) © Karl Weatherly, 1989, Allstock, (bottom left) © Philip Bailey, 1992, The Stock Market, Inc., (bottom right) © F. Stuart Westmorland, Allstock; **Fig. 1.5** © Susan Ruklin, Photo Researchers, Inc.; **Fig. 1.6** © Charles Gupton, Stock Boston, Inc.; **Fig. 1.7** © Brown Brothers; **Fig. 1.8** © Brown Brothers; **Fig. 1.9** © Brown Brothers; **Fig. 1.10** © Bettmann Archive; **Fig. 1.11** © Ted Polumbaum; **Fig. 1.12** © United Press International; **Fig. 1.14** © Furumoto and Scarborough, 1986, courtesy of Wellesley College; **Fig. 1.15** © Howard, et. al., 1986, courtesy of Columbia University; **Fig. 1.16** © Mardigan and O'Hara, 1992, courtesy of National Library of Medicine; **Fig. 1.17** © Bettmann Archive; **Fig. 1.18** © Ted Polumbaum; **Fig. 1.19** © Rudi VonBriel, 1994; **p. 121** Shannon Buckels; **Fig. 1.21** © Bill Aron, PhotoEdit; **Fig. 1.24** © Bettmann Archive; **p. 30** © 1993 Washington Post Writers Group. Reprinted with permission.

Chapter 2 © Lawrence Migdale, Photo Researchers, Inc.; **Fig. 2.1** © Charles Gupton, Stock Boston, Inc.; **Fig. 2.4** © *National Geographic Society Magazine*, photograph by Baron Hugo van Lawick; **Fig. 2.11** © Mike Kagan, Monkmeyer Press; **p. 36** van Lawick-Goodall, Jane. *In the Shadow of Man*, Houghton Mifflin Co. 1971, World rights: William Collins Sons & Co. Ltd., London; **p. 41** Cartoon courtesy of Pete Muller; **p. 48** © Richard Hutchings, PhotoEdit; **Fig. 2.14** © Lynn Goldsmith/LGI, 1986.

Chapter 3 © Cabisco, Visuals Unlimited; **Fig. 3.1** © Biophoto Associates/Science Source, Photo Researchers, Inc.; **Fig. 3.8** Fidia Research Laboratories, Pavda, Italy; **Fig. 3.14** Courtesy of Richard Haier, University of California, Irvine; **Fig. 3.16** Gazzaniga, M. S. *The Bisected Brain*. Plenum Publishing Co., 1970; **Fig. 3.17** Ornstein, R. E. *The Psychology of Consciousness*. W. H. Freeman and Co., 1972; **Fig. 3.24** © Michael Serino, The Picture Cube; **Fig. 3.25** © G. Giansanti, Sygma; **p. 80** © Mark Richards, PhotoEdit; **Fig. 3.26** © David Young-Wolff, PhotoEdit; **Fig. 3.29** © Custom Medical Stock Photo, 1990; **Fig. 3.31** Huntington Magnetic Resonance Center, Pasadena, California; **Fig. 3.32** © Charles Gupton, Stock Boston, Inc.; **Fig. 3.33** Graphics by EEG Systems; **Fig. 3.34** Washington University School of Medicine, St. Louis; **Fig. 3.35** Washington University School of Medicine, St. Louis.

Chapter 4 © John Kelly, The Image Bank; **Fig. 4.8** © Omikron, Photo Researchers, Inc.; **Fig. 4.11** (top) © Harvey Eisner, Taurus, (bottom) © David M. Campione, Taurus; **Fig. 4.14** © Jeffrey W. Myers, Stock Boston, Inc.; **Fig. 4.17** © Jon L. Barken, The Picture Cube; **Fig. 4.23** "La Sapienza", P. Motta University, Rome, © Photo Researchers, Inc.; **Fig. 4.26** © Richard Costaneo, *Discover Magazine*, 1993; **p. 110** © Tim Davis, Tony Stone Images; **Fig. 4.29** Chiras, D. *Human Biology: Health, Homeostasis, and the Environment*, © 1991 West Publishing Co; **Fig. 4.30** *After Cornsweet*, 1970; **Fig. 4.32** © Henry Wolf Productions, Inc.; **p. 116** © Tony Freeman, PhotoEdit; **Fig. 4.33** © Tim Barnwell, Stock Boston, Inc.; **Fig. 4.34** © NASA.

Chapter 5 © Mary Kate Denny, PhotoEdit; **Fig. 5.1** Yvaral, "Marilyn Numerisee #420," © Yvaral 1990, courtesy of Circle Gallery; **Fig. 5.5** © E. R. Degginger, Animals, Animals; **Fig. 5.9** Enrico Ferorelli, DOT; **Fig. 5.11** B. Julesz, Foundation of Cyclopian Perception, © 1971, University of Chicago Press; **Fig. 5.12** © 1994 N E Thing Enterprises, Distributed by Universal Press Syndicate; **Fig. 5.15** Dennis Coon; **Fig. 5.19** Dennis Coon; **Fig. 5.20** Bettmann Archive; **Fig. 5.22** © Baron Wolman; **Fig. 5.23** © Dan Francis, Mardan Photography; **Fig. 5.24** © David Austin, Stock Boston, Inc.; **Fig. 5.29** From "Cognitive Determinants of Fixation Location During Picture Viewing", by G. R. Loftus and N. H. Mackworth, *Journal of Experimental Psychology*. **Fig. 5.31** Held, Al, "The Big N" (1965) synthetic polymer paint on canvas 9′ 3/8″ × 9′. Collection, The Museum of Modern Art, New York, Mrs. Armand P. Bartos fund; **p. 146** © D. Goupy, Sygma; **p. 148** Kapleau, Philip, *The Three Pilars of Zen*, Harper and Row, 1966.

Chapter 6 © Orion SVC/TRDNG 1988; **Fig. 6.1** © Jean-Leo Dugast, Sygma; **p. 158** © Gary Larson, reprinted by permission of Chronicle Features, San Francisco, all rights reserved; **Fig. 6.4** © Yale Joel, *Life* Magazine, 1954, Time Inc.; **Fig. 6.5** © Martin M. Potker, 1981, Taurus Photos; **Fig. 6.7** Courtesy of Healthdyne, Inc.; **Fig. 6.8** Wide World Photos; **Table 6.3** Stanford Hypnotic Scale adapted from Weitzenhofler and Hilgard, Stanford University Press, 1959; **Fig. 6.9** © Dan Francis, Mardan Photography; **Fig. 6.10** © Dan Francis, Mardan Photography; **Fig. 6.12** "Spectrum of Continuum of Drugs", Dr. Robert W. Earle, University of California, Irvine; **Fig. 6.13** Illustration courtesy of the National Library of Medicine; **Fig. 6.14** Focus on Sports; **p. 179** © Gary Larson, reprinted by permission of Chronicle Features, San Francisco, all rights reserved; **Fig. 6.15** © P. Iovino/SAGA, 1991; **Fig. 6.18** "Marijuana and the Brain", *Science News*, vol. 143, p.88; **Fig. 6.19** "Beware Marijuana", courtesy of Dr. Lester Grinspoon, Harvard Medical School; **p. 186** Salvador Dali (Spanish, 1904–1989), *The Persistence of Memory* (*Persistence de la memoire*), 1931. Oil on canvas, 9 1/2″ × 13″ (24.1 × 23 cm.). Collection, The Museum of Modern Art, New York. Given anonymously. © 1994 Demart Pro Arte, Geneve/Artist Rights Society (ARS), NY; **Fig. 6.20** Courtesy of Maryanne Mott.

Chapter 7 © Tom Hugh, Photo Researchers, Inc.; **Fig. 7.6** © Dan Francis, Mardan Photography; **Fig. 7.11** Duomo Photography; **Fig. 7.12** Yale Joel, *Life* Magazine, © Time Inc.; **Fig. 7.14** "Chimp-O-Mat", Yerkes Regional Primate Research Center, Emory University; **Fig. 7.17** © Dan Francis, Mardan Photography; **Fig. 7.18** © Photo Researchers, Inc.; **Fig. 7.20** Photos by Barbara Martin, courtesy of the *Los Angeles Times*, © 1984; **Fig. 7.21** © Alain Dejean, Sygma; **Fig. 7.23** © David Weintraub, Photo Researchers, Inc.; **Fig. 7.24** "Effects of Punishment on Extinction". Chart from B. F. Skinner, *The Behavior of Organism*, 1938. Permission from Prentice-Hall, Inc.; **Fig. 7.26** © Ellis Herwig, The Picture Cube; **p. 225** Cartoon courtesy of Ed Arno and Science 80; **Fig. 7.31** Elena Rooraid, PhotoEdit; **Fig. 7.32** Nursery School Children, Dr. Albert Bandura, Stanford University; **Fig. 7.33** © Rick Smolan, Stock Boston, Inc.; **Fig. 7.34** © Michael Newman, PhotoEdit; **p. 225** © Tony Freeman, PhotoEdit; **Fig. 7.36** (left) © J. Albertson, Stock Boston, Inc., (right) Dennis Coon.

Chapter 8 © David Weintraub, Photo Researchers, Inc.; **Fig. 8.1** Courtesy of Apple Computers; **Fig. 8.3** From Wilder Penfield, *The Excitable Cortex in Conscious Man*, 1958. Courtesy of the author and Charles C. Thomas, Publisher, Springfield, IL; **Fig. 8.4** © Spencer Grant, Photo Researchers, Inc.; **Fig. 8.9** Photo courtesy of Larry Day; **Fig. 8.10** Redrawn from an illustration in Lewis Carroll's *Alice in Wonderland*; **p. 248** "Animal Crackers" cartoon reprinted with permission of Tribune Media Services; **Fig. 8.14** © J. L. Atlan, Sygma; **Fig. 8.19** © Rick Martin, *San Jose Mercury News*. **Fig. 8.20** © Andrew Lichtenstein, Impact Visuals; **Fig. 8.21** © Tulvig, 1989; **Fig. 8.22** © Animals, Animals; **p. 258** © David Young-

Wolff, PhotoEdit; **Fig. 8.23** © Joseph Nettis, 1991, Photo Researchers, Inc.; **Fig. 8.24** © AP/Wide World Photos.

Chapter 9 © A. Brucelle, Sygma; **Fig. 9.1** © Red Saunders, Four Walls Studio; **Fig. 9.4** Dennis Coon; **Fig. 9.7** Osgood, C. E., "The Nature and Measurement of Meaning." *Psychological Bulletin, 49.* © 1952 by the American Psychological Association, reprinted with permission; **Fig 9.11** "Teaching Language to an Ape," by Ann James Premack and David Premack, October 1972; **Fig. 9.12** © Enrico Ferorelli; **Fig. 9.16** (left) © ARCHIV/Photo Researchers, Inc., (right) Courtesy of Cray Computers; **Fig. 9.20** U. S. Patent No. 556,248. From *Absolutely Mad Inventions,* by A. E. Brown and H. A. Jefcott, Jr., Dover, 1970; **Fig. 9.21** (top) © Stacy Pick, Stock Boston, Inc., (center) © Dan Guravich, Photo Researchers, Inc., (bottom) © Thomas R. Fletcher, Stock Boston, Inc.; **p. 288** © Carl Purcell, 1989, Photo Researchers, Inc.; **Fig. 9.27** © Ralph Reinhold, Animals, Animals.

Chapter 10 © Mark Richards, PhotoEdit; **Fig. 10.1** © David Austen, Woodfin Camp; **Fig. 10.5** "Hyperphagic Rat", photograph courtesy of Dr. Neal E. Miller, Rockefeller University; **Fig. 10.6** © Bill Smith, *Sports Illustrated.* © Time, Inc.; **Fig. 10.7** (left) © Darlene Hammond, © Archive Photos, (right) © Kathy Banks, Sygma; **Fig. 10.8** © Peter Menzel, Stock Boston, Inc.; **Fig. 10.9** © Schiltman, Gamma Liaison; **Fig. 10.11** © Alain Evrard, Photo Researchers, Inc.; **Fig. 10.12** "Monkeys and Locks", Harry F. Harlow, University of Wisconsin Primate Laboratory; **Fig. 10.14** © David F. Hughes, The Picture Cube; **Fig. 10.18** © Ellis Herwig, The Picture Cube; **Fig. 10.19** © Doug Beghtel, *The Oregonian,* Sygma; **Fig. 10.21** Focus on Ethics; **Fig. 10.22** Courtesy of The Record, Hackensack, New Jersey; **Fig. 10.26** Photo courtesy of the Stoelting Co., Chicago, Il; **Fig. 10.27** Jack Fields, Photo Researchers, Inc.; **Fig. 10.28** Courtesy of The Record, Hackensack, New Jersey; **Fig. 10.29** © Richard Hutchings, Info. Edit; **Fig. 10.31** © Michael Grecco, Stock Boston, Inc.; **Fig. 10.32** © Dan Francis, Mardan Photography; **p. 332** © Michael Newman, PhotoEdit.

Chapter 11 © Mark Richards, PhotoEdit; **Fig. 11.2** (left) © Dennis Brack, Black Star, (right) © Sandy Herring, The Picture Cube; **Fig. 11.3** © Paul Marques, *Bienstar Health,* "Well-being and *Life* Style Choices for Pinal County", University of Arizona, 1982; **Fig. 11.4** © Liane Enkilis, Stock Boston, Inc.; **Fig. 11.5** © James Prince, 1988, Photo Researchers, Inc.; **p. 344** "Jump Start" cartoon reprinted with permission of UFS, Inc.; **Fig. 11.7** © Oscar C. Williams; **Fig. 11.10** © David Woo, Stock Boston, Inc.; **Table 11.2** Adapted with permission from "Social Readjustment Rating Scale," by T. H. Holmes and R. H. Rahe, *Journal of Psychosomatic Research,* 1967. Reprinted with permission from Pergamon Press, Ltd; **Fig. 11.12** © Bruce Robert, Photo Researchers, Inc.; **Fig. 11.13** © Photo Researchers, Inc.; **Fig. 11.14** © Owen Franken, Stock Boston, Inc.; **Fig. 11.15** © Comstock, Inc.

Chapter 12 © Steven W. Jones, 1988, FPG International; **Fig. 12.1** © Myrleen Ferguson Gate, PhotoEdit; **Fig. 12.2** From A. N. Meltzoff & M. K. Moore, "Imitation of facial and manual gestures by human neonates." *Science,* 1977, 198, 75–78; **Fig. 12.3a** "The Looking Chamber", Robert L. Fanz, © David Linton, 1961, Scientific American, Inc.; **Fig. 12.5** Bridges, K. M. B. "Emotional Development in Early Infancy." *Child Development,* 3 pp. 324–341, figure 2, p. 340. © 1932; **Fig. 12.6** © Biophoto Association, Photo Researchers, Inc.; **Fig. 12.9** © Bob Daemmrich, Stock Boston, Inc.; **p. 380** Table courtesy of Tom Bond; **Fig. 12.10** © Photo Researchers, Inc.; **Fig. 12.11** Photo courtesy of the University of Washington School of Medicine; **Fig. 12.12** © A. Glauberman, Photo Researchers, Inc.; **Fig. 12.13** © Ed Kashi; **p. 385** "Baby Blues" cartoon by Jerry Scott, Rick Kirkman and Creators Syndicate; **Fig. 12.15** © Nina Leen, 1964, Time, Inc.; **Fig. 12.16** © Michael Newman, PhotoEdit; **p. 390** "Baby Blues" cartoon by Jerry Scott, Rick Kirkman and Creators Syndicate; **Fig. 12.19** Jerome Bruner, *Child's Talk, Learning to Use Language,* W. W. Norton Co., 1981. Reprinted with permission; **Fig. 12.20** © Gilbert Lam, Sygma; **Fig. 12.21** © Stephen Frisch, Stock Boston, Inc.; **Fig. 12.22** © Yves Debraine, Black Star; **Fig. 12.23** © David Young-Wolff, PhotoEdit; **Fig. 12.25** © Michael Newman, PhotoEdit; **Fig. 12.26** © Angelina Lax, 1985; **Fig. 12.27** Courtesy of Harry F. Harlow, University of Wisconsin Primate Laboratory; **Fig. 12.28** © Joseph Nettis, Photo Researchers, Inc.; **p. 403** © David Young-Wolff, PhotoEdit; **Fig. 12.29** © Visuals Unlimited; **Fig. 12.30** © Philippe Phailly, Photo Researchers, *Discover Magazine.* **Fig. 12.31** © *Los Angeles Times.*

Chapter 13 © Ellan Young, 1988, Photo Researchers, Inc.; **Fig. 13.1** © Bettmann Archive; **Fig. 13.2** © Gabor Demjen, Stock Boston, Inc.; **Fig. 13.3** "Growing Up"; J. M. Tanner, © Scientific American, Inc., 1973; **Fig. 13.4** © Bob Daemmrich, Stock Boston, Inc.; **p. 418** "Far Side" © 1985 & 1990 Farworks, Inc./Dist. by Universal Press Syndicate. Reprinted with permission. All rights reserved; **Fig. 13.5** © David Woo, Stock Boston, Inc.; **Fig. 13.6** © Mark M. Walker, The Picture Cube; **Fig. 13.7** Courtesy of the Los Angeles County Department of Children's Services; **Fig. 13.9** © Michael Newman, PhotoEdit; **p. 427** " Quality Time" cartoon by Gail Machlis is reprinted by permission of Chronicle Features, San Francisco; **Fig. 13.10** © Rhoda Sidney, Monkmeyer; **Fig. 13.15** © R. Maiman, Sygma; **Fig. 13.17** © Bob Daemmrich, Stock Boston, Inc.; **Fig. 13.18** © Michael Newman, PhotoEdit; **Fig. 13.20** © A. Tannenbaum, Sygma.

Chapter 14 © Telegraph Colour Library; **Fig. 14.1** © Mimi Forsyth, Monkmeyer; **Table 14.3** Terman, L. & M. Merrill, "Stanford-Binet Intelligence Scale". 1937 (Revised ed. 1960b). Houghton Mifflin Co; **Fig. 14.4** © David Horan, Picture Group; **Table 14.4** Wechsler Scale, The Psychological Corporation, 1958; **Fig. 14.7** © Wide World Photos; **Fig. 14.8** (left) © Karen R. Preuss, Taurus, (center) © Dan Francis, Mardan, (right) © David M. Campione, Taurus; **Fig. 14.9** Photo courtesy of the California Special Olympics; **p. 466** © Custom Medical Stock Photo; **Fig. 14.12** Culture Fair Test Sample Items from R. B. Cattell, "Are I. Q. Tests Intelligent?" Reprinted by permission of Dr. R. B. Cattell.

Chapter 15 © Photo Researchers, Inc.; **Fig. 15.1** © "Wayne's World", 1991, Sygma; **Fig. 15.2** © Bertrand Explorer, Photo Researchers, Inc.; **p. 477** "Far Side", by Gary Larson, © Universal Press Syndicate; **Fig. 15.4** Cattell, R. B. "Personality Pinned Down." 1973. Reprinted by permission of Dr. R. B. Cattell; **Fig. 15.6** (left) © Alris Upitis, Black Star, (right) © Alris Upitis, Black Star; **Fig. 15.7** "All is Vanity", courtesy of Illusions, Park Ridge, IL; **Fig. 15.9** © UPI/Bettmann News Photo; **Fig. 15.10** © Lawrence Migdale, 1984, Photo Researchers, Inc.; **Fig. 15.11** © Bob Daemmrich, Stock Boston, Inc.; **Fig. 15.13** © Will & Deni McIntyre, Photo Researchers, Inc.; **Fig. 15.14** © Robert Brenner, PhotoEdit; **Fig. 15.15** © Richard Hutchings, Photo Researchers, Inc.; **Fig. 15.17** © Bob Daemmrich, Stock Boston, Inc.; **Fig. 15.19** © Comstock; **Fig. 15.20** Reproduced by permission. Copyright 1943, renewed 1970 by the University of Minnesota. Published by The Psychological Corporation, New York, NY. All rights reserved; **p. 505** © Ron Chapple, 1993, FPG International.

Chapter 16 "The Scream", Edward Munch (1863–1944), © Galleria Nazionale, Oslo, Scala, Art Resource; **p. 511** "Catch 22 Incident", Joseph Heller. Reprinted with permission of Simon and Schuster, Inc.; **Fig. 16.1** Photographs courtesy of Ulrike Kanton Gallery; **Fig. 16.3** © Jeff Greenberg/MRP; **Fig. 16.4** Dennis Coon; **Fig. 16.5** © Visuals Unlimited; **Fig. 16.6** © Sygma; **Fig. 16.7** © Dan Francis, Mardan; **Fig. 16.8** © Cary Wolinsky, Stock Boston, Inc.; **Fig. 16.9** (left) © UPI/Bettmann, (right) Dennis Coon; **Fig. 16.10** © Charles Gupton, Stock Boston, Inc.; **p. 532** © Peter Surel, Sygma.

Chapter 17 © Hank Morgan/Science Source, Photo Researchers, Inc.; **Fig. 17.1** © David Hanover; **Fig. 17.2** "The Mad Hatter" from Lewis Carroll's *Alice in Wonderland*, © Bettmann Archive; **Fig. 17.3** © Benyas, Black Star; **Fig. 17.4** © Grunnitus, Monkmeyer; **Fig. 17.6** © Derik Bayes/courtesy Guttmann-Maclay *Life* Picture Service; **Fig. 17.7** (left) © Dennis Brack, Black Star, (right) © Duke University Hospital; **Fig. 17.8** © The Brookhaven Institute; **Fig. 17.9** Dennis Coon; **Fig. 17.11** © Robin Thomas, NY, NY; **Fig. 17.13** © Will McIntyre, Photo Researchers; **Fig. 17.14** © Peter Southwick, Stock Boston, Inc.; **Fig. 17.15** © A. Tannenbaum, Sygma; **p. 559** © Tony Freeman, PhotoEdit.

Chapter 18 © Will and Deni McIntyre, Photo Researchers, Inc.; **Fig. 18.1** Courtesy of the Department of Library Services, American Museum of Natural History; **Fig. 18.2** (left) Courtesy of the New York Public Library, (right) © The Bettmann Archive; **Fig. 18.3** Demon from "The Temptation of St. Anthony", by Martin Schonganer. Treasury of Fantastic and Mythological Creatures by Richard Huber. Dover, 1981; **Fig. 18.4** © Historical Picture Service, Chicago; **Fig. 18.5** Michael Routgier, *Life* Magazine © Time, Inc.; **Fig. 18.6** © Curt Gunther, Camera 5; **Fig. 18.7** Teresa Zabula, © Uniphoto; **Fig. 18.8** Photograph courtesy of Albert Bandura and the American Psychological Association. © 1969 by the American Psychological Association. Reprinted by permission. From the *Journal of Personality and Social Psychology*, 1969, 13, pp. 173–199; **Fig. 18.9** Lovaas, O. I. and Simmons, J. Q., "Manipulation of Self-destruction in Three Retarded Children.: *Journal of Applied Behavior Analysis*, 1969, 2 pp. 143–157. Reprinted by permission; **Fig. 18.10** Token Economy photograph courtesy of Robert Liberman, M. D; **Fig. 18.11** © Stacy Pick, Stock Boston, Inc.; **Fig 18.13** © UPI/Bettmann; **p. 591** © Michelle Bridwell, PhotoEdit.

Chapter 19 © Alan Oddie, PhotoEdit; **p. 607** © Nick Hobart, Punch Publications, LTD; **Fig. 19.5** © Robert Caputo, Stock Boston, Inc.; **Fig. 19.6** © Elizabeth Zukerman, PhotoEdit; **Fig. 19.7** © Dan Francis, Mardan Photography; **Fig. 19.14** © Sygma.

Chapter 20 © Miro Vintoniv, Stock Boston, Inc.; **Fig. 20.1** © Richard Pasley, Stock Boston, Inc.; **Fig. 20.3** © Gregg Mancusco, Stock Boston, Inc.; **Fig. 20.5** © Bob Daemmrich; **Fig. 20.6** © Stacy Pick, Stock Boston, Inc.; **Fig. 20.7** © Bob Daemmrich; **Fig. 20.9** © Photo Researchers, Inc.; **Fig. 20.10** © Juneart 1983, The Image Bank; **Fig. 20.12** From the film "Obedience", by Stanley Milgram, The Pennsylvania State University, Audio Visual Services; **Fig. 20.15** © Robert Y. Eckert, Stock Boston, Inc.; **p. 654** © Tony Freeman, PhotoEdit.

Chapter 21 © David Young-Wolff, PhotoEdit; **Fig. 21.1** © C. Kuhn, The Image Bank West; **Fig. 21.2** © Mark Mittelman, Taurus; **Fig. 21.4** © Ellis Herwig, Taurus; **Fig. 21.5** © Rod Aydelotti, Waco *Tribune Herald*, Sygma; **Fig. 21.6** © Ellis Herwig, Taurus; **Fig. 21.7** © Bill Gallery, Stock Boston, Inc.; **Fig. 21.8** © Charles Gupton, Stock Boston, Inc.; **Fig. 21.9** © Dennis Brack, Black Star; **Fig. 21.10** © Chris Gueker, Picture Group; **Fig. 21.13** © The Photo Works, Photo Researchers, Inc.; **p. 682** © Jeff Greenberg, PhotoEdit.

Chapter 22 © David Hanover Photography; **Fig. 22.2** Photograph courtesy of the General Electric Company; **Fig. 22.3** © Lawrence Migdale, 1991, Stock Boston, Inc.; **Fig. 22.4** © Charles Feil, Stock Boston, Inc.; **Fig. 22.5** © Steve Hanson, Stock Boston, Inc.; **Fig. 22.7** © Brooks Kraft, Sygma; **Fig. 22.8** © Jeff Greenberg, Photo Researchers, Inc.; **Fig. 22.9** © Giannini, Sygma; **Fig. 22.11** © Charles Gupton, Stock Boston, Inc.; **Fig. 22.12** © Sygma; **Fig. 22.13** © Sygma; **p. 709** © David Young-Wolff, PhotoEdit; **Fig. 22.15** Art by Stan Jones, courtesy of NASA, Johnson Space Center; **p. 713** © J. Tiziou, Sygma.